J. PAUL SAMPLEY is Professor Emeritus of New Testament and Christian Origins, Boston University, and is the author of *Pauline Parallels* and "1 Corinthians" and "2 Corinthians" in the *New Interpreter's Bible*.

PAUL in the
Greco-Roman World

PAUL in the
Greco-Roman World

A HANDBOOK

EDITED BY
J. PAUL SAMPLEY

TRINITY PRESS INTERNATIONAL
A Continuum imprint
HARRISBURG • LONDON • NEW YORK

Copyright © 2003 J. Paul Sampley

Trinity Press International, P.O. Box 1321, Harrisburg, PA 17105

Trinity Press International is a member of the Continuum International Publishing Group.

Quotations from the New Revised Standard Version Bible are copyright 1989 by the Division of Christian Education of the National Council of the Churches of Christ in the United States of America. Used by permission. All rights reserved.

Cover art: Saint Paul discussing with Jews and Gentiles. Enamel plaque from a reliquary or altar in England. Victoria and Albert Museum, London, Great Britain. Erich Lessing/Art Resource, NY

Cover design: Wesley Hoke

Library of Congress Cataloging-in-Publication Data

Paul in the Greco-Roman world : a handbook / edited by J. Paul Sampley.
   p. cm.
  Includes bibliographical references and index.
  ISBN 1-56338-266-0
 1. Paul, the Apostle, Saint. 2. Civilization, Greco-Roman. I. Sampley, J. Paul.
BS2506.3 .P38 2003
225.9'2—dc21   2003010220

Printed in the United States of America

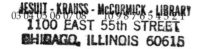

To Sally, my delightful partner these forty-seven years in love, in work, and in play.

To my students, in whom I delight.

CONTENTS

Acknowledgments ix

Abbreviations xi

Introduction 1

1. Paul and Adaptability
   Clarence E. Glad 17

2. Paul, Adoption, and Inheritance
   James C. Walters 42

3. Paul and Boasting
   Duane F. Watson 77

4. Paul and Commendation
   Efrain Agosto 101

5. Paul and Rhetorical Comparison
   Christopher Forbes 134

✓ 6. Paul, Hardships, and Suffering
   David E. Fredrickson 172

✓ 7. Paul and Greco-Roman Education
   Ronald F. Hock 198

8. Paul, Exemplification, and Imitation
   Benjamin Fiore, S.J. 228

9. Paul, Families, and Households
   David L. Balch 258

10. Paul and Frank Speech
    J. Paul Sampley 293

11. Paul and Friendship
    John T. Fitzgerald 319

12. Paul, Games, and the Military
    Edgar Krentz 344

13. Paul and Indifferent Things
    Will Deming 384

14. Paul, Marriage, and Divorce
    O. Larry Yarbrough 404

15. Paul and Maxims
    Rollin A. Ramsaran 429

16. Paul and *Pater Familias*
    L. Michael White 457

✓ 17. Paul, Patrons, and Clients
    Peter Lampe 488

18. Paul and Self-Mastery
    Stanley K. Stowers 524

19. Paul, Shame, and Honor
    Robert Jewett 551

20. Paul and Slavery
    J. Albert Harrill 575

21. Paul, Virtues, and Vices
    Troels Engberg-Pedersen 608

Contributors 635

Indexes 637

ACKNOWLEDGMENTS

This volume was the outgrowth of years of classes in which my students would become interested in a topic regarding Paul in the Greco-Roman world and look to me for some bibliographical assistance. In the process I found myself wishing there was one place where I could send a student for a good start on the selected issue. At the same time, though, I came to know who had done significant work on a given topic, so that when this book was conceived I knew the person who should contribute the article in question. So, as this book comes to completion, I thank my students.

When I decided to go ahead with the book, I approached a couple of publishers and received the usual, courteous assurance of interest with the predictable promise of a decision in a reasonable time. But it was Hal Rast, the director of Trinity Press International, who when he saw the prospectus and we talked a few moments said, "We want this book." Though he is since retired, I want to recognize him and his collegiality across my own career.

Henry Carrigan, Hal Rast's successor, has been a great support in realizing the volume. Throughout the navigation, from Trinity Press International's acceptance to the publication of the volume, he has been consistently helpful, with good counsel, patience, and encouragement.

To my colleagues who joined with me in making this book possible, I am most indebted. Not only did they agree to contribute essays, but they also conformed those works to the structure I proposed, and they bore with great grace my editorial suggestions and comments. I read each essay with a delight in how much my colleagues knew, in how much I learned from them, and in how much new light they were able to shed on our understanding of Paul.

Finally, I would like to thank Boston University for its support of me and of my research with a sabbatical leave during which I was able to do much of the editorial work on this volume.

Charlemont, Massachusetts
July 2002

ABBREVIATIONS

AB	Anchor Bible
ABD	*Anchor Bible Dictionary.* Edited by D. N. Freedman. 6 vols. New York, 1992
ABR	*Australian Biblical Review*
AJP	*American Journal of Philology*
AnBib	Analecta biblica
ANRW	*Aufstieg und Niedergang der römischen Welt: Geschichte und Kultur Roms im Spiegel der neueren Forschung.* Edited by H. Temporini and W. Haase. Berlin, 1972–
ANTC	Abingdon New Testament Commentaries
ATJ	*Ashland Theological Journal*
AUSS	*Andrews University Seminary Studies*
BAGD	Bauer, W., W. F. Arndt, F. W. Gingrich, and F. W. Danker. *Greek-English Lexicon of the New Testament and Other Early Christian Literature.* 2d ed. Chicago, 1979
BBB	Bonner biblische Beiträge
BCH	*Bulletin de correspondence hellénique*
BDAG	Bauer, W., F. W. Danker, W. F. Arndt, and F. W. Gingrich. *Greek-English Lexicon of the New Testament and Other Early Christian Literature.* 3d ed. Chicago, 1999
BDF	Blass, F., A. Debrunner, and R. W. Funk. *A Greek Grammar of the New Testament and Other Early Christian Literature.* Chicago, 1961
BETL	Bibliotheca ephemeridum theologicarum lovaniensium
BFCT	Beiträge zur Förderung christlicher Theologie
BGU	*Aegyptische Urkunden aus den Königlichen Staatlichen Museen zu Berlin, Griechische Urkunden.* 15 vols. Berlin, 1895–1983
BHT	Beiträge zur historischen Theologie
Bib	*Biblica*
BibInt	*Biblical Interpretation*
BJS	Brown Judaic Studies
BNTC	Black's New Testament Commentaries

BR	*Biblical Research*
BTB	*Biblical Theology Bulletin*
BZNW	Beihefte zur Zeitschrift für die neutestamentliche Wissenschaft
CBQ	*Catholic Biblical Quarterly*
CIL	*Corpus inscriptionum latinarum*
CJ	*Classical Journal*
ConBNT	Coniectanea biblica: New Testament Series
CP	*Classical Philology*
CQ	*Classical Quarterly*
CurTM	*Currents in Theology and Mission*
EDNT	*Exegetical Dictionary of the New Testament.* Edited by H. Balz and G. Schneider. ET. Grand Rapids, 1990–93
EKKNT	Evangelisch-katholischer Kommentar zum Neuen Testament
EPRO	Etudes préliminaires aux religions orientales dans l'empire romain
EvQ	*Evangelical Quarterly*
EvT	*Evangelische Theologie*
FB	Forschung zur Bibel
FRLANT	Forschungen zur Religion und Literatur des Alten und Neuen Testaments
GCS	Die griechische christliche Schriftsteller der ersten [drei] Jahrhunderte
GNS	Good News Studies
GR	*Greece and Rome*
HDR	Harvard Dissertations in Religion
HR	*History of Religions*
HSCP	*Harvard Studies in Classical Philology*
HTR	*Harvard Theological Review*
HTS	Harvard Theological Studies
HUT	Hermeneutische Untersuchungen zur Theologie
ICC	International Critical Commentary
IG	*Inscriptiones graecae. Editio minor.* Berlin, 1924–
IKZ	*Internationale kirchliche Zeitschrift*
Int	*Interpretation*
JAAR	*Journal of the American Academy of Religion*
JAC	*Jahrbuch für Antike und Christentum*
JBL	*Journal of Biblical Literature*
JECS	*Journal of Early Christian Studies*
JES	*Journal of Ecumenical Studies*
JESHO	*Journal of the Economic and Social History of the Orient*

JFSR	*Journal of Feminist Studies in Religion*
JHS	*Journal of Hellenic Studies*
JJS	*Journal of Jewish Studies*
JRH	*Journal of Religious History*
JRS	*Journal of Roman Studies*
JSJ	*Journal for the Study of Judaism in the Persian, Hellenistic, and Roman Periods*
JSNT	*Journal for the Study of the New Testament*
JSNTSup	Journal for the Study of the New Testament: Supplement Series
JTS	*Journal of Theological Studies*
LCL	Loeb Classical Library
LEC	Library of Early Christianity
LSJ	Liddell, H. G., R. Scott, and H. S. Jones. *A Greek-English Lexicon.* 9th ed. with revised supplement. Oxford, 1996
MEFR	*Mélanges d'archéologie et d'histoire de l'école français de Rome*
MTZ	*Münchener theologische Zeitschrift*
NA²⁷	*Novum Testamentum Graece,* Nestle-Aland, 27th ed.
NEAEHL	*The New Encyclopedia of Archaeological Excavations in the Holy Land.* Edited by E. Stern. 4 vols. Jerusalem, 1993
Neot	*Neotestamentica*
NICNT	New International Commentary on the New Testament
NIDNTT	*New International Dictionary of New Testament Theology.* Edited by C. Brown. 4 vols. Grand Rapids, 1975–85
NIGTC	New International Greek Testament Commentary
NJahrb	*Neue Jahrbücher für das klassische Altertum (1898–1925)*
NovT	*Novum Testamentum*
NovTSup	Novum Testamentum Supplements
NRTh	*La nouvelle revue théologique*
NTAbh	Neutestamentliche Abhandlungen
NTD	Das Neue Testament Deutsch
NTOA	Novum Testamentum et Orbis Antiquus
NTS	*New Testament Studies*
OCD	*Oxford Classical Dictionary.* Edited by S. Hornblower and A. Spawforth. 3d ed. Oxford, 1996
OEANE	*The Oxford Encyclopedia of Archaeology in the Near East.* Edited by E. M. Meyers. New York, 1997
OGIS	*Orientis graeci inscriptiones selectae.* Edited by W. Dittenberger. 2 vols. Leipzig, 1903–1905
PG	Patrologia graeca [= Patrologiae cursus completus: Series graeca]. Edited by J.-P. Migne. 162 vols. Paris, 1857–86

PRSt	*Perspectives in Religious Studies*
RAC	*Reallexikon für Antike und Christentum.* Edited by T. Kluser et al. Stuttgart, 1950–
RE	*Realencyklopädie für prostetantische Theologie und Kirche*
REA	*Revue des études anciennes*
REG	*Revue des études grecques*
ResQ	*Restoration Quarterly*
RevExp	*Review and Expositor*
RevPhil	*Revue de philology*
SB	*Sammelbuch griechischer Urkunden aus Aegypten.* Edited by F. Preisigke et al. Vols. 1– , 1915–
SBLDS	Society of Biblical Literature Dissertation Series
SBLMS	Society of Biblical Literature Monograph Series
SBLRBS	Society of Biblical Literature Resources for Biblical Study
SBLSBS	Society of Biblical Literature Sources for Biblical Study
SBLTT	Society of Biblical Literature Texts and Translations
SBS	Stuttgarter Bibelstudien
SCHNT	Studia ad corpus hellenisticum Novi Testamenti
SE	*Studia evangelica I, II, III* (= TU 73 [1959], 87 [1964], 88 [1964], etc.)
SNTSMS	Society for New Testament Studies Monograph Series
SP	Sacra pagina
StPatr	*Studia patristica*
SVF	*Stoicorum veterum fragmenta.* H. von Arnim. 4 vols. Leipzig, 1903–24
TAPA	*Transactions of the American Philological Association*
TBT	*The Bible Today*
TDNT	*Theological Dictionary of the New Testament.* Edited by G. Kittel and G. Friedrich. Translated by G. W. Bromiley. 10 vols. Grand Rapids, 1964–76
TLNT	*Theological Lexicon of the New Testament.* C. Spicq. Translated and edited by J. D. Ernest. 3 vols. Peabody, Mass., 1994
TU	Texte und Untersuchungen
TynBul	*Tyndale Bulletin*
USQR	*Union Seminary Quarterly Review*
WBC	Word Biblical Commentary
WMANT	Wissenschaftliche Monographien zum Alten und Neuen Testament
WUNT	Wissenschaftliche Untersuchungen zum Neuen Testament
ZAC	*Zeitschrift für antikes Christentum*
ZNW	*Zeitschrift für die neutestamentliche Wissenschaft und die Kunde der älteren Kirche*
ZPE	*Zeitschrift für Papyrologie und Epigraphik*

INTRODUCTION

Pauline studies have been a vigorous discipline for the last few decades. A sequence of events helps account for that vitality. First, Paul escaped the hegemony of Acts so that Paul could be read for the first time on his own grounds and not through Luke's lens. Second, Pauline studies benefited from insights and methods that we borrowed from our colleagues in social sciences—particularly anthropology and sociology. And third, we have always known and studied Paul the Jew, but it is only in the last few decades that renewed interest has been paid to setting Paul's letters in the Greco-Roman world, and this enterprise is clearly on the cutting edge of Pauline scholarship today. Now, Roman social, economic, and political practices, social conventions, and values are the common coin of Pauline studies. Even Greco-Roman patterns of rhetoric have emerged as a major research area.

This should be no surprise. Paul clearly understands himself as apostle to the non-Jews, and though he uses a Jewish expression to describe them (we translate it "Gentiles"), he dedicates himself to making the gospel available to those outside Judaism. We have no reason to deny that there might have been Jews in any Pauline congregation, but we have probably been too inclined to overestimate their numbers. And we can demonstrate that every undisputed Pauline letter (save Philemon) explicitly supposes that Gentiles are present among the recipients (a statement we cannot make equally regarding Jews). When Paul describes "his" churches in what I take to be his last authentic letter, Romans, he says that Prisca and Aquila have done so much that "all the churches of the Gentiles" are indebted to that couple. "All the churches of the Gentiles" is *Paul's* own characterization of them. So how can it be surprising that Paul, in his missionary efforts to "win some" of those "outside the Law" (1 Cor 9:21), had no choice but to employ categories, conceptions, perceptions, and inclinations that were familiar to his non-Jewish audiences? No doubt that is part of what he meant when he said he had become as "one apart from [the] Law"(1 Cor 9:21; cf. Gal 4:12) as a means of reaching those who are themselves apart from the Law.

In his missionizing to non-Jews, it would have made no sense to present the gospel in Jewish categories that had first to be explained and elucidated before he could preach and move an audience toward conversion. Communication begins with taking one's hearers precisely in their own context. Effective persuasion can move people from where they are, but it must always start with them where and as they are. Accordingly, Paul's addresses to non-Jews had to be cast, at least at first, in non-Jewish categories.

True, after Paul has gained a hearing with Gentiles, he can and does socialize them into the story of Israel as God's people. Then he can retell the exodus story in such a way as to include his Gentile auditors as persons who, with Paul, can identify the characters in the original exodus as "our ancestors" (1 Cor 10:1); they can come to understand that Christ is "our paschal lamb" (1 Cor 5:7), and they can begin to view themselves as part of the "Israel of God" (Gal 6:16).

The Governing Rationale for the Volume

This collection of essays takes with utmost seriousness that Paul, always the Jew (cf. Phil 3:5; 1 Cor 9:19–20; Gal 1:13–14), believed himself to be apostle set apart to evangelize those non-Jews (= Gentiles) and that he profoundly understood the social and cultural setting in which he and they lived.

The Topics and the Contributors

The subject matters to which the individual chapters are devoted are chosen because they are au courant in Pauline studies today. The contributors are among the leading Pauline scholars around the world. Each of the essays is fresh, original, and written for this volume; each offers a state-of-the-art treatment of its topic.

The Organization of Each Essay

Each study in this volume is structured in four parts. Part I, as much as two-thirds of the essay, details how the assigned pattern or convention or practice worked in the Greco-Roman world of Paul's time. References to Paul there are minimized. Part II, approximately one third of the chapter, assumes Part I as the context and looks at Paul's letters for instances in which the given pattern, convention, or practice seems to be in play. The Pauline passages are then interpreted in light of what has been learned about the Greco-Roman world. Part III lists passages in which the interested reader can take what has been learned and see other instances of it across the Pauline and Paulinist corpus. Part IV is an up-to-date bibliography of works on the assigned topic, works written either by researchers who are classicists in training or by New Testament scholars. As each of the chapters is fresh research, every essay bids to be the best and most authoritative treatment of the subject, and its bibliography will let the curious reader see what others have said on the matter.

The Seven Unquestioned Letters and the Paulinist Letters

Each of the studies assumes that Paul certainly wrote the following seven letters: Romans, 1 and 2 Corinthians, Galatians, Philippians, 1 Thessalonians, and Philemon. Hardly anyone disputes that those letters are authentic. Accordingly, the portraits of Paul and the passages discussed come primarily from those letters. The phrase "Paulinist letters" refers to those texts about which varying degrees of doubts have been raised as to whether in fact Paul wrote them. They include 2 Thessalonians, Ephesians, Colossians, and the Pastoral Epistles (1 and 2 Timothy and Titus) and are frequently mentioned in Part III of the essays where passages are listed for further consideration.

Ways to Use This Volume

1. Persons who want to learn more about Paul and the world of which he was a part will be treated to reading what some of the leading scholars in the world understand about Paul and his context.

2. Those who want to dig further on their own should go to Part III of any essay and look at the Pauline and Paulinist passages cited there for more references illustrating a given theme or topic.

3. One could also study a particular Pauline letter in light of the essays in this volume that treat that epistle. For example, several chapters deal in some detail with Galatians, admittedly with distinct questions in mind, but together they generate quite a conversation about how to read Galatians (compare the essays of Engberg-Pedersen, Walters, Ramsaran, Sampley). The same could be done for other letters, even Philemon (Hock, Harrill).

4. The book can also be read with a view to seeing the ways in which the modern world is at once like and at other times quite dissimilar from the world in Paul's time.

5. Occasionally the different essays will treat common topics; very seldom does that produce redundancy. Rather, most often the distinctive essays will stress particular nuances that call for some resolution. For a clear case in point,

note the different chapters that necessarily treat the very basic topic of education (Hock and Ramsaran) or the impact of house structures on family and social engagement (White and Balch).

6. At times different essays examine the same passages, from distinctive angles of vision and with different questions in mind.

7. The book could itself frame an extended Bible study or a class.

In each of the above instances, the question must arise whether there are any patterns in Paul's embrace of, dismissal of, or tweaking of social conventions and practices—a topic to which this introduction will turn at its conclusion.

Assumptions and Cautionary Remarks

The Mediterranean world in Paul's time was first Hellenized and then Romanized. Roman policy wisely allowed the continued practice of indigenous religions, especially if they were old, established ones; Roman authorities viewed new religions as suspect, much the same as many people today look at cults with jaundiced eyes. Cultic practice of indigenous religions may not have been systematically affected by the Romanization of the world, but nobody living in the Mediterranean basin escaped the day-to-day influence of Rome. It colored the economic and social transactions of everyone. For example, David Balch's essay shows how even house design was influenced across the area. Peter Lampe's essay demonstrates that everyone, Jews and non-Jews, found themselves in the vertical structure of the patronal system. And every essay could be mentioned in this same vein.

Among some scholars, there is an unspoken assumption that Paul's indebtedness to Judaism is safe and pure while the suggestion that Paul actually employed Hellenistic or Roman categories is somehow tainted and dangerous, theologically. Put in other terms, some Pauline interpreters have a theological prejudice in favor of seeing Paul's roots in Judaism and stressing those roots. I surely affirm Paul's Jewishness and salute his sense of freely embracing Jewish traditions as a means and even as a ground for his proclamation, and therefore for his self-expressions in his letters. Why, however, must the interpretation be either/or? Why should it be cast as better or worse? The supposition behind this book is both/and. The decision to affirm both Paul's Jewish *ethos* and at the same time his Greco-Roman *ethos* is not a theological choice offered over against what I have labeled a theological prejudice in favor of Judaism. On the contrary, the judgment that both must ultimately be considered is not an option but rather a necessity, given that all the Judaisms at the time of Christian beginnings are already Hellenized. They are already stamped in some measure by the all-pervasive influence of the Greco-Roman world and its *ethos*. Even Qumran, clearly the Judaism most determined to escape what it considered the contamination of the outside world, pictures the end-time staging of the apocalyptic army of the faithful in the model of the Roman army, with its centurions, its banners, and its organization of the troops (see the War Scroll). Accordingly, *among the many sources we have for studying the Greco-Roman world* in and around Paul's times are the contemporary Jewish writings themselves. For that reason, contributors were asked to consider Jewish traditions, documents, and other evidence *as part of* the Greco-Roman world (Watson's essay is exemplary in this way).

The Greco-Roman world was Paul's world. Accordingly, we cannot speak of Paul's having "borrowed" this or that Hellenistic or Roman tradition, convention, or practice. Neither can we use expressions that suggest that Paul is "adopting" the guise of a Roman; the encoded message in such claims is that Paul is reassuringly really a Jew after all. Paul was a Roman Jew, both together. To take him as anything else is to distort the realities of his letters. This volume's stress of Paul's free and ready capacities to engage his predominantly Gentile auditors in their own terms and on their own grounds is not a rejection of Paul's Jewishness; rather, it is an attempt to develop the larger picture with care.

One other consideration merits attention. In the nineteenth century, people used the metaphor of grain and talked about distinguishing the kernel—the essential, positive content—from the husk, that outer, superfluous case in which the most important part was sheathed. One underlying assumption was that the husk was a worthless, unnecessary over-layer that could be absolutely distinguished from the heart of the matter and cast aside, like chaff. Another supposition was that the kernel was not really affected by the husk, which was simply taken to be a neutral, often culturally contingent container.

A similar set of assumptions has sometimes been operative in interpretations of Paul. Under this line of thinking, Paul's "co-option" or "borrowing" of Hellenistic or Roman conceptions or conventions or practices was simply his creative way of packaging the gospel: he used Greek and Roman husks as ways of packaging what was the kernel, the real gospel that he wanted to preach. Far be it from me to argue that Paul was not an opportunist! He used whatever opening, opportunity, or situation that presented itself as an occasion to preach. Witness his preaching to the Galatians just because he fell sick while traveling through their province (Gal 4:13), or his preaching to the Pretorian guards because they happened to be the ones enforcing his captivity (Phil 1:13).

The gospel, however, has never been presented without some incarnation in socially viable conventions and assumptions. There is no such thing as a version of the gospel without culturally situated suppositions and conventions. Therefore the kernel-and-husk imagery is totally misleading and is a misrepresentation of what we face in Paul's letters. Perforce, the only valid gospel expressions are the ones pertinent to and viable for the speaker and the auditors. Communication, by its very nature, always works within the confines and employs the richness of the sociocultural assumptions of the communicators. Similarly, there is no gospel without its being cast in the conventions and assumptions of the times.

Therefore, the following essays do not offer a chance to cut through what might be deemed cultural dross to see the "real" gospel. Rather, each chapter is, in its second part, a study of Paul's creative expression of an aspect of his good news in the only means that Paul had at hand, namely in the social and cultural conventions of his time.

The Degree of Paul's Affiliation with Greco-Roman Conventions and Practices

If we were to imagine a continuum that ran from nearly complete Pauline identification with Greco-Roman practices and conventions to the most minimal connection we would find the following essays taking different places across the continuum. No doubt Engberg-Pedersen's essay would be far toward complete Pauline identification. Others find differing degrees of accommodation and identification.

Possible Patterns in the Way Paul Relates to the Social Conventions of His Time

We cannot dispute that Paul knew and incorporated social conventions—because, as I just argued, to live and to speak or write necessitates doing so. The critical issue, however, and the exciting window onto Paul comes when Paul takes the structure that the society offered him and changes it or tweaks it. For example, Paul embraces the patron-client configuration and places Christ or God at the apex, where the emperor normally resides. Paul's modifications and transpositions of contemporary cultural and social conventions and practices are the most telling junctures for identifying what Paul thinks is most important. So the reader or scholar of Paul does well to note where Paul abandons, transforms, opposes, or offers an alternative to what might have been expected in that time and in that culture. Precisely in the aberrations, in the points of dissonance, one may hope to take Paul's pulse.

In what follows I hope to make some initial steps toward identifying some of the patterns of Paul's relations to the cultural and social conventions and practices in which he and his auditors lived. I invite others to build on, and if need be correct, what is offered.

The Problem—Paul's Relation to Culture— and an Initial Sortie

Paul is thoroughly conversant with the conventions and practices of his day. The engaging issue is how far he accommodates and where and when and why he alters, differs, and departs from the practices (and of course the "why" question, even when it cannot clearly and obviously be answered, is the most telling one).

Surely, it is too early to arrive at the big picture in all its nuances, but the very collection of this many essays, each showing Paul in varying degrees of consonance and dissonance with the cultural values and practices of his time, raises the question whether we can discern any patterns in the times that Paul appears to embrace cultural notions and the times that he appears to distance himself from them. Put in different terms: can we figure out why Paul finds some conventions and practices thoroughly acceptable and modifies or even drops others? And to nuance the same question in an important way, can we discern why Paul uses some conventions and practices in some situations and does not employ them in others?

The word "culture" in the title of this section is used not as a technical term but as an umbrella designed to cover topics such as those noted earlier: social conventions, practices, values. In my pursuit of Paul's relation to culture, I want to assess how and in what ways he employs widely accepted practices and values and how and in what ways he seeks to separate himself from them.

The distinctiveness of Paul's apocalyptic vision is that the believers all live inescapably in two aeons, two ages, at the same time. Courtesy of God's grace, believers are already granted to be part of the new creation. Just as surely, however, they now live the new life in Christ in the middle of the old aeon, in the world marked by sin's corrupting power. There are the ways of faith (Paul identifies them as his own ways also; 1 Cor 4:17) and the ways of the world. Accordingly, Paul urges the Romans not to "be conformed to this aeon," understood as evil, but to "be transformed by the renewal" of their minds (12:2; cf. Gal 1:4). Likewise, he tries to counsel the Corinthians to live at an eschatological arm's length from the world when he writes: "I mean, brothers and sisters, the time is shortened; henceforth, let even the ones with wives comport themselves as if not, and the ones weeping, as if not weeping, the ones rejoicing, as if not rejoicing, and the ones frequenting the mall, as if not possessing, and the ones using the world, as if not using it" (1 Cor 7:29–31). He is after the same thing with the Galatians when he advises of his singular boast "in the cross of our Lord Jesus Christ," which provides him with a sort of double insulation from the world, as follows: "the cross has crucified the world to me and the cross has crucified me to the world" (Gal 6:14).

Paul notes what we might call a disconnect between what the world sees and knows and the reality of his life. The world's judgment about him and such apostles is that they are impostors whom nobody knows, who seem to be poor, punished, suffering, and dying. How wrong they are! In truth, Paul and other apostles like him are true, alive, and rejoicing; they are brokers of richness, and in fact possess everything. Superficial assessment that is content to rely on externals and appearances will inevitably err (cf. 2 Cor 4:16–18; 5:12). People who do not understand may remain in their darkness. Outsiders' views and assessments are never indicators of one's true worth.

Not only is there apocalyptic detachment for Paul; there is apocalyptic engagement. Stoics gained freedom by rehearsing what was under their control and being careful to distinguish all those things that were not under their control. Put differently, Stoics enhanced their freedom by a strategy of withdrawal from all those entanglements that bid to weave them into some sort of dependency, or that through their passions tied them to others. Stoic freedom employed the tactic of retreating from—minimizing—risk and the exposure to risk. For Stoics, the greatest freedom was achieved by risking the least, by exposing themselves to others to the minimum. Some of Paul's followers, in their Qumran-like eagerness to insure their holiness by withdrawal from society and its entanglements, would have raised the ante on the Stoic mentality.

The key: Once Paul understood that the gospel not only did not call for a wholesale retreat from the world and its practices but also allowed, even encouraged, engagement of the world, the door was open for his creative, even if ambiguous relation to the culture and its categories.

Two Models of Paul's Ambiguous Relation to Traditions and Conventions

One Model: Switch Social Patterns as Needed. Paul sometimes deals with cultural ambiguities by adopting distinctive cultural commonplaces that may be in tension with one another, using one for certain purposes and using another, distinctive commonplace to express another aspect of his convictions. For example, Paul employs the vertically ordered notions of patronage and the *pater familias,* the head of the household, for limited purposes when it suits him, but he clearly shifts to different social conventions when he wants to advance a radically different social structure—one of equality—among believers. Rather than critique either of these two social conventions, Paul simply shifts from the one to another when the first would neither meet his needs nor fit his convictions.

Let us briefly consider patronage and *pater familias,* two topics with chapters in this volume. As you will see, patronage makes the Roman world go 'round and weaves a web of social reciprocity, dependency, and obligation. As Seneca, a Roman moralist and rhetorician roughly contemporary with Paul, put it, "The giving of a benefit is a social act, it wins the good will of someone, it lays someone under obligation" (*Ben.* 5.11.1). Gratitude he considered simply "the first installment on his debt" (*Ben.* 2.22.1). The giving and receiving of gifts and associated honor build enduring social bonds and create the context for future, further actions of beneficence and patronage. Refusal of patronal gifts is unthinkable because it constitutes social rebuke; similarly, failure to reciprocate is inconceivable.

Paul embraces the patronal and patriarchal hierarchy with reference to God. God's eminence and power are assumed and affirmed across the corpus (see, just from 1 Corinthians, 8:6; 10:26; 11:3; 15:24–28). By linking all his cosmic claims about God's preeminence to God understood as Father (cf. all the letter salutations and 1 Cor 15:24), a notion not particularly well-represented in Israel's traditions (cf. Ps 2), Paul effectively personalizes the understanding of God, who might otherwise be thought of as distant and disconnected (cf. 2 Cor 1:3, in which God's pity/mercy/compassion is linked to God's being Father). Christ is God's son (Rom 1:9; 5:10; 8:3, 29, 32; 1 Cor 1:9; Gal 1:16; 4:4; 1 Thess 1:10), and believers, by the working of the Holy Spirit, are God's children who become God's heirs (Rom 8:15; Gal 4:6). God the ultimate Patron and the ultimate Father cares for the dependent ones and rightly deserves honor and thankfulness. Believers possess all things because they belong to Christ who belongs to God (1 Cor 3:21–23); believers inherit all things because they have God as their Father.

The Greco-Roman world is structured primarily vertically. By contrast, Paul's vision of the believing community, of the relations among believers, is decidedly not vertical. Rather, for Paul, believers stand on the common ground provided by God's grace equally given to each and to all.

Paul's ready employment of "father" nomenclature for God (and even for himself on occasion; cf. 1 Cor 4:15; 2 Cor 11:2; Phlm 10) inevitably carries hierarchical freight. Insofar as it does it makes it easier for Paul's followers to think that their relation to God (and to Paul) has great similarities to the rest of their vertically structured life that they know so well in the world. Furthermore, and this is critical, nowhere does Paul try to deny or even modify the hierarchical burden of the patriarchal language. The goals to which he directs the paternal claims are distinctively his own and express his own faith. Paul treats the father imagery as if it causes him no problem; he freely embraces it with respect to God (and in some circumstances to himself), and seems to find in it a helpful way of saying things about God (and about himself) and by extension about his dependent followers. So, Paul and his gospel do not manifest a critique of paternal references.

The believing community, as Paul sees it, is not hierarchical, ideally. All believers have the common definition as those for whom Christ has died, or, more specifically, as those who have died with Christ. In Paul's view, believers are *all alike* dependent on God's grace; they are all justified and reconciled by God and not by any performance or standing of their own. Any differences among them are not the signs of distinctions of status, but.of the diversity that enriches their unity in Christ and enhances their service of the common good.

In order to express his deep, abiding conviction that believers are those who all weep when one weeps, who all are incensed when one among them is caused to stumble, and who all celebrate when one rejoices, Paul must turn to a metaphor or image other than a culturally defined hierarchical image. His answer is to use familial terms and expressions of friendship.

In the family of God, no one has any special status over another. No charisma carries exalted status; instead, the charisma obligates service to the common good (1 Cor 12). Wisdom and wealth, and their associated worldly status, exalt no one in the community of faith. To express this mutuality and equality of believers, Paul turns to the socially and culturally available models of family and friendship. Rather than build an evidential base for these claims of mine in this space, I refer you to this volume's essays that treat the topics of family and friendship (also, compare Philemon, in which everybody in that little letter is a brother or sister to someone else).

In this first model, Paul takes cultural conventions and values, uses them when they help him, and shifts to another cultural convention or value when his needs change. Hierarchical structures function fine regarding God and even work at important times when Paul needs to take responsibility for the well-being of the communities of faith. When, however, Paul wants to discourse about the relations between and among believers, he readily turns to the picture of them as brothers and sisters—with God as Father. And he stays with the familial terminology even while he front-loads it with friendship conventions and even when he wants to make certain distinctions among the believers with regard to their charismata (or with regard to their measure of faith; cf. Rom 12:3). Admittedly, his occasional embrace of hierarchical categories probably encouraged some of his followers to drag hierarchical distinctions into the community (see 1 Cor 11:21–22).

In this first model Paul takes certain conventions and uses them for particular, but limited, purposes. And rather than critique those cultural values or practices, when they no longer fit his purpose, he simply shifts to a different cultural convention.

Another Model: Switch Social Patterns as Needed. In this model, Paul embraces the categories of values that all his readers or auditors would have known and uses the values' terminology, but his relation to them can indeed be quite complex. An illustrative dyad is shame and honor, the governing paradigm of the Greco-Roman world. Basically, the majority of people in that world, at whatever level of social status they found themselves, would be aiming to do whatever they could to garner praise and honor for themselves. Those same people would be just as intent on avoiding or at least minimizing blame and shame. All the transactions of life, the decisions one made, the goals to which one aspired, all of them passed through the honor-shame, praise-blame filter. And, universally, that filter was set assiduously to increase honor and decrease shame. Honor and shame were available in every human encounter, from the most public to the most intimate and private.

Paul's relation to this dominant social dyad is exquisitely complex. To grasp what Paul does with it, we have to do what parliamentarians would call dividing the question. First, we need to consider shame/blame and honor/praise discourse separately, because Paul relates to them distinctly. Further, at times he employs the cultural values of shame and honor and uses them in line with the widespread patterns; at other times, however, he keeps the terminology but basically alters the original values. First, then, to shame/blame.

At several points across the corpus, Paul uses shame as it would be employed in the larger world. At those points he expects shame to attract the same social opprobrium, and he embraces its culturally assumed negative value for its usefulness in eliciting a change of behavior. In short, Paul also uses shame and blame as a *social sanction* to discourage a particular behavior (e.g., 1 Cor 4:14; 5:11; 11:4–6, 17; 15:34; cf. 2 Thess 3:14). In all these instances, shame and dishonor function in Paul's letters as they do in the wider world. In the cited instances, he simply shares the culture's value of shame and uses it where he finds it helpful.

Paul's treatment of honor is different. He still employs the same terminology that his contemporaries used. He writes of honor and glory. He knows that *epainos*, which we may translate with a range of terms such as "praise," "approval," "recognition," is good and, when properly understood, desirable. In that he shares his culture's convictions. But what makes Paul's view on this matter distinctive is what we might call the proper understanding of honor, of its source, and of its significance.

To keep matters in perspective we must note that Paul's critique of cultural shame and honor is not the only dissenting voice in his time. From the Cynics through to Stoics like Seneca (*De Const.* 13.2, 5) and Epictetus (*Diatr.* 2.9.15), and indeed on to Dio Chrysostom, one can trace such critiques. But among them, Paul's appraisal is distinctive.

Something radical happened to the category of shame for Paul when he found the central claim of his gospel to be grounded in the cross where Jesus was crucified. Crucifixion was the ultimate Roman sanction; nothing was more shameful. By comparison, exile paled; so did being renounced by one's family or *polis* (city). Paul's whole-hearted embrace of the cross (and its inexorable Pauline connection with resurrection) necessitated a fundamental critique of its culturally associated shame. In what may almost be considered defiance, Paul declares himself not ashamed of the gospel that centers on the cross, that ultimate object of social disgrace. He is confident that he will not be shamed in preaching the gospel of the cross (2 Cor 10:8; Phil 1:20).

If no shame can be visited upon believers from those outside the faith because God is with and for them, then believers owe it to one another to love one another (Rom 13:8) and to make certain that whatever they say and do must not shame and dishonor others for whom Christ died. That is why Paul rebukes (itself a public shaming in this instance because the letter is presumably read aloud to the congregation) the wealthy Corinthians for shaming those who "have nothing" and who arrive later at the Lord's supper (1 Cor 11:22).

The cross, the ultimate marker of social shame in the Greco-Roman world, becomes the central symbol of the believers. Talk about turning the world upside down. And because honor is the reciprocal of shame, the same transvaluation has to be claimed for honor in the Pauline world. In fact the change on both fronts, honor and shame, is so profound that the terms could have proved unusable by Paul. We will consider a few of Paul's numerous honor references that are refracted in the light of the cross.

Paul's revisionist, totally alien view of honor can be laid out in this countercultural way: the honor that counts comes from God, not from others, and not from ourselves. Paul's ideal character, cast for his own purposes in Romans as one whose circumcision is inward and a matter of the heart, receives his praise "not from people but from God" (Rom 2:29). Similarly, to the Corinthians he declares that the only commendation that counts is the one from God (1 Cor 4:5).

Paul debunks comparison with others, the staple by which the shame-honor system of the Greco-Roman world operated (2 Cor 10:12). He also disparages self-commendation, affirming again that the only commendation that counts is from God (2 Cor 10:18). Paul's ironic view of worldly honor, praise, and commendation may understandably be seen when he commends himself by reference to his hardships and difficulties, which serve to show, as he says in 2 Corinthians, that the Lord's power is perfected in weakness (2 Cor 12:9).

Honor among Pauline believers is garnered by working hard for the propagating and inculcating of the gospel (for more on this, see Agosto's essay on commendation). The regular cultural drive to seek honor is condoned by Paul so long as two conditions are met: one should seek the true honor and seek it in appropriate ways.

Early in Romans, Paul addresses both of these issues together in 2:7–11. First, let me translate the text, and then we can analyze it.

> To those who are persisting in good work and seeking glory and honor and immortality, eternal life. To those who are factious and disobedient to the truth, who are obedient to wickedness, wrath and fury. Tribulation and anguish upon every last person who works evil, Jew first, also Greek. Glory and honor and peace to everyone who works the good, Jew first, also Greek. For there is no partiality with God.

The parallels within this passage are extraordinarily structured from beginning to end. In an *inclusio,* the text opens and closes with affirmations of good works and with rewards for the ones who do them. In contrast, note the parallel regarding the ones who work evil: their rewards are wrath, fury, tribulation, and anguish. The rewards awaiting the ones who do good are variously and richly described: eternal life, glory, honor, and peace. Those who persist patiently in doing good work and who seek the honor that counts are here assured that they will receive it. But this is not the honor that the world can give; rather, it is an honor available only from God. It is an honor that is appropriately associated with the glory and peace that only God can bestow. The only way appropriately to seek that God-given honor is by doing the good, by working the good, by persisting in good work. No wonder Paul affirms a divine judgment based on the works that love has generated (cf. Gal 5:6; 2 Cor 5:10).

The notion of believers pursuing rewards may seem strange in this post-Lutheran world where any sense of striving may seem out of order, but it is not strange for Paul or his communities. Paul knows that (even) he has not yet received the ultimate gift, resurrection from the dead; he knows that (even) he has not yet reached full maturity, but he does—and these are his own words—"pursue it so as to seize it, because I have been seized by Christ Jesus; brothers and sisters, I do not reckon that I have seized it; but one thing I do . . . I pursue the prize that is the object of the upward call" (Phil 3:12–14). Note well that Paul's pursuing and striving originates *in his having already been seized* by Christ Jesus. That same linkage lies behind his call for the Philippians to "work out their salvation with fear and trembling"—which sounds totally un-Pauline unless you also read the rest of the sentence: "because God is at work in you, both to will and to work for God's good pleasure" (2:13). Pursuing awards, in particular pursuing honor, would not have seemed strange to Paul's audiences. His grounding of all the pursuing and seizing, however, in believers having been seized by Christ Jesus would have sounded strange to them at first.

In a section of Romans (14:18–19), Paul tells the Romans that they should stop judging one another (echoed from 2:1–5), that they should determine not to put stumbling blocks or hindrances in the way of other brothers or sisters, in short that they should "walk in love" (14:15). In that context he addresses the honor question in two directions, before God and in relation to one's fellow human beings. "The one who is thus enslaved to Christ [that is, who is walking in love] is pleasing to God and approved by humans" (Rom 14:18). That is straight honor talk, but recast in Paul's categories. The first, what is pleasing to God, echoes Rom 12:1–2, in which Paul appealed to the Roman believers to "present your bodies as a living sacrifice" and coupled that with his call for them to "figure out and do" (*dokimazein*) what is pleasing to God (12:2). In 14:13–19, Paul details what pleases God: no longer judging one another (stated in the negative) but presently walking in love (declared positively). To walk in love is pleasing to God and thereby places the love-walker in the position of honor before God. Coincidentally, not only is love the occasion for God's pleasant honor, it also gains the favor of people, Paul claims (Rom 14:18). In this text, Paul uses the adjective *dokimos* (translated there as "approved"), which I have elsewhere translated as "tried and true," to describe the proper recognition and honor bestowed by other believers.

Paul caps off his argument with the appeal: "Therefore, then, let us pursue [that same verb again] the things that make for peace and the things that build up one another" (Rom 14:19). So much is encapsulated in this little verse. First, Paul supposes that the human pursuing he urges is grounded in proper servitude to Christ. Second, because believers have peace with God, as he has argued earlier in Rom 5:1, they must become agents of peace; they must pursue the things that bear on peace. And in his call for attention to the things that "build up one another," he is using his own personal code language for love. Love and edification are hand in glove in Paul's thought-world, as he expresses it directly to the Corinthians: "Knowledge puffs up; love builds up" (1 Cor 8:1). Later in the same letter, he directly encourages the Corinthians: "Pursue love" (14:1). It is not only okay to pursue the honor that comes with the expression of love; the pursuit of love is an obligation, it is the proper expression of faith, of one's relation to God. As Paul writes the Galatians, circumcision and uncircumcision do not matter, but faith working itself out in love does matter (Gal 5:6). So it turns out that, in the Pauline circle, *proper, enduring honor is the by-product of the proper exercise of love.*

With regard to shame and honor, Paul rejiggers the values; he adulterates the currency. Shame and honor are no longer reckoned on one's achieved or inherited status; honor is not a product of one's endless and energetic efforts to enhance one's standing through manipulation of the system. Honor is simply and profoundly bestowed by God. It is reckoned on God's terms. It is allocated as God pleases. And no believer is left out of the honor. Accordingly, believers no longer calculate human relations on what they can get out of the engagement; instead, they ask what love requires in this and that circumstance. Radically and even subversively, they seek the advantage of the other; they seek what builds up or edifies the neighbor. And most surprisingly, and requiring an incredible amount of trust in God, they come to realize that their own self-interests are cared for *not* by securing themselves first but by honoring their neighbors in love.

So we have seen two models that Paul uses in his ambiguous relation to the culture around him. There surely must be more, but these two are the predominant models and can be demonstrated time and again across the corpus.

At every point, though, it is Paul's convictions that govern and trump the cultural conventions and social values of his world. Never the other way around. The gospel is his filter, his lens through which he sees and evaluates all things. Paul is convinced that believers already live in the new creation, even while walking in the evil aeon. They have a new lord; they have to live in such a way as to please their new lord. Paul is confident that each believer, like a proper house servant, will be enabled to stand before that Lord and his judgment (2 Cor 5:10).

I

PAUL AND ADAPTABILITY

Clarence E. Glad

The purpose of this chapter is to draw attention to some of the ways in which the idea of *adaptability* was understood in Greco-Roman antiquity and in Paul. The study of adaptability in Paul is a complicated task for several reasons. One is that the term "adaptability" does not lend itself to precise definition. That difficulty is not unique; it is part of any thematic analysis. A second reason is more equivocal and is related to established conventions in Pauline scholarship. One searches in vain for the entry "adaptability" in indexes of scholarly publications on Paul; it is simply not a household word in Pauline scholarship, as are concepts such as *law, the righteousness of God, faith in/of Jesus, covenant, salvation, eschatology,* and *apocalypticism.*

"Theology" is also a word that most scholars do not have any qualms about using when explicating Pauline thought. Fewer scholars would use the term "religion" for the same purpose. That has not always been the case. Around the turn of the nineteenth century, for example, German scholars were more prone to use the term "religion" than "theology"; indeed, a lively debate took place as to which term better suited Paul. Such a debate keeps alive an important question, namely, to what extent should terms not used by persons in the past be used when we try to explain what those persons meant? This question applies to the terms "theology" and "religion" as well as to the term "adaptability." The topic of adaptability is not necessarily absent, although the term is absent.[1] Indeed, the concept of adaptability captures a social convention that was part of the Greco-Roman context in which Paul and his audiences were at home, a convention that has not received due attention in previous Pauline scholarship.

Part I. Adaptability in the Greco-Roman World

The idea of adaptability in the Greco-Roman world was common during Paul's time among different segments of society throughout the Mediterranean basin.

Although it is impossible to measure with precision the presence of cultural mores in the common consciousness of the general public, the different contexts in which the ideal and requirement of adaptability manifested itself show how widespread the concept was, at least among the cultured elite. It was a concern of politicians, public speakers, philosophers, religious leaders, and even stage actors. The pervasiveness of discussions about variability across different periods, genres, styles, and schools is unquestionable, reflecting a general cultural preoccupation of Greco-Roman Hellenism. As such we can speak of it as a social convention. The many possible ramifications of this widespread tradition for different segments of the population, or how, for example, it might relate to the ethical positions of the philosophical schools of the Hellenistic period, have still to be mapped out.[2]

Today adaptability is discussed, for example, inside ecological anthropology, focusing on human adaptability to the environment in the light of both cultural and biological factors. Adaptability is also discussed in theoretical educational literature and among psychologists with regard to human development and the importance of appropriate pedagogical methods at different life stages. In order to survive, a person must develop skills in order to maximize the possibility for successful adjustment, making use of natural or acquired aptitudes and appropriate training. The same is true of influencing others in their development; one must know when and how to appropriately adjust to the respective dispositions of the recipients.

"Adaptation" is a relational term; one must adapt or adjust something to something else, as for example one's conduct or speech to others in specific circumstances. As a relational concept the term refers to that which needs to be adapted and that to which it needs to be adapted. It relates to a person's character, task, and goals, and the various circumstances and types of persons encountered. These reflections draw attention on the one hand to the adaptable person and to the necessary requisites for successful adaptation, including the person's natural or acquired aptitudes and rhetorical, philosophical, or religious training. On the other hand, whatever needs to be adapted must be adjusted appropriately to that to which it is accommodated. This second focus centers on different characters and their dispositions.

In Greco-Roman discussions of these issues, different character types emerge in view of idealized characteristics. Before discussing these idealized character types, I first discuss briefly one aspect of adaptability. The importance of adaptability as a literary and rhetorical *topos* can be seen in the rhetorical handbooks. Language was an instrument of persuasion. Indeed, the first duty of an orator was to speak suitably in order to persuade.[3] Three kinds of proofs contributed to successful persuasion: the moral character of the speaker (*ethos*), the speech (*logos*) itself with its arguments, and the rousing of the hearers to emotion (*pathos*). The rhetorical handbooks included extensive discussions of ways to arouse hearers to specific emotion in light of their dispositions and psychological states, to which the rhetor needed to adapt.[4]

Adaptation in speech, often discussed under the rubrics of propriety of speech and character portrayal, had to factor in the various conditions of the addressees in an attempt to be discriminating. Rhetoricians were acutely aware of the extent to which their delivery could affect the reception of their discourses. Orators needed to know how to speak appropriately at the "opportune moment" in order to have the desired impact on their audiences. A certain coordination of the orator, the subject matter, and the audience was necessary according to the time, occasion, place, and circumstances of delivery of a discourse. Other aspects which orators needed to keep in mind regarding the auditors included age, sex, family relations, social status or position, vocation, previous experience and achievements, aspirations, disposition, and character types displaying certain passions, habits, beliefs, or opinions. Finally, the texture of the audience was important, for example, whether it consisted of a single person or a group, whether it was the senate, the populace of a city, judges, or private individuals.

The same concern is evident among progymnasmatic writers and letter writers who discussed various forms of elementary exercises and epistolary types. Both elementary exercises and different epistolary types were analyzed from the perspective of their persuasiveness in specific settings, as can be seen, for example, in Pseudo-Libanius's and Pseudo-Demetrius's description of epistolary types.[5] Elementary exercises were also discussed with a view to their contextual suitability and use in epideictic oratory, for training in the assembly, or for the court orator. Theon's discussion of resources for argumentation in personification points out that such resources all center upon the persuasiveness of character portrayal in specific settings. These argumentative techniques could maximize the persuasive effect of a discourse by, for example, lending a voice to people of different nationality, race, or community, or to characters of specific dispositions.[6]

The adaptability *topos* is structured on diametrically opposed character types and professions, each of which came to have quite precise collocations in Greco-Roman society during Hellenistic times among pagan, Jewish, and early Christian writers. The most common positive examples were teachers, fathers, and doctors. Other related types were mothers, nurses, philosophers, generals, pilots, counselors, friends and moral guides, and the orator. The most common negative examples were flatterers, demagogues, and "the friends of many."

Reflection on these idealized types in different contexts clarifies the requirements such persons needed to be successful in their tasks. All of these persons were involved in persuading, guiding, supervising, or caring for others. All had to descend to the level of their respective addressees, for example the teacher tutoring his or her students, the father bringing up his child, and the physician attending a sick patient. They all had to be adequately prepared for their respective tasks. Physicians needed to know the symptoms of various diseases in order to be able to diagnose patients correctly. They also needed to know the different types of drugs and when and how to apply them. Pilots needed to know the ship's equipment as well as the weather conditions in order to be able to bring the ship safely to her destination. And, finally, moral guides needed to know the human condition in order to be able to apply their words appropriately in the task of reforming others.

These individuals had not only to be well-prepared in their particular vocation but also with regard to their moral standing. They had to go through a period of introspection and self-scrutiny in order to know that their motives were honorable and true. Their behavior under all circumstances had to be genuinely directed at the well-being of others. They had to be trustworthy and to display a perfect conformity of word and deed. This harmonization of speech and behavior draws attention to an important aspect of the topic of adaptability, namely, the question of stability and change in personal appearance, customs, convictions, beliefs, and language.

Ideally, the above characters were viewed as "one and the same" persons regardless of their involvement with people in different situations. As such they were considered reliable and trustworthy. That, however, was not the case with characters of the opposite pole. Flatterers and related character types, such as the obsequious person, the pretentious person, the self-deprecator, the charlatan, and "the friends of many," brought to the fore the negative side of variability. In their ability to adapt both in speech and behavior, flatterers came to epitomize the multidimensional, hypocritical, and unscrupulous persons whose behavior was depreciated by moralists who valued consistency of character:

> . . .[T]he flatterer, since he has no abiding-place of character to dwell in, and since he leads a life not of his own choosing but another's, moulding and adapting himself to suit another, is not simple, not one, but variable and many in one, and, like water that is poured into one receptacle after another, he is constantly on the move from place to place, and changes his shape to fit his receiver.[7]

Several additional characteristics can be identified as recurring features in discussions of the flatterer in Greco-Roman antiquity. Flatterers have only their personal advantage in view. They speak in order to please, praise indiscriminately, are charming, affable, and witty. In rendering their "services" they accommodate themselves to those they flatter, and are cunning in their versatility. In their multiform manifestations the all-adaptable flatterers had learned to "play the second part in word and in deed." This proverbial phrase referred to mime-players acting a second part, imitating the chief actor in word and gesture. Changeable creatures, such as the chameleon, the polyp, the cuttlefish, and the sea god Proteus, were often cited for comparison in criticism of flatterers. Flatterers were also likened to ticks, gadflies, woodworms, vultures, ravens, puppies, or apes. Professions such as prostitution and cookery were also used to enhance the comparison. Culinary art was a form of flattery; the purpose of cooks, as that of prostitutes and flatterers, was to provide pleasure.

In addition to these analogies, flatterers were compared to the friends of many, as for example in Plutarch's *On Having Many Friends.* Flatterers and friends of many, as well as politicians, were contrasted with true, stable, dependable friends. Although occasionally the conduct of flatterers and genuine friends, themselves belonging to these opposite poles, might be the same, there were distinctive, more characteristic or permanent features that separated them. Friends who say something positive might thereby provide pleasure, but that, contrary to flatterers, was not their sole or even primary purpose. Friends mainly had the advantage of others in view. In order to achieve the well-being of others they might even have to impart some pain.[8] At times, they also had to be willing to behave, like flatterers, in a manner that could be construed by outside observers as an unscrupulous variability.

The inherent ambiguity in the ethic of adaptability shows itself clearly in reactions to Homer's versatile hero, Odysseus, "the man of many turns," who was either criticized for changing his character or hailed for his chameleon-like adaptability in social intercourse. Odysseus's detractors interpreted the term πολύ-τροπος (*polytropos*), used in the first line of Homer's *Odyssey*—"Tell me, Muse, of the polytropic man"—pejoratively in the ethical sense of often changing one's character, hence being unprincipled and unscrupulous. Others rallied to Odysseus's defense, interpreting the term as denoting his skill in adapting his figures of speech ("tropes") to his hearers at any particular time. On the whole, the negative ethical interpretation was more prevalent, comparing the deceitful Odysseus with the *homo duplex* type who hides his true motives, in contrast to the *homo simplex* type like Achilles who speaks candidly. The same ambiguity was present in the Greek terms used to describe human behavior; these equivocal terms were used both positively and negatively, depending on whether the activity in question was valued as resourcefulness or as a manifestation of the duplicity of a trickster. The ambiguity is understandable, because the border between adaptability and hypocrisy is easily crossed, and the intentions of the actors are inaccessible to outside observers.[9]

Responses to Odysseus through the centuries before and after the Common

Era among both pagan and early Christian writers reveal that we are dealing with long-standing traditions and patterns, regardless of whether or not individuals were aware of them through direct exposure to Homer's writings.[10] The ongoing debate about the character Odysseus captures some of the more essential features associated with the adaptability *topos,* especially those centering on idealized character types. During Paul's time, reflections on these opposing character types appear in writings describing the conduct and speech of flatterers and friends. The main contours of the discussions on how to distinguish flatterers and related characters from friends had already been set in the fifth and fourth centuries B.C.E. But that independent works dealing with this issue were composed shows its resurgence during late Republican times and under the early empire. We can see examples of it in Plutarch's *How to Tell a Flatterer from a Friend* and in Maximus of Tyre's work with the same title. Works on flattery by Philodemus also focus on the comparison, as do the works of authors such as Horace, Dio Chrysostom, Epictetus, and Lucian, even though they did not write separate treatises on the topic.[11]

The social matrix of patronage is the context for understanding not only the practices of flatterers and friends but also for comprehending how adaptability is regarded with respect to both types of people. Whether by flatterers or by friends, adaptive association with others has serious social ramifications. Flatterers belonged to the entourages of the rich and powerful; they slavishly accommodated themselves to those of a superior social position.[12] The question of what was involved when people of different social standing came together had been discussed earlier by philosophers in relation to various forms of friendship. They asked specifically whether people of different social and moral standing could become friends. Also, could humans and the gods become friends, given the vast difference in their status? The main questions revolved around equality and inequality, likeness and difference; the attachment of characters from different walks of life, gender, and age; and the proportional responsibilities involved in relationships between people who were not equals.[13]

These questions had to do with cultural norms regarding acceptable behavior, and centered upon habits, customs, and manners that both unite and separate people. In a status-oriented patronal society in which conventions relating to one's social position and occupation were firmly in place, questions regarding the permissible extent of variability in crossing social boundaries were pressing. How should one mingle appropriately with others from different walks of life? Barriers established by one's social role were not to be crossed lightly. Such barriers were not limited to social standing but applied to moral stature as well. Although members of high society might have thought that their social status secured their moral standing, others were quick to note any discrepancy between the two. Association with many was thought to ruin good moral behavior; hence, there were hazards in having many friends or in associating indiscriminately with people from different walks of life.[14] The previously noted ideal of harmonization of word and deed draws attention to the delicate matters of consistency and change in conduct when people of different social and moral standing mingle. One might assume a guise or need to conceal one's true identity when associating with people in circles different from those in which one customarily participated.

Traditional issues associated with the adaptability *topos* converge in works on flattery and the friendship of many. This can be seen in Plutarch's *On Having Many Friends,* in which the issue of association is also crucial:

> [I]t is not a fit thing to be . . . unsparing of our virtue, uniting and intertwining it now with one and now with another, but rather only with those who are qualified to keep up the same participation . . . who are able, in a like manner, to love and participate. For herein plainly is the greatest obstacle of all to having a multitude of friends, in that friendship comes into being through likeness. . . . [H]ow is it possible for friendship to be engendered in differing characters, unlike feelings, and lives which hold to other principles? . . . [I]n our friendship's consonance and harmony there must be no element unlike, uneven, or unequal, but all must be alike to engender agreement in words, counsels, opinions, and feelings, and it must be as if one soul were apportioned among two or more bodies. What man is there, then, so indefatigable, so changeable, so universally adaptable, that he can assimilate and accommodate himself to many persons, without deriding the advice of Theognis when he says: "Copy this trait of the cuttle-fish, which changes its colour / So as to seem to the eye like the rock where it clings?" However, the changes in the cuttle-fish have no depth, but are wholly on the surface, which, owing to its closeness or looseness of texture, takes up the emanations from objects which come near to it; whereas friendships seek to effect a thoroughgoing likeness in characters, feelings, language, pursuits, and dispositions. Such varied adaptation were the task of a Proteus . . . who by magic can change himself often on the very instant from one character to another, reading books with the scholarly, rolling in dust with wrestlers, following the hunt with sportsmen, getting drunk with topers, and taking part in the canvass of politicians, possessing no firmly founded character of his own. . . . [T]he possession of a multitude of friends will necessarily have . . . a soul that is very impressionable, versatile, pliant, and readily changeable. But friendship seeks for a fixed and steadfast character which does not shift about, but continues in one place in one intimacy. For this reason a steadfast friend is something rare and hard to find.[15]

In this text and others Plutarch mixes traditions connected to Odysseus, the sea god Proteus, demagogues, and politicians. Terminology traditionally applied to "the variable and many-sorted man," namely, Odysseus, is now used to sharpen the contrast between servile and multidimensional flatterers and friends of many, on the one hand, and steadfast friends on the other hand.[16]

Plutarch's mundane examples of adaptability all have to do with associating in certain activities with others. Plutarch is not alone in this; similar issues may be found in Seneca's letter *On the Dangers of Association with Our Fellow-Men*[17] and in Epictetus's discourses *That One Should Enter Cautiously into Social Intercourse* and *Of Social Intercourse*. For example, both of the cited treatises of Epictetus include the term *symperifora* in their titles, and the verb *synkatabainein* occurs in both documents—conclusive proof that issues relating to the association with others were part of the adaptability *topos*.[18] Hence the same topics of beguilement, truthfulness, consistency, and change in behavior surface in these discourses as well. When discussing issues relating to the social interaction of people, moralists emphasized that the activity in which one is engaged has an impact on one's feelings, language, disposition, and general character. They also stressed that character is contagious; good and bad manners rub off in a relationship. Two short quotes from Epictetus succinctly exemplify the problem:

> The man who consorts frequently with one person or another either for conversation, or for banquets, or for social purposes in general, is compelled either to become like them himself, or else to bring them over to his own style of living; for if you put by the side of a live coal one that has gone out, either the dead coal will put the live one out, or the latter will kindle the former. Since the risk, then, is so great, we ought to enter cautiously into such social intercourse with the laymen, remembering that it is impossible for the man who brushes up against the person who is covered with soot to keep from getting some soot on himself.[19]

> To this topic you ought to devote yourself before every other, how, namely, you may avoid ever being so intimately associated with one of your acquaintances or friends as to descend to the same level with them; otherwise you will ruin yourself.[20]

In light of such perceived dangers, moralists were concerned with one's personal mien and the best way to adjust to others in different contexts. One occupies, by accident or by training, a certain social position that sets fixed standards and anticipations as to what role one should play under different circumstances and how to interact with persons in different positions. One should not interact lightheartedly with others, at least not too frequently, in order not to lose one's identity. Neither should one enter into a profession without proper preparation, because the role of individuals was demarcated according to fixed patterns of behavior. Preferably, one should stay in the position in which one finds oneself and act one's part appropriately in word and deed, according to established social norms, not "ostensibly" but "in reality."[21]

Concerning association with all and sundry, moralists also discussed how forthcoming one should be toward others and whether and to what extent one should enter into a new relationship with another. One should divulge one's secrets only to those whom one could truly trust. Sparing speech was considered a virtue. The character of the one who speaks much, the babbler, and the poly-pragmatist, who does many things and desires to learn the troubles of others, were depreciated. In light of the perceived tendency of the age to speak ill of others and to expose their shortcomings, these concerns are understandable.[22]

Moralists not only warned of the dangers in associating with people from different walks of life. They also addressed the importance of being flexible when associating with various types of people, for example, when assisting others:

> Practice at some one time a style of living like an invalid, that at some other time you may live like a healthy man. No, that is not our way, but we wish to live like wise men from the very start, and to help mankind. Help indeed! What are you about? Why, have you helped yourself? But you wish to help them progress. Why, have you made progress yourself? Do you wish to help them? Then show them, by your own example, the kind of men philosophy produces, and stop talking nonsense. As you eat, help those who are eating with you; as you drink, those who are drinking with you; by yielding to everybody, giving place, submitting—help men in this way, and don't bespatter them with your own sputum. [23]

This preoccupation with both the positive and negative aspects of adaptability in a wide variety of social settings gives us a sense for the world in which Paul and his readers lived and breathed.

Part II. Adaptability in Paul

Paul's life was indeed multifaceted. Ethnically a Jew, Paul wrote in Greek and was a Roman citizen. He had an agenda that included non-Jews. In his travels as an itinerant recruiter, and through his speaking and writing to various culturally mixed groups, he doubtless encountered common expectations toward transient public speakers and toward psychagogic nurture. As such, Paul was probably aware of his receivers' "horizon of expectations,"[24] regardless of his "formal" education, whether or not it, for example, reached the tertiary level of rhetorical training. We should examine Paul's rhetorical and literary strategies employed in his letters for the general requirement of letter writers to take into account the circumstances of their addressees. Indeed, it has been amply demonstrated that Paul's letters are not haphazard literary productions; they display formal literary and rhetorical features, many of which were developed precisely in order to increase the persuasiveness of a speech or a letter. As such the value of formal literary and rhetorical features was discussed by the ancient writers themselves in light of circumstantial requirements for the delivery of a discourse.[25]

The various circumstantial aspects pointed out by orators, epistolary theorists, and progymnasmatic writers were important for all who employed speech in any type of teacher-student relationship. Differences among students required both sensitivity and adaptability to accommodate them in one's discourse. Regardless of how we classify Paul, throughout his career he was a leader who needed to be attentive to different aptitudes among his converts so that he could adapt his methods in a manner appropriate to their condition. It therefore comes as no surprise to find issues related to psychagogic guidance throughout the Pauline corpus, such as a classification of different types of adherents and the flexible use of hortatory means and techniques. Knowing when, how, and on whom to apply harsh and gentle methods of instruction was paramount, especially when dealing with neophytes, for whom a mixed method of praise and blame was required.[26]

One might be tempted to infer that Paul must have been aware of the concerns regarding adaptability as he faced the task of integrating the ideological viewpoints of his converts. Although such an inference is possible, I resist that temptation because it still has to be demonstrated that Paul shared these concerns and therefore that some of the issues mentioned above can be brought to bear on the interpretation and possible explanation of Pauline texts. My discussion will remain mainly at the level of description, as I draw attention to some of Paul's self-reflective remarks. In particular, I discuss how the issue of association with others is integrated in the larger literary context of the most explicit statement on adaptability in the Pauline corpus, namely, 1 Cor 9:19–23.

The topic of adaptability belongs to the larger context of variability in ancient Greco-Roman sources. It is precisely within the context of the long-standing debate about the uses, abuses, and permissible extent of variability that we should understand Paul's self-avowed adaptability, as one who is "all things to all people" (9:22b). Scholars have tried to identify more precisely the strand within Greco-Roman traditions that influenced this Pauline self-characterization. The major proposals are (1) the epic tales of Odysseus; (2) the Proteus legends; (3) friendship conventions (in particular that of the servile flatterer and the friend of many); (4) Cynic-Stoic arguments about true freedom; (5) the demagoguery *topos* of the enslaved leader; (6) political lore about politicians and factionalists; (7) psychagogic practices; and, finally, (8) divine condescension.[27]

I do not intend to discuss which of these sources may have exerted an influence on Paul, but it is difficult to see how the idea of divine condescension might have been crucial in this regard. First, by Paul's time these various "sources" of adaptability were not easily separable. Indeed, they overlapped to a great extent, notably in their uses of traditional, idealized character types and moral attributes. This mixture of traditions is nowhere better represented than in the previously discussed literature on flattery and friendship. Even in discussions of divine condescension, the same moral attributes were used as a basis for reflection on the nature of God. Although divine manifestations at different times in history reveal a remarkable flexibility in descending to the level of humans, due to their frailty, God still is reckoned unchangeable and reliable.[28]

Second, available evidence indicates that the topic of divine condescension was not prevalent before Paul's time. The terms *synkatabainein* and *synkatabasis*, which were later closely connected to the idea of divine condescension, were not common and were used more often than not by pagan authors to describe human condescension, for example in the questionable crossing of social boundaries or in the accommodation of a person of higher social standing to one of a lower standing.[29] It is not until Clement of Alexandria that the vocabulary associated with the adaptability *topos,* and especially that associated with divine accommodation, begins to appear in early Christian authors reflecting on Paul's practice.[30] There, divine accommodation became both a hermeneutical key for early Christian incarnational christology and an interpretative device that not only defused negative interpretations of Paul's self-characterization but also helped foster a particular view of Christianity as a superior form of religion, particularly as contrasted with Judaism.[31]

Despite such negative applications of divine condescension, the concept itself was a complex mixture of Greco-Roman, Jewish, and early Christian ideas during the first centuries of the Common Era. Philo, for example, refers to Homer to support his reflections on the variability of Israel's God. Like Josephus, Philo applies Odyssean epithets to ancient Hebrew figures, especially Joseph. Early Christian writers such as Clement of Alexandria, Origen, and John Chrysostom, while never mentioning Odysseus or other Hellenistic figures in connection with Paul's self-characterization, all regard it as an instance of condescension, an activity which they found to be characteristic of the God of Israel (and of God's Logos) and therefore legitimate behavior for the apostle to the Gentiles.[32] Pagan authors as well used the adaptability *topos* to reflect on the nature of God's accommodating behavior toward humans.[33]

Divine accommodation was, then, simply one of many issues raised within the adaptability *topos,* receiving its sharpest edge among early Christian writers in their defense of Paul and in Hellenistic Jewish writers contemporaneous with Paul. It is also clear that Paul used the topic of divine accommodation in his letters, as for example in Phil 2:5–11; Gal 4:4–5; and 2 Cor 8:9. Perhaps we should be willing to credit Paul with some originality as a participant in the general complex of development. In his argumentative strategy in 1 Corinthians, he at least integrates more completely than any other author the moral and divine perspectives on accommodation. Here indeed appears Paul's unique stamp on these matters. It would also seem to have been this mixture of divine and human accommodation as well as the moral implications of the adaptability *topos* that was problematic for later writers. Thus, instead of attempting to identify the source of Paul's reflections, it is more appropriate to acknowledge the conflation of traditional themes associated with issues of versatility within the adaptability *topos*[34] and then to attempt to explicate the configuration of such a mixture in specific contexts. Below I describe briefly how Paul builds upon such a synthesis in 1 Corinthians.

Paul's self-reflective remarks in 1 Cor 9:19–23 occur in a context in which he himself is engaged in psychagogic guidance but is reflecting at the same time on conflicting views on the guidance of the immature and on the question of association with all and sundry. This is of course not a full description of Paul's program of recruitment and guidance. However, in the employment of adaptability in this pericope, Paul's views on variability surface as he underlines the two most common issues of adaptability, namely, that of unreserved openness in associating with all types of people and flexibility in dealing with neophytes (cf. Rom 1:13–15).[35] Although the former was especially tied to a proselytizing strategy and the latter to psychagogic nurture, these two components of positive adaptability are intricately woven throughout 1 Corinthians, revealing the close connection of the religious and moral perspectives in Paul's reasoning as he attempts to distinguish those who belong to the community from others.

The reference to the various "groups" of people to which Paul adapts—Jews, law-abiders, the lawless ones, and the weak—and the inclusive nature of Paul's voluntary slavery and adaptation suggest the motif of unrestricted association with all. This is also accentuated by the reference to "the many" or "all" in 9:19, 22, and 10:33, and by the contrast between personal and communal advantage in the larger context. Paul distinguishes the "weak" referred to at the end of the pericope from the other groups by the repetition of γενωμαι (*genōmai*) and by the omission of ὡς (*hōs*) before the "weak" (9:20, 22b). The precise identity of the groups might be debatable, but the twofold focus on flexibility in light of human diversity and adaptation in light of different dispositions can hardly be questioned.

This same twofold emphasis can be seen, for example, in Philo's description of Joseph's political career in *On Joseph* 32–34 and 75–79, in which Philo compares the political man to a pilot and to a physician. In the first text the analogy is used to accentuate the need for resourcefulness and the importance for the political man, like the pilot, to be flexible and to adapt to diverse circumstances and conditions. The latter text uses the analogy of the physician to emphasize the need for the good statesman's adaptability, because the treatment employed by the physician is applied in view of, and adapted to, the particular sickness. Maximus of Tyre's defense of versatility in *That a Philosopher's Discourse Is Adapted to Every Subject* also emphasizes the importance of flexibility when associating unreservedly with all and in psychagogic adaptation (*Discourse* 1 [1,5–18,3 Hobein]). In Paul's case this twofold perspective is evident in his discussion about the "weak" (1 Cor 8; 10:23–11:1) and in his reflections on the association of different types of people, reflections that surface throughout 5:1–11:1. Regarding the latter question, people in Corinth did not see eye to eye, both with each other and with Paul.

Matters relating to association with others are clearly part of Paul's concerns. The language of "becoming" in 9:19–23 suggests a *change* in one's customary practice involving association, as for example when one is present at a dinner party with a previously shunned member of society. Such behavior reminds us of the practice of flatterers and friends of many and of the common animal analogies used to characterize them. A text from the author of *Barnabas,* as he explains a Jewish food law that forbade the consumption of a lamprey, a polyp, or a cuttlefish, is apropos (Lev 11:10). This law, he argues, means not to "consort with or become like such men who are utterly ungodly and who are already condemned to death, just as these fish alone are accursed."[36] Such a text, linking food laws and association, alerts us that, although the overt issues Paul addresses (in the chapters that begin in 1 Cor 8:1) have to do with the consumption of food offered to idols, a culturally sensitive reading suggests that what is at stake relates as much to the social context of such practices and to the association with other people in such contexts. Similar notions in Gal 2:11–14 show that Paul had earlier faced comparable issues.

Throughout 1 Cor 5:1–11:1, Paul comments on various types of relationships as he develops the themes of freedom and rights of individuals in a communal setting. First, Paul remarks on relationships with immoral people, both inside and outside the community. Specific examples include immoral behavior, the union of a man with his stepmother, and immoral people (οἱ ἄδικοι, *hoi adikoi*) inside the community. Paul counsels a withdrawal of association from such persons, from any "so-called brother or sister" who is "sexually immoral or greedy, or is an idolater, reviler, drunkard, or robber" (5:11 NRSV). The incestuous man should be judged within the community; the same holds true if there is dispute among members. Disputes should not be taken outside of the community (6:1–11). Then Paul comments on a relationship of a prostitute and a presumably enlightened person who claims to have the right to do whatever he wishes with his own body and to form whatever type of relationship he desires. Paul rejects such a conduct as characteristic of immoral persons (6:12–20).

Paul reflects next on obligations of individuals in marriage (7:2–5, 10), on whether the unmarried and widows should stay single or establish a new relationship (7:8–9). Paul reflects as well on obligations in a relationship of partners before and after a divorce (7:10–11), and on a relationship in marriage in which one is a believer and the other is not (7:12–16). The question whether the partners should change and adapt to the condition of the other or not, in view of their spouses' beliefs and convictions, receives a negative answer. Having addressed the question regarding the relationship of believers and unbelievers in marriage, Paul turns his attention to specific examples of possible change in conduct and status of individuals before and after they had joined the Corinthian community (7:17–24).

Paul asks first whether persons should remove or acquire the marks of Jewish ethnicity through circumcision, after they had been persuaded by Paul's "word of the cross" about "Christ crucified" (cf. 1:23; 2:2). The answer is no.[37] What matters is keeping "God's command" (7:18–20). Then Paul asks the same question regarding slaves. Should they avail themselves of the opportunity to gain freedom? The answer in that case is a qualified yes. Grasp the chance of liberty if it presents itself; otherwise, be content in that state and think of yourself as the "Lord's freedman," as those who are free are in reality "slaves in the service of Christ" (7:21–24).

Next Paul discusses celibacy and the various relationships of the celibate man, the married person (7:27), the divorced or unmarried person (7:27), and the one who wishes to marry (7:28). Paul also reflects on virgins who marry (7:28) and on the relationship of people in marriage (7:28) now when "the present form of this world is passing away" (7:31). This last point signals the main thrust of Paul's directives: Because the present time is short (7:29), one should live "as if" one is "not" in the state or condition one happens to be in. While the foreshortened time lasts, married men should be "as if" they had no wives, mourners "as if" they had nothing to grieve (7:30), the joyful "as if" they did not rejoice (7:30).[38] Wealth and acquisitions are also considered transitory (7:30); hence, one's attachment to external things should be tempered (7:31).

Paul wants the Corinthians to be "free from anxious care" in order that their attention may be undivided toward things of significance (7:32). Thus the unmarried man is able to devote his attention to "things of the Lord" and "how to please" the Lord while the married man has to care for "worldly things" and how "to please his wife." In that sense his mind is divided (7:32–34). The same holds true for the unmarried or celibate woman and the married woman (7:34). Paul claims that his ruminations are for the Corinthians' own benefit and that his aim is "to promote good order and unhindered devotion to the Lord" (7:35).

Paul ends this chapter with reflections on a man who has a partner in celibacy and on the obligations of a wife (7:36–40). Paul suggests that people should remain in the condition in which they were when "called" (7:17, 20, 24) but that they can change their social or marital status under certain conditions. Paul's conservative directives are understandable in light of concerns regarding the hazards of crossing established social boundaries and adopting a different mode of life than that previously entertained. His directives are also understandable, given his objective of preserving the unity of a socially mixed religious community in common worship. The diversity of "members," including Jews and non-Jews, both men and women, possibly from different social strata, gives an added poignancy to matters relating to the interaction of people in different relationships.

Because the topic of association with others formed part of the adaptability *topos*, it comes as no surprise in this epistolary context to find terms—such as *symphoros* (benefit, advantage), *euschemon* (proper, good order), and *kalos* (good, useful; 5:12; 7:1, 8, 26, 35, 37, 38; cf. 10:23; 12:7)—that relate to circumstantial requirements in the delivery of a discourse. These words were described by rhetoricians as "common topics" relating to the aim of a discourse, including the expedient, the honorable, the just, the possible, greatness, and their contraries. Such topics are situational and take seriously the contingencies of the addressees' lives. The concern with the beneficial, advantageous, edifying, decent, and good, in an epistolary context that combines dissuasion and persuasion, underscores Paul's concern with adaptation and the practical consequences of his directives.

In his nonrigid approach to various forms of relationships, Paul has emphasized different applications of a common tradition, his overall concern being the welfare of the Corinthians united in worship. Having discussed the rights of husbands and wives, widows, the unmarried, and slaves in various forms of relationships, Paul focuses on the interaction between the "wise" and the "weak" who share the same confession but draw different behavioral inferences from the same belief. Some felt they could eat meat sacrificed to idols, others did not. The behavior of those who were convinced they could eat meat offered to idols should be modified only if it became harmful to others (8:4–11).[39]

In chapter 9, Paul sets himself forth as one who voluntarily restricts his freedom for the good of others. In such an endeavor, both flexibility and self-discipline are needed (9:19–27). After a dire warning and a discussion of the dangers of participating in sacrificial meals and idolatry (10:1–13, 14–22), Paul argues that individual freedom of association must be restricted by communal advantage (10:23). He then gives his readers two criteria of conduct. First, "whatever you do, do everything for the glory of God." Second, "give no offense to Jews or to Greeks or to the church of God, just as I try to please everyone in everything I do, not seeking my own advantage, but that of many, so that they may be saved" (10:32–33).

Although Paul's twofold focus on adaptation in psychagogic nurture and on flexibility in associating with the "multitude" suggests a differentiation between recruitment and psychagogy, such a distinction is heuristic. The two lie on a continuum. Both novices and nonbelievers could, for example, be affected by the word of prophetic utterance in worship, showing the fluid state of affairs regarding communal boundaries in Corinth (14:23–24). The purpose of Paul's ethical guidelines for an accommodating behavior is, however, clear: namely, recruitment and ultimately salvation. When Paul spoke of salvation he probably had more than moral consequences in mind; it is, however, interesting how concerned he was with the moral fabric of the community, with why one should and should not continue to associate with immoral people. Indeed, the question with whom one could associate became a way of demarcating the blurred boundary between "insiders" and "outsiders," thus qualifying the nature of the community in Corinth (cf. 1 Cor 14:16).

Paul is explicit as to behavior one abides from "outsiders" and what one does not tolerate in "brothers," thus delineating obligations toward people within and outside the community by reference to their moral conduct. Paul thus attempts to throw light on the purpose of both association and disassociation, by clarifying why one should or should not associate with certain people. The continual presence of immoral people in the community reflects the success of Paul's recruitment, which probably involved acceptance of such a claim as "Christ died and lived again, so that he might be Lord of both the dead and the living" (Rom 14:9; cf. 1 Cor 1:23; 2:2; 8:6; 12:3; Gal 4:8–10; 1 Thess 1:9). In a letter such as 1 Corinthians, Paul works out the behavioral consequences of the acceptance of such a claim. Some had displayed vices before joining the community; now a reformation of character is required because οἱ ἄδικοι, the unrighteous, "will not inherit the kingdom of God" (1 Cor 5:8; 6:9, 11, 19–20). Paul's low entrance requirements regarding moral conduct resulted in a conflict with his communal ideal and required him to attempt to remedy the situation. In 1 Corinthians we witness the tension between Paul's ideal of associating unreservedly with all and his clarification of a communal ideal in formation.

The vices Paul lists are various forms of immoral behavior that he held to be grossly damaging and ungodly.[40] Such vices could not be condoned. The Corinthians had misconstrued Paul's advice from his previous letter to mean that they should stop associating with immoral persons such as the greedy, robbers, or idolaters "of this world," as he calls them (5:9–10). In 5:11, Paul makes clear that he meant for them not to "associate with anyone who bears the name of brother or sister" who continues to behave immorally; they should "not even eat with such a one." What is advised for the moral betterment of the vice-ridden persons is withdrawal; the purpose of shunning is reform of character by shaming into repentance.[41] Paul attempts as well to set clear limits to the Corinthians' association with "outsiders." They should not, for example, associate with a prostitute or participate in pagan cultic activities (6:18; 10:7, 8, 14). But Paul also recognizes continual, acceptable social interaction with people outside the community. "Insiders" can, for example, continue to dine with "outsiders" regardless of their moral attributes (10:27), although they are forbidden to dine with a believer who continues to behave immorally!

Paul's willingness to associate with persons of different moral standing probably encountered strong objections among those who emphasized the total separation from the immoral both inside and outside the community. That willingness probably contributed to the strain in the relationship between Paul and some Corinthian persons of societal status who valued friendships of equality among the aristocracy[42] and might even have suggested as legitimate some of the associations addressed as unacceptable. Paul emphasizes, however, that although associating with people of different moral standing could be seen as ungodly (cf. Lev 11:10; *Barn.* 10.5, above), it is indeed upright and law-abiding, congruent with "Christ's law" and accommodating behavior (9:21; 11:1; Gal 6:2).[43] Paul also explains the need for associating with all kinds of people for recruitment purposes. Association with the lawless and immoral might lead to their salvation.[44] That is also the reason why an "insider" may associate in marriage with an "unbeliever" (7:12–16). Finally, "unbelievers" may witness the various religious activities of the Corinthians and might be recruited because of them (14:22–25).

A nonrigid recruitment criterion was, however, followed by a more stringent set of criteria regarding morally desirable behavior within the community. The latter apparently did not entail unified beliefs on all matters or a unified code of behavior. Differences were, for example, recognized concerning beliefs that had different behavioral ramifications, such as convictions concerning the magical effect of food offered to idols (8:4–13; 10:27–28). Indeed, Paul's emphasis falls on the social interaction of different types of people as he attempts to shape the moral and religious views of his readers, and that attempt sharpens the distinction between *insiders* and *outsiders* and reveals the close connection of the religious and moral perspectives in Paul's reasoning.

Religion and ethics are indissolubly connected in Paul's argumentative strategy. Such a connection is apparent in his use of a proverb from a Greek tragedy— "Bad company ruins good morals"[45]— immediately after his reference to the reasoning of some in Corinth—"if the dead are not raised, 'Let us eat and drink, for tomorrow we die' "—and before his overt attempt to shame these people: "Come to a sober and right mind, and sin no more; for some people have no knowledge of God. I say this to your shame" (15:32–34). Paul's blame aims to change an immoral behavior in the light of God's present and future intervention in human destiny. In accord with such a belief, moral carelessness is inappropriate; others should not cultivate the bad company of these people because to do so ruins good moral character. The above proverb was closely related to the issue of association and had, more likely than not, implications for relationships in the community.

These reflections near the end of the letter, in a highly religious context, show that Paul's earlier issues relating to the moral fabric of the religious community are still in the forefront of his mind. Regardless of our estimation of the social composition of the Pauline communities or the social consequences of Paul's concerns,[46] the issues of "boundary-crossing" and adjustment through association with others of different standing were always present; the psychological, moral, and religious overtures of such associations are clearly visible in the Corinthian context.[47]

In 1 Corinthians, Paul does not describe himself as a truthful counselor as opposed to a flatterer. But as the spiritual father of the Corinthians and as their moral and religious leader and teacher, he assumes roles that bring out expectations among his recipients regarding the function and status of such persons. Paul's more specific utterances on different forms of association, and on his own accommodating conduct and desire to please everyone, tie his remarks to traditional issues of adaptability and connect his practice closely to the behavior of flatterers and obsequious persons. Earlier and later reflections in Paul's letters show that Paul was well acquainted with the contrast between flatterers and friends. In 1 Thess 2:2, 5, we find, for example, the first occurrence in early Christian literature of both "frankness" and "flattery" used together. Here Paul reflects on his ministry among the Thessalonians in terms of this contrast as he attempts to disassociate himself from the practices of flatterers. In 2 Corinthians we find reverberations of Paul's earlier debates with the wise in Corinth, in which some of the same concepts are used that were related to the comparison of idealized character types and behaviors.[48]

Although the concept of adaptability in Paul's world was primarily a moral-philosophical paradigm in the sense of desirable mode of conduct in various circumstances, it could hardly have excluded a transcendent dimension. At least, Paul's views on adaptability were integral to his views on the nature and function of God's dealing with humans. The incentive for Paul's behavior was found in a divine initiative and in the conduct of the founding figure of the message of which he was the herald. In the Philippian hymn, Paul used language associated with adaptability as he reflected on the self-abasement and change in the "status" of Jesus Christ, who was "in the form of God" but had taken on "the form of a slave." This change in Christ's "appearance," his voluntary slavery and willingness to take on different "forms" (μορφή, σχῆμα, morphē, schēma) in adapting to the condition of others, provided a model for Paul.[49] For Paul there was a distinct possibility that gods and humans could become friends in spite of the vast difference in their status.

Paul puts himself forward as an imitator of Christ and calls on the Corinthians to imitate his and, by implication, Christ's accommodating conduct (11:1). Although Paul does not ask his readers to imitate God,[50] his remarks on human "condescension" presuppose a divine model. Early Christian writers who used the idea of divine condescension to defuse the negative side of Paul's characterization made explicit what is latent in the Corinthian context. Paul recombines the Greco-Roman moralistic commonplaces connected to adaptability so as to give, by an implicit *theologoumenon,* support to a moral paradigm that had very specific communal implications for the church in Corinth. Paul weaves the divine and human perspectives, legitimizing conduct that was seen by many as socially reprehensible but ruling out some behavior that others would have condoned. Paul approves of association among people of different social and moral standing but attempts at the same time to be explicit as to the forms of association that are unacceptable.

The ethic of adaptability was an extension of divine condescension and was based on the adaptable behavior of Christ, who did not "please himself" (Rom 15:1–7).[51] This ethic served as a paradigm for social and ethical relations in the communities Paul founded; it was a constituent part of a community *ethos* to which all should conform. In fact, this ethic was integral to Paul's self-understanding as an apostle to the Gentiles, reflecting a willingness to cross established social, ethnic, and moral boundaries. In view of Paul's morally and religiously based idea of adaptability, we might perhaps also entertain the thought that Paul's theological reflections were also influenced by his adaptive and contextualized perspective in view of the transitory nature of things and the perceived imminent end of the present world.

Part III. Other Pauline and Paulinist Passages

This chapter has focused on one aspect of adaptability, namely, that of accommodation when associating with different types of people.[52] Paul used this perspective in his attempt to build up a community of morally committed individuals and to distinguish those who belonged to his fledgling communities from others in society. The emphasis falls on the past and present status of individuals and on the need for going through a moral and religious transformation that has implications for relationships toward both those who are outside and inside the community. This is a common perspective in Pauline thought and an ongoing discussion in later Pauline traditions. A good example of this perspective can be examined in Rom 12:1–15:14, in which issues relating to flexibility in associating with others both within and outside the community surface. Paul elaborates there on the nature of "rational" or "reasonable worship," which requires, instead of adapting oneself to the pattern of this present world, a transformation of one's mind that leads to spiritual insight and knowledge of that which is good, acceptable, and perfect (12:1–2). Such worship requires a recognition of the individually different appropriations of the same tradition and of the diverse functions of individuals in a religious community. People are urged to meet others on their level by sharing in their emotional experiences (12:15). The question of associating with outsiders, whether they are the socially humble, enemies, or the ruling authorities, is also addressed. Finally, Paul discusses the relationship between the mature and the immature.

The image of the body used both in Rom 12:4–5 and 1 Cor 12:12–27 to characterize different functions of individuals of a united religious community underscores the idea of diversity, the need for accommodation and a heightened sensitivity toward and acceptance of the differences (cf. Eph 4:1–16). Although we find the claim both in Paul and in later Pauline tradition that there are no distinctions anymore within the new community (Gal 3:27–29; Col 3:11), the continual mentioning of facts that in a patronal society were matters of distinction, such as ethnicity, gender, age, religious function, and social and moral status, raises the following question: To what extent did the ideal of communal solidarity and accommodation obliterate established social conventions or modify rules of conduct governing relationships in society in general?

In addition to passages referred to in this chapter, notice, for example, 1 Thess 3:12; 4:1–12; 5:13b–15, 22; 2 Cor 6:14–7:1. In the Paulinist tradition, consider Eph 2:1–22; 4:17–6:9; Col 1:21–23, 28; 3:5–4:6; 1 Tim 2:8–3:13; 4:11–6:2; 6:17–19; 2 Tim 2:20–3:5; 4:2; Titus 2:1–3:11.

Part IV. Bibliography

Benin, Stephen D. *The Footprints of God: Divine Accommodation in Jewish and Christian Thought.* SUNY Series in Judaica: Hermeneutics, Mysticism, and Religion. Albany: State University of New York Press, 1993.

Duchatelez, K. "La 'condescendance' divine et l'histoire du salut." *NRTh* 95 (1973): 593–621.

Glad, Clarence E. *Paul and Philodemus: Adaptability in Epicurean and Early Christian Psychagogy.* NovTSup 81. Leiden, New York, and Cologne: E. J. Brill, 1995.

Malherbe, Abraham J. "'In Season and Out of Season': 2 Timothy 4:2." Pages 137–45 in *Paul and the Popular Philosophers.* Minneapolis: Fortress Press, 1989.

Mitchell, Margaret M. "Pauline Accommodation and 'Condescension' (συνκατάβασις): 1 Cor. 9:19–23 and the History of Influence." Pages 197–214, 298–309 in *Paul beyond the Judaism/Hellenism Divide.* Edited by Troels Engberg-Pedersen. Louisville: Westminster John Knox Press, 2001.

Reumann, J. "*Oikonomia* as 'Ethical Accommodation' in the Fathers, and Its Pagan Backgrounds." *StPatr* 3 (1961): 370–79.

Stanford, W. B. *The Ulysses Theme: A Study in the Adaptability of a Traditional Hero.* 2d revised edition. New York: Barnes and Noble, 1968.

Notes

1. A cluster of terms in Greek expressed the concept of "adaptability" and "accommodation," including the words ἁρμόζω, ἐφαρμόζω, προσαρμόζω, ἐξομοιόω, συνεξομοιόω, συναφομοιόω, συμπεριφέρω, συμπεριφορά, συνκαταβαίνειν, συνκατάβασις, οἰκονομία. See the listings for these terms in LSJ.

2. The documentation in Clarence E. Glad, *Paul and Philodemus: Adaptability in Epicurean and Early Christian Psychagogy* (Leiden: E. J. Brill, 1995), enables us to claim that the topic of adaptability reflects a widespread tradition during Hellenistic times.

3. Cicero, *De Or.* 1.31.138 (LCL 348:96–97), "primum oratoris officium esse, dicere ad persuadendum accommodate."

4. See for example Aristotle, *Rhet.* 1.2.1–7 (LCL 193:14–19), and Heinrich Lausberg, *Handbook of Literary Rhetoric: A Foundation for Literary Study* (German original, 1973; Leiden: E. J. Brill, 1998), §§33, 257, 355.

5. As Pseudo-Demetrius succinctly argued: Letters "can be composed in a great number of styles, but are written in those which always fit the particular circumstances" (*Epistolary Types* 30, 3–4 and 20, in A. J. Malherbe, *Ancient Epistolary Theorists* [SBLSBS 19; Atlanta: Scholars Press, 1988]).

6. Theon, *Progymnasmata* 8.43–50, in James R. Butts, "The *Progymnasmata* of Theon: A New Text with Translation and Commentary" (Ph.D. diss., Claremont Graduate School, 1986).

7. Plutarch, *How to Tell a Flatterer from a Friend* (LCL 197:280–281). Here Plutarch uses language traditionally associated with Odysseus, whom he refers to shortly after this quote before discussing Alcibiades, the greatest of flatterers and demagogues. See also Athenaeus, *Sophists at Dinner* (LCL 224:160–61), "In fact, the flatterer, in one and the same person, is the very image of Proteus. At any rate, he assumes every kind of shape and of speech as well, so varied are his tones."

8. This problem is succinctly captured by Isocrates, who, in his defense of legitimate harshness, notes, "those who admonish and those who denounce cannot avoid using similar words, although their purposes are as opposite as they can be" (*Concerning Peace* 72; LCL 229:50–51). The intention was all-important. See also Clement, *Paed.* 66.1 (GCS 128, 26–29 Stählin-Treu): "Just as exhortation and encouragement are types of discourses akin to the advisory discourse, so is encomium akin to reviling and reproach. But this latter type is the art of censure, a form of censure which indicates good will, not hatred. For both a friend and a foe reproach, the latter out of contempt, the former out of good will."

9. For the Greek terms used to describe the behavior of these different types of persons, see Glad, *Paul and Philodemus*, 17–23.

10. W. B. Stanford traced the various reflections on Homer's Odysseus from the sixth century B.C.E. to the twelfth century C.E. in his *Ulysses Theme: A Study in the Adaptability of a Traditional Hero* (New York: Barnes and Noble, 1968). For discussions about Homeric knowledge among early Christians and Jews, see Günther Glockmann, *Homer in der frühchristlichen Literatur bis Justinus* (TU 105; Berlin: Akademie-Verlag, 1968); and Dennis R. MacDonald, *Christianizing Homer: The Odyssey, Plato, and the Acts of Andrew* (Oxford: Oxford University Press, 1994).

11. See Clarence E. Glad, "Frank Speech, Flattery, and Friendship in Philode-

mus," in *Friendship, Flattery, and Frankness of Speech,* ed. John T. Fitzgerald (NovTSup; Leiden: E. J. Brill, 1996), 21–59.

12. See Aristotle, *Magna Moralia* 2.3.3 (1199a14–18; LCL 287:576–77).

13. See the succinct statement in Aristotle's *Nichomachean Ethics* 1172a8–14 (LCL 73:574–75).

14. See Aristotle, *Nichomachean Ethics* 1157a17–24 (LCL 73:466–76), 1158a10–14 (LCL 73:472–73), 1170b23–1171a16 (LCL 73:564–69), 1172a2–14 (LCL 73:574–75); *Eudemian Ethics* 1239b10–15 (LCL 285:396–97); 1245b20–26 (LCL 285:444–45); and *Magna Moralia* 1213b3–18 (LCL 287:682–85). On this point, see further below.

15. Plutarch, *On Having Many Friends* (LCL 222:64–69). For Theognis's advice to Cyrnus, see Glad, *Paul and Philodemus,* 27.

16. See Plutarch's *Alcibiades* (LCL 80:4–7, 62–65) and the texts cited in Glad, *Paul and Philodemus,* 28–30.

17. Epistle 103 (LCL 77:186–89). See also Epistle 7, *On Crowds* (LCL 75:28–37).

18. *Discourse* 3.16 (LCL 218:104–5) and *Discourse* 4.2 (LCL 218:304–5), respectively. The verb *synkatabainein* occurs in 3.16.9 (LCL 218:106–7) and 4.2.1 (LCL 218:306–7).

19. *Discourse* 3.16.1–2 (LCL 218:104–5). See also 3.16.11 (LCL 218:106–9) and 3.16.16 (LCL 218:108–9). In the latter text, Epictetus advises his readers to flee from their former habits as well as from laymen (see 2 Cor 11:6).

20. *Discourse* 4.2.1 (LCL 218:304–7). See also 4.2.2 and 10 (LCL 218:306–9).

21. Cf. Epictetus, *Discourses* 1.2 (LCL 131:14–15); *How May a Man Preserve His Proper Character upon Every Occasion?* 1.19 (LCL 131:128–29); *How Ought We to Bear Ourselves toward Tyrants?* 4.8 (LCL 218:374–75); *To Those Who Hastily Assume the Guise of the Philosophers* 3.19 (LCL 218:114–15); *What Is the Position of the Layman, and What That of the Philosopher?* 3.21; *To Those Who Enter Light-Heartedly upon the Profession of Lecturing* (cf. 3.21.14 and 18–20 [LCL 218:126–27, 128–29]). See *Discourses* 2.9, *That Although We Are Unable to Fulfill the Profession of a Man, We Adopt That of a Philosopher* 19–22 (LCL 131:272–75): "Why, then, do you call yourself a Stoic, why do you deceive the multitude, why do you play the part of a Jew, when you are a Greek? Do you not see in what sense men are severally called Jew, Syrian, or Egyptian? For example, whenever we see a man halting between two faiths, we are in the habit of saying, 'He is not a Jew, he is only acting the part.' But when he adopts the attitude of mind of the man who has been baptized and has made his choice, then he both is a Jew in fact and is also called one. So we also are counterfeit 'baptists,' ostensibly Jews, but in reality something else, not in sympathy with our own reason, far from applying the principles which we profess, yet priding ourselves upon them as being men who know them. So, although we are unable even to fulfil the profession of man, we take on the additional profession of the philosopher—so huge a burden!" See also *Discourse* 3.24.119–110 (LCL 218:218–19), ". . . obedient to God, and that you are playing the part of the good and excellent man, not ostensibly but in reality." Just before this last quote Epictetus has emphasized the importance of adjusting to the "style of life" in the city in which one happens to be stationed.

22. Philodemus, *On Frank Criticism* frgs. 14, 39–42, 47–49, 53–55; Epictetus, *Discourse* 4.13 (LCL 218:428–29), *To Those Who Lightly Talk about Their Own Affairs;* Dio Chrysostom, *Discourse* 73, *On Trust* (LCL 385:194–205), *Discourse* 74, *On Dis-*

trust (LCL 383:208–37); Plutarch, *Concerning Talkativeness* (LCL 337:396–467), *On Being a Busybody* (LCL 337:472–517).

23. *Discourse* 3.13.21–23 (LCL 218:94–95). Cf. 1 Cor 10:31–33.

24. M. P. Thompson, "Reception Theory and the Interpretation of Historical Meaning," *History and Theory* 32 (1993): 248–72.

25 For literature on Paul's rhetorical techniques, see Duane F. Watson, "Rhetorical Criticism of the Pauline Epistles since 1975," *Current Research in Biblical Studies* 3 (1995): 219–48.

26. Glad, *Paul and Philodemus*, 53–59.

27. Margaret M. Mitchell identifies the first seven and argues for the last one in "Pauline Accommodation and 'Condescension' (συνκατάβασις): 1 Cor 9:19–23 and the History of Influence," in *Paul beyond the Judaism/Hellenism Divide* (ed. Troels Engberg-Pedersen; Louisville: Westminster John Knox Press, 2001), 197–214. Cf. also Peter Richardson, "Pauline Inconsistency: 1 Corinthians 9:19–23 and Galatians 2:11–14," *NTS* 26 (1980): 347–62, esp. 357–58.

28. Philo, *De confusione linguarum* 134–41 (LCL 261:82–87), and *De Somniis* 1.147, 232–233 (LCL 275:374–75, 418–21).

29. The examples of pre-Christian use of the terms *synkatabainein* and *synkatabasis* that K. Duchatelez cites ("La 'condescendance' divine et l'histoire du salut," *NRTh* 95 [1973]: 593–621; cf. 594–98) indicate their predominant "nonreligious" connotations. The verb *synkatabainein* was commonly used in the meaning to "descend together (with)" or "at the same time," but the substantive *synkatabasis* occurs for the first time in Philodemus's *Rhetoric* 2.25, in the first century B.C.E., with the meaning rhetorical adaptability (LSJ 1662). In the meaning of condescension of a person of a higher standing, such as God, to others of a lower standing, the noun is predominantly used by early Christian authors. It is used earlier only by Philo (with the possible exception of Aeschylus). In the meaning "accommodation" or "adaptation" of a person of a higher social standing to the level of an inferior, the verb is found in a Polybius fragment preserved in Athenaeus's *Deipnosophistae* 5.193D (LCL 208:376–77) about Antiochus Epiphanes, who "would condescend to men of the common people and converse with anybody, no matter whom, and he used to drink with travellers of the meanest sort who came to town." Epictetus has a similar use of the verb (*Discourses* 3.16.9, LCL 218:106–7; and 4.2.1, LCL 218:304–7; see n. 14, above). In this sense the terms came to be commonly applied, by Christian authors subsequent to Clement, to Christ's incarnation. It is not until the fourth century C.E. that Julian uses the noun *synkatabasis* of the condescension of a pagan god, namely Attis (*Oration* 5.171B–C; LCL 13:478–79). The pre-Christian use of *oikonomia*, a term nearly synonymous to *synkatabasis*, with the meaning "accommodation" or "expediency," is seen in three contexts, namely, in discussions of household management, rhetoric, and morals. See J. Reumann, "*Oikonomia* as 'Ethical Accommodation' in the Fathers, and Its Pagan Backgrounds," *StPatr* 3 (1961): 370–79.

30. Clement of Alexandria, *Strom.* 7.9 (GCS, *Clemens Alexandrinus* 3.39, ed. Otto Stählin and L. Früchtel).

31. In the first systematic study of the idea of religious accommodation—*The Footprints of God: Divine Accommodation in Jewish and Christian Thought*—Stephen D. Benin begins his survey with Christian authors of the second century

C.E., but observes the roots of the theme in Philo. Benin has been chided for paying only lip service to the fact that the application of the accommodationist principle among early Christian authors parented the *adversus Judaeos* tradition. See the review of John T. Pawlikowski in *JES* 34, no. 1 (1997): 144–45.

32. Mitchell, "Pauline Accommodation."

33. Although not necessarily using the terms *synkatabainein* or *synkatabasis.* See Plutarch, *On the Delays of the Divine Vengeance* (LCL 405:190–91, 264–65). I had noted the topic of divine adaptability in Glad, *Paul and Philodemus,* 39, 51, 216, 254, 256–58, 294, and 333. In the *Antiquities,* Josephus remarks: "how varied and manifold is the nature of God" (10.142; LCL 326:234–35). See also Eph 3:10 ("the wisdom of God in its rich variety"); 4:8–10 (God descended and ascended); Heb 1:1–2 ("Long ago God spoke to our ancestors in many and various ways by the prophets, but in these last days he has spoken to us by a Son . . ."); and Mark 16:12. Part of the larger issue addressed by pagan philosophers was the question of God's immutability. Note for example Plato, *Republic* 380D (LCL 237:380–81): "Do you think that God is a wizard and capable of manifesting himself by design, now in one aspect, now in another, at one time himself changing and altering his shape in many transformations and at another deceiving us and causing us to believe such things about him; or that he is simple and less likely than anything else to depart from his form?"

34. Glad, *Paul and Philodemus,* 273.

35. My views have been taken to imply that Paul provides here a full-scale description of his program of recruitment and guidance. In this Mitchell somewhat misconstrues my reading ("Pauline Accommodation," in *Paul beyond the Judaism/Hellenism Divide,* 197–214. In *Paul and Philodemus,* I used the psychagogic perspective of 1 Cor 9:19–23 as a stepping stone toward an investigation of Pauline psychagogy in general, for which I found that Epicurean psychagogy offered particularly illuminating comparative material.

36. *Barn.* 10.5.

37. If it is not to be construed as an instance of Acts' apologetic interests, Paul's circumcising of Timothy (Acts 16:3) in light of his expressed arguments against it elsewhere (Gal 5:2–6; Phil 3:2–6) might be seen either as a kind of variability or as an example of despicable opportunism.

38. See Epictetus, *Discourse* 3.22, *On the Calling of a Cynic* 50 and 54 (LCL 218:148–49). Cf. 2 Cor 11:19–20.

39. For a detailed exegetical reading arguing for this understanding of 1 Cor 8:4–11, see Clarence E. Glad, "Lestur og ritskýring 1. Korintubréfs 8: Deilur um kennsluaðferðir í Korintuborg," *Studia theologica Islandica* 8 (1994): 55–106.

40. The list of the "unjust" in 6:9–10 repeats a reference to fornicators or sexually immoral people, to the greedy, idolaters, robbers, drunkards, and revilers from the list in 5:9–11, adding adulterers, male prostitutes, sodomites, and thieves.

41. On such a reading the "offender" in 5:1–8 is not expelled forthwith; others should first attempt to shame him into repentance through disassociation and the practice of shunning. Compare Rom 16:17; 2 Thess 3:6, 14–15.

42. For an attempt to use the social grid of patronage to explicate one function of 1 Cor 9:19–23, see Glad, *Paul and Philodemus,* 264–72.

43. See Glad, *Paul and Philodemus*, 257–58. See also below.

44. Such a reading emphasizes the moral connotations of οἱ ἄνομοι in 1 Cor 9:21. See Glad, *Paul and Philodemus*, 257–58.

45. This proverb is often assumed to be from Menander's lost comedy *Thais*, but Robert Renehan has shown that the words "originally occurred in some tragedy, by Euripides more likely than not" ("Classical Greek Quotations in the New Testament," in *The Heritage of the Early Church: Essays in Honor of Georges Vasilievich Florovsky* [ed. D. Neiman and M. Schatkin; Rome: Pontifical Institute of Oriental Studies, 1973], 17–46).

46. Justin J. Meggitt has forcefully argued against the "New Consensus" that sees the early Pauline churches as incorporating individuals from a cross section of first-century society, including some from the higher social strata (*Paul, Poverty, and Survival* [Edinburgh: T. & T. Clark, 1998], 75–154).

47. Glad, *Paul and Philodemus*, 237–38, 309.

48. Ibid., 310–26.

49. See Phil 2:5–11; Gal 3:13; 4:3–5; 2 Cor 5:20–21; 8:9; and Rom 8:3 (contrast 2 Cor 11:13–15). Note *De Somniis* 1.232 (LCL 275:418–21), in which Philo reflects on God's different manifestations with the word ἑτερόμορφος (heteromorphos) and the previously noted passage in *Republic* 380D, in which Plato uses both the words εἶδος and μορφή as he reflects on the same issue. When people adapted to others they underwent a "metamorphosis," changing their "form," "shape," "appearance," or "character" (ὁ τρόπος, τὸ ἦθος, τὸ πλάσμα, τὸ εἶδος, ἡ μορφή, τὸ σχῆμα). Greek verbs used to describe a change included μετα/μορφόω and συ/μετασχηματίζω (Athenaeus, *Deipnosophistae* 258A [LCL 224:160–61]; Plutarch, *On Having Many Friends* [LCL 222:68–69], *How to Tell a Flatterer from a Friend* [LCL 197:284–85]; and *Alcibiades* [LCL 80:4–5, 62–65]). For similar language in Paul with positive religious connotations, see Gal 4:19; Phil 3:21; Rom 12:2; and 2 Cor 3:18 (cf. 1 Pet 1:14). The motif of "change" in order to "become" something else or stay as one "is," appears in 1 Cor 3:18 and 14:20, as well as in the previously discussed passage of 7:20–31, in which Paul uses the motif of living as if one is not (. . . ὡς μή) in the condition in which one finds oneself, now that "the present form (σχῆμα) of this world is passing away." See my discussion above. Although Rudolf Bultmann did not tie 9:19–23 to questions of adaptability, he did note that the view expressed reveals the attitude needed in the now–not yet situation of Christians ("Neues Testament und Mythologie: Das Problem der Entmythologisierung der neutestamentlichen Verkündigung" [1941], in *Kerygma und Mythos* [ed. Hans-Werner Bartsch; vol. 1; Hamburg: Herbert Reich, 1948], 29).

50. Contrast Eph 5:1.

51. See Glad, *Paul and Philodemus*, 257, 216n. 97, and 256n. 64. See above.

52. For passages relating to adaptability in psychagogic guidance, see Abraham J. Malherbe, "'In Season and Out of Season': 2 Timothy 4:2," in *Paul and the Popular Philosophers* (Minneapolis: Fortress Press, 1989), 137–45, and Glad, *Paul and Philodemus*, 185–332.

2
PAUL, ADOPTION, AND INHERITANCE

James C. Walters

Paul's use of the word "inheritance" is unparalleled in Greco-Roman usage outside of Judaism.[1] Paul's employment of legal-adoption terminology, however, and especially his association of adoption with inheritance, suggests the influence of Greco-Roman social and legal conventions. Υἱοθεσία (*huiothesia*), one of the Greek terms for adoption, occurs only five times in the entire Greek Bible (LXX + NT).[2] Four of these are in undisputed Pauline letters (Gal 4:5; Rom 8:15, 23; 9:4) while the fifth is in a Paulinist letter (Eph 1:5).[3]

Paul's close linkage of inheritance with adoption shapes this study, but the primary focus will be on adoption because this term especially suggests that Greco-Roman conventions shaped Paul's argument. Ascertaining the nature and purpose of adoption in the Greco-Roman world is of critical importance, lest modern notions affect interpretation.

Part I. Adoption and Inheritance in the Greco-Roman World

Whose Adoption Law?

Scholars have debated for years whether Jewish, Greek, or Roman law shaped Paul's adoption language.[4] Recently, J. M. Scott has advocated a Jewish background, saying that Paul uses the word with its Hellenistic meaning ("adoption as sons," not "sonship"), but with a Jewish background based on the "2 Sam. 7:14 tradition."[5] However, Scott's separation of the Hellenistic meaning from the Jewish background is problematic. Even if Paul sought to evoke Jewish expectations based on 2 Sam 7:14, he could not have removed himself from the Greco-Roman world.[6] Rather, as a Jew at home in the urban centers of the Greek East, Paul's usage would have been informed by his (and his readers') Greco-Roman context.[7]

Not only is υἱοθεσία (*huiothesia*) absent from the LXX, it does not occur in any other ancient Jewish literature, Josephus or Philo included. This is apparently not a term Paul appropriated from Jewish sources. Of course, Josephus and Philo—and other contemporary Diaspora Jews—were familiar with the practice of adoption. However, Joseph Fitzmyer is no doubt correct: "Υἱοθεσία is not found in the LXX, probably because adoption was not a normal institution among the Jews. . . . Normally, one could not be taken into a Jewish family in order to continue the line of the adopter."[8] Jews cared for orphaned children, but such care routinely fell to surviving family members, without any formal adoption procedure (cf. Esth 2:7, 15). Jewish writings prior to or contemporary with Paul exhibit no legal procedures parallel to those in Greek and Roman law whereby a son—usually as an adult, not a child—is adopted to supply an heir who will preserve a family line from extinction.[9] Treating orphaned children as if they were sons or daughters is quite different from actually making someone a legal son or daughter. The latter primarily involves filial rights, not providing a home for an orphaned child.

One should not automatically assume that Paul's usage reflects Roman law because Paul was a Roman citizen or because Roman adoption was "richer and more thoroughgoing."[10] Paul's earliest usage of adoption language is in Galatians, a letter to churches in the Greek East. Rome typically permitted cities there to adjudicate their own legal affairs. Roman law did form an overarching structure, but was an administrative umbrella that left intact Hellenistic and other local legal traditions.[11]

Rome did intervene in judicial matters, but not normally, as numerous ancient sources demonstrate.[12] Two examples illustrate the point. In the early second century C.E., Pliny served as the Roman governor of Bithynia, where he learned that fee structures varied widely from city to city. He wrote the emperor, suggesting that fees should be regularized. Trajan's reply is instructive:

> I can establish no general ruling as to whether all who become decurions in every city of Bithynia should be required to pay an entrance fee for the decurionate or not. I think therefore that—as is always the most prudent course—each city should conform to its own law. (Pliny, *Ep.* 10.112–13)

The second example is from Plutarch (a near-contemporary with Paul). It shows that locals most often prompted Roman intervention. Plutarch chastised fellow Greeks for referring every legal dispute to the emperors, thereby reducing local authority: "Those who invite the emperor's decision on every decree, meeting of a council, granting of a privilege, or administrative measure, force their emperors to be their masters more than they desire" (Plutarch, *Mor.* 8.14). Plutarch's protest, however, indicates that residents of the Greek East did employ Roman legal procedures when they thought it was to their advantage.[13]

It is unlikely that Paul or his Galatian readers had extensive knowledge of

Greek or Roman adoption and inheritance law. However, it is quite likely that both were familiar with the relationship between adoption and inheritance and the motives people had for adopting or giving their offspring up for adoption.

Because Paul was a native of the Greek East, and because he used adoption language in letters written to churches in the Greek East (Galatians) as well as to Christians in Rome (Romans), this essay explores both Greek and Roman legal conventions. The second part of the essay attempts to elucidate Paul's usage of adoption and inheritance language in light of these legal conventions, concentrating especially on his earliest use of adoption language, in Galatians.

Adoption and Inheritance in Greek Law

Sources. Sources for understanding Greek adoption in the ancient world are problematic. Greek adoption is known almost entirely from forensic speeches of disputed inheritance[14] from fourth-century B.C.E. Athens that are preserved in the works of the classical speechwriters, Isaeus and Demosthenes.[15] These speeches reflect atypical cases because surely most inheritances were not challenged. These sources, however, assume the more regular practices of adoption and inheritance, or at least shared values.[16]

Though these speeches reflect the wealthy Athenians who battled in court for their share of huge estates, the bias of these sources can be overstated because the speeches written by Isaeus and Demosthenes had to resonate with Athenian juries that were composed not only of the wealthiest citizens.[17] Rubinstein claims that we can neither "rule out nor confirm that adoption was practiced by Athenians belonging to all social strata of Athenian society."[18]

Arguably the most important single piece of evidence for Greek adoption and inheritance is the sixth-century B.C.E. Solonic law, apparently the basis for many Greek legal conventions. Though Isaeus refers to it, the best source for the law is Demosthenes (46.14; fourth century B.C.E.):

> Any citizen, with the exception of those who had been adopted when Solon entered upon his office, and had thereby become unable either to renounce or to claim an inheritance, shall have the right to dispose of his own property by will as he shall see fit, if he have no male children lawfully born, unless his mind be impaired by one of these things, lunacy or old age or drugs or disease, or unless he be under the influence of a woman, or under constraint or deprived of his liberty.

Comparing this law with later materials, a number of classical historians have put forward diachronic descriptions of Athenian inheritance and adoption that tend to see an evolution from a more religious and collectivist approach in the archaic period to a more secular and individualist approach in the Hellenistic period.[19] In this approach, the classical period is typically viewed as a time of great change in which old and new ideas clashed as Athenians increasingly attempted to control the destinies of their οἶκοι (*oikoi* can refer to the combination of property and persons making up Greek estates) by making wills.[20]

Despite classical scholars' increasing discomfort with suggestions that "Greek law" ever existed in the sense of a unified system,[21] Raphael Sealey argues persuasively for a certain unity of underlying ideas in Greek legal materials, especially with regard to rights and obligations of the individual. Inheritance law figures heavily in his argument. By looking at the similarities and differences between the laws of Athens and Gortyn (a Greek city on the island of Crete) and comparing the two with Roman law, Sealey shows that Athens and Gortyn have more in common than is often realized.[22]

Rather than seek to describe the legal procedures that were in effect across the first-century C.E. Hellenistic world, this essay seeks to discover the underlying ideas that shaped adoption and inheritance laws. A writer can use adoption as a metaphor only because communicating partners share certain underlying ideas.

Laws, social conventions, and procedure. The professional law-court speakers such as Isaeus and Demosthenes wrote speeches based on shared values relating to family, death, and inheritance. As we read the cases they argued it is impossible to say who was telling the truth, nor do we know how most of the cases were decided. Fortunately, this matters little because even when interested parties misrepresented facts in a speech, those misrepresentations appealed to the norms the speakers assumed would guide the decisions of jurors. It is these norms, and the underlying values, that concern us.

When a fourth-century Athenian father died, his estate passed directly to his son. No will was necessary; it was illegal for the father to give his property to anyone but his son.[23] For this reason, the speaker arguing for the estate of Philoctemon takes the existence of a will to be proof that the deceased did not consider reputed heirs to be his legitimate children.

> Euctemon was not dealing with them as legitimate children, as Androcles has declared in his evidence; for no one ever makes a gift by will of anything to the sons of his own body, because the law itself gives his father's estate to the son and does not even allow anyone who has legitimate children to dispose of his property. (Isaeus 6.28)

A legitimate son, born in wedlock to Athenian citizens, was not required to file any sort of legal petition to receive the estate of his father (Isaeus 3.59). He had what the Greeks called ἐμβατεύειν (*embateuein*), the right to "enter" into his father's estate without adjudication (ἐπιδικασία, *epidikasia*).[24] If the deceased left multiple sons the estate was divided evenly among them (partible inheritance as opposed to primogeniture).[25] Daughters did not inherit from their fathers nor did wives inherit from their husbands.[26] The wife of the deceased and any surviving daughters were part of the *oikos* inherited by the son(s). The heir was legally responsible for their continued care, including the responsibility to provide dowries for unmarried daughters.[27] Effectively, the son stepped directly into the shoes of the deceased father, inheriting the *oikos* and assuming all responsibilities for its continuation.

So Athenians assumed. However, it often did not work out this way. As demographic studies have illustrated, many families teetered on the brink of extinction.[28] Estimates of the average age at death for women and men in the classical period are usually the mid-thirties for women and mid-forties for men.[29] When these life-expectancy figures are coupled with a death ratio of five hundred infants per one thousand adults and family planning that required balancing desires to preserve the family line while not atomizing the estate—a danger in partible inheritance systems—it is no wonder that many families were threatened with extinction.

When for whatever reason a family had no male son to inherit the *oikos*—the incidence could be as high as four in ten families[30]—the legal strategy of adoption was used, and Athenian law treated adopted persons just as if they had been born into the family.[31] When families employed these strategies, disagreements and legal actions could arise.[32] Out of the twelve (mostly) complete extant speeches written by Isaeus, eleven involved lawsuits over estates with no surviving natural son.[33]

A number of restrictions limited who could adopt. According to Isaeus 10.10, women and minors were not permitted to adopt because of a law restricting them from entering certain contracts: "[A] minor is not allowed to make a will; for the law expressly forbids any child—or woman—to contract for the disposal of property more than a bushel of barley." Further, the already-cited Solonic law noted other restrictions: an Athenian male could not adopt if he already had a legal heir, that is, a legitimate son; neither could an adoption stand if the adopter was deemed to have lacked appropriate judgment when making the decision—either because of some sort of mental impairment or duress. Not surprisingly, charges that the deceased was "impaired," "influenced," or "constrained" often appear in legal cases seeking to annul an adoption or will. Isaeus has Menecles' adopted son begin his speech to the jurors: "I think, gentleman, that, if any adoption was ever made in accordance with the laws, mine was, and no one could ever dare to say that Menecles adopted me in a moment of insanity or under the influence of a woman" (Isaeus 2.1). Also, the adopter must be "master of his property," meaning that he must be free of outstanding debt (Isaeus 2.46; Demosthenes 44.49). Although a man could not adopt if he already had a legitimate son, he could adopt if he had a daughter (Demosthenes 46.14).

Only one limitation on candidates for adoption is apparent: the adoptee had to have Athenian citizenship—that is, both parents had to be Athenian citizens (Isaeus 7.16).

Three distinct adoptive arrangements would supply an heir to an Athenian man who lacked one: he could adopt an heir himself (adoption *inter vivos*); he could name an heir in his will (testamentary adoption); or, he could leave the selection of a suitable heir to his family after his death (posthumous adoption). Isaeus's law-court speeches reflect two *inter vivos*, eleven testamentary, and five posthumous adoptions.[34] Ratios based on these figures should not be taken to indicate relative popularity. The ratios more likely indicate that adoptions *inter vivos* were less likely to be contested—and therefore less likely to show up in the sources.

Inter vivos adoptions were not as easily challenged because the heir was selected and integrated into the adopter's household before the adopter died. Athenian law treated these adoptees just like natural sons: they had the right to enter their father's estate without adjudication. Other classes of heirs were required to have their rights adjudicated by the court prior to claiming the estate. The strength of the claim held by a son adopted *inter vivos* is manifest: "How could he be childless, when he adopted [*inter vivos*] and was survived by his own nephew, to whom the law gives the right of inheritance just as much as to children of his own body?" (Isaeus 6.63). Another text reveals the different status of one adopted by a will and the increased likelihood that the adoption would be challenged in court: "[W]hen testators leave legitimate issue, their children need not demand the adjudication of their patrimony; but, on the contrary, when testators adopt children by will [testamentary adoption], such children must obtain an adjudication of what is bequeathed to them" (Isaeus 3.60–61).

Because a son adopted *inter vivos* retained his right to a share of the father's inheritance even if the father produced natural heirs following the adoption, this form of adoption was probably unpopular with men until they were advanced in years (Isaeus 6.63). A younger man could protect the future of his *oikos* by naming an heir in his will (testamentary adoption) and later by amending his will if a son was born to him naturally. Consequently, men who were going away for military service sometimes used testamentary adoption as a precaution (Isaeus 6.5).

Though this strategy provided flexibility, it fostered numerous lawsuits, because such wills could displace the claims of closer relatives or even be forged. The appeal of the speaker to the jurors regarding the estate of Cleonymus reflects this:

[G]ive your verdicts on the grounds of affinity and the true facts of the case in favour of those who claim by right of kinship rather than of those who rely on a will. For you all know what a family relationship is, and it is impossible to misrepresent it to you; on the other hand, false wills have often to be produced—sometimes complete forgeries, sometimes executed under misapprehension. (Isaeus 1.41)[35]

The actual procedure of adoption is perhaps best reflected in a passage from Isaeus describing how Apollodorus adopted a son late in his life. The adopted son recounts that Apollodorus approached his mother

> and expressed a wish to adopt me and asked her permission, which was granted. He was so determined to act with all possible haste that he straightway took me to his own house and entrusted me with the direction of all his affairs, regarding himself as no longer capable of managing anything himself, and thinking that I should be able to do everything. When the Thargelia [an early summer festival] came round, he conducted me to the altars and to the members of the families and ward. Now these bodies have a uniform rule, that when a man introduces his own son or an adopted son, he must swear with his hand upon the victims [sacrificial animals] that the child whom he is introducing, whether his own or adopted son, is the offspring of an Athenian mother and born in wedlock; and, even after the introducer has done this, the other members still have to pass a vote and, if their vote is favourable, they then, and not till then, inscribe him on the official register. (Isaeus 7.14–16)[36]

A similar process—a private meeting and agreement followed by introductions—is reflected in the case of Menecles' estate, in which the adopted son of Menecles defends the legality of his adoption by describing what was done (Isaeus 2.14). The adoptive father's introduction of the adoptee as his son to family members, members of his deme, and his phratry seem to have been important features of the procedure based on the strategic recital of these introductions in defenses of adoptions. Rubinstein argues that it was these introductions that actually constituted the adoption procedure.[37] Introductions may have been the standard procedure in testamentary adoptions as well. If a father failed to make such overtures before his death, he greatly increased the chances of litigation.[38]

A man with daughters but no son had another avenue for securing an heir. At his death the dead man's property (*oikos*) passed to the nearest male relative (according to a fixed order).[39] That relative was required to marry the orphaned daughter in order to inherit the *oikos*. If he was already married he was expected to divorce his wife. If the nearest relative refused to marry her, the *oikos*—including the daughter—passed to the next relative in the fixed order. The relative who married her managed the estate until a son born to them reached the age of two years past puberty. At that point the son (or sons) born to the woman inherited the *oikos* of his grandfather with the requirement that he support his mother.[40]

In such a situation, the woman was said to be ἐπίκληρος (*epiklēros*, upon—or attached to—the estate). Although the arrangement provided protection for an orphaned daughter, its main function was to transmit the *oikos* of the dead man to his yet unborn descendants via his daughter and a near-kinsman. The obvious drawback of this approach was that the father was not able personally to control the destination of his *oikos*.

By the fourth century B.C.E., a more flexible arrangement emerged: adoption and bequest. The heirless father could adopt a son and bequeath his property to this chosen heir. An important caveat shows that this approach developed from the law of the *epikleros*: the adopted heir could only receive the estate if he married the daughter who had no brothers.

Although Solon's law, noted earlier, limited those who could make a will to fathers without sons, an exception permitted a father to do so and to name a guardian(s) if his son(s) was a minor. Just as adoption protected an *oikos* that lacked a son, guardianship (ἐπιτροπή, *epitropē*) protected an *oikos* that lacked a father. Because of high mortality rates and short life expectancies, a relatively large number of children became independent at an early age, upon the death of their fathers. The father could name a guardian while he was still alive, or—as was no doubt more common—he could appoint someone in his will.[41]

The appointee was generally a close relative, but such was not required (Dem. 27.4). If the father appointed no guardian, the closest male relative, according to the fixed order of intestate succession, was to be appointed. If no relative came forward, it was up to the archon to make the appointment.[42]

Guardians were to provide for the physical well-being of their wards, protect their legal interests, and see to their education. In the case against Diogeiton, Lysias includes food, shoes, laundry, haircuts, and even the cost of a *paidagōgos* (one—often a slave—responsible for the daily supervision of a young child) as items for which the guardian would have been responsible (32.20, 28). The guardian could provide money from his active management of the estate or he could invest the estate and support the ward(s) from its income. In charging Diogeiton with stealing from his wards, Lysias says, "[H]e might have farmed out the estate and so got rid of a load of cares, or purchased land and used the income for the children's support" (32.23). The guardian not only had charge of the child's property but even had control of the child himself. For instance it seems to have been the guardian's choice whether the child lived with its mother or with the guardian (Lysias 32.8, 16).

Although Greek laws pertaining to guardianship may have arisen to protect the *oikos* from being plundered, they also protected the child. When minors came of age, they could bring charges against their guardian(s) if they believed their estate was plundered or mismanaged—as the famous case of Demosthenes illustrates so well (Dem. 27).

Motives, values, and underlying assumptions. The typical reasons why a childless Athenian man might have chosen to adopt a son are most apparent in Isaeus 2.10. Here Menecles' adopted son offers the court the following reasons why he was adopted:

> [A]fter this [Menecles' divorce], some time passed; then Menecles began to consider how to avoid being childless, and how to have someone who would look after him in his old age while he was alive, and, when he was dead, would bury him and, in the future, perform the rites for him (at his tomb). (Isaeus 2.10)

Menecles' concern regarding his care in old age (γηροτροφία, *gērotrophia*) is understandable: in ancient societies responsibility for such care fell entirely on descendants or other close relatives.[43] If one's branch was the last in the family tree, one had reason for concern.[44]

Not surprisingly, therefore, insuring that one's *oikos* does not become "empty" (ἔρημος, *erēmos*) is the most common motive for adoption.[45] A continuing *oikos*, achieved by adopting a son *inter vivos*, would most securely guarantee Menecles' concerns. Because they take force only after death, testamentary or posthumous adoptions would not have created the same bonds or obligations that Menecles desired to insure his old age and burial.

Because the ultimate reason for adoption was to preserve the *oikos*, inheritance and adoption were always intricately interrelated in Athenian law. In modern times wills are a strategy for disposing of one's property, while adoption is a legal strategy for providing a permanent home for a child who lacks parents (or suitable parents). For the ancient Greeks, by contrast, wills were a legal strategy for naming an heir to preserve an *oikos* that was in danger of extinction. Concern for the welfare of a child was not the primary motive for most Greek adopters.

Thus far our focus has been on the reasons why Greeks adopted and the values underlying these reasons. We should also ask why some people were willing to give up their offspring for adoption. In many cases family ties motivated the decision: kinsmen worked together—especially evident in the adoptions involving nephews—to prevent an *oikos* from becoming empty.

Of course, financial considerations were also motivating factors. The adopted son of Menecles, for example, defended himself of the suspicion that he was only in it for the money (Isaeus 2.41–43). He responded to his opponents by pointing out that after being adopted *inter vivos* he cared for Menecles for twenty-three years.

Consider another financial motive. If a family was in serious debt, and had two or more sons, they could give one of the sons in adoption and still retain an heir, relieving an already debt-ridden family from financial obligations associated with positioning him for the future. Not only that, the adopted son would not inherit his natural father's financial burdens. In the lawsuit over the estate of Aristarchus, Isaeus writes, "Other people indeed, when they have monetary losses, introduce their children into other families in order that they may not share in their parents' loss of civic rights" (10.17).

Adoption and Inheritance in Roman Law

Sources. Whereas speeches written by lawyers and presented to Athenian juries represent the most important sources for Greek adoption and inheritance, the bulk of our information about Roman law comes from a professional class of jurists who provided legal opinions for magistrates. These jurists treated the law as an integrated system whose rules existed independent of social practice. By analyzing concrete cases, they sought to discover abstract legal principles that could then be applied to new situations.[46] The jurists produced commentaries on civil law and on the remedies that were contained in the magistrate's edict.

These juristic sources present the social historian with a number of formidable problems. First, determining what particular legal opinion obtained at a particular time can be very difficult because of interpolations in the sources. The *Digest* exemplifies this problem because it compiles excerpts from jurists from centuries earlier and abbreviates prior juristic works.[47] The problem, however, is not limited to the *Digest*; postclassical jurists were also interpreting the legal tradition for new situations and updating it to reflect changes in the law—often leaving modern scholars to guess when changes actually entered the law.

Another problem with the Roman juristic sources is that the texts by nature deal with technical legal issues that routinely lack sufficient description and context. Regarding adoption, for example, the juristic texts focus on the legal consequences of specific adoption cases—usually inheritance rights—but pay no attention to the motives of the parties involved. Literary materials—and to a lesser degree inscriptions—can shed some light here, but the relevant literary materials are mostly from the late republic, not the early empire. Furthermore, the adoptions mentioned in Roman literature typically involve the ruling elite. Thus the literary sources tell us little about the prevalence of adoption in Roman society at large.

Finally, in some literary and most epigraphic materials, adoptive status must be inferred from nomenclature. However, because nomenclature served a number of purposes, the form of a name can only suggest that a person may have been adopted; it cannot alone establish the fact.[48] Although the Roman legal sources for adoption and inheritance are difficult, the issues they present are not forbidding in light of our purpose: to search for underlying assumptions that shaped Roman law rather than to seek to establish specific legal practices and procedures that were operative in particular times and places.

Laws, social conventions, and procedures. When discussing adoption, the Roman jurists were concerned almost entirely with succession rights to property. In Roman law, as in Greek law, adoption and inheritance are closely linked because the starting assumption for Roman inheritance law was the succession of the *familia*. Jane Gardner offers a succinct characterization: "Essentially, Roman adoption is about property entitlement."[49] Roman law concerns itself with finding an heir who could step into the shoes of the deceased, assume all the rights and obligations of the dead *pater familias* (head of a family), and preserve the *familia* (the family and everything attached to it) with its *sacra* (sacred rites). Roman law looked for this heir first among the male children who became independent as a result of the death of the *pater familias*.[50] In contrast to Greek practice, Roman law permitted women to inherit; daughters were entitled to an equal share.[51]

Uniquely, Roman adoption must be considered in its relationship to the *pater familias* in the Roman *familia* because adoption in Roman law was a "device for taking a person out of one *familia* and placing him or her into another, under the *potestas* [power] of its *paterfamilias*."[52] Because the adopter had to possess *potestas*, the adopter had to be a *pater familias*, a male Roman citizen who was *sui iuris* (legally independent). The Roman *familia* is not equivalent to the modern conception of "family." Three differences stand out most clearly: first, the Roman *familia* included not only relatives but often slaves; second, descent and family membership were based on blood relation on the father's side only (agnatic, not cognatic descent); and third, and most important, legal control of the *familia* belonged to the *pater familias*, and his *potestas* was not terminated until his death.[53] Those under his *potestas* had no property of their own and could not take independent legal action.[54] In other words, adult men—and women—with their own families were unable to own any property if they had a surviving father or grandfather. So the death of the *pater familias* "signaled the end of a kind of slavery. The sons became adults, and the daughters, if they had not married or had divorced, became heiresses, free to marry whomever they wished."[55]

Roman legal texts reflect two distinct adoptive procedures, depending on the role of the *pater familias*.[56] In Roman law, free citizens were divided into two groups: those legally independent (*sui iuris*) and those under the *potestas* of a *pater familias* (*alieni iuris*). Notably, Gaius introduces adoption law and procedure as another way "children fall into our power [*potestas*]":

> We have just set out the rules under which our real children fall into our power. This also happens with those whom we adopt. Adoptions can be done in two ways, either by authority of the people [adrogation] or

through the jurisdiction of a magistrate, for instance, a praetor. (Gaius 1.97)

The first procedure, *adrogatio*, was used only for a person who was already *sui iuris* (legally independent), while the second, *adoptio*, was for a person who was still *in potestate* (under a *pater familias*). *Adrogations* were probably never very common. Not only was the process cumbersome, but the drawbacks associated with extinguishing a *familia* and surrendering one's independence and one's property to the adopting *pater* must have made it a relatively rare procedure.

The first stage of the process of *adrogatio* involved an enquiry by the college of pontiffs because a *familia* was being terminated along with its *sacra*.[57] If the pontiffs approved the proposed adoption, the curiate assembly *in Rome* had to approve by a formal vote. Gaius rightly calls adrogation "adoption by the authority of the people."[58]

Adoptio, the adoption of someone who was still *in potestas*, however, was relatively simple, because the adoptee was still under the authority of a *pater familias* who had the power to give him or her in adoption. This procedure involved two basic steps: first, the adoptee was released from the *potestas* of the natural father; second, the adoptive father received *potestas* over the adopted son or daughter by the magistrate's declaration. The first step required a classical emancipation formula wherein the natural father "sold" (mancipated) his son or daughter to an intermediary who manumitted the adoptee back to the natural father until the process was repeated three times. The father's *potestas* was broken after the third sale.[59] The second step was accomplished when the adoptive father claimed the adoptee as his son or daughter. If the natural father made no defense, the magistrate declared in accordance with the adopter's claim.

Because of the central role of the *pater familias* and its far-reaching legal implications, some historians have claimed that the purpose of Roman adoption was to create *patria potestas*.[60] In Roman law there was no way to perpetuate the *familia* without creating *patria potestas*.

For the Romans an adopted son had the same standing as a natural son, as Gaius notes: "Adoptive sons in their adoptive family are in the same legal position as real sons" (2.136). This legal status is reflected in adoptive formulae: "May it be your will and command that L. Valerius may be to L. Titius in right and in law his son, just as if he were born from him as *pater* and from his *materfamilias*, and that he [Titius] may have in relation to him [Valerius] the power of life and death, as there is to a father in the case of a son" (Gellius, *NA* 5.19.9).

Other restrictions affected who could adopt and who could be adopted. As noted earlier, women could not adopt because they did not possess *potestas* over other free persons. For the same reason, married couples did not adopt; rather, the

husband alone, as *pater familias,* adopted, and his adoptive children were not related to his wife, even as cognates.[61] Men who lacked the capacity to procreate
(*spadones*) could adopt (Gaius 1.103). Although exceptions can be cited, Romans
clearly expected the adopter to be older than the one adopted, and it appears that
a gap of eighteen years became the accepted convention (Justinian, *Inst.* 1.11.4).[62]
There was no minimum age for adopting someone *in potestate.* However, eighteen
years seems to have been the minimum age for adrogation, though this provision
was modified in the second century C.E. to allow adoption if there was a compelling reason (Gaius, 1.102).[63] An age restriction for adrogation protected the *impubes* (under-age) from exploitation because the adopter absorbed the entire property of the one adrogated. *Impubes* were in no position to make such a decision nor
was their guardian (*tutor impuberum;* Gellius, *NA* 5.19.10).

Protecting the estates of *impubes* was the role of the Roman institution of
guardianship (*tutela*). Guardianship receives considerable attention in Roman
legal sources and literature. Demographic studies suggest the reason: "[J]ust over
one-third of Roman children lost their fathers before puberty, and another third
then lost their fathers before age twenty-five."[64] Consequently, Romans treated
the protection of a minor as the most sacred of social responsibilities.[65] The tutor
was responsible for the management of the minor's property until the child
reached fourteen—when boys came of age. Although girls came of age at twelve,
they continued to have a tutor throughout their adult lives.[66]

Motives, values, and underlying assumptions. The original, primary purpose of adoption for the Romans was to allow an heirless father to co-opt someone to inherit his patrimony and prevent his family from dying out.[67] As Gardner
notes, "Wills were one method, but wills could fail; inheritance rights were more
secure."[68] Adoption was so regularly focused on perpetuating the line that there
are few examples of persons adopting someone who already had living sons or of
adopting females.[69]

Why would Romans give their sons up for adoption? An economically hard-
pressed *pater familias* could give one of his sons in adoption as a means of "maintaining a son's status from someone else's funds."[70] An example: L. Aemilius
Paulus had four sons and surrendered two for adoption. Those two later became
consuls. Aemilius thus assured those two sons' futures and left him able to enhance the futures of his two remaining sons.[71]

As in Greek law, a father might give a son in adoption to prevent him from
inheriting family debts that exceeded the value of the estate. However, a Roman
father had other options for achieving this goal. He could emancipate his son, or
he could leave a will in which he expressly disinherited his son. The son could
also protect himself by refusing to accept the inheritance.[72]

Conclusion. Greek and Roman conventions relating to adoption and inheritance reflect very similar motives, values, and underlying assumptions. Adoption and inheritance were closely related in both Roman and Greek law for a common reason: the continuation of the Roman *familia* and of the Greek *oikos*. There were differences of course, but if we focus on motives, values, and assumptions rather than on procedural matters, we may speak broadly of Greco-Roman adoption. Because many of the legal conventions noted above show up in Paul's employment of adoption and inheritance language, it is important to ask how they shaped his usage.

Part II. Adoption and Inheritance in Paul

Two Pauline texts feature adoption prominently: Rom 8:12–25 and Gal 4:1–7. In both, adoption language arose only after inheritance had already been mentioned, and in contexts where there was controversy regarding the status of Gentile believers vis-à-vis Jewish believers. So adoption functions for Paul as a metaphor that gives nuance to what he wishes to communicate about inheritance. If this observation is correct, we will understand Paul's use of adoption and inheritance only when we discover how the idea of adoption gives nuance to the idea of inheritance in Paul's argument—and not the other way around.

∞

This essay emphasizes Paul's usage in Galatians not only because it represents his first use of the term, but also because nowhere in the Pauline corpus does adoption and inheritance language play so key a role as in Galatians. Inheritance unites the argument of Gal 3:6–4:7. From the initial reference to "sons of Abraham" in 3:6 to the climactic affirmation that those baptized into Christ are "Abraham's offspring" and "heirs according to the promise" (3:27–29), the notion of inheritance is central to Paul's argument. Additional references to "heirs" in 4:1–7 are refinements of the argument of 3:6–29. In 4:1–7, Paul ties inheritance to adoption by making the heir an adopted son. Because the argument of 3:6–4:7 connects the Spirit to the "inheritance" by associating it with the "blessing of Abraham" and the "promise," it is possible to see 3:1–4:7 as one thematic unit within which inheritance is the central uniting concept.[73]

Donald Davidson argues that metaphors, by requiring us to see one thing as another, cause us to notice matters that would not otherwise be evoked.[74] Quintilian, an ancient rhetorical theorist, suggested that the role of metaphor should be to "move the feelings, give special distinction to things and place them vividly before the eye" (*Inst.* 8.6.19). These observations help us to focus the critical question: When Paul writes, "If a child (son), then an heir" (4:7), what did he want his

Galatian readers to notice by making the child an adoptee? What special distinction did he wish to communicate?

Points of Contact between Paul's Usage and Greco-Roman Conventions

Galatians reflects four points of contact between Greco-Roman adoption and inheritance practices and Pauline usage. Highlighting these and comparing them to Paul's argument is our best means of recognizing the special distinction Paul wanted his readers to notice.

The association of adoption and inheritance. Paul's linkage of adoption with inheritance in Gal 4:5 reflects Greco-Roman conventions.[75] Because the fundamental motive for adoption was the continuation of the *oikos/familia*, a Greco-Roman father thought first about his estate and what to do about his inheritance, and only secondarily about adoption. Likewise, for Paul in Gal 4:1–7 (and Rom 8:12–25), adoption enters the discussion because Paul is thinking about inheritance.

If a son, then an heir. Paul's "if a child (son), then an heir" (Gal 4:7) reflects an important Greco-Roman legal convention.[76] This principle is related to the one above: if the assumption that a son inherits his father's *oikos/familia* had not been so fundamental, adoption would not have been so closely associated with inheritance.[77]

The importance of the legal convention—if a son, then an heir—for Paul's argument is underscored by the structural role it plays in the development of the pericope. In the opening section Paul claims that it is believers who are the descendants (sons) of Abraham (3:7), only to conclude the argument by affirming that "if a son, then an heir" (4:7). Evidently Paul framed his argument on the basis of this legal assumption.

Certainty of the adoptee's right to inherit. Paul's argument in Gal 3:1–4:7 depends fundamentally on the adoptee's absolute right to inherit. Because the apostle shows that the Galatians are in fact already "sons," he establishes their status as full heirs by faith without circumcision or the Law, a status that Paul's opponents had apparently denied.

Adoption as a metaphor for status change. Paul's readers did not have to be masters of the legal nuances of adoption law to understand that adoption radically altered the adoptee's status. The status change resulted from severing all legal ties to the natural father and establishing legal ties with the adoptive father. Technically, the son was no longer the son of his natural father, but the son of the adopter, a change even his name—and that of his offspring—would reflect.[78]

Plutarch, a contemporary Hellenistic writer, uses adoption as a theological metaphor—a rarity outside of Paul—and shares Paul's awareness of this legal status change.[79] In his essay "The Divine Vengeance," Plutarch responded to Bion, who had critiqued God for punishing a descendant for the crimes of an ancestor.[80] Bion claimed that this instance of God's behavior was even more ludicrous than a doctor treating a descendant for an ancestor's malady. Plutarch countered that a preventative treatment can save a patient from an inherited disorder, and then attempted to show that God's actions had been known to cure inherited tendencies toward evil. Plutarch defended God's apparent inconsistency in this regard as the working of divine providence in providing "therapy for the soul" at the right time. After claiming that God does not always hold children accountable for the sins of their parents, Plutarch writes:

> But where a good man is born of a bad, as a healthy child may come of a sickly parent, the penalty attached to the family is remitted, and he becomes, as it were, *adopted* out of vice; whereas if a man's disorder reproduces the traits of a vicious ancestry, it is surely fitting that he should succeed to the punishment of that viciousness as to the debts of an estate. (Plutarch, *Mor.* 562F; emphasis added)

If evil tendencies are not inherited by the next generation, Plutarch believes it is because God intervened; God adopted the descendant out of an evil *oikos* (ἐκποίητος τῆς κακίας γενόμενος, *ekpoiētos tēs kakias genomenos*).[81] Clearly, adoption is the means by which the descendant is cleared from his original family's "debt" of vice.[82] Because an adopted child carried no debts from his father's *oikos* into the adopter's *oikos,* a family could give up a son for adoption as a means of freeing him from a burden of debt (Isaeus 10.17). Notably, Plutarch follows the above passage with an illustrative passage that has been called a "conversion" story.[83]

Plutarch reflects the same legal convention in another passage regarding the punishment of two Athenian traitors. The punishment's severity and its implications for the traitors' descendants is shown by the provision that, in their case, an adoption of one of their descendants will not free the adoptee from the ancestor's guilt and its results. Rather, the adopter himself will become guilty (Plutarch, *Mor.* 834B).

Plutarch's metaphorical usage provides an important comparison for Paul's employment of the adoption metaphor. First, Plutarch's text shows that the association of adoption with debt cancellation reflected in fourth-century B.C.E. Greek sources was known in Paul's time. Second, Plutarch assumed he could use this legal convention as a metaphor that would not only be understood by readers, but would also buttress his argument.[84] In fact, it was so well known that he could freely reverse the conventional understanding.

How do you free someone from inherited obligations? Adopt them! Consequently, when Paul used the metaphor of adoption he could reasonably assume that his Galatian readers would notice that, by virtue of their adoption as sons, their salvation involved a radical status change that freed them from inherited obligations. Significantly, Paul's adoption metaphor occurs in a passage that clarifies where the heirs stand vis-à-vis legal obligations. In fact, this is what especially binds 4:1–7 to the preceding argument, as is clear from Paul's use of ὑπό (*hypo*, under).[85] In 3:22, he declares that "scripture consigned all things to sin" (ὑπὸ ἁμαρτίαν, *hypo hamartian*) and then associates their "confinement" with the Law (ὑπὸ νόμον ἐφρουρούμεθα, *hypo nomon ephrouroumetha*). He then connects being ὑπὸ νόμον (*hypo nomon*, under the Law) with being ὑπὸ παιδαγωγόν (*hypo paidagōgon*, under a pedagogue, 3:24, 25), ὑπὸ ἐπιτρόπους καὶ οἰκονόμους (*hypo epitropous kai oikonomous*, under guardians and trustees, 4:2), and ὑπὸ τά στοιχεῖα τοῦ κόσμου (*hypo ta stoicheia tou kosmou*, under the elemental spirits of the universe, 4:3).

Paul's use of the verb ἐξαγοράζω (*exagorazō*, to redeem or buy back) earlier in the same verse (4:5) prepares the reader to notice this aspect of adoption because it suggests freedom by means of a payment.[86] Because Paul in 4:3–4 associated slavery with being under the Law and then presented God's Son as redeeming those under the Law, it is certain that ἐξαγοράζω (*exagorazō*) means more specifically to free a slave through paying a sum of money.[87] The language of slavery did not enter Paul's argument because the adoption of slaves by a god—as a means of securing their freedom—was a common Greco-Roman convention; rather, it entered as a rhetorical means of radicalizing the obligation of being under the Law.[88] Adoption is associated with Christ's role as redeemer in Gal 4:5 because the "heirs-to-be" had prior obligations out of which they needed to be adopted. By focusing on adoption as a means of freeing the adoptee from inherited debt, Paul shifts the perspective from how adoption benefits the adopter to how it benefits the adoptee. As noted earlier in this study, Greek and Roman sources do not view adoption primarily as a vehicle for protecting orphans, but rather as a vehicle for protecting fathers who lacked an heir. For Paul, this more typical view of adoption does not provide a useful analogy because God—the father in this case—is not in search of an heir to preserve an *oikos*/familia in danger of dying out. Rather, by focusing on the plight of the potential adoptees—those needing redemption from the debt hanging over their heads—Paul presents God as the adopter who intervenes on their behalf, freeing them from slavery.

The points of contact between Paul's use of adoption/inheritance language and Greco-Roman conventions are unambiguous. Determining more precisely how these conventions shaped Paul's use of adoption and inheritance requires a closer examination of Gal 4:1–7 in its historical and literary context.

Adoption and Inheritance in Light of Paul's Argument in Galatians 4:1–7

The historical context of Galatians. Pauline scholars commonly agree regarding the general setting of Galatians.[89] Subsequent to Paul's proclamation of the gospel in Galatia, other teachers entered the churches insisting that full membership in the people of God required circumcision and keeping the Law of Moses—or at least some of the Law's requirements. Although these teachers agreed that the coming of Jesus as Messiah meant Gentiles could be fully included in Israel, they did not believe this made the Law and circumcision irrelevant for Gentiles.

Paul's opponents insisted that Gentiles must keep the Law.[90] However, it is not so clear whether the primary issue was keeping the Law as a means of salvation (the traditional scholarly view) or as a requirement for living as a Christian (the more recent view).[91] Emphasizing 3:1–5 as the key text, Cosgrove has argued persuasively for the latter, claiming that the central issue is whether "believers can promote their ongoing experience of the Spirit by doing the law."[92] Paul's opponents say yes and apparently offer a thoroughly reasonable case for their position based on descent from Abraham. Beker argued persuasively that the opponents had constructed a "chain argument" featuring Abraham in order to persuade the Galatians to reevaluate Paul's gospel.[93] Abraham's status as the first proselyte, his circumcision, and Jewish traditions regarding his faithful keeping of the Law (prior to its revelation at Sinai) suggest how useful his example would have been to the rival teachers.[94] The argument establishes a line of continuity between Abraham, circumcision, the Law, and the Messiah that has obvious implications for Gentiles.[95] Consequently, Paul's discussion in Gal 3 attempts to disrupt the opponents' argument by driving a wedge between Abraham and the Law.

Literary analysis. Paul saw an opportunity to drive a wedge between Abraham and the Law by focusing on Abraham's descendants as heirs. It was not the inheritance itself that interested Paul here, but rather the basis upon which someone was designated an heir.

In Gal 3, Paul never describes the content of the inheritance itself. His association of the inheritance with Abraham, and especially with the "promise," indicates that Paul thought of inheritance in light of Jewish tradition.[96] However, Paul's usage has a strongly eschatological character.[97] In Galatians the most detailed statement of the inheritance's content comes in 5:21, in which Paul, after reciting a vice list, warns readers that "those who do such things shall not *inherit* the kingdom of God" (emphasis added). Using a different eschatological metaphor in 6:7–9, Paul tells the reader that the one who "sows to the Spirit will from the Spirit reap *eternal life*" (emphasis added). In a similar way Paul associates the inheritance with the "redemption of the body" in Rom 8:23, and with the resurrection of the body in 1 Cor 15:50.

Paul drives his wedge by establishing a cosmic order that has Abraham (and his descendants) and those "relying on the works of the Law" on opposite sides. Robert Hall's analysis of Galatians in light of the rhetorical argumentation of apocalypses elucidates Paul's strategy.

According to Hall, Gal 3:1–5; 3:7–29; 4:1–11; 4:21–5:1; and 5:16–6:10 reflect a common argument found in apocalypses: the revelation of cosmic order based on God's judgments.[98] Paul's revelation of this cosmic order discloses two spheres: "the wicked sphere in which angels enforce the law to curb sin and the recently established righteous sphere of Christ's faith."[99] Such an approach affords Paul the opportunity to urge readers to cling to the righteous sphere while rejecting the wicked sphere.

So the wedge Paul drives between Abraham and the Law in 3:6–29 is the revelation of cosmic order. Paul claims Abraham, and others of faith, for the righteous sphere (3:6–9) while those "relying on the works of the law are under a curse," a curse from which the righteous were redeemed by Christ's death, a death under the Law's curse (3:10–14). In 3:15–18, Paul justifies his disassociation of the Law from Abraham's promise.

Paul's argument in 3:15–18, together with his own association of the Law with the sphere of wickedness, requires him to explain the role of the Law and its relation to God's promises (3:19–22). But in 3:23–29 he reasserts the distinction between the sphere in which the Law operates and the sphere in which faith operates, and enjoins temporal limits for the period when the Law rightly functioned as a restraint: "the law was our disciplinarian [*paidagōgos*] until Christ came" (3:24).[100] Moreover, using a baptismal formula Paul connects the fulfillment of the Abraham promise with the believers' union with Christ effected in baptism, a union that results in the sonship of believers by virtue of their union with Abraham's singular seed, Christ (Gal 3:16). This union eliminates prior distinctions between Jew and Greek, as well as those between slave and free, and male and female. Paul's assertion that Christ is Abraham's singular seed, his one and only heir, is critical for his treatment of inheritance in Gal 3.[101]

The two-spheres framework is vital for interpreting Galatians. But we must note what most fundamentally distinguishes the two spheres. The primary antithesis on which Galatians is built is not Christ versus the law. Rather, as Gaventa put it, "the governing theological antithesis in Galatians is between Christ or the new creation and the cosmos; the antithesis between Christ and the law and between the cross and circumcision are not the equivalent of this central premise but follow from it."[102] Already in the salutation Paul associates the cross with cosmic invasion: "[The Lord Jesus Christ] gave himself for our sins to set us free from the present evil age, according to the will of our God and Father" (Gal 1:4). His hand-written conclusion to the letter (6:11–18, esp. vv. 14–15) makes an appropriate bookend when he identifies the cross as the means by which "the world has been crucified to me, and I to the world." Indeed, the assumption of the Christ-event as a cosmic invasion shapes the development of the entire letter. By interpreting descent from Abraham in light of the revelation of this cosmic order in 3:6–29, Paul prepares his readers for understanding the status change (and its effects) that his adoption language claims in 4:1–7.

Most interpreters read Gal 4:1–7 as a summary or restatement of the argument Paul made in chapter 3, especially in 3:23–29. Brendan Byrne is correct, therefore, when he claims that an examination of 4:1–7 "will be satisfactory only if it can explain why Paul doubles back in this way."[103] James Dunn communicated the overlap well in the following chart:[104]

3:23–29	4:1–7
(23) Before the coming of faith we were held in custody under the law confined until the coming of faith . . . (24) The law is our custodian until Christ . . . (25) But when faith came we were no longer under a custodian. (26) For all of you are sons of God . . . (27) You all were baptized into Christ . . . (29) So then you are Abraham's seed, heirs in accordance with promise.	(1) As long as the heir is a child . . . (2) He is under guardians and stewards. Until the time set by the father. (3) As children we were enslaved under the elemental forces . . . (4) But when the fullness of time came . . . (5) In order to redeem those under the law. In order that we might receive adoption. (5) God sent the Spirit of his Son . . . (7) So that you are no longer a slave but son, and if a son, then an heir through God.

Clearly the difference between the two paragraphs is not the subject matter! The following questions underscore the main difference: Why was characterizing the period prior to Christ/faith as confinement under the Law not sufficient for Paul? Why did he feel compelled to make the confinement "slavery," and why slavery under the "elemental spirits of the world" (*stoicheia tou kosmou*)? A more detailed look at 4:1–7 sheds light on these questions.

The structure of 4:1–7 is apparent: The metaphor of the "minor heir" is developed by Paul in verses 1–2 and then applied in verses 3–7.[105] The *paidagōgos* (disciplinarian) metaphor and that of the "minor heir" share three things in common. They are drawn from socio-legal practices that were common in cities of the Greek East.[106] Second, they feature restricted freedom. Third, they deal with a situation in which restricted freedom is appropriate at one time but inappropriate later.

The introduction of the "minor heir" in 4:1–7 allows Paul to use the term "heir" in verse 1 to connect to the "heirs" of 3:29 while at the same time refining the idea of inheritance in light of the situation in Galatia. When minor heirs were placed under guardians in the Greco-Roman world—or when fathers adopted sons—the parties involved were maneuvering through a maze of inheritance complications. Because of the interference of the opponents, Paul sees the Galatians as mired in inheritance complications as well. By using the metaphor of the minor heir, Paul restates the point he made in 3:23–25 to underscore the inappropriateness of using the Law as a guardian to supervise the behavior of believers. Moreover, by describing the minor heir as a virtual slave, he manages to put Jews in the same situation as Gentiles vis-à-vis the inheritance.

Several aspects of this illustration have troubled commentators. First, if Paul is constructing a metaphor from Greek or Roman legal conventions, why does he describe the heir as a νήπιος (*nēpios*, infant) rather than using a technical legal term for a minor (e.g., ἀφῆλιξ, *aphēlix*).[107] However, *nēpios* is a reasonable choice if Paul wants to include the pejorative note of immaturity in his description, an idea already implied by the *paidagōgos* analogy.[108] That Paul has this in mind is suggested by the ironic contrast he makes in 3:3 with the immaturity/maturity connotations of "beginning" and "ending," a text closely associated with 4:1–7.[109] Second, commentators often feel the need to explain apologetically Paul's reference to the young heir as "no different than a slave."[110] However, arguing that there are differences between young heirs and slaves misses Paul's use of the metaphor.[111] Paul nudges the reader to notice one aspect of the comparison: both young heirs and the slaves are subject to the control of others.

The third aspect of the analogy that has troubled commentators is the coupling of ἐπίτροποι (*epitropoi*, guardians) and οἰκονόμοι (*oikonomoi*, trustees) as those responsible for managing the affairs of a minor child; this combination is not typical of Greek or Roman legal arrangements.[112] However, *epitropos* is the standard Greek term for a guardian in this role.[113] *Oikonomos* usually denotes a person of slave status, and often refers to a household manager with fiscal duties.[114] Hence, these terms are descriptive of a commonplace in Roman tutelage: multiple guardians were often appointed while one exercises a management role vis-à-vis the others.[115] The best explanation for Paul's insistence on a plurality of persons managing the minor is that he is adapting his illustration to the point he wishes to make, namely, that young heirs and slaves are alike subject to others. He exercises considerable liberty in constructing this analogy because he already has framed these general terms through the *paidagōgos* metaphor in 3:23–25. By describing a plurality of managers who control the young heir's life, Paul is able to prepare readers for the analogy he will draw to the plural στοιχεῖα τοῦ κόσμου (*stoicheia tou kosmou*, elemental spirits of the world) in 4:3.

Fourth, the idea that a father's will could set the temporal limit of the guardianship (προθεσμίας τοῦ πατρός, *prothesmias tou patros;* 4:2) is unknown in Roman legal sources and rare in Greek sources.[116] Although the phrase does not correspond to Roman laws of guardianship, it does reflect a common Roman practice. Roman fathers increasingly made use of the *fideicommissum* (a kind of trust) to gain more flexibility in controlling their estates after death. Regarding this, Saller writes:

> Testators wishing to leave property to children sometimes felt that the ages established by law as the end of *tutela* (fourteen for boys and twelve for girls) were unsatisfactory. A testator uneasy at the thought of a teenage son making decisions about his patrimony could use the *fideicommissum* to raise the age at which the estate would be turned over to the child.[117]

Paul's reason for constructing his analogy in this manner is clear: By replacing "coming of age"—the conventionally expected end of guardianship—with "the date set by the father," Paul connects the end of the guardianship with the coming of Christ instead of the maturity of the ward. This strategy prevents Paul's opponents from using the immaturity of the Galatian believers as a means of justifying a continuing supervisory role for the Law.[118]

Finally, some object that the father in verses 1–2 does not correspond to the father in verses 3–7.[119] In the former the father is assumed to have died, leaving a minor child under the supervision of others, whereas in verses 3–7 the Father, God, is alive and active in sending the Son to redeem those under the Law.[120] As noted earlier with regard to metaphors, when Paul crafted analogies, he often adapted the phenomena on which his analogies were based to the point he wanted to illustrate.[121]

Many of the "irregularities" in the analogy that have troubled commentators in 4:1–7 actually contribute to the point Paul desires to make: the confinement under the Law (3:23–25) was (and is) more than the benign supervision of guardians, it was (and is) slavery to the elemental spirits of the world.

Paul's identification of Law and elemental spirits has profound implications for the interpretation of Galatians and for Paul's use of adoption and inheritance. Paul's association of the Law with slavery and the connection of that slavery to the *stoicheia tou kosmou* makes the decision confronting the Galatians not only a choice between slavery and freedom but also a choice between *this world* and God's *new creation.*[122] Following the negative use of slavery in 4:1–7, pejorative terms for slaves and slavery dominate in the rest of the letter.[123] Moreover, the radical alternatives established here are reinforced in the Sarah/Hagar allegory (4:21–5:1) and in the flesh/Spirit contrast (chs. 4 and 5).

Deciphering Paul's specific meaning for *stoicheia tou kosmou* has been problematic (4:3).[124] BDAG includes four basic meanings for *stoicheia*: (1) fundamental principles; (2) elemental substances; (3) elemental spirits; (4) heavenly bodies.[125] The dilemma is that when *stoicheia* occurs with *kosmos,* the meaning elemental substances (i.e., earth, air, fire, and water) seems to be the solid choice. However, the capacity of the *stoicheia* to enslave human beings, and Paul's reference to the enslaving *stoicheia* in 4:8–9 as "beings that by nature are no gods," suggest spiritual powers of some kind.[126]

What Paul associates with *stoicheia* is absolutely determinative for its interpretation. In 4:3–4, he associates slavery to the *stoicheia tou kosmou* with slavery under the Law; in 4:8–9, he associates slavery to the *stoicheia* with pagan enslavement to "beings that by nature are no gods." Paul's fundamental point is clear: Apart from Christ all human beings—both Jews and Gentiles—are enslaved to the *stoicheia tou kosmou.*[127]

Paul's reference to the *stoicheia tou kosmou* as enslaving powers and the letter's fundamental antithesis (*this world* versus the *new creation*) are critical for deciphering the role of the Spirit in adoption, and in Galatians more generally. This case has been persuasively argued by Lull:

> In short, in Paul's view the only adequate remedy for the human predicament . . . is a "new creation" in which the obstacles to human freedom—sin, the flesh and death—are deprived of their power. It is for this reason that the Spirit is not at the periphery but at the center of the new historical epoch.[128]

Paul began Gal 3 by reminding his readers that their journey began with the reception of the Spirit (Gal 3:2–3). In 4:1–7, Paul's summary, he returns to the arrival of the Spirit as God's power to overcome the human predicament. The Spirit's Abba-cry in 4:6 and the Galatians' experience of the Spirit in 3:1–5 both remind the readers that they were already sons.[129] Moreover, Paul's description of the human predicament and of the inability of the Law to remedy it—and especially his association of dual slaveries under the Law and under the *stoicheia tou kosmou*—encourages the Galatians to finish the journey the way they began it, with the Spirit, not with the works of the Law. Note, however, that Paul pictures the Galatian believers as in the middle of their faith journey; they are *already* beyond the reach of pedagogues or guardians (cf. 1 Cor 3:1–2; 4:14–21). Paul's *already*-claim contradicts his opponents' assertions that the Galatians were *not yet* full heirs of Abraham. The Galatians are not growing into an inheritance, they were adopted into one.

As noted above, the key to Paul's use of adoption in 4:1–7 is found in the differences between this paragraph's "restatement of the previous argument" and the previous argument itself.[130] Paul has gone to great lengths in the argument between 3:13–14 and 4:4–5 to depict Jews in the same pre-redemptive situation as Gentiles. Consequently, although the ethnic connections of Paul's pronouns may be tight in 3:13–14, they are loose in 4:4–7.[131] Why the difference? The change resulted from Paul's move to link the guidance of the Law as *paidagōgos* with slavery under the *stoicheia tou kosmou*, and his move to declare divine adoptive sonship more fundamental than descent from Abraham. After 3:29 Abraham is mentioned only once (4:22), to introduce the Sarah/Hagar allegory, while pejorative references to slaves and slavery are very common, beginning in 4:1 (one pejorative use prior to 4:1 [2:4]; fourteen in chs. 4 and 5). The question "who are descendants of Abraham" clearly gives way to the contrasting questions "who is a slave" and "who is free?" Galatians 4:1–7 is the bridge for this transition and adoption supports the span connecting the heir's status directly to God via God's cosmic invasion through Christ.

Paul's argument in Gal 3:1–4:7 owes much to his opponents' affirmation of *Abrahamic descent*. In chapter 3 Paul shapes his argument to theirs. However, in 4:1–7, Paul restates the argument in a way that seems to follow from the preceding discussion, but Abraham is missing there and in his place Paul features *descent from God*.[132] In other words, Gal 4:1–7 restates the previous argument, but in the frame of reference Paul prefers!

Comparing Romans

Space limitations compel abbreviated comments about Romans, which contains the only other occurrences of υἱοθεσία (*huiothesia*) in the undisputed Pauline letters. The occurrences in Romans demonstrate the flexibility with which Paul used *huiothesia:* in Rom 8:15, 23, he used it in referring to Jewish and Gentile Christians without ethnic distinctions, while in Rom 9:4 he unquestionably used it with reference to ethnic Israel, at the beginning of a list of privileges belonging to Israel— alluding to the exodus tradition and Israel's identity as a people chosen to be God's children (cf. Deut 14:1; Isa 43:6; Jer 31:9; Hos 1:10; Wis 9:7; *Jub.* 1:24–25).[133] Even here, however, we observe Greco-Roman nuances in the adoption metaphor. For example, the Greco-Roman assumption that "if a son, then an heir" supports Paul's insistence that Israel's election, viewed as a sort of divine adoption, is irrevocable (cf. 11:29).[134]

Romans 8:12–25 provides the closest parallel to Paul's use of adoption/inheritance language in Gal 4:1–7. Both of these texts use the same technical term for adoption; both associate adoption with inheritance;[135] both associate the Spirit closely with adoption; both refer to the Abba-cry as Spirit-prompted; both contrast the results of adoption with slavery; and both reflect the Greco-Roman assumption, "if a son, then an heir" (Gal 4:7; Rom 8:17).

Conclusion

The key to understanding Paul's incorporation of adoption and inheritance into his theological expression lies in noticing where this language occurs in his arguments in Romans and Galatians, not in comparing verbal parallels and differences between the two adoption passages. Paul introduced inheritance language in association with Abraham in Rom 4, the only other extended treatment of Abraham in Paul's letters besides Gal 3. As in Gal 3, Paul uses inheritance language with Abraham to dissolve distinctions between Jews and Gentiles: faith, not circumcision or Law-keeping, makes one an heir of Abraham.[136]

It is noteworthy that Paul did not use adoption language in conjunction with inheritance and Abraham in Rom 4; nor did he do so in the treatment of Abraham in Gal 3. In both letters, it was only after he collapsed Jewish-Gentile issues into an apocalyptic either/or (Rom 5–8 and Gal 4–6) that he associated inheritance with adoption.[137] After the Jew-Gentile issues are collapsed in Romans the question becomes whether "death has dominion" (5:14, 17) through Adam or "life has dominion" through Christ (5:17); in Galatians the question becomes whether one is a slave to the *stoicheia tou kosmou* or "in Christ."[138] These contrasting polarities flatten out the distinction between Jews and Gentiles and explain why, for Paul, "neither circumcision nor uncircumcision is anything; but a new creation is everything" (Gal 6:15)! In both Galatians and Romans, only after Paul has collapsed and reframed Jew-Gentile issues by means of the apostle's apocalyptic either/or does he employ the language of adoption to speak of how God makes heirs. It is no accident that Abraham drops out of the inheritance discussion when adoption comes in. In this apocalyptic drama one becomes an heir through God, not Abraham.

Part III. Other Relevant Pauline and Paulinist Texts

Adoption
> Rom 9:25–26
> 2 Cor 6:18
> Rom 1:3–4?
> Eph 1:5

Inheritance
> Gal 5:21
> 1 Cor 6:9, 10
> 1 Cor 15:50
> Eph 1:5, 11, 14, 18[139]
> Eph 5:5

Part IV. Bibliography

Classical Studies

Crook, John. *Law and Life of Rome*. Ithaca, N.Y.: Cornell University Press, 1967.

Gardner, Jane F. *Family and Familia in Roman Law and Life*. Oxford: Clarendon, 1998.

Harrison, A. R. W. *The Law of Athens*. 2 vols. Oxford: Clarendon, 1968.

Humphreys, S. C. *The Family, Women, and Death*. London: Routledge, 1983.

Johnston, David. *Roman Law in Context*. Cambridge: Cambridge University Press, 1999.

Lacey, W. K. *The Family in Classical Greece*. Ithaca, N.Y.: Cornell University Press, 1968.

Pomeroy, Sarah. *Families in Classical and Hellenistic Greece*. Oxford: Clarendon, 1997.

Rubinstein, Lene. *Adoption in iv. Century Athens*. Copenhagen: Museum Tusculanum Press, 1993.

Saller, Richard P. *Patriarchy, Property, and Death in the Roman Family*. Cambridge: Cambridge University Press, 1994.

Sealey, Raphael. *The Justice of the Greeks*. Ann Arbor: University of Michigan Press, 1994.

Todd, S. *The Shape of Athenian Law*. Oxford: Clarendon, 1993.

New Testament Studies

Beker, J. Christiaan. *Paul the Apostle*. Philadelphia: Fortress Press, 1980.

Betz, Hans Dieter. *Galatians: A Commentary on Paul's Letter to the Churches in Galatia*. Hermeneia. Philadelphia: Fortress Press, 1979.

Byrne, Brendan. *"Sons of God"—"Seed of Abraham": A Study of the Idea of the Sonship of God of All Christians in Paul against the Jewish Background*. Analecta biblica 83. Rome: Biblical Institute, 1979.

Dunn, James D. G. *A Commentary on the Epistle to the Galatians*. Black's New Testament Commentaries. London: A. & C. Black, 1993.

Gaventa, Beverly. "The Singularity of the Gospel: A Reading of Galatians." Pages 147–59 in *Pauline Theology*, vol. 1. Edited by Jouette Bassler. Minneapolis: Fortress, 1991.

Hafemann, Scott. "Paul and the Exile of Israel in Galatians 3–4." Pages 329–71 in *Exile: Old Testament, Jewish, and Christian Conceptions*. Edited by James Scott. Supplements to the Journal for the Study of Judaism 56. Leiden: Brill, 1997.

Hall, Robert. "Arguing Like an Apocalypse: Galatians and an Ancient *Topos* outside the Greco-Roman Rhetorical Tradition." *NTS* 42 (1996): 434–53.

Hays, Richard. *The Faith of Jesus Christ: An Investigation of the Narrative Substructure of Galatians 3:1–4:11*. SBLDS 56. Chico, Calif.: Scholars Press, 1983.

Hester, James. "The Heir and Heilsgeschichte: A Study of Galatians 4:1ff." Pages

123–24 in *OIKONOMIA: Heilsgeschichte als Thema der Theologie (Festschrift für Oscar Cullmann)*. Edited by Felix Christ. Hamburg: Herbert Reich, 1967.

Martyn, J. Louis. "Events in Galatia." Pages 160–79 in *Pauline Theology*, vol. 1. Edited by J. Bassler. Minneapolis: Fortress Press, 1991.

———. *Galatians*. AB 33A. New York: Doubleday, 1997.

Scott, J. M. *Adoption as Sons of God: An Exegetical Investigation into the Background of* ΥΙΟΘΕΣΙΑ *in the Pauline Corpus*. WUNT 2.48. Tübingen: J. C. B. Mohr, 1992.

Notes

1. So, Paul Hammer, "*KLERONOMIA* in Paul and Ephesians," *JBL* 79 (1960): 267–68: "[T]he term *kleronomia* does not occur as a theological term in either classical Greek or in hellenistic Gnosticism; in fact it occurs theologically in Hellenism only in writings with a strong Jewish orientation, e.g., Philo."

2. The meaning "adoption" as opposed to "sonship" has been persuasively demonstrated by J. M. Scott, *Adoption as Sons of God: An Exegetical Investigation into the Background of* ΥΙΟΘΕΣΙΑ *in the Pauline Corpus* (WUNT 2.48; Tübingen: J. C. B. Mohr, 1992), 13–57. Υἱοθεσία, the word Paul used, was more common in inscriptions than it was in literary usage.

3. Scripture quotations are from the NRSV unless otherwise noted; classical quotations are from the Loeb Classical Library unless otherwise stated.

4. For studies reflecting Greek and Roman contexts, cf. Scott, *Adoption*, 176–77n. 199.

5. Ibid., 186.

6. Pauline Christianity—like Judaism itself—was an urban Greco-Roman phenomenon. As Dale Martin put it, "[A]ny explanation of early Christian language that assigns concepts to sharply differentiate Greek and Jewish worlds should be suspect" (*Slavery as Salvation: The Metaphor of Slavery in Pauline Christianity* [New Haven, Conn.: Yale University Press, 1990], xvi).

7. Scott disagrees with Herbert Donner ("Adoption oder Legitimation? Erwägungen zur Adoption in Alten Testament auf dem Hintergrund der altorientalischen Rechte," *Oriens Antiquus* 8 [1969]: 87–119), who claims that adoption was not practiced in Israel. Scott highlights instances when something like adoption may be reflected in the Hebrew scriptures (e.g., Gen. 48:5; Exod 2:10; Esth 2:7, 15). But Donner's identifications require a loose, nonlegal definition of adoption.

8. Joseph Fitzmyer, *Romans* (AB 33; New York: Doubleday, 1993), 500.

9. Ibid., 500.

10. Francis Lyall, *Slaves, Citizens, Sons: Legal Metaphors in the Epistles* (Grand Rapids: Zondervan, 1984), 98. David Williams (*Paul's Metaphors: Their Context and Character* [Peabody, Mass.: Hendrickson, 1999], 64–65) also assumes Roman law without considering other options.

11. Under Roman rule, the cities of Galatia seem to have been organized in a manner similar to those of Bithynia. For details of the administrative arrangements and bibliography, see Stephen Mitchell, *Anatolia: Land, Men, and Gods in Asia Minor* (Oxford: Clarendon, 1993), 1:199. On Roman governance of the provinces, particularly with regard to indigenous law, see Andrew Lincott, *Imperium*

Romanum: Politics and Administration (London and New York: Routledge, 1993), 111–67.

12. Even in Egypt, where Roman control has been more extensive; see Alan Bowman and Dominic Rathbone, "Cities and Administration in Roman Egypt," *JRS* 82 (1992): 107–27.

13. For the example of a Jewish woman from Petra employing Roman legal options, see *Pyadin* 26 and Hannah Cotton, "The Guardianship of Jesus Son of Babatha: Roman and Local Law in the Province of Arabia," *JRS* 83 (1993): 96: "[T]he document assumes a high degree of Romanization in a native city that had just come within the Roman sphere of influence."

14. Four of the law-court speeches were written in defense of adoptions (Isaeus 2, 3, 6, 7) while six challenged adoptions (Isaeus 1, 4, 5, 9, 10; Demosthenes 44). Demosthenes 43 includes a description of an adoption, although adoption was not the main focus of the legal proceeding.

15. On judicial procedure and forensic oratory in Athens, see Christopher Carey, *Trials from Classical Athens* (London: Routledge, 1997), 1–25.

16. S. C. Humphreys, *The Family, Women, and Death* (London: Routledge, 1983), 9.

17. Sarah Pomeroy, *Families in Classical and Hellenistic Greece* (Oxford: Clarendon, 1997), 14.

18. Lene Rubinstein, *Adoption in iv. Century Athens* (Copenhagen: Museum Tusculanum Press, 1993), 31. Rubinstein is indebted to Humphreys (*Family, Women, and Death*, 79–130), who argued that the importance of adoption was tied to the significance citizens placed on the private tomb-cult. Humphreys believes that the private tomb-cult was not limited to the rich, but rather experienced a kind of "democratization" in the fifth and fourth centuries; it follows that incentives for adopting may have extended to other strata.

19. So early concern for the tomb-cult and issues of the larger city give way to more individual concerns to garner personal wealth or to control the future of one's *oikos*.

20. See, for example, L. Gernet, *Droit et société dans la Gréce ancienne* (Paris: Sirey, 1955). For other diachronic approaches, see the very helpful book by W. K. Lacey, *The Family in Classical Greece* (Ithaca, N.Y.: Cornell University Press, 1968), as well as A. R. W. Harrison, *The Law of Athens* (2 vols.; Oxford: Clarendon, 1968).

21. See S. Todd and P. Millett, "Law, Society, and Athens," in *Nomos: Essays in Athenian Law, Politics, and Society* (ed. P. Cartledge et al.; Cambridge: Cambridge University Press, 1990), 1–18.

22. Raphael Sealey, *The Justice of the Greeks* (Ann Arbor: University of Michigan Press, 1994), 81. Moreover, the evidence from Roman Egypt may not suggest as much evolution in Greek law as has been assumed by some; rather, as Sarah Pomeroy has argued, the differences may only be a reflection of the different legal systems that were permitted to function side by side (Pomeroy, *Families*, 193–229).

23. For a discussion of apparent exceptions, see Lacey, *Family in Classical Greece*, 132–37.

24. This is what Isaeus 8.34 calls "the incontrovertible title of lineal descent."

25. Todd, *Shape of Athenian Law*, 219.

26. Pomeroy, *Families*, 15.

27. A wife could not inherit because she was not within her dead husband's ἀγχιστεία (anchisteia). On women and property, see Todd, *Shape of Athenian Law*, 207–10.

28. For much of this demographic analysis I am indebted to Pomeroy, *Families*, 6, 7.

29. Thomas Gallant puts women at thirty-eight years and men at forty years (*Risk and Survival in Ancient Greece: Reconstructing the Rural Domestic Economy* [Stanford, Calif.: Stanford University Press, 1991], 20).

30. Pomeroy, *Families*, 6–7.

31. Sealey, *Justice of the Greeks*, 70.

32. Pomeroy, *Families*, 122.

33. The only exception is the lawsuit over the estate of Apollodorus (Isaeus 7).

34. Rubinstein, *Adoption*, 117–25, has cataloged a total of thirty-six adoptions from all fourth-century Athenian sources. Five adoptions were *inter vivos*, twelve testamentary, and ten posthumous. The nine remaining cases cannot be categorized from the extant data.

35. On the basis of such legal arguments, Rubinstein believes that a posthumous adoption was considered legal "only if the adopted son had already been recognized by the People's Court as the heir with the best claim to the inheritance of the adoptive father" (*Adoption*, 28).

36. Cf. Demosthenes, who also mentions a dissenter's obligation to remove the sacrificial victim from the altar if the adoptee was not legitimate (43.13–14).

37. Rubinstein, *Adoption*, 35–38.

38. See for example the testamentary adoption that included witnesses and introductions in Isaeus 9.7–8. Cf. Rubinstein, *Adoption*, 38–39.

39. This fixed order corresponds to the order of intestate succession and is recounted in the Hagnias case (Isaeus 11.1–3).

40. Cf. Isaeus 2.35–47. See also Sealey, *Justice of the Greeks*, 17.

41. Harrison, *Law of Athens*, 99. Apparently he could appoint as many guardians as he thought appropriate. Demosthenes' father appointed three (Dem. 27.4).

42. Harrison, *Law of Athens*, 103.

43. Cf. M. I. Finley, "The Elderly in Classical Antiquity," in *Old Age in Greek and Latin Literature* (ed. Thomas M. Falkner and Judith de Luce; New York: State University of New York Press, 1989), 1–20.

44. In Greece, sons were legally responsible for the care of their parents in ways that collateral relatives were not (Rubinstein, *Adoption*, 64–68).

45. Todd, *Shape of Athenian Law*, 221; Douglas MacDowell, "The *OIKOS* in Athenian Law," *CQ* 39, no. 1 (1989): 15.

46. David Ibbetson and Andrew Lewis, "The Roman Law Tradition," in *The Roman Law Tradition* (ed. David Ibbetson and Andrew Lewis; Cambridge: Cambridge University Press, 1994), 11.

47. For a brief but lucid introduction to the sources and the methodological problems they present, see David Johnston, *Roman Law in Context* (Cambridge: Cambridge University Press, 1999), 2–29. For a fuller treatment of the primary sources and interpretive problems, see Franz Wieacker, *Römische Rechtsgeschichte: Quellenkunde, Rechtsbildung, Jurisprudenz und Rechtsliteratur* (Munich: C. H. Beck, 1988), 63–182.

48. For an excellent discussion of these issues along with epigraphic examples, see Jane F. Gardner, *Family and Familia in Roman Law and Life* (Oxford: Clarendon, 1998), 134–35.

49. Ibid., 116.

50. John Crook, *Law and Life of Rome* (Ithaca, N.Y.: Cornell University Press, 1967), 118–22.

51. Partible systems could lead to the dividing of estates and the consequent loss of a family's ability to maintain its status (Richard Saller, *Patriarchy, Property, and Death in the Roman Family* [Cambridge: Cambridge University Press, 1994], 161).

52. Gardner, *Family and Familia*, 117.

53. Crook, *Law and Life of Rome*, 98–99.

54. Johnston, *Roman Law in Context*, 30.

55. Paul Veyne, "The Roman Empire," in *A History of Private Life: From Pagan Rome to Byzantium* (ed. Paul Veyne; Cambridge: Belknap Press, Harvard University, 1987), 29. Because of shorter life expectancies, only one in ten forty-year-olds may have still been in the power of a *pater familias* (Johnston, *Roman Law in Context*, 31).

56. For the procedures in ancient sources, see Cicero, *De domo* 34–38; Gellius, *NA* 5.19.1–14; Gaius 1.99–107; *Digest* 1.7.

57. Johnston, *Roman Law in Context*, 33.

58. An imperial rescript later replaced the assembly vote (Gaius 1.100) (Gardner, *Family and Familia*, 128).

59. Three sales were necessary because of a rule in the Twelve Tables that was probably intended to punish fathers who abused their power over their sons by repeatedly selling them into bondage (Gardner, *Family and Familia*, 11).

60. Crook, *Law and Life of Rome*, 112; Marek Kurylowicz, *Die adoptio im klassischen römischen Recht* (Studia antiqua 6; Warsaw: University of Warszawskeigo, 1981), 50.

61. Gardner, *Family and Familia*, 155.

62. Ibid., 148.

63. On ambiguity of evidence for legal age being fourteen or eighteen years, see Gardner, *Family and Familia*, 145–48.

64. Saller, *Patriarchy, Property, and Death*, 189.

65. On this, see Gellius, *NA* 5.13.5; for the awareness the Romans had of their mortality as it relates to guardianship, see Cicero, *Verr.* 2.1.153.

66. Tutors of adult women were more "authorizers" than "managers," so an *actio tutelae* could not be brought against a woman's tutor (Johnston, *Roman Law in Context*, 39). See also Gaius's comment that the authorization of a tutor in the case of a woman was a matter of form (1.190).

67. Crook, *Law and Life of Rome*, 111.

68. Gardner, *Family and Familia*, 203.

69. Ibid., 202–3.

70. Keith Hopkins, *Death and Renewal* (Cambridge: Cambridge University Press, 1983), 49. Cf. Gardner, *Family and Familia*, 136–38, for a debate whether freedmen's sons were given up for adoption to increase the son's chance of holding civic office.

71. Ironically, the two remaining sons died, with the result that his line was extinguished. On this case, see Valerius Maximus 5.10.2.; Cicero, *Off.* 1.121.

72. Johnston, *Roman Law in Context*, 45.

73. C. H. Cosgrove, *The Cross and the Spirit* (Macon, Ga.: Mercer University Press, 1988), 32.

74. Donald Davidson, "What Metaphors Mean," in *The Philosophy of Language* (ed. A. P. Martinich; Oxford: Oxford University Press, 1985), 448.

75. Of course, connecting adoption to inheritance immediately after two other analogies drawn from Greco-Roman social practices—the "disciplinarian" (*paidagōgos*, Gal 3:24–25) and the minor heir under guardians (4:1–2)—further supports the role of Greco-Roman conventions.

76. Paul's use of "son" in 4:7 rather than "child" (Rom 8:17) may reflect Greek legal conventions that prevented daughters from inheriting. On the other hand, it could be a generic usage that is not gender-specific. Either way, Paul's use of the more generic term "offspring" in 3:29—immediately after quoting a baptismal formula announcing the dissolution of gender barriers in 3:28—would have guided readers not to draw gender conclusions from the metaphor.

77. As noted earlier, a Roman father did have authority as *pater familias* to disinherit his son(s) and leave his property to whomever he chose; however, social expectations would have made passing over a son a radical move.

78. Isaeus 2.36; Rubinstein, *Adoption*, 55; Gardner, *Family and Familia*, 134–35.

79. For a survey of the various uses ancient writers made of adoption language, see Scott, *Adoption*, 13–57.

80. See the commentary in *Plutarch's Theological Writings and Early Christian Literature* (ed. Hans Dieter Betz; Leiden: E. J. Brill, 1975), 182–84.

81. Plutarch uses a different term for adoption (ἐκποίητος) than Paul uses, but as Scott noted in his analysis of the adoption word group, there is considerable overlap in the Greek usage of the various terms for adoption. Scott argues that the semantic field of υἱοθεσία includes the following word groups: εἰσποιεῖν, ἐκποιεῖν, ποιεῖσθαι, υἱοποιεῖσθαι, τίθεσθαι, and υἱοθετεῖν (*Adoption*, 13–57). He points out that this synonymy holds for both inscriptions and literary sources as well, noting that different terms are often used even in the same literary passage (56).

82. Plutarch probably generates this metaphor out of Greek adoption law and practice. His only other use of the metaphor occurs specifically in the context of Athenian legal history (*Mor.* 834B).

83. Betz, *Plutarch's Theological Writings*, 182.

84. Quintilian noted that metaphors drawn from nature were more persuasive because "every man applies to himself what he hears from others, and the mind is always readiest to accept what it recognizes to be true to nature" (*Inst.* 8.3.71). Many ancients, especially because of Stoic influence, considered social conventions themselves to be true to nature.

85. Linda Belleville, "Under Law: Structural Analysis and the Pauline Concept of Law in Galatians 3:21–4:11," *JSNT* 26 (1986): 54.

86. Victor Furnish, *Theology and Ethics in Paul* (Nashville: Abingdon, 1968), 165.

87. J. Louis Martyn, *Romans* (AB 33A; New York: Doubleday, 1997), 317. Cf. Paul's use of this term in Gal 3:13 and his elaboration of the image of redemption in 1 Cor 6:19–20.

88. On the unlikely association of Paul's use of adoption with *Adoptionsfreilassung* (sacral manumission followed by adoption), see Scott, *Adoption*, 85–87. See

also Derek R. Moore-Crispin, "Galatians 4:1–9: The Use and Abuse of Parallels," *Evangelical Quarterly* 60 (1989): 213–14. For Paul, to be in debt, or under obligation (ὀφειλέτης, *opheiletēs*), was closely associated with slavery. In Gal 5:3, Paul says that those submitting to circumcision are obligated (ὀφειλέτης) to keep the whole Law. Similarly, in Rom 8:12–17, the closest parallel to Gal 4:1–7, Paul associates being a "debtor to the flesh" (ὀφειλέτης again) with slavery, just prior to the adoption reference in 8:15. For another cluster of terms including debt cancellation, legal regulations, and the *stoicheia tou kosmou*, see Col 2:8–23.

89. Galatia could refer to the Roman province of Galatia that included south-central Asia Minor, or to the more northerly "Celtic" region from which the name of the province was derived. The long-standing debate over the location of the Galatian churches does not impact in any significant way the legal conventions that would have been familiar in the respective areas. See the discussion in Kümmel, *Introduction to the New Testament* (Nashville: Abingdon, 1973), 296–98.

90. On Paul's opponents in Galatia, see George Howard, *Crisis in Galatia* (Cambridge: Cambridge University Press, 1979).

91. E. P. Sanders, *Paul, the Law, and the Jewish People* (Philadelphia: Fortress Press, 1983), 20.

92. Cosgrove, *Cross and the Spirit*, 2.

93. J. Christiaan Beker, *Paul the Apostle* (Philadelphia: Fortress Press, 1980), 52.

94. For an insightful reconstruction of what the opponents' presentation may have included, see Martyn, *Galatians*, 303.

95. Beker, *Paul the Apostle*, 52.

96. Cf. Werner Foerster, "κληρονόμος," *TDNT* 3:785, and Paul Hammer, "A Comparison of *KLERONOMIA* in Paul and Ephesians," *JBL* 79 (1960): 269, though Hammer draws the contrast with Ephesians too sharply.

97. For the association of "inheritance" with "promise" and the development of a similar eschatological emphasis in the postbiblical Jewish tradition, see Brendan Byrne, *"Sons of God"—"Seed of Abraham": A Study of the Idea of the Sonship of God of All Christians in Paul against the Jewish Background* (Analecta biblica 83; Rome: Biblical Institute, 1979), 157.

98. For Hall, Galatians is not an apocalypse but it argues like one. I use the term "apocalyptic" with awareness of the difficulty involved in precisely defining the term. On this problem, see Leander Keck, "Paul and Apocalyptic Theology," *Int* 38 (1984): 229–41.

99. Robert Hall, "Arguing Like an Apocalypse: Galatians and an Ancient Topos Outside the Greco-Roman Rhetorical Tradition," *NTS* 42 (1996): 445.

100. On the *paidagōgos* image, see David Lull, "'The Law Was Our Pedagogue': A Study in Galatians 3:19–25," *JBL* 105 (1986): 481–98.

101. Richard Hays, *The Faith of Jesus Christ: An Investigation of the Narrative Substructure of Galatians 3:1–4:11* (SBLDS 56; Chico, Calif.: Scholars Press, 1983), 202.

102. Beverly Gaventa, "The Singularity of the Gospel: A Reading of Galatians," in *Pauline Theology* (ed. Jouette Bassler; Minneapolis: Fortress Press, 1991), vol. 1, 149.

103. Byrne, *Sons of God*, 174.

104. Dunn, *Galatians*, 210.

105. Contrary to Scott, who maintains that the relation between verses 1–2

and verses 3–7 is one of type and antitype. The first two verses present the first exodus while verses 3–7 construct the Galatian experience as a new exodus (*Adoption*, 149–55). However, the present-tense verbs in verses 1–2 argue decidedly against his claim.

Hafemann generally accepts Scott's analysis but he divides the argument of 4:1–11 differently. He has 4:1–5 referring not to Egypt but to Israel's continuing bondage as a result of the curse of the law (Scott Hafemann, "Paul and the Exile of Israel in Galatians 3–4," in *Exile: Old Testament, Jewish, and Christian Conceptions* [ed. James Scott; Supplements to the Journal for the Study of Judaism 56; Leiden: Brill, 1997], 347). For a general critique of using exodus typology as the key to interpreting Paul, see Mark Seifrid, "Blind Alleys in the Controversy over the Paul of History," *TynBul* 45 (1994): 73–95.

106. Lull, "Law Was Our Pedagogue," 481–98.

107. Scott, *Adoption*, 129.

108. *Nēpios* is the term Paul used to rebuke the Corinthians for their immaturity in 1 Cor 3:1. See also 1 Cor 13:11 and Eph 4:14.

109. David J. Lull, *The Spirit in Galatia* (SBLDS 49; Chico, Calif.: Scholars Press, 1980), 118.

110. Martin, *Galatians*, 386; Betz, *Galatians*, 20.

111. Paul's language in 4:7—"you are no longer a slave but a son"—clearly indicates his awareness of the substantive difference between a slave and a son/heir.

112. Scott makes much of this because he wants to show that these terms occur together in Egypt as titles for minor officials and correspond to those responsible for Israel's bondage. He ignores their joint occurrence in Lucian's satire on salaried posts in great houses (*Merc. Cond.* 12.23) because they play no role in the guardianship of minors (Scott, *Adoption*, 137n. 62).

113. This same term was used for the guardians in the Babatha Archive mentioned earlier. See also BDAG 303.

114. Martin, *Slavery as Salvation*, 15.

115. Saller, *Patriarchy, Property, and Death*, 186.

116. See the references to examples of fathers designating the time in Betz, *Galatians*, 204, and the discussion in Moore-Crispin, "Use and Abuse of Parallels," 208–9.

117. Saller, *Patriarchy, Property, and Death*, 176.

118. The adoptees in Galatians are beyond the control of pedagogues or guardians because the "date set by the father" (i.e., the coming of Christ) has already arrived (cf. 4:4)! Note that Paul made the same move with the *paidagōgos* analogy in 3:23–25.

119. Scott, *Adoption*, 123.

120. Cf. a similar problem in Paul's analogy in Rom 7:1–6, in which it is also impossible to match up all the roles in the analogy to parallel roles in the application. Joyce Little writes, "No matter how one distributes the roles, there is no way to get around the fact that these roles cannot be consistently applied throughout the first four verses" ("Paul's Use of Analogy: A Structural Analysis of Romans 7:1–6," *CBQ* 46 [1984]: 86).

121. Herbert Gale, *The Use of Analogy in the Letters of Paul* (Philadelphia: Westminster, 1964), 231.

122. This aim becomes absolutely clear in Paul's conclusion in Gal 6:11–15.

123. Δουλεία, *douleia* (4:24; 5:1); δουλεύω, *douleuō* (4:8, 9, 25; 5:13); δοῦλος, *doulos* (4:1, 7); δουλόω, *douloō* (4:3); παιδίσκη, *paidiskē* (4:22, 23, 30, 31). Three uses of slave terminology occur in the letter without pejorative connotations (1:10; 3:28; and 5:13).

124. For a historical review of the issue in scholarship, see Hans Hübner, "Paulusforschung seit 1945: Ein kritischer Literaturbericht," in *ANRW* II.25.4 (ed. Wolfgang Haase; Berlin: Walter de Gruyter, 1987), 2691–94.

125. BDAG 768–69.

126. Betz argues for a composite of the BDAG's third and fourth options (*Galatians*, 205).

127. See Martyn's well-founded stress on this conclusion (*Galatians*, 388–89; 393–406).

128. Lull, *Spirit in Galatia*, 104.

129. Whether to translate ὅτι (*hoti*; 4:6) as causal or declarative has been much debated, with the majority favoring causal. If it is translated "because," it makes the Spirit's Abba-cry a consequence of adoptive sonship, emphasizing the Spirit's role as the agent of adoption. If it is translated as a declarative, the emphasis is more on the Spirit's witness to the adoptive sonship of the Galatians. Both are possible. The latter fits the argument better, particularly the connection to 3:1–5. However, the former is the more natural reading grammatically. Cf. Dunn for the declarative translation (*Galatians*, 218–19); cf. Schlier for the causal translation and bibliography (Heinrich Schlier, *Der Brief an die Galater* [Göttingen: Vandenhoeck & Ruprecht, 1965], 197). Cf. Betz (*Galatians*, 210) for a poignant reminder of the role dogmatic commitments often play in this decision.

130. Although Hays has downplayed the differences between the redemptive formulas in 3:13–14 and 4:4–5 by positing a common underlying story, important differences remain (Hays, *Faith of Jesus Christ*, 116–18).

131. The identification of the pronouns' referents in 4:3–7 determines who Paul thinks receives adoption. Scholars have three fundamental choices for the identity of the adoptees: Christian Jews (Hafemann); Gentile Christians (Hays); or, all Christians without regard to ethnicity (Betz, Martyn, Scott). To consider Christian Jews the adoptees, the interpreter must make sense of the shift to "you" at the beginning of verse 6 and the shift back to "our" at the end of verse 6. To regard the adoptees as Gentile Christians, one must find a way to disassociate the "we" of verse 5b from "those under the law" in verse 5a. Hays attempts this by claiming that 4:4–5 shares an assumed sequence of salvation history with 3:13–14; namely, God redeems Israel from the Law so that Gentiles can receive the promise/adoption (Hays, *Faith of Jesus Christ*, 116–18). The pronouns cooperate with this in 3:13–14 but do not in 4:4–5 (especially the "we" of 5b in its close relation to "those under the law" in 5a). Hays is more committed to this sequence than Paul was. Paul may have reflected it in 3:13–14 only to move past it to a view that sees Jews and Gentiles in the same basic circumstance: Both stand in need of redemption and adoption because of their common slavery to the *stoicheia tou kosmou*. Neither of these options is tenable. It is impossible to read the pronouns with strict ethnic referents without accusing Paul of botching the very distinctions he was supposedly aiming to make. The third (and best) option is to loosen the eth-

nic moorings of the pronouns by either suggesting that Paul uses the various pronouns somewhat ambiguously because he has ethnic groupings in mind but not exclusively (Dunn, Cousar), or because he is intentionally alternating the pronouns as a means of undermining their expected ethnic associations (Martyn, *Galatians*, 333–34: "It is a rhetorical device, a language game, by which Paul seeks to erase all distinctions"). Although the evidence may favor the former option—ethnic groupings are in mind, but not exclusively—both of these readings yield similar interpretive results.

132. Martyn, "Events in Galatia," 167. James Hester points out that heir/inheritance language functions to emphasize continuity; however, he also recognizes that the context of 4:1–7 has a decided emphasis on discontinuity ("The Heir and Heilsgeschichte: A Study of Galatians 4:1ff.," in *OIKONOMIA: Heilsgeschichte als Thema der Theologie* (Festschrift für Oscar Cullmann) [ed. Felix Christ; Hamburg: Herbert Reich, 1967], 123–24).

133. Berger argues that Paul's use of the term to refer to all Christians in chapter 8 and then to Jews in chapter 9 was strategic (Kl. Berger, "Abraham in den paulinischen Hauptbriefen," *MTZ* 17 [1966]: 77–78).

134. C. E. B. Cranfield, *The Epistle to the Romans* (ICC; Edinburgh: T. & T. Clark, 1975), 1:397, correctly wrote, "Since adoption as a legal act was not a Jewish institution, Paul may reasonably be assumed to have had Greek or Roman adoption in mind. At the same time, in view of Gen 15:2–4; Exod 2:10; Esth 2:7; and also Exod 4:22f.; 2 Sam 7:14; 1 Chr 28:6; Ps 2:7; 89:26f.; Jer 3:19; Hos 11:1, it is unwise to claim that the background of the metaphor is exclusively Graeco-Roman."

135. The certainty of the adoptee's right to inherit receives even greater emphasis in Romans as compared to Galatians.

136. On the contours of the Jew-Gentile issues addressed in Romans, see Walters, *Ethnic Issues*.

137. My language here reflects Beker's characterization of Rom 5–8. Cf. Beker, *Paul the Apostle*, 87. The *stoicheia tou kosmou* in Gal 4:3, 9 play a similar role in Galatians to the role that Adam plays in Romans.

138. References to slavery or being a slave are especially concentrated in Rom 5–8 and in Gal 4–6.

139. Hammer, "A Comparison of *KLERONOMIA*," 267–72.

3

PAUL AND BOASTING

Duane F. Watson

In this chapter I examine the situations and conventions for boasting as understood in the Greco-Roman world of the first century C.E., including within Judaism. I then demonstrate in detail how Paul both used and modified these conventions of boasting in addressing the situation in Corinth. My focus will be on 2 Cor 10–13, in which, among all of Paul's letters, his boasting is most pronounced. I also look briefly at Paul's boasting in his other letters, especially the Epistle to the Romans. Finally, a brief bibliography of classical and current works on boasting is provided.

Part I. Boasting in the Greco–Roman World

Boasting in Israel's Scriptures and within Judaism

Paul derives his concept of boasting at least partially from Jer 9:23–24 (9:22–23 LXX; cf. 4 *Ezra* 7.98):

> Thus says the LORD: do not let the wise boast in their wisdom, do not let the mighty boast in their might, do not let the wealthy boast in their wealth; but let those who boast boast in this, that they understand and know me, that I am the LORD; I act with steadfast love, justice, and righteousness in the earth, for in these things I delight, says the LORD.[1]

Paul twice quotes Jer 9:23 in the context of boasting, "Let the one who boasts, boast in the Lord" (1 Cor 1:31; 2 Cor 10:17). In Jer 9:23–24, God commands that boasting should not be in any sense anthropocentric. Boasting is not to be based upon wisdom, strength, or wealth, that is, upon the three major things in which humanity can place its trust other than in God and thereby promote itself (cf. 1 Cor 1:26–31). Boasting about one's fragile and uncertain life circumstances in which God is not taken into account is excluded (1 Kgs 20:11; Prov 25:14; 27:1). In fact, such boasting is foolish ungodliness (Pss 52:1; 94:3–4).

God commands rather that boasting be theocentric, with its basis in an intimate relationship with and knowledge of God. There is no room for boasting before God, who is the creator, sustainer, and judge: "There is no Holy One like the LORD, no one besides you; there is no Rock like our God. Talk no more so very proudly, let not arrogance come from your mouth; for the LORD is a God of knowledge, and by him actions are weighed" (1 Sam 2:2–3; cf. Judg 7:2). Boasting in God's works is acceptable, particularly boasting about God's acts in sustaining the community of faith (1 Chron 16:28–29; 29:11; Pss 5:11; 89:15–18). As its incorporation into Psalms indicates (5:11; 89:15–18), such boasting is really worship and confession. Judaism continued this understanding of legitimate boasting as rooted only in God and God's work in the community of faith (Sir 17:9; 50:20), adding that boasting in the Law as God's gift was also legitimate (Sir 39:8). True boasting is in the fear of the Lord (Sir 1.11; 9.16; 10.22).

Boasting in the Greco-Roman World

Conventions for boasting and self-praise existed as early as 100 B.C.E. Popular philosophers and sophists were known for their self-praise. This self-praise could take the form of comparison with the abilities of other philosophers and sophists.[2] Self-praise was generally considered repugnant. Dionysius of Halicarnassus considered praise of one's own work "the most vulgar and most invidious of tasks."[3] Boasting was appropriately used in only a few well-defined circumstances: "[T]he educated Hellenistic world in which Paul moved knew of conventions of self-praise, but believed that they required great delicacy if they were not to be misused."[4]

In his *Fifty-seventh Discourse*, Dio Chrysostom, the first-century C.E. philosopher and orator, comments on Homer's *Iliad*.[5] Chrysostom defends Nestor's self-praise used in trying to stop a quarrel between Agamemnon and Achilles (*Iliad* 1.260–68, 273–74). Nestor refers to the deference that important men paid to him in order to convince Agamemnon and Achilles that his advice would benefit them and was worthy of their attention and obedience (3–5). Also, by praising these important men who were more important than Agamemnon and Achilles and who yet gave him deference, Nestor humbles these two. He accentuates their folly of not emulating better men who were willing to listen to him (6–9). This self-praise was considered acceptable because it secured the attention, compliance, and imitation of the audience (10).

Quintilian, the first-century C.E. orator, describes self-praise in his *Institutio oratoria* (11.1.15–28).[6] He observes that, in general, boasting disgusts and depreciates its audience (11.1.15–17). He particularly despises indirect boasting by denial of the opposite.

> And yet I am not sure that open boasting is not more tolerable, owing to its sheer straightforwardness, than that perverted form of self-praise, which makes the millionaire say that he is not a poor man, the man of mark describe himself as obscure, the powerful pose as weak, and the eloquent as unskilled and even inarticulate. But the most ostentatious kind of boasting takes the form of actual self-derision. (11.1.21)

However, looking to the example of Cicero, Quintilian does allow speakers boasting rights in specific instances: when defending others who have assisted them, when speaking in self-defense against those who accuse them out of envy (11.1.17–18), and when opposing enemies and detractors who denounce their actions as discreditable (11.1.23). Boasting about oneself can be tempered by presenting such boasting indirectly as the quotes of others (11.1.21), demonstrating that boasting was made necessary by another (11.1.22), and attributing one's success in part to others and the providence of the gods (11.1.23).

One of the most important extant works from the first century c.e. that informs us about boasting is Plutarch's *On Praising Oneself Inoffensively.*[7] This work outlines for statesmen what situations and purposes are appropriate for boasting and the content and devices to use to make such boasting acceptable to the audience. In general, Plutarch makes clear that self-praise is deplorable and shameless. The boaster is assigning to himself what others should bestow upon him, forcing others to agree with him in a public setting when they may not agree (539D).

Plutarch states that self-glorification is not acceptable when employed to gratify ambition and an appetite for fame (540A). This is particularly inappropriate when self-praise is done by comparison with others whose praise one wants to usurp: "But when they do not even seek to be praised simply and in themselves, but try to rival the honour that belongs to others and set against it their own accomplishments and acts in the hope of dimming the glory of another, their conduct is not only frivolous, but envious and spiteful as well" (540B). When people make claims for themselves that are undeserved, Plutarch advises that one should refute these claims by showing that they are pointless. Undermining these claims should not be done by self-praise. "If we hold them undeserving and of little worth, let us not strip them of their praise by presenting our own, but plainly refute their claim and show their reputation to be groundless" (540C).

However, self-glorification or boasting is acceptable under certain circumstances. The unfortunate can use self-praise and boasting, for it casts aside pity and attests to their ambition and courage in struggling to reach beyond their circumstances and ill-fortune (541A–C). Self-praise is also acceptable when "you are defending your good name or answering a charge" (540C). Boasting is permissible when pleading for justice to those who have dealt harshly with a speaker (541C–F). The examples that Plutarch gives are of prominent people who have given some great benefit to those speaking harshly against or turning their backs on them. In hopes of changing their detractors' attitudes, these prominent citizens then point to the benefits they have given their detractors in the past. Closely related to this pleading for justice is the use of self-glorification in contrasts to show that to do "the opposite of what one is charged with would have been shameful and base" (541F; 541F–542A).

When self-glorification works to build up the reputation of the speaker in order to facilitate some greater good, it is acceptable:

> [T]here are times when the statesman might venture on self-glorification as it is called, not for any personal glory or pleasure, but when the occasion and the matter in hand demanded that the truth be told about himself, as it might about another—especially when by permitting himself to mention his good accomplishments and character he is enabled to achieve some similar good. (539E–F)

Boasting is permissible when self-praise has some advantage and further end in view, like to inspire the audience with ambition and to emulate the speaker's own good example (544D–F).

Self-praise can be used "to overawe and restrain the hearer and to humble and subdue the headstrong and rash" (544F; 544F–545C). One example given by Plutarch is Aristotle, who told Alexander that those who have true opinions about the gods have the right to be proud (545A). When evil or unsound policy pertaining to important issues is being praised, and the audience is being swayed by the praise to adopt that policy, self-praise is acceptable to demonstrate the virtue of adopting an alternative policy. Plutarch says, "Where mistaken praise injures and corrupts by arousing emulation and evil and inducing the adoption of an unsound policy where important issues are at stake, it is no disservice to counteract it, or rather to divert the hearer's purpose to a better course by pointing out the difference" (545D; 545D–546A). "Such praise is best shown for what it is when true praise is set beside it" (545F).

The danger of self-praise becoming offensive and arousing envy is always present, but Plutarch advises that these dangers can be lessened by several techniques. Mix self-praise with the praise of the audience (542B–C). Ascribe some of the honor for what is praised to mere chance or to the gods (542E–543A). Use and amend the praise of others in self-praise so that the content of the praise is not self-ascribed (543A–F). Mention some personal shortcomings, but be sure that they are not degrading or ignoble: ". . . so some do not present their own praise in all its brilliance and undimmed, but throw in certain minor shortcomings, failures, or faults, thus obviating any effect of displeasure or disapproval" (543F). These shortcomings can be mistakes, ambitions, lack of information, or mention of poverty and low-birth (544A–B). Finally, mention the hardships that are inherent in whatever people are praising you for: "For it is with reputation and character as with a house or an estate: the multitude envy those thought to have acquired them at no cost or trouble; they do not envy those who have purchased them with much hardship and peril" (544C).

In summary, although generally repulsive, the conventions of Paul's era permitted boasting in certain prescribed situations. In these situations there was an acceptable content and approach to boasting that minimized the danger of offense always inherent in it. Boasting was acceptable when speakers mentioned overcoming unfortunate circumstances as a tribute to ambition and as a way to cast aside pity; defended their name against charges stemming from envy; spoke against enemies or detractors who denounced their actions as discreditable; pleaded their case for justice with those that have mistreated them; demonstrated that to do the opposite of the conduct being criticized would have been shameful; mentioned their accomplishments in order to achieve a similar good; built up their character in order to invite the audience in a similar worthy endeavor; showed an advantage or further purpose like arousing ambition and inspiring the audience to emulation; subdued the headstrong; and swayed the audience from unsound policy. Boasting was unacceptable when it was motivated by ambition, fame, self-glorification, or relied on comparison in order to usurp praise rightfully belonging to others. It was also unacceptable to use boasting to refute the unfounded claims of others.

Part II. Paul's Boasting

Boasting in 2 Corinthians 10–13

Paul's boasting in 2 Cor 10–13 has long been a source of difficulty for both the professional interpreter and casual reader alike.[8] How can Paul the apostle boast about his exploits and hold himself up as a model for imitation? Such a question cannot be answered merely by imposing our modern concepts of boasting upon Paul's letters. However, they can be answered by placing Paul's boasting within its first-century Mediterranean context and by analyzing his boasting by standards of his day. Was boasting ever acceptable? If so, in what contexts, and what was the appropriate content of boasting in each? When these questions are answered, we find Paul defending his honor and authority against the derision and challenge of others. We see a man who works within the conventions of his time, but in new and often surprising ways proffered by his Christian perspective and values.

The Situation in Corinth: An Honor Challenge

What situation had arisen in Corinth that prompted Paul to resort to boasting? Paul supported himself at Corinth by tent-making and working in leather. This support was supplemented by contributions from the newly established churches of Macedonia, particularly Philippi (2 Cor 11:9; Phil 4:15–16). In the course of his ministry some wealthy Corinthians wanted to become Paul's benefactors; that is, they would pay Paul to become their own private apostle. It had been Paul's position to freely preach the gospel to the Gentiles. He did not want to accept support for his preaching and become a burden to his congregations (2 Cor 11:9, 20–21; 12:16; 1 Cor 9:15–18). More important, acceptance of a gift from a benefactor would have changed his status to that of a client. He would have been considered a member of the household extending the benefaction. This dependent status could have become a hindrance to freely preaching the gospel.[9]

In the Greco-Roman honor culture, to deny such benefaction was a social affront to those extending it.[10] This was especially true when the refusal came from a social inferior, as was the case here. Paul was a tent-maker and thus of the artisan class near the bottom of society, while the Corinthians offering the benefaction were likely to be of the upper class. Paul had alienated a wealthy portion of the Corinthian church by refusing their benefaction. These alienated patrons found willing recipients of their benefaction in a group of itinerant preachers who came to Corinth (2 Cor 11:4) claiming to be apostles, workers, and ministers of Christ (11:13, 23).[11] They supported their apostolic status with recollections of visions and revelations (12:1). They treated Paul as a rival religious teacher or philosopher. As was often the case among teachers and philosophers of that day they compared themselves to Paul and found his claims unfounded and abilities lacking (10:12; 11:12). Their comparison involved self-praise and accusations hurled against Paul and ultimately denied his apostolic authority (see specific accusations below).

In 2 Cor 10–13, Paul is engaged in an apology or self-defense, and boasting was part of a leader's hortatory arsenal at that time (cf. 12:19). Quintilian and Plutarch would have said that, like anyone else, Paul was justified in boasting in self-defense against those who denounced his actions as discreditable and questioned his honor. Not only does Paul respond in a situation prescribed for boasting, but his boasting also has standard content and uses the techniques for mitigating self-praise with the audience. However, Paul does not slavishly follow social conventions. In light of the Christ-event, he transforms their content and shifts their emphases.

The interrelated matters of honor and challenge-response (riposte) are central to 2 Cor 10–13.[12] Paul's honor has been challenged by opponents.[13] Paul needs to respond to the challenge in order to reestablish his honor. A challenge is a claim to enter the social space of another and to dislodge that person from that social space. Paul's opponents want to acquire honor by comparing themselves with one another and with Paul and finding him lacking (10:1, 10, 12, 18; 11:12), as well as by making claims to Paul's work in Corinth (10:13–16). They want to be recognized at least as his equals (11:12).

Paul's opponents challenge his honor and authority on several fronts.[14] They have come to Corinth to minister in what Paul defines as his missionary field, assigned by God (10:13–16). They claim that Paul acts according to human standards, is worldly (literally, "walks according to the flesh"), that is, is not spiritual (10:2). They claim that he is humble when present, but bold when away (10:1). He is weak in person, but strong in letter (10:10). They have compared their rhetorical abilities and personal presence with that of Paul and found his wanting (10:1, 10, 12, 18; 11:5)—perhaps to the point of claiming that he does not manifest the gifts of an apostle. The Corinthians themselves have challenged Paul to prove that Christ speaks through him (13:3), because his speech is unimpressive (11:4–6; cf. 10:1, 10).

Paul's opponents have accused him of being socially dishonorable for not taking support from the Corinthians and for entering into a patron/client relationship. He is inconsistent for not taking money from the Corinthians while taking it from the Philippians. Refusing money from the Corinthians is a lack of love (11:7–11; 12:14–18). Support is a legitimization of an apostle, and Paul is not a true apostle because he refuses support (12:12–13). Perhaps they even accuse Paul of being cunning for using the collection for Jerusalem as a ruse for gaining support while denying that he receives such support (12:13–18).

Based on the inconsistency between Paul's strong letters and weak presence, and between his acceptance of support from Philippi and not from Corinth, Paul is a flatterer (*kolax*) and untrustworthy. This charge could be supported by Paul's own words in 1 Cor 4:12–13: "When reviled, we bless; when persecuted, we endure; when slandered, we speak kindly."[15] The flatterer is described in Plutarch's "How to Tell a Flatterer from a Friend":

> [S]ince he has no abiding-place of character to dwell in, and since he leads a life not of his own choosing but another's, moulding and adapting himself to suit another, is not simple, not one, but variable and many in one, and, like water that is poured into one receptacle after another, he is constantly on the move from place to place, and changes his shape to fit his

receiver. The changes of the flatterer . . . may be most easily detected if a man pretends that he is very changeable himself and disapproves the mode of life which he previously approved, and suddenly shows a liking for actions, conduct or language which used to offend him.[16]

The Corinthians were also part of the challenge to Paul's honor. They did not come to the defense of his honor when challenged by the opponents. "I have been a fool! You forced me to it! Indeed you should have been the ones commending me, for I am not at all inferior to these super-apostles, even though I am nothing" (2 Cor 12:11). In fact, they even asked for proof that Christ was speaking in him (13:3).

The public scrutinizes the reaction of the one challenged. Depending upon the reaction, the public can remove honor and give it to the challenger or once more affirm the honor of the one challenged. The challenge is a threat to the reputation of the one challenged, and he or she must respond to maintain that reputation. Not making a response is a forfeiture of honor and reputation. This perspective on an honor challenge explains Paul's motivation and the necessity to reestablish his honor, reputation, and the authority of his message.[17]

Paul's Boasting as Key Component in an Honor Defense

Paul vows not to be a flatterer and boasts of his God-given authority (2 Cor 10:1–11). Paul defends his honor against the challenge of the opposition that he is humble when face to face with the Corinthians, but bold when away (2 Cor 10:1, 10). He is accused of boldly defending himself from a distance with a letter, but that he is unable to do so in person because neither his personal presence nor speech exudes the same authority. He is thus accused of being a flatterer (*kolax*) and untrustworthy. Paul begins to boast of the boldness and weapons of divine power at his disposal that could be aimed at his opposition's challenge and the Corinthians' disobedience (vv. 3–6). He bases his boasting on the authority that the Lord gave him for building up the Corinthians (vv. 7–8). Paul anticipates his explanation that his boasting is legitimate because it is what the Lord has done through him (vv. 13–18). Paul assures the Corinthians that he will exercise the authority of which he boasts. What he writes in his letters will be implemented when he is present, and he will by no means be a flatter (v. 11).

The basis and limits of boasting (10:12–18). Paul does not rule out boasting as illegitimate, but rather defines its legitimate basis and limits. Ultimately he demonstrates that only he, and not his opponents, has the right to boast. While at first seeming to deny it, Paul is really comparing himself with his opponents. He is using irony to provide a negative comparison. By insinuation he proves that the opponents cannot compare themselves with him in their effort to claim authority in Corinth, because Corinth is his God-given territory for evangelism. The opposition does not have this legitimate basis for boasting.

Paul concedes that he is not so bold as to compare himself with his opponents, implying that they are clearly superior when judged by standards of personal presence and rhetorical finesse (v. 12). However, he then cleverly changes the basis for comparison and makes a comparison anyway. He will not compare himself with the opponents who are commending themselves by comparison with one another on rhetorical ability and status. Such an approach does not make good sense because, at least on one level, it violates social convention.

Paul sets a different basis and different limits for boasting and leaves it up to the Corinthians to conclude that the opponents do not have this basis for boasting. Adapting Jer 9:22–23, Paul bases proper boasting in the Lord and in what the Lord has done in and through the Lord's own people (v. 17; also quoted in 1 Cor 1:31). Although Paul's contemporaries viewed self-praise as legitimate in certain circumstances, he excludes it altogether. Self-praise is never legitimate because all boasting must be done in the Lord. Paul claims that his boasting is within the proper limits of boasting in the Lord: it occurs in his evangelization of the Corinthians as an exercise of his apostolic commission (vv. 13–15; cf. v. 8). They are the fruit of his call by Christ to proclaim the gospel to the Gentiles. The Corinthian church is what Christ has done in and through him. Paul plans to continue his missionary enterprise in areas that have not heard the gospel so that his boasting remains legitimate and not based on the work already done by others (v. 16), a rebuff to his opponents who are claiming Paul's work in Corinth as their own.

Paul's opponents cannot boast in the Corinthians because it was not through the opponents that Christ worked to evangelize them (2 Cor 3:2–3; 1 Cor 3:10). The content of their boasting is limited to their own accomplishments (v. 12) and trying to usurp Christ's work through Paul as their own (vv. 15–16). While they commend themselves, only those who are commended by the Lord are truly commended (vv. 12, 18). By establishing the basis and limits of boasting in the Lord, and demonstrating that he has the right to boast in the evangelization he performed among the Corinthians through his commissioning, Paul effectively removes the opponents' boasting to any authority over the Corinthians.

"Foolish" boasting (11:1–12:13). Having established that the basis of boasting must be in the Lord and confined to what the Lord does through a person (10:12–18), Paul moves to what has become known as the "Fool's Speech." Paul's foolishness is not in boasting per se, for he has established that there is legitimate boasting in the Lord. His culture has also established its own guidelines for legitimate boasting. Rather, Paul's foolishness is in the content of his boasting. Here, in response to the boasting of his opponents (11:1, 16–19, 21; 12:6, 11), Paul boasts in the flesh (11:18) and compares himself with the opposition. He has already established that such boasting does not make good sense and is useless for commending apostolic ministry, because it is not in the Lord (10:12–18).

However, Paul's boasting, while foolish in its content, is brilliant in its execution. He provides an ironic parody of the self-praise and comparison of the opponents (11:1). Paul compares himself with his opponents in an ironic counterattack that demonstrates the foolishness of their boasting in making comparisons to each other. By matching his opponents' claims point for point, Paul exposes their boasting to be in the flesh, foolish, and certainly not in the Lord. It is not legitimate boasting.

At 11:23 (cf. 11:21), Paul shifts the basis of his boasting to weakness. This is a further aspect of the irony. Rather than boasting in family background, education, wealth, power, and accomplishments—as his culture did—Paul bases legitimate boasting on weakness, something the Greco-Roman world found ludicrous. For Paul, the only content for boasting from oneself is in one's weakness, through which God can demonstrate power (12:9). This kind of boasting is in the Lord and not in one's own accomplishments. Boasting in suffering and weakness is the true basis of apostolic authority, because it is in the Lord. Paul undermines the claim to apostolic authority offered by his opponents in letters of recommendation (2 Cor 3:1–3) and speaking ability. Not only is the opponents' boasting based on comparison and self-commendation inappropriate, but so also is its content.

1. *Reason for an ironic, boastful comparison (11:1–6).* Paul's reason for making his ironic and foolish comparison is his "divine jealousy" for the Corinthians. As a father protects his daughter's purity during betrothal to present her pure at her wedding, so Paul protects the Corinthians to present them to Christ as a chaste virgin (v. 2). He is concerned that they are being deceived by the opponents whose message Paul disparages: it is the proclamation of another Jesus, another spirit, and another gospel (v. 4). His boasting is out of concern for the audience's being led astray by unsound policy—one of the permissible grounds for boasting in his culture.

Paul asserts: "I think that I am not in the least inferior to these super-apostles" (v. 5). This assertion provides the basis for the ironic comparison and boasting to follow. He concedes his opponents' charge that he is untrained in speech, but claims that he certainly makes up for it in his knowledge. Whereas they raise proud obstacles to the knowledge of God (10:5), Paul made that knowledge evident to the Corinthians (11:6). This is an example of *asteismos* (Lat. *urbanitas*), a form of "irony by which one urbanely displayed one's own rhetorical skill by affecting the lack of it."[18] Paul now goes on in the speech to demonstrate his rhetorical skill through his boastful comparison and through all of its ironic twists.

2. *Removing the opponents' basis for comparison and boasting (11:7–15).* In their

self-commendation and comparison, Paul's opponents were boasting that they had wealthy patrons within the Corinthian church while Paul did not (v. 12; 1 Cor 9:6–18). They did not insult their wealthy patrons, but rather accepted their patronage and the accompanying higher status that it afforded. They charged Paul with inconsistency in his dealings with the Corinthians. They noted that Paul accepted support from other churches, but not from the Corinthians. Paul acknowledges that he did receive support from the churches of Macedonia (Philippi and Thessalonica) and did not accept it from the Corinthians. He let the other churches be patrons and he their client, but he did not allow this Greek patronage system to operate in his relationship with the Corinthians. He appeals to his love for the Corinthians and his desire not to burden any of them (vv. 9–11; 12:15). Paul has changed the basis of boasting to denying support and patronage out of love. Denial on account of love is an unexpected basis for boasting in a client-patron culture, but such love is a basis for boasting in the Lord. Paul does not want this boasting silenced in Achaia. Should he accept support from the Corinthians he would not have his boast and a unique point of comparison with his opponents.

Having removed this one point of comparison with his opponents and shown that he is clearly the only one who loves the Corinthians, Paul widens his attack to deny the opponents any point of boasting of equality with Paul. They cannot boast because "such boasters are false apostles, deceitful workers, disguising themselves as apostles of Christ" (v. 13). Such activity certainly is not in the Lord and is at odds with Paul's own God-appointed ministry among the Corinthians.

3. Boasting in weakness in earthly things (11:16–33). Both Paul and his opponents are fools because they compare themselves with one another when there is no comparison, and their boasting is not in the Lord (vv. 16–18). Paul's boasting and irony make this foolishness obvious. "Paul is admitting comparability here only 'as a fool,' due to the fact that certain 'fools' in Corinth had been indulging in comparisons. He wishes to satirize their pretensions by use of the same form: in his view there is no such comparability."[19]

Up to this point in the Fool's Speech (v. 21), Paul has been boasting in the Lord, but now he joins with his opponents in boasting in the flesh, a tactic he had disavowed as not showing good sense (10:12). Paul's foolishness is that he dares to boast of the things that others boast, that is, not in the Lord (v. 21). However, because the comparison of the opponents was also with him, and this comparison was founded on accusations that denigrated his authority, Paul's boasting was legitimate according to the standards of Plutarch and Quintilian. It also helped reestablish his honor.

Paul's boasting is formulated as a comparison. As was typical in that culture he begins by comparing himself with his opponents on matters of birth and ethnic status. Paul notes that both he and his opponents are on equal footing when it comes to their Jewish background—they are all Hebrews, Israelites, and descendants of Abraham (v. 22). However, when comparing his ministry with that of his opponents, Paul claims superiority. He shifts to a completely different set of criteria than the set his opponents used for their boasting. He does not recount the numbers of souls saved, churches founded, letters of recommendation proffered, or accolades for speaking ability. His points of comparison would lessen his status in Hellenistic society—things like imprisonments and floggings and nakedness (vv. 23–29). Paul boasts of the opposite of the typical content of boasting, in what Judge calls a "parody of conventional norms."[20] Thus his boasting is foolish, not only because he boasts in human standards, but also in the wrong ones!

As with all features of Paul's boasting in this section, there is another perspective. The hardships suffered by a philosopher or teacher were understood to be evidence of the truth of their philosophy or teaching.[21] Paul is not so foolish, for while the content of his boastful comparison is foolish and unexpected, it is also reestablishing the authority of his message. Boasting in the flesh may be foolish, but Paul demonstrates that he can win at that game beyond question and, because that boasting is in hardship, also prove the truth of his message.

After the foolish comparison with his opponents, Paul enunciates the principle that has guided his boasting regarding his ministry. It is a principle that ultimately shows his boasting to be in the Lord and explains its atypical content: "If I must boast, I will boast of the things that show my weakness" (11:30). Paul's ministry has required a host of sufferings that his opponents have not experienced. Authority does not consist of personal presence, speaking ability, or patronage, but weakness. Paul is subtly saying that the opponents would surely find no point of comparison with him on the basis of weakness. "So far is Paul removing himself from the conventional attitudes of his opponents that, when 'forced' to boast, he will do so only ironically, in order to satirize precisely those kinds of achievements of which his opponents were most proud."[22]

Paul's boasting challenges the value system of the Corinthians through parody. Weakness in Christ is true strength: that is the main point of comparison (cf. 1 Cor 4:8–13). Weakness here is vulnerability in society, a lack of power and prestige. Paul shares the weakness of some of the Corinthians: "Who is weak, and I am not weak?" (11:29a; cf. 1 Cor 1:26–27). Weakness in Christ is something that the Corinthians can join Paul in boasting about.

Paul moves to specific instances from his ministry that provide the basis for boasting in weakness and in his apostolic authority. Because he is boasting in his weakness in the Lord, Paul swears an oath to underscore that God knows that he does not lie about what follows (vv. 30–31; cf. v. 10). Oaths like this were typically used when a person's honor was challenged. One instance of weakness was Paul's escape from King Aretas, the governor of Damascus (vv. 32–33). This is a parody of the *corona muralis,* an award for the first Roman soldier over the wall into a city under siege. In his weakness in Christ, Paul is persecuted by a king for his preaching and is the first over the wall and out of the city![23]

4. *Boasting in heavenly weakness and conclusions (12:1–13).* Paul brings his boastful comparison to the spiritual realm. He admits that boasting gains nothing (v. 1), but he proceeds anyway with a parody of his opponents and their comparison. Apparently they were boasting of visions and revelations of the Lord (v. 1). Paul discusses his experience with having been caught up into paradise and hearing things that no mortal is permitted to repeat (vv. 2–7a). He presents this example in the third person as if talking about someone else, to make his boasting more palatable while still providing a parody of his opponents (cf. Quint., *Inst.* 11.1.21). He could outdo his opponents in boasting of visions and revelations, but he chooses not to. He wants to be judged by what others can see in him or hear from him (vv. 6–7a).

Paul continues to boast in the weakness of having a thorn in the flesh. Paul will not boast except in his weakness, because it is there that Christ dwells in him and there that Christ's power is made perfect in him (vv. 7b–9). As Plutarch advised (*De laude* 541A), Paul is mediating his boasting by referring to a personal, physical weakness. However, in this case the weakness is interpreted as a strength. Thus a paradox—what typically would soften boasting in Greco-Roman society—is used to strengthen it within the Christian community. Paul's weakness is a paradoxical demonstration of strength as part of his apostolic imitation of Christ's own sufferings.

Paul concludes that the Corinthians forced him to boast as a fool (v. 11). He is justifying and tempering his boasting in a way advised by Quintilian: "I do not mean to deny that there are occasions when an orator may speak of his own achievements, as Demosthenes himself does in his defense of Ctesiphon. But on that occasion he qualified his statements in such a way as to show that he was compelled by necessity to do so, and to throw the odium attaching to such a proceeding on the man who had forced him to it" (*Inst.* 11.1.23). The entire enterprise of boasting should have been avoided, but could not because the Corinthians did not recognize the true signs of an apostle and were taken in by the opponents (v. 12). Paul performed the true signs of an apostle among them: "signs and wonders and mighty works." If his foolish boasting about his apostolic authority does not convince them, he points to another proof—signs (12:12).

Paul's Boasting in Relation to Contemporary Practice

Conformity, but with theological license. Convention condones Paul speaking in self-defense against those accusing him out of envy and denouncing his actions as discreditable, that is, challenging his honor (Quint., *Inst.* 11.1.17–18, 23). Paul's approach in these chapters seems, on other fronts, to violate social conventions. While he denies rhetorical power (11:5–6), he proceeds to demonstrate it in the Fool's Speech (11:16–12:13). He seems to be indirectly boasting by denial of the opposite, a tactic that Quintilian denounces (*Inst.* 11.1.21). However, because at least some of his audience does not appreciate his oratory (10:1, 10), what may be a denial of the opposite for him is a demonstration of irony meant to convince his audience of his rhetorical skill. From this perspective Paul has not violated rhetorical convention.

Also, he may appear to be the powerful person posing as weak, another of Quintilian's pet peeves (*Inst.* 11.1.21). Paul assumes that he is exercising divine power, yet stresses his weakness. Again, because his audience does not grant him strength and authority (10:1, 9–10), he is not perceived as a powerful person posing as weak. Rather, Paul has turned this on its head: He is powerful because he is weak, not a powerful person disguising himself as weak.

As outlined above, many accusations and charges have been made against Paul's honor. According to Plutarch, these provide ample warrant for Paul to boast to build up his reputation (*De laude* 540C). Plutarch warned that boasting that is motivated by ambition and fame and that seeks to dim the glory of another person is envious, spiteful, and not acceptable, especially when done by comparison (*De laude* 540A–B). This warning illumines Paul's statement about his opponents' comparisons with each other and with himself as not "show[ing] good sense" (10:12), because they were based on working in his sphere of action and trying to undermine his authority and honor (10:13–16). This warning also explains Paul's feigned reluctance to boast in comparison with his opponents (11:16–21), boasting that could be construed by the Corinthians as gratifying ambition and an appetite for fame.

Paul properly uses boasting to restrain the hearer and humble the headstrong opposition (*De laude* 544F–545C). Those who have true opinions about the gods were considered right to boast to restrain opposition (*De laude* 545A). Paul boasts of his knowledge of and relationship to God. Paul has been given visions and revelations (12:1–4). Divine power works through him (10:4; 12:9; 13:4). The Lord had given him authority (10:8; 13:10). Paul stresses that he is clearly trained in knowledge (11:6) and that "the truth of Christ is in me" (11:10).

Refuting the unwarranted claims of others should not be accomplished by boasting, but by showing their claims to be pointless and their reputation groundless (*De laude* 540C). Paul does not directly refute his opponents' claims by boasting about himself. Rather he defines the legitimate basis for boasting and the limits of boasting as weakness in the Lord. Paul uses a point-by-point comparison with his opposition based on the criterion of weakness, demonstrating that the opponents' comparison with Paul is groundless. They boast in strength, but he boasts on the legitimate basis of weakness. Through ironic comparison, Paul undermines all of his opponents' claims without directly refuting them (11:23–12:11).

Boasting is also acceptable when evil and unsound policy is swaying the audience, especially if boasting contrasts the unsound policy with what is worthy of true praise (*De laude* 545D–546A). Paul is boasting in part to sway the Corinthians from giving allegiance to what his opponents boast about—strength according to human standards (11:18), including trust in social conventions of benefaction, rhetorical finesse, and stunning delivery. He argues that boasting is not in strength as society defines it, but that weakness is true strength and the working of the power of Christ (11:23–33). True boasting is in the Lord and in weakness (12:9). His opponents' way is one of cunning that draws the church away from Christ (11:3) to enslavement and dishonor (11:20–21) and immoral behavior (12:19–13:2).

As convention advises, Paul demonstrates the necessity of boasting (Quint. *Inst.* 11.1.22). Boasting is necessitated by the Corinthians themselves. He tells them, "I have been a fool! You forced me to it" (12:11). They were not acknowledging his obvious apostolic status—a status demonstrated by knowledge (11:5) and signs, wonders, and mighty works (12:12)—because they were insulted by his refusal to receive support from them (11:7–11, 20–21; 12:14–18). Boasting can be used by speakers to plead for justice to those treating them harshly, especially if the speakers are prominent and have given a great benefit to those badly treating them (*De laude* 541C–F). The Corinthians are following his opponents and forgetting all Paul had done for them in the Lord. He was the first to bring the gospel to them (10:14). He did not charge them for his ministry among them (11:7–11; 12:13–18). Although he has been their benefactor, they do not acknowledge it. Rather, as Paul portrays it, they deem his bringing of the gospel free of charge a sin (11:7), as crafty (12:16). Even though he has left them a great benefit, he has to stress that not charging them is an expression of his love (11:10–11, 20–21; 12:15) and of building them up (12:19; cf. 10:8; 13:10). Paul's boasting is therefore necessary because his benefaction has been misinterpreted as malefaction.

Boasting can be used in contrasts to show that to do the opposite of what one had done would have been base and shameful (*De laude* 541F–542A). Paul contrasts his choice of not accepting support from the Corinthians with his opponents, who did not hesitate to do so. He tries to show that his behavior was one of love (11:11; 12:15) and of building the Corinthians up (12:19), but his opponents' behavior was to burden them (11:9; 12:16), to prey upon them, and to take advantage of them (11:20–21).

As it should according to Plutarch (De laude 539E–F), Paul's boasting has a greater good as its focus. He deals with the Corinthians in the power of God (10:4; 12:9; 13:4). The Corinthian church was part of his God-given mission (10:13–16). God gave Paul authority to build up the Corinthians (10:8; 12:19; 13:10). Paul is responsible to present the Corinthians to Christ corruption-free (11:3). They are being corrupted by another gospel (11:4) that may prevent them from living in the faith and meeting the test and thus cause them to fail (13:5–7). To solve this problem Paul must reestablish his authority and the authority of his gospel. The Corinthians may not perceive a greater good in his boasting, but Paul has included statements about mistreatment by his opponents (11:20) and their association with Satan (11:3, 13–15), statements the Corinthians should certainly want to evaluate in comparison with what Paul says about himself and his relationship with them.

Although Paul could emphasize that his self-praise has an advantage or further end in view, such as to inspire emulation (De laude 544D–F), he does not. His self-praise is aimed at reestablishing his honor, authority, and the respect of the Corinthians. Allegiance to Paul and his teaching has the advantage of building up the Corinthians (10:8; 12:19; 13:10) and has the end in view of rescuing them from the cunning and oppression of the opponents (11:3–4, 20–21), but Paul does not make this explicit. Neither does Paul ask the Corinthians to emulate him. He does discuss behavior that he expects to see and not to see from the Corinthians (12:19–13:10), but it is in obedience to what he has taught them rather than in emulation.

The unfortunate can boast to attest to their ambition and courage in struggling against circumstances and to cast aside pity (De laude 541A–C); Paul's boasting offers an interesting variation. He certainly makes clear that he has been struggling with ill-fortune—consult his list of hardships and sufferings (11:23–33) and the discussion of the thorn in his flesh (12:7–10), a discussion that ends with the expression, "Therefore I am content with weaknesses, insults, hardships, persecutions, and calamities for the sake of Christ; for whenever I am weak, then I am strong" (12:10). However, Paul understands his misfortune in the light of Christ's power. Paul is not suffering so that he can reach beyond his circumstances and ill-fortune, but presenting the state in which he revels and finds his strength. He is not trying to overcome these circumstances for something better, but something better, the power of Christ, arises out of this ill-fortune. Paul is also casting aside pity, for he may not have power and prestige as the opposition was defining these concepts, but he certainly cannot be pitied when his sorry circumstances work for the sake of Christ and the gospel.

Diffusing boasting. Paul uses techniques to diffuse his boasting so that the boasting seems less offensive, but, in light of his theological agenda, he uses the techniques in unusual ways. He never praises the audience in these chapters as his contemporaries advised (*De laude* 542B–C). His focus is on reestablishing his honor at the expense of the opponents' honor. Perhaps praise of the audience that has turned its allegiance away from him, in part because he is viewed as a flatterer (10:1, 10), would only reinforce that perception.

Nowhere in these chapters does Paul attribute his success to others, as advised in discussions of boasting (Quint., *Inst*.11.1.23), but, as advised, he does attribute his success completely to the providence of God, who works through his weakness (Quint., *Inst*.11.1.23; *De laude* 542E–543A). Paul's power is divine authority from the Lord (10:8; 11:4; 12:8, 19; 13:4, 10), his boasting can only be in the Lord (10:17–18; 12:9), and Christ's power is made perfect in Paul's weakness (12:9–10; 13:4). He can boast in his human weakness because God has chosen to use it for God's own power (11:21–12:10).

In this situation Paul has no praise from his audience or opponents to use and to amend in his boasting (*De laude* 543A–F). However, in league with the fact that Paul is the source of divine power through weakness (10:4; 12:9; 13:4), Paul uses God's praise as a way to make his boasting more acceptable: "He [God] said to me, 'My grace is sufficient for you, for power is made perfect in weakness'" (12:9).

Paul could lessen his boasting by mentioning some of his shortcomings (*De laude* 543F–544B). In light of his countercultural values, Paul does just the opposite. He actually refers to what is culturally degrading and ignoble in the midst of his boasting—his imprisonments, floggings, whippings, beatings with rods, and having been hungry, cold, and naked. Brushes with the law and lack of necessities were not virtues in his culture. Paul uses these degrading and ignoble items, not to lessen the arousal of envy or offense in his boasting, but to surprise the Corinthians into seeing that what they devalue is what Paul and God value—weakness. This is the glory—weakness, lack of personal presence, and persecution from the opposition. So although such weaknesses do lessen any boasting that Paul is making, they in fact become a proper boast in the Lord, furthering the glory of Christ: "So, I will boast all the more gladly of my weaknesses, so that the power of Christ may dwell in me" (12:9).

Paul could mention the hardships inherent in what people are praising him for (*De laude* 544C). However, the Corinthians are not praising Paul, so he does not have to obviate his boasting by using this technique. However, those convinced of the authority of Paul and the content of his boasting are less likely to be offended or envious because Paul obtained his authority through great hardships and a thorn in the flesh (11:22–33; 12:6–10).

In his honor defense in 2 Cor 10–13, Paul does a remarkable job of working with the conventions of his Jewish background and of the dominant Greco-Roman culture. In light of the charge that he lobs a strong letter from a safe distance and cannot back up that strength in person, he has to respond with an honor defense that is not perceived as "strong." To do this, he takes an indirect approach using boasting in an ironic mode, stressing his weakness. Ironic boasting is not a strong, confrontational approach. It is a nonthreatening way for Paul to defend his honor without opening him up to criticism of the discrepancy between his strong letters and his weak presence. However, such boasting still allows Paul to defend himself and to shame the Corinthians into seeing that his honor has been unduly challenged and that his opponents have dishonored the Corinthians as well.

Given the situation of challenge-riposte, Paul's honor defense conforms to the conventions prescribed by notables of his day. However, there is also a countercultural thread running throughout his honor defense. In league with countercultural groups Paul rejects the dominant culture's criteria for honor and offers a different set of criteria that he hopes will be its replacement.[24] Even while working within the fabric of social conventions, Paul surprises the Corinthians by boasting with nonconventional values. His emphasis upon weakness in the midst of an honor challenge to his strength and truthfulness would have been surprising if not "foolish." Paul's self-ascription of divine honor and the very working of Paul in weakness among the Corinthians, an approach that was successful in creating their churches, help the Corinthians see that weakness is strength. True honor is honor acquired from God as God works through weakness. Honor challenges based on matters of strength "do not make good sense" (10:12).

Conclusion. As we have seen in 2 Cor 10–13 and will see shortly in his other letters, Paul's understanding of boasting is a unique mix of boasting as understood within Judaism and within the dominant Greco-Roman culture. Paul uses boasting in the situations prescribed as appropriate by the Greco-Roman culture, and he uses boasting according to its conventions for those situations. However, his understanding of the content of boasting itself is borrowed from his Jewish heritage and his newfound faith in Christ. Boasting remains completely theocentric and only appears to be anthropocentric when Paul uses it ironically to defend his honor and challenge his opponents. Paul's boasting reorients the value system of his congregations so that their emphasis on boasting in earthly things is seen as foolishness and is replaced by boasting in the Lord and in his work in and through them. Paul's understanding of boasting is important in helping the young churches define themselves, both in continuity and discontinuity with Jewish and Greco-Roman backgrounds. Paul emphasizes that it is in the weakness of humanity that Christ's power is seen and that boasting resides in weakness. This basis for boasting relies on Judaism's understanding that boasting must be in the Lord because God alone is creator and sustainer, but this boasting is in opposition to the dominant culture, in which boasting is based on human strengths.

Boasting in Paul's Other Letters

Boasting in Paul's Epistle to the Romans. Boasting in Romans is an important component of Paul's understanding of justification. His understanding of boasting does not venture far from traditional Jewish conceptions. Boasting is discussed in terms of where faith is placed for salvation. Faith can be placed either in the self or in God. If faith is placed in the self, then boasting is an outgrowth of an effort to merit salvation by works. It is virtually synonymous with having confidence in the flesh (Phil 3:3–4). If faith is placed in God, then boasting in no way derives from personal effort or from a notion that human beings can in any way save themselves. Boasting derives from what God has and is doing for the justification of humanity. God has purposed that only faith in Christ is ultimately effective for salvation (3:27–28; cf. Eph 2:8–9). Even Abraham, father of the Jews and of the Gentiles who believe, was justified by faith and could not boast in works (4:1–3).

Boasting in works for salvation is self-delusion. Such boasting springs from a misdirected faith—a faith based upon an attempt to be justified by works independent of God. It prevents reception of justification by a faith based on God's grace. Such boasting is rebellion against God, even sin, because it rejects God's verdict that all are sinful and it spurns the offer of salvation through God's Son. Such boasting derives from a life that is a living declaration that God is a liar.

God-reliant boasting is ultimately confession and worship of God. It is the vanquishing of all self-praise. It springs from the exultant joy of repentant sinners who have accepted God's verdict upon them, and of God's act of redemption on their behalf in Jesus Christ (5:11). Such boasting trusts that God will ultimately fulfill promises that the redeemed will share God's glory (5:1–2). It is virtual praise, because God is so fully trusted to fulfill promises that the redeemed can dare to boast in them. Boasting in this hope can even be rooted in tribulation, because tribulation is a sign that what God has promised is nearing fulfillment (5:3; cf. 2 Cor 11:23–29).

Self-reliant boasting has already experienced or currently enjoys its object or basis, like, for example, the man who can count his meritorious deeds or take stock in his possession of the Law. God-reliant boasting must often await its object, like, for example, the glory of God (5:2). As such, proper boasting must remain theocentric, awaiting God's consummation and final fulfillment of God's promises to the redeemed.

Both self-reliant and theocentric boasting can be directed to others. However, the former issues in self-glorification before humanity and God. The latter is done legitimately because it engages others for their own sakes. Because theocentric boasting is based upon what God has done in and through the redeemed, its focus is heavenward, and it is in essence praise and confession to others and God. Take, for example, Paul's boasting in his Gentile mission that he directs to his Roman readers (15:17). The boasting is founded upon what Christ has done through him and not upon his own efforts. In essence, Paul's boast is a confession of and thanksgiving for Christ's power.

Legitimate theocentric boasting ironically may become improper anthropocentric boasting when boasting directed to God and others for God's gifts becomes boasting in the mere possession of the gifts. Legitimate boasting can be perverted when faith is no longer focused on God, but upon these gifts understood as an indication of merit. For example, Paul expects that the Jews could legitimately boast in their possession of the Law. However, he reprimands them because they boast against the Gentiles in the possession of the Law as a merit (2:23). Their boasting was merely a reliance upon the Law, as their lack of obedience indicates. Paul criticizes the Jews for boasting in their status of having a relationship with God as though it were a merit (2:17). Their boasting is focused on their status as a covenant people rather than upon the covenant-maker. Paul also accuses the Gentiles of similar anthropocentric boasting against the Jews. Gentiles have been grafted into God's people and treat their status with God as if it were a merit. God's gift has become a measure of status. They cannot boast because their status is due to God's kindness (11:18).

Boasting in 1 and 2 Corinthians. A blend of the Jewish and Greco-Roman understanding of boasting is found in 1 Corinthians. Paul reminds the Corinthians that God chose to bestow life in Christ upon those that were not esteemed by the values of society, but upon those who were not wise, powerful, or of noble birth (1 Cor 1:26–27). These are qualities of which the Greeks boasted among themselves and to their gods. The gift of wisdom, righteousness, sanctification, and redemption all belong to Christ, who gives them to the lowly Corinthians. Paul quotes Jer 9:23–24 that all boasting must be in the Lord. He affirms that because the Corinthians had nothing of which the world boasts, they can only boast in the Lord who has given them all things (1 Cor 1:26–31).

Love, the greatest Christian virtue, precludes boasting in the self. However, boasting in having given away all of one's possessions or oneself into slavery for another or as a martyr is a legitimate basis for boasting if it is done in love.[25] These are demonstrations of selfless love that are done in the *agape* love of Christ for others. It is, in essence, legitimate boasting in the Lord (13:1–7). Paul cannot boast in his proclamation of the gospel because he was called to it, but he does boast in doing so for free when he is entitled to support. This is a denial of himself for *agape* love toward the Corinthians (9:15–18; cf. 2 Cor 11:7–11).

The Corinthians did try to boast in their newfound freedom in Christ, and this could have been legitimate boasting in the Lord. However, their boasting was in sexual immorality as a demonstration of their newfound freedom, but such boasting did not demonstrate the lordship of Christ and was, as Paul understates, "not a good thing" (5:1–8).

Based on Greco-Roman conceptions, the Corinthians were boasting about one leader over another as a way to gain status for themselves. Paul undermines this boasting by reminding them that all leaders are provided by God and all leaders belong to all Christians (1 Cor 3:21–23). Boasting against others involves judgment and the assumption that the boaster has something that was not received from God and that can be claimed as personal merit. Paul reminds the Corinthians that judgment belongs to the Lord and that everything that they have is a gift of God (1 Cor 4:1–7). Unlike his opponents, Paul does not misplace his boasting on earthly wisdom (2 Cor 1:12–14) or on outward appearance rather than the heart (2 Cor 5:12).

Paul's boasts of a clear conscience forged by frankness and by godly sincerity in his work for the Lord at Corinth. The Corinthians are Paul's work, and each can boast in the other as works in the Lord (2 Cor 1:12–14; 5:11–13). Paul can boast about the works of the Corinthians because it is boasting in the Lord's work through them (2 Cor 7:4, 14; 8:24; 9:2–3; 1 Cor 15:31).

Boasting in Philippians, 1 Thessalonians, and Galatians. The Judaizing factions in Galatia and Philippi were stressing that circumcision and obedience to the Law were necessary for salvation. In other words, they were finding the basis for boasting before God in personal merit. In Philippians, Paul holds up himself and the Philippians as those who have no confidence in the flesh, but who boast in Christ Jesus (3:2–11). In Galatians he claims that the motivation of the Judaizers is the misplaced boasting in the flesh of the circumcised, whereas he will boast solely in the cross of Christ (Gal 6:13–14).

Paul anticipates sharing with the Philippians in boasting in their progress and joy in faith (1:25–26). By holding onto the word of life, Paul hopes to boast on the day of Christ that his labor for Christ was not in vain (2:16). This is proper boasting in the Lord's work through him. The Thessalonians as a work of Paul in the Lord are his crown of boasting before Jesus at his coming (1 Thess 2:19–20). The Galatians are told that their work for Christ in the community of faith is a legitimate source of boasting (6:4).

Part III. Relevant Pauline and Paulinist Texts

Eph 2:9

In Eph 2:8–10 the Paulinist understanding of boasting continues. Salvation is a gift of God and not the result of good works so that no one can boast. Human beings cannot save themselves and only faith is effective for salvation (cf. Rom 3:27–28). Boasting can only be in what God has done for their salvation. The absurdity of boasting in good works is that even these good works were created in Christ Jesus by God as the Christian way of life. The Jewish understanding of boasting reemerges that boasting before God is precluded because human beings are created by God and thus all they have is a gift of God.

Part IV. Bibliography

Barrett, C. K. "Boasting (καυχᾶσθαι, κτλ) in the Pauline Epistles." Pages 363–68 in *L'Apôtre Paul: Personalité, style et conception du ministère*. Edited by A. Vanhoye. BETL 73. Louvain: Louvain University Press, 1986.

Betz, Hans Dieter. *Der Apostel Paulus und die sokratische Tradition: Eine exegetische Untersuchung zu seiner "Apologie" 2 Korinther, 10–13*. BHT 45. Tübingen: Mohr [Siebeck], 1972.

———. *"De Laude ipsius (Moralia 539A–547F)."* Pages 367–93 in *Plutarch's Ethical Writings and Early Christian Literature*. Edited by H. D. Betz. SCHNT 4. Leiden: E. J. Brill, 1978.

Bosch, J. Sánchez. *"Gloriarse" segun San Pablo: Sentido y teologia de kauchaomai*. AnBib 40; Colentanea San Paciano 16. Rome: Biblical Institute; Barcelona: Facultad de Teologia [SSP], 1970.

Bultmann, Rudolf. "Καυχάομαι . . ." *TDNT* 3:645–54.

Dio Chrysostom. *The Fifty-seventh Discourse*. Translated by H. Lamar Crosby. LCL 376. Cambridge: Harvard University Press, 1946. [Pages 417–29.]

Fiore, Benjamin. "The Hortatory Function of Paul's Boasting." Pages 39–46 in *Proceedings: Eastern Great Lakes and Midwest Biblical Societies*. Edited by Phillip Sigal. Vol. 5. Otterbein, Ohio: Otterbein College, 1985.

Forbes, Christopher. "Comparison, Self-Praise, and Irony: Paul's Boasting and the Conventions of Hellenistic Rhetoric." *NTS* 32 (1986): 1–30.

Hafemann, Scott. "'Self-Commendation' and Apostolic Legitimacy in 2 Corinthians: A Pauline Dialectic?" *NTS* 36 (1990): 66–88.

Hahn, H. C. "Boast." *NIDNTT* 1:227–29.

Judge, E. A. "Paul's Boasting in Relation to Contemporary Professional Practice." *ABR* 16 (1968): 37–50.

Lambrecht, Jan. "Dangerous Boasting: Paul's Self-Commendation in 2 Cor. 10–13." Pages 325–46 in *The Corinthian Correspondence*. Edited by R. Beiringer. BETL 125. Louvain: Louvain University Press, 1996.

Marshall, Peter. *Enmity in Corinth: Social Conventions in Paul's Relations with the Corinthians*. WUNT 2.23. Tübingen: J. C. B. Mohr [Paul Siebeck], 1987. [See esp. pp. 341–95.]

Peterson, Brian K. *Eloquence and Proclamation of the Gospel in Corinth.* SBLDS 163. Atlanta: Scholars Press, 1998.

Plutarch. *On Praising Oneself Inoffensively (De se ipsum citra invidiam laudando).* Vol. 7 of *Moralia.* Translated by P. H. De Lacy and B. Einarson. LCL 337. Cambridge: Harvard University Press, 1959. [Pages 109–67.]

Quintilian. *Institutio Oratoria.* Translated by H. E. Butler. 4 vols. LCL 124–27. Cambridge: Harvard University Press, 1979. [11.1.15–28.]

Sampley, J. Paul. "Paul, His Opponents in 2 Corinthians 10–13, and the Rhetorical Handbooks." Pages 162–77 in *The Social World of Formative Christianity and Judaism: Essays in Tribute to Howard Clark Kee.* Edited by Jacob Neusner et al. Philadelphia: Fortress Press, 1988.

Spicq, Ceslas. "Καυχάομαι, καύχημα, καύχησις." *TLNT* 2:295–302.

Travis, S. H. "Paul's Boasting in 2 Corinthians 10–12." Pages 527–32 in *Studia Evangelica VI.* Edited by Elizabeth A. Livingston. [= TU 112.] Berlin: Akademie, 1973.

Zmijewski, J. A. "Καυχάομαι." *EDNT* 2:276–79.

———. *Der Stil der paulinischen "Narrenrede."* BBB 52. Köln: Peter Hanstein, 1978.

Notes

1. All biblical quotations are from the NRSV.

2. Christopher Forbes, "Comparison, Self-Praise, and Irony: Paul's Boasting and the Conventions of Hellenistic Rhetoric," *NTS* 32 (1986): 9–10.

3. Dionysius of Halicarnassus, *The Three Literary Letters* (ed. W. Rhys Roberts; Cambridge: Cambridge University Press, 1901), in the *Letter to Pompeius,* 92, lines 28ff.; cited by Forbes, "Comparison, Self-Praise, and Irony," 8.

4. Forbes, "Comparison, Self-Praise, and Irony," 10.

5. Dio Chrysostom, *The Fifty-seventh Discourse* (Crosby, LCL), 417–29.

6. Quintilian, *Institutio oratoria* (Butler, LCL), 124–27.

7. Plutarch, *De Se Ipsum Citra Invidiam Laudando* (De Lacy and Einarson, LCL), 109–67.

8. For analyses of 2 Cor 10–13, see Hans Dieter Betz, *Der Apostel Paulus und die socratische Tradition: Eine exegetische Untersuchung zu seiner 'Apologie' 2 Korinther, 10–13* (BHT 45; Tübingen: J. C. B. Mohr [Paul Siebeck], 1972); Scott Hafemann, " 'Self-Commendation' and Apostolic Legitimacy in 2 Corinthians: A Pauline Dialectic?" *NTS* 36 (1990): 66–88; Jan Lambrecht, "Dangerous Boasting: Paul's Self-Commendation in 2 Corinthians 10–13," in *The Corinthian Correspondence* (ed. R. Bieringer; BETL 125; Louvain: Louvain University Press, 1996), 325–46; Peter Marshall, *Enmity in Corinth: Social Conventions in Paul's Relations with the Corinthians* (WUNT 2.23; Tübingen: J. C. B. Mohr [Paul Siebeck], 1987), 341–95; J. Paul Sampley, "Paul, His Opponents in 2 Corinthians 10–13, and the Rhetorical Handbooks," in *The Social World of Formative Christianity and Judaism: Essays in Tribute to Howard Clark Kee* (ed. Jacob Neusner et al.; Philadelphia: Fortress Press, 1988), 162–77; S. H. Travis, "Paul's Boasting in 2 Corinthians 10–12," in *SE VI* (ed. Elizabeth A. Livingston [= TU 112]; Berlin: Akademie, 1973), 527–32; and J. Zmijewski, *Der Stil der paulinischen "Narrenrede"* (BBB 52; Cologne: Peter Hanstein, 1978).

9. John H. Elliott, "Patronage and Clientage," in *The Social Sciences and New*

Testament Interpretation (ed. Richard Rohrbaugh; Peabody, Mass.: Hendrickson, 1996), 144–56 (see excellent bibliography); Ronald F. Hock, *The Social Context of Paul's Ministry* (Philadelphia: Fortress Press, 1980), 59–64.

10. Peter Marshall, *Enmity in Corinth: Social Convention in Paul's Relations with the Corinthians* (Tübingen: Mohr-Siebeck, 1987), 1–34.

11. For a complete discussion of the opponents in these chapters, see, among many others, Dieter Georgi, *The Opponents of Paul in Second Corinthians* (Philadelphia: Fortress Press, 1986).

12. For more on honor and shame, see Halvor Moxnes, "Honor and Shame," in Rohrbaugh, *Social Sciences and New Testament Interpretation*, 19–40; Bruce J. Malina and Jerome H. Neyrey, "Honor and Shame in Luke-Acts: Pivotal Values of the Mediterranean World," in *The Social World of Luke-Acts: Models for Interpretation* (ed. Jerome H. Neyrey; Peabody, Mass.: Hendrickson, 1991), 25–65; Bruce J. Malina, *The New Testament World: Insights from Cultural Anthropology* (rev. ed.; Louisville: Westminster John Knox, 1993), 28–62; David A. deSilva, *The Hope of Glory: Honor Discourse and New Testament Interpretation* (Collegeville, Minn.: Michael Glazier, 1999).

13. For the role of honor in 2 Cor 10–13, see Arthur J. Dewey, "A Matter of Honor: A Social-Historical Analysis of 2 Corinthians 10," *HTR* 78 (1985): 209–17.

14. For full identification of Paul's opponents in this section and a reconstruction of their challenge and claims, see Jerry Sumney, *Identifying Paul's Opponents: The Question of Method in 2 Corinthians* (JSNTSup 40; Sheffield, England: Sheffield Academic Press, 1990), 149–79.

15. Forbes, "Comparison, Self-Praise, and Irony," 10.

16. Plutarch, *Quomodo Adulator Ab Amico Internoscatur* (Babbitt, LCL), 197, 52B, 52F–53A. Cited by Forbes, "Comparison, Self-Praise, and Irony," 10–11.

17. Vernon K. Robbins, *Exploring the Texture of Texts: A Guide to Socio-rhetorical Criticism* (Valley Forge, Pa.: Trinity Press International, 1996), 81.

18. E. A. Judge, "Paul's Boasting in Relation to Contemporary Professional Practice," *ABR* 16 (1968): 37.

19. Forbes, "Comparison, Self-Praise, and Irony," 18.

20. Judge, "Paul's Boasting," 47.

21. John T. Fitzgerald, *Cracks in an Earthen Vessel: An Examination of the Catalogues of Hardships in the Corinthian Correspondence* (SBLDS 99; Atlanta: Scholars Press, 1988), 44–51.

22. Forbes, "Comparison, Self-Praise, and Irony," 20.

23. Judge, "Paul's Boasting," 47.

24. Robbins, *Exploring the Texture of Texts*, 87; idem, *The Tapestry of Early Christian Discourse: Rhetoric, Society, and Ideology* (New York: Routledge, 1996), 169–70.

25. Some ancient texts refer to giving of the body "to be burned" (13:3).

4

PAUL AND COMMENDATION

Efrain Agosto

Commendation was an instrument of power in the Greco-Roman world. By means of commendation letters, powerful patrons endorsed clients and friends to their social peers throughout the Roman Empire, including Asia Minor and Greece, the heart of the Apostle Paul's missionary activities in the mid–first century C.E. Paul also used commendation in his letters to endorse supporters in his churches. This study compares and contrasts commendation texts in Paul's letters with those in the Greco-Roman world in order to understand how Paul employed the convention of commendation.

Part I. Commendation in the Greco–Roman World

The roots of commendation lie with the practice of "encomium," the praise of persons, which was taught in the rhetorical handbooks of the time. To praise someone, a writer or speaker first explained a person's birthplace and family origins in order to demonstrate the extent of that individual's noble beginnings. Second, encomia described a person's upbringing, nurture, and training, including general education, character formation, and training in the laws.

Typical encomia also observed the person's accomplishments in life, which included the noble actions that a good character produced. These could be divided into three areas: deeds of the soul or mind, deeds of body, and deeds of fortune or external circumstances such as wealth. Deeds of the soul included such virtues as wisdom, honor/shame, justice, and courage. Deeds of the body related to actions produced by such physical prowess as good health, beauty, speed, and strength.

With regard to fortune, encomia often extolled matters not necessarily under the control of the person being praised, but nonetheless indicative of divine favor (i.e., the goddess Τυχη, *Tychē*, Fortune). Thus land ownership, wealth, social connections, and such items added to a person's perceived character, even if the person simply acquired these from their parents or "good fortune." Finally, encomia often included comparison to others, usually in a positive sense, such as, "this person compares well to this other noble individual."[1]

Learning to speak and write encomia, then, was an essential part of a good rhetorical education. Commendation letters used encomium to enhance the reputation of the subject of the letter. As we shall see below, letter writers also enhanced their own reputations by writing commendation letters for other praiseworthy individuals.

Commendation Letters

The volume of extant Roman commendation letters in Latin is fairly large. In particular, the prolific Roman writers Cicero (106–43 B.C.E.), Pliny (ca. 61–ca. 120 C.E.), and Fronto (ca. 100–ca. 166 C.E.) left a significant number of commendation letters among their many writings. Though not abundant, commendation letters have been found among private correspondence in both Latin and Greek. Unfortunately for the study of Pauline commendation passages, very few Greek commendation letters have survived from the East, except for Greek papyri letters from Egypt.[2]

The structure of a commendation letter remains fairly similar across a variety of types, styles, and purposes. After opening greetings, most letters identify the person being commended, usually by including the person's family or household relationships, and thus begin to cite the person's credentials. In this initial section, the writer also often explains why the letter was written, such as the person recommended "asked me to write this letter."[3] The heart of the recommendation letter is the "request period." Here "the writer indicates the favor he is asking of the recipient on behalf of the recommended."[4] Usually, this involves some kind of "general assistance" for the recommended, such as an introduction of the person in question to influential friends of the letter's recipient.[5]

Commendation letters typically conclude with an "appreciation" statement and the final greeting. Usually this thanksgiving reads something like "by doing this you will have my gratitude."[6] Generally, this structure—identification and credentials, request and appreciation— appears both in the Greek papyri letters and also the Latin literary letters.

Latin Commendation Letters

Although they exhibit the basic structure for typical commendation letters of the first century C.E., the private, papyri letters, both Greek and Latin, are often "arid and schematic" in quality.[7] Thus, several scholars have questioned the usefulness of the papyri letters of commendation for understanding the genre as a whole.

Stanley Stowers describes Egyptian papyri letters, for example, as "rather stereo-typed and formulaic." Stowers argues that this most likely "reflects the standard practice of popular professional letter writers who tended to set the local standards for writers with little education." Stowers asserts that the literary letters, while reflecting similar structure as the papyri, "naturally show more variety and creativity since their authors usually had rhetorical educations."[8]

Therefore, a comparative analysis of the literary letters of commendation, rather than the Greek papyri letters, will be more useful in studying the commendations of the Apostle Paul:

> Although Paul employs language and certain formal features that parallel the rather schematized papyrus letters, his freedom in writing introductions, commendations and intercessions makes him better resemble the generally more educated writers of literarily transmitted letters.[9]

Indeed, along with the rhetorical handbooks of the time, the Latin literary writers of commendation, especially Cicero, Pliny, and Fronto, became the models for commendation-letter writing throughout the period of the early empire.

Common Elements in Greco-Roman Commendation Letters

Cicero, Pliny, and Fronto shared certain elements in their commendation letters. First, Greco-Roman commendation letters shared a history and purpose. In *Ad Amicos* 1.1, Fronto gives a historical accounting of commendation that is generally plausible, if not fully developed. Commendation, argues Fronto, began with the "good will" (*benevolentia*) of anyone who would want "to have his own friend made known to another friend and rendered intimate with him." In time, says Fronto, the practice became one of providing testimonials of persons in trial. In short, Fronto concludes, "these commendatory letters seemed to discharge the function of a testimony to character."[10] Thus commending character (ἦθος, *ēthos*) constituted a major factor in commendation letters.

Second, as "testimonies to character," Roman commendations introduced younger protégés to new patrons. For example, Fronto writes to a military leader, Naucellius, about Faustinianus, the son of a beloved friend: "Any attention you shew [sic] him will be paid with interest" (*Ad Amicos* 1.5). Fronto compliments Faustinianus by wishing he had a son worthy to send under Naucellius's supervision. In addition, Naucellius will receive benefit from a new alliance with this family, as well as from the "refined nature," "learning," and "military ability" of the young man in question. Both the young man's character and his family connections commend him to the letter recipient, Naucellius.

Thus this letter also illustrates another common element of Roman commendation: the importance of family origins and other connections. Fronto extols the native abilities and character of Faustinianus, but these proceed from the noble roots of a "dear father" (*Ad Amicos* 1.5). Mentioning the ties of the candidate *and* the letter writer to a good family (or, as in other cases, to powerful patrons and friends) enhances the attraction of the commendation for the letter recipient. The latter benefits from responding favorably to a commendation for a well-connected individual.

These common commendation elements—character, introduction, and connections—all helped to enhance honor, status, and opportunity for the family, protégés, and friends of the powerful. Thus, the parties involved in commendation—the person being commended, the letter writer, and the letter recipient—could expect benefits from a commendation letter.

The major beneficiary of a commendation, of course, was the commended person. However, effective commendations often depended more on the influence of the writer than upon the personal qualities of the commended. Thus, individuals sought out people of influence. When Cassio requests a commendation from Cicero, the latter writes: "As to your writing therefore that you are sure that some good can be done by influence and eloquence [*auctoritate et eloquentia*] . . ." (*Ad Fam.* 12.2).

Cicero asserts the importance of the writer's having influence with those in power in order for a commendation to benefit its subject. Only after this assertion does Cicero cite the personal qualities of Cassio (e.g., "patriotism," "speaking freely," and "being a relative" of the powerful) to support his commendation (*Ad Fam.* 12.2).

Cicero's recommendations were coveted because of his great power and influence:

> There are many reasons of long standing for the close attachment of Q. Pompeius, son of Sextus, to myself. As in the past it is in my recommendations that he has got into the habit of finding support for his fortunes, his reputation and influence, he certainly ought just now, when you are governor of the province, to profit by my letter so far as to be assured that there is nobody to whom he has ever more highly commended. (*Ad Fam.* 13.49)

Cicero asks Curius, a provincial governor, "to show my friends as much respect as your own" and to admit Pompeius into a "special friendship" with him (Curius). Such a relationship should convince Pompeius "that nothing could possibly have been of more service or more of a distinction to him than my [Cicero's] recommendation." Because of Cicero's influence and connections, Pompeius can expect his own "fortunes, reputation and influence" to be enhanced.

Similarly, Pliny's influence with the emperor Trajan benefited those whom he commended. In one letter to Trajan, after citing the personal qualities, family origins, and wealth of a candidate for senatorial rank, Pliny adds:

> In addition to this I trust that my own plea on his behalf will be a further recommendation to your kind interest. I pray you then, Sir, to enable me to congratulate Romanus, as I so much wish to do, and to gratify what I hope is a worthy affection. I can then be proud to think that your recognition of myself extends to my friend. (*Ep.* 10.4.6)

For his friend's advancement, Pliny trades on his favor and reputation with the emperor.

Commendation letters, as instruments of patronage, benefited not only the individual commended, but also the writer of the letter. For example, Cicero expects benefits in return for the favor of writing a recommendation for P. Cuspious: "I earnestly beg of you to see to it that the thanks I receive from Cuspious as a result of this recommendation may be as cordial, as prompt and as frequent as possible" (*Ad Fam.* 13.6).

Cuspious now has two patrons, not only the man to whom he is commended, but also the one who commended him, Cicero. Cicero benefits from this commendation by acquiring a new client, someone with a debt of gratitude to him.

Pliny commends the son of a loyal supporter and expects to benefit from his recommendation: "[A]ny increase of dignity [*honores*] which he [the youth] shall receive, will be an occasion of particular congratulation to myself [*meam gratulationem*]" (*Ep.* 10.87.3). Thus a commendation letter often proved to be as strategic for the status of the writer as for the subject of the commendation.

Letter recipients could also benefit by responding positively to commendation requests. In *Ad Fam.* 13.22, Cicero commends T. Manlius, a banker, to Sulpicius. Manlius has shown "marked respect" to Cicero. He has also earned the favor of another leading Roman citizen, Varro Murena, who asked Cicero for this commendation of Manlius. Cicero's request on Manlius's behalf draws on Sulpicius's sense of honor and "high position." Cicero assures Sulpicius that by "promoting the interests" of Manlius, he (Sulpicius) "will reap the reward . . . usually expect[ed] for services done to men of merit." Manlius's previous patronal connections ensure the benefits of patronage for Sulpicius as well.

These brief examples illustrate the dynamics of effective commendation. All parties involved benefit from the commendation, including the person commended, the letter writer, and the letter recipient. All of these sought commendation, wrote commendations, or received commended individuals in order to enhance their patron-client relations and status. In effect, then, commendations promoted patronage.

Character in Commendation

Commendations described the character, or *ēthos* (ἦθος), of an individual being commended as an important criterion supporting that person. Scholars concur: "In all periods and places the letter of recommendation was first and foremost a testimonial: it testified to the recommended person's good character and trustworthiness."[11] However, *ēthos* entailed more than personal character traits. All the factors of that person's life including personal traits, social status, and patronage connections (whether family, friends, or associates) constituted his or her *ēthos*.

Commendation writers did often begin with personal qualities. In his commendations, Fronto cited such character traits as hard work, energy, patriotism, and honesty. For example, Fronto commended a long-standing friend, Gavius, as "conscientious," "reasonable," and "generous," and for having "simplicity, continence, truthfulness, an honor plainly Roman, a warmth of affection [φιλοστοργία, *filostorgia*]." Fronto considered *filostorgia* ("warm affection") a rare virtue in Rome, "for there is nothing of which my whole life through I have seen less at Rome than a man unfeignedly *filostorgon* [warm in affection]" (*Ad Ver. Imp.* 2.7.6). Thus, in his commendations, Fronto often emphasized a person's virtues as important criteria, especially those rarely found in others.

However, despite his preferences, even Fronto could not limit his discussion of character to personal qualities. He often presented other, more pragmatic reasons for supporting a commendation, such as friendship: "Please pay him such attention as you would expect to be shown by another to your intimate friend, the sharer of your home and your counsels" (*Ad Am.* 1.3).

Similarly, Cicero lauded a candidate for a consulship as the "most admirable and gallant of citizens [*optimus et fortissimus civis*]"; "a man of great influence [*summa auctoritate*] and soundest sentiments [*optime sentiens*]" (*Ad Fam.* 12.2.3). People like these, wrote Cicero, are "the leaders of public policy [*auctores consili publici*]" (12.2.3). He refused to recommend as Roman consulars any without these character traits and, in fact, decried the paucity of them.

Yet Cicero ended this letter with an offer of support that reflected additional concerns beyond the candidate's personal qualities: "For myself, I never fail, and I never shall fail, to protect those dear to you; and whether they appeal to me for advice or whether they do not, I can in either case guarantee my love and loyalty [*benevolentur fidesque*] to yourself" (12.2.3).

Cicero expected that his protection, advice, goodwill, and loyalty for the letter recipient would secure the commendation. Thus commendations depended on the *ēthos* of patrons, both letter writers and letter recipients, as well as the personal qualities of the commended.

Family origins were another important "external circumstance" observed by many commendation writers. Pliny cited numerous aspects of personal character in his commendation letters. In a letter to the military commander Priscus, Pliny described the personal, professional qualities that he experienced firsthand from his friend Voconius Romanus: "No one could be a more faithful friend or more delightful companion. His conversation, voice and whole expression have a special charm, and he is gifted besides with a powerful and penetrating intellect, trained by his profession at the bar to express itself with ease and grace" (*Ep.* 2.13).

However, Pliny also emphasized the family origins of Romanus: "His father was distinguished in the order of knights" (2.13.4). Voconius's mother came from "a leading family" (*mater e primis*). Second, Voconius held a significant leadership post in Spain, namely a provincial priesthood of the highest order. The character of his family and his previous positions enhanced the *ēthos* of Voconius.

Pliny also cited his long friendship with Voconius as a significant criterion for this commendation: "Our friendship began with our studies, and we were early united in the closest intimacy. We live together in town and country; he shared with me my most serious and my gayest hours: and where, indeed, could I have found a more faithful friend, or more agreeable companion?" (*Ep.* 2.13.5)

In the eyes of Pliny shared roots imply similar and, therefore, commendable *ēthos*.

Thus, in commendation letters, other important criteria besides character traits, such as personal connections (e.g., friendship and patronage) and family origins, including the nobility and wealth of that family, all contributed to establishing one's *ēthos* as a whole. In fact, the strength of one's connections or the state of one's finances often determined, along with the qualities of one's personality, what aspect of *ēthos* would be emphasized in a given commendation.

Wealth, in particular, either its possession or lack, significantly affected written commendations. Whenever wealth was present, personal qualities seemed less important. Writers and readers believed that the character of the commended could be demonstrated by acquisition of wealth. Conversely, when an individual's financial resources were limited, other character traits were emphasized. When Pliny endorsed Voconius Romanus, he cited his friend's "cultivated interests," his kindness to his parents, but also that Romanus had an inheritance and had secured a strategic adoption from a wealthy stepfather after the death of his own father (*Ep.* 10.4). Pliny asserted that these financial strengths showcased the character of Romanus. Pliny wrote that the wealth and rank of the family of Romanus should also enhance his attractiveness. Romanus had received, from his mother, land and other holdings valued at four million sesterces. Thus Pliny had all the pieces in place to make a strong recommendation to the emperor for the senatorial ranking of his friend Voconius Romanus. Pliny's request depended on a character that included family background, good connections, and personal qualities, but, in Voconius's case, especially wealth.

If someone had financial problems, recommenders resorted to other emphases. In *Ep.* 10.12, Pliny acknowledged the financial limitations of Attius Sura, who had "fortune below mediocrity" (10.12.2). Instead, Pliny lauded the modest ambitions, noble birth, and great integrity of Attius. Pliny also had to depend on the favor of the letter's recipient, the emperor Trajan: "Though I am well assured, Sir, that you, who never forget any opportunity of exerting your generosity, are not unmindful of the request I lately made of you . . ." (10.2.1). The best chances for Pliny and Attius to receive favorable reply to this commendation rested on "the happiness of [Trajan's] reign" and his "kind interest" (10.12.2). Thus the risk factor involved in the commendation, limited wealth, was alleviated by the advantage of Pliny's connection with the emperor.

In conclusion, access to wealth, noble family roots, and the character of one's friends and patrons all indicated a character worthy of commendation. Relationships and loyalty to powerful and well-placed letter writers and letter recipients, those with worthy character and high status themselves, showed that the commended merited consideration for further enhancement of their status. Such persons as slaves, former slaves, and all but the most wealthy, independent women, could expect little weight to be given to their personal character unless their patrons, masters, and husbands were highly regarded.

The Nature of Commendation Requests

Generally, letters of commendation make ambiguous requests. For example, in the following Greek papyri letter, the writer asks for "general assistance": "You do well then if you take care of him in whatever he asks of you. For it is a favor you do for me. And write to me also for whatever purpose."[12]

Such generalities and ambiguities may have been intentional. The writer may have wanted "to leave the recipient enough leeway to interpret the request in a way which is commensurate with his own interests and dignity."[13] Thus general requests of "assistance" or "introduction" prevailed, with the "means and methods" of granting such assistance left up to the letter's recipient as a matter of good "decorum" in commendation letters.[14]

Pliny's commendation letters include many general requests. In *Ep.* 10.87, he commends the son of a longtime friend and associate to Trajan with a general petition: "That he is equal to any honor you shall think proper to confer upon him" (10.87.3). Pliny, too, keeps the options open for compliance from the emperor.

Nonetheless, in many instances, the commendation writers also make specific requests from the recipients. For example, in *Ad Fam.* 13.29, Cicero seeks direct intervention by Plancus on behalf of an inheritance due Capito:

> Now I ask you, my dear Plancus, in the name of our hereditary connexion, our mutual affection, our common pursuits, and the close resemblance of our whole lives . . . to spare no effort, no endeavour, and so to bring it about that through my recommendation, your own assiduity, and the kindness of Caesar, Capito may make good his claim to his relative's legacy. (13.29.5)

Financial, social, and political advancement thus constituted specific kinds of requests often made by the literary commendation writers. For example, Fronto makes this request for advancement:

> To Aegrilius Plarianus, greeting. I commend to you with all possible cordiality Julius Aquilinus, a man, if you have any faith in my judgment, most learned, most eloquent. . . . A man so learned and so cultured should naturally find from a man of your serious character and wisdom not only protection but advancement and honor [*provehi et illustrari*]. (*Ad Am.* 1.4)

Thus leadership advancement was a key request in many of the Roman commendation letters. As exemplified by Cicero, Pliny, and Fronto, the Roman letters had their raison d'être in the social and political advancement of friends, clients, and protégés of patronal elites in the Roman hierarchical social system. Moreover, those friends and protégés who were commended usually already had positions somewhere in the hierarchy. Commendation helped to boost them further in the system. It also helped their patrons maintain and enhance their honorable reputations, because they could place so many of their charges in positions of power.

Conclusion

I have argued that in the Greek papyri and, especially, the Roman literary commendations, the characteristics and qualities of the individuals being commended are quite similar. Moreover, most individuals commended have some combination of significant wealth, noble family origins, or appropriate previous leadership experience in the Roman system that enhances their personal qualities of integrity, loyalty, and patriotism (service to the empire).

Nonetheless, the most crucial aspect in these commendations relates to the connections and networks of the parties involved in the commendation. Whom did the commended parties know and how did they serve those whom they knew? The person recommending them invariably was a friend, political colleague, or someone to whom the letter's recipient owed some kind of obligation. In short, the recommender was a patron.

Thus the background for commendations was indeed patronage. The relations of patrons to clients were the social arrangements from which the commendation letter emerged.

Our task now is to study commendation in the letters of the Apostle Paul in light of these phenomena of patronage and status in Greco-Roman society as exemplified in the Roman commendation letters. Commendation structure, social dynamics, the benefits of commendation, and aspects of character must be explored in several Pauline commendation passages. We need to see how commendation functions as a factor in clarifying the overall exigence of the letters that contain such commendation. I will also consider the role of patronage in Pauline commendation.

Part II. Commendation in Paul

The Apostle Paul makes one of his few explicit statements about commendation in Second Corinthians:

> Are we beginning to commend ourselves again? Surely we do not need, as some do, letters of recommendation to you or from you, do we? You yourselves are our letter, written on our hearts, to be known and read by all; and you show that you are a letter of Christ, prepared by us, written not with ink but with the Spirit of the living God, not on tablets of stone but on tablets of human hearts. (2 Cor 3:1–3)[15]

Thus Paul claims independence from the need for letters of recommendation. That a community of faith has been formed in the city of Corinth under his direction should be enough to recommend him. The Corinthian church is Paul's "letter of recommendation" (see συστατικῶν ἐπιστολῶν, *systatikōn epistolōn*, in 2 Cor 3:1).

Yet despite distancing himself from the convention of commendation, Paul offers a self-commendation of his ministry in 2 Cor 3:4–6:13. Given the presence of rival leaders in Corinth, who apparently do have written letters of recommendation, Paul felt compelled to defend his ministry.[16] In addition, Paul also commends other leaders in significant ways in several key places throughout his letters, even though he claims that "it is not those who commend themselves that are approved, but those whom the Lord commends" (2 Cor 10:18).

The Structure of a Pauline Commendation

In his study of Greek commendation letters, Chan-Hie Kim identified seven passages of commendation in Paul's letters: Rom 16:1–2; 1 Cor 16:15–16, 17–18; Phil

2:29–30; 4:2–3; 1 Thess 5:12–13a; and the Letter to Philemon, the only complete commendation letter in the Pauline corpus.[17]

Like Greco-Roman commendations, Pauline commendations have a discernible form, although because Paul's commendation passages, except for Philemon, are contained within larger letters, their structure is simplified in comparison to the Greco-Roman letters. Pauline commendations have (1) an introduction naming the person or persons to be commended; (2) the credentials commending these individuals; and (3) the statement of desired action by the readers of the commendation.[18]

In what follows, I discuss, in varying degrees of detail, five instances of commendation in Paul, those which I believe best exemplify Pauline commendation in form and content: 1 Thess 5:12–13; 1 Cor 16:15–16, 17–18; Phil 2:29–30; and Rom 16:1–2. In the final section of this essay, I simply point out two other formal Pauline commendations, the Letter to Philemon and the passage commending Euodia and Syntyche in Phil 4:2–3. There also, I will mention envoy passages in Paul that, while formally distinct from commendation passages, still bear commendation elements.[19]

The study of Paul's commendation passages in this section briefly describes the immediate context of each pericope and its place in the argument of the letter in question. I point out the commendation aspects in them: (1) how Paul identifies the leaders, including the dynamics between the various parties involved (Paul, the letter recipient, the commended persons); (2) the criteria (aspects of *ēthos*) he invokes for commending them; and (3) the specific commendation request he makes of his readers.

1 Thessalonians 5:12–13. Paul places the commendation passage of 1 Thess 5:12–13 at the beginning of his final exhortation section in this letter to a young, struggling congregation. However, rather than general parenetic material, Paul has in mind certain needs specific to the Thessalonian situation, including the need to recognize the community's leaders. For the latter, he uses commendation.

Paul seeks recognition of persons he identifies, not by name, but by their functions, described with three present-active participles: κοπιῶντας, *kopiōntas;* προϊσταμένους, *proistamenous;* and νουθετοῦντας, *nouthetountas* (5:12). Paul employs only one article (τούς, *tous:* "those who") for all three participles. Thus he probably has in view one group of people who engage in these three activities rather than three different groups of persons, each of which undertakes a different task.[20] These individuals render activities or services on behalf of the church community at Thessalonica, as demonstrated by the second-person plural pronouns that follow each of the participles (ἐν ὑμῖν, *en hymin;* ὑμῶν, *hymōn;* and ὑμᾶς, *hymas*—"in" or "among you").

Most Pauline commendations, like Greco-Roman commendations, name the individuals being commended. First Thessalonians 5:12 is an exception. The participles, which give the credentials of the commended, also provide their identity. By not using names, Paul probably intends to generalize his commendation. Although he has specific individuals in mind, and the other church members know who they are, he wants to encourage others in the community to participate in the work of the church.

Paul frequently uses cognates of κοπιῶντες, *kopiōntes* ("those who labor"), especially the noun κόπος, *kopos,* with reference to the ministry in general and the hard work of ministry in particular (cf. 1 Thess 1:3; 2:9; 3:5), whether his ministry or that of his associates and other traveling workers and missionaries (cf. 1 Cor 15:10; Gal 4:11; Phil 2:16). Moreover, Paul also employs *kopos* when referring to the work of members of local churches (cf. 1 Cor 16:16; Rom 16:6, 12). While we cannot determine from the term itself what specific aspect of gospel work Paul refers to, the emphasis in the most frequent translation of *kopos*—"*hard* work"—lies on the *effort* of those who labor for the gospel.[21]

In fact, the effort in their work for the gospel helps establish the *ēthos* of gospel laborers. For example, in 1 Thess 2:1–12, Paul details the hardship (2:2), integrity (2:3–6), care (2:7–8, 11), and hard labor (2:9) that he and his associates undertook on behalf of the Thessalonians. In the face of possible opposition to the missionaries because of their early departure (2:17–18), Paul must reestablish their *ēthos* in the mind of the Thessalonians. Hard work is a key ingredient to an acceptable character. We find similar emphasis on hard work in several Roman commendation letters: "The man is hard-working, energetic, of a free and free-handed nature, a true patriot . . ." (Fronto, *Ad Am.* 1.3). Thus κοπιῶντας, *kopiōntas*—"those who labor"—in 1 Thess 5:12 focuses on the "hard work" of certain people within the church community. For Paul, their hard work illustrates a commendable *ēthos.*

Paul employs the second participle, προϊσταμένους, *proistamenous,* and its cognates, less frequently throughout his writings. Indeed, the word is rare in the whole of the New Testament. Moreover, it is difficult to define with precision. *Proistamenos* is the present-active participle of the verb προϊστημι, *proistēmi,* which literally means "place first" and, therefore, often refers to "presiding" or "leading."[22] Thus, the NRSV translates the term in 1 Thess 5:12 as "those who are in charge of you." However, the verb has a derivative—and equally frequent—sense: "to be concerned about" or "care for," "to help." In Rom 12:8, Paul provides a list of gifts, including the one who is προϊστάμενος, *proistamenos.* The latter appears between "generous contributors" and "those who do acts of mercy." The immediate context, therefore, indicates that the *proistamenoi* are those who provide special care for the church.

The other important occurrence of a *proistēmi* derivative is Rom 16:2. However, as we shall see below, the use of the noun form προστάτις, *prostatis,* has clearer connotations of leadership with its frequent appearance in the literature of the times, with reference to a "patron" or (less frequently) "patroness." Thus the NRSV refers to Phoebe in Rom 16:1–2 as a "benefactor" of the church and of Paul, and not just as a "helper," as in the RSV translation.[23]

The context of the *verb* form in 1 Thess 5:12 indicates an emphasis on the service and function of caring and providing help, more than on identifying the person as someone in charge. Paul commends these caregivers in 1 Thess 5:12–13 "on account of their work" (5:13b). Nonetheless, their service does result in their recognition as leaders (5:13a): "In most cases *proistēmi* seems to have sense *a.* 'to lead' but the context shows in each case that one must also take into account sense *b.* 'to care for.' This is explained by the fact that caring was the obligation of leading members of the infant church."[24]

Thus this text introduces a formula Paul will reiterate frequently in his commendations: service for the church results in commendation and recognition.

The third participle, νουθετοῦντας, *nouthetountas*, comes from the verb νουθετέω, *noutheteō*, which means "to instruct, teach" or "warn."[25] In 5:14, Paul appeals to the entire community, and not just the leaders, to "admonish the idlers [νουθετεῖτε τοὺς ἀτάκτους, *noutheteite tous ataktous*]." Perhaps Paul commends a particular group of *workers* in the church in 5:12–13 because the "nonworkers" or "idlers" resist the leadership, instruction, and admonishments of the *nouthetountoi*. Paul first endorses the leadership of the latter (5:12–13) and then encourages the whole community to straighten out the wayward path of the *ataktoi* ("idlers"; 5:14).[26]

In any case, with these three participles, 1 Thess 5:12 identifies a group within the Thessalonian church: those who work hard, care for, and instruct or admonish the community. In addition, the participles indicate the credentials commending these individuals: their work, care, and admonishment of the community commend them. These functions demonstrate their *ēthos*. Moreover, the persons performing these functions probably emerge as leaders because of their service. "Any group soon throws up natural leaders and there is no reason to doubt that such appeared in Thessalonica during Paul's time or soon after he left."[27] For those who have provided hard work, care, and vigilance for the young congregation, Paul provides support by means of commendation.

Paul presents his commendation request with two verbs of petition: εἰδέναι, *eidenai* ("recognize"), in 5:12 and ἡγεῖσθαι, *hēgeisthai* ("regard"), in 5:13. With *eidenai*, Paul emphasizes the need for *awareness* of the work of these local church leaders. With *hēgeisthai*, not only is the church to recognize the work of these individuals, but they are to hold the workers in high regard. Paul also adds the adverb ὑπερεκπερισσοῦ, *hyperekperissou* ("with all earnestness," "very highly indeed"), in order to highlight the respect and affection to be given these persons.

Paul calls the community to "have the highest regard" or "respect beyond measure" for these church workers. In other words, Paul expects honor for them.

Further, the community should have this high regard for its leaders ἐν ἀγάπῃ, *en agapē* ("in love"), that is, with the kind of disinterested love that Paul expects of believers. This parallels 5:12, in which the leaders work in the community and care for it "in the Lord [ἐν κυρίῳ, *en kyriō*]." Paul makes clear that the work of the local leaders is carried out under the authority of the church's Lord, Jesus Christ, and the community responds to that work with the appropriate regard and honor expressed in love.

In many instances, writers of Roman commendation letters sought social or political advancement for their clients. Fronto requested "not only protection but advancement and honor" for Julius Aquilinus (*Ad Fam.* 1.4). Paul requests recognition and honor for the Thessalonian leaders, but he does not indicate concern for advancement in a hierarchy.

Thus Paul's commendation has elements of a Greco-Roman commendation—leaders are identified (at least by the work they do), their credentials (*ēthos*) described, and honor requested. Moreover, a "lord" or "patron" is involved. However, Paul distinguishes his commendations somewhat: the Lord is Christ; so selfless love, and not individual quest for status or honor, should prevail.

Paul concludes this commendation passage by stating the reason the Thessalonians should honor their leaders: διὰ τὸ ἔργον αὐτῶν, *dia to ergon autōn* ("on account of their work"). The work of the leaders on behalf of the Thessalonian community motivates this commendation. Paul urges the highest regard for them "because of what they do."[28] In Greco-Roman commendation letters, patronage and friendship motivate commendation. For example, Cicero uses his influence with the letter recipient to exact patronal benefits for himself as well as the person recommended:

> For this reason I beg of you with exceptional earnestness, since in view of our close association it is incumbent upon you to show my friends as much respect as your own, to admit this gentleman to your special friendship in such a way as to convince him that nothing could possibly have been of more service or more of a distinction to him than my recommendation. (*Ad. Fam.* 13.49)

For Paul, service to readers of this letter, not advancement in a patronage network, constitutes the *ēthos* and engenders the endorsement for consideration as a leader.

Paul employs the convention of commendation in 1 Thessalonians to address needs and problems of the church to which the letter was written. A certain group of individuals in the church had responded to church needs with significant effort, concern, and instruction. This effective, caring work had caught the attention of the community's founder, who was at a distance but, nonetheless, heard about these efforts from his envoy (1 Thess 3:1–10). Therefore, within a larger letter of encouragement to the whole community, Paul endorses the caring service of these naturally developing leaders so that they continue to do the work they are already doing on behalf of the church.

At the same time, Paul seems to encourage a particular approach to leadership with this commendation; namely, those who work, lead. This approach probably encouraged others to participate in the work of the church because Paul offers recognition as a benefit to those who serve the church in similar ways. Indeed, by not naming the leaders specifically, Paul opens up participation and, therefore, recognition for others. In this way Paul seeks to solidify and build up the young congregation. Commendation plays a key role in this effort. It also helps to restore the confidence of the church members in their absent founder. "Here are leaders to be trusted because of their work, just like we are to be trusted for ours." So Paul receives benefits from a positive reaction to this commendation. Questions about his own leadership are mollified by pointing out comparable local leaders.

1 Corinthians 16:15–18. A second set of commendations, the two in 1 Corinthians 16:15–18, follows a similar pattern to 1 Thess 5:12–13. While placed in a fairly traditional epistolary location at the end of the letter, before final greetings and benediction (16:19–23), Paul's Corinthian commendations have strategic import in his response to the problems of discord in Corinth. Paul mentioned the subjects of the commendations, Stephanas and his household, at the beginning of the letter as persons baptized early in the church's history by Paul (1:16). In 1:12–17, Paul sought to minimize the importance of his early baptisms in order to emphasize community unity in Christ (1:13–15), rather than ties to particular leaders (for example, Paul, Apollos, or Cephas, 1:12–13), apparently one source of the discord.[29] However, that early mention of Stephanas strategically sets up the second mention, in the commendations of 1 Cor 16:15–18. In the latter passage, Paul now praises Stephanas and his household for their service to the church. Paul's commendation of Stephanas and company further assists Paul in his efforts to bring unity to the Corinthian church around the issues of leadership. In Stephanas, Paul has found someone worthy of leadership recognition.

First Corinthians 16:15–16 has an unusual construction, which demonstrates Paul's "singular emphasis on Stephanas":[30] "I urge you, brothers and sisters; you know [οἴδατε, *oidate*] the household of Stephanas, that it is ἀπαρχή [*aparchē*, "first fruits"] of Achaia and for service [εἰς διακονίαν, *eis diakonian*] to the saints they have set themselves apart [ἔταξαν ἑαυτούς, *etaxan heautous*]" (16:15, my translation).

The passage begins, as did 1 Thess 5:12–13, with a typical Pauline verb announcing the beginning of parenesis, in this case, παρακάλω, *parakalō*. However, one does not read the infinitive complement of *parakalō* until verse 16: "I urge you [v. 15] . . . that you be subject to such people . . . [v. 16]." In between the exhortation verb and the exhortation itself, Paul supplies the reasons for commending Stephanas. First, the community knows Stephanas and his household. Paul often used the Greco-Roman household (the οἶκος, *oikos*) as a starting point for his churches.[31] Heads of household like Stephanas, Philemon, Prisca and Aquilla (cf. 1 Cor 16:19 and Rom 16:3–5a), and Gaius (Rom 16:23) host Paul in their homes and/or travel on his behalf. Therefore, along with Phoebe (Rom 16:1–2; see below), they appear to be patrons or patronesses of Paul's work. Paul depends on them for the success of his ministry.[32]

Thus Paul commends Stephanas and his household as "first-fruits" (ἀπαρχή, *aparchē*) or "initial converts" of Paul's work in Corinth. The use of the metaphor *aparchē* probably also means that Paul expected positive results ("fruit") from early converts.

Paul also commends Stephanas and company for their διακονία, *diakonia*: "They have devoted themselves to service for the saints." The verb (τάσσω, *tassō*) has various related meanings, all with the idea of placing or appointing someone "in a fixed spot" or to an assigned position or office.[33] When used with a preposition, the term takes on connotations of authority: "*tassein tina epi tinos*—put someone over [or] in charge of someone or something."[34] For example, Paul uses the passive participle of the verb (τεταγμέναι, *tetagmenai*) with reference to the appointment by God of governing authorities (Rom 13:1). However, the reflexive form has a sense of self-appointment, usually by means of active demonstration, such as work or service. For example, in Plato's *Republic* (2.371C) and in Xenophon's *Memorabilia* (2.1.11), a form of τάσσω ἑαυτούς, *tasso heautous*, is related to δουλεία, *douleia*, or διακονία, *diakonia*. Thus, "to assign oneself" is to "devote oneself to service."

It is this sense of devotion to the ministry or service for the church community ("the saints"—v. 15) that Paul cites as one criterion for his recommendation in verse 16. He provides no further details on the nature of this service. Paul and the Corinthians know what that *diakonia* connotes in Stephanas's case. Paul is even more general than in 1 Thess 5:12–13, where he describes at least three aspects of service (hard work, care for the community, and instruction or admonishment). However, 1 Cor 16:15–16 echoes the same sense of commendation based on service to the community as 1 Thess 5:12–13. One commentator suggests that "the appeal of this brief paragraph (vv. 15–18) . . . has its precedent in 1 Thess 5:12–14."[35]

The commendation request in 1 Cor 16:15–16 exhibits further parallels to

1 Thess 5:12–13. Paul employs similar language in both requests: "I urge you [from v. 15] . . . that [ἵνα, *hina*] you also be submissive [ὑποτάσσησθε, *hypotassēsthe*] to such people [τοιούτοις, *toioutois*] and to all who work [συνεργοῦντι, *synergounti*] and labor [κοπιῶντι, *kopiōnti*]" (1 Cor 16:16, my translation). In 1 Thess 5:12, Paul requested recognition for those who labored (κοπιῶντας, *kopiōntas*) in the church, and he sought honor for them "because of their work [ἔργον, *ergon*]" (5:13). In 1 Corinthians, Paul uses the same general structure and language, but a stronger petition verb, "be submissive" (ὑποτάσσησθε, *hypotassēsthe*), and a call for support of all such workers.

The verb ὑποτάσσω, *hypotassō*, appears frequently in Paul with respect to submission or subjection to God, to the Law, to the will of God (1 Cor 15:27–28; Rom 8:7; 10:3), to government authorities, or to church prophets (Rom 13:1; 1 Cor 14:32). However, only in 1 Cor 16:16 is the term used with reference to the relation between the church community and those who serve it.[36] The sense of 16:16 is that because workers like Stephanas and his household have devoted themselves (ἔταξαν ἑαυτούς, *etaxan heautous*) to such service for the community, the community ought to respond in kind (καὶ ὑμεῖς, *kai hymeis*—"you also") and "put yourselves at the service [ὑποτάσσησθε, *hypotassēsthe*] of such people" (NRSV).

This play on words with τάσσω, *tassō*, and ὑποτάσσω, *hypotassō*, reflects reciprocity and exemplification.[37] Because Stephanas and his household have served the community, the community should likewise serve them. Paul sets up the household of Stephanas as an example for others to follow when he commends "everyone who works and toils" for the church "with them" (16:16c). Paul asserts that all who follow the example of service set by Stephanas and company merit the same recognition requested for them.

Paul repeats these same ideas in a second commendation (1 Cor 16:17–18), which has more specific identifications, additional credentials, and another request that invites exemplification.[38] In 16:17–18, Paul commends Stephanas, Fortunatus, and Achaicus, who are present with him: "I rejoice [χαίρω, *chairō*] at the coming [παρουσία, *parousia*] of Stephanas . . ." (16:17a). Paul often uses *chairō* to introduce a new section. Moreover, in a variety of New Testament and papyri letters, the verb simply expresses joy at the arrival of visitors.[39] Thus, Paul shifts focus in 1 Cor 16:17–18, from commending Stephanas and his household generally to celebrating their current presence with him.

Paul's main point in 16:17–18 is to show support for those who support him. Their presence with Paul and the effect of their presence becomes another point of commendation. These church representatives bring joy to the apostle (v. 17a). They fill the void (ἀνεπλήρωσαν, *aneplērōsan*) produced by the absence of any Corinthians and Corinthian news (ὑμέτερον ὑστέρημα, *hymeteron hysterēma*) (v. 17b). After all, this was a church founded by him and a people nurtured by him for some time now. Stephanas and the others "brought relief" or "refreshed" (ἀνέπαυ-σαν, *anepausan*, v. 18a) Paul's "spirit" like anyone "thus visited by longtime friends in the faith."[40]

In addition, Paul indicates further evidence that Stephanas and the others practice this ministry of "refreshment." To the assertion that they have refreshed his spirit, Paul adds καί, *kai*, το ὑμῶν, *hymōn*—"and yours also" (v. 18). Thus, once again, service to the community as a whole commends Stephanas and his colleagues. Whether in Corinth or with Paul, these individuals bring joy and refresh spirits.

Paul again employs exemplification in this second commendation. He encourages recognition of the worth of Stephanas and his colleagues, citing them as examples for others to follow: "Recognize [ἐπιγινώσκετε, *epiginōskete*], therefore, *such* people as these [τοὺς τοιούτους, *tous toioutous*]" (16:18b, my translation and emphasis). In a church full of strife, it is important to have models that can bring joy and refreshment. This *ēthos* commends Stephanas, Fortunatus, and Achaicus. Thus Paul requests recognition of them and modeling of them by others in the community.[41]

Therefore, in the first commendation (16:15–16), Paul cites the service and work of Stephanas and his household on behalf of the Corinthian church. In their service to this church, they set examples of the type of individuals Paul commends and that others should emulate. In the second commendation (16:17–18), Paul shifts focus to the actual presence with him of Stephanas and two other individuals from Corinth, Fortunatus and Achaicus. Thus Stephanas and the others are worthy of commendation wherever they go. Their presence brings joy and refreshment to a burdened apostle. This aspect of their *ēthos* should have a similar impact in the Corinthian community. Paul emphasizes the work and character of exemplary leaders in these two commendations. He challenges others to follow the same pattern.

Hard work and exemplary character highlight the leadership criteria cited by Paul in these commendation passages of 1 Thessalonians and 1 Corinthians. Both sets of leaders have demonstrated their worth to the community by service to their communities. In Thessalonica, hard work and care for the church community characterized such service; in Corinth, it was Stephanas and others bringing "devoted" service and a caring presence to the community. In the Corinthian commendation, in particular, Paul encourages others to follow the commended behavior.

Roman commendations rarely encourage emulation. After praising the personal qualities of a candidate for consulship, Cicero writes that people like these should be "the leaders of public policy" (*Ad Fam.* 12.3). Cicero recommends only people with similar qualities, but laments how few leaders like this exist. His only encouragement is that he will "protect those dear to" the letter recipient, whether they appeal for commendation to Cicero or not, because of his "love and loyalty" to his friend (12.4).

Roman commendation letters sought to preserve existing patronage connections among the elite, and not necessarily to encourage the emergence of new leadership, especially from among nonelite classes. Paul not only commends Stephanas and the others for exemplary character in service to the church, but also encourages *anyone* else who patterns his or her character similarly. Paul shows interest in everyone's improvement, not just a select few. However, these individuals must show support for Paul's causes—the gospel, the church, and Paul's missionary enterprise.

Philippians 2:25–30. Formally, the commendation of Epaphroditus appears in Phil 2:29–30. However, before that, Paul promises to send Timothy (2:19–24) and to return Epaphroditus (2:25–28) to the Philippians. Philippians 2:19–30 fits the rhetorical purpose of Paul in the entire Philippian letter. Paul endorses the ministry of Timothy and Epaphroditus as reflections of the servant ministry of Christ (2:1–11) and of Paul himself (1:12–26; 2:17–18). All of these (Christ, Paul, Timothy, and Epaphroditus) are models for what Paul expects of the Philippians in this letter: "Brothers and sisters, join in imitating me, and observe those who live according to the example [τύπον, *typon*] you have in us" (Phil 3:17). Epaphroditus has been an example worthy of commendation. As in 1 Cor 16:15–18, a Pauline commendation results in exemplification.

In Phil 2:25–28, Paul describes the service of Epaphroditus, both to Paul and to the Philippian church, by using several designations. To Paul, Epaphroditus has been "my brother and coworker [συνεργόν, *synergon*] and fellow-soldier [συστρατιώτην, *systratiōtēn*]." For the Philippians, Epaphroditus has been their ἀπόστολος, *apostolos* ("messenger"), and λειτουργός, *leitourgos* ("servant"), to Paul's needs. Paul calls anyone who is a fellow believer ἀδελφός, *adelphos*, a "brother" or "sister." Many of those who had traveled with Paul in his missionary journeys, or who had in some other way joined with Paul in the gospel ministry, are his "coworkers."[42] Συστρατιώτης, *systratiōtēs*, "fellow-soldier," was "a military term to describe those who fight side by side."[43] Paul often refers to his ministry with this military imagery (1 Cor 9:7; 2 Cor 10:3).

Epaphroditus has faced the conflicts and battles of the gospel ministry together with Paul. Paul writes the letter to the Philippians from prison (cf. Phil 1:12–14) and describes his situation as follows:

> For it has been granted to you that for the sake of Christ you should not only believe in him but also suffer for his sake [τὸ ὑπὲρ αὐτοῦ πάσχειν, *to hyper autou paschein*], engaged in the same conflict [ἀγῶνα, *agōna*] which you saw and now hear to be mine. (Phil 1:29–30, RSV)

Epaphroditus has personally participated in Paul's *agōna*.[44] Therefore, Paul designates him his συστρατιώτης, *systratiōtēs* ("fellow-soldier").

Two other designations indicate Epaphroditus's role with the Philippian church. The Philippians commissioned Epaphroditus as their ἀπόστολος, *apostolos*, with a specific mission to minister to Paul's needs on their behalf (Phil 2:25). On another occasion, Paul describes envoys who have a particular mission from a group of churches as ἀπόστολοι, *apostoloi* (cf. 2 Cor 8:18–19, 23). Thus Paul uses the term *apostolos*, not only with regard to the original twelve, or those with special commissions, like Paul himself, but also of official delegates from churches.[45]

Paul also designates Epaphroditus as a λειτουργός, *leitourgos* ("servant"), of the Philippians. In the Greco-Roman contexts, *leitourgos* and cognates such as λειτουργία, *leitourgia* ("service"), often refer to "all kinds of public service."[46] "Liturgies" in the Greco-Roman world entailed public-works projects that Roman and provincial officials took on, at their own expense, in order to advance their social status.[47] In one commendation letter, Pliny lauds Voconius Romanus for being a *flamen*, a provincial position that involved funding local ceremonies and communal games (Pliny, *Ep.* 2.13.4).

In Phil 2:17, Paul describes a cultic notion of *leitourgia*: "But even if I am being poured out as a libation over the sacrifice and the offering [*leitourgia*] of your faith, I am glad and rejoice with all of you." Thus *leitourgia* takes on the sense of "sacrificial service" on behalf of the community of faith.[48]

As the Philippian envoy, Epaphroditus has provided *leitourgia* for Paul on behalf of this community (2:30). This *leitourgia* included delivering a Philippian monetary offering to Paul for which Paul uses the language of sacrifice: "a fragrant offering, a sacrifice acceptable and pleasing to God" (Phil 4:18). Second, Epaphroditus's *leitourgia* includes his presence with Paul as a representative of the Philippian church. The Philippians could not realistically accomplish their partnership (κοινωνία, *koinōnia*) with Paul without a representative "to make up [ἀναπληρώσῃ, *anaplērōsē*] for those services [*leitourgias*] that you could not give [τὸ ὑμῶν ὑστέρημα, *to hymōn hysterēma*] me" (Phil 2:30).[49] This echoes the commendation of Stephanas and company, who "made up [ἀνεπλήρωσαν, *aneplērōsan*] for your [the Corinthians'] absence [ὑμέτερον ὑστέρημα, *hymeteron hysterēma*]" when they came to visit Paul (1 Cor 16:17). Similarly, Epaphroditus stands with Paul on behalf of the Philippians.[50]

Finally, the ministry of Epaphroditus had its risks: "For indeed he was ill, near to death" (2:27a). Paul asserts that Epaphroditus "came close to death for the work of Christ [τὸ ἔργον Χριστοῦ, *to ergon Christou*]" (2:30a). Specifically, this "risking of life" (παραβολευσάμενος τῇ ψυχῇ, *paraboleusamenos tē psychē*) came about because of his ministry to Paul on behalf of the Philippians (2:30b). Like Paul, Epaphroditus has experienced hardships on behalf of the gospel ministry.[51]

Epaphroditus also shows his *ēthos* by his concern for his church. He "longs" to see the Philippians and "is anxious" about them (2:26). These two participles carry strong emotional weight and illustrate Epaphroditus's strong ties to the Philippian community. Indeed, Epaphroditus has been concerned because he knows that the Philippians have heard about his illness (2:26b). In a striking image, Paul highlights the commendable character of Epaphroditus, who, although he has been ill, is more worried about the Philippians' distress over his illness.

Thus, Paul expects the Philippians to rejoice at the return of their envoy (2:28a). Moreover, Paul will be relieved of the anxiety over Epaphroditus's absence from Philippi (2:28b). Paul's relief could mean that the envoy was an important leader in the Philippian church and thus was needed in their time of distress, to which Paul turns immediately following the commendation of Epaphroditus: "Look out for the dogs, look out for the evil-workers, look out for those who mutilate the flesh. For we are the true circumcision . . ." (Phil 3:1–3).[52] Thus, in Phil 2:25–28, Paul has described the *ēthos* of Epaphroditus before he offers a formal commendation request in 2:29–30.

Paul's formal request parallels some of what we saw in the Greco-Roman commendations. First, Paul enjoins a welcome reception for Epaphroditus upon his return to Philippi: "Therefore receive [προσδέχεσθε, *prosdechesthe*] him in the Lord with all joy" (2:29a). The verb *prosdechomai* reflects one of those general requests often made in commendations. To "receive" someone entails hospitality.[53] Paul also indicates that Epaphroditus should be received "in the Lord with all joy" (cf. 1 Thess 5:12–13).

Second, Paul requests that the Philippians "hold in honor [ἐντίμους ἔχετε, *entimous echete*] such people as these [τοὺς τοιούτους, *tous toioutous*]" (2:29b). With this, Paul indicates that he expects high esteem for Epaphroditus, as the Roman commendation writers sought honor for their charges (e.g., Pliny, *Ep.* 3.2.5; Fronto, *Ad Am.* 1.4). Paul seeks honor for Epaphroditus, as he sought "recognition" and "high esteem" for the leaders in Thessalonica (1 Thess 5:12–13), and also for Stephanas, Fortunatus, and Achaicus (1 Cor 16:18).

However, Paul's request for honor differs from Roman commendations. First, as he did with Stephanas and company, Paul generalizes Epaphroditus's behavior as exemplary for others to follow: "Honor *such* people as these" (Phil 2:29, emphasis added). Anyone who would be willing to risk even life for the gospel and the gospel community deserves honor, recognition, and commendation. Second, Paul's reasons for honoring Epaphroditus parallel the reasons in 1 Thess 5:12–13 and 1 Cor 16:15–18: "Because, on account of the work [διὰ τὸ ἔργον, *dia to ergon*] for Christ, he came near to death, risking life so that he might fulfill what was lacking of your service to me" (Phil 2:30, my translation). Paul seeks recognition of and high esteem for the Thessalonian leaders "because of their work [ἔργον, *ergon*]" for the church (1 Thess 5:13). Stephanas and the others had "devoted themselves to the service [διακονία, *diakonia*] of the saints" (1 Cor 16:15); therefore, Paul requests reciprocal service and recognition (16:16, 18). Work (ἔργον, *ergon*), service (λειτουργία, *leitourgia*), and, in addition, risk demonstrate the *ēthos* of Epaphroditus such that he merits commendation from Paul and honor from the Philippians.

In sum, these three commendations present a consistent picture of Pauline commendation. First, all three of these passages commend work and service carried out on behalf of the gospel and of the gospel community. The Corinthian and Philippian passages also indicate that the ministry of the leaders to Paul himself merits commendation. Thus Paul benefits from the ministry of these individuals. Moreover, by commending *ēthos* that parallels his, Paul also receives benefit. For example, the Thessalonian leaders in 1 Thess 5:12–13 exhibit qualities (caring concern for the church) that Paul has claimed for himself and his associates in 1 Thess 2:1–12. Thus, the Thessalonian workers emulate the missionary workers, and thereby help solidify the missionaries' reputation in the Thessalonian church community.

At the end of the commendations in 1 Corinthians and Philippians, Paul requests recognition and honor for the commended, but also generalizes to include "all such persons" who follow the examples of these gospel workers. Anyone who works, serves, and even risks his or her life on behalf of the work of the gospel and the service to its community merits recognition. In addition, while the Thessalonian text addresses a specific group throughout, the effect of not mentioning names and focusing on their functions may have been to encourage others to labor, care for, and admonish the community (1 Thess 5:12).

Finally, only the commendation of Epaphroditus, among these three, cites the latter's risks taken on behalf of his service to Paul and the church. However, this risk parallels the hardships Paul cites about his own ministry, which further develops a coherent picture of Pauline commendation: Paul commends those, including himself, who work for the gospel and serve its community, without regard for personal risk or gain.

One final commendation rounds out this picture of Pauline commendation before we turn more fully to comparison and contrast with Roman commendations.

The Commendation of Phoebe: Romans 16:1–2

Romans 16:1–2 has a similar structure to the other Pauline commendations:

(a) *identification:* "I commend to you Phoebe,
(b) *credentials:* our sister, who has been a deacon of the church at Cenchreae,

(c) *desired action:* so that [ἵνα, *hina*] you may receive her in the Lord, in a manner worthy of the saints, and assist her in whatever matter [πράγματι, *pragmati*] she has need from you,

(b') *credentials:* for she has been a patroness [προστάτις, *prostatis*] of many and of me also."[54]

In addition, Rom 16:1–2 includes some typical terms from Greco-Roman commendation-letter writing: συνίστημι, *synistēmi* ("commend"); προσδέχεσθε, *prosdechesthe* ("receive"); and παραστῆτε, *parastēte* ("assist" or "help"). Paul clearly states Phoebe's credentials for commendation. She is a "sister," a διάκονος, *diakonos* ("servant"), someone "worthy [ἀξίως, *axiōs*] of the saints," and a προστάτις, *prostatis*. Except for the final term, Paul uses language found elsewhere in his letters, including commendation passages (cf. "service [διάκονια, *diakonia*] to the saints," 1 Cor 16:15; "receive [προσδέχεσθε, *prosdechesthe*] him in the Lord," Phil 2:29). Finally, the action Paul requests from the Roman churches on Phoebe's behalf is ambiguous. She is to be welcomed and assisted in whatever she needs. Such ambiguity is also typical of Greco-Roman commendation letters.

The most striking aspect of Paul's commendation of Phoebe is his reference to her as a προστάτις, *prostatis* (16:2). In my discussion of 1 Thess 5:12–13, I noted the paucity of this term and its derivatives in Paul. The verb προΐστημι, *proistēmi*, has two essential meanings: (1) to preside or lead, and (2) to help or protect. I argued above that, in the context of 1 Thess 5:12–13 and Rom 12:8, the participle for *proistēmi* (προισταμένους, *proistamenous*) best translates as "the one who cares for" the church. Many translators likewise interpret *prostatis* in Rom 16:2 as "helper."[55] However, the noun *prostatis*, both in its masculine and feminine form, appears in Greco-Roman literature with reference to patrons and benefactors.[56]

One example of a female patron, Junia Theodora, a contemporary of Phoebe of Cenchreae in nearby Corinth, has inscriptions dedicated to her patronage:

> [T]he council and people of Telemessos decreed . . . since Iunia Theodora, a Roman, a benefactress of the greatest loyalty to the Lycian federation and our city has accomplished numerous benefits for the federation and our city . . . displaying her patronage (*prostasian*) of those who are present . . . it is decreed that our city . . . to give honour and praise for all the above reasons to . . . Iunia Theodora and to invite her . . . to always be the author of some benefits toward us . . . in return our city recognizes and will acknowledge the evidence of her goodwill.[57]

The inscription also includes the broad range of patronal activities that Junia Theodora has carried out on behalf of her city, including financial support for building projects, hospitality for travelers, especially foreign dignitaries, and negotiations with Roman authorities on behalf of her region.[58] Perhaps Phoebe of

Cenchreae carried out similar activities, but maybe on a smaller scale for her city, although certainly in a significant way for Paul and for "many others" in the Pauline mission (Rom 16:2).

Thus the term *prostatis* in Rom 16:2 means "patron" or "benefactor" (NRSV). Phoebe's patronage to Paul and others commends her. Her status as a *prostatis* may mean that she had the financial resources and networks to provide benefaction for Christian churches, especially for the missionary work of the Apostle Paul. In the Greco-Roman letters, patronage capabilities like Phoebe's were attractive features in commendation.

Phoebe's status as a *prostatis* is the clearest instance of Greco-Roman patronage at work in a Pauline commendation. However, there are also two other factors. First, considering that direct use of patron titles for women is rare in Greek contexts, Paul's reference to Phoebe as *prostatis* stands out. As James Walters observes: "It is rather obvious that the terms Paul used to commend Phoebe are no different from those he would have used if he had been commending a man. He presents her to his readers as a *prostatis* worthy of their kindness and cites no familial relationships nor domestic virtues when he honors her."[59] Phoebe represents an independent woman acting for the good of the gospel, and Paul commends her as such.

When Paul also commends Phoebe as a διάκονος, *diakonos*, of the church at Cenchreae, he further clarifies the nature of her patronage. In texts such as 1 Cor 3:5–6; 2 Cor 3:6; and 6:4–5, Paul's use of *diakonos* emphasizes the *function* of service rather than an official status. Does Paul commend Phoebe as a *diakonos* of Cenchreae because of her functional service or official position? The answer lies somewhere in between. "The modifying clause 'of the church in Cenchrea' [sic] separates the Phoebe text from the general usages of *diakonos*."[60] However, it is difficult to know if Phoebe had an official designation as a *diakonos* from the church in Cenchreae, or whether that is simply how Paul designates her for this commendation.

A better avenue is to consider both designations together: her patronage and her service. Paul's discussion of gifts is instructive here:

> Having gifts that differ according to the grace given to us: . . . if for service [διακονίαν, *diakonian*], let us serve [διακονία, *diakonia*], . . . if for exhorting, let us exhort, if for sharing, do so with generosity, if for helping [προιστάμενος, *proistamenos*], with zeal, if to show mercy, do so with cheerfulness. (Rom 12:6–8, my paraphrase)

The appearance of both these terms—*diakonia* and a form of *prostatis*—a few chapters before Paul's commendation of Phoebe supports the picture of a patroness who serves the church by helping, giving financial support, and doing acts of compassion. Moreover, these duties are central to the functions leaders in churches do. Paul marks Phoebe "as leader in the church at Cenchrea [*sic*] because of her status and labor in behalf of the community."[61] Thus, taken together, *prostatis* and *diakonos* indicate patronage exercised functionally by an active church servant. They also signal Phoebe as an important leadership figure for Paul and for the church at Cenchreae.

Paul commends Phoebe to a group of churches that do not know her. Many in the Roman churches also do not know Paul. Thus it is important for Paul to greet the people in the Roman churches who do know him (Rom 16:3–16). It is also important that Paul state clearly Phoebe's credentials (Rom 16:1–2) to reduce any risks that his commendation request be rejected in Rome.

The terms of request are general:

> I commend to you Phoebe . . . so that [ἵνα, *hina*] you receive [προσδέξησθε, *prosdexēsthe*] her in the Lord [ἐν κυρίῳ, *en kyriō*] in a manner worthy [ἀξίως, *axiōs*] of the saints and [that] you assist [παραστῆτε, *parastēte*] her in whatever matter [πράγματι, *pragmati*] she has need of you. (Rom 16:1a, 2a, my translation)

Paul asks for a welcome reception to this sister in the Lord. The Roman churches should receive her in a manner worthy of all "saints" anywhere in the Roman Empire. Second, Paul asks for general assistance on behalf of Phoebe, "in whatever matter she has need of you," a circumstantial clause that parallels similar phrases attached to commendation requests: "Rejoice therefore upon hearing him and receive [ὑπωδείξας, *hypōdeixas*] him concerning whatever he stands in need [περὶ ὅν παραγέγονεν, *peri hon paragegonen*]."[62]

Therefore, Paul probably has no specific πρᾶγμα, *pragma*, deed, in mind in his commendation request for Phoebe. However, Paul's designation of Phoebe as a *prostatis* comes in a causal clause after this request for general assistance: "help her in whatever she may require from you, for she has been a benefactor of many and of myself as well" (16:2b).[63] Paul requests hospitality and assistance for Phoebe, in part, because she has been a *prostatis* of Paul's churches. Beyond her *ēthos* as a sister and one of the saints, Paul suggests to the Romans that her patronage—caring service and financial support for Paul and for many in the church—might extend to them as well upon their welcome reception and assistance in whatever her needs might be. Phoebe is a church leader worthy of attention, honor, and support because she has similarly supported other believers.

E. A. Judge concludes that the Phoebe passage "nicely illustrates the way in which [Paul] supported the system of patronage in return for the security it afforded him."[64] However, Paul is selective in his support of the patronage system. For example, he did not accept patronage from the Corinthian elite, although his opponents did.[65] Thus Phoebe, Paul's benefactor, merits commendation because of her service to Paul, his churches, including the one at Cenchreae, and others, but the "super-apostles" of 2 Cor 10–13 do not. Paul accepts hospitality and, therefore, patronage, from such house-church leaders as Philemon (Phlm 7, 22) and Gaius (Rom 16:23). He also accepts financial support and, therefore, a form of patronage from the Philippians (Phil 1:3–5; 4:10–20).[66] However, he refuses the financial support of the Corinthians (1 Cor 9:1–18; 2 Cor 11:7–11), even though the offer of support was probably extended forcefully by certain patrons of the church in Corinth.[67]

Thus Paul uses the system of patronage when needed for support of his mission, but avoids any client status that might compromise the gospel ministry and message. Moreover, when he employs an important vehicle of patronage, the convention of commendation, he considers how a commendation will benefit his standing among the churches. Ultimately, he commends leaders in order to benefit his ministry, his churches, and the whole gospel enterprise.

Conclusion: Paul's Commendations

In this study of Paul's commendations, I have pointed out some connections between them and the Greco-Roman commendation letters. Similarities include structure. Like Greco-Roman commendations, Paul follows a familiar pattern of identification, credentials, and request. He also uses similar vocabulary. The language of "receive," "recognize," and "honor" appears frequently in Pauline commendation, as in Greco-Roman commendation. Both Paul and the Romans also highlight the importance of character (*ēthos*): the letter writer's, the recipient's, and of those commended. Such personal qualities as love, loyalty, and persistence in the face of hardship and difficulty (especially financial hardship in the Roman letters) can be discerned in both Pauline and Roman commendations. Finally, aspects of patronage lie behind both Roman and Pauline commendation. On several occasions, Paul commends persons who have offered their patronage to him and his cause, such as Phoebe (Rom 16:1–2) and household leaders such as Stephanas (1 Cor 16:15–18).

However, several aspects of character and patronage in Paul deviate somewhat from Greco-Roman patterns. With regard to *ēthos*, Paul commends himself on the basis of his work and service for God, Christ, and his churches, even to the point of hardship (cf. 2 Cor 3:1–6:13). In the case of the Thessalonian leaders (1 Thess 5:12–13) and the household of Stephanas (1 Cor 16:15–18), their hard work and service for the church community commends their recognition and honor. Paul also recognizes the work of Phoebe as a *diakonos* ("servant") of the church at Cenchreae. Epaphroditus serves Paul on behalf of the Philippian church. Thus service and hard work for the church becomes the fundamental quality Paul extols in his commendation. The commended serve the church and the apostle, but ultimately God and the gospel. For the most part, Roman commendation letters extol service to patrons, and also to imperial and provincial governments. Although Paul commends Phoebe for her status as his benefactor (Rom 16:1–2), he points to God as his ultimate patron (2 Cor 10:18).

Paul's formal commendation requests parallel the Greco-Roman appeals. They are generally vague and, at most, usually request some kind of assistance, welcome reception, and also recognition or honor. However, while the honor the Roman letters usually request for the commended depends on family status, wealth, or patronage connections, Paul ascribes honor to those whom he commends because of their work for the church, including devotion and love. Epaphroditus "has been longing for" the church (Phil 2:26). The household of Stephanas is "devoted" in its service to the church (1 Cor 16:15). The Thessalonian leaders "care for" the church and "admonish" it when they need to (1 Thess 5:12). Thus on matters of character, patronage, and commendation requests, Paul's commendations distinguish themselves from Roman commendations.

When Paul commends others who are connected to him, his *ēthos* is also enhanced. Pauline commendation of others, as in the Greco-Roman literature, assumes self-commendation. Paul commends those who emulate his own behavior. Such commendation helps secure his status among the Thessalonians, for example (cf. 1 Thess 2:1–12; 5:12–13). However, in urging imitation of himself, Paul ultimately promotes another: "Be imitators of me, as I am of Christ" (1 Cor 11:1).

Pauline commendation also promotes the leadership of other, yet-to-be-determined individuals. Pauline commendation identifies models, a major difference from the Roman commendations. Paul presents himself as a model of the "true apostle" (2 Cor 12:12). Similarly, Paul depicts his commended leaders as persons "worthy of the saints" (Rom 16:2). Anyone with a similar *ēthos* should be commended as well: Stephanas, Epaphroditus, and "people such as these" should be given recognition and honor (cf. 1 Cor 16:16, 18; Phil 2:30). This opens the door for others to participate in church work because they know they too can anticipate honor and recognition for their service to the churches of God.

Thus Paul styles and structures his commendations in ways that parallel and contrast Greco-Roman commendations. The picture of a Pauline commendation that emerges is one that endorses local church leadership for its ongoing work on behalf of the gospel and their churches, and encourages emulation of both Paul and also of the commended leaders. All the parties involved, as in the Greco-Roman commendation, benefit from Paul's commendations: Paul, the letter recipients (the churches), and the commended. However, in a way that finds no parallel in the Roman letters, the *cause* that Paul espouses so forcefully remains the ultimate beneficiary, at least in Paul's mind, from a successful commendation: the gospel of Jesus Christ.

Part III. Relevant Pauline and Paulinist Texts

Other Pauline passages, including Paul's envoy passages, that commend leaders confirm and expand this picture. Envoy passages entail formal "sending," such as Timothy in Phil 2:19–24 and 1 Cor 16:10–11, and Titus and the "brothers" in 2 Cor 8:16–24.

Of course, the entire Letter to Philemon represents the only full commendation letter in the Pauline corpus. It merits attention that space in this essay would not allow.

The only Paulinist letter that carries a commendation is Col 4:7–9.

Part IV. Bibliography

Ancient Texts

Cicero. *Letters to His Friends (Epistulae Ad Familiares)*. Translated by W. Glynn Williams. 3 vols. LCL. Cambridge: Harvard University Press, 1972.

Fronto. *Correspondence*. Translated by C. R. Haines. 2 vols. LCL. London and New York: Wm. Heinemann and G. P. Putnam's Sons, 1920.

Pliny the Younger. *Letters and Panegyricus*. Translated by Betty Radice. 2 vols. LCL. Cambridge: Harvard University Press, 1969.

Plutarch. "On Praising Oneself Inoffensively." *Moralia* 539–547. Translated by Phillip H. DeLacey and Benedict Einarson. Vol. 7. LCL. Cambridge: Harvard University Press, 1959.

Quintilian. *Institutio Oratoria*. Translated by H. E. Butler. 4 vols. LCL. Cambridge: Harvard University Press, 1920–22.

Secondary Texts

Agosto, Efrain. "Paul's Use of Greco-Roman Conventions of Commendation." Ph.D. diss., Boston University, 1996.

Baird, William R. "Letters of Recommendation: A Study of 2 Cor 3.1–3." *JBL* 80 (1961): 166–72.

Belleville, Linda L. "A Letter of Apologetic Self-Commendation: 2 Cor 1:8–7:16." *NovT* 31 (April 1989): 142–63.

Chow, John Kingman. *Patronage and Power: A Study of Social Networks in Corinth.* Sheffield, England: Sheffield Academic Press, 1992.

Cotton, Hannah. *Documentary Letters of Recommendation in Latin from the Roman Empire*. Beiträge zur klassischen Philologie 132. Königstein, Germany: Anton Hain, 1981.

———. "Letters of Recommendation: Cicero–Fronto." Doctoral diss., Oxford University, 1977.

Forbes, Christopher. "Comparison, Self-Praise, and Irony: Paul's Boasting and the Conventions of Hellenistic Rhetoric." *NTS* 32, no. 1 (1986): 1–30.

Keyes, Clinton W. "The Greek Letter of Introduction." *AJP* 56 (1935): 28–48.

Kim, Chan-Hie. *Form and Structure of the Familiar Greek Letter of Recommendation.* SBLDS 4. Missoula, Mont.: Scholars Press, 1972.

Malina, Bruce J., and Jerome H. Neyrey. *Portraits of Paul: An Archaeology of Ancient Personality.* Louisville: Westminster John Knox Press, 1996.

Marshall, Peter. *Enmity in Corinth: Social Conventions in Paul's Relations with the Corinthians.* Tübingen: J. C. B. Mohr, 1987.

Mitchell, Margaret M. "New Testament Envoys in the Context of Greco-Roman Diplomatic and Epistolary Conventions: The Example of Timothy and Titus." *JBL* 111 (1992): 641–62.

Saller, Richard P. *Personal Patronage under the Early Empire.* Cambridge: Cambridge University Press, 1982.

Stowers, Stanley K. *Letter Writing in Greco-Roman Antiquity.* Philadelphia: Fortress Press, 1986.

Walters, James. " 'Phoebe' and 'Junia(s)'—Rom 16:1–2, 7." Pages 167–90 in *Essays on Women in Earliest Christianity,* edited by Carroll D. Osburn. Vol. 1. Joplin, Mo.: College Press Publishing, 1993.

Notes

1. These characteristics of encomia are found in several rhetorical handbooks, including Quintilian, *Institutio Oratoria* 3.7.10–18. See Bruce J. Malina and Jerome H. Neyrey, *Portraits of Paul: The Archaeology of Ancient Personality* (Louisville: Westminster John Knox, 1996), 23–33, for a helpful summary, with several sample texts from the handbooks in appendix 1 (219–24). See also Heinrich Lausberg, *Handbook of Literary Rhetoric: A Foundation for Literary Study* (ed. David E. Orton and R. Dean Anderson; trans. M. T. Bliss, A. Jansen, and D. E. Orton; Leiden: Brill, 1998).

2. See Chan-Hie Kim, *Form and Structure of the Familiar Greek Letter of Recommendation* (SBLDS 4; Missoula, Mont.: Society of Biblical Literature, 1972), which includes an appendix of eighty-three Greek papyri commendation letters. See also Clinton Keyes, "The Greek Letter of Introduction," *AJP* 56 (1935): 28–44; Hannah Cotton, "Greek and Latin Epistolary Formulae: Some Light on Cicero's Letter Writing," *AJP* 105 (1984): 409–25; idem, "Letters of Recommendation: Cicero-Fronto" (diss., Oxford University, 1977); and idem, *Documentary Letters of Recommendation in Latin from the Roman Empire* (Beiträge zur klassischen Philologie 132; Königstein, Germany: Anton Hain, 1981). Peter Marshall provides a good introduction to the practice of commendation, particularly as it relates to friendship, in *Enmity in Corinth: Social Conventions in Paul's Relations with the Corinthians* (Tübingen: J. C. B. Mohr, 1987), 91–129. Marshall relies, as I shall here, on the literary letters of commendation, especially those of Cicero.

3. Kim, *Form and Structure,* 56; on openings and closings, see 9–34; on the

background and identification of the recommended, 35–53; and on the reason for writing the letter, 53–58.

4. Ibid., 61.

5. Ibid., 68.

6. From Stanley Stowers, *Letter Writing in Greco-Roman Antiquity* (Philadelphia: Westminster, 1986), 154. Cf. Kim, *Form and Structure*, 89–97.

7. As argued by Cotton, "Greek and Latin Epistolary Formulae," 412, 424.

8. Stowers, *Letter Writing*, 153.

9. Ibid., 156.

10. *Ad Amicos* 1.1.1. Translations of Fronto, and also Cicero and Pliny below, come from the Loeb Classical Library editions. The Fronto edition includes such letter collections as *Ad Amicos*, *Ad M. Caesar* ("Marcus Aurelius as Caesar"), and *Ad Verum Imperator* (Lucius Verus, Emperor). For more on commendation testimonials in court, see Richard Saller, *Personal Patronage under the Early Empire* (Cambridge: Cambridge University Press, 1982), 152–53.

11. Cotton, *Documentary Letters*, 6.

12. P.Mich. 33 (third century b.c.e.), reproduced in Kim, *Form and Structure*, 169. Kim lists other texts that request similar "general assistance" (65–77).

13. Cotton, *Documentary Letters*, 30.

14. Ibid., 30–31: "It was considered advisable and tactful to leave it as vague as possible" (31).

15. This and all other biblical references are from the New Revised Standard Version (nrsv), unless otherwise noted.

16. See details of this self-commendation in Efrain Agosto, "Paul's Use of Greco-Roman Conventions of Commendation" (Ph.D. diss., Boston University, 1996), 122–38.

17. Kim, *Form and Structure*, 120.

18. Ibid., 126. Kim also placed the commendation passages within the formal structure of the entirety of the Pauline letter. Following Robert Funk's work on the "apostolic parousia" sections of Paul's letters, Kim argued that Pauline commendation passages typically followed Paul's statements of travel plans and/or the plans of his associates and envoys. These travel plans and commendations are followed by final exhortations and closing matters in most of Paul's letters (ibid., 120–23); cf. Robert Funk, "The Apostolic *Parousia*: Form and Significance," in *Christian History and Interpretation: Studies Presented to John Knox* (ed. W. R. Farmer, C. F. D. Moule, and R. R. Niebuhr; Cambridge: Cambridge University Press, 1967), 249–68.

19. See Margaret M. Mitchell, "New Testament Envoys in the Context of Greco-Roman Diplomatic and Epistolary Conventions: The Example of Timothy and Titus," *JBL* 111 (1992): 641–62, esp. 647–50n. 32, who notes the overlap between commendation and envoy passages. See also my study of envoy passages that commend Paul's associates in "Paul's Use of Greco-Roman Conventions," 196–223.

20. Most commentators agree on this point, following Ernest Best, *A Commentary on the First and Second Epistles to the Thessalonians* (Harper's New Testament Commentaries; reprint, Peabody, Mass.: Hendrickson, 1988), 118.

21. So I. H. Marshall, *1 and 2 Thessalonians* (New Century Bible Commentary; Grand Rapids: Eerdmans, 1983), 147.

22. See "προΐστημι (proistēmi)," BDAG 707, and Bo Reicke, "προΐστημι (prois-

tēmi)," TDNT 6:700–703. See also James Walters, "'Phoebe' and 'Junia(s)'—Rom 16:1–2, 7," in *Essays on Women in Earliest Christianity* (ed. Carroll D. Osburn; vol. 1; Joplin, Mo.: College Press, 1993), 167–90 (esp. 177–79), who shows the connection of the basic meanings (helping and leading) to the tasks of patronage.

23. Similarly, the NRSV shifts the sense of προιστάμενος ἐν τῇ παρακλήσει ἐν σπουδῇ, *proistamenos en tē paraklēsei en spoudē,* in Rom 12.8 from the one "who gives aid, with zeal" (RSV) to "the leader, in diligence." However, the immediate context requires "those who help" or "those who give aid," as in the RSV. Yet, see Walters, "'Phoebe' and 'Junia(s),'" 178, who relates the term to patronage: "The *proistamenos* is not the one who 'governs' but who 'protects' the interests of those who are socially vulnerable, a patron."

24. Reicke, "*proistēmi,*" 701. For a similar conclusion, see F. F. Bruce, *1 & 2 Thessalonians* (WBC 45; Waco, Tex.: Word, 1982), 119, who writes, "[T]he verb *proistasthai* combines the ideas of leading, protecting and caring for." Best, *Commentary on the First and Second Epistles,* 225, argues strongly for the meaning "caring for," because it contrasts well with the next participle νουθετοῦντας, *nouthetountas*— "admonishing." In Best's view the leadership element is one of several aspects of the "care" being requested, but not the predominant one.

25. See "νουθετέω (*noutheteō*)," BDAG 544.

26. See Robert Jewett, *The Thessalonian Correspondence: Pauline Rhetoric and Millenarian Piety* (Philadelphia: Fortress Press, 1986), 5–18, 168–78.

27. Best, *Commentary on the First and Second Epistles,* 227. So also Bruce, *1 & 2 Thessalonians,* 120–21.

28. As translated by Best, *Commentary on the First and Second Epistles,* 228.

29. See Stephen Pogoloff, *Logos and Sophia: The Rhetorical Situation of 1 Corinthians* (SBLDS 134; Atlanta: Scholars Press, 1992), 106–8, who argues that the baptism reference (1 Cor 1.13–17) functions in 1 Corinthians as an example of Paul's rhetoric against divisions.

30. Gordon Fee, *The First Epistle to the Corinthians* (NICNT; Grand Rapids: Eerdmans, 1987), 828–29.

31. See the studies on Pauline house churches by Abraham Malherbe, *Social Aspects of Early Christianity* (2d ed.; Philadelphia: Fortress Press, 1983), 60–91; and Robert Banks, *Paul's Idea of Community: The Early House Churches in their Historical Setting* (Grand Rapids: Eerdmans, 1980). Banks's revised edition (Peabody, Mass.: Hendrickson, 1994) expands on other dynamics with regard to Pauline community and limits the main discussion on house churches to pages 26–36.

32. On this point, see Wayne Meeks, *The First Urban Christians: The Social World of the Apostle Paul* (New Haven and London: Yale University Press, 1983), 51–73. Others who discuss the role of householders in church leadership roles include Gerd Theissen, *The Social Setting of Pauline Christianity: Essays on Corinth* (ed. and trans. John H. Schütz; Philadelphia: Fortress Press, 1982), 83–99; and Bengt Holmberg, *Paul and Power: The Structure of Authority in the Primitive Church as Reflected in the Pauline Epistles* (Philadelphia: Fortress Press, 1980), 99–109. On the basis of these studies, Charles Wanamaker, *Commentary on 1 and 2 Thessalonians* (NIGTC; Grand Rapids: Eerdmans, 1990), 193–96, argues for a "householder-as-leader" theory with regard to the leaders commended in 1 Thess 5:12–13. A stronger case can be made for Stephanas in 1 Cor 16.

33. See BDAG 805.

34. BDAG 806.

35. Fee, *First Epistle to the Corinthians,* 828.

36. Cf. ibid., 830.

37. Exemplification refers to following the example of others. In ancient rhetoric, examples (*exempla*) helped strengthen a particular argument. Paul uses his coworkers and associates as examples of good leadership. See J. Paul Sampley, *Walking between the Times: Paul's Moral Reasoning* (Minneapolis: Fortress Press, 1991), 88–91.

38. Because the structure—identification, credentials, request—repeats itself, Kim, *Form and Structure,* 130, writes: "1 Cor 16:15–18 has two passages of commendation appearing together."

39. See ibid., 130–31.

40. Fee, *First Epistle to the Corinthians,* 832.

41. See Sampley, *Walking between the Times,* 90. Cf. Margaret M. Mitchell, *Paul and the Rhetoric of Reconciliation: An Exegetical Investigation of the Language and Composition of 1 Corinthians* (Louisville: Westminster John Knox, 1991), 178–79, who argues that in 1 Cor 16:15–18, Paul follows the rhetorical practice that calls for "obedience" to exemplary leaders in order to end discord.

42. See E. Earle Ellis, "Paul and His Co-workers," *NTS* 17 (1971): 445–49, who posits that Paul's designation of his coworkers as "brothers" and "sisters" indicates a leadership term.

43. Peter T. O'Brien, *Commentary on Philippians,* NIGTC (Grand Rapids: Eerdmans, 1991), 331.

44. On this term and its significance for Paul, see Victor C. Pfitzner, *Paul and the Agon Motif* (Leiden: Brill, 1967).

45. See O'Brien, *Commentary on Philippians,* 332. With an ironic tone, Paul also designates his opponents in 2 Cor 10–13 as "super-apostles" (2 Cor 11:1–6; cf. 11:12–15; 12:11–13). They may in fact be commissioned from another church, because they do come with letters of recommendation (2 Cor 3:1).

46. Ibid., 322. See Max Zerwick and Mary Grosvenor, *A Grammatical Analysis of the Greek New Testament* (Rome: Biblical Institute Press, 1981), 553, for a suggestion that λειτουργία, *leitourgia,* has at its roots the words λαός, *laos* (people), and ἔργον, *ergon* (work). Thus, in their estimation, a "work" or "service" for "the people," whether in a religious or secular context, stands behind the meaning of this word.

47. See Henry G. Liddell and Robert Scott, *A Greek-English Lexicon* (Oxford: Clarendon, 1961), 1036–37.

48. See O'Brien, *Commentary on Philippians,* 308–9, for a fuller discussion, with references, of *leitourgia* and Paul's notion of "sacrificial service."

49. See J. Paul Sampley, *Pauline Partnership in Christ: Christian Community and Commitment in Light of Roman Law* (Philadelphia: Fortress Press, 1980), 51–72, who details the obligations of the Philippians to Paul in their mutual relationship of κοινωνία, *koinōnia* (partnership).

50. See O'Brien, *Commentary on Philippians,* 332–33, on the nature of Epaphroditus's mission as regards the term *leitourgia.* See also Gordon D. Fee, *Paul's Letter*

to the Philippians (NICNT; Grand Rapids: Eerdmans, 1995), 276, who describes the need for friends to assist and feed Roman prisoners.

51. On Paul's use of hardship lists to validate his ministry, see the detailed study by John T. Fitzgerald, *Cracks in an Earthen Vessel: An Examination of the Catalogues of Hardships in the Corinthian Correspondence* (SBLDS 99; Atlanta: Scholars Press, 1988).

52. As suggested by F. W. Beare, *The Epistle to the Philippians* (San Francisco: Harper & Row, 1959), 99.

53. See Kim's list of commendation texts with *prosdechomai* in *Form and Structure*, 76–77, 131–32.

54. Format adapted from ibid., 132; my translation.

55. See RSV ("helper"), NIV ("a great help"), GNB ("a good friend"), Phillips ("of great assistance"), and C. K. Barrett, *The Epistle to the Romans* (New York: Harper & Row, 1957), 283 ("protectress"). See also C. E. B. Cranfield, *A Critical and Exegetical Commentary on the Epistle to the Romans* (vol. 2; Edinburgh: T. & T. Clark, 1975–79), 782, who concludes that the term προστάτις, *prostatis*, "can hardly have here any technical legal sense such as the masculine form *prostates* could bear." Therefore the best translation, according to Cranfield, is something more general like "helper."

56. For examples of this literature see Walters, "'Phoebe' and 'Junia(s),'" 171–72.

57. Excerpted from ibid., 173–74, which cites the full inscription published in D. Pallas et al., "Inscriptions lyciennes trouvèes à Solômos près de Corinthe," *BCH* 83 (1959): 505–6.

58. Ibid., 174–75.

59. Ibid.

60. Ibid., 181.

61. Ibid., 185.

62. P. Cairo Goodspeed 4 (mid–second century B.C.E.), reproduced in Kim, *Form and Structure,* 193 (see also 78–80 for other examples).

63. See Kim, *Form and Structure,* 86–87, for causal clauses in several Greek commendation letters like this one in Rom 16:2.

64. E. A. Judge, "The Early Christians as a Scholastic Community: Part II," *JRH* 2 (1961): 125–37 (quote from 129).

65. See John K. Chow, *Patronage and Power: A Study of Social Networks in Corinth* (Sheffield, England: Sheffield Academic Press, 1992), 101–12, who posits that the problems cited in 1 Corinthians originate from the Corinthian search for patronage, which Paul rejects. Cf. Marshall, *Enmity in Corinth,* 165–257, who interprets Paul's problems with the Corinthians as a refusal of their financial support and, therefore, their "friendship." These problems continue to intensify in 2 Cor 10–13 when outside leaders do accept Corinthian patronage.

66. Although see Pheme Perkins, "Philippians: Theology for the Heavenly *Politeuma*," in *Pauline Theology,* vol. 1: *Thessalonians, Philippians, Galatians, Philemon* (ed. Jouette M. Bassler; Minneapolis: Fortress Press, 1991), 100–101, who argues that Paul avoids the status of client to the Philippians by invoking his self-sufficiency and contentment in Phil 4:11–13, even as he accepts their monetary gift.

67. See Chow, *Patronage and Power,* 173–75; Marshall, *Enmity in Corinth,* 218–58.

5

PAUL AND RHETORICAL COMPARISON

Christopher Forbes

Part I. Comparison in the Greco–Roman World

When a Greek or Roman schoolboy (or less commonly, schoolgirl) was asked to prepare a piece of work for presentation, it would normally take the form of a speech rather than a written essay. And whereas the mythical school student of the mid–twentieth century might have been asked to write on "What I Did in My Holidays," ancient topics, though equally stereotyped, were rather different. Alongside retelling a well-known fable or historical narrative, confirming or re-futing the truth of a fable or story, arguing the truth or falsehood of a moral gen-eralization, and writing an encomium of a famous person, the student might well be asked to prepare a σύγκρισις (*synkrisis*), a speech of comparison.[1] As their ed-ucation proceeded, they would move on from attempting these and other prelim-inary exercises (προγυμνάσματα, *progymnasmata*) for their own sakes, and begin applying the techniques they had learned in them to more practical and more dif-ficult topics.

Early Cases and Discussions of Rhetorical Comparison

The existence of προγυμνάσματα (*progymnasmata*), formalized elementary curric-ula for rhetorical education, is first mentioned in the pseudo-Aristotelian "Rhetoric to Alexander" (1436a25; fourth century B.C.E.). Other references, explicit and implicit, show that they remained the staple of elementary education throughout antiquity.[2] Comparison (σύγκρισις, *synkrisis*) in the προγυμνάσματα (*progymnasmata*) was primarily a set of techniques for the "amplification" (αὔξη-σις, *auxēsis*) of good and bad qualities in speeches involving praise and blame.[3] The technique of comparison was well enough known, at a simple level, to be

134

taught at the higher end of "secondary" education, under a *grammaticus,* or early in rhetorical school, that is, at the age of twelve to fourteen.[4] Like much of the rest of Greco-Roman rhetorical theory, it arose out of the systematization of "common sense" and actual practice.[5]

Later theorists identified comparisons as having been written as early as the fourth century. Aristotle argued that Isocrates misused the technique:

> If he [your subject] does not furnish you with enough material in himself, you must compare him with others [ἀντιπαραβάλλειν, *antiparaballein*], as Isocrates used to do, because of his inexperience in forensic speaking.[6]

For Aristotle, then, rhetorical comparison was more appropriate for epideictic than for forensic oratory. Although this became the majority view, writers did not exclude comparison from forensic and deliberative speeches, but epideictic was perceived as the most appropriate style for the widespread use of comparison. Quintilian, however, detected a particularly forceful example of comparison in Cicero's *pro Murena:* this demonstrates both that comparison could be used in forensic speech, and that such comparison could be ironic and critical in nature.[7]

> Again, in antitheses and comparisons the first words of alternate phrases are frequently repeated to produce correspondence. . . . [Quintilian now quotes Cicero] "You pass wakeful nights so that you may be able to reply to your clients; he that he and his army may arrive betimes at their destination. You are roused by cockcrow, he by the bugle's reveillé. You draw up your legal pleas, he sets the battle in array. You are on the watch that your clients be not taken at a disadvantage, he that cities or camps be not so taken. . . . He knows and understands how to keep off the enemy, you how to keep off the rainwater; he is skilled to extend boundaries, you to delimit them."

According to Menander Rhetor, Isocrates wrote a comparison of Theseus and Heracles.[8] Meleager of Gadara, writing shortly after the turn of the first century B.C.E., is said to have produced a work that contained "the *synkrisis* of pease-porridge and lentil soup."[9] The question was as to which of these was the worse! Dionysius of Halicarnassus identified comparisons in Isocrates and Demosthenes.[10]

Such identifications were not arbitrary. Aristotle not only identified cases of comparison; he and other writers laid down methods for using the technique, which were then taught. In the anonymous "Rhetoric to Alexander," methods of amplification in encomium are discussed as follows:

> The eulogistic species of oratory [τὸ ἐγκωμιαστικόν, *to enkōmiastikon*] consists, to put it briefly, in the amplification of creditable purposes and ac-

tions and speeches and the attribution of qualities that do not exist, while the vituperative species [ψεκτικόν, *psektikon*] is the opposite, the minimisation of creditable qualities and the amplification of discreditable ones. Praiseworthy things are those that are just, lawful, expedient, noble, pleasant and easy to accomplish. . . .

First you must show, as I lately explained, that the actions of the person in question have produced many bad, or good, results. This is one method of amplification. A second method is to produce a previous judgement—a favourable one if you are praising, an unfavourable one if you are blaming—and then set your own statement beside it and compare them [παραβάλλειν, *paraballein*] with one another, enlarging on the strongest points of your own case and the weakest ones of the other and so making your own case appear a strong one. A third way is to set in comparison [ἀντιπαραβάλλειν, *antiparaballein*] with the thing you are saying the smallest things that fall into the same class, for thus your case will appear magnified, just as men of medium height appear taller when standing by the side of men shorter than themselves. . . .[11] One must also argue one's case by employing comparison [συμβιβάζειν, *symbibazein*], and amplify it by building up one point on another, as follows: "It is probable that anyone who looks after his friends, also honours his parents; and anyone who honours his parents will also wish to benefit his own country."[12]

In discussing the various methods of αὔξησις [*auxēsis*], the "amplification" of material, Aristotle argued that

you must compare him [your subject, συγκρίνειν, *synkrinein*] with illustrious personages, for this affords grounds for amplification, and is noble, if he can be proved better than men of worth. . . . [I]f you cannot compare him with illustrious personages, you must compare him [παραβάλλειν, *paraballein*] with ordinary persons, since superiority is thought to indicate virtue.[13]

Likewise, in a more philosophical context, Aristotle argued that

we may place also in the category of "accident" comparisons [συγκρίσεις, *synkriseis*] of things with one another, when they are described in terms derived in any way from accident; for example, the questions "Is the honourable or the expedient preferable?" and "Is the life of virtue or the life of enjoyment more pleasant?"[14]

Thus philosophical comparisons of relative ethical value can be made. Such topics rapidly became "commonplaces" (τόποι [*topoi*], κοινοὶ τόποι [*koinoi topoi*], στοιχεῖα [*stoicheia*], *loci, loci communes*), standard popular philosophical generalizations, which were the bread and butter of various kinds of rhetorical exercises.

Comparisons [τὰς . . . συγκρίσεις, *tas . . . synkriseis*], then, of things with one another should be made in the manner described. The same commonplaces [τόποι, *topoi*] are useful for showing that something is simply worthy of choice or avoidance. . . . For sometimes, when we are actually comparing [κατὰ τὴν πρὸς ἕτερον σύγκρισιν, *kata tēn pros heteron synkrisin*] two things, we immediately assert that each or one of them is worthy of choice, for example, when we say that one thing is naturally good and another not naturally good. . . .[15]

Comparison from the First Century B.C.E., the "Genres" of Rhetoric, and Wider Literature

In the late Hellenistic and Roman period, in the second stage of rhetorical training, more-complex exercises, sometimes known as μελέται (*meletai*) or ἀναφωνήσεις (*anaphōnēseis*), or *declamationes*, were attempted.[16] Roman writers tended further to subdivide *declamationes* into those on legal or forensic topics (*controversiae*) and those on political or deliberative topics (*suasoriae*). Depending on the teacher, the student might also begin practicing epideictic, or ceremonial, "display" speeches.[17] However, Aristotle's three-way division of rhetoric into forensic, deliberative, and epideictic topics[18] was only one of several competing categorizations: others were also known.[19]

In these more advanced rhetorical exercises, once again, comparison was used. In Cicero's *de Inventione* 1.17, the following "deliberative" example is given:

A complex case is made up of several questions, in which several inquiries are made, such as: "Should Carthage be destroyed, or handed back to the Carthaginians, or should a colony be established there?" The case involves comparison [*comparatio*] when various actions are contrasted and the question is which one is more desirable to perform. . . .[20]

Quintilian, *Inst.* III.8.33–4, goes further:

Nor is expediency compared [*comparantur*] merely with inexpediency. At times we have to choose between two advantageous courses after comparison of their respective advantages. The problem may be still more complicated, as for instance when Pompey deliberated whether to go to Parthia, Africa or Egypt. . . . *as a rule all deliberative speeches are based simply on comparison* [*comparatio*], *and we must consider what we shall gain and by what means, that it may be possible to form an estimate whether there is more advantage in the aims we pursue or greater disadvantage in the means we employ to that end.* (Emphasis added)

Nor are forensic exercises without opportunities for comparison, whatever Aristotle may have thought of Isocrates' attempts.

Sometimes, if it is difficult to refute the statements made by our opponent, we may compare [*conferemus*] our arguments with theirs, at least if by such a procedure it is possible to prove the superiority of our own.[21]

However, it is clear that "epideictic" topics allow the greatest play to comparison. Menander Rhetor advises as follows: in royal panegyrics, when discussing the actions of the emperor,

Add also a comparison [σύγκρισις, *synkrisis*] to each of the main heads, comparing nature with nature, upbringing with upbringing, education with education, and so on, looking out (?) [*sic*] also examples of Roman Emperors or generals or the most famous of the Greeks.[22]

Having discussed all his virtues, and finally his Tyche (Fortune),

You should then proceed to the most complete comparison [σύγκρισις, *synkrisis*], examining his reign in comparison to [ἀντεξετάζων, *antexetazōn*] preceding reigns, not disparaging them (that is bad craftsmanship) but admiring them while granting perfection to the present. You must not forget our previous proposition, namely that comparisons [συγκρίσεις, *synkriseis*] should be made under each head; these comparisons, however, will be partial . . . whereas the complete one will concern the whole subject, as when we compare [συγκρίνομεν, *synkrinomen*] the reign as a whole and in sum with another reign, e.g., the reign of Alexander with the present one. After the comparison comes the epilogue.[23]

Finally, comparison was not merely a training exercise, but a living feature of literary culture. Students practiced encomia because real speeches of encomium were to be given;[24] students studied comparison because various forms of comparison had to be written. Orators and sophists compared themselves with one another in frequently acrimonious disputes.[25] Literary critics like Caecilius of Calacte and Dionysius of Halicarnassus developed a subtle comparative criticism;[26] Cicero compared the styles of Isocrates, Lysias, and Demosthenes, and M. Antonius, Crassus, and Scaevola.[27] "Longinus" developed comparisons of Demosthenes with Hyperides, and Plato with Lysias.[28] Quintilian, with some trepidation, even essayed a comparison of Demosthenes with Cicero.[29]

Most strikingly, and of course best known, Plutarch constructed several of his works, and the whole architecture of his *Lives*, on a comparative model. His early work, "On the Fortune of Alexander" (*Mor.* 326D–345B), dealt with the question whether luck or brilliance was more responsible for the greatness of Alexander's achievements. He also wrote on whether land animals or marine animals were more clever (*Mor.* 959A–985C), whether fire or water is more useful (*Mor.* 955D–958E), and an essay on whether Athens was more famous for warfare or wisdom (*Mor.* 345C–351B). His "On the Virtue of Women" is explicitly comparative: he argues that

> it is not possible to learn better the similarity and the difference between the virtues of men and women from any other source than by putting lives beside lives and actions beside actions, like great works of art, and considering whether the magnificence of Semiramis has the same charac-ter as that of Sesostris, or the intelligence of Tanaquil the same as that of Servius the King. . . .[30]

His "Dialogue on Love" is a detailed comparison of the relative virtues of het-erosexual and homosexual love, modeled in part on the famed "Symposium" of Plato. The speech of Protogenes (*Mor.* 750C) is a comparison designed to favor pederastic love, while the reply of Daphnaeus (*Mor.* 751B) is a countercompari-son, at first valuing both equally, but then inclining strongly to heterosexuality. Plutarch's comparison of the various human functions watched over by various gods (*Mor.* 757C–758C) is a more rhetorically developed example. *Moralia* 760D compares the power of Eros to that of Ares in some detail. This comparison is clearly an example of αὔξησις (*auxēsis*) by σύγκρισις (*synkrisis*). Further, the great majority of the pairs of lives, one Greek and one Roman, came with a detailed σύγκρισις (*synkrisis*). In many cases, it is clear that the lives in question had been carefully written to prepare for the main themes of the comparison.[31]

In the introductory section above I noted the evidence of the pseudo-Aris-totelian "Rhetoric to Alexander," and Aristotle's own contribution to the develop-ment of ideas of comparison. The verbs παραβάλλειν (*paraballein*) and συγκρίνειν (*synkrinein*) were used virtually synonymously for the process of rhetorical com-parison as a means of amplification. More generally, Aristotle, *Rhet.* 3.12.6, argues that "the epideictic style is especially suited to written composition; and next to it comes the forensic style." Speeches given orally and the written versions of those speeches had similar rhetorical features. Cicero, *De Or.* 2.341, makes the point that epideictic is to be read as well as heard. Quintilian, however, makes a related point, arguing (*Inst.* 12.10.51) that "there is absolutely no difference between writ-ing well and speaking well, and that a written speech is merely a record of one that has actually been delivered." In sections 53–55 he extends his point:

> Since those who are appointed to give sentence are frequently ill-edu-cated and sometimes mere rustics, it becomes necessary to employ every method that we think likely to assist our case, and these artifices must not merely be proclaimed in speech, but exhibited in the written version as well, at least if in writing it our design is to show how it should be spo-ken. If Demosthenes or Cicero had spoken the words as they wrote them,

would either have spoken ill? . . . Well, you ask, is an orator then always
to speak as he writes? If possible, always.

Clearly, for both Cicero and Quintilian the gap between oratory and written composition was not great.

In brief, then, literary comparison, at various levels, spoken or written, was a
living feature of Greco-Roman culture, and a feature of which anyone of any formal education would have been thoroughly aware. Further, because displays of
oratory were an extremely popular form of public entertainment, a high proportion of at least the male urban population would have had a good informal
knowledge of rhetoric. It is now time to examine the evidence for the practice in
greater detail. The task is complicated by the fact that the ancient terminology is
not uniform (see n. 3 above). It is also important to remember that the synthetic
picture to be presented is to a high degree artificial. Some students in ancient
times would have had access to one or more of these texts, or presentations based
on them, but not others.[32] Nonetheless, a chronological outline of the evidence
will demonstrate, at the least, the wide range of discussion on the topic.

Aristotle's analysis of rhetoric, probably due to its clarity and accessibility, as
well as its foundational nature, has been much used by New Testament scholars.
We cannot assume, however, that it was the model best known in the cultural environment in which Paul moved.[33] This survey, then, gathers its information from
a wide range of the ancient discussions. The aim is to show that "comparison"
was universally accepted as a feature of ancient rhetoric.

Chronological Overview of the Evidence

Discussions of comparison are found in the first-century B.C.E. *Rhetorica ad Herennium* 1.24–25. Discussing the forensic argument that could be described as "the
lesser of two evils" defense, the author argues that "a cause rests on Comparison
[*comparatione*] with the Alternative Course when we declare that it was necessary
for us to do one or the other of the two things, and that the one we did was the
better."

The example given is of a general who surrendered in humiliating circumstances, rather than have his army completely destroyed. The author has found
the place for comparison in forensic oratory that Aristotle denied to Isocrates.[34]

In *ad Herennium* 2.6, a different term is used for a feature of a speech for the
prosecution, in which

Comparison [*conlatio*] is used when the prosecutor shows that the act
charged by him against his adversary has benefited no-one but the defendant, or that no one but his adversary could have committed it, or that his

adversary could not have committed it, or at least not so easily by other means.

In other words, the advocate compares the probabilities of the defendant, and anyone else, having committed the act in question.

Ad Herennium 2.50 treats the more emotive use of the comparison (*comparatione*) of the adverse circumstances of the defendant with his previous good fortune, as a means of stirring the jurors to pity.[35] This seems as much an "epideictic" feature as a case of "forensic" speech as such, but that fact merely illustrates the artificiality of the categories.[36]

Cicero himself, writing in the same generation as the *Auctor ad Herennium*, likewise dealt with both the more limited and the more rhetorically elaborate forms of comparison. In his early *De Inventione* (ca. 89 B.C.E.), he defines *comparatio* in forensic oratory (2.72), discusses illustrative comparisons in forensic oratory (1.82, 2.75ff.), the use of comparison (*comparatio*) of the two cases in the peroration of a forensic speech (1.99), and comparing the crime in question with "other crimes which are by common consent regarded as crimes, and so by contrast it is shown how much more horrible and shameful is the offence now before the court" (1.104).

In his *Topica* 18:68–71 and 84–85, Cicero deals with comparative illustrations (see especially the second-to-last paragraph) and clearly draws on an earlier Hellenistic text that discussed the wider rhetorical practice of comparison:

> [68] Comparison is made [*comparantur*] between things which are greater, or less or equal. And in this connection the following points are considered: quantity, quality, value, and also a particular relation to certain things.

> [69] Things will be compared in respect to quantity as follows: more "goods" are preferred to fewer, fewer evils to more, goods which last for a longer time to those of shorter duration, those which are distributed far and wide to those which are confined to narrow limits, those from which more goods are generated, and those which more people imitate and produce.

> In comparing things in respect to their quality [*specie autem comparantur*] we prefer those which are to be sought for their own sake to those which are desired because they make something else possible; also we prefer innate and natural qualities to acquired and adventitious ones, what is pure to what is defiled, the pleasant to the less pleasant, what is honourable to what is profitable itself, the easy task to the difficult, the necessary to the unnecessary, our own good to that of others, things that are rare to those that are common, desirable things to those which you can easily do without, the perfect to the incomplete, the whole to its parts, reasonable actions to those devoid of reason, voluntary to necessary acts, animate

things to inanimate objects, the natural to the unnatural, that which is artistic to that which is not.

[70] In regard to value, distinctions are drawn in comparisons as follows: An efficient cause is weightier than one that is not; things which are sufficient in themselves are better than those that require help from others; we prefer what is in our own power to what is in the power of others; the stable to the uncertain; what cannot be taken from us to that which can.

Relation to other things is of this nature: the interests of leading citizens are of more importance than those of the rest; a similar value attaches to things that are pleasanter, that are approved by the majority, or are praised by all virtuous men. And just as these are the things which in a comparison [*in comparatione*] are regarded as better, so the opposites of these are regarded as worse.

[71] When equals are compared there is no superiority or inferiority; everything is on the same plane. But there are many things which are compared because of their very equality. The argument runs something like this: If helping one's fellow-citizens with advice and giving them active assistance are to be regarded as equally praiseworthy, then those who give advice and those who defend ought to receive equal glory. But the first statement is true, therefore the conclusion is also. . . .

[84] When the question is about the nature of anything, it is put either simply or by comparison [*aut simpliciter quaeritur aut comparate*]; simply as in the question: Should one seek glory?—by comparison as: Is glory to be preferred to riches? . . . [85] . . . [O]ne might ask whether eloquence or jurisprudence is more valuable.

Here, then, we have an analysis that predates the extant προγυμνάσματα (*progymnasmata*), but draws on very similar material.

Like other writers, Cicero draws on earlier "classic" speeches and detects comparisons within them.[37] But his real focus is on the contemporary use of oratory, whether forensic or deliberative. In his *De Partitione Oratoria* 49, he discusses the comparison of the reliability of witnesses: "and they must be compared [*comparandique*] with witnesses of higher authority who have nevertheless not been given credence." In section 66, in the context of deliberative speeches, he says that "the question asked is not only the simple inquiry, what is honourable, what is useful, what is equitable, but it also involves comparison [*comparatione*]—what is *more* honourable or useful or equitable, and also what is *most* honourable."

Discussing the topic of expediency in political decision making in section 95, he comments that "we must not only envisage the resources that we possess but the things that operate against us; and if on comparison [*ex contentione*] the balance is on our side, we must not only persuade our audience that the course we advise is feasible."

Compare section 98: in a court of law

> the subject at which a speech of this kind aims is equity, which occasion-
> ally is envisioned not in simple form but by means of a comparison [*ex
> comparatione*]. . . . [I]n these cases, the question is raised as to what is
> more, or most, equitable.

Finally, Cicero both bears witness to and practices a form of comparative criticism in his works on the history of oratory. In *Brut.* 229, he writes: "It is inevitable
in the case of men who live a long life of activity that they come into comparison
[*compararentur*] with men much older than themselves as well as with men much
younger." In section 301, he gives an example of this phenomenon:

> Though his [Hortensius's] beginnings fell in the period of Cotta and
> Sulpicius, who were ten years older, when Crassus and Antonius, then
> Philippus, and afterwards Julius, were still at the height of their reputa-
> tions, yet in renown as a speaker he was constantly compared [*compara-
> batur*] with these veterans.[38]

Turning to the first century C.E., the writings of Philo of Alexandria show that
the practice of comparison was not merely theorized about by rhetoricians, but
could be a powerful satirical weapon. In his *Legat.* 77–110, Philo notes that Gaius
assimilated various forms of cult to himself and ridicules his pretensions by comparing his deeds with the achievements of the mythical figures in question: the
Dioscuri, Dionysus, Heracles, Hermes, and Apollo.[39]

From the late first century C.E. we have the work of Aelius Theon, the first of
the extant "Progymnasmata." In the context of a general discussion of encomium,[40] students are given a broad definition of comparison, warned against
forced or artificial comparisons, and then given reasonably detailed instruction as
to how to compose their comparisons.

> Comparison [σύγκρισις, *synkrisis*] is a form of speech which contrasts
> the better and the worse. Comparisons are drawn between people, and
> between things: between people, for example Ajax and Odysseus; be-
> tween things, for example, wisdom and courage. When one distinguishes
> between people, one takes into consideration their acts, but if there is
> anything else of merit about them, then the one method would suffice for
> both.
>
> First, it should be noted that comparisons are not drawn between
> things which are vastly different from each other. It would be ridiculous
> to debate whether Achilles is more courageous than Thersites. Like
> things should be considered, things over which there can be disagree-
> ment as to whether a position should be taken up, because of the impos-
> sibility of distinguishing any pre-eminence of the one over the other.

In the comparison of people, one firstly juxtaposes their status, education, offspring, positions held, prestige and physique; if there is any other physical matter, or external merit, it should be stated beforehand in the material for the encomia.

Next one compares actions, preferring the finer ones and those responsible for more numerous and greater benefits; those which are more stable and durable; those which were especially opportune; those for which the failure to perform them would have resulted in the occurrence of great injury; those performed out of choice rather than of necessity or chance; and those performed by the few rather than the many. Commonplace and hackneyed things should not be singled out for praise. One should refer to those things done with effort rather than ease, and things done after the appropriate age and opportunity rather than those performed when the possibility was there.[41]

The writings of the great rhetorician Quintilian, likewise from the end of the first century, deal primarily with training in forensic oratory, but his discussion also encompasses the early stages of the rhetorical curriculum. For example, in 2.4.20ff., he illustrates the place of comparison in the early development of the skills of the student.

From this [narratives, and their confirmation and refutation] our pupil will begin to proceed to more important themes, such as the praise of famous men and the denunciation of the wicked. . . . It is but a step from this to practice in the comparison [comparationis] of the respective merits of two characters. . . .

But the method to be followed in panegyric and invective will be dealt with in its proper place, as it forms the third department of rhetoric.

He then proceeds to "commonplaces" (communes loci) and "theses" (2.4.24), which "are concerned with the comparison [comparatione] of things and involve questions such as 'Which is preferable, town or country life?' or 'Which deserves the greatest praise, the lawyer or the soldier?'" The incremental nature of the preliminary exercises is particularly visible here.

Quintilian also gives comparatio a central role in amplification of argument: "I consider . . . that there are four principal methods of amplification: augmentation [incremento], comparison [comparatione], reasoning [ratiocinatione] and accumulation [congerie]" (Inst. 8.4.3).

However, the term can have multiple meanings. Quintilian, like earlier authors, uses the term comparatio for a range of different comparative figures. In Inst. 8.6.69, he uses the term for a minor comparative metaphor. In 8.5.19, 21, he uses it in the context of "Sententiae" with comparative illustrations. In 8.6.4ff., he uses it for metaphors and similes, and in 9.2.2 for comparable precedents. In 5.10.125

and 5.11.7ff., he deals with arguments from historical parallels, which he says the Greeks call παράδειγμα (*paradeigma*), but the Romans *exemplum*. In 9.2.100, he discusses the precise nature of comparison, understood inclusively, dealing with the question whether it should be considered a figure of speech or a "figure of thought."[42]

Dealing with what we would call *a fortiori* arguments in a forensic context, *Inst.* 8.4.9 argues:

> Just as this form of amplification [augmentation] rises to a climax, so, too, the form which depends on comparison seeks to rise from the less to the greater. . . . (8.4.13) [W]hen amplification is our purpose we compare not merely whole with whole, but part with part, as in the following passage [he cites Cicero's First Catilinarian oration, 1.1.3:] "Did that illustrious citizen, the pontifex maximus, Publius Scipio, acting merely in his private capacity, kill Tiberius Gracchus when he introduced but slight changes for the worse that did not seriously impair the constitution of the state, and shall we as consuls suffer Catiline to live, whose aim was to lay waste the whole world with fire and sword?"
>
> Here Catiline is compared to Gracchus, the constitution of the state to the whole world, a slight change for the worse to fire and sword and desolation, and a private citizen to the consuls, all comparisons affording ample opportunity for further individual expansion, if anyone should desire so to do.

In simpler terms, *Inst.* 4.2.99 suggests that "arguments will be drawn from a comparison [*comparatione*] of the characters of the two parties."

In 5.10.91, reflecting on the whole topic, Quintilian muses that "the comparison of things is infinite: things may be more pleasant, more serious, more necessary, more honourable, more useful . . ." He goes on to discuss arguments from the greater to the lesser, from the general to the specific, and vice versa. In *Inst.* 7.2.10–11, discussing comparison as a feature of forensic argument in cases in which different persons may be claimed to be guilty of a crime, he suggests that

> we compare [*comparatio est*] characters, motives and other circumstances. . . . There is also a different form of comparison [*comparationis genus*], which comes into play when both parties claim the credit of some act, and yet another kind, when the question is not as between two persons, but as between two acts.
>
> 7.2.22: Further, such cases [where two people accuse one another of the same crime] consist of comparison [*comparatione*], which may be effected in different ways. For we may either compare our case in its entirety with that of our adversary, or we may compare individual arguments. . . .
>
> 7.2.25: Now just as in cases of mutual accusation where each party

shifts the guilt to his opponent, so in this case [where two people claim the reward for slaying a tyrant] we compare the characters, motives, means, opportunities, instruments and evidence of the persons who claim the reward. 26–27 [in the case where it is the action, not the actor, which is in question]: Does not the whole suit consist of comparison of the two cases and of two different and opposite sets of conjectures?

In a case for the defense, one might argue (7.4.12):

Under the same heading as the appeal to public or personal interest comes the plea that the act in question prevented the occurrence of some-thing worse. For in a comparison of evils [*comparatione malorum*] the lesser evil must be regarded as a positive good. . . . This form of defence is called ἀντίστασις [*antistasis*] by the Greeks, while we style it defence by comparison [*comparativum nostri vocant*].

In some legally complex cases, *Inst.* 7.6.2 suggests that

when two laws clash, they may be of a similar nature, as for instance if we have to compare two cases in which a tyrannicide and a brave man are given a choice of their reward, both being granted the privilege of choosing whatever they desire. In such a case we compare the deserts of the claimants, the occasions of the respective acts and the nature of the re-wards claimed.

In brief, then, Quintilian recognizes a wide variety of circumstances in which rhetorical comparison is a necessary and an effective tool.

Hermogenes of Tarsus, writing in the second century C.E., deals with the topic of comparison in two contexts: first, as a means of amplification within other top-ics; and, second, as a topic in its own right. First, under the topic of "Common-places," he says:

The so-called Commonplace is the amplification of a thing admitted, of demonstrations already made. For in this we are no longer investigating whether so-and-so was a robber of temples, . . . but how we shall amplify the demonstrated fact. . . . The procedure must be as follows: (1) analysis of the contrary, (2) the deed itself, (3) comparison [*synkrisis*]—Next go on to comparison. "He is more dangerous than murderers. . . . [T]hey have presumed against human life, but he has outraged the gods. He is like despots, not like them all, but like the most dangerous. For in them it ap-pears most shocking that they lay hands on what has been dedicated to the gods." And you will bring into the denunciation comparisons with the lesser, since they are destructive. "Is it not shocking to punish the thief, but not the temple-robber?"[43]

Clearly this relates to comparative illustrations of the kind discussed in such detail by Cicero as particularly appropriate in forensic speeches. Second, in the section on encomia, having listed the common topics for an encomium, he comments:

> But the greatest opportunity in encomia [of people] is through comparisons, which you will draw as the occasion may suggest. . . . [With animals] you will use throughout such comparisons as fall in with these topics. . . . [With plants] comparisons you will lay hold of everywhere.[44]

On the exercise of comparison itself, he writes:

> Comparison has been included both under *commonplace* as a means of our amplifying misdeeds, and also under *encomium* as a means of amplifying good deeds, and finally has been included as having the same force in censure. But since some [authors] of no small reputation have made it an exercise by itself, we must speak of it briefly. It proceeds, then, by the encomiastic topics; for we compare city with city as to the men who came from them, race with race, nurture with nurture, pursuits, affairs, external relations, and the manner of death and what follows. Likewise if you compare plants, you will set over against one another the gods who give them, the cultivation, the use of their fruits, etc. Likewise also if you compare things done, you will tell who first undertook them, and will compare with one another those who pursued them as to qualities of soul and body. Let the same principle be accepted for all.
>
> Now sometimes we draw our comparisons in terms of equality, showing the things we compare as being equal either in all respects or in several; sometimes we put the one ahead, praising also the other to which we prefer it; sometimes we blame the one utterly, and praise the other, as in comparisons of wealth and justice. There is even comparison with the better, where the task is to show the less to be equal to the greater, as in the comparison of Heracles with Odysseus. But such comparison demands a powerful orator and a vivid style; and the working out always needs vivacity because of the need to make the transitions swift.[45]

Hermogenes also deals briefly with the "comparative (συγκριτικόν, *synkritikon*) mode" of writing a narrative in his *Progymnasmata*, section 2. "The comparative is as follows: 'Medea, daughter of Æetes, instead of ruling her spirit, was enamored; instead of guarding the golden fleece, betrayed it; instead of saving her brother Absyrtus, slew him.'"[46]

Menander Rhetor of Laodicea wrote two treatises on rhetoric before or around 300 C.E.,[47] in which both the concept of comparison and the terms are used regularly. For example, in his section on praising cities, Menander advises that "if the place is hot, one should enumerate the evils of cold places, and if it is cold, the evils of hot places" (1.337.31–32): the comparison is implicit. In section II.380.9ff., however, discussing a speech to honor the arrival of a new governor, he suggests:

[W]e cannot adduce comparisons [συγκρίσεις, *synkriseis*] for the actions, because no actions by the governor have yet been seen, we compare his family to some lineage of great repute, the Heraclids or the Aeacids. In the section on virtues, however, we make no comparisons [οὐ συγκρίνο-μεν, *ou synkrinomen*]: how can we, when nothing has yet happened? We shall however adduce parallels [συγκρίναιμεν, *synkrinaimen*] by a device of technique.

And again, at sections II.380.25 and II.381.5: "The following is the manner of constructing comparisons [συγκρίσεις, *synkriseis*] relating to the subject as a whole. . . . You will then be able to mention demigods and generals in the comparison, seeing that you are here comparing all the virtues together."

The epilogue follows immediately. If the governor has been in office for some time, then one has wider play; comparisons again are undertaken for each virtue separately, and then in general (II.381.29–32). When one makes a speech for one's own arrival in a city (II.383.13ff.),

having described beauties of plains, rivers, harbours, mountains; in regard to the sea, say how convenient it is for visitors and by what seas it is washed—here there should be a description of the sea; in the section on climate, you should show that it is healthy. Under each of these heads, you should adduce a comparison. This may be of country against country. . . . In regard to climate, the comparison should be with Athens or Ionia.

When discussing the four cardinal virtues (II.386.10–22), the speaker

should work up individual συγκρίσεις [*synkriseis*] for each of the virtues, followed by an over-all σύγκρισις [*synkrisis*] of city with city, taking in everything, including the preceding sections (nature, nurture, accomplishments, actions). Wherever you find the city which is your subject to be on equal or superior terms, you should set out the contrast [ἀντεξετάσεις, *antexetaseis*] in your σύγκρισις [*synkrisis*]; where it is inferior, however, this is something you ought to pass over quickly. . . . After the σύγκρισις [*synkrisis*] should come the epilogue.

In the case of epithalamia, wedding speeches, Menander notes (II.402.21) that

After the passage on marriage, in which you have hymned the god, you will come to the encomium of those contracting the marriage. . . . You may link family with family, not making a comparative evaluation [οὐ συγκρίνων, *ou synkrinōn*], so as not to appear to disparage one family or overvalue the other, but none the less proceeding by a method of comparison [ἀντεξέτασιν, *antexetasin*], since like is being linked with like. . . . Alternatively, you may avoid both linking and the comparative method [οὐ συνάψεις μὲν οὐδ᾽ ἀντεξετάσεις, *ou synapseis men oud' antexetaseis*], but praise separately first the bridegroom's family, as it may be, and secondly the girl's.

Later (II.404.2ff.), discussing the bride and groom, he uses the term ἀντεξέτασις (*antexetasis*) in a different sense:

One can praise the couple by separating the praises of the two and keeping them distinct, though beauty must always be treated as regards both of them, in the form of a comparison [κατὰ ἀντεξέτασιν, *kata antexetasin*]: "Is she not like the olive, most beautiful of plants, and he like the palm?"

Even in birthday speeches (II.412.16ff.), during the encomium, comparison is appropriate: "With each of these headings, as I have often said, you should include a σύγκρισις [*synkrisis*]; and finally, after the individual comparisons that accompany the separate headings, there should come a comparison applying to the whole subject."

Once again, in speeches addressed to governors (II.416–17),

it is good craftsmanship to add appropriate συγκρίσεις [*synkriseis*] to each division of virtue, so that the speech acquires thereby a greater number of amplifications. . . . Proceed next to temperance. Here you should speak of his self-restraint in pleasures and laughter. Diomedes may be introduced πρὸς τὴν σύγκρισιν [*pros tēn synkrisin*], by way of comparison. . . . Courage should be admired on the ground of the governor's frankness to the emperors, his struggle against unpleasant circumstances for his subjects' sake, and his not bowing the knee or giving way in the face of fears. Here come the Ajaxes, Pericles, Alcibiades, and the like. You should not, however, dwell on these or go into them in detail. This belongs to the full encomium. . . . after the virtues, proceed to the σύγκρισις [*synkrisis*]. Over-all comparisons [τὸ συγκρίνειν, *to synkrinein*] and separate ones are distinct. An instance of a separate comparison is when we compare [συγκρίνωμεν, *synkrinōmen*] justice with justice, wisdom with wisdom. An over-all comparison is when we compare one whole tenure of office with another. . . . After all this, you will come to construct the epilogue.[48]

Likewise in the roughly contemporary work attributed to Dionysius of Halicarnassus, "On Epideictic Speeches,"[49] we find detailed instructions for speechwriters on how to make use of comparisons. When speaking at festivals (258), "institute a comparison with other games" (cf. 289); "[n]or will a comparison between the garland and those used elsewhere fail to confer prestige" (259). In section 260 we are advised that "one must in fact adopt a style that follows the lead of the thought, by treating narrative passages or those relating to myths with simplicity [ἀφελῶς, *aphelōs*], anything concerning emperors or gods with grandeur [σεμνῶς, *semnōs*], and anything involving contrasts or comparisons [παραβολῶν καὶ συγκρίσεων, *parabolōn kai synkriseōn*] in the style of public rhetoric [πολιτικῶς, *politikōs*],"[50] that is, in deliberative style. The author gives further instructions for use of comparison in birthday speeches (266) and speeches to governors (275).

Comparison, in various forms, was a topic dealt with in detail across the spectrum of rhetorical writing. It was both discussed in theory, and widely practiced. As far as the theoreticians were concerned, it was a crucial preliminary exercise, and as the student progressed could be used to amplify material in encomium and invective. Related to this was comparison's role in judicial speeches, whether for the prosecution or for the defense. Finally, the comparison of alternatives was an important aspect of deliberative speeches, as the comparative benefits of differing policies had to be evaluated. Some writers used the Greek term παραβάλλω [*paraballō*], others συγκρίνω [*synkrinō*], while in Latin a variety of terms were used. In Greek writers, the terms denoted primarily developed rhetorical comparisons. In Latin, the terminology was more diffuse, with meanings ranging from simple metaphor through comparative illustrations to developed comparison. The phenomenon of rhetorical comparison could occur, however, either with or without the use of the terminology.

Various scholars have raised doubts about the methodological validity of using information from technical rhetorical manuals, and about using Latin writers, neither of which Paul may have read, to illuminate the Pauline letters. It has also been pointed out that many of the technical manuals postdate Paul.[51] The criticism clearly has its point, though the deep conservatism of the rhetorical tradition strongly suggests that the later material has earlier roots, as I have suggested particularly for Cicero's discussion in his *Topica,* above. I have attempted here, however, to demonstrate that the broad convention of rhetorical comparison was so well-known and widespread in both the rhetorical tradition and in the wider literary culture, that it would be remarkable if Paul were *not* aware of it.

Part II. Rhetorical Comparison in the Pauline Letters

To what degree ought we to expect Paul's letters to evince ancient rhetorical forms, when ancient rhetoric's categories developed out of the analysis of oratory, not letter-writing? This difficult question has been examined by a number of recent writers.[52] Doubtless any number of reasonable analyses of rhetoric could be applied to the Pauline letters, and yield hermeneutically interesting results. But would such results resemble anything that Paul himself, or his first audience, might have recognized?[53]

My own suggestion is as follows. Paul is not, in Greco-Roman terms, a "man of letters" (ἀνὴρ λόγιος, *anēr logios*, Acts 18:24). It seems very unlikely that his formal education extended to the upper levels. Paul was, however, a highly experienced speaker and, from what we can tell, in his own time and place a persuasive one. He may or may not have had formal rhetorical training, but he knew from observation and experience what styles of argument would, and would not, hold the attention of his target audience. Arguments that his letters ought to be expected to conform more to epistolary than to rhetorical conventions have this weakness: Paul was not writing letters to individuals, to be read at their leisure.[54] He was writing letters to Christian assemblies, where his letter would be read aloud, often in quite polemical situations.[55] I know of no discussion of such letters in any Greco-Roman epistolary theorist.[56] Further, ancient oratorical conventions were far more accessible to the casual observer than were epistolary conventions, by the very fact that oratory was a prominent feature of public life.

We ought not look in Paul's letters for the elegance of the litterateur, or the tightly woven rhetoric of the trained and elegant Greco-Roman orator. At least in the Corinthian correspondence he claimed that he deliberately avoided such a style, though apparently even some of his opponents in Corinth found his letters impressive (2 Cor 10:10). But we are justified in looking for rhetorical patterns that were widely known and acceptable within his cultural environment. Further, in the specific case of rhetorical comparisons we can be confident that Paul was fully aware of the convention.

Rhetorical comparisons in the broad sense are quite common in Paul, though they are rarely fully developed in rhetorical terms. We identify them by their context, their formal characteristics, their function, and sometimes via technical vocabulary. In Rom 2:12–3:20, he compares the relative positions of Jews and Gentiles under the judgment of God. In Rom 5:12–17, he compares the "two Adams" and the very different results of their actions;[57] in Rom 8:18, he denies the comparability of the sufferings of the present with the coming glory. In 1 Cor 1–2, he compares the "wisdom of the world" (with its "persuasive words") with "God's secret wisdom"; in 1 Cor 4:1–13, Paul satirically compares the social situation of the apostles with that of the Corinthians; in 1 Cor 7:32–34, he compares marriage to celibacy. In 1 Cor 11:4–11, he compares "proper" male and female hairstyles, in 1 Cor 13 he compares the effects of the use of various χαρίσματα (*charismata*) with and without love, and in 1 Cor 14:2–25 he compares intelligible and unintelligible inspired speech. In 2 Cor 3:7–18, Paul compares the two ministries of the old and the new covenants. Most strikingly and explicitly, in 2 Cor 11:21b–12:13 Paul compares himself, with fierce irony, with the Corinthian "super-apostles." In Gal 3:15–4:11, Paul argues from the lesser to the greater, which presumes some degree of comparability between "the Law" and "the Promise," rather than developing it as a theme.[58] However, Paul only uses the technical term for rhetorical comparison, σύγκρισις (*synkrisis*), twice: once in the above-mentioned 2 Cor 10:12, and once in 1 Cor 2:13, where its meaning is not at all clear, and probably not related to rhetorical concerns.

Given the relative wealth of material in the Pauline corpus, it is surprising how little systematic scholarly discussion has been generated on the topic.[59] The four most recent major treatments of the subject of Paul's use of rhetorical models, though they touch briefly on aspects of the subject of comparison, do little to advance our understanding of it.[60] To complete this discussion, then, I examine a number of Pauline passages in more detail.

Romans 2:6–3:20. The exegetical complexities of the first few chapters of Romans are well known, and any attempt to survey the debate in a systematic way would take us far beyond the boundaries of this study. I will therefore adopt a reasonably mainstream interpretation, and focus on the ways that recognition of the rhetorical comparison in the text might be fruitful for that interpretation.[61] In Rom 2:11–3:20, Paul compares the relative positions of a theoretical Jewish interlocutor, and Gentiles of various kinds, under the judgment of God. His comparative evaluation starts with the implied rhetorical premise that the Jew has great advantages, but goes on to subvert much of that premise.

The previous section, verses 6–10, built a case with which many, both Jews and Gentiles, would have felt compelled to agree: that "God shows no partiality"[62] (v. 11). For Paul, however, it was still true that God's dealings are with "the Jew first, and also the Greek" (vv. 9, 10). This double focus structures the remainder of the section.

In verse 12, Paul formulates his first deduction from the premise of divine impartiality: All who sin ἀνόμως (*anomōs*) will also perish ἀνόμως (*anomōs*), and all who sin under the law will be judged by the law.[63] The σύγκρισις (*synkrisis*) has begun. The common Jewish preconception that their access to the Law of Moses would be an advantage on the day of judgment is given an uncharacteristic but thoroughly Jewish critique: it is obedience to the Law, not merely access to it, that is required.[64] Thus, Paul argues, one commonly understood comparative advantage of "the Jew" over "the Greek" may be illusory. *At least* theoretically, Gentiles might keep those aspects of the Law that were required of them.[65] Furthermore, in so doing they would demonstrate that the requirements of Law were "written on their hearts." With this formulation Paul is preparing to undercut the standard ethnic ("outward") definition of Jewish identity, though that section of his argument will have to wait for verses 28–29. This preliminary section ends with the cautious statement of verses 15–16. Despite the indictment of Rom 1:18–32, Jews might find themselves standing on equal terms with some Gentiles in the Day of the Lord. Contrary to their expectations, their Jewishness might be of no advantage to them.

Paul now turns to the (apparent) advantages of "the Jew." He formulates his case, using well-known rhetorical conventions, addressing a theoretical Jewish opponent.[66] A difficult question arises: what kind of Jew, or Jews, is Paul presenting and engaging here? It has often been taken for granted that the passage is intended to represent Jews in general, or even (anachronistically) typical rabbinic Jews. But the context requires that Paul present a type of Jew known to his Roman audience, and his expression in the passage (he addresses *a* Jew, in the singular) suggests that a particular type of Jew, not all Jews in general, is what he has in mind. At the least it seems clear that he is representing a type of Diaspora Jew, not a Judean Jew. In all likelihood he means to portray (or perhaps caricature?) a kind of Judaism that his audience will recognize, and will perhaps have found attractive, or even have been identified with. His rhetorical opponent, he suggests, relies on the Law and "boasts in God." Paul's response to such a person falls into two parts. First, in parallel with his critique of Greco-Roman society in chapter 1, he proposes that this kind of Jew may have characteristic moral faults as well.

> [21] you, then, who teach others, do you not teach yourself? You who preach against stealing, do you steal? [22] You who say that people should not commit adultery, do you commit adultery? You who abhor idols, do you rob temples [or: act sacrilegiously]? [23] You who brag about the law, do you dishonor God by breaking the law? [24] As it is written, "God's name is blasphemed among the Gentiles because of you."

Second, and consequentially, he argues in verses 25–29 that, because law-breaking of one kind or another is so common, it actually undermines the simple distinction between Jew and Gentile. A Gentile may be, in effect, more "Jewish," that is, Law-abiding, than his hypothetical Jewish opponent.

> [27] The one who is not circumcised physically and yet obeys the law will condemn you who, even though you have the written code and circumcision, are a lawbreaker. [28] A man is not a Jew if he is [only] one outwardly, nor is circumcision [merely] outward and physical. [29] No, a man is a Jew if he is one inwardly; and circumcision is circumcision of the heart, by the Spirit, not by the written code. Such a man's praise is not from men, but from God.

The privileges of Jewish identity, then, may be of no avail. Gentiles and Jews seem to stand on the one level before the judgment of God. Unexpectedly, the balance of the σύγκρισις (*synkrisis*) has come out even.

In chapter 3, Paul's hypothetical Jewish interlocutor poses the question: is Jewish identity, then, of no value? On the contrary, argues Paul: Jews have had, and continue to have, the benefit of the Law and the faithfulness of God to the promises. (This theme is taken up again in Rom 9.)

[3:1] What advantage, then, is there in being a Jew, or what value is there in circumcision? [2] Much in every way! First of all, they have been entrusted with the very words of God. [3] What if some of them did not have faith? Will their lack of faith nullify God's faithfulness? [4] Not at all! Let God be true, and every man a liar . . .

The relationship between verses 1–4 and verses 5–8 is unclear: who, in Paul's argument, makes the claim that is rejected in verse 6? It may be that verse 5 is the interlocutor's response to Paul's claim that "the Jew" has no advantage from his ethnic heritage at the day of judgment.

[5] But if our unrighteousness brings out God's righteousness more clearly, what shall we say? That God is unjust in bringing his wrath on us? (I am using a human argument.) [6] Certainly not! If that were so, how could God judge the world? [7] Someone might argue: "If my falsehood enhances God's truthfulness and so increases his glory, why am I still condemned as a sinner?" [8] Why not say, as we are being slanderously reported and as some claim that we say, "Let us do evil that good may result"? Their condemnation is deserved.

But in 3.9ff., Paul argues, with biblical citations, that "we" are as much under sin as the Gentiles: no one will be declared righteous by works of the Law. In this regard both Jews and Gentiles are on an even footing, despite what might appear.

[9] What shall we conclude then? Are we/they any better? Not at all![67] We have already made the charge that Jews and Gentiles alike are all under sin. [10] As it is written: . . . [19] Now we know that whatever the law says, it says to those who are under the law, so that every mouth may be silenced and the whole world made accountable to God. [20] Therefore no one will be declared righteous in his sight by works of the law; rather, through the law we become conscious of sin.

Paul's rhetorically imagined Jewish interlocutor, then, claims a privileged position for Jews before the judgment of God. Paul counters that the shared premise of God's impartiality necessitates a different view. Despite the great privileges of his ancestral covenant, which he does not deny, Paul's Jew (and indeed, all Jews, 3:19–20) still stands unable to be justified by "works of the Law." The Jews' privileges, though real, are irrelevant, as (1) "all, both Jews and Greeks, are under the power of sin" (v. 9); "no one will be declared righteous in his sight by works of the law" (v. 20), and (2) the true definition of Judaism is not ethnic: "a person is not a Jew who is one outwardly" (2:28). Paul's σύγκρισις (synkrisis), then, tends to equality despite the covenantal advantages of "the Jew."

Romans 5:12–21. In this passage Paul compares the effects of the actions of the "two Adams" on the conditions of human existence.[68] However, the comparison is not simply between Adam and Christ.[69] It is formulated in terms of the very different results of their actions.

> [15] But the gift is not like the trespass. For if the many died by the trespass of the one man, how much more did God's grace and the gift that came by the grace of the one man, Jesus Christ, overflow to the many! [16] Again, the gift of God is not like the result of the one man's sin: the judgment followed one sin and brought condemnation, but the gift followed many trespasses and brought justification. [17] For if, by the trespass of the one man, death reigned through that one man, how much more will those who receive God's abundant provision of grace and of the gift of righteousness reign in life through one man, Jesus Christ.

Comparability is found in the effects on wider humanity of the actions of each "man." But comparability is not equivalence.[70] Paul's comparison is obviously designed to point out that "the gift is *not* like the trespass," or its results, in all ways. Its effects were far greater. Sin increased, but grace increased even more. The comparison closely follows the pattern of Hermogenes' "comparative narration," discussed above.

1 Corinthians 4:1–13. In 1 Cor 4:1–13, Paul satirically compares the social situation of the apostles with that of the Corinthians.[71] Verses 1–7, and particularly 6b–7, set up the comparison:

> [6] Now, brothers, I have applied these things to myself and Apollos for your benefit, so that you may learn from us the meaning of the saying, "Do not go beyond what is written."[72] Then you will not take pride in one man over against another. [7] For what makes you different from anyone else? What do you have that you did not receive? And if you did receive it, why do you boast as if you did not?

Now begins the *synkrisis* proper:

> [8] Already you have all you want! Already you have become rich! You have become kings, and that without us! How I wish that you really had become kings, so that we might be kings with you! [9] For it seems to me that God has put us apostles on display at the end of the procession, like men condemned to die in the arena. We have been made a spectacle to the whole universe, to angels as well as to men.

Having compared the Corinthians and the apostles in broad terms, he moves to a sharp, point-for-point comparison:

> [10] We are fools for Christ, but you are so wise in Christ! We are weak, but you are strong! You are honored, we are dishonored! [11] To this very hour we go hungry and thirsty, we are in rags, we are brutally treated, we are

homeless. [12] We work hard with our own hands. When we are cursed, we bless; when we are persecuted, we endure it; [13] when we are slandered, we answer kindly. Up to this moment we have become the scum of the earth, the refuse of the world. [14] I am not writing this to shame you, but to warn you, as my dear children. [15] Even though you have ten thousand guardians in Christ, you do not have many fathers, for in Christ Jesus I became your father through the gospel. [16] Therefore I urge you to imitate me.[73]

As Witherington points out: "[A] synkrisis presupposes that an illustrious person is being held up as an example. The irony here is that Paul is notable for being a leading example of being last or of being a servant."[74]

This irony is crucial. Paul is using comparison as a tool of amplification in an inverted encomium of himself and his companions. He is boasting, with heavy irony, about the hardships and humiliations of his apostolic life. Such humiliations are the last things one would normally want to parade before a status-conscious audience such as the Corinthians. Note also that Paul is not merely boasting of hardships or struggles in a great cause, something a Greco-Roman audience would find perfectly comprehensible.[75] The theme is not the quality of his behavior under hardship, but the hardship and humiliation *itself*, as an indicator, Paul argues, of true apostolic status.[76]

Paul's disclaimer that he is not writing as he does to shame the Corinthians, but to warn them, makes clear that humiliation and anger were a likely response to the intensity of his implied critique of Corinthian values.

2 Corinthians 3:7–18. In this passage Paul compares the two "ministries" of the old and the new covenants.

[7] Now if the ministry that brought death, which was engraved in letters on stone, came with glory, so that the Israelites could not look steadily at the face of Moses because of its glory, fading though it was, [8] will not the ministry of the Spirit be even more glorious? [9] If the ministry that condemns men is glorious, how much more glorious is the ministry that brings righteousness! [10] For what was glorious has no glory now in comparison with [because of?] the surpassing glory. [11] And if what was fading away came with glory, how much greater is the glory of that which lasts!

G. A. Kennedy suggested that this passage "could be described as a synkrisis of Moses and Paul,"[77] but this is mistaken: the comparison here is between ἡ διακονία (*hē diakonia*, the ministry) of "Moses," representative of the "old covenant" as a whole, and ἡ διακονία (*hē diakonia*) of "we all" (3:18), that is, Christians. Ben Witherington aptly comments that Paul "begins his defense with a comparison. It was not uncommon in forensic rhetoric for a comparison 'to rise from the lesser to the greater, since by raising what is below it must necessarily exalt what is above' (*Inst. Or.* 8.4.9.)."[78] Witherington writes:

> It is often suggested that Paul is using a traditional form of Jewish argument, the *qal wāyyomer* [sic], that is, from the lesser to the greater. This form of argument is not from the bad to the good, but from the lesser good to the greater good. This Jewish background may be present, but as we have seen Quintilian also says that one should argue from the lesser to the greater when making a rhetorical comparison where one member of the two is to be preferred to the other.[79]

As I commented (n. 13 above), in no way should these two argumentative styles, Jewish and Greco-Roman, be seen as exclusive alternatives; rather, they go hand in hand.

2 Corinthians 11:21b–12:13. Since Peter Marshall and I identified 2 Cor 11:21b–12:13 as an elaborate parody of the conventions of comparison,[80] it has been widely accepted that the passage is a clear case of σύγκρισις (*synkrisis*).[81] Paul compares himself, with fierce irony, with the boastful claims of the Corinthian "super-apostles"; it is no coincidence that this, his most rhetorically developed comparison, is to be found in a parody of epideictic style and conventions. In 2 Cor 10:12, he tells us explicitly that his opponents in Corinth have been making rhetorical comparisons as a form of "self-commendation" (ἑαυτοὺς συνιστάνων, *heautous synistanōn*). He ironically comments: "We are not being so bold as to rank ourselves, or invite comparison, with certain people who write their own references."[82] He next derides the practice of such comparisons as lacking understanding, and then, in 11:16ff., takes on the persona of a fool in order to indulge ironically in precisely the same kind of boasting. As Ben Witherington points out, this comparison is not an isolated one:

> The argument section of 2 Corinthians began with a masterful comparison of the ministries of Paul and Moses (ch. 3), and now Paul closes it with an even more extended *synkrisis* comparing his and his opponents' ministries. The earlier comparison prepares for and points forward to the later one.[83]

But the difference is that this comparison is itself a biting parody of comparison. This point tends to be weakened by those who argue that Paul is seriously comparing his apostolic sufferings with the missionary sufferings of which, it is presumed, the "super-apostles" also boasted.[84] While it was certainly possible for a Greco-Roman orator to boast of the hardships and sufferings he had undergone in a great cause, I see no clear evidence that the "super-apostles" had been doing so. Paul does not boast to compete on agreed terms: he boasts "like a fool," of all the wrong things, (1) in order to subvert and ridicule self-commendatory boasting altogether, and (2) to reshape the Corinthian evaluation of status and humiliation. Further, as in the case of 1 Cor 4, above, Paul does not boast of his *endurance* of sufferings for the cause, but of the sufferings and humiliation themselves, "so that Christ's power may rest on me. That is why, for Christ's sake, I delight in weaknesses, in insults, in hardships, in persecutions, in difficulties. For when I am weak, then I am strong" (2 Cor 12:10).

Galatians 4:21–31. Study of Paul's allegorical interpretation of Gen 16 and 21 in Galatians has rightly focused heavily on the questions of (1) whether the argument is merely an afterthought to Paul's main argument, or the climax (thus Betz); (2) the probable prior use of the story by Paul's opponents; and (3) the nature of the allegorical reading by which Paul hopes to turn the tables on them.[85] Commentators such as Dunn have described the passage as "a sequence of antithetical correspondences . . . though this applies primarily to the comparison of the two women in the first part (verses 22–27)."[86] As far as I am aware, however, no commentator has noted that the passage is structured as a σύγκρισις (*synkrisis*) between the two forms of early Christianity metaphorically presented as the "two sons of Abraham."

> Tell me, you who want to be under the law, are you not aware of what the law says? [22] For it is written that Abraham had two sons, one by the slave woman and one by the free woman. . . . [25] Now Hagar stands for Mount Sinai in Arabia and corresponds to / stands in parallel with [συστοιχεῖ, *systoichei*] the present city of Jerusalem, because she is in slavery with her children. [26] But the Jerusalem that is above is free, and she is our mother. . . . [31] Therefore, brothers, we are not children of the slave woman, but of the free woman.

Notice that in verse 25 Paul describes Hagar/Mount Sinai as "standing in parallel" (συστοιχεῖ, *systoichei*) with "the present city of Jerusalem."[87] The term is used in Aristotle, *Rhet.* I.7.26–28, as follows: in comparative evaluations, comparing greater and lesser goods,

> Things that last longer are preferable to those that are of shorter duration, and those that are safer to those that are less so; for time increases the use of the first and the wish that of the second; for whenever we wish, we can make greater use of the things that are safe. And things in all cases follow the relations between co-ordinates [ἐκ τῶν συστοίχων, *ek tōn systoichōn*] and similar inflexions; for instance, if "courageously" is nobler than and preferable to "temperately," then "courage" is preferable to "temperance," and it is better to be "courageous" than "temperate." And that which is chosen by all is better than that which is not; and that which the majority choose than that which the minority choose. . . .

The term is also used in an anonymous *Art of Rhetoric,* dated to the third century C.E. Following Aristotle's analysis, the author deals with parallelism, giving cases of parallel verbal forms, or what we would call "cognate terms": "*Systoichia* [parallelism] shows commonality between actions, things or words. For example [in the case of words], we speak of the terms 'thought' and 'the thoughtful man' as being in parallel with each other."[88]

In the case of Galatians, a comparison is being made between two sets of parallel concepts. On the one hand a parallel is being drawn between Hagar/Sinai in Arabia and "the present city of Jerusalem" as the "mother" of one form of Christianity. On the other hand a parallel is implicitly drawn between Sarah and the "Jerusalem above." This rhetorical parallelism informs the basic allegorical structure of the passage. These two sets of parallel symbolic structures are then compared. The Sarah/"Jerusalem above" complex is presented as superior on two grounds: it is associated with freedom rather than slavery, and with "the promise" rather than descent "according to the flesh" (4:23). As a result the Galatians are urged not to fall back under "a yoke of slavery" (5:1).

We have seen in these examples that Paul is well-aware of the potential of rhetorical comparison. He makes forceful use of comparative structures of argument at several points in his letters. Some of these comparisons are of a theological kind (Romans, Galatians); others are more directly pastoral/personal (1 Cor 4). He had been on the "receiving end" of hostile rhetorical comparisons, and responded, in 2 Cor 10:9ff., with stinging irony. He rarely uses comparisons as ornamental flourishes. Rather, his use of σύγκρισις (*synkrisis*) is normally subservient to the purpose of his argument. Paul is not comfortable with the self-conscious use of rhetorical artistry (1 Cor 2:1–5), and will not be drawn into comparisons between people without considerable provocation, and even then only with strong (and usually ironic) reservations. All of this might be viewed as the natural eloquence of an able but untrained speaker. However, the precision and rhetorical skill Paul displays, particularly in 1 Cor 4 and in his parody of comparative self-recommendation in 2 Cor 10–12, suggests to me that his comments on his own rhetorical abilities in 2 Cor 11:6 ought not to be taken seriously. Self-deprecation in such matters was a well-recognized rhetorical form itself, as (for example) Dio Chrysostom's Oration 32.39 demonstrates.

Part III. Other Pauline and Paulinist Passages

1 Cor 1–2: Paul compares the "wisdom of the world" (with its "persuasive words") with "God's secret wisdom."

1 Cor 7:32–34: marriage to celibacy.

1 Cor 11:4–11: "proper" male and female hairstyles.

1 Cor 13: the effects of the use of various χαρίσματα (*charismata*) with and without love.

1 Cor 14:2–25 (closely related): intelligible and unintelligible inspired speech.

1 Cor 15:35ff.: different kinds of bodies.

2 Cor 5:1–4: earthly and eschatological bodies.

Gal 3:23–4:1–9: the era of the Law with the era of faith.

Gal 5:19ff.: the works of the flesh and the fruit of the Spirit.

Phil 3:4: "reasons to put confidence in the flesh" and "knowing Christ Jesus."

Col 2:8ff.: "hollow and deceptive philosophy" and "the fullness in Christ."

1 Thess 5:1ff. He compares the "children of the day" with "those who belong to darkness."

Part IV. Bibliography

Classical Studies

Anderson, R. Dean. *Glossary of Greek Rhetorical Terms*. Louvain: Peeters, 2000.

Baldwin, C. S. *Medieval Rhetoric and Poetic*. New York: Macmillan, 1928.

Burgess, T. C. *Epideictic Literature*. Chicago: University of Chicago Press, 1902.

Butts, J. R. *The Progymnasmata of Theon*. Ph.D. diss., Claremont Graduate School, 1987.

Gascó, F. "Menander Rhetor and the Works Attributed to Him." Pages 3110–46 in *ANRW* II.34.4. Berlin: de Gruyter, 1998.

Kennedy, G. A. *The Art of Rhetoric in the Roman World*. Princeton, N.J.: Princeton University Press, 1972.

———. *Greek Rhetoric under Christian Emperors*. Princeton, N.J.: Princeton University Press, 1983.

———. "Historical Survey of Rhetoric." Pages 3–50 in *Handbook of Classical Rhetoric in the Hellenistic Period*. Edited by S. E. Porter. Leiden: Brill, 1997.

———. *New Testament Interpretation through Rhetorical Criticism*. Chapel Hill: University of North Carolina Press, 1984.

Larmour, D. H. J. "Making Parallels: *Synkrisis* in Plutarch's 'Themistocles and Camillus.'" Pages 4154–74 in *ANRW* II.33.6. Berlin: de Gruyter, 1992.

Lausberg, H. *Handbook of Literary Rhetoric*. Edited by D. E. Orton and R. D. Anderson. Leiden: Brill, 1998.

McCall, M. H., Jr. *Ancient Rhetorical Theories of Simile and Comparison*. Cambridge: Harvard University Press, 1969.

Malherbe, A. J. *Ancient Epistolary Theorists*. Atlanta: Scholars Press, 1988.

Martin, H. M. "Plutarch." Pages 715–36 in *Handbook of Classical Rhetoric in the Hellenistic Period*. Edited by S. E. Porter. Leiden: Brill, 1997.

Porter, S. E., ed. *Handbook of Classical Rhetoric in the Hellenistic Period*. Leiden: Brill, 1997.

Roberts, W. Rhys. "Caecilius of Calacte." *AJP* 18 (1897): 302–12.

———, ed. *Dionysius of Halicarnassus, the Three Literary Letters*. Cambridge: Cambridge University Press, 1901.

Russell, D. A. *Greek Declamation*. Cambridge: Cambridge University Press, 1983.

Russell, D. A., and N. G. Wilson. *Menander Rhetor*. Oxford: Clarendon, 1981.

Spengel, L. *Rhetores Graeci*. 3 vols. Leipzig: Teubner, 1853–56.

Usener, H., and L. Radermacher, eds. *Dionysios von Halikarnassos, Opuscula*. Leipzig: Teubner, 1899–1929.

New Testament Studies

Aletti, Jean-Noël. "The Rhetoric of Romans 5–8." Pages 294–308 in *The Rhetorical Analysis of Scripture,* edited by S. E. Porter and T. H. Olbricht. Sheffield, England: Sheffield Academic Press, 1997.

Amador, J. D. H. "Revisiting 2 Corinthians: Rhetoric and the Case for Unity." *NTS* 46 (2000): 92–111.

Anderson, R. Dean. *Ancient Rhetorical Theory and Paul*. 2d ed. Louvain: Peeters, 1999.

Aune, D. E. *The New Testament in Its Literary Environment*. Philadelphia: Westminster Press, 1987.

Basevi, C., and J. Chapa. "Philippians 2:6–11: the Rhetorical Function of a Pauline 'Hymn.'" Pages 338–56 in *Rhetoric and the New Testament,* edited by S. E. Porter and T. H. Olbricht. Sheffield, England: Sheffield Academic Press, 1993.

Betz, H. D. *Galatians: A Commentary on Paul's Letter to the Churches in Galatia*. Hermeneia. Philadelphia: Fortress Press, 1979.

Botha, P. "The Verbal Art of the Pauline Letters: Rhetoric, Performance, and Presence." Pages 409–28 in *Rhetoric and the New Testament,* edited by S. E. Porter and T. H. Olbricht. Sheffield, England: Sheffield Academic Press, 1993.

Classen, C. J. "St. Paul's Epistles and Ancient Greek and Roman Rhetoric." Pages 265–91 in *Rhetoric and the New Testament,* edited by S. E. Porter and T. H. Olbricht. Sheffield, England: Sheffield Academic Press, 1993.

Donfried, K. P., and J. Beutler, eds. *The Thessalonian Debate: Methodological Discord or Methodological Synthesis?* Grand Rapids: Eerdmans, 2000.

Fitzgerald, J. T. *Cracks in an Earthen Vessel*. Atlanta: Scholars Press, 1988.

Forbes, C. B. "Comparison, Self-Praise, and Irony: Paul's Boasting and the Conventions of Hellenistic Rhetoric." *NTS* 32 (1986): 1–30.

Harding, M. *Tradition and Rhetoric in the Pastoral Epistles*. New York: Peter Lang, 1998.

———. *What Are They Saying about the Pastoral Epistles?* Mahwah, N.J.: Paulist Press, 2001.

Hughes, F. W. "The Rhetoric of Letters" and "The Social Situations Implied by Rhetoric." Pages 194–240 and 241–54 in *The Thessalonian Debate: Methodological Discord or Methodological Synthesis?* edited by K. P. Donfried and J. Beutler. Grand Rapids: Eerdmans, 2000.

Jewett, R. "Following the Argument of Romans." Pages 265–77 in *The Romans Debate*. Rev. ed. Edinburgh: T. & T. Clark, 1991.

———. "Romans as an Ambassadorial Letter." *Int* 36 (1982): 5–20.

Krentz, E. "1 Thessalonians: Rhetorical Flourishes and Formal Constraints." Pages 287–318 in *The Thessalonians Debate: Methodological Discord or Methodological Synthesis?* edited by K. P. Donfried and J. Beutler. Grand Rapids: Eerdmans, 2000.

Marshall, P. *Enmity in Corinth: Social Conventions in Paul's Relations with the Corinthians.* Tübingen: Mohr [Siebeck], 1987.

Mitchell, M. M. *Paul and the Rhetoric of Reconciliation.* Tübingen: Mohr [Siebeck], 1991.

Olbricht, T. H. "An Aristotelian Rhetorical Analysis of 1 Thessalonians." Pages 216–36 in *Greeks, Romans, and Christians,* edited by D. L. Balch et al. Minneapolis: Fortress Press, 1990.

S. E. Porter. "Paul of Tarsus and His Letters." Pages 533–85 in *Handbook of Classical Rhetoric in the Hellenistic Period.* Leiden: Brill, 1997.

———. "The Theoretical Justification for Application of Rhetorical Categories to Pauline Epistolary Literature." Pages 100–122 in *Rhetoric and the New Testament,* edited by S. E. Porter and T. H. Olbricht. Sheffield, England: Sheffield Academic Press, 1993.

Porter, S. E., and T. H. Olbricht, eds. *Rhetoric and the New Testament.* Sheffield, England: Sheffield Academic Press, 1993.

———. *The Rhetorical Analysis of Scripture.* Sheffield, England: Sheffield Academic Press, 1997.

Reid, J. T. "Using Ancient Rhetorical Categories to Interpret Paul's Letters: A Question of Genre." Pages 292–324 in *Rhetoric and the New Testament,* edited by S. E. Porter and T. H. Olbricht. Sheffield, England: Sheffield Academic Press, 1993.

Sampley, J. P. "Paul, His Opponents in 2 Corinthians 10–13, and the Rhetorical Handbooks." Pages 162–77 in *The Social World of Formative Christianity and Judaism,* edited by J. Neusner et al. Philadelphia: Fortress Press, 1988.

Segal, A. F. "Universalism in Judaism and Christianity." Pages 1–29 in *Paul in His Hellenistic Context,* edited by T. Engberg-Pedersen. Edinburgh: T. & T. Clark, 1994.

Smit, J. "Argument and Genre of 1 Corinthians 12–14." Pages 211–30 in *Rhetoric and the New Testament,* edited by S. E. Porter and T. H. Olbricht. Sheffield, England: Sheffield Academic Press, 1993.

Stowers, S. K. *The Diatribe and Paul's Letter to the Romans.* Chico, Calif.: Scholars Press, 1981.

———. *Letter Writing in Greco-Roman Antiquity.* Philadelphia: Westminster, 1986.

———. "Paul's Dialogue with a Fellow Jew in Romans 3:1–9." *CBQ* 46 (1984): 707–22.

———. *A Re-reading of Romans: Justice, Jews, and Gentiles.* New Haven: Yale University Press, 1994.

———. "Romans 7.7–25 as a Speech-in-Character." Pages 180–202 in *Paul in His Hellenistic Context,* edited by T. Engberg-Pedersen. Edinburgh: T. & T. Clark, 1994.

Watson, D. F. "A Rhetorical Analysis of Philippians and Its Implications for the Unity Question." *NovT* 30 (1988): 57–87.

Weima, J. A. D. "The Function of 1 Thessalonians 2:1–12 and the Use of Rhetorical Criticism: A Response to Otto Merk." Pages 114–31 in *The Thessalonians Debate,* edited by K. P. Donfried and J. Beutler. Grand Rapids: Eerdmans, 2000.

Welborn, L. L. "Paul's Appeal to the Emotions in 2 Corinthians 1.1–2.13; 7.5–16." *JSNT* 82 (2001): 31–60.

Witherington, Ben, III. *Conflict and Community in Corinth.* Grand Rapids: Eerdmans, 1994.

Wuellner, W. "The Argumentative Structure of 1 Thessalonians as a Paradoxical Encomium." Pages 117–36 in *The Thessalonian Correspondence,* edited by R. F. Collins. Louvain: Louvain University Press, 1990.

Notes

1. For this sequence of exercises, and more, see Quintilian, *Inst.* 2.4.1–21. Unless otherwise noted, all translations from the ancient sources are taken from the editions of the Loeb Classical Library.

2. For further indirect evidence of the existence of the progymnasmata before the first full extant work, that of Theon, see R. D. Anderson, *Ancient Rhetorical Theory and Paul* (2d ed.; Louvain: Peeters, 1999), 73–75.

3. The English term "comparison" is sufficiently broad to be used as a translation for quite a variety of ancient terms for figures of speech. Throughout this study we are considering not simple comparative figures of speech such as similes and metaphors, but those developed rhetorical comparisons that the ancients termed συγκρίσεις (*synkriseis*), and for the practice of which they used the verbs συγκρίνω (*synkrinō*) and παραβάλλω (*paraballō*). Various forms of similes, metaphors, comparative illustrations and such were known to the ancient rhetorical theorists, though M. H. McCall, Jr. (*Ancient Rhetorical Theories of Simile and Comparison* [Cambridge: Harvard University Press, 1969], chs. 1–2) makes clear that the relation between their terminology and ours is by no means simple. But σύγκρισις (*synkrisis*) and cognates are (as far as I know) never used for simple comparative figures of speech, but only for developed rhetorical comparisons. In Latin the terminology is broader, and *comparatio* is used of both simple comparative figures of speech and full-blown rhetorical comparisons.

4. G. A. Kennedy, "Historical Survey of Rhetoric," in *Handbook of Classical Rhetoric in the Hellenistic Period* (ed. S. E. Porter; Leiden: Brill, 1997), 18–19. Kennedy's judgment on this matter may well modify my earlier claim that "it seems to be extremely unlikely that anyone educated early in the first century would have been taught the *progymnasmata* earlier than under a rhetorician" (C. Forbes, "Comparison, Self-Praise, and Irony: Paul's Boasting and the Conventions of Hellenistic Rhetoric," *NTS* 32 [1986]: 7).

5. See the explicit statement to this effect by Quintilian, *Inst.* 5.10.120. Likewise, for Menander and Pseudo-Dionysius in particular, see D. A. Russell and N. G. Wilson, *Menander Rhetor* (Oxford: Clarendon, 1981), xviii. The comment of S. K. Stowers (*Letter Writing in Greco-Roman Antiquity* [Philadelphia: Westminster Press, 1986], 51) is apt: "Rhetorical theory was always a combination of what actually happened in practice and what the rhetoricians thought ought to be the case."

6. Aristotle, *Rhetoric* I.9.38, 1368a.

7. Quintilian, *Inst.* 9.3.32.

8. Menander Rhetor, II.386.19.

9. Athenaeus, *Deipnosophistae* 4.159A.

10. Dionysius of Halicarnassus, *Isocrates* 17, *Demosthenes* 17 and 21, cited by R. Dean Anderson, *Glossary of Greek Rhetorical Terms* (Louvain: Peeters, 2000), 111.

11. "Rhetoric to Alexander," 1425b37–1426a24.

12. "Rhetoric to Alexander," 1426b3–7.

13. Aristotle, *Rhet.* I.9.38, 1368a.

14. Aristotle, *Top.* 1.5.102b15.

15. Aristotle, *Top.* 3.4.119a1–11.

16. On the terminology see D. A. Russell, *Greek Declamation* (Cambridge: Cambridge University Press, 1983), 9ff.

17. Russell argues that "encomia and other 'epideictic' forms do not count" as μελέται (*meletai*), citing Menander Rhetor 331.16 (*Greek Declamation*, 10 and n. 34). Two points: first, that is not quite what Menander says. He says that "demonstrations" (ἐπιδείξεις, *epideixeis*) of public speeches (λόγων πολιτικῶν, *logōn politikōn*) are not true ἐπίδειξιν (*epideixin*). That practice demonstrations are not true epideictic does not mean that epideictic exercises cannot be μελέται (*meletai,* complex exercises). Second, even if the point held for Menander, it would not follow that it held for all, or even for most other writers.

18. Aristotle, *Rhet.* 1366a29ff.

19. See the full discussion below, in the section on Paul and rhetoric.

20. See *de Inventione* 2.114 for another example.

21. Quintilian, *Inst.* 5.13.12, and cf. 5.13.57.

22. Menander Rhetor, trans. Russell & Wilson, II.372.20ff.

23. Menander Rhetor, II.376.31–II.377.9.

24. It is quite incorrect to claim, as J. Smit does ("Argument and Genre of 1 Corinthians 12–14," in *Rhetoric and the New Testament* [ed. S. E. Porter and T. H. Olbricht; Sheffield, England: Sheffield Academic Press, 1993], 226), that "in the handbooks of rhetoric the *genus demonstrativum* [γένος ἐπιδεικτικόν, *genos epideiktikon*] is only schematically discussed. The reason for this is that public speeches of praise or censure rarely occurred. The attention this genre nevertheless receives is connected with the practice of including demonstrative excurses in judicial pleas and political addresses." There are two major problems with this formulation. First, it is simply not true that "in the handbooks of rhetoric" generally, epideictic is "only schematically discussed." The handbooks of both Menander Rhetor and Pseudo-Dionysius are almost exclusively concerned with epideictic oratory, and develop their material in great detail. Second, it is not true that "speeches of praise or censure rarely occurred." On the contrary, the public honoring of friends and benefactors, and invective against rivals, were major features of civic life. Is Smit perhaps overinterpreting the *Auctor ad Herennium*'s comments that "if epideictic is only seldom employed by itself independently, still in judicial and deliberative causes extensive sections are often devoted to praise and censure" (3.4.8)? Far more accurate is the comment of C. Basevi and J. Chapa, in the same volume (p. 352), that "encomiastic literature blossomed a good deal during the Empire," though they provide little evidence of its social location. Further, it may be true that "demonstrative excurses" were included in other types of speeches, or it may be better to formulate the matter differently: various features of actual oratory crossed the boundaries between the three broad categories of

rhetoric laid down by the mainstream theoreticians. On this matter see further below.

25. On this subject see C. Forbes, "Comparison, Self-Praise, and Irony," *NTS* 32 (1986): 7–8.

26. See, for example, W. Rhys Roberts, "Caecilius of Calacte," *AJP* 18 (1897): 302–12; Plutarch, "Life of Demosthenes" 3; *Dionysius of Halicarnassus, the Three Literary Letters* (ed. W. Rhys Roberts; Cambridge: Cambridge University Press, 1901), esp. 90–97; Dionysius of Halicarnassus, *On Isocrates* 3.17, *On the Style of Demosthenes* 2, 9–10, 17, 23, 33, and *On Thucydides* 16, 35, 36, 37, 41.

27. Cicero, *Brut.* 32–35, 138–150.

28. Ps.-Longinus, On the Sublime, 33–36.

29. Quintilian, *Inst.* 10.1.105ff.

30. Plutarch, "On the Virtue of Women," *Mor.* 243.

31. On this subject see the discussion of H. M. Martin, Jr., "Plutarch," in Porter, *Handbook*, 724–28, and D. H. J. Larmour, "Making Parallels: *Synkrisis* in Plutarch's 'Themistocles and Camillus,'" in *ANRW* II.33.6 (Berlin: de Gruyter, 1992), 4154–74.

32. As prime examples, we should note (1) the likelihood, argued by Anderson, *Ancient Rhetorical Theory*, 46–49, that Aristotle's work on rhetoric, so foundational to our understanding of the development of ancient rhetoric, was hardly read by rhetoricians in the Hellenistic and early Roman period; and (2) that Pseudo-Longinus, "On the Sublime," is not cited by any ancient writer on rhetoric or literature until the eleventh century C.E. (ibid., 86).

33. See, for example, T. H. Olbricht, "An Aristotelian Rhetorical Analysis of 1 Thessalonians," in *Greeks, Romans, and Christians* (ed. D. L. Balch et al.; Minneapolis: Fortress Press, 1990), 216–36; and D. F. Watson, "A Rhetorical Analysis of Philippians and Its Implications for the Unity Question," *NovT* 30 (1988): 57–87.

34. Compare 2.21, where, once again, it is the *comparatione* of alternative courses of action that is at issue. Cicero discusses the same use of *comparatio* in his *de Inventione* 1.15.

35. See also Cicero, *Part. Or.* 57.

36. *Ad Herennium* also discusses comparative similes and illustrative comparisons, which the author calls *comparationes,* at 4.44f., 4.46, 4.57, and 4.59ff.

37. In *Opt. gen.* 21, Cicero comments that the case between Demosthenes and Aeschines in "On the Crown" "involves a very nice interpretation of the law on both sides, and a comparison [*contentionem*] of the public services of the two orators which is extremely impressive."

38. See section 138 for Cicero's comparison of Demosthenes and Hyperides with Antonius and Crassus, and section 145 for his comparison of the styles of Crassus and Scaevola. Compare also section 294, and *De Or.* 3.53.205, 40.138.

39. See Anderson, *Ancient Rhetorical Theory*, 254n. 21. J. T. Fitzgerald, *Cracks in an Earthen Vessel* (Atlanta: Scholars Press, 1988), 145n. 95, suggests that Philo, *Quod Deterius* 34, is a *synkrisis* between lovers of virtue and the self-interested.

40. See the comments, by Russell and Wilson, *Menander Rhetor*, xxvi, on the context: Having defined encomium, "Theon proceeds then to give a list of further topics on which praise may be based: posthumous admiration, unbiased by flat-

tery or envy; disinterested or altruistic actions; success depending on effort rather than on fortune; being first in the field; receiving the praises of notable men; conjectures about achievements which death cut short; comparisons with others; even play on names. . . . Many of these topics can be found also in earlier texts; but the emphasis on comparison is an interesting addition. . . . After this, the encomiast proceeds to the acts [πράξεις, *praxeis*] of his subject—and so arranges them as to demonstrate his possession of the cardinal virtues."

41. The translation is that of R. J. Mortley, originally published in my "Comparison, Self-Praise, and Irony" (see n. 25 above). For a wider discussion, see J. R. Butts, *The Progymnasmata of Theon* (Ph.D. diss., Claremont Graduate School, 1987).

42. Surely Quintilian can only be uncertain in the case of very simple comparative figures: more complex comparisons could hardly be described as "figures of speech." On the distinction between these categories, see the note of G. L. Hendrickson in his Loeb edition of Cicero's *Brutus*, 124: "figures of language or words, such as alliteration, rhyming or assonant pairs; and figures of thought, in which an idea is given force or vividness by the form in which it is cast, as when a simple statement is put in the form of a rhetorical question, an appeal, a wish, a prayer, an oath . . ." For Quintilian's list of "figures of speech," see *Inst.* 9.3.1. For "figures of thought," see Cicero, *De Or.* 3.52.201–354.208, cited in Quintilian bk. 9, followed in bk. 9.2.102 by Quintilian's own list.

43. Spengel, *Rhetores Graeci*, vol. 2, 14–15; translation slightly adapted from that of C. S. Baldwin, *Medieval Rhetoric and Poetic* (New York: Macmillan, 1928), 28–30.

44. Baldwin, *Medieval Rhetoric*, 32.

45. Ibid., 33–34. It is worth pointing out in passing that the exercise that follows *synkrisis* in the progymnasmata is *ēthopoiia* (Hermogenes) or *prosōpopoiia* (Theon), which can be translated as "characterization": the exercise of placing a speech in the mouth of, or writing a letter in the persona of, a character. For further examples, see Quintilian 3.8.49, 4.1.66–69, and 4.2.106. For an exegetical application of this rhetorical category to a much-controverted Pauline passage, see S. K. Stowers, "Romans 7.7–25 as a Speech-in-Character," in *Paul in His Hellenistic Context* (ed. T. Engberg-Pedersen; Edinburgh: T. & T. Clark, 1994), and *A Rereading of Romans* (New Haven: Yale University Press), 1994, 16–21. For a less detailed suggestion to do with 1 Cor 1:12, see M. Mitchell, *Paul and the Rhetoric of Reconciliation* (Tübingen: Mohr [Siebeck], 1991), 86. As I pointed out in my discussion of *synkrisis* in 2 Cor 11–12 (Forbes, "Comparison, Self-Praise, and Irony"), given the developmental nature of the progymnasmata, it is entirely likely that, after learning comparison, students would practice using comparisons within speeches put into the mouths of historical or mythical characters.

46. Baldwin, *Medieval Rhetoric*, 25.

47. *Menander Rhetor*, ed. Russell & Wilson. See also F. Gascó, "Menander Rhetor and the Works Attributed to Him," in *ANRW* II.34.4, 3110–46, esp. 3113–16 on authorship and dating.

48. Similar material can be found in virtually every section of Menander's manual. See, for examples, in funeral speeches, II.421.2–10, and in speeches inviting a governor to a festival, II.425.8, II.427.1.

49. Trans. Russell and Wilson, *Menander Rhetor*.

50. *Dionysios von Halikarnassos, Opuscula* (ed. Usener-Radermacher; Leipzig, Teubner, 1899) *Ars Rhetorica* 1.8, 260 lines 14–15.

51. See, for example, E. Krentz, "1 Thessalonians: Rhetorical Flourishes and Formal Constraints," in *The Thessalonians Debate: Methodological Discord or Methodological Synthesis?* (ed. K. P. Donfried and J. Beutler; Grand Rapids: Eerdmans, 2000), 287–318, esp. 316–17.

52. See J. A. D. Weima, "The Function of 1 Thessalonians 2:1–12 and the Use of Rhetorical Criticism: A Response to Otto Merk," and the detailed comments of F. W. Hughes, "The Rhetoric of Letters," both in Donfried and Beutler, *The Thessalonians Debate,* 124ff., and most notably S. E. Porter, "The Theoretical Justification for Application of Rhetorical Categories to Pauline Epistolary Literature," in Porter and Olbricht, *Rhetoric and the New Testament,* 100–122, and Anderson, *Ancient Rhetorical Theory,* 117–21.

53. This is, of course, not the only possible approach to the topic. Hermeneutically interesting results may themselves be sufficient justification for some approaches, and the Pauline literature can be studied in any number of ways. The historian, however, will normally want to know about historical context, and it is within that context that this study is formulated.

54. In my view this point undercuts the otherwise strong case of Porter, "Paul of Tarsus and His Letters," in Porter, *Handbook,* 565–67. As Porter himself comments (540), "[I]t is somewhat surprising that more attention has not been given to delivery, since these letters were almost assuredly designed to be read before a church congregation." Likewise Anderson misses the point when he notes that "the rhetorical situation for the presentation of a speech is quite a different scenario to that of writing a letter" (*Ancient Rhetorical Theory,* 117). His discussion on pages 119–20 does, however, pick up the issue.

55. As F. W. Hughes shows ("Rhetoric of Letters," 202), this central insight goes back at least as far as J. Weiss in 1897. See particularly 1 Thess 5:27, though the same general point can and should be made of the entire corpus. Thus in my view C. J. Classen ("St. Paul's Epistles and Ancient Greek and Roman Rhetoric," in Porter and Olbricht, *Rhetoric and the New Testament,* 282) is only half right when he comments: "It is certainly advisable at this stage to remember that St. Paul was not making a speech, and that rules for speeches and other types of composition cannot be expected always to be easily applicable to letters." True: but neither was Paul writing a "pure" letter to an individual reader. The epistolary conventions of the literary elite may not have been easily applicable either, and may have been less accessible. As J. T. Reid observes, Cicero notes the distinction between the private and the public letter (*pro Flacco* 37), and various other kinds (*ad Fam.* 2.4.1, 4.13.1, 5.5.1). Oddly, Reid argues: "If the letter was read to a gathering of Christians, the speaker may have been concerned with these features [of rhetoric: memory and delivery] of speech. But it is doubtful that Paul the letter writer was" ("Using Ancient Rhetorical Categories to Interpret Paul's Letters: A Question of Genre," in Porter and Olbricht, *Rhetoric and the New Testament,* 206n. 14.). Far more persuasive is the view of P. Botha (in the same volume), "The Verbal Art of the Pauline Letters: Rhetoric, Performance, and Presence," 409ff., regarding the social context of the reception of Paul's letters. He argues forcefully: "Paul's dictation of his letter was, in all probability, also a coaching of the letter carrier and eventual

reader. The carrier of the letter would most likely have seen to it that it be read like Paul wanted it to be read" (417). See similarly Ben Witherington III, *Conflict and Community in Corinth* (Grand Rapids: Eerdmans, 1994), 36 and 38: "He may have chosen couriers such as Timothy or Titus who would be able to read aloud a letter in a way that conformed to his own rhetorical strategy and intent." Cf. 107, 387nn. 6–7, and 434.

56. The nearest approximation to such letters would probably be the "open letter," or letter written to a civic assembly. The letters of Isocrates to Philip of Macedon and Demosthenes' letter to the Athenians are possible examples, but the topic requires separate treatment. Demetrius, *De Elocutione* 233, notes: "Since occasionally we write to states [πόλεις, *poleis*] or royal personages, such letters must be composed in a slightly heightened tone." But he adds immediately: "It is right to have regard to the person [τοῦ προσώπου, *tou prosōpou*, singular) to whom the letter is addressed." (The translation is that of A. J. Malherbe, *Ancient Epistolary Theorists* [Atlanta: Scholars Press, 1988], 19.) In other words, nothing other than an individual recipient is considered in any detail at all.

57. That this passage (Rom 5:12–21) should be understood as a σύγκρισις (*synkrisis*) is suggested by Anderson, *Ancient Rhetorical Theory*, 209, with detailed analysis at 225ff.

58. Similarly ibid., 163.

59. Pauline σύγκρισις (*synkrisis*) is mentioned once by G. A. Kennedy, in his *New Testament Interpretation through Rhetorical Criticism* (Chapel Hill: University of North Carolina Press, 1984). D. F. Watson suggests that Paul uses "example and comparison of example" and "amplification by comparison" in Phil 2–3 and 4:7–8, "A Rhetorical Analysis of Philippians and Its Implications for the Unity Question," *NovT* 30 (1988): 67 and 74. However, Watson's claim is no more than a brief reference within his broader analysis, and neither example would seem to represent a full-blown σύγκρισις (*synkrisis*). R. Jewett suggests that Rom 9–11 functions in Paul's overall argument in Romans as a "comparatio," "a historical example or an imaginative case to demonstrate the superiority of the argument or case already established. . . . Paul takes up the case of unbelieving Israel to demonstrate that the righteousness of God will still be triumphant, that the Gospel in the end will not fail" (R. Jewett, "Following the Argument of Romans," in *The Romans Debate* [ed. K. P. Donfried; rev. ed.; Edinburgh: T. & T. Clark, 1991], 271–72). However, a "comparatio" is not the same as a full rhetorical σύγκρισις, *synkrisis*. And the case is not made in any detail. Most recently, Krentz, in his "1 Thessalonians," 309, suggests that in 1 Thess 2:5–12 "Paul uses an implied comparison" (σύγκρισις, *synkrisis*) between himself and wandering Cynic philosophers, and suggests (313–14) that 1 Thess 2:14–16 is a Pauline σύγκρισις (*synkrisis*) between the Thessalonian converts and their Jewish-Christian predecessors. But in the first case the implied comparison is a little too hypothetical, and, in the second, a simple illustrative comparison of this kind would not normally be termed a σύγκρισις (*synkrisis*).

60. These are the *Handbook of Classical Rhetoric in the Hellenistic Period* (ed. S. E. Porter; Leiden: Brill, 1997); *Rhetoric and the New Testament: Essays from the 1992 Heidelberg Conference* (ed. S. E. Porter and T. H. Olbricht; Sheffield, England: Sheffield Academic Press, 1993); *The Rhetorical Analysis of Scripture* (ed. S. E. Porter and

T. H. Olbricht; Sheffield, England: Sheffield Academic Press, 1997); and R. Dean Anderson, *Ancient Rhetorical Theory and Paul* (2d ed.; Louvain: Peeters, 1999). One of the few who does comment is M. Heath, in his treatment of "Invention," in Porter, *Handbook*, 96n. 18, though he does not attempt to locate any New Testament examples.

61. As far as I am aware, no commentator has developed an explicit understanding of this passage as a rhetorical comparison.

62. A broad variety of Jewish literature in this period acknowledged both that many sinful or apostate Jews would fall under God's judgment, likewise that "righteous Gentiles" would inherit a share in the "age to come." See, for example, A. F. Segal, "Universalism in Judaism and Christianity," in *Paul in His Hellenistic Context* (ed. T. Engberg-Pedersen; Edinburgh: T. & T. Clark, 1994), 1–29. On the Greco-Roman side, the impartiality of God was a central tenet of educated opinion.

63. The difficulties of the conventional translation, "without the Law," have been outlined by Stowers, *Re-reading*, 138–41. However, his solution, to translate "all who have sinned in a lawless manner shall perish in a manner befitting lawlessness" (139), seems to me to ignore the overall structure of the passage.

64. See, for example, *m. Abot* 1:17. For the full acceptance that obedience to the Law was required, notwithstanding the sense of privilege that access to the Law brought to Jewish self-identification, see *2 Bar.* 48:22–24, and the discussion of J. Dunn, *Romans 1–8* (WBC; Dallas: Word Books, 1988), 97.

65. For a discussion of the distinction between parts of the Law that Gentiles were, and were not, required to keep, see again Segal, "Universalism in Judaism and Christianity," 8–12, 21.

66. Our understanding of the rhetorical form of this passage has been greatly advanced by S. K. Stowers, in *The Diatribe and Paul's Letter to the Romans* (Chico, Calif.: Scholars Press, 1981), and in idem, "Romans 7.7–25 as a Speech-in-Character" (προσωποποιία, *prosōpopoiia*), and the wider application of this case in his *A Re-reading of Romans*. I remain unpersuaded, however, of his identification of the "persona" with which Paul speaks here.

67. This deliberately ambiguous translation is adopted to bring out the difficulty of verse 9: the verb is middle, and probably takes a passive sense, though the majority of translations render it as active: "do we excel?" rather than "are we excelled?" The middle sense, "do we have anything [i.e., an excuse] to put forward?" is also possible. On this passage see S. K. Stowers, "Paul's Dialogue with a Fellow Jew in Romans 3:1–9," *CBQ* 46, no. 4 (1984): 707–22.

68. That this passage (Rom 5:12–21) should be understood as comparative is commonplace. The more precise view that it constitutes a developed rhetorical comparison, a σύγκρισις (*synkrisis*), is suggested by (among others) Jean-Noël Aletti, "The Rhetoric of Romans 5–8," in *The Rhetorical Analysis of Scripture* (ed. S. E. Porter and T. H. Olbricht; Sheffield, England: Sheffield Academic Press, 1997), 294–308, esp. 304–6. For Aletti, "Synkrisis is thus the leading figure of the section" (Rom 5–8). In no way should this insight be taken as an alternative to the view that sees the argument as structured around a rabbinic *qal wahomer* or *a fortiori* argument. The two go hand in hand.

69. Compare Anderson, *Ancient Rhetorical Theory*, 209, with detailed analysis at 225–26. Anderson correctly emphasizes (225n. 75) that "although the precise

terms of the σύγκρισις [*synkrisis*] vary, the comparison is *not* between the persons Adam and Christ as such." Indeed, it is between "the trespass" (παράπτομα, *paraptoma*) and "the gift" (χάρισμα, *charisma*; 5:15), "the judgment" (κρῖμα, *krima*) and "the gift" (χάρισμα, *charisma*; 5:16), "the trespass (παράπτομα, *paraptoma*) of the one man" and the "abundant provision of grace and . . . the gift of righteousness . . . through the one man, Jesus Christ" (5:17), "one trespass" (παράπτομα, *paraptoma*) and "one act of righteousness" (δικαίομα, *dikaioma*; 5:18), and "the disobedience (παρακοή, *parakoē*) of one man" and "the obedience (ὑπακοή, *hypakoē*) of the one man" (5:19).

70. Thus, correctly, Moo, *The Epistle to the Romans* (Grand Rapids: Eerdmans, 1996), 315: "The actions of Adam and Christ, then, are similar in having 'epochal' significance. But they are not equal in power." Similarly, Dunn makes use of the term "epochal" (*Romans 1–8*, 293).

71. On this passage, see primarily Fitzgerald, *Cracks,* 132–48. See also Mitchell, *Paul and the Rhetoric of Reconciliation,* 219ff., including 220n. 181. She says: "The final section of epideictic proof, a very important part, is the σύγκρισις [*synkrisis*] or comparison. It is a standard rhetorical practice in an encomium or vituperation to compare the person or city under discussion with illustrious examples. In 4:1–13 Paul sets up and executes a comparison between the Corinthians and the apostles, the most illustrious Christian examples. . . . [220n. 181:] the rhetorical σύγκρισις *depends* upon Paul's assumed stature as an illustrious person worthy of comparison and emulation (along with all the apostles)" (219).

72. On the rhetorical meaning of μετασχηματίζω (*metaschēmatizō*), see the recent discussion of Witherington, *Conflict and Community,* 136, 140.

73. See also ibid., 142: "By means of a *synkrisis,* a standard rhetorical device (a comparison, used in this case to point out a contrast), Paul will offer both example and admonition."

74. Ibid., 142n. 20, citing Mitchell, *Paul and the Rhetoric of Reconciliation,* 220n. 181.

75. That self-praise was acceptable in such circumstances is made clear from, for example, Plutarch, *Mor.* 541–543. The topic is discussed in detail by Fitzgerald, *Cracks,* chapter 3, "The Hardships of the Sage."

76. As Fitzgerald observes, "[W]hereas Epictetus' ideal Cynic shares in the reign of Zeus as his servant (*Diss.* 3.22.95), Paul as God's servant does not even share in his converts' reign (1 Cor 4:1, 8). The irony is profound, and is designed to prompt the Corinthians to make a radical reassessment of their present status" (Fitzgerald, *Cracks,* 148).

77. Kennedy, *New Testament Interpretation,* 23.

78. Witherington, *Conflict and Community,* 375. The passage from Quintilian is cited in the first section of this chapter. On page 378, Witherington also mentions the "comparison with the Mosaic dispensation"; referring to 2 Cor 3:7, he comments that "Paul is comparing two different glories, the first of which has been annulled" (379n. 15).

79. Ibid., 380.

80. P. Marshall, *Enmity in Corinth: Social Conventions in Paul's Relations with the Corinthians* (Tübingen: Mohr [Siebeck], 1987), 53–55; C. Forbes, "Comparison, Self-Praise, and Irony."

81. See, for example, J. P. Sampley, "Paul, His Opponents in 2 Corinthians 10–13, and the Rhetorical Handbooks," in *The Social World of Formative Christianity and Judaism* (ed J. Neusner et al.; Philadelphia: Fortress Press, 1988), 162–77.

82. Thus, elegantly, the Jerusalem Bible. This translation perfectly catches the flavor of the Pauline barb.

83. Witherington, *Conflict and Community*, 429.

84. Thus Witherington (ibid., 450), citing J. Fitzgerald and D. Georgi, argues: "Paul is comparing his own hardships to those that the opponents claim to have endured. Self-praise by sages and philosophers for endurance of hardships was exceedingly common in the Greco-Roman world. . . . The difference between Paul and his adversaries was 'in his *interpretation* of his hardships, not in the fact that he suffered and they did not. The difference is, he saw his weakness as the primary sphere for the manifestation of divine power, and they "signs, wonders, and mighty works" (12:12).'" The value of the insight in the final sentence is not diminished by the weakness of the supposition in the first.

85. See particularly C. K. Barrett, "The Allegory of Abraham, Sarah, and Hagar in the Argument of Galatians," in *Essays on Paul* (Philadelphia: Westminster, 1982), 154–70; on the nature of Pauline allegory, R. N. Longenecker, *Galatians* (WBC; Dallas: Word Books, 1990), 208–10; or Ben Witherington III, *Grace in Galatia* (Edinburgh: T. & T. Clark, 1998), 321–40.

86. Dunn, *Galatians*, 244.

87. H. D. Betz, *Galatians*, Hermeneia (Philadelphia: Fortress, 1979), 245, points out that Lietzmann noted the correspondences in the allegory, describing them as a συστοιχία (*systoichia*), which Betz translates as "parallel columns of concepts" (249). Ditto J. Louis Martyn, *Galatians* (AB; New York: Doubleday, 1997), 393–406, 438, 449. Both cite various philosophical usages of the term, but no rhetorical usages.

88. The text of the so-called Anonymous Seguerianus can be found in Spengel, *Rhetores Graeci*, vol. 1; the passage cited is on page 449, lines 14–16. The translation is my own.

6

PAUL, HARDSHIPS, AND SUFFERING

David E. Fredrickson

I focus my examination of suffering on the concept of grief (λύπη, *lypē*), which in the Greco-Roman world was widely considered one type of passion. The Greek term for passion (πάθος, *pathos*) denotes the self being acted upon rather than acting upon the external world. To suffer (πάσχειν, *paschein*) is to be moved by externals.[1] From the philosophic perspective, it mattered little whether this movement was occasioned by grief or by the other main types of passion (fear, pleasure, lust, and, in some sources, anger). This association of suffering with passion in general, though correct, would indicate too broad a range of inquiry. For practical reasons, therefore, I limit this investigation to what English-speakers normally mean by suffering—emotional pain or grief.[2] Furthermore, I highlight aspects of the ancient discourse about grief that bear directly on the interpretation of Paul's letters: some pertinent forms of grief, hardships and hardship lists, the role of grief in moral reformation; two ancient letter types that make grief thematic; and the notion of shared suffering in friendship.

Part I. Hardships and Suffering in Greco-Roman Philosophy and Epistolography

The Psychology of Suffering

Grief as irrational contraction (συστολή, *systolē*) of the soul or heart is a commonplace in Stoic psychology (Diogenes Laertius 7.111,118; *SVF* 1.51.26–31; 3.94.14–15; 3.95.17–18, 24–25, 41–43; Epictetus, *frg.* 9; Plutarch, *Lib. aegr.* 1,7).[3] Cicero shows that the metaphor of grief as soul shrinkage was so well established in Greek writers that it survived the translation of philosophical terms into Latin: "*Distress* [*aegritudo*] then is a newly formed belief of present evil, the subject of which thinks it right to feel depression and shrinking of soul [*demitti contrahique animo*]" (Cicero, *Tusc.* 4.14; cf. *Tusc.* 1.90; 3.83; 4.66–67; *Quint. fratr.* 1.1.4; Seneca, *Ep.* 99.15). Some of the varieties of grief imply the idea of contraction. For example, groaning (στεναγμός, *stenagmos*) conveys the notion of contraction in the root στεν (*sten;* see Rom 8:23, 26; 2 Cor 5:2, 4).[4] Soul shrinkage accounts in the philosophers for the experience of grief at its most fundamental level.[5]

Not all types of emotional pain, however, exhibit contraction of soul. One such variety of grief often treated by the philosophers was regret (μεταμέλεια, *metameleia*), a particularly sharp form of suffering. The standard definition of regret was "grief over sins done as though happening through one's own self."[6] What makes regret so painful is self-hatred and self-condemnation: "Regret is a factious passion of the soul which brings unhappiness, for to the extent that the one is encompassed by regrets and is grieved at the things which have happened, to this degree he is angry at himself, since he became the cause of these things" (*SVF* 3.149.20–24; my translation). According to Plutarch, the soul that regrets a deed is filled with no other thought than "how it might escape from the memory of its iniquities, drive out of itself the consciousness of guilt, regain its purity, and begin life anew" (Plutarch, *Sera* 556A). Such persons condemn their lives, feel remorse, hate themselves, and are distressed over what they have done (Plutarch, *Sera* 566E). The notion that, as Seneca put it, "he who has sinned has already punished himself," echoed throughout ancient writings (Seneca, *Ira* 2.30.2).[7] Seneca comments further that "no man is more heavily punished than he who is consigned to the torture of remorse" (Seneca, *Ira* 3.26.2).

Philosophers used the notion of self-condemnation to explain the nature of regret. Aristotle formalized a connection probably found already in everyday speech: "But a good man does not rebuke himself either at the time, like the uncontrolled, nor yet his former self his later, like the penitent [ὁ μεταμελητικός, *ho metamelētikos*] . . . because when men blame themselves they are putting themselves to death" (Aristotle, *Eth. eud.* 7.6.14–15; modified translation).

Plutarch draws out the analogy between regret and punishment. Like prisoners sentenced to death, every wicked man suffers "terrors, forebodings, and the pangs of remorse" (μεταμελείας, *metameleias;* Plutarch, *Sera* 554E–F). He also writes that when "despots . . . desire to make miserable those whom they punish, [they] maintain executioners and torturers, or devise branding-irons and wedges; vice . . . fills the man with grief and lamentation, dejection and remorse" (μεταμελείας, *metameleias;* Plutarch, *An vit.* 498D; cf. *Sera* 554A–B). Consciousness of a sin "leaves behind it in the soul regret [μεταμέλειαν, *metameleian*] which ever continues to wound and prick it. For the other pangs reason does away with, but regret [μετάνοιαν, *metanoian*] is caused by reason itself, since the soul, together with its feeling of shame, is stung and chastised by itself" (Plutarch, *Tranq. an.* 476E–477B; cf. *Gen. Socr.* 592A–B).

This understanding of regret in juridical metaphors occurred frequently in discussions of conscience and repentance.[8] Writers used courtroom imagery for the self-examination of conscience (Seneca, *Ira* 3.36.3; Juvenal, *Sat.* 13.2–3). The notion of a self-imposed sentence of death figures prominently: "genuine repentance is utterly to root out of the soul the sins for which a man has condemned himself to death" (Clement of Alexandria, *Quis div.* 39; cf. *Strom.* 4.22.143).

Hardships and Hardship Lists

The work of John T. Fitzgerald on hardships and hardship lists in ancient moral philosophy has proven to be a rich resource for students of the Pauline epistles.[9] He summarizes what writers had in mind when recounting hardships:

> The intimate connection between virtue and adversity has been thoroughly documented in the preceding pages. Since *peristaseis* [difficulties] constitute a test of human character, they have both a revelatory and a demonstrative function. The man with little or no integrity collapses under the weight of his burdens. His *peristaseis* reveal and prove his deficiencies as a person. The *proficiens* [one who makes progress], by contrast, shows greater strength of character in dealing with his hardships, so that his *peristaseis* reveal his progress, what he is *becoming*. Since they help to form his character, they play a crucial role in his *paideia* [education]. For the *sapiens* [wise man], however, *peristaseis* no longer have this educative character. They provide the proof that he is educated. Consequently, they exhibit who he *is*, what he has *become*.[10]

Fitzgerald has accounted for two functions of the philosophic discourse about hardships. First, the philosophers taught that reason is superior to all the vicissitudes of life, and because the self is identified with reason, nothing external can cause harm.[11] Hardships provide an opportunity for this lesson to be illustrated in an actual life.[12] Second, by the time of Paul, most philosophers had abandoned the absolute distinction between the wise man and the fool and had settled on a doctrine of progress in moral virtue.[13] The notion that hardships train the *proficiens* (one who makes progress) in virtue and that suffering produces character in the one striving for wisdom had widespread appeal.[14]

We have seen that hardships demonstrate the sage's virtue or train the person aspiring to the serenity of the sage. There was yet a third function of representing the sage's endurance: to demonstrate his philanthropy (Epictetus, *Diatr.* 2.12.17–25; Lucian, *Peregr.* 18). Reminiscent of Antisthenes' depiction of Odysseus's dangers (Antisthenes, *frg.* 15.1–3, 9),[15] Dio Chrysostom distinguishes himself from philosophers who refused to associate with the crowd and face danger: "For some among that company do not appear in public at all and prefer not to make the venture, possibly because they despair of being able to improve the masses" (Dio Chrysostom, *Alex.* 8; cf. *Alex.* 24; *1 Tars.* 15).[16] The genuine philosopher "stands ready, if need be, to submit to ridicule and to the disorder and the uproar of the mob" (Dio Chrysostom, *Alex.* 32.11). He should be compared with Diogenes, whose free speech was often not endured (Dio Chrysostom, *Isthm.* 9.7–9).[17]

Grief and Moral Reformation

Harsh Cynic philosophers regarded moral failure as justification for causing grief (λύπη, *lypē*) (Ps.-Socrates, *Ep.* 24; Lucian, *Pisc.* 20).[18] From a text representing harsh Cynicism, we learn that the laughter of Democritus aimed to condemn humanity for its foolishness.[19] Not regarding laughter a strong enough measure against human vice, however, Democritus wished "to discover something even more painful [λυπηρόν, *lypēron*] to use against them" (Ps.-Hippocrates, *Ep.* 17.45 [Hercher, *Epistolographi Graeci* 304, my translation]). Cynic moral reproof was often painful because it was inopportune (Ps.-Hippocrates, *Ep.* 17.19–20, 34). Hippocrates protests that Democritus's laughter at others' misfortunes does not consider the circumstances of those he mocks (Ps.-Hippocrates, *Ep.* 17.20–21). Likewise, Plutarch denounces those who cause suffering when the circumstances of the hearer demand encouragement and consolation (Plutarch, *Adul. amic.* 69A).

In response to these criticisms, some Cynics sought to place their frank speaking in a better light by stressing philanthropic aims (Plutarch, *Virt. mor.* 452D; Stobaeus, *Flor.* 3.13.42).[20] They claimed that although words of truth are sometimes painful, in the end they are beneficial, because they are not motivated by hatred but by a desire to heal others (Seneca, *Vit. beat.* 26.5). It is the duty of the philosopher to benefit others, even if this requires a painful dose of truth-telling (Epictetus, *Diatr.* 3.1.10–11; cf. Dio Chrysostom, *Alex.* 5, 7, 11; Lucian, *Hermot.* 51).

In his introduction to Epictetus's *Discourses*, Arrian testifies to the concept of appropriate suffering in the reception of moral exhortation:

> He was clearly aiming at nothing else but to incite the minds of the hearers to the best things. If, now, these words of his should produce that same effect, they would have, I think, just that success which the words of philosophers ought to have; but if not, let those who read them be assured of this, that when Epictetus himself spoke them, the hearer could not help but feel [πάσχειν, *paschein*] exactly what Epictetus wanted him to feel [παθεῖν, *pathein*]. (*Arriani epistula ad Lucium Gellium* 5–7)

Epictetus himself compared the lecture hall of the philosopher to a hospital, from which students should not walk out in pleasure "but in pain" (Epictetus, *Diatr.* 3.23.30; cf. 3.1.10–11; 3.23.37).[21]

The role of pain in moral improvement was controversial. For the Epicureans, emotional pain (λύπη, lypē) was something to be avoided, because tranquillity, the goal of Epicurean mutual exhortation, was the opposite of grief.[22] In their view, pain was a sign of misapplied or misunderstood frank speech (Philodemus, *Lib.* 12, 13, 31, 61–62, XVA, XVIB, XXIIB). This Epicurean judgment is not far removed from the position of the earlier Stoics, who argued against the usefulness of pain in moral transformation. They considered regret over one's errors a characteristic of the bad person (*SVF* 3.100.33; 3.149.18–24; 3.150.24–27). The later Stoics, on the other hand, emphasized progress in the moral life and mitigated the absolute distinction between the wise man and the fool.[23] In this context, grief over one's errors was a good thing—the beginning of the moral life and a sign of progress (Cicero, *Amic.* 90; Lucian, *Nigr.* 4, 35; Plutarch, *Virt. prof.* 82C).

Plutarch illustrates the function of grief in moral transformation when he describes the way students should listen to the frank speech of philosophers.[24] Although cowardly grief is to be avoided, the student has to feel some pain (Plutarch, *Rec. rat. aud.* 46C). The student must see that the teacher's speech aims to reform character. Admonitions should be allowed to penetrate like a biting drug and cause humiliation, sweating, and dizziness, and a burning with shame in the soul (Plutarch, *Rec. rat. aud.* 46D). Yet Plutarch does not want the student to experience excessive grief:

> For this reason he who is taken to task must feel and suffer some smart, yet he should not be crushed or dispirited, but, as though at a solemn rite of novitiate which consecrates him to philosophy, he should submit to the initial purifications and commotions, in the expectation that something delectable and splendid will follow upon his present distress and perturbation. (Plutarch, *Rec. rat. aud.* 47A)

Grief and Epistolary Theory

In the epistolary handbook of Ps.-Libanius (fourth–sixth centuries C.E.) we discover the following definition of the grieving style: "The grieving style is that in which we present ourselves as being grieved."[25] More instructive is his sample letter:

> The letter of grief [Λυπητική, Lypētikē]. You caused me extremely much grief [λελύπηκας, lelypēkas] when you did this thing. For that reason I am very much vexed with you, and bear a grief [λυποῦμαι λύπην, lypoumai lypēn] that is difficult to assuage. For the grief [λῦπαι, lypai] men cause their friends is exceedingly difficult to heal, and holds in greater insults than those they receive from their enemies. (Ps.-Libanius, *Charact. Ep.* 90, in Malherbe, *Ancient Epistolary Theorists*, 80–81)

The grieving style has overtones of rebuke (Gregory of Nazianzus, *Ep.* 40.1–4; Basil, *Ep.* 44.1).[26] Friendship language calls attention to the unexpected pain the writer has suffered at the hands of his friend and thereby increases the force of the rebuke.

Two letters attributed to Demosthenes, both of doubtful authenticity, exhibit the grieving style. In Epistle 2, Demosthenes complains to the council and assembly of the unfair treatment he has received. The letter is full of indignation and reproach (Demosthenes, *Ep.* 2.1, 3, 8, 12). Demosthenes portrays himself as grief-stricken over the wrongs he has received from his readers (Demosthenes, *Ep.* 2.13, 21–22). Near the conclusion of the letter, he expresses his suffering one last time:

> Let not one of you think, men of Athens, that through lack of manhood or from any other base motive I give way to my grief from the beginning to the end of this letter. Not so, but every man is ungrudgingly indulgent to the feeling of the moment, and those that now beset me—if only this had never come to pass!—are sorrows and tears [λῦπαι καὶ δάκρυα, *lypai kai dakrya*], longing both for my country and for you, and pondering over the wrongs I have suffered, all of which cause me to grieve. (Demosthenes, *Ep.* 2.25; cf. *Ep.* 3.44)

Notice especially Demosthenes' reference to his tears and the rebuke they communicate.[27]

The conciliatory letter was another epistolary type that made suffering thematic. According to Ps.-Libanius, the conciliatory style was appropriate when the writer had grieved the letter's recipient: "The conciliatory style is that in which we conciliate someone who has been caused grief by us for some reason. Some also call this the apologetic style" (Ps.-Libanius, *Charact. Ep.* 19, in Malherbe, *Ancient Epistolary Theorists*, 68–69). As the example below will illustrate, the writer does not deny that he had caused the recipient pain. In fact, he acknowledges the pain his words had inflicted. He does, however, assert that causing pain had not been his intention. Furthermore, even if pain did arise, its real significance, so it is asserted, is the healing that it bestowed in the end:

> The conciliatory letter. In addition to making the statements that I did, I went on (to put them) into action, for I most certainly did not think that they would ever cause you sorrow [λυπηθήσεσθαι, *lypēthēsesthai*]. But if you were upset by what was said or done, be assured, most excellent sir, that I shall most certainly no longer mention what was said. For it is my aim always to heal my friends rather than to cause them sorrow [λυπεῖν, *lypein*]. (Ps.-Libanius, *Charact. Ep.* 66, in Malherbe, *Ancient Epistolary Theorists*, 76–77)

The conciliatory letter reflects the philosophic teaching concerning the reforming power of grief brought on by bold words uttered in friendship (Cicero, *Quint. fratr.* 1.2.12–13; Gregory of Nazianzus, *Epp.* 17.1–3; 59.1–4).

Shared Suffering and Friendship

The notion of friends sharing suffering was not the invention of philosophers. "Suppose the misfortunes of friends to be your own," Menander wrote, echoing what we can assume to be a widespread opinion.[28] Yet the philosophers explored shared suffering in friendship and, significantly, set limits upon it.

Aristotle recognizes as a friend "one who shares his friend's joys and sorrows" (Aristotle, *Eth. nic.* 9.4.1). Furthermore, he points out that suffering is indeed "lightened by the sympathy of friends" (Aristotle, *Eth. nic.* 9.10.2; cf. Cicero, *Amic.* 22). Aristotle hesitates to answer definitively whether the pain is actually *shared,* or whether it is simply the pleasure of comrades' company and "consciousness of their sympathy" that mitigates pain. He does maintain, however, that it is "womanish" for one person to allow another to share in pain (Aristotle, *Eth. nic.* 9.11.4).

Later writers enforce a similar limitation. On the one hand, it is necessary to risk danger on account of friendship (Cicero, *Amic.* 23; Plutarch, *Amic. mult.* 96A; Lucian, *Tox.* 7, 9). Yet shared suffering must not go so deep as to touch the soul of the friend who gives comfort (Epictetus, *Ench.* 16.1). It is also problematic whether a friend should share in another's disrepute (Cicero, *Amic.* 61), although some writers believe this to be the case with true friends (Plutarch, *Amic. mult.* 96B; Lucian, *Tox.* 46; Maximus of Tyre, *Or.* 14.5). In spite of these limits imposed by some philosophers, we find the complete sharing of adversity, even pain, sorrow, and grief, to be a commonplace pertaining to friendship (Cicero, *Amic.* 46–48). In fact, according to Lucian this sharing is the first thing that must be said about friendship (Lucian, *Tox.* 6). The ground for such a notion is that friendship is a kind of sharing, that friends have all things in common (Seneca, *Epp.* 6.2; 48.2–4; Themistius, *Or.* 22.269, 270, 274).

The ultimate demonstration of friendship was willingly to suffer death for another (Diogenes Laertius 10.120; Plutarch, *Amic. mult.* 96C–D; Lucian, *Tox.* 20,36–37; Maximus of Tyre, *Or.* 14.3).[29] Cicero reports that theatergoers were moved to standing ovation at scenes of such devotion (Cicero, *Amic.* 24), and we know from literary sources that the theme of death for friendship's sake was gaining great popularity in the first century B.C.E.[30] Again, however, there was a limit. The one for whom suffering and death are endured must be good. This qualification is based on the requirement that a friendship be established only with the good person. Friendship is possible only after testing to see if the potential friend possesses virtue (Cicero, *Amic.* 79, 85).

Part II. Hardships and Suffering in Paul's Letters
(2 Corinthians 1–7; Romans 5:1–11; and 8:18–39)

Grief and the Occasion of 2 Corinthians 1–7

Second Corinthians 1–7 is full of references to suffering and hardships. Paul's acknowledgment of the suffering of the Corinthian community opens (1:3–7) and closes (7:8–11) this portion of the letter. References to Paul's own suffering are fitted between the portrayals of the church's grief in two ways. First, he narrates his travel from Asia Minor into Macedonia (1:8–11; 2:12–16; 7:5–6). It is a journey of woe. Second, Paul employs the philosophic convention of hardship lists (4:7–12; 4:16–5:5; and 6:3–10). Our current task is twofold: to reconstruct the occasion of 2 Cor 1–7 and to understand its rhetorical strategy, using what we know about the ancient ways of speaking about suffering and hardships. We treat the occasion first.

In 2 Cor 2:4, Paul refers to a letter which has been named appropriately "the letter of tears": "For out of much affliction [θλίψεως, *thlipseōs*] and contraction of heart [συνοχῆς καρδίας, *synochēs kardias*] I wrote to you through many tears" (διὰ πολλῶν δακρύων, *dia pollōn dakryōn*, my translation). This letter was a critical event between the writing of 1 and 2 Corinthians.[31] Paul had made an emergency visit to Corinth to deal with the troubles in the church.[32] During this intermediate visit, an individual injured or insulted Paul (2 Cor 1:15, 23; 2:1–11; 7:12; 12:21–13:2).[33] The identity of this individual is unknown, but in the secondary literature he is frequently called ὁ ἀδικήσας (*ho adikēsas*, "the one who caused injury") after 2 Cor 7:12. After Paul left Corinth, he wrote a letter that rebuked the church for not taking disciplinary action against "the one who caused injury."[34]

Our knowledge of the grieving style in ancient epistolography (see above) allows us to see the rebuking function of this letter and to assess its impact on the Corinthian community. Paul portrayed himself as weeping and made his grief the stated motivation for writing. As we have seen, shrinking soul is a commonplace in Stoic psychology, in which expressions similar to Paul's "affliction and contraction of the heart" signify grief. We also know from 2 Cor 7: 8 that this letter caused pain to the congregation at Corinth.

There is more evidence that the pain caused by this letter was a factor in the occasion of 2 Cor 1–7. Many scholars agree that 6:11–13 states Paul's reconciling purpose in writing 2 Cor 1–7, although a full appreciation of his use of the psychology of suffering has not accompanied this correct insight.[35] In 6:11, Paul refers to his frank speech with the phrase "our mouth stands open toward you."[36] He then places his bold speech in the context of friendship. Paul's friendship for the Corinthians is indicated by the joy that accompanies his speech. Joy, understood by the philosophers as the opposite of grief, was often depicted as a widening of the heart (*SVF* 3.105.17–18; Seneca, *Ep.* 59.2). In 6:12, Paul reiterates his joy for the Corinthians by denying that they are the cause of any grief to him. Reflecting the philosophic definition of grief as soul shrinkage, he says that the church is not restricted (στενοχωρεῖσθε, *stenochōreisthe*) in his heart, even as he, as a friend, uses frank speech in moral admonition. Yet in 6:12b, Paul points out the narrowness in the church's affections toward him, and he exhorts his hearers to return his friendship by widening their hearts so that he might exist there. Shrinking soul covered a range of suffering, including annoyance. Indeed, the terms Paul employs to depict the church's attitude toward him in 6:11–13 are reminiscent of the definition of annoyance (Diogenes Laertius 7.111; *SVF* 3.100.29; Plutarch, *Sera* 564B–C; Seneca, *Dial.* 2.10.2–3; *Ira* 2.6.1; Marcus Aurelius 9.32).

So far, we have accounted for two ways in which the issue of suffering contributed to the occasion of 2 Cor 1–7. Paul suffered grief over the community's indifference to the injury that he had received, and the congregation was grieved at being rebuked by Paul through the letter of tears. Another grief must be considered as well. In 2 Cor 2:5–11, Paul skillfully minimizes the wrong that "the one who caused injury" had done to him and pleads with the congregation to affirm love for the man. Apparently, the "letter of tears" had worked too well. The Corinthian congregation had disciplined the offender too harshly, and now, alienated from the community, he suffered from excessive grief, possibly in danger of suicide. Paul's plea in 2:5–11 for the community to exhort, love, and forgive him parallels the philosophical concern for appropriate grief in the context of moral reformation.

To appreciate the grief "the one who caused injury" experienced, attention must be given to the term ἐπιτιμία (*epitimia*) in 2:6. Here ἐπιτιμία is synonymous with ἐπιτίμησις (*epitimēsis*, "rebuke").[37] Rebuke was defined as a type of moral exhortation (Isocrates, *Demon.* 1.38; Dio Chrysostom, *Alex.* 33; Lucian, *Demon.* 55; *Jupp. trag.* 23; *Fug.* 12; *Pseudol.* 3; Stobaeus, *Flor.* 3.13.42).[38] Philo draws up a list of the salutary forms of moral discourse:

> If I speak in the general assembly I will leave all talk of flattery to others and resort only to such as is salutary and beneficial, reproving [ἐπιτιμῶν, *epitimōn*], warning, correcting in words studied to shew a sober frankness without foolish and frantic arrogance. (Philo, *Ios.* 73; cf. Cicero, *Off.* 1.38.137; Seneca, *Ep.* 94.39; Clement of Alexandria, *Paed.* 1.9.75.1; 1.9.77.1)[39]

Striking is the inclusion of encouragement and comfort in the contexts in which rebuke is treated as a type of moral exhortation (Plutarch, *Superst.* 168C; Lucian, *Demon.* 7; Clement of Alexandria, *Paed.* 1.9.75.1; 1.9.87.2; Seneca, *Ira* 1.15.1; *Ep.* 99.32; Ps.-Demetrius, *Form. Ep.* 6; Julian, *Or.* 6.201C). Because the final goal of rebuke was moral improvement, once shame and grief had taken hold and repentance had been brought about, words of encouragement and comfort were to be added lest excessive suffering lead to alienation and even death (Plutarch, [*Lib. ed.*] 13D–E).[40] This is Paul's stated fear, and exhortation and affirmation of friendship is the remedy he pleads for the church to employ for the sake of the now grief-stricken "one who caused injury."

One last grief remains to be described. It is Paul's own grief, suffered as he made his way from Asia Minor to Macedonia in order to receive from Titus news of the congregation's reaction to the severe rebuke in the letter of tears: "We do not want you to be unaware, brothers and sisters, of the affliction [θλίψεως, *thlipseōs*] we experienced in Asia; for we were so utterly, unbearably crushed that we despaired of life itself" (2 Cor 1:8). Paul exaggerates his suffering for rhetorical purposes, which we will explore more fully below.[41] It is enough here to pinpoint the exact nature of the affliction.

In 1:9, Paul indicates to his hearers that he suffered from regret. He had passed the "sentence of death" (τὸ ἀπόκριμα τοῦ θανάτου, *to apokrima tou thanatou*) upon himself. We have learned that the metaphor of self-condemnation was a common way of speaking about regret, a variety of grief. Second Corinthians 7:8 confirms that the emotion he describes in 1:9 is regret: "For even if I grieved [ἐλύπησα, *elypēsa*] you with my letter, I do not regret [μεταμέλομαι, *metamelomai*] it, though I did regret [μεταμελόμην, *metamelomēn*] it, for I see that I grieved [ἐλύπησεν, *elypēsen*] you with that letter, though only briefly." The philosophical understanding of regret as self-condemnation allows us to connect chapters 1 and 7. Some of Paul's references to his pain in the intervening passages (2:13; 4:8–11; 7:4–7), which otherwise might be understood as allusions to the general sufferings of an apostle, can be seen as the regret he claims to have suffered after writing the letter of tears.

Suffering in the Rhetorical Strategy of 2 Corinthians 1–7

Having pointed out the way grief sets the stage for the letter, we turn now to Paul's rhetorical strategy within the letter itself. Paul adopts and adapts philosophic and epistolographic conventions to reconcile the Corinthian community, who had been stung by rebuke in the letter of tears. Paul employs four aspects of the ancient discourse about suffering: the notion that friends share both joy and sorrow; the epistolographic conventions of the conciliatory letter; the idea of appropriate grief in the reception of moral exhortation; and the endurance of hardships.

Second Corinthians 1:3–7 develops the notion that friends share both joy and suffering. The key term that connects Paul's rhetoric with the philosophic discourse about suffering is τὰ παθήματα (*ta pathēmata*):

1:5: the sufferings (τὰ παθήματα, *ta pathēmata*) of Christ abound in us

1:6: the same sufferings (παθημάτων, *pathēmatōn*) which we ourselves have (πάσχομεν, *paschomen*)

1:7: partners in the sufferings (κοινωνοί ἐστε τῶν παθημάτων, *koinōnoi este tōn pathēmatōn*, my translation)

Shared suffering is the necessary condition for true friendship. This goes to the heart of traditional teaching on friendship. Christ, Paul, and the church are one because they share emotions. Not only did this identity of emotions provide the ground for friendship, it also defined its task (Plutarch, *Adul. amic.* 49F; *Amic. mult.* 95F–96D; Dio Chrysostom, *3 Regn.* 3.100–103; *Gnomologium Vaticanum* 273; Cicero, *Amic.* 48, 64; Seneca, *Ep.* 6.3). Friends were to share sorrow, or in the Pauline idiom in 2 Cor 1:3–7, to share in affliction (θλίψις, *thlipsis*). It is no surprise, then, that in 1:7 Paul uses the key term for this sharing of emotion in friendship: κοινωνία (*koinōnia*) (Aristotle, *Eth. nic.* 8.9.1; 8.12.1; 9.12.1; *Eth. eud.* 7.9.1; Plutarch, *Amic. mult.* 96D; Lucian, *Tox.* 6–7; Julian, *Or.* 8.240A–B; 241C).[42]

Second Corinthians 1:3–7 underscores the friendship that Paul claims exists between the community and himself. Sharing suffering is proof that they are friends. Here Paul does not call attention to the fact that *he* caused the community its grief. The vocabulary of suffering is vague enough to allow Paul to categorize the sting of rebuke felt by the church and his own regret to be categorized under the same terms. Later in the letter (beginning in 2:1–4 and culminating in 7:9–10) Paul deals directly with the pain he caused, characterizing it as appropriate grief.

Before exploring that strategy in detail, however, we need to examine the ways 2 Cor 1–7 exhibits characteristics of the conciliatory letter. First, stating one's regret for acting offensively or having written in severe tones was an element in the letter of reconciliation (Cicero, *Quint. fratr.* 1.2.12–13; Chariton, *Chaer.* 4.4; Philostratus, *Vit. soph.* 562–563; Fronto, *Ad M. Ceas.* 5.59).[43] Paul makes such statements in 1:8–9 and 7:8. Second, Paul follows the conventions of the conciliatory letter by saying that the intention of his rebuke was not to cause pain but to demonstrate his friendship (2:4 and 7:3; see above). Finally, Paul claims that the intent and the effect of his severe words were to promote healing. In 7:8–12, Paul reviews for his readers the salutary effects of the rebuke conveyed in the grieving letter. Behind these verses stands the *topos* that a friend does not intend his frank speech to cause pain but to bring about repentance and moral healing. The progression in 7:9–10 from grief to repentance and then to salvation places Paul's characterization of his treatment of the church squarely in the psychagogic tradition (see above).

The distinction between godly grief and worldly grief in 7:9b–11a further demonstrates Paul's use of the Greco-Roman tradition of soul-care in order to justify the severity of the grieving letter. Godly grief and the grief of the world were distinguished in their effects: repentance leading to salvation on the one hand, and death on the other.[44] Plutarch contrasts the grief that God inflicts with the pain caused by humans. God causes pain in order to bring about repentance; humans simply punish without a view to moral improvement (Plutarch, *Sera* 551C–E).[45] Moreover, unlike humans who get angry, cause pain, and then regret their severity (Plutarch, *Cohib. ira* 464C–D; *Sera* 550E–F; 551C; Seneca, *Ira* 2.6.2), God knows no remorse and causes no damage (Philo, *Conf.* 171). In 7:9, Paul claims that godly grief caused by the grieving letter did the church no damage.

We have moved from the epistolographic conventions of 2 Cor 1–7 to the philosophical *topos* of appropriate emotional pain in the context of moral exhortation. This is natural, because the rhetoric of conciliation draws from the philosophic tradition of soul-care. Paul had already invoked the notion of appropriate grief in 2:5–11 and emphasized that the grief inflicted by moral admonition should be combined with exhortation and affirmations of friendship. He reiterates this theme in 7:2–4, only now to ameliorate the suffering he had caused the church. In 7:3a, he denies that his speech aims to condemn his readers (πρὸς κατάκρισιν οὐ λέγω, *pros katakrisin ou legō*).[46] The uses of frank speech for moral edification, on the one hand, and condemnation, on the other, were well-known (Stobaeus, *Flor.* 3.13.63; Isocrates, *Paneg.* 4.130; 8.72; Philodemus, *Lib.* 37–38, IB; Lucian, *Pseudol.* 3; *Deor. conc.* 2; *Icar.* 30; Ps.-Diogenes, *Ep.* 29.2–3; Marcus Aurelius 11.6.2.).[47] As we have seen, harsh Cynics were well-known for their unbridled use of free speech to condemn the ills of humankind. Democritus's laughter condemned humanity for its inconsistency (Ps.-Hippocrates, *Ep.* 17.40). The notion of the philosopher's rebuke of sin as the guilty verdict in a legal proceeding is found in Cynic self-description (Ps.-Heraclitus, *Epp.* 7.2; 9.8; *Gnomologium Vaticanum* 116,487). Similarly, the harsh Cynic understood bold speech as punishment of human error (Ps.-Diogenes, *Ep.* 29.1, 4; Ps.-Socrates, *Ep.* 12; Ps.-Heraclitus, *Epp.* 7.4; 9.3; Plutarch, [*Vit. X orat.*] 842D; Epictetus, *Diatr.* 3.22.94, 97–98; Dio Chrysostom, *Isthm.* 8).

Paul distances himself from these harsh practitioners of frank speech by opposing the excessive grief their words inflict. This brings us to the last of his rhetorical strategies in 2 Cor 1–7. Paul uses hardship lists to shape his image as a bold-speaking friend whose chief concerns are reconciliation and the salvation of his hearers.

In order to understand how the hardships in 4:7–15 shape Paul's image, I first consider his reliance on God and abasement for the sake of the church. Second Corinthians 4:5–6 anticipates the hardships in 4:7–15 by raising the issue of the source of Paul's authority. He claims not to preach himself but Jesus Christ as Lord, and himself as the church's slave. The hardships in 4:7–15 amplify these two claims. They depict the free and bold-speaking Paul, who nevertheless relies entirely on God, not his own virtue, and who subordinates himself to the Corinthian congregation.

An ambiguity in 4:7 prepares the reader to move from the theme of God as source of power (4:8–9) to Paul's abasement for the sake of the church (4:10–15). On the one hand, the term θησαυρός (*thēsauros*, "treasure") suggests Paul's illumined and transformed soul.[48] The phrase "in earthen vessels" evokes the fragility of his outer self in anticipation of 4:16–5:5, and the "transcendent power" points to God's power to preserve the fragile Paul in the midst of hardships.[49] On the other hand, "treasure" could also refer to Paul's ministry. Then earthen pottery denotes the abasement he accepts for the sake of the church,[50] and "transcendent power" evokes the life-giving power of Paul's ministry.[51] The ambiguity of 4:7 reflects the correlation of the salvation Paul has received from God and God's salvation of humanity through Paul's ministry (cf. 1:4; 4:1; 5:18–19).

The catalog of hardships in 4:8–9 illustrates the dangers of Paul's ministry, his endurance, and, most of all, his source of power—God.[52] That Paul's power derives not from himself but from God distinguishes him from the wise man whose authority depends upon his ability to make all things depend upon himself. By making himself dependent upon God in this way, Paul prepares for his self-presentation as a reconciler.

The hardships in 4:10–15, however, point no longer to Paul's God-given power to endure difficulties but to endurance of ignomiy and death for the sake of the church. Paul now becomes a suffering bold-speaker whose concern is the salvation of the church. The purpose clauses in 4:10–11 suggest the voluntary nature of Paul's suffering. Moreover, if παραδιδόμεθα (*paradidometha*, "we hand ourselves over") is in the middle voice, the voluntary quality of Paul's suffering finds further emphasis.[53] The philanthropic aspects of Paul's hardships come out clearly in 4:12: "So then, death is at work in us, but life is at work in you." The theme of Paul's voluntary enslavement to the Corinthian church also appears in 4:15, in which he asserts that all things he does are for its sake.

In 4:16–5:5, Paul's hardships no longer emphasize the enslavement theme but underscore his spiritual transformation. The renewal of Paul's inner self is treated in 4:16–17, while the renewal of his outer self is expressed in 5:1–5.[54] In both cases, Paul calls upon, yet also modifies, the philosophic theme of hardships as the sage's training in virtue. The theme of training is present in 4:17 when Paul claims that affliction produces glory. Yet hardships prepare a *future* weight of glory, not a sage trained and perfected in reason. Paul modifies the philosophic *topos* by stressing the eschatological dimension of the transformation that God is working in him. He does not yet possess the transformed self but points to God's daily renewal of his inner self and God's preparation of an eternal dwelling (cf. Phil 3:12–14). By stressing progress instead of perfection, Paul distinguishes himself from the notion in the philosophic tradition that bold speech derived from the moral superiority of the sage.

We turn to the last hardship list in 2 Cor 1–7. In 6:3–10, Paul uses a list of hardships to commend himself to the Corinthians.[55] Again, we see that Paul is not satisfied simply to reproduce a philosophic *topos*. In addition to the hardships that Paul enumerates in 6:4–5, 7b–10, which portray him as courageous and steadfast, we find terms in 6:6–7a that seem anomalous: "by purity, knowledge, patience, kindness, holiness of spirit, genuine love, truthful speech, and the power of God. . . ." These terms make sense if they are viewed in light of the Greco-Roman psychagogical tradition.[56] The phrases "truthful speech" and "genuine love" refer to frank speech. Paul describes himself, the servant of God, as a bold speaker.[57] Paul's creativity here consists of introducing insights from philosophic soul-care about the way moral criticism is to be applied to avoid excessive grief.

The notion of excessive grief is present in 6:3, although modern translations and exegesis obscure it. The NRSV reads: "We are putting no obstacle [προσκοπήν, *proskopēn*] in anyone's way, so that no fault may be found with our ministry." Exegetes have incorrectly regarded the term προσκοπή as equivalent to πρόσκομμα (*proskomma*, "obstacle").[58] A very different understanding emerges, however, if προσκοπή is seen in contexts associated with bold speech. In these instances, it designates arousal of hatred because of the grief inflicted by moral rebuke (Polybius 38.4.2–4; Sextus Empiricus, *Math.* 2.54; Cicero, *Amic.* 88–89).[59] Προσκοπή is the alienation caused by bold speech (Isocrates, *Ep.* 9.12; Dionysius of Halicarnassus, *Ant. rom.* 11.9.1; Ps.-Socrates, *Ep.* 1.7; Dio Chrysostom, *Diod.* 4; Lucian, *Hermot.* 51; Aristides Rhetor, *Or.* 3.668). If this lexical insight is brought to bear on 6:3, then the reason Paul adds the phrase "so that no fault may be found with our ministry" becomes clear. According to 5:18–19, Paul's ministry aims at reconciliation. He would subvert this purpose if his speech alienated those he aimed to win over. If his speech only caused suffering, it would be inconsistent with the ministry of reconciliation. In 6:3–10, Paul presents himself as one who combines words of truth with kindness and encouragement in order not to alienate those whom he has addressed with bold speech. Yet kindness and patience should not be mistaken for timidity, because the hardships he has endured demonstrate courage.

The Problem of Suffering Reconstructed: Romans 5:1–11 and 8:18–39

No passages better demonstrate Paul's familiarity with philosophic discourse concerning hardships and suffering than Rom 5:1–11 and 8:18–39. Familiarity is perhaps too weak a word. Paul is so acquainted with the philosophic tradition that he uses its commonplaces effortlessly. Yet Paul manipulates theses commonplace sayings and ideas in order to criticize philosophy's claim about the capacity of the wise man to endure suffering. In other words, Paul both employs *and subverts* the patterned discourse of philosophy with its confidence in reason to conquer hardships.

He does this for a purpose. In place of virtue or reason as the solution to the problem of suffering, Paul advances the notion of shared suffering. Although he derives from the philosophic tradition the idea that friends share joy, suffering, and even death, Paul radically expands the pool of friends to include God, Christ, the Holy Spirit, and all of creation. The controlling image in these two passages is not the sage, protected from hardships by his reason, but the friend surrounded by friends who share all things.

At first glance, Rom 5:3–4 simply reproduces the notion that hardships train the sage in virtue.[60] Suffering builds character (see above). Paul writes, "And not only that, but we also boast in our sufferings, knowing that suffering produces endurance, and endurance produces character, and character produces hope . . ." Paul recasts this commonplace philosophical notion in a familiar rhetorical figure, climax.[61]

Yet some unfamiliar aspects of Paul's argument would have frustrated the ancient reader's expectations. Notice that Paul completes the climax in 5:4 by saying that "character produces hope." From the philosophic standpoint, this is an odd conclusion to an account of the way suffering builds character.[62] Some philosophers regarded hope as a moral disease, because hope placed happiness in externals, over which no one has control. Pursuit of externals can only lead to shame (Seneca, *Epp.* 5.7; 13.13; 23.2; 24.1; 71.14; 99.5, 13; 101.4).[63] Thus, by introducing hope as the product of character, Paul begins his critique of the philosophic view of suffering as the training of reason.

In its place, Paul explores the relationship between friendship and suffering. I must point out the ways Paul works the friendship motif into the argument as a replacement of philosophic reason. In 5:5 we read that hope is secure, "because the love of God has been poured into our hearts through the Holy Spirit that has been given to us." The putative exegetical dilemma that would force a decision whether "love of God" is an objective genitive (the love we have for God) or a subjective genitive (God's love for us) likely is a false problem. The central metaphor of the sentence, love as a liquid, suggests a mutuality of love. The idea of love as a liquid poured into the heart is found in amatory literature. It depicts the beloved as the source of the lover's affection.[64] If Paul is using this notion of mutual love, then the reason why hope is secure and can replace reason in the face of hardships becomes clear: friendship with God means a mutual sharing of suffering and joy. Paul has already alluded to this sharing in 5:2 when he boasts on the hope of sharing the glory of God.

In 5:6–8, Paul reiterates the theme of friendship and suffering from a different angle: "For while we were still weak, at the right time Christ died for the ungodly. Indeed, rarely will anyone die for a righteous person—though perhaps for a good person someone might actually dare to die. But God proves his love for us in that while we still were sinners Christ died for us." This verse echoes the philosophic idea that the ultimate proof of friendship was to undergo hardships and even to die for the friend. Paul construes Jesus' death for others in just this way. Notice also that Jesus' death also demonstrates God's love (5:8). There are some important distinctions, however, which set Paul's argument apart from the usual discussion of this matter. The philosophers were careful to put a limit on friendship. Friendship is possible only between the virtuous (see above). Jesus (and by implication God) violates this canon of friendship. Jesus dies for the weak, sinners, and enemies.

The final way Paul works the friendship motif into the argument is the repeated use of καταλλάσσειν (*katallassein*) in 5:9–11. This term, translated somewhat misleadingly as "to reconcile," does not simply mean the cessation of animosity, although this is the way commentators invariably regard it. The term regularly referred to the establishment of friendship (Aristotle, *Eth. nic.* 8.6.7; Dio Chrysostom, *Nicom.* 11,41,47–48), and with friendship comes the notion of sharing all things. Thus, we have come again to the point that began the passage: Paul's confidence resides in his hope of sharing God's glory. Paul does not take the philosopher's approach of viewing suffering as the occasion to display or to train human reason. In the last analysis, human suffering is a test of divine friendship. Will the sharing between suffering humanity and God be complete? If there is to be a human boasting in God's glory will there also be God's participation in human suffering?

Romans 8:18–39 makes the case for divine participation in human suffering. This passage takes up the issue of suffering, as the opening verse clearly indicates: "I consider that the sufferings of this present time are not worth comparing with the glory about to be revealed to us." There are numerous parallels between 8:18–39 and 5:1–11. The most obvious is the hardship lists in 8:35–39 that remind the reader of 5:3–4:

> Who will separate [χωρίσει, *chōrisei*] us from the love of Christ? Will hardship, or distress, or persecution, or famine, or nakedness, or peril, or sword? As it is written, "For your sake we are being killed all day long; we are accounted as sheep to be slaughtered." No, in all these things we are more than conquerors [ὑπερνικῶμεν, *hypernikōmen*] through him who loved us. For I am convinced that neither death, nor life, nor angels, nor rulers, nor things present, nor things to come, nor powers, nor height, nor depth, nor anything else in all creation, will be able to separate [χωρίσαι, *chōrisai*] us from the love of God in Christ Jesus our Lord.

The items in the first list (8:35) are typical of the dangers endured by the wise man. The provocative aspect of both lists, however, is their rhetorical function. Neither list works in any of the three ways hardships were used in the ancient discourse about the wise man. Virtue is neither displayed nor trained here, nor is the philanthropy of Paul and his readers exhibited. Paul is putting these hardship lists to a novel use, and what he does not say about suffering might have seemed to his hearers to have as much importance as what he did say.

The novelty of Paul's use of these hardship lists is that he puts them in the context of friendship. Instead of calling attention to an individual's virtue or philanthropy, the lists name the things that cannot separate Paul and his readers from the love of God. Paul mentions separation twice (8:35, 39) thus putting his hearers in mind of a problem often treated in discussions of friendship (Aristotle, *Eth. nic.* 8.5.1; Plutarch, *Amic. mult.* 95A; Seneca, *Ep.* 55.8–11; 63.3). Separation was the greatest grief friends might suffer. Yet there was comfort. Even when physically absent from one another, friends were inseparable, because they were one soul in two bodies. Hardships in Paul's hands, then, serve the rhetorical purpose of reconstructing the problem of suffering. Suffering is not the occasion for the display or the training of virtue as would have been the case for Stoics and indeed for much of the Greco-Roman world. For Paul, hardships produce or exhibit nothing in themselves; rather, and simply, hardships do not obstruct the friendship among God, Paul, and his hearers.

Paul further challenges the understanding of suffering in the philosophic tradition when he employs the phrase "we are more than conquerors [ὑπερνικῶμεν, *hypernikōmen*] through him who loved us." To understand why this is a challenge, we need first to appreciate the claim the victory motif makes for the supremacy of reason in the face of misfortune. The victory motif was a popular metaphor in the philosophic portrayal of the wise man's superiority to hardships. The wise man conquers hardships (Seneca, *Dial.* 1.2.2; 2.10.4; *Polyb.* 17.1–2; *Helv.* 2.2), while he himself is invincible (ἀνίκητος, *anikētos*; Ps.-Diogenes, *Ep.* 33; Epictetus, *Diatr.* 1.18.21–23; *Ench.* 19.2; Seneca, *Ep.* 85.29; *Vit. beat.* 4.2; *Helv.* 5.5). Fortune vanquishes lesser souls (Seneca, *Helv.* 1.1). Both military and athletic victory served as a point of comparison for the sage's indomitable soul.[65] The victory could be over external dangers or over one's own passions.[66] Seneca, who used the metaphor extensively,[67] ends a discourse on suffering like Paul with the rhetorical flourish supplied by the victory motif:

> And when will it be our privilege to despise both kinds of misfortune? When will it be our privilege, after all the passions have been subdued and brought under our control, to utter the words "I have conquered [*vici*]!"? Do you ask me whom I have conquered [*vicerim*]? Neither the Persians, nor the far-off Medes, nor the warlike race that lies beyond the

Dahae; not these, but greed, ambition, and the fear of death that has conquered the conquerors of the world [*qui victores gentium vicit*]. (Seneca, *Ep.*
71.37)

The motif emphasized the importance of placing all of one's hopes in oneself and
not in others (*Ceb. Tab.* 22–24; Seneca, *Vit. beat.* 8.3). It also pointed to the capacity
of reason to protect the self from every misfortune (Cicero, *Tusc.* 5.52–54; Seneca,
Epp. 9.18–19; 78.15–21; *Dial.* 2.5.7; 2.6.6).

Paul seems to affirm the philosopher's confidence in reason by introducing
the victory motif into a discussion of hardships. Nevertheless, he dismantles the
philosophic view in two ways. First, he claims that "we are *more* than conquerors"
(emphasis added), implying that the metaphor of victory over suffering may not
be adequate. Second, victory over suffering comes not through an individual's
use of reason but through friendship with God: "we are more than conquerors
through him who loved us" (8:37). If anything is clear about the philosopher's use
of the victory motif, it is this: the individual soul has within itself all that is necessary to overcome suffering. Victory through another's agency would have appeared ludicrous and an insult to the providence of God, who saw fit to place a
fragment of divine reason in every human soul.

If Rom 8:35–39 is the high point of Paul's attempt to reconstruct the problem
of suffering from the perspective of friendship, then Rom 8:18–34 builds up to this
conclusion by advocating the power of a friend's sympathy (taken in the strong
sense of co-suffering) to console the sufferer.[68] In these verses, Paul explores the
consolation of friendship as an alternative to the philosophic method of dealing
with suffering through rational control.[69] He portrays four agents as friends who
share all things with human sufferers: creation (8:19–22), the Spirit (8:26), God
(8:31–33), and Christ (8:34). Space allows only for developing the theme of shared
suffering in terms of creation and the Spirit.

In 8:19–22, creation is conceptualized as a person with emotions desiring to
share both in humanity's future freedom and in its present suffering. In short, creation is a friend:

> For the creation waits with eager longing for the revealing of the children
> of God; for the creation was subjected to futility, not of its own will but
> by the will of the one who subjected it, in hope that the creation itself will
> be set free from its bondage to decay and will obtain the freedom of the
> glory of the children of God. We know that the whole creation has been
> groaning in labor pains [συστενάζει καὶ συνωδίνει, *systenazei kai synōdi-
> nei*] until now.[70]

Paul draws upon motifs found in Greek literature and philosophy to portray the
friendship of creation with humans. While for some modern readers it may be

reminiscent of the opening chapters of Genesis and the development of biblical themes in Jewish apocalyptic thought,[71] nature's subjection to futility and its bondage to decay was a stock theme in consolation philosophy (Philo, *Cher.* 77–78; Ps.-Crates, *Ep.* 35; Plutarch, [*Cons. Apoll.*] 104C–106C, 112D; Cicero, *Tusc.* 3.58–61; Seneca, *Ep.* 71.11–16; *Polyb.* 1.1–4; Menander Rhetor, Περὶ ἐπιδεικτικῶν 2.9).[72] It was thought that those grieving might derive some encouragement from the thought that all existing things must of necessity suffer and perish.

The second motif is decidedly not from philosophical sources. The characterization of nature or an aspect of nature as a person in sympathy with human suffering is an ancient literary figure known in modern parlance as the pathetic fallacy.[73] "Groan (στένειν, stenein)," and "be in anguish (ὠδίνειν, ōdinein)," were frequently employed in instances of the pathetic fallacy to communicate nature's sympathy and mourning for human suffering (*Greek Anthology* 7.10, 142, 241, 268, 292, 328, 393, 468, 476, 481, 547, 549, 599, 633; 8.3; Bion, *Epitaph. Adon.* 35).[74] Creation is a friend, groaning over humanity's suffering, subject to the same futility, yet hoping to share in the same freedom and glory.

In 8:26, we discover that the Spirit also groans. This is a remarkable statement, but fits with the overall purpose of the passage to assert the shared sufferings of friends as an alternative to consolation through rational self-control. The moral philosophers condemned groaning (στεναγμός, stenagmos) as a sign of weakness and the lack of reason (Plutarch, [*Cons. Apoll.*] 113A; Epictetus, *Diatr.* 2.6.16–17). No good man ever groans (Epictetus, *Diatr.* 1.1.12, 22; 1.6.29). It is a disgrace to groan (Cicero, *Tusc.* 2.30–33). Groaning must be resisted (Cicero, *Tusc.* 2.42–50). Paul, on the other hand, makes this particularly acute form of grief part of the Spirit's experience.[75] The Spirit shares human groaning and is therefore in solidarity with humanity. God's friendship with humanity is implied in suffering the loss of the Son, or more accurately, in handing the Son over to death (8:32). Finally, the circle of friends is completed. As in the case of 5:6–8, Christ's friendship is demonstrated through his death for others (8:34; see above). Paul's reconstruction of the problem of suffering is finished. He has employed rhetorical forms and commonplace ideas associated with philosophy's confidence that reason conquers suffering. Yet he has disarmed that confidence. In place of the virtue of self-control, he has advocated the shared suffering of friends, and the circle of Paul's friends includes all of creation and the divine community.

Part III. Other Relevant Pauline and Paulinist Texts

Rom 2:9, 15; 7:24; 8:17; 9:1–3; 12:12, 15, 21; 15:1–3, 30
1 Cor 4:9–12, 21; 5:2; 7:35; 12:25–26; 13:3; 15:30–33
2 Cor 2:12–16; 5:14–21; 8:2; 11:23–33; 12:7–10; 12:21

Gal 6:2
Phil 3:18
1 Thess 1:6; 2:1–2, 7–8, 13–16; 3:3–5; 4:13–18; 5:8, 14
2 Thess 1:4–10
Col 1:24
Eph 3:13; 6:10–17
1 Tim 1:18–20; 4:10
2 Tim 1:8–2:13; 3:10–13; 4:6–8

Part IV. Bibliography

Classical, Hellenistic, and Greco-Roman

Braund, S. M., and C. Gill, eds. *The Passions in Roman Thought and Literature.* Cambridge: Cambridge University Press, 1997.

Buller, J. L. "The Pathetic Fallacy in Hellenistic Pastoral." *Ramus* 10 (1981): 35–52.

Fowler, R. L. "The Rhetoric of Desperation." *HSCP* 91 (1987): 6–38.

Glibert-Thirry, A. *Pseudo-Andronicus De Rhodes:* ΠΕΡΙ ΠΑΘΩΝ. Corpus latinum commentariorum in aristotelem graecorum, Supplement 2. Leiden: Brill, 1977.

Gregg, R. C. *Consolation Philosophy: Greek and Christian Paideia in Basil and the Two Gregories.* Patristic Monograph Series 3. Cambridge, Mass.: Philadelphia Patristic Foundation, 1975.

Höistad, R. *Cynic Hero and Cynic King.* Lund, Sweden: Carl Blom, 1948.

Johann, H.-T. *Trauer und Trost: Eine quellen- und strukturanalytische Untersuchung der philosophischen Trostschriften über Tod.* Studia et Testamonia Antiqua 5. Munich: Wilhelm Fink, 1968.

Perkins, J. *The Suffering Self: Pain and Narrative Representation in the Early Christian Era.* New York: Routledge, 1995.

Strubbe, J. H. M. "Epigrams and Consolation Decrees for Deceased Youth." *L'Antiquité classique* 67 (1998): 45–75.

New Testament

Fitzgerald, John T. *Cracks in an Earthen Vessel: An Examination of the Catalogues of Hardships in the Corinthian Correspondence.* SBLDS 99. Atlanta: Scholars Press, 1988.

Glad, C. E. *Paul and Philodemus: Adaptability in Epicurean and Early Christian Psychagogy.* NovTSup 81. Leiden: Brill, 1995.

Malherbe, A. J. *Paul and the Popular Philosophers.* Minneapolis: Fortress Press, 1989.

———. *Paul and the Thessalonians: The Philosophic Tradition of Pastoral Care.* Philadelphia: Fortress Press, 1987.

Talbert, C. H. *Learning through Suffering: The Educational Value of Suffering in the New Testament and in Its Milieu.* Collegeville, Minn.: Liturgical Press, 1991.

Notes

1. A. Glibert-Thirry, *Pseudo-Andronicus De Rhodes:* ΠΕΡΙ ΠΑΘΩΝ (Corpus latinum commentariorum in aristotelem graecorum, Supplement 2; Leiden: Brill, 1977), 223.

2. Cicero limited the topic in the same way. See A. Erskine, "Cicero and the Expression of Grief," in *The Passions in Roman Thought and Literature* (ed. S. M. Braund and C. Gill; Cambridge: Cambridge University Press, 1997), 41–42.

3. See M. Pohlenz, *Die Stoa* (2d ed.; 2 vols.; Göttingen: Vandenhoeck & Ruprecht, 1959), 1:149; 2:77.

4. Philo (*Leg.* 3.111) cites what appears to have been a standard definition: "groaning is intense and excessive sorrow [λύπη, *lypē*]." Unless otherwise indicated, texts and translations of ancient works are from the Loeb Classical Library.

5. If we associate soul shrinkage with grief, we are more likely to recognize allusions to emotional pain in Paul's letters. In addition to the words with the root *sten*, contraction of soul is present in the following terms in the Pauline epistles; note, however, that the English translations provided by the various modern versions (the NRSV is cited here) fail to convey the physiological aspect of the emotion: "affliction" (θλῖψις, *thlipsis*; e.g., Rom 5:3; 8:35; 2 Cor 1:4, 6, 8; 2:4); "anguish of heart" (συνοχή καρδίας, *synochē kardias*; 2 Cor 2:4); "faint-hearted" (ὀλιγόψυχος, *oligopsychos*; 1 Thess 1:14).

6. Glibert-Thirry, *Pseudo-Andronicus De Rhodes*, 227, my translation.

7. See A. C. van Geytenbeek, *Musonius Rufus and Greek Diatribe* (Wijsgerige Teksten en Studies 8; Assen, the Netherlands: Van Gorcum, 1963), 138. See also Plato, *Gorg.* 472D–479D; Isocrates, *Nic.* 53; Juvenal, *Sat.* 13.192–198.

8. See H. Deku, "Selbstbestrafung: Marginalien zu einem sehr alten, aber noch nicht ganz lexikonreifen Begriff," *Archiv für Begriffsgeschichte* 21 (1977): 42–58. See also Epictetus, *Diatr.* 2.22.35; *Ench.* 34; Clement of Alexandria, *Strom.* 2.12.55; Marcus Aurelius, 8.53; 12.16; Lucian, *Merc. cond.* 42; 1 John 3:19–22.

9. John T. Fitzgerald, *Cracks in an Earthen Vessel: An Examination of the Catalogues of Hardships in the Corinthian Correspondence* (SBLDS 99; Atlanta: Scholars Press, 1988). Critics of Fitzgerald underestimate the power of the Greek philosophical tradition on the Jewish sources that, it is claimed, were more of an influence on Paul. Furthermore, they fail to understand Fitzgerald's main contribution, to show how the rhetorical use of hardship lists flowed out of the central teachings of the philosophers on the relation between virtue and endurance. See, for example, N. Willert, "The Catalogues of Hardships in the Pauline Correspondence: Background and Function," in *The New Testament and Hellenistic Judaism* (ed. P. Borgen and S. Giversen; Århus, Denmark: Århus, 1995), 217–43.

10. Fitzgerald, *Cracks in an Earthen Vessel*, 115.

11. Ibid., 51–55.

12. See J. Perkins, *The Suffering Self: Pain and Narrative Representation in the Early Christian Era* (New York: Routledge, 1995), 77–98.

13. Fitzgerald, *Cracks in an Earthen Vessel*, 55–70.

14. See N. C. Croy, *Endurance in Suffering: Hebrews 12.1–13 in Its Rhetorical, Religious, and Philosophical Context* (SNTSMS 98; Cambridge: Cambridge University Press, 1999), 139–59.

15. See R. Höistad, *Cynic Hero and Cynic King* (Lund, Sweden: Carl Blom, 1948), 97. For the readiness of the wise man to suffer indignities for the good of others, see Antisthenes, *frgs.* 14.5–6; 15.5, 9. See H. D. Rankin, *Antisthenes Sokratikos* (Amsterdam: Hakkert, 1986), 168–70.

16. For the dangers faced by bold speakers, see Lucian, *Pisc.* 20; *Peregr.* 32. See A. Malherbe, *Paul and the Popular Philosophers* (Minneapolis: Fortress Press, 1989), 38.

17. See Höistad, *Cynic Hero,* 195–96.

18. For Cynic misanthropy, see G. A. Gerhard, *Phoinix von Kolophon: Texte und Untersuchungen* (Leipzig: Teubner, 1909), 39, 165–67, 170–75.

19. Ps.-Hippocrates, *Ep.* 17.40 (in R. Hercher, *Epistolographi Graeci* [Amsterdam: Hakkert, 1965], 303).

20. See Gerhard, *Phoinix von Kolophon,* 32–45.

21. See A. Malherbe, *Paul and the Thessalonians: The Philosophic Tradition of Pastoral Care* (Philadelphia: Fortress Press, 1987), 21–28.

22. For the Epicurean care of souls, see C. E. Glad, *Paul and Philodemus: Adaptability in Epicurean and Early Christian Psychagogy* (NovTSup 81; Leiden: Brill, 1995), 101–81. Note the emphasis on reason, truth, and bold speech in Lucian's (*Alex.* 47) account of the Epicurean path to tranquillity; no mention is made of a conversion involving pain, leading in turn to repentance.

23. See I. Hadot, *Seneca und die griechisch-römische Tradition der Seelenleitung* (Berlin: Walter de Gruyter, 1969), 71–78.

24. See H. G. Ingenkamp, *Plutarchs Schriften über die Heilung der Seele* (Hypomnemata 34; Göttingen: Vandenhoeck & Ruprecht, 1971), 74–90.

25. Ps.-Libanius, *Charact. Ep.* 43. Text and translation is A. Malherbe, *Ancient Epistolary Theorists* (SBLSBS 19; Atlanta: Scholars Press, 1988), 72–73.

26. For expressions of grief as moral condemnation in the philosophic tradition, see the Cynic appropriation of Heraclitus and the philosophers who imitated his gloominess: Ps.-Heraclitus, *Epp.* 5.3; 7.2–10; Lucian, *Demon.* 6; *Vit. auct.* 7; *Fug.* 18.

27. For other examples of the grieving style, see Julian, *Ep.* 68; Gregory of Nazianzus, *Epp.* 7, 16; Basil, *Epp.* 45, 156, 204, 207, 212, 223, 224, 270.

28. *Menandri sententiae* 370. In the same work we read, "Suppose all the burdens of friends to be in common" (534), and, "When a friend suffers with a friend he suffers with himself" (803; my translations; see also 543K).

29. Both Plato (*Symp.* 179B–180B) and Seneca (*Ep.* 9.10–12) recognize blurring in the distinction between friendship and erotic love when it comes to dying for a friend.

30. S. Farron, *Vergil's Aeneid: A Poem of Love and Grief* (Leiden: Brill, 1993), 19n. 5.

31. See C. K. Barrett, "Ο ΑΔΙΚΗΣΑΣ (2 Cor 7.12)," in *Verborum Veritas: Festschrift für Gustav Stählin* (ed. O. Böcher and K. Haacker; Wuppertal, Germany: Theologischer Verlag Rolf Brockhaus, 1970), 149–57.

32. V. Furnish, *II Corinthians* (AB 32A; Garden City, N.Y.: Doubleday, 1984), 54–55, 143.

33. Barrett, "Ο ΑΔΙΚΗΣΑΣ," 149–52.

34. For arguments against identifying the letter with either 1 Corinthians or 2 Cor 10–13, see Furnish, *II Corinthians,* 163–68.

35. Ibid., 367–71.

36. D. Fredrickson, "Παρρησία in the Pauline Epistles," in *Friendship, Flattery, and Frankness of Speech: Studies on Friendship in the New Testament World* (ed. J. Fitzgerald; NovTSup 82; Leiden: Brill, 1996), 180.

37. Ancient exegetes viewed ἐπιτιμία here as ἐπιτίμησις and thus an aspect of moral exhortation. See, for example, Chrysostom, *Hom. 4 in 2 Cor.* 4 (PG 61.422).

38. For the goals of moral exhortation, and rebuke in particular, see Hadot, *Seneca und die griechisch-römische Tradition der Seelenleitung,* 168–69. Philodemus (*Lib.* 31, 82, XXIVA) understands ἐπιτίμησις as a form of frank speech.

39. See A. Malherbe, "'Pastoral Care' in the Thessalonian Church," *NTS* 36 (1990): 381–85.

40. For rebuke leading to shame and suicide, see Plutarch, *Adul. amic.* 70F–71C.

41. R. L. Fowler ("The Rhetoric of Desperation," *HSCP* 91 [1987]: 6–38) has identified a rhetorical form employed from Homer to Roman times, which he has named "desperation speech." Its identifying marks include indication of the extreme weight of suffering borne by the speaker, the impossibility of a solution (ἀπορία, *aporia*), questioning whether life is any longer possible, not knowing whether to chose life or death, and an exclamation about how wretched one has become (parodied in Epictetus, *Diatr.* 1.12.27). In addition to 2 Cor 1:8, two other passages in Paul fit this form very well: Rom 7:24–25 and Phil 1:21–26. Fowler (27–31) calls attention to the fact that Euripides introduces the sympathy of friends as a solution to the *aporia* of the speaker. Similarly, Paul introduces the notion of friendship in each instance of his use of desperation speech.

42. Friends have like emotions (see Plutarch, *Adul. amic.* 51E; *Amic. mult.* 97A). Friendship comes into being through likeness, and this includes the identity of emotions (see Aristotle, *Eth. nic.* 8.3.6–7; Plutarch, *Amic. mult.* 96E–F; Cicero, *Amic.* 50).

43. D. Fredrickson, "Paul's Sentence of Death (2 Corinthians 1:9)," in *God, Evil, and Suffering: Essays in Honor of Paul R. Sponheim* (ed. T. Fretheim and C. Thompson; Word and World Supplement Series 4; St. Paul, Minn.: Word & World, 2000), 103–7.

44. "Worldly grief" recalls Paul's description in 2:7 of the grief suffered by "the one who caused injury."

45. For the role of emotional pain or grief in God's intention to bring about moral reform, see Plutarch, *Sera* 549F–550A; 550E–F; 551C–E. Cf. Philo, *Det.* 144–146; *Conf.* 180–182; *Somn.* 1.91; Heb 12:10–11; Rev 3:19.

46. Other interpreters (e.g., C. K. Barrett, *The Second Epistle to the Corinthians* [BNTC; London: Black, 1973], 203; Furnish, *II Corinthians,* 369) regard this phrase as Paul's attempt to mitigate the severity of the previous denials (7:2), which they view as his accusations against the church.

47. See Gerhard, *Phoinix von Kolophon,* 36.

48. For the soul as treasure, see Philo, *Leg.* 3.104–106; *Cher.* 48; *Det.* 35, 43; *Deus* 42, 91–93; *Sobr.* 41, 68; *Conf.* 69; Plutarch, *An. corp.* 500D; Seneca, *Ep.* 92.31–32. Barrett (*Second Epistle to the Corinthians,* 137) gives good reasons to believe that Paul is alluding to his illumined soul; in the end, however, like other interpreters he does not come to this conclusion for fear of turning Paul's anthropology over to Hellenistic ideas about the body and soul. For Paul's ability to manipulate philosophic terminology, see n. 54 below.

49. So Fitzgerald, *Cracks in Earthen Vessels,* 167–69.

50. See H. B. Walters, *History of Ancient Pottery: Greek, Etruscan, and Roman* (2 vols.; London: Murray, 1905), 1:135–36; 2:455, 479. Cf. Rom 9:21 and esp. 2 Tim 2:20.

51. The power of God to give life through Paul's ministry is the theme of 5:12. Cf. 2 Cor 1:6; Gal 3:5; Phil 2:13; 1 Thess 2:13. For a similar notion, in the philosophic tradition, of divine power, see Dio Chrysostom, *Alex.* 15.

52. Fitzgerald, *Cracks in Earthen Vessels,* 169–76. Fitzgerald believes, however, that the divine power in Paul's weakness in 4:8–9 is "one of the ways in which the Corinthians are to know that he has been commissioned by God and the word that he speaks comes from God (172)." I would assert that Paul distinguishes himself from the popular conception of the philosopher, whose claim to authority rested on his own power.

53. So ibid., 180.

54. For Paul's use and critique in 2 Cor 4:16–5:5 of philosophic commonplaces such as "body as temporary dwelling" and "death as stripping the soul of the body," see D. Fredrickson, "Paul Playfully on Time and Eternity," *Dialog* 39 (2000): 21–23. For these commonplaces incorporated into discussions of hardships and suffering, see Seneca, *Epp.* 24.17–21; 92.30–35; 102.21–30; 120.13–19.

55. The view that 6:3–10 is apologetic has been challenged with good reason by Fitzgerald (*Cracks in Earthen Vessels,* 187–88). He has demonstrated (191–201) that 6:3–10 reflects the philosophic use of hardships to depict the sage's courage and constancy. I disagree, however, with his view that Paul's self-commendation fosters his hearers' confidence in him. Something more specific is at stake, namely, the integrity of the flexible approach to the care of souls suggested in 6:6–7. The constancy of Paul portrayed in 6:7–10 guards against any accusation that his gentleness is flattery. For the theme of adaptability in the care of souls, see Glad, *Paul and Philodemus,* 15–98.

56. Fredrickson, "Παρρησία in the Pauline Epistles," 179–80.

57. Ibid., 179.

58. See, for example, R. Martin, *2 Corinthians* (WBC 40; Waco, Tex.: Word Books, 1986), 170–71.

59. For the sense of hatred, see *SVF* 3.102.40; Cicero, *Tusc.* 4.23–24; 4.26; Seneca, *Ep.* 14.7.

60. Substitute "Christian" for "sage" and you have Paul's meaning. So C. H. Talbert, *Learning through Suffering: The Educational Value of Suffering in the New Testament and in Its Milieu* (Collegeville, Minn.: Liturgical, 1991), 21–22.

61. J. Wettstein, *Novum Testamentum Graecum* (2 vols.; Amsterdam: Ex officina Dommeriana, 1752; reprint, Graz, Germany: Akademische Druck- und Verlagsanstalt, 1962), 46.

62. A similar surprise awaits the reader in 1 Thess 5:8. The "armor of the sage" constructed out of reason was a widespread philosophic motif. See Malherbe, *Paul and the Popular Philosophers,* 95–103. Paul subverts the image, however, by constructing the armor out of faith, love, and hope. These make a person vulnerable to realities external to the soul. Paul's earliest interpreters were not so eager to abandon reason. Note the more conventional construction of armor in Eph 6:10–17 and 1 Tim 1:18.

63. Nevertheless, Paul's appeal to hope in affliction has parallels. For example, Menander (813K) writes, "In adversity a man is saved by hope." Does Rom 8:24a echo this saying? Cicero (*Amic.* 23, 59) believes that friendship provides hope for the future and does not let the spirit grow faint. This connection between friendship and hope is crucial for Rom 5 and 8.

64. See notes by M. Davies, *Hermes* 111 (1983): 496–97, and O. Vox, *Hermes* 120 (1992): 375–76. For additional examples, see D. Sider, *The Epigrams of Philodemus: Introduction, Text, and Commentary* (New York: Oxford University Press, 1997), 95–97.

65. Athletic victory: Ps.-Diogenes, *Ep.* 31; Epictetus, *Diatr.* 1.24.1–2; 3.25.1–6; 4.4.30–32; Philo, *Agr.* 110–21; *Mut.* 82.1; *Prob.* 26–27, 110–12. Military victory: Ps.-Diogenes, *Ep.* 5; and most of the instances in Seneca, including *Polyb.* 15.3; 16.3.

66. Victory over external hardships: Seneca, *Epp.* 98.12, 14; 104.27. Victory over passions: *SVF* 3.129.9; Ps.-Heraclitus, *Ep.* 4.3; Philo, *Abr.* 48–49; Epictetus, *Ench.* 34. External and internal are brought together in Ps.-Diogenes, *Ep.* 12; Cicero, *Tusc.* 2.63.

67. For a brief account, see C. E. Manning, *On Seneca's "Ad Marciam"* (Leiden: Brill, 1981), 62. Seneca reserves the victory motif for a final flourish in *Ep.* 67, a discourse on the endurance of hardships.

68. Compared with the other techniques for mitigating emotional pain, which focused on the irrationality of grief, a friend's sympathy was a little-utilized theme in Greco-Roman consolatory literature. See J. H. D. Scourfield, *Consoling Heliodorus: A Commentary on Jerome, Letter 60* (New York: Oxford University Press, 1992), 81. A few examples can be located: Plutarch, [*Cons. Apoll.*] 102A; Seneca, *Polyb.* 12.2. For the rational therapy of grief in philosophic consolation, see H.-T. Johann, *Trauer und Trost: Eine quellen- und strukturanalytische Untersuchung der philosophischen Trostschriften über Tod* (Studia et Testamonia Antiqua 5; Munich: Wilhelm Fink, 1968), and R. C. Gregg, *Consolation Philosophy: Greek and Christian Paideia in Basil and the Two Gregories* (Patristic Monograph Series 3; Cambridge, Mass.: Philadelphia Patristic Foundation, 1975). Outside of the philosophic writings, however, the notion that sharing emotional pain has consolatory power appears to have been widespread. See J. H. M. Strubbe, "Epigrams and Consolation Decrees for Deceased Youth," *L'Antiquité classique* 67 (1998): 45–75. Stobaeus (*Flor.* 5.48.16–31) provides a collection of texts around this theme.

69. We can be certain that Paul was aware of the forms of philosophic consolation, since he adopts some of them. See Malherbe, *Paul and the Thessalonians*, 57–58, and idem, *Paul and the Popular Philosophers*, 64–66.

70. The NRSV's "in labor pains" is too free a translation of συνωδίνει (*synōdinei*). The verbal aspect needs to be retained, and it is debatable whether the birth imagery should be given such emphasis. The term ὠδίνω (*ōdinō*) in the sense of "I am in anguish" was employed with "I groan" (στένω, *stenō*) in epitaphs without calling attention to birth imagery. The early association of the term with birth pain is no indication of actual usage in a later period.

71. O. Christoffersson, *The Earnest Expectation of the Creature: The Flood-Tradition as Matrix of Romans 8:18–27* (ConBNT 23; Stockholm: Almqvist & Wiksell International, 1990), 129–32.

72. See Johann, *Trauer und Trost*, 63–67, 119–64.

73. J. L. Buller, "The Pathetic Fallacy in Hellenistic Pastoral," *Ramus* 10 (1981): 35–52; J. M. Hurwitt, "Palm Trees and the Pathetic Fallacy in Archaic Greek Poetry and Art," *CJ* 77 (1982): 193–99; C. Segal, "Dissonant Sympathy: Song, Orpheus, and the Golden Ages in Seneca's Tragedies," *Ramus* 12 (1983): 229–51; J. D. Reed, *Bion of Smyrna: The Fragments and the Adonis* (Cambridge Classical Texts and Commentary 33; Cambridge: Cambridge University Press, 1997), 125, 215–16.

74. Nature's sympathy for human suffering should not be confused with the Stoic doctrine of συμπάθεια (*sympatheia*), which taught the impersonal, causal interconnection of all things. See H. R. Neuenschwander, *Mark Aurels Beziehungen zu Seneca und Poseidonios* (Noctes Romanae 3; Stuttgart: Paul Haupt, 1951), 14–23.

75. For groaning as a type of grief, see above, n. 4.

7

PAUL AND GRECO-ROMAN EDUCATION

Ronald F. Hock

Paul's early or formal education is a difficult subject to investigate. It is difficult for a variety of reasons. Paul himself says nothing about his early education, not even when he writes about his youth (Phil 3:5–6). Moreover, he self-consciously refused to incorporate worldly wisdom into his apostolic preaching (1 Cor 2:1–4) and even considered himself a rank amateur when it came to rhetoric (2 Cor 11:6), the content and goal of much of the educational curriculum in the Greco-Roman world.

But Paul protests too much. His status as an aristocrat[1] makes education a given, and the letters themselves betray such a command of the Greek language as well as a familiarity with the literary and rhetorical conventions of Greek education that only a full and thorough education in Greek on Paul's part makes sense of the evidence. This conclusion is in keeping with recent trends in Pauline scholarship, if stated more sharply.[2] Scholars, however, have not presented in sufficient detail just what such an education entailed nor have they taken account of the spate of scholarship on Greco-Roman education in recent years. Consequently, it may be helpful to survey Greco-Roman education in the light of this recent scholarship in order to gauge more precisely Paul's own level of education.

Part I. Greco-Roman Education in Recent Scholarship

The standard treatment of ancient education—from Homeric times to the end of antiquity—is Henri Irénée Marrou's *History of Education in Antiquity*,[3] and while this book remains indispensable, due to its scope, thoroughness, and use of primary sources, it is also true that scholarship on ancient education has progressed considerably beyond Marrou's analysis, especially for the first two stages of the curriculum, the primary and the secondary.

Scholars now have increased documentary evidence at their disposal[4] and, what is more, this evidence has been classified with greater precision and sophistication, as in Raffaella Cribiore's typology of school hands, that is, of handwriting skills, that distinguishes four grades: zero grade (least experienced), alphabetic, evolving, and rapid (most advanced).[5] She and other scholars, in particular Teresa Morgan, have argued for the primacy of this documentary evidence over the scattered and often idealized remarks about education in the literary sources, particularly when trying to establish exactly what and how well students learned to read.[6] Morgan has also emphasized a more developmental view of the curriculum, noting, for example, that the origins of the standard curriculum began shortly after—indeed, as a response to—Alexander's conquests[7] and developed over time, particularly with regard to the emergence of the study of grammar during the early Roman Empire as a new stage in the curriculum between learning to read and write and the study of rhetoric or philosophy.[8]

In addition, Morgan introduces the notion of core and periphery into the study of ancient education, emphasizing that most students were taught only a core of skills and authors during the primary and, to some extent, the secondary stages, while only very few moved beyond this core and received the sort of education prescribed by the literary sources.[9] Finally, scholars like Alan Booth have noticed greater fluidity and social differentiation in primary education than had been thought, leading to a revision of our picture of all students, from ages seven to eleven, learning to read from an elementary teacher; instead, some students, especially aristocratic boys, could have learned to read in as little as two years, and may have done so from a secondary-school teacher, who had accepted these younger children as a way of ensuring that he had students for his own grammatical curriculum.[10]

The following survey of Greco-Roman education will be organized around the tripartite curricular sequence of primary, secondary, and tertiary education, for, as Morgan points out, we know more about the curriculum than we do, for example, about places for classrooms, the numbers in a class, the ages of students at any one stage, the methods used by teachers, and the structure of the school day.[11]

Primary Education

In the first stage of the curriculum the elementary teacher taught students, starting at about age seven, to read, write, and compute.[12] Beyond the literary sources' sparse discussions about learning to read,[13] the sands of Egypt have preserved actual manuals that contain the primary curriculum. One such manual is Papyrus Bouriant 1, a student's notebook that covers most of the curriculum,[14] and there are more than two hundred other papyri, ostraca (pieces of clay pottery that were used as cheap writing surfaces), and waxed-wooden tablets that document specific exercises within this curriculum.[15]

From this evidence, both literary and documentary, we see that learning to read and write progressed from the simple to the ever more complex, from letters to syllables and then to words and finally to sentences and short poetic passages. Students first learned to recognize, pronounce, and write the letters of the alphabet and, also from the very beginning, to write their own names, as Cribiore has emphasized.[16] Recognizing the letters proved difficult for some,[17] and various ostraca and tablets illustrate the struggles students had when trying to copy letters of the alphabet, usually from models supplied by the teacher.[18] For example, one ostracon shows a student trying to copy several letters, especially Π, in a zero-grade hand,[19] whereas other ostraca preserve the alphabetic hand of one student writing the entire alphabet from alpha to omega[20] and another copying the alphabet not only from alpha to omega but also from omega back again to alpha.[21] Eventually, however, these students became proficient in writing the letters correctly, but, as Cribiore has emphasized, they also took special pride in writing them beautifully—calligraphically, as it were—a skill required of scribes, which explains a number of texts with letters and alphabets written by much older, experienced hands.[22] In other words, exercises at one stage continued after students moved on to other, more advanced, stages.[23]

Students then progressed to syllables and copied long and systematic lists of combinations of vowels with consonants, sometimes with the consonants preceding—as in βα, βε, βη, βο, βυ, and βω—and sometimes with the consonant preceding and following the vowels—as in βαβ, βεβ, βηβ, and so on.[24] Next came equally long lists of words, beginning with those of one syllable, then two, then three, and sometimes with as many as five syllables.[25]

It is at this point in the curriculum that P.Bour. 1 begins, where the young boy copies words of one to four syllables in alphabetical order. Thus, the list of one syllable words begins as follows: αἴξ (goat), βοῦς (bull), γύψ (vulture), δρῦς (oak), εὕς (brave), Ζεύς (Zeus), and so on.[26] The lists for two through four syllables are likewise in alphabetical order—beginning with Ἄμμων (Ammon) for two-syllable words, Ἀχιλλεύς (Achilles) for three syllables, and Ἀγαμέμνων (Agamemnon) for four—but these lists typically have four instances for each letter—for example, Ἄμμων (Ammon), Αἴας (Ajax), Ἄτλας (Atlas), and ἀκτίς (ray). As is evident from this small sample from P.Bour. 1, these lists contained a variety of words, including many proper names, mostly of deities (Zeus, Ammon, Atlas) and Homeric heroes (Achilles, Agamemnon, Ajax), but also, among those names not already cited, philosophers (Thales, Zeno, Xenophon), writers (Homer, Lysias, Menander), and even some characters from Menander's comedies (Demeas, Moschion, Sikon).[27] In the process, besides learning to read words of ever greater length, students were also being introduced to elements of Greek culture.[28] And, as Morgan has pointed out, the assimilation of this Greek culture would be easier for those students who came from Hellenized families than for those who did not, although the latter thereby had access to the dominant culture.[29]

After reading these lists of words students finally began, properly speaking, to read, that is, reading a series of words that made connected sense. Students' first reading experience usually involved poring over maxims and short poetic passages. Texts with maxims are especially numerous—indeed more numerous than any other literature preserved on school texts.[30] In P.Bour. 1, for example, there is a set of twenty-four maxims that form an acrostic; that is, the set begins with maxims whose first letters are alpha, then beta, then gamma, and so on through the entire alphabet. Here are the first five maxims, beginning, in the Greek, with the letters alpha through epsilon:

> The greatest beginning of wisdom is literature.
> A life without a livelihood is no life.
> Honor an old man as the image of the god.
> It is difficult to transplant an old tree.
> Eros is the oldest of all the gods.[31]

As is apparent from these examples, the purpose of these classroom maxims was not simply to teach reading but also, as Quintilian advised,[32] to inculcate some moral sentiment. Most maxims did just that, advocating, for the most part, a prudential ethic: valuing education, using wealth to help friends, showing hospitality to strangers, to name just a few. And yet there are also other maxims whose contents do not accord with these noble sentiments. Particularly noteworthy are those maxims vilifying women and marriage, as is apparent from the maxims in P.Bour. 1, beginning with the letters theta and iota:

> After the sea and fire a wife is the third evil.
> The savagery of a lioness and a wife is the same.[33]

The ethos inculcated by maxims, both noble and otherwise, helped students to begin to "identify with powerful and high-status Greek or Roman socio-cultural groups"[34] and hence to distinguish themselves from others, such as women and barbarians.

Secondary Education

When students had mastered the rudiments of reading and writing, they moved on, at about age ten or eleven and in much smaller numbers,[35] to the secondary curriculum of grammar and literature, taught by a secondary-school teacher.[36] In one sense this curriculum is similar to the primary curriculum, in that it, too, proceeded from letters to syllables, then to words and to literary texts. But in each stage the content to be learned was more complex, with the complexity coming, in part, from the relatively new discipline of grammar, which entered the curriculum, as already indicated, during the early Roman Empire and was codified in a textbook attributed to Dionysius Thrax.[37] Thus this grammatical analysis moved from merely recognizing and writing the letters of the alphabet to classifying them into consonants and vowels and the latter into long and short.[38] Similarly, students moved beyond merely reading lists of words to classifying them according to the eight parts of speech—nouns, verbs, participles, articles, pronouns, prepositions, adverbs, and conjunctions—along with numerous subdivisions of each, such as nouns into the genders, cases, and numbers, and verbs into tense, person, number, and voice.[39] Learning about declining nouns and conjugating verbs was invaluable, of course, because it allowed students to use them correctly—a skill that further differentiated these students from those below them. Finally, the goal of grammar was not merely the reading of maxims and short poetic passages but the κρίσις ποιημάτων, *krisis poiēmatōn,* or the interpretation of poetry.[40]

For example, a number of papyri, ostraca, and tablets preserve the attempts of students to study grammar by declining nouns and conjugating verbs[41] or by learning which cases go with which verbs.[42] The real complexity of declension, however, becomes apparent from a wooden tablet on which a student tried to decline an entire sentence through all the cases and numbers,[43] a declension that requires changes in various articles, nouns, verbs, and participles as the subject and verb of the sentence are manipulated by various formulae to allow these changes. To illustrate this complexity I quote just the nominative and genitive singular:

ὁ Πυθαγόρας φιλόσοφος ἀποβὰς καὶ γράμματα διδάσκων συνεβούλευεν τοις ἑαυτοῦ μαθηταῖς ἐναιμόνων ἀπέχεσθαι.
(Pythagoras the philosopher, once he had disembarked and was teaching letters, advised his students to abstain from red meat.)

τοῦ Πυθαγόρου φιλοσόφου ἀποβάντος καὶ γράμματα διδάσκοντος λόγος ἀπομνημονεύεται συνβουλεύοντος τοῖς ἑαυτοῦ μαθηταῖς ἐναιμόνων ἀπέχεσθαι.
(The statement of Pythagoras the philosopher, once he had disembarked and was teaching letters, is remembered for advising his students to abstain from red meat.)

In addition to mastering grammar, secondary students also continued to learn to read, although now it was not simply maxims and short passages that were assigned but lengthy literary works, most notably Homer, and especially the *Iliad.*[44] Students read and memorized a set number of lines daily, aided, at least at first, by what are called *scholia minora,* which gloss the many archaic words and phrases of Homer's Greek with their Koine equivalents.[45] Students also learned about the Homeric epics through making paraphrases of various episodes, as demonstrated by a tablet that retells *Iliad* 1.1–21 in prose at almost four times the length of the original.[46] Students also answered questions about the contents of the Homeric epics, as in these questions that Epictetus imagines a secondary teacher asking his students, who then provide the answers:

Q: Who was the father of Hector?
A: Priam.
Q: Who were his brothers?
A: Alexander and Deiphobos.
Q: Who was their mother?
A: Hecuba.[47]

As students read Homer they also studied grammatical matters. For example, as Dionysius Thrax's *Ars grammatica* suggests, teachers likely illustrated various subtypes of nouns when they appeared in their assignments from Homer. Thus, students learned what a patronymic noun was in the course of reading Homer, because Dionysius illustrates a patronymic noun with Πηλείδης (son of Peleus), which appears as early as *Iliad* 1.1, and similarly for a possessive noun, illustrated by Ἑκτόρεος χιτών (Hector's garment), which students encountered in *Iliad* 2.416.[48] Eventually, some commentator on Homer realized that one line in Homer (*Il.* 22.59) had particular significance for the study of grammar. This line, said by Priam to Hector, has eight words that represented each of the eight parts of speech:

πρὸς δ᾽ ἐμὲ τὸν δύστηνον ἔτι φρονέοντ᾽ ἐλέησον.
Have pity on me, the unfortunate one, while I am still alive.

The scholiast explained: "The word πρός is a preposition, δέ is a conjunction, ἐμὲ a pronoun, τόν an article, δύστηνον a noun, ἔτι an adverb, φρονέοντα a participle, and ἐλέησον a verb."[49] And for every line of Homer, the secondary-school teacher was concerned with all sorts of grammatical matters, some taken from Dionysius Thrax, such as pronunciation, accent, and punctuation,[50] and others taken from specialized treatments, such as those on tropes, in which students were introduced, among other things, to metaphor, allegory, enigma, periphrasis, pleonasm, and so on.[51] So, reading in the secondary-school room meant making a close, thorough, and complex investigation of literary works like the *Iliad* and the *Odyssey*.

What is more, even after they left the formal study of literature, students were encouraged to continue reading literature throughout life.[52] Indeed, as Dio Chrysostom put it, Homer was not only the first author to be read, but also the middle and last, by which he meant that Homer was of value to a boy, to an adult, and to an old man.[53] This perennial reading of Homer and of other authors like Euripides and Menander[54] would keep them fresh and familiar so that the secondary-school graduate could cite apt lines from them on virtually any occasion, thereby providing himself with a social marker as distinctive as his aristocratic clothing or his gymnasium-trained body. In short, the secondary-school curriculum, which taught a student to speak correct and often literary Greek, had a long-term cosmetic function that enabled the student to stand out linguistically from all others who did not have such training.

Tertiary Education

After finishing the secondary curriculum, students—very few of them, and virtually all of them aristocratic young men[55]—moved on, at about age fifteen, to the tertiary stage of education,[56] which typically meant study either with a philosopher or with an orator, and overwhelmingly with the latter.[57] Accordingly, the focus here will be on the rhetorical curriculum.[58]

The rhetorical curriculum began, as had the primary and secondary curricula, with relatively simple tasks and moved on to ever more complex ones. Students did not begin immediately with learning the standard rhetorical speeches—judicial, advisory, and epideictic—but with simpler compositional forms, called *progymnasmata*. This graded series of compositional exercises[59] taught students the essentials of style and argumentation, as is discussed in four extant *Progymnasmata*, beginning with Theon of Alexandria (late first century), Hermogenes of Tarsus (late second century), Aphthonius of Antioch (late fourth century), and Nicolaus of Myra (fifth century).[60]

As Theon explains, learning rhetoric from the rhetorical speeches is much like learning the potter's craft on a πίθος, or huge storage jar.[61] Thus it was thought necessary for students to begin with something more manageable, and the first progymnasma, the μῦθος, *mythos*, or fable, is a short, simple form that was familiar from childhood, so that composing a fable—for example, the fable of the crickets and the ants[62]—was a suitable task for students just leaving the poets and moving on to rhetoric.[63] But, as simple as a fable is, it was nevertheless thought to have value for the eventual task of composing a rhetorical speech. As John Doxapatres, a Byzantine commentator on the *Progymnasmata* of Aphthonius, says:

> Just as the task of the introduction to a speech is to make the audience attentive to what will be said in the narrative portion of the speech, so also the task of the fable is to prepare the audience for accepting the moral of the fable. Accordingly, the one who has been trained with the fable to make someone attentive to the advice in the moral of the fable would clearly not be at a loss to compose an introduction to a speech.[64]

As students progressed through the series of progymnasmata they learned still more skills that would help them later when composing rhetorical speeches. As an anonymous commentator on Aphthonius explains:

> The progymnasmata provide preliminary training in the kinds of rhetorical speech . . . insofar as some progymnasmata are akin to the deliberative speech (for example, fable, thesis, chreia, and maxim), others to the judicial speech (for example, confirmation, refutation, and commonplace), and still others to the epideictic speech (for example, encomium, condemnation, and comparison).[65]

By the time students had reached the end of the series they had honed their compositional skills to such an extent that they had, to use the imagery of Doxapatres, ascended the staircase to the very threshold of rhetoric.[66]

But the progymnasmata also inculcated certain habits of thought that transcended mere preparation for studying rhetoric. These habits lie in the very structure of the progymnasmata, in that each of the individual exercises teaches students to pay attention to matters of definition, classification, differentiation from similar forms, and etymology. Only after paying attention to these matters for one progymnasma did students try their hand at composition by learning the rules regarding the form and style of that progymnasma. Two progymnasmata, narrative and characterization, illustrate these habits.

Students learned to define a narrative as follows: "A narrative is the exposition of an event that has happened or could have happened."[67] They also learned to classify various types of narrative into fictional, historical, and political narratives.[68] In addition, the narrative (διήγημα, *diēgēma*) was differentiated from a related form, the narration (διήγησις, *diēgēsis*): "The narrative differs from a narration as an entire poem does from a portion of it, for an entire poem is the *Iliad*, whereas a portion of it is the preparation of Achilles' weapons."[69] Finally, regarding the composition of a narrative, students were told of its six constituent parts—the person who acted, the act that was done, the time when it was done, the place it was done, the way it was done, and the reason it was done—as well as the virtues of narrative—clarity, conciseness, plausibility, and purity of speech.[70] Only then did students compose a narrative, using as a model, in the case of Aphthonius, the fictional narrative of why roses are red.[71]

Similarly, when students moved on to characterization, they learned to define it as follows: "Characterization [ἠθοποιία, *ēthopoiia*] is the imitation of the character of the person in question."[72] Students also learned of several classifications, the basic one being the emphasis on emotion, disposition, or both.[73] An example of an emotional characterization would be what words Hecuba might say as she sees Troy in ruins. One example emphasizing disposition: what words a person of the interior might say on first seeing the ocean.[74] Other classifications include one in which the characterization is of a specific individual like Achilles or a type of individual like a householder.[75]

In addition, students differentiated characterization from εἰδωλοποιία (*eidōlopoiia*) and προσωποποιία (*prosōpopoiia*).

> Characterization involves a well-known person and only the character needs to be fashioned [by the writer]—for example, what words Herakles might say when given orders by Eurystheus. *Eidōlopoiia* also involves a well-known person but one who has died and ceased speaking—for example, as Eupolis does in "The Demos." *Prosōpopoiia*, in contrast, occurs when both the person and the character need to be fashioned, as Menander has done in "The Exposer."[76]

Students then learned the formal structure of a characterization, which is temporal. The writer first reflects on the person's present situation, then contrasts it with the past, and finally ponders the consequences of this situation for the future.[77] Aphthonius supplied as his model this emotional characterization: what words Niobe might say as her children lay dead.[78]

It should now be evident that even pre-rhetorical students learned various habits of thought as well as many specific and detailed rules that guided their efforts at composition. But the progymnasmata were only the beginning! Now the students were ready to study rhetoric proper, the preeminent intellectual discipline of the Greco-Roman world. Rhetoric involved learning to compose and deliver the three types of speech—the judicial, the deliberative, and the epideictic. They also learned how to compose and deliver the four parts of a speech—the introduction, the narration of the case, the proof, and the conclusion.

Various lengthy rhetorical treatises are readily available,[79] but a late-second-century epitome of rhetoric, attributed to Rufus of Perinthus, will illustrate the method.[80] Rufus begins, as expected, with a definition of rhetoric: "Rhetoric is the knowledge of how to compose artistically and persuasively each speech that is assigned."[81] Then follows, again as expected, a classification of speeches into the usual three—judicial, deliberative, and epideictic—along with a fourth, called historical.[82]

But the lion's share of the epitome is devoted to the four parts of a speech, especially as they pertained to the judicial speech.[83] Each of the parts of a speech is discussed in turn, beginning with a definition of that part, then a classification into subtypes, and finally suggestions on how this part can be composed, with almost all of them illustrated from the speeches of Demosthenes, the orator par excellence.

For example, Rufus defines the second part of a speech as follows: "A narration is a disclosure of the facts of a case told from the perspective of the speaker."[84] Then the virtues of this part, already familiar from the progymnasma, are identified: clarity, conciseness, and plausibility, complete with definitions of each.[85] Then Rufus moves beyond the progymnasma level by classifying the various ways a narration can be composed. He identifies four: (1) *narration proper,* a straightforward presentation of what happened; (2) *digressive narration,* an extraneous account added for its utility to the subject under discussion and used as an aside; (3) *preliminary narration,* an account as to why someone goes to trial, which is inserted before the narration proper; and (4) *implicit narrative,* an inclusion of the opinions and intentions of each person involved in the case, along with the events. Brief quotations from Demosthenes illustrate each of these subtypes.[86]

Rufus's discussion of the third part of a speech, the proof, is even more complex. After a definition of proof, Rufus identifies four kinds of proof—those based on the persons involved (their nationality, education, fortune, habits, deeds, and disposition), those based on the issues involved (in terms of their universal and individual features), those based on comparisons (examples from the past, analogies from daily life, and suppositions about the future), and those based on evidence not devised by the speaker (laws, contracts, wills).[87]

Once students had learned such an array of definitions, classifications, and illustrations they were finally ready to compose their own practice speeches, called declamations, that were often based on some typical situation or on an incident of Greek history.[88] And for these declamations, students once again had the models of their teachers. To cite but one example, the early-second-century sophist Polemo of Smyrna[89] is reported to have declaimed on certain themes, all historical: Demosthenes swears that he did not accept a bribe of fifty talents, as Demades alleged; the Greeks should take down their victory monuments after the Peloponnesian War; Xenophon decides to die after the execution of Socrates; and Demosthenes advises the Athenians to flee on their triremes at the approach of Philip.[90] None of these declamations is extant, but two others are. They are both historical, regarding the proposals of the fathers of two Greeks, Cynegrius and Callimachus, who fell at Marathon, for the honor of giving the funeral speech for all who had died at Marathon.[91]

Polemo represented the highest level an educated person could achieve in the Greco-Roman world. His talent, knowledge, and skills, so apparent in the extant declamations on Cynegrius and Callimachus, qualified him to speak as an ambassador on behalf of Smyrna before the emperor Hadrian; to address the Athenians gathered at the occasion of the completion, after more than five hundred years, of the Temple of Olympian Zeus; to receive numerous honors from the emperor; and, eventually, to be included by later sophists among the immortals themselves.[92]

Polemo's stature as the premier sophist of his time underscores the chasm that existed between him and a nameless small boy who tried "with extreme difficulty" to write the letter B five times on "cheap, coarse papyrus" in his "zero-grade" hand.[93] These are, of course, the extremes in educational achievement, but they do indicate the range within which to place Paul's own educational achievement.

Part II. Paul and Greco-Roman Education

Paul's own letters, despite his demurrers, betray a person who had passed through the curricular sequence of Greco-Roman education. It remains to confirm this claim with evidence, although only a sampling of texts can be discussed here.

The primary curriculum was so basic that anyone who possessed Greek literacy can be assumed to have been through this initial stage of education. Nevertheless, some traces of Paul's primary education are still visible in his letters. In Gal 6:11, for example, Paul refers to the large letters he was using when he himself penned the final eight verses of this letter.[94] The function of this autograph and its large letters has been variously explained,[95] but Paul's very reference to his handwriting recalls the primary child's pride in learning to write his letters clearly, correctly, and beautifully. Consequently, handwriting mattered, and Paul's reference to his own surely called the Galatians' attention to it and to some evaluation of it.

In 1 Cor 15:33, Paul cites a line of poetry—"Bad company ruins good morals." He does not cite the source, although later authors attributed the line either to Euripides or to Menander.[96] It has been argued that "conclusions in regard to Paul's literary education are not to be drawn" from this citation, presumably because the line had become detached from its source and hence was merely a popular maxim.[97]

But the line does allow us to draw some conclusions about Paul's education. Popular maxims were, as we have seen, the first sentences students used when learning to read as they reached the last parts of the primary curriculum. Given their numerical preeminence in the school texts, maxims also obviously became part of these students' early intellectual repertoire that they could draw upon throughout life. In addition, to use Morgan's terminology, Euripides and Menander were two of the core authors in Greek education, especially as sources for maxims at the primary stage but also as authors to read during the secondary curriculum.[98] In short, Paul's citing a poetic maxim, whether from Menander or Euripides, is precisely the habit of thought we should expect of someone who had been through the primary curriculum.[99]

Evidence of Paul's secondary education is also evident, although more obviously in his ability to cite and interpret literary texts—which were, in his case, the Greek Jewish scriptures, or Septuagint—than in the more technical study of grammar. Still, some signs of grammatical study appear, such as Paul's careful distinction between the singular and plural of a word in his understanding of the promises to Abraham (Gal 3:16). It is also possible that Paul's language and syntax in Gal 2:14 reflect knowledge of a form used in school, namely the form for an anecdote, or *chreia,* since Paul has expressed the incident in Antioch with Peter formally as a *chreia,* which is recognizable in the words "when I saw . . . , I said: . . ." *Chreiai* were used in secondary classrooms, as we have seen, and specifically as an advanced exercise in declension. But the habit of expressing oneself in the *chreia* form may have been learned as early as the primary curriculum, as illustrated by P.Bour. 1, where all five *chreiai* have the form "when Diogenes saw . . . , he said: . . ."[100] Still, the *chreia* form was certainly ingrained on the minds of students by the time they declined it during the secondary curriculum.

But it is Paul's many quotations from the Septuagint—almost ninety explicit quotations, according to Jerome Murphy-O'Connor[101]—that mark him as a product of the secondary curriculum and indeed as an educated person. Paul's familiarity with the Septuagint allowed him, as needed, to quote apt passages that would add persuasiveness and grace to his arguments. It is in this context that Paul's quoting of the maxim from Euripides or Menander in 1 Cor 15:33 should again be seen, as well as Luke's portrait of Paul in Athens, in which he has the apostle quote briefly from the philosopher Epimenides and the poet Aratus (Acts 17:28). The impression of Paul from his letters as well as from Acts, then, is of a person who would have been regarded as educated at least through the secondary curriculum.

That Paul's education went beyond the secondary stage, however, is also clear, and the letters themselves are again the evidence. These letters, given their length, complexity, and power, clearly point to an author who had received sustained training in composition and rhetoric, and it was only during the tertiary curriculum that such instruction was given. Accordingly, a fuller discussion of Paul's awareness of the forms of progymnasmata as well as the forms and rules of rhetorical speech and argumentation is required.

Learning the basic compositional skills began, as we have seen, with the progymnasmata, and the composition of letters is mentioned, if briefly, in one of the advanced progymnasmata, namely the eleventh exercise, characterization (*ēthopoiia*).[102] Such brief treatment suggests, however, that composing letters was not the primary exercise for learning characterization, although the applicability of skills learned in this school exercise to letter-writing is nevertheless obvious, in that here, too, the letter writer had to express his character, his *ethos,*[103] in response to a specific situation.

The prescribed method for composing a characterization was to structure it temporally, beginning with the present, then moving to the past, and, finally, looking to the future. That Paul was familiar with this advanced progymnasma is perhaps clearest in his shortest letter, the one to Philemon. Briefly, the situation is one in which Paul wants to send the slave Onesimus back to his master Philemon but also to have Philemon give his permission for Onesimus to return to help Paul. Aside from some epistolary conventions—address (vv. 1–3), thanksgiving (vv. 4–7), and closing greetings and benediction (vv. 23–25)—the Letter to Philemon betrays the conventions of an *ēthopoiia*. In fact, we could summarize the contents of the remainder of the letter (vv. 8–22) as if it were an *ēthopoiia:* what words Paul might say when trying to intercede on behalf of Onesimus.

In any case, Paul's argument on behalf of Onesimus unfolds, on the one hand, along a temporal scheme, and throughout the argument Paul assumes, on the other hand, a character, an *ethos,* that fitted precisely to the situation at hand. Paul begins his *ēthopoiia* with the present situation by saying that the letter is an appeal on behalf of his child Onesimus (vv. 8–10a). Then he recalls the past, mentioning Onesimus's conversion while with Paul (v. 10b), Onesimus's former uselessness to his master (v. 11), Paul's earlier desire to keep Onesimus that was overridden by his desire to do nothing without Philemon's consent (vv. 13–14), and Paul's suggestion as to why Onesimus had left his master in the first place (v. 15). Finally, Paul looks to a future in which Philemon might have Onesimus back forever, though as more than a slave (v. 16), might welcome him as though he were Paul himself (v. 17), and might be confident of having any debts incurred by Onesimus repaid by Paul himself, an assurance made stronger by Paul's repeating it in his own hand—"I will repay" (vv. 18–19). Paul ends with a glance toward a more distant future by praying that he might be able to visit Philemon and even asks him to have a room readied (vv. 21–22).

Throughout this appeal, in which Paul follows the prescribed temporal sequence, he also takes great care to characterize himself in a way that serves to advance his entreaty. Thus Paul presents himself as in dire need of Onesimus, stressing his current status as a prisoner (v. 9; cf. v. 1) and as an old man (v. 9), though not without hints of his long-term characterization as an apostle (cf. v. 8). Alongside Paul's self-depiction are his characterization of Onesimus as his child (v. 10; cf. vv. 11, 17) and his characterization of Philemon as having been generous in the past (v. 7), as still holding legal authority over Onesimus (vv. 14, 16), but also as indebted to Paul (v. 19). All these characterizations advance Paul's appeal to such a degree that Philemon could have done little else but return Onesimus to Paul so that he, Paul's child, could support him in his imprisonment and old age.[104] The progymnasmatic conventions of *ēthopoiia* are therefore analytically useful for reading Philemon and thus for indexing the level of Paul's formal education. Because this letter demonstrates Paul's knowledge of the conventions of writing an epistolary *ēthopoiia*, it betrays an education that reached the tertiary stage.

Ēthopoiia has also been proposed as a form for Paul's longest letter, the Letter to the Romans, but its use is sufficiently different there to merit further attention. Stanley K. Stowers's groundbreaking rereading of Romans argues,[105] among other things, that Paul used *prosōpopoiia*, a term Stowers takes from Theon but a term that was later superseded by *ēthopoiia* in Hermogenes, Aphthonius, and Nicolaus. Both terms, however, refer to much the same exercise. In any case, Stowers understands *prosōpopoiia* to mean the invention of a character by means of speech either for a known person or for an invented one, the latter being a type of person, such as a general or soldier.[106] But Stowers also turns to Quintilian's discussion of *prosōpopoiia*, which emphasizes that by this figure of thought an author can add variety to his oratory by introducing the inner thoughts of opponents, the conversations of others, or even conversations between the author and others. Quintilian also adds that it is not necessary to identify the shift in speakers.[107] Finally, Stowers refers to Hermogenes' discussion of *ēthopoiia*, which includes the formal structure of an *ēthopoiia* as involving the temporal sequence of present, past, and future.[108] With this understanding of *prosōpopoiia*, Stowers proposes that Paul made use of this technique in Rom 2:1–16; 2:17–29; and 7:7–25.[109] His analysis is intriguing and insightful at many points, but it is also not without problems. On the one hand, the first two passages cited are not really *prosōpopoiia*. For example, in Rom 2:1–16, Paul has not put words into the mouth of his imaginary *prosōpon* (literally, "face," and, by extension, "person"), a pretentious Gentile.[110] Rather, it is Paul who does virtually all the speaking, so that Quintilian's term *apostrophe*, discussed immediately after *prosōpopoiia*,[111] is more appropriate since Paul is *addressing* this imaginary *prosōpon*. *Apostrophe* is also the appropriate term for 2:17–27, because Paul continues to address an imaginary *prosōpon*, though now a Jewish teacher of Gentiles.

On the other hand, the proposal that Rom 7:7–25 is also an example of *prosōpopoiia* is more promising. Stowers follows modern scholarship in regarding the first-person singular of these verses as not being autobiographical and assumes instead a fictive "I," specifically a Gentile who lacks self-mastery even though he is trying to live according to the Law.[112] In addition, Stowers analyzes these verses in terms of Hermogenes' temporal structure for an *ēthopoiia*. To be sure, all three tenses appear in these verses, but their order does not follow Hermogenes because the sequence is past (7:7–11), then present (14–24a, 25), with virtually no future, save for a brief glance at the future toward the end of the section dealing with the present (24b).[113]

In other words, while someone other than Paul is speaking in Rom 7:7–25, which makes this passage conform better to the conventions of *prosōpopoiia*, the formal characteristics of this speech break with the temporal prescriptions of *ēthopoiia*, as not only are the present and past reversed, but the future is barely included and then inserted in the section on the present. This example of *prosōpopoiia* is thus rather irregular, and it remains to be seen how much divergence from the form was allowable before it was no longer recognizable as a *prosōpopoiia*.

Evidence of Paul's use of another progymnasma has also been proposed. Bruce J. Malina and Jerome H. Neyrey argue that Paul, when writing about himself, followed the conventions of encomium, a composition that sets out the excellent qualities of its subject.[114] Specifically, they analyze Gal 1:12–2:14; Phil 3:2–11; and 2 Cor 11:21–12:10, and in each passage they find correspondence between the contents and sequence of Paul's information about himself and those prescribed for an encomium.[115]

Malina and Neyrey consult various *Progymnasmata* but depend especially on Aphthonius for their understanding of the contents and sequence of an encomium. They thus give the following order of contents along with the respective Greek terms in transliteration: first, family background and birth (*eugeneia*); then, nurture and training (*anastrophē*); then, accomplishments and deeds (*epitēdeumata kai praxeis*); and, finally, comparison (*synkrisis*).[116]

Malina and Neyrey then compare the Pauline passages with the prescriptions for an encomium, but only one of the passages can be discussed here. Thus, in Gal 1:10–2:21, Paul's longest autobiographical account, they see him following these prescriptions and correlate them as follows:

> I. Introduction (1:10–12)—Paul's divine gospel
> II. Lifestyle (*anastrophē*) (1:13–17)—Paul's *ethos*
> A. 1:13–14—As persecutor of the church
> B. 1:15–17—As preacher of the gospel
> III. Deeds (*praxeis*) (1:18–2:10)—Paul's conduct
> A. 1:18–20—In Jerusalem
> B. 1:21–24—In Syria and Cilicia
> C. 2:1–10—In Jerusalem
> IV. Comparison (*synkrisis*) (2:11–21)—Cephas and Paul
> A. 2:11–14—Incidental: in Antioch
> B. 2:15–21—General: Paul and Judean Messianists
> V. Conclusion (2:21)—Paul and divine favor[117]

Their discussion of this structure and its contents emphasizes various points of contact with the encomium: Paul's use of the technical term *anastrophē* for "manner of life" (1:13); his reference to his *ethnos*, or ethnic group (1:13–14), and *genesis*, or birth (1:15); his account of his *paideia*, or education (1:18–24); his *epitēdeumata* and *praxeis*, or accomplishments and deeds that demonstrate his virtue, such as the courage he showed in the face of demands that he submit (2:5), or his fortune, such as the enhancement of his reputation through a meeting with the pillar apostles (2:7–9); and finally his use of *synkrisis*, or comparison, as evident in his confrontation with Peter in Antioch (2:11–14).[118] Accordingly, Malina and Neyrey conclude that "the encomium looms large as the model for Paul's remarks about himself in this passage from Galatians."[119]

At first glance this analysis of the contents and sequence of Paul's remarks about himself is intriguing and even persuasive. But on closer examination a number of problems arise. First, contrary to what Malina and Neyrey say, Paul's use of *anastrophē* (1:13) does not match the technical term used by Aphthonius for one of the structural heads of an encomium.[120] Aphthonius's term is ἀνατροφή, *anatrophē* ("upbringing").[121] Second, Paul's references to his *genos*, or race (v. 14), and to his birth (v. 15), do not belong under the heading of *anatrophē* anyway. In fact, Aphthonius does not mention birth; Hermogenes does, and he regards birth as a separate topic, one that comes before his term for upbringing, τροφή, *trophē*.[122] Third, *epitēdeumata* and *praxeis* do not belong together.[123] The latter is a separate heading,[124] and the former is, according to Aphthonius, a subhead of *anatrophē*.[125] In addition, *epitēdeumata* does not mean "accomplishments," but something akin to "career."[126] In other words, it seems more appropriate to consider Paul's former life as a persecutor (1:13) and his present one as an apostle (1:16, 23) as his *epitēdeumata*. Fourth, even the confrontation between Peter and Paul (2:11–14), which Malina and Neyrey categorize as a *synkrisis*, or comparison, is somewhat arbitrary, for they overlook Paul's other comparisons, such as those with his contemporaries in his zeal for the traditions of his fathers (1:14) and with the false brothers at Jerusalem (2:4–5). These latter two passages could also be termed *synkriseis*. What is more, *synkrisis* emerged as a structural part of an encomium only in the second century C.E., in Hermogenes' discussion of encomium, and even he includes it merely as the last of fifteen possible topics for an encomium.[127] Theon, a younger contemporary of Paul, makes only a passing reference to comparison among a myriad of other topics for an encomium.[128] Theon's structure for an encomium, moreover, is nothing like that which emerges in Hermogenes and that is standardized later in Aphthonius.

In short, Malina and Neyrey's analysis of Gal 1:10–2:21 fails, at least at the formal level, to convince, although their problematic analysis as well as Stowers's should not be interpreted as an argument against pursuing Paul's compositional techniques in terms of the progymnasmata, only a call for more careful and sophisticated analyses.

It remains, finally, to discuss Paul's likely rhetorical training, though much more briefly, in part because this aspect of Paul's education has recently received extensive, if indirect, attention. This recent surge of interest in rhetorical analysis of Paul's letters began with Hans Dieter Betz's proposal that Galatians conforms to the structure and arguments of a judicial speech and specifically to an apologetic letter.[129]

Betz noticed that previous scholars had outlined the contents of Galatians but had failed to give any criteria that justified their outlines.[130] He finds these criteria in the structure and rules governing a judicial speech, so he proposes that the epistolary situation Paul faced when writing the letter was judicial, in that Paul's Galatian opponents are the accusers, Paul the defendant, and the Galatians the jury.[131] Galatians is thus Paul's defense of his gospel and is organized according to the parts of a judicial speech, as follows:[132]

> I. The Prescript (1:1–5)
> II. The *Exordium,* or Introduction (1:6–11)
> III. The *Narratio,* or Statement of the Facts (1:12–2:14)
> IV. The *Propositio,* or Theme (2:15–21)
> V. The *Probatio,* or Proof (3:1–4:31)
> VI. The Parenesis (5:1–6:10)
> VII. The Postscript (6:11–18)

Betz compares what Paul says in each part to the requirements of that part as described in the rhetorical handbooks. For example, he cites the handbooks' definition of *narratio* as the exposition of what has been done; notes the qualities of clarity, brevity, and plausibility that were expected of a *narratio;* and then points out how Gal 1:12–2:14 functions as Paul's *narratio* and reflects the very qualities mentioned in the handbooks.[133] Betz's entire analysis of Galatians was sufficiently detailed, sophisticated, and fresh that his article prompted extraordinary interest, even if largely critical. This criticism, however, has not been to question the use of rhetorical categories[134] but rather to reject his specific proposal of Galatians as a judicial speech in favor of one in which this letter is recategorized and analyzed as deliberative speech.[135]

One problem that Betz's critics have with his analysis is his inability to incorporate the hortatory section of the letter (5:1–6:10) into a judicial outline. To be sure, Betz recognizes the problem, but his appeal to *parenesis* in philosophical letters does not resolve it.[136] And the problems do not stop there,[137] but essential to the criticisms is the conviction that Paul is not so much defending himself as trying to persuade the Galatians to continue to live out his gospel and not that of his opponents. With this view of the epistolary situation, Betz's critics have recategorized the letter as deliberative and have shown that it conforms to the structure and functions of a deliberative speech. One such deliberative outline for Galatians is that by Robert G. Hall:[138]

> I. Salutation/Exordium (1:1–5)
> II. Proposition (1:6–9)
> III. Proof (1:10–6:10)
>   A. Narration (1:10–2:21)

B. Further Headings (3:1–6:10)
IV. Epilogue (6:11–18)

Even if Betz's specific analysis of Galatians as judicial rhetoric has met with criticism, it has still been enormously influential within Pauline studies, for it has given rise to a flurry of studies that have applied rhetorical categories to Paul's other letters.[139] Especially notable is the recent effort to move beyond classification by rhetorical genre to focusing on careful analyses of Paul's argumentation in terms of rhetorical figures—for example, pleonasm, periphrasis, parenthesis, irony, hyperbole, rhetorical questions, personification, allegory, antithesis, to name just some of the figures that R. Dean Anderson finds in Gal 1:11–2:21 alone.[140]

Surprisingly, however, there has been a reticence on the part of scholars to attribute Paul's rhetorical sophistication to any formal education on his part. For example, in his book *New Testament Interpretation through Rhetorical Criticism*, George A. Kennedy says, "[I]t is not a necessary premise of this study that . . . Saint Paul had formally studied Greek rhetoric. . . . [T]here were many handbooks of rhetoric in common circulation which he could have seen."[141] And Stowers also stops short of assuming such study for Paul, saying that "Paul's Greek educational level roughly equals that of someone who had primary instruction with a *grammaticus*, or teacher of letters, and then had studied letter writing and some elementary rhetorical exercises."[142]

And yet, given the pervasive, varied, and accurate use of rhetorical forms and style in Paul's letters that Betz and others have pointed out, it is hard not to draw the conclusion that Paul had formal rhetorical training.[143] Such a conclusion is likely even if Luke's statement about Paul's having studied in Jerusalem with Gamaliel (Acts 22:3) is true, for Martin Hengel has assembled considerable evidence of rhetorical schooling in Jerusalem, where Paul may well have learned rhetoric and practiced it in the Greek-speaking synagogue(s).[144] Years of missionary preaching would certainly have honed Paul's rhetorical skills, but it seems best to assume that this preaching was built on much earlier study and practice under a rhetor.

Consequently, while Paul cannot be placed alongside a sophist like Polemo, which he himself admitted when he said he was a rank amateur when it came to speaking (2 Cor 11:6; cf. 10:10), he was certainly closer to Polemo in his educational achievements than he was to the boy just beginning to write his letters. Basic literacy itself was an accomplishment that would have already placed this boy into a small percentage of people who were literate. But Paul's much greater educational achievement—including not only primary schooling but also secondary and tertiary instruction—would therefore have put Paul into a very tiny elite indeed.

Part III. Other Relevant Pauline and Paulinist Texts

The reader is encouraged to read a number of other texts that betray Paul's educational experience and achievements. Here is a sample:

1 Cor 9:24–27 (cf. Gal 2:2; Phil 2:16; 1 Tim 6:12; 2 Tim 4:7; Titus 2:4): Paul mentions some activities that were typical of the gymnasium—running, boxing, and exercising. The gymnasium was also a principal site for educational instruction, so that Paul's specific and accurate depiction of these activities—for example, only one runner wins a prize (1 Cor 9:24)—points to his familiarity with this athletic and educational institution.[145]

2 Cor 11:6: Paul gives a self-deprecating assessment of his rhetorical abilities as being no better than those of a rank amateur (ἰδιώτης, idiōtēs). This assessment is often interpreted to mean that Paul lacked rhetorical training, but it could just as easily be a comparative assessment—whether Paul's abilities were less than those of his opponents at Corinth or of sophists generally. In either case, Paul may well have been relatively unskilled, but perhaps more in terms of his physical appearance than his skills, especially his ability to write impressive and powerful letters (2 Cor 10:10).[146]

Gal 1:14: Only here does Paul refer explicitly to his education, which he considered to have surpassed that of his contemporaries, at least in his knowledge of the Pharisaic traditions. Paul's familiarity with the Septuagint and its interpretation probably derives from this study, which would be equivalent to tertiary education.[147]

Gal 3:1: Paul says that when he first preached to the Galatians he portrayed Jesus Christ before their eyes as crucified (cf. 1 Cor 1:23; 2:2). His use of the verb προγράφειν, prographein, here translated by "portrayed," may hint at another progymnasma that Paul used as an apostle. This progymnasma is one of the most advanced, namely description (ἔκφρασις, ekphrasis). Knowledge of this progymnasma would have allowed Paul to give a vivid, detailed, and compelling description of Christ's crucifixion.[148]

Gal 3:24–25 (cf. 1 Cor 4:15): Paul characterizes the Law as a disciplinarian (παιδαγωγός, paidagōgos), a familiar social role in education. Specifically, a paidagōgos was an old slave whose task was, among other things, to accompany an aristocrat's son to and from school in safety and to monitor his overall behavior. Paul's use of this role as a metaphor for the Law in Galatians may very well have been drawn from personal experience.[149]

Acts 24:21: Paul is prosecuted before the governor Felix by a professional orator (ῥήτωρ, rhetōr) named Tertullus (vv. 1–8); Paul then defends himself (vv. 10–21), which suggests that the author of Acts regarded Paul as equally skilled in speaking in such a judicial setting.[150]

Titus 1:12: The saying "Cretans are always liars, vicious brutes, lazy gluttons," which may go back to the pre-Socratic philosopher Epimenides, reflects, in any case, the maxim habit learned at school. This maxim habit is repeated elsewhere—for example, "Love of money is the root of all evils" (1 Tim 6:10). But perhaps an especially telling example of Paul's education comes from an incident in Acts (see 21:27–40), in which, after Paul had nearly been beaten to death in front of the temple, he was rescued by a Roman tribune and asked, in order to learn his identity, whether he spoke Greek. Paul responds in a way that marked off the educated from the uneducated, by using a literary tag, in this case, a line that echoes Euripides' *Ion*: "I am a Jew, from Tarsus in Cilicia, a citizen of no mean city" (v. 39).[151] To be sure, there is at best an echo here, but it gains in probability when paired with a similar incident in Achilles Tatius, in which Clitophon, also in the midst of a beating at a temple, addresses the crowd that gathers as follows: "Gentlemen, what things I've suffered, I, a free man and from no mean city."[152]

Part IV. Bibliography

Classical Studies

Bonner, Stanley F. *Education in Ancient Rome: From the Elder Cato to the Younger Pliny*. Berkeley: University of California Press, 1977.

Cribiore, Raffaella. *Writing, Teachers, and Students in Graeco-Roman Egypt*. American Studies in Papyrology 36. Atlanta: Scholars Press, 1996.

Hunger, Herbert. *Die hochsprachliche profane Literatur der Byzantiner*. Handbuch der Altertumswissenschaft 12.5.1–2. Munich: C. H. Beck, 1978.

Marrou, Henri Irénée. *A History of Education in Antiquity*. Translated by G. Lamb. New York: Sheed & Ward, 1956. Reprint, Madison: University of Wisconsin Press, 1982.

Milne, J. G. "Relics of Graeco-Roman Schools." *JHS* 28 (1908): 121–32.

Morgan, Teresa. *Literate Education in the Hellenistic and Roman Worlds*. New York: Cambridge University Press, 1998.

Porter, Stanley E., ed. *Handbook of Classical Rhetoric in the Hellenistic Period, 330 B.C.–A.D. 400*. Leiden: E. J. Brill, 1997.

Robins, Robert H. *The Byzantine Grammarians: Their Place in History*. New York: Mouton de Gruyter, 1993.

Ziebarth, Erich. *Aus der antiken Schule: Sammlung griechischer Texte auf Papyrus, Holztafeln, Ostraka*. 2d ed. Bonn: A. Marcus & E. Weber, 1913.

New Testament Studies

Anderson, R. Dean. *Ancient Rhetorical Theory and Paul*. Contributions to Biblical Exegesis and Theology 18. Kampen: Kok Pharos, 1996.

Hengel, Martin. *The Pre-Christian Paul*. Philadelphia: Trinity Press International, 1991.

Kennedy, George A. *New Testament Interpretation through Rhetorical Criticism.* Chapel Hill: University of North Carolina Press, 1984.

Porter, Stanley E., and Thomas H. Olbricht, eds. *Rhetoric and the New Testament: Essays from the 1992 Heidelberg Conference.* JSNTSup 90. Sheffield, England: JSOT, 1993.

Notes

1. To be sure, Paul's social status as an aristocrat is problematic, in part due to his work as a tentmaker (Acts 18:3) while on his missionary journeys (1 Thess 2:9; 1 Cor 4:12; 9:6), an occupation that has led some to regard Paul as coming from a working-class background (see, most recently, Calvin Roetzel, *Paul: The Man and the Myth* [Minneapolis: Fortress Press, 1999], 23). But, while Paul surely marginalized himself by working at a trade during his years as a missionary, that does not preclude an aristocratic status during his pre-Christian years, precisely when he would have received an education. Particularly telling are the status terms that Paul used for his tent-making—for example, "slavish" (1 Cor 9:19) and "demeaning" (2 Cor 11:7)—which correspond to those that aristocrats used for working at a trade (see further Ronald F. Hock, "Paul's Tentmaking and the Problem of his Social Class," *JBL* 97 [1978]: 555–64). Paul was probably born into modest aristocratic circumstances, and only after his conversion and subsequent commitment to supporting himself as a tentmaker does he experience loss of status, much like Aegialeus, a privileged Spartan who because of his love for Thelxinoe gladly became a poor and marginalized fisherman to be with her (see Xenophon of Ephesus, 5.1.2–11).

2. See, e.g., Abraham J. Malherbe, *Social Aspects of Early Christianity* (Baton Rouge: Louisiana State University Press, 1977), 33–35; Martin Hengel, *The Pre-Christian Paul* (Philadelphia: Trinity Press International, 1991), 18–39; and Jerome Murphy-O'Connor, *Paul: A Critical Life* (Oxford: Clarendon Press, 1996), 46–51. Previous scholarship and to some extent today's scholarship tend to focus on where Paul received his education, in large part due to Willem Cornelis van Unnik's *Tarsus or Jerusalem? The City of Paul's Youth* (trans. G. Ogg; London: Epworth, 1962), which argued, on the basis of Acts 22:3, that Paul spent his earliest years in Jerusalem ("raised in this city [= Jerusalem]"), thereby making Paul's native language Aramaic and his education thoroughly Jewish. This view has been challenged recently. Murphy-O'Connor (*Paul*, 32–33) sees Acts 22:3 as reflecting Luke's own redactional concern to associate Paul ever so closely with Jerusalem rather than the city being a historical reminiscence. Hengel (*Pre-Christian Paul*, 34–39) doubts that Paul spent his early years in Jerusalem because his mastery of Greek and the Greek Bible makes it likely that Greek was his primary language, so that Paul must have gone to a good Greek elementary school, which was also a Jewish school. That Paul went as a youth to Jerusalem, "was educated at the feet of Gamaliel" (Acts 22:3), and in fact excelled his contemporaries in his zeal for the ancient traditions (see Gal 1:14; Phil 3:6) is likely, but beyond the scope of this essay (see further Murphy-O'Connor, *Paul*, 52–59, and Hengel, *Pre-Christian Paul*, 27–34).

3. See Henri Irénée Marrou, *A History of Education in Antiquity* (trans. G. Lamb; New York: Sheed & Ward, 1956; reprint, Madison: University of Wisconsin Press, 1982). See also Stanley F. Bonner, *Education in Ancient Rome: From the Elder Cato to the Younger Pliny* (Berkeley: University of California Press, 1977). Still useful are two older studies, notable for their use of documentary sources coming out of Egypt: Erich Ziebarth, *Aus der antiken Schule: Sammlung griechischer Texte auf Papyrus, Holtztafeln, Ostraka* (2d ed.; Bonn: A. Marcus & E. Weber, 1913), and Paul Collart, "A l'école avec les petits grecs d'Égypte," *Chronique d'Égypte* 21 (1936): 489–507.

4. For many years the standard reference to the documentary evidence on education has been Roger A. Pack, *The Greek and Latin Literary Texts from Greco-Roman Egypt* (2d ed.; Ann Arbor: University of Michigan Press, 1965), 137–40. For more recent and sophisticated attempts to collect the known educational texts, now totaling more than four hundred, see Janine Debut, "Les documents scolaires," *ZPE* 63 (1986): 251–78; Rafaella Cribiore, *Writing, Teachers, and Students in Graeco-Roman Egypt* (American Studies in Papyrology 36; Atlanta: Scholars Press, 1996), 175–284; and Teresa Morgan, *Literate Education in the Hellenistic and Roman Worlds* (New York: Cambridge University Press, 1998), 275–87.

5. See Cribiore, *Writing, Teachers, and Students*, 102–18, esp. 112, where she summarizes each hand. A student with a zero-grade hand does not yet know the letters and sometimes confuses them or writes them in peculiar ways—for example, a θ may have a vertical bar. A student with an alphabetic hand writes the letters accurately and without hesitation but has not yet developed eye-hand coordination, so that some letters are still written multistroke and the pace is slow. A student with an evolving hand shows much practice in writing but still writes with a clumsy or uneven look and has trouble maintaining alignment. A student with a rapid hand writes fluently and often cannot be distinguished from the hand of a teacher or of an adult who copies out a passage for his own use.

6. See Morgan, *Literate Education,* 67–73 and throughout.

7. See ibid., 21–25.

8. See ibid., 57–63.

9. See ibid., 71–73.

10. See Alan Booth, "Elementary and Secondary Education in the Roman Empire," *Florilegium* 1 (1979): 1–14. Cf. also Robert A. Kaster, "Notes on 'Primary' and 'Secondary' Schools in Late Antiquity," *TAPA* 113 (1983): 323–46.

11. See Morgan, *Literate Education*, 32.

12. See Marrou, *Education*, 150–59; Bonner, *Education*, 165–88; and Morgan, *Literate Education*, 90–151.

13. See, e.g., Dionysius of Halicarnassus, *De composit. verb.* 25, and Quintilian, *Inst. orat.* 1.1.24–29.

14. For this text, see Pierre Jouguet and Paul Perdrizet, "Le Papyrus Bouriant no. 1: Un cahier d'écolier grec d'Égypt," *Studien zur Palaeographie und Papyruskunde* 6 (1906): 148–61 (text: 150–56), and Paul Collart, *Les Papyrus Bouriant* (Paris: Éduard Champion, 1926), 17–27 (text: 21–26). This text is also reprinted in Ziebarth, *Aus der antiken Schule*, 21–24. References to lines of this papyrus will be according to those in Collart's edition.

15. For a handy sample of this evidence, see Ziebarth, *Aus der antiken Schule*,

3–9, and J. G. Milne, "Relics of Graeco-Roman Schools," *JHS* 28 (1908): 121–32. Cf. also Collart, "A l'école," 497–501. For a complete listing of letters and alphabets, see Cribiore, *Writing, Teachers, and Students*, 175–227, and Morgan, *Literate Education*, 275–85.

16. See Cribiore, *Writing, Teachers, and Students*, 40, 146–47.

17. See, for example, Kottalos in Herodas's third mime, who could not recognize the letter A unless it was shouted at him five times nor distinguish a Σ from a M (Herodas, 3.22–26). Philostratus tells of the sophist Herodes Atticus whose son had such difficulty recognizing the letters that he surrounded the boy with twenty-four σύντροφοι, or slave playmates, each named after a letter of the alphabet, such as Achilles for A (Philostratus, *Vit. Soph.* 588).

18. See the complete model alphabet in P.Mich. VIII 1099, published in Herbert Chayyim Youtie and John Garrett Winter, eds., *Papyri and Ostraca from Karanis* (Michigan Papyri 8; Ann Arbor: University of Michigan Press, 1951), 206.

19. O.Vindob.G. 565, published in Hermann Harrauer and Pieter J. Sijpesteijn, eds., *Neue Texte aus dem antiken Unterricht* (Mitteilungen aus der Papyrussammlung der Österreichischen Nationalbibliothek in Wien 15; Vienna: Verlag Brüder Hollinek, 1985), 36–37.

20. O.ROM inv. 906.8.522, published in Milne, "Relics," 121.

21. O.Vindob.G. 285, published in Harrauer and Sijpesteijn, *Neue Texte*, 26–27. For a complete listing of texts containing letters or alphabets—numbering, at latest count, seventy-seven—see Cribiore, *Writing, Teachers, and Students*, 175–91.

22. See, for example, the series of thirteen beta's by an experienced hand in P.Vindob.G. 23624, published in Harrauer and Sijpesteijn, *Neue Texte*, 31. Note also that Kottalos's mother, Metrotime, complains to his teacher that her son writes nothing beautifully on his oft-neglected tablet (Herodas, 3.18), a complaint made more poignant because she envisioned his becoming a scribe (cf. 3.26–28).

23. See further Cribiore, *Writing, Teachers, and Students*, 129–37.

24. See, e.g., P.Vindob.G. 36016, 26011b, 26011e verso, 26011m, and 26011c + d verso, published in Harrauer and Sijpesteijn, *Neue Texte*, 27–30. Cf. also Ziebarth, *Aus der antiken Schule*, 3–5, and Cribiore, *Writing, Teachers, and Students*, 191–96.

25. See Morgan, *Literate Education*, 101–4.

26. See P.Bour. 1, lines 1–13 (= Collart, *Les Papyrus Bouriant*, 21).

27. See P.Bour. 1, lines 1–140 (= Collart, *Les Papyrus Bouriant*, 21–23).

28. See further Janine Debut, "De l'usage des listes de mots comme fondement de la pedagogie dans l'antiquité," *REA* 85 (1983): 261–74, esp. 263–69.

29. See Morgan, *Literate Education*, 74–76.

30. See Morgan, *Literate Education*, 122 and 279–81. Cf. also Cribiore, *Writing, Teachers, and Students*, 204–27.

31. See P.Bour. 1, lines 169–89 (= Collart, *Les Papyrus Bouriant*, 24). My translation, as are all the others in this study.

32. See Quintilian, *Inst. orat.* 1.1.35.

33. See P.Bour. 1, lines 191–95 (= Collart, *Les Papyrus Bouriant*, 24). See further Morgan, *Literate Education*, 135–38.

34. Morgan, *Literate Education*, 150.

35. On the drastic decrease in numbers of students who moved on to the secondary curriculum, see Morgan, *Literate Education*, 163.

36. For fuller accounts than are possible here, see Marrou, *Education*, 160–85; Bonner, *Education*, 189–249; Robert H. Robins, *The Byzantine Grammarians: Their Place in History* (New York: Mouton de Gruyter, 1993); Morgan, *Literate Education*, 152–89; and Katherine Atherton, "Children, Animals, Slaves, and Grammar," in *Pedagogy and Power: Rhetorics of Classical Learning* (ed. Y. L. Too and N. Livingston; New York: Cambridge University Press, 1998), 214–44.

37. For the text, see G. Uhlig, ed., *Dionysii Thracis Ars Grammatica* (Grammatici Graeci 1.1; B. G. Teubner, 1883), 3–100; ET in Alan Kemp, "The TEKHNE GRAMMATICKE Translated in English," in *The History of Linguistics in the Classical Period* (ed. D. Taylor; Philadelphia: John Benjamins, 1987), 169–89. For related texts, see Alfons Wouters, *The Grammatical Papyri from Graeco-Roman Egypt: Contributions to the Study of the "Ars Grammatica" in Antiquity* (Brussels: Paleis der Academiën, 1979).

38. For details, see Dionysius Thrax, *Ars gram.* 6–10 (pp. 8, 4–22, G. Uhlig), and Robins, *Grammarians*, 52–57.

39. For details, see Dionysius Thrax, *Ars gram.* 11–22 (pp. 22, 3–100, G. Uhlig), and Robins, *Grammarians*, 57–86.

40. Dionysius Thrax, *Ars. Gram.* 1 (p. 6, 2 Uhlig).

41. See, e.g., PSI inv. 479, published in Giorgio Zalateo, "Papiri Fiorentini inediti," *Aegyptus* 20 (1940): 3–30, esp. 12–14, which declines σοφός (wise) with both masculine and feminine articles through all the cases and numbers. For other examples, see Ziebarth, *Aus der antiken Schule*, 16–17, 32, and Collart, "A l'école," 501–2. For a complete listing, see Cribiore, *Writing, Teachers, and Students*, 263–69, and Morgan, *Literate Education*, 285–86.

42. For a tablet which lists more than two hundred verbs and the case of their direct object, see Brit.Mus.Add. 37533, published in Frederic G. Kenyon, "Two Greek School-Tablets," *JHS* 29 (1909): 29–40, esp. 32–33. Cf. Ziebarth, *Aus der antiken Schule*, 24–27.

43. See Brit.Mus.Add. 37516, published in Kenyon, "School-Tablets," 29–31. Cf. Ziebarth, *Aus der antiken Schule*, 16–17, and Collart, "A l'école," 501–2.

44. See further Raffaella Cribiore, "A Homeric Writing Exercise and Reading Homer in School," *Tyche* 9 (1994): 1–8.

45. For examples of *scholia minora*, see P.Berol.inv. 5014, available in Ziebarth, *Aus der antiken Schule*, 13–14, and P.Mich.inv. 1588, published in Timothy Renner, "Three New Homerica on Papyrus," *HSCP* 83 (1979): 311–37, esp. 315–16. For a complete listing, see Cribiore, *Writing, Teachers, and Students*, 253–58. Cf. also John Lundon, "Lexeis from the Scholia Minora in Homerum," *ZPE* 124 (1999): 25–52.

46. See T.Bodl.Gr.Inscr. 3019, published in Peter J. Parsons, "A School-Book from the Sayce Collection," *ZPE* 6 (1970): 133–49, esp. 135–38. See further Cribiore, *Writing, Teachers, and Students*, 259–62.

47. Epictetus, *Diatr.* 2.19.7. For another example, see P.IFAO inv. 320, published in Jacques Schwartz, "Un manuel scolaire de l'époque byzantine," *Études de Papyrologie* 7 (1948): 93–109. On the latter, see also Marrou, *Education*, 166–69, and Bonner, *Education*, 240.

48. See Dionysius Thrax, *Ars gram.* 12 (pp. 26, 7–27, 1 Uhlig). That students learned the subdivisions of nouns through Homeric names and nouns is illustrated by Brit.Mus.Add. 37533, published in Kenyon, "School-Tablets," 32–39. Cf. also Ziebarth, *Aus der antiken Schule*, 27–28.

49. See Alfred Hilgard, ed., *Scholia in Dionysii Thracis artem grammaticam* (Grammatici Graeci 1.3; Leipzig: B. G. Teubner, 1901), 56, 16–19. Cf. Robins, *Grammarians*, 59.

50. See Dionysius Thrax, *Ars gram.* 2–4 (pp. 6, 5–8, 2 Uhlig). See further Bonner, *Education*, 220–23.

51. That all these exercises were illustrated from Homer, see the treatise attributed to Tryphon, *Trop.* (8.728–60, Walz). See further Bonner, *Education*, 229–37.

52. For the encouragement of students to continue their reading, along with specific recommendations, see Quintilian, *Inst. orat.* 1.8.1–12.

53. See Dio Chrysostom, *Orat.* 18.8.

54. Euripides and Menander are the next most likely texts that students read, on which see Morgan, *Literary Education*, 71 and 313. But there were exceptions, as in the case of the secondary-teacher Democritus who claimed that he had read and excerpted over eight hundred Middle Comedies (see Athenaeus, 13.610D). One of the best sources to get a sense of the way in which the grammatical ethos carried over into adult life is Athenaeus's *Deipnosophistae,* on which see my "Dog in the Manger: The Cynic Cynulcus among Athenaeus' Deipnosophists," in *Greeks, Romans, and Christians: Essays in Honor of Abraham J. Malherbe* (ed. D. L. Balch, E. Ferguson, and W. A. Meeks; Minneapolis: Fortress Press, 1990), 20–37, esp. 28–36.

55. Did women move to the tertiary stage of education? It is true that Stoics like Musonius Rufus, a contemporary of Paul, advocated philosophical education for both young men and women (see *Frags.* 3–4 [pp. 38–49 Lutz]), and perhaps it is significant that in Lucian's *Symposium* Aristaenetus has a son named Zeno and a daughter named Cleanthis (*Symp.* 5), names that recall two of the founders of Stoicism, Zeno and Cleanthes; Zeno is said to be studying philosophy with the Stoic Diphilus (*Symp.* 6, 26), and Cleanthis (the feminine form of Cleanthes) can be assumed to have heard many discussions of Stoic philosophy from her brother and intellectual father (*Symp.* 11). Indeed, Lucian's literary scenario may approximate what even Musonius intended, for Musonius's comments are consistent with women learning philosophy—the Stoic virtues only—from childhood, presumably from fathers like Aristaenetus. More generally, two factors made philosophical (or rhetorical) study unlikely for most aristocratic women: (1) tertiary education came at a time when they were more likely to be getting married than to continue their education, and (2) study at the tertiary stage often meant traveling to a city where a renowned intellectual resided, such as Epictetus's Nicopolis or Polemo's Smyrna. For survey on the evidence for the education of women at the primary and secondary stages, see Susan G. Cole, "Could Greek Women Read and Write?" in *Reflections of Women in Antiquity* (ed. H. Foley; New York: Gordon and Breach Science Publishers, 1981), 219–45, esp. 231–38.

56. On tertiary education, see Marrou, *Education*, 186–216, and Bonner, *Education*, 250–308.

57. On the preference for rhetoric over philosophy, see Marrou, *Education*, 194–96. Even students who chose philosophy often had first attended a school of rhetoric (see, e.g., Epictetus, *Diatr.* 2.27; 24.24–26; 3.1.1, 34).

58. That Paul was thoroughly conversant with philosophical language and issues has been especially emphasized by Abraham J. Malherbe, some of whose es-

says are collected in *Paul and the Popular Philosophers* (Minneapolis: Fortress Press, 1989). See also Martin Ebner, *Leidenslisten und Apostelbrief: Untersuchugen zu Form, Motivik und Funktion der Peristasenkataloge bei Paulus* (Würzburg, Germany: Echter Verlag, 1991); F. Gerald Downing, *Cynics, Paul, and the Pauline Churches* (New York: Routledge, 1998); and Troels Engberg-Pedersen, *Paul and the Stoics* (Louisville: Westminster John Knox, 2000).

59. The exercises are (1) fable (μῦθος), (2) narrative (διήγημα), (3) chreia (χρεία), (4) maxim (γνώμη), (5) refutation (ἀνασκευή), (6) confirmation (κατασκευή), (7) commonplace (κοινὸς τόπος), (8) encomium (ἐγκώμιον), (9) condemnation (ψόγος), (10) comparison (σύγκρισις), (11) characterization (ἠδοποιία), (12) description (ἔκφρασις), (13) thesis (θέσις), and (14) introduction of a law (νόμου εἰσφορά).

60. For the best introduction to the progymnasmata, see Herbert Hunger, *Die hochsprachliche profane Literatur der Byzantiner* (Handbuch der Altertumswissenschaft 12.5.1–2; Munich: C. H. Beck, 1978), 1.92–120. Cf. also Otmar Schissel, "Rhetorische Progymnasmatik der Byzantiner," *Byzantinisch-neugriechische Jahrbücher* 11 (1934): 1–11, and George A. Kennedy, *Greek Rhetoric under Christian Emperors* (Princeton: Princeton University Press, 1983), 54–66. For the standard text of Theon, see Leonard Spengel, ed., *Rhetores Graeci* (3 vols.; Leipzig: B. G. Teubner, 1853–56), 2:59–130; for Hermogenes, see Hugo Rabe, ed., *Hermogenis Opera* (Rhetores Graeci 6; Stuttgart: B. G. Teubner, 1913), 1–27; for Aphthonius, see Hugo Rabe, ed., *Aphthonii Progymnasmata* (Rhetores Graeci 10; Leipzig: B. G. Teubner, 1926), 1–51; and for Nicolaus, see Joseph Felten, ed., *Nicolai Progymnasmata* (Rhetores Graeci 11; Leipzig: B. G. Teubner, 1913), 1–79. Related material is also found in the commentaries on Aphthonius, such as those by John of Sardis, for which see Hugo Rabe, ed., *Ioannes Sardianus Commentarium in Aphthonium* (Rhetores Graeci 15; Leipzig: B. G. Teubner, 1928), and by John Doxapatres, for which see Walz, *Rhetores Graeci*, 2:81–564. Cf. also Hugo Rabe, ed., *Prolegomenon Sylloge* (Rhetores Graeci 14; Leipzig: B. G. Teubner, 1931), 73–183.

61. See Theon, *Progymn.* 1 (2.59, 5–11 Spengel).

62. See Aphthonius, *Progymn.* 1 (p. 2, 5–10 Rabe).

63. On the fable, see Hunger, *Literatur*, 1.94–96.

64. Doxapatres, *Hom. in Aphth.* (2.125, 15–22 Walz).

65. See Anonymous, *Prol. Syll.* 8 (p. 75, 7–13 Rabe).

66. See Doxapatres, *Hom. in Aphth.* (2.138, 16–17 Walz).

67. Aphthonius, *Progymn.* 2 (p. 2, 14–15 Rabe). For a survey of this progymnasma, see Hunger, *Literatur*, 1:96–98.

68. Aphthonius, *Progymn.* 2 (p. 2, 19–22 Rabe).

69. See Aphthonius, *Progymn.* 2 (pp. 2, 16–18 Rabe).

70. See Aphthonius, *Progymn.* 2 (pp. 2, 23–3, 4 Rabe).

71. See Aphthonius, *Progymn.* 2 (p. 3, 5–19 Rabe).

72. Hermogenes, *Progymn.* 9 (p. 20, 7–8 Rabe). For a survey of this progymnasma, see Hunger, *Literatur*, 1:108–16.

73. See Hermogenes, *Progymn.* 11 (p. 21, 10–18 Rabe).

74. See Aphthonius, *Progymn.* 11 (p. 35, 1–10 Rabe).

75. See Hermogenes, *Progymn.* 9 (pp. 20, 19–21, 5 Rabe).

76. See Aphthonius, *Progymn.* 11 (p. 34, 4–18 Rabe). Eupolis seems to have had long-dead people like Miltiades, Themistocles, and Pericles speak in his play, as

reported in a scholion on Aphthonius (2.646, 15–20 Walz). Menander gave the concept "exposure" a voice in this play (see John of Sardis, *Comm. in Aphth.* 11 [p. 205, 5–7 Rabe]). The commentators also point to an extant example, namely Lucian's giving a voice to a bed and lamp during Cyniscus's prosecution of Megapenthes (see Lucian, *Cat.* 27, and Doxapatres, 2.497, 12–24 Walz).

77. See Hermogenes, *Progymn.* 9 (pp. 21, 19–22, 3 Rabe).

78. See Aphthonius, *Progymn.* 11 (pp. 35, 15–36, 20 Rabe).

79. See Aristotle, *Rhetoric,* the *Rhetorica ad Alexandrum,* the *Rhetorica ad Herennium,* and Quintilian's *Institutio oratoria,* all available in the Loeb Classical Library. In addition, two previously untranslated rhetorical handbooks, one known as the Anonymous Seguerianus and the other attributed to Apsines of Gadara, are now available, with text and translation, in Mervin R. Dilts and George A. Kennedy, eds., *Two Greek Rhetorical Treatises from the Roman Empire* (Leiden: E. J. Brill, 1997). See also Heinrich Lausberg, *Handbook of Literary Rhetoric: A Foundation for Literary Study* (ed. D. E. Orton and R. D. Anderson; trans. M. T. Bliss, A. Jansen, and D. E. Orton; Leiden: Brill, 1998).

80. For the text of this treatise, see Leonard Spengel and Caspar Hammer, eds., *Rhetores Graeci* (3 vols.; Leipzig: B. G. Teubner, 1884), 1.2.399–407. On Rufus and his handbook, see Otmar Schissel, "Die rhetorische Kunstlehre des Rufus von Perinthus," *Rheinisches Museum* 75 (1926): 369–92, and Walter Ameling, "Der sophist Rufus," *Epigraphica Anatolia* 6 (1985): 27–33.

81. Rufus, *Rhet.* 1 (p. 399, 2–3 Spengel-Hammer).

82. See Rufus, *Rhet.* 2 (p. 399, 4–13 Spengel-Hammer).

83. See Rufus, *Rhet.* 3–41 (pp. 399, 14–407, 15 Spengel-Hammer).

84. Rufus, *Rhet.* 17 (p. 402, 13–14 Spengel-Hammer).

85. See Rufus, *Rhet.* 17–20 (p. 402, 14–22 Spengel-Hammer).

86. See Rufus, *Rhet.* 21–25 (pp. 402, 23–404, 8 Spengel-Hammer).

87. See Rufus, *Rhet.* 27–34 (pp. 404, 13–406, 9 Spengel-Hammer).

88. On declamation and the whole rhetorical ethos, see Donald A. Russell, *Greek Declamation* (New York: Cambridge University Press, 1983).

89. On Polemo, see Philostratus, *Vit. Soph.* 530–44.

90. See Philostratus, *Vit. Soph.* 542–43.

91. For text and translation of these two declamations, see William Reader, *The Severed Hand and the Upright Corpse: The Declamations of Marcus Antonius Polemo* (SBLTT 42; Atlanta: Scholars Press, 1996), 100–183.

92. See Philostratus, *Vit. Soph.* 531, 532–33, and 616.

93. See P.Vindob.G. 41103, published in Harrauer and Sijpesteijn, *Neue Texte,* 31 and Tafel 2. Quotations from Cribiore, *Writing, Teachers, and Students,* 180.

94. For other examples of Paul's closing a letter in his own hand, see 1 Cor 16:21–24; Phlm 19–25; cf. Col 4:18; 2 Thess 3:17–18. Cf. Rollin A. Ramsaran, *Liberating Words: Paul's Use of Rhetorical Maxims in 1 Cor 1–10* (Valley Forge, Pa.: Trinity Press International, 1996).

95. It has been argued that these large letters were due to hands deformed by his toil as a tentmaker (see Adolf Deissmann, *Paul: A Study in Social and Religious History* [trans. W. E. Wilson; 2d ed.; London: Hodder & Stoughton, 1926], 14) or that their size merely served to emphasize the contents of these last eight verses

(see Hans Dieter Betz, *Galatians: A Commentary on Paul's Letter to the Galatians* [Hermeneia; Philadelphia: Fortress Press, 1979], 314).

96. The line was used already by Diodorus Siculus (16.54.4) but again without attribution. For details on the attribution to Menander and specifically to his comedy entitled *Thais*, see Alfred Koerte, ed., *Menandrii quae supersunt* (Leipzig: B. G. Teubner, 1959), frg. 187. For Euripides, see Augustus Nauck, ed., *Tragicorum Graecorum Fragmenta* (2d revised ed. [B. Snell]; Hildesheim, Germany: Georg Olms Verlagsbuchhandlung, 1964), frg. 1024.

97. See Hans Conzelmann, *1 Corinthians: A Commentary on the First Epistle to the Corinthians* (trans. J. Leitch; Hermeneia; Philadelphia: Fortress Press, 1975), 278n. 139.

98. See Morgan, *Literate Education*, 71.

99. For Paul's habit of citing maxims, see, e.g., 1 Cor 5:6; 2 Cor 9:7; Gal 5:9; 6:7. Cf. Ramsaran, *Liberating Words*.

100. For five *chreiai* attributed to Diogenes, see P.Bour. 1, lines 141–67 (= Collart, *Les Papyrus Bouriant*, 23–24).

101. See Murphy-O'Connor, *Paul*, 47.

102. See Theon, *Progymn.* 10 (2.115, 20–22 Spengel), and Nicolaus, *Progymn.* 10 (p. 67, 2-5 Felten).

103. For this definition of character, see John of Sardis, *Comm. in Aphth.* 11 (p. 200, 18 Rabe).

104. See further Ronald F. Hock, "A Support for His Old Age: Paul's Plea on Behalf of Onesimus," in *The Social World of the First Christians: Essays in Honor of Wayne A. Meeks* (ed. L. M. White and O. L. Yarborough; Minneapolis: Fortress Press, 1995), 67–81, esp. 74–80.

105. See Stanley K. Stowers, *A Rereading of Romans: Justice, Jews, and Gentiles* (New Haven: Yale University Press, 1994). Much the same argument appears in his "Romans 7:7–25 as a Speech-in-Character (προσωποποιία)," in *Paul in His Hellenistic Context* (ed. T. Engberg-Pedersen; Minneapolis: Fortress Press, 1995), 180–202.

106. See Stowers, *Rereading of Romans*, 17.

107. See Quintilian, *Inst. orat.* 9.2.29–37. Cf. Stowers, *Rereading of Romans*, 20.

108. See Hermogenes, *Progymn.* 9 (pp. 21, 19–22, 3 Rabe). Cf. Stowers, *Rereading of Romans*, 270.

109. See Stowers, *Rereading of Romans*, 36–37, 39, 100–104, 143–50, 264–72.

110. See ibid., 100.

111. See Quintilian, *Inst. orat.* 9.2.38–39.

112. See Stowers, *Rereading of Romans*, 264.

113. See ibid., 270.

114. See Bruce J. Malina and Jerome H. Neyrey, *Portraits of Paul: An Archaeology of Ancient Personality* (Louisville: Westminster John Knox, 1996), 19–62. For this definition of an encomium, see Hermogenes, *Progymn.* 7 (p. 14, 17–18 Rabe); for a comprehensive survey of this progymnasma, see Hunger, *Literatur*, 1:104–6.

115. See Malina and Neyrey, *Portraits of Paul*, 34–60.

116. See ibid., 23–33. For full discussion, see esp. Aphthonius, *Progymn.* 8 (pp. 21, 20–21, 11 Rabe). Cf. Hermogenes, *Progymn.* 7 (pp. 15, 18–17, 4 Rabe).

117. See Malina and Neyrey, *Portraits of Paul*, 35–38.

118. See ibid., 38–50.

119. Ibid., 50. It should be pointed out that they use the encomium in this analysis of Galatians because they hold that this progymnasma gives access to an implicit model of Mediterranean personality. Hence the real aim of their analysis is to draw the further conclusion that "Paul presented himself as the quintessential group-oriented person, . . . utterly dependent on group expectations and the controlling hand of [external] forces: ancestors, groups, God" (51).

120. See ibid., 24, 27, 38.

121. See Aphthonius, *Progymn.* 8 (p. 22, 3 Rabe).

122. See Hermogenes, *Progymn.* 7 (pp. 15, 19–16, 1 Rabe).

123. See Malina and Neyrey, *Portraits of Paul,* 39.

124. See Aphthonius, *Progymn.* 8 (p. 22, 5–9 Rabe).

125. See Aphthonius, *Progymn.* 8 (p. 22, 3–4 Rabe).

126. The commentators on Aphthonius explain *epitēdeumata* as the life one chooses, such as being a philosopher, orator, or soldier (see John of Sardis, *Comm. in Aphth.* 8 [pp. 130, 21-131, 24 Rabe], and Doxapatres, *Hom.* 8 [2.429, 29–430, 22 Walz]).

127. See Hermogenes, *Progymn.* 7 (p. 17, 2–4 Rabe).

128. See Theon, *Progymn.* 8 (2.111, 1–3 Spengel).

129. See Hans Dieter Betz, "The Literary Composition and Function of Paul's Letter to the Galatians," *NTS* 21 (1974–75): 353–79. The rhetorical analysis of this article is carried over into his commentary *Galatians: A Commentary on Paul's Letter to the Churches of Galatia* (Hermeneia; Philadelphia: Fortress Press, 1979). See also the programmatic essay by Edwin A. Judge, "Paul's Boasting in Relation to Contemporary Professional Practice," *ABR* 16 (1968): 37–50.

130. See Betz, "Literary Composition," 353.

131. See ibid., 377.

132. See ibid., 355–77.

133. See Betz, ibid., 362–67.

134. For some cautions on the use of rhetorical categories, see Stanley E. Porter, "The Theoretical Justification for Application of Rhetorical Categories to Pauline Literature," in *Rhetoric and the New Testament: Essays from the 1992 Heidelberg Conference* (ed. S. E. Porter and T. H. Olbricht; JSNTSup 90; Sheffield, England: JSOT, 1993), 100–122. For an outright rejection of such analysis, however, see Philip H. Kern, *Rhetoric and Galatians: Assessing an Approach to Paul's Epistles* (New York: Cambridge University Press, 1998), 257–58: "Paul wrote Galatians independently of the rules of Graeco-Roman rhetoric."

135. See, e.g., George Kennedy, *New Testament Interpretation through Rhetorical Criticism* (Chapel Hill: University of North Carolina Press, 1984), 144–52; Robert G. Hall, "The Rhetorical Outline for Galatians: A Reconsideration," *JBL* 106 (1987): 277–87; and especially Joop Smit, "The Letter of Paul to the Galatians: A Deliberative Speech," *NTS* 35 (1989): 1–26.

136. See Betz, "Literary Composition," 375–76.

137. See especially Smit, "Deliberative Speech," 2–9.

138. See Hall, "Rhetorical Outline," 282–87.

139. For a summary of scholars' rhetorical analyses of the Thessalonian letters, the Corinthian letters, Philippians, and Romans, see Stanley E. Porter, "Paul

of Tarsus and his Letters," in *Handbook of Classical Rhetoric in the Hellenistic Period, 330 B.C.–A.D. 400* (ed. S. E. Porter; Leiden: E. J. Brill, 1997), 533–85, esp. 547–61. Even Philemon has not escaped such analysis, though missed by Porter; see F. Forrester Church, "Rhetorical Structure and Design in Paul's Letter to Philemon," *HTR* 71 (1978): 17–33.

140. See Anderson, *Rhetorical Analysis*, 130–37.

141. Kennedy, *Rhetorical Criticism*, 9–10.

142. Stowers, *Rereading Romans*, 17. Incidentally, as we saw above, the *grammaticus*, or secondary-school teacher, did not teach letters, that is, the primary curriculum, but grammar and literature, and teaching an elementary rhetorical exercise like *prosōpopoiia*, as Stowers proposes for Paul in Romans, was not the preserve of a *grammaticus* who taught the secondary curriculum, but of a teacher at the tertiary level, a teacher of rhetoric. Also stopping short of Paul's having had a rhetorical education is R. Dean Anderson, *Ancient Rhetorical Theory and Paul* (Contributions to Biblical Exegesis and Theology 18; Kampen: Kok Pharos, 1996). He concludes (p. 249): "It would seem rather unlikely that Paul enjoyed a formal rhetorical training. . . . Paul, *at the most*, will have become acquainted with certain *progymnasmata*" (emphasis his).

143. So also Murphy-O'Connor, *Paul*, 49–51.

144. See Hengel, *Pre-Christian Paul*, 57–62.

145. For there being just one prize, see, e.g., Chariton, 1.2.2. See further David J. Williams, *Paul's Metaphors: Their Context and Character* (Peabody, Mass.: Hendrickson, 1999), 266–73.

146. See Judge, "Paul's Boasting," 37.

147. See further Roetzel, *Paul*, 22–24.

148. See further Basil S. Davis, "The Meaning of προεγράφη in the Context of Galatians 3:1," *NTS* 45 (1999): 194–212.

149. See further David J. Lull, "'The Law Was Our Pedagogue': A Study in Galatians 3:19, 25," *JBL* 105 (1986): 489–95.

150. See further Bruce Winter, "The Importance of the *captatio benevolentia* in the Speeches of Tertullus and Paul in Acts," *JTS* 42 (1991): 505–31.

151. See Euripides, *Ion* 8, which has the phrase "no mean city," and F. F. Bruce, *The Acts of the Apostles: Greek Text with Introduction and Commentary* (3d ed.; Grand Rapids: Eerdmans, 1990), 453.

152. Achilles Tatius, *Leucippe and Clitophon*, 8.3.1.

8

PAUL, EXEMPLIFICATION, AND IMITATION

Benjamin Fiore, S.J.

In the undisputed letters, Paul explicitly urges his followers to imitate his example at 1 Thess 1:6 and 2:14; Phil 3:17; Gal 4:12; and 1 Cor 4:16 and 11:1. Wilhelm Michaelis's article[1] provided an overview of the Pauline usage as well as an introduction to the history of the practice of imitation in Greco-Roman and Jewish culture. He saw obedience to authority as primary in 1 Cor 4 and as an important feature of the call to imitation in the other passages. In light of more recent studies, this survey of the undisputed Pauline letters will reasses the meaning of Paul's call to imitate his own example. In order to understand the Pauline usage within the rhetorical context of his day, an overview of the theory and practice of the use of example and the call to imitation precedes the analysis of the Pauline texts.[2]

Part I. Exemplification in the Greco-Roman World

When Greco-Roman rhetoricians analyzed the rhetoric of persuasion, they distinguished various forms of exemplification. In addition to its use in the court and the assembly, the power of example was recognized in the area of moral exhortation as well. Example is a type of comparison, and early rhetorical discussions did treat εἰκών, *eikōn* (image), παραβολή, *parabolē* (analogy), and ὁμοίωσις, *homoiōsis* (simile). Παράδειγμα, *paradeigma* (example), corresponds with the Pauline usage. Its treatment in a technical sense, however, began with Anaximenes' *Rhetorica ad Alexandrum* and Aristotle's *Rhetoric,*[3] the latter constituting a continuing influence through subsequent Greek and Latin rhetors. In Anaximenes' definition of *paradeigma* as "actions that have occurred previously and are similar to, or the opposite of, those which we are now discussing" (8 [1429a.21]), two notions receive attention. First he explains negative examples, that is, ways of acting counter to the one proposed and errors committed by people in the past, both of which are to be avoided now (8 [1429a.29–31] and 14 [1431a.26–27]). Second, he supplements historical examples with recent examples, διὰ τῶν νῦν γενομένων, *dia tōn nyn genomenōn* (8 [1430a.7–9]), and παραδείγματα . . . ἐγγύτατα τοῖς ἀκούουσι χρόνῳ / *paradeigmata . . . engytata tois akouousi chronō* (examples that are nearest in time . . . to our hearers) in 32 (1439a.1–5). In the latter passage, Anaximenes also declares that examples must be well-known to the listeners (γνωριμώτατα, *gnorimōtata*) for them to have any impact.[4]

Anaximenes observes that in the organization (*inventio*) of the argument in a discourse, example (*paradeigma*) and previous judgment (κρίσις, *krisis*) are both appealed to. These are two different types of proof. *Krisis* expresses a judgment on a similar situation in the past, while *paradeigma* provides an illustration of a similar situation. Actually, however, the judgment on a similar situation in the past functions like a *paradeigma* for present action and attitude. The difference is that previous judgment, τὸ κεκριμένον, *to kekrimenon*, or *krisis*, is a procedure or method of argument, while *paradeigma* is a kind of proof (1 [1422a.23–27] and 32 [1439a.13–17]). In other words, *krisis* wants to lead the audience to a conclusion like that referred to, while *paradeigma* provides evidence that is expected to help the audience arrive at the desired conclusion.

Aristotle ranges more widely into rhetorical theory than the practice-oriented Anaximenes.[5] He considers *paradeigma* to be a form of induction; παράδειγμα . . . ἐστιν ἐπαγωγὴ καὶ περὶ ποία ἐπαγωγὴ εἴρεται, *paradeigma . . . estin epagōgē kai peri poia epagōgē eiretai* ("We have said that example is a kind of induction and with what kind of material it deals by way of induction"; *Rhet.* 1.2.19 [1357b]). Into the ranks of the historical examples Aristotle admits only real, previous events and their named protagonists. He does not, unlike Anaximenes, allow descriptions of habits, customs, and mores of peoples and states. Among the fabricated *paradeigmata* Aristotle lists *parabolē* (analogy) and λόγοι, *logoi* (sayings). The former is an analogy different from historical examples in its use of real-life circumstances in the everyday world. These analogies present types of people familiar to the audience rather than the past deeds of specific individuals. Furthermore, the analogy can be expressed hypothetically, for example, ὁμοίον γὰρ ὥσπερ ἂν ἐι τις, *homoion gar hōsper an ei tis* ("for instance, if one were to say"; 2.20.4 [1393b]). The latter are fables, and his recommendation of these is surprising in view of his lack of enthusiasm for myth or reports of poets.

In general, forensic (reckoning about past events, usually in a judicial setting) and deliberative (consideration of possible courses of action, usually in a public council) speeches preoccupy Aristotle when he recommends enthymemes (deductive proof based on a syllogism) for the first and *paradeigmata* for the second type of oratory. Margaret Mitchell points out that "deliberative proof by example functions with an implied or even explicit appeal to imitate the illustrious example (or avoid the negative example)." This appeal to imitate "is common in deliberative discourse, grounded as it is in proof by example."[6] From Isocrates (436–338 B.C.E.) and Demosthenes (384–322 B.C.E.) through Dio Chrysostom (ca. 40–112 B.C.E.) and well into the imperial period, Mitchell observes, the deliberative proof by example, often combined with a call to imitation, is found in deliberative texts.[7] Moreover, deliberative letters similarly employ proof by example and the call to imitation. Authors of such letters even add themselves as examples in addition to ancestors, deities, or historical persons.[8] In doing this, they are using a tactic sanctioned by theoretical treatises such as Plutarch's *De se ipsum citra invidiam laudando* (*Mor.* D–F). This leads Mitchell to conclude that "deliberative argumentation is characterized by proof from example, and often includes an entreaty that the audience imitate the behavior of the esteemed example (or not imitate a negative example)." In fact, this is a distinctive element in deliberative rhetoric.[9]

As for enthymemes, recommended by Aristotle for forensic oratory, example may be a source for these deductive proofs. The enthymeme makes a statement and offers a supporting reason. Thus, example can give a probably universal principle or truth from which one may then reason by the use of enthymeme to a particular conclusion. Example gives access to the universal by the flash of insight by which one passes from knowledge of a particular fact to a direct knowledge of the corresponding principle. In fact, if one discerns any relevance of the example to the universal principle in the first place, one has most likely already made a transition in one's mind from the example to the universal.[10]

An example can also function by analogy and move from particular to particular without expressing a universal, as a syllogism would. This characteristic of enabling the audiences to draw direct analogies from the exemplary situations to their own situations was well-suited for hortatory speeches and letters. Consequently, appeal to example became a distinctive feature of deliberative oratory and letters.

Addressing the advantages of using examples, Aristotle lauds the easy intelligibility and quick comprehension gained through the illustration of particulars—without losing the audience, as enthymemes might—in a demonstration of the whole (*Probl.* 18.3 [916.26–36]).[11] He also credits examples with stirring greater belief, standing as they do as corroborating witnesses to what is being proved.

Imitation, or *mimesis,* is obviously associated with example.[12] Aristotle finds that *mimesis* describes the aim of poetry and all art inasmuch as they reproduce the model or exemplary figure as faithfully as possible. In this understanding, *mimesis* shares the work of ποίησις, *poiēsis* (poetic composition), inasmuch as it goes beyond a slavish reproduction. *Poiēsis* in its turn is anchored in the reality of the model that inspires it. Plato railed against poetry because of the role poetry played, especially the Homeric epics, in education. It was παιδία, *paidia* (a game), and not παιδεία, *paideia* (education in true knowledge or philosophy; *Resp.* 606E).[13] He rejected the poets' and artists' abusive arrogation that they played the leading role in the moral and cultural tradition of the Greeks.

Of the three centuries between Aristotle and *Rhetorica ad Herennium* and Cicero's *de Inventione,* little evidence remains from the developing theory on *paradeigmata.* More is known of the *exempla* collections, which sprang up in late Republican and Augustan Rome, with the Romans' emphasis on exemplary figures. One of these, *Facta et dicta memorabilia,* a nine- (or ten-) book collection by Valerius Maximus (fl. 26 C.E.), is clearly a rhetorical sourcebook, and its examples are organized under, among other headings, virtues and vices. Other compilers of example collections were Nepos and Varro.[14]

Valerius Maximus, writing during the reign of Tiberius (14–37 C.E.), compiled his *Memorable Deeds and Sayings* for the use of students and future practitioners of declamation in the final stage of their education.[15] In the collection he supplied rhetorical illustrations for *exempla* in a wide range of rhetorical uses and explained how to introduce, correct, and conclude the example stories. His collection carried forward the Greek and Roman tradition—vital in constructing speeches since Aristotle—of using historical anecdotes as an aid to argument (2 [1356a.35–b.6]).[16] Valerius took Cicero as his precedent and preferred Roman over Greek examples as more suited to the audiences of his future orators. He accepted Cicero's examples as authoritative but recast them to suit use by a later generation of students. Not concerned with historical accuracy, Valerius instead celebrated the examples as demonstrating the custom of his audience's ancestors (*mos maiorum*). He also presented his examples by juxtaposing the good and bad. Those for whom he compiled his books hoped that the use of historical examples in their *suasoriae* (declamation exercises in composing speeches of advice) and *controversiae* (declamation exercises in composing disputations) would gain themselves recognition and advancement into high public positions.[17]

Clive Skidmore's study of Valerius Maximus found that examples were not only set pieces for declaimers' debates but were a significant source of moral guidance.[18] Valerius's aim was moral education achieved by imitation of great deeds. In his outline, he stressed the praise of virtue and reproach of vice and gave precedence to the praiseworthy.[19]

In this he stood on the sturdy shoulders of his Roman predecessors, trained by Greek tutors, in the use of examples for moral instruction. Strabo (*Geogr.* I.2.3–8), Isocrates (*Antid.* 84, *Evag.* 76), and Plutarch (*Lives*) used historical examples. Roman writers generally preferred history over poetry as a source of examples for moral education.[20] Even historians such as Livy (I.10) wrote to encourage noble deeds among good citizens.[21] Tacitus's *Agricola* was motivated by aims of moral education (see also Plutarch, *Pericles* 2.3–4). Tombstone inscriptions and funeral orations (Sallust, *Bell. Jug.* 4; Polybius VI.53–55) aimed to spur Romans to emulate the virtues expressed there.

Another method of fostering emulation of virtue was the institution in which a young aristocrat apprenticed to an elder statesman to learn to imitate his mentor (*tirocinium fori;* Plutarch, *Cat. Maj.* 3.4; Cicero, *Off.* II.13–46; Pliny, *Ep.* VI.11; VIII.23, VIII.14.4–6; Seneca, *Ep.* VI.5). For those without well-known forebears or aristocratic connections, the examples of great men of history served as common ancestors. In the latter circumstance, virtue was developed through character formation rather than through lineage. Even foreigners constituted models for imitation; in Valerius, one example in three was non-Roman.[22]

The *Rhetorica ad Herennium* treated *exemplum,* the Latin counterpart to the Greek *paradeigma,* as a figure of thought, *sententiarum exornatio* (4.13.18). As such, *exemplum* functions as a device in a speech's elaboration or refinement (*expolitio*) and as a figure in its own right.[23] Thus, two of the methods available for elaborating a theme were *simile* (comparison) and *exemplum* (4.43.56). *Ad Herennium* often mentions *simile* or *similitudo* (a comparison, a parallel case) together with *exemplum;* so do Cicero and Quintilian. A long discussion of *similitudo* (4.45.59–48.61) preceded *ad Herennium*'s treatment of *exemplum* and contained this definition:

> Comparison is a manner of speech that carried over an element of likeness from one thing to a different thing. This is used to embellish or prove or clarify or vivify. Furthermore, corresponding to these four aims, it has four forms of presentation: contrast, negation, detailed parallel, abridged comparison. To each single aim in the use of comparison we shall adapt the corresponding form of presentation. (4.45.59)[24]

Exemplum is "the citing of something done or said in the past along with the definite naming of the doer or author. It is used with the same motives as a comparison" (4.49.62). *Exemplum* is the same as *similitudo* in purpose, whether for ornament, proof, clarification, or demonstration.

Cicero defined example as "that which supports or weakens a case by the appeal to precedent or experience, citing some person or historical event" (*Inv.* 1.30.49).[25] He suggested (*Part. or.* xxvii.96 and cf. *De or.* 120) that the speaker should have a large supply of examples, with older examples lending delight, authority, and credibility. Cicero located *exemplum* in the *confirmatio* of a speech, where it, along with *imago* (a figurative representation) and *collatio* (a comparison, similitude), was a member of *comparabile,* itself, in turn, one of the four types of argument from probability. In addition to the use of an example to strengthen one's own or to weaken an opponent's argument, proper hortatory discourse used example in a parallel way. Bennet Price observed that *confirmat et infirmat* (corroborate and invalidate) were equal to the hortatory terms προτροπή, *protropē*/ἀποτροπή, *apotropē* (or *hortari/dehortari*, exhort/dissuade).[26]

In his discussion of induction (*inductio*), Cicero treated *exemplum* as a genus or type of argument belonging to the topic of similarity or comparison (*locus similitudinis; Top.* 10.41–45). It has two species: *facta* and *ficta exempla*. *Facta exempla* include legal precedents as well as historical examples. *Ficta exempla* are more than fables, and a look at *ad Her.* 4.53.66 is helpful in clarifying what they are. Here the author discusses *conformatio* or *prosōpopoiia* (personification, dramatization by putting speeches into the mouths of characters) and finds that it consists in "representing an absent person as present, or in making a mute thing or one lacking in form appropriate to its character." Often this rhetorical technique aims to lay out examples and compares past and present. As effective *loci* (grounds of proof) of amplification (*Part. or.* 55), *exemplum* and *similitudo* share the task of moving the audience's spirits and are identified as particularly stirring figures of thought (*maxime movent; De or.* 3.53.205).[27] They also make the point believable (*facit fidem; Part. or.* 40). Cicero affirms the persuasive power of historical examples (*Or.* 34.120) and claims that their use both enhances the credibility of the speaker and delights the audience. Of course, Cicero's main concern was with judicial speeches, and their requirements predominate in his treatment of *exemplum*. Despite his forensic (law-court) emphasis, Cicero's elaboration of the persuasive effects of using *exemplum* are applicable to other categories of oratory as well.

Whatever systematization Cicero lacked in his discussion of *exemplum*, Quintilian made up for (*Inst.* 5.11). Quintilian, the late-first-century C.E. educator, saw no difference except a terminological one between the Greek system's *paradeigma* with its subdivisions *paradeigma* and *parabolē* (comparison), Cicero's *inductio* (inductive reasoning)—divided into *exemplum* and *collatio* (comparison)—and his own *exemplum* with subdivisions *exemplum* and *similitudo* (comparison). Thus Greek and Roman rhetorical theorists agree on the function of example.[28]

Regarding examples, Quintilian reasoned that children should copy down great men's thoughts because the exercise would convey some moral lesson and form their character (*Inst.* 2.1.35–36).[29] Adult orators must already have developed their own moral character and acquired all that was just and honorable because otherwise they could be neither morally good nor skilled in speaking (12.2.1).

Mentoring and apprenticeship were elements of the aristocrat's education. The classroom too provided opportunities for imitation of examples. Quintilian explained:

> For however many models for imitation he may give them from the authors they are reading, it will still be found that fuller nourishment is pro-

vided by the living voice, as we call it, more especially when it proceeds from the teacher himself, who, if his pupils are rightly instructed, should be the object of their affection and respect. And it is scarcely possible to say how much more readily we imitate those whom we like. (*Inst.* 2.2.8)[30]

Quintilian emphasized the importance of moral admonition in a teacher's exemplification of a virtuous lifestyle. In this the teacher functions much like parents, who offer domestic examples for their children's formation (2.1–8).

These discussions and recommendations of example all share a pedagogical setting, and they look to example for the similar function of clarifying and encapsulating the point of the lesson and for encouraging emulation. The pedagogical use of example introduces the device into yet another setting besides the law court, the legislature, and the memorial site: namely, the classroom. In addition to teaching the theory on the usefulness of examples, and offering examples of the theory in practice, the rhetorical theorists expect the good rhetor himself to be an example of the art that he teaches. In exemplifying his rhetorical art, the rhetor was like master teachers in other disciplines who guided their students to learn the mores of an occupation or public function. The rhetor's art is both the art of speaking appropriately to the situation and the art of living well. The same can be said of the *mores*, that is, that they include both professional competence and qualities of character.

The teacher in the school is considered an extension of, or at least analogous to, the parent in the home. Both teacher and parent, expected to be good examples themselves, also propose particularly compelling models among the *domestica exempla* (examples from one's household or native place), the pupil's predecessors in civic or familial virtue. Finally, instruction, in this broader view, sees ethics as inextricably bound up with technical competence and virtuous living. Consequently, moral exhortation and admonition are intrinsic to professional preparation.[31]

In this usage, example is not primarily proof or a device in service of a proof, as it was with Aristotle and Cicero, but rather demonstration. Example finds its sources in the past and the present, in proverbs and sayings, in opinions and prior judgments, in commonly acknowledged customs and habitual actions, and in specific individuals and events.

Example expresses the best way, to be followed, or the worst, to be avoided. Moreover, it gives a precedent that shows the desired course can be followed or ought not be followed. In its character as delineating what should be chosen (protreptic) and avoided (apotreptic), example serves various types of discourse, of which one is deliberative oratory.

Whatever its source, the example cogently attests the desirability or advantage of a recommended action, attitude, or association, or the harm in those derogated. Similarly, the ability to provide an apt example bolsters the authority of the exhorter-admonisher or even offers vindication from undeserved criticism. As such, these attestations serve a forensic function, but are not at all restricted to the courtroom. Example as a hortatory device clearly demonstrates what a speech is getting at, but it is not employed just for the sake of better comprehension. The use of example in discourses aims to promote virtue and action that imitates or rejects that example.[32]

In practice, ethical exhortation and admonition by way of example found their place in the various forms of epideictic oratory (for praise or blame), be they triumphal odes (ἐπινίκια, *epinikia*) for victors, eulogies (ἐγκώμια, *encōmia*) for leaders and states, or funeral orations (ἐπιτάφια, *epitaphia*) for deceased relatives and people of note.[33] In epideictic literature, προτρέψις, *protrepsis* (admonition)—often expressed with a precept attached and focused on attaining a certain knowledge or ἀρετή, *aretē* (virtue or quality)—and παραίνεσις, *parainesis* (exhortation)—more wide-ranging and less specific in content—both found expression.[34]

In his biographical sketches, the *Lives,* Plutarch (ca. 46–120 C.E.) was able to paint vivid examples of virtue and vice and thereby to educate himself and his audience. His *Virtues of Women* likewise aimed to demonstrate feminine virtues by way of example stories.[35]

Historians such as Livy (59 B.C.E.–17 C.E.) could characterize their efforts as providing wholesome examples to imitate and shameful ones to avoid, both for individual and civic good (*A U C* 1 proem 10). Propertius (b. between 54 and 47 B.C.E.) even offered exemplary lessons for lovers in his poetry (3.11.5–8).

The spiritual guide par excellence, however, was Seneca (5/4 B.C.E.–65 C.E.), and his chosen literary vehicle was the epistle. In *Ep.* 98.13, he urged Lucilius to join him in aiming to be an exemplary figure (*simus inter exempla*).[36] The crown of life lived in accordance with virtue is to become an example oneself. In his prose writings, Seneca used historical examples, but in his letters he relied on the immediate experience of his correspondents for illustrations and preferred those that were spontaneous and easy (*inlaboratus et facilis; Ep.* 75.1). Seneca explained the value of examples to the moralist (*Ep.* 120): they allow the audience to conceptualize virtue with the remembrance of great men as powerful as their living presence (102.30; cf. 104.21–22). Examples show that the virtuous life is possible; they are more direct than precepts ("The journey is long through precepts, short and efficient through examples," *longum iter est per praecepta, breve et efficax per exempla* [*Ep.* 6.5]). Not only do examples show the doubting person that the moral life can be lived (*Ep.* 76.22), they become companions and guardians for the individual's self-examination and moral progress (*Ep.* 104.21).[37]

Seneca used both positive and negative examples along with precepts (*Ep.* 94.42; 95.65). The author's self-presentation in a tone and context of friendship belongs to the essence of his chosen instructional form, the letter. The letter, for all intents and purposes, becomes the personal presence of the friend who advises and instructs. Personal presence achieved through the letter may actually be more effective and pure than physical presence.[38] Along with references to Lucilius as the recipient of several of his letters, Seneca added personal testimony to the familiar epistolary conventions to create a more comprehensive and convincing epistolary presence in a pedagogical situation of teacher and learner. Moreover, Seneca's self-descriptions and personal notices attest to the measure of success or failure in his own effort to realize the good, the philosophical ideal. In this Seneca demonstrated the difficulty of the undertaking that he urged upon Lucilius.

Hildegard Kornhardt identifies a variety of functions for examples in Seneca and other classical authors.[39] In one function, the example is a *sample*, one instance of a category, a pattern for what is sought. The author constructs or fabricates the exemplar. The end envisaged is the discovery and recognition of that person or thing. The audience might be expected to join the search or at least to accommodate their perceptions and evaluations to those of the author.

Much like the first usage is that of the example as *specimen*. The difference is that the author does not construct the exemplar but finds an actual representative of a series of objects or persons. The end envisaged and the audience's reaction remain the same.

Example as *prototype* or *model* constitutes a third category. This resembles the first two functions in that the example can be a real specimen found by the author or an idealized construct. It differs from the preceding functions in that attention centers either on the person or thing that imitates or copies the prototype, or that at least strives to fashion itself after the model. Thus the end in view is the effort to imitate the example. As a means of accomplishing that imitation, the audience is expected to enter or continue a program of instruction and formation as outlined by the author.

In the final view, example provides an *instructional experience,* on the basis of a precedent in personal circumstances or historical events. The example directs attention toward an analogous set of circumstances or conditions in the present or future. The example is meant to be learned and to be an aid in formulating future decisions and therefore is ideal for deliberative rhetoric, which focuses directly on such future decisions.[40]

The rhetorical handbooks—used for training of students for public life— explained the χρεία, *chreia* (a concise reminiscence of a saying or action aptly attributed to some character)[41] and its use. The handbooks also describe the γνώμη, *gnōmē* (a summary saying, in a statement of general application, dissuading from something or persuading toward something).[42] In addition to the protreptic/apotreptic (delineating what should be chosen and what should be avoided) functions, the rhetorical development of the *chreia* and *gnōmē* employs examples and demonstration by comparison, criticizes contrary stances, and can include precept in its exhortation. In the rhetorical development of the *chreia* and *gnōmē*, example serves as a key device. The rhetorical handbooks give instructions and strategies for this development, instructions and strategies adapted by orators and writers to a variety of genres, including the letter.[43]

Because the hortatory epistle has already emerged above, the link between the rhetorical handbooks and the epistolary genres may be clarified. In general, the letter has been characterized as half a dialogue, and therefore could be expected to employ the same *genus dicendi* (mode of speaking) as appears in the dialogue.[44] Some rhetorically accomplished writers of epistles destined for the public eye held that the letter should be free of rhetorical elaboration. But this view was neither unanimously held nor rigidly adhered to.[45]

The use of example as a device to persuade or dissuade has been shown above to be constant in Greek and Roman usage. Those engaged in deliberative oratory found it to be a particularly appropriate strategy to move their audiences to action by illustrations with examples. Rhetorical devices found their way into letter-writing as well. It is not surprising then to find Paul making use of examples in his letters.

Part II. Exemplification in Paul's Letters

Paul's letters abound with examples. He names persons from his own mission team (Timothy in Phil 2:22) and from his communities (Epaphroditus in Phil 2:29–30) as well as his communities as a whole (Gal 4:14) to exemplify the desired attitudes and actions (Phil 3:17). He refers to scriptural examples (Abraham in Rom 4:3; cf. 1 Cor 10:6–11) as well as midrashic ones (1 Cor 10:4–6). In addition to actual and scriptural persons and events, Paul creates imaginary dialogues from typical work situations (the potter in Rom 9:20) or from human anatomy (the body in 1 Cor 12:14–21) and the natural world (a branch in Rom 11:17). Human behavior (1 Cor 12:23–24), typical situations (1 Thess 5:2–4, 7), or human activities (building in 1 Cor 3:10–15) all serve as a store of examples for Paul. Primary, of course, among his examples is Christ (Phil 2:5) and Paul himself as he follows Christ's example (1 Cor 11:1).

Paul uses example in a variety of rhetorical strategies. Stanley Stowers, for instance, has described the use of example as a formal feature in the diatribe and finds Paul's dialogic exchanges in Romans to reflect the usage in Epictetus, Dio, Seneca, and others.[46] Mitchell has found exemplification at the heart of deliberative discourse.

Brian Dodd's study of Paul's self-references analyzes the literary strategy behind the use of personal example.[47] He points out that Dio Chrysostom describes the follower and pupil as imitating the acts and words of the teacher to acquire the teacher's art (*Or.* 55.4–5). Epictetus similarly refers to himself as a model of the Cynic way of life that he hopes to have his pupils observe ("Look at me!") and imitate (this is his character and his plan of life; *Diat.* 3.22.45–50). Dodd concludes that the imitation of Paul can and should be understood both as a pedagogical technique and as an implied assertion of authority. The latter is the case in that the call to imitate is a summons to conform to the pattern set by Paul as a regulative model. Dodd also takes note of the exceptional instances of 1 Thess 1:6 and 2:14, in which the phrase "you became imitators" is used to compare the Thessalonians' experience with Paul's, Christ's, and the Judean churches' experience.[48] The content of Paul's own example includes the behavior he modeled when originally present with his readers (1 Cor 4:17; Gal 4:13–15; Phil 4:9).[49] Dodd[50] points out that Paul often structures his argument on the basis of his personal example, whether as a "thesis statement" of the argument that follows (Rom 1:16–17; Gal 1:10) or as a summary and transition (1 Cor 11:1).[51]

Galatians

In the undisputed Pauline letters, there are six passages in which Paul explicitly calls on his audience to be like him. At Gal 4:12, Paul urges the Galatians to be like him as he had become like them. The appeal introduces the argument section that follows, just as 2:19–21 introduces the first argument section, 3:1–5.[52] Commentators generally agree that in Gal 4:12 Paul refers to his becoming like the Gentile Galatians in behavior (cf. 1 Cor 9:21; Gal 2:19–20; Phil 3:5–6), in leaving aside his strict observance of Jewish Law.[53] The same commentators point out Paul's shift in tone here to friendliness from earlier harsh reproof and his contrast to his opponents' self-interest.[54] A friendly tone is useful for Paul's hortatory aim and is typical in epistolary exhortation, as Seneca's letters also demonstrate. While friendship often establishes the context for imitation,[55] Paul Nadim Tarazi is cautious in this matter as he detects inequality, because it was Paul's initiative in preaching the gospel that makes the friendship possible.[56] Frank Matera questions Hans Dieter Betz's suggestion that a succession of friendship τόποι, *topoi*, counterbalances the heavier and harsher sections of the letter. For Matera, Paul is more than a friend. He is a concerned parent (4:16–17) and a founder whom the Galatians received as an angel (4:14).[57]

Apart from the debate here about the importance of friendship, the nature of the imitation in Galatians can be clarified. Beverly Gaventa and Dodd agree that Paul does not want the Galatians to imitate his way of life.[58] Rather he wants them to imitate his single-minded response to the gospel's exclusive claim on him as

Christ lives within him. The christological implication is that they can be conformed to Christ (4:19), as they are crucified with Christ (5:24; 6:14–17).[59] The
model is actually far-ranging and includes Paul's autobiographical statements in
chapters 1 and 3 about his own call and life in Christ.[60] Dodd finds that Paul uses
comparison (σύγκρισις, synkrisis/comparatio) to denigrate the alternative model of
his rivals (2:4–5, 11–21).[61] Paul's own self-presentation includes being a slave of
Christ and of no other, a characteristic of baptismal freedom (1:10; 3:25; 5:24; and
cf. 1 Cor 7:22). The Galatians are thus to be like him and not to be enslaved by the
rival teachers (2:4).[62] Paul does not call the Galatians to imitate what he does, but
rather he wants them to absorb into their own attitudes the way Paul has allowed
the gospel of Christ to work in him.

I Thessalonians

The imitation passages in 1 Thess 1:5–6 and 2:14–16 also direct the audience beyond Paul to the experience of conversion to faith in Christ.[63] Paul does not look
for a further change in the Thessalonians but for two things: their correct appraisal of the power of the Holy Spirit behind their conversion and their own
apostolic effectiveness, similar to Paul's, in aiding the spread of the gospel in
Macedonia and Achaia by their model (τύπος, typos) of accepting the gospel
(1 Thess 1:7).[64] They accomplished this by putting others' interests ahead of their
own for the sake of the gospel.[65] Paul uses the indicative, "you have become"
(1 Thess 1:6), rather than the imperative to focus the Thessalonians on what is in
fact the case.[66] Here imitation involves a comparison of the Thessalonians' experience of suffering for the gospel with that of Paul, his colleagues (2:2; 3:3–5), and
the Judean churches (2:14). These all suffer.[67] The grace they received empowers
them not just to spread the word as Paul does, but also to build up their own community in responsibility and loving care for each other. In 1 Thessalonians, Paul
finds that the Thessalonians have embraced his example. His concern is that they
"stand firm in the Lord" (1 Thess 3:8). In this way, their modeling of acceptance
of the gospel will be sustained and will have ongoing effect (1 Thess 1:7–8; 4:12).

Paul further calls for ethical conformity to his own pattern of behavior: he
embodies what he expects of the Thessalonian community.[68] Paul works for his
own support (2:7, 9) and uses the language of recollection to direct the Thessalonians' attention to the various aspects of his example with which they are already
familiar, a common hortatory technique.[69] His self-portrayal is both paradigmatic
for those who conform to his model and also polemical, against those who di-
verge from it (5:14; the disorderly, ἄτακτοι, ataktoi).[70] In this regard, Paul's example also reinforces his authority, for he demonstrates the attitudes that he expects
from the Thessalonians (1:5; 2:10–11; 4:10b–12; 5:14). Paul expands the example

and increases its force by including in it the other senders of the letter (Silvanus and Timothy in 1:2, "us" in 2:15–16). This establishes a bond between Paul and the audience by way of an appeal to emulate those who have the desired characteristics.[71]

The imitation passages in 1 Thessalonians form a ring pattern or *inclusio*. The Thessalonians' mimetic endurance receives praise at 1:6–10. Paul and his fellow missionaries' noble intention and perseverance are highlighted at 2:1–12. And again the desired mimetic endurance takes the spotlight. Despite the mention of suffering, the emphasis falls on the Thessalonians' joy derived from the Holy Spirit at their welcome reception of the gospel (1:6).[72]

Philippians

The theme of imitation, Markus Bockmuehl suggests, recurs as an integrating focus in every major section of Philippians.[73] Only after his autobiographical remarks—outlining his change of focus from his Jewish birth (3:5–6) and describing how he shared Christ's suffering (itself an imitation) in hopes of sharing the resurrection of Christ (3:8–11)—does Paul call for his audience to imitate him (3:17).[74] Paul's renunciation of prerogatives—echoing Christ's renunciation (2:6–8) and total reliance on God's power offered through the gospel—is at the heart of what is to be imitated.[75]

Paul's call to imitate employs the term συμμιμηταί, *symmimētai* (3:17), and echoes the earlier call to unity at 1:7 and 2:2–4. By his addition of the prefixed preposition συν, *syn* (here *sym*, meaning "together with"), he connects himself with like-minded people (3:15), and contrasts himself with self-interested persons whom Paul contemns (1:28 and 3:18).[76]

Paul is not the only model in the letter. The Christ hymn and Paul's introduction to it place Christ at the heart of the *mimesis* context. In addition to the soteriological summary (2:9–11), the hymn illustrates the ethical principle of deferential service in Christ's actions (2:7–8). This, in turn, shapes Paul's conduct (2:17–18). The content of Christ's renunciation and its saving consequences are obviously beyond human imitation. Paul wants the Philippians to apply the principle of deferential service embodied by Christ's renunciation to their own behavior in conformity to, instead of in mimicry of, the example.[77] They cannot replicate what Jesus did, but they can look to others' interests before their own, as Jesus did. In fact, Paul is an imitator of Christ himself and wants to draw the Philippians into the same imitation (*mimesis*) as co-imitators (*symmimētai*).[78] In the concrete, Paul demonstrates different ways of imitation: preaching, community building, and service toward others.[79]

Beyond himself and Christ, Paul offers the selfless examples of Timothy

(2:19–24) and Epaphroditus (2:25–30).[80] Indeed, like himself (1:20, 2:17) Epaphroditus risked even death (2:30) to fulfill his mission of service, a selflessness that embodies his imitation of Christ, who humbled himself even to death (2:8). Thus Paul changes to the plural "us" (3:17b) from the singular "me" at 3:17a.[81] Paul has already included Timothy in the salutation and is about to send him to Philippi (2:23). The leadership team plus Epaphroditus seem to be referred to with "us."

Paul uses "I/me" more than fifty times in the Letter to the Philippians and begins to propose himself as the paradigm of *mimesis* as early as 1:12–26.[82] He and the Philippians, by virtue of their baptism, are to conform their words and deeds to their life in Christ. Baptized into Christ (Rom 6:34), they have to shape their lives to reflect their new identity. Paul can be an example because he is "in Christ" (1:1, 8, 13, 20–21; 3:7–10, 12).[83]

Paul is a type for the community because they, like him, are all "in Christ."[84] Self-emptying might well be an attitude that links Jesus as model (2:5) to Paul, Timothy, Epaphroditus, and the Philippians as imitators. In this letter, Paul stresses humility, which gives priority to others and their benefit as the way to conform to the image of Christ. Thus Paul hopes that the Philippians will press on with determination like his to be found perfectly in Christ.[85] The eschatological goal for Paul and the Philippians is still ahead of him (3:12, and them), while Jesus already enjoys heavenly glory (2:11).[86] The opponents see the cross or suffering as a curse, perhaps out of an attitude expressive of triumphalism or over-realized eschatology.[87]

The call to imitate Paul appears again at 4:9. Parenetic language abounds here, for example, "learned," "received," "heard," "saw."[88] All of these refer to Paul's previous presence, practice, and teaching among them as well as what they learned about him in his trials and imprisonment.[89] As such, the Christian life finds embodiment in Paul himself ("in me," ἐν ἐμοί, *en emoi*; 4:9). Behavior that runs counter to the saving significance of the cross is at issue, not doctrinal opposition to it (4:19). As a negative model, some indulge in sinful behavior and repudiate God's will (3:18–19).[90] Paul, on the other hand, displays godly contentment (4:11–13) and inner peace from God (4:7, 9, 19).[91]

I Corinthians

The last imitation passages with an explicit call to imitation in the authentic letters of Paul are at 1 Cor 4:16 and 11:1. In fact, 11:1 forms an *inclusio* with 4:16. At 4:6, 4:16–17, and 11:1 Paul stands as a paradigm for dealing with each of the major topics presented, that is, factionalism, boasting, and self-interest.[92] Moreover, throughout the letter Paul makes use of examples to advance his arguments, to correct the Corinthians' behavior, and to regain their allegiance.[93] In addition to its parenetic aim, 1 Corinthians also has a deliberative purpose, and both are served by Paul's example.[94] Paul inserts himself into each problem situation (5:12; 6:12; 8:13; 9:12–15, 19–23; 10:28–11:1; 12:31–13:3; 13:11–12; 14:11, 14, 18) and thereby offers himself as an example of a nondivisive course of action[95] that he hopes the community will follow.[96]

In the two explicit imitation texts, Paul addresses the problems that come up throughout the letter, that is, arrogance, false wisdom, idolizing chosen leaders (1:12; 3:13; 5:6), and self-vaunting superiority (11:1). Paul's counterlesson highlights the imitation of his humility and self-abasement as being like "rubbish of the world" (4:13 NRSV), for humility, paradoxically, is a true sign of spiritual maturity. It also models seeking, not one's own prerogatives (9:4–7, 15), but others' interests (9:22; 10:33).[97] As in Philippians, this stands at the core of the pattern set by Christ, a pattern on which Paul asserts his own actions are based. Paul tries to move the Corinthians from an anthropocentric view and an emphasis on personal rights to a theocentric perspective and emphasis on obedience and service, which he demonstrates in chapter 9.[98] The imitation is oriented toward the crucified Christ. Paul, as imitator of Christ and bearer of the gospel, in his whole being, embraces the task of the risen savior Christ in renunciation and suffering.[99] In this orientation toward Christ, Paul and all the Christians live in Christ and not just according to his model. Paul's apostolic existence is fashioned by Jesus crucified and risen, just as exemplary virtue derives from the inner influence of the grace of the Holy Spirit (Gal 5; 1 Cor 3).[100]

Paul asks for imitation only from communities that he founded.[101] In the imitation passages, Paul's relationship with Christ as follower and apostle is expressed and legitimated.[102] While Michaelis's *TDNT* article stresses this aspect of the Pauline example, most of the more recent studies have broadened the understanding of Pauline example and imitation. While Paul is concerned to reinforce his authority in Galatians and 1 Corinthians, exhorting his churches in a broader sense to follow his attitude and even his conduct dominates his efforts in Philippians, and in Galatians and 1 Corinthians as well.

The pedagogical and hortatory uses of example, particularly in the epistolary literature of the Greco-Roman world, find expression in Paul's letters. The imitation section in 1 Thessalonians shares the hortatory aim but does it by way of comparing what the Thessalonians have accomplished to what Paul has done, and these two in relation to the model established by the suffering Jesus. The christological dimension of imitation is consistent in all the instances surveyed, with selflessness standing out as a way of being patterned after Jesus.

The passages in which Paul calls attention to his example are specific instances of a more general program throughout his letters. Paul uses autobiographical recollections and self-references as a paradigm of Christian outlook and practice for his followers to learn from and imitate. Paul Sampley demonstrates how it is "not uncommon for Paul to recount his life or a carefully selected portion of his life with a view to its exemplary value for exhortation."[103] So the Galatians were reminded of Paul's and their life and radical conversion, his and their life under challenge by opponents, the opposition of once-allied colleagues, the threats of spiritual bondage, the meaning of Christ's crucifixion for him and them, and his fidelity to the crucified Christ, a fidelity that he urges on them.[104]

Likewise, in Philippians, the imprisoned Paul relates to the Philippians, who are also subject to affliction (1:15–17, 28–30). He chooses to serve the needs of others like Timothy and Epaphroditus (2:21–22, 30). He dramatically dismisses his heritage as he pushes to his spiritual goal, which he wants them to emulate (3:4, 13, 17).[105] Brian Dodd's monograph elaborates on this strategy in 1 Corinthians, Galatians, Philippians, Philemon, 1 Thessalonians, and Romans.[106] Similarly, George Lyons's study of Galatians stresses the paradigmatic function of the "formerly/now" and "man/God" dichotomies in Paul's conversion (1:13–2:21) and the Galatians' desertion and surrender to slavery under the Law (1:6; 2:4; 3:28; 4:1–9, 22–31; 5:1, 13).[107] Lyons finds Paul's exemplary ethos at work in eight ways in his parenesis in 1 Thessalonians: in the exhortation itself; his moral conduct; his commitment to please God; his constant love and friendship; his labor and self-support; his prayer of thanksgiving; his rejoicing in affliction; and his eschatological hope.[108]

Implied Examples

Paul refers to a variety of examples in addition to his own. At 1 Cor 1:12, the names Cephas, Apollos, Paul, and Christ might well refer to exemplary figures adopted by factional currents in the Corinthian churches.[109] Paul refers to Apollos together with himself at 1 Cor 4:6 as examples in his exhortation to the Corinthians against exaggerated self-importance and disunity.[110] At 1 Cor 7:7–8, Paul proposes himself as an example of remaining in one's current condition in view of the end time.[111] For Dodd, "Paul's self-presentation as a model is the skeletal structure of his argument in 1 Corinthians."[112] The paradigmatic statement at 1 Cor 8:13, which echoes the hortatory "I" at 5:12 and 6:12, proposes the model behavior Paul expects the Corinthians to emulate, namely, the practice of love that requires that the Corinthians not claim all their rights or exercise all their freedom. This exhortation continues through chapter 9, where Paul discusses the apostolic prerogatives that he forgoes. Paul's exhortation culminates in the "personal example for renunciation of freedom" at 1 Cor 10:23–11:1.[113] With his personal example in 1 Cor 13, which contains twenty-five first-person-singular references, Paul reinforces the exhortation to harmony in chapters 12 and 14, and he recapitulates themes from elsewhere in the letter.[114] In the last use of his example in 1 Cor 15:8–19, 30–32, Paul reinforces his argument in support of belief in the resurrection against the Corinthians' over-realized eschatology and denial of the necessity of suffering and death.[115] Galatians offers a variety of autobiographical references that constitute an example for the audience. Paul's self-characterization as a slave of Christ at 1:10 shows himself to be a pleaser of God rather than of humans.[116] In Philippians, Paul includes others as models or patterns, although his example is meant to be primary (3:17; 4:9).[117] The self-references in Philemon have hortatory power, and the community as a whole is in view as Paul makes his appeal to Philemon.[118] Paul's request combines an appeal to Philemon's free decision (Phlm 14) with implications of command and compulsion (vv. 8, 14). This appears to be the paradigmatic attitude of interaction that Paul wishes Philemon to adopt vis-à-vis Onesimus, Philemon's slave and now his brother, and also a surrogate for Paul himself (v. 17).[119] Paul paradigmatically renounces authority in favor of generosity, love, and compassion for others in the community.[120] In 1 Thess 2:12, Paul's self-presentation might well be "paradigmatic and polemical, modeling industry and chastising the indolent."[121] Paul opposes the indolent (5:14) and exemplifies industriousness (4:10b–12; 5:14). Some of the first-person references in Rom 7 have been shown to echo the story of Adam in Genesis. In general, the expressions of sinfulness before the Law do not fit Paul's self-confident declarations in Phil 3. However, an understanding of the style of diatribal argumentation helps give a more comprehensive perspective on the first-person references here. Nonetheless, the references to slavery echo Paul's remarks at 1:1 and in chapters 5–6. In 7:14–25, the first-person declarations are "a literary device that portrays the divided self's utter need for redemption."[122] Moreover, the "I" statement in Rom 7:14–25 is akin to 1 Cor 1–4, where Paul uses self-deprecation to focus the Corinthians on their unity in Christ. Here the self-deprecation demonstrates Christ's power to free the sinner by concentrating on a person enslaved to the Law.[123]

The Pauline correspondence liberally employs the rhetorical device of examples for imitation, both explicit and implicit. The aim in most instances is hortatory, to encourage the letter readers to adopt attitudes and actions in imitation of Paul's.

Part III. Other Relevant Pauline and Paulinist Texts

Three passages in the Pastoral Epistles offer Paul's example in the first person: 1 Tim 1:3–20; 2 Tim 1:3–18; 3:1–4:8. These three personal examples are a hortatory tool in the letters to urge the readers to hold to the teachings and virtues associated with Paul and to eschew the alternative doctrines and vices attributed to the false teachers.[124] Throughout the letters, Paul exhibits qualities and actions that embody qualities advanced in the letters. He thus becomes an implicit example of those qualities.[125]

In other places in these letters, Timothy and Titus are also expected to be models for the community. At 1 Tim 4:12, virtues dominate over teaching as constituents of the desired model (*typos*) to be imitated, the model that the letter advances.[126] As with Paul's example, a negative counterpart is outlined here as well. Titus, too, is to be a model (*typos*) of good works (Titus 2:7–8), in contrast to the antithetical example that precedes it at 1:10–16.[127] There is a rhetorical strategy at work here in proposing these examples to the readers. If the audience follows the virtuous and authentic example proposed, they will thwart the advance of the rival teachers. Furthermore, adopting the examples into their own lives, the audience will give authenticity to the positive teaching by the blameless lives that it produces (1 Tim 5:14; 6:14; 6:1). This in turn validates the criticism of the other teachers' failings.[128]

Part IV. Bibliography

Primary Sources

Aristotle. *Ars rhetorica.* Translated by J. H. Freese. LCL. London: W. Heinemann, 1927.

———. *Problems and Rhetorica ad Alexandrum.* Translated by H. Rackham and W. S. Hett. LCL. London: W. Heinemann, 1936.

Cicero. *Ad. C. Herennium libri IV; De ratione dicendi.* Translated by H. Caplan. LCL. Cambridge: Harvard University Press, 1954.

———. *De inventione, De optimo genere oratorum, Topica.* Translated by H. M. Hubbell. LCL. Cambridge: Harvard University Press, 1949.

———. *De officiis.* Translated by Walter Miller. LCL. Cambridge: Harvard University Press, 1913.

———. *De oratore III, De fato, Paradoxa stoicorum, De partitione oratoria.* Translated by H. Rackham. LCL. Cambridge: Harvard University Press, 1942.

Demetrius. *Demetrii et Libanii qui feruntur TYPOI EPISTOLIKOI et EPISTOLIMAIOI CHARAKTERES.* Leipzig: Teubner, 1910.

Nepos, Cornelius. *Vitae.* Edited by K. Halm and A. Fleckeisen. Leipzig: Teubner, 1916.

Philo. *Works.* Translated by F. H. Colson and G. H. Whitaker. 10 vols. LCL. Cambridge: Harvard University Press, 1956.

Plato. *The Republic.* Translated by Paul Shorey. 2 vols. LCL. Cambridge: Harvard University Press, 1956.

Pliny, The Younger. *Epistulae.* Translated by Betty Radice. 2 vols. Cambridge: Harvard University Press, 1969.

Plutarch. *Lives.* Translated by Bernadotte Perrin. 11 vols. LCL. Cambridge: Harvard University Press, 1914.

Quintilian. *Institutio oratoria*. Translated by Harold E. Butler. LCL. London: Heine-mann, 1920.

Seneca, The Elder. *Declamations*. Translated by M. Winterbottom. LCL. Cambridge: Harvard University Press, 1974.

Seneca, The Younger. *Ad Lucilium epistulae morales*. Translated by Richard M. Gummere. 3 vols. LCL. London: W. Heinemann, 1917.

Varro, Marcus Terentius. *Opere*. Edited by Antonio Traglia. Turin, Italy: Unione Tipografico Editrice, 1974.

Secondary Sources

Adinolfi, Marco. *La Prima Lettera ai Tessalonicesi nel mondo greco-romano*. Rome: Pontifici Athenaei Antoniani, 1990.

Alewell, Karl. *Über das rhetorische PARADEIGMA: Theorie, Beispielsammlung, Verwendung in der römischen Literatur der Kaiserzeit*. Leipzig: A. Hoffman, 1913.

Anderson, R. Dean. *Ancient Rhetorical Theory and Paul*. Kampen, the Netherlands: Kok Pharo, 1996.

Assion, Peter. "Das Exempel als agitatorische Gattung: Zu Form u. Funktion der kurzen Beispielgeschichte." *Fabula* 98 (1985): 72–92.

Baasland, Ernst. "Zum Beispiel der Beispielerzählungen: Zur Formenlehre der Gleichnisse und zur Methodik der Gleichnissauslegung." *NovT* 28, no. 3 (1986): 193–219.

Babut, Daniel. "Sur la notion d'"Imitation' dans les doctrines esthetiques de la Grèce classique." *REG* 98 (1985): 72–92.

Bloomer, W. Martin. *Valerius Maximus and the Rhetoric of the New Nobility*. Chapel Hill and London: University of North Carolina Press, 1992.

Borneque, Henri. *Les déclamations et les déclamateurs d'après Seneque le père*. Hildesheim, Germany: Georg Olms, 1902. Reprint, 1967.

Brant, Jo-Ann A. "The Place of *Mimesis* in Paul's Thought." *Studies in Religion/Sciences Religieuses* 22, no. 3 (1993): 285–300.

Burgess, Theodore. *Epideictic Literature*. Chicago: University of Chicago Press, 1902.

Cancik, Hildegard. *Untersuchungen zu Senecas epistuale morales*. Hildesheim, Germany: Georg Olms, 1967.

Carter, Howard Vernon. "The Mythological Paradigm in Greek and Latin Poetry." *AJP* 54 (1933): 201–24.

Castelli, Elizabeth A. *Imitating Paul: A Discourse of Power*. Louisville: Westminster John Knox, 1991.

Dodd, Brian. "Paul's Paradigmatic 'I' and 1 Cor 6.12." *JSNT* 59 (1995): 39–58.

———. *Paul's Paradigmatic "I": Personal Example as Literary Strategy*. Sheffield, England: Sheffield Academic Press, 1999.

Dornseiff, Franz. "Literarische Verwendung des Beispiels." *Bibliothek Warburg* 4 (1924–25): 206–28.

Eadie, John W., and Josiah Ober, eds. *The Craft of Ancient Historians: Essays in Honor of Chester G. Starr*. Lanham, Md.: University Press of America, 1985.

Eddy, Paul R. "Christian and Hellenistic Moral Exhortation: A Literary Comparison Based on 1 Thessalonians 4." Pages 45–51 in *Directions in New Testament*

Methods, edited by Martin C. Albl, Paul R. Eddy, and Renee Murkes, O.S.F. Milwaukee: Marquette University Press, 1993.

Fiore, Benjamin, S.J. *The Function of Personal Example in the Socratic and Pastoral Epistles.* AnBib 105. Rome: Biblical Institute Press, 1986.

Fraisse, Jean-Claude. "Imitation, Ressemblance et Metaphore dans la 'Poetique' d'Aristote." *Les Etudes Philosophiques* (1981): 9–18.

Gaventa, Beverly. "Galatians 1 and 2: Autobiography as Paradigm." *NovT* 28, no. 4 (1986): 309–26.

Getty, Mary Ann. "The Imitation of Paul in the Letters to the Thessalonians." Pages 277–83 in *The Thessalonian Correspondence,* edited by Raymond F. Collins. BETL 87. Louvain: Louvain University Press, 1990.

Grimaldi, William A., S.J. *Studies in the Philosophy of Aristotle's Rhetoric.* Wiesbaden, Germany: Franz Steiner, 1972.

Hadot, Ilsetraut. *Seneca und die griechisch-römischer Tradition der Seelenleitung.* Berlin: Walter de Gruyter, 1969.

Haight, Elizabeth H. *The Roman Use of Anecdotes in Cicero, Livy, and the Satirists.* New York: Longmans, Green, 1940.

Halliwell, Stephen. "Aristotelian Mimesis Revisited." *Journal of the History of Philosophy* 28 (1990): 487–510.

Hartlich, Paulus. "De exhortationum a Graecis Romanisque scriptarum historia et indole." *Leipziger Studien* 11 (1889): 207–36.

Hock, Ronald F., and Edward N. O'Neil, eds. *The Chreia in Ancient Rhetoric: The Progymnsasmata.* Vol. 1 of *The Chreia in Ancient Rhetoric.* Atlanta: Scholars Press, 1985.

Holloway, Paul A. "The Enthymeme as an Element of Style in Paul." *JBL* 120 (2001): 329–39.

Holmberg, Arne. *Studien zur Terminologie und Technik der rhetorischen Beweisführung bei lateinischen Schriftstellern.* Uppsala, Sweden: Almqvist & Wiksell, 1913.

Jaques, Mary V., and Kelly Walter. "Pauline Adaptation of Epistolary Conventions in Philippians 3:2–4:1." Pages 79–84 in *Directions in New Testament Methods,* edited by Martin C. Albl, Paul R. Eddy, and Renee Murkes, O.S.F. Milwaukee: Marquette University Press, 1993.

Johanson, Bruce C. *To All Brethren: A Text-Linguistic and Rhetorical Approach to 1 Thessalonians.* ConBNT 16. Stockholm: Almqvist & Wiksell, 1987.

Jost, Karl T. *Das Beispiel und Vorbild der Vorfahren bei den attischen Rednern und Geschichtschreibern bis Demosthenes.* Paderborn, Germany: F. Schöningh, 1936.

Kornhardt, Hildegard. *Exemplum, eine bedeutungsgeschichtliche Studie.* Göttingen, Germany: Robert Noske, 1936.

Lumpe, A. "Exemplum." *RAC* 6:1229–57.

Lyons, George. *Pauline Autobiography: Toward a New Understanding.* SBLDS 73. Atlanta: Scholars Press, 1988.

Maslakov, G. "Valerius Maximus and Roman Historiography: A Study of the Exempla Tradition." Pages 437–96 in *ANRW* II.32.1.

Mayer, Roland G. "Roman Historical Exempla in Seneca." Pages 141–76 in *Seneque et la Prose Latine,* edited by Oliver Reverdin and Bernard Grange. Fondations Hardt Entretiens sur l'antiquité classique 36. Geneva: Vandoeuvres, 1991.

Mitchell, Margaret M. *Paul and the Rhetoric of Reconciliation: An Exegetical Investigation of the Language and Composition of 1 Corinthians.* Tübingen: J. C. B. Mohr [Paul Siebeck], 1991.

Price, Bennet J. "*Paradeigma* and *Exemplum* in Ancient Rhetorical Theory." Ph.D. diss., University of California at Berkeley, 1975.

Reinhartz, Adele. "On the Meaning of the Pauline Exhortation: '*Mimetai mou ginesthe*—Become Imitators of Me.'" *Studies in Religion/Sciences Religieuses* 16, no. 4 (1987): 393–403.

Robinson, Arthur Wirt. "Cicero's Use of People as 'Exempla' in His Speeches." Ph.D. diss., Indiana University, 1986.

Römer, Franz. "Zum Aufbau der Exemplasammlung der Valerius Maximus." *Wiener Studien* 103 (1990): 99–107.

Sanders, Boykin. "Imitating Paul: 1 Cor 4:16." *HTR* 74, no. 4 (1981): 353–63.

Skidmore, Clive. *Practical Ethics for Roman Gentlemen: The Work of Valerius Maximus.* Exeter, England: University of Exeter Press, 1996.

Smith, Abraham. *Comfort One Another: Reconstructing the Rhetoric and Audience of 1 Thessalonians.* Louisville: Westminster John Knox, 1995.

Stadter, Philip A. *Plutarch's Historical Methods: An Analysis of the "Mulierum Virtutes."* Cambridge: Harvard University Press, 1965.

Stanley, David, S.J. "Imitation in Paul's Letters: Its Significance for His Relationship to Jesus and to His Own Christian Foundations." Pages 127–41 in *From Jesus to Paul: Studies in Honour of Francis Wright Beare,* edited by Peter Richardson and John C. Hurd. Waterloo, Ont.: Wilfrid Laurier University Press, 1984.

Stowers, Stanley Kent. *The Diatribe and Paul's Letter to the Romans.* SBLDS 57. Chico, Calif.: Scholars Press, 1981.

Suhl, Alfred. "Der Galaterbrief-Situation und Argumentation." Pages 3067–134 in *ANRW* II.25.4, edited by Wolfgang Haase. Berlin: Walter de Gruyter, 1987.

Thraede, Klaus. *Grundzüge griechisch-römischer Brieftopik.* Edited by Erik Burk and Hans Diller. Zetemeta: Monographien zur klassischen Altertumswissenschaft 48. Munich: C. H. Beck, 1970.

Trapp, M. B. *Maximus of Tyre: The Philosophical Orations.* Oxford: Clarendon, 1997.

Valgiglio, Ernesto. "Dagli 'Ethica' ai 'Bioi' in Plutarco." Pages 3994, 4010–13 in *ANRW* 33.6: II *Principat* 33.6. Edited by Wolfgang Haase. Berlin and New York: de Gruyter, 1992.

Vetschera, Rudolf. *Zur griechischen Paraenese.* Smichow and Prague: Rohlicek & Sievers, 1911–12.

Willms, Hans. *EIKON, eine begriffsgeschichtliche Untersuchung zum Platonismus.* Münster, Germany: Aschendorff, 1935.

Wuellner, Wilhelm. "Greek Rhetoric and Pauline Argumentation." Pages 177–88 in *Early Christian Literature and the Classical Intellectual Tradition: In Honorem Robert M. Grant,* edited by William R. Schoedel and Robert L. Wilken. Paris: Beauchesne, 1979.

Notes

1. Wilhelm Michaelis, "μιμέομαι, *mimeomai,*" *TDNT* 4:666–73. See Benjamin Fiore, S.J., *The Function of Personal Example in the Socratic and Pastoral Epistles*

(AnBib 105; Rome: Biblical Institute Press, 1986), 164n. 2, for bibliography. For a discussion of Michaelis's article, see 164–68.

2. Much of this overview is derived from Bennet J. Price, "Paradeigma and Exemplum in Ancient Rhetorical Theory" (Ph.D. diss., University of California at Berkeley, 1975). See also Arne Holmberg, *Studien zur Terminologie und Technik der rhetorischen Beweisführung bei lateinischen Schriftstellern* (Uppsala, Sweden: Almqvist & Wiksell, 1913); and Peter Assion, "Das Exempel als agitatorische Gattung: Zu Form u. Funktion der kurzen Beispielgeschichte," *Fabula* 98 (1985): 72–92.

3. Aristotle, *Problems and Rhetorica ad Alexandrum* (LCL; London: W. Heinemann, 1936).

4. By and large, Anaximenes' concern is with examples in forensic or legislative speeches, and so most of his remarks have little direct bearing on hortatory discourses. This is largely the case with all the rhetorical theorists surveyed here.

5. Aristotle, *Ars rhetorica* (Freese, LCL).

6. Margaret M. Mitchell, *Paul and the Rhetoric of Reconciliation: An Exegetical Investigation of the Language and Composition of 1 Corinthians* (Tübingen: J. C. B. Mohr [Paul Siebeck], 1991), 42.

7. Ibid., 43.

8. Ibid., 45.

9. Ibid., 46.

10. William A. Grimaldi, S.J., *Studies in the Philosophy of Aristotle's Rhetoric* (Wiesbaden, Germany: Franz Steiner, 1972), 104–5.

11. Aristotle, *Problems* (Hett, LCL).

12. Daniel Babut, "Sur la notion d'"Imitation' dans les doctrines esthetiques de la Grece classique," *REG* 98 (1985): 79. See also Stephen Halliwell, "Aristotelian Mimesis Revisited," *Journal of the History of Philosophy* 28 (1990): 487–510, and Jean-Claude Fraisse, "Imitation, Ressemblance et Metaphore dans la 'Poetique' d'Aristote," *Les Etudes Philosophiques* (1981): 9–18.

13. Clive Skidmore, *Practical Ethics for Roman Gentlemen: The Work of Valerius Maximus* (Exeter, England: University of Exeter Press, 1996), 6, and see also Plato, *Resp.* 378d (Paul Shorey, LCL).

14. Varro's *Hebdomades vel de imaginibus* contains one hundred portraits of great personalities of Greek and Rome with epigrams and short biographies. Nepos's *De viris illustribus* contains biographies organized in occupational categories. Here Greeks are contrasted with Romans.

15. W. Martin Bloomer, *Valerius Maximus and the Rhetoric of the New Nobility* (Chapel Hill and London: University of North Carolina Press, 1992), 1–4, 18. M. B. Trapp, *Maximus of Tyre: The Philosophical Orations* (Oxford: Clarendon, 1997), xxxvi–xxxvii, describes the source of examples in Maximus's orations from Homer to prose authors, mythology to history. All of these examples helped clarify and display a mastery of the cultural heritage and history. At page xli, Trapp notes that Maximus's audience, on the threshold of their public careers, used the essays to claim some acquaintance with the philosophical heritage as part of their general *paideia*.

16. See also Karl Alewell, *Über das rhetorische PARADEIGMA: Theorie, Beispielsammlung, Verwendung in der römischen Literatur der Kaiserzeit* (Leipzig: A. Hoffman, 1913); Howard Vernon Carter, "The Mytholographical Paradigm in Greek and Latin Poetry," *AJP* 54 (1933): 201–24; Elizabeth H. Haight, *The Roman Use of*

Anecdotes in Cicero, Livy, and the Satirists (New York: Longmans, 1940); G. Maslakov, "Valerius Maximus and Roman Historiography: A Study of the Exempla Tradition," in *ANRW* II.32.1, 437–96; Henri Bornecque, *Les déclamations et les déclamateurs d'après Seneque le Père* (Hildesheim, Germany: Georg Olms, 1902; reprint, 1967).

17. Bloomer, *Valerius Maximus,* 5, 7–17, 20–30, 83–89.

18. Skidmore's conclusion was contrary to Bloomer (Skidmore, *Practical Ethics,* 2–3). Franz Römer, "Zum Aufbau der Exemplasammlung des Valerius Maximus," *Wiener Studien* 103 (1990): 99–107, found a careful organizational plan behind the collection of examples in Valerius.

19. Skidmore, *Practical Ethics,* 3, 53–65.

20. Ibid., 7–11. Note also Polybius X.21; Strabo, *Geogr.* VII.3.9; Dionysius of Halicarnassus, *Pomp.* 6.

21. "History is wholesome and profitable because you behold lessons of every kind of experience. From these you may choose for yourself and for your own state what to imitate; from these mark from avoidance what is shameful in the conception and shameful in the result" (preface to *Ab urbe condita,* in Haight, *Roman Use of Anecdotes,* 38). See Skidmore, *Practical Ethics,* 13–18, and Tacitus, *Hist.* II.13, 47; III.51, 67; *Ann.* III.55; IV.33; XV.57; Livy V.51.8; XLV.40.6, 41.10.

22. Skidmore, *Practical Ethics,* 19–21.

23. Ancient rhetoric distinguished between figures of thought and figures of speech or elocution. Figures of speech refer to the beautification of verbal expression, such as accumulation of similarities or differences (*polysyndeton*), and elimination of otherwise necessary parts of a sentence (*ellipsis*). Figures of thought refer to sense relationships between parts of sentences, such as antitheses or rhetorical questions, and direct address (*apostrophē*).

24. Cicero, *Ad C. Herennium libri IV; De ratione dicendi* (Caplan, LCL).

25. Cicero, *De inventione, de optimo genere oratorum, topica* (Hubbell, LCL). See also Arthur Wirt Robinson, "Cicero's Use of People as "Exempla" in His Speeches" (Ph.D. diss., Indiana University, 1986), 5–7, 34.

26. Price, "Paradeigma and Exemplum," 104.

27. Cicero, *De oratore III, de fato, paradoxa stoicorum, de partitione oratoria* (Rackham, LCL). See also Price, "Paradeigma and Exemplum," 267n. 30; *De or.* 3.27.104–5; *Ad Her.* 2.30.47.

28. Quintilian said, "(1) [T]he third kind of proof, of those proofs which are brought into the matter under discussion and are not intrinsic to it, the Greeks call *paradeigma.* They have used this word both broadly/generally for every comparison of like with like and narrowly/specifically for those comparisons which rely on the authority of history. Roman writers generally have preferred to use the word *similitudo* for what the Greeks call *parabolē,* although the historical example involves similarity, while the *similitudo* is like an *exemplum.* (2) I, to make the matter simpler, would consider both (historical example and *similitudo*) species of the genus *paradeigma* and call them *exemplum*" (*Inst.* 5.11.1–2; as translated by Price, "Paradeigma and Exemplum," 132–33).

29. Skidmore, *Practical Ethics,* 22.

30. Quintilian, *The Institutio Oratoria of Quintilian* (Butler, LCL). See also *Ad Her.* 4.6.9 and Cicero, *de Or.* 2.2.88.

31. On teachers affecting the pupils' morals, see also *Inst.* 1.2.4–5. According to *Ep.* 8.32.2, Pliny formed the habits of Junius Avitus as if he were his teacher, standing in the relationship of love and respect that Quintilian here outlines. See Pliny, *Ep.* 8.14, and compare Horace, *Sat.* 1.4.103–29, especially 105–7. See also Seneca, *Con.* 10.2.16: "Solebas mihi, pater, insignium virorum exempla narrare, quaedam etiam domesticam. Aiebas: avum fortem virum habuisti, vide ut sis fortior" ("Father, you used to tell me of the feats of famous men, some actually taken from our family records. You would say, 'You had a hero for a grandfather; make sure you are braver'"; The Elder Seneca, *Declamations* [Winterbottom, LCL]); Pliny, *Ep.* 5.8.4–5; Seneca, *Clem.* 1.9.1; and Alewell, *Über das rhetorische PARA-DEIGMA*, 27.

32. See Cicero, *Resp.* 2.6.6; Quintilian, *Inst.* 12.2.2; Seneca, *Con.* 9.2.27: "Omnia autem genera corruptarum quoque sententiarum de industria pono, quia facilius et quid imitandum et quid vitandum sit docemur exemplo" ("Indeed, I purposely quote all kinds even of decadent epigrams; it is easier for you to learn by example both what to imitate and what to avoid"); and also Seneca *Ep.* 6.5.

33. Franz Dornseiff, "Literarische Verwendung des Beispiels," *Bibliothek Warburg* 4 (1924–25): 206–28.

34. For a fuller discussion, see Fiore, *Function of Personal Example*, 39–42. See also Theodore Burgess, *Epideictic Literature* (Chicago: University of Chicago Press, 1902); Paulus Hartlich, "De exhortationum a Graecis Romanisque scriptarum historia et indole," *Leipziger Studien* 11 (1889): 207–36; and Rudolf Vetschera, *Zur griechischen Paraenese* (Smichow/Prague: Rohlicek & Sievers, 1911–12).

35. John W. Eadie and Josiah Ober, eds., *The Craft of the Ancient Historians: Essays in Honor of Chester G. Starr* (Lanham, Md.: University Press of America, 1985), 377–80; Ernesto Valgiglio, "Dagli 'Ethica' ai 'Bioi' in Plutarco," in *ANRW* II *Principat* 33.6 (ed. Wolfgang Haase; Berlin and New York: de Gruyter, 1992), 3994, 4010–13; and Philip A. Stadter, *Plutarch's Historical Methods: An Analysis of the "Mulierum Virtutes"* (Cambridge: Harvard University Press, 1965), 125, 131. Plutarch, *Aem.* 1.1–3, serves as a programmatic declaration for all his parallel *Lives*. Plutarch states that he planned, with the help of history, like a mirror, to adorn his life and conform it to virtues of which the historical personages were the actors: "[G]athering memories of better and more illustrious men, I prepare myself to free myself from them, chasing them away, if something evil or ignoble insinuates itself in me and to turn happy and gentle in mind to better examples."

36. Seneca, *Ad Lucilium epistulae morales* (Gummere, LCL). See also Roland G. Mayer, "Roman Historical Exempla in Seneca," in *Seneque et la Prose Latine* (ed. Oliver Reverdin and Bernard Grange; Fondation Hardt: Entretiens sur l'antiquité classique 36; Geneva: Vandoeuvres, 1991), 141–49, 158–59.

37. Mayer, *Roman Historical Exempla*, 165–69; Cicero, *De or.* 2.226; and Seneca, *Ep.* 64.9 ("quidni ego magnorum virorum et imagines habeam incitamenta animi" "why should I not keep statues of great men to kindle my enthusiasm").

38. See Hildegard Cancik, *Untersuchungen zu Senecas epistulae morales* (Hildesheim, Germany: Georg Olms, 1967), 25, 48; Klaus Thraede, *Grundzüge griechischrömischer Brieftopik* (ed. Erik Burk and Hans Diller; Zetemata: Monographien zur klassischen Altertumswissenschaft 48; Munich: C. H. Beck, 1970); and Ilsetraut Hadot, *Seneca und die griechisch-römischer Tradition der Seelenleitung* (Berlin: Walter

de Gruyter, 1969). See also Ernst Baasland, "Zum Beispiel der Beispielerzählungen: Zur Formenlehre der Gleichnisse und zur Methodik der Gleichnissauslegung," *NovT* 28, no. 3 (1986): 198.

39. Hildegard Kornhardt, *Exemplum: Eine bedeutungsgeschichtliche Studie* (Göttingen: Robert Noske, 1936), 10–47.

40. See also Karl T. Jost, *Das Beispiel und Vorbild der Vorfahren bei den attischen Rednern und Geschichtschreibern bis Demosthenes* (Paderborn, Germany: F. Schöningh, 1936); Hans Willms, *EIKON, eine begriffsgeschichtliche Untersuchung zum Platonismus* (Münster, Germany: Aschendorff, 1935); and A. Lumpe, "Exemplum," *RAC* 6:1229–57.

41. Aphthonius, *Progymnasmata* 139.

42. Ronald F. Hock and Edward N. O'Neil, eds., *The Progymnasmata* (vol. 1 of *The Chreia in Ancient Rhetoric*; Texts and Translations 27; Greco-Roman Religion Series 9; Atlanta: Scholars Press, 1986).

43. Donald L. Clark, *Rhetoric in Greco-Roman Education* (New York and London: Columbia University Press, 1957), 186–88, and Leonhard von Spengel, ed., *Rhetores graeci* (Leipzig: B. G. Teubner, 1853).

44. Demetrius, *Eloc.* 223, and see Weichert's introduction to his edition of Demetrius and Libanius xii, in which he refers to Synesius, *Ep.* 138, p. 724 (Hercher) and Philostratus, *Vit. Apoll.* 4.25 (Valentine Weichert, ed., *Demetrii et Libanii qui feruntur TYPOI EPISTOLIKOI et EPISTOLIMAIOI CHARAKTERES* [Leipzig: B. G. Teubner, 1910]).

45. While Seneca in *Ep.* 75 presumes that a letter should be as spontaneous and free from artifice as a heart-to-heart conversation, Demetrius, 224, allows a degree of elaboration, and Weichert observes (*Demetrii et Libanii*, xv) that, after Demetrius, a good deal of art found its way into the letter, with the sanction of rhetors.

46. Stanley Kent Stowers, *The Diatribe and Paul's Letter to the Romans* (SBLDS 57; Chico, Calif.: Scholars Press, 1981), 157, 167–71.

47. Brian Dodd, *Paul's Paradigmatic "I": Personal Example as Literary Strategy* (Sheffield, England: Sheffield Academic, 1999), 17–18.

48. Ibid., 29.

49. Ibid., 32, and compare "way" and "walk" in the LXX for a person's conduct offered for imitation at Judg 2:17; 1 Sam 8:3; 1 Kgs 3:14; 9:4; 11:33, 38. Note also Phil 3:17; 1 Cor 4:16–17.

50. R. Dean Anderson finds that Paul's method of argumentation and use of example does not follow the norms of Hellenistic rhetoric. Paul, he finds, simply states rather than defends his arguments and does not use carefully constructed epicheiremes (syllogisms). Indeed, Paul's argumentation is obscure and raises more questions than answers. In classical Greco-Roman rhetoric, examples often concluded the presentation of arguments, to bolster them (Aristotle, *Rhet.* 2.20; 8). Anderson notes, however, that examples at times could serve as proofs in the absence of enthymemes. But then multiple examples are put first, and so the argument might seem to be an inductive proof (Cicero, *Inv* 1.51–56; *Top* 42; Quintilian, *Inst* 5.10.73). This does not appear to be Pauline practice (R. Dean Anderson, *Ancient Rhetorical Theory and Paul* [Kampen, the Netherlands: Kok Pharos, 1996], 252 and 311). The rhetorical theorists, however, had speeches in mind and not letters, and so Paul's rhetorical deficiencies come as no surprise. Paul A. Holloway, "The

Enthymeme as an Element of Style in Paul," *JBL* 120 (2001): 329–39, finds enthymemes that accord with Greco-Roman rhetorical conventions in 1 and 2 Corinthians, Galatians, and Romans.

51. George Lyons, *Pauline Autobiography: Toward a New Understanding* (SBLDS 73; Atlanta: Scholars Press, 1988), 164–68.

52. Alfred Suhl, "Der Galaterbrief-Situation und Argumentation," in *ANRW* II.25.4 (ed. Wolfgang Haase; Berlin: Walter de Gruyter, 1987), 3131.

53. L. Ann Jervis, *Galatians* (Peabody, Mass.: Hendrickson, 1999), 117; Dieter Lührmann, *Galatians* (trans. C. Dean, Jr.; Minneapolis: Fortress Press, 1992), 86; Leon Morris, *Galatians: Paul's Charter of Christian Freedom* (Downers Grove, Ill.: InterVarsity, 1996), 136–37; Paul Nadim Tarazi, *Galatians: A Commentary* (Crestwood, N.J.: St. Vladimir's Seminary Press, 1994), 226–27; Timothy George, *Galatians* (Nashville: Broadman & Holman, 1994), 318; Udo Borse, *Der Brief an die Galater* (Regensburg, Germany: Friedrich Pustet, 1984), 149; Frank J. Matera, *Galatians* (Collegeville, Minn.: Liturgical, 1992), 164; Beverly Gaventa, "Galatians 1 & 2: Autobiography as Paradigm," *NovT* 28, no. 4 (1986): 321.

54. Jervis, *Galatians,* 117; Tarazi, *Galatians,* 226.

55. Fiore, *Function of Personal Example,* 12n. 9.

56. Strictly speaking, friendship is between equals. See Benjamin Fiore, S.J., "The Theory and Practice of Friendship in Cicero," in *Greco-Roman Perspectives on Friendship* (ed. John T. Fitzgerald; Atlanta: Scholars Press, 1997), 66n. 19.

57. Matera, *Galatians,* 162, 166.

58. Gaventa, "Galatians 1 & 2," 313; Dodd, *Paul's Paradigmatic "I,"* 163–64.

59. Dodd, *Personal Example,* 163–64.

60. Gaventa, "Galatians 1 & 2," 322.

61. Dodd, *Paul's Paradigmatic "I,"* 133.

62. Ibid., 150–55. Paul is Christ's slave (1:10), and he resisted the rivals' efforts to take away the freedom he and Titus enjoy (2:4). Paul expects the Galatians to show the same boldness toward them that he himself showed (1:8–9).

63. See Mary Ann Getty, "The Imitation of Paul in the Letters to the Thessalonians," in *The Thessalonian Correspondence* (ed. Raymond F. Collins; BETL 87; Louvain: Louvain University Press, 1990), 277, where she notes that 1 Thess 1:7–8 applies the word *typos* to the Thessalonians. Their being called a *typos* is the result of their imitation.

64. Lyons, *Pauline Autobiography,* 190–201.

65. Jo-Ann A. Brant, "The Place of *Mimesis* in Paul's Thought," *Studies in Religion/Sciences Religieuses* 22, no. 3 (1993): 291–93; Arland J. Hultgren, Donald H. Juel, Jack D. Kingsbury, eds., *All Things New: Essays in Honor of Roy A. Harrisville* (Word and Work Supplement Series 1; St. Paul, Minn.: Luther Northwestern Seminary Press, 1992), 141–45; Earl J. Richard, *First and Second Thessalonians* (Sacra pagina 11; Collegeville, Minn.: Liturgical, 1995), 67–68; Paul R. Eddy, "Christian and Hellenistic Moral Exhortation: A Literary Comparison Based on 1 Thessalonians 4," in *Directions in New Testament Methods* (ed. Martin C. Albl, Paul R. Eddy, and Renee Murkes, O.S.F.; Milwaukee: Marquette University Press, 1993), 49; Getty, "Imitation of Paul," 280–81; Adele Reinhartz, "On the Meaning of the Pauline Exhortation '*mimetai mou ginesthe*—Become Imitators of Me,'" *Studies in Religion/Sciences Religieuses* 16, no. 4 (1987): 402.

66. Dodd, *Paul's Paradigmatic "I,"* 212–13. Dodd agrees here with Michaelis and Castelli (Elizabeth A. Castelli, *Imitating Paul: A Discourse of Power* [Louisville: Westminster John Knox, 1991]) that the imitation consists in what is already a fact rather than an exhortation to be like Paul. See David Stanley, S.J., "Imitation in Paul's Letters: Its Significance for His Relationship to Jesus and to His Own Christian Foundations," in *From Jesus to Paul: Studies in Honour of Francis Wright Beare* (ed. Peter Richardson and John C. Hurd; Waterloo, Ontario: Wilfrid Laurier University Press, 1984), 133–35, and also Gaventa, "Galatians 1 & 2," 16, who explains that the indicative serves to encourage and reinforce similar behavior in the future.

67. See Bruce C. Johanson, *To All the Brethren: A Text-Linguistic and Rhetorical Approach to 1 Thessalonians* (ConBNT 16; Stockholm: Almqvist & Wiksell, 1987), 96–97, who asserts that Paul makes a quasi-logical appeal supporting the genuine character of the Thessalonians' Christian experience of the gospel. Paul finds suffering to be the identifying mark for Christians.

68. Charles A. Wanamaker, *The Epistle to the Thessalonians: A Commentary on the Greek Text* (Grand Rapids: Eerdmans, 1990), 283, and cf. 1 Cor 4:16; 11:1; and Phil 3:17.

69. Fiore, *Function of Personal Example,* 16n. 17.

70. Dodd, *Paul's Paradigmatic "I,"* 214–19; Stanley, "Imitation in Paul's Letters," 137; Gaventa, "Galatians 1 & 2," 17; Abraham Smith, *Comfort One Another: Reconstructing the Rhetoric and Audience of 1 Thessalonians* (Louisville: Westminster John Knox, 1995), 72. Paul expands the polemical tone at 2:15–16, a *vituperatio* (reproof) against obdurate and hostile opponents; see Johanson, *To All the Brethren,* 98, who says that the *pathos* (a play upon feelings) appeal is strengthened by the blame and judgment against the persecutors. See also Wanamaker, *Epistle to the Thessalonians,* 118; Gaventa, "Galatians 1 & 2," 129–30; and Marco Adinolfi, *La Prima Lettera ai Tessalonicesi nel mondo greco-romano* (Rome: Pontifici Athenaei Antoniani, 1990), 92–102. See also Smith, *Comfort One Another,* 34–36, who observes that the denigration of an ethnic group was a standard method of ancient invective to create boundaries between the audience, orator, and the identified opponent.

71. Johanson, *To All the Brethren,* 84.

72. Smith, *Comfort One Another,* 80; Richard, *First and Second Thessalonians,* 67–68.

73. Markus Bockmuehl, *The Epistle to the Philippians* (Peabody, Mass.: Hendrickson, 1998), 254.

74. Mary V. Jaques and Kelly Walter, "Pauline Adaptation of Epistolary Conventions in Philippians 3:2–4:1," in Albl, Eddy, and Murkes, *Directions in New Testament Methods,* 83–84. Gordon D. Fee, *Paul's Letter to the Philippians* (Grand Rapids: Eerdmans, 1995), 363–64, notes that imitation of the teacher was an ideal in the Jewish tradition and cites Philo, *Virt.* 66 and *Congr.* 70: "For the practicer must be the imitator of a life, not the hearer of words, since the latter is the characteristic mark of the recipient of teaching, and the former of the strenuous self-exerciser" (LCL 4.493).

75. Stanley, "Imitation in Paul's Letters," 141, and Reinhartz, "Pauline Exhortation," 400–401. Τοῦτο φρονῶμεν, *Touto phronōmen* ("Let us adopt this attitude," 3:15), refers to Paul's own striving for maturity (3:15), detachment (3:8), and hope for resurrection (3:10–11), as well as referring to 2:5 (τοῦτο φρονεῖτε, *touto phron-*

eite, "Have among yourselves the same attitude") and the Christ hymn. Defense of his own authority does not seem to be an issue for Paul in this letter, contrary to Michaelis. Peter T. O'Brien, *The Epistle to the Philippians: A Commentary on the Greek Text* (Grand Rapids: Eerdmans, 1991), 446, says that it is not Paul's authority but aspects of his attitude and behavior that he wants the Philippians to imitate.

76. O'Brien, *Epistle to the Philippians,* 444; Moises Silva, *Philippians* (Chicago: Moody, 1988), 208; Reinhartz, "Pauline Exhortation," 401.

77. Brant, "Place of *Mimesis,*" 296–97; Richard R. Melick, Jr., *Philippians* (Nashville: Broadman, 1991), 142.

78. Silva, *Philippians,* 208; O'Brien, *Epistle to the Philippians,* 445; *mou* here would be possessive. O'Brien, however, takes it as objective.

79. Brant, "Place of *Mimesis,*" 299.

80. O'Brien, *Epistle to the Philippians,* 443; Dodd, *Paul's Paradigmatic "I,"* 190–91.

81. O'Brien, *Epistle to the Philippians,* 447.

82. Dodd, *Paul's Paradigmatic "I,"* 171. Dodd finds that Paul's proposal of himself as a model goes far beyond the specific passages in which he urges imitation and includes the multiple references to himself, his attitudes and experiences.

83. Ibid., 187–88, 192–94.

84. Dodd, in ibid., 188–94, does not see Paul as imitating Christ or reflecting Christ's model because most of Christ's story is inimitable. Nonetheless, he does agree that Jesus' self-abnegation is exemplary for the Philippians in their community relations and that Christ is an archetype for Paul and the Philippians.

85. O'Brien, *Epistle to the Philippians,* 446–47, states that 2:12–16 prepares for the call to imitation while 2:8–11 provides the groundwork for it.

86. Brant, "Place of *Mimesis,*" 298–300, and Fee, *Letter to the Philippians,* 363–64.

87. Dodd, *Paul's Paradigmatic "I,"* 177–80.

88. Silva, *Philippians,* 229–30.

89. O'Brien, *Epistle to the Philippians,* 510–11.

90. Ibid., 454–55.

91. Dodd, *Paul's Paradigmatic "I,"* 186.

92. Brian J. Dodd, "Paul's Paradigmatic 'I' and 1 Cor 6.12," *JSNT* 59 (1995): 42, 49.

93. Ibid., 51, and Mitchell, *Rhetoric,* 47–48, where she indicates the use of both positive and negative examples. Paul proposes negative examples at 10:6; various occupations as paradigms at 9:7; examples from scripture at 5:6–8; 6:16–17; 9:8–10, 13; 10:18; 11:2–16; 14:21; 15:32; voice, speech, and communication in chapter 14; seeds and heavenly bodies in chapter 15; and Christ himself at 11:1.

94. Mitchell, *Rhetoric,* 50–60; Reinhartz, "Pauline Exhortation," 398. In 1 Corinthians, Paul is a teacher/father (4:15, 17), while the Corinthians are infants (3:1; 2:6) and immature (3:2).

95. Similarly in Philippians, Paul proposes his example as a model to diffuse the divisiveness of the rivals at 1:14, 17–18, 20, 30; 2:17–18; 3:3–4 (Mitchell, *Rhetoric,* 50–54; Dodd, "Paul's Paradigmatic 'I,'" 53–54; Dodd, *Paul's Paradigmatic "I,"* 32).

96. Michaelis stresses that Paul's call to imitation is an expression of his authority. The implied assertion of authority in Paul's proposing himself as an example for imitation is a pedagogical technique. He is a regulative model (Dodd,

Paul's Paradigmatic "I," 29), advanced to promote unity in the community (ibid., 33–48). His example serves to encourage his audience that the ends can be attained (ibid., 103). For this use of example as an encouragement of success, see Plutarch, *Mor.* 7:539–47. The verb *nouthetein* (admonish) also expresses Paul's aim of correction in view of improved behavior and attitude (see Christian Wolff, *Der erste Brief des Paulus an die Korinther* [Leipzig: Evangelische Verlagsanstalt, 1996], 93).

97. Brant, "Place of *Mimesis*," 294–95; Reinhartz, "Pauline Exhortation," 397–98; Boykin Sanders, "Imitating Paul: 1 Cor 4:16," *HTR* 74, no. 4 (1981): 358–59; Carl Holladay, *The First Letter of Paul to the Corinthians* (Austin, Tex.: Sweet, 1979), 138. There is *accumulatio* (accumulation of arguments) from 10:23 to 11:1, in which Paul gathers points made from 8:1 on. The principle of not seeking one's own prerogatives is also demonstrated at Phil 2:6–11; 2 Cor 8:9; 13:4.

98. Richard A. Horsley, *I Corinthians* (Nashville: Abingdon, 1998), 142.

99. See Wolff, *An die Korinther,* 94, 242, who finds parallel comments about Jesus' exemplary renunciation and suffering at Rom 15:2; 2 Cor 8:9; Phil 2:6–8. See also Jose Maria Casciaro, ed., *St. Paul's Epistle to the Corinthians* (Dublin: 4 Courts, 1991), 69, and Gerhard Sellin, "Haupt Probleme des ersten Korintherbriefes," in *ANRW* II 25.4 (ed. Wolfgang Haase; Berlin and New York: Walter de Gruyter, 1987), 3023.

100. Giuseppe Barbaglio, *La prima lettera ai Corinzi* (Bologna, Italy: EDB, 1995), 241–49; Jerome Murphy-O'Connor, *I Corinthians* (New York: Doubleday, 1998), 37; John J. Kilgallen, S.J., *First Corinthians: An Introduction and Study Guide* (New York and Mahwah, N.J.: Paulist, 1987), 92. Wilhelm Wuellner, "Greek Rhetoric and Pauline Argumentation," in *Early Christian Literature and the Classical Intellectual Tradition: In Honorem Robert M. Grant* (Paris: Beauchesne, 1979), 187, says that the "digression" at 9:1–10:13 with Paul himself as model is meant to assure that salvation reaches not some, but all, and that the commitment to sacrifice is the point of the metaphor and the scriptural appeal.

101. Franz Josef Ortkemper, *1 Korintherbrief* (Stuttgart: Katholisches Bibelwerk, 1993), 54.

102. Reinhartz, "Pauline Exhortation," 403.

103. J. Paul Sampley, "Reasoning from the Horizon of Paul's Thought World: A Comparison of Galatians and Philippians," in *Theology and Ethics in Paul and His Interpreters: Essays in Honor of Victor Paul Furnish* (ed. Eugene H. Lovering and Jerry L. Sumney; Nashville: Abingdon, 1996), 125.

104. Ibid., 125.

105. Ibid., 127.

106. Dodd, "Paul's Paradigmatic 'I.'"

107. Lyons, *Pauline Autobiography,* 171, 174–75.

108. Ibid., 218–19, 224–25.

109. Dodd, *Paul's Paradigmatic "I,"* 37–40.

110. Ibid., 45–48.

111. Ibid., 94–95.

112. Ibid., 95.

113. Ibid., 98–101.

114. Ibid., 114–25.

115. Ibid., 125–29.

116. Ibid., 148–51, and see 2:4–5, 11–14. Dodd also describes Paul's "participationist language" in reference to Christ and his sufferings (156–61, referring to Gal 2:19–20).

117. Ibid., 183.

118. See ibid., 200–201, where Dodd notes the references to coworkers and the church (Phlm 2–3, 22–25) and the liturgical setting implied by the "grace and peace" formula (vv. 3, 25).

119. Ibid., 203–4.

120. Ibid., 205.

121. Ibid., 215–19.

122. Ibid., 222–32.

123. Ibid., 233–34.

124. Fiore, *Function of Personal Example,* 198–208.

125. Ibid., 209–11.

126. Ibid., 213–16.

127. Ibid., 211.

128. Ibid., 212–13.

9

PAUL, FAMILIES, AND HOUSEHOLDS

David L. Balch

The archaeology of domestic, urban living quarters is basic for understanding social relationships in Pauline families and communities.[1] For example, one cannot accurately understand whether family life was public or private, the importance of meals, or the place of slaves in the household without investigating the architecture of actual Greek, Roman, and Palestinian houses. Therefore, I survey selected studies of Greco-Roman housing in urban settings, focusing on archaeological observations that might illuminate social relationships in first-century households and also in the Pauline house churches that worshiped in these same architectural settings. The second part of the essay examines selected, specific topics in relation to Greco-Roman families: sexuality, home schooling of young and old, the status of slaves in the household, and family customs at meals, especially women at meals.[2]

Families that owned a house lived in the same domestic spaces with their slaves, which had consequences for sexual activity. Only a wealthy *pater familias* could afford a teacher for the children of the household. Slaves worshiped at the same household altars as did their masters, but they served the meals while the owners reclined in the dining room(s). This raises the question whether family eating customs were followed when Pauline ἐκκλησίαι, *ekklēsiai,* worshiped and celebrated the Eucharist in the same domestic spaces. These and other questions are treated in the following essay on Pauline families and households.

Part I. Archaeology of Greco-Roman Housing

Archaeology helps us understand the social, cultural, and religious environment of the households in which families in Pauline churches lived and worshiped. To achieve this aim, the study cannot be limited to tracing the footsteps of Paul in Asia Minor and Greece.[3] We cannot archaeologically investigate actual houses in which the Pauline churches met. We can learn more about contemporary Greco-Roman domestic culture by examining houses in cities other than those in which Paul preached, because those cities and houses are better preserved. Professor Osiek and I have suggested that the atrium houses in Pompeii are comparable to those that would have been found in other Greco-Roman cities. On the assumption that houses in Pompeii are to some extent typical, additional questions need discussion. Assuming that some Pauline churches also met in apartment buildings,[4] how widespread was the building of atrium houses and apartment buildings in the first century C.E., and were Greek houses qualitatively different from Roman ones?

Peter Lampe has written about early Christians in Rome, concluding that they met in Trastevere,[5] a poor region of the city populated by immigrants. Even in this poorer region, however, there was no zoning; that is, *domus* (atrium houses) and *insulae* (apartment buildings) were built in the same regions.[6] Therefore, an analogy with apartment buildings in our run-down city slums misleads interpreters. One apartment house excavated in Pompeii, the Sarno Bath compound, was not lower-class housing, but rather a condominium with a private bath for the wealthy.[7] Wallace-Hadrill argues that the poor were to be found also in atrium houses, perhaps in greater numbers than in the apartment buildings. Poor clients visited or lived with their wealthy patrons in the atrium houses, which means that rich and poor persons may have had more occasions for social interchange in houses than in apartment buildings.[8] In his new paper (n. 4), Wallace-Hadrill observes that for Rome we would best think in terms of a "neighborhood" (*vicus*) with a mixture of interrelated, wealthy and poor housing, slave quarters, and shops, not in terms of isolated houses or apartment buildings.

Many in Pauline households were poor (1 Cor 1:26–29), but one would be mistaken to assume that this was true of all the earliest Christians. Prisca and Aquila were wealthy enough to have an assembly meeting in their house (1 Cor 16:19 and Rom 16:5, houses in Ephesus and Rome). Both have been identified as freed persons or children of freed persons of the Acilius family. A. Acilius Glabrio, consul in 91, was executed by Domitian with a group of nobles charged with practicing atheism and adopting Jewish customs (Dio Cassius 67.14).[9] Stowers also argues that "those who belong to Aristobulus" (Rom 16:10) belong to the household of the grandson of Herod the Great and the brother of Agrippa I, a friend and client of the emperor Claudius.[10] Paul next mentions "my relative Herodian" (Rom 16:11), who, because freed persons carried their master's name, Stowers suggests, probably belonged to the same larger family. "One can plausibly imagine writings of Philo circulating among the dependents of Agrippa's and Aristobulus's households and Paul having gentile followers in their households."[11]

Wallace-Hadrill's and Zanker's characterizations of housing in Pompeii and

Herculaneum are helpful in attempting to understand the social possibilities and challenges faced by Christian families in Rome, Corinth, and Ephesus. "Pompeii was by no means an important urban center; it was only one of many medium-sized country towns in Italy."[12] Houses in this city varied dramatically in size: the House of the Faun in Pompeii covered an entire city block, 31,000 square feet, with two peristyle courtyards and two atria at the entrances.[13] By contrast many shops had an attached small room on the ground floor or a cramped living quarters on the second reached by stairs, quarters that might be 220 square feet. We do not know the size, for example, of the houses of Lydia (Acts 16:40), Prisca and Aquila (1 Cor 16:19; Rom 16:3–5), Stephanus (1 Cor 1:16; 16:16–17), Philemon with Apphia and Archippus (Phlm 2), or Nympha (Col 4:15). Gaius's house was large enough so that the members of several house churches could meet in his home in Corinth (Rom 16:23; 1 Cor 14:23; see 1:11). The hundreds of atrium houses in Pompeii give us some idea of the range of possibilities. Not until the middle or end of the second century C.E. did Christians begin to remodel houses into buildings specifically adapted for their assembly and worship.[14]

The social functions of these Greco-Roman houses were dramatically different from those of North America and Europe. During the day the front doors of Roman houses were left open to invite visitors in![15] "Our homes are private spaces, in which we live for the most part in nuclear families, screened from the public gaze in every sense. . . . The Roman house, by contrast, was a center of social communication. . . . During the day, when the front door stood open, the lines of sight were purposely designed to allow glimpses deep into the interior of the house from the entrance."[16]

In the twenty-first century we typically separate our living from our working spaces, but the Romans did not. Business was conducted at home, and the aesthetic beauty of the home attracted visitors into the business. "The area open to visitors in a Roman house offered no privacy, and there were clearly no separate rooms for the women and children of the household, for instance, or for guests. . . . [T]he intense social activity . . . cannot be adequately described with our terms 'public' and 'private'" (12). The more people who crowded into the house, the more influence the owner of the house had. "Influence spread from the residences of powerful families into the public sphere and not vice versa, as was the case in Greek cities" (6). These customs would dramatically affect a family or a worship service in such a house. Paul asks what unbelievers would think when they entered the house/worship service (1 Cor 14:23), probably assuming that visitors would simply walk in the front door, whether specifically invited or not.

Paintings dominated domestic interiors, so that to us they would seem like museums. "Even ceilings and floors were treated as large surfaces to be covered systematically with bands and fields of decoration, very much in contrast to our homes, where furniture blocks most of the walls" (11–12). Zanker devotes a chapter to the meaning of these mosaics, paintings, and sculptures, suggesting that they are a better way to gauge the tastes and aspirations of the population than are literary and epigraphic sources (136). Zanker concludes: "[P]articularly in medium-sized and smaller residences in Pompeii" (20; see 126, 140–41, 174, 184, 193, 199), despite their limitations of space, the owners imitated the new domestic architecture and aesthetic decor of larger, wealthy villas. Unless the houses were very small, we can assume that the owners of houses who hosted Christian assemblies typically would have internalized the values and aspirations of those who were wealthy. In the climate of competition in Greco-Roman society, "everything the upper classes did was imitated" (141). "In a competitive society with relatively extensive upward mobility, the powerful create models for less wealthy and powerful contemporaries through their habits and the style in which they live, at least when they place themselves on display as ostentatiously as Roman aristocrats did" (13). The cultures of local peoples were giving way to a new and unified Roman culture (4). Those with medium- and small-sized houses redesigned them to include a peristyle courtyard with as many impressive reception and dining rooms around the courtyard as possible, decorated with real or imitation marble, thereby identifying themselves with the Roman way of life (13, 21, 117). This is self-Romanization,[17] which means they lived in a world of imagination, not simply in their own everyday world.[18]

The slave quarters of such houses, however, were not painted with frescoes, but sometimes with stripes. Service areas of the house where slaves worked, such as kitchens, were marginalized, pushed away to a corner of the house. Wallace-Hadrill has stressed that there were hierarchical social distinctions not merely between households, but within the social space of the house.[19] Foss studied the relationship between beautiful dining rooms and undecorated slave kitchens in these houses, finding that owners placed them as far from each other as possible.[20] The wealthier the house, the farther the slaves had to go to serve the food; owners wanted those sights, sounds, and smells far from their beautiful dining rooms. The architecture of the house where Christians lived and assembled would thus have been in tension with the pre-Pauline baptismal formula that proclaimed "there is no longer . . . slave or free" (Gal 3:28b).[21]

Zanker and Trümper both point to the work of the American sociologist Veblen, who gave us the category of "conspicuous consumption."[22] The architects' and owners' extravagance, luxury, exaggeration in scale, and excessive use of expensive materials exhibits their focus on the pleasures of life. Zanker's thesis is based especially on the study of medium and small houses, the size house in which Christians may have lived and worshiped. Zanker concludes that these houses are evidence of the materialistic values of life that dominated Roman society. He refers to Petronius's picture of Trimalchio, a freedman, as the prototype of a common figure in the empire.[23]

But how typical are the Roman houses of Pompeii? I make some preliminary observations by summarizing studies, by Monika Trümper, of Greek houses on the island of Delos; the following paragraphs summarize her conclusions.[24] Delos freed itself from Athens in 314 B.C.E. and flowered during independence for the following 150 years, due to busy trade through a good harbor. Foreigners arrived from all over the Mediterranean. The Romans declared Delos a free port and gave it back to Athens in the period 168–165. Athenians returned to the island and ruled until 88 B.C.E.; many merchants migrated to do business, but Delians were exiled. Between 130–88 B.C.E. Delos attained its greatest economic success. However, in 88 it was sacked by a general of Mithridates, who slaughtered twenty thousand residents. Delos lost its leading role in commerce, so that, in the time of the Caesars, Delos was forgotten and its population dwindled.[25]

The inhabitants of Delos, immediately after attaining independence, focused on building in the public sector, in contrast to contemporary, simple houses in the Quartier du theatre. The city plan was systematically enriched with public gathering and entertainment buildings (theater, gymnasium, palaestra, stadium, and agora with halls). The Delian citizens seem to have subordinated their personal, private needs for high-status houses until they gave their city an appropriate appearance.[26] Romans looked down on all who did not dwell in "cities," considering them barbarians. When Strabo (*Geog.* 3.4.14) describes the Celtiberians, who were famous for dwelling in cities, he remarks that these were only villages.[27] But the Allobroges of the middle Rhone developed their township into a "city," Vienna, a consequence of the Roman conquest (Strabo 4.1.11).[28]

Trümper interprets the building and remodeling of the Greek houses on Delos in light of Veblen's categories: the builders had a desire not only for display, but also for "cultural belonging."[29] Owners installed peristyle courtyards, columns, vestibules, richly equipped rooms, latrines, and baths, even when their houses were small. Even national minorities on Delos accepted these norms of taste. This is not true of the earliest houses built in the third century B.C.E., which Trümper names "canonical Delian normal [typical?] houses." Few rooms in those early houses opened directly on the courtyard, and there was little possibility of variation. But after 166 B.C.E. the colonists and businesspeople began to build houses with as many rooms—at least three—around the courtyard as possible, so that they opened directly on the courtyard. This required a certain length and width, but there was no strict correlation between size and wealth. Even middle-sized houses were decorated with mosaics, wall paintings, and marble. The contrast between size and luxury was even greater in a small house like TH VI O (86)[30] that had different living quarters on the ground and upper floors, but that included quality bronze statues, a frieze with figures, and good furniture. Trümper suggests that the change in Delian architecture, that is, the building of larger, richer, more luxurious houses with peristyle courtyards, occurred through the immigration of rich merchants beginning in 166, with a second change in luxury houses occurring in relation to the series of historical events around 130 B.C.E.

Specific uses of rooms could be determined only in relation to latrines, baths, and kitchens, which were placed as far as possible from the courtyard, in corners, in the vestibule, or in their own section of the house; in this respect, Trümper's observations match those of Foss in Pompeii. In larger homes, some researchers have argued for a separation between "private living" and "public presentation" spaces. But Trümper concludes that a separation between living and public presentation spaces cannot be observed in the archaeological remains, even in houses with multiple courtyards.[31] Instead, Delians built upward, but even then, not in order to separate different functions. The upper floors were consistently more richly decorated than were the ground floors, so it is not believable to interpret them as private living areas.[32] Even in rich houses, separate inhabitants occupied the upper floors; all aspects of living were united on the upper floor.

There is some grouping of the earliest, simple, "normal [typical] houses," which may suggest a relationship between lower social status and living in the Quartier du theatre. But for a building like the Ilot de la maison des masques, Trümper observes that socially diverse inhabitants must have been anticipated from the beginning. More research remains to be done on whether there is a correlation between social levels and the different blocks (*insulae*) of the city.

Trümper concludes that the best comparative material for Greek houses in Delos lies in the Vesuvian cities of Pompeii and Herculaneum. But whether this similarity results from direct Roman influence or from Athenian or oriental influence would go beyond archaeological evidence.

The second Greek city whose houses I will characterize briefly is Pergamon, summarizing and quoting the study by Wulf-Rheidt.[33] Early houses, some of which had the earliest courtyards, are in an area of Pergamon built in the early third century B.C.E. by Philetairos. But huge peristyle houses were built in the early second century B.C.E. by Eumenes II,[34] about the same time as analogous changes occurred on Delos. The older building plot measured an average of 130–200 square meters, but the newer peristyle courtyard houses occupied 1,200 square meters.[35] A large hall-like room,[36] the dining hall, along the east or west side of the courtyard was an indispensable feature of the later peristyle houses. The upper floors had lavishly decorated rooms (308), as did some basements with marble revetments and lavish wall paintings—so they were not service rooms (309).

Earlier researchers identified two major types of dwelling. The first included houses with the main rooms arranged around an oblong courtyard in a "U"-

shaped configuration (around three sides of the house). The second consisted of a group with almost square ground plans with rooms arrayed around a courtyard in the shape of an "L" (around two sides of the house) (301). Wulf-Rheidt disputes this, seeing rather three different types: (1) houses with a dining hall that may connect with additional smaller chambers; (2) a three-room group that generally has two secondary rooms; and (3) smaller, almost square rooms connected with neither a three-room group nor a dining hall (311). The model from the second century B.C.E. was a square peristyle courtyard; deviations from this were due to the steep hill on which Pergamon was built (309–10). The most important aim determining both dimensions of peristyle halls and their design was the desire for symmetry. The desire for a great peristyle courtyard may be the reason some houses do not show a "U"-shaped arrangement, which would have made the peristyle too small.

The dining halls were always located close to the entrances of the houses or next to the service areas in order to link the latter with the house's public areas (311), a significant architectural and social difference from Pompeii and Delos. The hall-like rooms are banqueting halls. Halls facing each other served as a summer and a winter triclinium (dining room), respectively, because the climate in Pergamon would not allow a banquet in an open room during the winter months. The center room of the three-room groups with columnar opening seems to have been a reception room, in which valuable silver dishes were displayed on a buffet (312). Adjoining rooms were triclinia available for symposia. Small rooms off the peristyle courtyard were also triclinia. All the main rooms arrayed around the peristyle courtyard were, therefore, used for different occasions, whether great banquets or more-private dinners. Service and secondary rooms were arranged outside the peristyle courtyard at the entrance of the houses or were detached. Wulf-Rheidt assumes that living rooms and other private rooms of family were located on the upper floor, a basic disagreement with Trümper.

In a large peristyle house the dining hall is the most important room (313). Such halls are always located on the side opposite the entrance, providing an axial vista, also typical of the peristyle houses of Pompeii and Delos. Some houses have both two dining halls and a group of three rooms on the north, but these three-room units do not have a columnar opening; the emphasis is still on the dining halls, which are large. The main vista between entrance and three-room group also played a role, but was not as important as in those houses in which the dining hall was central. The desire for opulence did not find expression simply in size of rooms, but in their number and lavish furnishings (314), as on Delos.

To summarize, by the mid–second century B.C.E. Roman culture had begun to unify even domestic architecture in Italy, on a Greek island such as Delos, and in Asia Minor as illustrated by Pergamon. Christian families, just like Jewish and pagan families, would have experienced the cultural attractions and pressures of living in Greco-Roman cities and houses. It was "civilized" to live in cities, not merely in villages. In cities even small or middle-sized houses were built or remodeled to include symmetrical peristyle courtyards with as many rooms, especially a dining room, opening onto the courtyard as possible. In Roman peristyle houses, the front door was open in the daytime, and those passing by could see deep into the house. Because Roman houses were social and political centers, clients and strangers were welcome to enter, often far into the house, even without a specific invitation. The key room was the triclinium, the dining room, or, in the house of a wealthier owner, several dining halls, often facing each other, along with other rooms whose function could be changed quickly. Because there was far less furniture than in modern houses, changing the function of such rooms was easy. Trümper argues that upper floors were not private living quarters either, because they were highly decorated; upper floors unified all the functions of domestic living. A Christian family that hosted a Pauline *ekklēsia* might have lived on an upper floor (see Acts 1:13; 9:37, 39; 20:8). Zanker develops the thesis that these houses, particularly small and middle-sized ones, had aesthetic ornamentation that imitated wealthy villas. Those whose income was moderate aped the tastes of the wealthy, crowding paintings, sculptures, and mosaics into the rooms in their houses, often in a confusing and contradictory fashion, attempting to demonstrate that they belonged to Roman society, even if they were foreigners. The quarters of the slaves, however, were undecorated, in which nobodies lived and worked.[37] In Pompeii and Delos the slave kitchens were placed as far as possible from the dining rooms, although in Pergamon they were built in proximity to each other.

Paul's mission, aimed at converting these households, moved between the cities of Greece/Asia Minor and Jerusalem (see, e.g., Gal 1:18; 2:1; Rom 15:25); a cultural contrast between Greece/Asia Minor and Palestine can be observed even in domestic architecture. The four-room Israelite house, common from the earliest settlements until the Babylonian exile, differed dramatically from the Greco-Roman peristyle house in function, art, and architecture. The first floor was for work and animals, while humans apparently lived on the upper floor.[38] But during Jesus' lifetime, Herod the Great had transformed Palestine from a world of small villages into one with all the architecture of Greco-Roman cities, including temples, gymnasia, theaters, amphitheaters, stadia, and hippodromes.[39] The Herodian building program in Palestine is a prime example of the watershed in art and architecture of the Augustan age generally.[40] In the Herodian Quarter of Jerusalem itself, archaeologists have excavated a peristyle house decorated with mosaics and with frescoes painted in the first and second Pompeian style on imitation marble with colored panels and floral patterns![41] When Josephus was sent to

Galilee in 66 C.E., just before the outbreak of war with Rome, he informed the leaders of Tiberius that he had been commissioned by authorities in Jerusalem to demolish Herod's palace; it contained representations of animals, forbidden by the laws (Josephus, *Life* 64–65; compare *Ant.* 15.267–79).[42]

Scholars debate just how, when, and where a form of Judaism developed that accepted the artistic depiction of animals and humans. Archaeological excavations of Beth-She'arim in Lower Galilee have revealed Jewish representational art in the catacombs where Rabbi Judah I (beginning of the third century C.E.) was buried.[43] When discussing Paul and family household relationships, it is crucial to observe that Greco-Roman domestic culture in the form of a peristyle house with Pompeiian frescoes had invaded Herodian Jerusalem. Further, some Jewish authors in the diaspora, for example, the author of the Gospel of Matthew (22:20), were deemphasizing the prohibition of images legislated in the Decalogue.[44] How would various audiences hear—and see—the Pauline gospel in the diverse domestic settings in Rome, Corinth, and Jerusalem?

Greco-Roman Families' Sexual, Educational, Slave, and Meal Customs

Families and sexuality. Greco-Roman medical handbooks, frescoes on the walls of Pompeii, and contemporary literature help modern interpreters conceptualize sex in the Greco-Roman world. The medical handbooks, written both by doctors and by laypeople, for example, Celsus, "helped men take possession of the female body."[45] They reflect a mixture of philosophical and contemporary scientific information. "Sexual intercourse, they [Epicurean philosophers] say, has never done a man good, and he is lucky if it has not harmed him" (Diog. Laert. 10.118 [Hicks, LCL]). Celsus, writing in the early first century C.E., advised that "sexual intercourse neither should be avidly desired, nor should it be feared very much. Rarely performed, it revives the body, performed frequently, it weakens. . . . [S]exual union is recognized as not harmful when it is followed by neither apathy nor pain. The weak, however, among whom are a large portion of townspeople, and almost all those fond of letters, need greater precaution" (Celsus, *On Medicine* 1.1.4; 2.1).[46]

The physician Soranus reports a debate in the late first century C.E. between two medical schools over sexual abstinence, both agreeing with Epicurus's opinion that abstinence is ideal. Soranus himself argues that "permanent virginity is healthful, because intercourse is harmful in itself" (*Gynecology* 1.7.32).[47] Few medical sources explain why contemporary physicians thought intercourse was harmful. But Galen, a physician writing in the second century C.E., explains that sperm is identical with spirit, and therefore, when sperm is ejected, the person loses vital spirit and becomes weaker.[48] An excess of sexual activity, according to the doctors, produces physical and spiritual weakness.

Sexually ascetic Therapeutae are described by the Alexandrian Hellenistic Jew Philo. He writes of aged virgins who, because of their yearning for wisdom, have of their own free will kept their chastity. Males, too, possessed like Dionysiac bacchanals and desiring the vision of God, soar above the senses. They abandon their property, leave their families and cities, and go to Jewish monasteries.[49] Philo's description is complemented by, or perhaps written in response to, that of the contemporary Stoic philosopher and Egyptian priest Chaeremon, who similarly praises some Egyptian priests who renounce their income and devote their whole life to contemplation of the divine. These priests practice self-control, do not drink wine, abstain from animal food, vegetables, and above all from sexual intercourse with women or men.[50]

Roman Stoics, on the other hand, typically supported marriage, but some opposed the widespread assumption that the man owns the woman. Musonius taught: "The husband and wife . . . should come together for the purpose of making a life in common and of procreating children, and furthermore, of regarding all things in common between them, and nothing peculiar or private to one or the other, not even their own bodies" (frg. 13A, trans. Lutz).

There was a contemporary debate about the relationship between friendship and sex. In Plutarch's *Amatorius*, Protogenes praises pederasty because it includes friendship (*Mor.* 750D), but denounces the housebound love for women as devoid of it (ἀφίλοι, *aphiloi*, 751B). Daphnaeus and Plutarch argue the opposite, against older views of friendship with boys, that a wife is a suitable, more graceful, and constant friend (769A–D, 751C).

But some contemporary biologists contrasted male and female nature.

All females are less spirited than the males, except the bear and leopard: in these the female is held to be braver. But in the other kinds the females are softer [μαλακότερα, *malakotera*], more vicious, less simple, more impetuous, more attentive to the feeding of the young, while the males on the contrary are more spirited, wilder, simpler, less cunning. There are traces of these characters in virtually all animals, but they are all the more evident in those that are more possessed of character and especially in man. For man's nature [φύσιν, *physin*] is the most complete, so that these dispositions too are more evident in humans. Hence a wife is more compassionate than a husband and more given to tears, but also more jealous and complaining and more apt to scold and fight. The female is also more dispirited and despondent than the male, more shameless and lying, is readier to deceive and has a longer memory; furthermore she is more wakeful, more afraid of action, and in general is less inclined to move than the male, and takes less nourishment. The male on the other hand, as we have said, is a readier ally and is braver than the female. (Aristotle, *History of Animals* IX.1 608a32–608b18 [Balme, LCL])

Women are by nature softer, men stronger.

The relationship between the sexes in these centuries was not static. One conclusive sign that their relationship was changing dramatically in the first century is architectural. (1) In Republican times, men and women went to public baths segregated by gender; (2) during the empire, beginning in the first century C.E., the baths were remodeled so that men and woman bathed together nude; but (3) in the fourth century C.E., men and women were separated again.[51] The culture shock of moving from one practice to the other would have been deep and is a sign that the cultural roles being played by women were changing. This cultural change toward more friendship between men and women and the acts that symbolized this development, such as bathing together, generated conflict (Pliny, *Hist. Nat.* 33.153; Quintilian, *Inst.* 5.9.14).

The pleasure of sex was to be limited by satisfaction, just as a wise person with a full stomach limits eating.[52] Greek discussions of what is "natural" and how to "use" it do not raise the question of the gender of either the subject or the object of sexual desire. Plutarch (*Advice to Bride and Groom* 144B) even refers to the wife's "use" of the husband.[53] Greco-Roman discussions of household management are one source of this terminology, which advised the householder about the "use" of possessions, including the "use" of a wife. "Use" focuses on "the psychological significance of the act for the subject [not the object] of sexual desire,"[54] a focus that differs from modern debates.

Education in households. The Villa dei Papyrii near Herculaneum is an example of a house that was a center of education. In 79 C.E., when Vesuvius covered it with volcanic lava, it contained a large library of books by the resident teacher-philosopher, Philodemus.[55]

There are four tractates on education under Plutarch's name, two actually by Plutarch and two by his students (*Mor.* 1A–48D and 1131B–1147A). All four are enlightening, but here I will dwell on Plutarch, *How to Study Poetry* (14E–37B), which covers what the grammarian teaches teenage children at home. Plutarch recommends that one study Homer's poetry, but also includes Hesiod, Pindar, Theognis, Aeschylus, Sophocles, Euripides, and Menander. Plutarch recommends blending philosophy with poetry, because "many the lies the poets tell" (16A [Babbitt, LCL]). "Whenever, therefore, in the poems of a man of note and repute some strange and disconcerting statement either about gods or lesser deities or about virtue is made by the author, he who accepts the statement as true is carried off his feet, and has his opinions perverted" (16D). Whenever one reads in the *Iliad* that Zeus weighed the fates of Achilles and Hector and predetermined

Hector's death, Plutarch suggests that this is obviously myth fabricated to please the hearer, but one does not need to share the poet's delusion regarding the gods (17AB; see 34A). When one reads of visits to Hades, of blazing rivers, and of grim punishments, this too is myth and falsehood, even if believed by Homer, Pindar, and Sophocles (17B). Such feelings are disturbing, but the young should be equipped with the maxim that "poetry is not greatly concerned with the truth" (17E), and with the reassurance that such questions stagger even philosophers such as Plato.

Poetry is analogous to painting, which may depict unnatural acts. In this case, Plutarch commends the art, but repudiates the actions (18BD). Authors create unnatural and mean persons to discredit their actions and words, and sometimes, Plutarch observes, the poet himself hints that these actions and words are distasteful (19A). Another method of interpretation, Plutarch suggests, is to notice the mutual contradictions among the poets. When Euripides writes that the gods defeat our plans, the interpreter may quote his other line to the contrary: "If gods do aught that's base, they are no gods" (21A). If Sophocles praises wealth, he also writes that "to beg [πτωχεύω, *ptōcheuō*] does not degrade a noble mind" (21B). If the poet does not offer a solution himself, one may cite declarations of other well-known writers (21D). When Theognis wrote, "[A]ny man that is subject to poverty never is able either to speak or to act," Bion replied, "How is it then, that you, who are poor, can talk much nonsense and weary us with this rubbish?" (22A). The grammarian teaches teenagers about philosophy, that is, about theology and ethics in ancient and contemporary literature, as does Paul, although he focuses on Torah. Teenagers may find that Pythagoras and Plato agree with what they read in poetry (35F). So from Plato they will learn that "to do wrong is worse that to be wronged" (*Gorgias* 473A) and "to do evil is more injurious than to suffer evil" ([*Republic* I 351–352D and IV]; Plutarch 36A). So the child will not be "stuffed with what he has heard always from his mother and nurse, and I dare say, from his father and tutor [παιδαγωγός, *paidagōgos*] as well, who all beautify and worship the rich, who shudder at death and pain, who regard virtue without money and repute as quite undesirable and a thing of naught" (36E).

The Hellenistic Jew Philo agrees with his middle-Platonist colleague Plutarch about the function of "grammar," the study of literature in the poets and historians (*Preliminary Studies* 15; see 74, 142, 148). Education's whole goal, with wisdom at its apex, is theology (49, 105, 133) and ethics (65, 79–107), to have the "courage to say, God and God alone must I honor, not anything that is below God" (133).

I conclude with a final comment on teaching/preaching in house churches: teachers interpreted classical texts in light of frescoes and sculptures in such houses. A contemporary rhetorician, Lucian, writes that the art in such "a splendid hall/house excites the speaker's fancy and stirs it to speech, as if he were somehow prompted by what he sees. No doubt something of beauty flows through the eyes into the soul, and then fashions into the likeness of itself the words that it sends out" (*De domo* [The hall or house] 4 [Harmon, LCL]). Lucian promises his audience as he speaks in a house with frescoes on the walls that he will "paint you a word-picture [γράψομαι . . . τῷ λόγῳ, *grapsomai . . . tō logō*] . . . despite the difficulty of representing pictures [συστήσασθαι τοσαύτας εἰκόνας, *systēsasthai tosautas eikonas*] without color, form, or space" (*De domo* 21).

Postclassical, baroque[56] art portrayed human suffering and death with significant analogies to Jesus' passion. For example, sculptures of the hanging Marsyas are known from more than twelve copies. The myth is that Marsyas, a satyr or silenus, learns to play pipes discarded by Athena, then challenges Apollo to a musical contest with his life as forfeit. The Hellenistic sculpture group shows the forfeit, a gruesome divine punishment of vanity and hubris. The old man Marsyas is strung from a tree about to be flayed alive by a Scythian, who sharpens his knife for the task and looks up menacingly. Fleischer's interpretation makes the group an allegory of Seleucid Asia Minor: the usurper Achaios was savagely punished by the young Antiochus III. Achaios was captured in 213 B.C.E., mutilated, decapitated, and crucified (Polybius 8.21).

The relationship between domestic wall paintings and the Pauline gospel, as far as I know, has never been studied, but as we saw above (n. 18), Zanker claims that these frescoes are a better way to gauge the tastes and aspirations of the population than are literary and epigraphic sources. One example is Euripides' tragedy, *Iphigenia at Aulis*. Sam Williams has shown that Euripides' language is quite close to Paul's soteriology.[57] I quote some lines from the play, presented in 405 B.C.E., then show the image painted on a Pompeiian wall. Iphigenia willingly sacrificed her body for Greece, bowing to the will of the gods:

> "Resolved I am to die" (1375) for "Phrygia's overthrow" (1379). "Lo, if Artemis hath willed to claim my body as her right, what, shall I, a helpless mortal woman, thwart the will divine? . . . My body unto Hellas I resign, sacrifice me, raze ye Troy" (1395–1398). "I die—O freely I die for thee" (1503).

> "But to her father's side she came, and stood, And said: 'My father, at thine hest I come, And for my country's sake my body give [1551–1553], . . . willingly, and sacrificed. . . . [1555]. Then let no Argive lay a hand on me; Silent, unflinching, will I yield my neck.'" (1559–1560; Euripides, *Iphigenia at Aulis* [Heinemann, LCL])

After Euripides' death, Timanthes, a contemporary, painted a picture of Iphigenia's willing sacrifice (Cicero, *Orat.* 22.74; Quintilian, *Inst.* 2.13.13), a fresco reproduced more than four centuries later on a Pompeiian wall (see fig. 1).[58] With Artemis's temple behind her and to the right, Iphigenia stands independently, not

Fig. 1. House of Modesto (?), Pompeii: with Artemis's temple behind her, Iphigenia voluntarily offers herself for Greece. Agamemnon, her sorrowful father, sits on the viewer's right, pulling his robe over his eyes, while the priest, Calchas, cuts a lock of her hair with a knife. (Published with permission of the Soprintendenza per i Beni Archeologici delle province di Napoli e Caserta.)

forced by anyone, while the priest Calchas cuts a lock of her hair with the sacrificial knife. In Greco-Roman oral/visual culture, this domestic fresco would have generated both understanding and misunderstanding of the Pauline gospel (see below).

Slaves in households. Aristotle was the first to make slavery as a social institution within the political system an object of systematic philosophical thought.[59] The city, he observed, is composed of houses, which in turn are composed of "master and slave, husband and wife, father and children" (*Politics* I.1253b 6–7).[60] Garnsey observes two essential characteristics of Aristotle's theory: (1) the slave is subhuman, and (2) the slave/master relationship is mutually beneficial.[61] Neither assertion is plausible, Garnsey argues, nor easy to establish by argument.

Stoics discussed legal slavery only marginally, not debating its causes, origins, or justification. Epictetus, for example, explores the nature of freedom and slavery, which for him were moral, not legal, questions: the Stoic wise man should adopt an attitude of extreme indifference toward such externals (*Diss.* 4.1.76–79).[62] Epictetus does discuss some externals, wealth/poverty and health/sickness, but hardly mentions legal slavery (see 4.1.33–37), which is peculiar because he himself had been a slave.[63]

There was some discussion of how to treat slaves: Seneca pleaded for masters not to be cruel to their slaves (*Ep.* 47). Sexual harassment has become a crime in modern Western societies but was not in the Roman world: "[U]nchastity [*impudicitia*] is a crime for the freeborn, a necessity for a slave, and a duty [*officium*] for the freeman" (Seneca, *Controversiae* 4 preface 10).[64] "A much repeated way of teasing a slave is to remind him of what his master expects of him, i.e., to get down on all fours."[65] Several laws of the first and second centuries C.E. apparently aimed to restrict the cruel punishment of slaves; for example, Claudius granted freedom to sick slaves abandoned by their masters.[66] But in contrast to their severe treatment of slaves, Romans frequently manumitted them, and freed persons could become Roman citizens. This provided incentive for slaves to work and to behave in a manner approved by the masters.[67] Scholars dispute how frequently Roman slaves were manumitted.[68]

The Jewish Essenes, as described by Philo (*Prob.* 79; *Hypoth.* 11.4), condemned slavery and did without it, but were regarded as fulfilling a utopian dream beyond the frontiers of usual society.[69] Some early Christian writers on monasticism, Augustine (354–430 C.E.) and Basil (ca. 330–379 C.E.), required monks and nuns to do without slaves in order to keep the rule of poverty, but did not condemn the social institution. One early Christian writer, Gregory of Nyssa (died 394), did attack owning slaves itself as an aspect of the sin of pride:[70]

> For what is such a gross example of arrogance in the matters enumerated above [Eccl. 2:7]—an opulent house, and an abundance of vines, and ripeness in vegetable-plots, and collecting waters in pools and channeling them in gardens—as for a human being to think himself the master of his own kind? . . . So when someone turns the property of God into his own property and arrogates dominion to his own kind, so as to think himself the owner of men and women, what is he doing but overstepping his own nature through pride, regarding himself as something different from his subordinates? . . . You have forgotten the limits of your authority, and that your rule is confined to control over things without reason. . . . But has the scrap of paper, and the written contract, and the counting out of obols deceived you into thinking yourself the master of the image of God? What folly! (*Homilies* IV on Eccl. 2:7, late fourth century C.E.)[71]

Gregory seems, however, to have been unique.

Slaves were property to be bought and sold, transactions over which they had no control. Bradley examined such transactions recorded on Egyptian papyri, the great majority of which documented the sale of individual slaves. "The Egyptian evidence offers no example at all of the sale together of a husband and wife, or of a husband, wife and children."[72] Slave owners seem not to have considered preserving family ties when selling their property, which would then be an aspect of the slaves' psychology that could be manipulated negatively by their masters. The slaves' hopes for a family and for manumission gave owners significant means of social control.

The whole issue of slaves' social status, however, is more complex than one might imagine. Wax tablets found in the Pompeiian house of a banker, Julius Caecilius Jucundus, give a fascinating example.[73] Five of these tablets record a series of loans to C. Novius Eunus, who borrowed ten thousand sesterces from Ti. Iulius Evenus Primianus, an imperial freedman. Hesychus, his managerial slave, handled the whole affair, making the loan, accepting grain as collateral, and arranging the interest. Later, Hesychus rented a portion of a warehouse to store the grain from C. Novius Cypaerus, not directly, but through the warehouse owner's slave manager. The same day Novius borrowed an additional three thousand sesterces, but this time from the slave Hesychus, not from his master. Hesychus's profession and social position were more important than and inconsistent with his legal status. Hesychus the slave became the patron of Novius, his client, a free, wealthy businessperson. Such status inconsistency must have been duplicated often in many cities of the Roman Empire.

Family meals. Greek *symposia*, Roman *convivia*, philosophical banquets, sacrificial meals, communal meals of clubs, Jewish[74] and Christian meals all had a common form in the first century C.E.[75] All adopted the posture of reclining for formal afternoon or evening meals while slaves served the food. It is "womanish and weak to sit on a chair or on a stool" according to Alcidamus the Cynic (Lucian, *Symp.* or *Carousal* 13–14 [Harmon, LCL]). In that honor-shame culture, whether one was invited to recline on the most prestigious couch was a recurrent problem (see Plutarch, *Table Talk* 615D–619A). Once annually at the Roman Saturnalia, banquet customs were reversed. One of the first laws of the festival was, "let every man be treated equally, slave and freeman, poor and rich" (Lucian, *Sat.* 13 [Kilburn, LCL]). But this was contrary to the practice in Roman peristyle houses that were built to reinforce status. "Roman domestic architecture is obsessively concerned with distinctions of social rank, and the distinctions involved are not merely between one house and another . . . but within the social space of the house."[76] Servile areas of a house, rooms where cooking, washing, and working occurred, were socially "dirty," marginalized, pushed away to the far corners of otherwise beautiful spaces (see above). Drinking, entertainment, and discussion would follow the meal itself. Friendship was deepened, sometimes with disruptive, drunken behavior. Philo critiques these Greco-Roman banquets (*The Contemplative Life* 40–63), especially those described by Xenophon and Plato (57–62), but he eulogizes the banquets among Jewish Therapeutae (24–39, 64–89).[77]

Past assumptions have been that men presided at these meals. Household management and symposia literature from Greco-Roman culture were written by men, for men, and assumes that men are in charge. Pompeii, however, gives other clues. The largest business building (ca. 60-x-40 meters) on the forum (VII.ix.1/67) has the inscription, "Eumachia, daughter of Lucius, public priestess in her own name and that of her son, Marcus Numistrius Fronto, built at her own expense the outside porch, the cryptoporticus, and the porticoes and dedicated them to Concordia Augusta and Pietas" (*CIL* 10.810 and 811).[78] The father had been *duovir,* one of two key city officials, in 2/3 C.E., and the son became *duovir* later. Eumachia had some connection with fullers, dyers of wool, and she shipped large pottery jars of goods as far away as Carthage. She would have had a voice in her own business affairs. Another woman, Julia Felix, owned the largest Pompeiian residence thus far excavated (Region II, insula iv). She placed this advertisement: "In the property of Julia Felix, daughter of Spurius, to lease: The Venus baths, fitted up for the best people, taverns, shops and second story rooms, for the space of five years, from the ides of next August to the ides of the sixth August thereafter" (*CIL* 4.1136). We may realistically imagine her in the *tablinum* (office) of her house advising clients, freedmen, and slaves operating shops in her house, at her baths, or managing her extensive gardens. The inscriptions of Eumachia and Julia Felix do not defer to any male authority; the women run their own businesses and exercise feminine authority, in Eumachia's case as far away as Africa.

If Vetruvius (*De architectura* 6.7.1–5) is accurate, Greek houses segregated the family's women from the male activities of business and entertaining. Roman houses were built not to segregate women, but rather to display social status in which women participated. Honor-shame codes operated and affected women differently from men, but there were geographical and cultural variations.[79] Osiek questions not only the usual assumption, that the more imposing the peristyled *domus,* the more hierarchical and patriarchal the social structure would be, but also its counterpart, that in less formal meeting situations in apartment buildings, more flexible leadership structures could be presumed.[80] Rather, the evidence of voluntary associations and private cults suggests highly organized leadership structures, with less evidence of women as actual leaders.

Earlier Eastern, Greek tradition has women present with men for meals only in family circles; formal dinners would find them absent. In the early first century C.E., Valerius Maximus (2.1.2) describes the traditional Roman way of dining: women are seated next to their husbands' couches; but, he writes, at contemporary banquets Roman women recline with their men. At their wedding, Livia reclined in the new way next to Augustus, but on formal occasions, she still gave separate banquets for women (Dio Cassius, *Hist. Rom* 48.44.3; 55.2.4, 8.2; 57.12.5). In the last reference, however, Livia gave a separate dinner for the women because her son Tiberius wanted to remove her from public affairs.

Part II. Paul, Families, and Households

Sexuality and Families

Given the current medical opinions cited above (those of Epicurus, Celsus, Soranus, and Galen, cited under "Greco-Roman Families' Sexual, Educational,
Slave, and Meal Customs"), the Corinthian Christian ascetics may have rejected
sexual activity in relation to their desire for spiritual gifts (1 Cor 7, 12, and 14; see
Paul's concession at 7:5a).[81] The theological and philosophical values of the mid–
first century C.E. (Therapeutae, Philo, and Chaeremon, all ascetics seeking a vision
of the divine) match those of the contemporary medical doctors and provide a
context for understanding Corinthian sexual asceticism. Some Corinthians had
written Paul their opinion that "it is well for a man not to touch a woman" (1 Cor
7:1b NRSV). Earlier in the letter Paul had made a Jewish connection between sexual immorality and idolatry (5:9, 11); he discusses the former in chapters 5–7 and
the latter in chapters 8 and 10. Paul had also had an oral report that "a [Christian]
man is living with his father's wife" (5:1), about which they were arrogant (5:2).
Paul criticizes the church, saying, "your boast is not good" (5:6; compare 1:29, 31;
3:21; 4:7), and demands that they "hand this man over to Satan for the destruction
[ὄλεθρον, olethron] of the flesh, so that his spirit may be saved in the day of the
Lord" (5:5). A. Y. Collins interprets this last phrase communally and eschatologi-
cally.[82] In 1 Thess 5:2–3, Paul refers to the "sudden [eschatological] destruction
[ὄλεθρος, olethros] that will come upon them," a trial of creation in which the
"flesh" hostile to God will be "destroyed." Paul is not judging the eternal fate of
the son who has taken his father's wife, but insisting, in view of the coming eschatological crisis, that those who are sanctified act appropriately to their sanctification, a typical linkage of the indicative with the imperative in Paul.

Paul then condemns Christians' going to court before the "unjust," because
the "unjust," whether pagans or Christian, will not inherit the kingdom of God
(6:1, 7a, 8, 9a). Connecting the topics with the term "unjust," Paul repeats the six
vices of 5:11 and adds four more in 6:9–10, including μαλακοί, malakoi, and
ἀρσενοκοῖται, arsenokoitai, terms of uncertain meaning.[83]

Paul quotes Corinthian slogans, "all things are lawful for me" (6:12a) and
"food is meant for the stomach and the stomach for food" (6:13a), which he wants
to nuance. Greeks typically drew parallels between passion for food and for sex
(see nn. 52, 90), but Paul rejects the idea that they are equally important before
God (1 Cor 8:8). True, Paul agrees, neither a kosher Jewish diet (e.g., Lev 11) nor
Hellenistic vegetarianism (e.g., Plutarch, *The Eating of Flesh* I and II [*Mor.* 993A–
999B]) will present people to God. However, "the body is meant not for fornication [πορνεία, porneia, sexual immorality], but for the Lord, and the Lord for the
body" (6:13b). The final phrase, "the Lord is for the *body*," is the astounding

phrase in a Philonic, Middle Platonic culture. Paul exhorts Corinthian males rather to cleave to the Lord, not to cleave to prostitutes (6:15–18). Here the public morality of the ancient world differs from that of modern times. Males in the Greek world thought it unremarkable to be sexually active with more than one woman. For example, Plutarch exhorts Pollianus, soon to become Eurydice's husband, to send her away after dinner if he is going to impose himself sexually on a slave woman, to which she should not object (*Advice to Bride and Groom* 140B). To explain male, Corinthian Christians continuing to use prostitutes, we need only assume their slogan "all things are lawful" (6:12), which could have been their interpretation of Paul's earlier preaching that the gospel saves apart from the Law (see 1 Cor 7:19 and 15:56), and also assume some (Plutarchian) defensiveness about sexual partners. But Paul rejects the philosophy and practice of husbands' sex with prostitutes as entertainment after meals.[84]

Paul does not argue but assumes that a male should not act in a way that is feminine, "soft" (μαλακός, *malakos;* 1 Cor 6:9). This biological assumption is in high tension with the baptismal confession employed in his churches ("there is no longer . . . male and female," Gal 3:28) and with modern biology. Many modern Christians have rejected these ancient Greek biological male/female polarities and their ethical corollaries.

The Corinthians had written Paul a letter agreeing with Epicurean, medical, Stoic (Chaeremon), and Hellenistic Jewish (Philo's Therapeutae) opinion that "it is well not to touch a woman" (7:1). Is sex to be allowed at all? Continuing the concern for sexual immorality about which he had written in chapters 5–6, Paul argues the opposite of the ascetics' slogan in gender-fair language: "but because of cases of sexual immorality, each man should have his own wife and each woman her own husband" (7:2). "For it is better to marry than to burn" (7:9). Paul does not score high marks here with modern persons who are concerned about the quality of marriage relationships. Barré observes, however, that although "to burn" in verse 9 may indeed in other contexts mean to be aflame with passion, it is not used absolutely with this meaning, except in association with a noun that specifies the emotion, which is absent here.[85] Paul is referring rather to the "fiery" eschatological judgment of Yahweh. Verse 9 is not proposing marriage as a cure for being "inflamed" with passion, as the NRSV and other translations suggest, but rather is warning converts with ascetic ideals about the eschatological consequences of acting as if they had none.

The husband and wife mutually have each other's body (7:3–4). Paul's exhortations correspond with the domestication of morality and friendship in the empire (compare Musonius and Plutarch). This cultural change toward more friendship between men and women and the acts that symbolized this development, bathing together and women's charismatic speech in worship, generated conflict in the Corinthian house churches. Paul was ambivalent. He accepted women's charismatic speech (1 Cor 11:5) and their leadership of house churches (Rom 16:1, 3–5 [where Prisca is named first], 6, 12; Phil 4:2), but rejected women's removing their veils in worship, a powerful symbol of the change (1 Cor 11:5–16).[86]

A preference for celibacy may have motivated some Corinthians to separate from their spouses (7:10–16), as among Philo's Therapeutae. In response, Paul cites the Lord's prohibition (see Mark 10:2–12), interpreting this as a prohibition of separation. He is, however, not focused on legal rules: "but if she does separate, let her remain unmarried or else be reconciled to her husband" (7:11). Although Paul repeatedly uses mutual, gender-fair language in this chapter, this exhortation concerns only a woman, who may have been seeking social and religious freedom. Paul then reverses the usual understanding of purity (that a clean person is contaminated by touching an unclean person) and argues instead that a believer's sanctity would make a spouse holy, as it does children (7:14). But if the unbelieving spouse separates, the brother or sister is not "enslaved" (7:15).

Later in the chapter, Paul insists that the husband and wife are not to lose their individuality (7:29), that the relationship is to reduce anxiety, that each is to make efforts to please the other, that marriage is for the benefit of both, and that it is not to result in distraction from the affairs of the Lord (vv. 32–35).[87] Paul's approach, encouraging each believer to decide whether marriage or celibacy makes him or her anxious and to act accordingly, contrasts both attitudes with the Roman emperors' concern that all citizens marry and have children[88] and with the Corinthian ascetics' concern that sex is a sin (7:36). For Paul there is more than one way to live a sanctified life: married, mutually active sex is holy (7:3–4, 14), but so is the celibate life (7:34), and Paul prefers the latter (7:7, 38). Most contemporary Protestants deemphasize Paul's preference.

Another key text for understanding Paul's attitude toward sexuality is Rom 1. Focusing on Greco-Roman philosophic and literary ways of conceptualizing sexual matters, Fredrickson concludes that "in Romans 1:24–27 Paul points to the problem of passion without introducing the modern dichotomy of homo-heterosexuality."[89] Like his contemporaries, Paul writes about "natural use" (φυσικὴν χρῆσιν, *physikēn chrēsin*) and "unnatural use" (χρῆσιν . . . τὴν παρὰ φύσιν, *chrēsin . . . tēn para physin*) of sexual desire (1:26, 27), which was thought to be analogous to the natural use of hunger.[90] The pleasure of sex, then, is to be limited by satisfaction, just as a wise person with a full stomach limits eating. As we saw above, this use of "natural" does not raise the question of the gender of either the subject or the object of sexual desire. Plutarch (*Advice to Bride and Groom* 144B) also refers to the wife's "use" of the husband, to which Paul probably refers in Rom 1:26 ("Their females exchanged natural use for that which is against nature"), which is not then a reference to lesbian sexual activity.[91] Greco-Roman discussions of household management are one source of this terminology, which advised the householder about the "use" of possessions, including the "use" of a wife. "Use" focuses on "the psychological significance of the act for the subject [not the object] of sexual desire."[92] Fredrickson agrees with Martin: by "against nature" (παρὰ φύσιν, *para physin*), Paul means not "disoriented desire" but "inordinate desire."[93] When desire is insatiable, addictive, it is "against nature." Paul uses a string of terms that point toward the problem of ἔρος, *eros:* "desire" (1:24), "passion" (1:26), "inflame," "appetite," and "error" (1:27), each of which plays a role in the contemporary discussion of erotic love.[94] When humans refuse to give God glory and gratitude, God is wronged and dishonored. God delivers into dishonor those who dishonor the creator. Erotic, insatiable passion brings the lovers into dishonor, which itself is punishment (1:27).[95]

Education of Young and Old

Paul seldom alludes to children.[96] He is more focused on ethnic, Jew/Gentile issues than on legal families with sexual or blood ties. After discussing the few sentences that mention children, I examine teachers in early Christian houses in the context of Philo's and Plutarch's discussions of teachers doing home schooling.

Paul's references to children are mostly metaphorical. He mentions two biological children, Rufus (Rom 16:13) and the man living with his father's wife (1 Cor 5:1–5). The only debate concerns children of "mixed," Christian/pagan marriages, where his focus concerns the relationship between the married partners (1 Cor 7:12–16). Paul never argues that the purpose of sex is to have children, a surprising contrast to other contemporary Jewish, Stoic, and Roman authors.[97]

Metaphorically the Corinthians are his children (1 Cor 4:14), so that they do not have many fathers (4:15). He cannot address them as adults, but only as babies in Christ (3:1–2). In a different sense Timothy is his beloved, faithful child in the Lord (4:17), and the slave Onesimus, "begotten" in chains, is his very own child (Phlm 10, 12). Intimacy is the dominant motif in Paul's metaphorical reference to this relationship.

I turn from these few verses to the question of teachers in the Pauline households, a question related to home schooling in the Greco-Roman world. Paul himself may have been taught by the methods Philo and Plutarch outline for reading the Bible and Homer, and he taught his house churches in this manner. The content of Paul's education stressed the Bible, as Philo emphasizes.

There are similarities between Philo's and Plutarch's discussion of teachers in Jewish[98] and Hellenistic home schooling, on the one hand, and Paul's discussion of prophets and teachers in Christian houses on the other. Paul directs, "Let two or three prophets speak, and let the others weigh [διακρινέτωσαν, *diakrinetōsan*] what is said" (1 Cor 14:29). Plutarch repeatedly emphasizes this "weighing" of what is said to students in schools: "[L]et us observe this . . . discrimination [διά-κρισιν, *diakrisin*] of words in greater and more serious matters, and let us begin with the gods" (23A). "In making his examination and forming his judgment [κρίσιν, *krisin*] of the lecture he [the hearer] should begin with himself and his own state of mind" (42A). Paul further exhorts, "Test everything!" (δοκιμάζετε, *dokimazete*, 1 Thess 5:21). Plutarch too wants "to remind our sons that authors write them [poetic epics or tragedies], not because they commend or approve [δοκιμάζοντες, *dokimazontes*] them, but with the idea of investing mean and unnatural characters and persons with unnatural and mean sentiments" (18F).[99] First Corinthians 14:24–25 observes that an outsider can be reproved, just as students were in school. Plutarch gives advice on how to receive such rebukes (44C–E). Most important, Paul is himself willing to read even holy scripture with a critical eye. For example, he criticizes Lev 18:5, a key text in Mosaic covenantal promises, in Gal 3:12–13, Rom 7:10, and 10:5. Not even Christ did the works of the Law and lived by them, as Leviticus promises, but rather he was cursed by the Law. Righteousness comes not from the Law, but from faith.

One consequence of the critical theological reading of ancient canonical texts, whether Homer or Leviticus, is that theological confessions, which are among the earliest in history, are found in Philo and Paul, confessions probably written down within a decade of each other. The critical interpretation of ancient, sacred texts assumes that the teacher has criteria, and early confessions served that function.[100] Philo makes five points: "Firstly, that the Deity is and has been from eternity. . . . Secondly, that God is one. . . . Thirdly, . . . that the world came into being. . . . Fourthly, that the world too is one as well as its Maker. . . . Fifthly, that God also exercises forethought on the world's behalf" (*On the Creation* 170–172 [Colson and Whitaker LCL]).[101] Analogously, Paul taught the Corinthians that "no idol in the world really exists" and that "there is no God but one" (1 Cor 8:4). "Yet for us there is one God, the Father, from whom are all things and for whom we exist, and one Lord, Jesus Christ, through whom are all things and through whom we exist" (8:6).[102]

Finally, Greco-Roman homes were filled with art, with frescoes, mosaics, and sculptures, seen by more (illiterate) people in a household than were written texts. Preaching perhaps in such a house, Paul too reminded his audience that "before your eyes, Jesus Christ was publicly exhibited [προεγράφη, *proegraphē*] as crucified" (Gal 3:1 NRSV).[103] Paul's oratorical art and his own life as a suffering apostle ("I carry the marks of Jesus branded on my body," Gal 6:17) had analogies in contemporary domestic sculptures and frescoes. Baptismal and eucharistic confessions in Paul (1 Cor 15:3; 11:23–26) focus on the meaning of Christ's voluntary death for us. Schefold compares the popular sculptures and domestic paintings of

Marsyas's suffering with Christ's.[104] A crucial difference is that Marsyas impiously challenged Apollo, while Christ died submitting to the will of God (see Gal 1:4; 2:20; 2 Cor 5:14–15).

Christ willingly gave his body as a sacrifice for others (Rom 3:25–26), a theology that has close analogies in Euripides' play *Iphigenia at Aulis,* first performed in 405 B.C.E. but painted on the walls of Pompeii in the first century C.E. (see nn. 57–58 and fig. 1). When Paul preached Christ crucified, as one who willingly died for others, some of his auditors could have been familiar with wall paintings of Iphigenia; both he and they could even have been viewing one while he preached in a home with this picture on the wall. There are other examples,[105] but this image of Iphigenia shows how many families would have been educated and influenced, perhaps more by domestic frescoes than by texts they read or plays they saw in local theaters. Euripides' *Iphigenia at Aulis,* however, legitimizes ethnic conflict (e.g., lines 1395–1401), while the Pauline baptismal pronouncement (Gal 3:28) confesses that ethnic contrasts have no value before God and in the *ekklēsia.*

Like the sculptures and frescoes of Marysas and Iphigenia, Jesus' cross was multivalent, ambiguous,[106] depending on whether one understood it from above or from below.[107] Romans punished Jesus and the disciples as criminals (Suetonius, *Nero* 16.2; Tacitus, *Ann.* 15.44), but from a different perspective Paul felt "crucified with Christ" (Gal 2:19; 6:14; Rom 6:6; compare Josephus, *War* 5.449–50; *Ant.* 13.380; *Life* 420). Further, Iphigenia died so that Phrygians and not Greeks would be slaves (Euripides, *Iph. Aul.* 1379–80, 1395–1401), whereas those baptized in early Pauline churches denied the value of such ethnic distinctions (Gal 3:28).

The Status and Function of Slaves

Under the supervision of the head of the house, the household gods were worshiped, and they were expected to protect all inhabitants, including slaves.[108] This worship was performed in diverse rooms, most often in courtyards, but also in dining or other rooms. There seem to have been few boundaries between slave and free in household worship; the domestic cult of the Lares became, as no other, a cult controlled by slaves.

Lampe offered strong evidence that Onesimus was not a runaway slave.[109] Proculus, an important Roman jurist in the early first century C.E., stated that a slave in difficulty, who suddenly sought out a third party to become the slave's advocate to the angry owner, was not a fugitive. Lampe notes the irony: a non-Christian slave slips away to the apostle hoping that Paul would influence his Christian master. Paul wins him for Christ, which Philemon had not done. Paul's epistles to Philemon and to Philippians are often interpreted in relation to each other. The dynamic, temporal christological hymn in Phil 2:6–11 might indeed move a slave toward conversion more than the static, spatial deutero-Pauline hymn in Col 1:15–20.[110] In the former, Christ emptied himself, taking the form of a slave (2:7), whom God exalted, a christology open to a slave's hope for manumission. But in deutero-Pauline theology, Christ is the all-powerful creator of a static social order; the confession that Christ became a humble slave was repressed—and a household code (Col 3:18–4:1) added.

Harrill emphasizes verse 16:[111] Philemon is to receive back his newly converted slave Onesimus "no longer as a slave, but more than a slave, a beloved brother—especially to me but how much more to you, both in the flesh and in the Lord." This probably, but not certainly, suggests manumission. Paul wants the gifted slave (compare Hesychus of Pompeii) for ministry (διακονία, *diakonia*, v. 13) in place of Philemon.

Galatians 3:28 ("there is no longer Jew or Greek, there is no longer slave or free, there is no longer male and female; for all of you are one in Christ Jesus") functioned in early Christian baptismal practice. Did this baptismal declaration have any practical consequences in church or social life, especially in light of 1 Cor 7:21, which some translate: "Were you a slave when called? Do not be concerned about it. Even if you can gain your freedom, make use of your present condition now more than ever" (NRSV). With that reading slaves should continue functioning as slaves. Bartchy argues that this translation incorrectly assumes that slaves had some choice about their manumission.[112] Harrill, however, cites a number of instances in which slaves were offered freedom, for example, by generals in war and by Roman senators in political contests.[113] He also analyzes seventeen examples of the Greek construction μᾶλλον χρῆσαι, *mallon chrēsai*, that Paul employs in 1 Cor 7:21, successfully arguing for the alternative translation: "You were called as a slave. Do not worry about it. But if you can indeed become free, use instead [freedom]." With that reading, slaves should function as freed persons.

But Harrill gives a unique meaning to being "called": it "refers to the situation and circumstances in which one was called at the time of baptism."[114] Paul, for whom Christ's cross has put distance between him and the world (Gal 6:14), gives advice about lifestyle also in view of the "impending [eschatological] crisis" (1 Cor 7:26), in a time that has "grown short" (v. 29), advice to which he, however, allows a number of exceptions. A married woman is not to separate from her mate (v. 10), "but if she does . . ." (v. 11). Believers should live with their unbelieving mates, "but if the unbelieving partner separates . . ." (v. 15). Paul advises a single male not to seek a wife, "but if you marry . . ." (v. 28). And if one is not behaving properly toward a woman, "let him marry"! (v. 36). In these four situations in the same chapter, Paul gives wise advice, but allows the possibility of a change in social or marital status, despite the eschatological crisis. Paul even demands a change in marital status (v. 36), just as he demanded that Peter change his kosher eating habits for "the truth of the gospel" (Gal 2:11–14). Paul allowed Corinthian Christians to change their social/legal status, to separate from a mate or to marry. Roman social conservatives, for example, Seneca, did not oppose manumission; if Paul had opposed slaves' manumission, he would have been unique in that culture.[115] If the interpretation given above of Paul's Letter to Philemon is correct, Paul encouraged Philemon to manumit Onesimus. Then, in such an interpretation, "calling" refers to one's relationship to God, as in Rom 11:29 and Phil 3:14, "I press on toward the goal for the prize of the upward call of God in Christ Jesus." First Corinthians 7:17, 20, and 24 exhort "each" Corinthian Christian to remain in his or her calling by and to God, a call to God that is simultaneously experienced in "each" one's own concrete social situation that might not change, or, on the contrary, that sometimes must change.

Meals

Osiek describes five options for women at the common meal of a house church: (1) to be absent, (2) to eat in separate dining rooms, (3) for women and children to be seated next to their reclining male relatives, (4) for women and children to be seated apart from the reclining men, and (5) for women and men to recline together, with children seated or eating separately.[116] The first option is unlikely at the common ritual meal, and the second is also, if all were supposed to share from the same table (1 Cor 10:17; see 11:33; Matt 14:21; 15:38; Did. 9.4; Justin, 1 Apol. 67). All the remaining options are plausible, depending on culture and geography, Greek/Eastern or Roman/Western. In Roman colonies like Philippi and Corinth, Christian women and men in some of the house churches may have reclined together, but in more Eastern churches, they probably did not. Paul explicitly writes, however, that some or all "sat" during worship (1 Cor 14:30), although he knows that those eating meals in the temple "reclined" (κατακείμενον, katakeimenon; 8:10). It probably follows from their sitting posture that not all the Christian worshipers were in the dining room on couches; further, triclinia often had space for only a few (cf. Rom 16:23). Some worshipers must have sat in the courtyard and/or in the atrium. Practice must also have varied between the times that an individual house church met and times when all the house churches in a city met together. Given the differences noted above between Vetruvius (De architectura 6.7.1–5) and Valerius Maximus (2.1.2), practice would have differed again depending on whether the meeting of the whole was in a more Latin city (1 Cor 14:23) or a more Greek one (Acts 15:22, Jerusalem).

Women found their voices at these meals. The instruction that "women should be silent in the churches" (1 Cor 14:34) is a later interpolation into Paul's epistle, not plausible in the houses of Eumachia or Julia Felix in Pompeii,[117] or for the Christians Prisca, Lydia, or Junia. Osiek "surmise[s] that . . . these women hosted formal dinners and presided at them, including the assembly of the *ekklesia*."[118] This social role would have been possible for women householders like Prisca (1 Cor 16:19; Rom 16:3–5, where she is named before her husband), Phoebe (Rom 16:1–3), Lydia (Acts 16:14–15), and Nympha (Col 4:15). Conservative males disapproved, as is evident in Juvenal's sixth satire, in which we hear echoes of the Roman male voices that influenced deutero-Pauline churches, against Paul's practice, to silence women ministers (1 Tim 2:12).

> But the most intolerable of all is the woman who as soon as she has sat down to dinner commends Virgil, pardons the dying Dido, and pits the poets against each other, putting Virgil in the one scale and Homer in the other. The grammarians make way before her; the rhetoricians give in; the whole crowd is silenced; no lawyer, no auctioneer will get in a word in, no, nor any other woman; so torrential is her speech that you would think that all the pots and bells were being clashed together. . . . She lays down definitions, and discourses on morals, like a philosopher; thirsting to be deemed both wise and eloquent. . . . Let not the wife of your bosom possess a special style of her own; let her not hurl at you in whirling speech the crooked enthymeme! Let her not know all history; let there be some things in her reading which she does not understand. I hate a woman who is for ever consulting and poring over the "Grammar" of Palaemon, who observes all the rules and laws of language, who like an antiquary quotes verses that I never heard of, and corrects her unlettered female friends for slips of speech that no man need trouble about: Let husbands at least be permitted to make slips in grammar! (Juvenal, *Sat.* 6.434–56 [Ramsay, LCL])

Part III. Other Relevant Pauline and Paulinist Texts

Other possible topics include Paul's being a father to his converts (1 Cor 4:15; Gal 4:19; Phlm 10), that believers are to grow up (τέλειος, *teleios*; 1 Cor 14:20; Phil 3:15), and the *ekklēsia* as the converts' adoptive family, the family of God (readily to be observed in 1 Thessalonians).[119] The discussion of family in the Greco-Roman world and Paul could include attitudes toward abortion and infanticide.

Part IV. Bibliography

Studies by Classicists

Bradley, K. *Slaves and Society at Rome: Key Themes in Ancient History.* Cambridge: Cambridge University Press, 1994.

Clarke, J. R. *Looking at Lovemaking: Constructions of Sexuality in Roman Art, 100 B.C.–A.D. 250.* Berkeley: University of California Press, 1998.

Cohen, Shaye J. D., ed. *The Jewish Family in Antiquity.* BJS 289. Atlanta: Scholars Press, 1993.

Dixon, S. *The Roman Family.* Baltimore: Johns Hopkins University Press, 1992.

———. *The Roman Mother.* London: Routledge, 1988.

Eyben, E. *Restless Youth in Ancient Rome.* London: Routledge, 1993.

Finley, M. I. *Ancient Slavery and Modern Ideology.* New York: Viking, 1980.

Golden, M. "Did the Ancients Care When Their Children Died?" *Greece and Rome* 35 (1988): 152–63.

Hallett, J. P., and M. B. Skinner, eds. *Roman Sexualities.* Princeton, N.J.: Princeton University Press, 1997.

Joshel, S. R., and S. Murnaghan, eds. *Women and Slaves in Greco-Roman Culture: Differential Equations.* London: Routledge, 1998.

Murray, O., ed. *Sympotica: A Symposium on the Symposium.* Oxford: Clarendon, 1990.

Rawson, B., ed. *Marriage, Divorce, and Children in Ancient Rome.* Oxford: Clarendon, 1991.

Richlin, A. *The Garden of Priapus: Sexuality and Aggression in Roman Humor.* New Haven: Yale University Press, 1983.

Saller, R. *Patriarchy, Property, and Death in the Roman Family.* Cambridge: Cambridge University Press, 1994.

Slater, W. J., ed. *Dining in a Classical Context.* Ann Arbor: University of Michigan Press, 1991.

Treggiari, S. *Roman Marriage: Iusti Coniuges from the Time of Cicero to the Time of Ulpian.* Oxford: Oxford University Press, 1991.

Wiedemann, T. *Adults and Children in the Roman Empire.* London: Routledge, 1989.

Studies by New Testament Scholars

Alexander, L. C. A. "Paul and the Hellenistic Schools: The Evidence of Galen." Pages 60–83 in *Paul in His Hellenistic Context,* edited by T. Engberg-Pedersen. Minneapolis: Fortress Press, 1995.

Bartchy, S. S. *Mallon Chresai: First-Century Slavery and 1 Corinthians 7:21.* SBLDS 11. Missoula, Mont.: Scholars Press, 1973.

Bobertz, C. A. "The Role of Patron in the *Cena Dominica* of Hippolytus' *Apostolic Tradition.*" *JTS* 44 (1993): 170–84.

Braun, W. *Feasting and Social Rhetoric in Luke 14.* Society of New Testament Studies Monograph Series 85. Cambridge: Cambridge University Press, 1995.

Collins, J. N. *Diakonia: Re-interpreting the Ancient Sources.* New York: Oxford University Press, 1990.

Harrill, J. Albert. *The Manumission of Slaves in Early Christianity.* HUT 32. Tübingen: J. C. B. Mohr [Paul Siebeck], 1955.

Martin, Dale. *The Corinthian Body.* New Haven: Yale University Press, 1995.

Moxnes, H., ed. *Constructing Early Christian Families: Family as Social Reality and Metaphor.* London: Routledge, 1997.

Osiek, Carolyn, and David L. Balch. *Families in the New Testament World: House-holds and House Churches.* Louisville: Westminster John Knox, 1997.

Notes

1. For surveys of cities in the Pauline mission, see John E. Stambaugh and David L. Balch, *The New Testament in Its Social Environment* (Philadelphia: Westminster, 1986), chs. 4 and 6; R. Wallace and W. Williams, *The Three Worlds of Paul of Tarsus* (London: Routledge, 1998), pt. 4; Bradley Blue, "Acts and the House Church," in *The Book of Acts in Its First-Century Setting*, vol. 2: *Graeco-Roman Setting* (ed. David W. J. Gill and Conrad Gempf; Grand Rapids: Eerdmans, 1994), 119–222.

2. I will summarize and update Carolyn Osiek and David L. Balch, *Families in the New Testament World: Households and House Churches* (Louisville: Westminster John Knox, 1997). Compare *Constructing Early Christian Families: Family as Social Reality and Metaphor* (ed. Halvor Moxnes; London: Routledge, 1997). See David L. Balch and Carolyn Osiek, eds., *Early Christian Families in Context: An Interdisciplinary Dialogue* (Grand Rapids: Eerdmans, 2003).

3. Helmut Koester, "Preface," in *Ephesos, Metropolis of Asia: An Interdisciplinary Approach to Its Archaeology, Religion, and Culture* (ed. Helmut Koester; HTS 41; Valley Forge, Pa.: Trinity Press International, 1995), xviii. The architecture of the Pauline mission is discussed by L. Michael White, *The Social Origins of Christian Architecture*, vol. 1: *Building God's House in the Roman World: Architectural Adaptation among Pagans, Jews and Christians* (HTS 42; Valley Forge, Pa.: Trinity Press International, 1990), 102–10.

4. See Robert Jewett, "Tenement Churches and Communal Meals in the Early Church: The Implications of a Form-Critical Analysis of 2 Thessalonians 3:10," *BR* 38 (1993): 23–43. I incorrectly wrote (Osiek and Balch, *Families*, 21) that we lack archaeological evidence of such apartment buildings in the first century C.E. See J. J. Deiss, *Herculaneum: Italy's Buried Treasure* (2d ed.; Malibu, Calif.: J. Paul Getty Museum, 1989), 114–15, based on A. Maiuri, *Ercolano: I Nuovi Scavi (1927–1958)* (Rome: Istituto Poligrafico dello Stato, 1959), 1:113ff. (on the palestra) and 449–69 (on shops and apartments) with figs. 91–111 and 401–19. Maiuri's work describes a complex like the second- and third-century C.E. apartment buildings in Ostia. It is 113-x-80 meters (p. 113), a unified edifice (pp. 116, 449), built in the early first century C.E. (p. 116). The insulae in Ostia have internal courtyards, but the Herculaneum edifice has instead an internal, private palestra-gymnasium (p. 449). The ground floor has shops facing a main street, cardo 5, running from the *decumano inferiore* to the *decumano massimo* (p. 116). These shops have internal wooden stairs ascending to the next floor (fig. 419). Nothing is left of the upper, third floor of apartments, but it had entrances separate from the other two floors (fig. 449). Maiuri has a second volume of plates: plates XXXVIII and XL picture reconstructions of the commercial complex. A. Wallace-Hadrill, "*Domus* and *insulae* in Rome: Families and Housefuls," discusses first-century apartment buildings in Rome in *Early Christian Families in Context: A Cross-Disciplinary Dialogue* (Grand Rapids, Mich.: Eerdmans, 2003), 1–18.

5. Peter Lampe, *Die städtrömischen Christen in den ersten beiden Jahrhunderten* (WUNT 2.18; Tübingen: J. C. B. Mohr [Paul Siebeck], 1987; 2d ed., 1989), 30; on the early "title" churches of St. Prisca and St. Clement, see pp. 11–12. Lampe also notes that Philo, *Leg.* 155, 157, locates the Jewish community in Trastevere. White, *Social Origins,* vol. 2: *Texts and Monuments for the Christian Domus Ecclesiae in Its Environment* (1997), 210–11, concludes that the oldest construction under SS. Giovanni e Paolo in Rome is second century C.E. Christians began meeting in an edifice now under S. Clemente in Rome in the third century C.E. (White, *Social Origins,* 2:224, 226). The mithraeum now under S. Prisca in Rome was introduced ca. 195 (ibid., 2:406). See his table 3.1, listing the earliest Christian archaeological sites (ibid., 2:442).

6. See Osiek and Balch, *Families,* 23n. 65, citing Marion E. Blake, *Roman Construction in Italy from Tiberius through the Flavians* (Washington, D.C.: Carnegie Institution of Washington, 1959), 125.

7. Ibid., 21, with bibliography.

8. Ibid., 23, citing A. Wallace-Hadrill, *Houses and Society in Pompeii and Herculaneum* (Princeton: Princeton University Press, 1994), 45–47.

9. Cited by Stanley K. Stowers, *A Rereading of Romans: Justice, Jews, and Gentiles* (New Haven: Yale University Press, 1994), 75, with nn. 80, 82, 94.

10. Ibid., 77, citing C. E. B. Cranfield, *A Critical and Exegetical Commentary on the Epistle to the Romans* (Edinburgh: T. & T. Clark, 1979), 2:791–92.

11. Ibid.

12. Paul Zanker, *Pompeii: Public and Private Life* (Cambridge: Harvard University Press, 1998), 20; see 29.

13. Ibid., 34, 142. See Osiek and Balch, *Families,* 15, 201–3.

14. White, *Social Origins* (cited in n. 3), 1:102–10. See, however, James F. Strange, "Ancient Texts, Archaeology as Text, and the Problem of the First-Century Synagogue," in *Evolution of the Synagogue: Problems and Progress* (ed. H. C. Kee and L. H. Cohick; Harrisburg, Pa.: Trinity Press International, 1999), 27–45, who discusses four buildings of the first century in Palestine that "are indeed synagogues" (45).

15. Osiek and Balch, *Families,* 24, with n. 72 citing Wallace-Hadrill, *Houses and Society,* 45, 47.

16. Zanker, *Pompeii,* 10. The several subsequent page citations in the text are from Zanker's volume.

17. On the term "Romanization," see L. Michael White, "Urban Development and Social Change in Imperial Ephesos," in Koester, *Ephesos* (cited. n. 3), 31–33, who defines it as "internal social change through urbanization."

18. Zanker, *Pompeii,* 188–89, 199, 202.

19. Osiek and Balch, *Families,* 29, 183, 199, citing Wallace-Hadrill, *Houses and Society,* 10, 36, 39.

20. Ibid., 201, 205–6, citing Pedar William Foss, "Kitchens and Dining Rooms at Pompeii: The Spatial and Social Relationship of Cooking to Eating in the Roman Household" (Ph.D. diss., University of Michigan, 1994). How meals were organized in apartment buildings needs treatment.

21. On the centrality of this text, see Elisabeth Schüssler Fiorenza, *Rhetoric and Ethic: The Politics of Biblical Studies* (Minneapolis: Fortress Press, 1999), ch. 7.

22. Zanker, *Pompeii,* 12 (see 131, 141, 146, 188–89, 192, 200); Monika Trümper, *Wohnen in Delos: Eine baugeschichtliche Untersuchung zum Wandel der Wohnkultur in hellenistischer Zeit* (Internationale Archäologie 46; Rahden and Westfalen: Marie Leidorf, 1998), 152.

23. Zanker, *Pompeii,* 198–200, although he modifies his earlier stress on freedmen (240n. 165).

24. Compare B. Hudson McLean, "The Place of Cult in Voluntary Association and Christian Churches on Delos," in *Voluntary Associations in the Graeco-Roman World* (ed. John S. Kloppenborg and Stephen G. Wilson; London: Routledge, 1996), 186–225; also White, *Social Origins,* 1:32–37.

25. McLean, "Place of Cult," 186–89.

26. Trümper, *Wohnen in Delos,* 155.

27. A. N. Sherwin-White, *Racial Prejudice in Imperial Rome* (Cambridge: Cambridge University Press, 1970), 4.

28. Ibid., 8; see p. 21.

29. Trümper, *Wohnen in Delos,* 152.

30. For the system of designating houses on Delos, see ibid., xxi.

31. Ibid., 153.

32. Ibid., 154.

33. Ulrike Wulf-Rheidt, "The Hellenistic and Roman Houses of Pergamon," in *Pergamon, Citadel of the Gods: Archaeological Record, Literary Description, and Religious Development* (ed. Helmut Koester; Harrisburg, Pa.: Trinity Press International, 1998), ch. 12. On art in Pergamon, see Andrew Stewart, *Greek Sculpture: An Exploration* (New Haven: Yale University Press, 1990), 1:205–16 and 2:662–717.

34. Wulf-Rheidt, "Hellenistic and Roman Houses," 304.

35. Ibid., 309. Subsequent page citations in the text come from Wulf-Rheidt's study.

36. Designating the dining room a "hall" may confuse English-speaking readers.

37. Osiek and Balch, *Families,* 29n. 11 and 199, citing Foss, "Kitchens and Dining Rooms," 54–56.

38. John S. Holladay, Jr., "Four-Room House," *OEANE* 2:337–42. See also idem, "House: Syro-Palestinian Houses," *OEANE* 2:110–14, and A. M. T. Moore, "Villages," *OEANE* 5:302.

39. David F. Graf," Palestine," *OEANE* 4:225. Also S. Freyne, "Cities," *OEANE* 2:32, and S. Guijarro, "The Family in First-Century Galilee," in Moxnes, *Constructing Early Christian Families* (n. 2 above), 42–65, esp. 49–55 on types of houses.

40. Paul Zanker, *The Power of Images in the Age of Augustus* (Ann Arbor: University of Michigan, 1988), and H. Mielsch, "Funde und Forschungen zur Wandmalerei der Prinzipatszeit von 1945 bis 1975," in *ANRW* 12.2 (1981), 244.

41. A. Mazar, "Architectural Decoration," *OEANE* 1:193; C. Kondoleon and L. A. Roussin, "Mosaics," *OEANE* 4:51. See Nahman Avigad, "Jerusalem," *NEAEHL* 2:730–34, at p. 730 for a map of the Herodian Quarter, and p. 734 for the House of Columns. See N. Avigad, *The Herodian Quarter in Jerusalem* (Wohl Archaeological Museum; Jerusalem: Keter, 1989), 9, 18, 21, 32–37, 61, 66, on the peristyle house, and Klaus Fittschen, "Wall Decorations in Herod's Kingdom: Their Relationship with Wall Decorations in Greece and Italy," in *Judea and the Greco-Roman World in the Time of Herod in the Light of Archaeological Evidence* (ed. K. Fittschen and G. Foer-

ster; Göttingen: Vandenhoeck & Ruprecht, 1996), 139–61, with twenty-six figures. See Eccl 2:4–9 and the discussion by S. Applebaum, *Judea in Hellenistic and Roman Times: Historical and Archaeological Essays* (Leiden: Brill, 1989), ch. 3. See n. 71 below on Eccl 2:7 and Greek household values.

42. Lee I. Levine, *Judaism and Hellenism in Antiquity: Conflict or Confluence?* (Peabody, Mass.: Hendrickson, 1998), 56–58. Archaeologists have found animals depicted in Herodian Sepphoris and in houses on Mount Zion in Herodian Jerusalem, but *not* in Herodian palaces. See Silvia Rosenberg, "The Absence of Figurative Motifs in Herodian Wall Painting," in *I Temi Figurativi nella Pittura Parietale Antica (IV sec. A.C.–IV sec. D.C.)* (ed. D. S. Corlàita; Bologna, Italy: Bologna University Press, 1997), 283–85, 415–16, at 284.

43. L. I. Levine, "Beth-She'arim," *OEANE* 1:311, and Levine *Judaism and Hellenism*, ch. 4.

44. J. M. G. Barclay, *Jews in the Mediterranean Diaspora* (Edinburgh: T. & T. Clark, 1996), 342, discusses the omission of the prohibition of images from the Decalogue in pseudo-Phocylides 3–8, possibly written in Syria. Matthew, also written in Syria, repeatedly refers to the Decalogue (5:21, 27; 12:2; 15:4; 19:18–19). It is hardly an accident in Greco-Roman culture that Matthew fails to refer to Exod 20:4//Deut 5:8.

45. Aline Rousselle, *Porneia: On Desire and the Body in Antiquity* (Oxford: Basil Blackwell, 1988), 21–22.

46. Osiek and Balch, *Families*, 105, with bibliography.

47. Owsei Tempkin, trans., *Soranus' Gynecology* (Baltimore: Johns Hopkins University Press, 1956), 23.

48. Rousselle, *Porneia*, 14–15; Osiek and Balch, *Families*, 107, citing Galen, "On Sperm," an excerpt in U. C. Bussemaker and Ch. Daremberg, trans., *Oeuvres d'Oribase* (Paris: L'imprimerie Nationale, 1851–58), 3:40–52, here 3.40.13 and 3.46, 1–47, 14.

49. Philo, *On the Contemplative Life* 6, 11–13, 18–19, 65, 90.

50. P. W. van der Horst, *Chaeremon, Egyptian Priest and Stoic Philosopher: The Fragments Collected and Translated with Explanatory Notes* (EPRO; Leiden: E. J. Brill, 1984), 9, 56.

51. Osiek and Balch, *Families*, 115, citing Roy Bowen Ward, "Women in Roman Baths," *HTR* 85, no. 2 (1992): 125–47, esp. 131–34.

52. David E. Fredrickson, "Natural and Unnatural Use in Romans 1:24–27: Paul and the Philosophic Critique of Eros," in *Homosexuality, Science, and the "Plain Sense" of Scripture* (ed. David L. Balch; Grand Rapids: Eerdmans, 2000), 197–222, at 199–200.

53. Ibid., 201 with n. 14; see 199–207.

54. Ibid., 205.

55. See David L. Balch, "Philodemus, 'On Wealth' and 'On Household Management': Naturally Wealthy Epicureans against Poor Cynics," in *Philodemus and the New Testament World* (ed. John T. Fitzgerald; NovTSup; Leiden: Brill, forthcoming).

56. R. R. R. Smith, *Hellenistic Sculpture: A Handbook* (London: Thames and Hudson, 1991), ch. 7: "Baroque Groups: Gauls and Heroes"; for interpretation of Marsyas, see pp. 106–7 with figs. 135.1–2 and 136. Smith supports the suggestion of R. Fleischer, "Marsyas and Achaios, "*Jahreshefte des Österreichischen archäologi-*

schen Instituts in Wien 50 (1972–75), 103–22. See Stewart, *Greek Sculpture* (cited n. 33), 1:216; Karl Schefold, *Der religiöse Gehalt der antiken Kunst und die Offenbarung* (Kulturgeschichte der Antiken Welt 78; Mainz: Philipp von Zabern, 1998), 432, on Marsyas and the gospel in Greco-Roman culture.

57. Sam K. Williams, *Jesus' Death as Saving Event: The Background and Origin of a Concept* (HDR 2; Missoula, Mont.: Scholars Press, 1975), ch. 4.

58. *Pompei: Pitture e Mosaici* (9 vols.; Rome: Enciclopedia Italiana, 1990–99), here 4:290–93; the room is located in Pompeii at VI 5,2, perhaps related to a shop connected to Casa VI 5,3.

59. See Peter Garnsey, *Ideas of Slavery from Aristotle to Augustine* (Cambridge: Cambridge University Press, 1996), 107–27, and idem, "The Middle Stoics and Slavery," in *Hellenistic Constructs: Essays in Culture, History, and Historiography* (ed. P. Cartledge, P. Garnsey, and E. Gruen; Berkeley: University of California Press, 1997), 159–74.

60. These same three household pairs are exhorted by deutero-Pauline authors in Col 3:18–4:1 and Eph 5:21–6:9.

61. Garnsey, *Ideas of Slavery,* 125.

62. Ibid., 134.

63. Ibid., 135.

64. M. I. Finley, *Ancient Slavery and Modern Ideology* (New York: Viking, 1980), 95–96.

65. Paul Veyne, "Homosexuality in Ancient Rome," in *Western Sexuality* (ed. P. Ariès and A. Béjin; Oxford: Oxford University Press, 1985), 29.

66. Garnsey, *Ideas of Slavery,* 94 and 90, citing Modestinus in Dig. 48.8.11.1–2; 40.8.2

67. Ibid., 97–101.

68. Cf. ibid., 99n. 12, with J. A. Harrill, "Ignatius, Ad Polycarp, 4.3 and the Corporate Manumission of Christian Slaves," *JECS* 1 (1993): 107–42.

69. Garnsey, *Ideas of Slavery,* 240.

70. Ibid., 240, 243: "the hero of my narrative is Gregory of Nyssa, who, perhaps uniquely, saw that slavery itself is a sin."

71. Ibid., 81–82, quoted from Stuart George Hall, ed., *Gregory of Nyssa, Homilies on Ecclesiastes: An English Version with Supplementary Studies* (Proceedings of the Seventh International Colloquium on Gregory of Nyssa; St. Andrews, Scotland, 5–10 Sept. 1990) (Berlin: de Gruyter, 1993), 73–75.

72. K. R. Bradley, *Slaves and Masters in the Roman Empire: A Study in Social Control* (Collection Latomus 185; Brussels: Revue d'études latines, 1984), 58.

73. Osiek and Balch, *Families,* 77.

74. For influence of the *symposium* on the Passover Seder see Levine, *Judaism and Hellenism,* 119–24.

75. Osiek and Balch, *Families,* 193–204. See Dennis E. Smith, *From Symposium to Eucharist: The Banquet in the Early Christian World* (Minneapolis: Fortress Press, 2003).

76. Ibid., 29, 183, 199, quoting Wallace-Hadrill, *Houses and Society,* 10, 36, 39.

77. Ibid., 196–98.

78. Ibid., 27–28, 202. See Zanker, *Pompeii,* 93–101 with figs. 45–50, and Roy Bowen Ward, "The Public Priestesses of Pompeii," in *The Early Church in Its Con-*

text: Essays in Honor of Everett Ferguson (ed. A. J. Malherbe, F. W. Norris, and J. W. Thompson; JSNTSup 90; Leiden: Brill, 1998), 318–34, at 323–27.

79. Carolyn Osiek, "Women in House Churches," in *Common Life in the Early Church: Essays Honoring Graydon F. Snyder* (ed. Julian V. Hills et al.; Harrisburg, Pa.: Trinity Press International, 1998), 300–315, at 307.

80. Ibid., 309.

81. Contrast Will Deming, *Paul on Marriage and Celibacy: The Hellenistic Background of 1 Corinthians 7* (SNTSMS 83; Cambridge: Cambridge University Press, 1995).

82. A. Y. Collins, "The Function of 'Excommunication' in Paul," *HTR* 73 (1980): 251–63, at 259.

83. Osiek and Balch, *Families,* 103, citing Peter S. Zaas, "Catalogues and Context: 1 Corinthians 5 and 6," *NTS* 34 (1988): 622–29.

84. Jennifer A. Glancy, "Obstacles to Slaves' Participation in the Corinthian Church," *JBL* 117, no. 3 (1998): 481–501, discusses Christian slaves whose masters forced them into sexual activity. She defines sexual continence as "celibacy in the single life and fidelity in the married life" (497), a modern political slogan read into Paul as exegesis. She then concludes that "sexual obligations incumbent on many slaves would have presented sometimes insuperable barriers to their participation in churches of the Pauline circle" (501), a conclusion that misunderstands Pauline christology and ecclesiology, beginning with the confession that Christ "emptied himself taking the form of a *slave*" (Phil 2:7a).

85. M. Barré, "To Marry or to Burn: *Purousthai* in 1 Cor 7:9," *CBQ* 36 (1974): 193–202, at 195.

86. This assumes that 1 Cor 14:33b–36 is an interpolation by a deutero-Pauline editor (see n. 117). See Osiek and Balch, *Families,* 117. Contrast Antoinette Clark Wire, *The Corinthian Women Prophets: A Reconstruction through Paul's Rhetoric* (Minneapolis: Fortress Press, 1990), 149–52, 229–33. See W. A. Meeks, "The Image of the Androgyne: Some Uses of a Symbol in Earliest Christianity," *HR* 13 (1974): 165–208.

87. See D. L. Balch, "1 Cor 7:32–35 and Stoic Debates about Marriage, Anxiety, and Distraction," *JBL* 102 (1983): 429–39.

88. Zanker, *Power of Images,* 156–59.

89. Fredrickson, "Natural and Unnatural Use," 199. See David L. Balch, "Romans 1:24–27, Science, and Homosexuality," *CurTM* 25, no. 6 (1998): 433–40.

90. Fredrickson, "Natural and Unnatural Use," 199–200, 202, 204, 207n. 7, citing Aristotle, *Nicomachean Ethics* 3.11.1–3.

91. Ibid., 201 with n. 14.

92. Ibid., 205.

93. Ibid., citing Dale Martin, "Heterosexism and the Interpretation of Romans 1:18–32," *BibInt* 3 (1995): 332–55, at 342.

94. Fredrickson, "Natural and Unnatural Use," 208–15.

95. Ibid., 216.

96. For more detail on the information in this section, see Osiek and Balch, *Families,* 64–74 and 156–62.

97. Larry O. Yarbrough, "Parents and Children in the Letters of Paul," in *The Social World of the First Christians: Essays in Honor of Wayne A. Meeks* (ed. L. M. White and O. L. Yarbrough; Minneapolis: Fortress Press, 1995), 126–41.

98. A marble plaque found on the Acrocorinth refers to a "teacher (*didas[kalos]*) and *arch[isynagog]os* of the [synagogue of Corinth?]," discussed by G. H. R. Horsley, *New Documents Illustrating Early Christianity* (Marrickville, Australia: Maquarie University Press, 1987), 4:213–14.

99. Osiek and Balch, *Families,* 158 with nn. 12–13.

100. See J. N. D. Kelly, *Early Christian Doctrines* (New York: Harper & Row, 1960), ch. 2.

101. E. R. Goodenough, *An Introduction to Philo Judaeus* (Oxford: Blackwell, 1962), 35, refers to this as the first creed in history.

102. H. Conzelmann, *1 Corinthians* (Hermeneia; Philadelphia: Fortress Press, 1976), 142n. 26 and 144n. 46, compares Ps.-Aristotle, *Mund.* 6 379b 14–15, and Marcus Aurelius Ant., *Medit.* 7.9.

103. Compare H. D. Betz, *Galatians* (Hermeneia; Philadelphia: Fortress Press, 1979), 131–32, and contrast B. S. Davis, "The Meaning of *proegraphe* in the Context of Galatians 3.1," *NTS* 45, no. 2 (1999): 194–212.

104. Schefold, *Der Religiöse Gehalt,* 432. For example, the House of T. Dentatius Panthera (IX 2,116) in Pompeii (*Pompei: Pitture e Mosaici* [cited n. 58], IX, p. 10, fig. 15).

105. See David L. Balch, "The Suffering of Isis/Io and Paul's Portrait of Christ Crucified (Gal 3:1): Frescoes in Pompeiian and Roman Houses and in the Temple of Isis in Pompeii," *Journal of Religion* 23, no. 1 (2003): 24–55, and "Paul's Portrait of Christ Crucified (Gal 3:1) in Light of Paintings and Sculptures of Suffering and Death in Pompeiian and Roman Houses," in *Early Christian Families in Context.*

106. See, e.g., Doug Adams, *Transcendence with the Human Body in Art: George Segal, Stephen De Staebler, Jasper Johns, and Christo* (New York: Crossroad, 1991), 13–14, 21, 27, 34–36, on Segal's "The Holocaust."

107. On the "democratization" of an aristocratic ethic or the "aristocratization" of a popular mentality, that is, on exchanges between upper-class and lower-class virtues, see Gerd Theissen, *The Religion of Earliest Christianity: Creating a Symbolic World* (Minneapolis: Fortress Press, 1999), 82; also 49–50.

108. For more information on the material in this section, see Osiek and Balch, *Families,* 72–82, 174–85. For household gods specifically, see ibid., 81–82, citing F. Bömer and P. Herz, *Untersuchungen über die Religion der Sklaven in Griechenland und Rom, Erster Teil: Die wichtigsten Kulte und Religionen in Rom und im Lateinischen Westen* (2d ed.; Forschungen zur Antiken Sklaverei 14.3; Stuttgart: Franz Steiner, 1981), 46–47, 52, 54–56.

109. Peter Lampe, "Keine 'Sklavenflucht' des Onesimus," *ZNW* 76 (1985): 135–37. This is contested by J. Albert Harrill, "Using the Roman Jurists to Interpret Philemon: A Response to Peter Lampe," *ZNW* 90 (1999): 135–38.

110. Osiek and Balch, *Families,* 177, 182–83.

111. J. Albert Harrill, *The Manumission of Slaves in Early Christianity* (HUT 32; Tübingen: J. C. B. Mohr [Paul Siebeck], 1995), 3.

112. S. Scott Bartchy, *Mallon Chresai: First Century Slavery and 1 Corinthians 7:21* (SBLDS 11; Missoula, Mont.: Scholars Press, 1973), 134–43.

113. Harrill, *Manumission,* 89.

114. Ibid., 123.

115. Ibid., 74, 121.

116. Osiek, "Women in House Churches" (cited n. 79), 310. Compare Osiek,

"The Family in Early Christianity: 'Family Values' Revisited," *CBQ* 58, no. 1 (1996): 1–24, at 18–20.

117. Despite traditionalist ideology, these two women in the Roman city of Pompeii (see n. 78) were hardly silent in their own houses. In 1 Cor 14:32, Paul, discussing charismatic speaking in tongues, writes that "the spirits of the prophets are subject [ὑποτάσσεται, *hypotassetai*] to the prophets." An editor saw this verb, the key verb in deutero-Pauline household codes (e.g., Col 3:18; Eph 5:21; cf. 1 Pet 3:1), and interpolated a familial subordinationist ethic into 1 Corinthians. Further, Paul wrote that when one charismatic receives a revelation, another is to be "silent" (1 Cor 14:30), a second key idea in traditional, misogynist ethics (Aristotle, *Pol.* I 1260a 31; 1 Tim 2:11–12), which the deutero-Pauline editor read into 1 Cor 14:35, despite the contradiction with 11:5.

118. Osiek, "Women in House Churches," 312.

119. Abraham J. Malherbe, *Paul and the Thessalonians: The Philosophic Tradition of Pastoral Care* (Philadelphia: Fortress Press, 1987).

10

PAUL AND FRANK SPEECH

J. Paul Sampley

In the Greco-Roman world, how did one correct, or even affect, the conduct of another person or of a group? Demetrius, of "probably . . . late Hellenistic or early Roman"[1] times, concluded that an orator, and we may equally assume a letter-writer, had only three alternatives: flattery, figured speech (alternately referred to as covert hint or oblique speech), and adverse criticism (*Style* 294), which we may take to be a functional overlap with παρρησία, *parrēsia*, direct speech or frank speech, the focus of this essay.

Plutarch, a moralist born before 50 C.E., and therefore roughly contemporary with Paul, condemns flattery as notoriously useless, even counterproductive, in any and all circumstances. The second option, oblique or indirect speech—in which the speaker treats a ticklish issue or problem by transferring the discussion to an analogous matter about which passions are not inflamed and positions are not already established—was most commonly and widely used in Paul's time, if for no other reason than that it provided safety from retribution in the public arena and that it was known by rhetoricians to be powerfully effective, because it depended on the auditors to make self-application.[2]

In Paul's time, direct or frank speech (*parrēsia*, frankness) was less frequently employed in public deliberation but was surely part and parcel of the way social dynamics played themselves out all the way down the social pyramid. Where there was friendship, frank speech was crucial to its maintenance.

In the following, I first establish the understanding of *parrēsia*'s function in Paul's time—its goals, its risks, and the range of responses the frank speaker might expect. The second part of the essay considers some examples of *parrēsia* in Paul's letters.

Part I. *Parrēsia* in the Greco-Roman World of Paul's Time

Translating *parrēsia* presents a challenge. The problem, in part, is historical. In earlier Greek times, the term referred to a citizen's right to speak out and to be heard

293

in public assembly. With the Cynics the term came to mean the freedom to say whatever was on one's mind. In Paul's time, however, the term's social context[3] was friendship, and *parrēsia* was what friends owed one another. So the definition is that *parrēsia* is the frank speech delivered by a friend, and its aim is the friend's improvement—and it can range in form from the harshest rebuke to what Philodemus, a first-century C.E. educator, moralist, and rhetorician, called "the gentlest of stings" (*On Frank Criticism*, col. VIIIb).

By Paul's time, one cannot understand *parrēsia* apart from friendship. But friendship had also changed by Paul's time. Prior to the Common Era, friendship assumed "that friends were more or less of equal station, and that the obligations that friendship might impose were in principle mutual and symmetrical."[4] But by the turn of the eras, the notion of friendship had come to operate more frequently "between people of unequal station and power."[5] Of course, flattery also flourished in that same social setting and provided a ready contrast with genuine friendship, as Plutarch's title shows so clearly: "How to Tell the Difference between a Flatterer and a Friend."

Parrēsia is what most clearly distinguishes a friend from a flatterer. Plutarch calls *parrēsia* "the language of friendship" ("How to Tell" 51C [Babbitt, LCL]).[6] Philodemus recognizes that *parrēsia* is "performing the office of a friend" (φιλικὸν ἔργον, *philikon ergon*; *On Frank Criticism*, col. XIXb).[7] Friends keep "close watch" on one another "not only when they go wrong but also when they are right" ("How to Tell" 73D). True friends will endeavor to "foster the growth of what is sound and to preserve it" ("How to Tell" 61D). *Parrēsia* is a "fine art" and requires the greatest of care in its application ("How to Tell" 74D).

Analogies with the physician-patient relationship abound: *parrēsia* is "the greatest and most potent medicine in friendship" ("How to Tell" 74D); "the true frankness such as a friend displays applies itself to errors that are being committed; the pain which it causes is salutary and benignant, and, like honey, it causes the sore places to smart and cleanses them too" ("How to Tell" 59D).

Though it is more desirable to have a friend "commend and extol us," it is more difficult to find and probably more important to have "a friend to take us to task, to be frank with us, and indeed to blame us when our conduct is bad. For there are but few among many who have the courage to show frankness rather than favour to their friends" ("How to Tell" 66A). *Parrēsia* is a duty, an obligation, and the ultimate sign of friendship. *Parrēsia* can be a vital aid in self-correction, in the emendation of one's ways. It is an invaluable help to keeping one on the right track and to maintaining perspective not only on one's self, but also on surrounding matters and events.

Parrēsia is a delicate social transaction. It can degenerate into a source of enmity if it is applied (1) at the wrong time (*On Frank Criticism* frg. 62, col. XVIIb;

"How to Tell" 66B, 68C–D, 69A–C); (2) in the wrong way ("How to Tell" 66B); (3) in a fashion that gilds the reputation of the dispenser (*On Frank Criticism* col. XXIIIb); (4) in anger (*On Frank Criticism* frgs. 2, 12, 38, 70); (5) if it is an expression of self-interest ("How to Tell" 71D); (6) if it is not in proportion to the problem (*On Frank Criticism* frg. 84); (7) if it is generated "out of envy" (*On Frank Criticism* col. XXIIIa); or (8) if it "derives from some hurt that has been received or from some personal eagerness to get even" ("How to Tell" 66E–67A).[8]

The appropriateness of frank speech is clearly an issue of great importance, and it can be tested by asking some key questions: does it come from "their entire heart," and is it genuinely aimed at achieving the proper goals of *parrēsia* (*On Frank Criticism* col. XVIb)? Though always painful, is the frankness helpful, beneficial, advantageous ("How to Tell" 51C [ὠφέλιμον, *ōphelimon*], 64C [ὠφέλειαν, *ōphelian*]; *On Frank Criticism* frg. 32, col. XVIIb; cf. Dio Chrys., *Or.* 32.5, 7, 11)? Does it bring the "patient to one state—that which is for his good" (ἐπὶ τὸ συμφέρον, *epi to sympheron*; "How to Tell" 55B, 63B; *On Frank Criticism* frg. 1, col. Xb)?

Indeed, analogies with medicine are not without point. Frank speech is applied to problems, to deviances, to matters that if not changed can lead to an even further deterioration in "health." The dispenser of frankness, like the surgeon, must have a vision of the desired change, and, while recognizing the intermediate pain, the surgeon anticipates a time beyond the pain when the wholeness is restored and gratitude is forthcoming. The frank speech is not itself the goal, but the desired change is. Similarly, educational analogies abound in the literature about frank speech and appropriately so, because frankness can be the occasion for an individual to benefit and to improve.[9]

Frank speech does not settle for the status quo; it seeks another level of performance. In some instances it urges increased maturity. Or, if the recipient has ventured onto a dubious or dangerous path, it calls for a change in direction. The frank speaker values the aspirations and goals enough to risk that the recipient may reject not only the frank speech but the speaker as well. The willingness to risk one's own standing with another for the good of the other is why frank speech can only be understood in the context of genuine friendship.[10]

As surely as life's problems come in all degrees of difficulty, from the most minor to the seemingly earth-shattering, so *parrēsia* varies in degree from harsh to gentle.[11] At one extreme lies harsh *parrēsia* (using a form of σκληρός, *sklēros*, as the descriptor, *On Frank Criticism* frg. 7; or using a form of πικρός, *pikros*, frg. 60; Plutarch makes the same point with σφροδρός, *sphrodros*, "severe," "How to Tell" 69E) whose focus is on blame alone, without any praise. Harsh frank speech has as its nearest neighbor insult (λοιδορία; *On Frank Criticism* frg. 60), which itself is no longer *parrēsia*. The "line between ridicule and reproach was a thin one indeed."[12] At the other extreme of the continuum lies "mixed" frank speech (μεικτός, *meik-*

tos; On Frank Criticism frg. 58).[13] The neighbor just beyond the lightest sting of frank criticism is flattery, which itself is no longer *parrēsia*. The taxonomy of *parrēsia* can be charted along a continuum as follows:

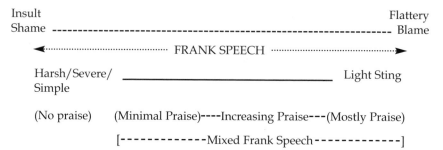

All frank speech finds itself somewhere along that continuum, inside insult and flattery. The determination of *parrēsia*'s harshness lies in identifying how much praise accompanies it. The more praise, the lighter the sting; the absence of praise, probably a most rare occurrence, indicates harsh or severe frank speech. The question arises: how and when would one use harsh or severe frankness?— and to that question we turn shortly.

Human exchanges can be ranged along a continuum such as may be seen in the chart above, from insult on one extreme to flattery on the other. True *parrēsia* functions in varying degrees along but within that continuum, not reaching insult and falling short of flattery, ranging from harsh/severe/simple on the one extreme to what Philodemus calls "the gentlest of stings" (*On Frank Criticism*, col. VIIIb; frg. 58) on the other extreme. All speech short of harsh, simple criticism is what he calls "mixed" *parrēsia* (κατὰ μεικτὸν τρόπον; frg. 58) because it interlaces criticism and praise. The former is straightforward and direct, having no praise intermixed, but consisting simply of blame. In like fashion blame-to-praise should also be considered a continuum between the extremes and allowing a supposedly infinite variety of admixtures of the two. Accordingly, if one wanted to assess just how harsh is the *parrēsia* in a given document, one could look for the amount of praise that accompanies the frank speech. The more praise one finds alongside the call for a change of conduct or for the avoidance of a contemplated course of action, the further to the right on the continuum one would place the document and its *parrēsia*.

Outside the extremes of genuine *parrēsia* lie the fakes. To the left one makes "a parade of harshness and of being acrimonious and inexorable in his bearing towards others" ("How to Tell" 59D) or "seek[s] for glory in other men's faults, and to make a fair show before spectators" (71A). Beyond the border in the other direction is a frankness that is "soft and without weight or firmness" ("How to Tell" 59C) and that is tantamount to flattery.

When does one use harsher criticism? When does one employ only the slight-est corrective? Philodemus is especially helpful as he addresses the problem of how to nurture his most obstinate young students whom he likens to horses/stal-lions (*On Frank Criticism* frg. 71; cf. frg. 83 and Philo, "On Husbandry" 34). The harshest criticism, that is, *parrēsia* without praise, is reserved for such people, as an ultimate measure, as an effort of last resort when all else has failed. Plutarch agrees: "In what circumstances, then, should a friend be severe . . . in using frank speech? It is when occasions demand of him that he check the headlong course of pleasure or of anger or of arrogance, or that he abate avarice or curb inconsider-ate heedlessness" ("How to Tell" 69E–F). On the other hand, the gentlest of cor-rectives is applied between friends who have the highest regard for one another (*On Frank Criticism* col. VIII). Philodemus imagines the mildest frank speech be-tween two sages who are already attuned to high standards for themselves and who enjoy one another's company and mutual respect: "[T]hey will be reminded pleasurably by one another in the ways we have made clear, as also by them-selves, and they will sting each other with the gentlest of stings and will acknowl-edge gratitude [for the benefit]" (*On Frank Criticism* col. VIIIb). Clearly, one of the challenges facing the dispenser of frankness is proportionality, how to make the frankness appropriate to the crisis.

Those who engage in *parrēsia* come under special scrutiny. Many of the re-quired characteristics are identical with those of friendship—and the issue quickly comes down to a question of character or *ēthos*, as Greek writers ex-pressed it. How should one describe what *ēthos* denotes in antiquity?[14] *Ēthos* is a comprehensive term describing an individual's total bearing or character: his or her distinguishing hallmark or core identity, those specific qualities that betoken who a person really is—particularly those moral qualities that are strongly devel-oped and strikingly displayed with an abiding consistency. All of one's actions and statements contribute to one's *ēthos*.[15] Plutarch puts it succinctly: "but frank-ness of speech ought to have seriousness and character [σπουδὴν . . . καὶ ἦθος, *spoudēn . . . kai ēthos*]" ("How to Tell" 68C).

The issue of one's *ēthos* becomes more critical as the addressed problem or cri-sis becomes greater: "[E]very man's frank speaking needs to be backed by charac-ter, but this is especially true in the case of those who admonish others and try to bring them to their sober senses" ("How to Tell" 71E). Weak or diminished *ēthos* permits little or no frankness: "But the speech of a man light-minded and mean in character [*ēthos*], when it undertakes to deal in frankness, results only in evoking the retort: 'Wouldst thou heal others, full of sores thyself!'" (How to Tell" 71F).

Parrēsia draws upon a reservoir of goodwill built up by a consistent life whose values govern the behavior of the one who speaks frankly. What Plutarch calls one's "supply of frankness" depends on how full one's reservoir of goodwill is

("How to Tell" 73B). The following questions are the sort to ask if one wants to assess someone's reserve of goodwill: Do the frank critics apply the same standard of scrutiny to their own actions as they do to those of others? Do they correct "their friends precisely as they correct themselves" ("How to Tell" 72A)? At the heart of the issue is consistency and continuity: "[I]t is necessary to observe the uniformity and permanence of his [the frank critic's] tastes, whether he always takes delight in the same things, and commends always the same things, and whether he directs and ordains his own life according to the one pattern" ("How to Tell" 52A). Frank speech will backfire if the frank speaker seems eager for his or her own reputation ("How to Tell" 52B; *On Frank Criticism* col. XXIIIb) or if the speaker seems to be serving selfish aims.

Further, a true friend is concerned with the whole scope of the other's behavior, from good to bad, celebrating the former and lamenting the latter. Again, Plutarch: "[W]e ought to keep close watch upon our friends not only when they go wrong but also when they are right, and indeed the first step should be commendation cheerfully bestowed" ("How to Tell" 72D).

Frank critics hope for a response that is gracious (*On Frank Criticism* frg. 36), and if they are indeed fortunate their recipients "will receive the reminder with total gratitude" (col. XIVb). But most of all they yearn for an emendation of behavior (or, using a medical analogy, a return to health or wholeness; cf. "How to Tell" 55B–E) or to "foster the growth of what is sound and to preserve it" ("How to Tell" 61D). But frank critics must be prepared for rejection: "[S]o it is the duty of a friend to accept the odium that comes from giving admonition when matters of importance and of great concern are at stake" ("How to Tell" 73A).

Frank speech always risks the friendship upon which it depends. The one dispensing the frankness must sufficiently value the desired good for the recipient friend to hazard possible rejection. Philodemus recognizes that some people take frank speech more readily than others. He wonders: "Why is that, when other things are equal, those who are illustrious both in resources and reputations abide [frank speech] less well?" (*On Frank Criticism* col. XXIa). He understands that old people bridle at frankness because "they think that they are more intelligent because of the time [they have lived]" (col. XXIVa).

Flattery plays to emotion, frank speech to "the thinking and reasoning powers" ("How to Tell" 61E). Frank speech calls for moral reasoning; it asks the recipient to engage in reflection, in deliberation, in self-reflective weighing whether to continue in the present direction or to change. Frank speech provides the context for self-evaluation and suggests self-correction. *Parrēsia* does not force change. It does call for change, but the recipient remains the moral agent and must weigh the matter so as to decide what response is appropriate.

Those who do the work of friendship, that is, who apply frank speech to others, are most frequently depicted as warning or instructing or appealing to them. Forms of νουθετέω, *noutheteō*, and ἐπιτιμάω, *epitimaō*, are widely used in the descriptions of what the frank critic does. The semantic range of these two terms is vast, ranging from admonition to warning to instruction for the former term,[16] and from rebuke, to reproof, to censure, to warning, and to speaking seriously for the latter.[17] But *parrēsia* does not require the use of any set terminology. *Parrēsia* occurs whenever anyone directly questions or calls for reexamination of another's—or of a group's—behavior, practice, or contemplated action. Its range goes from appeal to rebuke, with multifarious variations in between.

We now turn to an examination of *parrēsia* in Paul's letters. Though we will not take time for a detailed survey of Paul's use of the term *parrēsia*,[18] we note the term's varied functions when it appears in the passages we consider. The study's focus now turns to selected instances of frank speech in Paul's letters (whether the term *parrēsia* appears or not). The essay concludes by evaluating the harshness and gentleness of the instances of frank speech we study in Paul's letters.

Part II. Some Instances of Frank Speech in the Pauline Correspondence

First we turn to the two most obvious examples of Pauline *parrēsia*, Galatians and 2 Cor 10–13. After we have analyzed those, we examine a few other Pauline instances.

No one can doubt that Galatians and 2 Cor 10–13 represent frank speech. What we seek to determine is how severe the frank speech is in each and how little or much Paul follows the conventions of *parrēsia* noted in the first section.

Galatians

Paul writes the Galatian churches because he sees them inclined to move toward what he considers a dangerous precipice. Outsiders have come into the Roman province of Galatia and have interfered with Paul's churches, insisting that the men should be circumcised and that all should commit themselves to what the intruders consider proper fidelity to the Law. Paul hears of this development and because he is not free to go to Galatia in person, he sends this peppery letter.

Signs of Paul's distress flash across the letter. Even the salutation (1:1–5) is defensive. Where the Galatians might have expected a thanksgiving to God, they hear instead Paul chide them: "I am astonished . . ." (1:6–9). He mentions another, rival gospel (1:6–9). He forcefully reminds them of his earlier warnings (1:9). He calls them "foolish" or "stupid" (ἀνόητοι, *anoētoi*) and suggests that they may have fallen under some spell (3:1, 3).

Soon it becomes clear that the issue before Paul's predominantly Gentile churches in Galatia is obedience to the Law and undergoing circumcision, the ancient Jewish ritual signifying covenant participation: circumcision is the subject of the Jerusalem conference (2:1–10); withdrawal from fellowship with Gentiles involves a non-Pauline way for believers to behave (2:11–21); and, skipping much other evidence along this same line, we note in 5:12 that he hopes those so eager to circumcise will have the knife slip!

Paul knows that the Galatian believers have received the Holy Spirit, for him the hallmark of anyone's being a believer (3:1). He was there, and his preaching occasioned their reception of the Spirit (3:2–5). He knows they converted from their idolatry and slavery to cosmic powers (4:3, 8) and now he asks in astonishment whether they are not on the brink of re-converting, reverting to their former slavery (4:8–10). He concludes that section of the letter with a sharp rebuke: "I am afraid that all my hard work on you may have been wasted" (4:11).

Galatians is Paul's warning cry to believers whom he fears are dangerously near a precipice. So far, no Galatians seem to have fallen over the cliff; but at least some of them are near it and appear to deliberate moving forward. Plutarch distinguishes two uses of frankness. One "reclaim[s] a wrongdoer" while the other "stir[s] a man to action" ("How to Tell" 74A). In the former, one lightly charges "'You acted unbecomingly' rather than 'You did wrong' . . ." (73A). In the latter, "we should turn around and ascribe their action to some unnatural or unbecoming motives" (74A). Because the Galatian believers have not yet done the wrong, Paul does question their purposes (4:8–11; cf. 3:1, 3; 5:12).

Paul engages his frank speech with them on three fronts: (1) their relation to the gospel and to Paul; (2) their inaccurate self-assessment as to how they are doing and where they are heading (prime issues for frank speech); and (3) the implications if they were to proceed.

The Galatians' relation to the gospel and to Paul. Frank speech draws upon a reservoir of goodwill built up by the friend who speaks frankly; consistency of behavior and genuine concern are required of the frank friend. Consider the numerous ways Paul reminds the Galatians of his *ēthos* by reference to his past performance and present concern. The burden of Gal 1–2 is the refinement and burnishing of Paul's *ēthos* and his offering of himself as a model to be emulated in their current crisis.[19] From the details of his past, Paul selects those snapshots that not only will encourage Galatian identification with him but also will help them see more clearly that Paul has manifested the true friend's dependability and consistency. So, from the outset, Paul establishes that God, not other human beings, has been in control of his life.

The recounted scenes from his life invite the Galatians to identify with him. He, like them, has experienced a transformation of his life. They were "slaves to elemental spirits" and alienated from God (4:8–9); Paul attacked the gospel and its adherents (1:13–14). The Galatians were called (1:6); so was Paul (1:1, 15). The Galatians now have to deal with the issue whether Gentiles have to become circumcised to be part of God's people; Paul had to confront the very same issue at the Jerusalem conference (2:1–10). If anything, Paul's past predicaments were on an even grander scale than the Galatians are now experiencing: the very people who pressured him to change, as the Galatians are now being pressured, were none other than James, Cephas, and John—and this compulsion Paul experienced while on *their* turf. The encoded message: you Galatians can stand, indeed you must stand against those who would now enslave you again. Finally, in Antioch, when even Barnabas, Paul's right-hand man, caved in to the pressure, Paul stalwartly resisted what he considered Cephas's compromising withdrawal from fellowship with Gentiles (Gal 2:11–21).[20]

Philodemus and Plutarch would have recognized immediately that, in Paul's recounting of these vignettes of his own life, we have someone eminently qualified as a true friend, tried and true through all the tests that life could provide. By this Paul endeavors to persuade the Galatian believers that he merits their trust in "the truth of the gospel" and in delineating the comportment appropriate to it. His opening chapters position him as one eminently qualified to carry out the "work of friendship" by using frankness to warn them of the dangers of their contemplated action.

Paul contrasts the Galatian readiness to change again with his own stalwartness and dependability. He and they already share that fundamental change that moved them from outsiders to full participation in the gospel—the reception of the Spirit. For Paul, the Galatians' contemplated accommodation to the intruders is a move backward to slavery from freedom, and is simply unthinkable. The first change, their conversion, was formative of who they are now; the sort of change that the Galatians are pondering is destructive. On that basic premise Paul structures much of the remainder of the letter into praise for their present standing in the faith and into warnings against the change they are weighing.

Paul does praise the Galatians. To their credit, the Galatians began just as they should have—with the Spirit (3:3). With one of his beloved athletic metaphors he praises them for "running well"; they got off to a good start and were headed in the right direction until intruders impeded their progress (5:7). The Galatians' reception of Paul and the gospel were exemplary (4:14–15). A final blessing caps the letter: "peace and mercy upon them and upon the Israel of God"—on those who decide to "follow in the footsteps of this rule" (5:16).

Warnings and statements of shame, however, predominate. Paul uses florid language to gain attention: the Galatian believers are "deserting" God (1:6); they may have started with the Spirit, but they will "end up with the flesh" (3:3); their fate will come to nothing (3:4); they will become slaves again (4:9); and they stand to lose their "blessedness" (ὁ μακαρισμὸς ὑμῶν, *ho makrismos hymōn*; 4:15). Warnings include a repeat of what he had said before: those who do works of the flesh shall not inherit God's kingdom (5:19–21). Paul also gives a warning about self-deception, because God will repay according to what they sow (5:15, 26). And finally, Paul warns that the Galatians are not relating to one another in an appropriate way (6:1–5).

At the heart of the letter and at the center of this issue of Paul's friendship and frankness with the Galatians lies a critical, rich passage (4:12–20) that can be appreciated fully only in the context of friendship and frank speech. The verses are laced with signs of friendship from start to end. First, Paul calls them brothers (ἀδελφοί, eleven times in this letter), itself a term used among friends, and reflecting the Galatians' having been resocialized into a new family with God as Father (1:3). Paul's imploring "Become as I am" is a call for them to imitate those characteristics that he has exemplified in the earlier recounting of scenes from his life (chs. 1 and 2). Beyond that, in the passages that intervene between Paul's own exemplary story in Gal 1–2 and 4:12–20, Paul has told the common story of the origins of his and their faith in such a way as to include himself in it with them, or, as he puts it in 4:12, "as" them: "Before faith came *we* were confined under the law, *mutually* restrained [συγκλειόμενοι, *synkleiomenoi*] until faith should be disclosed . . ." (3:23; emphasis added). Once again he includes himself with his auditors, when he writes about how the heir must grow up before receiving the estate: "Just so with *us*, when *we* were children, *we* were slaves to the elemental spirits of the cosmos . . . in order that *we* might receive sonship" (4:3–5; emphasis added).

Paul's unequivocal declaration that the Galatians have done him no wrong (4:12) clarifies that his frank speech in the letter is not a reprisal for something they had done to him, because that would have been an inappropriate context for *parrēsia* ("How to Tell" 66F–67A). By this means Paul forestalls any suggestion that his frankness on either side of this passage is self-servingly motivated, a charge he readily alleges about the intruders (4:17; 6:12–13).[21] Here *synkrisis*, comparison, serves Paul's purpose well and strengthens his ground for the frank speech of this letter.[22]

In 4:12–20, Paul recounts the foundational story of the believing communities in the Roman province of Galatia. It is at once a narrative of God's grace having its way and of the origin of an intense friendship between Paul and the Galatian believers. Paul's sickness laid him up there, and he shared the gospel with them. By the description in 4:14–15, their response to the gospel and indeed to Paul surmounted whatever trial his illness was to them—an early sign of genuine friendship on their side—and bound them into a friendship relationship with him: they were eager even to give of themselves for the well-being of their new friend, Paul. Why, he writes, they would have plucked out their eyes and given them to him—surely a metaphorical and rhetorically exuberant way of describing that genuine and deep friendship in which nothing matters more than the well-being of one's friend. He asks, in effect, what has changed since that foundation time that was characterized by such enthusiasm? Not Paul. Not his gospel. Once again (cf. chs. 1–2) he stresses his dependability and consistency. By calling their exuberance "blessedness" (4:15), Paul understands it as an effervescence of God's love through them and back to Paul. What further do they need to do than simply to live out that blessedness in their lives together?

With this careful and powerful recounting of their rich and genuine friendship, its origins and the bonds it has created between them and Paul, Paul frames the question of how the Galatians will receive this letter of frank speech, in which he has taken them to task for their temptation to follow the intruders' urgings that they need to be circumcised. Will they reckon that his frankness is not genuine, that he is not carrying out the truest "office of friendship" (*On Frank Criticism* col. XIXb)? He puts the issue directly to them: Will they view Paul as no friend at all, in fact as an *enemy* because he cares enough about them to risk the friendship (4:16)?[23]

In the next verse and in a contrast with himself, Paul depicts the intruders as Plutarch's flatterers, who praise others for the benefits they can wrest from them (4:17); then he moves his discourse to a new level, namely to his maternity. Mother Paul affectionately and directly addresses the Galatians: "My little children [τέκνία μου, *teknia mou*], again I am in labor until Christ be formed in you" (4:19). Friendship categories are overlaid with family ties. Maybe the intruders could also claim to be friends with the Galatian believers, but nobody but Paul can claim to have suffered labor pains over them!

The passage concludes with Paul's open reflection about his frank speech. Paul expresses a double wish: that he could be with them and that he could change his tone or voice (φωνή, *phōnē*) because he is perplexed with them (4:20). Paul is passionately involved with them and seeks their well-being, as any genuine friend and good mother would. Plutarch would have thought Paul perfectly in line here to show passionate feeling about the Galatians' predicament: "[I]f it concern matters of greater moment, let feeling also be evident" ("How to Tell" 68C). Paul's frankness here passes the test of "weight and firmness" (59C); it also has a little praise mixed in (72C).

Paul knows the risk of frank speech, as his question about becoming the Galatians' enemy indicates (4:16), but he clearly cares enough about them to take the chance: "the man who by chiding and blaming implants the sting of repentance is taken to be an enemy and an accuser" ("How to Tell" 56A); "it is the duty of a friend to accept the odium that comes from giving admonition when matters of importance and of great concern are at stake" (73A). As a friend, also as an apostle and mother, Paul simply cannot allow the Galatians to go further down the wrong road without his challenge (64C).

We are now in a position to evaluate what sort of frankness Paul has used in Galatians. Because praise is scattered here and there it cannot be simple, harsh frank criticism. So it is mixed *parrēsia,* and therefore not as harsh as it could have been; we could even dare to make up a new, Pauline category of affectionate but strong *parrēsia.* Because the harshest frank speech is reserved for those who are perceived to be beyond hope (*On Frank Criticism* frg. 71), and such criticism is not employed in Galatians, we can say with some conviction that (1) Paul is ultimately not troubled that the Galatians will split from him now that they have been given a proper warning and (2) he must therefore have good reason to expect that his mixed *parrēsia* will bring them around.

2 Corinthians 10–13

In order to set a context for considering 2 Cor 10–13, we look at Paul's prior correspondence with the Corinthians with regard to the question of his employment of frank speech.

The "previous" letter (Paul's first letter to the Corinthians). Paul's actual first letter to the Corinthians is lost to us, but we know about it from what we call 1 Corinthians. In 1 Cor 5:9–11, Paul reminds them of his earlier letter. Apparently it was concerned with immoral persons and questions regarding association with them; we learn about this letter because Paul refers to it and, quite intriguingly, because it apparently caused some confusion as to what Paul really meant. We know too little about it to say anything about its relation to frank speech.

1 Corinthians (Paul's second letter to the Corinthians). What we now call 1 Corinthians, though really Paul's second letter, seems to have been prompted by several developments: (1) the Corinthians have written a letter to Paul (cf. 1 Cor 7:1), in which they inquire for his guidance (cf. also perhaps, 1 Cor 8:1; 12:1; 16:1); (2) reports Paul has received from "Chloe's people" and maybe from others (1:11; cf. 16:17); (3) and, in what may be a straightforward result of the reports, Paul has some concerns about what he thinks is going on among the believers in Corinth.

There is some praise of the Corinthians in this letter. Let us here confine ourselves to a representation rather than a full catalog of that praise. The Corinthians possess knowledge and can express it (1:5). They do not lack any charismata, spiritual gifts (1:7). Paul repeatedly calls them "brothers and sisters" (see 1:10; 2:1; etc.). Though they are more childish than he would wish, they are still beloved by him (3:14). There is no confusion about paternity; Paul is their father, and they are his children (4:14). They are, if anything, overly enthusiastic about the freedom that they genuinely have in Christ (6:12–20; 10:23–11:1). They are eagerly excited about the charismata that they have been given (ch. 12). But every instance of praise seems to have an edge of reproof. Every item noted here has to do with something that is only partially right in the Corinthians; in each instance, Paul goes on to instruct them in such a way that they get it right or move beyond their partial realization. Here also should be mentioned ironic praise that seems directed against some who may be on the brink of understanding important matters but who fumble it because they think too highly of themselves (4:8–13). Paul's description of the Corinthians as babies seems apropos, because they eagerly try to live the life and to do the exercises of faith that Paul has taught them, but they always seem to get just enough to drop it in such a way that even the milk he gives them is spilled!

So there is a persistent edge of criticism across this letter. The Corinthians are quarrelsome and divisive (1:10–13) when they should not be. They are supposed to be people of the Spirit (as all believers are, by definition); they should be ready for meat but they really are yet only babies, and therefore Paul has to give them milk (3:1–4). They have immorality within the community (5:1–8), and they do not use frank speech against it. They have taken differences among believers to civil courts for adjudication and gotten verdicts from judges who are unaware of what real justice (righteousness) is (6:1–11). They either are consorting with prostitutes, or Paul uses that charge as a metaphor describing the way they are not singularly faithful to Christ (6:12–20). They have confusion about marriage and sexuality (ch. 7) and meat offered to idols (ch. 8). Matters related to worship are a nightmare: the Lord's Supper is a travesty, and their worship services are chaos (chs. 11–14). They should indeed be excited about resurrection, but some of them at least have misunderstood even something so basic (ch. 15). Paul will not close the letter until he urges them to give his agent, Timothy, a warm reception and, when he is ready to leave, to send him off with "your blessing" (16:10–11). Likewise, he seems not to have full confidence that the Corinthians, left to themselves, will properly honor three of their own whom Paul thinks are leadership-quality, so he tweaks them about that (16:15–18).

Where does this letter of frank speech fall along the continuum? The presence of some praise, measured as it is, means that the letter should be classified as "mixed frank speech." But it is strong in its frankness. It appears that the Corinthians—or, to be more precise, some of the Corinthians—see themselves as persons who already have "arrived" (see esp. 4:8–11, but the problem is not expressed only in that passage). Put in another way, some of the Corinthian believers have understood freedom in Christ better than they have understood the love that must always be factored into the equation. Some Corinthians have taken even their spiritual gifts and made of them a way to establish superiority. Paul is astonished by this pervasive inclination among the Corinthian believers, and he tries across the letter to counterbalance it (cf. his own self-portrait as the person of the most extensive rights, but who will not employ them if someone might be harmed [ch. 9]; cf. 10:31–11:1). First Corinthians is, therefore, a continual case study of Paul's efforts to keep the hierarchy-driven structures of the outside world from penetrating the community of believers. Because Paul employs mixed *parrēsia,* we can deduce that he thought the Corinthians could successfully be called to growth and improvement.

    2 Corinthians 1–9.[24] Paul was prompted to write this letter fragment by several factors, most of which have worked, at least with some of the Corinthians, to damage Paul's *ēthos* as the trustworthy friend/mother/apostle: (1) he promised them a visit and failed to show; (2) he made an unannounced visit that was a disaster because some individual at Corinth (we know him from Paul as "the one who did the wrong"; 2 Cor 7:12) attacked Paul, and, to Paul's shame, no one came to his defense; (3) stung by this, Paul wrote a letter that he acknowledges was frank speech, calling the Corinthians to task; (4) Titus has reported to Paul that the frank letter had the desired result and that the Corinthians were therefore realigned with Paul (in fact "a majority" of the believers had disciplined the one who did the wrong by shunning him; 2:6–11); but (5) there was enough residual displeasure and mistrust that (some of?) the Corinthians had lost their desire to take part in the collection, that goodwill, one-time offering that Paul had been gathering from among the Gentiles, which Paul hoped to see delivered to Jerusalem. So when Paul writes 2 Cor 1–9, he has a diminished *ēthos* with the Corinthians and, at least from the collection, he knows that not all of them are delighted with him, even though Titus has reported some improvement in their relation to Paul. Before looking at 2 Cor 1–9, I need to comment on a few matters about the above (item 3) letter of acknowledged frank speech that Paul wrote between 1 Corinthians and 2 Cor 1–9.

    "The painful letter" (Paul's third letter to the Corinthians, now lost). We know about this letter only by its mention in 2 Cor 2:1–4 and 7:6–13. It is generally called the "painful" letter because of the pain and grief it caused the Corinthians (2:2–4), or the "tearful letter," because Paul describes himself as having written it in tears (2:4). Paul acknowledges that the letter was *parrēsia,* that it caused the Corinthians pain and grief (2:4; 7:8–12). He said the letter was to show them Paul's extraordinary love (2:4) and how devoted they are to him (7:12). In line with Plutarch and Philodemus, Paul assures the Corinthians that he did not write with the intention to hurt them; he is not happy because of the pain or grief, but because of their resulting reaffiliation with him (7:8–9).

Because we do not know whether there was any praise in the painful letter, we cannot be sure just how unmitigated was the harshness of speech. But Paul's great anxiety over its reception (cf. 7:5–7) suggests that it may have been quite harsh. In any case, the residual tenderness among (some of) the Corinthians is a significant factor that Paul must have considered (obliquely, of course) in writing 2 Cor 1–9.

2 Corinthians 1–9 (Paul's fourth letter to the Corinthians). Most of 2 Cor 1–9 is focused on two things: highlighting Paul's long, solid history with the Corinthians, particularly his having brought the gospel to them; and an indirect magnifying of Paul's ministry (of which the Corinthians are prime beneficiaries) through three laudatory portraits (ministry of the new covenant, 3:1–4:6; ministry of affliction and mortality, 3:7–5:10; and ministry of the new creation, 5:11–21).[25] Those passages function to refurbish Paul's *ēthos* and thereby to renew the Corinthians' attachment to him. They have no explicit appeals within them. But as the letter fragment comes toward its end, Paul does make an overt appeal—and it will be no surprise that the appeal is on the basis of friendship and of his paternity of them, Paul's having "spoken frankly to" them and "opened" his heart to them (6:11). Denials consistent with the contemporary conventions of friendship—"we have wronged nobody, ruined nobody, exploited nobody" (7:2)—frame Paul's reiteration of his desire that they should make room for him in their hearts (7:2). Paul, in his doubled appeal for greater affection (6:13; 7:2), acknowledges that he is using frank speech with them: "We have spoken very frankly to you, friends in Corinth" (6:11 REB; and 7:4). These appeals for closer filiation with him are acknowledged frank speech, but of what sort?

The answer lies in realizing how much the frankness is framed in substantial praise of the Corinthians. The letter reaches a climax in his doubled appeal for increased affection (6:13; 7:2). For praise, one need look only at the way chapter 7 concludes by lavishing exuberant commendations upon them (perhaps overly: "I rejoice that in everything I have confidence in you"; 7:16). Paul's earlier boasts to Titus about the Corinthians have proven true (7:14–16).[26] The way Paul ties his appeal for great affection to lavish praise of the Corinthians identifies 2 Cor 1–9 as a relatively light sting of frank speech.[27]

One other matter relating to frank speech deserves attention. Titus informed Paul that the majority of the Corinthians had disciplined "the one who did the wrong" (2:5–7). Paul's counsel regarding this man tells us something about his understanding of the limits of frankness. Paul declares that, "in the face of Christ," Paul has forgiven the one who did the wrong, and he urges the Corinthians to "reassure him of your love for him" (2:8). In this matter Paul exemplifies and indeed telegraphs his own readiness to let bygones be bygones with the Corinthians and to embrace them, which he does explicitly in chapters 6–7. So, for

Paul, frank speech is never to be seen as an end in itself; it is always and only a means to alter, to recover, and to redirect.

2 Corinthians 10–13 (a fragment of Paul's fifth letter to the Corinthians). In these chapters, the sting of frankness is anything but light. Paul and the Corinthians have serious troubles. Are matters beyond repair? Paul is determined to have a showdown visit with them. He wishes that his "sphere of influence"[28] (κανών, *kanōn*) among them would increase (10:15), but he openly declares his fears that he will find them other than he hoped (12:20). He even notes the concern that God may humble him because the Corinthians, likened to a bride, are not as they should be—and Paul knows that he, as the bride's father, is obligated to present a pure bride to Christ (11:2). As he closes the fragment, he prays for their "being made complete"[29] and adds a sententious appeal for change (2 Cor 13:11).

From beginning to end, 2 Cor 10–13 is unadulterated frank speech. In it Paul (twice) reminds the Corinthians, in an emphatic *inclusio* or ring device, that God has given him the power to build up and the power to tear down (10:8; 13:10). From that position of authority and responsibility, he calls on them to realign with him and his gospel and challenges them to undertake a serious self-assessment to see whether they are still living the life of faith and whether Christ is still among them (13:5)—a fundamental challenge. The entire letter fragment contains not one instance of praise for the recipients.[30] Accordingly 2 Cor 10–13 is what Philodemus and Plutarch called "pure," "simple," or "harsh" frank speech.

Severe frank criticism is invoked only in the direst circumstances, as a last resort, and when all else has failed. "In what circumstances, then, should a friend be severe, and when should he be emphatic in using frank speech? It is when occasions demand of him that he check the headlong course of pleasure or of anger or of arrogance, or that he abate avarice or curb inconsiderate heedlessness" ("How to Tell" 69E–F). Philodemus also knows that harsh frank speech is reserved for those "somewhat more in need of restraint . . . the strong who will scarcely change [even] if they are shouted at" (*On Frank Criticism* frg. 7). Paul's resort to such harshness indicates that Paul thinks matters with the Corinthians have come to a head, so that he has no alternative.

Paul's imminent arrival will be a confrontation on his terms. Particularly important since his earlier visit to Corinth, when "the one who did the wrong" (2:7) single-handedly and publicly upbraided Paul and no one came to Paul's defense, Paul now prescribes that any allegation must be supported by the Deuteronomic canon of two or three witnesses (2 Cor 13:1; Deut 19:15). Throughout these chapters Paul makes the claim that, in Paul, the Corinthian rebels will come face to face with God's power (2 Cor 13:3–4; 10:3–6, 8; 12:9, 12; 13:10).

Part and parcel of Paul's frank speech is a recitation of his past acts on the Corinthians' behalf, in other words, of his previous and consistent acts of friendship.

God gave the Corinthians into his care (10:13). Paul extended himself ("all the way," for emphasis) and therefore the gospel to them (10:14). He charged no fee (11:7) and burdened nobody (11:9). He performed the signs of a true apostle among them (12:12). And he did what the good Jewish father is supposed to do; he was obligated to present the Corinthians as a pure bride to Christ (11:2).

Like a true friend, he was consistent and dependable—and he forcefully says as much to them: "And what I do, so shall I [continue to] do" (11:12). He never took advantage of them (11:20; 12:14), nor did Titus, Paul's agent (12:17). He has always spoken the one truth to them (13:2; 12:6; 13:8). He has always preached the same way (11:4). He has never used the God-given authority to destroy but has always worked for their edification (10:8; 13:10). And when we recall that "love edifies" (1 Cor 8:1), we can see that his claim always to have worked for their edification is equivalent to his affirming that he has consistently loved them. In fact, statements of his love punctuate the chapters (11:11; 12:19; 12:15).[31] What more could anyone ask of a good friend?

Matters with the Corinthians have come to a worrisome head. Paul seems to expect that his projected visit will be a showdown. His explicit call for their self-examination and self-testing—implicit or relatively more hidden in all frank speech, but unmistakable in this example of pure frankness—is designed to provide a basis for their imminent meeting with Paul.[32] We may hope that the letter continued beyond chapter 13 so that it does not climax on such a strong sting, namely, with Paul telling the Corinthians to check if Christ was still in or among them (13:5). Unless the letter did not end with chapter 13, Paul has violated Plutarch's cautions against ending an interview—and one may suppose the same would apply to a letter—on a "painful and irritating . . . final topic of conversation" ("How to Tell" 74E). But, in fairness, Plutarch assumes a conversation when he writes; he is not contemplating a letter of the harshest possible frank speech as we have in 2 Cor 10–13.

We do not have a record of how this last effort at frankness played out with the Corinthians, but oh, to have been on hand when Paul and his entourage arrived in Corinth! We do have a few clues that this showdown may have gone rather well for Paul. Let me list the clues. (1) Romans was written from Corinth. (2) Paul stayed in Gaius's home, which is said to have room for "the whole church" at Corinth (which indirectly affirms that there is a whole church; Rom 16:23–24). (3) Achaia, the Roman province in which Corinth stands, did contribute to the great symbolic collection for the poor in Jerusalem (Rom 15:26). And there was still a church at Corinth and it was still associated with Paul's name when Clement wrote the Corinthian Christians a half-century later. Curiously and aptly, Clement points out in his letter that Paul surely had depicted the Corinthian believers' *ēthos* correctly when he showed them to be contentious and difficult.

Frank Speech in Philippians

To round out the study, I examine frankness in Philippians. No other Pauline church had been on better relations with Paul across the years than the church at Philippi.[33] "From the first day until now" the Philippians have joined with Paul in a partnership in the gospel (1:5; 4:15). They have been and are a source of joy for Paul. The signs of friendship run through the entire document:[34] Paul holds the Philippians in his heart (1:7); he longs for them (1:8); though he would rather be unfettered by concerns in this world, he chooses to stay for their sake (1:19–26);[35] he sees them as persons who can fill out his joy (2:2); they are his beloved (2:12; 4:1); they are addressed as his "brothers" [ἀδελφοί, nine times]); they have sent an ἀπόστολος (apostolos), an agent of their own, Epaphroditus, to him (2:25–30); they have sent Paul support (4:10–20); and, in the ultimate sign of friendship, Paul is even ready to be sacrificed for them and their well-being if necessary (2:17).[36] Like a physician, a true friend strives, just as Paul does across this letter, "to foster the growth of what is sound and to preserve it" (Plutarch, "How to Tell" 61D).

Philippians is structured around four exemplars whose shared characteristic is their willingness to seek the well-being of others, even if it is at some cost or risk to themselves. This characteristic is itself a sublime test of friendship. The four, in sequence as they appear in the letter, are Paul, Christ, Timothy, and Epaphroditus. Paul describes himself as preferring to depart from the world to be full-time with Christ (1:23; 2 Cor 4:14; 5:2) but as having decided to stay around for the Philippians' "progress and joy in the faith" (1:25). Christ, though being on a par with God, made common cause with people, "taking on the form of a servant" (δοῦλος, doulos; 2:7), even to the point of his death (2:5–8). The characteristics of Timothy that Paul features are his being "tried-and-true," as the Philippians know (δοκιμή, dokimē; 2:22), his specially close relation to Paul (ἰσόψυχος, isopsychos, a "double" of himself and like a son; 2:20, 22), and, most important here, his genuine anxiousness "for your welfare" (2:20 NRSV). Epaphroditus fits the same picture because he risked his life to finish up the Philippian service to Paul (2:30).

Paul's references to himself in his letters serve many purposes.[37] Most frequently they are for exemplification,[38] as they surely are here in Philippians. Of course, self-reference always serves as ēthos enhancement. In Philippians, Paul's self-references show an eagerness to establish as much common ground with the Philippians as possible. Like them, he has reason to look back with pride (3:4–14), but he openly urges them to imitate him (3:17) as he focuses on God's culminating work. Surely Paul's self-references shore up his ēthos, though one gets the impression from this letter that not much is needed in this regard with the

Philippians. In fact, the most comprehensive call to emulation in the Pauline corpus appears in Phil 4:9 and should lead us to see that the primary concern with Paul's self-references in Philippians is exemplification: "Whatever you have learned and received and heard and seen in me, do these things."

Paul's call for modification of their behavior, that is, his *parrēsia*, is very limited with the Philippians because they are—and always were—doing so well. In this letter, most of his frankness comes as the most gentle of reminders to keep on doing as they have, or, at worst, to do more fully what he urges. His comment in 3:1 that to write the same things is not burdensome to him suggests that he knows that his urgings have become rather commonplace between him and them. They could complete his joy if they were even more unified than they are (2:2); they can keep watching for the dogs who would advocate circumcision (3:2–11; taking 3:1 as bracing the Philippians for more of what they have heard from him in the past); and they could be steadfast (again, just as they have a noteworthy history of being). That leaves the most obvious place—and the one unprecedented matter—in Philippians in which Paul delivers frank speech, and it is what Philodemus would call the "gentlest of stings" (*On Frank Criticism* col. VIIIb): Paul's double entreaty of the two women, Euodia and Syntyche (4:2–3).

Paul and the Philippians know what problems these two ladies have had. Paul does not have to recite what provoked this carefully doubled appeal to them. We see Paul beseech each of them "to agree with one another in the Lord" (τὸ αὐτὸ φρονεῖν ἐν κυρίῳ, *to auto phronein en kyriō*; 4:2). From the earlier use of the identical formulation τὸ αὐτὸ φρονεῖν, *to auto phronein*, in the general appeal to complete Paul's joy by being of one mind (2:2), we can take Paul's appeal in 4:2 as a specification of one place where the problem of disunity needs special attention. The person either named "Yoke-fellow" or nicknamed something analogous to "Comrade" (σύζυγος, *syzygos*)[39] is characterized as γνήσιος, *gnēsios*, genuine or true, and is specially asked by Paul to bring these two women together (συλλαμβάνω, *syllambanō*, is a term that implies the use of enough effort to make it happen).[40] The rest of the passage details, in a very laudatory way, the lofty standing of these two women. Significantly, the chief description of the two women, namely that they have "contended/struggled" alongside Paul (συνήθλησαν, *synēthlēsan*; 4:3), echoes the same verb Paul used when he earlier implored the Philippians to "stand in one spirit, *contending/struggling* as one for the faith of the gospel" (1:27, emphasis added; cf. "to write the same things," 3:1).

Euodia and Syntyche have a creditable history of doing just what Paul hoped all the Philippians would do, but they have come into some disagreement. The two women have been counted to stand with Paul, with Clement, "and the rest of my fellow workers whose names are in the book of life" (4:3). So there can be no confusion: Euodia and Syntyche have been and are leaders in Paul's coterie. In his recitation of their great history of proper comportment in service of the gospel (4:3), Paul has done precisely what Plutarch recommended: when the reproof reminds the hearers of their own past "honourable actions," they may strive to be like their better selves ("How to Tell" 72D). So praise and the gentlest of stings are woven in Paul's entreaty of these two women leaders.

With the gentlest frankness, Paul calls for the two women to end their strife and asks a third party to broker the resolution. The entire letter has set the occasion for this frank appeal.[41] Paul's own forgetting of what lies behind (3:13) and his pressing forward "to the prize of the upward call of God in Christ Jesus" (3:14) becomes the model of how these two women should "let bygones be bygones" and focus on God's future. Paul's—and Christ's and Timothy's and even their coreligionist Epaphroditus's—search for what is the best for others is a pattern that should also guide these two women as they receive Paul's frank call for them to be of one mind.

Conclusion

Paul knows and employs *parrēsia,* frank speech, as a powerful tool of social transaction within the conventions of his time. The Pauline examples of frank speech that we have studied manifest the varying degrees of frank speech known at the turn of the eras. The examples also show Paul exercising extreme care to fit the degree of harshness to the situation.

If we consider these Pauline instances of frank speech with regard to (1) how much praise they intermingle with the call for an emendation of conduct or of contemplated action, and (2) how harsh and fundamental is the "sting," we can make relative distinctions among the instances. Of those usages considered in this study, clearly the harshest criticism is found in the letter fragment, 2 Cor 10–13, in which no praise of the Corinthians is to be found. In our study the other extreme, the lightest of stings, is represented in Philippians, which is dominated by praise and in which Paul celebrates the joy in the gospel that he has had across the years with them. Even though he is proud of them and finds their conduct generally appropriate, he is nevertheless concerned that Euodia and Syntyche overcome their recent difficulty.

In between those two extreme examples, we can place the frank speech in 2 Cor 1–9 and in Galatians. In 2 Cor 1–9, Paul is thankful that his frank speech of the "painful letter" has wrought a powerful, positive change in the Corinthians' disposition, but he is not satisfied that their response is as full or whole-hearted as it can be, so he applies a gentle but very basic sting.[42] It is one thing to urge two people to get over a spat (Philippians); it is another to call for greater affection. The former is subject to leverage and intervention; the latter situation does not necessarily respond to entreaty. The former is relatively easier to deliver; the latter must spring forth on its own power if it is to come at all. Accordingly, I would rank the frank speech of 2 Cor 1–9, couched as it is in considerable praise, as a bit harsher than that of Philippians.

The frank speech of Galatians lies somewhere between that of 2 Cor 1–9 and 2 Cor 10–13. Prior to this study, the frank speech of Galatians might have been considered as harsh as that of 2 Cor 10–13, but now we can see that the two, though related, are readily distinguishable. Though 2 Cor 10–13 sits directly in the blame column and lacks praise, Galatians praised the recipients even while pointing out a very fundamental problem with what they, or, more accurately, some of the them,[43] were tempted to do.[44]

Certain factors complicate Paul's application of frank speech. First, Plutarch seems reasonably to suppose that much or most frank speech takes place between one individual and another,[45] face to face. Granted, Philodemus spends a fair amount of time considering frank speech between a teacher and his students. But neither Philodemus nor Plutarch contemplates delivering frank speech in a letter, when the writer is absent from the recipient(s). Both Plutarch and Philodemus allow for the frank speaker to observe the responses that the frank speech is generating and to make midstream accommodation by altering course, modulating voice, or by offering some other sign of friendship. Paul as letter writer has no such recourse. No wonder he agonized over the response of the Corinthians to his "painful letter" and found no rest until Titus brought news of their favorable response (2 Cor 7:5–7). With a letter, the load of frankness is delivered in one shot, as packaged; the situation allows no midcourse amelioration, short of a follow-up letter or visit.

Second, Paul's frank speech always occurs in connection with a group, his followers. Sometimes his frank speech is focused on individuals (as in Philippians with the two women, in 2 Cor 2 with the "wrong-doer," or in Philemon), but it always engages the entire community along with the individuals. On other occasions, Paul's frank speech surely engages the community but has bearings on outsiders who bid for allegiance in competition with Paul. In such instances, Paul's frank speech not only calls directly for a change in his followers, but often, sometimes indirectly, involves a critique of or a comparison with the outsiders. Galatians, 2 Cor 1–9, and 2 Cor 10–13 all have this triangulation in some degree; in each instance, the frank speech, a critique of the community, is intertwined with a criticism of the outsiders, and the two need to be distinguished.

Finally, though friendship (the social matrix of *parrēsia*) in Paul's time functioned more typically between persons of different social standing and status, Paul's employment of the concept is so thoroughly reshaped into his own thought-world as to be assimilated to the family of God. Paul's relations with his communities are fundamentally ambivalent, and that ambivalence appears in a study of his use of frank speech. On the one hand, Paul and his followers are equal in Christ; they are equally dependent on God's grace; they are all alike freed from sin's power; and they will all have to give account of themselves before God or Christ at the judgment day. In all those respects, Paul and his followers are no different. However, when it comes to their moral and spiritual development— and we certainly notice when his followers have even the slightest problem in that regard—Paul is ultimately responsible for them, like a father or mother for children. So Paul's resorts to frank speech are always couched in this fundamental ambiguity: he, like the letter recipients, is on the road to maturity, but he, distinctively, feels himself responsible for their proper continuance and development; he is at once their friend and at the same time their apostle. All the instances of frank speech in this study are situated in that ambivalence.

Part III. Other Relevant Pauline and Paulinist Texts

Rom 12:1–5; 15:14–16; 16:17–20
Gal 6:1–5
1 Thess 3:1–5; 4:1–12
Philemon
Eph 4:1–6
Col 2:6–8

Part IV. Bibliography

Ahl, Frederic. "The Art of Safe Criticism in Greece and Rome." *AJP* 105 (1984): 174–208

Fitzgerald, John T., ed. *Friendship, Flattery and Frankness of Speech: Studies on Friendship in the New Testament World.* Leiden: Brill, 1996.

———. *Greco-Roman Perspectives on Friendship.* SBLRBS 34. Atlanta: Scholars Press, 1997.

Fürst, Alfons. *Streit unter Freunden: Ideal and Realität in der Freundschaftslehre der Antike.* Stuttgart: Teubner, 1996.

Konstan, David. *Friendship in the Classical World.* Cambridge: Cambridge University Press, 1997.

Konstan, David, et al., eds. *On Frank Criticism.* SBLTT. Atlanta: Scholars Press, 1998.

Sampley, J. Paul. "Paul's Frank Speech with the Galatians and the Corinthians." Pages 265–321 in *Philodemus and the New Testament World,* edited by J. T. Fitzgerald, G. S. Holland, and D. Obbink. NovTSup. Leiden: E. J. Brill, 2003.

Notes

1. D. A. Russell, "Demetrius," *OCD* 326.

2. Frederic Ahl, "The Art of Safe Criticism in Greece and Rome," *AJP* 105 (1984): 174–208. In figured speech, "the text is incomplete until the audience completes the meaning" (187). For a Pauline example, consider his explicit identification of his rhetorical purpose in 1 Cor 4:6, in which he tells his readers that, in the previous sections, he has applied his comments to himself and Apollos for their benefit. See my "1 Corinthians" in *The New Interpreter's Bible* (Nashville: Abingdon, 2002); B. Fiore, "'Covert Allusion' in 1 Corinthians 1–4," *CBQ* 47 (1985): 85–102; D. R. Hall, "A Disguise for the Wise: METASCHEMATISMOS in 1 Corinthians 4:6," *NTS* 40 (1994); P. Lampe, "Theological Wisdom and the 'Word about the Cross': The Rhetorical Scheme in 1 Corinthians 1–4," *Int* 44 (1990): 117–31. J. T. Fitzgerald, *Cracks in an Earthen Vessel: An Examination of the Catalogues of Hardships in the Corinthian Correspondence* (SBLDS 99; Atlanta: Scholars Press, 1988), traces the identification of this as covert allusion back to J. B. Lightfoot in 1895 (119n. 10). For another Pauline example, see my "The Weak and Strong: Paul's Careful and Crafty Rhetorical Strategy in Romans 14:1–15:13," in *The Social World of the First Christians: Essays in Honor of Wayne A. Meeks* (ed. L. M. White and O. L. Yarbrough; Minneapolis: Fortress Press, 1995), 40–52.

3. See David Konstan's description of the "new" understanding of friendship that was operative by the turn of the eras, "Friendship, Frankness and Flattery," in *Friendship, Flattery and Frankness of Speech: Studies on Friendship in the New Testament World* (ed. J. T. Fitzgerald; Leiden: Brill, 1996), 7–10. For more on friendship's shift "from the political to the moral sense" (ibid., 7–19), see David Konstan, *Friendship in the Classical World* (Cambridge: Cambridge University Press, 1997).

4. Konstan, "Friendship, Frankness and Flattery," 8–9.

5. Ibid., 9.

6. Other treatments of *parrēsia* appear in Cicero, *Amicitia* 88–100; Maximus of Tyre, *Orationes* 14; Dio Chrysostom, *Or.* 77/78.38, 33.9; Philo, *Her.* 19; Julian, *Or.* 6.201A–C.

7. All quotations of Philodemus are from *On Frank Criticism* (edited and translated by D. Konstan et al.; SBLTT; Atlanta: Scholars Press, 1998). On *parrēsia* as a "duty" of friendship, see Konstan, "Friendship, Frankness and Flattery," 10; as a "sign of goodwill," see C. Glad, "Frank Speech," in *Friendship, Flattery, and Frankness*, 31–32.

8. Philodemus is concerned about excesses, about *parrēsia* beyond the fringe (frgs. 37, 78 [= 80N]), about frankness that deteriorates into "foolish harshness" (frg. 79 [81N]).

9. See Konstan's discussion of Philodemus's *On Frank Criticism* in "Friendship, Frankness, and Flattery," 12–13. Plutarch captures the connection of frankness with education in his declaration that the "sons of the wealthy and sons of kings do learn to ride on horseback, but they learn nothing else well and properly; for in their studies, their teacher flatters them with praise . . . whereas the horse . . . throws headlong those who cannot ride him" ("How to Tell" 58F).

10. The connection of *parrēsia* with friendship dates at least from Aristotle: see A. Fürst, *Streit unter Freunden: Ideal and Realität in der Freundschaftslehre der Antike* (Stuttgart: Teubner, 1996), 133–34.

11. Here I follow the interpretation of N. W. de Witt, "Organization and Procedure in Epicurean Groups," *CP* 31 (1936): 205–211, and C. Glad, *Paul and Philodemus: Adaptability in Epicurean and Early Christian Psychagogy* (Leiden: Brill, 1995), 143–46. See also Glad, "Frank Speech," 35n. 74. Though these authors' interests are focused on Epicureans, a similar picture emerges in Plutarch, as we shall see.

12. Peter Marshall, *Enmity in Corinth: Social Conventions in Paul's Relations with the Corinthians* (Tübingen: J. C. B. Mohr, 1987), 79n. 59.

13. So also Plutarch: ". . . among the most useful helps is a light admixture of praise" ("How to Tell" 72C).

14. A group or community also has an *ēthos:* see M. Wolter, "Ethos und Identität in paulinischen Gemeinde," *NTS* 43 (1997): 430–44.

15. For example, "arrogance, ridicule, scoffing, and scurrility" are inimical to frank speech ("How to Tell" 67E).

16. BDAG 544.

17. BDAG 302–3.

18. D. E. Fredrickson, "ΠΑΡΡΗΣΙΑ in the Pauline Epistles," in *Friendship, Flattery, and Frankness*, 163–83, does that.

19. Cf. George Lyons, *Pauline Autobiography: Toward a New Understanding* (SBLDS 73; Atlanta: Scholars Press, 1985).

20. Interestingly, the account is itself a description of Paul's frank speech to Cephas. Philodemus wrote that one can "persuade also through [deeds], and not just [through speaking]" (*On Frank Criticism* frg. 16).

21. Cf. the rhetorical traditions concerning how one discredits opponents by impugning their motives, particularly by declaring that such persons serve their own self-interest: Sampley, "Paul, His Opponents in 2 Corinthians 10–13, and the Rhetorical Handbooks," in *The Social World of Formative Christianity and Judaism: Essays in Tribute to Howard Clark Kee* (Philadelphia: Fortress Press, 1988), 162–77.

22. Christopher Forbes, "Comparison, Self-Praise, and Irony: Paul's Boasting and the Conventions of Hellenistic Rhetoric," *NTS* (1986): 2–8. Cf. also Marshall, *Enmity in Corinth*, 53–55, 348–53.

23. See Marshall, *Enmity in Corinth*, 35–51, for a good depiction of the enmity that Paul has risked by his frankness.

24. Adopting V. P. Furnish's understanding of the sequence and scope of the Corinthian correspondence in *2 Corinthians* (Garden City, N.Y.: Doubleday, 1984), 35–48.

25. For more detail on this breakdown, see Sampley, "Second Corinthians," in *The New Interpreter's Bible* (vol. 11; Nashville: Abingdon, 2000), 14, 56–99.

26. For other instances of praise in 2 Cor 1–9, see 1:7; 2:3; 3:2–3.

27. For an assessment of the problems Paul generated by following the harsher frank speech of the painful letter with another sting, be it ever so gentle, and for Paul's light-sting appeal for more affection as a wrongful use of frank speech by the conventions of that time, see Sampley, "Paul's Frank Speech with

the Galatians and the Corinthians," in *Philodemus and the New Testament World* (ed. J. T. Fitzgerald, G. S. Holland, and D. Obbink; NovTSup; Leiden: E. J. Brill, 2003).

28. BDAG 403.

29. BDAG 418.

30. Certainly this is only a letter fragment, so there might have been some praise in the missing parts, but nowhere in the Pauline corpus do we have another four chapters without a single note of praise.

31. In this particular, Paul parts company slightly from Philodemus, who, for sharp *parrēsia*, expects that one may "forget 'dearest' and 'sweetest' and similar things" (*On Frank Criticism* frg. 14).

32. Frankness helps keep perspective as to what is important and what is indifferent; see Plutarch, "How to Tell" 59F.

33. I am not convinced by partition theories with regard to Philippians; the letter coheres, as one may see in R. A. Culpepper, "Co-workers in Suffering: Philippians 2:19–30," *RevExp* 77 (1980): 349–58.

34. S. K. Stowers, "Friends and Enemies in the Politics of Heaven: Reading Theology in Philippians," in *Pauline Theology* (ed. J. M. Bassler; vol. 1; Minneapolis: Fortress Press, 1991), 114–21; A. J. Malherbe, "Paul's Self-Sufficiency (Philippians 4:11)," in *Friendship, Flattery and Frankness*, 126–28; J. T. Fitzgerald, "Philippians in the Light of Some Ancient Discussions of Friendship," in *Friendship, Flattery and Frankness*, 144–47. For a dissenting voice, see John Reumann, in that same volume.

35. See James Jaquette, "A Not-So-Noble Death: Figured Speech, Friendship, and Suicide in Philippians 1:21–26," *Neotestamentica* 28 (1994): 177–92.

36. For comparison, see Konstan, *Friendship in the Classical World*, 118–20, for a recounting of some extravagant signs of friendship in classical times.

37. See my discussion of how this works in Galatians and Philippians: "Moral Reasoning from the Horizons of Paul's Thought World: A Comparison of Galatians and Philippians," in *Theology and Ethics in Paul and His Modern Interpreters: Essays in Honor of Victor Paul Furnish* (ed. Eugene H. Lovering, Jr., and Jerry L. Sumney; Nashville: Abingdon, 1996), 114–31.

38. Margaret Mitchell, *Paul and the Rhetoric of Reconciliation: An Exegetical Investigation of the Language and Composition of 1 Corinthians* (Louisville: Westminster John Knox, 1991), 39–60.

39. BDAG 776. For "yoke" as a metaphor of friendship in antiquity, see Fitzgerald, "Philippians in the Light," in *Friendship, Flattery and Frankness*, 149–51.

40. BDAG 776–77 suggests "take hold of together, then support, aid, help."

41. N. A. Dahl, "Euodia and Syntyche and Paul's Letter to the Philippians," in *The Social World of the First Christians*, 3–15. Another noteworthy feature is Paul's ready but open dismissal of any reason he might have had for concern or distress that the Philippians had been a long time in sending him support (4:10). This fits what Plutarch says: "And if one also makes it clear that in speaking frankly he is leaving out of all account or consideration a friend's lapses toward himself, but taking him to task for certain other shortcomings . . . the force of such frankness is irresistible" ("How to Tell" 67B).

42. Plutarch notes that a good time for "admonition [νουθεσίας, *nouthesias*] arises when people, having been reviled by others for their errors, have become

submissive and downcast" ("How to Tell" 70D)—though in the Corinthian instance it was *Paul* who had used the earlier frank speech.

43. Does my own self-correction in this sentence raise yet another possible distinction between 2 Cor 10–13 and Galatians? May we not suppose that an ingredient in the harshness gradient between these two letters is that a higher percentage of the Corinthians than Galatians were tempted to stray from Paul and his understanding of the gospel?

44. We simply know too little about the "painful letter" to place it with certainty.

45. Troels Engberg-Pedersen, "Plutarch to Prince Philopappus," in *Friendship, Flattery, and Frankness* (see esp. 64).

11

PAUL AND FRIENDSHIP

John T. Fitzgerald

Friendship is a universal phenomenon, practiced and discussed to varying degrees by all cultures. For both intellectual and social history, it has few rivals in importance, having evoked not only ecstatic praise for its benefits but also anguished laments over its failures and attendant problems. In both theory and praxis, certain aspects of friendship have remained fairly constant through the centuries, while others have varied significantly. This was already true by the time of the Greco-Roman period, so that friendship as understood and practiced by Paul and his contemporaries cannot be adequately appreciated without giving attention to what was both old and new in their theory and praxis. For that reason, I provide in the first part of this essay a brief and highly selective history of friendship from Homer to imperial Rome.[1]

Attention to the terminology, theory, and practice of friendship prior to the first century C.E. is crucially important, for inhabitants of the Greco-Roman world were the beneficiaries of their predecessors' ruminations on the subject and continued to practice many of the ancestral forms of friendship. That is, many if not most of their ideas about friendship were neither new nor unique to that time period but had arisen in earlier periods and had been passed down from generation to generation. Furthermore, these ideas never existed in a social or ideological vacuum but were shaped and sustained within specific historical contexts that conditioned the ways in which friendship was practiced.

At the same time, antiquity's notions about friendship were closely associated with many other concepts. Consequently, they were not transmitted from one generation to another in isolation but collectively, so that recipients inherited them as a group of interconnected ideas. It is useful to think of this nexus of ideas as a "linkage group," a term that I am adapting from the field of genetics, in which it is used of the tendency of some genes to remain linked and to be inherited as a unit. Thus a linkage group is "a group of hereditary characteristics which remain associated with one another through a number of generations."[2] When applied to concepts, the expression "linkage group" thus indicates certain terms and ideas that remain associated with one another through a number of generations. For example, from the very earliest period friendship was closely linked to the practice of hospitality, so that these two ideas belong to the same linkage group. Although the ways in which both friendship and hospitality were practiced changed over the centuries, the two ideas remained closely linked. Antithetical concepts can also belong to the same linkage group, and in the case of friendship, its traditional antonym was enmity. As early as the archaic period, this antithesis was enshrined and inculcated in the moral dictum that one should help friends but harm enemies. The archaic linkage between friendship and enmity was still vibrant in the first century and appears, for example, in the Gospel of John, where the theme of friendship with Jesus (15:12–17) is followed by its axiomatic corollary, namely, the world's enmity (15:18–25).

Although inhabitants of the Greco-Roman world owed much to traditional wisdom about friendship, their own understanding and practice reflected the specific values and concerns of their own age. Consequently, they transmitted to later antiquity not only what they themselves had received but also their own insights and innovations. As we shall see, some of these are of crucial importance for understanding the New Testament.

Part I. The Terminology, Theory, and Practice of Greek and Roman Friendship: A Brief History

The standard Greek word for "friend" in the classical and Greco-Roman periods was φίλος (philos), an old term that appears already in Homer. There is considerable debate about the original meaning of this term, with some scholars arguing that it indicated possession and others that it indicated emotion. Those who assert the priority of the possessive sense usually argue that the substantive φίλος originally indicated relationship rather than affection and designated a person who was "one's own," such as a member of one's family, household, or larger social group. Its chief antonym in this case would have been ξένος (xenos), that is, "the stranger" who does not belong to "one's group." Scholars who regard φίλος as originally or exclusively emotive typically argue that the term φίλος, when used as a substantive in the Iliad and the Odyssey, expresses affection and friendship, and that in certain cases the emotive sense of φίλος may even be reciprocal, designating someone who is involved in a relationship that is both mutual and reciprocated. If this claim is correct, the common classical and Greco-Roman idea that friendship (φιλία, philia) involves mutuality and reciprocity is present already in Homer. Indeed, one of the major claims advanced by David Konstan in his recent history of Greek and Roman friendship is that the substantive φίλος is normally used in *all* periods of ancient Greek history to indicate a "friend"[3] and that "the abiding image of friendship" throughout these periods is that of "an intimate relationship predicated on mutual affection and commitment."[4]

Although the controversy over the original meaning of φίλος (*philos*, "friend") and its use in Homer is far from settled, this debate should not obscure the fact that the *idea* of friendship is already present in Homer. As is frequently the case in the history of ideas, practice precedes theory, and, in this case, even vocabulary. The emergence of φίλος as the standard Greek word to designate a friend is clearly post-Homeric, but the kind of relationship later celebrated by φίλος is vividly portrayed by Homer, above all in the case of Achilles and Patroclus. In the Greco-Roman period, these two comrades were widely recognized as being special friends (e.g., Chariton, *Chaer.* 1.5.2) and were regularly cited in the "canon" of those joined closely together in "a yoke of friendship" (ζεῦγος φιλίας, *zeugos philias*). Plutarch, for instance, cites them along with Theseus and Peirithous, Orestes and Pylades, Phintias and Damon, and Epaminondas and Pelopidas (*Amic. mult.* 93e). Each of these five pairs of friends had acquired canonical status by the Greco-Roman period and thus served as models of friendship. For certain streams of Jewish tradition, the friendship between David and Jonathan had a similar status.[5]

In addition to inheriting various *exempla* of friendship from previous ages, the inhabitants of the Greco-Roman world inherited a considerable body of popular, philosophical, and rhetorical literature devoted to friendship. These contained numerous ideas about what constituted friendship and reflections on many of the problems connected with its practice. Already in Homer, for example, one finds the idea that "oneness of mind" is decisive for the existence of friendship, that without a genuine unity of mind and purpose two people cannot truly be friends (*Il.* 4.360–361; 22.262–265; *Ody.* 6.180–185; 15.195–198). The claim that concord (ὁμόνοια, *homonoia, concordia, consensio*) is essential to friendship is frequently repeated in the classical period and had become largely axiomatic by the Greco-Roman period (see, for example, Cicero, *Amic.* 4.15; Dio Chrysostom, *Or.* 4.42; Plutarch, *Amic. mult.* 96e–f; Philo, *Spec.* 1.70). In other cases, later ideas and concerns about friendship were seen as already anticipated by Homer. For instance, the prominent Greco-Roman conviction that frankness of speech (παρρησία, *parrēsia*) is indispensable to friendship was seen as having already been practiced by Patroclus to Achilles (*Il.* 16.21–45).[6] Similarly, the Hellenistic concern with distinguishing the true friend from the pseudo-friend resulted in the identification of certain Homeric characters as parasites and flatterers, not genuine friends (see Athenaeus, *Deipn.* 6.236C–E).

Homer also bequeathed to later generations a concern with certain problems related to friendship. Of these, three may be noted here. First and foremost was the problem of abuse in friendship, seen above all in the case of guest-friendship (ξενία, *xenia*). Paris's seduction of Helen occurred within the context of guest-friendship and led ultimately to the Trojan War. A second problem was the death of a friend, seen particularly in Achilles' response to Patroclus's death. A third problem was the loss and restoration of friendship, dramatized especially in the collapse of friendly relations between Agamemnon and Achilles and all the subsequent efforts to restore amicability between the two warriors. All three of these problems continued to be a concern in subsequent centuries; indeed, reflection on all three continues to this day.

In commenting on friendship, post-Homeric writers in archaic Greece focused especially on the problem of the disloyal and faithless friend. Preoccupation with this problem was doubtless the result of too many instances in which friends had failed to act in a fitting manner. Charges of duplicity, insincerity, anger, betrayal, and bad counsel were common, and various suggestions were offered on how to deal with the failures of one's friends. The problem of the false and unreliable friend is a particular concern in the Theognidea, a corpus of poetry traditionally associated with Theognis of Megara, but it is also seen in other writers, such as Hesiod. As a result of attention to this problem, certain convictions about friendship were crystallized. First, loyalty became a chief criterion in defining friendship, and this characteristic was even celebrated in ancient *skolia* (songs sung at banquets). One of these drinking songs extols the loyal friend with the lyrics: "He who does not betray a man who is his friend has great honor among mortals and gods, in my judgment."[7] The true friend was someone who could be trusted, especially in a time of crisis, and who never left the other in the lurch.

Second, care needed to be exercised in the formation of friendships because it was so easy to make mistakes in the realm of personal relations. To be certain about another person's true character was difficult, if not impossible. As another Athenian drinking song laments, "If only it were possible to know without being deceived what sort of person each man is who is a friend, cutting open his chest, looking into his heart, and locking it up again."[8] Because so many people lacked integrity or acted duplicitously, it was foolish to be indiscriminate in the establishment of friendships; a lack of discernment in regard to friendship was bound to lead to disaster and disappointment. To protect oneself from harm and to enjoy the benefits of friendship, one needed to avoid associations with worthless companions and to cultivate relationships with those who were worthy and least likely to betray one's confidence.

Third, caution and selectivity in forming friendships meant that one individual did not become the friend of another instantaneously but only after a period of time and testing. During that period those worthy of friendship gave proof of their capacity to be trustworthy companions. Fourth, the number of worthy companions with whom one had time to associate was necessarily limited, so one could and should restrict oneself to a few close friends. While many people in archaic and later Greece adopted these convictions about friendship, others continued to establish friendships quickly with a wide circle of people and for various purposes.

The cultural and social context in which friendship is practiced is an important factor in both its definition and scope. "Recent archaeological studies suggest that at the end of the eighth century B.C., Greek society predominantly took the form of small independent communities of fifty families or fewer."[9] The rise of the Greek *polis* was to alter that context decisively, especially in places like classical Athens, which had an estimated population of at least 150,000 people at the outbreak of the Peloponnesian War in 431 B.C.E. The precise effect of urbanization on the theory and practice of friendship is difficult to calculate, but it was likely quite profound.[10] It contributed, among other things, to a politicization of friendship in certain circles, with the cultivation of partisan bonds among those of the same social class and ideological persuasion, and with disloyalty now defined in terms of political treachery. It is perhaps significant that it was Solon, the Athenian politician and poet, "who first associates mistreatment of friends with civil dissension (fr. 4.21–2), and he too who articulates for the first time the ideal of being sweet to one's friends and bitter to one's enemies (13.5)."[11] In short, with the rise of the *polis*, the practice of friendship gained a new political dimension, though the extent of this dimension is sharply debated.[12] Yet one important element of continuity during this transitional period was provided by the meal, where friends gathered together to eat and drink. Indeed, the meal—whether the archaic feast or the classical and Hellenistic supper (δεῖπνον, *deipnon*) followed by the symposium—was a primary *Sitz im Leben* for the establishment and cultivation of friendship in all periods of Greek and Roman history.

The classical period in Greek history saw new ideas about friendship arise as well as elaborations and modifications of traditional ideas. In regard to the latter, for example, the archaic period's concern with the rupture and restoration of friendship was shared by those who lived in the classical city. Experiences in the realm of personal relations caused people who lived in both periods to be highly suspicious of others and thus to counsel moderation in behavior toward both friends and foes. One of the most influential archaic apothegms about friendship was attributed to Bias of Priene, one of the Seven Sages of ancient Greece. It occurs in two basic forms in writers from later periods, one involving friends, and one dealing with both friends and foes. According to the first form, Bias advised others "to love their friends as if they would some day hate them, for most people are evil" (Diogenes Laertius 1.87 [Hicks, LCL, modified]). The second form provides similar counsel about foes: "[A]ccording to the precept of Bias, they love as if they would one day hate, and hate as if they would one day love" (Aristotle, *Rhet.* 2.13.4 [Freese, LCL]). Ancient tradition also attributed to Bias a context in which this change in relationship typically occurred. "He said that he would rather decide a dispute between two of his enemies than between two of his friends; for in the latter case he would be certain to make one of his friends his enemy, but in the former case he would make one of his enemies his friend" (Diogenes Laertius 1.87 [Hicks, LCL]).

These sentiments were adopted and elaborated by classical Greek authors. For example, Euripides has the nurse in his *Hippolytus* apply the Delphic maxim about moderation (265: μηδὲν ἄγαν, *mēden agan*, "nothing in excess") to friendship:

> I have learned much
> from my long life. The mixing bowl of friendship,
> the love of one for the other, must be tempered.
> Love must not touch the marrow of the soul.
> Our affections must be breakable chains that we
> can cast them off or tighten them.[13]

In the storms of life, friendship all too often proved an unreliable harbor in which to take refuge (Sophocles, *Ajax* 683). Friends often became foes, and enemies occasionally became friends (1359). In view of the potential transposition of relations, therefore, the conventional morality of simply helping friends and harming enemies was increasingly viewed as problematic by people in the classical period; the moral dictum should not be applied absolutely, but with a view toward a possible change in relations. The archaic code was not only rejected on ethical grounds by philosophers such as Plato but also exposed as deficient in various ways by playwrights such as Sophocles in his *Ajax*.[14] The latter depicts Ajax as feeling utterly betrayed by the Atreidae, whom he had helped without reservation as their ally and friend (1053). Because his mighty exploits on their behalf have been neither appreciated nor reciprocated but fallen "unloved among the unloving" (620: ἄφιλα παρ' ἀφίλοις, *aphila par' aphilois*) kings, he vows never again to make the same mistake:[15]

> I now know this, that while I hate my enemy
> I must remember that the time may come
> When he will be my friend; as, loving my friend
> And doing him service, I shall not forget
> That he one day may be my enemy. (678–682)[16]

Later in the same play, Sophocles provides an example of the former of these two possibilities. After Ajax has committed suicide, Agamemnon and Menelaus forbid the burial of his body. Teucer, the half-brother of Ajax, defies the Greek leaders by insisting on a proper burial for Ajax. To everyone's surprise, Odysseus steps forward and takes Teucer's side in the dispute and prevails. With permission to bury Ajax now secured, Odysseus speaks the following words to Teucer:

> Teucer,
> I have this to say to you: I am your friend
> Henceforth, as truly as I was your enemy. (1376–1377)

In keeping with his new status, Odysseus offers to assist in the burial (1378–1380). Although Teucer refuses the offer for fear that Ajax would not approve, he has nothing but praise and gratitude for Odysseus, who earlier had been extremely hostile to Ajax (1383), and ends his speech by inviting him to the burial and calling him a good man (1381–1399).

This elaboration and modification of the ancestral wisdom about proper behavior toward friends and foes was embraced by other Greeks (such as Demosthenes, *Or.* 23.122) and became a conventional sentiment. Indeed, centuries later, Philo of Alexandria was still advocating this manner of dealing with friends and enemies: "It is a very admirable saying of the ancients that in joining friendship we should not ignore the possibility of enmity, and conduct our quarrels with future friendship in view" (*Virt.* 152 [Colson, LCL]). But others, such as Scipio Africanus the Younger (*apud* Cicero, *Amic.* 16.59–60) and the Neopythagoreans, attacked the idea of treating friends as potential foes. In doing so, the latter may well have been following Pythagoras, to whom later antiquity attributed the following counsel: "He also directed them to be so disposed in their associations with one another, that they never become enemies to their friends, but become, as quickly as possible, friends to their enemies."[17]

If the attack on Bias's precept does go back to Pythagoras, he was not alone in finding fault with it. Others who criticized it included Aristotle (*Rhet.* 2.21.13–14), who was the first to take all the varying ideas and practices associated with friendship and to subject them to systematic analysis. In discussing friendship, he presupposed the *polis* as the context in which friendship was practiced, and his ideas about friendship, mediated partly through his own works and partly through those of his successor Theophrastus, were enormously influential in shaping subsequent Greek thought on this subject. Given the brevity of this essay, it is obviously impossible to do justice here to Aristotle's treatment, and a few brief remarks must suffice.

First, the word that Aristotle uses to designate friendship is φιλία (*philia*), a word that essentially indicates "affection" or "affectionate attachment." Therefore, while φιλία includes what most people in the twenty-first century usually mean by "friendship," it is much broader and includes other kinds of affectionate relationships, such as that which ideally exists in various kinship relations.[18] The element that is common to all the varieties of φιλία is κοινωνία (*koinōnia*), that is, shared activity and purpose. "All affection (φιλία) consists in partnership (κοινωνία)" (*Eth. nic.* 8.12.1). Without partnership, there can be no affection and thus no friendship. Those who are partners in some common enterprise, such as business, are not necessarily fond of one another, but those who are fond of one another, including those who are friends, participate together in activities of various kinds. Those who are friends will share a common life.

Second, in regard to friendship proper, Aristotle distinguishes three kinds in accordance with what grounds the relationship. The first is grounded in utility, the second has its source in pleasure, and the third is based on virtue. Mutuality is common to all three forms. Unless the affection that arises from usefulness, pleasure, and excellence of character is reciprocated, friendship will not exist. There will only be εὔνοια (*eunoia*), the good will that one individual feels toward another, not friendship. "To be friends, therefore, people must (1) feel good will for each other, that is, wish each other's good, and (2) be aware of each other's good will, and (3) the cause of their good will must be one of the lovable qualities mentioned above," namely, usefulness, pleasure, or character.[19] In short, as with κοινωνία (*koinōnia*), εὔνοια is indispensable to friendship, but good will by itself does not constitute friendship; rather, it marks the inception of friendship.

Third, of the three forms of friendship, the highest is that which is based on mutual admiration of character. "The perfect [τελεία, *teleia*] form of friendship is that between the good, and those who resemble each other in virtue [ἀρητή, *arētē*]" (*Eth. nic.* 8.3.6 [Rackham, LCL]). Those whose friendship is grounded in virtue will experience pleasure in each other's company and will find their relationship to be extremely useful, but the joy and the utility are the consequences of their friendship, not their source. Character friendship is the most permanent form of friendship; those associations grounded in utility or pleasure dissolve more quickly, indeed, as soon as one person ceases to find the other useful or a source of delight. Virtue is infinitely more permanent than pleasure and utility, so friendships grounded in virtue are inherently more stable and long-lasting. Friendships founded on mutual admiration of character can also founder and fail, but only when one of the friends ceases to act virtuously or is discovered to be lacking in virtue. Friendship involves reciprocity, and when friends are able to reciprocate and do not, that failure raises questions about their personal integrity and places the friendship in jeopardy.

Fourth, Aristotle gives emphasis to various features of character friendship. It is, above all, altruistic rather than egoistic; it seeks the good of the friend for the friend's sake and acts in order to promote that good. Because friends seek one another's good, they do not (or at least should not) wrong one another. On the contrary, they help each other morally by not only striving to prevent one another from doing wrong but also by correcting one another when they do err. Furthermore, friends desire the same things, and chief among these is the desire to spend time with each other. As a result of living together, their relationship is marked by concord (ὁμόνοια, *homonia*), equality (ἰσότης, *isotēs*), intimacy (συνήθεια, *synētheia*), and confident trust in one another. Those who are friends are consequently "one soul" (μία ψυχή, *mia psychē*), sharing not only material possessions but also joys and sorrows. In short, a friend is one's *alter ego*, "another self" or "second self," on whose behalf one is willing even to die.

Just as there was both continuity and discontinuity in the understanding and practice of friendship between the archaic and the classical periods, the same is true of the transition from the classical to the Hellenistic and later Roman periods. Many of the old convictions about friendship, such as the need for care in the selection of friends, the prudence of testing potential friends before establishing close relationships with them, and the importance of fidelity as the bond of friendship, remained fixtures in Greco-Roman reflections on friendship, as did attention to the problem of the rupture and restoration of friendship. All these notions and concerns, for instance, appear in Cicero's *On Friendship* (*De amicitia*), the major work on friendship in the Greco-Roman period. Many of them also appear in other extant Greco-Roman discussions of friendship, including those by Arius Didymus, Valerius Maximus, Seneca, Dio Chrysostom, Epictetus, Plutarch, Lucian, Alcinous, Apuleius, Maximus of Tyre, and later writers and orators, including Themistius. Interest in friendship is not restricted to rhetoric and philosophy, for the theme appears in a wide variety of other works, such as histories, letters, novels, inscriptions, and the papyri. In these works some classical ideas about friendship assumed even greater importance. For instance, the common idea that "there is no possession lovelier than a friend" (Menander, *Sent.* 575 Jäkel) and that "a good and sincere friend is the most precious of all possessions" (Xenophon, *Mem.* 2.4.1; see also Euripides, *Orest.* 1155–1158) was developed into the thesis that a friend is a "treasure" (θησαυρός, *thēsauros*). Indeed, a widespread Greco-Roman *chreia* about Alexander the Great has this as its subject: "Alexander the Macedonian king, on being asked by someone where he kept his treasures, pointed to his friends and said: 'In these.' "[20] This same *chreia* appears in the *Progymnasmata* of the orator Libanius, who elaborates it by giving an encomium on friendship and its benefits (see *Progym.* 3, Chreia Elaboration 1).

While there was continuity in certain of the ideas about friendship, the context in which friendship was practiced was markedly different. Politically, one of the major differences was the rise of regional Hellenistic dynasties in the wake of Alexander the Great's triumphs, and later, the emergence of Rome as a world empire. The *polis*, which had served as the presupposition for Aristotle's analysis of

friendship, of course still existed, but it was not only eclipsed in political importance by the rise of these new powers but also internally transformed by them
and other forces. Thanks to increased physical and social mobility, for instance,
the population of the typical Hellenistic *polis* was much more heterogeneous and
transient than its classical predecessor. In this altered context, new phenomena in
regard to friendship began to arise. Two of these call for comment.

First, the Greco-Roman world witnessed the emergence of several kinds of
"unequal" friendships, that is, friendships between people from different socioeconomic groups. This phenomenon was so widespread that "[i]t can probably be
taken for granted that, to the eyes of Romans, the two parties to a friendship
would rarely have looked like equals."[21] This is quite different from what Aristotle had presupposed or envisioned. The philosopher, to be sure, had argued that
the three kinds of φιλία (*philia*, "friendship") exist in relationships of both equality (e.g., citizen-citizen) and inequality (ruler-subject, father-son, husband-wife,
benefactor-beneficiary), but he had denied that those in the latter category are
truly φίλοι (*philoi*, "friends") and illustrated his point by discussing the father's
relationship to his child:

> There being then . . . three kinds of friendship, based on goodness, utility,
> and pleasantness, these are again divided into two, one set being on a
> footing of equality and the other on one of superiority. Though both sets,
> therefore, are friendships [φιλίαι, *philiai*], only when they are on an equal-
> ity [κατὰ τὴν ἰσότητα, *kata tēn isotēta*] are the parties friends [φίλοι, *philoi*];
> for it would be absurd for a man to be a friend [φίλος, *philos*] of a child,
> though he does feel affection [φιλεῖ, *philei*] for him and receive it
> [φιλεῖται, *phileitai*] from him. (*Eth. eud.* 7.4.1–2 [Rackham, LCL])[22]

According to Aristotle, in situations where the friends are socioeconomic
equals, the benefits given and received are regarded by them, over time, as quan-
titatively equal. In unequal friendships, by contrast, there can never be any numerical equality in benefits given and received. There can only be proportionate
equality, "where the superior party bestows more benefit (of whatever kind) than
he receives, and equality is only restored by his receiving [from the inferior party]
more affection than he bestows."[23] The inferior's affection and honor correspond
to the value or worth (ἀξία, *axia*) of the superior's actions, and this proportionate
response by the inferior "establishes equality and preserves the friendship" (*Eth.
nic.* 9.1.1). While both of the partners in an unequal relationship can have affection for each other, they are not, strictly speaking, friends. Aristotle's restriction of
the term "friend" to those in a symmetrical relationship was doubtless influenced
by the ethos of democratic Athens, in which friendship "was a relationship between equals who fiercely resisted any imputation of social or financial dependency. Where long-term labor for hire on a private basis was considered

tantamount to servitude, friendship was constituted as a sphere free of domination and subordination, and in this respect was a paradigm of relations in the democracy."[24]

Aristotle's reluctance to apply the term "friends" to those in an unequal relationship all but vanished in the Greco-Roman period, where such relationships flourished. This happened in part because friendship was now often based not so much on economic parity as on ethical congruence: one chose as friends those whose ideals and morals paralleled one's own.[25] In keeping with this social reality, Greco-Roman authors tended to emphasize the unifying aspects of the unequal relationship. Cicero, for example, "can present friendship as a more or less uniform phenomenon by focusing on the *studia* [pursuits], *mores* [moral habits, character], and *officia* [duties] which unite the partners rather than on status differences which divide them."[26] One conspicuous example of these unequal friendships is to be found in the courts of the Hellenistic rulers, where groups of advisers known as "Friends" conversed with the king and offered him counsel. A second is that which existed between patrons and their clients, a relationship which the Romans often designated as *amicitia* ("friendship").[27] While some of these relationships were doubtless marked more by deferential "friendliness" than by authentic affection, others were much deeper. Indeed, "in Latin sources, language expressing friendship, affection, and love . . . is not subsidiary to some other representation of the relationship, but is itself the preeminent expression of it."[28]

For unequal partners, friendship language has an important social function. By defining the friends' relationship in terms of their common aims, attitudes, and activities, it puts into eclipse their socioeconomic differences. As Peter White perceptively notes, "In a Roman context, the emphasis on friendship serves to blunt the consciousness which each of the two parties has of belonging to a particular lineage, census-class, or order, and to refocus attention on particular pursuits and ideals which they share."[29] However great the difference between them in social status and wealth, they are affectionate collaborators within their shared sphere of aspirations, activities, and values.

Furthermore, in support of the potential for people of a different socioeconomic status to become true friends, Greco-Roman writers could point not only to instances from the Roman Republic (e.g., Cic., *Amic.* 19.69) but also to the unequal pairs in the traditional canon of famous Greek friends. Patroclus, for example, was the henchman or squire (θεράπων, *therapōn*) of his lord Achilles and thus hardly his true equal (Homer, *Il.* 23.89–90). In a similar way, Pylades was not the equal of Orestes, and the economic disparity between Pelopidas and Epaminondas was enormous; the former was wealthy whereas the latter was poor (Plut., *Pel.* 3). The same inequality holds true in an even more striking way for that most famous pair of ancient Israelite friends, David and Jonathan. At the time of their friendship, Jonathan was the son of King Saul, and David was the king's servant, not yet king himself. Josephus, in recounting the story of their oaths of "life-long mutual affection and fidelity" (*A.J.* 6.275), makes a point of having David speak to prince Jonathan "of that friendship for which you have seen fit to receive pledges from me and to grant me the like yourself, though you are the master, and I your servant" (*A.J.* 6.228 [Thackeray and Marcus, LCL, modified]).

Second, the Greco-Roman period witnessed the emergence of the "flatterer" as a key problem in the practice of friendship. The appearance of this figure as a central concern was related to the flourishing of unequal friendships in the post-classical period. The flatterer was viewed as a socioeconomic inferior who feigned friendship with his superior in order to exploit the latter. In response to this problem, moralists of the period endeavored to give the rich and powerful advice on how they might differentiate the flatterer from the true friend. One of the standard means for distinguishing between the two was παρρησία (*parrēsia*) or "frankness of speech." Whereas the flatterer tended to lavish praise and to avoid criticism in his dealing with his "friends," the true friend was valued as someone who was willing to speak frankly to his companions when the latter merited candid criticism and could profit from it. Such candor was the mark of both sincerity and affection, and therefore the hallmark of friendship.

The invocation of frank speech (παρρησία, *parrēsia*) as the touchstone of genuine φιλία (*philia*, "friendship") marked a major departure from its use in classical Athens, where it was a sign of freedom and a civic right; by speaking his mind freely and fearlessly, a free man was exercising both his right and his responsibility as a citizen. It was a right forfeited by exiles and never attained by slaves. In the Greco-Roman period, however, frankness of speech also became an indispensable private virtue that was practiced and encouraged within the philosophical schools as a moral obligation on the part of friends. Its use was appropriate to all forms of friendship, not just unequal ones, because it was hailed as an effective therapeutic method in dealing with the passions (πάθη, *pathē*), which were a chief area of philosophical concern. Individuals who were prone to anger, could not control their desires, or were paralyzed by grief over the death of a friend were engaged in conduct that was self-destructive. Genuine friends could not sit idly by and let that happen to people for whom they cared. By speaking candidly to their angry or grieving companions, true friends hoped to persuade them to cease from their ruinous behavior and thereby to improve the quality of their lives. Although those who used frank speech ran the risk of angering their friends and jeopardizing the friendship, their willingness to do so was crucial to their friends' fulfilling their potential as individuals. Without self-control in regard to the passions, there could be no moral or spiritual progress (προκοπή, *prokopē*); indeed, without frank speech, there would only be regress in the moral and spiritual life.

In short, in the Greco-Roman world both παρρησία (*parrēsia*, "frankness of speech") and προκοπή (*prokopē*, "progress") belong to the same linkage group as φιλία (*philia*, "friendship"). The same is true of a host of other terms and concepts, such as κοινωνία (*koinōnia*) and all that implies, such as partnership in common projects, the sharing of possessions, participation in one another's experiences of joy and sorrow, and, of course, reciprocity. Other terms belonging to friendship's linkage group include ἀρητή (*arētē*, "virtue"), εὔνοια (*eunoia*, "good will"), ἰσότης (*isotēs*, "equality"), συνήθεια (*synētheia*, "intimacy"), and ὁμόνοια (*homonoia*, "oneness of mind"), including the various ways in which this was expressed, such as having μία ψυχή (*mia psychē*, "one soul"). Especially important also are the various terms for fidelity (such as πίστις, *pistis*), for the friend's faithfulness, as demonstrated over time and in countless tests, means that he or she is someone who has been fully attested (δόκιμος, *dokimos*) as worthy (ἄξιος, *axios*) of another's trust; consequently, such a person can be relied on not to betray or to abandon one's confidence (πεποίθησις, *pepoithēsis*, "trust," "confidence").

Similarly, friendship's linkage group includes the host of terms that indicate the true friend's sincerity and integrity in both word and deed. Even flattery (κολακεία, *kolakeia*), though it stands outside acceptable practices among friends, is linked to the group by negative association, by defining what friendship is not. Indeed, there are other key terms, less obvious than flattery but no less important, that also belong to friendship's linkage group. These include the terms for self-sufficiency (αὐτάρκεια, *autarkeia*) and reconciliation (καταλλαγή, *katallagē*, διαλλαγή, *diallagē*), whose importance for the ancient understanding of friendship is indicated in the following part of this essay.

Friendship was thus a highly vibrant social institution in the Greco-Roman world, one whose great importance evoked comment by both Jews and Gentiles. No one in that world who was concerned for ethical obligation and the moral or spiritual life could have failed to take seriously the ways in which friendship was practiced and the ideas associated with it. Indeed, those who reflected on friendship were themselves involved in friendships of various kinds. Not only Paul but also his converts and colleagues belonged to this group, and Paul's interactions with his contemporaries helped him refine his notions of friendship within the Christian community.

Part II. Paul and Friendship

Because the terms φιλία (*philia*, "friendship") and φίλος (*philos*, "friend") do not occur in the Pauline corpus, some have wrongly inferred that friendship was not an important factor in the apostle's work. It is often said in this connection that Paul prefers kinship language to characterize relations within the Christian community. That is, of course, true, but it misses two important points: kinship was a widely recognized kind of φιλία, and kinship terms were often used to describe friendship, not lineage. It is thus more accurate to say that Paul's use of affect-laden language is more frequent with kinship than with friendship proper.

But terminology associated with the latter does occur in Paul, who uses it as both a complement and a substitute for kinship language. Nor is Paul alone in using the language of both fraternity and friendship; pagan authors such as Dio Chrysostom do the same (*Or.* 38.11, 15, 22, 45–47). Three additional points merit emphasis at the outset. First, letters were the chief means by which friends who were apart from each other endeavored to overcome their physical separation and to preserve each other's good will. Furthermore, letters functioned as the means by which they fulfilled their obligations as friends, offering each other counsel, consolation, and exhortation. Paul's letters do precisely that. Second, some of the standard ancient definitions and descriptions of friendship occur in his letters. For example, Paul makes use of the "one soul" (μία ψυχή, *mia psychē*) definition of friendship in Phil 1:27, where he exhorts the Philippians to strive side by side "with one soul," that is, as friends. Third, although the word φιλία (*philia*, "friendship") does not occur in Paul's correspondence, many of the terms or concepts in its linkage group do. The most frequent of these linked terms is κοινωνία (*koinōnia*, "partnership"), which is also, as we have seen, a standard component in the definition of friendship. Regarding exegetical method, the presence of a term from a particular linkage group should alert one to the possibility that associated ideas may be present. When several terms from the same linkage group are present in a text, the probability is strong that linked notions are also implicitly at work.

An instance where Paul uses multiple terms associated with friendship will serve to illustrate the point. The passage is Phil 4:10–20, in which Paul begins by conveying his joy at the Philippians' expression of concern for him (τὸ ὑπὲρ ἐμοῦ φρονεῖν, *to hyper emou phronein*, 4:10). Such concern was not only a quintessential element of the care friends were expected to exercise for one another but also one of the chief practical reasons why having many friends was viewed as problematic. Paul uses the imperfect tense of the verb φρονεῖν (ἐφρονεῖτε, *ephroneite*, "you were concerned") to assert that the Philippians' concern was long-standing, but he switches to the aorist of another verb (ἀναθάλλειν, *anathallein*, "to bloom again") to express his joy at its most recent manifestation.

In keeping with the cultural penchant to use agricultural and horticultural imagery to describe both friendship and its services, he says that the Philippians' concern has now "bloomed again" (ἀνεθάλετε, *anethalete*). Later in this pericope (4:17) he uses the word "fruit" (καρπὸν, *karpon*), another horticultural image, to describe the interest that accrues to their "account" (4:17). Like other writers, Paul thus mixes agricultural and commercial language when discussing friendship. A second instance of this commercial terminology occurs in 4:15, where he uses the language of credits and debits, of "giving and receiving," to describe his interaction with his friends at Philippi. Since the time of Aristotle, friendship had been commonly viewed as an exchange relationship, and Paul's use of this terminology reflects the reciprocal nature of the relationship that he enjoys with the Philippians.

Indeed, Paul points to the inaugural period of their friendship by recalling how they had already sent similar gifts to him in Thessalonica, doing so on more than one occasion (4:15–16). The Philippians' κοινωνία (*koinōnia*, "partnership") with him is not only unique (4:15) but also has stood the test of time, the mark of any true friendship. It is true that there had been no recent gesture by the Philippians, but far from reproaching them for any neglect on their part (which would have violated the ethics of friendship), he graciously notes that until now they had no opportunity (ἠκαιρεῖσθε, *ēkaireisthe*) to express their care (4:10). By mentioning their lack of opportunity, he invokes one of the widely recognized reasons for a friend to be slow in repaying a benefit (see, for instance, Seneca, *Ben.* 4.40.3: "I am not responsible for the delay if I lack either the opportunity or the means" [Basore, LCL]).

The concentration of friendship terms in 4:10 leads in 4:11 to Paul's denial of need and assertion of self-sufficiency. Both of these concepts played a significant role in discussions of friendship. Need was a widely viewed ground of φιλία (*philia*), connected especially with utilitarian kinds of friendships. But many philosophers, such as Aristotle and the Stoics, denied that it was the basis for true friendship, reserving that distinction for virtue. In denying that he is in need, Paul is rejecting any suggestion that his friendship with the Philippians is utilitarian. In asserting his self-sufficiency, he broaches the issue of how φιλία is related to αὐτάρκεια (*autarkeia*, "self-sufficiency"), a concept that had been firmly linked to friendship since the time of Aristotle. Both were widely lauded as moral values, yet their precise relation was problematic because they were viewed as logically in tension with each other. Paul follows in the train of those philosophers (like Cicero and Seneca) who wanted to assert both friendship and self-sufficiency, but he departs from them by grounding both phenomena in God, the former implicitly and the latter explicitly.

He does so in 4:12 by means of a catalog of vicissitudes, a form of the *peristasis* catalog that gives both favorable and unfavorable circumstances in life and indicates how an individual responds to drastically different situations as well as to fluctuation in fortune itself. The theme of vicissitude looms large in discussions of friendship, being closely tied to the conviction that friends share one another's lives. To do so necessarily entails sharing each other's joys and sorrows, the inevitable ups and downs of human existence. Friends are important in times of prosperity, for they sweeten life and make it more pleasant. Yet they are crucial in times of adversity. Indeed, friendship, like virtue, is particularly associated with adversity. Prosperity tends to hide the worthless, the lucky, and the charlatan, but adversity lifts the veil and reveals all such people for what and who they are. Therefore, just as adversity is virtue's opportunity, so is the plight of a friend. Adverse circumstances constitute a test—of the individual's character and of the friend's loyalty. The base person is crushed by adversity and the feckless friend leaves one in the lurch, but the person of integrity stands firm in the midst of life's fiercest storms, and the genuine friend loyally shares another's dangers and humiliations. Valerius Maximus is thus typical of ancient thought when he says, "Truly loyal friends are most recognized in time of trouble, when whatever is rendered proceeds entirely from steady goodwill" (4.7 praef. [Shackleton Bailey, LCL]).

That the Philippians have not abandoned Paul in the time of his affliction (4:14; cf. 1:12–19) is thus glowing proof of the reality of their friendship with the apostle and their continuing joint participation (κοινωνία, koinōnia) with him in the gospel. Yet it is not to his friends in Philippi that Paul attributes his capacity to experience the vicissitudes of life. He rejoices in their loyalty and he praises them for having acted appropriately (4:14), but he denies that their gift is what sustains him and that their relationship is what empowers him. The enabling power he attributes to God (4:13; cf. 1:19d), who uses godly wealth to satisfy both Paul's own need and that of his Philippian friends (4:19). In short, Paul here (as well as elsewhere) attributes to God the role that others assign to virtue and friendship.

The claim that Paul regards God as his friend is controversial, as is the assertion that he views the church as a community of friends. Yet the evidence of the apostle's letters can sustain both claims. Their chief basis is Paul's use of the term "reconciliation" (καταλλαγή, katallagē) to describe God's action in Christ.[30] As previously noted, the words "friendship," "enmity," and "reconciliation" belong to the same linkage group. The basic meaning of both καταλλάσσειν (katallassein) and διαλλάσσειν (diallassein) is "to change from enmity to friendship."[31] They are commonly used to mark both the inception of friendship between those previously hostile to one another and the resumption of friendship between those whose affectionate bonds had been ruptured. It is thus not surprising that Hesychius of Alexandria gives φιλία ("friendship") as one of the two meanings he offers for καταλλαγή ("reconciliation"). Similarly, he defines ἀδιάλλακτος (adiallaktos, "irreconcilable") as ἀφιλίωτος (aphiliōtos, "not to be made a friend of"), and gives φίλον ποιῆσαι (philon poiēsai, "to make a friend") as the meaning of the verb ἀποκαταλλάξαι (*apokatallaxai*, "to reconcile"), the deutero-Pauline verb used for reconciliation (Eph 2:16; Col 1:20, 22).[32]

As a lexicographer, Hesychius is only making explicit what was everywhere assumed in the Greek-speaking world and had been axiomatic for centuries. Already in the *Symposium*, for instance, Plato has Aristophanes argue that in order to avoid harm and attain bliss, humans ought to be pious toward the gods. Whoever acts otherwise "is hateful to the gods" (θεοῖς ἀπεχθάνεται, *theois apechthanetai*); "if," on the other hand, "we become dear to [φίλοι, *philoi*] and are reconciled with the god" (διαλλαγέντες τῷ θεῷ, *diallagentes tō theō*), we shall have the felicity of finding our true loves (193B). The same connection between terms for reconciliation and words for friendship appears centuries later in Dio Chrysostom. In a speech on ὁμόνοια (*homonia*), Dio says that concord "is both friendship [φιλία, *philia*] and reconciliation [καταλλαγή, *katallagē*] and kinship, and it embraces all these" (*Or.* 38.11). In another speech on ὁμόνοια (*homonia*), this one dealing with the need for concord between his native city of Prusa and the neighboring city of Apameia, Dio says, "I did not go to them or speak any word of human kindness in anticipation of the official reconciliation [καταλλαγῆναι, *katallagēnai*] of the city and the establishment of your friendship [φίλους, *philous*] with them"; rather than act independently, "I preferred to make friends [φίλος, *philos*] with them along with you" (*Or.* 40.16).[33]

The same close connection between terms for friendship, enmity, and reconciliation appears in a speech of debated authorship and date that most likely derives from the Second Sophistic (ca. 60–230 C.E.) and that the manuscript tradition attributes to the famous Herodes Atticus (ca. 110–177 C.E.). Here the speaker denounces his adversary (apparently Archelaus of Macedon), declaring that "this man will never be our friend [φίλον, *philon*], nor will there be a reconciliation [διαλλαγήν, *diallagēn*] of that man with us. For although he has not been injured by us, he is our enemy [ἐχθρὸς, *echthros*], wishing to injure us" (*On Government* 6).

Given this nexus of ideas, it is not surprising that the terms for friendship and reconciliation are often used as synonyms in accounts that depict the process of negotiating a truce between hostile camps. For example, in book 2 of his *Roman Antiquities*, which depicts conflicts between the Sabines and the Romans, Dionysius of Halicarnassus uses synonymously such expressions as "to bring together the nations into one and establish friendship" (συνάξειν εἰς ἓν τὰ ἔθνη καὶ ποιήσειν φιλίαν, *synaxein eis hen ta ethnē kai poiēsein philian*: 2.45.3), "to bring together the nations into friendship" (εἰς φιλίαν συνάξουσι τὰ ἔθνη, *eis philian synaxousi ta ethnē*: 2.45.4), "to make the reconciliation" (ποιεῖσθαι τὰς διαλλαγάς, *poieisthai tas diallagas*: 2.46.1), and to form a "treaty of friendship" (συνθῆκαι περὶ φιλίας, *synthēkai peri philias*: 2.46.1). Later in 5.49.2, he says that "the Sabines sent ambassadors . . . to treat for friendship [φιλίας, *philias*], . . . and after many entreaties obtained with difficulty a reconciliation [διαλλαγὰς, *diallagas*]."[34]

Similarly, in book 3 Dionysius recounts the story of a conflict between the Albans and the Romans. The Alban leader Fufetius takes the initiative in trying to bring about a reconciliation (καταλλαγὰς, *katallagas*: 3.5.4) and friendship (φιλίας, *philias*: 3.7.5), arguing that the grounds for dissolving "so great a friendship [τοσαύτην φιλίαν, *tosautēn philian*]" had been far too trivial (3.7.3). He calls for laying aside their mutual enmity (τὰ κοινὰ ἔχθη, *ta koina echthē*: 3.8.3, 5) and offers two options for their reconciliation. The first would grant amnesty to everyone and the second would require punishment for those individuals who were found guilty of inflicting injury. Fufetius recommends the first option: "For my part, I hold that mutual reconciliation [διαλλαγὰς, *diallagas*] is the best and the most becoming to kinsmen and friends [φίλοις, *philois*], in which there is no rancor nor remembrance of past injuries, but a general and sincere remission of everything that has been done or suffered on both sides" (3.8.4). Tullus, the Roman king, agrees with his recommendation, arguing that the Romans "will forgive every injury and offence we have received from the city of Alba" and will no longer have any memory of past injuries (3.9.2, 3). But Tullus is not simply concerned with "how we may dissolve our present enmity [ἔχθραν, *echthran*] toward one another," but also with how the two cities may preserve their friendship in the future. He thus proposes taking various steps to ensure "that we may be friends [φίλοι, *philoi*] both now and for all time" (3.9.3).

The same connection between friendship and reconciliation appears in Jewish writers as well. Sirach (22:20), for instance, recognizes that "one who reviles a friend [φίλον, *philon*] destroys friendship [φιλίαν, *philian*]," but he does not believe that abusive speech should forever rupture the relationship. Therefore, he exhorts his readers, "If you open your mouth against a friend [φίλον, *philon*], do not worry, for reconciliation [διαλλαγή, *diallagē*] is possible" (22:22). For Philo this linkage is also axiomatic. In discussing Joseph's reconciliation with his brothers, he notes that "his brethren will make with him covenants of reconciliation [καταλλακτηρίους, *katallaktērious*], changing their hatred [τὸ μῖσος, *to misos*] to friendship [φιλίαν, *philian*], their ill-will to good-will" (*Somn.* 2.108 [Colson, LCL]).

In short—in theory if not always fully in actual practice—reconciliation brings about a change of both affection and relationship. It marks the end of hatred and the inception or return of affection. Good will replaces ill will, and with that change, enemies are transformed into friends. As noted previously, there was a widespread ideal that one should treat enemies moderately so as not to preclude the possibility of becoming friends in the future. Indeed, that ideal was so widespread that it had become a proverb: "our friendships should be immortal, but mortal our enmities" (*amicitias immortales, mortales inimicitias debere esse*: Livy

40.46.12 [Sage and Schlesinger, LCL]). Furthermore, in philosophical circles, the emphasis on nonretaliation was often part of a strategy designed to bring about both reconciliation with one's enemy and his moral transformation. Among those who stressed the transformation of enemies into friends were the Neopythagoreans, who did so as part of their emphasis on universal φιλία (*philia*, "friendship"). In his *Preambles to the Laws*, for example, Zaleucus argued that "no one should consider anyone of the citizens whom the laws allow to participate in the rights of citizenship, an irreconcilable enemy" (ἐχθρὸν ἀκατάλλακτον, *echthron akatallakton*).[35] Accordingly, he is said to have urged that

> they should consider no one of their fellow citizens as an enemy [ἐχθρὸν, *echthron*] with whom there can be no reconciliation [ἀκατάλλακτον, *akatallakton*], but that the quarrel [ἔχθραν, *echthran*] be entered into with the thought that they will again come to agreement and friendship [φιλίαν, *philian*]; and that the one who acts otherwise should be considered by his fellow citizens to be savage and untamed of soul.[36]

Given the widespread linkage between friendship, enmity, and reconciliation, Paul's depiction of God's action in Christ is revealing. God acted "while we were enemies" (ἐχθροί, *echthroi*), at a time of human hostility to the divine. That inimical relationship has now been terminated, for "we were reconciled [κατηλλάγημεν, *katēllagēmen*] to God through the death of his son" (Rom 5:10). This is paradigmatically the case in regard to Paul himself, profoundly transformed from adversary to envoy by the action of "God, who reconciled [καταλλάξαντος, *katallaxantos*] us to himself through Christ and gave us the ministry of reconciliation [καταλλαγῆς, *katallagēs*]" (2 Cor 5:18).

Inherent in the use of such terminology is the implication that God has transformed Paul into his friend and entrusted him with the task of bringing God's gift of friendship to others. The terms of reconciliation offered by God are, to use the language of Fufetius and Tullus, "the best and the most magnanimous" (Dionysius of Halicarnassus, *Rom. ant.* 3.8.4; 3.9.2), for God grants a blanket amnesty to all who will accept the offer of friendship, "not counting their trespasses against them" (2 Cor 5:19). To be reconciled to God (2 Cor 5:20) means concretely to become the friend of God. Of all the unequal friendships of the Greco-Roman world, friendship with God was the most extreme and important example. In a world in which friends were counted as treasures, Paul's designation of his gospel as a "treasure" (2 Cor 4:7) may well derive from the notion that it centered on God's act and offer of friendship.

In establishing friendship with the world, both God and Christ have gone far beyond what was ordinarily imagined. To emphasize this fact, Paul invokes the idea—common in theory but rare in practice—that friends are willing to die for each other. "Indeed, rarely will anyone die for a righteous person—though perhaps for a good person someone might actually dare to die" (Rom 5:7). The highest ideals of human friendship thus pale in comparison to what God has done through Christ's death for ungodly, hostile sinners (5:6, 8, 10). This extraordinary feat is evidence to Paul of God's unfathomable love (5:8; cf. Rom 11:33–36, esp. v. 35), which is the ultimate ground of human friendship with God.

While the manifestation of this love is exceptional, the linking of friendship with love is not. In both Greek and Latin, the words for love and friendship are cognates, and love is often seen as the fount of friendship. Cicero, for instance, says that "it is love [amor], from which the word 'friendship' [amicitia] is derived, that leads to the establishing of goodwill" (Amic. 8.26).[37] Paul's radical claim thus builds upon a common cultural connection.

God's friendship with Paul underlies other passages in Paul's correspondence. For example, it plays a part in his depiction of God's absolute fidelity. Friends, as Aristotle says, do not abandon (μὴ ἐγκαταλείποντας, mē enkataleipontas) each other (Rhet. 2.4.26), especially in adversity. Similarly, Paul asserts in his peristasis catalog of 2 Cor 4 that he has not been left in the lurch (οὐκ ἐγκαταλειπόμενοι, ouk enkataleipomenoi), namely, by God as his faithful divine friend (2 Cor 4:9). Even Paul's paradoxical style here and in 2 Cor 6 recalls one of Cicero's descriptions of the paradoxes of friendship: "Wherefore friends, though absent are at hand; though in need, yet abound; though weak, are strong; and—harder saying still—though dead, are yet alive" (Amic. 7.23). That Paul was still strong whenever he was weak (2 Cor 12:10) was due to God's friendship with him.

Paul's interactions with all of his churches reflect, to varying degrees, the conviction that God has established in Christ a community of friends. Within this sphere, differences of ethnicity, social status, and gender are put into eclipse, for all are one in Christ (Gal 3:28) and share in God a common father and friend.[38] Given the socioeconomic diversity within Pauline communities, it was imperative to stress elements of commonality, and friendship language was useful in identifying what Christians shared. That such language is especially prominent in Philippians was to be expected. Philippi was the apostle's first European church, and if, as it is likely, Philippians is a single letter written during Paul's Roman imprisonment, it reflects more than a decade of interactions as friends. Yet even 1 Thessalonians, written less than a year after the founding of the church in Thessalonica, employs a friendly parenetic style, contains language from friendship's linkage group, such as flattery (2:5) and frankness of speech (2:2), and addresses perennial problems in friendship, such as physical separation from each other (2:17–3:10) and the death of dear friends (4:13–5:11). Galatians, written at a moment when Paul's friendship with the Galatians was in danger of being ruptured, contains a moving appeal that is replete with friendship terminology (4:12–20).

His Corinthian correspondence is even more so. The presupposition with which he addresses the problem of communal division in 1 Corinthians, for instance, is that of ὁμόνοια (*homonia*, "oneness of mind"), that friends have the same mind and the same opinion (1:10). Later in the letter he quotes Menander's warning about the deleterious consequences of forming friendships with the wrong kinds of people (15:33). As subsequent events in that city demonstrate, the Corinthians failed to heed that warning; they formed friendships with Christians who were hostile to Paul and raised doubts about his character and the nature of his friendship with the Corinthian church. One factor involved was Paul's staunch refusal, contrary to the norms of friendship and to his own practice with the Philippians, to accept financial support from the Corinthians (9:1–23). Thus in 2 Corinthians he must confront the charge that he, like Gnatho in Terence's play *The Eunuch* (2.12.21; see also Cic., *Amic.* 25.93–94), is not a sincere or constant friend, but rather someone whose "yes" and "no" vacillates with the occasion (2 Cor 1:17). He responds by stressing his integrity and sincerity as a person (1:12; 2:17), opening up his heart (6:11) to show that he is neither a fawning, fickle flatterer nor a power-mongering tyrant lording over their faith (1:24).[39] He is instead their collaborator and friend, fully attested (δοκιμή, *dokimē*, "proof") by God and entrusted with God's gospel, and he speaks to them as befits a true friend, with full παρρησία (*parrēsia*, "frankness of speech": 3:12).

The way in which Paul writes to Philemon presupposes that they are involved in a reciprocal relationship, that Paul has received great joy and comfort from Philemon (7) and that Philemon owes him a great deal, including his own self (19). Paul even uses the practice of mutual benefaction in friendship to craft a pun involving the name of Onesimus ("beneficial"), who now truly merits the name (11). Inasmuch as Philemon owes Paul his very self, Paul asks his friend to reciprocate by giving him the "benefit" (20) he wants, namely, Onesimus himself.

Finally, in Romans, though he writes to churches that he has never visited, Paul still makes use of friendship language, especially in chapter 12. Here, among other exhortations, he urges the Romans to share one another's lives by rejoicing with those who rejoice and weeping with those who weep (12:15). It is not simply because he has old friends in Rome (16:3–15) that he can make use of friendship language. More fundamentally, it is because he presumes that, owing to God's reconciling activity in Christ (5:6–10), all Christians are implicitly friends, even those who have not yet met one another. In this regard, Christian friendship resembles that among the Neopythagoreans, who regarded each other as friends even when they had not met and even undertook to assist financially their unseen friends (see esp. Iamblichus, *VP* 237–239).

The most conspicuous Christian counterpart to the expression of friendship among those who do not yet know one another is the Gentile collection for the Jerusalem church, an endeavor uppermost in Paul's mind when he writes to the churches in both Rome and Corinth. For Paul, there is no greater expression of Christian friendship, of the unity and equity in Christ, than the collection. Involving κοινωνία (koinōnia, "partnership"), reciprocity (Rom 15:27), and ἰσότης (isotēs, "equality": 2 Cor 8:13–14), it both symbolizes and actualizes what it means to be friends in Christ.

Part III. Other Relevant Pauline and Paulinist Texts

The following list of passages is suggestive rather than exhaustive:

Rom 1:9–15; 5:6–11; 12:9–21; 15:1–7, 14, 22–32; 16:1–2, 3–16, 17–23

1 Cor 1–4; 5; 6:1–8; 9:1–23; 11:17–34; 15:33

2 Cor 1:3–7, 12–14, 15–24; 2:1–10, 17; 3:12; 4:7–9; 5:18–20; 6:11–13, 14–18; 7:2–4, 7; 8:13–14; 10–13

Gal 4:12–20; 6:1–2

Eph 2:14–18

Phil 1:21–26, 27, 30; 2:2, 6–11, 25–30; 3:18; 4:1–3, 10–20

Col 1:20–22

1 Thess 2:2, 5, 9, 17; 3:6–8; 4:9–12, 13–18; 5:3, 11, 12–15

2 Thess 3:13–15

Phlm 7, 9–14, 17, 19–20

Part IV. Bibliography

Fitzgerald, J. T., ed. *Friendship, Flattery, and Frankness of Speech: Studies on Friendship in the New Testament World*. NovTSup 82. Leiden: Brill, 1996.

_____. *Greco-Roman Perspectives on Friendship*. SBLRBS 34. Atlanta: Scholars Press, 1997.

Konstan, David. *Friendship in the Classical World*. Key Themes in Ancient History. Cambridge: Cambridge University Press, 1997.

Marshall, Peter. *Enmity in Corinth: Social Conventions in Paul's Relations with the Corinthians*. WUNT 2.23. Tübingen: Mohr Siebeck, 1987.

Peachin, Michael, ed. *Aspects of Friendship in the Graeco-Roman World: Proceedings of a Conference Held at the Seminar für Alte Geschichte, Heidelberg, on 10–11 June, 2000*. Journal of Roman Archaeology Supplementary Series 43. Portsmouth, R.I.: Journal of Roman Archaeology, 2001.

Notes

1. My understanding of the history of friendship in the ancient Mediterranean world has been highly influenced by the work of David Konstan and other members of the SBL's Hellenistic Moral Philosophy and Early Christianity Section, and I draw freely on their studies in writing this essay. See esp. David Kon-

stan, *Friendship in the Classical World* (Key Themes in Ancient History; Cambridge: Cambridge University Press, 1997), and the two volumes that I have had the honor of editing: *Friendship, Flattery, and Frankness of Speech: Studies on Friendship in the New Testament World* (NovTSup 82; Leiden: Brill, 1996), and *Greco-Roman Perspectives on Friendship* (SBLRBS 34; Atlanta: Scholars Press, 1997). The reader is referred to these three volumes for fuller discussion and documentation of many of the ideas presented in this study.

2. J. A. Simpson and E. S. C. Weiner, eds., *The Oxford English Dictionary* (2d ed.; 20 vols.; Oxford: Clarendon, 1989), 8:996 (s.v. "linkage"), citing *Chambers's Techn. Dict.*

3. Konstan, *Friendship in the Classical World*, 9.

4. Ibid., 19. Konstan's claim about the normal meaning of substantive φίλος (*philos*, "friend") does *not* extend to the verb φιλέω (*phileō*, "to love," "to have affection for," "to be a friend to") and the noun φιλία (*philia*, "affection," "friendship"), both of which have a much broader semantic range than the notion of friendship. See ibid., 9, 12, and 55–56.

5. See, for example, Josephus, *A.J.* 6.206, 225, 228, 236, 239, 276; 7.111.

6. Plutarch, *Adul. am.* 67a. See also 66f–67a for Odysseus speaking frankly to Agamemnon.

7. 908 Page = Athenaeus, *Deipn.* 15.695F. The translation is that of Konstan, *Friendship in the Classical World*, 45. References to the Attic *skolia* are cited according to D. L. Page, ed., *Poetae Melici Graeci* (Oxford: Clarendon, 1962).

8. 889 Page = Athenaeus, *Deipn.* 15.694D–E. The translation is a modified version of that given by Konstan, *Friendship in the Classical World*, 45. According to Eustathius, "This scolion comes from a Fable of Aesop, in which Momus finds fault with Prometheus because when he made man he did not add gates to the breast so that when they were opened we might see his heart, but allowed him to be a dissembler" (1574.18 [Edmonds, LCL; rev. ed.]).

9. Konstan, *Friendship in the Classical World*, 26.

10. The effect of the *polis* on the practice of guest-friendship is debated. For the view that citizens' obligations to their own city-states conflicted sharply with their obligations to their guest-friends, see Gabriel Herman, *Ritualised Friendship and the Greek City* (Cambridge: Cambridge University Press, 1987). For a different view, see Konstan, *Friendship in the Classical World*, 83–87.

11. Konstan, *Friendship in the Classical World*, 48–49.

12. The politicization of friendship is seen already in the Theognidea, as Konstan (ibid., 51–52) persuasively argues. He denies, however, that friendship had a central role in Athenian democratic politics (60–67). For a quite different view of the role of friendship in politics, see W. R. Connor, *The New Politicians of Fifth-Century Athens* (Princeton: Princeton University Press, 1971), and Horst Hutter, *Politics as Friendship: The Origins of Classical Notions of Politics in the Theory and Practice of Friendship* (Waterloo, Ontario: Wilfrid Laurier University Press, 1978). See also B. S. Strauss, *Athens after the Peloponnesian War: Class, Faction, and Policy, 403–386 BC* (Ithaca, N.Y.: Cornell University Press, 1986), 20–31.

13. Euripides, *Hipp.* 252–257. The translation is that of David Grene in *Euripides I* (ed. D. Grene and R. Lattimore; The Complete Greek Tragedies; Chicago: University of Chicago Press, 1955), 173.

14. For the philosophic rejection of the conventional morality, see J. T. Fitzgerald, *Cracks in an Earthen Vessel: An Examination of the Catalogues of Hardships in the Corinthian Correspondence* (SBLDS 99; Atlanta: Scholars Press, 1988), 103–7. For Sophocles' treatment of this moral code in his *Ajax,* see esp. Bernard Knox, *Word and Action: Essays on the Ancient Theater* (Baltimore: Johns Hopkins University Press, 1979), 125–60, and M. W. Blundell, *Helping Friends and Harming Enemies: A Study in Sophocles and Greek Ethics* (Cambridge: Cambridge University Press, 1989), 60–105.

15. See Malcolm Heath, *The Poetics of Greek Tragedy* (Stanford, Calif.: Stanford University Press, 1987), 188.

16. Except for line 620, all translations of Sophocles' *Ajax* are those of E. F. Watling, *Sophocles: Electra and Other Plays* (Harmondsworth, England: Penguin, 1953).

17. Iamblichus, *VP* 40. The translation is that of John Dillon and Jackson Hershbell, *Iamblichus, "On the Pythagorean Way of Life": Text, Translation, and Notes* (SBLTT 29; Atlanta: Scholars Press, 1991), 65. See also Diogenes Laertius 8.23: "and so to behave one to another as not to make friends into enemies, but to turn enemies into friends" (Hicks, LCL). Neopythagoreans emphasized the transformation of enemies into friends, but the idea was not unique to them; see, for instance, the *chreia* in *Gnom. Vat.* 82 (p. 38 Sternbach): "Alexander, on being asked what kind of king seemed to be the best, said: 'The one who keeps his friends with gifts and who makes friends of his enemies through benefactions'" (trans. R. F. Hock). For the latter, see Ronald F. Hock and Edward N. O'Neil, *The Chreia in Ancient Rhetoric* (SBLTT 27; Atlanta: Scholars Press, 1986), 6. See also Dionysius of Halicarnassus, *Ant. rom.* 5.30.2, and for the idea of renouncing our friends when they harm us and becoming friends with our enemies when they bestow benefits on us, see *Ant. rom.* 8.34.2.

18. See Konstan, *Friendship in the Classical World,* 68–72.

19. Arist., *Eth. nic.* 8.2.4 (Rackham, LCL, modified).

20. The first extant appearance of this *chreia* is in Theon, who probably wrote in the second half of the first century C.E. For other authors who quote this *chreia,* see Hock and O'Neil, *Chreia in Ancient Rhetoric,* 302. I have slightly modified their translation.

21. Peter White, *Promised Verse: Poets in the Society of Augustan Rome* (Cambridge: Harvard University Press, 1993), 276n. 20.

22. See also *Eth. nic.* 8.7.4 and Konstan, *Friendship in the Classical World,* 68, 94–95.

23. The quotation is Rackham's comment in the LCL (pp. 516–17).

24. Konstan, *Friendship in the Classical World,* 82; see also pp. 101 and 136.

25. With some slight alterations, I am here paraphrasing and reproducing the statement of White, *Promised Verse,* 14.

26. Ibid., 276n. 20. The bracketed English definitions of the Latin terms are mine.

27. Like the Greek term φιλία (*philia,* "friendship"; see n. 4 above), the Latin word *amicitia* ("friendship") was applied to a wide variety of amicable relationships. See Konstan, *Friendship in the Classical World,* 122–24.

28. White, *Promised Verse,* 13.

29. Ibid., 14.

30. See J. T. Fitzgerald, "Paul and Paradigm Shifts: Reconciliation and Its Linkage Group," in *Paul beyond the Judaism/Hellenism Divide* (ed. T. Engberg-Pedersen; Louisville: Westminster John Knox, 2001), 241–62; 316–25.

31. See, for example, LSJ 401 (s.v. "διαλλάσσω," III) and 899 (s.v. "καταλλάσσω," II); G. Abbott-Smith, *A Manual Greek Lexicon of the New Testament* (3d ed.; Edinburgh: T. & T. Clark, 1937), 109 (s.v. "διαλλάσσω," 2) and 236 (s.v. "καταλλάσσω"); C. Spicq, *TLNT* 2.262; and BDAG 521 (s.v. "καταλλάσσω").

32. The other definition that Hesychius gives for καταλλαγή (*katallagē*, "reconciliation") is εἰρήνη (*eirēnē*, "peace"), another term that belongs to φιλία's linkage group and that often occurs together with it (see, e.g., Polybius 4.52.6; 21.16.9; Dionysius of Halicarnassus, *Ant. rom.* 5.34.4; Dio Chrysostom, *Or.* 38.22). I draw the references to Hesychius from Cilliers Breytenbach, *Versöhnung: Eine Studie zur paulinischen Soteriologie* (WMANT 60; Neukirchen-Vluyn: Neukirchener Verlag, 1989), 47.

33. The translations of Dio Chrysostom are those of Crosby, LCL.

34. Here and in the following paragraph I have slightly modified the translations of Cary, LCL, usually in order to emphasize Dionysius's use of the language of friendship and reconciliation. See also *Ant. rom. 7* 5.30.1–5.31.4.

35. Zaleucus, *Prooem.* 227.29–31 Thesleff.

36. Zaleucus, *Prooem.* 226.18–21 Thesleff = Diodorus of Sicily 12.20.3 (Oldfather, LCL).

37. All translations of Cicero's *De amicitia* are those of Falconer, LCL.

38. For the idea that worship of the same gods (including participation in the same rites and festivals) provides a basis for friendship and concord between humans, see Dio Chrysostom, *Or.* 38.22, 46; 40.28; 41.10. For the Jewish monotheistic version of this same idea, see Philo, *Spec.* 1.69–70 and *Virt.* 35.

39. Whereas the flatterer is almost always the inferior in an unequal relationship, the more powerful partner can be characterized by such terms as "king," "lord," and "patron." For instances of the latter terms in Latin poetry, see White, *Promised Verse,* 280n. 47. Paul denies that his relationship to the Corinthians falls into either of these two categories.

12

PAUL, GAMES, AND THE MILITARY

Edgar Krentz

Part I. Games and the Military in the Greco-Roman World

In 174 B.C.E., the Oniad Jason purchased the high priesthood and Hellenized Jerusalem with the permission of Antiochus IV Epiphanes. He established the gymnasium and enrolled the upper-class youth in the *ephebeia* (military organization and school for young men between eighteen and twenty years of age). Young men took to wearing the πέτασος (*petasos*), the typical Greek hat, and a symbol of their commitment to the Greek way of life. They exercised as Greek athletes, in the nude. Adherence to the temple and the Torah declined. Priests neglected the temple sacrifices in favor of exercise in the palestra, practicing the discus throw, and wrestling, thus placing the highest value on Greek mores (2 Macc 4:7–15).[1]

Many Palestinian Jews regarded this as desertion of their ancestral mores and religion. They held that the quadrennial games in Tyre in honor of Herakles, formed on the model of the Olympic and Pythian games, were an idolatrous abomination, as 2 Macc 4:18 makes clear. Ultimately, according to 1 and 2 Maccabees, this led to the Jewish revolt, motivated both religiously and culturally. From that time on many Palestinian Jews saw a sharp cleft between Greek culture and Jewish commitment to the worship of God and ancestral mores.[2]

Hellenistic Jews reacted quite differently, so far as we can tell. The Jews in Miletus had reserved seats in the fifth-row center of the theater. Though late, to be sure, the great synagogue in Sardis was right next to the gymnasium with its huge palestra. The Jews of Aphrodisias were involved in public life, as a long inscription demonstrates.[3] Philo of Alexandria is well-read in Greek philosophy. Paul's activity, according to the New Testament, was carried out in the Hellenized cities of the eastern Mediterranean, from Antioch on the Orontes, through Galatia and Asia to Macedonia and Achaia. On the one hand there is no critique of Greek or Roman athletics or militarism in Paul's letters; on the other, he makes significant use of athletic and military language. Like Philo, Paul has the attitude of a Diaspora Jew who lives in an essentially early Roman Empire context.

Athletics and military training were interrelated in the Greek world. The contests in the Greek games were military in nature in many cases: consider for example the foot race in full armor. Homer already bears witness to this relationship in the games celebrated by the Greek army at the death of Patroclus, Achilles' friend, before Troy. Thus the terminology for the games and for military battle was often similar. For example, ἀγών (*agōn*) was used both for a contest in the games and for military engagement. Hence it makes sense to treat them together.

The Culture of Greek Athletics

Athletics played a much larger role in the Greek world than modern people would expect.[4] More than one reason for this can be given. One is the simple fact that ancient Greek culture was agonistic through and through, that is, highly competitive.[5] Athletic imagery permeated Greek literature. In the Roman Empire no city was without the facilities for public entertainment: theaters, odea (covered music halls), baths (including for exercise a palestra, the Greek establishment for educational and athletic training of young men),[6] stadia, amphitheaters, and hippodromes (or circuses).[7]

There were many games, both Panhellenic and local, such as the ones at Tyre mentioned in 2 Maccabees above, in which men and boys competed. The Greek Panhellenic games at Olympia, the Corinthian Isthmia, Delphi, and Nemea had distinguished histories. The Olympic games, traditionally dated to 776 B.C.E., were the oldest.[8] The other three, while probably founded earlier, were refounded in the sixth century B.C.E.: the Isthmian ca. 582 B.C.E.,[9] the Pythian in 582 B.C.E.,[10] and the Nemean in 573 B.C.E.[11] In each case there was a strong religious element to the games. Each was related to a precinct with a major temple.[12] Athletes swore an oath to compete fairly[13] and made dedications in the sacred precinct if victorious. By the time of the early Roman Empire there were local games throughout the Mediterranean world, for example, at Aegae, Dion, Ephesus, Caesarea Maritima, Aphrodisias, and Nicopolis, to name only a few.[14]

Greek athletics were closely interrelated with military matters, though not identical.[15] Training in sports was also training in the arts of war. There is no ancient Greek term equivalent in meaning to the English word "game." The term ἀγών, frequently used, has the root meaning of "assembly" or "gathering." Greeks used it of the assembly for one of the Panhellenic games, for example, in Olympia,[16] or of the contest itself.[17] It was also used of any struggle, including battle in war, the teacher's attempt to win one to a life of philosophy, and the like. At Olympia there were foot races of various lengths (some in full armor),[18] the long jump, the pentathlon,[19] the three combat sports of wrestling, boxing, and the pankration (a form of anything-goes wrestling),[20] chariot racing, horse races, and mule-cart racing (for only fourteen Olympiads), the javelin throw, and the discus throw.[21] The games also included competition in music and other nonathletic events, but they remained primarily athletic.

The winner of an event in a Panhellenic contest was rewarded with a crown of leaves.[22] Victory conferred great distinction (δόξα, *doxa*), as the Epinician Odes of "the Theban eagle," Pindar, made clear in the early fifth century B.C.E.[23] This honor was not temporary, but lived on, memorialized with a statue in the precinct or with an inscription or statue in his home city.[24] His home city might welcome him with money, civic honors, or even with dining at civic expense for the rest of his life.[25] The same was true of a victory in the quadrennial Panathenaic games, where one or more amphorae of fine olive oil was the prize.

One delivers a speech to athletes for the same purpose one does to an army, to stimulate strength. "For speech is appropriate for all purposes, and gives strength for any effort: soldiers need the speech and exhortation of the general for war or battle, and then excel themselves in strength. Athletes particularly need the encouragement and exhortation of speech."[26] The athlete competes under conditions similar to those of an army at the moment of conflict. "For just as in an army, the most genuine soldiers, having heard speeches from their commanders, are most ambitious for victory, so it is with those who receive exhortations in the proper spirit at the games: they will be most anxious to win."[27] The general's speech stimulates to noble deeds; so does the trainer's.

There was criticism of this elevation of the victor early[28] and again later. Dio Chrysostom ridicules athletes who die in the games for a crown of olive.[29] On the other hand philosophers frequently used athletic imagery as an ethical *topos*. Thus Cicero uses the observance of the rules in racing as a simile for moral rectitude.[30] Epictetus, a century and a half later, uses numerous illustrations from athletics in his diatribes to urge acting in accordance with reason.[31] Maximus of Tyre contrasts the Olympic competition for a perishable prize with "the labor that is the soul's own and the contest [ἀγωνίσμα, *agōnisma*] that is the soul's own" for the prize of virtue.[32] Athletic contexts are thus a familiar philosophic *topos* to urge living a good life, though one must train for it and labor at it. All of life is a race for the prize.

Roman Athletics and Entertainment (The Ludi)

Greek athletic competitions continued in the early Roman Empire, but declined in popularity, though the Romans did not disturb the Greek games in the east.[33] Some emperors favored the games, for example, Augustus, Nero, and Hadrian in the second century C.E., while local games were founded, above all, in Greek cities in the east. The Romans participated in vigorous exercise, but did not have the agonistic attitudes of the Greeks, being much devoted to spectator sport.

Romans traditionally preferred the *ludi* or *munera* (games).[34] These games took place in the arena (amphitheater), the circus (hippodrome), or the theater. Gladiatorial games were in origin honorific military funeral games presented by the family of a distinguished dead man. They employed gladiators to fight in honor of the deceased. As time went on, they lost this funereal association. They were not for citizen participation, but for professionals, slaves, criminals, or prisoners of war. Participants in the games in the arena (gladiators) or the theater had very low social status—though some were lionized by members of the Roman urban elite.[35] A citizen who fought in the arena suffered ultimate disgrace, *infamia*, loss of status and citizenship.

Roman institutions spread throughout the empire, speeded up by the establishment of Roman colonies under Julius Caesar and Caesar Augustus.[36] Colonists in the eastern provinces brought Roman institutions with them, including the arena, the circus, and the Roman bath.[37] The baths included an exercise ground (*palestra*), but this was now largely for personal exercise, not preparation for athletic contests or warfare.[38] Romans liked various kinds of ball games[39] which they often played before bathing; therefore some baths had a *spheristerium* (a ball game court).[40] The sponsorship of gladiatorial games demonstrated the genuine Roman character of a city, and thus also was a social and political statement. Accordingly, the Corinthians built a hippodrome (*circus*) and an arena.[41] Apollonius of Tyana criticized the Athenians for their games in which they made gladiators of adulterers, fornicators, burglars, cutthroats, kidnappers, and such criminals and set them to fight in the theater of Dionysus.[42]

The Roman Army

Athletes, gladiators, and charioteers competed as individuals; soldiers by definition had to act in concert, not as individuals. While athletic imagery was useful in calling individuals to commitment or action, military language could be used either to encourage an individual or to promote social, political, intellectual, or religious unity. The army was a major Romanizing force in the Greek east as Julius Caesar and Caesar Augustus spread the legions throughout the Roman Empire, and later emperors followed their model.[43] They also followed a similar policy in their establishment of colonies and so spread Roman law, mores, and social patterns throughout the empire.[44] Between them they established both citizen and military colonies especially in the east. Julius Caesar was responsible for Buthrotum, Dyme, and Corinth in mainland Greece, and for Sinope, Apamea Myrleia, and Parium. After defeating Antony in the battle in the Bay of Aktion (2 September 31), Octavian (soon to be called Augustus) began an extensive program of colonization.[45] He claims to have founded twenty-eight colonies in Italy itself,[46] as well as colonies in Africa, Sicily, Macedonia, both Spanish provinces, Achaia, Asia, Syria, Gallia Narbonensis, and Pisidia.[47] Augustus planted colonies at Patrae, Dyrrachium, Dion, Casandreia (first established by Brutus) and Philippi (first founded by Antony). In all these colonies, the army turned out to be a major Romanizing force both in war and in peace.[48]

Augustus changed the character of the Roman army from a group of civilians to a force with essentially nonprofessional officers leading soldiers who looked on military service as a lifelong career.[49] The legionnaire normally served for twenty years and was subject to recall for five years after that.[50] Augustus took care to bond the legions to himself. He was their patron, they his client. He gave donatives of money, recognized the army's accomplishments on his coinage, and celebrated their victories as his personal triumphs.[51] Whereas soldiers in the republic took an oath to serve the commander and not desert him, under the empire their oath was to "place the safety of the emperor above everything,"[52] swearing to die rather than disobey.[53] The oath to the emperor (*sacramentum*, πίστις, *pistis*), their Lord (*dominus*, κύριος, *kyrios*), renewed annually, was "to serve the emperor and his appointed delegates and obey all orders unto the death and recognize the severe punishment for desertion and disobedience."[54] The baptismal confession "Jesus is Lord" is clearly analogous. On being mustered out, usually after twenty years of service, soldiers received Roman citizenship. Thus the army was a major mode of social advancement.

The senators and equites (knights) provided the commanders and upper officers of the army.[55] The general[56] in a campaign was not a professional soldier, but a member of the elite. Onasander[57] describes the role of a general well. As Oldfather says in his introduction, the "burden of the treatise is really ethics, morale, and the general principles of success in arms."[58] The general should be an able speaker (ἱκανος λέγειν, *hikanos legein*, 1.1), able to encourage before battle (1.13), should purify the army by sacrifice (5) and take omens (10) before battle, should personally lead in military formation (6), should show himself as gay, cheerful, and undaunted (ἱλαρὸς, γεγηθὼς καὶ ἀκατάπληκτος, *hilaros gegēthōs kai akataplēktos*) when in danger of loss (13), and recognize the value of fear (φόβος, *phobos*) to make soldiers steady, whether cowardly or rash (14). Plato, much earlier, says that a general will know what words to say to soldiers to encourage them (στρατιώταις παραινοῦντι, *stratiōtais parainounti*)[59] better than a rhapsodist.[60]

Onasander refers to two genres of generals' speeches to troops—before and after battle.[61] In his post-battle speech a general should encourage the survivors (παραμυθησάμενος τοὺς ἀνασωθέντας, *paramythēsamenos tous anasōthentas*), if defeated; if victorious he should guard against suffering harm through the soldiers' negligence (36.2). He also suggests that a general should encourage his army when losing by shouting out good news, even if it is false (23)![62]

The other genre is the harangue before battle (4.3–6). Onasander describes the kind of speech a general gives before war and the reasons for doing so. Burgess gives the most extensive list of pre-battle speeches found in Greek historians known to me.[63] Burgess points out that, although neither Menander nor Pseudo-Dionysius of Halicarnassus[64] lists the general's speech as a separate division of epideictic oratory, one can argue that the frequency and importance of such a speech are great "and it preserves its identity even more thoroughly, than many of those which have unquestioned recognition and detailed rhetorical presentation." Pseudo-Dionysius' section describing the προτρεπτικὸς ἀθληταῖς (*protreptikos athlētais*, speech encouraging athletes) comes close to giving an outline of the general's speech.

Military harangues follow a standard outline and use standard τόποι (*topoi*, traditional forms of argumentation) including: (1) a reminder of their ancestry; (2) a call not to disgrace their heritage; (3) a comparison of forces; (4) an appeal to patriotism; and a series of assertions that (5) valor, not numbers, wins; (6) great rewards await the victors; (7) the auspices are favorable; (8) death is glorious for the brave; (9) defeat is a disgrace; (10) they have conquered this enemy before; (11) the war is just, because we have suffered from the enemy; and (12) our commander is superior to the enemy's.[65] Polyaenus refers to such speeches a number of times. Thus Chabrias exhorted his soldiers, "Since we are about to fight, let us not in any event think that we are engaging the enemy's gods, but men who have flesh and blood and have shared the same nature we do."[66]

Generals fought alongside their troops in ancient warfare. Generals were not far-off officers in a command post; they genuinely wanted to fight beside and share the dangers of their soldiers. Archilochus described the ideal commander as follows: "Give me a man short and squarely set upon his legs, a man full of heart, not to be shaken from the place he plants his feet."[67] Later theorists were less certain that commanders should undergo such danger.[68]

One result was that "a Greek commander's absence on occasion could set off panic among the men at his side who watched him go down."[69] Xenophon advised his officers (στρατηγοί, ταξίαρχοι καὶ λοχαγοί, *stratēgoi, taxiarchoi kai lochagoi*) that they should be braver than their troops, exercise forethought for their good, and set an example of enduring hardship.[70] The commander was in many ways another soldier, fighting alongside his troops. The description of Epaphroditus as an ἀδελφὸς καὶ συνεργὸς καὶ συστρατιώτης (*adelphos kai synergos kai systratiōtēs*, Phil 2:25) reflects this side of ancient warfare.

The army's functions were to win wars, to enforce peace, to patrol the borders (the *limes*), and to carry out many tasks in peacetime. The organization, training, and discipline of the army made it an effective tool for all these functions. In peacetime it served as the engineer corps, building roads, aqueducts, bridges, and so forth.[71] This is one of the ways in which the army was a force for the Romanization of the empire.

It was an effective war machine.[72] The armies of Rome had brought peace to the empire, so that wars were normally waged on a distant frontier.[73] Men were trained to obedience, to working not as individuals, but as part of a unit. Massed soldiers, not individual prowess, won battles. Individual skills were not as important.[74] Legionnaires were trained to keep in place, not to leave the line. Vegetius (of the fourth to fifth century C.E.) describes training for battle formation (single line, double line, square, wedge, and circle) as follows:

> There is nothing which has proved to be of greater service in action than for the men to learn by constant practice to keep their allotted positions in the line, and nowhere to close or to open their ranks disadvantageously. Men packed closely together have no room for fighting and merely get in one another's way. Similarly, if they are scattered and there is too much daylight between them they give the enemy an opportunity of breaking through. Inevitably, if the line is cut through and the enemy attacks the fighting troops from behind, there is immediate panic and universal disorder. . . . If the young soldiers perfect these movements by constant practice they will more easily keep their ranks in real fighting.[75]

Polyaenus illustrates the necessity to "keep the line" with an anecdote: Cleandridas taught his soldiers that the Lucanians lost because they scattered and did not hold their ground as his soldiers did.[76]

Commands were given both by voice and, more audibly in battle, by trumpet (σάλπιγξ, tuba) or horn (*cornu*).[77] Soldiers were also to watch the standard, the eagle carried by the *aquilifer* (eagle bearer), to note the direction of movement. The term that Aeneas Tacticus uses for battle is ἀγών (*agōn*, also used for athletic contests), for victory σωτηρία (*sōtēria*, usually translated salvation in the New Testament: cf. Rom 1:16; 10:1, 9; 13:11; 2 Cor 1:6).[78]

Victories were celebrated in two ways.[79] First, victors erected a τρόπαιον (*tropaion*), a memorial in which the armor of the defeated commander was hung on a pole, sometimes with a cross bar. The lower band of the Gemma Augustea illustrates the procedure very well, as it shows Roman soldiers erecting the pole decorated with the defeated general's armor and nude captives under the harsh control of legionnaires.[80] The second was with a triumph, a procession in which the victorious general and his army were feted.[81] Part of the procession included prominent captives taken in war along with the riches that the victory brought to Rome. The Arch of Titus in the Roman forum illustrates this well, with Titus pictured in the chariot (on one interior wall) and the booty from the Jerusalem temple on the other interior wall. Augustus celebrated two triumphs (ἐθριάμβευσα, *ethriambeusa*) with an ovation and three curile triumphs, was proclaimed αὐτοκρά-τωρ (*autokratōr*, sole ruler) twenty-three times, and was frequently voted triumphs (θρίαμβοι, *thriamboi*) by the senate.[82] Such repeated triumphs exalted the emperor in the mind of the troops.

The Military Topos

Moral philosophers found military language useful for stressing the importance of moral action.[83] This has a long history with Plato's Socrates already comparing proper living to the soldier's obedience to orders (Plato, *Apol.* 28.d5–29a.1). The Stoic Epictetus compares the soldier's oath of allegiance to the emperor to the philosophic student's "oath" never to disobey god or to find fault with anything that god has given.[84] The philosopher's duty, like that of a soldier, is to obey when the general gives the signal to retreat, following him and praising him.[85] Seneca too uses this *topos* to describe the philosophic life in his moral letters to Lucilius.[86] Maximus of Tyre describes god as a general who posts people properly.[87] Or he says that "Whoever refuses to allow the philosopher to seize every opportunity to speak seems to me to be doing the same as someone who selects a single station from the whole chancy, fluctuating, unstable business of war, and there confines the versatile soldier who knows how to fight both as hoplite and as archer, and can shoot as effectively on horseback as he can from a chariot."[88] Valerius Maximus praises the severity of military discipline because it leads to the support of the empire.[89] The *topos* is used to urge life in conformity with one's philosophic tenets.

Part II. Pauline Use of Athletic and Military Imagery

Imagery from the Greek Panhellenic Games

Corinth controlled the Isthmian games in the first century and, during Paul's time there, may even have celebrated them in the city itself.[90] Paul never mentions the site of any of the Panhellenic games by name. But he lived in Corinth, the city that controlled the Isthmian games; so it is not surprising that 1 Corinthians contains passages that use imagery from the Greek games in a manner similar to ethical thinkers. In 1 Cor 9:24–27[91] Paul uses a clear foot-race-in-a-stadium metaphor (οἱ ἐν σταδίῳ τρέχοντες, *hoi en stadiō trechontes*, "those running in a stadium," one of his few references to an architectural structure!), to describe life as a contest (ἀγ-ωνιζόμενος, *agōnizomenos*, competing).[92] "Every athlete [πᾶς δὲ ὁ ἀγωνιζόμενος πάντα ἐγκρατεύεται, *pas de ho agōnizomenos panta enkrateuetai*] must exercise self control in all respects. All run, but only one wins the prize [πάντες μὲν τρέχουσιν, εἷς δὲ λαμβάνει τὸ βραβεῖον, *pantes men trechousin, heis de lambanei to brabeion*], a wreath that deteriorates" (φθαρτὸν στέφανον, *phtharton stephanon*). He then shifts to a boxing metaphor (οὕτως πυκτεύω, *houtōs pykteuō*), claiming that he does not shadow-box (ὡς οὐκ ἀέρα δέρων, *hōs ouk aera derōn*, "not as one boxing the air"), but "pommels his body and enslaves it" (ὑπωπιάζω[93] μου τὸ σῶμα καὶ δουλα-γωγῶ, *hypōpiazō mou to sōma kai doulagōgō*). He rejects a comparison with shadow-boxing in order to stress the reality of his struggle for the gospel. He does not want to be disqualified for competing unfairly (ἀδόκιμος, *adokimos*).[94] Paul's description is accurate for contemporary practice.

There is a similar use of the foot race in Phil 3:12–14, where Paul speaks of concentrating on what is before, not behind him (τὰ μὲν ὀπίσω ἐπιλανθανόμενος τοῖς δὲ ἔμπροσθεν ἐπεκτεινόμενος, *ta men opisō epilanthanomenos tois de emprosthen epekteinomenos*), as he strives to get to the goal (κατὰ σκοπὸν διώκω, *kata skopon diōkō*) and the prize (τὸ βραβεῖον, *to brabeion*). Lucian uses similar language as he describes how an outstanding athlete competes fairly, but an inferior, unsports-manlike athlete cheats.[95] The good runner forgets the starting line, thinks only of getting ahead, and strains his mind toward the goal.[96]

Paul may refer to someone's unfairly breaking the rules in a race, where Paul says that the Galatians were running well (Gal 5:7). Williams translates "someone tripped you up," taking it as a statement rather than a question. This is the only passage in which Paul applies the race metaphor to his hearers.[97]

While it is, strictly speaking, not athletics, 1 Cor 14:7 uses language that would make sense within the games. There was competition in both music and dance at the Isthmia and Delphi, but not at Olympia.[98] The instruments were the lyre (κιθάρα, *kithara*) and the flute (αὐλός, *aulos*). Paul refers to both. If they give no clear distinction in their notes (διαστολὴν τοῖς φθόγγοις, *diastolēn tois phthongois*), how can one recognize what is blown or played? Greeks recognized different scales and assigned them differing value and influence.[99] Paul plays on this musical understanding as he discusses glossolalia (speaking in tongues).

Paul uses imagery from the Roman arena a number of times. In 1 Cor 4:9, he describes apostles as "sentenced to death," and therefore as ones who have become a spectacle; the language speaks as if they are condemned criminals.[100] He speaks of "fighting with wild animals in Ephesus" (ἐθηριομάχησα, *ethēriomachēsa*; 1 Cor 15:32) to describe how the hope of resurrection enables his disregard of death. While Paul probably was not a combatant in the arena, he describes himself as a gladiator who was expected to be willing to die.[101]

In 2 Cor 4:8–12, Paul uses an extended gladiatorial image to describe his on-going expectation of death as he proclaims the reconciling Christ. His language is highly rhetorical, putting four contrasts before his reader. He is

(1) pressured in every way, but not cornered (ἐν παντὶ θλιβόμενοι ἀλλ᾽ οὐ στενοχωρούμενοι, *en panti thlibomenoi all' ou stenochōroumenoi*)

(2) at a loss, but not in despair (ἀπορούμενοι, αλλ᾽ οὐκ ἐξαπορούμενοι, *aporoumenoi all' ouk exaporoumenoi*);

(3) chased around, but not deserted (διωκόμενοι ἀλλ᾽ οὐκ ἐγκαταλειπόμενοι, *diōkomenoi all' ouk enkataleipomenoi*);

(4) struck down, but not destroyed (καταβαλλόμενοι αλλ᾽ οὐκ ἀπολλύμενοι, *kataballomenoi all' ouk apollymenoi*).

These four contrasts describe him as a losing gladiator, whose continuing life is given by his Lord. He is constantly in danger of death for Christ ("we are always being given up to death," εἰς θάνατον παραδιδόμεθα, *eis thanaton paradidometha*; 2 Cor 4:11), yet does not give in to evil (2 Cor 4:16), and does not despair (2 Cor 4:16).[102]

Paul uses the language of Greek and Roman sports (and entertainment) consistently to describe his own struggles as apostle for Christ. The language is most frequent in the Corinthians letters (a reflection of the Isthmian games?), where he stresses how seriously he takes his labor, how little he strives for recognition, and how humble his own situation often is. He uses the language of Roman entertainment (the gladiatorial games) to stress his suffering of hardships without being defeated. He never critiques any aspect of ancient athletics or the gladiatorial games, while using imagery drawn from them. He thus demonstrates both his immersion in the culture of his time and his freedom from it.[103]

Pauline Passages with Military Imagery

Like the philosophers, Paul uses military imagery to urge fitting activity.[104] Scattered passages illustrate this well. Readers are urged to be victorious, for example, in Rom 12:21, "Do not be conquered by evil, but conquer evil with good," using forms of the verb νικάω, *nikaō*.[105] Romans 13:11–14 uses an extended metaphor: now Christians need to be awake (i.e., on guard; ὥρα ἤδη ὑμᾶς ἐξ ὕπνου ἐγερθῆναι, *hōra ēde hymas ex hypnou egerthēnai*), armed, not with the works of darkness, but "the weapons of light" (τὰ ὅπλα τοῦ φωτός, *ta hopla tou phōtos*),[106] for their victory (ἡ σωτηρία, *hē sōtēria*) is closer than when they first came to believe.[107] Paul refers to armor again in 1 Thess 5:7–8, naming the breastplate (θώραξ, *thōrax*) and the helmet (περικεφαλαία, *perikephalaia*), the hope of salvation, while he urges staying awake. Once again "salvation" here may mean victory.

The Corinthian letters use military language extensively. Paul describes his own life as a battle: he is hemmed in every way, "battles [μάχαι, *machai*] outside, fears inside." One finds a similar motif in Rom 7:23, where a principle (*nomos*, law?) in Paul's body parts wars (ἀντιστρατευόμενον, *antistrateuomenon*) against the principle in his mind and takes him captive to the principle of sin.[108] Paul refers to going to war (στρατεύεται, *strateuetai*) in 1 Cor 9:7 as well as to the soldier's rations (ὀψώνιον, *opsōnion*).[109] In discussing the (non-)utility of glossolalia Paul asks how one can prepare for war (πόλεμος, *polemos*) if the trumpet does not give a clear signal (1 Cor 14:8). According to 1 Cor 15:57–58, God gives the victory (τὸ νῖκος, *to nikos*) in the war Christians wage; therefore they should "stand firm, immovable," like soldiers in the line, since they know their toil (ὁ κόπος ὑμῶν, *ho kopos hymōn*) will win in the end. In 1 Cor 16:13, Paul's closing imperatives play on acting like a soldier on guard duty or preparing for battle: "Stay awake, stand firm in the faith, be courageous,[110] use your power!" (γρηγορεῖτε, στήκετε ἐν τῇ πίστει, ἀνδρίζεσθε, κραταιοῦσθε, *grēgoreite, stēkete en tē pistei, andrizesthe, krataiousthe*; 16.14, πάντα ὑμῶν ἐν ἀγάπῃ γινέσθω, *panta hymōn en agapē ginesthō*). Paul stresses the need to be constantly alert, but fills his commands with his own particular meaning by adding in verse 14, "Let all that you do be done in love."[111]

Second Corinthians 2:14 uses the verb θριαμβεύω (*thriambeuō*, "to celebrate a triumph") to describe God as the victorious general who leads Paul in a triumphal procession, using the same verb that Caesar Augustus used.[112] Paul (ironically?) casts himself as a captive led in the train of God as victorious general. He plays on the death awaiting most captives as he describes himself as an odor of death for some, life for others. In this way he also prepares the reader of 2 Corinthians for the extensive discussion of his difficulties. In 2 Cor 7:7 he refers to the weapons of righteousness (justice, δικαιοσύνη, *dikaiosynē*) on the right and on the left. The Roman legionnaire normally wore a dagger on his left side, his sword on the right, and carried a lance. Paul describes a well-armed warrior, omitting the lance. Second Corinthians 10:3–6 describes the Corinthians as warring, but not by a fleshly standard:

> For though we live in the world we are not carrying on a worldly war [οὐ κατὰ σάρκα στρατευόμεθα, *ou kata sarka strateuometha*], for the weapons [τὰ γὰρ ὅπλα, *ta gar hopla*] of our warfare [τῆς στρατείας ἡμῶν, *tēs strateias hēmōn*] are not worldly but have divine power to destroy strongholds. We destroy [ἐπαιρόμενον, *epairomenon*] arguments and every proud obstacle to the knowledge of God, and take every thought captive [αἰχμαλωτίζοντες, *aichmalōtizontes*] to obey Christ, being ready to punish [ἐν ἑτοίμῳ ἔχοντες ἐκδικῆσαι, *en hetoimō echontes ekdikēsai*] every disobedience [παρακοήν, *parakoēn*], when your obedience is complete.

All the Greek terms are at home in war texts.[113]

This strikingly pervasive application of military metaphors in scattered passages shows how much Paul is indebted to military metaphors. Paul uses them either to describe his own struggles to live out his faith or to encourage his hearers to actions in accord with the gospel. Paul's language is analogous to the language of the moral philosophers who use military metaphors to urge life in accordance with their philosophic positions.

Philippians, the Parade Example

Philippians is distinctive among Paul's letters as the only one that uses a combination of military and political language as the conceptual framework for the entire letter.[114] That is not surprising, because Octavian recolonized Philippi after the battle at Aktion with a second contingent of Roman soldiers and named it *Colonia Augusta Julia Philippensis*.[115] It bore that name until at least the first half of the third century C.E., as its coinage and inscriptions confirm.[116] Inscriptions testify to an ongoing military presence in Philippi down into the first century C.E.[117]

One can interpret much of Philippians as the pre-battle harangue of a general, who, we have noted, was normally present with the troops. The key passage is Phil 1:27–2:18; I shall restrict myself to a few comments on Phil 1:27–30, which I have discussed in detail elsewhere.[118] The term πολιτεύεσθαι (*politeuesthai*, "to live as a citizen," 1:27) puts one into the realm of life in the *polis*. Πολιτεύεσθε (1:27) is echoed in the term *politeuma* ("commonwealth," 3:20) and together the two terms form an *inclusio*, a ring device, 1:27–4:1; both are related to the word πόλις (*polis*, city).[119] I translate these verses to indicate the military cast to the language:

> Only live your life in the polis in a way that corresponds to the good news, in order that whether I come and observe you or, absent, hear about your affairs, that you are standing [firm] in one spirit, with one mind,[120] fighting together for the oath to the gospel,[121] not terrified by the opponents drawn up in line against you, which is a demonstration of defeat for them, but of your victory—and that from God; because that which is on Christ's behalf has been granted to you, not only the matter of swearing an oath to him, but also to suffer for him,[122] since you have the same battle of the sort you saw in me and now hear of in me.

Paul uses military language in Phil 1:27–30 to summon the Philippians to unity as they struggle on behalf of Christ. That correlates with the social situation of the city as a military colony and with Paul's convictions that Christians are engaged in God's war. There is further, extensive use of military and political language in other sections of Philippians.

In what follows I call attention to specific military terminology or motifs that are found in 2:1–3:21 and scattered in other parts of the letter. Paul, as the general, desires to be with them (Phil 1:25–26). But he needs to account for his absence from them in the battle they wage. Twice he notes his absence (Phil 1:27; 2:12), in the former urging them to stand firm, in the latter exhorting to obedience—as a general would.

Philippians 2:1–4 continues the exhortation Paul began in 1:27–30, as the "therefore" of 2:1 makes clear. Paul's use of the terms παράκλησις (*paraklēsis*, "exhortation") and παραμύθιον (*paramythion*, "encouragement") urges the Philippians to think the same thing (τὸ αὐτὸ φρονεῖν, *to auto phronein*),[123] recalling 1:27–30, and expands that by urging them to unity of love, of enthusiasm (σύμψυχοι, *sympsychoi*), and of thought (τὸ ἓν φρονοῦντες, *to hen phronountes*; 2:1–2). There is no room for self-advancement in the army; rather, each must think of the things related to others (μὴ τὰ ἑαυτῶν ἕκαστος σκοποῦντες ἀλλὰ καὶ τὰ ἑτέρων ἕκαστοι, *mē ta heautōn hekastos skopountes alla kai ta heterōn hekastoi*, Phil 2:2–4). After the discussion of 1:27–30 the implications are clear: unity of mind is achieved by considering the well-being of others ahead of individual survival or glory (κενοδοξία, *kenodoxia*, "empty reputation"), what Shakespeare calls the "bubble reputation." War is not an occasion for personal rivalry (ἐριθεία, *eritheia*); rather "in humility to regard others as your superiors, concerned not for your own interests, each one for the interests of others" (2:4). Onasander advises the commander how to put men in the line: "It is the part of the wise general to station brothers to rank beside brothers, friends beside friends, and lovers beside their favorites. For whenever that which is in danger near by is more than ordinarily dear the lover necessarily fights more recklessly for the man beside him."[124] Paul reminds the Philippians of this military truism, without invoking any aspect of homosexual love—in part, at least, because some of the leaders in Philippi are women (4:2–3).

The stress on humility leads Paul to quote the hymn in Phil 2:6–11 as an illustration of this self-denying mind that leads to concern for others. Arnold Ehrhardt thought the hymn in Phil 2:6–11 used an ancient *Herrscherideal*, a description of the ideal ruler.[125] His interpretation fits this military stress. How did Jesus become the Lord, the κύριος to whom they swear allegiance in baptism? Jesus was obedient to the point of dying. Therefore he was exalted to the position where the whole creation confesses "Jesus is Lord!" Paul uses the hymn to call the Philippians to similar obedience and to unity. Philippians 2:12 reminds the Philippians that they have obeyed Paul in the past (καθὼς πάντοτε ὑπηκούσατε, *kathōs pantote hypēkousate*). The good soldier obeys authority. Paul summons the Philippians to "produce their own salvation" (σωτηρία, *sōtēria*). "Salvation" here cannot mean religious salvation at the eschaton, but must mean "victory," as is normal in a military context. Epictetus calls for good order and obedience to God (ἐκπληρώσῃ εὐτάκτως καὶ εὐπειθῶς τῷ θεῷ, *ekplērōsē eutaktōs kai eupeithōs tō theō*), reinforcing it with a reference to Socrates, who preferred to be killed rather that leave the place in which God had ordered him to be (3.24.95). Paul uses the familiar philosophic *topos*, but with a new twist. Obedience is necessary to achieve victory. This reading obviates what appears otherwise to be an un-Pauline statement that one must produce his own ultimate salvation.

Paul also assures the Philippians that they will have the power to do what he asks because they have a powerful God who is working in them (2:13). God is the one who produces in them both the will and the power to act (τὸ θέλειν καὶ το ἐνεργεῖν, *to thelein kai to energein*). This is Paul's modification of a standard *topos* in military harangues. Because of their superior, mediated power, they can really be certain of victory.

But they should fight without complaints and arguments (χωρὶς γογγυσμῶν καὶ διαλογισμῶν, *chōris gongysmōn kai dialogismōn*, 2:14). Discipline in battle is essential; there is no room for disputing or discussing orders. Therefore soldiers must be accustomed to obey orders immediately, without question. For such orders bring safety to those who follow them, danger to those who disobey. So also one must not fight against that which nature brings; as Seneca says: "It is best to suffer what you cannot change, and to go with god, by whose authorship all things occur: an evil soldier is one who follows his commander, grumbling."[126] Paul opposes quarrelling and urges unity in other letters, but the directive here is in unusual language that fits well into a military harangue. They are to obey without complaints, as Seneca has urged.

Paul's use of the language of a libation poured out over a sacrifice also fits a military harangue: "But if I am being poured out as a libation [σπένδομαι, *spendomai*] on the sacrifice and liturgy of your oath [ἐπὶ τῇ θυσίᾳ καὶ λειτουργίᾳ τῆς πίστεως ὑμῶν, *epi tē thysia kai leitourgia tēs pisteōs hymōn*], I rejoice and have joy together with all of you" (Phil 2:17).[127] This probably is a reference to the sacrifices made before battle. The use of the term λειτουργία (*leitourgia*) supports this view, because a liturgy was a deed done in service of the state. Their liturgy was to work out their victory. Sacrifice was the responsibility of the commanding general. Onasander says that no general should fight a battle unless he has first sacrificed and taken the omens, and knows they are favorable to his side.[128]

There is multiple attestation for such sacrifice in ancient historians. Cyrus the Great asked his officers to have all, man and horse alike, breakfast while he sacrificed prior to the great battle against the Persians.[129] Sacrifices often included libations. Paul says that his death in defense of the gospel should not cause them to lose heart, but should be regarded as a favorable sacrifice. He clearly reckons with the possibility of his death in 1:19–26. There he says that his death or his life will magnify Christ (Phil 1:20). Paul later speaks of the "partnership in his [Christ's] sufferings" (3:11), as he had said that it was a gift for them to suffer on behalf of Christ (1:29).[130] If he dies, his death will be evidence of God's favor in their battle (Phil 2:13).

As for the rest (3:1), says Paul, he only writes what is not at all irksome to him and what aids their safety (ἀσφαλές, *asphales*). But Paul deserts this apparent conclusion and, instead, opens an attack on opponents (3:2–4) whom he later names "enemies of the cross of Christ" (ἐχθροι τοῦ σταυροῦ τοῦ Χριστοῦ, *echthroi tou staurou tou christou*, 3:18). Such a description of the enemy fits well into a military harangue. It implies the superiority of Paul's forces.

Philippians 3:6–11 introduces righteousness (or justice, δικαιόσύνη, *dikaio-synē*) into the discussion, a bit abruptly. Interpreters understandably tend to read it in the light of Paul's argument in Galatians and Romans. But Onasander allows an enrichment of that understanding. He argues that a general must marshal (συνίστασθαι, *synistasthai*) the causes of war most prudently. "It should be evident to all that one fights on the side of justice."[131] Then the gods are more kindly disposed, become comrades in arms, and soldiers fight more eagerly (προθυμό-τερον, *prothymoteron*). Paul makes very clear the priority of the δικαιοσύνη (or "justice," *dikaiosynē*) of Christ over his own, which makes the loss of everything else and participation in the sufferings (παθήματα, *pathēmata*) of Christ a good that determines all of his actions (3:12–15). Christ's justice is clearly superior to that of the enemies (Phil 3:2–4, 18–19).

In Phil 3:17–4:1, Paul picks up the language and the motifs of 1:27–30 and thus rhetorically provides closure to the argument by a form of ring composition. The passage first recalls Paul's self-references (3:17; cf. 1:7–26; 3:4b–14), then pointedly sums up the statements about the opposition (3:18–19; cf. 3:2–4a), and concludes by recapitulating the language and exhortation of 1:27–30 (3:20–4:1). One finds in the immediate context the nouns "God" (θεός, *theos*), and "savior" (σωτήρ, *sōtēr*, referring to Jesus); God is described as able to subject everything to Christ as savior (3:21).

Brewer pointed out that Philippi, a Roman colony governed by *ius Italicum*, included *Augustales*, freedmen especially devoted to the worship of the divine Augustus, and that ruler cult continued throughout the first century C.E.[132] He held that Paul formulated Phil 1:27–30; 2:9–11, and 3:20 in conscious opposition to the ruler cult of the emperor Nero. He summarizes his interpretation as follows:

> Read in the light of the three passages referred to they [the terms πολιτ-εύεσθε, *politeuesthe*, in 1:27 and πολίτευμα, *politeuma*, in 3:20] seem to be chosen deliberately and for a good reason. Paul seems to have employed these words to say, "Continue to discharge your obligations as citizens and residents of Philippi faithfully and as a Christian should; but do not yield to the patriotic pressure to give to Nero that which belongs to Christ alone. Remember that while you are members of a Roman colony you are also a colony of heaven from which you are awaiting the return of your divine Lord and Savior. So stand firm. Never waver in the conflict. You may have to suffer for Christ, but remember that he is your deliverer too."[133]

Brewer's insistence on interpreting Philippians in the light of public life in a

Roman colony, especially his insistence on Roman ruler cult, is entirely persuasive. Army veterans would continue to live in strong fealty to the emperor.

In Phil 3:17, Paul uses language that presents him as a model (τύπον, *typon*)[134] and at the same time asks the Philippians to join him in imitation (συμμιμηταί μου γίνεσθω, *symmimētai mou ginesthō*)! Imitation (μίμησις, *mimēsis*) played a great role in antiquity.[135] Notice that Paul asks them to imitate him in observing the "enemies of the cross of Christ" (ἐχθροι τοῦ σταυροῦ τοῦ Χριστοῦ, *echthroi tou staurou tou christou*, 3:18). The usual term for enemy in battle narratives is πολέμιοι, *polemioi*. But ἐχθρος (*echthros*) is also possible. They will be defeated (ἀπώλεια, *apōleia*, cf. 1:28).[136]

Paul describes the enemy according to a stereotype that contrasts them with the ideal soldier in 2:1–4. They do not have their minds fixed on that which gives unity and victory. "Their god is their gut" (3:19). Most commentators suggest that this is either a reference to sexual immorality or to a rather stylized complaint.[137] The reference is rather to a luxurious diet (the Roman soldier normally ate no meat!) and to an unsoldierly demeanor.[138] Some Romans held that soldiers should make do "with an evening meal of biscuits washed down with water."[139] These enemies rather think of "things below" (οἱ τὰ ἐπίγεια φρονοῦντες, *hoi ta epigeia phronountes*, 3:19); they find their glory (δόξα, *doxa*, their citizens' repuation) in the wrong things.

This description forms a clear contrast to the "commonwealth in heaven" (πολίτευμα ἐν οὐρανοῖς, *politeuma en ouranois*; 3:20). The enemies fight for the wrong values. The Philippians, however, are under oath to one who is their savior. Paul rarely uses σωτήρ (*sōtēr*, savior) of Jesus; Phil 3:20 is the only occurrence in the generally accepted Pauline epistles.[140] This term has its place in Roman ruler cult, but it also fits well into a military context. The Calendar inscription of Priene calls Caesar Augustus "savior" because he brought peace to the world.[141] Soldiers acknowledged him as *dominus*, that is, lord.

But Paul reminds the Philippians of another loyalty and another Lord. Sherwin-White points out that the term πολίτευμα (*politeuma*, "commonwealth") technically denoted self-sufficient, self-governing communities of non-citizens (especially Jews) "who were under the general authority of the citizen body, but organized their own internal affairs" in great cities such as Alexandria and Seleucia on the Tigris.[142] We should recall that the soldier "belonged" to the emperor. Augustus talked of "my soldiers" (*milites mei*). Paul recalls for the Philippians their baptismal *sacramentum*, their confession that "Jesus the Lord" is the Philippians' savior, that their allegiance is not to Rome, but to a *heavenly* πολίτευμα (*politeuma*) where their Lord now is (a conscious antithesis to the description of their enemies in 3:19). And, as believers, they have a future, a reward better than a donative. Once again motifs of the military harangue are present: know for whom you fight and win glory for yourselves at the eschaton. It is Christ as Lord "who will transform our humble body to the same shape as his glorious body." Philippians 3:20 promises a future reward.

This military ambiance in Philippi may shed light on the term ἐπίσκοποι (episkopoi, "overseers"), though not on καὶ διάκονοι (diakonoi, servants) in Phil 1:1. Martin Dibelius translates this phrase "samt Verwaltern und Gehilfin" ("together with the administrators and assistants") and justifies his translation with extended notes and a long excursus on the two terms.[143] He argues that Paul uses terms common in Philippi ("ortsüblichen Terminus"). Dibelius does not ask whether these terms have currency in military circles. John Reumann presents the case that the term ἐπίσκοπος (episkopos) "describes a supervisory office in the state, in various societies and in other groups in the Graeco-Roman world, often with financial responsibilities."[144] But there is some evidence to suggest military usage. Xenophon describes Clearchus as τυχὼν τότε τὰς τάξεις ἐπιοσκοπῶν (tychōn tote tas taxeis 'episkopōn, "overseeing the arrangement") of his troops, when his guards informed him that heralds from the Persian king were there. He ordered the camp guards to tell the heralds to wait until he had some leisure,[145] while he credits Cyrus the Great with ordering his officers to "inspect the weapons of your horses and yourselves" (ἐπισκέψασθε, episkepsasthe, "oversee") before battle.[146] The term is at home also in a military context. At present, however, I know of no evidence for διάκονος (diakonos) as a military title.[147]

The reference to the πραίτοριον ("pretorium") in Phil 1:13 is, in the first instance, a reference to an elite military unit stationed in Rome as the emperor's bodyguard.[148] A series of coins from Philippi picture the goddess Victoria with the legend VIC(toria) AVG(usta) on their obverse. Their reverse shows three Roman military standards ringed by a beaded "milling," with the legend COHOR(s) to the left and PRAE(toria) to the right, and below the standards PHIL.[149] Collart points out that "Ces pièces apportent la preuve que Philippies fut colonisée aussi par une cohorte de prétoriens."[150] Descendants of those original colonists might well have a special interest in members of the Pretorian guard who became Christian.[151] Plate XXXI in Collart shows coinage of the early imperial period (Claudius, Nero, Vespasian, Domitian, etc.); almost all the coins carry on the reverse the same iconography as the Augustan coins, the emperor on the left crowned by the genius of the town from the right, with the legend identifying the coinage as coming from the COL(onia)AVG(usta) IVL (ia) PHILIP(pensis).[152]

Paul's extended treatment of his own imprisonment (Phil 1:18–26), and hence absence from Philippi, is also illuminated by military customs and language. A general should not be absent from a battle, but should exhort the troops and lead them into war. Paul's letter fulfils the former obligation; his absence is a problem.

Moreover, as Aeneas Tacticus says, a leader "will inspire [his] friends with courage by [his] initiative and fearlessness and arouse fear in [his] enemies so that they will remain quietly at home."[153]

Paul's imprisonment might well appear to raise an impediment to his ministry for Roman citizens. In Roman law a prisoner of war lost his status as citizen, recovering it only when freed.

> When a Roman citizen had been captured in war he was automatically reduced to slavery. As far as the Roman legal system was concerned he was civilly dead. However, if he returned to Roman territory thereafter (provided that his capture was genuine, i.e., that he had not deserted to the enemy), most of his former rights were revived. This was known as the *ius postliminium, limen* being the Latin for "threshold"; the term thus refers to crossing back over the threshold of the Roman state.[154]

But Paul's lack of fear before death (1:21–24) will encourage the Philippians to greater efforts on behalf of the gospel, just as his imprisonment has served to advance the gospel (εἰς προκοπὴν τοῦ εὐαγγελίου ἐλήλυθεν, *eis prokopēn tou euangeliou elēlythen*, 1:12), for which they are to battle (1:27). The term προκοπή (*prokopē*, "advancement;" 1:25) is at home in many contexts; it occurs in Stoic philosophers to denote ethical progress.[155] But it also occurs in military contexts; Polybius uses it in relation to the war of the Achaeans, Philip, and their allies against the Aetolians and of Asdroubus against Karchedon.[156] Paul here describes the progress of the gospel like the advance of an army (1:25).

Paul argues that his imprisonment will actually end in victory (ἀποβήσεται εἰς σωτηρίαν, *apobēsetai eis sōtērian*, 1:26). Paul's words in 1:21–26 gain new poignancy when read against this background. Does μενῶ καὶ παραμενῶ (*menō kai paramenō*, "I remain and will remain along [with you]," 1:25) suggest that Paul will remain steadfast in line (see the references to μένειν above)? Or does it pick up the theme of the absent commander? Perhaps both. Paul will do whatever is necessary; he anticipates his being with the Philippians "once again" (1:26). If he remains (i.e., does not die), it is for their benefit, that is "for their advance and joy of faith" (εἰς τὴν ὑμῶν προκοπὴν καὶ χαρὰν τῆς πίστεως, *eis tēn hymōn prokopēn kai charan tēs pisteōs*; 1:25). Paul's experience parallels theirs. Their forward march will benefit from his remaining alive.

Paul's Co-workers (Phil 2:19–30)

Paul discusses his personal plans and situation in relation to Timothy and Epaphroditus in 2:19–30. He describes Timothy as ἰσόψυχος (alter-ego)"[157] who will recall them γνησίως (*gnesios*, "nobly") to the things that concern them. Paul describes him as a general would describe a trusted aide, an alter ego, a friend who carries out necessary commissions.

Paul takes up the case of Epaphroditus in Phil 2:25–30. His name is interesting, suggesting that his parents dedicated him to Aphrodite (Venus). The Julian line of emperors claimed descent from Venus through Aeneas. Dedication to Venus might, then, imply dedication or fidelity to the emperor. Paul identifies Epaphroditus as a brother, a coworker, and fellow soldier (ἀδελφὸν καὶ συνεργὸν καὶ συστρατιώτης, adelphon kai synergon kai systratiōtēs; Phil 2:25). Epaphroditus served as their emissary (ἀπόστολος καὶ λειτουργός, apostolos kai leitourgos) who carried out a liturgy, a public service to the state, though this time it is to Paul's need (2:25).[158] Paul reports on Epaphroditus's health because the Philippians had heard he was sick (2:26). Xenophon points out that Cyrus was concerned about the health of his soldiers, even to setting up clinics for them.[159] Paul sends him back to Philippi in order to give them joy and to make his own mind ἀλυπότερος (alypoteros, "free from anxiety," 2:28). The Philippians are urged to welcome him joyfully (2:29) and to regard people like him as worthy of civic honors. The term ἔντιμος (entimos, "worthy of public honor") belongs to the linguistic field of Greek honorific inscriptions set up for people who performed a "liturgy" (a public benefaction) to the city, often to people who served as ambassadors.[160] Paul asks the Philippian Christians to recognize Epaphroditus's "public service" on their behalf. He has filled up what was lacking in their liturgy.

In Phil 4:2–4, Paul urges Euodia and Syntyche to have the same mind, just what he had urged upon all the letter recipients in 1:27–2:4. These two women have struggled (συνήθλησαν, synēthlēsan) alongside Paul, that is, been coworkers along with others in Philippi (τῶν λοιπῶν συνεργῶν μου, tōn loipōn synergōn mou). These leaders are Paul's fellow soldiers, like Epaphroditus (2:25) who risked his life (2:27).

Paul calls the Philippians "my joy and crown" (4:1). The στέφανος ("crown") has rich associations and significance in the ancient world.[161] Ancients placed crowns on sacrificial animals, on cult statues and altars, and on priests. Magistrates at times wore them. They were used in symposia and weddings. At times corpses were crowned at burial. The crown is a symbol of victory in the games, in war (worn in triumphs), and a reward to soldiers. The Gemma Augustea (the Augustan Cameo) shows the deified Augustus seated on a throne in the process of being crowned. Paul is reminding the Philippians that their actions determine whether or not he will receive a military crown as a victor welcomed into the heavenly commonwealth. Paul suggests that the Philippians' struggle will determine whether his victory crown will be a military or political award from a grateful Lord Jesus and his heavenly commonwealth.[162] Therefore he calls on them to "stand firm" (στήκετε, stēkete); the verb forms an inclusio, a ring with 1:27 by recalling the fundamental interpretation of life in the polis as standing firm.

Twice near the close of the letter Paul links God with peace. Philippians 4:7

says the "peace of God" will guard (φρουρήσει, *phrourēsei*) hearts and minds; in 4:9 Paul promises that "the God of peace will be with you" (4:9). A statue base from the forum of Philippi is dedicated to the *Quies Augusti* ("the quiet of Augustus").[163] A fragmentary inscription from the *macellum* (meat market) south of the forum area mentions the *aequitas Augusti* ("impartiality of Augustus").[164] One might add to these local inscriptions the public recognition of the *pax Romana* by the Priene calendar inscription. The Roman army under the imperator was the guarantor of peace and the guardian of the borders. Paul couples ἡ εἰρήνη τοῦ θεοῦ (*hē eirēnē tou theou*, "the peace of God") with the verb φρουρήσει (*phrourēsei*), "will guard." Herodotus speaks of guarding the land[165] or a bridge,[166] Thucydides of garrisoning Potidaea.[167] A φρούριον (*phrourion*) is a hill-top fort,[168] a term applicable to the fortification of Akro-Philippi, which towers high over the city. As Caesar Augustus brought peace to the Roman world, so the Lord Jesus brings peace to his Philippian army, an excellent closure to this highly military letter.[169]

Philippians corresponds to the genre of military harangue. Paul compares the Philippian Christians with their enemy, to the enemy's disadvantage. He urges them to fight valiantly. He holds out before them the award of glory when their Lord Jesus comes. He implies that they fight, as he did, for δικαιοσύνη (*dikaiosunē*), "justice." He appeals to their citizenship in the heavenly commonwealth. And their Lord is superior to the enemy. So, Phil 1:27–4:1 uses many of the features of the military harangue.

Military language also occurs in other parts of the letter, though not with such equal density. Paul, probably also uses the language of friendship, though the term itself never occurs.[170] Such language was well known in the ancient world, treatises being written on it.[171] John Reumann has been critical of identifying the genre as a letter of friendship, though he agrees that the vocabulary of the *topos* is probably present.[172] There is also evident use of the language of the polis, of commercial language, and possibly or Roman legal language.[173] But I am convinced that the greatest of these is military language.

Part III. Other Relevant Pauline and Paulinist Texts

Pauline texts: Rom 16:20
Paulinist texts: Eph 6:10–17; 2 Tim 4:6

Part IV. Bibliography

Web Sites for Athletics

http://www.perseus.tufts.edu/Olympics/ [Perseus (search for Olympic Games)]
http://depthome.brooklyn.cuny.edu/classics/dunkle/courses/clsscs22.htm [Roger Dunkle (course materials on Greek athletics)]

RELIGIOUS GAMES

http://www.csun.edu/~hcfll004/sportbib.html [sport in antiquity: a brief bibliography]

http://www.trinity.edu/mgarriso/Vases/VaseProjects/EB/greekweb8.html [athletics and vases in ancient Greece, Eliza Blum]

http://www.novaroma.org/ludi/ [Roman Ludi (games)]

http://abacus.bates.edu/~mimber/Rciv/gladiator.htm [the gladiator]

Greek and Roman Athletics

Dodge, Hazel. "Amusing the Masses: Buildings for Entertainment and Leisure in the Roman World." Pages 205–55 in *Life, Death, and Entertainment in the Roman Empire,* edited by D. S. Potter and D. J. Mattingly. Ann Arbor: University of Michigan Press, 1999.

Gardiner, E. Norman. *Athletics of the Ancient World.* Chicago: Ares; Oxford: Clarendon Press, 1978.

Harris, Keith. *Sport in Greece and Rome.* Aspects of Greek and Roman Life. London: Thames and Hudson; Ithaca, N.Y.: Cornell University Press, 1972.

Matz, David. *Greek and Roman Sports: A Dictionary of Athletes and Events from the Eighth Century B.C. to the Third Century A.D.* Jefferson, N.C.: McFarland, 1991.

Miller, Stephen. *Arete: Greek Sports from Ancient Sources.* 2d ed. Berkeley and Los Angeles: University of California Press, 1991.

———. *Nemea: A Guide to the Site and Museum.* Berkeley: University of California Press, 1990.

Poliakoff, Michael R. *Combat Sports in the Ancient World: Competition, Violence, and Culture.* New Haven: Yale University Press, 1987.

Potter, David S. "Entertainers in the Roman Empire." Pages 256–325 in *Life, Death, and Entertainment in the Roman Empire,* edited by D. S. Potter and D. J. Mattingly. Ann Arbor: University of Michigan Press, 1999.

Reed, Nancy B. *More Than Just a Game: The Military Nature of Greek Athletic Contests.* Chicago: Ares, 1998.

Sansone, David. *Greek Athletics and the Genesis of Sport.* Berkeley, Los Angeles, and London: University of California Press, 1998.

Scanlon, Tom. *Greek and Roman Athletics.* Chicago: Ares, 1984.

Swadling, Judith. *The Ancient Olympic Games.* Austin: University of Texas Press, 1981.

Sweet, Waldo E. *Sport and Recreation in Ancient Greece: A Sourcebook with Translations.* Oxford and New York: Oxford University Press, 1987.

Gladiatorial Games

Barton, Carlin. *The Sorrows of the Ancient Romans: The Gladiator and the Monster.* Princeton, N.J.: Princeton University Press, 1993.

Futrell, Alison. *Blood in the Arena: The Spectacle of Roman Power.* Austin: University of Texas Press, 1997.

Hopkins, Keith. *Death and Renewal*. Cambridge: Cambridge University Press, 1983.

Humphrey, John. *Roman Circuses: Arenas for Chariot Racing*. Berkeley: University of California Press, 1986.

Kyle, Donald G. *Spectacles of Death in Ancient Rome*. London and New York: Routledge, 1998.

Plass, Paul. *The Games of Death in Ancient Rome*. Madison: University of Wisconsin Press, 1995.

Veyne, Paul. *Bread and Circuses: Historical Sociology and Political Pluralism*. London: Allen Lane, Penguin Press, 1990.

Wiedemann, Thomas. *Emperors and Gladiators*. London and New York: Routledge, 1992.

The Greek and Roman Armies

WEB SITES

http://www.fiu.edu/~eltonh/warfare/gwarfare.html [warfare in the Greek world]

http://www.csun.edu/~hcfll004/armybibl.html [the Roman army, a bibliography (John Paul Adams's massive bibliography]

http://webpages.charter.net/brueggeman/ [the Roman army, tactics (Gary Brueggeman)]

http://www.roman-empire.net/army/army.html [the Roman army]

ANCIENT WRITERS AND MILITARY DOCUMENTS[174]

Aeneas Tacticus. *On the Defense of Fortified Positions*. Translated by the Illinois Classical Club. LCL. 1928. Reprint, Cambridge: Harvard University Press, 1986.

———. *How to Survive under Siege*. Translated by D. Whitehead. Oxford: Oxford University Press, 1990.

Arrian, Flavius. *TEXNH TAKTIKA (Tactical Handbook) and EKTAXIS KATA ALANWN (The Expedition against the Alani)*. Translated and edited by James G. DeVoto. Chicago: Ares, 1993.

Asclepiodotus. *Tactics*. Translated by the Illinois Classical Club. LCL. 1928. Reprint, Cambridge: Harvard University Press, 1986.

Belopoeica. Pages 105–84 in *Greek and Roman Artillery: Technical Treatises*, edited and translated by E. W. Marsden. Oxford: Clarendon Press, 1971.

Devine, A.M. "Aelian's Manual and Hellenistic Military Tactics: A New Translation from the Greek with an Introduction." *Ancient World* 20 (1989): 31–64.

Frontinus, Sextus Julius. *The Stratagems*. Translated by Charles E. Bennett. LCL. Cambridge: Harvard University Press, 1925.

Onasander. *The General*. Translated by the Illinois Classical Club. LCL. 1928. Reprint, Cambridge: Harvard University Press, 1986.

Polyaenus. *Stratagems of War*. Edited and translated by Peter Krentz and Everett L. Wheeler. 2 vols. Chicago: Ares, 1994.

Sage, M. *Warfare in Ancient Greece: A Sourcebook*. London, 1996.

Valerius Maximus. *Memorable Doings and Sayings*. Edited and translated by D. R. Shackleton Bailey. 2 vols. LCL. Cambridge: Harvard University Press, 2000. [2.7: "Of Military Discipline"; 2.8: "Of Triumphal Law"; 4.4: "Stratagems."]

Vegetius Renatus, Flavius. *Epitoma Rei Militaris*. Edited with an English translation by Leo F. Stelten. New York: Peter Lang, 1990.

———. *Epitome of Military Science*. Translated with notes and introduction by N. P. Milner. Translated Texts for Historians 16. 2d ed. Liverpool, England: Liverpool University Press, 1996.

Xenophon. *Anabasis*. Translated by Carleton L. Brownson. LCL. Cambridge: Harvard University Press, 1922.

———. *Hellenica*. Translated by Carleton L. Brownson. 2 vols. LCL. Cambridge: Harvard University Press, 1918.

Ancient Warfare

Connolly, Peter. *Greece and Rome at War*. Englewood Cliffs, N.J.: Prentice-Hall, 1981.

Dawson, Doyne. *The Origins of Western Warfare: Militarism and Morality in the Ancient World*. Boulder, Colo.: Westview Press, 1996.

Hackett, John, Sir, ed. *Warfare in the Ancient World*. New York: Facts on File, 1989.

Greek Warfare

Adcock, F. E. *The Greek and Macedonian Art of War*. Berkeley: University of California Press, 1957.

Anderson, John Kinloch. *Military Theory and Practice in the Age of Xenophon*. Berkeley: Unversity of California Press, 1970.

Ducrey, P. *Warfare in Ancient Greece*. Translated by Janet Lloyd. New York: Schocken Books, 1986. [Translation of French original.]

Hanson, Victor Davis, ed. *Hoplites: The Classical Greek Battle Experience*. London and New York: Routledge, 1991.

———. *The Western Way of War: Infantry Battle in Classical Greece*. New York: Alfred A. Knopf, 1989.

Pritchett, W. K. *The Greek State at War*. 5 vols. Berkeley: University of California Press, 1971–91.

Snodgrass, A. M. *Arms and Armour of the Greeks*. Ithaca, N.Y.: Cornell University Press, 1967.

Worley, Leslie J. *Hippeis: The Cavalry of Ancient Greece*. Boulder, Colo.: Westview Press, 1994.

The Roman Army

Baus, Karl. *Der Kranz in Antike und Christentum*. Theophaneia 2. Bonn: Peter Hanstein, 1940.

Bishop, M. C., and J. C. N. Coulston. *Roman Military Equipment: From the Punic Wars to the Fall of Rome*. London: B. T. Batsford, 1993.

Campbell, Brian. *The Emperor and the Roman Army, 31 B.C.–A.D. 235*. Oxford: Clarendon Press, 1984.

———. *The Roman Army: 31 B.C.–A.D. 337*. London: Routledge, 1994. [A source book.]

Davies, R. W. "The Daily Life of the Roman Soldier under the Principate," "Duties of Officers and Men," and "Administration." Pages 299–338, 305–10, and 312–14 in *ANRW* II.1. Berlin and New York: de Gruyter, 1974.

Elton, Hugh. *Warfare in Roman Europe, A.D. 350–425*. Oxford: Clarendon Press, 1996.

Goldsworthy, Adrian Keith. *The Roman Army at War, 100 B.C.–A.D. 200*. Oxford: Clarendon Press, 1996 [1997].

———. *Roman Warfare*. London: Cassell & Co., 2000.

Grant, Michael. *The Army of the Caesars*. New York: Charles Scribner's Sons, 1974.

Holder, Paul I. *The Auxilia from Augustus to Trajan*. BAR International Series 70. Oxford: Archaeopress, 1980.

Keppie, Lawrence. *The Making of the Roman Army: From Republic to Empire*. New edition. Norman: University of Oklahoma Press, 1998.

Le Bohec, Yann. *The Imperial Roman Army*. New York: Hippocrene Books; London: B. T. Batsford, 1993.

MacMullen, Ramsay. "The Legion as Society." *Historia* 33 (1984): 440–56.

———. *Soldier and Civilian in the Later Roman Army*. Cambridge and London: Harvard University Press, 1963.

Rich, John, and Graham Shipley, eds. *War and Society in the Roman World*. Leicester-Nottingham Studies in Ancient Society 5. New York and London: Routledge, 1993. [Collection of twelve papers.]

Speidel, Michael P. *Riding for Caesar: The Roman Emperors' Horse Guards*. Cambridge: Harvard University Press, 1994.

Watson, G. R. *The Roman Soldier*. Ithaca, N.Y.: Cornell University Press, 1969.

Webster, Graham. *The Roman Imperial Army of the First and Second Centuries A.D.* 3d ed. Norman: University of Oklahoma Press, 1998.

Whittaker, C. R. *Frontiers of the Roman Empire*. Baltimore: Johns Hopkins University Press, 1994.

New Testament Metaphors: Athletics and Warfare[175]

Bultmann, Rudolf. *Der Stil der paulinischen Predigt und die kynisch-stoische Diatribe*. FRLANT 13. Göttingen: Vandenhoeck und Ruprecht, 1910.

Geoffrion, Timothy. *The Rhetorical Purpose and the Political and Military Character of Philippians*. Lewiston, N.Y.: Mellen Biblical, 1993.

Harnack, Adolf von. *Militia Christi: The Christian Religion and the Military in the First Three Centuries*. Translated by David McInnes Gracie. Philadelphia: Fortress Press, 1983.

Krentz, Edgar. "De Caesare et Christo." *Currents in Theology and Mission* 28 (2001): 340–45.

———. "Military Language and Metaphors in Philippians." Pages 105–27 in *Origins and Method: Towards a New Understanding of Judaism and Christianity, Essays in Honour of John C. Hurd*, edited by Bradley H. McLean. JSNTSup 96. Sheffield, England: Sheffield Academic Press, 1993.

Pfitzner, Victor C. *Paul and the Agon Motif.* NovTSup 16. Leiden: E. J. Brill, 1967.

Stowers, Stanley K. "Friends and Enemies in the Politics of Heaven." In *Thessalonians, Philippians, Galatians, Philemon.* Vol. 1 of *Pauline Theology,* edited by Jouette M. Bassler. Minneapolis: Fortress Press, 1991.

Straub, Werner. *Die Bildersprache des Apostels Paulus.* Tübingen: J. C. B. Mohr [Paul Siebeck], 1937.

Williams, David J. *Paul's Metaphors: Their Content and Character.* Peabody, Mass.: Hendrickson, 1999.

Appendix: A List of Military Harangues

(*a*) Thucydides reports a number: Pericles, as general, to the Athenian assembly (2.60.4), general to army (2.87), Phormio to army (2.89), Demosthenes to army (4.10; 4.93.1), Hippocrates to army (4.95), Brasidas to army (4.126.1; 4.127.1; 5.9.10), to the Mantineans (5.69.1–2), Meias to army (6.68), Nicias to navy (7.63.3), Gylippus to navy (7.66), mutual encouragement of army (8.76.3).

(*b*) Xenophon, *Anab.* 3.2.8–32; 3.1.20–24, 42–44; Cyrus in Xenophon, *Cyr.* 1.4; Cyrus in *Cyr.* 6.4.12.

(*c*) Polybius: general to army (1.27); Hannibal to army (3.44); Hannibal and Scipio (3.63–64); Aemilius to his army (3.108); Hannibal (3.111); Scipio (11.28; 11.31); Hannibal (20.10); Scipio and Hannibal (15.10–111).

(*d*) Dionysius Halicarnassus: Posthumius (*Ant. rom.* 6.6); Fabius (9.9).

(*e*) Diodorus Siculus: Nicias at Syracuse (13.15; 18.15); Callicratides (13.98).

(*f*) Arrian: Alexander before Issus in Arrian, *De ex. Alex.* (2.83); Alexander at the Hyphasis (5.25); Alexander to soldiers proposing to return (7.9).

(*g*) Dio Cassius: Caesar before battling Ariovistus (38.36–46); Caesar to discontented army (41.27); Antony before Actium (50.16–24); Caesar Augustus before Actium (50.24–30); three brief speeches of generals in 62.9–11.

(*h*) Appian: Caesar to his army (*De bello civ.* 2.73); Cassius to army (4.90); Brutus to army (4.117); Antony to army (4.119); Scipio to army (*De bello Punico* 8.19 and 116).

(*i*) Herodianus: Severus to his army (3.6); others in 2.10 and 8.3.

(*j*) Josephus: Herod to his army (*Ant.* 15.5).

(*k*) Theophylact 22.13–14; 3.13.[176]

Notes

1. Emil Schürer, *The History of the Jewish People in the Age of Jesus Christ (175 B.C.–A.D. 135),* a new English version revised and edited by Geza Vermes and Fergus Millar (Edinburgh: T. & T. Clark, 1973), 1:148–49. Robert Doran, "The High Cost of a Good Education," in *Hellenism in the Land of Israel* (ed. John J. Collins and Gregory E. Sterling; Christianity and Judaism in Antiquity 13; Notre Dame, Ind.: University of Notre Dame Press, 2001), 94, describes all the facilities and the costs involved in building such a gymnasium.

2. There was, nonetheless, much influence from Hellenism in Palestine. See Martin Hengel, *Hellenism and Judaism: Studies in Their Encounter in Palestine during*

the Early Hellenistic Period (2 vols.; Philadelphia: Fortress Press, 1974); idem, *The Hellenization of Judaea in the First Century after Christ* (Philadelphia: Trinity Press International, 1989); and the essays in John J. Collins and Gregory E. Sterling, eds., *Hellenism in the Land of Israel* (Christianity and Judaism in Antiquity 13; Notre Dame, Ind.: University of Notre Dame Press, 2001).

3. See J. Reynolds and R. Tannenbaum, *Jews and Godfearers at Aphrodisias* (Cambridge Philological Society, Supplementary Volume 12; Cambridge: Cambridge Philological Society, 1987), 3–131, for text and discussion of the inscription, excavation inventory no. 76.1.

4. David Sansone, *Greek Athletics and the Genesis of Sport* (Berkeley, Los Angeles, and London: University of California Press, 1988), 76–77. By "culture" in the subheading I mean the aura surrounding athletics and athletic victories. The only ancient treatise on athletics is Philostratos, "On Athletics." Waldo E. Sweet, *Sport and Recreation in Ancient Greece: A Sourcebook with Translations* (New York and Oxford: Oxford University Press, 1987), gives an English translation on pp. 212–30. Other important sources are Pausanias, Lucian, numerous inscriptions, and incidental remarks in many ancient writers.

Two excellent collections of ancient sources in translation are Sweet, *Sport and Recreation*, and Stephen G. Miller, *Arete: Greek Sports from Ancient Sources* (Berkeley, Los Angeles, and London: University of California Press, 1991). Both include texts from the early Roman Empire.

5. Greeks held contests in drama, oratory, dancing, lyre playing, and even in drinking (symposia). Even Greek prose was often structured antithetically, as in the case of the rhetor Gorgias.

6. It was not surprising that Plato should select the Academy, which included a gymnasium, for teaching philosophy.

7. See the excellent discussion by Hazel Dodge, "Amusing the Masses: Buildings for Entertainment and Leisure in the Roman World," in *Life, Death, and Entertainment in the Roman Empire* (ed. D. S. Potter and D. J. Mattingly; Ann Arbor: University of Michigan Press, 1999), 205–55.

8. E. Norman Gardiner, *Athletics of the Ancient World* (corrected edition; Oxford: Clarendon, 1955), 33–36. Standard works on Olympia are Alfred Mallwitz, *Olympia und seine Bauten* (Darmstadt, Germany: Wissenschaftliche Buchgesellschaft, 1972; licensed printing from Prestel Verlag, Munich); H.-V. Hermann, *Olympia: Heiligtum und Wettkampfstätte* (Munich: Hirmer Verlag, 1972).

9. N. J. Richardson, "Isthmian Games," *OCD* 772.

10. Ibid., 1285.

11. Ibid., 1033; Stephen G. Miller, ed., *Nemea: A Guide to the Site and Museum* (Berkeley: University of California Press, 1990), 2–3.

12. To Zeus at Olympia, Apollo at Delphi, Poseidon at Isthmia, and to Zeus at Nemea.

13. One can still read the text of the oath at Delphi in the inscription on the southern wall of the stadium.

14. Marcus Aurelius Asclepediades speaks of competing in Italy, Greece, and Asia, winning at Pisa, Delphi, Nemea (twice), Argos, Rome, Puteoli, Naples, Nikopolis, Athens (five times), Smyrna (five times), Pergamum (three times), Ephesus (three times), Epidauros, Rhodes, Sardis, Sparta, Mantinea, and others,

retiring at age twenty-five, never having lost. *IG* XIV.1102 (Greek inscription, dated to 181 C.E., found in Rome); cited in Sweet, *Sport and Recreation*, 146–47; additional epigraphic evidence on 148–50.

15. Nancy B. Reed, *More Than Just a Game: The Military Nature of Greek Athletic Contests* (Chicago: Ares, 1998); Judith Swaddling, *The Ancient Olympic Games* (Austin: University of Texas Press, 1980), 57; Michael B. Poliakoff, *Combat Sports in the Ancient World: Competition, Violence, and Culture* (New Haven and London: Yale University Press, 1987).

16. Herodotus 6.127. References from Henry George Liddell and Robert Scott, *A Greek-English Lexicon* (revised and augmented by Henry Stuart Jones, with assistance of Roderick McKenzie; Oxford: Clarendon Press, 1940; reprint, with revised supplement edited by P. G. W. Glare, with assistance of A. A. Thompson, Oxford: Clarendon Press, 1996).

17. Herodotus 2.91; Plato, *Leg.* 658A.

18. The term for the starting line was γραμμή (LSJ, s.v.) or ὕσπληξ (LSJ, s.v.), when a rope or bar was dropped, as in the early starting line at the Isthmia, as interpreted by Oscar Broneer. Thus the term ἀφορμή (*aphormē*) in Gal 5:13 has nothing to do with racing; it rather means pretext or, in a military context, base camp.

19. The five events of pentathlon included discus throw, jumping, javelin throw, running, and wrestling, all held in one afternoon. It tested more comprehensive athletic ability. Swaddling, *Ancient Olympic Games*, 49; Gardiner, *Athletics of the Ancient World*, 177–80.

20. See Poliakoff, *Combat Sports*.

21. These are well described by a number of authors: Gardiner, *Athletics of the Ancient World*, 128–221; H. A. Harris, *Sport in Greece and Rome* (Aspects of Greek and Roman Life; Ithaca, N.Y.: Cornell University Press, 1972); Swaddling, *Ancient Olympic Games*, 44–73. See Miller, *Nemea*, 4–7, for a listing of events there.

22. At Olympia of wild olive, at Delphi of laurel (bay leaves), at the Isthmia of wild celery, at Nemea of parsley; Pausanias 8.48.2–3; Miller, *Arete*, 77; Gardiner, *Athletics of the Ancient World*, 33–37. These crowns would deteriorate over time; inscriptions often were used to record victory more permanently.

23. The subsequent honor still survived in the Roman era, as two victory stelae at Isthmia make clear. I am not aware of photographs or publications of these inscriptions.

24. In the Roman Empire often erected by the athlete himself, for example, the inscription of T. Flavius Archibius, 107 C.E. (*IG* XIV.747), Miller, *Arete*, no. 150, p. 168; that of Markos Aurelios Demetrios in ca. 200 C.E. (*IG* XIV.1102), cited by Miller, *Arete*, no. 153, p. 171; cf. n. 14 above for the inscription of Marcus Aurelius Asclepediades.

25. Evidence for Athens in *IG* I (2d ed.) 77, cited in Waldo E. Sweet, *Sport and Recreation in Ancient Greece: A Sourcebook with Translations* (New York: Oxford University Press, 1987), 125–27.

26. Pseudo-Dionysius, p. 285.5–10 Usener-Radermacher; D. A. Russell and N. G. Wilson, *Menander Rhetor* (edited with translation and commentary; Oxford: Clarendon, 1981), 377: λόγος γὰρ εἰς πάντα ἐπιτήδειος καὶ προς πᾶν ἐπιρρώνυσιν· οὕτως καὶ ἐπὶ πολέμου καὶ ἐπὶ παρατάξεως δέονται στρατιῶται τοῦ παρὰ τῶν

στρατηγῶν λόγου καὶ τῆς προτροπης, καὶ αὐτοὶ αὐτῶν ἐρρωμενέστεροι ἐγένοντο. μάλιστα δὲ οἱ ἀθληταὶ δέοιντο ἄν τῆς ἀπὸ τοῦ λόγου προτροπῆς καὶ ἐπικελεύσεως.

27. Pseudo-Dionysius, p. 286.5–9 Usener-Radermacher; Russell and Wilson, *Menander Rhetor*, 378: ὥσπερ γὰρ καὶ ἐν στρατοπέδῳ οἱ γνησιώτατοι παρὰ τῶν στρατηγῶν λόγους ἀκούσαντες μάλιστα φιλοτιμοῦνται περὶ τὴν νίκην, οὕτως καὶ οἱ ἐν τοῖς ἀγῶσι προτρεπτικοὺς λόγους οἰκείως ἀναδεξάμενοι· μάλιστα γὰρ ἄν ὀρέγονται τοῦ περιγενέσθαι. Theodore C. Burgess, "Epideictic Literature," in *Studies in Classical Philology* (vol. 3; Chicago: University of Chicago Press, 1902), 209, calls attention to these two passages.

28. In his discussion of athletics, Athenaeus, *Deipn.* 10.413–14, cites Euripides, who says that there is nothing worse than the genus of athletes "who will neither learn how to live well nor can they." He next cites Xenophanes, who complains that the athlete is honored for a victory, when he is not as good as the wise man. Both in Sweet, *Sport*, 121–22.

29. Dio Chrysostom, *Or.* 66.5 (*1 Glor.*). In *Or.* 31.110 (*Rhod.*) he praises athletes. See C. P. Jones, *The Roman World of Dio Chrysostom* (Cambridge: Harvard University Press, 1978), 110, for additional references.

30. Cicero, *Off.* 3.10.42, possibly borrowed from a Greek source (Chrysippus?).

31. For example, Epictetus, *Diatr.* 1.2.25–29, 37; 1.4.13; 1.24.1–2; 2.17.29–33, and throughout. See the indices in Epictetus, *Diat.* [Oldfather, LCL, vols. 1 and 2].

32. Maximus Tyrius, *Diss.* 1.4. See M. B. Trapp, ed., *Maximus Tyrius Dissertationes* (Stuttgart and Leipzig: B. G. Teubner, 1994); idem, *Maximus of Tyre: The Philosophical Orations*, translation with introduction and notes (Oxford: Clarendon, 1997), 8–9.

33. See ch. 2, "Greek Athletics in the Roman World," 44–74, in H. A. Harris, *Sport in Greece and Rome* (Aspects of Greek and Roman Life; Ithaca, N.Y.: Cornell University Press, 1972); Gardiner, "Roman Sports," in idem, *Athletics in the Ancient World*, 46–52.

34. Harris, *Sport in Greece and Rome*, does not mention them, nor does Gardiner, "Roman Sports," 117–27; both refer to the circus and chariot racing. The arena and the *ludi* do not fit their definition of sport!

35. Thus Martial 5.24 writes an epigram in praise of the gladiator Hermes. Good discussions of this ambivalent status in Carlin A. Barton, *The Sorrows of the Ancient Romans: The Gladiator and the Monster* (Princeton: Princeton University Press, 1993), 11–46; Thomas Wiedemann, *Emperors and Gladiators* (London: Routledge, 1992), 27–30. There has been extensive publication on the gladiators in recent years: Roland Auguet, *Cruelty and Civilization: The Roman Games* (London: George Allen and Unwin, 1972; reprint, London: Routledge, 1994); Paul Plass, *The Games of Death in Ancient Rome* (Madison: University of Wisconsin Press, 1995); Alison Futrell, *Blood in the Arena: The Spectacle of Roman Power* (Austin: University of Texas Press, 1997); Donald G. Kyle, *Spectacles of Death in Ancient Rome* (London: Routledge, 1998); D. S. Potter and D. J. Mattingly, eds., *Life, Death, and Entertainment in the Roman Empire* (Ann Arbor: University of Michigan Press, 1999).

36. See the chapter "Eastern Colonies," 62–72, in G. W. Bowersock, *Augustus and the Greek World* (Oxford: Oxford University Press, 1965), for a brief overview of the many Augustan colonies in the eastern Mediterranean.

37. "[I]n the eastern half of the empire too, gladiatorial games spread hand-in-hand with the identification by elites of their place within the Roman empire" (Wiedemann, *Emperors and Gladiators*, 43).

38. Erika Brodner, *Die römische Thermen und das antike Badewesen* (Darmstadt, Germany: Wissenschaftliche Buchgesellschaft, 1983), gives plans of numerous baths with *palaestrae*.

39. Martial 7.82, satirizing the sycophantic Monogenes at the baths, names hand-balls and bladder balls; 14.45–48, four different balls (cf. 7.32); 14.163 implies ball games before one bathes. Harris, *Sport in Greece and Rome*, 75–111, has an extensive discussion, with numerous references to Latin texts. Garrett G. Fagan, *Bathing in Public in the Roman World* (Ann Arbor: University of Michigan Press, 1999), 25, gives the Latin text of the Monogenes reference with a fresh translation and brief discussion. Brodner, *Römische Thermen*, 92, cites Martial on various ball games—without giving precise references.

40. Fagan, *Bathing in Public*, 9n. 21, notes the possibility for part of the *palaestra* in the Stabian Baths at Pompeii; see also p. 57.

41. See David G. Romano, "Post–146 B.C. Land Use in Corinth, and Planning of the Roman Colony of 44 B.C.," in *The Corinthia in the Roman Period* (ed. Timothy E. Gregory; Journal of Roman Archaeology, Supplementary Series 8; Ann Arbor, Mich.: Journal of Roman Archaeology, 1994), figs. 1 and 2. According to Donald Engels, *Roman Corinth: An Alternative Model for the Classical City* (Chicago: University of Chicago Press, 1990), 49–50, the theater and odeon were both modified for gladiatorial games before the arena was built in the third century C.E.

42. Philostratus, *Vit. Apol.* 4.22; reference from Widemann, *Emperors and Gladiators*, 43.

43. Lawrence Keppie, *The Making of the Roman Army from Republic to Empire* (Norman: University of Oklahoma Press, 1984; new preface and bibliography, 1998), lists twenty-eight legions under Augustus.

44. See Bowersock, *Augustus and the Greek World*, 62–72.

45. E. T. Salmon, *Roman Colonization under the Republic* (Aspects of Greek and Roman Life; Ithaca, N.Y.: Cornell University Press, 1970), 134, claims that Octavian demobilized more than 120,000 men after Aktion.

46. Augustus, *Res Gestae* 28.2: "Italia autem XXVIII [colo]nias, quae vivo me celeberrimae et frequentissimae fuerunt, me[a auctoritate] deductas habet" ("Italy moreover had twenty-eight colonies founded, which were famous and very crowded during my lifetime"). Cited according to *Res Gestae Divi Avgvsti: Das Monumentum Ancyranum* (ed. Hans Volkmann; 2d ed.; Kleine Texte 29/30; Berlin: Walter de Gruyter, 1964). Suetonius, *Aug.* 46, noted that "Divus Augustus adsignata orbi terrarum pace exercitus, qui aut sub Antonio aut Lepido militaverant, pariter et suarum legionum milites colonos fecit, alios in Italia, alios in provinciis" ("The divine Augustus, peace of the army having been given to the circle of lands, which either under Antony or Lepidus had waged war, founded colonies of soldiers, equally of their and also his own legions, some in Italy, others in the provinces").

47. *Res Gestae* 28.1. Volkmann, *Res Gestae*, 49, comments that these colonies of veterans served to hold the new empire together—as the context in which Augustus mentions them suggests. Salmon's "List of Roman Colonies," in idem, *Roman*

Colonization under the Republic, 158–64, includes Byllis, Cassandrea, Dium, Dyrrhachium, Pella, and Philippi as Macedonian colonies founded by Julius Caesar or Caesar Augustus. Thessalonica did not achieve colony status until the time of Valerian (253–60 C.E.).

48. Useful here are the works of Ramsay MacMullen, *Soldier and Civilian in the Later Roman Empire* (Harvard Historical Monographs 52; Cambridge: Harvard University Press, 1963); Yann Le Bohec, *The Roman Imperial Army* (New York: Hippocrene Books; London: B. T. Batsford, 1994); and John Rich and Graham Shipley, eds., *War and Society in the Roman World* (Leicester-Nottingham Studies in Ancient Society 5; London: Routledge, 1993).

49. Keppie, *Making of the Roman Army*, 146–71, describes this change well.

50. Brian Campbell, *The Roman Army, 31 BC–AD 337: A Sourcebook* (London: Routledge, 1994), gives more than four hundred texts in English translation.

51. Keppie, *Making of the Roman Army*, 149.

52. The phrase comes from Epictetus, *Diatr.* 1.14.15, comparing the soldier's oath to the emperor to the philosophic student's oath to God to live *kata physin* ("according to nature").

53. Sextus Julius Frontinus, *Strategemata* 4.1.4 [LCL, Bennett], says that the oath (*Sacramentum*) was the original name, but it became the *iusiurandum* in 216 B.C.E. Frontinus gives its content as a pledge "not to quit the force by flight, or in consequence of fear, and not to leave the ranks except to seek a weapon, strike a foe, or save a comrade." See Brian Campbell, *The Emperor and the Roman Army: 31 B.C.–A.D. 235* (Oxford: Clarendon Press, 1984), 23–32, for an extended discussion of the *sacramentum*. It is not surprising that early Christians adopted this term for the confession of Jesus as Lord in baptism.

54. The formulation is modern; see Graham Webster, *The Roman Imperial Army of the First and Second Centuries A.D.* (3d ed.; Norman: University of Oklahoma Press, 1998), 120 and 137. G. R. Watson, *The Roman Soldier* (Ithaca, N.Y.: Cornell University Press, 1969), 49n. 95, cites Dionysius of Halicarnassus, *Ant. rom.* 10.18.2; 11.43, on the oath.

55. See the section "The Officer Corps" in Le Bohec, *Roman Imperial Army*, 36–42.

56. Scholars perforce use modern, technical military language to describe the Roman army—though it is anachronistic and one should not press it.

57. Onasander is a contemporary of Paul, writing his treatise *Strategicus* (*The General*) under Claudius. He dedicated the work to Q. Veranius, consul in 49 C.E., who died in Britain in 59 C.E. See Alfred Neumann, "Onasandros," in *Der kleine Pauly: Lexikon der Antike* (ed. Konrat Ziegler and Walther Sontheimer; 5 vols.; Muenich: Alfred Druckenmüller Verlag, 1972), 4:300; F. A. Wright, *A History of Later Greek Literature* (New York: Macmillan, 1932), 260. The best edition is that of W. A. Oldfather, *Aeneas Tacticus, Asclepiodotus Onasander* (ed. The Illinois Classical Club, LCL; Cambridge: Harvard University Press, 1928).

58. Oldfather, *Aeneas Tacticus, Asclepiodotus Onasander*, 350.

59. Παραίνεσις ("exhortation") is the technical term for a general's speech.

60. Plato, *Ion* 540D.

61. Cf. E. Norden, *Die Antike Kunstprosa* (Leipzig: B. G. Teubner, 1915), 87n. 1, who comments: "Anreden an die Soldaten (παρακελεύσεις, παραινέσεις heißen sie

in unsern Thukydidesscholien) waren so üblich, daß die Kriegsschriftsteller vor-schreiben, zum Feldherrn zu wählen einen ἱκανὸν λέγειν ("Addresses to soldiers [called παρακελεύσεις, παραινέσεις in our Thucydides scholia] were so customary that the writers on military affairs prescribe choosing as commander one who is ἱκανὸν λέγειν [good at speaking]"). Norden also cites S. Dehner, *Hadriani reliquiae* (vol. 1; Bonn, 1883), 10.

62. Onasander 36:2 and 23.

63. Burgess, "Epideictic Literature," 209. He claims that more than forty exist in Greek literature alone. See the list in the appendix.

64. Burgess refers to Pseudo-Dionysius of Halicarnassus, *Ars Rhetorica. I. Artis generis demonstrativi capita selecta*. The standard edition of the Greek text is by Her-mann Usener and Ludwig Radermacher, *Dionysii Halicarnassei Opuscula* (Leipzig: B. G. Teubner, 1899–1904; reprint, 1965), 2.253–292. There is a good English trans-lation in Russell and Wilson, *Menander Rhetor*, 362–81.

65. This list is given by Burgess, "Epideictic Literature," 212–13, with reference to the speeches that contain them. Theon (2.115 Spengel) talks about the general's speech in his *Progymnasmata*. He says that a general who speaks to his soldiers about dangers must have the proper προσωποποιίς· στρατηγὸς τοῦς στρατιώταις ἐπὶ τοὺς κινδύνους ("persona: a general to his soldiers in relation to dangers").

66. Polyaenus collected military stratagems from many ancient sources in his *Strategemata*, dedicated in 161–66, during the Parthian War, to Marcus Aurelius and Lucius Verus. Quote from 3.11.1.

67. Fr. 93 [= Fr. 60, Diehl, Fr. 58 Bergk]: ἀλλά μοι σμικρός τις εἴη καὶ περὶ κνήμης ἰδεῖν; ῥοικός, ἀσφαλέως βεβηκὼς πόσσι, καρδίης πλέος. See *Archiloque Fragments* (text edited by François Lassere; translation and commentary by André Bonnard; Collection des Universités de France; Paris: Société d'édition "Les Belles Lettres," 1958), 30. Translation from Victor David Hanson, *The Western Way of War: Infantry Battle in Classical Greece* (New York: Alfred A. Knopf, 1989), 110. The first two lines of Archilochus read, "I don't like the towering captain with the spraddly length of leg, one who swaggers in his lovelocks and clean shaves be-neath his chin."

68. See Xenophon, *Mem.* 3.1; Onasander 33.1: "The general should fight cau-tiously rather than boldly, or should keep away altogether from a hand-to-hand fight with the enemy."

69. See Hanson, *Western Way of War*, 109.

70. Xenophon, *Anabasis* 3.1.37. On the relation of leader to soldier in classical Greece, see Everett L. Wheeler, "The General as Hoplite," in *Hoplites: The Classical Greek Battle Experience* (ed. Victor Davis Hanson; London and New York: Rout-ledge, 1991), 121–70. Wheeler gives extensive documentation from both classical and later Hellenistic historians such as Polybius and Plutarch and from the tacti-cian Polyaenus. This volume also has a short glossary of Greek military terms dis-cussed in the book. A dictionary of Greek military terms is a desideratum.

71. Vegetius 2.11, in describing the duties of the prefect of engineers, lists "en-gineers, carpenters, masons, wagon-makers, blacksmiths, painters, and other ar-tificers, ready-prepared to construct buildings for a winter camp, or siege-engines, wooden towers and other devices for storming enemy cities or defending our own, to fabricate new arms, wagons and the other kinds of torsion-

engines, or repair them when damaged." Cited from Vegetius, *Epitome of Military Science* (translation with notes and introduction by N. P. Milner; 2d ed.; Translated Texts for Historians 16; Liverpool: Liverpool University Press, 1996), 43. Mac-Mullen, *Soldier and Civilian*, 23–48, provides the most extensive discussion of the army's peacetime activity.

72. Sources for reconstructing this description include the one surviving manual from Latin antiquity: Flavius Vegetius Renatus, *Epitoma Rei Militaris* (edited with an English translation by Leo F. Stelten; New York: Peter Lang, 1990); see also Milner's translation, above, n. 71. Two other writers in Latin deal with special topics: Sextus Julius Frontinus, *The Stratagems* (LCL [Bennett]; Cambridge: Harvard University Press, 1925), treats sieges, while Valerius Maximus, *Memorable Doings and Sayings* (2 vols.; LCL [Shackleton Bailey]; Cambridge: Harvard University Press, 2000), discusses military discipline in 2.7, triumphal law in 2.8, and strategies in 4.4.

All three draw on earlier Greek writers of history and, especially, of military tactics. These include A. M. Devine, "Aelian's Manual and Hellenistic Military Tactics: A New Translation from the Greek with an Introduction," *Ancient World* 20 (1989): 31–64; Aeneas Tacticus, *On the Defense of Fortified Positions* (1928; LCL [Illinois Classical Club]; reprint, Cambridge: Harvard University Press, 1986); idem, *How to Survive under Siege* (trans. D. Whitehead; Oxford: Oxford University Press, 1990); Flavius Arrian, *ΤΕΧΝΗ ΤΑΚΤΙΚΑ (Tactical Handbook) and ΕΚΤΑΞΙΣ ΚΑΤΑ ΑΛΑΝΩΝ (The Expedition against the Alani)* (trans. and ed. James G. DeVoto; Chicago: Ares, 1993); Asclepiodotus, *Tactics* (1928; LCL [Illinois Classical Club]; reprint, Cambridge: Harvard University Press, 1986); Onasander, *The General* (1928; LCL [Illinois Classical Club]; reprint, Cambridge: Harvard University Press, 1986); Polyaenus, *Stratagems of War* (ed. and trans. Peter Krentz and Everett L. Wheeler; 2 vols.; Chicago: Ares, 1994); M. Sage, *Warfare in Ancient Greece: A Sourcebook* (London: Routledge, 1996).

73. Celebrated by Aelius Aristides, *Or.* 26, throughout. Critical Greek text in *Aelii Aristidis Smyrnaei Quae Supersunt Omnia* (ed. Bruno Keil; 2d ed.; Berlin: Weidmann, 1957), 91–124; ET: in Aelius Aristides, ΕΙΣ ΡΩΜΗΝ, *To Rome* (trans. Saul Levin; Glencoe, Ill.: Free Press, 1951). James H. Oliver, *The Ruling Power: A Study of the Roman Empire in the Second Century after Christ through the Roman Oration of Aelius Aristides* (Transactions of the American Philosophical Society, n.s., 43/4; Philadelphia: American Philosophical Society, 1953), provides an extensive introduction, translation, commentary, critical Greek text, and other relevant essays.

74. John Lazenby, "The Killing Zone," in *Hoplites: The Classical Greek Battle Experience* (ed. Victor David Hanson; London: Routledge, 1991), 103. Peter Connolly, *Greece and Rome at War* (Englewood Cliffs, N.J.: Prentice-Hall, 1981), 126–34, gives a good overview of the change in formations and tactics that differentiates the Roman legion from the Macedonian phalanx. See also H. D. M. Parker, *The Roman Legions* (New York: Dorset Press, 1992), 9–20, esp. 18–20.

75. Vegetius 1.26, as translated in Watson, *Roman Soldier*, 70–71. Watson gives the Latin text in a footnote. The best critical edition is now Flavius Vegetius Renatus, *Epitoma Rei Militaris* (ed. and trans. Leo F. Stelten; American University Studies, ser. 17, Classical Languages and Literature 11; New York: Peter Lang, 1990).

Asclepiadotus, *Tactics*, illustrates different formations used earlier by the phalanx, though he wrote in the first century B.C.E.

76. Polyaenus, *Stratagems of War* 2.10.2.

77. Le Bohec, *Imperial Roman Army*, 49–50. P. Krentz, "The *salpinx* in Greek Warfare," in Hanson, *Hoplites*, 110–20.

78. Aeneas, in his introduction to his treatise *On the Defense of Fortified Positions*.

79. See Edgar Krentz, "De Caesare et Christo," *CurTM* 28 (2001): 340–45.

80. The Gemma Augustea is a sardonyx cameo, Inv. no. IX A 79, in the Kunsthistorisches Museum in Vienna. The upper band portrays the apotheosis of Augustus. There is a good illustration with discussion in Karl Galinsky, *Augustan Culture: An Interpretive Introduction* (Princeton: Princeton University Press, 1996), 120–21; see Larry J. Kreitzer, *Striking New Images: Roman Imperial Coinage and the New Testament World* (JSNTSup 134; Sheffield, England: Sheffield Academic Press, 1996), 76–78, for a line drawing of the piece.

81. Ernst Künzl, *Der römische Triumph: Siegesfeiern im antiken Rom* (Munich: C. H. Beck, 1988). Campbell, *Emperor and the Roman Army*, 133–42, describes the significance of imperial triumphs.

82. *Monumentum Ancyranum* 4. A triumph with ovation was a minor triumph with the triumphator walking; a curile triumph was a major triumph in which he rode in a chariot. See *Res Gestae Divi Augusti* (LCL [Shipley]; Cambridge: Harvard University Press, 1924), 349 note d and 351 note a.

83. See H. Emonds, "Geistliche Kriegsdienst: Der Topos der militia spiritualis in der antiken Philosophie," in *Heilige Überlieferung* (ed. O. Casels; Münster, Germany: Aschendorff, 1938), 21–50, and Harry Sidebottom, "Philosophers' Attitudes to Warfare under the Principate," in *War and Society in the Roman World* (ed. John Rich and Graham Shipley; New York: Routledge, 1993), 241–64.

84. Epictetus, *Diss.* 1.14.13–17; see also 3.24.95–99. *Diss.* 1.9.16 may also use military language.

85. *Diss.* 3.26.29. The signal to retreat here is to commit suicide.

86. See *Ep. Mor.* 59.7–8, which praises a philosopher named Sextius, and 96.5: "And so, Lucilius, to live is to serve as a soldier. Therefore those who are tossed about and who go up and down through toilsome and harsh circumstances and go to meet most perilous military operations are brave men and the most illustrious of those in the fortresses." For additional references see Timothy C. Geoffrion, *The Rhetorical Purpose and the Political and Military Character of Philippians: A Call to Stand Firm* (Lewiston, N.Y.: Mellon Biblical, 1993), 39–42.

87. Maximus Tyrius 5.3 (Trapp, 44).

88. Maximus 1.3. See the index under "images, war" in Trapp's translation, 352, for many additional uses of military metaphors or similes.

89. Valerius Maximus, *Memorable Doings and Sayings* 2.7 (LCL, Shackleton Bailey, 2000). Cf. Clive Skidmore, *Practical Ethics for Roman Gentlemen: The Word of Valerius Maximus* (Exeter, England: University of Exeter Press, 1996), 53–58, esp. 58.

90. See Elizabeth R. Gebhardt, "The Isthmian Games and the Sanctuary of Poseidon in the Early Empire," in Gregory, *Corinthia in the Roman Period*, 82–89. She concludes: "In summary, representations of the victor's wreath and the deities of the sanctuary on the early duoviral coinage of Corinth tell us that the Isthmian

festival returned to the city's control almost immediately after the colony was founded. The absence of substantial archaeological remains around the temenos of Poseidon and the theater in the Isthmian sanctuary makes it likely that the actual celebration of the games remained largely in Corinth until the principate of Nero" (88).

The most extensive treatment of Pauline metaphors is David J. Williams, *Paul's Metaphors: Their Context and Character* (Peabody, Mass: Hendrickson, 1999). Williams provides excellent, terse descriptions of each area of investigation and extensive documentation, both from ancient sources and modern scholarship. Werner Straub, *Die Bildersprache des Apostels Paulus* (Tübingen: J. C. B. Mohr [Paul Siebeck], 1937), 115, notes the use of athletic and military imagery, but gives no extended discussion.

91. Key athletic terminology inserted in Greek.

92. Calvin Roetzel, *Paul: The Man and the Myth* (Columbia: University of South Carolina Press, 1998), 127, holds that the footrace metaphor is used in Rom 9:30–33; 11:11–12, 26–27; the only basis I can see is the use of the term "pursue" (διώκω, *diōkō*) in Rom 9:30–32. This is possible, but one term is not enough to be sure of metaphoric use. As the old Greek proverb puts it, "One swallow does not make a spring."

93. The term literally means to hit one under the eye, to give a black eye. LSJ, s.v., cites Diogenes Laertius 6.89 (Hicks, LCL) of Crates, who was struck in the face. Plutarch, *Fac.* 921–22 (Cherniss, LCL), speaks of giving the moon a black eye by describing the moon's face as murky air and smoldering fire (see BDAG, s.v.).

94. Romans 9:16 may use racing metaphorically. Straub, *Bildersprache des Apostels Paulus*, 102, notes that Paul often places two metaphors next to each other. Rudolf Bultmann, *Der Stil der paulinischen Predigt und die kynisch-stoische Diatribe* (FRLANT 13; Göttingen: Vandenhoeck & Ruprecht, 1910), 38, identifies this as a characteristic of the diatribe.

95. Lucian, *Cal.* 12 (Harmon, LCL); reference from Sweet, *Sport and Recreation*, 28.

96. See Gardiner, *Athletics of the Ancient World*, illustrations 89, 91, 92, and 93, and Sweet, *Sport and Recreation*, plate 3, p. 9 (Panathenaic amphora), and plate 4, p. 28 (a black-figured amphora), for ancient depictions of dashes and long-distance foot races. The runners are "straining" as they pursue the leader in the short race. Paul does not use the imagery of the long-distance race in discussing endurance (ὑπομονή, *hypomonē*).

97. Williams, *Paul's Metaphors*, 272. There is an extended race metaphor in Heb 12:1–2, also applied to life as Christian; there the stress is on endurance.

98. Sweet, *Sport*, 183; plate 61 shows a man playing a *diaulos* (flute) and carrying a *kithara* (lyre).

99. See the excellent article on "Music" by Andrew D. Barker, *OCD* 1003–12.

100. Williams, *Paul's Metaphors*, 260, called this to my attention.

101. This fits well with Paul's continued stress on his suffering and humilty throughout 2 Corinthians. He has no reputation (δόξα, *doxa*) according to human criteria, no letters of recommendation, and so on. See Abraham Malherbe, "The Beasts at Ephesus," in *Paul and the Popular Philosophers* (Minneapolis: Fortress

Press, 1989), 79–89. The gladiator took an oath (*sacramentum*, πίστις, *pistis*) that he was willing to die. See Barton, *Sorrows of the Ancient Romans*, 15–17; Wiedemann, *Emperors and Gladiators*, 107–8. Seneca, *Ep.* 37.1–2, gives the oath as a model for moral struggle.

102. Williams, *Paul's Metaphors*, 266, supports this interpretation. Alfred Plummer suggested the arena or a military interpretation in his ICC commentary (Edinburgh: T. &. T. Clark, 1915), 129. Margaret Thrall, in the new ICC commentary (Edinburgh: T. & T. Clark, 1994), 1:952, recognizes the possibility, but suggests that it could be boxing or even a statement of actual persecution. Victor Furnish, *II Corinthians* (AB 32A; Garden City, N.Y.: Doubleday, 1984), 255, notes the possibility but rejects it on the basis of Septuagint usage.

103. Williams, *Paul's Metaphors*, 270, interprets the verb "labor" in Phil 2:17, in the context of run, as "train" for competition. This is possible, but the larger context is military.

104. Some scholars think that Rom 11:11 contains military language. The case is weak.

105. See also the use of ὑπερνικῶμεν (*hypernikōmen*) in Rom 8:37.

106. The deutero-Pauline letter Ephesians expands the metaphor to include almost the entire weaponry of the legionnaire (ἡ πανοπλία, *hē panoplia*): mail around the hips, breastplate, boots, shield, helmet, and sword (6:10–18). The lance and dagger are missing. There is much additional military language in the passage. For illustrations of this weaponry see M. C. Bishop and J. C. N. Coulston, *Roman Military Equipment from the Punic Wars to the Fall of Rome* (London: B. T. Batsford, 1993), throughout.

107. Or is it when they "first pledged their oath," interpreting *episteusamen* as reflecting an oath, that is, their baptismal confession to Jesus as Lord? I am not aware of any interpreter of Rom 13:11 who construes the verb in this sense.

108. In Rom 6:13, Paul speaks of his members as weapons of injustice.

109. Cf. Rom 6:23; 2 Cor 11:8.

110. Courage, acting like a man (ἀνδρεία, *andreia*), is one of the four cardinal virtues. The other three are prudence (φρόνησις, *phronēsis*), sobriety or temperance (σωφροσύνη, *sophrosynē*), and justice (δικαιοσύνη, *dikaiosunē*). Wisdom of Solomon 8:7 lists them as virtues (ἀρεταί, *aretai*).

111. Some of Williams's arguments about military metaphors are not persuasive. He finds a reference to "proper battle array" in 1 Cor 14:40, really based only on the one term τάξις (*taxis*, 215). The one term στοιχάω (*stoichaō*, "to be in line with a person or thing . . . to hold to, agree with, follow, conform," BDAG, s.v.) in Gal 5:25, translated "walk in step" by Williams (*Paul's Metaphors*, 213), is not enough to show a military metaphor. Nor is the reference to the trumpet in 1 Thess 4:16 enough to warrant a military metaphor, because the context is that of a royal parousia (see ibid., 218).

112. See citation of the *Res Gestae* in the description of the Roman military above. Colossians 2:14–15 combines the images of the τρόπαιον (*tropaion*, the "monument of an enemy's defeat"; LSJ, s.v.), the victory trophy, with the triumphal procession to interpret the significance of the crucifixion as military trophy leading to triumph, not defeat.

113. Williams, *Paul's Metaphors*, 215, has a good discussion of this passage.

114. This does not rule out other linguistic fields, for example, the use of friendship language, along with military language.

115. After the defeat of Brutus and Cassius in 42 B.C.E., Mark Antony colonized Philippi with army veterans, giving it a new status with the *ius Romanum*, local government by Roman law. Salmon, *Roman Colonization under the Republic*, 128, notes that Velleius (1.15.5) says that all Roman colonies after the foundation of Eporedia were *coloniae militares*. After 100 B.C.E., "provision for veterans became the principal, as distinct from an incidental, aim of colonization." Julius Caesar and Augustus together seem to have founded as many *coloniae*, many outside Italy, as all other Roman emperors combined.

116. P. Collart, *Philippes Ville de Macédoine depuis ses origines jusque à la fin de l'époque romaine* (Travaux et Mémoires publiés par les professeurs de l' Institut superior d'Études françaises et les membres étrangers de l'École francais d'Athenes 5; Paris: E. de Boccard, 1937), 237–38, plate XXXI, 1–9. Plate XXXII, 1, shows the name on an architrave block from the forum. Peter Pilhofer has now gathered all known inscriptions from Philippi (767), in *Philippi*, vol. 2: *Katalog der Inschriften von Philippi* (WUNT 119; Tübingen: Mohr Siebeck, 2000).

117. E.g., no. 202 in Pilhofer, *Katalog der Inschriften von Philippi*, honorary inscription for Lucius Tatinius Cnosus, dated before 96 C.E. clearly identifies him as a *beneficarius tribuni*, a sign that he had been an officer. He dedicated a statue base in the forum (no. 203, Pilhofer) to the *Quieti Aug(ustae) col(oniae) Philippiens(is)*, "the quiet of the Augustan colony of the Philippians."

118. I treated Phil 1:27–30 in detail in Edgar Krentz, "Military Language and Metaphors in Philippians," in *Origins and Method: Towards a New Understanding of Judaism and Christianity: Essays in Honour of John C. Hurd* (ed. Bradley H. McLean; JSNTSup 96; Sheffield, England: Sheffield Academic, 1993), 105–27. See also Geoffrion, *Rhetorical Purpose* (see n. 86 for full citation).

119. Thus Paul sees this military language as a subset to political language that describes life in the city or political entity of which one is a citizen. Philippians 3:20 makes clear what this entity is.

120. See BDAG, s.v. "ψυχή" (*psychē*), 2.c, citing as parallel Dio Chrysostom, *Or. (Borysth.)* 36.30, where it is parallel to δύναμις, *dynamis*, "power."

121. Williams, *Paul's Metaphors*, 265, thinks this reflects the arena. But the language of the paragraph is much more that of warfare.

122. Πάσχω may here mean "die," playing off the soldier's oath. Danker, BDAG, s.v. 3.a.b., calls attention to Appian, *Bell. Civ.* 1.15.63, as a parallel and cites Justin, *Dial.* 121.2—ὑπὲρ τοῦ μὴ ἀρνεῖσθαι αὐτόν (*hyper tou mē arneisthai auton*, "on behalf of not denying him")—as a military metaphor.

123. Plutarch implies that "presence of mind" (φρονεῖν) is important for a military commander (*Pyrrh.* 16.7–8): καὶ διὰ φροντίδος ἔχων ἤδη τὸ μέλλον, ἔγνω τοὺς συμμάχους ἀναμένειν ("And grasping the future already through his presence of mind, he knew that he should wait for his allied fighters"). See also Dio Chrysostom 34.20; Dionysius of Halicarnassus, *Ant. rom.* 4.20.4.2; 2.59.7.4; 8.15.1.8.

124. Onasander 24. Oldfather (LCL, 343) points out that this is a frequently stated idea. He points to Homer, *Il.* 2.362ff., Xenophon, *Symp.* 8.32, and Plato, *Symp.* 178Eff.

125. Arnold Ehrhardt, "Jesus Christ and Alexander the Great," in *The Frame-*

work of the New Testament Stories (Cambridge: Harvard University Press, 1965), 37–43 [= *JTS* 46 (1947)]; idem, "Eine Antikes Herrscherideal: Phil 2,5–11," *EvT* 8 (1948/49): 101–10; and idem, "Nochmals: Ein antikes Herrscherideal," *EvT* 8 (1948/49): 569–72.

126. Thus Seneca, *Ep. Mor.* 107.9–10, where he says: "the soldier who follows his commander grumblingly is evil."

127. In 2 Tim 4:6–8, the much later author of the Pastorals uses the same libation language, along with reference to a good battle, keeping one's oath, and receiving a crown—all good military metaphors.

128. Onasander 5 (speaks of purification by correct ritual) and 10.25–28, which directs both sacrifice and taking the omens: Μήτε δὲ εἰς πορείαν ἐξαγέτω τὸ στράτευμα μήτε πρὸς μάχην ταττέτω, μὴ πρότερον θυσάμενος ("And let him not lead out the army for forage or draw it up in line for battle, if he has not first sacrificed"). He ought to have both experts in sacrificing (θύται, *thytai*) and seers (μάντεις, *manteis*) along with him to read the omens (τὰ ἱερά, *ta hiera*). For the earlier period, see Michael H. Jameson, "Sacrifice before Battle," in Hanson, *Hoplites*, 197–227.

129. Xenophon, *Cyr.* 6. 3.21: αὔριον δὲ πρῴ, ἕως ἂν ἐγὼ θύομαι . . . (*aurion de prō, heōs an egō thyomai*, "early tomorrow, after I sacrifice . . .").

130. Paul may use this figure to avoid speaking of his death as human sacrifice before battle—shades of Agamemnon at Aulis.

131. 4.1: τὰς δ᾽ ἀρχὰς τοῦ πολέμου μάλιστά φημι χρῆναι φρονίμως συνίστασθαι καὶ μετὰ τοῦ δικαίου πᾶσι φανερὸν γίγνεσθαι πολεμοῦντα.

132. R. R. Brewer, "The Meaning of πολιτεύεσθε in Phil 1:27," *JBL* 73 (1954): 76–83. He cites a Neapolis inscription which refers "to an unnamed Roman magistrate [*duumvir*] at Philippi as *pontifex, flamen, divi Claudi Philippi*," cited from Lightfoot's commentary (51n. 4). Surprisingly Brewer nowhere cites Collart's magisterial work, which notes seven inscriptions relevant to the ruler cult at Philippi from before the time of Vespasian. Collart cites the fuller text of the Neapolis inscription: "P. Cornelius Asper Atiarius Montanus / equo publico honoratus, item ornamentis decu / rionatus et IIviralicis, pontifex, flamen divi Claudi Philippis, / ann. XXIII, h. s. e." ("Publius Cornelius Atiarius Montanus, honored with a public horse, that with decurinal and dumviral decorations, priest, flamen of the divine Claudius of Philippi, was placed here in [his] twenty-third year," *CIL* III.650). Note the reference to public honors, equivalent to the ἔντιμος (*entimos*, "worthy of public recognition") of Phil 2:29.

133. Brewer, "Meaning of πολιτεύεσθε in Phil 1:27," 83.

134. Paul uses the noun τύπος (*typos*, "type, model") of himself only here, probably to distinguish himself from Christ whom they are to imitate with him (cf. 1 Cor 11:1). He applies the term to the Thessalonians in 1 Thess 1:7. In Rom 5:14, he speaks of Adam as a type of Christ, in 1 Cor 10:6 of events in the wilderness as types of Christian pneumatic food and drink. See BDAG, s.v.

135. See H. Koller, *Die Mimesis in der Antike: Nachahmung, Darstellung, Ausdruck* (Dissertationes Bernenses, ser. 1, fasc. 5; Bern: A. Francker, 1954).

136. The use of enemy language also shows up in deutero-Pauline Col 1:20–22, which speaks of making peace by reconciling enemies.

137. Martin Dibelius, *An die Thessalonicher I, II; An die Philipper* (3d ed.; Tübin-

gen: J. C. B. Mohr, 1937), 93, supports the latter ("eine beiläufig vorgebrachte Klage"); by citing 3 Macc 7:11 (τοὺς γαστρὸς ἔνεκα τὰ θεῖα παραβεβηκότας προστάγματα), he suggests that the reference to shame supports a sexual interpretation and that "stomach" might then refer to carousing.

138. Jean-Michel Carrié, "The Soldier," 100–137, in *The Romans* (ed. Andrea Giardina; trans. Lydia B. Cochrane; Chicago: University of Chicago Press, 1993), 118, describes the Tacitean view that soldiers are men "ruled by desires, impulses, and appetites."

139. Florence Dupont, *Daily Life in Ancient Rome* (trans. Christopher Woodall; Oxford and Cambridge, Mass.: Blackwell, 1992), 270, citing Horace, *Sat.* 2.2.23.

140. The term occurs frequently in the deutero-Paulines, Eph 5:23; 1 Tim 1:1; 2:3; 4:10; 2 Tim 1:10; Titus 1:3, 4; 2:10, 13; 3:4, 6; and elsewhere in 2 Pet 1:1, 11; 2:20; 3:2, 18.

141. *OGIS* 2:458.

142. A. N. Sherwin-White, *Roman Society and Roman Law in the New Testament* (Oxford: Clarendon, 1965 = corrected ed., 1963), 185.

143. " 'Bischöfe' und 'Diakonen' in Philippi," in Dibelius, *An die Thessalonicher I, II; An die Philipper,* 61–62.

144. John Reumann, "Church Office in Paul, Especially Philippians," in *Origins and Method: Towards a New Understanding of Judaism and Christianity* (*Essays in Honour of John C. Hurd*) (JSNTSup 86; Sheffield, England: Sheffield Academic Press, 1993), 82–91, citation from p. 83 summarizing the position of Hans Lietzmann. Markus Bockmuehl, *The Epistle to the Philippians* (BNTC; Peabody, Mass.: Hendrickson, 1998), 53–55, provides a useful summary of modern interpretations.

145. Xenophon, *Anab.* 2.3.2.

146. *Cyr.* 6.3.21. Cyrus also set up a board of health, comprised of the best physicians and outfitted with all medical instruments and medicines. "Whenever any one fell sick in whose recovery he was interested, he would visit him and provide for him whatever was needed" (ἐπεσκόπει καὶ παρεῖχε πάντα ὅτου ἔδει, *epeskopei kai pareiche panta hotou edei, Cyr.* 8.2.24–25). Aeschylus, *Eum.* 296. See also Aeschylus, *Eum.* 296, and LSJ, s.v., for other references.

147. I have not seen Prokopios (Metropolitan of Philippi). ἡ ὀργάνωσις τῆς ἐκκλησίας τῶν φιλίππων κατὰ τὴν ἀποστολικὴν καὶ μεταποστολικὴν ἐποχήν. Οἱ πρεσβύτεροι τῆς ἐκκλησίας τῶν φιλίππων, *Delton Biblikon Meleton* 9 (1980): 56–62.

148. See Le Bohec, *Imperial Roman Army,* 20–21, on the praetorian cohort, and the many references in his index under "cohort, praetorian."

149. Collart, *Philippes,* 232, plate XXX, 8–11.

150. "These pieces carry the proof that Philippi was colonized also by a cohort of pretorians."

151. No commentary I have consulted has made use of Philippian coinage or called attention to its possible significance for understanding Phil 1:13.

152. Collart, *Philippes,* 237–39, interprets this coinage. This iconography is also relevant for interpreting the στέφανος (*stephanos,* "crown") of Phil 4:1.

153. Aeneas Tacticus 9.3.

154. Francis Lyall, *Slaves, Citizens, Sons: Legal Metaphors in the Epistles* (Grand Rapids: Zondervan, 1984), 169, with reference to William W. Buckland, *The Roman Law of Slavery* (1908; reprint, Cambridge: Cambridge University Press, 1970), 307–17.

155. For example, Epictetus, *Diss.* 1.4, is titled περὶ προκοπῆς, "On Progress" (in ethical living).

156. Polybius 2.37.10; 2.13.1. See also 8.15.6

157. Compare this to σύμψυχοι (*sympsychoi,* "unified in feelings") in 2:2.

158. Polyaenus, *Stratagems of War* 8.23.15, says that Caesar called soldiers "fellow soldiers" (or "comrades," συστρατιῶται, *systratiōtai*), but when they mutinied, he called them simply "citizens." When they said they wanted to be called "comrades," he said then they should serve together as soldiers, quelling the mutiny. In 8.23.22, Polyaenus says that Caesar, by calling his soldiers "fellow soldiers," raised their eagerness to fight, because the term implied equality of honor.

159. Cf. *Cyr.* 8.2.24–25.

160. Cf. Plato, *Resp.* 5462B; Seneca, *Ep. Mor.* 107.9. See Anthony Bash, *Ambassadors for Christ* (WUNT 92; Tübingen: J. C. B. Mohr [Paul Siebeck], 1997), for a study of ambassadors, and Frederick W. Danker, *Benefactor: Epigraphic Study of a Graeco-Roman and New Testament Semantic Field* (St. Louis: Clayton, 1982), on honorific inscriptions. Danker discusses Phil 2:25–30 on pp. 425–26.

161. See Karl Baus, *Der Kranz in Antike und Christentum: Eine religionsgeschichtliche Untersuchung mit besonderer Berüksichtigung Tertullians* (Theophaneia 3; Bonn: Peter Hanstein, 1940), and Michael Blech, *Studien zum Kranz bei den Griechen* (Religiongeschichtliche Versuch und Vorarbeiten 38; Berlin and New York: Walter de Gruyter, 1982).

162. The term βραβεῖον (*brabeion,* "prize, award"; Phil 3:14) supports this interpretation, though its military use is not immediately clear. Demosthenes' greatest oration was περὶ τοῦ στεφάνου ("On the [golden] crown"), regarding the golden crown awarded him by the Athenians on a motion made by Ctesiphon to recognize Demosthenes' contributions to the state; it was a response to Aeschines, who contested the award in his oration *Against Ctesiphon.* See LSJ, s.v., 2.b.

163. It bears the following inscription: "Quieti Aug. / col. Philippiens. / L. Tatianus L. f./ Vol Cnosus, sta/torum, sua pecu/nia posuit" ("Lucius Tatianus, son of Lucius, of the tribe Voltinia, a centurion *statorum* placed this statue to the quiet of the Augustan Colony at Philippi at his own expense"). Collart, *Philippes,* 411, and plate LXIV, 2. See also Collart, "Inscriptions de Philippes," *BCH* 56 (1932): 220ff., no. 9.

164. The full inscription is "aequitatem Augusti / et mensuras / M. Cornelius P. f. Vo. Niger, / P. Valerius P. f. Vol. Niger, / aed., d. s. p. f. c. / In id opus coiectum est ex mensuris / iniquis aeris p (ondo) / / XXXXIII (Collart, *Philippes,* 363n. 5, and 411–12).

165. Herodotus 3.90.

166. Herodotus 4.133.

167. Thucydides 3.17. Cf. Xenophon, *Cyr.* 6.1.17. References from LSJ, s.v.

168. Thucydides 7.28: ἀντὶ τοῦ πόλις εἶναι φρούριον κατέστη, *anti tou polis einai phrourion katestē;* cf. 2.18; Lysias 12.40; Xenophon, *Cyr.* 1.4.16. References from LSJ, s.v.

169. This does not exhaust the possibilities. "Forgetting behind, straining forward" in 3:13 could describe the forward thrust in battle. Does 4:8–9 suggest that the Philippians are a civilizing force like the Roman army? Perhaps.

170. Stanley Stowers, "Friends and Enemies in the Politics of Heaven," in *Pauline Theology,* vol. 1: *Thessalonians, Philippians, Galatians, and Philemon* (ed. Jouette M. Bassler; Minneapolis: Fortress Press, 1991), 105–21; Ken L. Berry, "The

Function of Friendship Language in Philippians 4:10–20," in *Friendship, Flattery, and Frankness of Speech: Studies on Friendship in the New Testament World* (ed. John T. Fitzgerald; NovTSup 82; Leiden: E. J. Brill, 1996), 107–24; John T. Fitzgerald, "Philippians in the Light of Some Ancient Discussions of Friendship," in ibid., 141–60.

171. David Konstan, *Friendship in the Classical World* (Key Themes in Ancient History; Cambridge: Cambridge University Press, 1997); John T. Fitzgerald, *Greco-Roman Perspectives on Friendship* (SBLRBS 34; Atlanta: Scholars Press, 1997).

172. John Reumann, "Philippians, Especially Chapter 4, as a 'Letter of Friendship': Observations on a Checkered History of Scholarship," in Fitzgerald, *Friendship, Flattery, and Frankness*, 83–196.

173. See J. Paul Sampley, *Pauline Partnership in Christ* (Philadelphia: Fortress Press, 1980), 51–77.

174. These are primarily military documents, excluding historians.

175. This short bibliography lists only works that treat these topics at length.

176. Most, but not all, these references are from Burgess, "Epideictic Literature," 211–14.

13

PAUL AND INDIFFERENT THINGS

Will Deming

Ἀδιάφορον (*adiaphoron*) is the Stoic term for an "indifferent thing." What the Stoics intended by this term, and what role it played in their understanding of ethical behavior is our focus in the first part of this chapter. The second part explores the possibility of better understanding certain passages from Paul in light of these Stoic teachings. This is followed by a selection of passages from Paul for further study and a short bibliography.[1]

Part I. Stoic Views on Indifference

The Stoics held that every thing in existence was either a "good thing" (ἀγαθόν, *agathon*), a "bad thing" (κακόν, *kakon*), or an "indifferent thing" (ἀδιάφορον, *adiaphoron*).[2] Because they used "good" as the equivalent of "morally beautiful" (καλόν, *kalon*),[3] good things, or simply "goods," for the Stoics consisted of virtue and all things that "participated" in virtue. Although they envisioned virtue as a unified whole,[4] they often spoke of four cardinal virtues with many sub-virtues below these.[5] Thus goods consisted of virtues like discernment, prudence, courage, and justice, and things that participated in virtue like true joy, cheerfulness, and confidence. Bad things were the opposite of good things, consisting of vice (parsed into four cardinal vices and sub-vices)[6] and all things that participated in vice.[7]

Everything else in the world was an "indifferent." Thus, indifferents were neither virtue nor vice, nor did they participate in virtue or vice. They included things like health and sickness, wealth and poverty. While the Stoics classed all such things as indifferents, they held that indifferents could nonetheless differ from one another on the basis of "value." Some indifferents, like health and wealth, had an appreciable amount of value (ἀξία, *axia*), while indifferents like sickness and poverty had an appreciable amount of negative value, or disvalue (ἀπαξία, *apaxia*).[8] Then there were indifferent things whose value was scant or in-

384

significant, like whether one had an odd or even number of hairs on his or her head. Here, for example, is Antipater's understanding of value, as cited by Arius in a review of different definitions of value:

> Value is spoken of in three ways . . . ; and the third type, which Antipater calls selective, through which, when things allow, we rather choose these particular things instead of those, such as health instead of sickness, life instead of death, and riches instead of poverty. (Stobaeus, *Ecl.* 2.7.7f. [Pomeroy])

If an indifferent had an appreciable amount of positive value, the Stoics called it a "preferred indifferent." An appreciable amount of disvalue earned it the title "rejected" or "avoided indifferent"; and an indifferent whose value was insignificant was inconsequential. Again, Arius gives us a summary:

> [O]f indifferent things, some have more value and others have less. . . . And some are preferred, others dispreferred, while others are neither. Preferred are whatever indifferent things have much value—to the extent that this exists among indifferent things. Likewise dispreferred are whatever have much lack of value. Neither preferred nor dispreferred are whatever have neither much [value nor] much lack of value. (Stobaeus, *Ecl.* 2.7.7b [Pomeroy])[9]

Although many in antiquity, including some Stoics, took issue with these views, arguing that things with positive value such as health and wealth should be classified as "goods,"[10] most Stoics stood by this distinction between goods and preferred indifferents. Goods, they contended, were always "beneficial,"[11] and consequently of the "greatest" value. Preferred indifferents, by contrast, had only "much" or "little" value. In the normal course of life they were "in accord with nature" and "useful," but never "beneficial" in their own right; and under some conditions they could even be an impediment to one's moral development. Theirs was thus an "assigned" value, not an inherent one; a value that was relative to something good, and variable, depending on circumstances. Diogenes Laertius and Arius offer us these accounts:

> For as the property of hot is to warm, not cool, so the property of good is to benefit, not to injure; but wealth and health do no more benefit than injury, therefore neither wealth nor health is good. Further, they say that that is not good of which good and bad use can be made; but of wealth and health both good and bad use can be made; therefore wealth and health are not goods. (Diogenes Laertius 7.103 [Hicks, LCL])

No good thing is a preferred, because they have the greatest value in themselves. But the preferred, having the second rank and value, to some extent come close to the nature of the good. . . . The preferred are so called, not because they contribute some things to happiness and work in partnership towards it, but because it is necessary to make the selection from these things instead of the dispreferred. (Stobaeus, *Ecl.* 2.7.7g [Pomeroy]).

The practical significance for the Stoics, and there was one, of insisting on this complicated and rather counterintuitive classification of *things* comes into view when we consider their understanding of ethical *actions*. For them, the process by which humans become moral and progress toward moral perfection depended on a person's interaction with *things*, especially indifferent things. It is through selecting preferred indifferents, avoiding rejected indifferents, and maintaining equanimity toward the other indifferents that one developed his or her moral disposition and, if able, became completely virtuous. Thus, for the Stoics, a *thing* might be indifferent, but the use one made of it was not a matter of indifference. Depending on a thing's assigned value relative to gaining virtue, selecting, rejecting, or being neutral toward it became one's moral imperative in life. As Seneca explains to his friend Lucilius:

> "[I]f good health, rest, and freedom from pain are not likely to hinder virtue, shall you not seek all these?" Of course I shall seek them, but not because they are goods,—I shall seek them because they are according to nature and because they will be acquired through the exercise of good judgment on my part. What, then, will be good in them? This alone,—that it is a good thing to choose them. For when I don suitable attire, or walk as I should, or dine as I ought to dine, it is not my dinner, or my walk, or my dress that are goods, but the deliberate choice which I show in regard to them . . . if I have the choice, I shall choose health and strength, but . . . the good involved will be my judgment regarding these things, and not the things themselves. (Seneca, *Ep.* 92.11–13 [Gummere, LCL])

Likewise, Plutarch reports:

> [T]he prudent selection and acceptance of those things is the goal, whereas the things themselves and the obtaining of them are not the goal but are given as a kind of matter having "selective value." (Plutarch, *De comm. not.* 1071B [Cherniss, LCL])[12]

Part II. Ἀδιάφορα in Paul's Letters

In considering whether Paul's ethics can be better understood in light of Stoic "indifferent things," we must acknowledge that almost any system of ethics will distinguish between what is good, what is bad, and what is neither, or "indifferent."

Specifically in the Greco-Roman context, the Stoic definitions of these notions were preceded by and competed with Platonic and Aristotelian positions.[13] One task of this investigation, therefore, beyond simply locating discussions of indifferents in Paul, must be to demonstrate that it is *Stoic* notions about indifferents, not those from some other system of thought, that are important for understanding Paul.

This task is complicated by the fact that Paul rarely uses the principal terms of the Stoic discussions, and rarely, if ever, in a manner that would mark their usage as distinctively Stoic. Αδιάφορον and ἀπαξία, for example, never occur in Paul. Likewise, Paul never identifies the good, τὸ ἀγαθον, solely with the morally beautiful, τὸ καλόν, and it is an open question as to whether any of the occurrences in Paul of the term "wise" (σοφος, *sophos*) owe any debt to Stoic thought or are even better understood in light of Stoic usage (e.g., 1 Cor 1:20–25).

Likewise, an attempt to demonstrate Stoic influence on Paul by comparing Paul's lists of indifferent things (e.g., Phil 4:12) with those used by Stoics also seems to offer little promise. The problem here is that much of what these lists contain is common philosophical material, not anything exclusively Stoic; these lists are never complete, either in Paul or the Stoics; in the Stoa they change over time and between teachers;[14] and Paul's lists, quite naturally, have a Christian emphasis, which further frustrates comparison with the Stoics.[15]

In light of these considerations, I will use two somewhat indirect approaches. In the first instance, I will examine three passages in which Paul discusses things that are in some sense "indifferent" for the purpose of identifying Stoic parallels *generally*, not just with respect to Stoic ideas about indifferents. These passages are Phil 1:20–26; 1 Cor 7:25–38; and 1 Cor 7:20–23. On the strength of my success in uncovering Stoic influence per se, I will suggest that Paul's treatment of indifferents in these passages is likely to owe a debt to Stoicism as well, even if the evidence with regard specifically to indifferents is too weak to make the case on its own.

In the second set of passages, which pertain to circumcision, my argument will rely even less on the presence of material parallels with Stoic texts. Rather, I will attempt to show that there exist conceptual similarities between the basic assumptions of Stoic thinking on indifference and the way in which circumcision functions as an indifferent for Paul. From this I will suggest that it is helpful to interpret Paul's approach as a "functional" or "dynamic" equivalent of the Stoic approach, even if the evidence for material parallels is scant.[16]

But before I begin, let me pause for some clarification and to point out the obvious. For an author to be "influenced" by a particular stream of thought can mean many things. From Paul actively seeking out Stoic expressions for their potential rhetorical impact on his audiences, to his inadvertently using a phrase that was introduced into the Greek language centuries before him, there is a long and subtle continuum of "influence." As far as I know, no scholar has been so rash as to argue that Paul was a Stoic or studied under a Stoic teacher, but this does not rule out the many other possibilities for Stoic influence on Paul.

Most Americans, for example, assume that they have a "subconscious," a notion that can be traced back to the work of Sigmund Freud. Yet this does not mean that Americans are Freudians, or that most Americans have even heard of Freud. It does mean, however, that our way of thinking about ourselves has been profoundly influenced by Freudian thought. Likewise, Paul may have been influenced by Stoic thought regardless of whether he attended a Stoic lecture or met a Stoic. How profound this influence was on Paul—that is, what difference it should make in our understanding of Paul—is a another matter, and something scholars will need to debate, and perhaps for some time. But this is no reason to gainsay the presence of "influence" in the first place.

In one form or another, Paul treats many things as indifferents: social class, ethnic identity, gender, food, education, speaking in tongues, life and death, marriage, slavery, and circumcision.[17] Of these, it is the last five, in my view, that have the most potential for being better understood in light of Stoic teachings on indifference. Let us begin with Paul's discussion of life and death in Phil 1:20–26.[18]

From a Stoic perspective, biological life and death were indifferent things: as they had no share in virtue or vice, one could be virtuous (or vicious) with either.[19] But as we have indicated, this did not mean that life and death were without value for the Stoics. In the natural flow of things, life was a highly valued, preferred indifferent, while its opposite, death, was a highly disvalued, rejected indifferent.[20] Under normal circumstances it was against nature, reason, and God to select death over life. So, while life and death as *things* were indifferent, the *selection* of one over the other was a matter of great ethical concern, requiring careful consideration. Here, for example, is Cicero's summary of Stoic theory:

> But since these neutral things [i.e., indifferents] form the basis of all appropriate acts, there is good ground for the dictum that it is with these things that all our practical deliberations deal, including the will to live and the will to quit this life. When a man's circumstances contain a preponderance of things in accordance with nature, it is appropriate for him to remain alive; when he possesses or sees in prospect a majority of the contrary things, it is appropriate for him to depart from life. . . . Therefore the reasons for both remaining in life and for departing from it are to be measured entirely by the primary things of nature aforesaid. . . . And very often it is appropriate for the wise man to abandon life at a moment when he is enjoying supreme happiness, if an opportunity offers itself for making a timely exit. For the Stoic view is that happiness, which means life in

harmony with nature, is a matter of seizing the right moment. (Cicero, *Fin.* 3.19.60–61 [Rackham, LCL]).[21]

Yet not only was the topic Paul addresses in Phil 1:20–26, whether he should choose life or death, popular among Stoics, but his approach—his appraisal of the alternatives—is also in line with Stoic treatments. As he makes clear, his goal is not to gain either life or death, necessarily, but to act with moral purpose. He is determined to conduct himself "boldly" (ἐν πάσῃ παρρησίᾳ, *en pasē parrēsia*) and not be "put to shame" so that Christ will be honored through his body, "whether by life or by death" (εἴτε . . . εἴτε, *eite . . . eite*, v. 20). Paul's moral dilemma in this passage stems from the fact that life and death both offer attractive advantages: life is "Christ" and "fruitful labor," and death is "gain" (κέρδος, *kerdos*). "I do not know which I will choose (αἱρέομαι, *haireomai*)," he states. "I am hard pressed between the two" (vv. 21–23a). In Stoic thought this would be seen as an attempt to select between two preferred indifferents on the basis of their value with respect to one's moral duty.

Beyond this, Paul's resolution of the question is quite similar to the pronouncements of his Stoic contemporaries Musonius Rufus and Seneca. In a letter Seneca writes to Pauline, his second wife, he reasons that even though he is very sick and in much pain, he must choose life over death for the sake of those he holds dear:

> . . . because the good man should not live as long as it pleases him, but as long as he ought. He who does not value his wife, or his friend, highly enough to linger longer in life—he who obstinately persists in dying—is a voluptuary.[22]

Likewise, Musonius states:

> It is not allowed for one who is benefiting many to die if he is living in a fitting manner, unless by dying he benefits more.[23]

Paul, in turn, reasons that it is "more necessary" (ἀναγκαιότερον, *anankaioteron*, v. 24) for him to remain alive for the sake of his church at Philippi, to further their "moral progress" (προκοπή, *prokopē*, v. 25). In making his choice on their account, rather than for honor, or wealth, or even so that he might "be with Christ," which is his own "desire" and "far better" for him (v. 23b), he comes very close to these Stoic views.

Finally, throughout this passage Paul relies on a terminology that is well documented in philosophical discussions and, in some cases perhaps, more at home there than in Paul's own theology.[24] Thus, the notion of "necessity" (ἀνάγκη, *anankē*) has a long history in philosophical considerations of "noble death,"[25] and according to Antipater of Tarsus, head of the Stoa at the end of the second century B.C.E., the superlative "most necessary" (ἀναγκαιότατος, *anankaiotatos*) designated a special category of Stoic duties.[26] Προκοπή is a term so integral to their concept of the moral life, that both Seneca and Epictetus devoted short works to it,[27] and as Paul Holloway notes, Paul's expression εἴτε . . . εἴτε in 1:20 ("whether . . . or whether . . .") was also used by Musonius, Epictetus, and Seneca to compare indifferents.[28] When Paul states that dying is "gain" (κέρδος, v. 21), he is using a word that occurs both in Epictetus, as part of a specialized Stoic vocabulary,[29] and in Phil 3:7–8, several features of which also argue for a comparison with the Stoic doctrine of indifferents (see below).

Even Paul's statement "to live is Christ" (τὸ ζῆν Χριστός, *to zēn Christos*, v. 21) is of interest in this respect. It is possible that Paul intended this awkward expression as a wordplay between Χριστός and the similar sounding χρηστός (*chrēstos*, "good, useful").[30] If this is so, Paul's choice of words has reference to a moral concept used by Musonius to describe the character of the good person;[31] and this, in turn, accords well with Paul's use of αἱρέομαι in 1:22, a word favored by Stoics when describing a wise man's choice of indifferents.[32]

In sum, there appears to be sufficient reason to conclude that what Paul writes in Phil 1:20–26 has been shaped by Stoic discussions of indifferents and that we bring further clarity to this passage if we interpret it in light of those discussions.

A second passage in which it may be possible to detect the impact of Stoic thinking about indifferents upon Paul is 1 Cor 7:25–38. Because I have dealt with this passage at length in another context,[33] I will simply summarize those points that are relevant to our investigation here. As in Phil 1:20–26, we find in 1 Cor 7:25–38 a topic much favored by the Stoics[34] as well as several terms that suggest a Stoic provenance. Among these are "free from concern" (ἀμέριμνος, *amerimnos*) and "to worry" (μεριμνάω, *merimnaō*) in verses 32–34; "benefit" (σύμφορον, *symphoron*) and "undistractedly" (ἀπερισπάστως, *aperispastōs*) in verse 35; and the pair "propriety/ to act shamefully" (τὸ εὔσχημον/ἀσχημονέω, *to euschēmon/aschēmoneō*) in verses 35–36.[35] In 7:27–28, moreover, Paul uses a diatribe pattern that was popular in the first and second centuries among both Stoics and authors influenced by Stoicism, including Philo, Seneca, Plutarch, and Epictetus.[36] The function of this pattern, significantly, was to highlight the indifference of certain things such as old age, holding political office, slavery (see below), and *marriage*, which is Paul's topic here. Thus, for example, we may compare this passage to one from Epictetus:

> Are you bound to a wife? —Do not seek release! Have you been released
> from a wife?—Do not seek a wife! (1 Cor 7:27–28)

> Your little child died?—It was given back! Your wife died?—She was
> given back! (Epictetus, *Ench.* 11)

Paul also approaches the issue of marriage as a Stoic might. For the Stoics, marriage was a preferred indifferent, which meant that in the normal course of one's
life it was a moral "duty" to marry. If poverty, war, or some other adverse circumstance intervened, however, a person's moral allegiances might call him or her
away from the responsibilities of marriage. In these cases marriage became a "rejected indifferent," and *not* marrying became the fitting course of action.[37] As Hierocles explains:

> [M]arried life is "preferred" for the wise man, although life without a
> wife is preferred when there are mitigating circumstances. And so, since
> we need to imitate the man of reason in whatever ways we can, and for
> him marrying is "preferred," it is clear that it would be "fitting" for us as
> well, unless some circumstance is impeding. (Hierocles in Stobaeus, *Ecl.*
> 4.22a.22 [4.502.9–14 W.-H.])

In 1 Cor 7:25–31, Paul frames his discussion in a manner that appears to owe a
great deal to this perspective. He considers what is "good for a man" in light of
the adverse circumstances that were pressing in on the Corinthians.[38] While he rejects the Stoic notion that selecting marriage under these circumstances is "making a mistake" or "sinning" (ἁμαρτάνω, *hamartanō*, vv. 28, 36),[39] he nevertheless
outlines the drawbacks of marriage in terms of one's allegiance to Christ over
against the distractions of a spouse (vv. 32–35).[40] Here we may compare Paul with
Epictetus:

> The unmarried man is anxious about the affairs of the Lord, how to
> please the Lord; but the married man is anxious about the affairs of the
> world, how to please his wife, and his interests are divided. . . . I say this
> for your benefit . . . to promote good order and undistracted devotion to
> the Lord. (1 Cor 7:32b–35)

> [P]erhaps it is necessary that the Cynic be undistracted, completely en-
> gaged in the service of God, able to make his rounds to men, not attached
> to private duties nor involved in social relations. (Epictetus, *Diss.* 3.22.69)

Paul then concludes the passage by contrasting the Christian who marries with
the Christian who does not, using expressions that Stoics commonly employed to
characterize the wise man (vv. 36–38).[41] As with Phil 1:20–26, it would be difficult,

I would argue, to understand Paul's reasoning in 1 Cor 7:25–38 without some reference to Stoic materials on indifference.

∞

Next we turn to 1 Cor 7:20–23, where Paul gives advice on slavery and freedom. Like the topics of life and death and marriage, this was also a popular topic among Stoics in Paul's day.[42] The Stoics, along with most other Greco-Roman moralists, made a distinction between legal slavery, or physical bondage, and "real" slavery, or bondage of the spirit. They considered the former an indifferent thing, the latter a bad thing. Likewise, they distinguished between legal freedom and "real" freedom, the former being an indifferent, the latter a good. It is on this basis, for example, that Philo introduces his subject in *Every Good Man Is Free*:

> Slavery then is applied in one sense to bodies, in another to souls; bodies have men for their masters, souls their vices and passions. No one makes the first kind the subject of investigation. . . . Casting aside, therefore, specious quibblings and the terms which have no basis in nature but depend on convention, such as "homebred," "purchased" or "captured in war," let us examine the veritable free man, who alone possesses independence, even though a host of people claim to be his masters. (Philo, *Prob.* 17–19 [Colson, LCL])[43]

Thus, the Stoics held that legal slavery and legal freedom were neither good nor bad in themselves. One could be virtuous as a slave or as a freeman. What was important, rather, was that one pursued the true freedom of the spirit and rejected spiritual enslavement.

In 1 Cor 7:20–23, Paul appears to reproduce this line of thought in a Christianized form. On the one hand, he states that neither legal slavery nor legal freedom is a matter of any real concern for people "in the Lord," because they can fulfill their obligations to God in either condition (vv. 21a, 22). The important thing, rather, is that believers avoid becoming "slaves of men" (v. 23b), by which he means human ideologies that are opposed to God.[44] Further, while we find nothing that is distinctly Stoic in Paul's word choice in this passage, we may point out that 7:21–22 is couched in the same diatribe pattern we noted in our discussion of 7:27–28.[45] On several counts, then, it can be argued that 1 Cor 7:20–23 draws on Stoic traditions about the indifference of slavery and freedom.

It may even be the case that Paul's particular use of the diatribe pattern in 1 Cor 7:21–22 can give us insight into the pedigree, so to speak, of the Stoicism reflected in this passage. As I have argued elsewhere, Paul modifies the way in which this diatribe pattern was typically used, adding the phrase ἀλλ' εἰ καὶ δύνασαι ἐλεύθερος γενέσθαι, μᾶλλον χρῆσαι (*all' ei kai dynasai eleutheros genesthai, mal-*

lon chrēsai) in 7:21b, which in the context of this pattern seems to mean, "but if you are able to become free, take advantage of the opportunity."[46] If this is correct, then Paul is offering advice, based on solid Stoic principles, that is unparalleled among his Stoic contemporaries. In Stoic terms, Paul has categorized legal slavery not only as an indifferent thing, but more specifically as a *rejected* indifferent, and thus something that normally should be de-selected when the opportunity arises. This conclusion is well within the logic of Stoic ethical theory,[47] although, somewhat curiously, we have no record of a Stoic taking this position, nor do we possess a text that includes legal slavery in a list of rejected indifferents (along with poverty and illness, for example), or legal freedom in a list of preferred indifferents (along with wealth and health, for example).[48]

In attempting to understand how Paul might have come to this conclusion on the basis of Stoic ethics, even though we have no record it was ever supported by the Stoics themselves, we should note that a philosophical position against slavery such as *could* have developed among the Stoics is documented as early as the fourth century B.C.E. In *Politics* 1253b, Aristotle records the view of some of his contemporaries that legal slavery is wrong because it is unjust (οὐδὲ δίκαιον, *oude dikaion*), against nature (παρὰ φύσιν, *para physin*), and based on compulsion (βίαιον, *biaion*). This is a view that is both congenial to Stoic teachings on justice, nature, and freedom, and one that may even have influenced some early Stoics;[49] yet it was never embraced by the middle or late Stoa. It is, however, reflected in this later period in Philo. Thus, in *Special Laws*, Philo declares that no one is a slave by nature (ἐκ φύσης, *ek physēs*);[50] and in *Contemplative Life*, he reports of the Therapeutae that these "philosophers" regard slave ownership as an injustice (ἀδικία, *adikia*) and against nature (παρὰ φύσιν, *para physin*), and so they choose to serve one another without compulsion (οὐ πρὸς βίαν, *ou pros bian*).[51] Consistent with this, in *Rewards and Punishments*, Philo comes very close to treating legal slavery as a *rejected* indifferent, calling it a "lesser evil" that should be avoided.[52] As we saw earlier, of course, Philo is already familiar with the notion that legal slavery is an indifferent.

In Philo, therefore, whose treatment of slavery in Stoic terms has been said to "anticipate" the Stoicism of Seneca,[53] we find a rationale congenial to Stoic principles that may explain the position Paul takes in 1 Cor 7:21–22, namely, that legal slavery should be treated as a rejected indifferent.[54] This observation, in turn, seems to indicate that the Stoicism reflected in 1 Cor 7:20–23 has affinities with Stoic thought as it was transmitted or developed in Jewish theological circles, rather than with the dominant school-tradition of Stoicism that we know from Arius, Musonius, Seneca, Plutarch, Epictetus, and Hierocles.

This hypothesis is strengthened, moreover, in light of another parallel between Paul and Philo. In his *Every Good Man Is Free*, a work whose Stoic leanings are beyond dispute, Philo reports that Jewish philosophers known as the Essenes reject slave ownership because it annuls "the statute of Nature, who mother-like has born and reared all men alike, and created them genuine brothers, not in mere name, but in very reality."[55] Here Philo has grounded the philosophy of the Essenes in Stoic universalism, a fact made apparent not only by the Stoic bent of this tractate, but also by Seneca's advocacy for the humane treatment of slaves, based on the notion that "Heaven is the one parent of us all."[56]

Thus, in accord with Stoic universalism—which did not advocate universal equality, of course, but the equality of those seeking wisdom[57]—Philo's Essenes and Seneca agree that the measure of a person should not be birth or legal status, but his or her allegiance to wisdom, even though, unlike Philo's Essenes, Seneca does not come to the conclusion that slave ownership is bad. Paul, however, seems to have been led precisely in this direction when he states in Phlm 16 that he expects Philemon to accept the slave Onesimus back as "a beloved brother . . . both in the flesh and in the Lord." If this is a request for Onesimus's manumission, as some New Testament scholars surmise,[58] then Paul's argument can be read as a Christianized extension of the Stoic universalism that underlies the "Essene" view found in Philo. Just as Philo's Essenes, on the basis of Stoic universalism, take the position that individuals become "genuine brothers . . . in reality" by virtue of their devotion to wisdom, so also Paul asks Philemon to regard Onesimus as a brother "in the flesh and in the Lord" because of the latter's devotion to Christ (Phlm 10–11). Indeed, generalizing this (Stoic) reasoning may have contributed to Paul's declaration in his other letters that *all* distinctions of status and birth and social identity are irrelevant for those "in Christ," including not only the distinction between slave and freeman, but also that between Jew and Greek, and male and female (e.g., Gal 3:28; cf. Rom 10:12–13; and see below).

To return to 1 Cor 7:20–23, there is reason to believe that this passage not only draws on Stoic traditions, but, more precisely, on Stoic traditions as they developed or were transmitted by some of Paul's Jewish (and Jewish-Christian?) contemporaries.

Paul's advice on slavery and freedom in 1 Cor 7:20–23 is immediately preceded in 7:18–19 by his remarks on circumcision and its opposite, "uncircumcision," both of which he declares to be "nothing" (οὐδέν ἐστιν, *ouden estin*). This raises the possibility that Paul may have envisioned circumcision, too, along the lines of a Stoic indifferent, especially when we observe that his discussion of circumcision in 7:18–19 is cast in the same diatribe pattern as 7:21–22 and 7:27–28. Against this, however, is the fact that Paul readily joins the pairs Jew/Greek (i.e., circumcised/uncircumcised) and slave/free elsewhere in his letters (1 Cor 12:13; Gal 3:28).

To explore this possibility, therefore, it will be necessary to examine Paul's statements on circumcision outside of 1 Cor 7:18–19, as this passage offers too little with which to work. When we do this we find no certain evidence of Stoic vocabulary or phraseology, but we do discover two potentially important things. First, in Galatians Paul also declares circumcision and uncircumcision to be "nothing" (οὔτε τί εστιν, *oute ti estin,* 6:15) and "of no avail" (οὔτε τι ἰσχύει, *oute ti ischyei,* Gal 5:6); and similarly, in Gal 3:28 and Rom 10:12 he states that both Jewish and Greek identities are irrelevant.[59] There is reason to think that these statements depend, in part, on Stoic notions of universalism. Second, Paul refers to circumcision as having moral value and disvalue. In Rom 2:25, he states that circumcision benefits one who keeps the law; and, in Rom 3:1–2, he asks, "What benefit has circumcision?" answering, "Much, in every way!" Yet Paul can also place circumcision among the things he counts as "loss" since becoming a Christian (Phil 3:5–8); he holds that receiving circumcision "estranges" one from Christ such that Christ, on whom salvation depends, will be of *no* benefit (Gal 5:2–4); and consistent with this he objects passionately to gentile Christians receiving circumcision (Gal 2:3; 5:12; Phil 3:2–3).

While many scholars find it possible to explain Paul's reasoning in these passages without reference to Stoic ethics, I would suggest that the potential inconsistency we find here can be understood, if not best understood, if we bring to mind some of the peculiarities of Stoic ethics. First, let us remember that Stoics made a sharp distinction between *things* and *actions.* A *thing* could be an "indifferent," meaning that it had no real or inherent value with respect to what was truly good; but moral *actions,* which involved selecting and rejecting things, were either "fitting" or "not fitting." From this perspective we can understand Paul as speaking about circumcision as a "thing" that has no moral significance—for one can be made righteous whether or not he has circumcision (Rom 3:30)—but "receiving circumcision" or "becoming circumcised" as an *action* that is sometimes appropriate and sometimes not.

Second, and following naturally from this, Stoics spoke of indifferent things as having an assigned value, which was a value based on their potential for enabling someone to act morally and work toward moral perfection. This value was variable, moreover, depending on circumstances. In a given situation an indifferent could be preferred, rejected, or inconsequential. In speaking about circumcision, Paul seems to envision a variety of circumstances. For someone who is *already* a Jew, circumcision can have great value (Rom 3:1–2).[60] Likewise, circumcision has value for someone who intends to observe the Law (Rom 2:25),[61] for as Paul implies in Gal 5:3–4, receiving circumcision is tantamount to seeking justification under the Law (ἐν νόμῳ δικαιοῦσθε, *en nomō dikaiousthe*). Since the time of Christ's resurrection, however, God's justification has been available through faith in Christ, not through works of the Law (e.g., Gal 2:16), and thus it is now both inconsequential if one *already has* circumcision, and at the same time unfitting for one to *receive* circumcision, for then Christ is of no benefit (Gal 5:2).

Finally, we have seen that Stoics spoke of indifferents as having "much" or "little" value, whereas goods had "the greatest" value. This, in turn, might be the conceptual framework for Phil 3:5–8. Here Paul explains that in view of the "surpassing greatness" (ὑπερέχον, *hyperechon*) of knowing Christ, things that he formerly counted as "gain" (κέρδος), including circumcision, he now considers "loss" (ζημία, *zēmia*),[62] so that he might "gain Christ" (ἵνα Χριστὸν κερδήσω, *hina Christon kerdēsō*). And to this we need only add that κέρδος and ζημία, while not uniquely Stoic, do occur in Epictetus as part of his ethical vocabulary.[63]

I realize that to a modern reader this interpretation of Paul's views on circumcision may seem overly technical and artificial. But the Stoics did employ these ethical categories, and they became popular among many non-Stoics, especially in the period from ca. 150 B.C.E. to ca. 150 C.E. (i.e., from Arius and Cicero to Epictetus and Hierocles). I stress this point here because of the potential importance of this understanding of circumcision in Paul. Unlike life and death, marriage, and slavery, circumcision was *not* a topic that was discussed by the Stoics. This means that if Paul is, in fact, treating circumcision in these passages as an indifferent thing, then he is not doing so by borrowing or imitating an existing Stoic treatment. Rather, either he or a Jewish, or Jewish-Christian, contemporary has integrated basic elements of Stoic ethical theory into the very heart of Christian theology and applied them to issues facing the early church. And if the integration of Stoic and Christian ethics has taken place at such a foundational level in Paul's theology, then several exciting possibilities come into view.

First, it is possible that Paul's indifference to the other things on our original list—for example, food, education, and speaking in tongues—may also depend on a Stoic approach to the world, even though there is little or nothing in what Paul says about them to suggest the presence of Stoic reasoning. Second, if the rationale of Paul's arguments depends to some measure on Stoic premises, then a basic understanding of these premises must have been part of the intellectual and moral world of his audiences, if we are to assume that his arguments were effective.

Third, and quite beyond this, we must consider the implications of this integration of Stoic and Christian ethics for mapping out a theoretical basis for Paul's ethics. After all, if there is a category of "indifferent things" in Paul's ethics, are there also "good" and "bad things" or virtues and vices—and if so, what are they? To some extent, these questions have already been taken up by Paul Sampley,

James Jaquette, and, most recently, Paul Holloway.[64] The latter, for example, on the basis of a careful exegesis of Philippians, has identified several "things that matter" in Paul (τὰ διαφέροντα, *ta diapheronta*, Phil 1:10), which, for the Stoics, would be the equivalent of "goods." These include: "the progress (προκοπή) of the gospel" (Phil 1:12–18a), "Paul's own anticipated salvation (σωτηρία, *sōtēria*)," "the boldness (παρρησία, *parrēsia*) of the gospel messenger" (both Phil 1:18b–21), and "the surpassing greatness of the knowledge of Christ" (Phil 3:8–14).[65] To these, in turn, we could add love (1 Cor 13:1–13), "faith working through love" (Gal 5:6), and the "new creation" (Gal 6:15), all of which Paul explicitly contrasts with things of relative worth and, consequently, indifference.

Fourth, if Paul has treated circumcision as an indifferent, it is not impossible that he viewed other commandments of the Mosaic Law as indifferent things. We know, for instance, that Paul devalued all "works of the Law" by comparison with grace and faith (e.g., Gal 3:2); and the striking statement he makes in 1 Cor 7:19b might also point in this direction. In 1 Cor 7:18–19a, as we are contending, Paul seems to treat circumcision, a prominent commandment of the Law in his theological circles, as an indifferent. In verse 19b, he then justifies this position, in part, by stating: "circumcision is nothing and uncircumcision is nothing; *but obeying the commandments of God is everything*." Evidently, "what matters" here is the "commandments of God," which are somehow distinct from circumcision, an (indifferent) work of the Law.[66]

Has Paul employed or been influenced by Stoic notions of indifference in his thinking on life and death, marriage, slavery, and circumcision? Based on his choice of words and phrases, there is reason to think so. In addition, a case can be made that Paul shares certain conceptual assumptions with the Stoics, even if he expresses these assumptions in his own theological idiom.

Yet perhaps determining the extent of Stoic influence on Paul should not be our primary concern. After all, if Paul's writings make better sense to us in light of Stoic ideas, then Stoic thought is relevant for understanding Paul, whether or not we can demonstrate influence. It has, in other words, heuristic value for interpreting Paul. The more important question, therefore, seems to be: "Does Paul make better sense in light of Stoic ethics?"—and as I suggested above, this is a matter that scholars will need to debate, perhaps for some time.[67]

Part III. Other Relevant Pauline and Paulinist Texts

Rom 8:35–39; 14:5, 6–8, 14–17, 20
1 Cor 1:26; 3:21–23; 4:10–13; 6:7–8, 12–13a; 8:8; 9:3b–7, 15–18; 10:23–24; 13:1–3;
    14:18–19
2 Cor 5:8–10
Gal 2:6–9
Phil 3:4–8, 12–16; 4:10–13

Part IV. Bibliography

Primary Texts, Translations, and Commentaries

Dyck, Andrew R. *Commentary on Cicero, De Officiis.* Ann Arbor: University of
    Michigan Press, 1996.
Griffin, M. T., and E. M. Atkins, eds. *Cicero: On Duties.* Cambridge: Cambridge
    University Press, 1991.
Hicks, R. D., trans. *Diogenes Laertius: Lives of Eminent Philosophers.* Cambridge:
    Harvard University Press, 1931. [See 2:110–319.]
Inwood, Brad, and L. P. Gerson, trans. *Hellenistic Philosophy: Introductory Readings.*
    2d ed. Indianapolis: Hackett, 1997. [Pp. 190–260.]
Johannes [Hans] von Arnim, ed. *Stoicorum Veterum Fragmenta.* Stuttgart: B. G.
    Teubner, 1968. [See 3:117–68.]
Long, A. A., and D. N. Sedley. *The Hellenistic Philosophers.* Cambridge: Cambridge
    University Press, 1987–88. [See 1:346–86, 394–410; 2:343–82, 389–404.]
Pomeroy, Arthur J., ed. *Arius Didymus: Epitome of Stoic Ethics.* SBLTT 44. Graeco-
    Roman Series 14. Atlanta: Society of Biblical Literature, 1999.
Wright, M. R., ed. and trans. *Cicero: On Good and Evil.* Warminster, England: Aris
    and Phillips, 1991.

Secondary Literature

Deming, Will. Review of *Discerning What Counts,* by James L. Jaquette. *JBL* 115
    (1996): 758–60.
Holloway, Paul A. *Consolation in Philippians: Philosophical Sources and Rhetorical
    Strategy.* SNTMS 112. Cambridge: Cambridge University Press, 2001.
Inwood, Brad. *Ethics and Human Action in Early Stoicism.* Oxford: Clarendon Press,
    1985.
Jaquette, James L. *Discerning What Counts: The Function of the Adiaphora Topos in
    Paul's Letters.* SBLDS 146. Atlanta: Scholars Press, 1995.
Long, A. A. *Hellenistic Philosophy: Stoics, Epicureans, Skeptics.* New York: Charles
    Scribner's Sons, 1974. [Pp. 179–209.]
Long, A. A., and D. N. Sedley. *The Hellenistic Philosophers.* Cambridge: Cambridge
    University Press, 1988. [See 2:505–10.]

Malherbe, Abraham J. "Determinism and Free Will in Paul: The Argument of 1 Corinthians 8 and 9." Pages 231–55 in *Paul in His Hellenistic Context*, edited . by Troels Engberg-Pedersen. Minneapolis: Fortress Press, 1995.

Rist, J. M. *Stoic Philosophy*. Cambridge: Cambridge University Press, 1969.

Sandbach, F. H. *The Stoics*. New York: W. W. Norton, 1975. [Pp. 28–68.]

Notes

This essay is dedicated to Frank Reynolds, for his instruction in comparative religious ethics.

1. My thanks to Abraham Malherbe for his help with these two parts, and to Paul Sampley for his valuable editorial suggestions.

2. E.g., Stobaeus, *Ecl.* 2.7.5a; Diogenes Laertius 7.101–102. For this sketch of Stoic ethics see A. A. Long and D. N. Sedley, *The Hellenistic Philosophers*, vol. 1: *Translations of the Principal Sources with Philosophical Commentary* (Cambridge: Cambridge University Press, 1987), 344–437. Long and Sedley's volume includes documentation and further discussion.

3. E.g., Philo, *Post.* 133: "Indeed, it was from virtue that the Stoic canon sprang that the morally beautiful alone is good" (Colson and Whitaker, LCL). See also Cicero, *Fin.* 3.27, 29; and Diogenes Laertius 7.100–101.

4. E.g., Diogenes Laertius 7.125; Stobaeus, *Ecl.* 2.7.5b5, 7; Philo, *Mos.* 2.7; Plutarch, *Stoic. rep.* 1046E.

5. E.g., Stobaeus, *Ecl.* 2.7.5b2; Diogenes Laertius 7.92.

6. E.g., Diogenes Laertius 7.93.

7. For other examples of what Stoics considered good and bad things, and their relation to virtue and vice, see Stobaeus, *Ecl.* 2.7.5a-5b2; and Diogenes Laertius 7.95–99.

8. E.g., Stobaeus, *Ecl.* 2.7.7; Cicero, *Fin.* 3.21.69.

9. See also Stobaeus, *Ecl.* 2.7.7f–g; and Diogenes Laertius 7.105–107.

10. See Long and Sedley, *Hellenistic Philosophers*, 1:401–410.

11. E.g., Stobaeus, *Ecl.* 2.7.5d; and Diogenes Laertius 7.94, 98–99.

12. See also Seneca, *Ep.* 82.10–11; and Cicero, *Fin.* 3.58.

13. See above, n. 10, and A. A. Long and D. N. Sedley, *The Hellenistic Philosophers*, vol. 2: *Greek and Latin Texts with Notes and Bibliography* (Cambridge: Cambridge University Press, 1987), 350.

14. See Damianos Tsekourakis, *Studies in the Terminology of Early Stoic Ethics* (Hermes: Zeitschrift für klassische Philologie, Einzelschriften 32; Wiesbaden, Germany: Franz Steiner, 1974), esp. 38–44.

15. On Paul's lists, see David E. Aune, *The New Testament and Its Literary Environment* (Philadelphia: Westminster, 1987), 194–96; John T. Fitzgerald, *Cracks in an Earthen Vessel: An Examination of the Catalogues of Hardships in the Corinthian Correspondence* (SBLDS 99; Atlanta: Scholars Press, 1988); and Anthony C. Thiselton, *The First Epistle to the Corinthians: A Commentary on the Greek Text* (Grand Rapids: Eerdmans, 2000), 561–62. The nature of our sources is a further problem. With the Stoics we have primarily lectures and handbooks that treat ethics in a theoretical and systematic fashion. With Paul we have occasional correspondence that

treats ethics practically and unsystematically. We could wish for better dialogue partners in a comparison.

16. Cf. the discussion in Troels Engberg-Pedersen, "Stoicism in Philippians," in *Paul in His Hellenistic Context* (ed. Troels Engberg-Pedersen; Minneapolis: Fortress Press, 1995), 269–74.

17. See Part III, below.

18. Cf. the discussion in James L. Jaquette, *Discerning What Counts: The Function of the "Adiaphora Topos" in Paul's Letters* (SBLDS 146; Atlanta: Scholars Press, 1995), 110–20.

19. E.g., Epictetus, *Diss.* 4.1.133, "'Life is not a good, is it?'—'No.'—'Death is not a bad thing, is it?'—'No.'"

20. E.g., Diogenes Laertius 7.106; cf. Cicero, *Fin.* 5.7.18–20; and Stobaeus, *Ecl.* 2.7.7d.

21. See also J. M. Rist, *Stoic Philosophy* (Cambridge: Cambridge University Press, 1969), 233–55; David Seeley, *The Noble Death: Graeco-Roman Martyrology and Paul's Concept of Salvation* (JSNTSup 28; Sheffield, England: Sheffield Academic, 1990), 113–41; Anton J. L. van Hooff, *From Autothanasia to Suicide: Self-Killing in Classical Antiquity* (London and New York: Routledge, 1990), passim; Arthur J. Droge and James D. Tabor, *A Noble Death: Suicide and Martyrdom among Christians and Jews in Antiquity* (San Francisco: HarperSanFrancisco, 1991), 29–39; and J. L. Jaquette, "A Not-So-Noble Death: Figured Speech, Friendship, and Suicide in Philippians 1:21–26," *Neot* 28 (1994): 177–92. And see the brief mention in Stobaeus, *Ecl.* 2.7.7f (cited above), of the choice of life over death as having "selective value" for the Stoics.

22. Seneca, *Ep.* 104.3 (Gummere, LCL); cf. *Ep.* 78.1–2. The first passage continues in 104.4: "It gives proof of a great heart to return to life for the sake of others; and noble men have often done this. But this procedure also, I believe, indicates the highest type of kindness. . . . one should watch over one's old age with still greater care if one knows that such action is pleasing, useful, or desirable in the eyes of a person whom one holds dear. This is a source of no mean joy and profit" (Gummere, LCL).

23. Musonius, *frag.* 29, my translation. Epictetus 4.1.167 provides an interesting variant of this tradition, especially in light of 2 Cor 11:32–33: "[words of a coward:] 'If I save my life I shall be useful to many persons, but if I die I shall be useful to no one.'—[Epictetus]: 'Yes, indeed, and if we had had to crawl out through a hole to escape, we should have done so!'" (Oldfather, LCL)

24. For the possibility of philosophical, and specifically Stoic, terminology elsewhere in Philippians, see Engberg-Pedersen, "Stoicism in Philippians," 261–64; and Abraham J. Malherbe, "Paul's Self-Sufficiency (Philippians 4:11)," in *Friendship, Flattery, and Frankness of Speech: Studies of Friendship in the New Testament World* (ed. John T. Fitzgerald; NovTSup 82; Leiden: E. J. Brill, 1996), 125–39. On *parrēsia*, see David E. Fredrickson, "ΠΑΡΡΗΣΙΑ in the Pauline Epistles," in Fitzgerald, *Friendship*, 163–83. On Stoic notions of "things that matter" (τὰ διαφέροντα)—i.e., "goods" as a counterpart to "indifferents"—see Paul A. Holloway, *Consolation in Philippians: Philosophical Sources and Rhetorical Strategy* (SNTMS 112; Cambridge: Cambridge University Press, 2001), 74–83, 94–99, 103, 130–32, and the discussion below.

25. Beginning with Plato, *Phaedo* 62C (cf. *Laws* 873C); see Arthur J. Droge, "*Mori lucrum:* Paul and Ancient Theories of Suicide," *NovT* 30 (1988): 283–84; and Droge and Tabor, *Noble Death*, 21–22, 35–36, 122–24.

26. Antipater of Tarsus, *SFV* 3.255.5 (Stobaeus 4.508.2–3 W.-H.), speaks of "the most necessary and primary actions that are fitting" as a distinct category of duties (see also Hierocles in Stobaeus, *Ecl.* 4.22a.21 [4.502.2 W.-H.]). On other possible Stoic uses of ἀνάγκη in Paul, see Ernst Baasland, "ἀνάγκη bei Paulus im Lichte eines stoischen Paradoxes," in *Geschichte—Tradition—Reflexion: Festschrift für Martin Hengel zum 70. Geburtstag*, vol. 3: *Frühes Christentum* (ed. Herman Lichtenberger; Tübingen: J. C. B. Mohr [Paul Siebeck], 1996), 357–85; and Will Deming, *Paul on Marriage and Celibacy: The Hellenistic Background of 1 Corinthians 7* (SNTSMS 83; Cambridge: Cambridge University Press, 1995), 207–9.

27. Seneca, *Ep.* 32; Epictetus, *Diss.* 1.4. The word is also used by Philo in a Stoic sense (e.g., *Leg.* 2.81; *Det.* 46). Elsewhere in Paul only at Phil 1:12 (on which, see Holloway, *Consolation in Philippians*, 141–42, and the discussion below); and in the Pauline collection at 1 Tim 4:15.

28. Holloway, *Consolation in Philippians*, 104–5, 110.

29. Epictetus, *Diss.* 1.28.13; 3.22.37; 3.26.25 (with χρήσιμον, *chrēsimon*—see n. 31); and 4.5.8. Not in the LXX. Elsewhere in the Pauline collection only at Titus 1:11. It is possible that κέρδος also reflects the Socratic tradition found in Plato's *Apology* 40D–E. See D. W. Palmer, "To Die Is Gain (Philippians 1.21)," *NovT* 17 (1975): 203–18; cf. also Josephus, *Ant.* 15.158.

30. See Droge, "*Mori lucrum*," 279–80; and Phlm 11.

31. Musonius, *frag.* 3.42.10; 8.66.11; 10.78.16; 14.92.31; 16.104.33 Lutz. Elsewhere in Paul: in Rom 2:4 as an attribute of God, which coincides with both LXX and Stoic usage; and in 1 Cor 15:33, in a philosophical adage that Paul quotes.

32. When speaking technically, Stoics made a distinction between "choosing" (αἱρέομαι) and "selecting" (λαμβάνω), the former describing only the actions of the wise man (e.g., Stobaeus, *Ecl.* 2.7.5o). In informal contexts, however, the words could be interchangeable, as in Musonius, *frag.* 1.32.24–26 and 18B.118.5–7 Lutz. It is possible, therefore, that through his choice of αἱρέομαι, Paul is suggesting that his decision to live is a "right action," consistent with perfect reason. Otherwise αἱρέομαι occurs in the Pauline collection only at 2 Thess 2:13 (God choosing the Thessalonians, which may derive from LXX usage).

33. Deming, *Paul on Marriage and Celibacy*, 173–210.

34. Ibid., 67–89.

35. Ibid., 173–210, 212–13.

36. Ibid., 159–64; Seneca, *Ep.* 42.9; 47.17 (see below, n. 45); 70.8–9; 96.1; 99.2; *Brev. vit.* 17.5–6; *Ira* 2.24.2–4; 2.30.1; *Prov.* 5.5; *Tranq.* 11.10, 12. While much has been written on the style and content of the diatribe, no one, to my knowledge, has investigated diatribe patterns. On Paul's use of diatribe style, see Stanley Kent Stowers, *The Diatribe in Paul's Letter to the Romans* (SBLDS 57; Chico, Calif.: Scholars Press, 1981); and Thomas Schmeller, *Paulus und die "Diatribe": Eine vergleichende Stilinterpretation* (NTAbh 19; Münster, Germany: Aschendorff, 1987).

37. See Deming, *Paul on Marriage and Celibacy*, 73–87.

38. Ibid., 173–97; cf. 110–12.

39. So Arius: "everything that happens among rational animals contrary to

that which is fitting is a sin [ἁμάρτημα, *hamartēma*]" (Stobaeus, *Ecl.* 2.7.8a); and ps.-Ocellus Lucanus, "many sin [ἁμαρτάνω, *hamartanō*] by forming marriages without regard for the excellence of a person's soul or for the benefit of the community" (*De univ. nat.* 48). These, naturally, are informal ways in which Stoics discussed "error," or "sin." According to strict Stoic orthodoxy, *every* action contrary to the perfect reason of the wise man was a sin (e.g., Stobaeus, *Ecl.* 2.7.11a).

40. Deming, *Paul on Marriage and Celibacy*, 197–205.

41. Ibid., 205–10.

42. E.g., Philo, *Quod omnis probus liber sit*; Seneca, *Ep.* 47; Epictetus, *Diss.* 3.24.64–77; 4.1; and Dio Chrysostom, *Or.* 14 and 15. For discussion see Deming, *Paul on Marriage and Celibacy*, 164–65; Samuel Vollenweider, *Freiheit als neue Schöpfung* (FRLANT 147; Göttingen: Vanenhoeck & Ruprecht, 1989), 23–104; and Peter Garnsey, *Ideas of Slavery from Aristotle to Augustine* (Cambridge: Cambridge University Press, 1996), 128–52.

43. See also Stobaeus, *Ecl.* 2.7.11i; and Diogenes Laertius 7.121–22.

44. E.g., Raymond F. Collins, *First Corinthians* (SP 7; Collegeville, Minn.: Liturgical, 1999), 286; and Thiselton, *First Epistle to the Corinthians*, 561–62.

45. See especially Seneca, *Ep.* 47.17: "He is a slave!—But his soul may be that of a freeman. He is a slave!—But shall that stand in his way?" [Gummere, LCL].

46. Will Deming, "A Diatribe Pattern in 1 Cor 7:21–22: A New Perspective on Paul's Directions to Slaves," *NovT* 37 (1995): 130–37.

47. So also Garnsey, *Ideas of Slavery*, 150–51, 163.

48. On this, see the excellent discussion in ibid., 129–31, 134–52.

49. See Diogenes Laertius 7.122, where slave ownership is equated to tyranny and judged "bad" (φαύλη, *phaulē*).

50. Philo, *Spec.* 2.69; and see Miriam T. Griffin, *Seneca: A Philosopher in Politics* (Oxford: Clarendon Press, 1976), 459.

51. Philo, *Contempl.* 70–71. Likewise, Josephus, *Ant.* 18.21, reports that the Essenes do not have slaves because slavery is a source of injustice (ἀδικία, *adikia*).

52. Philo, *Praem.* 137–38.

53. Garnsey, *Ideas of Slavery*, 171.

54. It has been a source of frustration to many modern theologians that Paul does not simply condemn slavery as "bad," but this would not have been the Stoics' or Paul's understanding of a rejected indifferent.

55. Philo, *Prob.* 79 (Colson, LCL).

56. Seneca, *Ben.* 3.28.1–2 (Gummere, LCL); "Heaven" in this translation is the word *mundus*, "heaven, the earth, the universe." See also *Ep.* 47.10: "[H]e whom you call your slave sprang from the same stock, is smiled upon by the same skies, and on equal terms with yourself breathes, lives, and dies" (Gummere, LCL).

57. E.g., Seneca, *Ben.* 3.18.2.

58. See Joseph A. Fitzmyer, *The Letter to Philemon: A New Translation with Introduction and Commentary* (AB 34C; New York: Doubleday, 2000), 113–16.

59. Gal 3:28, οὐκ ἔνι Ἰουδαῖος οὐδὲ Ἕλλην (*ouk eni Ioudaios oude Hellēn*); and Rom 10:12, οὐ γάρ ἐστιν διαστολή . . . (*ou gar estin diastolē . . .*), where διαστολή ("difference, distinction") carries a rather scholarly or philosophical meaning not found in the papyri (see BDAG, s.v. "διαστολή" [p. 237], and cf. Rom 3:22).

60. Paul uses ὠφέλεια/ὠφελέω (*ōpheleia/ōpheleō*) to indicate this value—terms

that Stoics consistently reserve to describe the "benefit" of goods only (e.g., Diogenes Laertius 7.102; cf. Seneca, *Ep.* 87.36–37), using χρεία (*chreia*), "utility," for both goods and indifferents (e.g., Diogenes Laertius 7.98–99, 107). That Paul, a non-Stoic, would use a technical term in a casual way, however, poses no problem. Even Stoics sometimes (although not in this case) used their terminology somewhat casually (see above, n. 32).

61. Which, interestingly, Paul phrases with the "you" singular of the diatribe (ἐὰν νόμον πράσσῃς, *ean nomon prassēs*).

62. That Paul's former gain is now considered loss rather than simply indifferent may be due to his having redefined the good as "knowing Christ"; see Holloway, *Consolation in Philippians*, 136–38, and the discussion below.

63. On κέρδος, see above, n. 29. Ζημία occurs only here in Paul and is seldom in the LXX. In Epictetus: 1.11.11 (twice); 1.20.11; 2.10.15, 19 (thrice, with κερδαίνω, *kerdainō*); 3.25.10; 3.26.25 (with κέρδος); 4:1.120; 4.4.32; 4.9.10 (twice); 4.12.18. Also Musonius, *frag.* 9.74.2; 15.96.19 Lutz. On the unusual expression "to gain Christ," see Phil 1:21, "to live is Christ," and the discussion above.

64. J. P. Sampley, *Walking between the Times: Paul's Moral Reasoning* (Minneapolis: Fortress Press, 1991), 77–83; and Jaquette, *Discerning What Counts*, 213–25. For Holloway, see next note.

65. Holloway, *Consolation in Philippians*, 101–45.

66. On this understanding of the "law of God," see Deming, *Paul on Marriage and Celibacy*, 169–73; and John J. Collins, *Between Athens and Jerusalem: Jewish Identity in the Hellenistic Diaspora* (2d ed.; Grand Rapids: Eerdmans, 2000), 229–30, 246. Nonetheless, Paul believes that the Mosaic Law still enables one to discern "the things that matter" (τὰ διαφέροντα). This information is found in Rom 2:18, which is couched in diatribe style.

67. See the remarks by Engberg-Pedersen, "Stoicism in Philippians," 277–80.

14

PAUL, MARRIAGE, AND DIVORCE

O. Larry Yarbrough

In the Greco-Roman world of the first century C.E., marriage and divorce were threads in an intricate web of social relations, the patterns of which varied widely. Each had both a public and private aspect, simultaneously. Even the most intimate relations of a married couple had implications for the wider public. And the values and customs of the wider public determined much of how a couple perceived its private relations. Thus, when we seek to understand marriage and divorce in the Greco-Roman world, we must take into account a wide variety of evidence drawn from many and disparate sources. Furthermore, we must evaluate that evidence with considerable care lest our own presuppositions cause us to over-emphasize one kind of evidence and undervalue another.

The sources for the study of marriage and divorce in the Greco-Roman world are both literary and archaeological. The literary evidence is drawn from law codes and judicial literature, wills, letters, drama, poetry, philosophical essays, histories, novels, and medical texts. Archaeological evidence includes the remains of domestic architecture (villas, houses, and apartments), epitaphs, papyrus fragments, and art.

If each body of evidence makes a unique contribution to the study of marriage and divorce, each also presents its own peculiar methodological problems. Most of the literary evidence, for example, derives from men in elite circles and thus reflects their values and points of view. We have little literary evidence from women and the lower classes. Both philosophical essays treating marriage and references to marriage in standard Greek and Roman histories reflect the values of the well-educated, propertied men in Greek and Roman society.[1] They were written by them and for them. The same can be said of medical texts, even those written about women.[2] Most of the references to marriage in Greek and Roman drama occur in comedy; most of the references in poetry appear in satires. The question here is the extent to which comedy and satire reflect reality. Both forms create effect through exaggeration and reversal of the normal order. Can their treatment of marriage and divorce be trusted? Were divorces really as common as Juvenal claims? Were fathers really as doting as Plautus suggests?[3] The same kind of question can be asked of ancient novels. Although marriage is a major element in the plots of both the plays and the novels, the marriages depart from the norms derived from other sources in a number of striking ways. For example, while most sources suggest that marriages were arranged by parents without concern for what we would call "romance," the plot of ancient novels demands that a young couple meet accidentally, fall violently in love at first sight, marry, and, after a period of trial, live happily ever after.[4]

The legal material is problematic because the codes were drawn up long after our period and do not always reflect laws as they existed in the first century.[5] Furthermore, the question of when and how Roman law was put into effect in the provinces is difficult to determine. Because Roman citizenship was extended to the whole of the empire only after our period, we cannot assume Roman laws applied in the cities of the provinces when Pauline Christianity was developing.[6] Although Roman wills were legal documents concerned with the distribution of property, they reflect sentiments also. Romans wanted to be well regarded in death. But because wills derive predominantly from the propertied classes, they must be used with caution in determining more widely held values.[7]

The archaeological evidence presents a different set of challenges. While many of the numerous epitaphs scattered throughout the Greco-Roman world derive from predominately wealthy mourners, a significant number reflect the sentiments of people further down the social ladder. They also record the voices of women. Reading them, however, is problematic, and not simply because so many of them are in fragments. While the peoples of the ancient Mediterranean wrote considerably more on their tombstones than modern Westerners, they were not always as detailed in recording the data as scholars would want. Still, they come as close to census data as we are likely to get for the Greco-Roman world and present the same kind of challenges—how to correlate and categorize a wealth of disparate information. And then there is the question of how much to believe. Many of the sentiments reflected on ancient tombstones were clearly commonplaces, so that to save time and money a grieving husband could inscribe on his wife's tombstone that he had lived with her forty years *s. u. q.* and be confident that everyone would know he meant *sine ulla querella* ("without any quarrels").[8] But, though passersby would have known what he meant, would they have believed him? And should we? The funerary inscriptions of slaves present a similar problem. There are numerous examples of slaves commemorating the deaths of their husbands, wives, and children. The problem here is that according to Roman law slaves could not marry! How is it then they use familial language when burying their dead?

Archaeological excavations of villas, houses, and apartment complexes are corroborating, and adding to, what we know of living arrangements from the literary sources. For our purposes, the excavations and reconstructions of apartment complexes and living quarters attached to street-side shops are especially revealing, because Paul's mission apparently drew from the population who lived in them.[9]

Wall paintings and gold-glass medallions portraying married couples, and children, also contribute to our understanding of marriage in the Greco-Roman world, though it is sometimes hard to know just what to make of them. They clearly portray people from the wealthier strata of society, for such works of art were expensive. Furthermore, the iconography and symbolism of the portraits are not always clear. Other wall paintings and household furnishings may also tell us something about marriage, or, more precisely, about attitudes to sexuality. For while most examples of "erotic" art in antiquity are found in brothels and public baths, it does show up in Roman domestic architecture. In addition, there are the remains of numerous oil lamps, vases, porcelain pieces, and mirrors with erotic scenes. Here again "reading" these examples of artistic expression is difficult, for the iconography must be understood in its own terms and not ours. Indeed, as John R. Clarke has recently shown, the iconography of erotic art changed decidedly from the Hellenistic to the Roman period, so that we must treat examples from antiquity with care, lest we transfer the meanings of one time and place to those of another.[10]

Thus far, we have treated traditional issues with regard to marriage as an institution with legal, political, and social dimensions. The last fifteen years have seen the development of other lines of inquiry with significant implications for the understanding of marriage in antiquity, though their concerns are broader than the study of marriage itself. I refer here to studies exploring the "construction" of sex and gender. There is great potential in these studies, though the approach is not yet fully developed and debates over its fundamental categories are sharp. Thus, the methods, categories, and questions deriving from them will be useful only to the extent they cohere with the evidence of antiquity. The results, moreover, must be placed alongside that derived from other approaches and assessed accordingly. But this is no more than what we require of all approaches. As we shall see, there is much to learn from these new lines of inquiry, both in the study of the Greco-Roman world and in the study of Paul's place in it.[11]

Part I. Marriage and Divorce in the Roman World

The purpose of Roman marriage was to produce legitimate children—*liberorum quaerundorum causa*. This phrase, or one similar to it, shows up in legal documents, in epitaphs, in poetry, and in comedies. Because marriage had such a prominent role in promoting the public good, it was not simply a private affair between a man and a woman—or even between the two households that arranged their marriage. Augustus was among the first to attempt social engineering through legislation designed to reward citizens for marrying and producing children and to punish those who did not.[12] Other emperors changed the laws when new times required new measures. But everyone recognized this purpose, even if they chose not to carry it out.

Because of the power (*potestas*) they had as head of the household, fathers determined the selection of a spouse, or so it was said.[13] The emperors regularly wielded this power to arrange marriages within their own households. No doubt it worked in other households of the privileged classes as well. Richard Saller has shown, however, that by the beginning of the empire the power of the *pater familias* was greatly limited. Arrangements for the marriages of Cicero's daughter suggest that no pattern worked for all situations even in the same family. Cicero apparently chose Tullia's first two husbands. But neither marriage lasted. The first ended in the death of the husband; the second in divorce. Tullia and her mother decided on a third husband while Cicero was abroad on a diplomatic mission. Their choice was not much better, however, for the third marriage ended in divorce also. Thus, while it might have been traditional, and in keeping with familial *pietas*, for a son or daughter to acquiesce to a father's choice, there were options. Mothers, other family members, and even the couple itself had a voice. And as Susan Treggiari notes, the couple's role may have been greater the lower we look on the social ladder. Indeed, Augustus' legislation decreed that a father could not force a child to marry or refuse his consent for a child's marriage if all else were in order. In fact, the free consent of both partners was one of the few requirements for a legal marriage.[14]

The other crucial requirement for marriage was proper legal standing. Some aspects used to determine legal standing will be familiar enough to modern readers. For example, while the degrees of kinship prohibited by Roman law may differ from those set in modern societies, the existence of such laws is widely accepted. Also similar to Rome, most Western cultures have established a minimum age for marriage. In Rome the minimum legal age for females was twelve; for males, fourteen. It was probably very rare, however, for either sex to marry at such an early age. Based on his analysis of tens of thousands of inscriptions, Richard Saller has set the median age for first marriage at twenty for females and thirty for males. But there were regional differences. This evidence, moreover, is for the wider populace. Among those of senatorial rank, marriage tended to occur earlier.[15] The difference in age between the husband and wife was common for all classes, meaning, among other things, that if the wife survived childbirth she was likely to outlive her husband for a considerable time. It also meant that relatively few fathers would have lived to see the marriages of their children.[16]

The most unusual requirement for legal standing, from a modern point of view at any rate, was *conubium*, which was based on notions quite foreign to most Western cultures. In essence, *conubium* was the capacity (*facultas*) to enter into a legal marriage based on a person's social status. As stated in the *Tituli Ulpiani* 5.3–5, "*Conubium* is the capacity to marry a wife in Roman law. Roman citizens have *conubium* with Roman citizens, but with Latins and foreigners only if the privilege was granted. There is no *conubium* with slaves."[17]

At issue here is the legal status of the children. In effect, if the parents did not have *conubium* the child was illegitimate. Significantly, however, while illegitimacy appears not to have had any moral connotations, the legal implications were significant indeed, having to do with rights of succession, inheritance, and all the privileges afforded by Roman citizenship. Consequently, *conubium* was a highly desired commodity; the preservation of family wealth depended upon it. As Roman influence expanded with the acquisition and annexation of more and more territory, moreover, claims to citizenship and thus to *conubium* became the subject of debate and numerous lawsuits, especially with regard to marriages between a Roman citizen and a "foreigner." Late in the Republic and early in the principate, the tendency was toward preserving boundaries. The Minician Laws, for example, decreed that children of "mixed marriages" took the status of the parent with the more inferior status.[18] Augustus's legislation on marriage went so far as to limit the right of *conubium* for senators and soldiers.[19] The effect of the laws regarding *conubium*, therefore, was to preserve the boundaries between Roman and non-Roman and between Romans of high social status and those of low status.

Roman law and the prejudices of the upper classes protected the "authorized marriages" (*iusta matrimonia*) of citizens. Other classes (and the elite who offended society) were consigned to "unauthorized marriages" (*iniusta matrimonia*), or relationships that had no legal standing at all. Couples whose marriage was unauthorized had limited rights of inheritance; their children were illegitimate.

Yet another kind of "marriage" was *concubina*, which involved a man and a woman living together without intent of marriage. There is no indication that in the first century there was any moral stigma attached to this relationship in Roman society. Indeed, it could be long lasting, satisfying, and beneficial for both partners. Neither partner, however, had any legal rights with respect to the other; the children were illegitimate.[20]

Finally, there was *contubernium*, which designated a relationship in which one or both partners were slaves. Such relationships had no legal standing at all. *Contubernium* existed at the discretion of owners (who of course could benefit from them through ownership of any children the couple might have) and could be ended by the sale of one or both of the partners. What is most striking about this category is that couples commonly referred to one another with traditional terms for family. "Husbands" buried "wives"; "wives" buried "husbands"; and "fathers" and "mothers" buried their "sons" and "daughters." What is more, the same intimate terms we see elsewhere appear on their tombstones also. Thus we have evidence that many who could not contract legal marriages nonetheless entered relationships that they regarded as tantamount to marriage.[21]

When marriage did take place, engagements and weddings could be very elaborate, with invitations, wedding gowns, rings, veils, vows, a homily, and parties with lots of well-wishers—just the sort of thing one might see in a wedding today.[22] Other parts of the ritual are not so familiar—sacrifices, omens, the bride's smearing fat on the door posts of the groom's house, and an elaborately decorated bed in the house's entryway. None of this was necessary, even for a legal marriage. Nor was a "marriage license." A simple declaration of intent to live together as husband and wife was sufficient. And, it was not always clear, even to the couple itself, when the marriage began. This question appears as a set topic in legal debates.

Negotiating over a dowry and concern with arranging financially and politically advantageous matches were standard features of upper-class marriages. That does not mean, however, that sentiment was lacking in them. As Treggiari shows, there is abundant evidence to show that feelings of respect, kindness, and even affection were both the ideal and the reality for many marriages. And this was true for all forms of "marriage," at all social levels.[23]

Still, marriages did not always work. The frequency of divorce, especially among the privileged classes, continues to be debated. Susan Treggiari concludes that, "[o]n balance the divorce-rate seems much less rapid and the habit of divorce less widespread than has commonly been thought."[24] Keith Bradley reads the evidence quite differently, arguing that in the upper classes divorce and remarriage were common and that the constant reconfiguring of households must be taken into account when defining the Roman family.[25]

Whatever the rate may have been among the elite, we know even less about the rest of Roman society, for the sources are almost completely lacking. Divorce, after all, is not the kind of subject likely to show up in funerary inscriptions. Because Roman law was less concerned with unauthorized forms of marriage and informal relationships, moreover, ending them would not have involved complicated legal maneuvering as it did among the elite. "Divorce" took place by mutual agreement, or when one partner abandoned the other.

Whenever and wherever divorce occurred, the most "dispensable" member of the family was the wife/mother, because she was the one to leave since the children of legal marriages belonged to the father.[26] Consequently, in upper-class households where remarriage was common, a child could have numerous mothers while growing up,[27] and servants frequently provided the physical and emotional support for most children.[28] So, divorce could be painful for a child, as Cicero's nephew Quintus showed when he broke down upon learning, at the age of fourteen, that his parents were contemplating divorce.[29]

Scholars still debate the makeup of the households in antiquity. The evidence suggests that there was a wide range of possibilities. Because the family is treated elsewhere in this volume, we will not explore it here.[30] However, marriage *must* be seen in the context of the larger family, which includes both parents and children on the one hand and the more broadly defined *domus* (complete with slaves and relatives) on the other. For Saller is correct in arguing that much of the debate on the "nuclear family" has been too narrowly focused.[31] Still, the Romans clearly had a notion of husband, wife, and children as an identifiable unity. They sculpted images of them, painted pictures of them, told stories of them, and reflected on their obligations and concerns for one another. In all likelihood, however, husband, wife, and children seldom lived alone, unless, that is, they belonged to the working people who inhabited rooms behind roadside shops or cubicles on the upper stories of tenements. The rest, both the wealthy families of senatorial or equestrian rank and the families of slaves who served them, lived together in villas and houses, along with all the others who worked in the household or were in and out of it on a daily basis as clients.[32] Even in death the Roman family was not alone, for when its members died, they were often buried and memorialized along with others from the larger household.[33]

Thus far, we have examined marriage as most Romans knew it. There were other voices, especially among popular moralists and physicians. Some of the moralists, echoing debates about the value of marriage from earlier Greek traditions, questioned whether it was good to marry. For others, the focus of the debate shifted from whether one should marry to how one could control sexual passions. Physicians, who were themselves closely linked to the philosophers, were especially interested in the latter question.[34] It is difficult to say how many Romans took either question seriously. Augustus' marriage legislation, directed toward the elite, suggests that many in their circles were not marrying and producing children. Though we cannot be certain of the extent to which the moralists and physicians influenced their decisions, they doubtless played a role. For the moment, however, it is enough to point out the questions and to locate them among the elite. As we shall see when we examine 1 Corinthians, their concerns may well play a deciding role in the way Paul addressed questions of marriage and sexuality.

As diverse as the attitudes and customs regarding marriage were among Romans, Paul would have encountered still others when he traveled through the empire. Unfortunately, we do not know as much about them as we do about the attitudes and customs of Rome. Although studies of marriage in classical Athens are of some help, the world had changed decidedly since that time, and customs changed with it. Scholars are just beginning to gather and sort through the evidence of the Hellenistic world.[35]

Paul would also have encountered Jewish households, which were very much part of the Greco-Roman world. Indeed, in the cities to which he wrote his letters, the structure of Jewish households was probably quite similar to all the others, even if Jewish moralists claimed superior ethics.[36] Here again, we will have occasion to note some of the similarities and differences as we work through Paul's references to marriage and divorce.

Part II. Marriage and Divorce in Paul

We do not have sufficient evidence to determine precisely what Paul thought about marriage and divorce. Furthermore, the evidence we do have is frequently conflicting. In the seven letters treated in this volume, there are only four explicit references to marriage and divorce: Rom 7:1–6; 1 Cor 7 and 9:5; and 2 Cor 11:2–4.[37] None of them is a systematic presentation of Paul's thought. Indeed, only 1 Cor 7 is expressly about marriage, the others referring to it in the course of his treatment of other issues. Furthermore, because 1 Cor 7 is part of a larger rhetorical argument and highly polemical in nature, it must be used with caution. Before looking at 1 Cor 7, therefore, it will be helpful to examine the incidental references, because they are likely to reflect Paul's presuppositions about marriage and thus prepare us for the more polemical arguments. Similarly, it will be instructive to look at Paul's comments regarding the married couples he knew. Here again, such comments, reflective of his own experiences, provide a context for the polemical arguments.

Prisca and Aquila are the most noteworthy of the couples Paul mentions, not only because we can identify them with certainty, but also because of their long relationship with him.[38] Paul mentions Prisca and Aquila twice in concluding sections of his letters. In 1 Cor 16:9, he sends *their* greetings to the church in Corinth; in Rom 16:3–5, he sends *his* greetings to them in Rome. In both cases, Paul makes reference to "the church in their house," suggesting they are among the more prosperous of Paul's associates. The greeting in Romans tells us even more, for here Paul indicates that they "risked their necks" on his behalf. Just what Paul means by this rather dramatic phrase, he does not say. Perhaps we are to think of an incident like those in the narrative of Acts 18, which were said to have happened while Paul was staying with Prisca and Aquila in Corinth. But he gives no details in Romans. Whatever may have happened, there is no question about Paul's opinion of Prisca and Aquila. He mentions them first in the long list of former associates that makes up Rom 16, and extends thanks to them on behalf of himself and all the churches of the Gentiles. He also refers to them as "coworkers" (συνεργοί, synergoi), the same term he uses to describe such prominent members of his mission as Timothy and Titus.[39] Prisca and Aquila, therefore, appear to be a married couple engaged in the Pauline mission at very high levels, possibly in Rome to help prepare the way for Paul's own visit.[40]

Andronicus and Junia appear to have been another married couple in the Roman house churches.[41] The way Paul links their names and describes them together just as he does Prisca and Aquila certainly suggests they were married. And interestingly enough, we may actually know as much about them as we know about Prisca and Aquila, at least if we are limited to the evidence in Paul's own letters. Indeed, we may know more. Paul greets Andronicus and Junia as "kinsmen" and "fellow prisoners" (τοὺς συγγενεῖς μου καὶ συναιχμαλώτους μου; tous syngeneis mou kai synaichmalōtous mou).[42] He also says they were "in Christ" before he was. Apparently, therefore, Andronicus and Junia were Jewish-Christians who at some point had met, joined, and were imprisoned with Paul in the course of his mission. Because Paul does not refer to them as hosts of a house church, they may not have had the same social and economic standing as Prisca and Aquila. But his regard for them does not appear to be any less. Indeed, Paul refers to Andronicus and Junia as "prominent among the apostles" (ἐπίσημοι ἐν τοῖς ἀποστόλοις, episēmoi en tois apostolois). Here again, he offers no details. But they must have done something to warrant arrest and imprisonment. Paul would likely have assumed the Roman churches already knew their story, just as they knew of Prisca and Aquila. We have, therefore, two married couples who had been actively engaged in mission with Paul. One had risked their necks on his behalf; the other had been imprisoned with him.

Two other couples may appear in Rom 16:15: Philologus and Julia and Nereus and his "sister." The linking of their names and the common use of "sister" to describe wives in papyrus letters makes it possible they were married. But we know nothing of them, except that Olympas and a number of "saints" were with them in Rome. Because Paul does not mention any kind of house here, we should perhaps think of their living together, or near one another, in one of the many high-rise apartments that catered to the urban poor in Rome. Perhaps Philologus and Julia and Nereus and his "sister" were among the many slaves in Rome who could not marry but did.[43]

Finally, we have the apostles and their wives mentioned in 1 Cor 9:5. As Galatians makes clear, there were tensions between Paul and the apostles. But there is no indication there or here that marriage was a factor in those tensions. The presence of Aquila and Prisca and Andronicus and Junia among Paul's co-workers suggests, rather, that both missions employed the strategy of using married couples. Unfortunately, apart from the passing references in Rom 16, corroborated to some extent by the accounts of Prisca and Aquila in Acts, we do not know much about how such couples worked. In all likelihood, the social status and economic ability of the couple would have determined what they did. Prisca and Aquila, as patrons of house churches, again provide one model. If Cephas and the other apostles were itinerants, they and their wives provided another.

Paul's references to these couples provide a striking background for considering his attitude to marriage and divorce in the more polemical writings. Prisca and Aquila and Andronicus and Junia appear to be people for whom he had genuine respect. What is more, even if Prisca and Aquila were the only married couple in Paul's mission, his account of their risking their lives for him is enough to make us look more closely at his claim that married couples were concerned only with pleasing one another and not the Lord (cf. 1 Cor 7:32–35). In real life, he knew better.

Romans 7:2–6 and 2 Cor 11:2–6 are Paul's two incidental references to marriage. They may well reflect common presuppositions, because the references to marriage are in the service of other arguments and thus require acceptance by his readers. In Rom 7, Paul uses marriage as an analogy to the role of the Law in salvation history. The analogy works because of Paul's assumption that a wife is bound to her husband until his death.[44] Interestingly, however, when he continues the argument in 7:4–6, he switches metaphors. Instead of saying that having died to the Law believers are free to marry Christ, he says that having been "discharged" from the Law the believer becomes a slave "in the new life of the Spirit."

We should not take this switch in metaphors to mean that Paul wanted to avoid the image of marriage to Christ, however, for he does use it in 2 Cor 11:2: "I promised you in marriage to one husband, to present you as a chaste virgin to Christ." Here Paul's assumptions are in keeping with common opinion, both Roman and Jewish. The father plays a prominent role in arranging marriage; the daughter is presented to her husband; and the bride is presumed to be chaste. Furthermore, the type of fear that Paul expresses, that as Eve was deceived by the serpent the Corinthians will be "corrupted" by the false apostles who follow him, is a topic that drives the plots of many comedies and novels. Here again the metaphor breaks down, because by the end of the argument it is not clear whether the offended husband is Christ or Paul. But the effect is the same: Young brides must be protected, lest they fall prey to unscrupulous suitors who would lead them into adultery.

Romans 7:2–6 and 2 Cor 11:2–6 suggest, therefore, that Paul held many conventional ideas about marriage. They also suggest that Paul is capable of shifting metaphors in the midst of an argument, using them only insofar as they suit his purpose. We should be prepared, therefore, for such shifts and the mixture of the conventional and unconventional in other arguments. We turn then to 1 Cor 7, the most complex of Paul's statements about marriage.

Every paragraph, every verse, every phrase, and every word in 1 Cor 7 has been the subject of numerous, and frequently conflicting, studies. Some of the challenges of reading 1 Cor 7 derive from the ambiguity of the situation(s) Paul is addressing. Others derive from the ambiguity of Paul's response. Still other challenges derive from the complexity of the Greco-Roman world of the first century, and our still incomplete understanding of it. While consensus has been reached on some parts of Paul's argument, on others, opinions remain widely divergent. The same can be said with regard to the interpretation of the chapter as a whole. I make no attempt here to survey all the literature dealing with 1 Cor 7. But in keeping with the theme of this volume, we should point out some of the recent efforts to find similarities and differences between Paul and the Greco-Roman world. These studies have made great contributions to our understanding of Paul's view of marriage and divorce.

Will Deming, in a detailed analysis of the language and ideas of 1 Cor 7, grounds Paul's arguments concerning marriage in the Cynic-Stoic debates of the centuries just before and after the turning of the eras.[45] According to his reconstruction, the early Stoics, as supporters of traditional social values, argued that a man should marry and have children because this was one of his prime responsibilities toward the city, the gods, and the universe. If men failed in these obligations, the world as they knew it would collapse. The Cynics, on the other side of the debate, agreed that the world would collapse but were not bothered by the prospect. In fact, they welcomed a collapse, claiming that it would lead to greater freedom to pursue philosophy. By our period, Deming argues, an "inner-Stoic" debate had developed, with some holding to the early Stoic position and others borrowing from the Cynic position. The result was a third way which held that marriage is appropriate for the wise man, but only if circumstances permit. When circumstances are not advantageous, it is a "sin" to marry, because the wise man will be distracted from his greater purpose.

Deming demonstrates that both Paul and the Corinthians knew the Cynic-Stoic debates over marriage and claims that Paul sought to restrain the Corinthians' radical Cynic views by drawing on the mediating arguments of the inner-Stoic debate, adding to them elements of Jewish apocalypticism and wisdom traditions.[46] Deming's conclusion is that Paul's use of Cynic-Stoic arguments precludes treating him as an ascetic. Paul was not concerned with a rigorous system of denial, but with the practicalities of serving God. Paul's advocacy of celibacy, therefore, is only "the necessary by-product of two things, a desire to live the unencumbered, single life, and the Judeo-Christian prohibition of extra-marital relations."[47]

Other recent studies of ancient debates on marriage argue for a quite different interpretation of the evidence drawn from the philosophical tradition. Two factors contribute to the differences: the use of ancient medical texts as a supplement to the philosophical treatises and the use of theoretical models developed in contemporary feminist and gender studies.

For our purposes, Dale Martin's *The Corinthian Body* is perhaps the best example of these studies, because, as the title suggests, it is concerned specifically with the Corinthian correspondence. Here again, although the details of the argument are too complex and too numerous to treat here, it must be read along with Deming's study by anyone interested in 1 Cor 7.[48] Martin's work is concerned with the "construction" of sexuality among the elite of Greco-Roman society. He draws on the medical texts of Soranus, Galen, and Oribasias, and links their arguments to those of the moral philosophers, including, but not limited to, the Cynics and Stoics Deming treats. Martin finds in this literature—all written for the privileged elite—a concern for maintaining the ideal of the male body, which necessitated, among other things, preserving balance in the life forces. Sex, in this view, was a driving passion that had to be controlled, lest excessive loss of semen lead to a weakening of the body. Excessive passion, he shows, was regarded as a disease and treated accordingly. In applying this assessment to 1 Cor 7, Martin argues that while Paul and the Corinthians agreed that "it is good for a man not to touch a woman," their reasons were different, though equally ascetic. Like the physicians, the Corinthians were concerned with the weakening of the body through the loss of vital powers in sexual intercourse. They saw celibacy as a way of maintaining strength, both for themselves and the community.

Paul, however, was concerned with *porneia* (sexual immorality) and desire. And because he regarded both as a threat to the community, he argued that both should be avoided. Avoiding *porneia*, Martin points out, was Paul's major concern in 1 Cor 5–6, reflected in his treatment of the man living with his stepmother (5:1–5) and those who visited prostitutes (6:12–20). In chapter 7, Martin argues, Paul's main concern was with desire. His goal was to suppress it, even in marriage, so that the danger from *porneia* could be eliminated. For Martin, therefore, the strong in Corinth would have shared the views of a growing elite in the Greco-Roman world. Paul, however, would have been the odd man out. While everyone else wanted to control desire; he wanted to eliminate it.

David E. Fredrickson's treatment of "natural use" in Rom 1:24–27, though concerned with another text, covers some of the same ground as Deming and Martin and thus contributes to an understanding of Paul's language in 1 Cor 7. Fredrickson's reconstruction of the argument in Rom 1:24–27 suggests that Paul was more concerned with controlling desire than Martin allows. He shows, more-over, that the goal may not have been so unusual. Indeed, his survey of Greco-Roman philosophers leads him to conclude that Paul's argument "follows a pat-tern established by the moral philosophers whose concern was to make passion and its control the core ethical problem in all matters of life." Citing Epictetus, Musonius Rufus, Seneca, and others, he finds "copious references to nature in de-scriptions of the ideal life spent in pursuing necessities without indulging pas-sion."[49] These observations are as applicable to 1 Cor 7 as they are to Rom 1:24–27, which would suggest that Paul's concern with avoiding desire was perfectly in keeping with moral traditions of the philosophers.[50]

Stan Stowers's recent study of Romans also argues that Paul was concerned with controlling desire. His treatment of "Readers in Romans and the Meaning of Self-Mastery" makes an important contribution to the study of 1 Corinthians be-cause it places Paul's arguments regarding the control of desire in a broader con-text.[51] He draws on many of the same philosophical and medical texts we find in the other studies and adds to them a systematic treatment of Jewish moral tradi-tions. He also emphasizes the political implications of the debate. For our pur-poses, however, it is especially striking that Stowers makes his case with only one reference to 1 Cor 7![52] He shows, therefore, that Paul's concern with sexual desire is only one aspect of self-mastery. Even more importantly, Stowers's treatment of "the cooperative virtues under the rubric of love" found in Rom 5, leads him to the following conclusion:

> [Paul] deemphasizes the ethic of self-mastery and denies that any of the
> virtues can be had through the performing of works from the law. Paul
> does not deny a place to self-control, but he does not, as his competitors
> were likely to have, center his ethic on self-mastery.[53]

In these and other recent studies of marriage and sexuality in the Greco-Roman world, numerous aspects of Paul's arguments in 1 Cor 7 have been clari-fied. For example, the meaning of Paul's claim that "it is better to marry than to burn" in verse 9 and the term "strong passions" (ὑπέρακμος, hyperakmos) in verse 36 have been firmly fixed within the discussions of the physical aspects of the body.[54] His references to agreement between husband and wife (v. 5), the concern with anxiety and the burdens of marriage (vv. 32–35), and having a wife as if not having her (v. 29)—all these, and many others, resonate with contemporary dis-cussions. Perhaps more important than these observations about individual pieces of Paul's argument in 1 Cor 7, however, is the consensus among most re-cent studies that Paul's concern with self-control places him squarely in the elite circles of Greco-Roman society for whom it was a key issue. But in the end, as

Stowers shows, concern with self-control does not determine Paul's ethics. The recognition of this drives us back to 1 Cor 7 and Paul's own arguments.

The structure of 1 Cor 7 is very complex. The chapter begins with reference to a letter from the Corinthians, and Paul's initial response to it in verses 2–7. In verses 8–16, Paul addresses three different groups: "the unmarried and widows," "the married," and "the rest." A discussion of circumcision and slavery follows in verses 17–24. Although in verse 25 Paul appears to introduce a new topic, "the virgins," it is not clear how much of verses 26–40 relate to it. Verses 39–40, for example, return to the treatment of widows first mentioned in verse 8. Indeed, throughout the chapter Paul inserts comments to one group in the context of his treatment of another, moving back and forth in his argument. He treats those who *have been married* in verses 8–9, 27b, and 39–40; he treats those who *are married* in verses 10–11, 12–16, 27a, and 29–31; and he treats those who *have not been married* in verses 25–26, 28, 32–35, and 36–38. In spite of the complexity in 1 Cor 7, however, there are a number of consistencies in Paul's arguments.

The most striking consistency is Paul's advice to "remain as you are." Paul himself emphasizes the consistency of his advice in the excursus on circumcision and slavery in verses 17–24. In verse 17, he writes, "[L]et each person walk in the status the Lord has allotted, each as God has called. This is what I decree in all the churches" (ἑκάστῳ ὡς ἐμέρισεν ὁ κύριος, ἕκαστον ὡς κέκληκεν ὁ θεός, οὕτως περιπατείτω. καὶ οὕτως ἐν ταῖς ἐκκλησίαις πάσαις διατάσσομαι, *hekastō hōs emerisen ho kyrios, hekaston hōs keklēken ho theos, houtōs peripateitō. Kai houtōs en tais ekklēsiais pasais diatassomai*). He repeats the advice in verse 20: "Let everyone remain in the calling they were in when called" (ἕκαστος ἐν τῇ κλήσει ᾗ ἐκλήθη, ἐν ταύτῃ μενέτω, *hekastos en tē klēsei hē eklēthē, en tautē menetō*). In verse 24 he gives it a third time: "Brothers and sisters, let all remain with God in whatever status they were in when called" (ἕκαστος ἐν ᾧ ἐκλήθη, ἀδελφοί, ἐν τούτῳ μενέτω παρὰ θεῷ, *hekastos en hō eklēthē, adelphoi, en toutō menetō para theō*). The threefold repetition of his advice and Paul's claim that it expresses what he taught "in all the churches" demonstrate that "remaining as you are" is a fundamental principle for him.[55]

Although Paul applies the principle "remain as you are" to circumcision and slavery in the excursus of verses 17–24, these are not his primary concerns in 1 Cor 7. Rather they are illustrations of what he has argued throughout the chapter thus far and will return to again in verses 25–40. The links between the excursus and the rest of the chapter are the transitional phrase in verse 17 (Εἰ μή, *ei mē,* "However that may be"), the repetition of the word "remain" in verses 8, 11, and 40, and the arguments for the status quo in verses 10–11, 12–13, 25–27, and 37–38.[56] Every situation Paul addresses in 1 Cor 7:8–40 is governed by this principle.

As we have already seen, Paul refers to the dominical saying regarding divorce in 7:10–11 when he addresses believers who *are* married.[57] Explicitly basing his position on a word of the Lord, he declares that the wife should not leave her husband and the husband should not send away his wife.[58] This, of course, is tantamount to saying that they should remain as they are. Paul adds, however, that if a woman is divorced, she should remain unmarried or be reconciled to her husband.

In 7:12–16, Paul writes to those who are married to unbelievers, noting this time that *he* is speaking, not the Lord. The position, however, is fundamentally the same: a brother or sister should not divorce an unbelieving partner who is content with the marriage. They should remain as they are. Here again, however, Paul adds a qualification, saying that, in the event the unbelieving partner does not consent to live with a believing spouse, the believer may consent to the divorce.

The other segments in 1 Cor 7:8–40 address those whose marriages have ended in the death of a spouse (vv. 8–9 and 39–40) and those who have never married (vv. 25–28 and 36–38). In every instance he advises against getting married. In effect, that is, he advises unmarried Corinthians to remain as they are. The situation is clearest in verses 39–40, where Paul advises widows "to remain" as they are, because, in his opinion, they will be "more blessed" if they do. He does not explain what being more blessed may mean here, perhaps believing he has made his point clear enough in the earlier examples in the chapter. It is important to note, however, that he grants a concession here too. His opinion notwithstanding, he says, the widow is free to marry whomever she wishes, only in the Lord.[59]

The situation in verses 25–28 is less clear, but appears to conform to the pattern we have noted. In treating the topic of "virgins," Paul again gives his "opinion" that it is good for them, and those who are contemplating marriage with them, to remain as they are (καλὸν ἀνθρώπῳ τὸ οὕτως εἶναι, *kalon anthrōpō to houtōs einai*). Significantly, moreover, "the impending crisis" (τὴν ἐνεστῶσαν ἀνάγκην, *tēn enestōsan anangkēn*) is not an argument for avoiding marriage, but for remaining in one's present status, whether married or single.[60] But here too Paul grants a concession, "If you do marry you do not sin [οὐχ ἥμαρτες, *ouch hamartes*]; if the virgin marries, she does not sin [οὐχ ἥμαρτεν, *ouch hēmarten*; 7:28]." Because the concession deals only with those who are not married, however, Paul supports his argument with another reason, this time dealing only with the question of whether one should marry. "Those who marry," he writes, "will have tribulation in the flesh [θλῖψιν τῇ σαρκὶ, *thlipsin tē sarki*], and I would spare you that."

The situation Paul addresses in verses 36–38 is even less clear, though again his argument follows the pattern. I accept here the view that verses 36–38 deal with a special case related to the theme of the virgins begun in verse 25 and that

Paul addresses a man who is concerned about the way he is behaving toward the young girl to whom he is betrothed.[61] Paul's advice differs in this situation only in the order he gives it. Here he begins with the concession (v. 36) and only then states that the one who is able to remain as he is (and keep the virgin as she is) does well (v. 37). This forces him to restate his opinion in verse 38, this time more clearly: "The one who marries his virgin does well; the one who does not marry does better."

In verses 8–9, addressed to those whose marriage ended in the death of a spouse, the basic pattern we have seen throughout the chapter also appears, though with an interesting twist. Here Paul does not write that the unmarried should remain as *they* are, but that they should remain as *he* is. The effect, of course, is the same. For as the concession that follows makes clear, Paul has in mind that widows and widowers remain unmarried. But the conditional element in the concession suggests that more is at stake for Paul than merely remaining unmarried. "If they do not exercise self-control," he writes, "let them marry. For it is better to marry than to burn" (εἰ δὲ οὐκ ἐγκρατεύονται, γαμησάτωσαν, κρεῖττον γάρ ἐστιν γαμῆσαι ἢ πυροῦσθαι, *ei de ouk engkrateuontai gamēsatōsan, kreitton gar estin gamēsai ē pyrousthai*). The language clearly echoes the elite arguments regarding self-control we saw in the philosophical and medical texts. This is not a strong argument in favor of marriage. But it is the only one Paul gives in the whole chapter.

By contrast, Paul gives four reasons for not marrying: "tribulation in the flesh" (28), freedom from the "anxiety" marriage brings (32), the promotion of good order, and unhindered devotion to the Lord (35). Furthermore, when he allows marriage in verses 9 and 36, he clearly accepts it as a secondary good. What are we to make of this?

Paul's view of marriage and divorce, along with his understanding of sexual desire, was complex—to the extent we can determine it. There were tensions, if not contradictions, in his thinking. He worked closely with married couples such as Prisca and Aquila and recognized the risks they took for his mission and his life. Yet he could also argue that married people were concerned about one another and not the Lord. He presupposed the traditional patriarchal model of relations between husbands and wives and yet advocated their sharing responsibility over each other's bodies. He could argue that sexual intercourse with a prostitute is defiling (1 Cor 6:12–20) and that a married believer sanctifies an unbelieving partner (1 Cor 7:14).

These tensions in Paul's arguments probably have many sources. Some derive from the world around him, some from his own experiences in that world, and some from the situations he faced when writing his letters. The situation in Corinth, I maintain, contributed most to the formulation of Paul's response to their letter and to the reports he had heard. Moreover, Dale Martin is probably right in arguing that marriage is one of the conflicts that divided the Corinthians along fault lines of social status.[62] The "strong," as Paul calls them, regard themselves as superior to those who lack self-control, just as they considered themselves superior with regard to knowledge and spiritual gifts. Here, as elsewhere in 1 Corinthians, therefore, Paul confronted them because they were destroying the body of Christ. In Paul's view, they were doing as much damage to the Corinthian body as *porneia*. Clearly then there is a polemical edge to Paul's argument throughout 1 Cor 7.

If the interpretation of what Paul says about marriage in this chapter hinges on the recognition of this polemical edge, the application of what he says is affected by it even more. What, we might ask, would Paul have written to the "weak" if they had written the letter to which he was responding? It would hardly have looked like 1 Corinthians as we have it. Just as we would expect a different treatment of the question of food sacrificed to idols, for example, so we should expect a different treatment of marriage. I do not mean to suggest that Paul would have changed his fundamental position. He would still have argued that believers should remain as they are. But his treatment of relations between husband and wives would doubtless look different. Prisca and Aquila might even have served as an example of married couples who served the Lord. Similarly, Paul might have dealt with the question of children, especially if it had appeared in the letter itself. Here he might have said more about how parents ought to care for their children, a theme he will take up in a different context later in his correspondence with the Corinthians.[63] All of this is speculation, of course, but it should give us pause in our interpretation of the polemical elements in Paul's treatment of marriage.

Throughout 1 Cor 7 Paul refuses to allow the strong to determine how the others will live. In verse 7, he refuses to assume that authority for himself. He may "wish" everyone were like himself and may have opinions about how they should live. But he acknowledges that this is not his to determine. God gives the gifts with regard to sexuality just as God makes the calls with regard to social status.

Part III. Other Relevant Pauline and Paulinist Texts

Of the other passages that might deal with marriage in Paul's letters, 1 Thess 4:3–8 is the most important. I have argued elsewhere that, like a number of examples from the Jewish parenetic tradition, it advocates marriage as a way to abstain from immorality. The arguments for reading it this way are still strong.[64] But if Paul *is* arguing this way in 1 Thessalonians, he must have changed his mind before writing 1 Corinthians. For there, as we have seen, he claims categorically that "remain as you are" is the principle he lays down in all the churches. A change is certainly possible, though it would result in a tension even more pronounced than the others we noted. Consequently, I am now inclined to treat the metaphorical language in 1 Thess 4:4 as a reference to behaving toward a wife (which would be in keeping with the reading of 1 Cor 7:2 given above) or to controlling the body and its passions. However, we take it, 1 Thess 4:3–8 clearly contributes to the discussion of marriage and sexuality in Paul's thought, for it provides another example of his concern to control "the passion of desire."

Marriage remained a concern for Paul's followers. In the Paulinist literature, the household codes of Col 3:18–4:1 and Eph 5:21–6:9 reflect the socially more traditional aspects of Paul's thought. First Timothy 2:8–3:13 and 5:1–6:2 and Titus 2 continue this trajectory. Outside the canon *The Acts of Paul and Thecla* reflects the more ascetic aspects of Paul's thought. The history of interpretation demonstrates that the tensions between the two trajectories have never been resolved. And they probably never will be, for if we do not understand our own "constructions" of marriage and sexuality are we ever likely to understand Paul's?

Part IV. Bibliography

Classicists

Balsdon, J. P. V. D. *Roman Women: Their History and Habits*. London: Bodley Head, 1962.

Bradley, Keith R. *Discovering the Roman Family*. New York and Oxford: Oxford University Press, 1991.

Corbett, P. E. *The Roman Law of Marriage*. Oxford: Oxford University Press, 1936.

Dixon, Suzanne. *The Roman Family*. Baltimore: Johns Hopkins University Press, 1992.

———. *The Roman Mother*. Norman: University of Oklahoma Press, 1988.

Gardner, Jane. *Women in Roman Law and Society*. Bloomington: Indiana University Press, 1986.

Hallett, Judith P. *Fathers and Daughters in Roman Society: Women and the Elite Family*. Princeton, N.J.: Princeton University Press, 1984.

Pomeroy, Sarah B. *Families in Classical and Hellenistic Greece: Representations and Realities*. Oxford: Clarendon, 1997.

Rawson, Beryl. "Family Life among the Lower Classes at Rome in the First Two Centuries of the Empire." *Classical Philology* 61 (1966): 71–83.

———. "Roman Concubinage and Other *De Facto* Marriages." *Transactions of the American Philological Association* 104 (1974): 279–305.

———, ed. *The Family in Ancient Rome: New Perspectives*. Ithaca, N.Y.: Cornell University Press, 1986.

———, ed. *Marriage, Divorce, and Children in Ancient Rome*. Oxford: Clarendon, 1991.

Rawson, Beryl, and Paul Weaver. *The Roman Family in Italy: Status, Sentiment, Space*. Canberra, Australia: Humanities Research Centre, 1997.

Rouseselle, Aline. *Porneia: On Desire and the Body in Antiquity.* New York: Basil Blackwell, 1988.

Saller, Richard P. "*Patria potestas* and the Stereotype of the Roman Family." *Continuity and Change* 1 (1986): 7–22.

———. *Patriarchy, Property, and Death in the Roman Family.* Cambridge: Cambridge University Press, 1994.

Treggiari, Susan. *Roman Marriage: "Iusti Coniuges" from the Time of Cicero to the Time of Ulpian.* Oxford: Clarendon, 1991.

Wallace-Hadrill, Andrew. *Houses and Society in Pompeii and Herculaneum.* Princeton, N.J.: Princeton University Press, 1994.

New Testament and Early Christian

Balch, David L. "1 Corinthians 7:32–35 and Stoic Debates about Marriage, Anxiety, and Distraction." *JBL* 102 (1983): 429–39.

———. *Let Wives Be Submissive: The Domestic Code in 1 Peter.* SBLMS 26. Chico, Calif.: Scholars Press, 1981.

Baumert, Norbert. *Ehelosigkeit und Ehe im Herrn: Eine Neuinterpretation von 1 Kor 7.* FB 47. Würzburg, Germany: Echter, 1984.

Countryman, L. William. *Dirt, Greed, and Sex: Sexual Ethics in the New Testament and Their Implications for Today.* Philadelphia: Fortress Press, 1988.

Deming, Will. *Paul on Marriage and Celibacy: The Hellenistic Background of 1 Corinthians 7.* SNTSMS 83. Cambridge: Cambridge University Press, 1995.

Elliott, John H. *A Home for the Homeless: A Sociological Exegesis of 1 Peter, Its Situation and Strategy.* Philadelphia: Fortress Press, 1981.

MacDonald, Margaret Y. "Early Christian Women Married to Unbelievers." *Studies in Religion* 19 (1990): 221–34.

———. "Women Holy in Body and Spirit: The Social Setting of 1 Corinthians 7." *NTS* 36 (1990): 161–81.

Martin, Dale B. *The Corinthian Body.* New Haven and London: Yale University Press, 1995.

Osiek, Carolyn, and David L. Balch. *Families in the New Testament World: Households and House Churches.* Louisville: Westminster John Knox, 1997.

Sampley, J. Paul. *"And the Two Shall Become One Flesh": A Study of Traditions in Ephesians 5:21–33.* SNTSMS 17. Cambridge: Cambridge University Press, 1971.

Ward, Roy Bowen. "Musonius and Paul on Marriage." *NTS* 36 (1990): 281–89.

Wimbush, Vincent L. *Paul the Worldly Ascetic: Response to the World and Self-Understanding according to 1 Corinthians 7.* Macon, Ga.: Mercer University Press, 1987.

Wolbert, Werner. *Ethische Argumentation und Paränese in 1 Kor 7.* Moraltheologische Studien, systematische Abteilung 8. Düsseldorf: Patmos, 1981.

Yarbrough, O. Larry. *Not Like the Gentiles: Marriage Rules in the Letters of Paul.* SBLDS 80. Atlanta: Scholars Press, 1985.

Notes

1. Many Greek and Roman popular moral philosophers wrote essays "on marriage" or discussed it in the context of other topics. Two recent studies are Susan Treggiari, *Roman Marriage: Iusti Coniuges from the Time of Cicero to the Time of Ulpian* (Oxford: Clarendon, 1991), chs. 6–7, and Will Deming, *Paul on Marriage and Celibacy: The Hellenistic Background of 1 Corinthians 7* (SNTSMS 83; Cambridge: Cambridge University Press, 1995), ch. 2. Both have extensive bibliographies.

2. Readily available editions of ancient medical texts that have a bearing on marriage include Soranus's *Gynecology* (Baltimore: Johns Hopkins University Press, 1956), and Galen's *Hygene* (Springfield, Ill.: Charles C. Thomas, 1951).

3. See, for example, Juvenal's Satire 6 and any of the plays of Plautus.

4. The period of trial could actually occur before the marriage, but the effect is the same. For a survey of marriage in the ancient novels, see Brigitte Egger, "Women and Marriage in the Greek Novels: The Boundaries of Romance," in *The Search for the Ancient Novel* (ed. James Tatum; Baltimore and London: Johns Hopkins University Press, 1994), 260–80. According to Egger's figures, in the five "ideal type" novels (those of Chariton, Xenophon of Ephesus, Achilles Tatius, Longus, and Heliodorus) there are seventeen weddings and twenty-three proposals of marriage. In addition to these, forty other marriages are mentioned. This comes to one marriage for every seven pages in *The Collected Greek Novels,* ed. B. P. Reardon (Berkeley: University of California Press, 1989).

5. The same problem, of course, obtains for the study of the Mishnah and Talmud. The main codifications of Roman law are those of Gaius and Justinian. The literature on Roman law is vast. For a useful introduction, see Andrew Borkowski, *Textbook on Roman Law* (2d ed.; London: Blackstone, 1994). For special studies on Roman marriage law, see the bibliography at the end of this essay.

6. Corinth and Philippi, for example, were officially Roman colonies. But we do not know the extent to which Roman law applied with regard to marriage and divorce. On the question of the use of Roman law in the provinces, see the comments and bibliography by David Johnston in *Roman Law in Context* (Cambridge: Cambridge University Press, 1999), 9–11.

7. For a treatment of wills in Roman society, see Edward Champlin's *Final Judgments: Duty and Emotion in Roman Wills, 200 B.C.–A.D. 250* (Berkeley: University of California Press, 1991), and J. A. Crook's essay "Women in Roman Succession," in *The Family in Ancient Rome: New Perspectives* (ed. Beryl Rawson; Ithaca, N.Y.: Cornell University Press, 1986).

8. See number 8156 in Hermann Dessau, *Inscriptiones latinae selectae* (Berlin: Weidmann, 1954).

9. See the works of Andrew Wallace-Hadrill in the bibliography for this essay and chapters 11–13 in Beryl Rawson and Paul Weaver, *The Roman Family in Italy: Status, Sentiment, Space* (Canberra, Australia: Humanities Research Centre, 1997), each of which has useful bibliographies.

10. John R. Clarke's *Looking at Lovemaking: Constructions of Sexuality in Roman Art, 100 B.C.–A.D. 250* (Berkeley: University of California Press, 1998), provides a thoughtful interpretation of Roman erotic art, with bibliography. On the question

of "reading" family art (with a focus on children), see the two parts of chapter 9, "The Iconography of Roman Childhood" and "Iconography: Another Perspective," by Beryl Rawson and Janet Huskinson in Rawson and Weaver, *Roman Family in Italy*.

11. See, for example, John J. Winkler, *The Constraints of Desire: The Anthropology of Sex and Gender in Ancient Greece* (New York: Routledge, 1990); David Halperin et al., *Before Sexuality: The Construction of Erotic Experience in Ancient Greece* (Princeton: Princeton University Press, 1990); Page DuBois, *Sowing the Body: Psychoanalysis and Ancient Representations of Women* (Chicago: Chicago University Press, 1988); and Michel Foucault, *The History of Sexuality*, vol. 2: *The Use of Pleasure* (New York: Random House, 1985). Studies treating Paul will be noted below.

12. The literature on Augustus's legislation is vast, with interpretations of its purpose differing. For a recent survey, with references to the earlier literature, see Treggiari, *Roman Marriage*, 60–80. Treggiari (59) suggests that Julius Caesar may also have sought to encourage marriage and increased fertility at Cicero's prodding. In addition to the literature cited by Treggiari, see J. H. W. G. Liebeschuetz, *Continuity and Change in Roman Religion* (Oxford: Clarendon, 1979), 90–100. As Liebeschuetz shows, Augustus's legislation on marriage and divorce was part of a sweeping moral reform program. Augustus was intentionally harking back to an earlier (idealized) time when citizens married and produced children for the good of the city-state. Moral philosophers made this a central theme in their treatises on marriage. The philosophers also referred to the benefits children provided parents when they were older. See n. 1 above for recent bibliography.

13. A father could, of course, be under his father's *potestas* and thus subject to his decree. *Potestas* belonged to the oldest living male in direct line. Mothers also had a voice. See Suzanne Dixon, *The Roman Mother* (Norman: University of Oklahoma Press, 1988), 62–63.

14. Treggiari, *Roman Marriage*, 122–24.

15. See chapters 2 and 3 in Richard P. Saller, ed., *Patriarchy, Property, and Death in the Roman Family* (Cambridge: Cambridge University Press, 1994). On age of marriage for the privileged classes, see Keith Hopkins, "The Age of Roman Girls at Marriage," *Population Studies* 18 (1965): 309–27, but in light of the comments in Saller.

16. On this and the issue of age at marriage, see Dixon, *Roman Mother*, ch. 2, and Richard Saller, "Men's Age at Marriage and Its Consequences in the Roman Family," *CP* 82 (1987): 21–34.

17. Cited and translated by Treggiari, *Roman Marriage*, 43.

18. These laws were promulgated sometime before 90 B.C.E. "Mixed marriage" does not refer to interracial marriage but to marriage between persons of different social (and legal) status.

19. Augustus disallowed marriages between any member of a senatorial family and a person who was not freeborn. The morals of a potential spouse should also be unquestionable. Lower on the social scale, Augustus forbade soldiers to marry while in active service.

20. See Beryl Rawson, "Roman Concubinage and Other *De Facto* Marriages," *Transactions of the American Philological Association* 104 (1974): 279–305.

21. See, for example, Beryl Rawson, "Family Life among the Lower Classes at

Rome in the First Two centuries of the Empire," *CP* 61 (1966): 71–83. Here at 78–79.

22. See the more detailed descriptions in J. P. V. D. Balsdon, *Roman Women: Their History and Habits* (London: Bodley Head, 1962), 180–85, and Treggiari, *Roman Marriage*, chs. 4 and 5. I compare the "solemn words" of the *auspex* (whom Baldsdon, *Roman Women*, 183, describes as "a cross between a family priest and a best man") to the modern homily.

23. Treggiari, *Roman Marriage*, ch. 8.

24. See ibid., 473–82, and appendices 5 and 6 on 516–19. The quotation is on 482.

25. Keith Bradley, "Remarriage and the Structure of the Upper-Class Family at Rome," in *Discovering the Roman Family* (New York and Oxford: Oxford University Press, 1991), 172.

26. See Dixon, *Roman Mother*. She also shows that a divorced woman could still maintain ties with her children (9, 11).

27. If a man remarried late in life, the new mother could even be younger than her children, given the usual age of girls at first marriages. The story of Knemon in Heliodorus's novel "An Ethiopian Story," which has explicit echoes of Euripides' tragedy "Hippolytus," teasingly relates what could happen when a young wife becomes stepmother to a sexually mature, and attractive, young man. See bk. I, 9–17.

28. See chapters 2–4 in Bradley's *Discovering the Roman Family*. The servants were frequently called *mamma* and *tata*, that is, "mamma" and "daddy."

29. See Bradley, "A Roman Family," in his collection of essays, *Discovering the Roman Family*, 195. This essay is very revealing of the range of relationships within a "family."

30. See the article by David Balch ("Paul, Families, and Households," ch. 9) in this volume.

31. See his comments in the preface to *Patriarchy, Property, and Death*, ix, and chs. 4 and 5.

32. There is a growing body of literature on domestic space in the Greco-Roman world. See the essays (with bibliographies) by Lisa Nevett, Michele George, and Penelope Allison in Rawson and Weaver, *Roman Family in Italy*.

33. See Dale B. Martin, "The Construction of the Ancient Family: Methodological Considerations," *JRS* 86 (1996): 40–60. Paul Gallivan and Peter Wilkins argue, however, that their survey supports the claim that nuclear families were the rule. See their "Familial Structures in Roman Italy: A Regional Approach," in Rawson and Weaver, *Roman Family in Italy*, 239–79, esp. 240n. 4.

34. For surveys of the philosophers, see n. 1 above. For the physicians, see Dale B. Martin, *The Corinthian Body* (New Haven: Yale University Press, 1995), and Aline Rousselle, *Porneia: On Desire and the Body in Antiquity* (Oxford: Blackwell, 1988).

35. See, for example, Sarah B. Pomeroy, *Families in Classical and Hellenistic Greece: Representations and Realities* (Oxford: Clarendon, 1997). Cynthia B. Patterson treats marriage and the family in Menander's plays in chapter 6 of *The Family in Greek History* (Cambridge and London: Harvard University Press, 1998).

36. See the essays in Shaye J. D. Cohen, *The Jewish Family in Antiquity* (BJS 289; Atlanta: Scholars Press, 1993).

37. Notice also Paul's quotation of the commandment against adultery (Exod 19:14) in Rom 2:22 and 13:9. Although 1 Thess 4:3–8 may well refer to marriage, Paul's metaphorical language in verse 4 precludes certainty. Other possible references include 1 Cor 11:2–16 and 14:34–35; and 2 Cor 6:14–7:1. Because of the problems associated with all these passages, I will make use of them only secondarily.

38. If Paul did meet Prisca and Aquila in Corinth in 50 c.e. as Acts 18:1–17 suggests, he would have known them for between four and seven years by the time he sends greetings to them in Rome, the length of time dependent on the dating of Romans. Furthermore, if we follow the account in Acts, he would have lived with them for eighteen months in Corinth and traveled with them to Ephesus. Under such conditions, Paul clearly would have known them well.

39. For Timothy, see Rom 16:21; 2 Cor 1:24; and 1 Thess 3:2. For Titus, see 2 Cor 8:23. See also the reference to Apollos in 1 Cor 3:9. Other "coworkers" include Epaphroditus (Phil 2:25); Mark, Aristarchus, Demas, and Luke (Phlm 23); and Euodia, Syntyche, Clement, and the others "whose names are in the book of life" (Phil 4:3).

40. According to Acts 19:21–22, Paul sends Timothy and Erastus to Macedonia to prepare for his stop there on his impending trip to Jerusalem. Peter Lampe also raises the possibility of Prisca and Aquila's having a role in preparing the way for Paul in "The Roman Christians in Romans 16," in *The Romans Debate* (ed. K. P. Donfried; 2d ed.; Peabody, Mass.: Hendrickson, 1991), 220.

41. Paul greets them in 16:7. On the name Junia, see C. E. B Cranfield's commentary, *Epistle to the Romans* (2 vols.; ICC; Edinburgh: T. & T. Clark, 1979), 2:788. For a discussion of the evidence, with references to other scholars who accept this reading, see Peter Lampe, "Junias," *ABD* 3:1127. For a very different view of the relationship between the men and women in the Pauline mission (and elsewhere in the early Christian community), see Ross S. Kraemer, *Her Share of the Blessings: Women's Relations among Pagans, Jews, and Christians in the Greco-Roman World* (Oxford: Oxford University Press, 1992), 136–38, and M. R. D'Angelo, "Women Partners in the New Testament," *JFSR* 6 (1990): 65–86.

42. In 16:11, Paul describes Herodian as a "kinsman" (*syngenē*). Lucius, Jason, and Sosipater, who were with Paul when he wrote the letter to Rome and asked that their greetings be included in it, are also described as *syngeneis* (16:21). The meaning of the term is fixed by Rom 9:3, where Paul uses it in the phrase,"my brothers, kindred according to the flesh." Epaphras is said to be a "fellow-prisoner" in Phlm 23. See also Col 4:10, which refers to Aristarchus as a "fellow-prisoner."

43. It also seems likely, though again far from certain, that Philemon and Apphia, who are mentioned in Phlm 1–2, were husband and wife. Even if they were, however, Paul makes nothing of it. In contrast to the way he describes Prisca and Aquila, he uses the term "coworker" only in reference to Philemon; and in contrast to the use of "his" to describe Nereus's "sister," he does not use a possessive pronoun in reference to Apphia. She is simply "the sister." Given the purpose of the letter, it is understandable that Paul describes the house as belonging only to Philemon, because, as the one having *potestas*, he owned it and everything in it. This also explains why Paul's request on behalf of Onesimus was addressed to Philemon alone.

44. In Roman law this was not true, of course, because divorce provided a woman another means to end marriage. It may not have applied to Jewish law either, though the question of whether a Jewish woman could initiate divorce is debated. Among earlier studies, see J. D. M. Derrett, *Law in the New Testament* (London: Darton, Longman & Todd, 1970), 386–88; Bernadette Brooten, "Konnten Frauen im alten Judentum die Scheidung betreiben? Überlegungen zu Mk 10, 11–12 und 1 Kor 7, 10–11," *EvT* 42 (1982): 65–80; and idem, "Zur Debatte über das Scheidungsrecht der jüdischen Frau," *EvT* 43 (1983): 466–78. More recently, see the series of articles treating Papyrus Se'elim 13: Tal Ilan, "Notes and Observations on a Newly Published Divorce Bill from the Judean Desert," *HTR* 89 (1996): 195–202; Adriel Schremer, "Divorce in Papyrus Se'elim 13 Once Again: A Reply to Tal Ilan," *HTR* 91 (1998): 193–202; and David Instone Brewer, "Jewish Women Divorcing Their Husbands in Early Judaism: The Background to Papyrus Se'elim 13," *HTR* 92 (1999): 349–57. Instone Brewer makes reference to his forthcoming book on the Jewish background of divorce and remarriage, which I have not seen. In considering the evidence, we must allow for a wide range of approaches to Jewish law. No doubt a woman who wanted a divorce would make use of whatever code helped her achieve her goal, if she had the option. Salome's use of Roman law to divorce her husband, Castobarus, gives just such a case (Josephus, *Ant.* 15.259–260). But because Paul's citation of the dominical saying on divorce in 1 Cor 7:10–11 suggests that he understands it as absolute, at least with regard to believers, marriage does serve as an analogy in his argument here. I examine Paul's use of the dominical saying in 1 Cor 7:10–11 below.

45. He gives a history of interpretation of 1 Cor 7 in his first chapter (*Paul on Marriage and Celibacy;* see n. 1, above, for citation), including references to other scholars who recognize Cynic and Stoic influence.

46. Deming, *Paul on Marriage and Celibacy,* lists the most important parallels between Paul and the Cynics and Stoics on p. 213. There is an index of select Greek words on p. 265. The details of Deming's argument are too complex and too numerous to treat here, though the significance of his broad outline should be readily apparent. Anyone seriously interested in 1 Cor 7 must take notice of Deming's work, for he meticulously works through the Cynic and Stoic literature citing parallels to Paul's terminology and arguments.

47. Ibid., 221.

48. Whether one agrees with Martin (*Corinthian Body;* see n. 34 for citation) or not, his reading forces a fresh look at the evidence. My primary problem with the book is that Martin seems to be fighting on several fronts simultaneously, with the result that his arguments are not as carefully worked out as they might have been. I find this especially true in chapter 8.

49. David E. Fredrickson, "Natural and Unnatural Use in Romans 1:24–27," in *Homosexuality, Science, and the "Plain Sense" of Scripture* (ed. David L. Balch; Grand Rapids: Eerdmans, 2000), 197–222. See p. 206 for the quotations. For another interpretation, see William Schoedel's essay "Same-Sex Eros: Paul and the Greco-Roman Tradition" in the same volume, 43–72.

50. Martin dismisses the kind of argument Fredrickson develops by claiming that "Greco-Roman authors occasionally mention the possibility of sex or marriage without desire; they probably do not mean, however, a complete absence of

desire; and they are a small minority in any case" (see Martin, *Corinthian Body*, 293n. 56).

51. This is the title of chapter 2 in Stanley Stowers, *A Rereading of Romans: Justice, Jews, and Gentiles* (New Haven: Yale University Press, 1994).

52. Stowers, in ibid., cites 1 Cor 7:5 parenthetically on p. 45.

53. Ibid., 73. The competitors here are Jewish-Christian missionaries who employ Jewish parenetic traditions that use the Torah to teach self-mastery.

54. See Martin, *Corinthian Body*, 219–28, for a convincing argument that ὑπέρ-ακμος applies to the woman.

55. Cf. Rollin Ramsaran, *Liberating Words: Paul's Use of Rhetorical Maxims in 1 Corinthians 1–10* (Valley Forge, Pa.: Trinity Press International, 1996), 43–46.

56. Paul's use of the phrase "you are bought with a price" in verse 23 echoes 6:20 and thus is one of the many links between 1 Cor 7 and the two preceding chapters.

57. Because in the next section he addresses believers who are married to "unbelievers," verses 10–11 treat those who are married to believers.

58. Paul's language here echoes conventional language about divorce. Though numerous terms could be used to describe the actions of divorce, transitive verbs regularly define the role of the husband; intransitive verbs, frequently in the middle voice, describe the role of the wife. See Treggiari, *Roman Marriage*, 435–41.

59. Most likely, Paul means by this last phrase that she should choose a partner from within the community of believers.

60. Verse 27 should be taken as an explanation of the phrase τὸ οὕτως εἶναι ("to be so"), thus making the verses read something like "I reckon that because of the impending crisis it is good for all to remain as they are. If you are bound to a wife, do not seek to be loosed from her. If you are loosed from a wife, do not seek another."

61. The betrothal scenario reflects the current consensus regarding verses 36–38; its relation to verses 25–28 is more widely interpreted.

62. See Martin, *Corinthian Body*, 70–76.

63. See O. Larry Yarbrough, "Parents and Children in the Letters of Paul," in *The Social World of the First Christians: Essays in Honor of Wayne A. Meeks* (ed. L. Michael White and O. Larry Yarbrough; Minneapolis: Fortress Press, 1995), 126–41.

64. See O. Larry Yarbrough, *Not Like the Gentiles: Marriage Rules in the Letters of Paul* (SBLDS 80; Atlanta: Scholars Press, 1985), ch. 3. For the most recent treatment of 1 Thess 4:3–8 as a *topos* on marriage, see Abraham Malherbe, *The Letters to the Thessalonians* (AB 32B; New York: Doubleday, 2000), 224–41. If Paul does refer to "obtaining" a wife in verse 3, I would be inclined to consider verse 6a as a reference to negotiating dowry rather than adultery. The commercial language would be appropriate to both interpretations.

15

PAUL AND MAXIMS

Rollin A. Ramsaran

Part I. Maxims in the Greco–Roman World of Paul's Time

Investigation of Paul's use of rhetorical maxims is still a relatively new endeavor. Interest in the subject has been sparked by the ongoing investigation of the wisdom sayings of Jesus and the rediscovery of rhetoric as a key framework out of which to view and interpret the NT writings.[1] In what follows, I seek to demonstrate (1) how maxims functioned in Paul's time and (2) how Paul made excellent use of their persuasive value in his letters.

The Persuasive World of Paul's Time

Paul lived and traveled in a lively world. Acquainted with Judea's major urban center, Jerusalem, Paul moved on to preach a message of good news in Arabia, in the regions of Syria and Cilicia, and, then, in major cities along the Roman road system from Antioch on the Orontes to Rome.[2] From every indication the former Saul of Tarsus, a Diaspora Jew, moved about easily in the Greco-Roman urban world.

This lively world was inherently persuasive. The deep social, intellectual, and political changes wrought by Alexander the Great and his successors included the movement of Greek rhetorical theory and practice into the imperial period.[3] The ability to speak well was connected to the Greco-Roman educational system. Techniques for persuasion were built upon the firm foundation of received παι-δεία, *paideia* (culture)—indeed, rhetoric was in the service of propagating, defending, and making a convincing case for the retention of Greco-Roman ways.[4]

Paul, though at many points critical of Greco-Roman ways, found rhetoric redeemable as a means to convince community members to progress in their faith and moral behavior.[5] As did other NT writers, Paul certainly understood his role as one who brought into being competent moral communities—new covenant communities in line with the expressions of the people of God found in Israel's scriptures.[6] For Paul, believers made up deliberative assemblies (ἐκκλησίαι, *ekklēsiai*) who along with the Spirit of God worked out among themselves the will of God in the present (Phil 2:12–13; Rom 12:2; 1 Cor 2:6–16).[7] Rhetoric provided linguistic patterns and argumentative strategies for persuasive deliberation; Paul and others engaged in its use.

To the rhetorician, speaking well could never be viewed apart from the perceived character (ἦθος, *ēthos*) of the one speaking. Moral integrity was connected to honor, self-mastery, consistency in word and deed, loyalty in friendship, moral wisdom, and freedom.[8] Who was speaking, how one spoke, what one spoke, where one spoke, and to whom one spoke were not incidental. Also of prime importance were attention to proper conventions and appeals to the common bond between speaker and audience.

Rhetorical speech and practices were carried on in the private and public spheres.[9] In private, rhetorical expression might take either an informal or formal shape through conversations, debates, or speeches at symposia (dinner parties) and elsewhere. Furthermore, in a lively city like Corinth, for instance, public demonstrations of rhetoric might be connected with formal debates, declamation (fully composed speech exercises), speeches connected with civic duties, religious festivals, or the biennial athletic games, and, of course, local assembly gatherings. The public orientation of much rhetoric, along with its frequency of occurrence, was a major factor in developing rhetorical competency throughout the various levels of Greco-Roman society.[10]

Maxim Persuasion in Three Forms

Maxims—a pervasive, basic feature of rhetoric in antiquity—were concisely expressed, stylized, and memorable principles or rules of conduct. Greeks called such sayings γνῶμαι, *gnōmai*; Romans called them *sententiae*. The content of maxims is drawn largely from recurrent, observable, and taken-for-granted experiences common to the world of the intended hearers. As a rhetorical device, the maxim at the time of Paul was particularly valued for its persuasive power and for its character-building qualities.

Maxims had a long history of development and usage from the Greek classical period to the early empire.[11] The use of maxims altogether, and the moral *sententia* (see below) in particular, was intensified in the time of Paul with the rise of declamation exhibitions.

In his *Institutio Oratoria* 8.5.3–34, the late-first-century C.E. rhetorician, Quintil-

ian, brings together the current traditions, forms, and uses of the maxim. Quintilian's work suggests that Paul and his contemporaries had access to three different
maxim forms: the gnomic maxim, the gnomic sentence, and the moral *sententia*.[12]

The gnomic maxim, at home in poetry and prose, was encapsulated wisdom,
an expression of general, traditional, and moral truth. The truth of the gnomic
maxim was generally thought to be universal and indisputable. In Paul's time the
gnomic maxim would be heard in the exhortations of everyday speech, childhood
instruction, the quotation of the poets, and as a well-chosen argumentative component in rhetorical speeches. An example of a gnomic maxim is "The chances of
war are the same for both [sides]."[13] Compare 1 Cor 4:2: "Moreover, it is required
of stewards that they be found trustworthy."[14]

The *gnomic sentence* was an individual's expression of recognized wisdom
based on general observations or decrees of judgment, but always *applied to particular circumstances of the moment*. Such a maxim could certainly be tested for its
truth, usefulness, and applicability to any given situation. Rather than being simply considered indisputable (cf. the gnomic maxim), the gnomic sentence could
be affirmed or refuted. As a move from the universal to the particular, the gnomic
sentence is not simply traditional, but it is rhetorical. The gnomic sentence brings
recognized wisdom to bear in a deliberative context and as such must be framed
in light of one's stature, one's ability to move the audience, and the pertinence of
the counsel to the particulars of the situation.[15] In Paul's time the gnomic sentence
was most prominent in formal deliberative discussions, debates, and speeches
where persuasive moral reasoning was imperative. An example of the gnomic
sentence is "There is no man who is really free, for he is the slave of either wealth
or fortune [τύχη, *tychē*]."[16] Compare 1 Cor 1:25, "For God's foolishness is wiser
than human wisdom, and God's weakness is stronger than human strength."
Here, Paul's maxim reflects the apocalyptic intervention of God's power in
human history through the cross of Christ (1:18–31)—a striking reversal and sub-
version of human norms about the acquisition of strength and power.

According to Quintilian (*Inst.* 8.5.9–34), general moral truth could be shaped
in the form of a "newer," *moral sententia*: a statement that is brief, well-rounded,
memorable, employing a striking figure, having an aesthetic-emotional appeal,
and often placed as a *clausula* (conclusion). The popularity of this moral *sententia*[17]
paralleled the rise and extensive practice of declamation exercises. Declamation
sessions moved from the school rooms and private homes and became "an entertaining and stimulating social activity in their own right," offering recreation, entertainment, intellectual excitement, friendly competition, and the practice,
maintenance, and improvement of oratorical skills and criticism.[18] The use of styl-
ish and proper *sententiae* increased the ἦθος, *ēthos*, of the speaker even to the point
that "an exceptionally good one [moral *sententia*] passed swiftly among the de-

claimers and could confer an instant reputation upon its author."[19] An example of the moral *sententia* is "All happiness is unstable and uncertain."[20] Compare 1 Cor 4:20, "The kingdom of God does not consist in talk but in power" (RSV) or 1 Cor 10:23, "'All things are permissible'" (my translation).

Navigating Effectively with Maxims

What strategies would Paul's contemporaries use to increase the persuasive value of maxims in communication? First, moral maxims were deemed appropriate for speakers of good character. The rhetor's ἦθος, *ēthos*, contributed to the persuasiveness of spoken maxims; and interestingly enough, the use of such maxims further built up that same *ēthos*. The establishment of good rapport between audience and speaker was important to the introduction of moral maxims. Once introduced, further moral maxims continued to enhance the speaker or writer's *ēthos* as the communication proceeded.[21]

Second, the persuasive power of a maxim came not only through its content, but also through the expressive techniques used in its construction. The maxim finds its power to draw attention, distinguish itself as a rhetorical and poetic form, and become memorable through its stylistic markings. This is most noticeable with the moral *sententia* described above. Gnomic maxims, however, were also singled out and appreciated for presenting wisdom in an aesthetically pleasing way with poetic figures of speech.[22] And rhetoricians took exceptional care to catalog stylistic markings that would aid in formulating gnomic sentences, as evidenced in *Ad Alexandrum, Ad Herennium*, Ps. Hermogenes' *Progymnasmata*, and Quintilian's *Institutio Oratoria*.[23] Brevity and the employment of a figure of speech or thought characterized most maxims.

Third, their position, clarity, and elaboration enhanced the persuasiveness of maxims. Strictly speaking, the maxim may appear in any position in argumentation, but placement at the beginning or the end highlights particular usage patterns. The rhetorical exercise handbook of Theon points to the use of the maxim to confirm a thesis.[24] Hence, in advancing argumentation for or against a thesis, the maxim may be the ground from which argumentation is introduced. In that case, it would occupy the lead position in the argument. Popularity for using the moral maxim in the final (end) position is characteristic of the new *sententia* usage from at least the time of the Elder Seneca (fl. 80 B.C.E.–35 C.E.) forward. The maxim in final position (*clausula*) provides summation, reiteration, and emphasis.[25]

A skilled rhetorician expressed maxims in a way that focused clarity. Some maxims are self-evident: described by Aristotle as "already known" and "no sooner are they uttered than they are clear to those who consider them."[26] Some maxims are in need of a supplement (ἐπίλογος, *epilogos*) or reason: namely, those

"contrary to general opinion," "disputable," "paradoxical," or where the statement is "obscure."[27] In addition, when the maxim is offered as a guide for moral
conduct, a supplement may be added to focus the interpretation of the maxim's
more general truth to the particular situation. In this way the supplement may
clarify the motivations of the speaker and the desired response.[28] If the language
of the proposed maxim is very general, a supplement should be offered to pinpoint "the moral purpose."[29]

Good rhetoricians bolstered their maxim argumentation with, among other
things, expansion or condensation, illustrations, examples, contrast, enthymeme
proof, objection, and refutation.[30] We do not have specific instructions for using
all of these methods of elaboration with the maxim. Presumably some methods
were taught in the course of education and required little explanation for use. The
rhetorical strategies of refining, refutation, and commonplace preparation of maxims, however, require further comment.

In *Ad Herennium*[31] 4.42.54–4.43.56, *expolitio,* or refining, takes two argumentative patterns. In the first place it "consists in dwelling on the same topic and yet
seeming to say something ever new." It is accomplished by repetition with
changes in words, in delivery, and in treatment by "form of dialogue" or "form of
arousal" (4.42.54).[32] In the second place, refining is, as a fuller argumentative pattern, the discoursing on a theme with a treatment in seven parts: simple pronouncement, reason(s), second expression in new form, contrary, comparison,
example, and conclusion (4.42.54–4.44.58).[33]

Porcius Latro's training regime is instructive for maxim use and elaboration.[34]
Competent rhetoricians had a set of moral *sententiae* that were their "stock." These
moral *sententiae* were of a general nature and truth, forming a repertoire of commonplaces to fit a variety of moral questions, deliberations, or τόποι, *topoi* (common topics). A supply of moral maxims readily at hand was impressive,
especially in spontaneous situations such as debate or declamation displays.

Finally, maxim sentences and moral *sententiae* were subject to refutation.
Aelius Theon of Alexandria (ca. C.E. 50–100) and Aristotle provide some counsel
on maxim refutation. Theon tells us that refutation of the maxim was an important *progymnasma* (practice exercise) for schoolboys. Theon offers a list of helpful
commonplace arguments (for obscurity, for incompleteness, for impossibility, and
so forth) from which the refutation of a maxim might be established.[35] Aristotle
discusses the refutation of maxims in his *Rhetorica* (2.21.13–14), *immediately after
he has given* advice about confirmation by supplement or reason. Aristotle points
out that maxims should be used "even when contrary to the most popular sayings" (2.21.13). Success is gained when doing so makes one's character appear
better or when the contrary maxim is spoken with passion.[36] In using a maxim for
refutation, the response should have its moral purpose made clear by the language; otherwise a reason should be added.[37]

∞

This now completes our depiction of the contemporary persuasive world and the types, functions, and options for the use of maxims within it. We must now consider factors in identifying maxims in Paul's letters and, then, Paul's persuasive argumentation using three maxims in Gal 5–6 and 1 Cor 7.

Part II. Maxims in Paul's Letters

Paul's Commonplace Maxim Formulations

Our understanding of maxims in Paul's letters needs to be expanded along a number of avenues.[38] In this section, I (1) discuss factors that help to identify maxims in Paul's letters; (2) examine the relationship between commonplaces or common topics (τόποι, *topoi*) and maxims; (3) make a brief survey of commonplace maxims in Paul's letters; and (4) examine more fully the argumentation of three recurrent commonplace maxims focused on ἀδιάφορα, *adiaphora*: Gal 5:6; Gal 6:15; and 1 Cor 7:19.

Identifying Maxims in Paul's Letters

Ancient speakers and writers did not necessarily call attention to their use of maxims. Rhetoricians and philosophic moralists considered it a sign of maturity and stature to compose maxims for proper living, commonly neither citing their sources nor prefacing their created wisdom outright.

In Paul's letters, maxims appear in two ways: embedded maxims and maxim stacks. Embedded maxims (our main focus in this study) denote those maxims that, standing independently, are woven into a written text as an important part of its argumentation. Maxim stacks or *gnōmologia* (γνωμολογία) are collections or anthologies of gnomic sayings written alongside one another, usually for didactic purposes.

Identification of maxim stacks in Paul's letters is relatively easy. Paul uses stacks near the end of some of his letters for the didactic purpose of "painting pictures" of proper community relationships.[39] Identifying individual embedded maxims, however, is a bit more challenging.

The classification of embedded maxims of any of the three types (moral *sententia*, gnomic sentence, or gnomic maxim) begins with three factors.[40] First, one establishes that a proposed maxim contains *traditional moral content* derived from either (1) the social stock of knowledge recognizable in the wider Greco-Roman society or (2) the common (in-group) social stock of knowledge recognizable to a participant in a Pauline community. Second, one considers the *brevity* or *con-*

ciseness of the statement. Moral *sententiae* are usually brief. Gnomic sentences, while concise, tend to be longer, with the addition of particularizing characteristics such as the supplement or reason. Gnomic maxims vary with the types of stylistic features chosen. Third, maxims have a *figured form*. One or more figures or stylistic markers (e.g., comparison, antithesis, interrogation, or even brevity itself) attract the hearer's attention and mark the maxim off from everyday speech.

Two further, supporting factors for maxim identification are argumentation and recurrence. Rhetorical handbooks provide known argumentative patterns for maxim usage: establishment of the rhetorician's character, refutation of another maxim, detailed elaboration, and inclusion in diatribal style (raising and answering objections in a school [teacher and pupil] or other instructional context). A statement of traditional moral content, expressed in a concise and figured form, found in one of these argumentative contexts gives strong indication of being a maxim. Recurrence of a maxim within the same or another Pauline letter also strengthens identification. To some degree, rhetoricians treated their maxims as commonplaces.[41] Useful maxims were ready at hand for certain moral situations and could be flexibly applied according to the needs of the particular circumstances.

Common Topics (Τόποι, Topoi) and Maxims

Paul, like other rhetoricians of his time, often structured his argumentation around common topics (*topoi*). The τόπος, *topos*, is a "place" around which certain recurring themes come together to support argumentation on a specific moral subject (e.g., civil concord, marriage, anger, and slavery versus freedom).[42] *Topoi* can form combinations with one another in support of a larger subject: *topoi* on civic responsibility, the household, and covetousness could, for example, pertain to a treatise on the state. As part of rhetorical invention, the rhetorician creatively selects, shapes, and applies the traditions chosen from any *topos* or *topoi*. Rhetoricians could find maxims in connection with certain *topoi* or develop their own maxims as support of themes within a *topos*.[43]

Paul, of course, also developed *topoi* on moral subjects peculiar to the thought world of believers in Christ. Paul's preaching of the gospel was in service of bringing into being faithful and just moral communities before God. Indeed, it was the gospel that formed the core of Paul's own identity and the focus of his mission endeavors to others. Simply put, then, one would expect Paul to use both traditional *topoi* and newly developed *topoi* which argued for the truth and vitality of the gospel—at these "places" (*topoi*), Paul often constructed maxims from scratch and from traditional materials. Therefore, among the many Pauline commonplaces one often finds maxims.

A Brief Survey of Commonplace Maxims in Paul's Letters

Let us now briefly consider recurrent maxims that are connected with some prominent topics related to Paul's gospel. Close to the core of Paul's gospel is the topic of peace. In the present, through Christ's death, there is peace between two parties: God and faithful humanity (Rom 5:1). Using maxims relating to peace, Paul capitalizes on the character of God as peaceful and deduces moral counsel for three very different social settings. From the maxim "It is to peace that God has called you" (1 Cor 7:15) he derives counsel concerning the maintenance or dissolution of marriage bonds between believers and unbelievers. Based on the maxim "For God is a God not of disorder but of peace" (1 Cor 14:33) he offers guidelines for proper conduct in worship. By the maxim "For the kingdom of God is not food and drink but righteousness and peace and joy in the Holy Spirit" (Rom 14:17; cf. 14:19) Paul addresses differences of opinion.

As the Rom 2:11 maxim, "God shows no partiality," avers, the God of peace who advances to meet humanity is also the God who shows no distinction by accepting and bestowing gifts on those who respond in faith. Again, the perceived character of God sets the moral nature and agenda for a believing community's relationships with one another. In Gal 3:28, the extended maxim, again declaring impartiality—"There is no longer Jew or Greek, there is no longer slave or free, there is no longer male and female; for all of you are one in Christ Jesus"—serves Paul's redrawing of the boundary lines for God's new people, God's family. Divine impartiality is once more expressed in the maxim "For there is no distinction between Jew and Greek; the same Lord is Lord of all and is generous to all who call on him" (Rom 10:12) as an assurance that because they are confessing believers they will not be shamed at the judgment seat of Christ.[44]

For Paul, the gracious movement of God toward humanity and God's acceptance of renewed relationship with humanity always took a covenantal shape. Hence, human responsibility and faithfulness were also an important part of the moral nature of God's people. Paul expected believers to return gratitude to God, to express dependence on God's provisions for daily living, and to exercise proper and just social relationships within and among the communities. Paul sometimes delivers community reminders concerning "human obligation" by way of maxims: "For whatever a person sows, that he or she will also reap" (Gal 6:7, my translation based on RSV) appears in a discussion of moral boundaries defined by flesh and Spirit; and "The one who sows sparingly will also reap sparingly, and the one who sows bountifully will reap bountifully" (2 Cor 9:6) bolsters Paul's appeal for monetary support for "the poor" in Jerusalem.

Paul realized that human obligation could easily be misconstrued into human achievement apart from dependence on God, leading to pride, self-conceit, and boasting. Rather than working together with God and keying in on God's values, human beings might choose forms of idolatry and dependence on other human beings. In order to bridle this tendency, Paul uses a gnomic maxim from Israel's scriptures when counseling the Corinthians on proper boasting: "Let the one who boasts, boast in [what] the Lord [has done through him or her]" (my translation, 1 Cor 1:31, again verbatim in 2 Cor 10:17).[45]

Finally, we would be remiss not to make a comparison of the maxim stacks in 1 Thess 5:12–22 and Rom 12:9–18. In each of these two letters, Paul paints a picture of vibrant and functioning community. Pauline believers are invited to reflect upon this *topos*, join into "the picture," and further grow in true community expression. In 1 Thess 5:12–22 and Rom 12:9–18, the maxim overlap around this common topic of proper community life is striking: love genuinely; be in harmony, at peace; care for the weak and faint-hearted; repay no one evil with evil; rejoice together; be constant in prayer; be open to the Spirit's guidance; keep hold of the good and direct it toward others.[46]

A Detailed Study of Three Maxims Marked by Ἀδιάφορα, Adiaphora: Galatians 5:6; Galatians 6:15; 1 Corinthians 7:19

I now consider three of Paul's maxims in more detail. These three merit study together because they share similar opening clauses: "For in Christ Jesus neither circumcision nor uncircumcision counts for anything; the only thing that counts is faith working through love" (Gal 5:6); "For neither circumcision nor uncircumcision is anything; but a new creation is everything!" (Gal 6:15); Circumcision is nothing, and uncircumcision is nothing; but obeying the commandments of God is everything" (1 Cor 7:19). Important to the discussion of each statement is (1) its maxim shape; (2) its *adiaphora* (indifference) content; and (3) its rhetorical use in Paul's larger argumentation.

Maxim Features

I begin my analysis by providing the Greek transliteration of the three statements followed by my own English translation. After that, we can consider similarities and differences, the shape of the statements, and the use of stylistic devices.

Gal 5:6:
(ἐν γὰρ Χριστῷ Ἰησοῦ) οὔτε περιτομή τι ἰσχύει οὔτε ἀκροβυστία, ἀλλὰ πίστις δι᾽ ἀγάπης ἐνεργουμένη,

(En gar christō Iēsou) oute peritomē ti ischyei oute akrobystia, alla pistis di' agapēs energoumenē.

(For in Christ Jesus,) neither circumcision enables anything nor uncircumcision [enables anything], but [what enables something is] faith working through love.

Gal 6:15:

οὔτε (γὰρ) περιτομή τί ἐστιν οὔτε ἀκροβυστία, ἀλλὰ καινὴ κτίσις

oute (gar) peritomē ti estin oute akrobystia, alla kainē ktisis.

(For) neither circumcision is anything nor uncircumcision [is anything], but [what is something is] a new creation.

1 Cor 7:19:

Ἡ περιτομὴ οὐδέν ἐστιν καὶ ἡ ἀκροβυστία οὐδέν ἐστιν, ἀλλὰ τήρησις ἐν-τολῶν θεοῦ

Hē peritomē ouden estin kai hē akrobystia ouden estin, alla tērēsis entolōn theou.

Circumcision is nothing and uncircumcision is nothing, but [what is something is] doing the commandments of God.

First, each of the statements includes *traditional moral content*. The issue of circumcision, introduced in the first clause of each of our statements, was a moral issue debated both in movements of Second Temple Judaism and in the early Christian communities.[47] Following ἀλλά, *alla* ("but"), each second clause speaks of moral direction: faith working through love; new creation; doing the commandments of God.

"New creation" (Gal 6:15b) is not as self-evident as the other two regarding moral direction; thus I comment on it briefly. Paul's reference to "new creation" is, in its larger context, surely a moral statement. In 6:16, Paul references his maxim in 6:15 as a "straight (measuring) rod" (κανών, *kanōn*, "standard") from which the people of God follow (στοιχεῖν, *stoichein*) a course to peace and mercy before God. The maxim in 6:15 summarizes the Spirit-led versus the flesh-led life Paul has outlined in chapter 5. This "new creation" (a new *community* of individuals to be enfolded into the redemption of all creation, Rom 8:18–25) stands on the basis of a new reality and power, over and against the worldly structures of the day (Gal 6:14).

Second, the maxim core of each of the three statements is marked by *brevity*. I have placed transitional material in parentheses, leaving the maxim core for analysis. The maxim cores of Gal 5:6 and 6:15 are identical with the exception of the verb used in the first clause and, of course, the second clauses. Both are marked by abbreviation through ellipsis of the verb and object ("enables/is anything") in the second half of the first clause and by ellipsis of the subject and verb ("what enables/is something is") in the second clauses. These have been added in the bracketed portions of the English translations. First Corinthians 7:19 is not abbreviated in the first clause (this, however, provides stylistic balance, as we will see), but has ellipsis of the subject and verb ("what is something is") in the second clause. The structure of the maxim core in 1 Cor 7:19 drops the positive indefinite pronoun (τί, *ti*; "something") used with two negative coordinating conjunctions (οὔτε . . . οὔτε, *oute . . . oute*; "neither . . . nor") as found in Gal 5:6 and 6:15. In its place Paul uses the nominal indefinite negative pronouns (οὐδέν . . . οὐδέν, *ouden . . . ouden*; "nothing . . . nothing") with the positive coordinating conjunction (καί, *kai*; "and"). Although the grammatical structure is slightly different, the sense remains the same as in Gal 5:6 and 6:15. In sum, then, all three maxim cores are marked by brevity and a similar structure.

Third, certain stylistic features mark out these three statements from ordinary speech. Common to all three is brevity, as just discussed. In addition, each statement is marked by *antithesis*[48] where "what is not important" is more drawn out, only to be followed by a strong, quick *movement to climax* concerning "what is important."

First Corinthians 7:19 is the most artfully constructed: there are no introductory particles or phrases; there is almost perfect balance on either side of the καί, *kai* ("and") (nine syllables and ten syllables respectively), forming an *isocolon*[49] in the first clause and a *period*[50] overall; there is the same structure on both sides of the *kai* ("and"), with repetition of three out of four words producing *epanaphora*[51] and *antistrophe*[52] (*interlacement*);[53] there is a double use of emphatic ἐστιν, *estin* ("is"). In Greek, the first *estin* is not strictly necessary. Its inclusion, however, makes the second *estin* doubly unnecessary, as any native hearer would supply it in the parallel grammatical construction. Hence, the inclusion of both uses of *estin* should be judged as intentionally placed for stylistic balance.

Both Gal 5:6 and 6:15 use *conjunction*[54] with *epanaphora* to maintain a similar balance on either side of the predicate-verb combination (τι ἰσχύει, *ti ischyei*/τί ἐστιν, *ti estin*; "[neither] . . . enables anything/is anything") and, then, move more quickly from first clause to second clause. Galatians 5:6 is drawn out a bit by the explanatory clause ("For in Christ Jesus"), but 6:15 is notable for its brevity and quick movement overall (only minimally hindered by the explanatory particle, "For"). Galatians 6:15 concludes with a tight *alliteration*.[55]

The analysis demonstrates that these three statements, Gal 5:6, Gal 6:15, and 1 Cor 7:19, are indeed maxims. In a fashion that sets them apart from normal speech, these maxims give us traditional content, brevity, balance, and stylistic figures to produce a form that is memorable.

Finally, variations in the maxim forms (including the second clauses) should not be viewed as a problem for maxim identification but as normal. Rhetoric is the "hidden art"[56] and this dictate is appropriate for isolated, embedded maxims. Paul's use of maxims, in line with the world we have described, telegraphs encapsulated wisdom *naturally*. The rhetorician formulates a gnomic sentence with strong attention to the particular situation being addressed. Adaptation to distinct situations leads to variation, to be sure, but also provides the proper criteria for assessing the truth of the maxim. In his use of these three maxims marked by *adiaphora*, Paul exemplifies Seneca the Elder's portrait of Porcius Latro as one prepared with a supply of moral maxims to fit a variety of moral questions, deliberations, and common topics (*Controversiae 1. pr.* 24).

Recurrent Maxims Marked by Adiaphora

Moralists in Paul's time, particularly those connected with Stoicism, shaped their moral reasoning on the basis of virtues, vices, and things of indifference (*adiaphora*). The flourishing life was achieved by focusing on what was important, namely, virtue; by laying aside vice; and by setting aside or using rightly indifferents. *Adiaphora* or indifferents were regarded as largely neutral morally; however, Stoics divided indifferents into matters "preferred" and "unpreferred," based on whether they helped or hindered the individual along the path to virtue. Paul's own moral reasoning followed suit by clarifying matters of importance through the identification of indifferent matters such as ethnic background, gender identification, social status, life and death, and the amount of one's possessions or comfort.[57]

The three statements, Gal 5:6, 6:15, and 1 Cor 7:19, demonstrate that Paul takes this classic pattern of moral reasoning ("is not anything" and "is nothing" = "is a matter of indifference") and uses it as a framework for creating moral statements regarding what truly matters. Given our above analysis of these statements, we can rightly refer to them as recurrent maxims marked by *adiaphora*. We can paraphrase our maxims as follows: "Circumcision and uncircumcision are both matters of indifference, but what is truly important is faith working through love (—a new creation, —doing the commandments of God)."

The foundation of Paul's *adiaphora* reasoning differed from that of other moralists of his time. For Paul, the attainment of virtue by living in accord with nature or reason is not principal. Rather, what is truly important is that believers have been granted a proper relationship to God so that they can live according to the gospel with power: they are part of the new creation; their faith therefore expresses itself in love; and they do the commandments. Hence, as we examine Gal 5:6, Gal 6:15, and 1 Cor 7:19 below, we must seek to understand the second clauses of each in such a way that they encapsulate or move the believer toward "living according to the gospel."

Paul's Rhetorical Argumentation

Galatians 5 and 6. Paul's Letter to the Galatians is a deliberative letter in which a future change of action is argued for and anticipated.[58] The issue at hand is whether the Galatian communities will change or add anything to the sufficient gospel proclaimed by Paul or whether they will stand firm at present in the faith they received in the not-too-distant past (1:6; 3:1–5; 4:8–9; 5:1; 5:7).[59] Three issues are pertinent to understanding the maxims in Gal 5:6 and Gal 6:15: (1) the supreme importance and truthfulness of Paul's gospel; (2) the Galatians' already-established commitment to nondistinctions in status; and (3) the function of Gal 5:6 and 6:15 in Paul's overall argumentation.

In Galatians, Paul states straightforwardly that his call and his gospel, having their source in a revelation of Jesus Christ, are of supreme importance. Neither the content of Paul's gospel nor the commission to proclaim it have human beings as their source (1:1–2; 11–12). Paul chastises the Galatian believers: "I am astonished that you are so quickly deserting him who called you in the grace of Christ and turning to a different gospel—not that there is another gospel, but there are some who trouble you and want to pervert the gospel of Christ" (1:6–7). Of course, the "different gospel" of certain "Teachers" is,[60] according to Paul's rhetorical construction, the gospel with an addition—the demand that Gentile believers be circumcised and that, possibly, they also adopt other Jewish cultural patterns. Put another way, the *important* and sufficient (i.e., dependence on God's gracious giving of the Spirit and the human act of faith in response; 3:1–4) had been or was about to be abandoned, as Paul construes it, by the addition of inconsequential, indifferent matters (i.e., dependence on "works of the Law" such as circumcision and possibly cultic eating patterns and times; 3:2; 5:2; 4:8–10).[61]

Paul addresses this conflict over priorities by using exemplification in Gal 1–2. Consistent with the gospel, Paul ate with all believers in Antioch regardless of distinction. But when Peter came and remained apart from Gentile believers (contrary to the agreed upon gospel; 2:1–10), being led astray by false brothers, Paul stood his ground against Peter and for the "truthfulness of the gospel" (2:11–14). The Galatian believers, in line with Paul's example, are now to do the same: not to follow after present false Teachers or those who follow them but to stand their ground for the truthfulness of the gospel (4:12; 5:1). The truth of the gospel, for Paul, is evident in the Galatians' coming-to-faith experience: God's grace and purposive power (Spirit) were extended to Gentile believers who, apart from circumcision, heard the gospel and responded in faith (Gal 3:1–4).

The Galatians' already-established commitment to non-distinctions in status also stems from their coming-to-faith experience that is rooted in their words of baptismal performance:[62]

> But now that faith has come [to us], we are no longer subject to a disciplinarian, for in Christ Jesus you are all children of God through faith. As many of you as were baptized into Christ have clothed yourselves with Christ. There is no longer Jew or Greek, there is no longer slave or free,

there is no longer male and female; for all of you are one in Christ Jesus. And if you belong to Christ, then you are Abraham's offspring, heirs according to promise. (Gal 3:27–29)

Among believers there are no distinctions according to ethnic lines, social placement, or gender. Instead, inclusion is by the promise to Abraham brought forward in Christ (3:29) and by a response of faith based on Christ's faithfulness (2:16, 20; 3:22).[63]

In chapters 3–5, Paul emphasizes, in a variety of ways, the following key points concerning all children of God: (1) they share a common heritage—being the people of God through Abraham, (2) they share a common entry point—receiving the grace of God with a response of faith, and (3) they share a common endowment to live rightly—being guided by the Spirit of God.

Having established God's impartiality toward Gentile believers and the inclusion of Gentiles in the heritage of Israel by faith apart from "works of the Law," Paul addresses, in chapters 5–6, their common endowment through the Spirit and its resulting moral course. The following basic outline of Gal 5–6 will guide the analysis:

A. Setting Forth the Thesis: "Faith Working through Love"—5:1–12
B. Repetition and Further Elaboration of the Thesis: Energizing and Doing Love—5:13–6:10
C. Letter Closing and Reiteration of Thesis: The Stance of a "New Creation"—6:11–18

Having concluded that the true people of God are according to promise, through the free woman (4:21–31), Paul develops this theme of freedom versus slavery by setting down a thesis statement: "For freedom Christ has set us free; stand fast therefore, and do not submit again to a yoke of slavery" (5:1). In what follows, Paul comments on the second half of his thesis statement in 5:2–4; the first half in 5:5–7a; and the second half again in 5:7b–12.

"Do not submit again to a yoke of slavery." In 5:2–4, Paul "testifies" that subsequent dependence on circumcision and other customs of the Law will separate the Galatians from God's present and more apocalyptically-driven plan of hope that they have experienced through dependence on the Christ-event and its effects (3:1–4; 5:2b). The Galatians are turning from the "truth" of God's gospel, from the power that operates by grace in the present time.[64] Paul's testimony is firmly grounded in his example (cf. the exemplary sections in 1:11–2:21 and 4:12–20).[65] His comportment is marked by the Spirit-driven, self-giving love of Christ (5:5–6 with 2:19–20) and his persuasion is through a faithful proclamation of the cross of Christ (5:11 with 6:14–17). In the cross of Christ is found the power that breaks slavish, sinful, and worldly bonds and resists their alignments and standards in the present (2:17–21; 5:24; 6:14).

"For freedom Christ has set us free; stand fast therefore" (5:1). The positive pole of Paul's thesis statement is picked up in 5:5 with a key clarifying statement: "For through the Spirit, by faith, we wait for the hope of righteousness." Freedom comes through the Spirit and by faith—and as we will see, through continual responsiveness to the Spirit and the continual exercise of faith—as one stands fast and waits. In 5:6, Paul further clarifies (*gar;* "for") 5:5, and therefore also 5:1a, by formulating a maxim: "For in Christ Jesus neither circumcision nor uncircumcision counts for anything; the only thing that counts is faith working through love." The Galatian believers had made a good start and had been functioning well (v. 7a), but now they are in danger of being led astray (vv. 7b–12).

Paul's use of this maxim in 5:6 is significant for five reasons. First, by reasoning according to *adiaphora*, the maxim negates the Teachers' urging of circumcision for Gentiles. Second, the maxim demonstrates the active, dynamic, covenantal quality of the "wait for the hope of righteousness." The biblical idea of righteousness contains within it the expectation that believers' moral actions in community will align with the character, plans, and actions of God[66]—"faith working through love." Third, given the context of 5:5, the maxim in 5:6 implies a cooperation between the Spirit and the human response of faith. One might paraphrase: ". . . but what enables something is the Spirit and faith together working through love."[67] Fourth, the maxim's expected outcome sets the agenda for Paul's discussion in 5:13–6:10 (see below). Finally, the maxim has a memorable shape which forms a definitive link with Gal 6:15.

In Gal 5:13, Paul restates his thesis from 5:1a: "For freedom Christ has set us free" becomes "For you were called to freedom"; and "do not submit again to a yoke of slavery" (5:1c) becomes "do not use your freedom as an opportunity for the flesh" (5:13b). Next, in 5:13c, Paul clarifies the positive pole of his thesis, using the key term, "love," which was introduced by his maxim in 5:6.

The rest of the section, 5:13–6:10, indicates that Paul's thought and argument conform to his maxim in 5:6—as if to say, "with the guidance of the Spirit, exercise your faith so that 'through love [you become] servants of one another.'" Paul reinforces his point with a quotation from Lev 19:18: "You shall love your neighbor as yourself." Paul claims that his maxim and counsel *do* what the Galatian Teachers encourage—he pays proper attention to the whole Law (5:14a; cf. Rom 8:4). By contrast, what the Teachers have precipitated among the Galatians is divisive and destructive (5:15).

The argumentative structure of Gal 5:16–6:10 can be divided into two parts:

Gal 5:16–26—Conduct your life by the Spirit
Gal 6:1–10—Put love in action

Two structural features mark 5:16–26 as a unit:[68] (1) the repeated use of "live/be led/be guided by the Spirit" (5:16, 18, 25; note the similar expressions at 5:16 [πνεύματι περιπατεῖτε, *pneumati peripateite*] and 5:25 [πνεύματι, *pneumati . . .* στοιχῶμεν, *stoichōmen*]), and (2) the antithesis between "flesh" and "Spirit" and their structural elaboration through vice (5:19–21) and virtue (5:22–23) lists respectively.

The Spirit's interaction with human faith is essential to Paul's maxim in 5:6. In 5:16–26, Paul emphasizes the Spirit's role in motivating and guiding the moral life. As can be seen within the section, faith is ever present in the call for believers to respond to God's Spirit (5:16, 18, 25, 26). Believers can resist and even avoid the internal and external pressures of the flesh, because faith, inaugurated by the Christ-event, joins itself to the guidance of the Spirit (5:24–25).[69] The result is the development of character and the exercise of appropriate moral decisions based on love. Hence, Paul's virtue list ("the fruit of the Spirit") *begins* with the desired outcome (love) and then provides the contributing virtues (joy, peace, patience, kindness, generosity, faithfulness, gentleness, and self-control).[70]

Galatians 6:1–10 provides general parenesis that is modestly shaped to the Galatians' situation. Paul's "Spirit" language (6:1; 6:8) builds upon the previous section. Paul reinforces his earlier point: the true meaning of the Law is to love or "bear one another's burdens;" indeed, this fulfills the standard of conduct set down by Christ (6:2).

Using a series of maxims,[71] much of Paul's counsel in 6:1–10 connects to the virtue list in 5:22–23: gentleness (6:1a); self-control (6:1b, 4–5, 7–8); love (6:2, 10); generosity (6:6); patience/faithfulness (6:9); also compare 5:26 with 6:3.[72] In this section, Paul provides a picture of believers living in effective and proper community, with the actions of love abounding.[73]

Paul moves quickly to his letter closing in 6:11–18. Two recognizable features from Paul's other letters are present: (1) Paul picking up the pen to close (6:11), and (2) the concluding prayer (6:18). By and large, though, the closing is concerned with the summation of Paul's position and argument to the Galatian communities.

This summation or peroration[74] continues to contrast the Galatian Teachers with Paul's own example and *ēthos*. The Teachers do not value law for how it defines God's will and purposes for humanity and for the world; rather, they selectively use the Law to boast about their superior knowledge and to instruct others toward circumcision (6:12–14; reiterating 2:3, 14; 3:3; 4:17; 5:11–12). Apparently, according to Paul, this suits their purpose, for other Jewish groups, even Christ-believing ones, might be inclined to persecute them for neglecting circumcision as a boundary marker of God's present communities.

Paul, in contrast to the stance of the Teachers, claims that the cross of Christ has utterly reshaped reality. God has chosen to renew God's promises through the cross of Christ, and in doing so to reorient how the promises will be accomplished. As God reclaims the full heritage of Abraham (now including Gentile believers), this movement of grace is accomplished apart from the Law—even against the Law (Gal 3:13)! Now God's new reality stands beyond and above all standard expectations and power structures within the present cosmos (world).

The heart of Paul's peroration comes in 6:14–16. Paul's own example is to boast (and therefore to live/walk) in the cross of Christ "by which the world has been crucified to me, and I to the world." By this, Paul means that he perceives and acts within a new reality, one in which he refuses to let the world (now passing away; cf. 1 Cor 7:31) set his standards and values. Instead, he aligns himself with God's present transformation of humanity and of the cosmos. One world is crucified as another is reborn. A believer's proper boast requires the claim for and fully participating in this ongoing transformation of reality brought into being by the cross of Christ.

Speaking as a wise moralist, Paul, in Gal 6:15, restates his point in maxim form: "For neither circumcision nor uncircumcision is anything; but a new creation is everything!" In its final position (*clausula*), the maxim is the capstone statement to Paul's argument. Old standards, if they have any value, are largely indifferent. What is of true importance is the new reality—a new way of seeing the world and humanity's place within it as being transformed.

Two factors indicate that Paul's full argument is not simply that of "perception." First, because this *adiaphora* maxim is recurrent with the opening clause of 5:6, one can be assured that laying hold of this new reality involves a response of "faith [guided by the Spirit] working through love." Paul's concluding maxim casts its insightful shadow back over every part of chapters 5 and 6. Second, the remarkable blessing in 6:16 also indicates that the desired response to the 6:15 maxim requires proper action. Paul states, "And whoever follows (στοιχήσουσιν, *stoichēsousin*) [the Spirit][75] according to this standard (from κανών, *kanōn*; cf. Eng. "canon"), let peace and mercy be upon them, and upon the Israel of God" (my translation).

Paul's rhetorical argumentation in Galatians 5 and 6 is skillfully constructed, using appropriate devices: thesis statement and restatement, warning, proverb (5:9), personal example, virtue and vice lists, parenesis, blessing. It is, however, Paul's maxim argumentation that ties chapters 5 and 6 together from beginning (elaboration of the thesis statement in 5:1 and setting the moral agenda to be discussed) to end (summary conclusion in maxim form, followed by exhortation and promised blessing).[76] Appropriately, Paul has strengthened his *ēthos* by placing his maxims at the two points in the letter where he takes strongest issue with these faltering Galatians over the matter of circumcision (5:2–12; 6:11–17)!

1 Corinthians 7. First Corinthians 7 considers the appropriateness of women (certainly) and men (possibly) to renounce normal marriage obligations for either alternative spiritual arrangements or separation (7:1–16). Furthermore, Paul considers the appropriateness of single persons to marry in a traditional or spiritual manner or remain single as a religious vocation (7:25–40).[77]

In 1 Cor 7:17, Paul states: "Therefore, unless peace is at stake [7:15c],[78] each person should seek to live properly[79] within the context assigned by the Lord when God called. And this is a directive[80] I give in all the churches" (my translation). *The basis of this "directive"* is an important starting point, as opposed to an ending point (it contains an exception!), for Paul's argument, as is evidenced by its *varied* repetition at 7:20 and 24.[81]

Paul's primary counsel in 7:17, then, is to address *how persons should walk or conduct their lives appropriately in differing circumstances.*[82] This being the case, the moral appeal to a maxim (7:19) supports Paul's purposes much better than a commandment. Paul's counsel is not a "rule" about "remaining in the state [social situation] in which one was called." Rather, Paul's "directive" is qualified by a maxim in 7:19 that both gives a definitive answer in one specific situation (circumcision/uncircumcision) and suggests an open-ended deliberation process for other areas.[83] In this way, the function of the maxim mirrors the counsel of the chapter as a whole.[84]

How does one walk according to 1 Cor 7:17–24? The structure of the unit pinpoints the answer in two places:

A   Directive: Live appropriate to place/call—v. 17
B   Illustration: Circumcision/uncircumcision mark ethnic indifferences; neither is a "preferred"[85]—v. 18
C   *How to walk*: Maxim = "Circumcision is nothing and uncircumcision is nothing, but what is something is *doing the commandments of God*"—v. 19
A'   Repetition of directive, focused on maintaining ethnic statuses of indifference at call—v. 20
B'   Illustration: Being set apart to God makes social status an *adiaphoron*; however, social movement from slavery to freedom *is a "preferred"*[86]—vv. 21–22
C'   *How to walk*: Exhortation = "You were bought with a price; *do not become slaves of human beings*"[87]—v. 23
A"   Repetition of directive focused on remaining with God *in whatever situation*[88]—v. 24

"Keeping the commandments of God."[89] Apparently Paul has previously instructed the Corinthians concerning the Law and the traditions of Israel. He appeals to these traditions in relationship to Christ's death ("our paschal lamb," 5:7); he draws a "patterned example" from the Exodus story to guide present behavior within the community (10:1–22); and the Corinthians appear to have been informed about the corrupting power of the Law controlled by sin ("the power of sin is the Law," 15:56). Paul's maxim, however, frames "keeping the commandments" as the very foundation (that which is most important!) for the *believer's* relationship to God.

In addition, a correlation of the concluding statements from the other two recurrent *adiaphora* maxims (faith working through love; a new creation) argues for a very positive appreciation of the counsel provided in Paul's final phrase in 1 Cor 7:19. Paul's use of "the commandments" represents God's instruction and telic purposes for all humanity, now redeemed in Christ. Characteristic of the obedient life of believers is the breaking down of distinctions; the opening up of God's call of grace to all; the furthering of humanity's ability to love one another; and the initiation of a realm of peace and solidarity for human creation as a whole.

"Circumcision and uncircumcision are matters of indifference; what is truly important is keeping the commandments of God" (my translation). In the ongoing context of deliberation begun in chapter 7, Paul's maxim reinforces the long-standing covenantal social obligations required of God's people—here, emphasizing social obligations between marriage partners (7:1–16). In its immediate context, as a self-contained maxim, 7:19 demands full social obligations and contact across ethnic lines. In its larger context (7:17–24), the maxim's refrain, "keeping the commandments," echoes the first commandment (Exod 20:3), no doubt important to Paul: maintaining a single-minded, proper stance before God negates connection with other idolatrous spiritual and human influences. Fidelity to God provides a springboard to a number of issues that lie ahead in 1 Corinthians (7:23, 35; 10:20–22; 11:27–30; 12:2–3; 15:24–28, 34; 16:13, 22). To keep the commandments of God, to ascertain what is most important in any of a number of situations, is to have the "mind of Christ" (1 Cor 2:16b; cf. Rom 12:2; Phil 1:9–11).[90] Thus, the elaboration of Paul's directive, through two illustrations and a *very significant* maxim in 1 Cor 7:17–24, is important for Paul's argumentation before (7:1–16) and after (7:25–40, and beyond).[91]

At the point of *what is most important*, then, the three maxims come into focus together. For a husband and wife to maintain covenantal bonds of marriage, as God has done for God's people, is to "*keep the commandments of God*" (7:10–11). For a believer to remain yoked to an unbelieving spouse, so long as peace can be maintained, is truly "faith working through love" (7:12–16). To recognize holiness in the offspring of a believer and an unbeliever is to be able to see, believe in, and experience the coming *"new creation"* (7:14). To maintain "set-apartness" to God by marrying rather than "burning" which could lead to impropriety (7:36) or by remaining single in order to achieve "maximum devotion to God" (7:32–35) or by not sharing sacred space and rituals with idols (10:14–22) is to *"keep the commandments."* Not to violate another's conscience in matters of eating or worshiping (1 Cor 8–14) is "faith working through love." And to crucify a world and be crucified to it; to die daily; to be willing to live courageously by faith and for love, even to death, is to glimpse one's part in a complete and unbounded new creation (1 Cor 15).

Part III. Other Relevant Pauline and Paulinist Texts

Paul's Letters

Gnomic maxims. 1 Cor 1:31; 4:2; 9:7a, 7b, 7c, 9a, 10b; 2 Cor 9:6; Gal 6:7b.

Gnomic sentences. Rom 6:23; 10:12; 13:7; 14:7–8, 22b, 23b; 1 Cor 1:25; 3:21–23; 4:15; 6:12, 13; 7:1b, 19, 26, 40a; 8:1c, 8; 9:15b (καλὸν γάρ, *kalon gar . . .*), 19; 10:23, 31; 2 Cor 8:21; Gal 2:20; 3:28; 4:12a (Gr.), 18a; 5:6; 6:8, 15.

Sententiae. Rom 2:11; 14:17; 1 Cor 3:21b, 22b; 4:20; 6:12a, 13a; 7:15c; 8:1b; 8:4b; 8:4c; 9:25a; 10:23a; 11:12b; 13:6b; 14:26c; 14:33; 14:40; Phil 1:21; 4:13.

Gnomologia (maxim stacks). Rom 12:9–18; 1 Cor 16:13–14; 2 Cor 13:11b; Gal 6:2–6; Phil 4:4–9; 1 Thess 5:12–22.

Paulinist Writings

Gnomic maxims. 1 Tim 5:18; 2 Tim 2:4–6; Titus 1:12.

Gnomic sentences. 1 Tim 1:8; 4:8; 6:6, 10; 2 Tim 2:19.

Part IV. Bibliography

Rhetorical Handbooks and Progymnasmata
(Loeb Classical Library editions, unless otherwise noted)

Anaximenes, *Rhetorica ad Alexandrum.*

Aristotle. *The Art of Rhetoric.*

Butts, James R. "The *Progymnasmata* of Theon: A New Text with Translation and Commentary." Ph.D. diss., Claremont Graduate School, 1987.

Demetrius. *On Style.*

Elder Seneca. *Controversiae* and *Suasoriae.*

Kennedy, George A. *Progymnasmata: Greek Textbooks of Prose Composition and Rhetoric.* Vol. 10 of *Writings from the Greco-Roman World.* Translation by George A. Kennedy. Atlanta: Society of Biblical Literature, 2003.

Longinus, *On the Sublime*.
Quintilian. *Institutio Oratoria*.
Rhetorica ad Herennium.
Seneca. *Epistulae Morales*.

General Reference

Horna, K., and K. von Fritz. "Gnome, Gnomendichtung, Gnomologien." *RE*, suppl. 6 (1935): 74–90.
Lausberg, Heinrich. *Handbook of Literary Rhetoric: A Foundation for Literary Study*. Foreword by George A. Kennedy. Translated by Matthew T. Bliss et al. Leiden: E. J. Brill, 1998.
Martin, Josef. *Antike Rhetorik: Technik und Methode*. Munich: C. H. Beck, 1974.
Porter, Stanley E., ed. *Handbook of Classical Rhetoric in the Hellenistic Period: 330 B.C–A.D. 400*. Leiden: E. J. Brill, 1997.

Classical Studies

Bonner, Stanley F. *Education in Ancient Rome: From the Elder Cato to the Younger Pliny*. Los Angeles: University of California Press, 1977.
———. *Roman Declamation in the Late Republic and Early Empire*. Berkeley: University of California Press, 1949.
Clark, Donald Lemen. *Rhetoric in Greco-Roman Education*. New York: Columbia University Press, 1957.
Clarke, M. L. *Rhetoric at Rome: A Historical Study*. London: Cohen and West, 1953.
Delarue, F. "La sententia chez Quintilien." *La Licorne* 3 (1979): 97–124.
Henderson, Ian H. "Quintilian and the *Progymnasmata*." *Antike und Abendland* 37 (1991): 82–99.
Karavites, Peter. "*Gnōmē's* Nuances: From Its Beginning to the End of the Fifth Century." *Classical Bulletin* 66 (1990): 9–34.
Kriel, D. M. "The Forms of the Sententia in Quintilian VIII.v.3–24." *Acta Classica* 4 (1961): 80–89.
Lardinois, André. "Modern Paroemiology and the Use of *Gnomai* in Homer's *Iliad*." *CP* 92 (1997): 213–34.
Levet, J. P. "RHĒTOR et GNŌMĒ: Présentation sémantique et recherches isocratiques." *La Licorne* 3 (1979): 9–40.
Marrou, H. I. *A History of Education in Antiquity*. 3d ed. Translated by George Lamb. Madison: University of Wisconsin Press, 1982.
Russell, D. A. *Greek Declamation*. Cambridge: Cambridge University Press, 1983.
Searby, Denis. *Aristotle in the Greek Gnomological Tradition*. Studia graeca upsaliensia 19. Stockholm: Gotab, 1998.
Sinclair, Patrick. "The *Sententia* in *Rhetorica Ad Herennium*: A Study in the Sociology of Rhetoric." *AJP* 114 (1993): 561–80.
———. *Tacitus the Sententious Historian: A Sociology of Rhetoric in Annales 1–6*. University Park, Pa.: Pennsylvania State University Press, 1995.
Sussman, Lewis A. *The Declamations of Calpurnius Flaccus*. Leiden: E. J. Brill, 1994.

————. *The Elder Seneca*. Leiden: E. J. Brill, 1978.

Villemonteix, J. "Remarques sur les sentences homériques." *La Licorne* 3 (1979): 83–96.

New Testament Studies

Betz, Hans Dieter. *Galatians: A Commentary on Paul's Letter to the Churches in Galatia*. Hermeneia. Philadelphia: Fortress Press, 1979.

————. *2 Corinthians 8 and 9: A Commentary on Two Administrative Letters of the Apostle Paul*. Hermeneia. Philadelphia: Fortress Press, 1985.

Henderson, Ian H. *Jesus, Rhetoric, and Law*. Biblical Interpretation Series 20. Leiden: E. J. Brill, 1996.

Ramsaran, Rollin A. *Liberating Words: Paul's Use of Rhetorical Maxims in 1 Corinthians 1–10*. Valley Forge, Pa.: Trinity Press International, 1996.

Sampley, J. Paul. *Walking between the Times: Paul's Moral Reasoning*. Minneapolis: Fortress Press, 1991.

Snyder, Graydon F. "The 'Tobspruch' in the New Testament." *NTS* 23 (1976): 117–20.

Snyman, Andreas H. "On Studying the Figures (*schēmata*) in the New Testament." *Bib* 69 (1988): 93–107.

Wilson, Walter T. *Love without Pretense: Romans 12.9–21 and Hellenistic-Jewish Wisdom Literature*. WUNT 46. Tübingen: J. C. B. Mohr, 1991.

Notes

1. See the discussion in Rollin A. Ramsaran, *Liberating Words: Paul's Use of Rhetorical Maxims in 1 Corinthians 1–10* (Valley Forge, Pa.: Trinity Press International, 1996), 74–77.

2. On the urban settings for Paul's early missionary work in Arabia, Syria, and Cilicia, see Martin Hengel and Anna Maria Schwemer, *Paul between Damascus and Antioch: The Unknown Years* (Louisville: Westminster John Knox, 1997), 106–26; 151–77.

3. George A. Kennedy, *A New History of Classical Rhetoric* (Princeton: Princeton University Press, 1994), 81–127.

4. Ramsaran, *Liberating Words*, 5, and the literature cited therein.

5. It is now widely recognized that Paul's letters, written to believers, are rhetorically shaped. See ibid., 1, with nn. 2 and 3; 79, with n. 147.

6. Wayne A. Meeks, *The Origins of Christian Morality: The First Two Centuries* (New Haven: Yale University Press, 1993), esp. 3–7.

7. See Richard A. Horsley, "Building an Alternative Society: Introduction," in *Paul and Empire: Religion and Power in Roman Imperial Society* (ed. Richard A. Horsley; Valley Forge, Pa.: Trinity Press International, 1997), 209.

8. On ἦθος (*ēthos*) in general, see George A. Kennedy, *New Testament Interpretation through Rhetorical Criticism* (Chapel Hill: University of North Carolina, 1984), 15.

9. For what follows, see Ramsaran, *Liberating Words*, 5, 13. Cf. the background

in M. L. Clarke, *Rhetoric at Rome: A Historical Study* (London: Cohen and West, 1953), 7–22; 85–108.

10. Ramsaran, *Liberating Words*, 79–80, with nn. 14 and 15.

11. Notice that with Quintilian the two generic terms for "maxim" (Greek: γνώμη, and Latin: *sententia*) form descriptive *subcategories* as the two cultures move together. For a complete discussion, see ibid., 5–29.

12. The following discussion of the three maxim forms follows closely the more detailed investigation in ibid., 9–17.

13. Aristotle, *Rhetorica* 2.21.11. All translations from classical sources are from the Loeb Classical Library (LCL) unless otherwise specified.

14. All biblical translations are from the NRSV unless otherwise specified.

15. See Aristotle, *Rhet.* 2.21.2–16.

16. Aristotle, *Rhet.* 2.21.2.

17. For the moral *sententia* as a subset of *sententiae* in general, see Ramsaran, *Liberating Words,* 14–15.

18. Lewis A. Sussman, *The Elder Seneca* (Leiden: Brill, 1978), 13–17. Cf. Ramsaran, *Liberating Words*, 12–17.

19. Sussman, *Elder Seneca*, 38. Cf. Seneca the Elder, *Controversiae* 2.4.9; 7.6.15; 9.2.23; 10.1.14; 10.2.10.

20. Seneca the Elder, *Controversiae* 1.1.3.

21. Ramsaran, *Liberating Words*, 17; 35–37.

22. For Homer's stylistic influence on the gnomic-maxim tradition, see ibid., 9–10.

23. Rhetoricians show a propensity for classification and attention to stylistic instruction. Anaximenes suggests hyperbole and parallel (*Ad Alexandrum* 1430b.10–11). *Ad Herennium* 4.17.24–25 points out single and double forms. Ps.-Hermogenes proposes categorizing maxims into true, plausible, simple, compound, or hyperbolic. Finally, Quintilian sums up classification under ten heads before listing his own favorites: opposition, simple statement, transference of the statement from the general to the particular, and giving the general statement a personal turn (*Institutio Oratoria* 8.5.5–8).

24. Ramsaran, *Liberating Words*, 8.

25. Ibid., 14–15, with nn. 108 and 110.

26. Aristotle, *Rhet.* 2.21.5. Also *Rhet. ad Alex.* 1430b.3–4; Seneca, *Ep.* 94.10, 27, 44.

27. Aristotle, *Rhet.* 2.21.3–7. Also *Rhet. ad Alex.* 1430b.3–7; *Ad Herennium* 4.17.24; Seneca, *Ep.* 94.10, 27, 44.

28. E.g., Aristotle, *Rhet.* 2.21.13–14, "Nor do I approve the maxim 'Nothing in excess,' for one cannot hate the wicked too much," and Quintilian, *Inst.* 8.5.7, "Caesar, the splendour of your present fortune confers on you nothing greater than the power and nothing better than the will to save as many of your fellow-citizens as possible."

29. Aristotle, *Rhet.* 2.21.14.

30. Ramsaran, *Liberating Words*, 7–8.

31. The writer of *Ad Herennium* is unknown. The work is generally thought to date from the first century B.C.E. and is falsely attributed to Cicero.

32. For refining in a Pauline text, see the discussion of 1 Cor 10:23–31 in Ramsaran, *Liberating Words*, 56–62.

33. See H. Caplan, *Ad Herennium*, LCL, lviii.

34. Elder Seneca, *Controversiae* 1.pr.24, and Ramsaran, *Liberating Words*, 14, 20.

35. James R. Butts, "The 'Progymnasmata' of Theon: A New Text with Translation and Commentary" (Ph.D. diss., Claremont Graduate School, 1987), 217.

36. "It would be an instance of the latter if a man in a rage were to say, 'It is not true that a man should know himself; at any rate, such a man as this, if he had known himself, would never have claimed the chief command.' And one's character would appear better, if one were to say that it is not right, as men say, to love as if one were bound to hate, but rather to hate as if one were bound to love" (*Rhet.* 2.21.14).

37. "[B]y saying 'that it is right to love, not as men say, but as if one were going to love for ever, for the other kind of love would imply treachery'" (*Rhet.* 2.21.14). Note how maxim refutation can be a reformulation, using common vocabulary, of the maxim in dispute (*dei philein*).

38. Two major studies have been Ramsaran, *Liberating Words*, an investigation of the moral maxims of Paul and some Corinthians within the context of open maxim debate in 1 Cor 1–10; and Walter T. Wilson, *Love without Pretense: Romans 12:9–21 and Hellenistic-Jewish Wisdom Literature* (WUNT 46; Tübingen: Mohr, 1991), an analysis of the form, function, and argumentation of Paul's *gnōmologium*, or "maxim stack," in Rom 12.

39. See J. Paul Sampley, *Walking between the Times: Paul's Moral Reasoning* (Minneapolis: Fortress Press, 1991), 96–97. A definitive and complete analysis is Wilson, *Love without Pretense*.

40. The following two paragraphs follow Ramsaran, *Liberating Words*, 23–25, closely.

41. See The Elder Seneca, *Controversiae* 1.pr.24, and the discussion in Ramsaran, *Liberating Words*, 14.

42. See Margaret M. Mitchell, *Paul and the Rhetoric of Reconciliation: An Exegetical Investigation of the Language and Composition of 1 Corinthians* (HUT 28; Tübingen: Mohr/Siebeck, 1991), 67n. 8.

43. On the definition of *topos* and its creative and flexible use by the rhetorician or moralist, see Abraham J. Malherbe, "Hellenistic Moralists and the New Testament," in *ANRW* II 26.1, 320–25; idem, *Moral Exhortation: A Greco-Roman Handbook* (Philadelphia: Westminster, 1986), 144–45; and Luke T. Johnson, "James 3:13–4:10 and the *Topos PERI PHTHONOU*," *NovT* 25 (1983): 334–35.

44. Cf. 1 Cor 12:12–13; Col 3:11. Space will not permit me to draw out the relationship between "no distinction," "the body" *topos,* and "giftedness" as expressed in 1 Cor 12–14 and Rom 12–15.

45. For an extensive discussion of the maxim form and function of 1 Cor 1:31 and its connection with boasting, see Ramsaran, *Liberating Words*, 30–38.

46. Also cf. 1 Thess 4:9–12 with Rom 12:9–18.

47. Robert G. Hall, "Circumcision," *ABD* 1:1029–31.

48. *Ad Herennium* 4.15.21: "*Antithesis* occurs when the style is built upon contraries, as follows: 'Flattery has pleasant beginnings, but also brings on bitterest endings.'" Note the maxim as illustration.

49. *Ad Herennium* 4.20.27. The *isocolon* is the figure made up of two or more cola—a colon or clause being a part of a sentence that is brief and complete but

needing another colon to complete the entire thought—that "consist of a virtually equal number of syllables."

50. *Ad Herennium* 4.19.27: "A *period* is a close-packed and uninterrupted group of words embracing a complete thought. We shall best use it in three places: *in a maxim*, in a contrast, and in a conclusion" (emphasis mine).

51. *Ad Herennium* 4.13.19: "*Epanaphora* occurs when one and the same word forms successive beginnings for phrases expressing like and different ideas."

52. *Ad Herennium* 4.13.19: "In *antistrophe* we repeat, not the first word in successive phrases, as in *epanaphora*, but the last."

53. *Ad Herennium* 4.14.20. *Interlacement* combines *epanaphora* and *antistrophe*.

54. *Ad Herennium* 4.27.38: "*Conjunction* occurs when both the previous and the succeeding phrases are held together by placing the verb between them."

55. "The repetition of the same letter or syllable at the beginning of two or more words in close succession" (*homoepropheron*) (E. W. Bullinger, *Figures of Speech Used in the Bible* [Grand Rapids: Baker, 1968], 171).

56. Note Longinus, *On the Sublime* 17.1–3.

57. See the texts and discussion in Sampley, *Walking between the Times*, 77–83.

58. See Kennedy, *New Testament Interpretation*, 144–52. I am sympathetic to J. Louis Martyn's analysis of the letter's genre and structure (*Galatians: A New Translation with Introduction and Commentary* [AB 33A; New York: Doubleday, 1997], 20–23). He considers it an "extended sermon" in which Paul re-preaches the gospel to the Galatians as a performative speech-act that argues for the death of the old cosmos and the arrival of a new one. One can maintain Martyn's strong points *and* also speak of the structure of the letter in rhetorical terms as basically deliberative with judicial elements interspersed.

59. See J. Paul Sampley, "Reasoning from the Horizons of Paul's Thought World: A Comparison of Galatians and Philippians," in *Theology and Ethics in Paul and His Interpreters: Essays in Honor of Victor Paul Furnish* (ed. Eugene H. Lovering, Jr., and Jerry L. Sumney; Nashville: Abingdon, 1996), 117–18.

60. For background and agenda of these "Teachers" who have threatened Paul and persuaded some in the Galatian communities, see Martyn, *Galatians*, 14, 18, and esp. 117–26. The designation "Teachers" is adopted from Martyn.

61. See Hans Dieter Betz, *Galatians: A Commentary on Paul's Letter to the Churches in Galatia* (Hermeneia; Philadelphia: Fortress Press, 1979), 262–63. Martyn (*Galatians*, 123) also suggests that the Teachers may connect reception of the Spirit with proper interpretation of and obedience to the Law.

62. Betz, *Galatians*, 186–201; Martyn, *Galatians*, 373–83.

63. See Richard B. Hays, "Jesus' Faith and Ours: A Rereading of Galatians 3," in *Conflict and Context: Hermeneutics in the Americas* (ed. Mark Lau Branson and C. René Padilla; Grand Rapids: Eerdmans, 1986), 257–80.

64. Cf. Rom 3:21–26; 4:16–25; 5:15–21. See the insightful description of Paul's apocalyptic theology in Martyn, *Galatians*, 97–105; 570–74.

65. George Lyons, *Pauline Autobiography: Toward a New Understanding* (SBLDS 73; Atlanta: Scholars Press, 1985), 138–68.

66. Bruce C. Birch, *Let Justice Roll Down: The Old Testament, Ethics, and Christian Life* (Louisville: Westminster John Knox, 1991), 153–55; 176–78; 259–61.

67. This point has already been important to Paul. See especially Gal 3:1–4: where faith took root, the Spirit had preceded. The point remains vital to Paul's argument in chapter 5: for faith to remain authentic and growing, it must be guided by the Spirit.

68. Siding with the text division in NA[27] and contra the 5:25–6:10 of Betz, Martyn, James D. G. Dunn (*The Epistle to the Galatians* [BNTC; Peabody, Mass.: Hendrickson, 1993]), and others. It is difficult to ignore Paul's use of *adelphoi* ("brothers and sisters") as a subsection marker in Galatians (cf. 1:11; 3:15; 4:12; 4:28, 31 [marking an inclusion for the subsection that makes application of the allegory]; 5:13; 6:1). No doubt 5:25–26 is transitional to 6:1–10, but its connection is stronger to what comes before, as I argue here. Galatians 5:26 stands as a refrain to 5:15, as does 5:25 to 5:16.

69. See Martyn's insights (*Galatians*, 524–36) on this point.

70. Victor Paul Furnish, *Theology and Ethics in Paul* (Nashville: Abingdon, 1968), 87–88.

71. The fine analysis of *sententiae* in chapter 6 by Betz (*Galatians*, 291–311) has been followed up with insightful commentary by John M. G. Barclay (*Obeying the Truth: Paul's Ethics in Galatians* [Minneapolis: Fortress Press, 1991], 146–77) and Martyn, *Galatians*, 541–54. In my estimation, Paul's commonplace maxim stack of *sententiae* (see n. 39 above with discussion in text) has been particularized to the Galatian situation and to Paul's redefined worldview (rightly Barclay and Martyn) in Christ *through a transformation to gnomic sentences.* A similar move on Paul's part is made in Phil 4:4–9.

72. Cf. the similar observations and list in Martyn, *Galatians*, 543.

73. Hence, the section functions as a maxim stack. See the discussion at the beginning of Part II with nn. 39 and 46.

74. The peroration "summarizes the argument and seeks to arouse the emotions of the audience to take action or make judgment" (Kennedy, *New Testament Interpretation*, 24).

75. The catchword στοιχήσουσιν ("follows"), connected to πνεύματι καὶ στοιχῶμεν ("let us also follow the Spirit") in Gal 5:25, and the overall argument based upon the Spirit in Gal 5–6 warrant this clarification in translation.

76. At these points, then, Paul's maxim argumentation is according to the counsel of the rhetorical handbooks as discussed in Part I above: Paul's maxims form memorable, well-crafted statements with recurrent opening clauses; give guidance for moral conduct; elaborate a thesis statement; focus clarity in thinking through *adiaphora* reasoning; provide a summary of the larger argument; and reinforce his *ēthos.*

77. Studies on 1 Cor 7 abound. For recent readings, see Will Deming, *Paul on Marriage and Celibacy: The Hellenistic Background of 1 Corinthians 7* (SNTSMS 83; Cambridge: Cambridge University Press, 1995); Judith M. Gundry-Volf, "Controlling the Bodies: A Theological Profile of the Corinthian Sexual Ascetics (1 Cor. 7)," in *The Corinthian Correspondence* (ed. R. Bieringer; Louvain: Louvain University Press, 1996), 519–41; and Richard A. Horsley, *1 Corinthians* (ANTC; Nashville: Abingdon, 1999). For my larger interpretive framework and other sources, see Ramsaran, *Liberating Words*, 38–46.

78. The translation "Therefore, unless peace is at stake" gives true recognition

to εἰ μὴ ("nevertheless") as a continuative connector of exception ("Since this usage 'excepts' a preceding negative, it almost certainly goes back to v. 15b: 'The brother or sister is not bound in such cases. . . . Nevertheless . . .'" [Gordon D. Fee, *1 Corinthians* (NICNT; Grand Rapids: Eerdmans, 1987), 309]). Paul and the Corinthian community are participating in a give-and-take deliberative discussion of real-life situations in which varying circumstances do matter.

79. *Peripatein* ("to walk") has the strong metaphorical sense of "to conduct one's life." See BAGD 649. The translation "*seek* to live *properly*" is justified by the deliberative nature of the chapter as a whole (cf. 7:1, 8, 10, 12, 25–26, 35, 40) and the inclusive nature of the directive for all Paul's churches (v. 17c).

80. *Diatassomai* ("make arrangements," LSJ 414; cf. "order, direct, command," BAGD 189) is a word Paul uses when ordering proper community life (see 11:34). Nominalizing, then reifying, the lexical value of *diatassomai* makes for the unhappy translation of "this is my rule" (RSV, NRSV), which fits neither the deliberative context of this chapter, nor 1 Corinthians, nor Paul's generally preferred method of moral counsel (see Ramsaran, *Liberating Words*, 68–73).

81. Verse 20 is specific to circumcision and uncircumcision; verse 24 widens the directive to be a starting point from which a variety of situations can be deliberated (i.e., the manumission opportunity before [7:21b] and the issues of engaging or refraining from marriage after [7:25–40]).

82. The Greek syntax with οὕτως περιπατέιτω in final position gives emphasis: "thus, he/she should walk/live!"

83. Sampley, *Walking between the Times*, 97: "[Maxims] demand direct and active participation and provide the individual with a resource that in some future situation may yield an insight into how to live in faithfulness to God."

84. Commentators generally agree that this chapter contains a series of positions that are qualified by exceptions. See Horsley, *1 Corinthians*, 102.

85. A "preferred" is that which among the *adiaphora* is determined to help one along the way to virtue. See "Recurrent *Adiaphora* Maxims" in this section, above.

86. With regard to Paul's views on slavery, we need to ask how and in what ways "free status" might function as a "preferred" in helping one along to the full power of God's good news (or in Paul's own terms: doing the commandments of God; faith working through love; a new creation). See for example, Jennifer A. Glancy, "Obstacles to Slaves' Participation in the Corinthian Church," *JBL* 117 (1998): 481–501. Cf. S. Scott Bartchy, *Mallon Chrēsai: First Century Slavery and the Interpretation of 1 Corinthians 7:21* (SBLDS 11; Missoula, Mont.: Society of Biblical Literature, 1973), 127–59; and Neil Elliott, *Liberating Paul: The Justice of God and the Politics of the Apostle* (Maryknoll, N.Y.: Orbis Books, 1994), 31–54.

87. Whether as slave or free person, one can give up proper freedom in Christ by following others who conform to worldly standards—an underlying problem in the Corinthian congregations. The antidote is to accept one's place as a proper location to live out one's call before God (7:24), that is, to maintain proper freedom by owning all things, but belonging to Christ and God alone (3:21–23). See Ramsaran, *Liberating Words*, 30–46; 66–68.

88. The directive has been broadened with the change after *en* to a relative pronoun (ἐν ᾧ; "in what[ever] [situation]") and with the addition of παρὰ θεῷ ("before God"). See the discussion in Fee, *1 Corinthians*, 320–22, and n. 87 above.

89. The following comments are probing and exploratory—that is, the kind of thinking generated by a maxim. By necessity I leave aside the vast topic of Paul and the Law.

90. Note how, at the conclusion of chapter 7, Paul states, "And I too believe I have the Spirit of God." This is surely equivalent to "the mind of Christ" based on a reading of 1 Cor 2.

91. Ramsaran, *Liberating Words*, 42–43.

16

PAUL AND *PATER FAMILIAS*

L. Michael White

Part I. *Pater Familias* in the Greco–Roman World

The Latin term *pater familias* is properly translated "father of the family," meaning roughly "head of the household." In the social and cultural milieu of the Greco-Roman world, however, it carried a broader range of meaning than either of these translations can communicate simply. The reason, in part, is the difference in meaning of the word *familia*; next, the definition and role of the "father" within the *familia* and in the society at large.

Pater *and* Familia *in Context*

The term *familia* was not limited to the "nuclear family" consisting of parents and children, as it is commonly applied in the modern world.[1] Instead, the *familia* in the Roman world was both a legal and social designation for the larger "household" (or *domus*), modeled after the patrician social structure of Republican Rome. Thus, the *familia* normally included parents and children, along with other relatives (agnates and cognates), the domestic slaves, and a coterie of other dependents, freedmen, or clients. From a strictly legal perspective the word *familia* could also mean the property of an estate that was inherited by the heirs or other agnate kin.[2] When applied to persons rather than property it could designate all the agnate kin or just the domestic slaves.[3] When these two concepts are combined, *familia* refers to all the persons who are under the power (*potestas*) of the *pater familias* either by nature or by law; its definitions and workings were closely bound up with laws governing inheritance.[4] At times the word *domus* (meaning either the house itself or the household, kinship, and patrimony) was virtually

457

synonymous with *familia*. Hence, the terms *familia* and *domus* both refer to a set of relationships extending vertically over several generations.[5]

The *pater familias* stood as the ultimate source of power and authority in the household. This notion, called *patria potestas* ("paternal power"), was the father's hereditary rule over the goods, possessions, and people belonging to his patrimonial estate.[6] In legal discussions, many of the concepts of public law, administration, and statecraft were patterned after this idealized notion of paternal rule over the household. At root stood the conception of the extended *familia* and its social structure as a microcosm of the state.[7]

The Powers and Responsibilities of the Pater Familias

Roman familial life was extremely patriarchal and exclusively patrilineal. The autocratic and despotic nature of *patria potestas* is a commonplace in discussions of the Roman family.[8] From the legal perspective the *pater familias* held the right to punish slaves at will, and he had the power of life and death over newborn children. Even freeborn children were virtually slaves to their father's estate until his death.[9] At the very least, *patria potestas* provided the *pater familias* with both strict disciplinary authority and sexual dominion over the members of his extended *familia*.[10] Even so, the discussions of the Roman jurists may be somewhat misleading in regard to the social reality; the *pater familias* had moral obligations as well.[11] The quintessential Roman virtue of *pietas* ("piety, loyalty") described both the duties of children to obey parents and the devotion of fathers to wives and children.[12]

The duties and responsibilities of the *pater familias* toward the household were extensive. First and foremost, he had to provide food and care for all persons under his power, whether slave or free. He also provided monetary allowances for his freedmen and other clients. He was required to oversee the estate, not only in day-to-day operations, but also in terms of guarding the *patrimonium* (or *familia*) for succeeding generations. He might delegate individual management responsibilities in the operation of the household to his chief slave, a son, or his wife, but ultimately he was responsible. A son's share of the inheritance was held and managed as *peculium* ("private purse") by the father until such time as it was released, either by action of the father or by execution of the father's will. The father had to give formal approval for both sons and daughters to marry. Disposal of any and all properties, including chattel slaves, was his province, no matter to whom he might delegate the actual negotiations.

At the same time laws regarding patrimony and inheritance placed some restrictions on the powers of the *pater familias*. By the end of the Republic, most Roman marriages fell under the legal category *sine manu* ("without hand" or "handless"). It meant that when she entered the marriage, a woman did not actually enter into the "hands," that is, the agnatic kinship line, of the husband. Instead, she remained tied to the *familia* of her own father. This had important implications for property rights and inheritance.[13] A woman's inheritance, therefore, did not pass over to the ownership of her husband; instead, it remained technically the property of her father's *familia* or *patrimonium*.[14] Such restrictions did not apply to funds or properties given to the husband as dowry, but once her father was deceased, a woman had *de iure* control of her own property. In practical terms this meant that a woman could manage her own properties even within marriage while technically under the *patria potestas* of her husband. Numerous cases indicate that many a husband felt compelled to accede to his wife's wishes in financial and other matters because of her independent property rights. Sons might even "borrow" from the mother's estate in order to advance their own careers, but legally they might have to repay her from their own *peculium* or the inheritance from the father's *patrimonium*.[15]

Depending on the relative wealth of the familial lines joined by marriage, the mother's inheritance might be more or less important. By the time of the empire, women were increasingly in control of larger personal estates that they were able to manage either within the marital family or on their own. A woman whose father and husband had both died, was functionally, at least, an independent agent, and the term *mater familias* has come to designate the fact that some women were becoming "heads of households" even in the old Roman aristocracy.

The *pater familias*, as a public figure, was also responsible for obligations to the city and the state. These duties included holding public magistracies, sponsoring annual festivals or games, and serving in the civic *curia* (the senate at Rome itself, or the *decurionate* or "council" in other cities). Such duties carried significant financial responsibilities as well. The *dignitas* ("dignity," meaning the repute or "good name") of the *familia* was viewed as a trust that had to be managed, just like the *patrimonium* itself, for the benefit of future generations. A family's status was multidimensional, depending on several distinct and related factors. Wealth and land were very important, to be sure, but other factors were also at work, including social prestige (e.g., intermarriage of elite families), political success, and the number of clients one could command. Thus, there was a greater degree of social mobility in the Roman world than is sometimes imagined. At the same time, each successive generation encountered some risk of losing status and fostered intense competition to maintain and acquire status.[16] The bulk of this competition necessarily fell on the *pater familias* as public figure.

Two examples with opposite outcomes will illustrate the problem. The first is a legendary case from earlier Republican times and relates the failing fortunes of the Scipioni. Publius Scipio Nascia was first cousin of the brothers Scipio Africanus and Scipio Asiaticus and served as consul in 191 B.C.E. Writing during the early principate, Valerius Maximus explained the family's political misfortunes as follows:

> Publius Scipio Nascia was a famous and powerful figure in ruling circles . . . who took pride in being leader of the senate for many years. As a young man, when he was seeking election to the curule aedileship, he shook the hand of a certain peasant somewhat assiduously, as candidates often do. He noticed that the man's hand was hardened by his country work, and making a joke asked him if he normally walked on his hands. The bystanders took exception to this jibe, which spread among the country people and led to Scipio losing the election.[17]

Valerius's account epitomizes the responsibilities toward social inferiors of those who aspire to nobility. Mobility, both upward and downward, was possible, and a family's good name took constant care.

Another example comes from the inscription over the entrance to the Iseum at Pompeii.

> Numerius Popidius Celsinus, son of Numerius, at his own expense rebuilt from its foundations the Temple of Isis, which had collapsed by reason of the earthquake. On account of his generosity, the decurions of the city have received him without cost into their own order, even though he is six years old.[18]

The occasion for the rebuilding project was the great earthquake of 62 C.E., but a child of six can hardly be thought of as initiating such a project. Nor should a six-year-old boy be a candidate for the decurionate, the city's leading council or *curia*. The situation becomes intelligible if we recognize that the boy's father, Numerius Popidius Ampliatus, was an aspiring freedman of the prominent *gens Popidii*.[19] A freedman was prohibited by law from being admitted to the decurionate, but the son of a freedman could be. So, the father has paid for the renovations of the Iseum in the name of his son in order to advance him into the ranks of the local aristocracy; he made an investment in the fortunes of his *familia* for posterity. There was a complex calculus to the life of a *pater familias* built around his networks of social and political relationships.[20]

Between Public and Private: The Pater Familias at Home

The cultural resonances of Roman familial structure can be seen in the plan and ordering of daily life at home, explicitly in the provisions made by and for the *pater familias*. The rhythm and the rules (many of them unspoken) of daily life are often difficult for moderns to grasp. In particular we must be cautious of the notion of the home as the seat of "private" life alone. Just as we have already seen

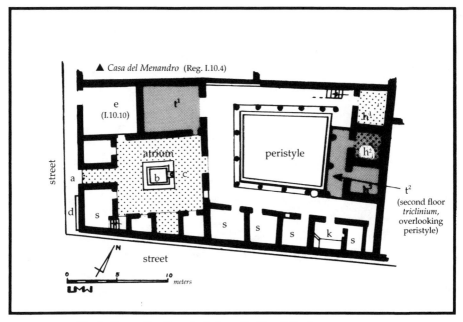

Fig. 1: Pompeii. *Casa degli Amanti* **(Reg. I.10.11)**
a - Main entrance, b - *impluvium*, c - seat of the *pater familias*,
d - bench for clients, e - shop space, t - dining rooms (*triclinium*),
k - kitchen (with *lararium*), h - master bedrooms (*cubiculum*),
s - service areas   (drawing by the author, adapted from O. Elia)

that the modern term "family" does not map so easily onto the ancient social structures of *familia* and *domus*, so too a traditional western dichotomy of home/ private versus work/public does not aptly describe the daily life of the *pater familias.*

New perspectives on the physical setting of the Roman house and the life of the household[21] help to decipher encoded elements of Roman daily life; as a result we are better able to understand their implicit moral template of household order. For example, the "typical" Roman houses found in Pompeii and Herculaneum do not have areas that are easily labeled as men's areas, women's areas, or slave quarters.[22] Most domestic spaces were assumed to have multiple functions depending on the time of day and the people involved. Even within the house, architectural forms were "obsessively concerned with distinctions of social rank"[23] both for those who resided there and those who merely visited. Slaves were virtually omnipresent throughout the house during most hours of the day and night, but the social encoding of the architecture often masks their presence. Domestic space reinforced the ideological superiority of the *pater familias* and his pattern of movements and functions within the house.[24]

There were two key areas of the house where the role and status of the *pater familias* was encoded architecturally. They are the atrium and the triclinium. The atrium was the site of daily rituals surrounding the *salutatio* and worship of the *Penates* (household deities); the *triclinium*, the site of evening hospitality and social dining, the *cena* (see fig. 1 on previous page).[25] With the introduction of the Hellenistic peristyle there was a two-stage entry into the inner confines of the house.[26]

It was the outer court, the atrium proper, that served as the public reception hall of the *pater familias* in his daily ritual of "greetings" (*salutatio*) by clients, well-wishers, and suppliants. He usually sat in a small chair (fig. 1, locus *c*)—sometimes fixed in place, sometimes portable, a *sella curulis* (or "magisterial seat")—opposite the front door (*a*) with the *impluvium* (*b*, the central basin open to the sky) in between. From six to eight o'clock in the morning, the "callers" would gather outside the front door (*d*) along the street.[27] The chief household servant, the master's trusted chamberlain (Latin *cubicularius*), would stand at the main door to admit and announce each of the clients or suppliants in turn. On entering, the clients would then approach the seated *pater familias* with a gesture of obeisance (*obsequium*) and devotion (*pietas*). This show of loyalty and respect signaled the client's willingness to serve at the patron's bidding, for example, to show up and voice support if he were in court on some matter. In turn, they might ask for a particular favor from the patron. Most freedmen and clients received a daily allowance (called *sportula*) of either food or money as part of the *salutatio*. Those clients who were especially trusted or favored might serve in some other capacity in business or public life for the patron and, in turn, might receive special rewards for their services.[28]

Beginning at the *salutatio* and for much of the day, the main doors of the house were expected to stand open to the street; the atrium of the house was considered a part of the *pater familias'* public domain, an extension of his activities as a public citizen. The line of demarcation between public and private was not drawn neatly at the front door; rather, the atrium marked an intentionally "open" space that was used for a variety of ordinary household functions, including commercial production, as well as for the formal receptions of the *pater familias*. For anyone entering the atrium of such a house there was an accepted (but rarely stated) etiquette, a set of social cues and conventions by which one negotiated the domestic space. Rooms with doors closed or areas guarded from direct view by a person in the atrium were being "marked" as more private. Sheer distance sometimes served as a marker, too.[29] Accordingly, visitors had to be alert to the signs of where the private domain of the *pater familias*—the spaces reserved for his household and staff—began.

No single room or type of space stood for privacy alone in the Roman house. Rather, privacy was more a function of time of day, status, and social context.[30] Such functions help to explain the lavish decorations one finds so commonly in the bedrooms of elite houses at Pompeii.[31] The visitor to the house had to know his or her own place and how to "negotiate" the spatially marked areas by time and circumstance.

The other principal arena of the *pater familias* in domestic activity was as host and patron at dinner parties. Here Petronius's satirical "*Cena* of Trimalchio" provides ample evidence of the social interplay that might take place at such a gathering with the *pater familias* thoroughly in charge of the proceedings. Usually, the most honored guest and the host were stationed strategically so that they had the most impressive view of the house.[32] Increasingly in the imperial period, such dinners were not only for respected friends but also for clients and others who viewed such occasions both as dole and duty. Two accounts, one satirical and the other a letter, illustrate the ways that status and dependency were orchestrated at the meal by the host and *pater familias*.[33] The first comes from an epigram of Martial:

> Since I am asked to dinner, no longer as a purchased guest [i.e., a client] as before, why is not the same dinner served to me as to you? You take oysters fattened in the Lucrine lake, I suck a mussel through a hole in the shell; you get mushrooms, I take hog-fungus; you tackle turbot, but I brill. Golden with fat, a turtledove with its bloated rump gorges you; there is set before me a magpie that has died in its cage. Why do I dine without you, even though, Ponticus, I am dining with you. The dole has gone; let us have the benefit of it—let us eat the same fare.[34]

The second comes from a letter of Pliny the Younger:

> It would take too long to recount how it happened that I, though not one of his familiars, was with a certain man for a dinner that seemed to him to be lavish though frugal but which seemed to me to be meager yet extravagant. The best dishes were for himself and a select few, while cheap morsels were served to the rest. He even assigned the wine in tiny little flasks into three categories, not so that a person might be able to choose, but so that he might not have the right to refuse what he was given. One was for himself and for us; another for his lesser friends (even his "friends" have grades); and another for his and our freedmen. The man who was reclining closest to me took note [of this] and asked whether I approved. I said, "No." "What procedure do you follow, then?" he asked. "I serve the same to everyone," [I replied], "for I invite people to a dinner, not to make a show of inequalities; rather, I make them equals at the same table and with the same treatment." "Even the freedmen?" [he asked]. "Certainly, for then they are my fellow-diners, not just freedmen."[35]

Both comments show that food and the seating arrangements were symbols of status. Moreover, the point of Pliny's letter, addressed to a young aristocrat named Junius Avitus, was to instruct him on how not to fall into such bad habits in social entertaining. It assumes, however, that similar shows of snobbery took place with some frequency, even though there were higher ideals to be found.

Part II. *Pater Familias* in Paul's Churches

A Note on Greek Equivalents

The *pater familias* was a product of Roman social and cultural construction. So, a question still remains on how, if at all, these ideas might have been present outside of Italy, and especially in the predominantly Greek-speaking world of Paul. We may begin with a note on terminology. The Greek words οἶκος (*oikos*) and οἰκία (*oikia*, both meaning "house or home") were used to translate both *familia* and *domus* in Latin; they can thus mean house, household, family, or estate depending on the context.[36] A good example is the term *familia Caesaris*, the designation for the imperial bureaucracy made up of clerks and bookkeepers who were technically slaves of the emperor. The typical Greek equivalent for this group, which was extensive in Greek cities under Roman rule, was οἶκος/οἰκία Καίσαρος (*oikos/oikia Kaisaros*) as in Phil 4:22.[37] On the other hand, there is no exact Greek equivalent for *pater familias*, even thought there is such for the Latin *pater patriae* using the Greek πάτηρ πατρίδος (*patēr patridos*), an honorific epithet meaning "father of the fatherland."[38] More common in Greek usage might be πάτηρ τῆς πόλεως (*patēr tēs poleōs*, "father of the city"), regularly found as an honorific title for civic benefactors.

While the term *pater familias* does not occur in normal Greek usage, the concept seems still to be alive in Greek cities under Roman rule. The common form in Greek that reflects such patriarchal household order is οἰκοδεσπότης (*oikodespotēs*) or just δεσπότης (*despotēs*, both meaning "ruler of the house"). That it was thought of as the Greek equivalent to *pater familias* is perhaps best illustrated by a comment from Cicero; writing in Latin to his friend Atticus, he refers to efforts to find a new house for himself:

> [B]ut what is wanted except an opening for a purchaser? And that could be gotten through any of the heirs. But I think Mustela will arrange that, if you ask. You will have provided me not only with the very place I want for my purpose, but a place to grow old in as well. For those [houses] of Silius and Drusus do not seem to be sufficiently οἰκοδεσποτικά (*oikodespotika*) for me. (*Letters to Atticus*, 12.44.2, dated 45 B.C.E.)

So, in this Latin text, when Cicero is referring to the suitability of a house for the life of a *pater familias*, he opts into the Greek, perhaps partly because it has a viable adjectival form. But Cicero's letters to Atticus are liberally sprinkled with Greek terminology meant to reflect the Latin equivalent. The term οἰκοδεσπότης (*oikodespotēs*) shows up frequently in the New Testament where the context clearly means "householder" (as it is usually translated) or "head of the household."[39] The usual Greek term for the chief household slave (Latin *cubicularius* or "chamberlain") is οἰκονόμος (*oikonomos,* often translated "steward").[40] A good example of the usage is found in Luke 12:39–45, where οἰκοδεσπότης (*oikodespotēs*) designates the householder, and οἰκονόμος (*oikonomos*), the chief steward. As the parable continues two other terms are given as synonyms that further elucidate the usage: in 12:43 the οἰκονόμος is called a δοῦλος (*doulos,* "slave"), while the οἰκοδεσπότης is called κύριος (*kyrios,* here meaning "lord, master, or sir"). The term κύριος (*kyrios*) is probably the most common way of designating the *pater familias* in Greek, perhaps as a shorthand for something like ὁ κύριος τοῦ οἴκου (*ho kyrios tou oikou,* or "master of the house"), as seen in the papyrus letter (*PGiss.* 17), where a slave uses κύριος (*kyrios*) and δεσπότης (*despotēs*) interchangeably in addressing her master. The clearest use of this terminology to describe a typical familial structure in Paul is Gal 4:1–3:

> I am saying that the *heir* (κληρονόμος, *klēronomos*), so long as he is a *child* (νήπιος/ *nēpios*), is no better than a *slave* (δοῦλος/ *doulos*), even though he is *master of all* [the estate] (κύριος πάντων ὤν, *kyrios pantōn ōn*). Rather, he is under *overseers and stewards* (ἐπιτρόπους . . . καὶ οἰκονόμους, *epitropous . . . kai oikonomous*) until the time set by his *father* (προθεσμίας τοῦ πατ-ρός, *prothesmias tou patros*).

Thus, Paul too is using κύριος (*kyrios*) and πατήρ (*patēr*) to define the role of the *pater familias.*

Compare also Dio Chrysostom's terminology for household relationships in *Or.* 38.15:

> While the salvation of households [οἴκων, *oikōn*] lies in the like-mindedness of the masters [τῇ τῶν δεσποτῶν ὁμοφροσύνῃ, *tē tōn despotōn homophrosynē*] and in the obedience of domestic slaves [τῇ τῶν οἰκετῶν πειθ-αρχία, *tē tōn oiketōn peitharchia*], yet discord between master and mistress [literally, *masterly discord*—ἥ τε δεσποτικὴ στάσις, *hē te despotikē stasis*] has destroyed as many households [οἴκους, *oikous*], as has the bad character of slaves [ἡ κακοδουλία, *hē kakodoulia*].

The context indicates that the plural "masters" (δεσποτῶν, *despotōn*) refers to the husband *and* wife, viewed jointly as head of the household. This discussion of the proper relations in the household also reflects the broader social expression of the so-called "household duty code" that shows up in the later Paulinist writings (see below).

We know less about the legal provisions concerning the rights or powers of the "head of the household" among Greek-speaking provincials during the

Roman Empire. In most cases, one would assume that local customs of household organization and management persisted. The Greek family from Classical to Hellenistic times was, like the Roman, decidedly patriarchal.[41] Indeed, there was even more separation between men and women in the traditional Greek house, where there was an *andron* (including the dining room) for the men and the *gynaikeon* for the women.[42] Also, women more typically were kept under the care of a male guardian, either father, husband, or adult son; unlike the Romans, women did not originally inherit property to manage on their own. On the other hand, women from leading families in Greek cities commonly held high civic offices, such as the head of the *prytaneion* (chief magistrate) in Ephesus or the priest of the imperial cult in Pergamon or Akmoneia.

It appears that Roman rule had an effect on some of these practices by subtle accommodation to Roman models. Two factors may have contributed: the presence of Roman *colonia* ("colonies") in Greece and Anatolia and the adlection of provincial aristocrats from major Greek cities to the Roman senate. Considerable research has been done on Greek senators and their role in the early and middle principate. For the present discussion, it will suffice to note that many aspiring Greek provincials took on Roman styled family names (the *trinomen*) and followed the standard *cursus honorum* ("course of honors," i.e., the offices of pubic career) of a Roman aristocrat. It suggests, therefore, that they would have operated within the household much like a traditional Roman *pater familias* and *patronus*.[43]

Three colonies in particular should be mentioned in relation to the career of Paul; they are Corinth, Philippi, and Pisidian Antioch. All three had been refounded as colonies under Julius Caesar or Augustus; as such, they held the legal status of Roman cities.[44] Their administrative structures combined typically Italian civic offices (such as *duovirs* and *aediles*) with Greek offices (*agonothete* and *strategos*).[45] A high proportion of inscriptions from Corinth, Philippi, and Antioch are in Latin, especially for the earlier periods; it appears that these *colonia* became more Greek in language and culture as time went on.[46] In this light, we should expect that traditional familial structures around the *pater familias* would have been present there, too.

Paul's House-Church Patrons: Pater and Mater Familias

As in Greek literature more generally, the Latin term *pater familias* does not occur in Paul's letters. Nonetheless, the social place of the "father," and in some cases the "mother" of the household, are apparent in the social organization of Paul's churches. It was part of Paul's missionary strategy that he organized his congregations around local households.[47] His letters are regularly addressed to "so-and-so and the church in his/her/their/your house."[48] It would appear that there were multiple house-church cells in the larger cities. In greater Corinth, for example, there may have been as many as six during Paul's time there; three were led by men (Crispus, Gaius, and Stephanus), two by women (Chloe, Phoebe), and one by a married couple (Prisca and Aquila) where the woman is mentioned first.[49] Similarly, the Roman letter seems to offer greetings to as many as eight different house-church cells.[50]

The most direct points of contact with the role of the *pater familias* are the Pauline house-church patrons, both men and women. Paul and his coworkers regularly stayed in the homes of house-church patrons while visiting in each city.[51] Consequently hospitality and patronage were important virtues in the social dynamics of congregational life (cf. Rom 12:13b); the dinner gathering for the eucharistic meal or "Lord's supper" (κυριακὸν δεῖπνον, *kyriakon deipnon*, 1 Cor 11:20) would have been hosted by them as well.[52] It also appears that Paul typically baptized only the head of the household, who in turn baptized the rest of the group.[53] This practice would have been in keeping with the prerogatives of a *pater/mater familias* over the rest of the household members.

Especially noteworthy is the appearance of a number of women house-church patrons within Paul's Aegean mission sphere. They must be women of independent means who manage their own households as *mater familias*. In addition to Phoebe, Chloe, and Prisca there are implicit references to Euodia and Syntyche at Philippi (Phil 4:1–2) and an explicit one to Nympha at Laodicea (Col 4:15, if genuine).[54] Among the list in Rom 16:5–16 are several other women who are prominently noticed for their "labors" (ἐκοπίασεν/*ekopiasen*, κοπιώσας/*kopiō-sas*) on behalf of the churches (Mary, 16:6; Tryphaena and Tryphosa, 16:12) as well as a "renowned" apostolic couple, Andronicus and Junia (16:7). While it is not certain that these are also women house-church patrons (as Phoebe clearly was for the congregation at Cenchreae—Rom 16:1–2), it is at least possible, because Paul regularly uses terms associated with labor, work, and struggle to value the efforts of his patrons, the house-church leaders.[55]

So we may compare 1 Thess 5:12 where the exhortation to acknowledge "those who labor among you" (εἰδέναι τοὺς κοπιῶντας ἐν ὑμῖν, *eidenai tous kopi-ōntas en hymin*) is supplemented with the additional descriptors "who *preside* over you and admonish you in the Lord" (καὶ προϊσταμένους ὑμῶν ἐν κυρίῳ καὶ νουθε-τοῦντας ὑμᾶς, *kai proïstamenous hymōn en kyriō kai nouthetountas*). The verb προϊ-στημι (*proïstēmi*) here is also of note since it can mean to "stand before" or "preside over" and especially in the middle voice where it means "to take as leader or guardian." The term "patroness" (προστάτις, *prostatis*) found in reference to Phoebe, the house-church leader at Cenchreae (Rom 16:2), is a cognate of this same verb. We should thus think of the reference in 1 Thess 5:12 as referring to the "presidents and patrons" of the house churches, that is, the *pater* or *mater familias* who owned the house and opened it for hospitality to the churches.[56] There is no direct indication of resistance to their leadership here; this admonition is a rhetorical commonplace that reaffirms the traditional social expectations for behavior toward a *pater/mater familias* who provides hospitality in their home.[57] Paul, again following social convention, regularly uses language regarding their laborious service as a means of acknowledging and honoring them.[58]

Paul as Client

Paul also relied on these house-church patrons for financial support of his missionary activities, especially as he traveled to new locations. Phoebe's embassy to the churches in Rome should be seen in this light as Paul prepared to end his Aegean mission and move on to a new territory, Spain.[59] He seems to be relying on the same patterns of financial support he had developed among the house churches of the Aegean. Paul's reliance on such financial support can best be seen in his "thank you note" of Phil 4:10–20. Here Paul uses the language of "partnership" (κοινωνία, *koinōnia*; κοινωνέω, *koinōneō*)[60] to refer explicitly to the financial arrangements between himself and the Philippian congregation (esp. 4:15: ἐκοινώνησεν εἰς λόγον δόσεως καὶ λάμψεως, *ekoinōnēsen eis logon doseōs kai lampseōs*, "entered into partnership for an account of giving and receiving"). This language of partnership or sharing is closely connected to two other rhetorical *topoi* in cultural ideals of that day. First, it is found in legal contract language in reference to business arrangements.[61] Second, it is closely connected to the ideals of friendship in Greek culture, but could imply patronal relations as well.[62] Especially the latter semantic context places this terminology in the social matrix of activities for a *pater/mater familias*. Even though Paul phrases his "financial partnership" as a relation to the church in Philippi, one must guess that the bulk of the funds came from the house-church patron(s).

Paul's financial dependence also places him in a difficult position relative to the power of such patrons. It may be for this reason that Paul refused to accept financial support at times, as in the case of at least some of the house churches at Corinth (2 Cor 11:7–10). Even so, it has been argued convincingly by Peter Marshall that this refusal also created tensions, even enmity, with house-church patrons who expected to offer such aid and to be accorded corresponding honor.[63] Accepting financial support, or even hospitality, placed Paul in the position of a client to the patron; the social conventions associated with such a relationship demanded obsequious respect on the part of the client. In both Philippi and Corinth, where the social and administrative climate was even more heavily informed by Roman models of the *pater familias*, these conventions could hardly be ignored.[64]

Contravening the Powers of a Pater Familias

Perhaps the clearest case where dependency on a house-church patron created a delicate situation for Paul comes in his dealings with Philemon over the matter of the slave Onesimus. Because Paul seems to be intervening in the powers of a *pater familias* in matters of a household slave, this case is particularly instructive. The situation of the Philemon letter is generally well known, even though some of the key details remain unclear. Philemon was a house-church patron (Phlm 2) who afforded Paul hospitality when he came to visit (v. 22). It would appear that Paul himself had baptized Philemon (v. 19), and he established the congregation around the nucleus of Philemon's household (v. 2, assuming that Apphia and Archippus are the wife and son, respectively). Also among the members of Philemon's household was the domestic slave, Onesimus, who had not been baptized. The occasion for the letter arose after Onesimus had been sent to Paul while in prison in Ephesus, perhaps with a gift of financial aid from Philemon.[65] While there, Paul had also baptized Onesimus (v. 10). Apparently Paul wanted to keep Onesimus with him, but dared not do so without the permission of the slave's master.[66] The letter then was written as a recommendation for Onesimus' return, and in it Paul made a plea for Onesimus to be welcomed back "no longer as a slave but as above a slave, a beloved brother, especially to me, but how much more to you, both in the flesh and in the Lord" (v. 16). Most commentators think this means that Paul was asking for Philemon to free Onesimus, because manumission was an institutional expectation for many slaves in the Roman world, but it remains unclear.[67]

What has gone largely unnoticed in most discussions of the letter is the way that Paul calls on Philemon to take Onesimus back into the household, but with some sort of new status. Even as a friend, Paul could hardly *command* a *pater familias* in such a matter, much less as a client, and less so still if Philemon had somehow been "wronged" (v. 18) by Onesimus's and/or Paul's actions. Yet such is the implication of Paul's statement to "charge it to my account" (τοῦτο ἐμοὶ ἐλλόγα, *touto emoi elloga*), namely that Paul had accepted financial support from Philemon, especially while in prison.[68] Now he says, in effect, "Just write off the Onesimus affair to what you would have given me as your client." Next, Paul employs similar patronage language regarding his spiritual relationship to Philemon (vv. 18–19) as a ploy in order to claim that Philemon owes him this favor. This is a rhetorical tour de force that relies precisely on the implicit and accepted notions of patronage and the status of the *pater familias* in order for it to work. By calling Philemon to account to the one who baptized him, Paul was claiming rights that accrued from being Philemon's "spiritual patron." This also has the effect of placing Philemon and Onesimus on a more equal footing, because Paul had personally baptized both of them. It is also significant, therefore, that Paul used "birth-ing" language (v. 10) in reference to having baptized Onesimus. Now Paul has be-come patron, if not *pater familias,* to both Onesimus and Philemon.

Paul as Pater Familias *and Spiritual Patron*

Paul seems to use both patronage and *pater familias* language of himself in a selec-tive way to refer to his special relationship to his Gentile converts (cf. 1 Thess 2:7, 9, 11). As in the case of the letter to Philemon, it often occurs in rhetorically charged passages. One of these is 1 Cor 4:14–21, in which Paul delivers a stern re-buke as to wayward children: "I do not write this to make you ashamed, but to admonish you, as my beloved children" (v. 14). In verse 15, he even contrasts his role as their father "through the gospel" (i.e., by converting them) to that of ordi-nary "guides" (παιδαγωγούς, *paidagōgous,* literally the household slave who tu-tored the master's children). Next, he urges them to imitate him (v. 16), and he delegates Timothy, his "faithful child" (v. 17), to show them the proper path. Fi-nally, he cautions against arrogance or recalcitrance on their part by threatening them with his *patria potestas,* that is, his apostolic presence and "power" (v. 20), and so he concludes (v. 21) with the prerogatives of a *pater familias*: "What do you wish? Shall I come to you with a rod or with love and a spirit of gentleness?"

Another example occurs in Gal 4:11–20; once again Paul is delivering a re-buke, but the case is more serious, because his converts are threatening to aban-don Paul's "gospel." We find key terms that cluster around Paul's "labors" on their behalf (v. 11), friendship ("enmity," v. 16), imitation (v. 12), and his apostolic "presence" (v. 20). The rebuke reaches its rhetorical peak with Paul's exasperated outburst: "My little children, with whom I am once again in travail[69] until Christ be formed in you!" (v. 19). The use of birthing imagery, again, refers to his efforts in converting them, just as in Phlm 10. Yet here, Paul is also accusing them of turn-ing their back on his spiritual patronage.[70]

Paul's "spiritual patronage" may also be connected to his use of "father" lan-guage in reference to God. Paul regularly calls God "father," as in his epistolary greetings. Not all of these explicitly employ imagery or social conventions from the Roman *pater familias,* but some do. One of these is Gal 4:1–9, where Paul uses the model of adoption to discuss the status of those who are "in Christ." The pas-sage opens (vv. 1–2), as noted earlier, with very traditional language of Roman household relations under the father. Next, the new status of heirs by adoption is affirmed by the "Spirit" which allows one to call on God as "Abba, Father!" (vv. 6–7). Romans 8:14–17 employs a very similar formulation regarding the role of the Spirit in adoption as heirs who receive the ability to call on God as "Abba, Father!"

But if God is now the *pater familias* and the converts his adopted children, what is Paul's role? Paul's use of such metaphors for his theological reflections is not always consistent; it is noteworthy that he sometimes opts into maternal or birthing language for his role in conversion (as in Gal 4:19, by contrast to 1 Cor 4:14–21 and 1 Thess 2:11). He thus becomes, in some sense, an intermediary or functionary relative to the "fatherhood" of God. Worth noting in these passages is the prominent place of the "Spirit" as a gift received from God at baptism, as a sign of adoption (Gal 4:6). Galatians 3:1–5 may be taken to suggest that Paul saw himself as the one who supplied the Spirit by his role in preaching and conversion.[71] Taken together, these elements point to Paul's declaring himself as the benefactor (or "broker," for God as *pater familias*) of their reception of the Spirit through his own presentation of the gospel.[72]

Managing the Household: Paul on Sexuality

Paul's advice on marriage and sexuality in 1 Cor 7 also enters into the traditional domain of the *pater familias*. The key passage is 1 Cor 7:2–6. The context for this discussion is an interest on the part of at least some of the Corinthian Christians in sexual asceticism; indeed, the appeal to asceticism as a superior mode of life seems to come from Paul himself.[73] Even so, it reflects a view of sexuality widely known in ancient philosophical and medical circles.[74] In Jewish contexts, Philo had already adopted similar injunctions.[75] Typically, these discussions tend to take the male perspective with regard to matters of the sexual control required and medical benefits to be derived. So too, the opening slogan that Paul repeats in 1 Cor 7:1 ("It is good for a man not to touch a woman") comes from this dominant male perspective.

Given this view, however, it seems surprising at first that Paul should give such balance in regard to a woman's rights regarding marital sexuality. It has been argued, for example, that the degree of reciprocity and parallelism voiced by Paul in 1 Cor 7:3–5 marks a significant departure from the patriarchal rights of the *pater familias* in the ancient world.[76] But, in fact, there were similar arguments for sexual "mutuality" in the marriage, especially among Stoics. The Roman Stoic Musonius Rufus advised:

> For a husband . . . and a wife should come together each with the other, on the one hand so that they make a life together with one another, and on the other so that they together procreate children, and furthermore to consider all things in common and [to consider] nothing one's own alone, not even their own bodies.[77]

Musonius reflects a persistent theme among the moralist philosophers of the day regarding the ideals of household management.[78] They stem from the basic conception of the family as a microcosm of the state. Consequently they often decry excesses and abuses in the exercise of *patria potestas* in treatment of slaves (e.g., anger and brutality). They also advocated a kind of mutuality in marriage that often ran counter to the traditional sexual mores. In this case, Musonius advocates a marital mutuality built on the ideal of friendship, as seen in his adaptive use of the slogan "to hold all things in common (κοινά, *koina*)," which comes from the traditional Greek definition of friendship. As noted above, friendship language figures prominently in other aspects of Paul's dealings with his house-church patrons. Also, such Stoic moral ideals were widely disseminated in the early empire.[79] In the final analysis, then, while Paul calls for ethical constraints on the traditional powers of the *pater familias* in sexual matters, his is not an entirely unusual stance by the moral standards of the day. Here as elsewhere Paul fits well within the realm of contemporary moralist advice aimed at improving people's lives, albeit with some differences on the theological underpinnings of that advice.

Part III. Other Relevant Texts in Pauline and Paulinist Literature

In many ways Paul stands in an ambiguous position in relation to the traditional powers of the *pater familias*. He adopts many of the critical views of contemporary moralists, but at the same time he rarely challenges the traditional familial structure in any overt way. It may be suggested, however, that in some ways this more conservative aspect of Paul's thought actually served to expand and protect the social position of women, especially the women house-church patrons who were so central to his missionary activities around the Aegean. On the other hand, when we turn to the literature of the later Paulinist tradition, there appears an even more traditional and conservative turn with regard to the exclusively patriarchal role and power of the *pater familias*, both as head of the family and as head of the church.

God as Father

In addition to the greeting formulas (cf. Rom 1:7; 1 Cor 1:3; 2 Cor 1:2; Gal 1:3–4; Phil 1:2; 1 Thess 1:1; Phlm 3), the usage occurs sporadically.[80] It is found frequently in doxological (1 Cor 8:6; 2 Cor 1:3; Phil 2:11; 4:20) or benedictory formulations (Rom 15:6; 1 Thess 3:11), but also occurs in the apocalyptic description of 1 Cor 15:24. The other distinctive usage in Paul is in reference to the death/resurrection of Jesus (Rom 6:4), which may well anticipate his symbolic use of the Akedah (or "binding of Isaac") in Rom 8:32.

In the context of adoption, see Rom 8:12–17 and Gal 4:1–5 (see above).

These ideas are extended and systemized in the Paulinist tradition. Compare Eph 3:14–19. One of the recurring themes in the Pastorals is the image of the church as the "household of God" (οἶκος τοῦ θεοῦ, *oikos tou theou*), and the model of leadership by the *pater familias* is central to this image.[81] The bishop is even called "God's household manager" (Titus 1:7: θεοῦ οἰκονόμον, *theou oikonomon*), using the standard designation for the chief slave of the *pater familias* in a Greek/Roman household.

Paul as Father/Mother

1 Thess 2:11 (compare 1 Thess 2:7, "gentle as a nurse").[82]

1 Cor 4:14–21; Gal 4:19 (discussed above). See also Phil 2:22 (Paul to Timothy) in comparison to Phlm 10.

By contrast, Paul generally uses the verb form κυριεύειν (*kyrieuein*, "to lord it over or master someone") in the typical sense of hierarchical or power relationships, often with a negative sense; cf. Rom 6:9 (death), 14 (sin); 7:1 (Law); 14:9 (Christ); 2 Cor 1:24 (Paul).

Patronage, Hospitality, and Household Management

House(hold) churches. Rom 16:2, 5; 23; 1 Cor 16:15–17, 19; Phlm 2; cf. Col 4:15.

Patronage. Rom 16:2 (see above); cf. 1 Thess 5:12; Rom 16:12 (see above).

Hospitality. Rom 12:8–13 (see above); Phlm 22; Rom 16:23.

There are other indications that later Pauline Christians made apologetic accommodations in relation to Roman household mores.[83] Perhaps the best example of this tendency is the so-called *Haustafel* or Household Duty Code (Col 3:18–4:1; Eph 5:22–6:9; cf. Titus 2:4–10); compare the deutero-Petrine tradition (1 Pet 2:18–3:7). It reflects a fixed formula of household relationships that circulated widely in Hellenistic moral philosophy.[84]

The pattern is best seen in Col 3:18–4:1. In each case the focus ultimately is on submission of other members of the household to the *pater familias*.[85] This model is now used as an image of the cosmic order but with Christ at its "head" (Col 1:18; 3:15; Eph 1:22; 4:4), like a well-ordered household. As a result "the church came more and more to resemble an extended household, characterized by patriarchal leadership, high expectations of cohesiveness, and exclusive claims to honor by some over other members."[86]

By the second century, there were even stronger tendencies to reassert the traditional patriarchal models of household organization for church governance, as seen in the Pastoral Epistles. In addition to introducing prohibitions on women's public roles in the church (1 Tim 2:11–12), they also oppose any form of asceticism (1 Tim 4:3) and assert the value of marriage for women (1 Tim 5:14; cf. 2:15). These texts reflect an intensification of patriarchal structures within the family but also within the organization of the church.[87] In particular, one sees for the first time explicit lists of qualifications for male church offices of bishop/elder and deacon that are patterned after the model *pater familias* (1 Tim 3:2–13; Titus 1:7–9). In Titus 2:4–5, we have a convergence of the household duty codes, already at work in earlier deutero-Pauline letters, with a more rigidified and hierarchical power structure. In the case of both elders and deacons the need to "manage their children and household well" (1 Tim 3:12: τέκνων καλῶς προϊστάμενοι καὶ τῶν ἰδίων οἴκων, *teknōn kalōs proïstamenoi kai tōn idiōn oikōn*) is a clear criterion for judging him fit to manage the church (1 Tim 3:4–5; Titus 1:11).[88]

Part IV. Bibliography

Classical Studies

Allison, Penelope. "Roman Households: An Archaeological Perspective." Pages 112–46 in *Roman Urbansim: Beyond the Consumer City*, edited by H. Parkins. London: Routledge, 1997.

Berry, Joanne. "Household Artifacts: Towards Reinterpretation of Roman Domestic Space." Pages 183–95 in *Domestic Space in the Roman World*, edited by R. Laurence and A. Wallace-Hadrill. Journal of Roman Archaeology Supplements 22. Portsmouth, R.I.: Journal of Roman Archaeology, 1997.

Bloomer, W. Martin. *Valerius Maximus and the Rhetoric of the New Nobility.* Chapel Hill: University of North Carolina Press, 1992.

Clarke, John R. *The Houses of Roman Italy, 100 BC–AD 250: Ritual, Space, and Decoration.* Berkeley: University of California Press, 1991.

Crook, John A. *Law and Life of Rome, 90 BC–AD 212.* Ithaca, N.Y.: Cornell University Press, 1967.

———. *"Patria Potestas." Classical Quarterly*, n.s., 17 (1967): 113–22.

D'Arms, John. *Commerce and Social Standing in Ancient Rome.* Cambridge: Harvard University Press, 1981.

Dickmann, Jens-Arne. "The Peristyle and the Transformation of Domestic Space in Hellenistic Pompeii." Pages 121–36 in *Domestic Space in the Roman World*, edited by R. Laurence and A. Wallace-Hadrill. Journal of Roman Archaeology Supplements 22. Portsmouth, R. I.: Journal of Roman Archaeology, 1997.

Flandrin, J. L. *Families in Former Times.* Cambridge: Cambridge University Press, 1979.

Foss, Pedar. "Watchful *Lares:* Roman Household Organization and the Rituals of Cooking and Eating." Pages 197–218 in *Domestic Space in the Roman World*, edited by R. Laurence and A. Wallace-Hadrill. Journal of Roman Archaeology Supplements 22. Portsmouth: Journal of Roman Archaeology, 1997.

Franklin, James L. *Pompeii: The Electoral Programmata, Campaigns, and Politics, AD 71–79.* Papers and Monographs of the American Academy at Rome 28. Rome: American Academy at Rome, 1980.

George, Michele. "*Servus* and *domus:* The Slave in the Roman House." Pages 15–24 in *Domestic Space in the Roman World,* edited by R. Laurence and A. Wallace-Hadrill. Journal of Roman Archaeology Supplements 22. Portsmouth: Journal of Roman Archaeology, 1997.

Grahame, Mark. "Public and Private in the Roman House." Pages 137–161 in *Domestic Space in the Roman World,* edited by R. Laurence and A. Wallace-Hadrill. Journal of Roman Archaeology Supplements 22. Portsmouth: Journal of Roman Archaeology, 1997.

Hopkins, Keith. *Death and Renewal.* Cambridge: Cambridge University Press, 1983.

Jongman, Willem. *The Economy and Society of Pompeii.* Amsterdam: J. C. Gieben, 1988.

Koukouli-Chrysantaki, Chaido. "Colonia Iulia Augtusta Philippensis." Pages 5–27 in *Philippi at the Time of Paul and after his Death,* edited by H. Koester and C. Bakirtzis. Harrisburg, Pa.: Trinity Press International, 1998.

Lacey, W. K. *The Family in Classical Greece.* Ithaca, N.Y.: Cornell University Press, 1968.

———. "*Partia Potestas.*" Pages 121–44 in *The Family in Ancient Rome: New Perspectives,* edited by Beryl Rawson. Ithaca, N.Y.: Cornell University Press, 1987.

Laurence, Ray. "Space and Text." Pages 7–14 in *Domestic Space in the Roman World: Pompeii and Beyond,* edited by R. Laurence and A. Wallace-Hadrill. Journal of Roman Archaeology Supplements 22. Portsmouth: Journal of Roman Archaeology, 1997.

Levick, Barbara. *Roman Colonies in Southern Asia Minor.* Oxford: Clarendon, 1967.

Nielsen, Hanne Sigismund. "Men, Women, and Marital Chastity: Public Preaching and Popular Piety at Rome." Pages 525–55 in *Early Christianity and Classical Culture: Comparative Studies in Honor of Abraham J. Malherbe,* edited by J. T. Fitzgerald, T. H. Olbricht, and L. M. White. NovTSup 110. Leiden: E. J. Brill, 2003.

Nussbaum, Martha. *The Therapy of Desire: Theory and Practice in Hellenistic Ethics.* Princeton: Princeton University Press, 1994.

Pomeroy, Sarah. *Families in Classical and Hellenistic Greece: Representations and Realities.* Oxford: Clarendon, 1997.

Riggsby, Andrew M. "Public and Private in Roman Culture: The Case of the *Cubiculum.*" *Journal of Roman Archaeology* 10 (1997): 36–56.

Roller, Matthew. "Pliny's Catullus: The Politics of Literary Appropriation." *TAPA* 128 (1998): 265–304.

Romano, David. "A Tale of Two Cities: Roman Colonies at Corinth." Pages 83–104 in *Romanization and the City: Creations, Transformations, and Failures,* edited by E. Fentress. Journal of Roman Archaeology Supplements 38. Portsmouth: Journal of Roman Archaeology, 2000.

Saller, Richard P. "*Familia, Domus,* and the Roman Conception of the Family." *Phoenix* 38 (1984): 336–55.

———. *Patriarchy, Property, and Death in the Roman Family.* Cambridge: Cambridge University Press, 1994.

Shaw, Brent D. "The Family in Late Antiquity: The Experience of Augustine." *Past and Present* 115 (1987): 3–51.

Veyne, Paul. *A History of Private Life: From Pagan Rome to Byzantium*. Cambridge: Harvard/Belknap, 1987.

Wallace-Hadrill, Andrew. *Houses and Society in Pompeii and Herculaneum*. Princeton: Princeton University Press, 1994.

Weaver, P. R. C. *Familia Caesaris: A Study of the Emperor's Freedmen and Slaves*. Cambridge: Cambridge University Press, 1972.

White, L. Michael. "Counting the Costs of Nobility: The Social Economy of Roman Pergamon." Pages 331–72 in *Pergamon: Citadel of the Gods*, edited by H. Koester. HTS 46. Harrisburg, Pa.: Trinity Press International, 1998.

New Testament Studies

Ascough, Richard S. *What Are They Saying about the Formation of Pauline Churches?* New York: Paulist, 1998.

Balch, David. "Backgrounds of I Cor VII: Sayings of the Lord in Q, Moses as Ascetic Theios Aner in II Cor III." *NTS* 18 (1971/72): 351–64.

———. "Household Codes." Pages 25–50 in *Graeco-Roman Literature and the New Testament*, edited by D. E. Aune. SBLSBS 21. Atlanta: Scholars Press, 1988.

———. *Let Wives Be Submissive: The Domestic Code in 1 Peter*. SBLMS 26. Chico, Calif.: Scholars Press, 1981.

Balch, David, and Carolyn Osiek. *Families in the New Testament World: Households and Housechurches*. Louisville: Westminster John Knox, 1997.

Bartchy, S. Scott. "Philemon, Epistle to." *ABD* 5:305–10.

Berry, Ken L. "The Function of Friendship Language in Philippians 4.10–20." Pages 107–24 in *Friendship, Flattery, and Frankness of Speech: Studies on Friendship in the New Testament World*, edited by J. T. Fitzgerald. Leiden: E. J. Brill, 1996.

Betz, Hans Dieter. *Galatians*. Hermeneia. Philadelphia: Fortress Press, 1979.

Chow, John K. *Patronage and Power: A Study of Social Networks in Corinth*. JSNTSup 75. Sheffield, England: JSOT Press, 1992.

Dahl, Nils A. "Euodia and Syntyche and Paul's Letter to the Phiilippians." Pages 3–15 in *The Social World of the First Christians: Essays in Honor of Wayne A. Meeks*, edited by L. M. White and O. L. Yarbrough. Minneapolis: Fortress Press, 1995.

Danker, Frederic W. *Benefactor: Epigraphic Study of a Graeco-Roman and New Testament Semantic Field*. St. Louis: Clayton, 1982.

Fitzgerald, John T. "Philippians in the Light of Some Ancient Discussions of Friendship." Pages 141–60 in *Friendship, Flattery, and Frankness of Speech: Studies on Friendship in the New Testament World*, edited by J. T. Fitzgerald. Leiden: E. J. Brill, 1996.

Gaventa, Beverly Roberts. "The Maternity of Paul: An Exegetical Study of Gal 4:19." Pages 189–201 in *The Conversation Continues: Studies in Paul and John in Honor of J. Louis Martyn*, edited by R. T. Fortna and B. R. Gaventa. Nashville: Abingdon, 1991.

Harrill, J. Albert. *The Manumission of Slaves in Early Christianity*. HUT 32. Tübingen: Mohr-Siebeck, 1995.

Jewett, Robert. "Paul, Phoebe, and the Spanish Mission." Pages 142–61 in *The Social World of Formative Christianity and Judaism: Essays in Tribute to Howard Clark Kee,* edited by J. Neusner et al. Philadelphia: Fortress Press, 1982.

———. *The Thessalonian Correspondence: Pauline Rhetoric and Millenarian Piety.* Minneapolis: Fortress Press, 1986.

Joubert, Stephan. *Paul as Benefactor: Reciprocity, Strategy, and Theological Reflection in Paul's Collection.* WUNT 2.124. Tübingen: Mohr-Siebeck, 2000.

Klauck, Hans-Josef. *Hausgemeinde und Hauskirche im frühen Christentum.* Stuttgart: Katholische Bibelwerk, 1981.

Knox, John. *Philemon among the Letters of Paul.* Nashville: Abingdon, 1959.

Lampe, Peter. "Keine 'Sklavenflucht' des Onesimus." *ZNW* 76 (1985): 135–47.

Malherbe, Abraham J. *The Letters to the Thessalonians.* AB. New York: Doubleday, 2000.

———. *Paul and the Popular Philosophers.* Minneapolis: Fortress Press, 1991.

———. *Paul and the Thessalonians.* Minneapolis: Fortress Press, 1987.

———. *Social Aspects of Early Christianity.* 2d ed. Philadelphia: Fortress Press, 1983.

Marshall, Peter. *Enmity in Corinth: Social Conventions in Paul's Relations with the Corinthians.* WUNT 2.23. Tübingen: Mohr-Siebeck, 1987.

Martin, Dale. *The Corinthian Body.* New Haven: Yale University Press, 1995.

Martyn, J. Louis. *Galatians.* AB. New York: Doubleday, 1997.

Meeks, Wayne A. *The First Urban Christians: The Social World of the Apostle Paul.* New Haven: Yale University Press, 1983.

Sampley, J. Paul. *Pauline Partnership in Christ: Christian Community and Commitment in the Light of Roman Law.* Philadelphia: Fortress Press, 1980.

Schüssler Fiorenza, Elisabeth. *In Memory of Her: A Feminist Theological Reconstruction of Christian Origins.* New York: Crossroad, 1982.

Scroggs, Robin. "Paul and the Eschatological Woman." *JAAR* 40 (1972): 283–303.

Shaw, Teresa. *The Burden of the Flesh: Fasting and Sexuality in Early Christianity.* Minneapolis: Fortress Press, 1998.

Varner, David C. *The Household of God: The Social World of the Pastoral Epistles.* SBLDS 71. Chico, Calif.: Scholars Press, 1983.

White, L. Michael. "Finding the Ties That Bind: Issues from Social Description." *Semeia* (Atlanta: Scholars Press) 56 (1991): 1–20. [The issue theme is "Social Networks in the Early Christian Environment," edited by L. M. White.]

———. "Morality between Two Worlds: A Paradigm of Friendship in Philippians." Pages 188–215 in *Greeks, Romans, and Christians: Studies in Honor of Abraham J. Malherbe,* edited by D. L. Balch, E. Ferguson, and W. A. Meeks. Minneapolis: Fortress Press, 1990.

———. "Rhetoric and Reality in Galatians: Framing the Social Demands of Friendship." Pages 307–49 in *Early Christianity and Classical Culture: Comparative Studies in Honor of Abraham J. Malherbe,* edited by J. T. Fitzgerald, T. H. Olbricht, and L. M. White. NovTSup. Leiden: E. J. Brill, 2003.

———. *The Social Origins of Christian Architecture.* 2 vols. HTS 42. Harrisburg, Pa.: Trinity Press International, 1996–97.

———. "Visualizing the 'Real' World of Acts 16: Towards Construction of a Social Index." Pages 234–61 in *The Social World of the First Christians: Essays in Honor of Wayne A. Meeks,* edited by L. M. White and O. L. Yarbrough. Minneapolis: Fortress Press, 1995.

Winter, Sara C. "Methodological Observations on a New Interpretation of Paul's Letter to Philemon." *USQR* 39 (1984): 203–12.

———. "Paul's Letter to Philemon." *NTS* 33 (1987): 1–15.

Woyke, Johannes. *Die neutestamentlichen Haustafeln: Ein kritischer und konstuktiver Forschungsüberblick.* Stuttgart: Katholisches Bibelwerk, 2000.

Notes

1. Richard P. Saller, "*Familia, Domus,* and the Roman Conception of the Family," *Phoenix* 38 (1984): 336–55; also idem, *Patriarchy, Property, and Death in the Roman Family* (Cambridge: Cambridge University Press, 1994), 74–77. Regarding the changed meanings of the term between ancient Roman and modern times, Saller follows the groundbreaking work of J. L. Flandrin, *Families in Former Times* (Cambridge: Cambridge University Press, 1979), 4–10.

2. The definition of *familia* by Ulpian in *Digest* 50.16.195.1–4 opens with a legal maxim, drawn from an archaic Roman law regarding inheritance in the Twelve Tables: "[L]et the nearest agnate [kin] have the *familia*" (*adgnatus proximus familiam habeto*). It is meant to show that the term *familia* here means "things or property" (*res*), rather than persons.

3. Thus, one of the standard meanings of the term *familia* as found in certain contexts is explicitly the household slaves. While this meaning reflects the broader notion of the "extended family," it may also result from homonymy with the more specific term for slave, *famulus,* and the cognate verb *famulo,* meaning "to serve" or "make serviceable."

4. See Saller, *Patriarchy, Property, and Death,* 75, again based on the passage in the *Digest* cited above: "Someone is called *pater familias* if he holds dominion in the house, and he is rightly called by this name even if he does not have a son, for we do not only mean his person but his legal status" ("pater autem familias appllatur, qui in domo dominium habet, recteque hoc nomine appellature, quamvis filium non haveat: non enim solam personam eius, sed et ius demonstramus"). The passage continues a few lines later: "We designate a *familia* consisting of all the agnates under a single legal rule, for even if all of them have their own families after the death of the *pater familias,* nonetheless all of them who were under the power of a single person will rightly be called by the same *familia* since they come from the same house and *gens*" ("commune iure familiam dicimus omnium adgnatorum: nam etsi patre familias mortuo singuli singulas familias habent, tamen omnes, wui sub unius potestate fuerunt, recte eiusdem familiae appellabuntur, qui ex eadem domo et gente proditi sunt").

5. Brent D. Shaw, "The Family in Late Antiquity: The Experience of Augustine," *Past and Present* 115 (1987): 3–51.

6. Consequently, the concept of the *pater familias* influenced a number of other key terms and ideas in Roman culture, including *dominium* ("dominion"), *imperium* ("sovereign authority") of emperors and magistrates, and *patrocinium* (or "protection, patronage") of a person or the state over another. The word *dominium*

itself comes directly from *domus*, and thus signifies one's rule over something, like that of the *pater familias* over the household.

7. This notion is found extensively in Stoic discussions; cf. Cicero, *De officiis* 1.17.54: "[T]he first bond of union is that between husband and wife; the next, that between parents and children; then we find one home [*domus*] with everything in common; and this is the foundation [*principium*] of the city and, as it were, the seedbed [*seminarium*] of the state." See also the article by W. K. Lacey, "*Patria Potestas*," in *The Family in Ancient Rome: New Perspectives* (ed. Beryl Rawson; Ithaca, N.Y.: Cornell University Press, 1987), 121–44. For the way this idea is taken over in St. Augustine's thought, with a slight modification, see Shaw, "Family in Late Antiquity," 10–11.

8. Saller (*Partiarchy, Property, and Death,* 103–4) comments on the commonplace.

9. Cf. Paul Veyne, *A History of Private Life: From Pagan Rome to Byzantium* (Cambridge: Harvard/Belknap, 1987), 16–17 (deciding whether the child should live), 29 (children as slaves to the father), 65–67 (mistreatment of slaves). In general on the powers of life and death, see Saller, *Patriarchy, Property, and Death,* 115–22.

10. Shaw, "Family in Late Antiquity," 29, with some special notes on Augustine's attitudes in regard to sexual mores. See also Hanne Sigismund Nielsen, "Men, Women, and Marital Chastity: Public Preaching and Popular Piety at Rome," in *Early Christianity and Classical Culture: Comparative Studies in Honor of Abraham J. Malherbe* (ed. J. T. Fitzgerald, T. H. Olbricht, and L. M. White; NovTSup 110; Leiden: E. J. Brill, 2003), 525–51.

11. Saller, *Patriarchy, Property, and Death,* 105; cf. John A. Crook, "*Patria Potestas*," *CQ,* n.s., 17 (1967): 113–22. For a summary of the laws governing *patria potestas,* see John A. Crook, *Law and Life of Rome, 90 BC–AD 212* (Ithaca, N.Y.: Cornell University Press, 1967), 107–13.

12. Saller, *Patriarchy, Property, and Death,* 109.

13. The practice seems to have evolved as a mechanism for protecting the patrimonies of elite families from inheritance by marriage. This was especially true in circumstances in which there were more daughters than sons, or where there was no male heir to the patrimony. Roman families developed strategies to accommodate these contingencies through adoption and other mechanisms. For a discussion, see Keith Hopkins, *Death and Renewal* (Cambridge: Cambridge University Press, 1983), 99–117. See also the discussion by Saller, *Patriarchy, Property, and Death,* 36–42, 66–69.

14. See Crook, *Law and Life of Rome,* 103–4.

15. Saller, *Patriarchy, Property, and Death,* 128–29.

16. Hopkins, *Death and Renewal,* 107–17.

17. *Memorable Deeds and Sayings* 7.5, as quoted by Hopkins, *Death and Renewal,* 107. One problem is that Valerius Maximus sometimes seems to confuse characters with similar names. It is not altogether clear whether this episode applies to the son or grandson among the three individuals with the name P. Scipio Nascia. On this point see W. Martin Bloomer, *Valerius Maximus and the Rhetoric of the New Nobility* (Chapel Hill: University of North Carolina Press, 1992), 152.

18. *CIL* X.846 (= *Inscriptions latinae selectae* 6367), my translation. For the text and other discussion, see L. M. White, *Social Origins of Christian Architecture,*

vol. 1: *Building God's House in the Roman World* (HTS 42; Valley Forge, Pa.: Trinity Press International, 1996), 31 and 157n. 18.

19. The father's full name appears in two other benefactor inscriptions in the Iseum (*CIL* X.847–848). His wife's name, Cor(n)elia Celsa, also appears in the first of these inscriptions. For the *gens Popidii* among the leading citizens of Pompeii at this time, we may cite the brothers L. Popidius Ampliatus and L. Popidius Secundus, both of whom ran for public office in the 70s C.E. (cf. *CIL* IV.1041; 2966; 7418). For the Popidii in public life at Pompeii, see Willem Jongman, *The Economy and Society of Pompeii* (Amsterdam: J. C. Gieben, 1988; reprint, 1991), 260–64, 284–89; James L. Franklin, *Pompeii: The Electoral Programmata, Campaigns, and Politics, AD 71–79* (Papers and Monographs of the American Academy at Rome 28; Rome: American Academy at Rome, 1980), 105–11.

20. On the topic of social networks, see my article "Finding the Ties That Bind: Issues from Social Description," *Semeia* 56 (1991): 16–18 and throughout. This issue of *Semeia,* edited by L. M. White, focused on the theme "Social Networks in the Early Christian Environment."

21. An excellent introduction to the problems and the new perspectives appears in Ray Laurence, "Space and Text," in *Domestic Space in the Roman World: Pompeii and Beyond* (ed. Ray Laurence and Andrew Wallace-Hadrill; Journal of Roman Archaeology Supplements 22; Portsmouth, R.I.: Journal of Roman Archaeology, 1997), 7–14.

22. See Andrew Wallace-Hadrill, *Houses and Society in Pompeii and Herculaneum* (Princeton: Princeton University Press, 1994), 9–13. The following paragraph is largely based on the observations of Wallace-Hadrill, supplemented by additional studies as noted.

23. Ibid., 10.

24. Michele George, "*Servus* and *domus*: The Slave in the Roman House," in Laurence and Wallace-Hadrill, *Domestic Space in the Roman World*, 22–24.

25. Due to the diversity and variations of domestic planning found at Pompeii and elsewhere, it is difficult to demonstrate all of the features of a "typical" Roman atrium-peristyle house with just one example. For purposes of this discussion, I have chosen the Casa degli Amanti (Reg. I.10.11) from Pompeii, because it represents a none-too-lavish version of the atrium-peristyle house, a stark contrast with its immediate neighbor to the north, the Casa del Menandro (I.10.4), one of the grandest villas of Pompeii. The original portions of the Casa degli Amanti lay to the west, in the area of the atrium. Cf. Wallace-Hadrill, *Houses and Society*, 38–43 and fig. 3.7. For other comments on this house, see the article by Pedar Foss, who classifies the Casa degli Amanti as a *casa media*: "Watchful *Lares*: Roman Household Organization and the Rituals of Cooking and Eating," in Laurence and Wallace-Hadrill, *Domestic Space in the Roman World*, 197–218, esp. 209 and fig. 15.

26. For this development, see Andrew Wallace-Hadrill, "Rethinking the Roman Atrium House," in Laurence and Wallace-Hadrill, *Domestic Space in the Roman World,* esp. 236–40. On the introduction of the peristyle, see Jens-Arne Dickmann, "The Peristyle and the Transformation of Domestic Space in Hellenistic Pompeii," in Laurence and Wallace-Hadrill, *Domestic Space in the Roman World*, 121–36. Dickmann concludes (135–36) that the Hellenistic peristyle could not sim-

ply replace or be integrated into the atrium itself due to the established symbolic status of the atrium. This observation further reinforces the architectural articulation of its cultural function within the emerging Roman patron-client system in relation to the extended *familia.*

27. Roman satirists provide frequent comments on the earliness of the hour or the crowds at the door, as well as the affronts to one's dignity when even freeborn citizens had to make such calls; cf. Juvenal, *Satires* 1.95–102; 3.127–130, and esp. Martial, *Epigrams* 4.8.1: "prima salutantes atque altera conterit hora" ("the first hour—and even the next—wears out those making the salutation rounds," my translation).

28. On the role of freedmen as agents of commercial activity for their patrons, see John D'Arms, *Commerce and Social Standing in Ancient Rome* (Cambridge: Harvard University Press, 1981), 121–48. D'Arms makes the further point that such service both to patrons and to cities created its own kind of *cursus honorum* ("course of honor") for social advancement among freedmen.

29. See Mark Grahame, "Public and Private in the Roman House: The Spatial Order of the *Casa del Fauno*," in Laurence and Wallace-Hadrill, *Domestic Space in the Roman World*, 137–61; Penelope Allison, "Roman Households: An Archaeological Perspective," in *Roman Urbanism: Beyond the Consumer City* (ed. Helene M. Parkins; London: Routledge, 1997), 112–46; idem, "Artifact Distribution and Spatial Function in Pompeian Houses," in *The Roman Family in Italy: Status, Sentiment, Space* (ed. Beryl Rawson and Paul Weaver; Oxford: Clarendon, 1997), 321–54; and Joanne Berry, "Household Artifacts: Towards a Re-interpretation of Roman Domestic Space," in Laurence and Wallace-Hadrill, *Domestic Space in the Roman World,* 183–95.

30. Andrew M. Riggsby ("'Public' and 'Private' in Roman Culture: The Case of the *cubiculum,*" *Journal of Roman Archaeology* 10 [1997]: 36–56) provides an excellent study of different ways or circumstances in which the *cubiculum* was considered private space and so defined both legally and culturally in Roman thought and literature. Cf. Matthew Roller, "Pliny's Catullus: The Politics of Literary Appropriation," *TAPA* 128 (1998): 265–304.

31. So observed in the master bedrooms h1 and h2 in the Casa degli Amanti (fig. 1 above). In general on the way art and decoration were used as "roadsigns" and social cues for moving around the house, see John R. Clark, *The Houses of Roman Italy, 100 BC–AD 250: Ritual, Space, and Decoration* (Berkeley: University of California Press, 1991), 99–101.

32. For sight lines in architectural planning among Pompeiian houses, see L. Bek, "From Eye-Sight to View Planning: The Notion of Greek Philosophy and Hellenistic Optics as a Trend in Roman Aesthetics and Building Practice," in *Aspects of Hellenism in Italy: Towards a Cultural Unity* (ed. P. Guldager Bilde, I. Nielsen, and M. Nielsen; Copenhagen: Institute for Study of Antiquity, 1993), 127–50.

33. Horace (*Sat.* 2.8.7) uses the term *pater cenae* to mean the "host" of an extravagant dinner party where Maecenas was guest of honor. The text is also useful for the way it depicts the seating arrangements (2.8.18–24).

34. *Epigr.* 3.60, my translation.

35. *Ep.* 2.6.1–4.

36. In Greek texts of the Roman Empire, such as census records from Egypt,

οἰκία (*oikia*) is the term most often used to designate the "house" as physical dwelling place, but it can also mean "household." So see the census list of buildings from Panopolis in the Thebaid, *P.Gen. Inv.* 108 (= *SB* VIII [1967] 9902). Οἶκος (*oikos*) often means "household" in the Roman period; however, when used of physical structures, it can mean a "building" of any type and does not refer exclusively to domestic edifices.

37. P. R. C. Weaver, *Familia Caesaris: A Social Study of the Emperor's Freedmen and Slaves* (Cambridge: Cambridge University Press, 1972), throughout.

38. Compare Cicero, *In Pisonem* 6 (in reference to himself as *parentem patriae*), with Plutarch, *Cicero* 23.3 ("*patera patridos* . . . the first to receive this title"). For nonliterary texts, see BGU 1074.1 (a papyrus from the first century C.E.); *Inscriptiones Graecae ad Res Romanas Pertinentes* 3.176–177 (Greek inscriptions from Ankyra under Trajan); and *Inscr. Corinth* VIII.3.99 and 106 (Greek inscriptions referring to Trajan).

39. So Matt 13:27, 52; 20:1, 11; Mark 14:14 // Luke 22:11; Luke 12:39; 13:25; 14:21. Interestingly, the term does not occur in the LXX.

40. So Luke 12:42; 16:1, 8; Rom 16:3 (Erastus, the city treasurer); 1 Cor 4:1–2; Gal 4:2; Titus 1:7; 1 Pet 4:10.

41. W. K. Lacey, *The Family in Classical Greece* (Ithaca, N.Y.: Cornell University Press, 1968), 21–25; Sarah Pomeroy, *Families in Classical and Hellenistic Greece: Representations and Realities* (Oxford: Clarendon, 1997), 22–23.

42. Pomeroy, *Families*, 29–33.

43. For some case studies with substantial bibliography, see L. M. White, "Counting the Costs of Nobility: The Social Economy of Roman Pergamon," in *Pergamon, Citadel of the Gods,* ed. Helmut Koester, HTS 46 (Harrisburg, Pa.: Trinity Press International, 1998), 331–72.

44. On the civic status and administrative structures, see Barbara Levick, *Roman Colonies in Southern Asia Minor* (Oxford: Clarendon, 1967), 29–40 and 68–91; Chaido Koukouli-Chrysantaki, "Colonia Iulia Augusta Philippensis," in *Philippi at the Time of Paul and after His Death* (ed. Charalambos Bakirtzis and Helmut Koester; Harrisburg, Pa.: Trinity Press International, 1998), 5–27; David Romano, "A Tale of Two Cities: Roman Colonies at Corinth," in *Romanization and the City: Creations, Transformations, and Failures* (ed. Elizabeth Fentress; Journal of Roman Archaeology Supplements 38; Portsmouth: Journal of Roman Archaeology, 2000), 83–104.

45. Cf. *Inscr. Corinth* VIII.2.67, 68, 80, 81; VIII.1.66, 76, 80. In the last two, it appears that the Greek *stratēgon pentaetērikon* is the equivalent of the Latin *duovir quinquennalis.*

46. Levick, *Roman Colonies,* 130–44.

47. The secondary literature on the "house church" is now quite extensive. See inter alia Wayne A. Meeks, *The First Urban Christians: The Social World of the Apostle Paul* (New Haven: Yale University Press, 1983), 74–90; Abraham J. Malherbe, *Social Aspects of Early Christianity* (Philadelphia: Fortress Press, 1983), 60–91; Richard S. Ascough, [What Are They Saying about] *The Formation of Pauline Churches?* (New York: Paulist Press, 1998), 5–9; David L. Balch and Carolyn Osiek, *Families in the New Testament World: Households and Housechurches* (Louisville: Westminster John Knox, 1997), 91–102; Hans-Josef Klauck, *Hausgemeinde und*

Hauskirche im frühen Christentum (Stuttgart: Katholische Bibelwerk, 1981), 30–40; and White, *Social Origins of Christian Architecture,* 1:11–25, 102–23.

48. Rom 16:5; 1 Cor 16:19; Phlm 2; cf. Col 4:15.

49. The respective references are 1 Cor 1:14 (Crispus and Gaius); Rom 16:23 (Gaius); 1 Cor 16:15 (Stephanus; cf. 1:16); 1 Cor 1:11 (Chloe's "household"); Rom 16:1–2 (Phoebe); 1 Cor 16:19 (Prisca and Aquila; cf. Rom 16:5; Acts 18:1–3).

50. Rom 16:5–16.

51. Rom 16:23; Phlm 22; Rom 16:1–2.

52. Cf. Meeks, *First Urban Christians,* 60–67; Malherbe, *Social Aspects,* 92–112; Osiek and Balch, *Families in the New Testament World,* 206–14.

53. This is an inference drawn from 1 Cor 1:14–17, *contra* the picture given in Acts (e.g., 16:15, 33, etc.); see also below, n. 65.

54. On the likelihood that Euodia and Syntyche are house-church patrons who have had some disagreement over Paul, see L. M. White, "Morality between Two Worlds: A Paradigm of Friendship in Philippians," in *Greeks, Romans, and Christians: Studies in Honor of Abraham J. Malherbe* (ed. David L. Balch, Everett Ferguson, and Wayne A. Meeks; Philadelphia: Fortress Press, 1990), 214; Nils A. Dahl, "Euodia and Syntyche and Paul's Letter to the Philippians," in *The Social World of the First Christians: Essays in Honor of Wayne A. Meeks* (ed. L. M. White and O. L. Yarbrough; Minneapolis: Fortress Press, 1995), 3–15.

55. Elisabeth Schüssler Fiorenza, *In Memory of Her: A Feminist Theological Reconstruction of Christian Origins* (New York: Crossroad, 1983), 181–82.

56. The sense of "presiding" here does not imply a hierarchical office of elder or bishop; that is a later development to be seen in the Pastoral Epistles (see below). Rather, here it is a functional designation for service within the congregation; so Abraham J. Malherbe, *The Letters to the Thessalonians* (AB 32B; New York: Doubleday, 2000), 311–13. Malherbe elsewhere (*Paul and the Thessalonians* [Minneapolis: Fortress Press, 1987], 15) suggests that this might likely be a person of some means, like Jason in Acts 17:6, 9, who posted bond and hosted the congregation in his house. Compare also Rom 12:8, in which προϊστάμενος (*proïstamenos*) occurs in the context of other financial services (μεταδιδούς, *metadidous;* ἐλεῶν, *eleōn*) to the congregation listed among the hierarchy of charismatic gifts.

57. Robert Jewett (*The Thessalonian Correspondence: Pauline Rhetoric and Millenarian Piety* (Philadelphia: Fortress Press, 1986], 103) argues more explicitly for these leaders to be "house-church patrons and patronesses" based on the social profile of other congregations, but he sees in the exhortation of 5:12 evidence of resistance to their leadership.

58. The image of a patron or benefactor who "gives 'til it hurts" is, in fact, a commonplace in inscriptions honoring benefactors. Frederick Danker rightly identifies this as "the endangered benefactor motif" (*Benefactor: Epigraphic Study of a Graeco-Roman and New Testament Semantic Field* [St. Louis: Clayton, 1982], 417–35).

59. Robert Jewett, "Paul, Phoebe, and the Spanish Mission," in *The Social World of Formative Christianity and Judaism: Essays in Tribute to Howard Clark Kee* (ed. Jacob Neusner et al.; Philadelphia: Fortress Press, 1982), 142–61.

60. These pregnant Pauline terms may also be translated "communion" or "sharing," but the financial and patronal implications of the terms are often overlooked.

61. See J. Paul Sampley, *Pauline Partnership in Christ: Christian Community and Commitment in Light of Roman Law* (Philadelphia: Fortress Press, 1980), 11–20, 51–77.

62. See the discussion in White, "Morality between Two Worlds," 210–15; cf. Ken L. Berry, "The Function of Friendship Language in Philippians 4:10–20," in *Friendship, Flattery, and Frankness of Speech: Studies on Friendship in the New Testament World* (ed. John T. Fitzgerald; Leiden: E. J. Brill, 1996), 107–24; John T. Fitzgerald, "Philippians in the Light of Some Ancient Discussion of Friendship," in ibid., 141–60.

63. Peter Marshall, *Enmity in Corinth: Social Conventions in Paul's Relations with the Corinthians* (WUNT 2.23; Tübingen: Mohr-Siebeck, 1987), 130–64.

64. For the importance of the Roman colonial framework for understanding the patronal elements in the Corinthian situation, see John K. Chow, *Patronage and Power: A Study of Social Networks in Corinth* (JSNTSup 75; Sheffield, England: JSOT Press, 1992), 38–81.

65. For this reading and against the traditional interpretations that Onesimus was a runaway slave, see especially John Knox, *Philemon among the Letters of Paul* (Nashville: Abingdon, 1959), throughout; Sara C. Winter, "Methodological Observations on a New Interpretation of Paul's Letter to Philemon," *USQR* 39 (1984): 203–12; idem, "Paul's Letter to Philemon," *NTS* 33 (1987): 1–15; S. Scott Bartchy, "Philemon, Epistle to," *ABD* 5:305–10; Peter Lampe, "Keine 'Sklavenflucht' des Onesimus," *ZNW* 76 (1985): 135–37; Osiek and Balch, *Families in the New Testament World*, 175–78. I am not convinced, however, by Winter's proposal that Paul wanted Onesimus to work with him as a minister because of his gifts as a speaker. Paul also regularly uses *diakonia* to refer to the services of a patron, and this seems to me to be the implication of Phlm 13: ἵνα ὑπὲρ σοῦ μοι διακονῇ, *hina hyper sou moi diakonē* ("in order that he might serve me on your behalf"). Winter also argues that Onesimus had been delegated by the church to go to Paul in prison; however, even if such were true, one would guess that verse 13 (with its singular "you"; compare vv. 2, 5–6) suggests that Philemon himself was the real source. So, it may be that Philemon decided to help Paul in prison and sent his own domestic slave to carry out the task. On this we may well compare the situation of Epaphroditus (who is called ἀπόστολον καὶ λειτουργόν [*apostolon kai leitourgon*—"apostle and minister for my need" in prison]) on behalf of the church at Philippi (Phil 2:25–30, esp. v. 25). Lampe's interpretation (followed by Bartchy and Osiek and Balch) differs in suggesting that Onesimus had gotten in trouble with Philemon at home and had sought out Paul to intervene on his behalf. The crux for this interpretation is that Philemon has apparently suffered some "wrong" because of Onesimus (v. 18). While there is evidence for slaves seeking out a third party to mediate situations (as shown by Lampe), it is difficult to see how this would fit as easily with the occasion of Onesimus traveling to Ephesus on behalf of Philemon.

66. So notice especially verses 13–14: "[Onesimus] whom I wished to retain for myself, in order that he might minister on your behalf to me in my imprisonment for the gospel, but without your consent I wished to do nothing . . ." (my translation). It is possible that Paul's strong language here implies that he wanted to retain Onesimus as his own personal servant; cf. Osiek and Balch, *Families in the New Testament World*, 177.

67. See J. Albert Harrill, *The Manumission of Slaves in Early Christianity* (HUT 32; Tübingen: Mohr-Siebeck, 1995), 2–3, 127; Bartchy, "Philemon," 309.

68. The famous "I owe you" statement in verse 19 is part of this arrangement. The financial relationship between Philemon and Paul is also the implication of the "partnership" language in verse 17, where Paul asks for Onesimus to be welcomed back hospitably. Here I disagree with Bartchy ("Philemon," 308–9), who assumes that Paul was already acknowledged as Philemon's "patron" from the outset, because he had baptized him. In fact, it seems to me that this gambit on Paul's part is the central rhetorical twist of the letter.

69. For other interpretations of the birthing imagery here, see J. Louis Martyn, *Galatians* (AB 33A; New York: Anchor/Doubleday, 1997), 430–31; cf. Beverly Roberts Gaventa, "The Maternity of Paul: An Exegetical Study of Gal 4:19," in *The Conversation Continues: Studies in Paul and John in Honor of J. Louis Martyn* (ed. R. T. Fortna and B. R. Gaventa; Nashville: Abingdon Press, 1991), 189–201.

70. Hans Dieter Betz (*Galatians* [Hermeneia; Philadelphia: Fortress Press, 1979], 236–37) takes the passage as rhetorical artifice without much relevance either for Paul's theological conceptions or for the actual situation of the letter. For this reading of the passage, see L. M. White, "Rhetoric and Reality in Galatians: Framing the Social Demands of Friendship," in *Early Christianity and Classical Culture: Comparative Studies in Honor of Abraham J. Malherbe* (ed. J. T. Fitzgerald, T. H. Olbricht, and L. M. White; NovTSup 110; Leiden: E. J. Brill, 2003), 307–49.

71. Most commentators take this as a reference to God as "the one who supplies the Spirit"; so Betz, *Galatians,* 135; Martyn, *Galatians,* 285–86. Paul would surely say God is the ultimate source (so Gal 4:6; cf. 2 Cor 5:5). Yet, the parallelism with Gal 3:2 in reference to their "receipt" of the Spirit and the parallelism with the participial constructions of Gal 1:6 and 5:8, where Paul is clearly referring to himself as the active agent who "called" them to God, offer the possibility of reading Gal 3:5 as a reference to Paul's role in supplying the Spirit. See the discussion in White, "Rhetoric and Reality in Galatians," 332–36.

72. For "supply" (ἐπιχορηγεῖν, *epichorēgein*) as benefaction language, see Frederick W. Danker, *Benefactor: Epigraphic Study of a Graeco-Roman and New Testament Semantic Field* (St. Louis: Clayton, 1982), 331; for the phrase "the one who called you" (τοῦ καλεσάντος ἡμας, *tou kalesantos hēmas*) as reference to benefactor, see ibid., 452. Even if Paul views God as the ultimate source of these benefits, this still puts Paul in a position of supplying benefaction. The recent study of Stephan Joubert, *Paul as Benefactor: Reciprocity, Strategy, and Theological Reflection in Paul's Collection* (WUNT 2.124; Tübingen: Mohr-Siebeck, 2000), should be mentioned here, because he also sees Paul using the ideology and language of benefaction, especially in formulating ideas about the collection for Jerusalem. Joubert, however, distinguishes between the "systems" of patronage and benefaction based on their hierarchical versus reciprocal relations, respectively. He also argues that Roman patronage was not as operative in the Greek East (65). In keeping with this distinction, he finds Paul using the language of benefaction, not patronage, but his citation of evidence from Roman colonies such as Corinth is far too limited. For an alternative view see White, "Rhetoric and Reality in Galatians," 336n. 108.

73. Thus, the slogan in 7:1 may depend on his own earlier instructions on the subject, for which they are now seeking clarification. Paul's own view that the un-

married and ascetic life is better is clearly stated in 7:7, 9. For the situation in 1 Co-rinthians and its relation to ancient notions of sexuality, see Dale Martin, *The Co-rinthian Body* (New Haven: Yale University Press, 1995), 200–212.

74. For a good introduction to this ancient medical discussion, see Osiek and Balch, *Families in the New Testament World*, 103–11; see also Martha Nussbaum, *The Therapy of Desire: Theory and Practice in Hellenistic Ethics* (Princeton: Princeton University Press, 1994), throughout; and Teresa Shaw, *The Burden of the Flesh: Fasting and Sexuality in Early Christianity* (Minneapolis: Fortress Press, 1998), 27–77.

75. So David L. Balch, "Backgrounds of I Cor VII: Sayings of the Lord in Q, Moses as Ascetic *Theios Aner* in II Cor. III," *NTS* 18 (1971/72): 351–64.

76. Robin Scroggs, "Paul and the Eschatological Woman," *JAAR* 40 (1972): 283–303; cf. Schüssler Fiorenza, *In Memory of Her*, 224.

77. Musonius Rufus, *Dis.* 13A (ed. Hense, 67.6–68.1), my translation.

78. See n. 8 above.

79. Compare Plutarch, *Amatorius* (*Mor.* 750D–771C); cf. Osiek and Balch, *Families in the New Testament World*, 115.

80. It does not occur in the closing formulas in any of the genuine letters.

81. So 1 Tim 3:15 (cf. 3:5; 5:4; 2 Tim 2:20). See David C. Verner, *The Household of God: The Social World of the Pastoral Epistles* (SBLDS 71; Chico, Calif.: Scholars Press, 1983), 13–25, 83–111.

82. See Abraham J. Malherbe, " 'Gentle as a Nurse': The Cynic Background to Paul's Metaphor in 1 Thess. 2.7," in *Paul and the Popular Philosophers* (Minneapolis: Fortress Press, 1988), 35–48.

83. This is perhaps most clearly seen in a characteristic feature of the conversion stories in Acts, especially prominent in Acts 16–18. At the end of each of these episodes, Paul (or earlier, one of the other disciples) has encountered a main character, either male or female, who is won over by his preaching and/or miracles and is "baptized together with all his/her household" (Acts 7:10; 10:2; 11:14; 16:15, 31, 33; 17:33; 18:8). Taken together with the passages in Acts, it appears, then, that the author has constructed the conversion stories to show that Christian missionaries had not intruded into the household in inappropriate ways. Instead, Paul (and Peter) dealt directly with the *pater* or *mater familias*, who, in turn, authorized the new cult for the rest of the household. This thematic tendency reflects the new social plateau that Pauline Christianity had reached by the end of the first century, and the resultant apologetic point for the author of Luke–Acts was to show that Christians do not transgress the traditional boundaries of *patria potestas*. See L. M. White, "Visualizing the 'Real' World of Acts 16: Towards Construction of a Social Index," in *The Social World of the First Christians: Essays in Honor of Wayne A. Meeks* (ed. L. M. White and O. L. Yarbrough; Minneapolis: Fortress Press, 1995), 234–61.

84. David L. Balch, "Household Codes," in *Greco-Roman Literature and the New Testament* (ed. David E. Aune; SBLSBS 21; Atlanta: Scholars Press, 1988), 25–50. The formula originally came from Aristotelian political theory on household management. It was used extensively in religious and philosophical discussions and often carried an apologetic intent to show adherence to the accepted mores of society. See also Balch, *Let Wives Be Submissive: The Domestic Code in 1 Peter* (SBLMS 26; Chico, Calif.: Scholars Press, 1981), 68–82. See also Johannes Woyke,

Die neutestamentlichen Haustafeln: Ein kritischer und konstruktiver Forschungsüber-blick (Stuttgart: Katholisches Bibelwerk, 2000), 23–38.

85. Following Osiek and Balch, *Families in the New Testament World*, 118–19. Notice that the section on slaves (Col 3:22–25) has been expanded and gives even greater emphasis to *patria potestas*.

86. Osiek and Balch, *Families in the New Testament World,* 220. Cf. Schüssler Fiorenza, *In Memory of Her,* 250–70.

87. Cf. Schüssler Fiorenza, *In Memory of Her,* 286–94.

88. See also the discussion above under Part II ("Paul's House-Church Patrons: *Pater* and *Mater Familias*"). Cf. Malherbe, *Letters to the Thessalonians,* 313, and idem, *Social Aspects,* 99.

17

PAUL, PATRONS, AND CLIENTS

Peter Lampe

Part I. Patrons and Clients in the Greco-Roman World

When describing modern societies, we tend to think in horizontal categories: in social strata, in lower, middle, or upper classes. Horizontal layers also characterized the ancient society of the Roman Empire. At the same time, however, interaction between these strata divided society into vertical sections as well. The individual inhabitants of the Roman Empire lived in vertical relationships of dependency. These relationships were characterized by the reciprocal exchange of services and goods between those of lower social status and those above them. In fact, these vertical relationships defined a person's identity much more than his or her social contacts on the horizontal level. "I belong to Caesar's household," or, "This senator is my patron, and I support his political causes, while he protects my economical and legal interests." Such statements defined a person's identity, not statements such as "I belong to the working class." In general, class consciousness hardly existed in the Roman Empire. The cohesion, for example, among slaves or among lower-class people was very weak. Only the small social elite, the members of the three noble classes (senators, equestrians, and, to some extent, the *decuriones,* the local elite), developed cohesion among themselves and a "class consciousness."

The smallest vertical units in society were the individual households, the so-called *oikoi* (see "Paul, Families, and Households" [ch. 9] and "Paul and *Pater Familias*" [ch. 16] in this volume). At the hierarchical top resided the "father of the household," the *pater familias,* or, in some cases, a (widowed) woman, a *mater familias.*[1] All members of the household—wives, children, slaves, freed persons— were reverently and obediently oriented toward this patron at the top and were dependent on him (or her) in all crucial aspects of life,[2] while the patron was ex-

488

pected to protect, support, and love these dependents. The early Christian household codes followed this societal pattern.[3]

The small unit of the household for its part was tied into larger vertical-dependency relationships. If the *pater familias* was a freedman (*libertus*) or a so-called client (*cliens*), he was personally bound in his loyalty to another, even more superior patron.[4]

1. Freed slaves (*libertus, liberta*), even if they moved out of the former master's house and founded households and businesses of their own, were expected to remain respectful and loyal to him as a patron for the rest of their lives. Most of them stayed under the care of his legal guardianship, and most were obligated to fulfill unpaid services (*operae*) for their patron after manumission.[5] The patron, in return, was obliged to keep faith with his freed persons by providing them with legal aid, supporting them in need, and developing economic opportunities for them. The mutual loyalty went so far that neither the patron nor the freed person could be forced to testify against each other in court.

Although many of the freed persons were economically independent from their patron, sometimes accumulating great wealth for themselves, they nevertheless often also continued to work as agents or associates for their patron's businesses. In this way, large business clusters could emerge, "associations of households," which were involved in big, often supraregional businesses. These clusters included a great many freed persons who were active for their patron in many places in the empire. The family of the *Faenii,* for example, traded with fragrances and had business branches run by the family's freed persons in Capua, Puteoli, Rome, Ischia, and Lyon. With their freed slaves, the *Olitii* family was in business both in Rome and Narbo, the *Aponii* family both in Narbonne and Sicily. Freed persons of the senatorial *Laecanii* family owned large land tracts near (modern) Trieste; these freed persons in turn employed their own freed slaves in businesses in Italian ports—all of these businesspeople were extensions of the economically powerful senatorial family of the *Laecanii*. Other families of senators and the local aristocrats had freed persons or slaves working in the production and sales of textile materials or in the construction business. Thus, noble family masters, who as rich landowners were proud of not being "tainted" by craft or trade, nevertheless were able to participate in "dirty" but lucrative businesses through their slaves and freed persons. A business cluster of this caliber, based on patron-client relations, could profit from a whole production circle in one area: the landowner's flocks of sheep, for example, produced the wool, which was subsequently woven into fabric and sold by the landowner's slaves and freed persons.[6] Obviously, the patron-client relationships, which made these clusters possible, were of the highest economic importance—not only for the families involved but also for the entire society.

2. A *cliens*, on the other hand, usually was a freeborn person who entered a relationship of dependency with an influential patron. The two made a contract based on mutual trust and loyalty (*fides*). This meant that the client was expected to show respect and gratitude to the patron, to render certain services to him (*operae* and *obsequium*) and to support his political, economic, and social activities.[7] In return, the influential patron protected the client's economic, social, and legal interests by letting him profit from the patron's social connections and by allowing him access to the patron's resources.[8]

Patron-client relationships had existed for a long time in many places in the ancient Mediterranean world. Dionysius of Halicarnassus (*Ant. rom.* 2.9.2) mentions them, for example, in early Athens and Thessaly as well as in early Rome. Early Rome, however, was unique in that it clearly defined the rights and duties of clients and protected their status in relation to the patron; this was recorded already in the fifth-century B.C.E. Law of the Twelve Tables (8.21). In early Roman times, the contract between patron and client often involved the lending of land. Italian patricians established personal dependency relationships by giving small parcels of land (a *precarium*) to settlers for an indefinite period, maintaining the right to revoke this agreement at any time. With increasing urbanization, agricultural land became less important in patron-client relations. Whether land utilization was part of the contract or not, a client voluntarily[9] (or involuntarily)[10] subjected himself to the authority of the patron (*in fidem se dare*) who then accepted him (*in fidem suscipere*).

The voluntary client did not lose his personal freedom or his legal capacity but was obliged to allegiance and to carry out services for the patron.[11] He strengthened the patron's social prestige and supported his political goals. The patron in return vowed to protect and help the client in all his needs, provided free legal advice and representation,[12] and offered economic advantages. "To put the matter briefly," the patron was expected "to secure for them [the clients] both in private and in public affairs all that tranquillity of which they particularly stood in need," Dionysius writes.[13] Because both parties to the voluntary and private contract could be Roman citizens,[14] and because the client retained his freedom and legal responsibility, the aspect of power (*potestas*) of the patron over an inferior, obedient client increasingly faded into the background, while the moral aspect of reciprocal loyalty (*fides*) increased.[15]

On the basis of this system of vertical-dependency relationships between patrons and clients or freed persons, large portions of the society were tied to a few influential families during the Roman Republic: not only the masses of slaves and freed persons, but also numerous freeborn persons, sometimes even entire communities in Italy. Powerful and wealthy Roman families secured their societal and political influence through droves of clients in Italy and the provinces.[16] In fact, during the Roman Republic, political power to a large extent was based on the number of supporting clients one could count on in several strata of the society.[17]

In imperial times, the political influence of the noble families faded. Consequently, clientage became less a political factor but remained a social and economic institution. Unlike the freed persons who were tied to their patrons by clearly defined legal relations, clients' bond to their patrons was a very loose, *merely moral, social, and economic* dependency. Juridical implications were negligible; the patron-client relationship was legally irrelevant during imperial times.[18] Both sides voluntarily agreed upon it, and although it usually was hereditary,[19] it could be dissolved at any time. Often one client served several patrons at the same time.[20] Conversely, a patron usually had many clients—as a symbol of his power to provide for social inferiors. Dionysius (*Ant. rom.* 2.10.4) put it this way: "It was a matter of great praise to men of illustrious families to have as many clients as possible and not only to preserve the succession of hereditary patronages but also by their own merit to acquire others." In the first two-thirds of the first century C.E., the influential families still were very eager to increase their prestige through their clientele (Tacitus, *Ann.* 3.55.2; *Hist.* 1.4). The clients were a retinue for a rich patron, whose social status was reflected in the size of this following.[21] The patron in return saved the clients from unemployment and starvation.

In the morning, the clients presented themselves in the atrium of the patron's house and made their obeisances. In Rome, they were required to dress up in a toga for this occasion. During the day, they surrounded the patron as his entourage, accompanied him to the Forum, to the bath, or to his visits, joined him for his travels, clapped for his public speeches, and walked behind his sedan-chair.[22] They addressed him as *dominus* ("sir") or even *rex* ("king") and sometimes honored him with a statue.[23] In Pompeii, some actively supported their patrons' election campaigns for city offices.[24] These were time-consuming services. And most often clients were not enthusiastic about their "job." In cold weather, they cursed the early-morning walks across the city to the patron's house. They frowned when they were ranked lower than other clients at the patron's receptions or dinners. They deplored the lack of *fides* (loyalty). Martial, Juvenal, Lucian, and Epictetus continually report these numerous complaints.[25]

For their services, the clients were paid a *sportula* each day that they came to the patron's house. Originally, the *sportula* had been "a little basket," as the word is literally translated, containing food. In imperial times, however, the *sportula* often was pocket money. At the time of Martial, in the second half of the first century C.E., this usually amounted to twenty-five *asses*. For that amount of money, one could buy twelve and a half loaves of bread or six liters of good wine.[26] In other words, the *sportula* was a sort of private support for the unemployed.

In addition to the *sportula,* the patrons occasionally invited the clients to dinner. This was especially done at the festival of the Saturnalia. Now and then the clients were given a piece of clothing or some extra money. Sometimes they were offered a loan, legal aid, or a surety. Very rarely did they receive a whole farm as a gift or free lodging.[27] At the Saturnalia or on a birthday, clients usually offered little gifts, such as candles, to the patron in order to receive more valuable presents in return.[28]

In the realm of financial activities, there was no sophisticated banking system. Therefore, people tended to turn to friends, patrons, or clients rather than to banks in order to obtain advice, loans, or gifts. Aristocratic landowners, for example, when lacking cash for the financing of their careers, games, or electoral bribery, often asked not only superior patrons or equal friends but also inferior clients for loans. On the other hand, aristocrats exercised influence as creditors to friends and clients. Thus, an exchange between patrons and clients took place, both groups taking on the roles of creditors and borrowers. The social bond created by financial favors cannot be overestimated.[29] Loans and gifts helped raise the status both of the receiver *and* of the donor. The latter's prestige was raised by his or her generosity. And the former's need for money to finance a career or other status-raising activities was met.

At times the patron also helped a client retrieve money that had been lent to a third person. In order to protect the client's interests in these cases, the patron used his social connections to exercise social pressure on the borrower until everything was repaid.[30]

We are best informed about clients in the city of Rome. However, this form of patron-client relationship also existed in smaller Italian towns, such as Pompeii and in the provinces.[31]

Private support for the unemployed or financial gifts and loans were only one side of patronage and clientage in imperial times. Another was the active sponsoring of (talented) individual persons—much the same way that it is done today. This was an even looser form of patronage, without the daily *sportula,* and it could be found throughout the Roman Empire. A senator, for example, sponsored a sophist,[32] and a matron named Phoebe sponsored and supported the apostle Paul.[33] Naturally, patronal relations between teachers and students also developed, for example, between physicians and their students[34] or sophists and their students.[35]

In summary, *vertical* units of different sizes constituted society and prevented the development of horizontal class consciousness below the ranks of the nobility. These vertical units prevented the lower population from developing homogeneous interests. Neither the freed persons nor the clients formed a "class."[36] To a large extent, the members of the non-noble societal strata were distinguished from each other by *vertical* demarcation lines, created by the dependencies on different patrons and their households.[37]

These vertical connections helped increase the clients' chances for *upward social mobility*. Personal social advancement was largely influenced by the loyalty toward a patron whose connections and resources could be helpful for ambitious clients. Municipal aristocrats, for example, had no chance of moving up socially without the patronal protection of some members of the senatorial or equestrian ranks.[38]

One important characteristic of the patron-client relation was that power (*potestas*) was much less emphasized than mutual loyalty (*fides, πίστις [pistis]*). The latter confined the display of power. In this way, reciprocal give-and-take relationships could develop that suited the interests of both partners in this vertical interaction. In the middle of the first century C.E., these relationships still served the superiors' interests in prestige and the inferiors' desire for social protection. Later, patron-client relationships increasingly failed in meeting these goals.

3. Not only individual persons were clients. Also clubs, entire communities, even provinces could obtain the client status. Rome's supremacy over subjected territories often was interpreted as patronage (*deditio in dicionem et fidem populi Romani*).[39] Conquerors of provinces and founders of colonies became their "patrons."[40] Cities selected influential senators, former municipal authorities, or other distinguished personalities to be their patrons. These patrons represented the community's political and legal interests, sponsored its various activities, particularly its building projects, and were generous with donations.[41] Sometimes a city selected several patrons simultaneously.[42] We are able to identify more than 1,200 city patrons of this kind between about 70 B.C.E. and 300 C.E. in the Roman Empire.[43] In addition, patrons of religious and professional associations (*collegia,* clubs) were numerous. They excelled in donations, gifts, and the financing of banquets. And the more distinguished they were, the more they raised the social prestige of the club and its members. Women, too, often were the patrons of religious associations.[44] The profit that the patrons received from these relationships was prestige: their grateful clients praised them in inscriptions and immortalized them in statues.

4. The emperor, of course, was considered the most prestigious patron. His clientele included his freed persons, the urban Roman *plebs,* the soldiers of the army and fleet, and the members of the local elite in the provinces. Senators and equestrians were often called *amici,* friends on an equal level. However, this was mere diplomatic language, because they were in fact clients, too.

Finally, the entire population of the Roman Empire was seen as being in a patronal relationship with the emperor, who was considered the *pater patriae,* the "father of the country." Dion of Prusa depicted the ideal ruler as someone who "sees the social care for the people not as a triviality or a mere hassle . . . , but rather as his personal task and his profession. If he is busy with something else, he feels that he is doing something unimportant" (Or. 3.55).[45] Of course, many emperors did not live up to this ideal. Nevertheless, as *defensor plebis* ("defender of the common people"), the emperor looked after the *plebs* in the city of Rome with donations of money and grain; after earthquakes, he offered financial help to communities for rebuilding. The examples are well known and could easily be augmented.

Also in this special patron-client relationship, the clients were of course obliged to show their loyalty to the patron, by rendering "to Caesar the things that are Caesar's"—by paying taxes, also by taking oaths of allegiance (e.g., ILS 190), or worshiping the emperor in the imperial cult (e.g., ILS 112). But it is clear that the second half of the above-quoted early Christian text, "give to God the things that are God's" (Matt. 22:21), focuses on a second, competing pyramid, with God at the apex. In times of political stress, such as the threat that the writer of Revelation perceived in Domitian, who wanted to be worshiped by pagans as well as Christians, this second patron-client relationship competed mightily with the first. The *Clausula Petri* (Acts 5:29) also did not exclude such a competition. The early Christians developed the concept of an alternative pyramid with alternative loyalties. It was explosive, and, in Revelation, it led to the provocative thesis that the pagan pyramidal Greco-Roman system, with Satan, the emperor, and the priests of the imperial cult at the apex, merely mimicked the triad of God, Christ, and the Holy Spirit.[46]

There is no doubt that the alternative pyramid with God and Christ at the top was just as real for the early Christians as was the pyramid presided over by the emperor. For them, the risen *Kyrios* represented just as real a personal and social entity as the emperor himself. Thus, according to their perception, both pyramids were on the same level. The possible modern reproach that different categories are mixed here, and that human society and the religious world cannot be placed in competition with each other on the same level, would have perplexed the early Christians, leaving them shaking their heads.

Part II. Patron and Client in Paul's Letters

Pagan sources that illuminate patron-client relationships most often focus on aristocratic patrons from Rome and the provinces. Patrons and clients of lower social standing left less record of their activities; these have been found mainly in the inscriptions and the Egyptian papyri, but also in Pauline Christianity. In Pauline

Christianity, patron-client relationships can be found both between individuals and between individuals and groups. However, at the same time, these vertical relationships were also questioned as being problematic. Two seemingly contradictory tendencies therefore coexisted in Pauline Christianity.

Egalitarian Tendencies

In Gal 3:27–28, Paul refers to the early Christian understanding of baptism. In baptism and in the postbaptismal existence, worldly differences among the baptized become irrelevant; regardless of their worldly status, all who are baptized are assured of the same closeness to Christ. Without differentiation, all Christians are "children of God through faith" (3:26).[47] Whatever the worldly differences among the Galatians may be, they are abolished. "There is neither Jew nor Greek, slave nor free, male nor female" (3:28).

The text differentiates between two social contexts that stand both beside and in opposition to each other. On the one hand, there is the worldly, Hellenistic-Roman context in which Jews and Greeks are differentiated from each other, as well as the not legally free from the free, and the men from the women. On the other hand, the Christian community has changed the paradigm. In the new social context of the Christians, these differentiations among people were no longer made. In the house churches and in the Christians' interactions with each other, such worldly differences, vertical or horizontal, were considered irrelevant, so that the one person stood equal to the other.[48]

This was the egalitarian maxim in Pauline Christianity. On the other hand, however, there *were* vertical relationships even within Pauline Christianity. And we will have to ask how far the principal of equality radiated into these social relationships and possibly modified them.

Patrons as a Basis of Early Christian Church Life

The Christian patrons and their private households played a most vital role in the life of the early church. In the first two centuries C.E., almost the only real estate that the church used was the private rooms of patrons.[49] Church-owned buildings and land did not exist before the third or even fourth centuries. Only in the third century C.E. were so-called "homes of the church" (*domus ecclesiae*) set up, that is, special rooms that were reserved exclusively for worship purposes. In the first two centuries, the Christian congregations or "house churches" met in private rooms in the homes of patrons. These rooms, of course, were used for everyday purposes by their owners or tenants during the week.[50] Thus, in the first and second centuries the church existed not *beside* Christian patrons' private households,

it existed exclusively *in* them. This service rendered by the Christian house owners was praised accordingly, and the virtue of hospitality was emphasized. Those
who opened their homes were greatly appreciated—whether they had houses or
only apartments such as the one on the third floor of a tenement house in Troas
(Acts 20:8–9) or Justin's rental apartment "above Myrtinus' bath" in Rome.[51]

Usually, all of the Christians in a city could not fit into one private household.
Therefore, several house churches coexisted in the bigger cities in New Testament
times. In Corinth and its harbor satellite town Cenchreae, groups crystallized in
the homes of Stephanas, Gaius, Titius Justus, Crispus, and Phoebe. In the capital
city of Rome, at least seven Christian circles can be identified in the middle of the
first century C.E. In the Lycus Valley in Asia Minor, in the area of Colossae-
Laodicea-Hierapolis, Christians met at the dwelling of Nympha or at Philemon's
house.[52]

We know of only one early central meeting place where all the Christians of
one city sometimes assembled: Gaius's home in Corinth.[53] Other cities did not
have plenary meetings of several house churches, certainly not Rome. The structure of the early church was thus fragmented; *several* house churches met in one
city. That is, *several* patrons hosted church meetings, and no single patron gained
a monopoly of the leadership in one city. This fragmented church structure was indeed one of the reasons why a central church government headed by a city bishop
evolved relatively late. In Rome, for instance, it was not until the second half of the
second century C.E. that city bishops emerged who at least *tried* to subject all Christian groups of the city of Rome to their leadership and patronage. They were not
always successful in their attempts, not even Victor, whose tenure fell into the last
decade of the second century. Before the middle of the second century, we only encounter leaders of individual house churches in Rome, but no sole, central
bishop.[54] A similar development can be observed in the eastern part of the Roman
Empire. There, the city bishops did not emerge before the first decades of the second century. Ignatius, for example, called himself the only bishop of Antioch. But
whether these sole city bishops of early times were always acknowledged as such
by all of the Christians in the town is doubtful; also in the east, some Christians
did not want to be under the "bishop."[55] And still at the end of the second century,
at least the church of Ancyra in Asia Minor was led by a group and not by a single city bishop.[56] Neither from the New Testament documents nor *First Clement*
nor the *Shepherd of Hermas* can it be proved that the term "bishop" implied a sole
central leader of the Christians in one city. All these writings still reflect a collegial
church leadership: a number of people governed the church in each city.[57] And this
had to do with the fragmented structure of the church, represented by multiple
house churches that were hosted by *multiple* patrons.

To summarize, *the hosts of congregational meetings,* of house churches, can be construed as patrons of these congregations. As parallels in the Hellenistic world we see political communities and pagan religious associations that enjoyed the patronage of individual (often female) benefactors and sponsors. It would be fair to say that all early Christian hosts who opened their homes for Christian house-church gatherings were "patrons."[58]

Did these patrons of small house churches hold a position *over* the other church members in Pauline Christianity? As far as we know, the answer is no. There was no static vertical subordination under these patrons. Christian patronage did not automatically imply a hierarchical structure. The early Christian social relationships were more dynamic and less clearly defined.

1. It would be a misconception to infer from their role as hosts that these patrons also were the leaders of the congregational meetings. According to 1 Cor 12 and 14, especially 12:28, the function of steering and leading the Corinthian congregation was not yet tied to one specific person, not even to a fixed group of persons. No one presided at the Corinthian worship services. No individual leader was responsible for its order, for its beginning, for the sequence of its elements (cf. also 1 Cor 11:17–32). The *whole* congregation was responsible (14:26ff.). Thus, the worship service was spontaneous and sometimes even chaotic. The Holy Spirit led. And everybody whom the Spirit inspired could perform "leading acts" (12:28, κυβερνήσεις [*kyberneseis*]) in the congregation. Without a doubt this included the hosts, but was not exclusive to them. The task of leading was still in many hands.

2. Paul had not a vertical but a symmetrical model in mind when he asked all Christians for *mutual respect*, for *mutual love*, and for φιλαδελφία (*philadelphia*, Rom 12:10; cf. Gal 5:13). It is significant that this symmetrical model stands in the immediate context of the "patrons" who take care of the economically weak Christians and who open their houses as hosts (Rom 12:13).

3. More than once, Paul had to admonish congregations to *respect* their leaders who had worked hard for them and to subordinate themselves (ὑποτάσσησθε [*hypotassesthe*]) to them (1 Thess 5:12–13; 1 Cor 16:16). Apparently, there was a lack of proper respect for those who performed "leading acts" (κυβερνήσεις [*kyberneseis*; cf. 1 Cor 12:28]). Did the maxim of Gal 3:28 play a role in this? This is very probable. According to 1 Tim 6:2, Christian slaves often tended to show less respect for their masters if the latter were Christian brothers. The maxim of Gal 3:28 (cf. Col 3:11, also James 2:1–5) seems to have been realized to a certain extent in the life of the congregations—even to such an extent that Paul and the author of 1 Timothy felt obliged to steer in the opposite direction once in a while. Even though pa-

trons and leaders were merely "brothers" and "sisters" in the house-church context, some subordination and respect for those who performed "leading acts" and opened their homes for worship meetings seemed appropriate in Paul's eyes. For love among equals also entails "serving" others and self-denial (1 Cor 8; 13; Phil 2:5ff., etc.). Whoever *insists* on his or her rights and status, insisting that she or he is "equal" to (or even "better" than) others, does not live according to Christ's example of being ready to renounce his status for the benefit of others.

To summarize, in early Pauline Christianity, there were no clear-cut and rock-solid static vertical relationships. Things were more dynamic. The same can be observed once we look at the social relationships in which Paul himself worked and lived.

Patrons of Paul

Like the early church as a whole, Paul in his missionary work relied on several patrons who supported his apostolic mission by hosting and encouraging him, by providing helpers for him[59] and an audience that also included the dependents of these patrons. Lydia in Philippi, a well-to-do importer of luxury textiles, was baptized by Paul, hosted him and his entourage in her house, and also arranged the baptism of her dependents (Acts 16:14–15). She certainly was one of the sponsors who enabled the Philippian congregation to send money to Paul more than once to support his missionary work in other cities (Phil 4:10, 14–18; 2 Cor 11:9). In Thessalonica, a certain Jason supported Paul and Silas by hosting them in his house and shielding them against the local mob (Acts 17:5, 7). Several ladies of the local aristocracy in Thessalonica, several respected women and men in Beroea, and some of the local elite in Athens such as Dionysius and Damaris allegedly also became adherers of Paul's preaching (Acts 17:4, 12, 34) and may well have supported him, although we do not have direct information about this.[60] In Corinth, a certain Titius Justus opened his house for Paul's teaching activities (Acts 18:7), and Gaius hosted him when he wrote the Letter to the Romans (Rom 16:23). The mother of Rufus in Rome also was once a "mother" to Paul when she stayed in the east of the empire (Rom 16:13).[61]

The only person for whom Paul explicitly used the term "patron" (προστά-τις/*prostatis*) was Phoebe in Cenchreae, as we already saw (Rom 16:1–2). As a "patroness," she supported and sponsored "many" Christians, including Paul. Paul may have enjoyed the hospitality of her house in Cenchreae for a while when he was working in Corinth. She also seems to have opened her house for the meetings of the local house church of Cenchreae (16:1b).

However, Phoebe's support for local Christians did not really establish a vertical relationship. In the same passage she is also called "our sister" and "servant" (διάκονος/ *diakonos*) of the house church in Cenchreae. And when she traveled to Rome, the Roman Christians were supposed to support her dealings in Rome—as a patron would do. Thus, the roles of patron and client were reversed in this case, with Phoebe being the "client," if one really wanted to apply the patron-client model to this support relationship. The same is even truer for the relationship between Paul and Phoebe. On the one hand, Phoebe was a "patroness" for Paul (16:2c). On the other hand, Paul was an apostle, the founder of the Corinthian church, and, in Rom 16:1–2, he writes a short letter of recommendation in favor of Phoebe. That is, *he* assumes the role of patron here, wanting to make sure that the Roman Christians receive her well and support her in all that she needs during her visit in Rome. Thus, the roles of patron and client were not static, vertical-dependency relationships in early Pauline Christianity, but could even be reversed. This fact underscores that the principal equality of all Christians formulated in Gal 3:28 was no mere theory in the Pauline churches.

Because Phoebe was the only one for whom the technical term "patron" was specifically used, we may assume that this dynamic character of patron-client relationships also held true for the other patrons of Paul listed above.

It certainly held true for Paul's relationship to Prisca and Aquila. As patrons they supported his missionary work in Corinth by housing him and giving him a job in their workshop (Acts 18:2–3). As patrons they hosted house churches in Ephesus (1 Cor 16:19) and Rome (Rom 16:5). They "risked their necks" for Paul's life (Rom 16:4); this probably occurred during their stay in Ephesus, where Paul was exposed to serious dangers (1 Cor 15:32; 2 Cor 1:8–9). "All" Gentile Christian churches owed them thanks (Rom 16:4). On the other hand, Paul was more than just their "client." In 1 Cor 16:19, it sounds like that they were more Paul's coworkers in Ephesus than his "patrons." And in Rom 16:3, just one verse after Phoebe had been called a "patron," the couple was *not* labeled with this term but with the attribute "my coworkers." At least at the time of the Letter to the Romans, a *symmetrical* relationship had evolved between Paul and this couple. "Coworker" could even be used for helpers *subordinate* to Paul.[62] Thus, again, the vertical relations could be turned upside down, exemplifying the principle of the equality of all Christians.

This can be also illustrated for Gaius and Paul: Gaius on the one hand sponsored Paul's activities in Corinth and hosted the apostle (Rom 16:23). The apostle, on the other hand, had baptized this "patron" (1 Cor 1:14) and thus had sponsored his faith.[63]

The flexibility of relationships can also be illustrated by Paul's relationship to Barnabas. Barnabas was older than Paul and seems to have called Paul to Antioch, introducing him to the Christians of that city (Acts 11:25–26; cf. 9:26f.). He seems to have been a patron for Paul in these early years. Being more experienced and influential in the church than the newly converted Saul, Barnabas might even have played a fatherly role for Paul at the beginning.[64] Paul, however, soon seems to have turned out to be the more successful missionary, and this changed their relationship into a symmetrical one, as we can see during the so-called apostolic council (Gal 2:1, 7–9).[65] Paul even seems to have become the speaker and leader (Gal 2:2, 5–8) until they separated (Gal 2:13; cf. Acts 15:36–40).

The ambiguity of this example is due to dynamic developments within the relationship of the two men. And this is the main point that we learn from this ambiguity: the patron's position in Pauline Christianity is not rigid, with one always over the other. Sometimes the patron appears equal to the client; sometimes the "patron" and "client" can even change roles.

Other Apostles as Patrons of Paul?

How did Paul define his relationship to the other apostles who had been disciples of Jesus of Nazareth during his lifetime and who had been apostles long before Paul was converted? In 1 Cor 15:8–9, Paul confesses: "Last of all, as to one untimely born, He appeared to me also. For I am the least of the apostles, and not fit to be called an apostle, because I persecuted the church of God." Two to three years after his conversion, Paul traveled to Jerusalem, where he talked with Peter for fifteen days and met James. Were these two apostles therefore "patrons" of the newcomer Paul, instructing him, teaching him what it was like to be an apostle, and sending him into his missionary work? No, although being the least of all, Paul claimed to be an apostle *directly* dependent on Christ and not on any of the other apostles (Gal 1:11–12, 16–17). Only to Christ and God did he feel responsible and accountable as a "slave," "servant," or "steward" (Rom 1:1, 9; 1 Cor 4:1–2); that is, only in this relationship was there a vertical subordination that could be compared to patron-client structures.

Paul as Patron of Coworkers and Congregations

How is Paul's relationship to his other coworkers (besides Prisca and Aquila) and to his congregations to be defined?[66] What kind of leadership style did he exercise? Were these relationships strictly vertical, or did they also incorporate symmetrical elements that reflected the principal equality of all Christians? Did he leave room for situations in which equality was made manifest?

After the separation from Barnabas, Paul surrounded himself with helpers who traveled with him, preached with him, coauthored letters with him, and who were sent by him to congregations: Silas, Timothy, Titus, Erastus, Urbanus, Epaphroditus, Sosthenes, Tertius, Clement, Euodia, Syntyche, the travel companions Aristarchus, Gaius from Derbe, Sopater, Secundus, Tychicus, and Trophimus, along with anonymous persons.[67] Some of them were sent by congregations.[68]

The question of Paul's leadership style has often been addressed and answered along the lines of a predominantly "democratic" style.[69] However, after Walter Rebell's thorough analysis using social-psychological categories, a damper has been put on this optimism.[70] There is no room here to go into the details of this extended discussion. To sum up its result: the material that reflects Paul's leadership behavior sends out ambiguous signals. On the one hand, the apostle leaves room for his congregations to develop a certain degree of independence. They may, for instance, choose on their own among alternative ethical options.[71] Paul also stressed the φιλαδελφία (*philadelphia*), the love between equal brothers and sisters, which should dominate life within the churches.[72] But on the other hand, Paul styles himself as their "father,"[73] to whom they owe "service" (λειτουργία/*leitourgia,* Phil 2:30) and "lasting obedience," as Walter Rebell words it.[74] He locates Paul in "a middle position between democratic and authoritarian leadership style," but he also has serious doubts that we really may speak about a "leadership style" in view of Paul's complex and ambiguous leadership behavior.

The ambiguity of Paul's leadership can be illustrated by his relationship to Philemon. As "coworker," Philemon was subordinate to the apostle, for Paul had initiated Philemon into Christianity and could have "ordered" Philemon "to do what is proper" if he had wanted to (Phlm 1, 8, 19). Paul, however, refrained from "ordering": "For love's sake I rather appeal to you" (v. 9); "without your consent I did not want to do anything, so that your goodness would not be, in effect, by compulsion but of your own free will" (v. 14). This "appeal" at first glance seems to have put less pressure on Philemon, but at second glance it did not. The pressure only became more subtle and less direct this way. A little later Paul makes clear that he "has confidence" in Philemon's "*obedience*" (v. 21)—a statement that kept up the level of pressure to comply with Paul's wishes. The ambiguity of the relationship becomes even more obvious once we see Philemon taking on the role of patron. As a host of a house church (vv. 1–2) and as a host of Paul himself (v. 22), Philemon also was a "patron" not only of other Christians, but also of Paul. In Paul's eyes, the ambiguity of this relationship was best summarized by the symmetrical terms "brother" (vv. 7, 20) and "partner" (v. 17).[75]

Paul as Onesimus's Patron

The Letter to Philemon confronts us with still another type of patronage. Philemon had suffered a material loss in his household; we do not know the details (maybe something precious was broken). Philemon accused his slave of this damage. Onesimus, the slave, was afraid of his master's wrath and chose to do something that often was done by slaves in similar situations, as legal texts show:[76] He left the master's house not in order to run away but to go to a friend of his master, in this case to the apostle Paul, and asked him to take a mediating role in this conflict. Paul was asked to put in a good word for Onesimus; that is, he was asked to take on a temporary patronage or advocate's role. Paul accepted this role and wrote the Letter to Philemon, vigorously asking Philemon to swallow his anger and to accept Onesimus with love as a brother.

This temporary patron-client relationship between Paul and Onesimus was clearly vertical. And Paul used his patronage to convert the slave to Christianity and to teach him the Christian faith. However, in the course of his letter, Paul puts these vertical categories in another perspective by using symmetrical terms, thus undermining the absoluteness of vertical structures. The apostle claims that Onesimus is equal to him, "a beloved brother, especially to me, but how much more to you" (v. 16). Paul even identifies with Onesimus: "If then you regard me a partner, accept *him* as you would *me* (v. 17); "I have sent him back to you in person, that is, sending *my* very heart" (v. 12); "if he has wronged you in any way or owes you anything, charge that to *my* account" (v. 18). Also by emphasizing his own imprisonment frequently (vv. 1, 9, 10, 13, 23), Paul puts himself on the same level as the enslaved Onesimus. In Christ, those who in worldly eyes are super- or subordinated to each other become equal brothers. Philemon therefore is expected to receive Onesimus as an equal and beloved brother (vv. 16–17). He is expected to redefine his social relationship with Onesimus—not only during worship services but also "in the flesh" (v. 16), in everyday life. That is, he is expected to put aside his secular social role as master of a slave or (in case he decided to free Onesimus) as patron of a freed man. He is expected to make this continuing worldly difference irrelevant in his interactions with Onesimus—which corresponds exactly to the maxim of Gal 3:28. This maxim can be filled with life when superordinate persons such as Paul and Philemon renounce their privileged status.

To sum up the paradoxical result: in the Letter to Philemon, Paul *uses* his role as advocate and patron to *abolish* the relevance of such vertical hierarchies in inner-Christian social life.

Congregations as Patrons?

In Rom 15:24, 28, Paul hopes that the Roman Christians will sponsor his missionary work in Spain, possibly by providing travel companions, food or money for the trip, perhaps also by arranging means of transportation (προπέμπω/*propempō*). Such sponsoring of travel activities by local congregations can also be seen elsewhere. Paul expects the Corinthians to support Timothy's trip from Corinth to Ephesus (1 Cor 16:11) and his own trip to Judea (2 Cor 1:16; cf. 1 Cor 16:6). On this journey to Judea, with the money collected for Jerusalem in his bags, he is indeed accompanied by representatives of the congregations that had donated money for Jerusalem. These delegates of Macedonian and Achaian churches supported him on this trip. Through their presence, they also guaranteed and documented to any possible critics that everything in connection with this money transaction was handled properly (2 Cor 8:19–23; Acts 20:4–6).

When Paul founded the Thessalonian and Corinthian churches, the Philippian congregation sponsored these missionary activities (2 Cor 11:8–9; Phil 4:14–16). From a one-sided perspective, this sponsoring of apostolic journeys by congregations—through personnel or materials—could be interpreted as temporary *patronage,* with Paul or his coworker Timothy being *clients* of the sponsoring churches. However, and here the above-mentioned ambiguity starts again, Paul also was the founder, the "father," of the same congregations (see above). Thus, the patron-client roles were exchangeable. There was no one-sided vertical relationship between Paul and his churches. Once again, this fact illustrates the principle of equality in early Christian social life. The more adequate category, therefore, would not be the patron-client model but rather that Paul and his congregations were partners connected by friendship (*amicitia,* φιλαδελφία/*philadelphia;* see above). Of course, symmetrical relationships could include sponsoring activities; friends in the Greco-Roman world supported and helped each other. Especially the Philippians, who sponsored Paul's work more than any other congregation did, had a warm *amicitia* relationship with Paul, which was based on equality and reciprocity (Phil 2:25–30).[77]

In Corinth, Paul refused to take money from the local Christians when he founded their church; they did not understand this brusque refusal (1 Cor 9; 2 Cor 11:9–12; 12:13). What were his motivations? He preached the gospel about God's free gift of grace, and he did this at no charge; the content and form of his preaching corresponded. By refusing support, Paul also avoided any dependencies on local donors that could be misunderstood as patron-client relationships. As a preacher, he remained free of having to please anybody to whom he "owed" something.[78] Whether these aspects were only subconscious motivations of his refusal or deliberate intentions, we do not know. Several other factors motivated his refusal as well. By preaching at no cost, he wanted to avoid any obstacle to the spread of the gospel (1 Cor 9:12b; 2 Cor 11:9). Furthermore, God's will and not Paul's own forced him to preach; therefore, he felt uncomfortable taking reimbursement for his work (1 Cor 9:16–17). Also, he wanted to demonstrate that a Christian has to be free to forgo the use of one's rights if necessary—in this case, he did not insist on the missionary's right to be fed by those for whom he preached (1 Cor 9 in the context of chs. 8 and 10). Whatever Paul's conscious motivation might have been to refuse any support from the Corinthians during his stay in Corinth, his refusal in any case prevented the development of a patron-client relationship with any local donor in Corinth.

The relationship between the church in Jerusalem on the one hand and the Pauline congregations on the other was a problematic case. According to 2 Cor 9:12, 14 and Rom 15:26–27, 30–31, the purpose of the money collection in the Pauline churches of Macedonia and Achaia was to ease the economic need of the Jerusalem Christians. At first glance, it seems that the Pauline congregations took on the role of a patron for the Jerusalem church. However, this was not Paul's intention. His aim was a symmetrical, egalitarian relation. In 2 Cor 9:14 and Rom 15:27, he emphasized that the Jerusalem church, being older, let the Pauline congregations "share in their spiritual things"[79] and often prayed for the Pauline Christians. Therefore, the latter were "indebted" to the Jerusalem church (Rom 15:27). In Paul's eyes, reciprocity was guaranteed. Even more important, Paul understood the collection of money as an economic balancing on the horizontal level; according to him, the money collection specifically aimed at *equality* (ἰσότης/*isotēs*) in economic things (2 Cor 8:13–14). For in the future, when the Jerusalem Christians might perhaps have more financial means than the Pauline churches, they would donate in return: "this present time your abundance is a supply for their need, so that their abundance also may become a supply for your need, that there may be equality."

However, the Jerusalem Christians looked at the Pauline collection of money differently. From what we know, they most likely *rejected* this financial gift,[80] even though they were in need of money. In Rom 15:31, Paul had feared this disastrous outcome of the collection. And Luke did not know anything about a successful ending of it, although he knew about the offering (Acts 24:17) and although he usually liked to report success stories, even where it was inappropriate to do so.[81]

In the first place, Jerusalem's rejection of the money offering was theologically motivated. In the time since the apostolic council (Gal 2:3, 5–9), antagonism had started to color the relationship between the apostle of the Gentiles and the Jerusalem Christians. In the explosive situation in Palestine before the Jewish War, the Jewish Christians of Judea felt increasing pressure from their Jewish neighbors to prove their Jewish identity, especially in their obedience to the Torah. In this situation, a gospel free from the Law increasingly did not fit into the picture, and it became more advisable for the Jerusalem Christians to begin to distance themselves from Paul and his congregations. Presumably, this was one of the reasons they rejected Paul's money offering, which was meant to be a symbol of *koinōnia* and unity between Jerusalem and Paul's Torah-free congregations (Gal 2:9–10).

A second reason for the rejection of Paul's money offering is also plausible.[82] By accepting the support, the Jerusalem church would have run the risk of becoming a recipient of charity, of becoming a client of the economically stronger Pauline congregations in Macedonia and Achaia. The symmetry, the status of equals that was once established at the Jerusalem council (Gal 2), would have been lost. Consciously or subconsciously, the Jerusalem church avoided such a patron-client relationship when it rejected the offering of the Pauline churches.[83]

To summarize, wherever we encountered vertical patron-client structures in the social life of Pauline Christianity, they were in conflict with the strong early Christian feeling that horizontal symmetry and equality should govern the social interactions of Christians. This maxim constantly questioned and undermined top-to-bottom social structures and often led to ambiguity in social relationships.

The early Christian communities were not unique in this respect. Pagan Greco-Roman clubs also often combined hierarchical and egalitarian elements and thus departed from the strongly hierarchical patterns of their social environment.[84] The Christians' religious reasons for this departure, however, were unique. The vertical structures were a given in the Hellenistic world in which the early Christians continued to live. Equality, on the other hand, characterized the coming of the new world that was expected by the Christians and that was believed to have manifested itself partially already in the present. According to the early Christians, since the coming of Jesus of Nazareth, the old and the new aeons overlapped until the coming of the eschaton, when the old aeon with its worldly structures would disappear. Thus, wherever the new aeon became manifest already in the present time, wherever people interacted lovingly in relationships of equality, the eschaton was realized at least in a fragmentary way.

The theological reason for the early Christians' equality was their relationship to God: all were considered equally close to God. Thus, the only theologically legitimate vertical structure was God's relation to humanity.

God and Christ as Patrons

An analogy can be drawn between the patron-client model and the relationship that Christ has with Christians. Christ is their Lord (e.g., Rom 1:4; 10:9, 12; 14:6–9, 14; 1 Cor 1:3). They are joined to him (Rom 7:4; cf. 1 Cor 3:23). They live for him and not for themselves (Rom 14:7–8; 2 Cor 5:15). Christ intercedes for the Christians before God (Rom 8:34; cf. 8:27), as a patron seeks the advance of his client in forensic and other social contexts.

The nexus between Christ and the Christians can also be expressed in the category of "corporate representation" (1 Cor 15:20–22; Rom 5:12–19). This category exhibits at least similarities to a patron-client relationship. According to Paul, both Adam and Christ represent two different aeons. They embody whole groups. Each one of them represents many people, and the acts of each determine the destiny of many: Adam sinned, and therefore all humans are unable to evade sin and must die. Christ's act of righteousness on the cross, on the other hand, leads to justification of many, provided that they accept *Christ as their representative* and make Christ's attribute of being righteous their own attribute. Their righteousness then comes from Christ and not from their own achievements. Applied to resurrection, the category of "corporate representation" means that because God raised Christ from the dead, and because Christ is the *representative* of a whole new aeon, all people of this new aeon—the Christians (1 Cor 15:23b)—will be raised by God, too.

Thus, Christ elevates the eschatological status of Christian persons: they will be eternally saved, reigning with Christ, and made similar to Christ. That is, like a secular patron, Christ promotes the upward mobility of his clients—an upward mobility that depends on the loyalty (πίστις/*pistis, fides*) of the clients toward the patron *and* on the loyalty of the patron toward the clients.

Because loyalty is a *mutual* attitude in patron-client relationships, the question whether the expression πίστις Ἰησοῦ Χριστοῦ (*pistis Iesou Christou*, Phil 3:9; Gal 2:16, 20) represents a subjective or an objective genitive might pose false alternatives, because it is both. Not by *our* "works of the Law," but because *Christ* was faithful and loyal and because *we* faithfully believe in this Christ, we are justified.[85]

All these statements establishing a vertical patron–client-like relationship between Christ and the Christians, however, are counterbalanced by texts that emphasize Christ's "brotherhood" in regard to the Christians,[86] his humility, which allowed him to "empty himself" for the benefit of the Christians, and to "take upon him the form of a servant" (e.g., Phil 2:6–8). So even here in the Christ–Christian relationship, an *ambiguity* arises. The Christian idea of lordship and patronage includes the willingness to serve and to break open static, vertical structures (cf., e.g., 2 Cor 8:9; Phil 2:7).

Last but not least, God's role as it is pictured in Rom 1–5 can be interpreted in analogy to the patron-client-model,[87] although Paul himself does not use these technical terms. As creator, God expects exclusive loyalty (πίστις/*pistis*) from all human beings. Like clients, they are expected to "praise" and "thank" God (Rom 1:21), and if they fail to do so the patron's wrath is legitimate (1:18). The divine patron for his part shows his own loyalty by bestowing an act of beneficence (χάρις/*charis*): God reconciles humanity through the death of Christ (e.g., Rom 3:25; 5:8; 8:3) and "provides the believer with a new status (δικαιόω [*dikaioō*]) and unprecedented access (προσαγωγή [*prosagōgē*])."[88] In human patron-client relationships, acts of benefaction reinforce the difference in status between the benefactor and the client. This is also Paul's concern in Rom 1:23, 25: in the realm of sin, the distinction between the Creator and creature was blurred, and this alienated humanity from God. Thus, God's beneficial act of reconciliation reestablishes this distinction. Like all acts of patronage, this benefaction carries with it the obligation to honor the divine patron as sovereign God.[89]

Part III. Other Pauline and Paulinist Texts

Rom 16:3, 7, 9, 21; 1 Cor 1:1; 3:21–22; 12:28; 16:10–11, 15–16, 18–19; 2 Cor 1:1, 11, 19; 2:13; 3:1; 4:5; 7:6–7, 13–15; 8:6, 13–14, 16–19, 22–23; 9:3, 5; 11:7, 12, 20, 28–29; 12:10, 17–18; 13:4, 9a; Gal 1:10; 2:1, 3, 7; 4:13–18; 6:6; Phil 1:1; 2:19–23, 25, 29–30; 3:17; 4:1–3, 9–19; 1 Thess 1:1, 6–7; 2:6–9; 3:2, 5–6; 4:11–12; 5:12–14; 2 Thess 1:1; 3:7–12; Col 1:1, 7; 4:1, 7–14, 17; Eph 6:9, 21; 1 Tim 3:1–13; 4:13f.; 5:1–2, 4, 8, 16–17; 6:17–19; 2 Tim 1:16–18; 4:10–12, 19–20; Titus 1:5–9; 3:12–13; and see the cross-references in the footnotes.

Part IV. Bibliography

Albertini, A. "Un patrono di Verona del secondo secolo d.C.: G. Erennio Ceciliano." Pages 439–59 in *Il territorio veronese in età romana: Convegno del 22–23–24 ottobre 1971*. Verona, Italy: Accademia di Agricoltura, Scienze e Lettere, 1973.

Albertini, E. "La clientèle des Claudii." *Mélanges d'archéologie et d'histoire de l'école française de Rome* 24 (1904): 247–76.

Alföldy, G. *Römische Sozialgeschichte*. 3d ed. Wissenschaftliche Paperbacks 8: Sozial- und Wirtschaftsgeschichte. Wiesbaden, Germany: Steiner, 1984.

Allen, W. "Cicero's *salutatio* (In Catilinam 1,9)." Pages 707–10 in *Studies Presented to David Moore Robinson on His Seventieth Birthday*, edited by G. E. Mylonas and D. Raymond. St. Louis: Clayton, 1953.

Anderson, G. *Sage, Saint, and Sophist: Holy Men and Their Associates in the Early Roman Empire*. London and New York: Routledge, 1994.

Ardevan, R. "Un patronat inconnu de Sextus Cornelius Clemens." Pages 213–16 in *Actas del Coloquio International A.I.E.G.L. sobre Novedades de epigrafía jurídica romana en el ultimo decenio*, edited by C. Castillo. Pamplona, Spain: Servicio de Publicaciones de la Universidad de Navarra, 1989.

Badian, E. *Foreign Clientelae (264–70 B.C.)*. Oxford: Oxford University Press, 1958.

Beschaouch, A. "Uzappa et le proconsul d'Afrique Sex: Cocceius Anicius Faustus Paulinus." *MEFR* 81 (1969): 195–218.

Bitto, I. "La concessione del patronato nella politica di Cesare." *Epigraphica* 32 (1970): 172–80.

Bonneville, J.-N. "Les patrons du municipe d'Emporiae (Ampurias, Espagne)." Pages 181–200 in *Hommage à Robert Etienne*. Publications du Centre Pierre Paris 17 [= *REA* 88 (1986)]. Paris: Boccard, 1988.

Bormann, L. *Philippi: Stadt und Christengemeinde zur Zeit des Paulus.* NovTSup 78. Leiden: Brill, 1995.

Braund, D. "Function and Dysfunction: Personal Patronage in Roman Imperialism." Pages 137–52 in *Patronage in Ancient Society,* edited by A. Wallace-Hadrill. London and New York: Routledge, 1989.

Brunt, P. A. "Clientela." Pages 382–442 in *The Fall of the Roman Republic,* by P. A. Brunt. Oxford: Oxford University Press, 1988.

———. "Patronage and Politics in the 'Verrines.'" *Chiron* 10 (1980): 273–89.

Buonocore, M. "C. Herennius Lupercus patronus Larinatium." *Tyche* 7 (1992): 19–25, 96.

———. "Varia epigraphica abruzzesi. III: A proposito delle due tabulae patronatus di Amiternum." *Miscellanea greca e romana: Studi publ. dall' Istituto italiano per la storia antica* 9 (1984): 234–45.

Carter, T. L. "'Big Men' in Corinth." *JSNT* 66 (1997): 45–71.

Chow, J. K. *Patronage and Power: A Study of Social Networks in Corinth.* JSNTSup 75. Sheffield, England: Sheffield Academic Press, 1992.

Christol, M. "Hommages publics à Lepcis Magna à l'époque de Dioclétien: Choix du vocabulaire et qualité du destinataire." *Revue Historique de Droit français et étranger,* ser. 4, 61 (1983): 331–43.

Clarke, A. D. "The Good and the Just in Romans 5:7." *TynBul* 41 (1990): 128–42.

Clemente, G. "Il patronato nei collegia dell'Impero Romano." *Studi classici e orientali* 21 (1972): 142–29.

Cloud, D. "The Client-Patron Relationship: Emblem and Reality in Juvenal's First Book." Pages 205–18 in *Patronage in Ancient Society,* edited by A. Wallace-Hadrill. London and New York: Routledge, 1989.

Corbier, M. "Usages publics du vocabulaire de parenté: Patronus et alumnus de la cité dans l'Afrique romaine." Pages 815–54 in *L'Africa romana: Atti del VII convegno di studio Sassari, 15–17 dicembre 1989,* edited by A. Mastino. Vol. 2. Sassari, Italy: Gallizzi, 1990.

Corell, J. "Nueva tabula patronatus procedente de la Baetica." *Epigraphica* 56 (1994): 59–67.

Cotton, H. M. *Documentary Letters of Recommendation in Latin from the Roman Empire.* Beiträge zur klassischen Philologie. Königstein, Germany: Hain, 1981.

———. "Mirificum genus commendationis: Cicero and the Latin Letter of Recommendation." *AJP* 106 (1985): 328–34.

———. "The Role of Cicero's Letters of Recommendation: *Iustitia* versus *gratia?*" *Hermes* 114 (1986): 443–60.

Crampon, M. "Le parasitus et son rex dans la comédie de Plaute: La revanche du langage sur la bassesse de la condition." Pages 507–22 in *Forms of Control and Subordination in Antiquity,* edited by T. Yuge and M. Doi. Tokyo and Leiden: Brill, 1988.

Cumont, F. "Patrobouloi." *Revue de Philologie* 26 (1902): 224–28.

Danker, F. W. *Benefactor: Epigraphic Study of a Greco-Roman and New Testament Semantic Field.* St. Louis: Clayton, 1982.

D'Arms, J. H. "Control, Companionship, and *clientela:* Some Social Functions of the Roman Communal Meal." *Échos du Monde Classique* 28, n.s., no. 3 (1984): 327–48.

De Martino, F. "Clienti e condizioni materiali in Roma arcaica." Pages 679–705 in

Philias charin: Miscellanea di studi classici in onore di Eugenio Manni, edited by
M. J. Fontana. Vol. 2. Rome: Bretschneider, 1980.

———. "Nota minima sulla clientela." *Index* 22 (1994): 343–59.

Deniaux, E., *Clientèles et pouvoir à l'époque de Cicéron.* Collection de l'École Française de Rome 182. Rome and Paris: École Française de Rome, 1993.

———. "Commendatio, recommandations, patronages et clientèles à l'époque de
Cicéron." *L'Information Historique* 49 (1987): 194–96.

———. "Les hôtes des Romains en Sicile." Pages 337–45 in *Sociabilité, pouvoirs et
societé: Actes du Colloque de Rouen, 24/26 Novembre 1983,* edited by F. Thelamon.
Rouen, France: Université de Rouen, 1987.

Deniaux, E., and P. Schmitt-Pantel. "La relation patron-client en Grèce et à Rome."
Opus 6, no. 8 (1987/89): 147–63.

DeSilva, D. A. "Exchanging Favor for Wrath: Apostasy in Hebrews and Patron-
Client Relationships." *JBL* 115 (1996): 91–116.

———. "Patronage and Reciprocity: The Context of Grace in the New Testament." *ATJ* 31 (1999): 32–84.

De Visscher, F. "Jules César patron d'Alba Fucens." *L'Antiquité Classique* 33 (1964):
98–107.

Drummond, A. "Early Roman *clientes.*" Pages 89–115 in *Patronage in Ancient Society,* edited by A. Wallace-Hadrill. London and New York: Routledge, 1989.

Duthoy, R. "Le profil social des patrons municipaux en Italie sous le Haut-Em-
pire." *Ancient Society* 15, no. 7 (1984/86): 121–54.

———. "Quelques observations concernant la mention d'un patronat municipal
dans les inscriptions." *L'Antiquité Classique* 50 (1981): 295–305.

———. "Scenarios de cooptation des patrons municipaux en Italie." *Epigraphica*
46 (1984): 23–48.

———. "Sens et fonction du patronat municipal durant le Principat." *L'Antiquité
Classique* 53 (1984): 145–56.

Eck, W. "Abhängigkeit als ambivalenter Begriff: Zum Verhältnis von Patron und
Libertus." *Memorias de Historia Antiqua* [Actas del Coloquio 1978: Colonato y
otras formas de dependencia no esclavistas] 2 (1978): 42.

———. "Wahl von Stadtpatronen mit kaiserlicher Beteiligung?" *Chiron* 9 (1979):
489–94.

Edgar, D. "The Theology of Luke's Gospel." *Search* 20 (1997): 115–20.

Edlund, I. E. M. "Invisible Bonds: Clients and Patrons through the Eyes of Polybius." *Klio* 59 (1977): 129–36.

Eilers, C. F. "Cn. Domitius and Samos: A New Extortion Trial (IGR 4, 968)." *ZPE*
89 (1991): 167–78.

———. "A Patron of Myra in Ephesus." *Tyche* 10 (1995): 9–12.

Eisenstadt, S. N., and L. Roniger. *Patrons, Clients, and Friends: Interpersonal Relations and the Structure of Trust in Society.* Cambridge: Cambridge University
Press, 1984.

Elliott, J. H. "Patronage and Clientism in Early Christian Society: A Short Reading
Guide." *Forum* 3 (1987): 39–48.

Ellis, E. E. "Paul and His Co-workers." *NTS* 17 (1971): 437–52.

Engesser, F. "Der Stadtpatronat in Italien und in den Westprovinzen des römischen Reiches bis Diokletian." Diss., Freiburg, 1957.

Enríquez, J. A. "Una nueva tabula patronatus." Pages 299–306 in *Actas del Coloquio International A.I.E.G.L. sobre Novedades de epigrafía jurídica romana en el ultimo decenio*, edited by C. Castillo. Pamplona, Spain: Servicio de Publicaciones de la Universidad de Navarra, 1989.

Espinosa Ruiz, U. "Iuridici de la Hispania citerior y patroni en Calagurris." *Gerión* 1 (1983): 305–25.

Evans, J. K. "Political Patronage in Imperial Rome: The Appointment of Marius Celsus as Governor of Syria in A.D. 72." *Epigraphische Studien* 12 (1981): 215–24.

Ferenczy, E. "Über die alte Klientel." *Oikumene* 3 (1982): 193–201.

Folcandn, E. "Il patronato di comunità in Apulia et Calabria." Pages 51–137 in *Epigrafia e territorio. Politica e società*, edited by M. Pani. Temi di antichità romane 3. Bari, Italy: Adriatica, 1994.

Franciosi, G. "Una ipotesi sull'origine della clientela." *Labeo* 32 (1986): 263–81.

Freis, H. "Zwei lateinische Inschriften aus Albanien." *ZPE* 61 (1985): 224–28.

Frei-Stolba, R. "Zur tessera hospitalis aus Fundi (CIL I 2 611)." *ZPE* 63 (1986): 193–96.

Friedländer, L. *Darstellungen aus der Sittengeschichte Roms in der Zeit von Augustus bis zum Ausgang der Antonine*. Aalen, Germany: Scientia, 1979. [See 1:225–35; 2:241 ff., 246.]

Gagé, J. "Les 'clients' de M. Manlius Capitolinus et les formes de leur 'libération.'" *Revue Historique de Droit français et étranger*, ser. 4, 44 (1966): 342–77.

Gallego Franco, M. H. "Los términos epigráficos amicus/a y hospes como indicadores de dependencia en el ámbito social de la mujer hispanorromana." *Hispania Antica: Revista de historia antiqua* 19 (1995): 205–16.

Ganido-Hory, M. "Le statut de la clientèle chez Martial." *Dialogues d'Histoire Ancienne* 11 (1985): 380–414.

Garnsey, P., and G. Woolf. "Patronage of the Rural Poor in the Roman World." Pages 153–70 in *Patronage in Ancient Society*, edited by A. Wallace-Hadrill. London and New York: Routledge, 1989.

Gregori, G. L. "Gaio Silio Aviola, patrono di Apisa Maius, Siagu, Themetra e Thimiliga." Pages 229–37 in *L'Africa romana: Atti dell'VIII convegno di studio Cagliari, 14–16 dicembre 1990*, edited by A. Mastino. Vol. 1. Sassari, Italy: Gallizzi, 1991.

Grelle, F. "Patroni ebrei in città tardoantiche." Pages 139–58 in *Epigrafia e territorio: Politica e società*, edited by M. Pani. Temi di antichità romane 3. Bari, Italy: Adriatica, 1994.

Guido, R. "Liberi e dipendenti nella 'Geografia' di Strabone." *Index* 11 (1982): 245–56.

Guttenberger Ortwein, G. *Status und Statusverzicht im Neuen Testament und seiner Umwelt*. NTOA 39. (Freiburg, Germany: Univ. Verlag Freiburg; Göttingen: Vandenhoeck & Ruprecht, 1999.

Harmand, L. *Un aspect social et politique du monde romain: Le patronat sur les collectivités publiques des origines au Bas-Empire*. Paris: Presses Univ. de France, 1957.

Heinze, R. "Fides." *Hermes* 64 (1929): 140–66.

Hendrix, H. "Benefactor/Patron Networks in the Urban Environment: Evidence from Thessalonica." *Semeia* 56 (1991): 39–58.

Herrmann, P. "Cn. Domitius Ahenobarbus—Patronus von Ephesos und Samos." *ZPE* 14 (1974): 257–58.

Horsley, R. A., ed. *Paul and Empire: Religion and Power in Roman Imperial Society.* Harrisburg, Pa.: Trinity Press International, 1997.

Jewett, R. "Tenement Churches and Communal Meals in the Early Church: The Implications of a Form-Critical Analysis of 2 Thessalonians 3:10." *BR* 38 (1993): 23–43.

Jones, F. L. "Martial, the Client." *CJ* 30 (1934/35): 355–61.

Joubert, S.J. "*Patronatus* as dominante sosiale sisteem in die Romeinse wêreld gedurende die Nuwe-Testamentiese era" (Patronage as the dominant social system in the Roman world during the New Testament era). *Skrif en Kerk* 21 (2000): 66–78.

Judge, E. A. "The Early Christians as a Scholastic Community." *JRH* 1 (1960–61): 4–15, 125–37.

Kajava, M. "A New City Patroness?" *Tyche* 5 (1990): 27–36.

Katzoff, R. "Suffragium in Exodus Rabbah 37.2." *CP* 81 (1986): 235–40.

Kea, P. V. "Paul's Letter to Philemon: A Short Analysis of its Values." *PRSt* 23 (1996): 223–32.

Kirner, Guido O. "Apostolat und Patronage (I): Methodischer Teil und Forschungsdiskussion." *ZAC* 6 (2002): 3–37.

Kleiner, D. E. E. "Women and Family Life on Roman Imperial Funerary Altars." *Latomus* 46 (1987): 545–54.

Konstan, D. "Patrons and Friends." *Classical Philology* 90 (1995): 328–42.

Krause, J.-U. "Das spätantike Städtepatronat." *Chiron* 17 (1987): 1–80.

Lampe, P. "Die Apokalyptiker—Ihre Situation und ihr Handeln." Pages 59–115 in *Eschatologie und Friedenshandeln,* edited by U. Luz et al. 2d ed. SBS 101. Stuttgart: Katholisches Bibelwerk, 1982.

———. "Der Brief an Philemon." Pages 203–32 in *Die Briefe an die Philipper, Thessalonicher und an Philemon,* edited by N. Walter, E. Reinmuth, and P. Lampe. NTD 8/2. Göttingen: Vandenhoeck & Ruprecht, 1998.

———. "'Family' in Church and Society of New Testament Times." *Affirmation* 5, no. 1 (1992): 1–20.

———. "Keine 'Sklavenflucht' des Onesimus." *ZNW* 76 (1985): 135–37.

———. *Die stadtrömischen Christen in den ersten beiden Jahrhunderten: Untersuchungen zur Sozialgeschichte.* 2d ed. WUNT 2/18. Tübingen: J. C. B. Mohr, 1989. ET: *From Paul to Valentinus.* Minneapolis: Augsburg Fortress, 2003.

Leach, E. W. "Patrons, Painters, and Patterns: The Anonymity of Romano-Campanian Painting and the Transition from the Second to the Third Style." Pages 135–73 in *Literary and Artistic Patronage in Ancient Rome,* edited by B. K. Gold. Austin: University of Texas Press, 1982.

Le Gall, J. "La 'nouvelle plèbe' et la sportule quotidienne." Pages 1449–53 in *Mélanges d'archéologie et d'histoire offerts à André Piganiol,* edited by R. Chevallier. Vol. 3. Paris: S.E.V.P.E.N., 1966.

Lemosse, M. "L'aspect primitif de la fides." Pages 39–52 in *Studi in onore di P. de Francisci.* Vol. 2. Milan: Giuffrè, 1956.

———. "Hospitium." Pages 1269–81 in *Sodalitas: Scritti in onore di Antonio Guarino.* Vol. 3. Biblioteca di Labeo 8. Naples, Italy: Jovene, 1984/85.

Levi, M. A. "Da clientela ad amicitia." Pages 375–81 in *Epigrafia e territorio: Politica e società*, edited by M. Pani. Temi di antichità romane 3. Bari, Italy: Adriatica, 1994.

———. "Familia, servitus, fides: Indagación en torno a la dependencia humana en la sociedad romana." *Gerión* 1 (1983): 177–213.

———. "Liberi in manu." *Labeo* 22 (1976): 73–80 = M. A. Levi, *Né liberi né schiavi: Gruppi sociali e rapporti di lavoro nel mondo ellenistico-romano* (Milan: Cisalpino-Goliardica, 1976), 87–96.

Lintott, A.W. "Cliens, clientes." *Der Neue Pauly* 3 (1997): 32f.

———. *Imperium Romanum: Politics and Administration*. London and New York: Routledge, 1993.

Maier, H. O. "Purity and Danger in Polycarp's Epistle to the Philippians: The Sin of Valens in Social Perspective." *JECS* 1 (1993): 229–47.

Malina, B. J. "Patron and Client: The Analogy behind Synoptic Theology." *Forum* 4 (1988): 2–32.

———. *The Social World of Jesus and the Gospels*. London and New York: Routledge, 1996.

Mangas, J. "Clientela privada en la Hispania Romana." *Memorias de Historia antigua* 2 (1978): 217–26.

———. "Hospitium y patrocinium sobre colectividades públicas: Términos sinónimos? (De Augusto a fines de los Severos)." *Dialogues d'Histoire Ancienne* 9 (1983): 165–83.

Marache, R. "Juvénal et le client pauvre." *Revue des études latines* 58 (1980): 363–69.

Martina, M. "Grassatores e carmentarii." *Labeo* 26 (1980): 155–75.

Martini, R. "Su alcune singolari figure di patroni." Pages 319–26 in *Atti dell'Accademia Romanistica Costantiniana: X convegno internazionale in onore di Arnaldo Biscardi*, edited by G. Crifò and S. Giglio. Naples: Edizioni Scientifiche Italiane, 1995.

May, J. M. "The Rhetoric of Advocacy and Patron-Client Identification: Variation on a Theme." *AJP* 102 (1981): 308–15.

Mommsen, Th. "Das römische Gastrecht und die römische Clientel." *Sybels historische Zeitschrift* 1 (1859): 332–79 = Th. Mommsen, *Römische Forschungen*, vol. 1 (Berlin: Weidmann, 1864), 319–90.

Moxnes, H. "Patron-Client Relations and the New Community in Luke-Acts." Pages 241–68 in *The Social World of Luke–Acts: Models for Interpretation*, edited by J. H. Neyrey. Peabody, Mass.: Hendrickson, 1991.

Neri, C. "Suffragium: Per la storia di un'idea." Pages 115–37 in *Hestíasis: Studi di tarda antichità offerti a Salvatore Calderone*. Vol. 5. Messina, Italy: Sicania, 1995.

Neyrey, J. H. *2 Peter, Jude: A New Translation with Introduction and Commentary*. AB 37C. New York and London: Doubleday, 1993.

Nicols, J. "The Caecilii Metelli, patroni Siciliae?" *Historia* 30 (1981): 238–40.

———. "The Emperor and the Selection of the *patronus civitatis*: Two Examples." *Chiron* 8 (1978): 429–32.

———. "Patrona civitatis: Gender and Civic Patronage." Pages 117–42 in *Studies in Latin Literature and Roman History*, edited by C. Deroux. Vol. 5. Collection Latomus 206. Brussels: Latomus, 1989.

———. "Patrons of Greek Cities in the Early Principate." *ZPE* 80 (1990): 81–100.

————. "Patrons of Provinces in the Early Principate: The Case of Bithynia." *ZPE* 80 (1990): 101–8.

————. "Patronum cooptare, patrocinium deferre: Lex Malacitana c. 61." *Zeitschrift der Savigny-Stiftung für Rechtsgeschichte* 96 (1979): 303–6.

————. "Pliny and the Patronage of Communities." *Hermes* 108 (1980): 365–85.

————. "Prefects, Patronage, and the Administration of Justice." *ZPE* 72 (1988): 201–17.

————. "Tabulae patronatus: A Study of the Agreement between Patron and Client-Community." Pages 535–61 in *ANRW* 2.13. Berlin and New York: de Gruyter, 1980.

————. "Zur Verleihung öffentlicher Ehrungen in der römischen Welt." *Chiron* 9 (1979): 243–60.

Panciera, S. "I patroni di Aquileia fra la città e Roma." *Antichità altoadriatiche* 30 (1987): 77–95.

Pani, M. "Le raccomandazoni nell'epistolario di Plinio." Pages 141–47 in *Potere e valori a Roma fra Augusto e Traiano*, edited by M. Pani. Documenti e studi 14. Bari, Italy: Edipuglia, 1992.

Parma, A. "Un presunto vir inlustris patrono di Minturnae (AE 1954, 27)." *ZPE* 79 (1989): 188–90.

Pavis d'Escurac, H. "Pline le Jeune et les lettres de recommandation." Pages 55–69 in *La mobilité sociale dans le monde romain: Actes du colloque de Strasbourg (novembre 1988)*, edited by E. Frézouls. Contributions et travaux de l'Institut d'Histoire Romaine 5. Strasbourg: AECR, 1992.

Pflaum, H.-G. "Clients et patrons à la lumière du cimetière de l'Autoparco sous le Vatican à Rome." *Arctos* 9 (1975): 75–87.

Pickett, R. W. "The Death of Christ as Divine Patronage in Romans 5:1–11." Pages 726–39 in *Society of Biblical Literature 1993 Seminar Papers*, edited by E. H. Lovering. Atlanta: Scholars Press, 1993.

Poinssot, C. "M. Licinius Ruffis patronus pagi et civitatis Thuggensis." *Bulletin du Comité des Travaux Historiques et Scientifiques*, n.s., 5 (1969): 215–58.

Rajak, T., and D. Noy. "Archisynagogoi: Office, Title, and Social Status in the Greco-Jewish Synagogue." *JRS* 83 (1993): 75–93.

Rawson, E. "The Eastern *clientelae* of Clodius and the Claudii." *Historia* 22 (1973): 219–39 = E. Rawson, *Roman Culture and Society: Collected Papers* (Oxford: Clarendon, 1991), 102–24.

————. "More on the *clientelae* of the Patrician Claudii." *Historia* 26 (1977): 340–57 = E. Rawson, *Roman Culture and Society: Collected Papers* (Oxford: Clarendon, 1991), 227–44.

Rebell, W. *Gehorsam und Unabhängigkeit: Eine sozialpsychologische Studie zu Paulus.* Munich: Kaiser, 1986 = "Paulus—Apostel im Spannungsfeld sozialer Beziehungen: Eine sozialpsychologische Untersuchung zum Verhältnis des Paulus zu Jerusalem, seinen Mitarbeitern und Gemeinden" (diss., Bochum, 1982).

Rich, J. "Patronage and International Relations in the Roman Republic." Pages 117–35 in *Patronage in Ancient Society*, edited by A. Wallace-Hadrill. London and New York: Routledge, 1989.

Roda, S. "Polifunzionalità della lettera commendaticia: Teoria e prassi nell'epistolario simmachiano." Pages 177–207 in *Colloque genèvois sur Symmaque à l'occasion du mille six centième anniversaire du conflit de l'autel de la Victoire*, edited by F. Paschoud. Paris: Belles Lettres, 1986.

Rodríguez Neila, J. F., and J. M. Santero Santurino. "Hospitium y patronatus sobre una tabla de bronce de Canete de las Torres (Córdoba)." *Habis* 13 (1982): 105–63.

Rohrbaugh, L., ed. *The Social Sciences and New Testament Interpretation*. Peabody, Mass.: Hendrickson, 1996.

Roldàn Hervas, J. M. "La comunidad romana primitiva, la clientela y la plebe." *Memorias de Historia antigua* 2 (1978): 19–39.

Rouland, N. *Pouvoir politique et dépendance personnelle dans l'Antiquité romaine: Genèse et rôle des rapports de clientele*. Collection Latomus 166. Brussels: Latomus, 1979.

———. "I rapporti clientelari." Pages 150–64 in *La rivoluzione romana: Inchiesta tra gli antichisti*. Biblioteca di Labeo 6. Naples: Jovene, 1982.

Saavedra Guerrero, M. D. "La cooptatio patroni e el elogio de la virtus en el patronato colegial." *Athenaeum* 83 (1995): 497–507.

Sabbatini Tumolesi, P. "Una nuova tabula patronatus da Paestum." *Miscellanea greca e romana: Studi publ. dall'Istituto italiano per la storia antica* 15 (1990): 235–56.

Saller, R. P. "Martial on Patronage and Literature." *CQ*, n.s., 33 (1983): 246–57.

———. "Patronage and Friendship in Early Imperial Rome: Drawing the Distinction." Pages 49–62 in *Patronage in Ancient Society*, edited by A. Wallace-Hadrill. London and New York: Routledge, 1989.

———. *Personal Patronage under the Early Empire*. Cambridge: Cambridge University Press, 1982.

Sartori, M. "Un frammento di tabula patronatus del collegium centonariorum Laudensium." *Athenaeum* 65 (1987): 191–201.

Schmeller, T. *Hierarchie und Egalität: Eine sozialgeschichtliche Untersuchung paulinischer Gemeinden und griechisch-römischer Vereine*. SBS 162. Stuttgart: Katholisches Bibelwerk, 1995.

Schumacher, L. "Das Ehrendekret für M. Nonius Balbus aus Herculaneum (AE 1947, 53)." *Chiron* 6 (1976): 165–84.

Schütz, J. H. *Paul and the Anatomy of Apostolic Authority*. Cambridge: Cambridge University Press, 1975.

Seguí Marco, J. J. "Un aspecto particular en las relationes hispano-africanas durante el Alto Imperio: Los patrocinios públicos." Pages 1547–64 in *L'Africa romana: Atti dell'XI convegno di studio Cartagine, 15–18 dicembre 1994*, vol. 3, edited by M. Khanoussi, P. Ruggeri, and C. Vismara. Ozieri, Italy: Il Torchietto, 1996.

Serrao, F. "Patrono e cliente da Romolo alle XII Tavole." Pages 293–309 in *Studi in onore di Arnaldo Biscardi*. Vol. 6. Milan: Istituto Editoriale Cisalpino/La Goliardica, 1987.

Shaw, B. D. "Tyrants, Bandits, and Kings: Personal Power in Josephus." *JJS* 44 (1993): 176–204.

Sloan, I. "The Greatest and the Youngest: Greco-Roman Reciprocity in the Farewell Address, Luke 22:24–30." *Studies in Religion/Sciences Religieuses* 22 (1993): 63–73.

Smith, A. *Comfort One Another: Reconstructing the Rhetoric and Audience of 1 Thessalonians.* Literary Currents in Biblical Interpretation. Louisville: Westminster John Knox, 1995.

Soffredi, A. "Il patronato in Italia alla luce delle iscrizioni latine." *Epigraphica* 18 (1956): 157–72.

Soltau, W. "Grundherrschaft und Klientel in Rom." *NJahrb* 29 (1912): 489–500.

Sordi, M. "Ottaviano patrono di Taranto nel 43 a.C." *Epigraphica* 31 (1969): 79–83.

Sperber, D. "Patronage in Amoraic Palestine (c. 220–400): Causes and Effects." *JESHO* 14 (1971): 227–52.

Stoops, R. F. "Christ as Patron in the Acts of Peter." *Semeia* 56 (1991): 143–57.

Susini, G. "Q. Pompeius Senecio, console nel 169 d.C.: Alcune note." Pages 289–99 in *Mélanges d'archéologie et d'histoire offerts à André Piganiol*, edited by R. Chevallier. Vol. 1. Paris: S.E.V.P.E.N., 1966.

Taylor, W. F. "Cultural Anthropology as a Tool for Studying the New Testament." *Trinity Seminary Review* 18, no. 1 (1996): 13–27, and 18, no. 2 (1997): 69–82.

Torjesen, K. J. *When Women Were Priests: Women's Leadership in the Early Church and the Scandal of Their Subordination in the Rise of Christianity.* San Francisco: HarperCollins, 1993.

Trisoglio, F. "La lettera di raccomandazione nell'epistolario ciceroniano." *Latomus* 43 (1984): 751–75.

Van Berchem, D. "Les 'clients' de la plèbe romaine." *Rendiconti della Pontificia Accademia Romana di Archaeologia* 18 (1941/42): 183–90.

———. "Note sur les diplômes honorifiques du IVe siècle: A propos de la Table de patronat de Timgad." *RevPhil* 60 (1934): 165–68.

Voigt, M. "Über die Clientel und Libertinität." *Berichte über die Verhandlungen der Königlich Sächsischen Gesellschaft der Wissenschaften zu Leipzig, phil.-hist. Kl.* 30 (1978): 147–220.

von Premerstein, A. "Clientes." *Pauly/Wissowa* 4 (1901): 28–51.

Vyhmeister, N. J. "The Rich Man in James 2: Does Ancient Patronage Illumine the Text?" *AUSS* 33 (1995): 265–83.

Waldstein, W. *Operae Libertorum: Untersuchungen zur Dienstpflicht freigelassener Sklaven.* Stuttgart: Steiner, 1986.

Wallace-Hadrill, A. "Patronage in Roman Society: From Republic to Empire." Pages 63–87 in *Patronage in Ancient Society*, edited by A. Wallace-Hadrill. London and New York: Routledge, 1989.

Warmington, B. H. "The Municipal Patrons of Roman North Africa." *Papers of the British School at Rome* 22, n.s., 9 (1954): 39–55.

Whelan, C. F. "Amica Pauli: The Role of Phoebe in the Early Church." *JSNT* 49 (1993): 67–85.

White, L. M. "Social Authority in the House Church Setting and Ephesians 4:1–16." *ResQ* 29 (1987): 209–28.

———. "Social Networks: Theoretical Orientation and Historical Applications." *Semeia* 56 (1991): 23–36.

Wilkins, P. I. "Legates of Numidia as Municipal Patrons." *Chiron* 23 (1993): 189–206.

Winter, B. W. "'If a Man Does Not Wish to Work . . .': A Cultural and Historical Setting for 2 Thessalonians 3:6–16." *TynBul* 40 (1989): 303–15.

————. *Seek the Welfare of the City: Christians as Benefactors and Citizens.* First-Century Christians in the Graeco-Roman World. Grand Rapids: Eerdmans, 1994.

Notes

1. For references, see P. Lampe, "Family in Church and Society of New Testament Times," *Affirmation* (Union Theological Seminary in Virginia) 5, no. 1 (1992): 2, 14n. 5. For a definition of "household," see ibid., 1–2.

2. Even the dignity of the individual household members depended on that of the *pater familias.* This was true since Homer's time (*Od.* 1.234ff.; *Iliad* 22.483–499) and can still be observed in modern-day cultures.

3. Col 3:18–4:1; Eph 5:22–6:9; 1 Pet 2:18–3:7; 1 Tim 2:8–15; Titus 2:1–10; Pol., *Phil* 4.2–6.3; cf. *Did.* 4.9–11; *Barn.* 19.5–7; *1 Clem.* 21.6–9.

4. The slave–master relationship is a topic for itself with its own legal implications. It will not be discussed in this essay.

5. At manumission, a certain number of days' service to the patron was stipulated. Freed persons with Roman citizenship and with two children of their own, however, were freed from these services. Cf. Paulus, *Dig.* 38.1.37 pr.

6. Cf. the literature reviewed by H. W. Pleket, "Wirtschaft," in *Europäische Wirtschafts- und Sozialgeschichte* (ed. F. Vittinghoff; Handbuch der Europäischen Wirtschafts- und Sozialgeschichte 1; Stuttgart: Klett, 1990), 40–41, 84, 125, 132.

7. *Obsequium* means "obedience" and "subordination." The literal translation of *cliens* is "the obedient" (participle of *cluere*). Plutarch (*Rom* 13) and others translated "client" into the Greek by πελάτης (*pelatēs*), which denotes a person who seeks protection and becomes dependent.

8. The loyalty could extend so far that one was allowed to testify in favor of a client against a blood-related person (Gellius 5.13.4; cf. 20.1.40). Neither patron nor client could sue the other in court or testify against the other (*CIL* 12.583.10; 33). For these duties of both clients and patrons, see especially Dionysius Halic., *Ant. rom.* 2.9f.

9. The voluntary submission of a client looking for protection was called *applicatio ad patronum* (Cicero, *De or.* 1.177). It implied that the client could choose on his own to whose power (*potestas*), protection, and loyalty (*fides*) he wanted to submit himself. This entirely private contract between client and patron was based on mutual consent. Inheritable but always-revocable land utilization (*precarium*) could be part of the contract but was not a prerequisite. Cf. Dionys. Halic., *Ant. rom.* 2.9.2 (one could choose a προστάτην [*prostatēn*] one wanted), 2.10.4; Terence, *Eun.* 885, 1039; Gellius 5.13.2 ("clientes . . . sese . . . in fidem patrociniumque nostrum dediderunt"), 20.1.40 ("clientem in fidem susceptum").

10. Often these settlers belonged to conquered populations and were given land that they previously had owned. The involuntary submission of defeated or conquered persons was not part of a private contract but a matter of public law; the submission under the power of a conqueror and the latter's vow to loyalty (*fides,* which was under the protection of the gods to whom the patron vowed) were rooted in international law, which regulated the relations between citizens and noncitizens. Contrary to the voluntary clientage, this submission could imply

serious limitations to the legal capacity of the client. He, for example, had to accept the *nomen gentile* of the patron; the power of the *pater familias* was replaced by the patronage; he could not marry whomever he wanted; the patron often inherited his estate after his death; and so on. Such limitations did not confront voluntary clients. See A. v. Premerstein, "Clientes," *Pauly/Wissowa* 4 (1901): 28–30, 33, 38f., 41ff., 51.

11. For military service until the second century B.C.E., see ibid., 37. For financial contributions to the patron, see Dionys. Halic., *Ant. rom.* 2.10; Livius 5.32.8 (cf. 38.60.9; Dionys., ibid. 13.5.1). These payments helped to cover extraordinary expenses of the patron. Apart from this, financial gifts to the patron were frowned upon, but they could occur (Dionys., ibid. 2.10.4; Plutarch, *Rom* 13; Gellius 20.1.40; Livius 34.4.9; the *lex Cincia de donis*, probably from 204 B.C.E., had ruled that only very small presents to the patron were allowed; cf. A. W. Lintott, "Cliens, clientes," *Neue Pauly* 3 [1997]: 32). For the personal freedom of the clients, see, e.g., Proculus, *Dig.* 49.15.7 §1: "clientes nostros intellegimus liberos esse, etiamsi neque auctoritate neque dignitate neque viribus nobis pares sunt."

12. This was called *patrocinium*. Cf., e.g., Cicero, *De or.* 1.177, 3.33; Livius 34.4.9; Tacitus, *Ann.* 11.5; *Dial.* 3; Horace, *Ep.* 2.1.104; Dionys. Halic., *Ant. rom.* 2.10.1; Gellius 5.13.6. This task of the patrons, however, became less and less important the more complicated law and trials became. Already in late Republican times, professional upper-class lawyers often were consulted, and during a trial a *temporary* patron-client relationship was established between the professional attorney and the litigant (cf. Cicero, *Att.* 15.14.3). This form of clientage has survived until today, when "clients" put their legal dealings in the hands of lawyers. The original patrons' loss of legal competence contributed, of course, to the loosening of the ties between clients and patrons already in Republican times.

13. Dionys. Halic., *Ant. rom.* 2.10.1.

14. A client could even be of the equestrian rank, such as the poet Martial.

15. Fittingly, since Republican times, a patron and a client could marry one another. Cf., e.g., Gellius 13.20.8; Plutarch, *Cat. Maj.* 24; Pliny, *Nat.* 7.61. The reciprocity between patron and client was idealized by Dionysius Halic. (*Ant. rom.* 2.10.4): "It is incredible how great the contest of good will was between the patrons and clients, as each side strove not to be outdone by the other in kindness, the clients feeling that they should render all possible services to their patrons and the patrons wishing by all means not to occasion any trouble to their clients." Although talking about earliest Roman times here, Dionysius insists that the patron-client relations described in 2.10 "long continued among the Romans." Satirical authors such as Martial (see n. 22 below) counterbalance this idealized picture.

16. Cf., e.g., Livy 5.32.8; Dionys. Halic., *Ant. rom.* 9.41.5; Plautus, *Men.* 574ff.

17. It is not clear, however, to what extent the patrons in Republican times could control their clients' behavior at the polls. Bribery increased in the second century B.C.E., and this indicates that the ties between patrons and clients had loosened already in Republican times. See also n. 12, above, and Lintott, "Cliens," 32: From the *lex Gabinia* in 139 B.C.E. onward, the Roman legislation contributed to the loosening of these ties.

18. The *ius civile* proper did not regulate the clientage, and in the domain of

public law these private relationships, of course, did not play any role either. Their only meager legal protection was provided by the criminal law, which punished the *fraus patroni,* the patron's violation of loyalty (cf. Servius, *Aen.* 6.609, and v. Premerstein, "Clientes," 39–40, 46). The obligations of these give-and-take relationships, rooted in mutual loyalty (*fides*), were of a moral nature. They were not legally enforceable but rather were governed by custom and by reverence for the gods who protected the *fides.* Cf. Dionys. Halic., *Ant. rom.* 2.9.3: θέμις (*themis*) and ὅσιον (*hosion*) established the basis.

19. Cf. Dionys. Halic., *Ant. rom.* 2.10.4; 4.23.6; 11.36; Plutarch, *Mar.* 5.

20. Cf., e.g., v. Premerstein, "Clientes," 38, 52–53. Even freed persons could choose an additional patron besides their former slave master (cf., e.g., Cicero, *Sex. Rosc.* 19; *Att.* 1.12.2).

21. Therefore even less wealthy patrons aimed for a large entourage, with some getting into debt in order to finance this status symbol (Martial, *Ep.* 2.74).

22. For Roman clients, cf., e.g., Martial, *Ep.* 12.68.1–2; 9.100.2; 6.88; 4.40.1; 3.38.11; 3.36; 2.74; 2.18; 1.108; 1.59; 1.55.5–6; also Seneca, *Ben.* 6.33f.; Livy 38.51.6; Juvenal 1.95ff.; Suetonius, *Vesp.* 2.2.

23. Cf., e.g., Horace, *Ep.* 1.7.37. For a statue: *CIL* 6.1390; cf. Pliny, *Nat.* 34.17.

24. *CIL* 4.593, 822, 933, 1011, 1016.

25. Cf. n. 22 above and L. Friedländer, *Darstellungen aus der Sittengeschichte Roms in der Zeit von Augustus bis zum Ausgang der Antonine* (vol. 1; Aalen, Germany: Scientia, 1979), 227f.

26. For prices, see P. Lampe, *Die stadtrömischen Christen in den ersten beiden Jahrhunderten: Untersuchungen zur Sozialgeschichte* (2d ed.; WUNT 2/18; Tübingen: Mohr, 1989), 163. For twenty-five *asses,* cf. Martial, *Ep.* 1.59. Under Trajan, twenty-five *asses* were the amount of the usual *sportula.* Martial (*Ep.* 9.100.2) also knows of a *sportula* of three *denarii* (= 48–54 *asses*).

27. Cf. *Dig.* 7.8.2 §§1, 3; 9.3.5 §1; Tacitus, *Ann.* 16.22; and see Friedländer, *Sittengeschichte,* 1:227.

28. Cf. Macrobius, *Sat.* 1.7.33 (*lex Publicia,* probably 209 B.C.E.).

29. For the financial exchanges between patrons and clients, see the material collected by R. P. Saller, *Personal Patronage under the Early Empire* (Cambridge: Cambridge University Press, 1982), 120ff., 205.

30. See Pliny, *Ep.* 6.8.

31. *CIL* 3.6126. For further epigraphical evidence, particularly concerning Gaul, cf., e.g., v. Premerstein, "Clientes," 54. For North Africa, see Saller, *Patronage,* 145ff.

32. See the inscription in R. Merkelbach and J. Stauber, eds., *Steinepigramme aus dem griechischen Osten* (vol. 1; Stuttgart and Leipzig: Teubner, 1998), no. 03/02/28: The sophist Hadrianos of Tyre honors the consul Claudius Servius (second century C.E.) with a statue, thanking him for his patronage (προστασίης, προστάτην [*prostasiēs, prostatēn*]).

33. See below for Rom 16:2, where the same term is used: προστάτις (*prostatis*).

34. Cf., e.g., the inscription in Merkelbach, *Steinepigramme,* no. 06/02/32: A medical doctor from Pergamon praises his deceased teacher, who left him behind "as a son, worthy of your art." Greek physicians were like fathers to their stu-

dents. According to our inscription, the student even gave a burial place to his teacher in his own tomb.

35. Cf., e.g., the gift from students in the inscription Merkelbach, *Steinepigramme*, no. 03/02/31. For our purposes we will leave out the rural *coloni*, farmers who rented land from landowners and who were highly dependent on these landlords. Usually they were bound by heredity to the place where they were born and which they rented, being burdened by high rents and losing more and more rights. Sometimes these vertical relationships were considered client-like: Hermogenianus, *Dig.* 19.1.49 pr. ("colonum . . . in fidem suam recipit"). But the often oppressive relationships were governed more by solid, legally defined obligations than by the moral value of loyalty.

36. For a definition of "class," see G. Alföldy, *Römische Sozialgeschichte* (3d ed.; Wiesbaden: Steiner, 1984), 126–27.

37. Vertical borderlines also distinguished among *slaves, freed* persons, and *freeborn* persons, and between *rural* and *urban* lower-class people. A free person, for example, did not automatically have a higher social position than a slave. Often it was the other way around. Any idea of horizontal borderlines between these groups would be misleading. Cf., e.g., G. Alföldy's pyramid model of the society of the Roman Empire (*Sozialgeschichte*, 125).

38. Cf., e.g., Saller, *Patronage*, 120.

39. Cf. Paulus, *Dig.* 49.15.7 §1; Cicero, *Off.* 2.27; Livy 26.32.8; 37.54.17.

40. Lex col. Gen. 97; Cicero, *Off.* 1.11.35: "ut ii, qui civitates aut nationes devictas bello in fidem recepissent, eorum patroni essent more maiorum"; Valerius Maximus 4.3.6; Livy 37.45.2; Dionys., *Ant. rom.* 2.11.1: "each of the conquered towns had . . . προστάτας [*prostatas*, patrons]." The term parallels προστάτις (*prostatis*) in Rom 16:2.

41. Tacitus, *Dial.* 3; Cicero, *Sest.* 9; *Pis.* 25; Pliny, *Ep.* 4.1. Cf. also, e.g., the consul Cn. Claudius Severus, who in about 165 C.E. was honored as "protecting the city" of Ephesus. See the inscription in Merkelbach, *Steinepigramme*, no. 03/02/28.

42. E.g., Inscriptiones Latinae Selectae (ed. Hermann Dessau, Berlin 1,1892–3.2, 1916), 6121.

43. See J. Nicols, "Prefects, Patronage, and the Administration of Justice," *ZPE* 72 (1988): 201n. 3.

44. See F. Vittinghoff, ed., *Europäische Wirtschafts- und Sozialgeschichte in der Römischen Kaiserzeit* (Handbuch der Europäischen Wirtschafts- und Sozialgeschichte 1; Stuttgart: Klett, 1990), 203, 211.

45. Cf. also Pliny, *Pan.* 2.21.

46. Cf. Rev 5:6 with 13:3, 12, 14, and 13:15 with 11:11 as well as 13:2, 4; 13:11; 16:13; 20:10; 7:3; 13:16. See also P. Lampe, "Die Apokalyptiker—Ihre Situation und ihr Handeln," in *Eschatologie und Friedenshandeln* (ed. U. Luz et al.; 2d ed.; SBS 101; Stuttgart: Katholisches Bibelwerk, 1982), 95.

47. For the Christians as children of God, see also, e.g., Rom 8:14–17, 19, 21, 23. Christ, consequently, can be called their brother (v. 29), although he also appears as the vertically superordinated lord (see below).

48. This is what is meant by "you all are one" (εἷς [*heis*]) in 3:28. You are all together one and the same; nothing differentiates you. A paraphrase capturing

the meaning would be: "You all are the same as each other." Contrary to popular assumption, the masculine εἷς (*heis*) cannot mean that they all are "one [church] body." The neuter of σῶμα (*sōma*, "body") contraindicates this.

49. Exceptions: At the very beginnings of Judeo-Christianity, the Christian life also took place in the Jerusalem temple and in the synagogues. In Ephesus, Paul preached in a rented lecture room (Acts 19:9).

50. For literary and archaeological evidence, see, e.g., Lampe, *Die stadtrömischen Christen*, 307–10.

51. For the services of house owners, see, e.g., 2 Tim 1:16–18; Phlm 2, 5, 7; 1 Cor 16:15; compare also Mark 10:30 and 1:29–35; 2:15; 14:3. For hospitality, see, e.g., Rom 12:13; 1 Tim 3:2; Titus 1:8; 1 Pet 4:9; *1 Clem.* 1:2; compare also 1 Tim 5:10; 2 John 10. For Justin, see *Acta Iustini* 3.3.

52. For Asia Minor, see Phlm 2; Col 4:15; 1 Cor 16:19 (Ephesus); possibly 2 Tim 4:19. For Corinth, see 1 Cor 1:16; 16:15; Rom 16:1, 23; Acts 18:7; 18:8; and 1 Cor 1:14. For Thessalonica, see possibly 1 Thess 5:27 (Paul implores that the letter be read to all Christians in the city; this makes sense if at least two different house churches existed in town). For Rome, see Lampe, *Die stadtrömischen Christen*, 301–13.

53. Rom 16:23; cf. 1 Cor 11:18; 14:23.

54. For the relatively late emergence of a monarchic bishop in the city of Rome, see in detail Lampe, *Die stadtrömischen Christen*, 334–45.

55. Ignatius, *Phil* 7–8 (cf. *Magn.* 6–8).

56. Eusebius, *Hist. Eccles.* 5.16.5.

57. Cf., e.g., Lampe, *Die stadtrömischen Christen*, 336–39.

58. The same can be said about those economically stronger Christians who took care of fellow Christians in need. In Rom 12:13, they are listed side by side with the hosts. Often both groups would probably have been identical. The "good person" in Rom 5:7 probably was considered a patron, too: it was easily conceivable for people to give up their lives for their benefactor because of the ties of patronage (compare A. D. Clarke, "The Good and the Just in Romans 5:7," *TynBul* 41 [1990]: 128–42).

59. Cf., e.g., Tertius, to whom Paul dictated the Letter to the Romans in the house of Gaius in Corinth (Rom 16:22–23). Gaius hosted Paul and probably also arranged Tertius's job as secretary.

60. The same is true about the Jewish-Christian Crispus (Acts 18:7; 1 Cor 1:14) and about Stephanas (1 Cor 1:16; 16:15). Both were masters of households and supported church life in Corinth, thus indirectly also Paul's apostolic mission.

61. For other examples of patronage: if 2 Tim 1:16–18 preserves an accurate tradition, a certain Onesiphorus had a patronage role for the Christians in Ephesus and also tried to care for Paul when the apostle was in prison in Rome. Acts 19:31 mentions some leaders in the Province of Asia as "friends" of Paul. They were not Christians but tried to protect him from the turmoil that had been stirred up by the silversmiths in Ephesus.

62. 2 Cor 8:23 (Titus); cf. Gal 2:1–3; Rom 16:21 (Timothy); Rom 16:9 (Urbanus); Phil 2:25 (Epaphroditus); Phlm 24 (Mark, Aristarchus, Demas, and Luke); Phlm 1, 8 (Philemon); Phil 4:3. After the Emperor Claudius's death in 54 C.E., Prisca and Aquila had returned to Rome. This move may have been strategically motivated:

They were possibly sent by Paul as his vanguard to Rome, where he wanted to gain a firm footing with his gospel before continuing to Spain.

63. Also, Rufus's mother "mothered" Paul like a patron (Rom 16:13), probably by hosting Paul, but that did not make the apostle a subordinate "client."

64. See, e.g., S. Tarachow, "St. Paul and Early Christianity: A Psychoanalytic and Historical Study," in *Psychoanalysis and the Social Sciences* (ed. W. Muensterberger and S. Axelrad; vol. 4; New York: International University Press, 1955), 240; B. E. Redlich, *S. Paul and His Companions* (London: Macmillan, 1913), 62. Barnabas also was one of the patrons of the early Jerusalem church (Acts 4:36–37).

65. Cf. also Acts 13–14. From 13:13 on, most of the time Paul is even mentioned before Barnabas.

66. I will not take into consideration the parties mentioned in 1 Cor 1–4: Corinthian Christians, who had been initiated into Christianity by Paul, Peter, or Apollos, had formed three parties that were puffed up against each other. Similar to pagan teacher-student relationships, these parties looked up to their respective apostles as to patrons and venerated them and their respective theological wisdom. Paul scolds this practice as a perversion. One can only adhere to *Christ* as a patron and venerate him—not human apostles. See, e.g., P. Lampe, "Theological Wisdom and the 'Word about the Cross:' The Rhetorical Scheme in I Corinthians 1–4," *Int* 44 (1990): 117–31.

67. *Silas* and *Timothy* (1 Cor 4:17; 16:10; 2 Cor 1:1, 19; 1 Thess 1:1; 3:2; Phil 1:1; 2:19, 22–23; Rom 16:21; cf. Acts 15:40; 16:1–3; 17:14f.; 20:4); *Titus* (2 Cor 8:17, 23; Gal 2:1–3); *Erastus* (Acts 19:22); *Urbanus* (Rom 16:9); *Epaphroditus* (Phil 2:25, 28–30); *Sosthenes* (1 Cor 1:1); *Tertius* (Rom 16:22); *Clement, Euodia,* and *Syntyche* (Phil 4:2–3); the travel companions *Aristarchus, Gaius* from Derbe, *Sopater, Secundus, Tychicus,* and *Trophimus* (Phlm 24; Acts 19:29; 20:4; cf. Eph 6:21–22; Col 4:7–8, 10), plus *anonymous persons* (Gal 1:2; 2 Cor 8:22, 18–19; Phil 4:3).

68. 2 Cor 8:18–19; Phil 2:25, 30. In Paul's temporary entourage, see also Andronicus and Junia (Rom 16:7), some anonymous "brothers" (Phil 4:21), Epaphras (Phlm 23; cf. Col 1:7–8; 4:12), Mark, Luke, Demas, Onesimus, and Jesus Justus (Phlm 23; cf. Col 4:9–11, 14; 2 Tim 4:10–11), Lucius, Jason, and Sosipater (Rom 16:21). The latter might be identical with Sopater (Acts 20:4).

69. Cf., e.g., A. Schreiber, *Die Gemeinde in Korinth: Versuch einer gruppendynamischen Betrachtung der Entwicklung der Gemeinde von Korinth auf der Basis des ersten Korintherbriefes* (NTAbh, n.s., 12; Münster, Germany: Aschendorff, 1977), 100–103; K. Stalder, "Autorität im Neuen Testament," *IKZ* 67 (1977): 1–29, esp. 4; E. Berbuir, "Die Herausbildung der kirchlichen Ämter von Gehilfen und Nachfolgern der Apostel," *Wissenschaft und Weisheit* 36 (1973): 110–28, esp. 116; J. Eckert, "Der Apostel und seine Autorität: Studien zum zweiten Korintherbrief" (Habilitationsschrift, Munich, 1972), 494ff.; G. Friedrich, "Das Problem der Autorität im Neuen Testament," in *Auf das Wort kommt es an: Gesammelte Aufsätze* (ed. J. H. Friedrich; Göttingen: Vandenhoeck & Ruprecht, 1978), 374–415, esp. 392; J. A. Grassi, *A World to Win: The Missionary Methods of Paul the Apostle* (New York: Maryknoll, 1965), 135ff.; R. Pesch, "Neutestamentliche Grundlagen kirchendemokratischer Lebensform," *Concilium: Internationale Zeitschrift für Theologie* 7 (1971): 166–71, esp. 170; G. Schille, "Offenbarung und Gesamtgemeinde nach Paulus," *Zeichen der Zeit* 24 (1970): 407–17, esp. 409; R. Schnackenburg, "Die Mitwirkung

der Gemeinde durch Konsens und Wahl im Neuen Testament," *Concillium* 8 (1972): 484–89, esp. 486f.; J. D. G. Dunn, *Jesus and the Spirit* (London: SCM, 1975), 278; J. Hainz, *Ekklesia: Strukturen paulinischer Gemeinde-Theologie und Gemeinde-Ordnung* (Biblische Untersuchungen 9; Regensburg, Germany: Pustet, 1972), 54, 291; W. Schrage, *Die konkreten Einzelgebote in der paulinischen Paränese* (Gütersloh, Germany: Mohn, 1961), 113; R. Baumann, *Mitte und Norm des Christlichen: Eine Auslegung von 1 Korinther 1,1–3,4* (NTAbh, n.s., 5; Münster, Germany: Aschendorff, 1968), 248; H. Ridderbos, *Paulus: Ein Entwurf seiner Theologie* (Wuppertal, Germany: Brockhaus, 1970), 326; and, already, E. von Dobschütz, *Die urchristlichen Gemeinden* (Leipzig: Hinrichs, 1902), 51.

70. W. Rebell, *Gehorsam und Unabhängigkeit: Eine sozialpsychologische Studie zu Paulus* (Munich: Kaiser, 1986), esp. 104–45.

71. E.g., 1 Cor 6:5, 7 and 1 Cor 7. See also 2 Cor 8:17 (about Titus).

72. E.g., 1 Thess 4:9; Rom 12:10.

73. E.g., 1 Cor 4:14–16. See also 1 Cor 4:17 (Phil 2:22): Timothy as Paul's "child." In 1 Cor 16:10–11, Paul writes a recommendation for Timothy just as a patron does. The same is true for Epaphroditus, for whom Paul writes a recommendation and who "serves" the apostle (Phil 2:29–30).

74. Rebell, *Gehorsam und Unabhängigkeit,* 130. Cf. above the founders of colonies as patrons of these political communities.

75. See also Phlm 1, 3–4, 8–9, 20: Both are equals. Κοινωνία (*koinōnia*) in Phlm 6, 17 clearly is a symmetrical term; see P. Lampe, "Der Brief an Philemon," in *Die Briefe an die Philipper, Thessalonicher und an Philemon* (ed. N. Walter, E. Reinmuth, and P. Lampe; NTD 8/2; Göttingen: Vandenhoeck & Ruprecht, 1998), 212–32, with references. The ambiguity can be also seen in other relationships. Sosthenes and the "coworkers" (Rom 16:21; Phil 2:25), Timothy and Epaphroditus, too, were "*brothers*" (1 Cor 1:1; 2 Cor 1:1; Phil 2:25), although the apostle could "send" these coworkers wherever he wanted to and Epaphroditus "served" him (e.g., Phil 2:30, 25, 28). Paul called Titus not only a "coworker" but also a "partner" (2 Cor 8:23) who to a certain extent could make his own decisions (8:17). On the other hand, being younger than Paul, Titus was clearly subordinated to Paul at the apostolic council (Gal 2:1, 3). In all of these relationships, the ambiguity prevailed.

76. Dig. 21.1.17.4–5; 21.1.43.1; 21.1.17.12; Pliny, *Ep.* 9:21, 24. For this analysis of the situation behind the Letter to Philemon, see P. Lampe, "Keine 'Sklavenflucht' des Onesimus," *ZNW* 76 (1985): 135–37; idem, "Der Brief an Philemon," 203–32.

77. See esp. Rainer Metzner, "In aller Freundschaft: Ein frühchristlicher Fall freundschaftlicher Gemeinschaft (Phil 2.25–30)," *NTS* 48 (2002): 111–31.

78. Cf. Gal 1:10.

79. Κοινωνέω (*koinōneō*), like κοινωνία (*koinōnia*), has an egalitarian aspect; see above, n. 75.

80. See, e.g., P. Achtemeier, *The Quest for Unity in the New Testament Church: A Study in Paul and Acts* (Philadelphia: Fortress Press, 1987), 60, 109.

81. Especially at the end of Acts, where Luke seems to suppress the negative news of Paul's martyrdom (cf., e.g., 1 Clement 5) in favor of an optimistic tone (Acts 28:31). In the same way he apparently suppressed the news of the disastrous ending of the Pauline collection.

82. See especially W. Rebell, *Gehorsam und Unabhängigkeit: Eine sozialpsychologische Studie zu Paulus* (Munich: Kaiser, 1986) = "Paulus—Apostel im Spannungsfeld sozialer Beziehungen" (diss., Bochum, 1982), esp. pt. 1.

83. Seneca reports an analogous case (*Ben.* 2.21.5f.). When receiving money from friends to pay for his praetorian games, Iulius Graecinus refused to accept anything from two particular persons whom he considered infamous. He did not want to be socially bound and obligated to such people.

84. This is the main conclusion of T. Schmeller, *Hierarchie und Egalität* (Stuttgart: Katholisches Bibelwerk, 1995).

85. The context (Gal 1:23; 3:6,9) seems to indicate that Paul himself was more focused on an objective genitive. However, the author's intention is not always congruent with the text's entire potential. Galatians 3:20, especially, can also be read as a subjective genitive, with the participles at the end of the verse expressing beautifully Christ's loyalty toward his clients.

86. See above, n. 47.

87. See R. W. Pickett, "The Death of Christ as Divine Patronage in Romans 5:1–11," in *Society of Biblical Literature 1993 Seminar Papers* (ed. E. H. Lovering; Atlanta: Scholars Press, 1993), 726–39. For God as benefactor and patron and Jesus as mediator of God's favor in the New Testament, see also, e.g., D. A. DeSilva, "Patronage and Reciprocity: The Context of Grace in the New Testament," *ATJ* 31 (1999): 32–84; A. Smith, *Comfort One Another: Reconstructing the Rhetoric and Audience of 1 Thessalonians* (Louisville: Westminster John Knox, 1995); B. J. Malina, "Patron and Client: The Analogy behind Synoptic Theology," *Forum* 4 (1988): 2–32.

88. Pickett, "Death," 736. For the προσαγωγή (*prosagōgē*), see Rom 5:2.

89. Pickett (ibid., 738f.) also suggests: "By depicting God as divine patron in Rom 1–5, . . . Paul may . . . have been challenging the emperor's role as great patron of all." There may be some truth to it, if the singular in Rom 1:23 (ἀνθρώπου [*anthrōpou*]) really alludes to the imperial cult. In Rom 13, however, we look in vain for such challenging allusions.

18

PAUL AND SELF-MASTERY

Stanley K. Stowers

Part I. Self-Mastery in the Greek and Roman Worlds

The Greek notion of self-mastery (ἐγκράτεια, *enkrateia*) is central to a network of moral discourse that is prominent in Paul's letters and in the broader Greco-Roman culture. This moral discourse of Paul's day first took its characteristic form in classical Greece, although it has older roots in wider Greek and Mediterranean folk psychology and moral practices. The classical heritage remained strong in Paul's time because the larger culture looked to the art, literature, philosophy and history of the classical period for its dominant cultural models. The notion also has a broader context in the larger arena of ancient Mediterranean cultures for which the idea of restraint was important. In a society and economy nearly the opposite of our capitalistic consumer culture that produces new goods and services, all of the land and goods available through the ancient technology were already distributed. Thus the social order was based on maintaining inherited social status and property and passing it on to heirs. The morals of the ancient Mediterranean revolved around an ethic of restraint that could be expressed: "Do not desire more than is your due by your station of birth." Thus the central ancient moral precepts were like the ancient Israelite "thou shall not covet" and the Greek "in nothing too much."

Self-Mastery in the Greek Ethical Tradition

The Greeks of the fourth and fifth centuries B.C.E. possessed a very rich vocabulary for talking about feeling, emotions, thinking, believing, deliberation, and in general what we describe as mental activity. The vocabulary was enriched by literature, especially the tragic and comic stage, and by the growing work of medical doctors and natural philosophers. But Plato and Aristotle reflect an important broader Greek cultural trend that added a new element to this vocabulary by talking about people as political animals and describing citizens as political entities. Greek orators, writers, and philosophers began to use concepts such as that of ruler and ruled, power, authority, stable rule and revolt in order to talk about the person and the self.[1]

The adjective ἐγκρατής (*enkratēs*, "having control over") originally applied only to political or physical control over something. The noun first appears in Plato and Xenophon and it may have been Socrates who first used the term as an attribute for a person's character.[2] Our long Western heritage of such vocabulary runs so deep that it is difficult for us to imagine a time and cultures for which there was no explicit concept of self-control.[3] Thus we must exercise our imaginations to understand just how revolutionary was Socrates' idea that the person had a distinct self and that there could be a science of the self.

After Socrates, philosophers would articulate teachings about the person, of what the person consisted, and offer techniques that aimed to give people authority and control over the directions of their lives as wholes. Socrates also became the great model for self-mastery and that model had lost none of its power in Paul's day. According to Xenophon (Mem. 1.2.1), "[R]egarding sexual desire and the stomach he was the most self-mastered [ἐγκρατέστατος, *enkratestatos*] of all men; and possessed the most endurance of cold and heat and every sort of toil; and regarding needs he was trained in moderation so that he was content with very little."[4] Above all, the paradigm of Socrates' self-mastery was his willingness to stand and die for his teachings rather than give into the desires for safety, comfort, and survival.

The opposite of self-mastery was ἀκρασία (*akrasia*), lack of self-mastery. Isocrates (15.221), for example, writes that "many people because of their failures of self-mastery [*akrasiai*] do not abide by their reasonings, but neglect their interests and follow their impulse to pleasure." Plato, and especially Aristotle, analyzed "the problem of *akrasia*" and "the type of person who lacked self-mastery," thereby establishing themes that became prominent in literature, philosophy, and the common discourse.

Lack of self-mastery (*akrasia*) might exhibit itself in psycho-ethical conflict and the great cultural paradigm for such conflict became Medea in Euripedes' *Medea*. In view of the context in the play, the famous words in 1077–80 should probably be translated along the lines of Christopher Gill's translation, "I know that what I am about to do is bad, but anger is master of my plans, which is the source of human beings' greatest troubles."[5] Here Medea affirms that the reasons for her anger, and thus revenge, are persuasive even though her reason also tells her that the plan is horrible. But the Platonic and popular understanding soon came to construe the lines as about irrational passion overcoming reason. The following translation along traditional lines captures that view: "I realize what I am about to do is evil, but passion is stronger than my reasoned reflection; this is the cause of the worst evils for humans." Chrysippus, the Stoic, discussed the text extensively and defended the first interpretation. Throughout antiquity the passage was much written about and discussed by philosophers, moralists, and in literature. Paul's Stoic contemporary, Seneca, wrote a play about Medea and forms of the saying very close to Paul's in Rom 7:15, 19 appear in Epictetus, Ovid, and other writers.[6]

Because Paul explicitly discusses *akrasia*, knows the philosophical vocabulary, and even alludes to Medea's famous words, understanding the philosophical debate about *akrasia* is essential for interpreting the texts and grasping the significance and larger cultural location of the apostle's discussions. The discussion began with Socrates, Plato, and Aristotle.[7]

As on so many topics Plato has left not one coherent position regarding *akrasia*, but at least two distinct views that would influence later opposing interpretations. In the *Protagoras*, Socrates argues against the popular view that people can be overcome by pleasure so as to act against what they believe to be good or most pleasant. People may be mistaken about what is good/pleasant, but they will always do what they believe to be best or most pleasurable.

In the *Republic*, Plato reverses himself by accepting the popular view in the context of a very different account of knowledge. He also now has the famous tripartite soul that would be so important to Platonism in the late Roman Empire. The soul consists of the reasoning part, the spirited part, and the appetitive part. Reason is the natural ruler, but an emotion like anger of the spirited part can disobey or rebel against reason and may even side with the appetites. The primarily civic metaphors such as rule, disobedience, and rebellion often impart an ethos of violence to the soul. The three parts have desires and beliefs of their own almost as if the individual consisted of three different inner persons who had an inherent tendency to fight among themselves. Recent scholarship has shown that Plato's three-part soul overemphasizes the division in the self as compared to his discussions of the soul in terms of sets of beliefs and reasonings.[8]

Even though Plato's metaphors may have misrepresented his theory of the soul by exaggerating division and conflict, the images and metaphors made an enormous impression on the culture of the later Roman Empire and, after Clement and Origen, Platonism became the unofficially official philosophy of Christianity.

One of Plato's most vivid and influential images comes from book 9 (588C–591B) of the *Republic*. There Plato likens the soul to the inside of a person that consists of a large, untamable and always changing many-headed beast in the lowest part; a somewhat smaller lion in the middle, and a yet smaller person at the top. The person inside, representing the reasoning part, is what has often been translated as the "inner man" (hereafter, "inner person"). Paul uses the expression in 2 Cor 4:16 and in Rom 7:22.[9] Although one can be fairly certain that Paul's image originated in book 9 of the *Republic,* how he uses it is a matter of much dispute.[10] At any rate, Plato's image of the soul makes a fierce struggle for self-mastery inherent to human nature. Reason (the inner person) can soothe the lion and suppress the beast, but never totally tame them. Thus *akrasia* is normal for all but a few philosophers who have become so fixated on the divine ordering of the universe that only the desire for its beauty can be active, the lower emotions and appetites having no object on which to direct themselves.

Although one frequently hears New Testament scholars speak of "Platonic dualism" as if it were the dominant philosophical or even Greek view, neither Plato's tripartite soul of the *Republic* nor his dualism of the *Phaedo* had much influence for about four hundred years, even in the Platonic academy.[11] It was only during Paul's own time that these doctrines based on a certain way of reading Plato were just beginning to become influential. The earliest important figure in this new kind of Platonism was Paul's Jewish contemporary, Philo of Alexandria. The dominant school in Paul's time was Stoicism. Discussions about whether Paul had a unitary or dualistic view of the person generally confuse a number of issues and naively presuppose modern so-called Cartesian conceptions. Descartes, one of the founders of modernity, and Plato were dualists. For Descartes there is the natural material universe that is subject to the laws of science and the supernatural realm that is totally other. The human body belongs to the first and the human soul or mind to the second. In antiquity, only Plato and the Platonists defended a view that was similar to Descartes in its dualism with regard to humans.[12] Especially in the *Phaedo,* Plato claims that the soul is separate from the body and of an entirely different order of existence. But these views had very little influence until the first or second century C.E. All of the other schools of philosophy were so-called materialists or physicalists. Everything in the universe, including God or the gods, is one part of the "natural" or physical order and can in principle be investigated by humans. All of this raises questions about how to understand Paul's views of the person and the universe at a time when the common view was physicalist, but a few intellectuals were beginning to promote a protodualism. It is not clear that anyone, including Jews, in Paul's time were fully dualists of this sort. That may have come only with Plotinus (205–269/70 C.E.). And it is important to remember that this is only one kind of dualism. Paul certainly has ethical and temporal dualisms and dualisms of substance that are part of larger hierarchies of being (e.g., flesh/spirit; mind/body; heavenly stuff/earthly stuff).

The Stoics were strong opponents of dualism and of the divided Platonic soul. They took a major interest in the problem of *akrasia* and revived Socrates' attack on the paradox of how people could do what they did not want to do.[13] In contrast to the Platonists, the Stoics argued for a model of the person as a unified physical entity including what we would call the mind or psyche. Their very complex theory has a number of significant similarities to contemporary philosophical and scientific views.[14]

For the Stoics, emotions are not to be contrasted with reason. In fact, emotions are rational in the sense of involving, or even being, judgments and beliefs with accompanying psychophysical reactions. People who feel angry, for instance, may believe that someone has insulted them. If they perceived no insult, there could be no anger. A person who is afraid believes that some circumstance poses a danger. Take away the mistaken belief that a bear is on the trail and the fear disappears.

But the Stoics went further and argued that virtue is the only true good, and therefore, what people ordinarily experienced as emotions, in society that was generally corrupted by false values, involved false beliefs, and was morally bad. The person grieves when the stock market crashes because he falsely believes that wealth is a good rather than an indifferent matter that one might rightly prefer to have, when in truth wealth has no bearing on what is truly good. Thus Stoics advocated ἀπαθεία (apatheia), the elimination of ordinary emotions or passions based on false values. Instead, the wise would have certain rational "good emotions": most important was joy; "wish" instead of desire (ἐπιθυμία, hereafter epithymia); and "caution" instead of fear.

If Stoics could not subscribe to the popular and Platonic idea of emotion and appetite as coming from a distinct irrational part of the person, how did they explain akrasia, especially akrasia with strong mental conflict? Ironically, some of the most important sources for answering this question come from the writings of Platonists who lived shortly after Paul's time and who reflect earlier debates. Because Platonism became the philosophy of Christianity, almost none of the major Stoic writings have survived intact. Instead we must often depend upon reports and quotations in the writings of Platonists such as Plutarch and Galen who are attacking Stoicism. They especially attack Chrysippus (280–207 B.C.E.), the most important Stoic and third head of the school, who had a great interest in the problem of akrasia. Chrysippus saw in Medea and the Medean saying an especially interesting and challenging case for his theory of the emotions.

For Chrysippus, Medea's mental conflict was not a conflict between reason and irrational emotion, but between different sets of reasonings and beliefs with the appropriate accompanying impulses and bodily manifestations.[15] Medea, in Stoic terminology, has "assented to the impression" that it is appropriate to take revenge on her husband who has horribly betrayed her, that vengeance is even better than the lives of her children. In the normative sense of reason, her decision

is irrational and based upon false beliefs about what is good, but in involving beliefs and reasoning, her anger is an expression of reason in the sense of a functional capacity. Medea wavers back and forth as her beliefs and reasonings about
revenge conflict with those about the value of her children. In attacking the Stoics, Plutarch (*On Moral Virtue* 446F) correctly describes their view of mental conflict as temporal alteration rather than a struggle of distinct parts:

> [Stoics] say that emotion is not different from reason, and that there is no
> dispute or conflict between the two, but a turning of the same reason in
> two directions, which we do not notice because of the suddenness and
> speed of change. We do not see that it is the nature of the same function
> of the soul to desire and to change one's mind, to feel anger and fear, and
> which being carried toward what is shameful by pleasure, while being
> moved, recovers itself again.

Chrysippus argued that the fresh false belief/psychophysical impulse of
which an emotion consists could be so strong that one lost the capacity for reflective decision-making, but one could not truly do what one did not want to do.
Lack of self-mastery (*akrasia*), however, in another sense is a part of all emotion
because, on the one hand, all humans have "a natural tendency to develop toward virtue" (οἰκείωσις, *oikeiōsis*), but on the other hand, they have false beliefs
due to social environment.[16] Thus all typical emotions or passions (except the
"good emotions") involve an inner conflict between the two tendencies. In the
Stoic view, only wisdom constituted a complete consistency of beliefs, and wisdom is an enlarged view of the world that puts everything in its true relation.

Thus the Stoics defined self-mastery (ἐγκράτεια, hereafter *enkrateia*) not as in
the popular conception of control over irrational and rebellious internal forces,
but as "an unconquerable character with respect to what is according to right reason" (*SVF* 3.67.20–22; cf. 67.45–68.2). Self-mastery is constancy over time by following what appears as true to reason and according to right reason (cf. Rom
1:18–20). As in Rom 1:21–28, *akrasia* is foolishness (e.g., ἀφροσύνη, *aphrosynē*; cf.
2:20), a lack of constancy based on a failure to act according to what is true, a state
of passion. Epictetus writes: "One time you think of these things as good, and
then of the same things as bad, and later as neither; and constantly you experience pain, fear, envy, turmoil, and change. This is why you admit that you are
foolish [ἄφρων, *aphrōn*]" (*Diss.* 2.22.6–7).

The Politics of Self-Mastery in the Wake of the Augustan Revolution

Self-mastery was not only central to the work of philosophy in articulating a self,
creating practices of self-cultivation, and formulating ethics, but was also an im-

portant principle for constructing social hierarchies in the Greco-Roman cultures. Self-mastery concerns power over self and the potential for power or lack of it over others. As Xenophon's (*Mem.* 1.5.1–6) Socrates teaches, if you want a general to save the city, or a guardian for your children, or a manager of your estate, you will want someone who is "stronger than his belly," having subdued his appetite for wine, sexual pleasure, and sleep. In the *Alcibiades,* Socrates tells an ambitious young man that to succeed as a politician he must first master himself by overcoming passion and desire. Mastery of oneself to the degree possible, given one's "natural" endowments, places a person on the social hierarchy, indicating whom one is fit to rule and by whom one is ruled. Aristotle is only following the common ancient assumption when he says that lack of self-mastery is innate, that is natural, to some people. The examples he gives are of barbarians and women as compared to men (*Eth. Nic.* 7.7 1150b). In the cultures using this kind of discourse, a series of dualities created a hierarchy of the more self-mastered who are fit to rule others and those without enough mastery to rule or fully rule themselves: for example, mind/body, humans/animals, men/women, soft men/hard men, free/slaves, Greeks/barbarians, Israelites/Canaanites, Judeans/Gentiles.

The successful effort led by Augustus to transform the Roman Republic and its colonies into a great empire united under him as monarch made much use of the ethic of self-mastery in its propaganda and as a principle of social organization.[17] Paul's era, the early empire, was a time when the connection between self-mastery and ambition seems to have reached its apex. Augustus's laws on morals and marriage set the tone for the age. The ruling elites would have to show that they exercised firm control over themselves, their families, and their dependents if Rome was successfully to rule the world. Local aristocracies and the elites of ethnic minorities all over the empire vied to demonstrate to Rome their fitness to rule. The Judeans were no exception.

The Republic ended and the imperial age began with a massive propaganda effort that centered on an exaggerated form of the myth that while early Rome had been disciplined in all things, recent times had seen a dramatic loss of public and private discipline, an age of sin. Romans 1–3 plays on a major theme of the first century. In the war for the empire, Augustus and his followers had depicted Anthony as a lust-crazed slave of Cleopatra who led a life of sensual gratification (e.g., Plutarch, *Ant.* 60; Josephus, *Ant.* 15.93). Augustus, by contrast, was the very model of self-mastery.

Self-mastery also proved an essential ingredient in the justification of Rome's conquests. Cicero claims that in the past the magistrates of Rome exercised such great self-control that other nations had willingly relinquished self-rule in order to be ruled by the Roman people. Those whom Pompey conquered were so impressed by his self-mastery that they thought him a god (*Manilian Law* 14.41). In his *Republic,* Cicero gives Laelius the task of justifying Roman imperialism: certain people lack the natural endowments to govern their own lives; these people are better off as the slaves of others; thus self-disciplined Rome rules subject peoples for their own good.

Some scholars believe that Cicero derived this argument from the Stoic philosopher Panaetius.[18] Panaetius not only supported Roman rule in opposition to the earlier Stoa's democratic and anti-monarchical teachings, but also revised the unitary Stoic psychology that denied conflict in the healthy person between soul and body or between reason and emotion. Panaetius may have posited the inherent irrationality and rebelliousness of the passionate part of the soul. The rational part of the soul must subdue and master the emotional and instinctive part of the soul just as self-mastered peoples must rule irrational nations. Augustus explicitly appealed to philosophy and many, but not all, philosophers helped to supply an ideology for his new, yet supposedly ancient, order of virtue. Judeans and Christians also claimed to have an affinity with philosophy and to possess effective routes to self-mastery.

Augustus made Egypt into a lesson for subjected peoples who were not self-mastered.[19] Augustus, his successors in the first century, and writers and speakers depicted Egypt as an irrational mass of native Egyptians and corrupted Greeks who were drenched in wicked passion. Thus the epic battle between Augustus and Antony with Cleopatra could be depicted as a struggle for virtue and the good itself. Augustus punished Egypt by denying it self-rule and by imposing a system of apartheid that segregated native Egyptians, Jews, and Greeks, with the Egyptians on the bottom of the hierarchy. Ethnic peoples, including Judeans, knew that Egypt was a lesson for them. The self-mastered would be rewarded; the passion-ruled punished.

Judaism as a School for Self-Mastery

Jewish writers did indeed depict Judaism as a philosophy for the passions, a school for self-mastery. The most extensive evidence for this understanding of Judaism comes from Philo, the Jewish aristocrat from Alexandria. "The law exhorts us to philosophize and thereby improve the soul and the ruling mind. Therefore each seventh day stand open thousands of schools in every city; schools of wisdom, self-restraint, courage and all the other virtues" (*Spec. leg.* 2.61–2). Philo's schools are, of course, what we would call synagogues. He emphasizes that these schools stand open not only to Jews but also to Gentiles. Judeans inhabit the world because they have a mission to be to the whole world as the priest is to the whole Jewish people. This sacred office of the Judean people is evident because they purify both body and soul, obeying the divine laws that control "the pleasures of the belly and the parts below it . . . setting reason as charioteer of the irrational senses and . . . the wild and extravagant impulses of the soul . . . with philosophical exhortations" (*Spec. leg.* 2.162–3). The mission of the Jewish people consists in teaching the truth of the one God and the virtues that God has ordained when reason rules over the passions. Why do the Jewish laws win such approval among Gentiles? What makes the Law of Moses superior to other laws? "The law requires that all who assent to the sacred constitution of Moses must be free from every irrational passion and all vice to a greater degree than those who are governed by other laws" (*Spec. leg.* 4.55). The Jewish Law is superior because it better produces self-mastery. In contrast, the idolatry-promoting laws of other peoples "nourish and increase" the passions and vices (*Sacr. Abel* 15).

Above all, the Law for Philo solves the greatest of human problems, the treachery of desire (ἐπιθυμία, *epithymia*). Desire is a "treacherous enemy and source of all evils" (*Virt.* 100). "Moses put off emotion, loathing it as the vilest thing and the cause of evils, above all denouncing desire as like a destroyer of cities to the soul which itself must be destroyed and made obedient to the rule of reason" (*Spec. leg.* 4.95). Desire causes relatives to become bitter enemies and is

> why large and populous countries are decimated by civil wars, and both land and sea are constantly filled with new catastrophes caused by sea and land battles. For all the wars of Greeks and barbarians, among themselves and among each other, that are the subject of tragic drama, spring from one source, desire, desire for money, glory or pleasure. These are the things that bring destruction upon the human race. (*Dec.* 151–53)

Desire and emotion serve as general explanations for human evil.

Philo, Paul, and 4 Maccabees all understand the tenth commandment (Exod 20:17; Deut 5:21; 4 Macc 2:6; Philo, *Dec.* 142) as a prohibition of desire. They read it as "you shall not desire." Just as we modern interpreters of the Bible unconsciously read modern psychology, values, and institutions into the text, so Jews in the Greco-Roman world saw their assumptions about human nature in the writings of ancient Israel. For Judeans like Paul and Philo, the tenth commandment showed that the Law was concerned with the Greco-Roman ethic of self-mastery. As one might expect, the writings of Philo, Paul's letters, and 4 Maccabees are written from the perspective of male ruling elites in this ethnic subculture of the Greco-Roman world. The discourse of desire and self-mastery is the language of their social location. This discourse embodies not only the psychology of social and gender hierarchy but also the ideology of the ethnic other. As barbarians are represented by Greeks as dangerously different and of being incapable of controlling passions and desires, so Gentiles including Greeks suffer the same depiction at the hand of Jewish writers. As we shall see below, Paul and Philo also pick out desire (*epithymia*) as the most dangerous of the passions. In both cases, but most clearly in Philo, this seems to come from the way that they combined Stoic and Platonic influences. Desire is no worse than any other passion in Stoicism because all passions derive in the same way from false beliefs and judgments. But in the Platonic tripartite soul, the spirited passions can listen to reason and be persuaded, but the appetites (for which he uses *epithymia*) are a many-headed wild beast. It appears that Jews in the first century found congenial a basically Stoic approach to the soul with some key Platonic modifications. The way that they read scripture may have been their critical principle. Above all, the claim that true beliefs about the divine were the foundation for proper ethical behavior made a Stoic framework congenial in ethics, even though Jews and Christians favored a Platonic cosmos because it had a transcendent god.

Philo views the Law as an antidote to desire in several ways. Commandments like the tenth serve as exhortations addressed to the rationality of individuals. The Law also contains the constitution of the ideal commonwealth where all of the institutions and offices are designed to promote self-mastery. The tenth commandment

> stops that fountain of injustice, desire, from which flow the most lawless acts, both public and private, both small and great, sacred and profane, concerning both bodies and souls and things called external. For nothing escapes desire, and as I have said before, like a flame in wood, it spreads and consumes and destroys everything. Many parts of the Law come under this heading which is for the admonition of those who can be reformed and for the punishment of those who rebel by making a lifelong surrender to emotion. (*Dec.* 173–74)

Philo explains that the Law prohibits eating the meat of certain animals because they are most appetizing. Eating them would encourage desire and pleasure, whereas abstaining develops self-mastery. Such prohibitions embody further symbolic meaning. Animals, for example, that crawl on their stomachs represent the life of the belly, that is, the passions (*Spec. leg.* 113). Philo also describes (*Spec. leg.* 4.92–100) the laws pertaining to marriage, food, and drink as laws of self-mastery (*enkrateia*) and restraint (σωφροσύνη, *sōphrosynē*).

Scholars have long wondered what attracted Gentiles to Jewish practices and especially to food laws. But if one understands the enormous attraction exerted by the ideal of self-mastery and the powerful interpretation of the Jewish Law as a means to it, then the popularity of Jewish practices for certain Gentiles becomes understandable. Some Jews, and even some Gentile writers, represented Judean culture as unique, exotic, and strict, giving the appearance of a uniquely disciplined nation of philosophers to some non-Jews.[20]

Josephus also presents Judaism to Gentiles as a philosophy offering a better way to self-mastery. While Greek philosophy addresses only the few, Judaism addresses the many (*Ag. Ap.* 2.168–71). Judaism is a philosophy for the masses. Josephus stresses that Gentile religious practices lead to a lack of self-control (*Ag. Ap.* 2.193) and what great discipline the Judean Law requires (*Ag. Ap.* 2.234). Nevertheless, beginning with the Greek philosophers, Gentiles have increasingly adopted Jewish laws (2.282). In striking contrast to the Qumran writings themselves, which display no interest at all in an ethic of ascetic self-mastery but instead have an ethic of purity and pollution, Philo and Josephus depict the Essenes as austerely self-mastered philosophers. "They shun pleasures as evil and consider self-mastery (*enkrateia*) and resisting the power of the passions as virtue. . . . They do not reject marriage on principle . . . but wish to protect themselves against the sexual depravity of women being convinced that no woman ever remains faithful to one man" (*J.W.* 2.120–21). Similarly, but with less extremity, the Pharisees lead a simplified life and staunchly resist any concessions to luxury (*Ant.* 18). The accounts of the Essenes, Pharisees, and Therapeutae in Philo and Josephus undoubtedly serve as attempts to claim that Jewish philosophical groups outdo Greeks and others in their degree of self-mastery.[21] Philo, Josephus, and other Jewish writings from the Second Temple period provide extensive evidence of Jews who wanted to attract Gentiles into a sympathetic relationship with the Jewish community by advertising Judaism as a superior school for self-mastery. Paul's letters argue that Gentiles through identification with Christ can attain self-mastery apart from works of the Law.

Part II. Self-Mastery in Paul's Letters

Paul's letters use all of the major terms that philosophers used in their discussions of self-mastery and its opposite: self-mastery (ἐγκράτεια, *enkrateia*; Gal 5:23); to practice self-mastery (ἐγκρατεύομαι, *enkrateuomai*; 1 Cor 7:9; 9:25); lack of self-mastery (ἀκρασία, *akrasia*; 1 Cor 7:5); passion/emotion (πάθη, πάθος; *pathē, pathos*; Rom 1:26; 7:5; 8:18; 2 Cor 5:5, 6, 7; Gal 5:24; Phil 3:10; 1 Thess 4:5); desire or passionate desire (ἐπιθυμία, *epithymia*) and to experience desire (ἐπιθυμέω, *epithymeō*; numerous instances of the noun and verb); endurance (ὑπομονή, -έω, *hypomonē, -eō*; numerous instances); to be restrained or moderate (σωφρονέω, *sōphroneō*; Rom 12:3; 2 Cor 5:13).

Romans is by far the most important site for the discourse of self-mastery in Paul's letters. The letter is a useful place to begin because it gives a fairly clear account of his normative conception, the role that self-mastery and its opposite play in his gospel. The issue of self-mastery serves an important function in the letter's argument and relates closely to the fact that the apostle addresses the letter to Gentiles and tells a story about the past, present, and future of these non-Judean (non-Jewish) peoples. Romans 1:18–32 narrates how humans (no Jews yet) gave up a true understanding of God, failed to worship God, and instead turned to gods made with human hands (i.e., Gen 1–11, as read by Paul). The passage three times says that in response, God fittingly punished these idolaters by "handing them over" (1:24, 26, 28) to desires (*epithymiais*), passions, or emotions (πάθη, *pathē*), and an unfit mind (ἀδόκιμον νοῦν, *adokimon noun*). Because of the latter cognitive state, these peoples characteristically came to perform "inappropriate acts" (μὴ καθήκοντα, *mē kathēkonta*, 1:28). The latter is a technical Stoic term for the kinds of behavior that become natural—a kind of common decency—for all humans as individuals habituate themselves in their social worlds. The whole passage also has a strongly Stoic flavor in the way that it makes a false understanding of people's larger view of the world the cause of passions and passionate desire.

Paul never attributes such domination by passions and desire to Judeans generally. The asymmetry is remarkable.[22] But *akrasia* and worse characterize the non-Jewish peoples as in 1 Thess 4:3–4 where the apostle urges that the Thessalonians "abstain from sexual immorality; that each one of you ought to possess his own wife [lit., vessel] in holiness and honor, not with passion of desire like the Gentiles who do not know God." Just as the traditional ethnic-religious other of Greeks was barbarians who could by definition lack self-mastery, so the ethnic-religious other of Judeans was Gentiles who also typically failed in self-mastery.

Paul identifies his audience in Romans as Gentiles (1:13–14; 11:13; 15:14–21) who have turned to Christ so that the story of 1:18–32 is about their past and their culture. This recent past of his readers is made more dramatically personal when Paul suddenly turns away from his audience to address an imaginary Gentile in 2:1–16. Using the common ancient rhetorical technique of apostrophe that was especially popular with moral philosophers, the passage characterizes this Gentile as a person who says one thing, but inconsistently does another. In this case, the person sets himself up as a judge of the kind of people who perform "inappropriate acts" due to idolatry when he "does the same things" (1:32; 2:1, 2, 3) because he is yet another worshiper of false gods who has been "handed over" to passion and desire. Confirmation that this person whom Paul sharply warns is an akratic Gentile like those in chapter 1, appears in 2:15.[23] There the apostle not only explains that God will judge Jews and Gentiles impartially, but that God will look into the mental record of even the best Gentiles who have done much of what the Law requires and find a conflicted mind of accusing and excusing self-judgments.

The letter returns to this classic picture of strong *akrasia* as mental conflict in chapter 7. Thus 1:18–2:16 argues that the fundamental condition of the non-Jewish peoples is a general endemic tendency toward vice and the inconsistency of *akrasia*, even among the best who somehow "by nature" try to do what God's Law requires. The failure to understand (false beliefs) that God has created and rules the universe, and therefore to serve God, has led to a mental state that allows passion and desire to run rampant. The assumptions here are both Jewish and Stoic.

The issue of self-mastery and its opposite reemerges in chapters 6–8. Traditional readings take what is said of Jews and Gentiles in 1:18–3:21 as an argument about a fallen essential and timeless human nature beyond culture. In my judgment, Paul argues that due to God's just impartiality toward both Judeans and the other peoples, God has sent Christ as a solution to the just condemnation of the Gentiles and a rectification of an apocalyptic moment of world-wide sinfulness (chs. 3–5). That current sinfulness has caused a powerful leveling so that God can display impartial mercy equally on all (3:9–31). Chapters 6–8 go on to argue that the Law which Jewish teachers have offered to Gentiles (2:17–3:8) as a solution to passion and *akrasia* cannot and was never meant to produce sinlessness and un-conflicted self-mastery. Only identification with Christ in his death and new life, and God's spirit, can bring about sinlessness and self-mastery. That Paul truly meant sinlessness and self-mastery has been controversial in Western Christianity since Augustine launched his massive and momentous attack on the idea and sought to overthrow more than three hundred years of Christian interpretation of Paul's letters.

Paul says that the readers of the letter have died to sin (6:2). The old person has been crucified in identification with Christ so that the body of sin might be destroyed and the person is no longer enslaved to sin (6:6). The readers are to think of themselves as dead to sin (6:11) and not to let sin rule over their mortal bodies so as to obey its desires (*epithymiais*, 6:12). Paul's language seems to be definitive—they are dead to sin—and yet he urges them to be dead to sin. Troels Engberg-Pedersen has powerfully argued that this makes good sense in light of Stoicism in which virtue or goodness was an all-or-nothing affair.[24] Once a person had come to the decisive insight and self-understanding that reordered every value in relation to that insight, then one was qualitatively different, even if one still might have to work out in detail how this newness might apply in specific cases. This situation called for parenesis in which one is urged fully to realize the implication of the new state.[25]

If Paul's understanding of Christ was at major points shaped by these Stoic conceptions, then his seeming insistence on *apatheia* (Gal 5:24; Rom 6:11–12), that is, the elimination of ordinary emotions or passions, also makes sense. Up until the Protestant Reformation, Christians widely understood Paul to teach the elimination of passion, even if they had come to see this as a practical goal only for saints and monks who followed the higher calling. According to Gal 5:24, "those who are of Christ have crucified the flesh with its passions and desires." In 1 Cor 7, Paul wishes that everyone could be celibate like him, but he allows marriage because of the temptation to *porneia*. *Porneia*, as we have seen, is a characteristic of Gentiles who experience passionate desire when they have sex with their wives (1 Thess 4:4). Marriage is needed because of *akrasia,* lack of self-mastery that would otherwise ensue for most people (1 Cor 7:1–5). If the unmarried cannot exercise self-mastery, they should marry because it is better to marry than to burn (7:9). Burning was a common description in Paul's time for sexual desire (e.g., Chariton 5.9.9; Alciphron 4.10.5) and Paul uses it for sexual desire in Rom 1:27. Paul seems to advocate the ancient, but to modern sensibilities bizarre, idea of passionless sex, an idea found in Philo, Stoicism, and a number of other sources.[26]

Thus Pauline parenesis, appealing to the identification with Christ's death that eliminates passion and desire and the tendency to sin, forms a preface to the discussion of *akrasia* and the Law in Rom 7. The passage is one of the most contested and exegetically complex in the New Testament. Ancient and medieval commentators generally recognized that Paul's discussion in 7:7–24 was carried out in the terms of the ancient moral tradition and sometimes specifically of *akrasia.*[27] After the Protestant Reformation, this was often forgotten or denied for theological and apologetic reasons.[28] An unfortunate result of removing the interpretation of the passage from the context of the Greco-Roman moral tradition is that it has typically been interpreted in a historically naïve way in terms of post-Cartesian and Kantian psychology that differs in important ways from any known ancient conception of the person.[29]

Ancient commentators widely believed that the words of 7:7–24 were not Paul's own, but the common rhetorical technique of προσωποποιία, *prosōpopoiia,* in which speech is crafted so as to represent the character of some individual or some type of person.[30] A recent important interpretation of 7:7–24 by Troels Engberg-Pedersen argues that Paul here gives a fundamentally Stoic treatment of *akrasia* and its cure.[31] The text aims to show that life under the Law as seen from Paul's new perspective issues in a conscious self-understanding. Such a person understands her- or himself as constantly running the risk of sinning. Awareness of *akrasia* constantly threatens those who try to keep the Law.

The "I" of 7:14 ("I am sold under sin") and 7:24 is the whole person. Paul then divides the self into its different parts to illustrate the problem. The "I whole" has different relationships with its different aspects. The "I whole" identifies with the mind/reason (νοῦς, *nous*) or inner person that rejoices in God's Law, but not with the limbs and flesh so that it sometimes does not even identify with its own acts. According to Engberg-Pedersen, such *akrasia* and awareness of disassociation comes about when the people understand themselves from an egoistic, self-directed perspective. Identification with Christ resembles the enlarged objective view of the world in Stoicism that is wisdom and that eliminates the inconsistency in the self that issues in passion and desire, lack of self-mastery. Thus the

Law alone cannot produce consistent sinlessness; only identification with Christ and the gift of the spirit of God can do that.

Engberg-Pedersen's important reading fits with a number of Stoic-like features of Paul's discourse, and especially with texts supporting the idea that those in Christ have crucified the passions and desires of the flesh. But that reading does not easily explain all of the evidence. Some language seems rather to support a Platonic-like divided person with inherently rebellious, irrational parts. As discussed above, the image of the inner person comes from book 9 of Plato's *Republic*. The image is antithetical to the unitary soul of Stoicism. Paul uses the image in a characteristically Platonic way in Romans. He also employs the image of passions and appetites as beasts in 1 Cor 15:32. The inner person represents the reasoning part of the person with its own desires and the whole person also has typically contradictory desires that belong to the lower, fleshly part of the person. On a Stoic interpretation, all passion and desiring would be states of the reasoning ability. There is no intrinsically irrational or fleshly thinking, willing or desiring part. If Paul is giving a Stoic interpretation, he has done so by employing terms and images uncongenial to the task.

Texts from other letters are also difficult to square with Stoicism. In 1 Cor 9:24–27, Paul speaks of pummeling and enslaving his body so as to attain self-mastery. This fits well with a divided soul, but poorly with a Stoic position in which the body is not intrinsically rebellious and self-mastery is attained by making the reasoning consistent with right reason, or put a bit differently, of understanding who one truly is and how one fits into the scheme of the universe. Similarly, Paul's advice that Corinthian followers should marry to avoid *akrasia*, if they cannot attain self-mastery, is not aimed at the understanding as, for example, in Rom 6:11 when he says, "consider yourself dead to sin." The advice is go ahead and be akratic if necessary, but at least within marriage so that you will not be a passion-consumed adulterer.

The solution to this mixed evidence about Paul's understanding of self-mastery, *akrasia*, and the person may come from concluding that he did not have a pure philosophical heritage regarding these concepts. The idea is broadly plausible because the late Republic and early empire was a time that saw different attempts to combine Stoic and Platonic teachings about the person. To say this is not to fall into the highly discredited notion of an age of eclectic philosophy and syncretism. From the Stoic side, three examples are most prominent, Panaetius, Posidonius, and possibly Paul's exact contemporary, Seneca. Although the evidence is not very clear, a number of scholars have thought that Panaetius (ca. 185–109 B.C.E.) accepted an Aristotelian-like bipartite soul or that he was open to Platonic influences.[32] Posidonius (ca. 135–ca. 51 B.C.E.) seems to have accepted either an inherent irrational part to the soul or at least some kind of inherent tendency to the irrational.[33] It used to be thought that Seneca was either "eclectic" and perhaps influenced by Platonic ideas or that he followed, or sometimes followed, Posidonius in accepting an irrational part to the soul. In light of current scholarship, it seems that either Seneca (4 B.C.E. to 1 C.E.–65 C.E.) was Chrysippean (i.e., "orthodox") with some minor concessions to dualism or that he was merely in the habit of using images, analogies, and metaphors (through literary custom) that falsely seem to imply dualism, if not read from a strictly Stoic point of view.[34] This latter possibility might support Engberg-Pedersen's reading of Rom 7:7–24 by providing an example of a Stoic picture of the person depicted with easily misleading and Platonic-like images. All three illustrate that a fundamentally Stoic picture of the person was sometimes combined with Platonic or dualist elements.

In the second century B.C.E., Antiochus of Ascalon had given a strongly Stoic interpretation to Platonism and later Platonism typically incorporated Stoic elements.[35] Cicero, an admirer of Antiochus, tried to combine a Stoic view of the emotions with a Platonic divided soul in the *Tusculan Disputations* 4.

But the most interesting evidence comes from Jews contemporary with Paul who found a combination of Stoicism and Platonism congenial to imagining and interpreting a biblical world. The naming and condemnation of desire in the interpretation of the tenth commandment is just one among many commonalities that have scarcely been explored in Pauline scholarship. Philo was a Platonist, but for him the tripartite soul is just a further elaboration of the Aristotelian bipartite soul that he explains in detail with Stoic doctrines (e.g., *Spec. Leg.* 4.92; *Leg. All.* 2.6; *Opif.* 117). He holds to the Stoic idea of the elimination of the passions and replacement by the Stoic "good emotions" (e.g., *Leg. All.* 3.129; *Agr.* 10). Like Paul, he speaks of the reasoning part as the inner person, but with some difficulty and inconsistency, has a Stoic conception of the good and of virtue. The writer of 4 Maccabees also seems to take a basically Stoic conception of the single good, but a Posidonian or Platonically influenced view of the passions.[36] One can conclude that reading scripture through the lens of Greek philosophy and combining Stoic and Platonic elements in ethics and on the nature of the person were intellectual currents in the air that Jews like Paul breathed.

In Engberg-Pedersen's Stoic interpretation of Rom 7:7–24, he makes Paul's talk of the body, flesh, members, passions and desires, into the representation of a self-understanding from the perspective of the egoistic bodily self. This preserves the Stoic interpretation in which there is only one cognitive-bodily ruling element, but I find it implausible in light of Paul's language. Engberg-Pedersen struggles when he tries to explain how 8:1–13 provides a solution to *akrasia,* the attainment of self-mastery, so that one no longer runs the risk of sinning. A Stoic interpretation would expect a solution like the one in chapter 6 whereby understanding themselves to have died with Christ, such people would consider that

the perspective of the old sinful self has been eliminated. But 8:1–13 speaks of invasion by the spirit as the solution. Engberg-Pedersen argues that the passage
overall appeals to the self-understanding brought about by the Christ event, but
as he admits, that does not eliminate the reference to substantive effects of the
spirit.[37] The reading need not be either/or and it is possible to construe Paul's solution as congruent with the mixed Stoic-like and Platonic-like picture of *akrasia*
in 7:7–24. The central and dominant solution to *akrasia* would, as Engberg-Pedersen argues, be Stoic-like in the identification with Christ's death in chapter 6 and
the overall parenetic quality of 8:1–13. But Paul posits an inherently irrational tendency to the body that can only be fully eliminated by a substantive change
caused by the divine *pneuma* (spirit). If the person depicted in chapter 7 represents
the Gentiles of 1:18–32 whom God handed over to their passions and desires
(1:24, 26, 28), then the Platonic-like picture of intrinsically rebellious passions and
desires makes sense. Gentiles who try to keep moral teachings from the Law are
unable to do so without a change of nature.

Paul and the Politics of Self-Mastery

Paul was a participant of his culture and did not escape the politics of self-mastery. One finds such discourse especially on these topics: ethnicity, gender, sex,
opponents, and his own character. Paul represents himself as maintaining control
over his passions and desires by means of a vigorous struggle. He quite explicitly
commends this picture of himself as a model for his followers. The most vivid
passage is 1 Cor 9:24–27:

> Do you not know that all those in a race compete, but only one receives
> the prize? So run that you might win! Everyone who is an athlete exer-
> cises self-mastery [ἐγκρατεύεται, *enkrateuetai*] in all things. They do it to
> win a perishable wreath, but we for one imperishable. So then I pummel
> my body and subject it to slavery, lest after preaching to others I myself
> not meet the test.

Here self-mastery is emphatically involved in attaining the goal(s) that Paul
preaches. This Cynic-sounding passage employs an athletic metaphor for the
struggle to subdue the passions and desires of the body in a way typical of many
types of philosophers. For Stoics, however, passions and desires are not distinctly
bodily problems and the way to self-mastery lies through obtaining true beliefs
with reasonings rather than with ascetic suppression of the body. This passage
confirms my reading of Romans in which the defeat of *akrasia* and the attainment
of self-mastery is *one* central goal of the gospel. The surprise is that Paul represents himself as still violently struggling rather than having reached the calm victory of the wise man.

The image in 1 Cor 15:32 of Paul fighting with wild animals at Ephesus also accords with this picture. As Abraham Malherbe has shown, the wild animals are the passions.[38] Indeed, the image is coupled with an antithesis, "let us eat drink and be merry for tomorrow we die." The common philosophical image of life as a moral contest or struggle (ἀγών, *agōn:* mistranslated as "opposition" in the NRSV) appears in 1 Thess 2:2. Paul then characteristically goes on to say that he had resisted error, impurity, guile, the desire to flatter, greed, and the desire for reputation (2:3–6), all very typical false desires against which philosophers claimed to struggle. These last two passages highlight the tendency of modernist (as opposed to ancient and medieval) interpreters to read passages about an internal moral struggle as describing human opponents of Paul.

Paul's hardship lists also make the point that the apostle is inwardly strong and continues his work in spite of circumstances such as hunger, thirst, hard labor, persecution, and so on (e.g., 2 Cor 6:4–10; 11:23–29).[39] In other words, Paul has mastered his desires for pleasure, comfort, good repute, and so on and has attained the self-rule (*autarkeia*) by his mind that in Phil 4:11–12 he touts as a gift from God.

Paul presents his self-mastery in sexual desire as a higher norm in 1 Cor 7. He wishes that all people could be unmarried and, like him, not involved in any sexual activity (7:7). The whole discussion equates the unmarried and sexless life with self-mastery and married life with *akrasia.* Marriage is a concession by God for those who cannot exercise self-mastery and therefore is not sinful, but it shares the state of unmastered passion and desire with *porneia* (illegitimate sexual activity). Paul recommends marriage due to the temptation to *porneia* (7:2, 5). Even short periods of abstinence for married partners poses a threat of *porneia* because married people are characterized by *akrasia* (7:5). Marriage manages desire, but does not cure the disease. Widows and the unmarried are to marry if they cannot exercise self-mastery (ἐγκρατεύονται, *enkrateuontai*) because it is better to be married than to burn with desire (7:9). Protestant and modernist attempts to make Paul give an unqualified approval of marriage and a validation of sexuality completely ignore the words, concepts, and logic of self-mastery in the chapter. Traditional Christian readings in which Paul claims celibacy as a higher way are much closer to the ethos of the language in its context.

A crucial point for understanding Pauline thought comes from seeing that he has two sets of norms for judging behavior. The first is whether the activity in question is recommended or condemned by the Judean Law (e.g., marriage, sex outside of marriage) and the second whether the activity involves uncontrolled appetites or emotions. Regarding the latter, Jews in Paul's era appealed especially to the tenth commandment. In their reading shaped by the standard Greek ethical assumptions of their day, unlike the other commandments that prohibited actions, the tenth commandment prohibited an internal condition of the soul, unmastered passion, and desire. Other commandments (e.g., "thou shall not steal.") would not work for Paul's argument in Rom 7 or for the interests of the other Jewish sources.[40] That is because Paul and his Jewish contemporaries are interested in the moral and psychological state itself and the tenth commandment can thus validate the Greek moral tradition which was the moral psychology of their day.

If in Paul's representation, he is the model of self-mastery, then his opponents epitomize enslavement to the passions of the flesh. Philippians 3:18–19 speaks of undefined and unnamed "enemies of the cross" whose god is the stomach (*koilia*). The stomach is a standard metaphor for the appetitive desires and a bodily reference to the seat of the appetites.[41] In Rom 16:17–18, those who cause dissension and teach a different message than Paul serve their stomach. As is typical of so much Greco-Roman thought, the ultimate motivations for those who differ on intellectual or political matters gets attributed to unmastered appetites.

Much of the discourse of ethnicity and self-mastery in Paul's letters comes interwoven with the discourse of self-mastery, sex, and gender. According to Paul, except for the Judeans (e.g., Gal 2:15), all of the other peoples are characterized by lack of self-mastery. The narrative of the turn from God to idols in Rom 1 describes the bondage to passion and desire of the peoples who do not worship the Judean god as a punishment by God for false worship (1:24, 26, 28). In a way reminiscent of Greek representations of barbarians, and especially Persians after the Persian wars,[42] Paul follows Jewish writers who represent other ethnicities as inherently ruled by strong passions and therefore immoral. In this Judean representation, other peoples are especially characterized by *porneia*, sexual, gender, and kinship error. When he wants to humiliate the Corinthian group of followers, Paul admonishes that a case of sexual and kinship error in the group is so bad that such *porneia* is not even seen among the Gentiles (1 Cor 5:1).

One root of this myth of the immoral Gentile lies in the Hebrew Bible's treatment of the Canaanites and other nations of the land. There texts justify the Israelite conquest and possession of the land, and even the extermination of the native inhabitants, by claiming that the natives were given to constant sexual, gender, and kinship activity that was abhorrent (e.g., Deut 20:17–18; 7:2–5; Lev 18:24–25; 20:22–25). *Jubilees* (25:1) describes "all the deeds" of the Canaanites as impure, immoral, and lustful and as a reason not to intermarry with them. Paul, like Philo, generalizes this tradition and interprets it as the problem of inherent *akrasia*.

First Thessalonians 4:4 explains that in order to be holy, the Thessalonian men should possess their own wives (literally "vessels") in holiness and honor and not like the Gentiles, ignorant of the true god, who act with desiring passion (πάθει ἐπιθυμίας, *pathei epithymias*) toward their wives. Here Paul uses the same language as in Rom 1:24–28. The implication as in 1 Cor 7 is that Paul's Christ-believing followers should be married due to *akrasia,* but have sex in marriage without desire or strong desire, an idea found among some philosophers.[43] Paul may envisage three moral levels: *akolasia,* complete domination by one's passions and desires; *akrasia,* lack of consistent self-mastery that consists of struggling against passion and desire; and the ideal of complete self-mastery that does not consist in a constant struggle. Some scholars following the Augustinian/Lutheran tradition have thought that Paul is denying the role of reason and instead replaces reason with knowledge of God. Thus while a philosopher would say that Gentile passion was caused by a lack of reason, Paul attributes its cause to an ignorance of God. This interpretation constitutes a very serious misunderstanding of both Greek philosophy and of Paul. One must be clear about the two overlapping, but ultimately distinct senses of reason. For the philosophers, reason was a function or faculty of the human being, the ability to formulate premises and draw inferences. It also, as in English usage, meant for them norms in the sense of beliefs that have a normative force. Paul's frequent reference to reasoning and the mind (e.g., Rom 7:22, 23, 25) show clearly that he understood humans to operate with a reasoning function or faculty. For a Stoic, belief in god might be one of those norms of which reason consists. Paul understood true beliefs about God not in opposition to reason, but as a component of reason. His claim is that somehow false beliefs about divinity on the part of the non-Judean peoples make them incapable of exercising their reason in such a way that they can master passions and desire.

Paul's letters, as one would expect, also evince the ancient constructions of sex and gender that were heavily implicated in the ethic of self-mastery. In Greco-Roman antiquity, it was assumed that every person could be ranked on a spectrum of femaleness and maleness.[44] Some males could have predominantly female characteristics and some women male characteristics. Physical, psychological, and more narrowly moral characteristics were all thought to be mutable. A female child nursed by a woman who had previously had a boy or a woman who led a rigorous life would acquire masculine traits, both physical and moral/psychological. All female traits were by nature inferior to male traits, even if natural for women. Women were by nature deemed to be more passionate, less able to master themselves, and therefore needed to be under the rule and protection of men. Thus women were to stay indoors, enjoy softer occupations and, in the Greek East, to wear veils. For men, maleness was a constant achievement that could be lost by lack of toughness and self-mastery. Manly men were dry, hard, active, and had weak passions and desires. Women were by nature passive, soft, damp, and had strong passions and desires.

Paul's discussion in 1 Cor 7 is written from the point of view of ruling men, beginning with the declaration that it is good for a man to touch a woman (7:1).

Much of the advice, however, may not be entirely typical in treating the dangers of desire and *akrasia* as equal for men and women. The exception is the discussion of virgins (7:36–38) where the language speaks of the insatiable sexual desire of young women—an ancient cliché—and the possibility of men who have control over the young women handling the situation due to their own self-mastery.[45]

Still, Paul would prefer that followers not marry. The common claim that he advocated celibacy because Christ's return and the events ushering in the new age were near (7:29–31) does not explain his position because his fundamental reasons stem from a moral condemnation of desire and passion. Along with many writers of his age, he views passion and desire as moral and physical states in which reason—both the reasoning function and the normative beliefs of one's rationality—has lost control of its proper role as the true self. Thinkers in this ancient ethical tradition agreed that the social and communal goals about which they were concerned when they spoke of virtues such as justice could not be achieved unless people followed reason instead of their individual passions and desires. Texts like Gal 5:22–26 show that Paul also understood self-mastery within the context of a larger social ideal, even if he never clearly articulates the relation between self-mastery and the communal virtues: "The fruit of the spirit is love, joy, peace, patience, goodness, kindness, faithfulness, gentleness, and self-mastery. Concerning such [habits of character], no law applies, but those who are of Christ have crucified the flesh with its passions and desires." Paul seems to imply that mastery over passions and desires is necessary to eliminate individual interests that compete against the virtues of social solidarity (cf. 5:26, 16–21).[46]

Paul in 1 Cor 6:9 says that soft men (μαλακοί, *malakoi*; mistranslated as "male prostitutes" in the NRSV) will not inherit the kingdom of God. Ancient sources say that soft men (*malakoi*) were particularly fond of sex with women.[47] Male homoeroticism was considered manly for the active partner and an expression of femaleness by the passive partner. Paul's language in Rom 1:26–27 strongly suggests that he saw two problems with homoerotic activity. First it involved passion out of control and second an overturning of the "natural order" that lawful sex must involve a passive woman and an active man.[48] Why the example of homoeroticism? The most likely answer seems to come from contemporary or near-contemporary moralists and philosophers such as Musonius Rufus, Dio Chrysostom, and Philo, who paint a picture of how passionate desire gets out of control. Theirs is a domino theory of the emotions. Or in another figure, if one opens the gates of the fully mastered self, then the wild ponies will escape and keep running and running. All of these moralists draw on established traditions when they give male homoerotic sex as an illustration of how passionate this uncontrolled condition could become. The assumption here is that, while moderate or even passionless sex is possible with women, the love of beautiful boys is an objective fit for great passion. Paul, as elsewhere (cf. 1 Cor 7:2–5), in a way uncharacteristic for his culture, extends the parallel to women, but typically stresses the greater passion of the men by speaking of their "burning up with impulsive desire" and the damage to their bodies/selves (Rom 1:27).[50] The latter is almost certainly a reference to the physical/moral changes that were thought to come about from allowing passion to run wild and from experiencing pleasure. Such men become soft and weak, although as we have seen, soft effeminate men are not particularly linked to homosexuality, but to desire for sex in general, especially with women. Face, voice, gait, posture, complexion, and character all change when a man loses strict control over desires.[51]

To understand the ancient Mediterranean ethic of self-mastery, as found in the discourses of the texts that were preserved by later Christian culture, one must envisage a social and economic order different from our own.[52] The construction of moral character in the ethic of self-mastery is the reverse of our moral economy of consumption.

Paul's Jewish contemporary, Philo of Alexandria, writes that the Gentile inhabitants of Canaan, among whom were the Sodomites, and the inhabitants of later Syria

> were characterized by the uncontrolled quest for pleasure that was caused by the continual and unfailing abundance available to them; for being deep-soiled and well-watered, the land had bountiful harvests every year of all kinds of fruits, and the greatest cause of evils, as has aptly been said is, "goods in excess." Incapable of bearing this burden [of dealing with the goods of an abundant economy], bolting like animals they threw off the law of nature and pursued drinking much unmixed wine and eating fine foods and unlawful forms of intercourse. Not only in their desire for women did they violate the marriages of others, but men got on top of men without respecting the common nature [i.e., that men must always be active and women passive] that the active partner shares with the passive and so when they tried to conceive children they where unable due to ineffective seed.[53] Yet the discovery was of no benefit, so much more powerful was the desire [ἐπιθυμία, *epithymia*] by which they were conquered. (*De Abr.* 134–35)

Modern types of Christianity, such as Protestant evangelical and bourgeois Roman Catholic, whose values are designed to support capitalism, neatly reverse the basic structure of values manifest in early Christianity. Capitalism is founded on massive consumption stimulated by the hundreds, even thousands, of advertisements seen by individuals each day that are designed to arouse desire and to construct a way of life aimed at working, buying, and consuming: a house in the suburbs on three acres with a mall nearby, fast cars, big sport-utility vehicles, television, professional sports, constant entertainments, and so on. The central goal of our culture of consumption, often co-opting religious validation, is the stimulation of desire for all of the sorts of things and goals that ancient moralists deplored. By contrast, the goal of the ancient and early Christian ethic is the limitation of desire for things, experiences, and pleasures: "thou shall not desire." Paul inhabited this world and developed his own distinctive yet familiar interpretation of its moral possibilities.

Part III. Other Relevant Pauline and Paulinist Texts

Galatians 5:16–24 is an important text for Paul's conception of self-mastery, if read in relation to Greco-Roman moral thought rather than supposed "apocalyptic powers."

The following passages show that the ethic of self-mastery was very much alive in the decades after Paul's death when the works below were written in his name by those who tried to extend his teachings and appeal to his authority for their own purposes. The texts from Colossians and Ephesians pick up and reinterpret Paul's idea of the Gentile bondage to passions and desire that is overcome in Christ.

Eph 2:3–4; 4:19–24; Col 3:5–11; 1 Tim 6:9–10; 2 Tim 1:7; 2:22; 3:6; Titus 1:8, 12; 2:2, 5–7, 12; 3:3.

Part IV. Bibliography

The Greco-Roman World

Cooper, John. *Reason and Emotion.* Princeton: Princeton University Press, 1999.

Dover, Kenneth. *Greek Popular Morality in the Time of Plato and Aristotle.* Berkeley: University of California Press, 1974.

Engberg-Pedersen, Troels. "Philo's DE VITA CONTEMPLATIVA as a Philosopher's Dream." *Journal for the Study of Judaism* 30 (1999): 40–64.

Erskine, Andrew. *The Hellenistic Stoa: Political Thought and Action.* Ithaca, N.Y.: Cornell University Press, 1990.

Gill, Christopher. "Did Galen Understand Platonic and Stoic Thinking on Emotions?" Pages 114–23 in *The Emotions in Hellenistic Philosophy,* edited by Juha Sihvola and Troels Engberg-Pedersen. Dordrecht, the Netherlands: Kluwer Press, 1998.

———. *Personality in Greek Epic, Tragedy, and Philosophy: The Self in Dialogue.* Oxford: Clarendon Press, 1996.

Gosling, Justin. *Weakness of the Will.* London: Routledge Press, 1990.

Inwood, Brad, "Seneca and Psychological Dualism." Pages 449–84 in *Passions and Perceptions,* edited by J. Brunschwig and M. Nussbaum. Cambridge: Cambridge University Press, 1999.

Laqueur, Thomas. *Making Sex: Body and Gender from the Greeks to Freud.* Cambridge: Harvard University Press, 1990.

Long, Anthony. "Hellenistic Ethics and Philosophical Power." Pages 138–67 in *Hellenistic History and Culture,* edited by Peter Green. Berkeley: University of California Press, 1993.

Long, Anthony, and David Sedley. *The Hellenistic Philosophers.* Cambridge: Cambridge University Press, 1987.

Markschies, Christoph. "Innerer Mensch." *RAC* 18:266–312.

Martin, Dale. *The Corinthian Body.* New Haven: Yale University Press, 1995.

North, Helen. *Self-Knowledge and Self-Restraint in Greek Literature.* Ithaca, N.Y.: Cornell University Press, 1966.

Price, Anthony. *Mental Conflict.* London: Routledge, 1995.

Paul and Self-Mastery

Betz, Hans Dieter. "The Concept of the 'Inner Human Being' (ὁ ἔσω ἄνθρωπος) in the Anthropology of Paul." *NTS* (2000) 46: 315–41.

Engberg-Pedersen, Troels. *Paul and the Stoics.* Louisville: Westminster John Knox Press, 2000.

Fitzgerald, John T. *Cracks in an Earthen Vessel.* SBLDS 99. Atlanta: Scholars Press, 1998.

Heckel, Theo. *Der innere Mensch: Der paulinische Verarbeitung eines platonischen Motivs.* WUNT 2.53. Tübingen: Mohr Siebeck, 1993.

Malherbe, Abraham J. *Paul and the Popular Philosophers.* Minneapolis: Augsburg Fortress Press, 1989.

Martin, Dale. *The Corinthian Body.* New Haven: Yale University Press, 1995.

———. "Paul without Passion: On Paul's Rejection of Desire in Sex and Marriage." Pages 201–15 in *Constructing Early Christian Families,* edited by Halvor Moxnes. London: Routledge, 1997.

Stowers, Stanley. *A Rereading of Romans: Justice, Jews, and Gentiles.* New Haven: Yale University Press, 1994.

Theissen, Gerd. *Psychological Aspects of Pauline Theology.* Philadelphia: Fortress Press, 1987.

Ziesler, J. A. "The Role of the Tenth Commandment in Romans 7." *JSNT* 33 (1998): 47–49.

Notes

1. Kenneth Dover, *Greek Popular Morality in the Time of Plato and Aristotle* (Berkeley: University of California Press, 1974), 124–26, 208.

2. Anthony Long, "Hellenistic Ethics and Philosophical Power," in *Hellenistic History and Culture* (ed. P. Green; Berkeley: University of California Press, 1993), 143–45.

3. Helen North, *Self-Control and Self-Restraint in Greek Literature* (Ithaca, N.Y.: Cornell University Press, 1966), together with Long, "Hellenistic Ethics," 143.

4. All translations are my own unless otherwise noted.

5. Christopher Gill, *Personality in Greek Epic, Tragedy, and Philosophy: The Self in Dialogue* (Oxford: Clarendon, 1996), 223.

6. Stanley Stowers, *A Rereading of Romans: Justice, Jews, and Gentiles* (New Haven: Yale University Press, 1994), 260–64.

7. Justin Gosling, *Weakness of the Will* (London: Routledge, 1990), 7–47; Anthony Price, *Mental Conflict* (London: Routledge, 1995).

8. Gill, *Personality*, 245–60.

9. Theo Heckel, *Der innere Mensch: Der paulinische Verarbeitung eines platonischen Motivs* (WUNT 2.53; Tübingen: Mohr Siebeck, 1993); Christoph Markschies, "Innerer Mensch," *RAC* 18 (1997): 266–312; see also Betz in n. 11 below. Although helpful, I do not find any of the treatments of this image by New Testament scholars satisfactory, either on the philosophical traditions or on Paul's use of the metaphor. The discussions tend to be dominated by apologetic attempts to guard Paul's uniqueness, among other problems.

10. For bibliography, see the two works in n. 9 and Betz in n. 11.

11. The Old Academy had very little interest in the soul, and Plato's ideas on it were very strongly attacked by the other schools. The skeptical New Academy rejected all such doctrines and held sway until the formal end of the Academy in 87 B.C.E. So-called Middle Platonism was based upon systematic doctrines derived from Plato's unsystematic dialogues and began to revive dualism and the tripartite soul in the first and second centuries C.E. These facts are well known by scholars of ancient philosophy, but do not seem to have been noticed by New Testament scholars. For examples of the apologetic use of "Platonic dualism" as a foil for a supposedly unitary view by Paul, see Hans Dieter Betz, "The Concept of the 'Inner Human Being (ὁ ἔσω ἄνθρωπος)' in the Anthropology of Paul," *NTS* 46 (2000): 315–41. This aspect of Betz's erudite article is typical of a widespread phenomenon.

12. The context and purposes of the two dualisms are, of course, quite different. Descartes wanted to create autonomous realms for the new science and secular human activity over against religion, thereby protecting both. Plato and later Platonists still have a universe that is united and fully interactive, but with a great hierarchy of qualities and substances.

13. Gosling, *Weakness of Will*, 48–68; Price, *Mental Conflict*, 145–78; Gill, *Personality*, 229–32.

14. Anthony Long and David Sedley, *The Hellenistic Philosophers* (Cambridge: Cambridge University Press, 1987). For texts in translation and commentary, see vol. 1, 266–74, 313–22, 410–22, and vol. 2, 264–70, 310–20, 404–18. For the Greek and Latin texts with bibliography, see pp. 491–510.

15. Christopher Gill, "Did Galen Understand Platonic and Stoic Thinking on Emotions?" in *The Emotions in Hellenistic Philosophy* (ed. Juha Sihvola and Troels Engberg-Pedersen; Dordrecht, the Netherlands: Kluwer, 1998), 114–23.

16. The major work on this theory is Troels Engberg-Pedersen, *The Stoic Theory of Okeiosis: Moral Development and Social Interaction in Early Stoic Philosophy* (Århus, Denmark: Århus University Press, 1990).

17. For a more detailed discussion of this topic, with bibliography, see Stowers, *Rereading of Romans*, 52–65.

18. Andrew Erskine, *The Hellenistic Stoa: Political Thought and Action* (Ithaca, N.Y.: Cornell University Press, 1990), 192–200.

19. Stowers, *Rereading of Romans*, 52–53.

20. Ibid., 62–64.

21. Troels Engberg-Pedersen, "Philo's DE VITA CONTEMPLATIVA as a Philosopher's Dream," *JSJ* 30 (1999): 40–64.

22. In a desperate attempt to find texts that would make Judeans as sinful as Gentiles, some have appealed to 1 Cor 10:1–22, where Paul discusses the dangers of desire, but Paul does not generalize Israel's disobedience at Sinai to Judeans in general as he does the evil of Gentiles.

23. I owe this basic interpretation to Troels Engberg-Pedersen (*Paul and the Stoics* [Louisville: Westminster John Knox, 2000], 203 and n. 43). Engberg-Pedersen, I believe, confuses the issue when he describes the passage as depicting the mental conflict of *akrasia,* but then goes on to describe the person as the "self-mastered" individual who regularly struggles and succeeds in doing the right thing, but with internal conflict. This introduces a definition of the "self-mastered" person from Aristotle that does not easily fit Stoic thought.

24. Ibid., 225–39.

25. As far as I know, however, the progress in Stoicism was only for those who were progressing toward wisdom, and not for the wise.

26. Dale Martin, "Paul without Passion: On Paul's Rejection of Desire in Sex and Marriage," in *Constructing Early Christian Families* (ed. Halvor Moxnes; London: Routledge, 1997), 201–15.

27. E.g., Stowers, *Rereading of Romans,* 267–69.

28. Engberg-Pedersen, *Paul and the Stoics,* 368–69n. 27.

29. On modern versus ancient conceptions, see Christopher Gill, *Personality in Greek Epic, Tragedy, and Philosophy: The Self in Dialogue* (Oxford: Clarendon, 1996). Unfortunately a clear example of assuming a basically Cartesian, and more specifically Freudian, view of the person is Gerd Theissen's fascinating and erudite study *Psychological Aspects of Pauline Theology* (Philadelphia: Fortress Press, 1987).

30. See Stowers, *Rereading of Romans,* 264–69, and on the technique, 16–21. See also Stanley Stowers, "Apostrophe, Προσωποποιια, and Paul's Rhetorical Education," in *Early Christianity and Classical Culture* (ed. J. Fitzgerald and M. White; Trinity Press International, forthcoming).

31. Engberg-Pedersen, *Paul and the Stoics,* 239–53.

32. Long and Sedley, *Hellenistic Philosophers,* 1:316 (J), 321.

33. Recently there has been considerable debate about Posidonius's position: see Price, *Mental Conflict,* 175–78, and for an argument that Galen read a Platonic soul into Posidonius, who only added an emphasis on irrational movements in the soul to Chrysippus's view, see John Cooper, *Reason and Emotion* (Princeton: Princeton University Press, 1999), 449–84.

34. Brad Inwood, "Seneca and Psychological Dualism," in *Passions and Perceptions* (ed. J. Brunschwig and M. Nussbaum; Cambridge: Cambridge University Press, 1993), 150–83.

35. John Dillon, *The Middle Platonists* (Ithaca, N.Y.: Cornell University Press, 1996), 52–105.

36. Richard Renehan, "The Greek Philosophic Background of Fourth Maccabees," *Rheinisches Museum für Philologie* 115 (1972): 221–38; Stanley Stowers, "Fourth Maccabees," in *Harper's Bible Commentary* (San Francisco: Harper & Row, 1988), 924.

37. Engberg-Pedersen, *Paul and the Stoics,* 247–50.

38. Abraham Malherbe, *Paul and the Popular Philosophers* (Minneapolis: Augsburg Fortress Press, 1989), 79–89.

39. John T. Fitzgerald, *Cracks in an Earthen Vessel* (SBLDS 99; Atlanta: Scholars Press, 1988).

40. A very important point that I have only seen made by J. A. Ziesler, "The Role of the Tenth Commandment in Romans 7," *JSNT* 33 (1988): 47–49.

41. Stowers, *Rereading of Romans,* 49–50.

42. Edith Hall, *Inventing the Barbarian: Greek Self-Definition through Tragedy* (Oxford: Clarendon, 1989).

43. See n. 26 above.

44. There is now an extensive bibliography on this and on my following remarks about gender. An accessible introduction to the material is Thomas Laqueur, *Making Sex: Body and Gender from the Greeks to Freud* (Cambridge: Harvard University Press, 1990), whom I follow here.

45. Martin, *Corinthian Body,* 217–27.

46. This text seems to me to be one of the strongest pieces of evidence for Engberg-Pedersen's interpretation (*Paul and the Stoics*) of Pauline thought as aimed at eliminating the self-directed perspective.

47. Martin, *Corinthian Body,* 33.

48. Stowers, *Rereading of Romans,* 94–95, and Dale Martin, "Heterosexism and the Interpretation of Romans 1:18–32," *BibInt* 3 (1995): 332–55.

49. Martin, "Heterosexism," 332–55.

50. Especially on the women in 1:27, see Bernadette Brooten, *Love between Women: Early Christian Responses to Female Homoeroticism* (Chicago: University of Chicago Press, 1996).

51. For much material on changes brought about by softness leading to effeminacy, see Maud Gleason, *Making Men* (Princeton: Princeton University Press, 1995), esp. 55–81, and Martin, *Corinthian Body,* 33.

52. I write the sentence this way because we should not assume that the ideals and prescriptions of the elite sources transmitted by Christians accurately represent actual behavior, even if surely influencing behavior to some extent, for some people.

53. This passion leads to intercourse that is unlawful precisely because one man, in this construction, must always play a passive role and thus act as a woman. Philo also assumes that such softness would so attack the body that it would render the man incapable of having children, probably in virtue of "weak seed."

19

PAUL, SHAME, AND HONOR

Robert Jewett

A number of scholars have reflected on the social issues of honor and shame in Paul's letters. This research makes clear that the audience of Paul's letters consisted largely of persons with low social status, persons who would have been demeaned from birth on prejudicial grounds, not because of what they had done but because of their social, cultural, sexual, or religious identity. The rhetoric of shame in New Testament usage refers both to shameful deeds and shameful status imposed by others.[1] In Rom 1:14, for example, the latter dimension surfaces as the gospel relates both to shameful "barbarians" and honored "Greeks," both to the "educated" and the "uneducated" (Rom 1:14). These social distinctions correlate with other categories of honor and shame such as Jew/Gentile, weak/strong, which assume crucial significance in the theology and ethic of the letter.[2] A case can be made that each of the Pauline letters offers an antidote to shameful status, conveying that in Christ's ministry of grace, those held in contempt by society were raised to a position of righteousness and honor. We begin with a sketch of basic studies of honor and shame by social scientists and classicists.[3]

Part I. Examples of Honor Discourse in Greco-Roman and Jewish Culture

On the basis of sociological, anthropological, and historical information, Bruce Malina defined the ancient view of honor as "the value of a person in his or her own eyes . . . *plus* that person's value in the eyes of his or her social group. Honor is a claim to worth along with the social acknowledgement of worth."[4] In the competitive environment of the Mediterranean world, such honor was gained "by excelling over others in the social interaction that we shall call challenge and response."[5] This occurs only between persons of the same class, because superiority over those of lower status was assumed and did not have to be proved. The goal of a challenge, in arenas ranging from political power to religious reputation, was "to usurp the reputation of another. . . . When the person challenged cannot or does not respond to the challenge posed by his equal, he loses his reputation in the eyes of the public. . . . every social interaction that takes place outside one's family or outside one's circle of friends is perceived as a challenge to honor, a mutual attempt to acquire honor from one's social equal. . . . anthropologists call it an *agonistic* culture."[6]

Competition was a distinctive feature of ancient Greek culture, as perceived by classicists. For example in the *Iliad*, Glaucus boasts in a typical manner:

> Son of Hippolochus I; and he, I declare, was my father.
> He unto Ilium sent me and charged me instant and often
> Ever to be of the best, preeminent over all others.
> Neither bring shame on the house of my fathers, who were the
>   noblest
> Born in Ephyra town or in the broad kingdom of Lycia.
>   (Homer, *Iliad*, bk. 6, 206–10)[7]

Competition for honor occurred on all levels, in education, oratory, politics, poetry, music, athletics, and war. This resulted in the organization of formal competitions in most of these arenas, in which prizes honored superior performances.

In page after page, Pausanius describes the monuments honoring the famous victors in the Olympic competitions. Here is a typical excerpt:

> The statue of Astylus of Crotona is the work of Pythagoras; this athlete won three successive victories at Olympia. . . . There is also set up in Olympia a slab recording the victories of Chionis the Lacedaemonian. . . . Similarly in renown to Chionis was Hermogenes of Xanthus, a Lydian, who won the wild olive eight times at three Olympic festivals, and was surnamed Horse by the Greeks. Polites also you will consider a great marvel. . . . For from the longest race, demanding the greatest stamina, he changed, after the shortest interval, to the shortest and quickest, and after winning a victory in the long race, he added in the same day a third victory in the double course. . . . However, the most famous runner was Leonidas of Rhodes. He maintained his speed at its prime for four Olympiads, and won twelve victories for running. (Pausanius, *Description of Greece*, bk. 6, 13.1–4)[8]

This competitive orientation continued in various venues from the classical through the Hellenistic and Roman periods. N. R. E. Fisher's definitive study of classical Greek usage shows that *hybris* is "the deliberate dishonouring of those one should honour."[9] He concludes by stressing

> the importance of honour-based values inside and between Greek states; analysis needs to recognize the extent to which the drive for personal honour operated very strongly on all those engaged in public life, and even more the extent to which the loss of citizen status, and violent or sexual attacks on a person's honour, and that of his family or social group, aroused the very deepest feelings among Greeks of every status, and potentially very violent reactions.[10]

Aristotle provides a basic analysis of this widespread competition for honor. There are three levels of "slighting" others, holding them to be persons unworthy of honor. The first is "contempt," which indicates that someone has no value at all; the second is "spite," which places obstacles in the path of the unworthy other; the third is *hybris,* which Aristotle describes as follows:

> The man committing *hybris* also slights; for *hybris* is doing and saying things at which the victim incurs shame; not in order that one may achieve anything other than what is done but simply to get pleasure from it. . . . The cause of the pleasure for those committing *hybris* is that by harming people, they think themselves to be superior. . . . Dishonour is characteristic of *hybris,* and he who dishonours someone slights him, since what has no worth has no honour, either for good or for bad. That is why Achilles says when angry: "He dishonoured me; for he has himself taken my prize, and keeps it" [*Iliad* 2.356] and "He treated me as if I were a wanderer without honour" [*Iliad* 9.648 = 17.599], since he is angry for those reasons.[11]

As the examples from the *Iliad* show, honor involved not just approbation from others but also the possession of material advantages. As Thomas Fatheuer indicates, "The central conflict in the *Iliad,* the conflict between Achilles and Agamemnon, is a struggle about *timē* ("honor"), about the position and honor of each and simultaneously a struggle about the spoils of war, about the captive woman, Briseis."[12] Achilles feels dishonored and even deprived of his free citizenship as a Greek because his general insisted on a superior right to the spoils. After sulking for a season, Achilles resorts to a supreme act of *hybris* in dishonoring the body of the slain Hector as a way to retrieve his honor, with predictably tragic consequences.

The classicist E. A. Judge confirms the broad cultural tradition that viewed the earning of honor as the only suitable goal for life, despite its dangers. He describes the social attitudes that continued from the classical period down to the later Greco-Roman culture:[13]

By New Testament times the predominant Stoic school of philosophy had raised the estimate [of the value of glory] to a very high level, apparently in response to the cult of glory among the Roman nobility. It was held that the winning of glory was the only adequate reward for merit in public life, and that, given the doubt as to the state of man after death, it was the effective assurance of immortality. It therefore became a prime and admired objective of public figures to enshrine themselves, by actually defining their own glory, in the undying memory of posterity. What was more, a man was thought the meaner for not pursuing this quest for glory. . . . Self-magnification thus became a feature of Hellenic higher education, and by no means merely a caricature of its aims.

The honorific monuments throughout the Roman Empire illustrate this yearning for immortal glory. A well-known example is Augustus's *Res Gestae,* placed on the walls of the mausoleum in Rome and in temples at Ancyra and Pisidian Antioch, in which his public honors are listed in extraordinarily extensive detail. In Ekkehard Weber's words, it is "the product of a typical Roman quest for *gloria,* a reputation extending far beyond his own death, which represents the highest goal of every public life."[14] After describing his selfless rise to power and his triumph over the murderers of his father, Augustus begins to list the honors that he received:

Twice I triumphed in the form of Ovatio and thrice in curulic form [different forms of triumphs]; twenty-one times I was called to be Imperator. The Senate voted yet more triumphs for me which I declined. . . . Because of the victories won by me and my generals on land and water the Senate voted thanksgivings to the immortal gods fifty-five times. The total number of days on which such Senatorial celebrations were held was 890. In my triumphs nine kings or children of kings were led before my chariot. Up until the time I write this, I have been counsel thirteen times and am in the thirty-seventh year of the *tribunicia potestas.* . . . I belonged to the triumvirate for the new order of the state without interruption for ten years. I was the highest ranking Senator . . . for forty years; I held the office of Pontifex maximus and of Augur, belonged to the college of the sacred Quindecemviri and the sacred Septemviri, was a brother of the Arval, a member of the Titius and Fetiale societies. . . . Votive offerings for my well-being every five years were voted by the Senate to be performed by the Consuls and the members of the priesthood. On the basis of these offerings the four highest priestly colleges and the Consuls frequently organized festivals. As individuals as well as city assemblies all citizens with one accord unceasingly prayed in every holy place for my salvation. By senatorial decree my name was placed in the Salier cultic hymn, and by law decreed that I should be forever exempt from accusations and that I should have the protection of the people's tribunal as long as I lived. . . . By senatorial decree a delegation of a portion of the Praetorian Guard and the people's tribunal with Consul Q. Lucretius and leading representatives was sent to Campanian, an honor that never before had been granted except for me. When I returned to Rome from Spain and Gaul after successful activities in these provinces under the Consulship of Ti. Nero and P. Quintilius, the Senate dedicated an Altar of Augustan Peace in the Marsfield on the occasion of my return; there it was decreed that the officials, the priesthood, and the Vestal Virgins should make yearly sacrifices.[15]

Only politicians of totalitarian bent in the modern world would dream of listing their accomplishments and honors in such detail, but in the honor-shame culture of the Greco-Roman world it was perfectly natural. It ensured the memory of Augustus, which was the only sure form of immortality, and it served to stimulate emulation in others in the quest for honor, which was thought to be supremely virtuous.

The social function of claiming honor is particularly visible in the funeral oration of Pericles, which extols the courage of fallen soldiers in order to make their immortal fame and the preservation of their city a desirable goal for the current audience to emulate. Thucydides reports that Pericles lauded Athens in extensive detail: "Such, then, is the city for which these men nobly fought and died, deeming it their duty not to let her be taken from them; and it is fitting that every man who is left behind should suffer willingly for her sake" (Thucydides, *History of the Peloponnesian War,* II, 41.5).[16] The honor these soldiers gained in death undergirds the quest for honor among survivors:

> For they gave their lives for the commonweal, and in so doing won for themselves the praise which grows not old and the most distinguished of all sepulchres—not that in which they lie buried, but that in which their glory survives in everlasting remembrance, celebrated on every occasion which gives rise to word of eulogy or deed of emulation. . . . Do you, therefore, now make these men your examples, and judging freedom to be happiness and courage to be freedom, be not too anxious about the dangers of war. (*History of the Peloponnesian War,* II, 43.2–5)

To those who grieved over the loss of family members, Pericles urged that they be "comforted by the fair fame of these your sons. For the love of honor alone is untouched by age, and when one comes to the ineffectual period of life it is not 'gain' as some say, that gives the greater satisfaction, but honor" (*History of the Peloponnesian War,* II, 44.4). That the attainment of honor is the proper goal of life was never more clearly stated.

David deSilva confirms that the competitive orientation remained dominant in the New Testament period: "[T]he culture of the first-century world was built

on the foundational social values of honor and dishonor."[17] He provides a survey
of classical and rhetorical texts that constitute "honor discourse" aimed at reinforcing behavior that conforms to the "court of reputation" of one's particular
group.[18] For example:

> When the dominant, Greco-Roman culture held a group like the Jews in
> contempt the effect was a constant pressure on individual Jews to give up
> their Jewishness and join in those behaviors that would be greeted as
> honorable by the members of the dominant culture. Jewish authors
> would urge their fellow Jews to set their hearts on the opinion of the con-
> gregation and the opinion of God and so be able to resist the pull of the
> Gentile world.[19]

Sirach provides an example of this kind of discourse in lauding the genuine
honor to be gained by adhering to the values of Jewish culture, namely proper devotion to God and adherence to the Torah; here the honors accessible to Jews are
contrasted with the honors that can be gained by the rest of the human race:

> What race is worthy of honor? The human race.
> What race is worthy of honor? Those who fear the Lord.
> What race is unworthy of honor? The human race.
> > What race is unworthy of honor? Those who
> > transgress the commandments.
> The nobleman, and the judge, and the ruler will be honored,
> but none of them is greater than the man who fears the Lord.
> > > (Sir 10:19, 24)

Just as with Pericles in the classical period, examples of praiseworthy figures
from the past are lifted up to encourage current audiences to conform to their
virtues. In Sirach, for example, the author concludes with a hymn to the Jewish
ancestors that is intended to lead his readers to emulate their behavior; here is an
excerpt of such honor discourse:

> Let us now praise famous men,
> and our fathers in their generations.
> The Lord apportioned to them great glory,
> > his majesty from the beginning.
> There were those who ruled in their kingdoms,
> > and were men renowned for their power,
> > giving counsel by their understanding,
> > and proclaiming prophecies;
> all these were honored in their generations,
> > and were the glory of their times.
> But these were men of mercy,
> > whose righteous deeds have not been forgotten;

> their prosperity will remain with their descendents,
> > and their inheritance to their children's children.
> Their descendents stand by the covenants;
> > heir children also, for their sake.
> Their posterity will continue for ever,
> > and their glory will not be blotted out.
> > > (Sir 44:1–13)

And with that Sirach praises a list of worthies that begins with Enoch and runs through Abraham, Moses, Elijah, and Adam, among others (Sir 44:1–3, 7, 10–13, 16, 19; 45:1–2, 4, 16).

Although dissenting minorities such as Jews or early Christians could not gain honor in the manner lauded by Pericles, and were in fact usually viewed as dishonorable by the mainline Greek and Roman cultures, the desire to achieve honor by some other means remained dominant. DeSilva proposes a method for investigating honor discourse in this dissenting mode, by examining the language that reinforces adherence to the courts of reputation of particular groups. By seeking to please their God, such groups were able to defend the honor of members who were under pressure to conform to the dominant cultural norms. DeSilva concludes that early Christian writers such as Paul proclaim a message that differed from "core values within the dominant Greco-Roman culture as well as the Jewish subculture" concerning how to gain honor.[20] This conclusion can be elaborated by examining the peculiar discourse employed by Paul.

Part II. Examples from the Pauline Letters

I Corinthians 1–2

A typical form of competition for honor is expressed in the boasts of the Corinthian parties that Paul cites in 1 Cor 1:12: "I belong to Paul," "I belong to Apollos," and so on. These claims of "party allegiance"[21] contain implicit claims of superior honor, which explains why Paul develops the contrast between Greco-Roman/Jewish boasting and the new orientation required by faith in Christ. The entire system of honor and shame has been overturned by God's election of the "weak," the "low and despised in the world," to receive the gospel, which "puts to shame" the strong and wise, who would ordinarily be given precedence (1 Cor 1:26–28).[22] It follows that the only legitimate form of boasting is to "boast in the Lord" (1 Cor 1:30).[23] Only the divine court of reputation established by the crucified Christ remains valid.

The foundation of this new evaluation of honor and shame is the cross event (1 Cor 1:18–25), which "brought an end to human self-sufficiency as it is evidenced through human wisdom and devices."[24] While the Greeks seek validation through "wisdom" and the Jews through "miraculous signs" (1:22), the cross of Christ is folly and a stumbling block. It contradicts every human system of seeking superior status and gaining honor through religious and philosophical practice. Thus in Gordon Fee's formulation, whereas "*messiah* meant power, splendor, triumph, *crucifixion* meant weakness, humiliation, defeat."[25] The consequence is drawn by Richard Hays, that "the cross is the key to understanding reality in God's new eschatological age. Consequently, to enter the symbolic world of the gospel is to undergo a conversion of the imagination, to see all values transformed by the foolish and weak death of Jesus on the cross."[26] The values transformed here were central for Greco-Roman and Jewish societies, namely how to gain the honor that made life meaningful. The new age brought by Christ crucified grants honor to the lowly and brings shame to the boastful, eliminating the social system of "challenge and response" in the competition for honor. The gospel addresses the wounds of "toxic unwantedness" experienced by those who failed to gain or maintain honor.[27]

Autobiographical References in Galatians and Philippians

In Paul's autobiographical statements, his former participation in the intense competition that marked the Greco-Roman world comes clearly to expression. In Gal 1:14, he describes his achievements in explicitly competitive form: "I advanced in Judaism beyond many of my own age among my people, so extremely zealous was I for the traditions of my fathers." While the enumeration of achievements is smaller than that of Augustus, the competitive framework is defined by the word προέκοπτον (*proekopton*, "make progress, go against"), to advance by "going ahead in a contest between several young Jews who are faithful to the Law."[28] The basis of comparison is συνηλικιώτας (*synēlikiōtas*, "contemporary"), which appears here for the only time in the New Testament, referring to "a person of one's own age"[29] with whom such competition for honor would ordinarily be waged. In this instance, the competition was in "ardent" observance of the Torah.[30] As Jerome Murphy-O'Connor observes, "the combative tone and competitive spirit" of this statement "are equally characteristic of elite groups" such as students in the Pharisaic movement.[31]

The competition for honor is also visible in Paul's self-description in Philippians, in which, according to Peter O'Brien, there is a claim that "his heritage and achievements as grounds for personal boasting were second to none:"[32]

> If any other man thinks he has reason for confidence in the flesh, I have more: circumcised on the eighth day, of the people of Israel, of the tribe of Benjamin, a Hebrew born of Hebrews; as to the law a Pharisee, as to

zeal a persecutor of the church, as to righteousness under the law blameless. (Phil 3:4–6)

Here we find a list of status markers that were typical for Jewish members of the Greco-Roman world: a pedigree from an honorable family marked by piety, as shown by their proper circumcision of their son on the eighth day, according to the Law; impeccable national descent, with an honorable tribal identity without admixture of other blood lines or "any assimilation to Gentile customs and culture."[33] Paul's own achievements are listed in threefold fashion: a member of the Pharisee party that was noted for its strict observance of the Torah; zeal for the Torah even to the point of persecuting Torah violators in the early church; and flawless performance[34] of the demands of righteousness. This entire recital is couched in competitive terms, as verse 4 reveals: compared with any other claims of religious honor, "I have more." In Peter O'Brien's assessment, "Paul's grounds for boasting in his own pedigree and achievements are in fact greater than the credentials any Judaizer could produce. . . . no one can equal his claims."[35] Yet all of this is now counted as "loss" and "refuse" because of Christ's replacement of the system of gaining honor through performance of the Law; henceforth, honor comes only through faith in the crucified one (Phil 3:8–10). Since such honor is a gift rather than an achievement, it eliminates every system of "confidence in the flesh" (Phil 3:3).

Romans 3

This chapter provides the climax of an argument beginning in Rom 1:18, demonstrating that no group has a legitimate claim of superior honor because all have participated in suppression of the truth by glorifying humans rather than God. The goal of this argument is to shatter the presumption of superiority that Romans felt toward barbarians, and that the members of various house and tenement churches in Rome felt about each other. Paul makes a sweeping case that "from works of the law no flesh will be set right before God" (Rom 3:20). James D. G. Dunn has moved the discussion of this verse beyond the denunciation of Jewish Law popularized by the interpretative tradition undergirded by the Reformation to what he calls "the function of the law as an identity factor, the social function of the law as marking out the people of the law in their distinctiveness." The problem is that "works of the law" served as an identity marker for those "whom God has chosen and will vindicate," providing a method of "maintaining his [the obedient person's] status within that people."[36] However, Dunn does not link these insights with the systems of gaining honor and avoiding shame in the Mediterranean world, which would allow a broader grasp of Paul's argument. It is not just the Jewish Law that is in view here, but law as an identity marker for any culture. Σάρξ (*sarx*, "flesh") in this verse was not selected by Paul to expose "the equation of covenant membership with physical rite and national kinship,"[37] but because it includes the entirety of the human race. In the face of the impartial righteousness of God, no human system of competing for glory and honor can stand.

The climactic formulation in 3:23, that "all have sinned and fallen short of the glory of God," has a bearing on Jewish and Greco-Roman systems of shame and honor that has not been noticed. That Adam and Eve were originally intended to bear the glory of God, but lost it through the fall, is widely acknowledged. However, the use of the verb ὑστερεῖν (*hysterein*, "fall short") has not been sufficiently explained, because an equivalent term is not employed in any of the Jewish parallels. This is a comparative term relating to the failure to reach a goal, to be inferior to someone, to fail, to come short of something.[38] The basic connotation is that of "deficit, which consists either in remaining below the normal level, or in being behind others,"[39] hence placing one in a position of deserving shame.

An important parallel in Pauline usage is 2 Cor 11:5; 12:11, in which ὑπερλίαν (*hyperlian*), "super," is used in connection with the competition between Paul and the super-apostles. To fall short is shameful; this term resonates with the competition for honor within and between groups in the Greco-Roman world; and it echoes the wording of Rom 1:18–32 in refusing to grant honor to God by choosing to worship the creature rather than the creator. Despite the claims of Jews and Greeks to surpass each other in honor, and despite their typical claims that the other groups are shameful because of their lack of wisdom or moral conformity, Paul's claim is that *all* fall short of the transcendent standard of honor. If all persons and groups fail to reflect the ultimate standard of honor that they were intended to bear, that is, "the glory of God," then none has a right to claim superiority or to place others in positions of inferiority.

It follows that to be "set right through a gift by his grace through the redemption that is in Christ Jesus" (3:24) should also be understood in terms of honor discourse. "Righteousness," "honor," and "glory" can be used as virtually synonymous terms, a point whose relevance can only be grasped if the traditional English translation for δικαιούμενοι (*dikaioumenoi*), "being justified," is replaced with its more adequate verbal equivalent, "being set right." To be "set right" in the context of the "righteousness of God" (3:21), and with reference to humans who have fallen short of the "glory of God," is to have such glory and honor restored, not as an achievement but as a gift. Paul is not suggesting that believers gain a comparative form of honor, so that they can continue to compete with others who remain shameful. Rather, in Christ they are given an honorable relationship that results in what 2 Cor 3:18 refers to as an actual transformation derived from the mirror image of Christ, in which believers change "from one degree of glory to another." In being honored by God through Christ who died for all, the formerly shamed are integrated into the community of the saints in which this transformation process occurs, under the lordship of Christ. This could be correlated with the work of Stuhlmacher, Dunn, and Hays, stressing that the righteousness given to the converted Jews and Gentiles is understood "primarily in terms of the covenant relationship to God and membership within the covenant community."[40] However, in place of a largely theological construct elaborated by biblical theologians, Paul has in mind a new social reality: within the community of the shamed made right by the death and resurrection of Christ, there is no longer the possibility of any "distinction" (Rom 3:22) in honor. Redefining the theological issue in terms of shame and honor avoids the pitfalls of the ethical theory of justification, that humans are made righteous so that they come to deserve divine approbation; it avoids the artificiality of imputed justification, in which believers are treated as righteous although they remain sinners; it avoids the narrow scope of forgiveness as acquittal from charges arising against individual sins, or the individual experience of relief from guilty conscience, which limits being set right through Christ to those whose problem is guilt; it moves past the existentialist limits of merely providing a new self-understanding for believers as accepted by God despite all evidence to the contrary; and it takes account of the actual makeup of the audience of Romans, consisting largely of the urban underclass experiencing a wide range of deprivations deriving from shameful status.

Paul's crucial contention is that in Christ, rightful status is not achieved on the basis of any human effort. The threefold reference in Rom 3:24 to divine "grace," to the "gift," and to "redemption" through Christ makes it plain that no one gains this honorable, righteous status by outperforming others or by privilege of birth or wealth. In contrast to the hypercompetitive environment of the Greco-Roman world, including its Jewish component, this new status is granted by Christ only to those who have fallen short, and who would therefore have to recognize that their shame is manifest. By its very nature, honor granted through grace alone eliminates the basis of human boasting, which Paul explicitly states in 3:27: "Where is the boast? It is excluded!" In Halvor Moxnes's words, the result is "to exclude false claims to honour."[41]

The competitive center of the ancient systems of shame and honor was what Paul called "boasting," which poisoned relations not only between individuals and ethnic groups in the ancient world but also between the "weak" and "strong" in the congregations in Rome, as the later chapters of the Roman letter make clear. Such tensions have a profound theological implication, for as Rom 3:29–30 shows, boasting threatens the oneness of God. In his earlier study of this material, Halvor Moxnes showed that the doctrine of monotheism in Rom 3 addressed the "problem of divisions between Jews and non-Jews within Christian communities. . . . In this context, 'God is one' served as an argument for the inclusion and co-existence of both Jews and non-Jews in the same community, on the basis of faith."[42] Moxnes pointed out that the argument in these verses concerning God as the God of the uncircumcised as well as the circumcised constitutes "a conscious effort to include" the less popular Jewish Christians in a hostile Gentile Christian majority in Rome. In sum, "The Confession that 'God is one' was meant to serve as a bond of unity between Christians."[43] Moxnes's more recent studies of honor and the analysis of this study may help to elucidate the link between monotheism and unity. As long as the competitive system of honor prevailed, claims of superior status entailed competing assertions of divine approbation. God was in effect divided up and reduced to a function of social systems. Unity and equality between groups and persons was only possible when the ancient system of competing for honor was abandoned, following the logic of the gospel. Because Paul moves on to devote the final chapters of his letter to the question of mutual welcome and honor between competing groups in the Roman church, this theme clearly stands at the center of the theology and ethic of the letter.

Romans 5:1–11

The new system of honor and shame produced by the gospel of Christ crucified is clarified in this passage. In Rom 5:2, the verb καυχῶμεθα (kauchōmetha) can either be translated as an indicative ("we boast"), which most commentators prefer, or as a hortatory subjunctive ("let us boast"), matching the subjunctive verb in the preceding verse.[44] The indicative is particularly inappropriate in this instance, because it places both Paul and the Romans in the position of continuing to act contrary to his previous critique of boasting (2:17, 23; 3:27; 4:2). If the verb is in the subjunctive, it clearly indicates that he is recommending a revolutionary new form of boasting to replace the claims of honorable status and performance that marked traditional religion in the Greco-Roman world. While boasting was criticized in 2:17 and excluded because of divine impartiality in 3:37, it is now allowed in a new form, not in what the groups in Rome claim as their superiority over one another but "only in what God has accomplished through Christ."[45] Rather than boasting in present status and past achievements, Paul recommends a form of boasting consistent with the realm of grace that concentrates on two things: in "hope of the glory of God" (5:2) and in the next verse, "in our afflictions." Neither was a suitable basis for boasting in the mainstream honor discourse of the first century.

In Rom 5:3, the verb καυχώμεθα (kauchōmetha, "let us boast") is reiterated, focusing on experiences within the human realm that would never otherwise provide grounds for boasting.[46] The phrase "in our afflictions" designates the ground of boasting, as in 2 Cor 12:9, in which Paul evidently developed this idea in opposition to the super-apostles: "I will all the more gladly boast in my weaknesses, that the power of Christ may rest upon me." The formulation in Romans is noteworthy in several regards. First and foremost, some Greco-Roman and Jewish attitudes toward honor and shame, success and adversity are reversed here. This reversal continues to counteract a congregational situation of competitive boasting, which was culturally consistent with such attitudes.[47] Rather than boasting in superior virtue and status, Paul recommends boasting in "afflictions," that is, in hardships, persecutions, eschatological troubles, or daily trials[48] that unite all believers in "covenantal mutuality"[49] under the lordship of the crucified one. The definite article attached to "afflictions" is also noteworthy and should be translated with "our."[50] Whereas commentators tend to generalize afflictions as if there were no specifying article,[51] Paul evidently has specific hardships in mind that are known to himself and the Roman congregation. The difficulties related to the expulsion of Jewish-Christian leaders under Claudius and their return from exile after 54 C.E. would certainly have been included along with whatever portion of Paul's own sufferings that were known in Rome. In the extreme version of an honor/shame environment present in Rome, where triumphs over enemies were celebrated on every side, to boast in a group's adversities not only was countercultural in the general sense but also probably countered specific interpretations of such adversities by the competing churches in Rome.[52] Whereas the Greco-Roman and Jewish cultures viewed perseverance and tested character as virtues about which one could legitimately boast, Paul removes them from human causation. It is "sufferings" that "produce fortitude," whereby the verb κατεργάζομαι (*katergazomai*) has the sense of "complete, accomplish, bring about" or "produce,"[53] without reference to the human factor. Even though the wording of Phil 2:12–13 may be more satisfactory in accounting for both the divine and the human factors, Paul has a specific rhetorical goal in mind in Rom 5. By eliminating human participation in the creation of ὑπομονή (*hypomonē*, "fortitude, patience, perseverance"), Paul is able to carry through with his argument that ordinary boasting is disallowed before God. In Greco-Roman ethics, ὑπομονή (*hypomonē*) was the virtue of manly resistance to contrary pressure, thought to be necessary for the soldier or citizen.[54] The high value assigned to fortitude and endurance by the culture makes it all the more striking that Paul eliminates the element of human volition in his argument that "this[55] affliction produces perseverance." The formulation of 5:3 reflects Paul's extraordinary effort to detach boasting from any arena of human accomplishment.

The conclusion of the rhetorical climax in Rom 5:5 reiterates the theme of hope and claims that hope "does not put to shame," a formulation that provides a satisfying correlation with boasting in verses 2c–3a. If the normal goal of boasting is to achieve honor and avert shame, here it is claimed that the avoidance of shame is accomplished in a revolutionary manner. The theme of shame in the context of the hope of deliverance is clearly articulated with the verb καταισχύνει, *kataischynei*, drawn from the language of the Psalms (for example, LXX Pss 20:6; 24:20; 30:2; 70:1).[56] In all such examples, the faithful worshipers hope for a concrete restoration of fortune and a relief from adversity. When they triumph over their enemies, it becomes clear that they have not been put to shame. Their honor requires Yahweh's victory over their adversaries or, at least, the compensation of a blessed life after death, a theme that provides the basis for much commentary on Rom 5:5.[57] However, compensation, whether worldly or otherworldly, is conspicuously absent from Rom 5:1–11, and herein lies part of the remarkable revolution. By employing what should be read as a present-tense verb, "does not put to shame," Paul points to the overcoming of shame in the present experience of righteousness by faith, in the current stand of believers in grace. The divine court of reputation justifies their divergence from the majority culture. In this case the eschatological fulfillment is in the present.

When placed in the context of the honor discourse of the Greco-Roman society, the material in Rom 5:3–5 is counterintuitive at many points. Paul provides a fresh and creative admonition about how to live out the "peace with God," namely by changing the form of one's boasting in the light of salvation by grace alone. Given the mind-set produced by Greco-Roman and Jewish cultures, Paul cannot eliminate boasting altogether; it is bred in the bone, so to speak. Nevertheless he hopes to change its form into a celebration of the glory of God and of the love of Christ that sustains believers through every adversity. The traditional forms of boasting are no longer needed to gain and sustain their honor in the face of a hostile world. Christ's blood that was shed for the undeserving fills that need, and its consoling message is conveyed by the Spirit directly to the vulnerable hearts of believers, who thereby are enabled to live in confident hope no matter how badly they are treated. In Christ, adversity has lost its power to shame.

Romans 14–16

The closing chapters of Romans bring honor discourse directly into the life of the Roman house and tenement churches. Three Pauline admonitions—"welcome" each other (Rom 14:1 and 15:7), "greet" so and so in chapter 16, and the reference to the "holy kiss"—merit special attention. Because, from a rhetorical point of view, these admonitions appear in the peroration, thus comprising the climax of the letter, their significance in the argumentative development is indisputable. Yet commentators have lacked the theological and social sensitivity to understand what was at stake in these prominent references. The preoccupation with issues of guilt and forgiveness, which has dominated the theology of Romans since Augustine's time, has rendered our interpretive tradition oddly uninterested in the pervasive social issues of shame and welcome.

There is certainly no difficulty at the superficial level of understanding these typical formulas of welcoming and honoring guests and family members, which were well-known in the culture but nowhere used with this frequency in literary materials. Romans contains the most extensive list of such references in the annals of ancient letters. Paul's selection of the second-person plural imperative form, ἀσπάσασθε (*aspasasthe*, "you should greet"), in 16:3–16 was surely intentional and should not be translated as "I send greetings to . . ."[58] As Otto Michel points out, "The ones being greeted are at the same time those whom the Roman congregation should grant recognition."[59] When one observes the random sequence of the requested greetings and the interweaving of established Christian cells (16:3–5, 10b, 11b, 14, 15) and individual Christian leaders, it becomes clear that the recognition is to be mutual. In this context, to greet is to honor and welcome one another, probably with the hug, kiss, handshaking, or bowing that gave expression to greeting in the ancient world; the original meaning of the Greek term ἀσπάζομαι (*aspazomai*) was to wrap one's arms around another.[60] As Hans Windisch observed, the Pauline command to greet one another "expresses and strengthens the bond of fellowship with those who are engaged in the same task and who serve the same Lord, i.e., with saints and brothers."[61] The social context for these commands was the love feasts of various house and tenement churches.

In Rom 16:16, all the members of the various house and tenement churches as well as the returning refugees in Rome are admonished to "greet one another with a holy kiss," which implies a deep level of unity and mutuality between all Christians in Rome,[62] thereby overturning the normal boundaries of honor and shame. In the case of the Roman Christians, caught in a competition between the "weak" and the "strong" in which mutual denunciations had become routine, this gesture had transforming significance. Paul passes on greetings from "all the churches of Christ," the only time in the entire Pauline corpus that he presumes to speak so inclusively. Given the missional focus of the letter, these greetings have an integral purpose of embodying the inclusive righteousness of God so that the gospel of impartial love can be passed on in a credible manner to the barbarians in Spain and to others at the limits of the known world. It is highly significant that Paul's final letter closes on this note of overcoming the boundaries of honor and shame for the sake of the gospel.

Part III. Other Relevant Pauline and Paulinist Texts

Rom 1:5–7; 2:6–11, 12–16, 17–24; 4:9–12, 18–24; 8:1–8; 31–39; 9:30–33; 10:10–13; 11:17–32; 12:15–16; 13:7–10; 14:1–15:13

1 Cor 1:10–31; 2:1–13; 3:4–15, 18–23; 4:6–13; 7:36–40; 9:1–23; 11:2–16, 17–34; 12:14–33; 13:1–13; 14:26–39; 16:15–20

2 Cor 1:12–14; 2:14–17; 3:1–6, 18; 4:5–12; 5:11–21; 6:3–10; 8:16–24; 9:1–5; 10:5–18; 11:5–11, 16–33; 12:1–10, 19–21; 13:9–14

Gal 1:10–14; 2:11–21; 3:6–9, 10–14, 26–29; 4:21–31; 5:13–15, 19–26; 6:3–4, 11–16

Phil 1:15–18, 27–30; 2:1–11; 3:3–11

1 Thess 2:1–12, 19–20; 4:1–8; 5:12–22, 26–28

Phlm 1–3, 10–20, 23–25

Part IV. Bibliography

Classical and Social-Scientific Studies

Adkins, A. W. *Merit and Responsibility: A Study in Greek Values*. Oxford: Oxford University Press, 1960.

Alföldi, Andreas. "Die zwei Lorbeerbäume des Augustus." Pages 403–22 in *Römischer Kaiserkult*, edited by A. Wlosok. Wege der Forschung 372. Darmstadt, Germany: Wissenschaftliche Buchgesellschaft, 1978.

Balsdon, J. P. V. D. *Romans and Aliens*. Chapel Hill: University of North Carolina Press, 1979.

Bettini, Maurizio. *Anthropogy and Roman Culture*. Baltimore: Johns Hopkins University Press, 1991.

Cairns, Douglas. *Aidos*. Oxford: Oxford University Press, 1993.

Chance, J. K. "The Anthropology of Honor and Shame: Culture, Values, and Practice." *Semeia* 68 (1994): 139–51.

Cracco Ruggini, L. "Intolerance: Equal and Less Equal in the Roman World." *Classical Philology* 82 (1987): 187–205.

Cunliffe, B. *Greeks, Romans, and Barbarians: Spheres of Interaction*. New York: Metheun, 1988.

Cuss, Dominique. *Imperial Cult and Honorary Terms in the New Testament*. Paradosis, Contributions to the History of Early Christian Literature and Theology 23. Fribourg: Fribourg University Press, 1974.

Danker, Frederick W. *Benefactor: Epigraphic Study of a Graeco-Roman and New Testament Semantic Field*. St. Louis: Clayton, 1982.

D'Arms, John H. *Commerce and Social Standing in Ancient Rome*. Cambridge: Harvard University Press, 1981.

Dover, K. J., ed. *Perceptions of the Ancient Greeks*. Oxford: Blackwell, 1992.

Drexler, Hans. "*Gravitas*." *Aevum* 30 (1956): 291–306.

———. "*Honos*." *Romanitas* 3 (1961): 135–57. Reprint, pages 446–67 in *Römische*

Wertbegriffe, edited by H. Oppermann. Darmstadt, Germany: Wissenschaftliche Buchgesellschaft, 1983.

Fatheuer, Thomas. *Ehre und Gerechtigkeit. Studien zur gesellschaftlichen Ordnung im frühen Griechenland.* Münster: Westfael. Damphboot, 1988.

Fears, J. Rufus. "The Cult of Jupiter and Roman Imperial Ideology." Pages 1–141 in *ANRW* 17.1. 1981.

———. "The Cult of Virtues and Roman Imperial Ideology." Pages 828–948 in *ANRW* 17.2. 1981.

———. "Ruler Worship." Pages 1009–26 in *Civilization of the Ancient Mediterranean: Greece and Rome,* vol. 2, edited by M. Grant and R. Kitzinger. New York: Scribners, 1988.

———. "The Theology of Victory at Rome: Approaches and Problems." Pages 737–826 in *ANRW* 17.2. 1981.

Ferguson, John. "Ruler-Worship." Pages 766–84 in *The Roman World,* vol. 2, edited by J. Wacher. 2 vols. London and New York: Routledge & Kegan Paul, 1987.

Fisher, N. R. E. *Hybris: A Study in the Values of Honour and Shame in Ancient Greece.* Warminster, England: Aris & Phillips, 1992.

Garnsey, Peter D. A. "Patronal Power Relations." Pages 96–103 in *Paul and Empire: Religion and Power in Roman Imperial Society,* edited by R. A. Horsley. Harrisburg, Pa.: Trinity Press International, 1997.

Garnsey, Peter D. A., and Richard P. Saller. *The Roman Empire: Economy, Society, and Culture.* London: Duckworth, 1987.

Gilmore, David D., ed. *Honor and Shame and the Unity of the Mediterranean.* Washington: American Anthropological Association, 1987.

Hallett, J. P. "Women as *Same* and *Other* in Classical Roman Elite." *Helios* 16 (1989): 59–78.

Hassall, Mark. "Romans and Non-Romans." Pages 685–700 in *The Roman World,* vol. 2, edited by J. Wacher. 2 vols. London and New York: Routledge & Kegan Paul, 1987.

Hendrix, Holland. "Thessalonicans Honor Romans." Ph.D. diss., Harvard University, 1984.

Hertzfeld, M. "Honor and Shame: Problems in the Comparative Analysis of Moral Systems." *Man* 15 (1980): 339–51.

Hiltbrunner, Otto. "*Vir Gravis.*" Pages 195–207 in *Sprachgeschichte und wortbedeutung: Festschrift für Albrecht Debrunner.* Bern, Switzerland: Francke, 1954. Reprint, pages 402–19 in *Römische Wertbegriffe,* edited by H. Oppermann. Darmstadt, Germany: Wissenschaftliche Buchgesellschaft, 1983.

Hopkins, K. *Conquerors and Slaves.* Cambridge: Cambridge University Press, 1978.

Jones, C. P. "*Stigma*: Tattooing and Branding in Graeco-Roman Antiquity." *JRS* 77 (1987): 139–55.

Judge, Edwin A. "The Conflict of Educational Aims in New Testament Thought." *Journal of Christian Education* 9 (1966): 32–45.

———. "Cultural Conformity and Innovation in Paul: Some Clues from Contemporary Documents." *TynBul* 35 (1984): 3–24.

———. "The Early Christians as a Scholastic Community." *JRH* 1 (1960): 4–15, 125–37.

————. "Moral Terms in the Eulogistic Tradition." *New Documents Illustrating Early Christianity* 2 (1982): 105–6.

————. "Paul's Boasting in Relation to Contemporary Professional Practice." *ABR* 16 (1968): 37–50.

————. *Rank and Status in the World of the Caesars and St. Paul: The Broadhead Memorial Lectures 1981.* Christchurch, England: University of Canterbury Press, 1982.

————. "St. Paul and Classical Society." *JAC* 15 (1972): 21–36.

Kamtekar, R. "AIDWS in Epictetus." *Classical Philology* 93 (1998): 136–60.

Knoche, Ulrich. "Der römische Ruhmesgedanke." *Philologus* 89 (1934): 102–34. Reprint, pages 420–45 in *Römische Wertbegriffe,* edited by H. Oppermann. Darmstadt, Germany: Wissenschaftliche Buchgesellschaft, 1983.

Lendon, J. E. *Empire of Honour: The Art of Government in the Roman World.* Oxford: Clarendon, 1997.

MacMullen, Ramsay. *Roman Social Relations 50 B.C. to A.D. 284.* New Haven: Yale University Press, 1974.

Momigliano, Arnaldo. "How Roman Emperors Became Gods." *American Scholar* 55 (1986): 181–93.

Montgomery, H. "Women and Status in the Greco-Roman World." *Studia Theologica* 43 (1989): 115–24.

Oppermann, H., ed. *Römische Wertbegriffe.* Darmstadt, Germany: Wissenschaftliche Buchgesellschaft, 1983.

Parker, Robert. *MIASMA: Pollution and Purification in Early Greek Religion.* Oxford: Clarendon, 1985.

Pattison, Stephen. *Shame: Theory, Therapy, Theology.* Cambridge: Cambridge University Press, 2000.

Perella, Nicholas James. *The Kiss: Sacred and Profane: An Interpretative History of Kiss Symbolism and Related Religio-Erotic Themes.* Berkeley: University of California Press, 1969.

Peristiany, Jean G., ed. *Honour and Shame: The Values of Mediterranean Society.* London: Weidenfeld and Nicolson, 1966.

Saller, Richard P. "Poverty, Honor, and Obligation in Imperial Rome." *Criterion* (Chicago) 37 (1998): 12–20.

————. "Roman Class Structures and Relations." Pages 549–73 in *Civilization of the Ancient Mediterranean: Greece and Rome,* vol. 1, edited by M. Grant and R. Kitzinger. New York: Scribners, 1988.

Sherwin-White, A. N. *Racial Prejudice in Imperial Rome.* J. H. Gray Lectures, 1966. Cambridge: Cambridge University Press, 1967.

Stier, Hans Erich. "Augustusfriede und römische Klassik." Pages 3–54 in *ANRW* II.2. 1975.

Tenny, Frank. *Aspects of Social Behavior in Ancient Rome.* Cambridge: Cambridge University Press, 1932. Reprint, New York: Cooper Square Publications, 1969.

Weber, Ekkehard, ed. *Augustus: Meine Taten. Res Gestae Divi Augustus.* Munich: Heimeran Verlag, 1970.

Williams, Bernard. *Shame and Necessity.* Berkeley: University of California Press, 1993.

Zanker, Paul. "The Power of Images." Pages 72–86 in *Paul and Empire: Religion and*

Power in Roman Imperial Society, edited by R. A. Horsley. Harrisburg, Pa.: Trinity Press International, 1997.

Studies of Honor and Shame in the Pauline Epistles

Atkins, Robert A. "Pauline Theology and Shame Affect: Reading a Social Location." *Listening* 31 (1996): 137–51.

Barrett, Charles Kingsley. "I Am Not Ashamed of the Gospel." Pages 19–41 in *Foi et salut selon saint Paul (Épître aus Romains 1,16): Colloque oecuménique a l'Abbaye de S. Paul hors les Murs, 16–21 avril 1968,* edited by M. Barth et al. AnBib 42. Rome: Pontifical Biblical Institute, 1970. Reprint, pages 116–43 in *New Testament Essays.* Edited by C. K. Barrett. London: SPCK, 1972.

Benko, Stephen. "The Kiss." Pages 79–102 in *Pagan Rome and the Early Christians,* by S. Benko. Bloomington: Indiana University Press, 1984.

Clark, Elizabeth A. "Sex, Shame, and Rhetoric: En-gendering Early Christian Ethics." *JAAR* 59 (1991): 221–45.

Corrigan, Gregory M. "Paul's Shame for the Gospel." *BTB* 16 (1986): 23–27.

deSilva, David Arthur. *Honor, Patronage, and Purity: Unlocking New Testament Culture.* Downers Grove, Ill.: InterVarsity, 2000.

———. *The Hope of Glory: Honor Discourse and New Testament Interpretation.* Collegeville, Minn.: Liturgical, 1999.

———. "'Worthy of His Kingdom': Honor Discourse and Social Engineering in 1 Thessalonians." *JSNT* 64 (1996): 49–79.

Dewey, Arthur J. "A Matter of Honor: A Social-Historical Analysis of 2 Corinthians 10." *HTR* 78 (1985): 209–17.

Downing, F. Gerald. "'Honour' among Exegetes." Pages 19–42 in *Making Sense in (and of) the First Christian Century,* edited by F. G. Downing. JSNTSup 197. Sheffield, England: Sheffield Academic Press, 2000.

Ellington, John. "Kissing in the Bible: Form and Meaning." *Bible Translator* 41 (1990): 409–16.

Esler, Philip F. *The First Christians in Their Social Worlds: Social-Scientific Approaches to New Testament Interpretation.* London: Routledge, 1994.

Fiorenza, Elisabeth Schüssler. "Missionaries, Apostles, Co-workers: Romans 16 and the Reconstruction of Women's Early Christian History." *Word and World* 6 (1986): 420–33.

Fuchs, Ottmar. "Die Entgrenzung zum Fremden als Bedingung christlichen Glaubens und Handelns." Pages 240–301 in *Die Fremden,* edited by O. Fuchs. Theologie zur Zeit 4. Düsseldorf, Germany: Patmos, 1988.

Glombitza, Otto. "Von der Scham des Gläubigen: Erwägungen zu Rom i 14–17." *NovT* 4 (1960): 74–80.

Grayston, Kenneth. "'I Am Not Ashamed of the Gospel': Romans 1:16a and the Structure of the Epistle." *Studia Evangelica* 2 (1964): 569–73.

Herr, Larry G. "Retribution and Personal Honor." *Biblical Archaeologist* 44 (1981): 230–34.

Hofmann, Karl-Martin. *Philema hagion.* BFCT 38. Gütersloh, Germany: Bertelsmann, 1938.

Hooker, Morna D. *Not Ashamed of the Gospel: New Testament Interpretations of the Death of Christ.* Grand Rapids: Eerdmans, 1994.

Jewett, Robert. "Ecumenical Theology for the Sake of Mission: Rom 1:1–17 + 15:14–16:24." Pages 89–108 in *Pauline Theology,* vol. 3, edited by D. M. Hay and E. E. Johnson. Minneapolis: Augsburg Fortress Press, 1995 [1996].

———. "Honor and Shame in the Argument of Romans." Pages 257–72 in *Putting Body and Soul Together: Essays in Honor of Robin Scroggs,* edited by A. Brown, G. F. Snyder, and V. Wiles. Valley Forge, Pa.: Trinity Press International, 1997.

———. "Impeaching God's Elect: Rom 8:33–36 in Its Rhetorical Situation." Pages 37–58 in *Paul, Luke, and the Graeco-Roman World: Essays in Honour of Alexander J. M. Wedderburn.* Edited by A. Christophersen, et al. JSNTSup 217. Sheffield, England: Sheffield Academic, 2002.

———. *Paul the Apostle to America: Cultural Trends and Pauline Scholarship.* Louisville: Westminster John Knox, 1994.

———. *Saint Paul Returns to the Movies: Triumph over Shame.* Grand Rapids: Eerdmans, 1999.

Kee, Howard C. "The Linguistic Background of 'Shame' in the New Testament." Pages 133–47 in *On Language, Culture, and Religion: In Honor of Eugene A. Nida,* edited by M. Black and W. A. Smalley. The Hague: Mouton, 1974.

Klassen, William. "The Sacred Kiss in the New Testament." *NTS* 39 (1993): 122–35.

Lampe, Peter. "Der Konflikt zwischen Starken und Schwachen in Rome." Pages 87–89 in *"Sie aber hielten fest an der Gemeinschaft . . .": Einheit der Kirche als Prozess im Neuen Testament und heute,* edited by C. Link et al. Zurich: Benziger, 1988.

Malina, Bruce J. *Christian Origins and Cultural Anthropology: Practical Models for Biblical Interpretation.* Atlanta: John Knox, 1986.

———. *The New Testament World: Insights from Cultural Anthropology.* Atlanta: John Knox, 1981. [See pp. 25–50.]

Malina, Bruce J., and Jerome H. Neyrey. *Portraits of Paul: An Archaeology of Ancient Personality.* Louisville: Westminster John Knox, 1996.

Marshall, Peter. "A Metaphor of Social Shame: ΘRIAMBEUEIN in 2 Cor. 2:14." *NovT* 25 (1983): 302–17.

Mason, Steve. "'For I Am Not Ashamed of the Gospel' (Rom 1.16: The Gospel and the First Readers of Romans." Pages 254–87 in *Gospel in Paul: Studies on Corinthians, Galatians, and Romans for Richard N. Longenecker,* edited by L. A. Jervis and P. Richardson. JSNTSup 108. Sheffield, England: Sheffield Academic, 1994.

Matthews, Victor H., and Don C. Benjamin, eds. *Semeia* (Atlanta: Scholars Press) 68 (1996). [The theme of the issue was "Honor and Shame in the World of the Bible."]

Moxnes, Halvor. "Honor and Shame." Pages 19–40 in *The Social Sciences and New Testament Interpretation,* edited by R. L. Rohrbaugh. Peabody, Mass.: Hendrickson, 1996.

———. "Honor and Shame: A Reader's Guide." *BTB* 23 (1993): 167–76.

———. "Honor, Shame, and the Outside World in Paul's Letter to the Romans." Pages 207–18 in *The Social World of Formative Christianity and Judaism: Essays in*

Tribute to Howard Clark Kee, edited by Jacob Neusner et al. Philadelphia: Fortress Press, 1988.

————. "Honour and Righteousness in Romans." *JSNT* 32 (1988): 61–77.

————. "The Quest for Honor and the Unity of the Community in Romans 12 and in the Orations of Dio Chrysostom." Pages 203–30 in *Paul in His Hellenistic Context,* edited by Troels Engberg-Pedersen. Minneapolis: Fortress Press, 1994.

Neyrey, Jerome H. *Paul in Other Words: A Cultural Reading of His Letters.* Louisville: Westminster John Knox, 1990.

Plevnik, Joseph. "Honor/Shame." Pages 95–104 in *Biblical Social Values and Their Meanings: A Handbook,* edited by J. J. Pilch and B. J. Malina. Peabody, Mass.: Hendrickson, 1993.

Reasoner, Mark. "*Potentes* and *Inferiores* in Roman Society and the Roman Church." Pages 1–17 in *Society of Biblical Literature Seminar 1993 Papers,* edited by Eugene H. Lovering, Jr. Atlanta: Scholars Press, 1993.

————. *The Strong and the Weak: Romans 14.1–15.13 in Context.* SNTSMS 103. Cambridge: Cambridge University Press, 1999.

Seely, David. *The Noble Death: Graeco-Roman Martyrology and Paul's Concept of Salvation.* JSNTSup. Sheffield, England: Sheffield Academic, 1990.

Seeman, Chris. "Prominence." Pages 147–50 in *Biblical Social Values and Their Meanings: A Handbook,* edited by J. J. Pilch and B. J. Malina. Peabody, Mass.: Hendrickson, 1993.

Wilson, Walter T. *Love without Pretense: Romans 12.9–21 and Hellenistic-Jewish Wisdom Literature.* WUNT 46. Tübingen: Mohr [Siebeck], 1991.

Winter, Bruce W. "The Public Honouring of Christian Benefactors." *JSNT* 34 (1988): 87–103.

Notes

1. See A. Horstmann, "αἰσχύνομαι, be ashamed," *EDNT* 1:42–43, which highlights the public sense of persons "being put to shame" by others in contrast to the subjective meaning of "be ashamed" of what one has done, found especially in the use of ἐπαισχύνομαι. Howard Clark Kee, "The Linguistic Background of 'Shame' in the New Testament," in *On Language, Culture, and Religion: In Honor of Eugene A. Nida* (ed. M. Black and W. A. Smalley; The Hague: Mouton, 1974), 141–43, shows that three of the four categories of shame in the New Testament relate to public humiliation, the efficacy of promises, and eschatological vindication, while a small group of passages refer to shameful behavior.

2. R. Jewett, "Paul, Phoebe, and the Spanish Mission," in *The Social World of Formative Christianity and Judaism: Essays in Tribute to Howard Clark Kee* (ed. P. Borgen et al.; Philadelphia: Fortress Press, 1988), 144–64.

3. A skeptical evaluation of this line of research is provided by Downing, "'Honour' among Exegetes," 19–42. Downing concludes, "The issue of honour, of respect in community, is important, and may even *on occasion* be of prime importance. It does not help to assume—irrespective of the evidence—that it always must be dominant."

4. Bruce J. Malina, *The New Testament World: Insights from Cultural Anthropology* (Atlanta: John Knox, 1981), 27.

5. Ibid., 29.

6. Ibid., 32.

7. Translation by William Benjamin Smith and Walter Miller, *The Iliad of Homer* (New York: Macmillan, 1944), 130–31.

8. Translation by W. H. S. Jones (Cambridge: Harvard University Press, 1966), 75–77.

9. N. R. E. Fisher, *Hybris: A Study in the Values of Honour and Shame in Ancient Greece* (Warminster, England: Aris & Phillips, 1992), 193; see also p. 10.

10. Ibid., 498.

11. Aristotle, *Rhetoric* 1378b23–35, cited by Fisher, *Hybris,* 8.

12. Thomas Fatheuer, *Ehre und Gerechtigkeit: Studien zur gesellschaftlichen Ordnung im frühen Griechenland* (Münster, Germany: Westfael. Damphboot, 1988), 15.

13. E. A. Judge, "The Conflict of Educational Aims in New Testament Thought," *Journal of Christian Education* 9 (1966): 38–39; he cites Sallust, *Bellum Jugurthinum* 85:26, "Reticence would only cause people to mistake modesty for a guilty conscience."

14. Ekkehard Weber, ed., *Augustus: Meine Taten. Res Gestae Divi Augustus* (Munich: Heimeran Verlag, 1970), 52.

15. Ibid., 13–21 (translation mine).

16. This translation and subsequent ones for Thycidides are by Charles Forster Smith, *The History of the Peloponnesian War* (vol. 1; bks. 1–2; LCL; Cambridge: Harvard University Press, 1928), 331–33.

17. David Arthur deSilva, *Honor, Patronage, and Purity: Unlocking New Testament Culture* (Downers Grove, Ill.: InterVarsity, 2000), 23.

18. David Arthur deSilva, *The Hope of Glory: Honor Discourse and New Testament Interpretation* (Collegeville, Minn.: Liturgical, 1999), 1–33, esp. 4–7.

19. Ibid., 6.

20. DeSilva, *Honor, Patronage, and Purity,* 43.

21. Hans Conzelmann, *A Commentary on the First Epistle to the Corinthians* (trans. J. W. Leitch; Philadelphia: Fortress Press, 1976), 33.

22. See Raymond F. Collins, *First Corinthians* (Collegeville, Minn.: Liturgical, 1999), 110–11.

23. See Charles Kingsley Barrett, "Boasting (καυχάσθαι κτλ) in the Pauline Epistles," in *L'Apôtre Paul: Personalité, Style et Conception du Ministère* (BETL 73; Louvain: Louvain University Press, 1986), 367; Rudolf Bultmann, "καυχάομαι κτλ," *TDNT* 3:649: "faith implies the surrender of all self-glorying." See also Josef Zmijewski, "καυχάομαι κτλ," *EDNT* 2:278–79.

24. Gordon D. Fee, *The First Epistle to the Corinthians* (Grand Rapids: Eerdmans, 1987), 67.

25. Ibid., 75.

26. Richard B. Hays, *First Corinthians* (Louisville: John Knox, 1997), 31.

27. Stephen Pattison, *Shame: Theory, Therapy, Theology* (Cambridge: Cambridge University Press, 2000), 182–83.

28. See Gustav Stählin, "προκοπή," *TDNT* 6:714.

29. Hans Dieter Betz, *Galatians* (Philadelphia: Fortress Press, 1979), 68.

30. Ibid., 68.

31. Jerome Murphy-O'Connor, *Paul: A Critical Life* (Oxford: Clarendon, 1996), 60.

32. Peter T. O'Brien, *The Epistle to the Philippians* (Grand Rapids: Eerdmans, 1991), 365.

33. Ibid., 371–72.

34. The term ἄμεμπτος means "blameless, faultless" according to BDAG, thus claiming a standard of performance that could not be surpassed; "Paul had no 'blemishes' on his record as far as lawkeeping is concerned," according to Gordon D. Fee, *Philippians* (Downers Grove, Ill.: InterVarsity, 1999), 40.

35. O'Brien, *Philippians*, 368.

36. James D. G. Dunn, *Romans 1–8* (Dallas: Word, 1988), 159.

37. Ibid., 160.

38. See BDAG 849.

39. See Fréderic Godet, *Commentary on St. Paul's Epistle to the Romans* (trans. A. Cusin; revised and edited by T. W. Chambers; New York: Funk & Wagnals, 1883; reprint, Grand Rapids: Kregel, 1977), 148.

40. Richard B. Hays, "Justification," *ABD* 3:1131; see Peter Stuhlmacher, *Paul's Letter to the Romans: A Commentary* (trans. S. J. Hafemann; Louisville: Westminster John Knox, 1994), 31.

41. Moxnes, "Honour and Righteousness in Romans," *JSNT* 32 (1988): 61–77, here 71. Unfortunately Moxnes goes on to claim that "it is the particular boasting of the Jew, not something which is common to Jews and Gentiles, which Paul attacks. . . . Paul sees a direct connection between boasting and the Jewish Law." This overlooks the clear implication of the earlier argument of Romans, which makes it plain that all humans are involved in seeking honor that belongs to God alone, and that they all thereby forfeit their share of the "glory of God."

42. Halvor Moxnes, *Theology in Conflict: Studies in Paul's Understanding of God in Romans* (Boston: Brill, 1980), 223.

43. Moxnes, *Theology in Conflict*, 224.

44. See Otto Kuss, *Der Römerbrief übersetzt und erklärt* (Regensburg, Germany: Pustet, 1957–78), 2:200, 203; Theodore Pulcini, "In Right Relationship with God: Present Experience and Future Fulfillment: An Exegesis of Romans 5:1–11," *St. Vladimir's Theological Quarterly* 36 (1992): 68–69.

45. Marty L. Reid, *Augustinian and Pauline Rhetoric in Romans Five: A Study of Early Christian Rhetoric* (Mellen Biblical Press Series 30; Lewiston, N.Y.: Mellen, 1996), 100; see also Marc Schoeni's description of the "outrageous" nature of this admonition, in "The Hyperbolic Sublime as a Master Trope in Romans," in *Rhetoric and the New Testament: Essays from the 1992 Heidelberg Conference* (ed. S. E. Porter and T. H. Olbricht; JSNTSup 90; Sheffield, England: JSOT, 1993), 178.

46. See Schoeni, "Hyperbolic Sublime," 178.

47. See Reid, *Augustinian and Pauline Rhetoric*, 101.

48. See Jacob Kremer, "θλίψις, θλίβω," *EDNT* 2:152–53; Ulrich Wilckens, *Der Brief an die Römer* (EKKNT 6; Zürich: Benziger; Neukirchen-Vluyn: Neukirchener Verlag, 1978–82), 1:291; see also A. J. Mattill, Jr., "The Way of Tribulation," *JBL* 98 (1979): 535–39.

49. Reid, *Augustinian and Pauline Rhetoric*, 101.

50. See Joseph A. Fitzmyer, *Romans: A New Translation with Introduction and Comentary* (New York: Doubleday, 1993), 379.

51. See, for example, Kuss, *Römerbrief,* 1.204; Leon Morris, *The Epistle to the Romans* (Grand Rapids: Eerdmans, 1998), 220; Dunn, *Romans 1–8,* 250; Douglas J. Moo, *The Epistle to the Romans* (Grand Rapids: Eerdmans, 1996), 302–3; Brendan Byrne, S.J. (*Romans* Sacra Pagina Series 6; Collegeville, Minn.: Liturgical Press, 1996), 170.

52. See R. Jewett, "Impeaching God's Elect: Rom. 8:33–36 in Its Rhetorical Situation," in *Paul, Luke, and the Graeco-Roman World: Essays in Honor of Alexander J. M. Wedderburn* (ed. A. Christophersen et al.; JSNTSup 217; Sheffield, England: Sheffield Academic, 2002), 37–58.

53. "Κατεργάζομαι," *EDNT* 2:271; Georg Bertram, "κατεργάζομαι," *TDNT* 3:634–35.

54. See Friedrich Hauck, "ὑπομένω, ὑπομονή," *TDNT* 4:581–82; Ceslas Spicq, "ὑπομένω, ὑπομονή," *Lexicon* 3 (1994): 414–15.

55. The use of the article in the reduplicated members of the climax is translated as "this," reflecting the origin of the article in Greek as a demonstrative pronoun (BDF §§249, 252), referring back to an item just mentioned. Most translations and commentators simply skip the article in ἡ θλίψις, thus implying that any affliction produces fortitude, but Paul has the specific, previously mentioned affliction in mind.

56. See Rudolf Bultmann, "αἰσχύνω κτλ," *TDNT* 1:189–99; C. E. B. Cranfield, *A Critical and Exegetical Commentary on the Epistle to the Romans* (Edinburgh: T. & T. Clark, 1990), 262; Dunn, *Romans 1–8,* 252; Reid, *Augustinian and Pauline Rhetoric,* 104.

57. For example, Godet, *Commentary on St. Paul's Epistle to the Romans,* 189: "This hope will not be falsified in the end by the event." See also Heinrich Schlier, *Der Römerbrief* (Freiburg: Herder, 1987), 149; John Ziesler, *Paul's Letter to the Romans* (Philadelphia: Trinity Press International, 1989), 129; Dunn, *Romans 1–8,* 252.

58. Barclay M. Newman and Eugene A. Nida, *A Translator's Handbook on Paul's Letter to the Romans* (Stuttgart: United Bible Societies, 1973), 291.

59. Otto Michel, *Der Brief an die Römer* (Kritisch-exegetischer Kommentar über das neue Testament 4; Göttingen: Vandenhoeck und Ruprecht, 1978), 474.

60. See Hans Windisch, "ἀσπάζομαι κτλ," *TDNT* 1:497.

61. Ibid., 1:501.

62. See Stephen Benko, "The Kiss," in *Pagan Rome and the Early Christians* (Bloomington: Indiana University Press, 1984), 79–102; and Nicholas James Perella, *The Kiss, Sacred and Profane: An Interpretative History of Kiss Symbolism and Related Religio-Erotic Themes* (Berkeley: University of California Press, 1969), 12–17.

chrome institution without respect to the distinct manifestations in classical antiquity. In classical studies, *Greek slavery* designates the institution in the world of classical Athens (fifth and fourth century B.C.E.), and *Roman slavery* specifies the institution in the world (mostly in Italy and Sicily) of the middle Republic to the end of the Principate (200 B.C.E.–235 C.E.). It is important to keep the evidence from Athens and Rome separate, for Athenian slavery differed markedly from the institution in the Roman context. Although some Athenian material can illumine the history of the development of later Hellenistic practices in the East, classical Athens in fact has little to do with Paul's situation in Roman colonies of the empire.[3]

The importance of keeping the Athenian and Roman evidence separate becomes apparent in the attempt to define slavery. Aristotle calls a slave a "living tool" and claims that some human bodies, by virtue of their very anatomy, were biologically built for servitude (*Politics* 1.1–7 [1252a–56a]; see also *Nicomachean Ethics* 8.11). However, such a theory of natural slaves did not convince the Romans. In Roman law, slavery is an institution of the law of nations (*ius gentium*) by which, contrary to nature (*contra naturam*), one person is subjected to the power (*dominium*) of another, remarkably the only case in the entire extant corpus of Roman law in which the *ius gentium* and the *ius naturale* are in conflict (Justinian, *Institutes* 1.3.2; *Digest* 1.5.4.1). Likewise, Roman Stoic philosophy argues for a shared humanity between slave and free, making no natural distinction between the two, and avers slavery to be the product of fate and not nature: slaves were fellow human beings who just happened to have had bad luck (Seneca, *Letters* 47).

Yet this did not mean that slavery was considered morally wrong. Although the Roman jurists and Stoic philosophers understood slavery to be against nature, they clearly presumed slavery to be legitimate, proper, and morally right. They just did not share Aristotle's view about natural slaves; accordingly Aristotle has limited value for defining slavery in Paul's specific situation in the Roman world.[4]

Constructing a definition of slavery can take two interpretive approaches. The conventional approach begins with the Roman juridical concept of absolute ownership (*dominium*) and proceeds to define slavery as the treatment of human beings and their offspring as property (or "chattel") capable of being bought and sold by private owners. Hence, the term *chattel slavery* distinguishes it from other forms of dependent labor—debt bondage, indentured servitude, clientship, peonage, helotry, serfdom—which ancient writers may also describe with the language of slavery. For example, the helots of ancient Sparta are often called "slaves" in ancient literature, yet helots (unlike chattel slaves) were not imported from outside but were subjected collectively within their own territories and could not be bought or sold.[5] Because "slave" in both Latin (*servus*) and Greek (δοῦλος, *doulos*) does not always refer to what we would call a slave (but ranges in meaning from the metaphorical, such as a senator as a political or moral slave, to the generic, such as a laborer generally), the term *chattel slavery* helps clarify what the actual institution is—absolute ownership of a human being as a tangible object that can be bought and sold. This law-oriented approach, however, begs a larger methodological question about the use of legal evidence in historical inquiry. Law codes at best provide only inexact knowledge about social practice and, at worst, can build a highly misleading model of slavery.

Fortunately, a second, sociological approach to slavery offers a solution. It rejects the centrality of property ownership in the definition, even for the Roman period. While not denying slaves to be property objects, this interpretation argues nonetheless that to define slaves *only* as property fails to specify a distinct category of persons, because many who are clearly not slaves (spouses, children, or professional athletes, for example) can also be objects of a property relation. Rather, the concept of absolute power is key.

In this sociological approach, slavery is less a static institution of property law and more a dynamic process of total domination, an absolute kind of mastery that denies the slave access to autonomous relations outside the master's sphere of influence—in effect, reducing the slave to an alienated outsider, socially "dead" to the free population. Slavery is defined as *social death*. The historical sociologist Orlando Patterson, this definition's pioneer, identifies three necessary forces that must be present, and combined in a permanent way, before a phenomenon of domination may be called *slavery*: (1) direct and insidious violence (a social force); (2) nameless and alienating social death (a psychological force); and (3) general dishonor (a cultural force).[6] The impact of the first item on the Pauline material is minimal, not because Greco-Roman slavery lacked violence (far from the case), but because the Pauline evidence provides a non-representative sample of the slave condition in early Christianity. Here and there we find momentary glimpses of slavery's inherent violence, through metaphorical imagery—the "slap on the face" (2 Cor 11:20), the daily reality of corporal punishment (1 Cor 9:27), the slave's agony as "groaning in labor pains" (Rom 8:21–23)—but Paul nowhere in his undisputed letters remarks about slavery's direct and insidious violence with the attention and zeal that the deutero-Pauline material does (Eph 6:5–9; 1 Tim 6:1–2; Titus 2:9–10; cf. 1 Pet 2:18–25).

Given the honor/shame structure of Greco-Roman society, the third item, general dishonor, may also seem problematic if not outright lacking the nuance required for defining slavery in Paul's world. While an example of this dishonor is the common address of male slaves of any age as "boy" (Greek: παῖς, *pais*; Latin: *puer*), denigrating them as infantile adults, counterexamples are also found. Classical sources, to be sure, do mention high-ranking slaves and freedpersons having "honor" (Greek τιμή, *timē*; Latin *honor*), notably wealthy managerial slaves (*oikonomoi*) and imperial freedmen (*familia Caesaris*), many of whom had slaves of their own (*vicarii*, underslaves of slaves). However, in these ancient contexts the term *honor* carried specific and limited meaning: the bureaucratic nuance of holding rank associated with administrative office; or the commercial value of being expensive goods (1 Cor 6:20; 7:23; cf. Acts 19:19; Matt 27:9). Although the emperor Augustus, for example, "held many of his freedmen in high honor [*in honore*] and close intimacy," he did so "as patron and master": Augustus "put in chains" his slave Cosmos "who spoke of him most insultingly," forced his favorite freedman Polus to commit suicide for "adultery with Roman matrons," broke the legs of his secretary Thallus for accepting a bribe "to betray the contents of a letter," and had the pedagogue and attendants of his son Gaius "thrown into a river with heavy weights around their necks" because of their "acts of arrogance and greed" (Suetonius, *Aug.* 67 [Rolfe, LCL]). From a historical perspective, then, any honor conferred even on high-ranking servile persons was always fragile, as Thallus discovered when Augustus broke his legs. Subject to corporal punishment, limited in power, and existing solely at the whim of the master, servile *honor* was not aristocratic Roman *dignitas*.[7]

One might, nonetheless, object that Suetonius is an upper-class author and not representative of lower-class values and perceptions. Because of the status-by-association in the wider Greco-Roman patron-client system, the freeborn lower class might have granted a measure of honor (in the sense of dignity/prestige) to slaves and freedpersons of the managerial and imperial elite, in contrast to the fundamental dishonor given them by the aristocratic upper-class.[8] Problematic to this claim is that it elides the difference between the patron-client system and the slave-master dynamic.[9] Furthermore, funerary epitaphs among the lower social orders at Rome reveal clear recognition of the divide between the humble freeborn and the freed.[10] Most freedmen were humble men and they married women of the same rank; only imperial freedmen were capable of overcoming the awkward contradiction between rank and status to marry freeborn aristocratic women.[11] Such evidence is, I think, the best refutation of the view that the "lower class" somehow saw less dishonor in slavery than did the aristocratic elite. Patterson argues, furthermore, that members of the *familia Caesaris* were elevated to their positions not *in spite of* but *because* they were bereft of true honor. In this way, according to Patterson, the *familia Caesaris* share the fundamental dishonor found in palace (or "palatine") slaves generally, such as the Byzantine court eunuchs and the Islamic <u>Ghilmān</u> (some of whom were grand viziers of the Ottoman Empire), extreme examples of elite slaves which take Patterson to the very limit of, and still confirm, his concept of slavery as "social death."[12]

The denigration began with the enslavement process. Enslavement of (usually) foreigners relied on a variety of sources, including natural reproduction of the existing slave population, capture in warfare, import from overseas trade, piracy, brigandage, kidnapping, infant exposure, and the punishment of criminals (penal slavery). Ancient slavery was not based on race or skin color. The Romans acquired their slaves from all over the Mediterranean world—from Egypt, Asia Minor and Syria, Spain and Greece, Arabia and Ethiopia, Scythia and Thrace, Gaul and Britain. To get an idea of the ubiquity and inconspicuousness of slaves in Roman society, consider Seneca's remark about a bill requiring slave uniforms: "A proposal was once made in the Senate to distinguish slaves from free men by their dress; it then became apparent how great would be the impending danger if our slaves should begin to count their number" (Seneca, *On Mercy* 1.24.1 [Basore, LCL]).

As Seneca's remark reveals, even the Romans themselves did not know the absolute number of slaves. Despite the inadequacy of evidence, some scholars estimate that in urban areas of Roman imperial society slaves made up one-third of the population, but others place the figure lower, within the range 16.6 to 20 percent.[13] We do not know for sure. The ratio is perhaps comparable to demographics of modern periods where census data are available: in 1860, slaves made up 33 percent of the total population of the southern United States, with a slightly lower percentage in the Caribbean and Brazil. Yet demographic generalization based on American slavery is problematic because Roman slavery was an *open* system into which new slaves continued to be imported, unlike American slavery in 1860, which was a *closed* system that required the slave population to reproduce itself. Natural reproduction served as one source of new slaves in the Roman empire, but its importance is a matter of debate.[14]

Warfare and overseas trade were major sources of new slaves throughout the Roman period. Captives by the tens of thousands poured into the slave markets of Sicily and Italy as early as the First Punic War (264–241 B.C.E.), a direct result of the annual pattern of warfare and military expansion of Rome's borders during the Republic. In his campaigns in Gaul alone, Julius Caesar shipped back to Italy nearly one million Gallic prisoners of war (Plutarch, *Life of Caesar* 15.3; Appian, *Gallic History* 1.2). Parasitic military "camp followers"—traders, veterans, and vagabonds—facilitated the traffic and sale of plentiful war captives. In addition to war captives, other foreigners were imported to the Roman heartland as slaves from barbarian suppliers operating on the remote edges of the empire, the outlying areas of the Black Sea being particularly attractive.[15]

The international slave trade relied on not only foreign but also domestic supply, both legitimate and illegitimate. One legitimate source came from infant exposure, which involved the circulation of unwanted babies left at visible places known for foundlings (like a municipal dunghill or a temple of the healer god Asclepius). Traders were also not above obtaining their chattel by means deemed illegitimate by Greco-Roman custom, such as piracy, brigandage, and kidnapping of individuals in the free population. Whatever the method of procurement, the regular means of actual sale was by auction, either at a seasonal market or a year-round slave emporium in one of the major metropolitan ports, such as Ostia or Corinth; the island of Delos at its height reportedly received and dispatched "tens of thousands of slaves" on any given day (Strabo 14.5.2). Because the price of slaves was not prohibitively high, slave ownership went far down the social scale; most Roman families, not just the very wealthy, could have afforded to purchase slaves. The slave for sale usually stood in a single garment on a rotating platform, with a placard around his or her neck bearing origin, talents, and (by a Roman law known as the Aedilician Edict) any defects. Auctioneers typically used chalk to mark the feet of fresh overseas slaves to set them apart from the more domesticated, homebred ones.

Caution was advised when buying a slave. Seneca warns, "When you buy a horse, you order its blanket to be removed; you pull off the garments from slaves that are advertised for sale, so that no bodily flaws may escape your notice" (*Letters* 80.9 [Gummere, LCL]. The Elder Pliny reports that the infamous dealer Toranius sold, for a good price, two slave boys to the triumvir Mark Antony as twins, even though one came from Asia Minor and the other from Gaul (*Natural History* 7.12.56). Such dishonest practices gave slave dealers a reputation in the Greco-Roman world similar to that of used-car sellers today.[16]

Once enslaved and sold, a slave might later become freed by his or her master. The process of liberating a slave is called *manumission*, a legal procedure that should not be confused with *emancipation*, an attempt to effect political change. In Latin, a Roman householder "emancipated" (*emancipo*) an adult child from paternal power (*patria potestas*), but "manumitted" (*manumitto*) a slave. Ancient sources never use the term *emancipation* (the end of legal subordination) in connection with slaves. The *emancipation of slaves* is a modern coinage coming from the eighteenth-century European Enlightenment to express the moral and political conviction that slavery, both as an institution and ideology, is repugnant to the aims of all civilized and just societies of human beings. As such, *emancipation* becomes synonymous with abolition.[17]

The distinction between emancipation and manumission is important because Roman manumission was a limited form of enfranchisement that made the ex-slave a *freedman* or *freedwoman* who nonetheless still owed the ex-master a specific number of work days (*operae*) and respectful deference (*obsequium*), including forfeiture of the right to sue. The freed slave, therefore, entered into a patron-client relationship with the former master, now the patron. The patron-client relationship began by the very act of manumission itself, which took both formal and informal forms. The formal ceremony was either a public legal proceeding with all parties before a magistrate (*manumissio vindicta*) or an official publication in the master's valid will (*manumissio testamento*). If the form was done properly and the master a Roman citizen, the manumitted slave became a Roman citizen. Informal manumission took place in a private domestic gathering before friends serving as witnesses (*manumissio inter amicos*) or in a private letter stating that the slave was liberated (*manumissio per epistulam*).

There were also several degrees of Roman manumission ranging from full enfranchisement (Roman citizen) to partial (Junian Latin). A Junian Latin had the right to enter into Roman contracts (*commercium*) but neither the right to a recognized marriage (*conubium*) nor the capability to make or to inherit from a Roman will (*testamenti factio*). The creation of Junian Latins became common under the early Empire because of efforts to bar slaves from full Roman citizenship. In Hellenized areas of the Greek East, the enfranchisement obligations took the form of a *paramonē* contract, which required the former slave to remain with and serve the ex-master, often "as a slave" until the master's death.[18]

An unusual feature of Roman slavery, compared with the institution in classical Athens or in the Hellenized East, is that the Romans often manumitted their urban slaves. In fact, manumission was incorporated into Roman slavery as a structured and highly conventional practice. Urban manumission became so accepted by the upper orders that the Emperor Augustus had to enact laws curtailing manumission practices by citizens: the *lex Fulfia Caninia* (2 B.C.E.) set limits on the number of slaves that owners could manumit in their will, and the *lex Aelia Sentia* (4 C.E.) set minimum age requirements of twenty for the slave owner and thirty for the slave before formal manumission could occur. However, the frequency of manumission in the Roman context should not be exaggerated or pressed too far. A common mistake in New Testament scholarship is to assume manumission to be relatively automatic after six years of servitude or when the slave turned thirty years of age, often as evidence for humane treatment of slaves under the Roman Empire.[19] The only literary support for this claim is Cicero (*Eighth Philippic* 32), who writes that after six years a slave captured as a prisoner of war could expect to be freed. But Cicero's remark is more rhetoric than social description. He does not mention six years because it is a statistical minimum (or average); these are the six years from Julius Caesar's crossing of the Rubicon River in January 49 to February 43, during which the Roman state was politically enslaved (from the perspective of Cicero). Any Roman senator would understand and accept Cicero's argument even if it would never occur to him to manumit his own slaves after six years. Cicero himself did not manumit his personal domestic, Tiro, until 53 B.C.E., Tiro's fiftieth birthday.[20]

When manumission suited the master's interests and because it reinforced both the institution and the ideology of slavery, many Romans saw manumission as *the* customary reward for their deserving urban slaves. Although only a fraction of slaves actually were freed in Roman society—most, especially those laboring in agriculture or the mines, never saw freedom—the possibility, nonetheless, proved to be a powerful incentive for slave obedience.

Although the motives for manumission varied according to the whims of individual owners, it would be a mistake to assume kindness as a major factor. Often a liberated slave proved more useful to the master as a Roman citizen who could legally make contracts as an agent (*procurator*) in the master's commercial affairs. Additionally, in the Roman understanding of aristocratic virtue, greater honor (*dignitas*) came to the person who had a "crowded house" swelled with many clients and protégés instead of slaves who were forced by violence to be there.[21]

Slaves were vulnerable to physical abuse and violence. Both male and female domestics suffered rape and other forms of harm, including forced prostitution. Field hands working on large agricultural estates (*latifundia*), when disobedient, were chained up in prison-houses (*ergastula*) and left to starve. But the worst conditions were in the mines and mills, where slaves toiled to death. In his Greek romance, Apuleius provides one of the most haunting accounts. The protagonist, in the form of a donkey trapped in a flour mill, narrates the full horror:

> The men were indescribable—their entire skin was coloured black and blue with the weals left by whippings, and their scarred backs were shaded rather than covered by tunics which were patched and torn. Some of them wore no more than a tiny covering around their loins, but all were dressed in such a way that you could see through their rags. They had letters branded on their foreheads, their hair had been partially shaved off, and they had fetters on their feet. They were sallow and discoloured, and the smoky and steamy atmosphere had affected their eyelids and inflamed their eyes. Their bodies were a dirty white because of the dusty flour—like athletes who get covered with fine sand when they fight.[22]

Although admittedly a piece of fiction and highly rhetorical, Apuleius's account is confirmed by a historical narrative mentioning slave living conditions in the mines. There slaves "wear out their bodies both by day and by night in the diggings under the earth, dying in large numbers because of the exceptional hardships they endure" (Diodorus Siculus 5.38.1 [Oldfather, LCL]).

Torture, which Roman law required in the questioning of slaves for any court testimony, involved flogging, burning, and racking the body. The whip had metal pieces attached to its thongs and was meant to make deep, cutting wounds: the victim was either hung up, with feet weighted down, or stood with arms tied to a beam across the shoulders. Burning called for boiling pitch, hot metal plates, and flaming torches applied directly to the skin. Racking by the "little horse" (*eculeus*) or "lyre-strings" (*fidiculae*) meant tearing the body limb from limb. Slave owners weary of the effort could hire the services of professional torturers. The services of one torture-and-execution business survives in an inscription from Puteoli, offering flogging and crucifixion as standard options for a flat, low rate.[23]

Scholars of comparative slavery distinguish between genuine slave societies and societies that simply contained slaves. Genuine slave societies bear this designation not for the slaves' actual numbers so much as for the slaves' integration into their economies and societies. On this criterion, classical Italy (including Roman colonies such as Corinth) qualifies as a genuine slave society.

Roman slaves were not segregated from freeborns in work or type of job performed, with the notable exceptions of military service and mining. This integration of slaves into all levels of the ancient economy marks an important contrast with modern slavery. Modern slavery, for example, often required slave illiteracy by law, whereas ancient masters prized educated slaves. In cities throughout the Mediterranean, slaves were trained and served as physicians, engineers, artisans, shopkeepers, architects, artists, thespians, magicians, prophets (e.g., Acts 16:16–24), teachers, professional poets, and philosophers.

In such occupations, some slaves accumulated and administered a *peculium*, a potentially large fund of assets including money, tools, goods, land, and even other slaves. Although technically belonging to the master, the *peculium* often provided the means for a slave to bargain for manumission by offering to pay the cost of a replacement. In addition to a large *peculium*, some slaves and freedmen belonging to the household of the Roman emperor (*familia Caesaris*) also possessed royal power and privilege, a phenomenon known as palatine slavery. These imperial slaves and freedmen held administrative posts throughout the Empire. Felix, for instance, who served as procurator of Judea and whom the author of Acts reports as presiding initially over the trial of Paul (Acts 24:22–27), was an imperial freedman in the household of the emperor Claudius. However, most slaves were of quite modest means and worked as ordinary laborers or as specialized domestics. Because slaves could be found at all economic levels of society, they had no cohesion as a group and lacked anything akin to class consciousness.[24]

The very wealthiest of slave owners managed a large atrium-style house that contained hundreds of domestic slaves. The architecture kept slaves in their place, housed in small cells (*cellae, cellulae*) that also doubled as storage rooms.[25] In contrast to the situation in the American South, which typically had slaves living in separate "slave quarters" outside the master's manor, ancient slaves lived under the same roof as their owners, and this close-living arrangement heightened slave influence on Roman family relations.[26] Within the aristocratic house, slaves had jobs of extraordinary specialization. There were bath-attendants, masseurs, hairdressers, barbers, announcers of guests, waiters, tasters, choristers, cooks, child minders (*paedagogi*), secretaries, business managers (*procuratores*), and physicians.[27] Some scholars suggest a model for the early Christian house church that relies heavily on Roman atrium-style villas, such as those found at Pompeii and Herculaneum.[28] Tenement apartment buildings (*insulae*), another probable setting for Christian congregations, also had specialized integration of slaves into each activity of domestic life.

The religious life of domestic slaves, whether in houses or apartments, required participation in the daily ritual of the household cult, which centered around the family guardian spirits (*lares*) that represented the ancestral spirit (*genius*) of the estate owner (*pater familias*). During one January rite (the *Compitalia*), the family hung male and female dolls for each free member of the household (*domus*) but a woolen ball for each slave. While the ritual integrated slaves as family members, the representation nonetheless also subordinated them as dehumanized, genderless balls. The interplay of gender and status distinctions also was part of religious festivals for the benefit of slaves, the *Saturnalia* in December and the slaves' holiday on 13 August (*servorum dies festus*). Both celebrations "recognized the permeability of the boundary between master and slave status in the household, but only as the exception that confirmed that boundary."[29]

Greco-Roman polytheism allowed slaves to observe religions in addition to, and different from, that of the domestic cult of the master's household. Outside the *domus*, some slaves were also devotees and functionaries in a variety of international cults (of Mithras and of Isis, for example). Others joined and even served as magistrates in the voluntary associations of the "lower orders" (*collegia tenuiorum*). Public slaves, those owned by the state, served as temple liturgical attendants in municipal and imperial ceremonial religion.[30]

Joining a foreign cult was not only a sign of slave independence but also of some resistance to the social death imposed by the master's realm. Other forms of slave resistance included flight, truancy, theft, black marketeering, sabotage, random violence, uppity or slovenly behavior, feigned illness, murder, and even suicide. Seneca reports a large number of suicide cases: one runaway slave jumped off a roof; another stabbed himself rather than face recapture (*Letters* 4.4). A certain gladiator suffocated himself by ramming a latrine sponge down his throat; another placed his head between moving chariot-wheel spokes, decapitating himself to avoid fighting in the arena (*Letters* 70.19–26). One Spartan slave-boy even smashed his head against a stone wall to end having to perform menial tasks (*Letters* 77.14–15). Outright armed rebellions of slaves were seldom. This is not surprising because the comparative history of slavery shows slave revolts to be extremely rare occurrences. Only four outright slave wars are known: one in modern Haiti (1791, the French colony of Saint-Domingue); two in ancient Sicily

(136–132 B.C.E. and 104–101 B.C.E.); and the one led by Spartacus in ancient Italy (73–71 B.C.E.). The Romans never forgot the legacy of Spartacus, who had ravaged Italy in a war that took three years and ten legions to suppress (a size comparable to what Julius Caesar used to conquer all of Gaul). Yet all the ancient revolts occurred in a very limited time span in the context of massive military expansion and political upheaval under the Roman late Republic, and they coincided with relaxation—not tightening—of control over the slave population.[31]

The absence of slave revolt in the Roman imperial period does not indicate that slavery was then "humane" or that slaves had "relative contentment" with their lot.[32] Rather, the paucity of rebellion represents what the political theorist James Scott has called "the public transcript," the actions and words that dominant and subordinate groups use in open interaction.[33] In this public transcript, the Romans defined slavery as only part of a continuum of domination in the hierarchies of a society in which everyone was subordinated in some sense. Mastery over slaves was an absolute, personalized form of power, known in Latin as *auctoritas*, which involved a series of specific modes of domination to make the subordinate not only comply with individual orders but also to anticipate the master's wishes.[34] By broadening our understanding of rebellion to contain a whole range of practices (flight, truancy, theft, suicide), we begin to see the "hidden transcript" of slave resistance under the public transcript of *auctoritas*, the quintessentially Roman form of domination that was extremely effective in its repressive aims.

Slavery in the Greco-Roman world, therefore, should be understood in light of several factors. First is careful consideration of the available evidence, which is meager. Second is evaluation of comparative definitions of slavery, whether based on legal notions of property or on sociological theories of social death. In the end, slavery is best understood as a combination of violence, social death, and dishonor in a dynamic process that begins with enslavement (from multiple sources) and ends either with biological death or manumission, a limited form of freedom that created a social order of *freedpersons* beneath that of the freeborn population. The third factor is the separation of the ancient and the modern contexts, especially regarding the idea of emancipation. Although there were some opportunities for high status or resistance for a select group of the most resourceful and fortunate slaves, most slaves lived and died under a brutal system that never questioned the morality of enslaving fellow humans and had no abolitionist movement.

Part II. The Apostle Paul on Slaves and Slavery

Paul's letters exemplify the difficulty that Greco-Roman writing as a whole presents to the study of ancient slavery. There is little about slaves. The paucity of references is not due to a lack of slaves in the congregations, but to the biases and occasional nature of the evidence itself. Paul mentions slaves only incidentally and in passing, or metaphorically to make a theological point. Ethical inferences about slavery as a general phenomenon of the Greco-Roman world should be drawn from Paul's words only with great caution. The material yields little evidence for a reconstruction of Paul's ethic of slavery (assuming he had one); his outlook, as deduced from his letters, hardly differed from that in the wider Greco-Roman culture. The present essay will focus on the three main passages where a case for reference to actual slaves in Pauline congregations is clearest and easiest to establish: 1 Cor 7:20–24; Philemon; and Gal 3:28 (with parallel in 1 Cor 12:13).

The most important passage is 1 Cor 7:20–24, the only place in his authentic letters where Paul addresses slaves directly. It is among the most contested passages in the Christian Bible. The debate centers on verse 21, a sentence ambiguous in the original Greek and difficult to translate because Paul does not complete his final clause. The verse reads, "Were you called a slave? Do not worry about it. But if you can become free, rather use ———" (my translation). The reader is left to ask, Use *what*? Does Paul mean to use *being a slave*? Or does he mean the opposite, *becoming free*? In the first option, Paul would be telling his audience to "remain slaves," closing opportunities for freedom; the second has Paul urging slaves to "take liberty," the precise opposite advice. Comparison among frequently referenced English translations reveals the contradiction and current dilemma:

Remain a Slave	Take Liberty
Were you a slave when called? Do not be concerned about it. Even if you can gain your freedom, make use of your present condition more than ever. (NRSV, 1989)	Were you a slave when called? Never mind. But if you can gain your freedom, avail yourself of the opportunity. (RSV, 1946)
Wast thou called being a bond-servant? care not for it: nay, even if thou canst become free, use *it* rather. (American Standard Edition, 1885)	Were you a slave when called? Do not let that trouble you; though if a chance of freedom should come, by all means take it. (REB, 1992)
If you were a slave when you were called, never mind. Even if you can gain your freedom, make the most of your present condition instead. (Edgar J. Goodspeed, *New Testament: An American Translation*, 1923)	You were a slave when called? Never mind. Of course, if you do find it possible to get free, you had better avail yourself of the opportunity. (James Moffatt Version, 1954)
Were you a slave when you were called? Do not be concerned but, even if you can gain your freedom, make the most of it. (NAB, rev. ed., 1986)	If, when you were called, you were a slave, do not let this bother you: but if you should have the chance of being free, accept it. (JB, 1974)[35]

Yet even many of these versions remain ambiguous: the NRSV, the previous RSV, the NEB, the American Standard Edition, and the REB each has a note to this verse that presents the opposite translation as a possible alternative. Such contradictory readings demonstrate 1 Cor 7:21 to be a genuine interpretive problem, a puzzle beginning on the lexical level, which many scholars consider insoluble.[36]

There may be a possible solution. First, the passage's grammar and syntax heavily favor the "take liberty" interpretation. The verse contains two conditional clauses, each expressing a different situation. The first conditional clause asks "Were you called a slave?" Given this first situation Paul then advises the slave not to be concerned about slavery. The second conditional sentence expresses a new situation: "But if you can gain your freedom." Given this second, new situation Paul changes his advice toward a new course of action, that the slave should "take liberty." This kind of grammatical construction—the depiction of one situation followed by a direction, then the depiction of a second situation followed by a new direction with the clause "rather use" (μᾶλλον χρῆσαι, *mallon chrēsai*)—finds parallel in a number of Greek authors. They in fact use the same Greek words as Paul does. A pattern therefore emerges. When Paul sets up one premise (*being a slave*), he urges one action (*do not be concerned*). However, when he sets up a subsequent, different premise (*if you can become free*), he urges a different action (*be concerned and take it*).[37]

The distinctive formula of Greek diatribe that Paul employs in the passage's context is a second reason to favor the "use liberty" interpretation. The formula consists of a predictable stylistic pattern of three elements: (1) a statement of fact given in the form of a rhetorical question; (2) an imperative whose main purpose is to deny the statement of fact's significance for a person's life; and (3) an explanation for why the statement of fact should be treated with such indifference (sometimes omitted in the pattern).[38] The full context of 1 Cor 7 addresses slavery as part of larger themes of marriage and circumcision. Paul asks rhetorically, "Was anyone at the time of his call already circumcised?" (1 Cor 7:18a NRSV), issues an imperative, "Let him not remove the marks of circumcision," and provides an explanation, "Circumcision is nothing, and uncircumcision is nothing; but obeying the commandments of God is everything" (1 Cor 7:19).[39] He repeats this pattern for those uncircumcised at the time of baptism (1 Cor 7:18b) and for those married ("Were you bound to a wife?" Paul asks, followed by an imperative, "Do not seek to be free") or single ("Are you free from a wife? Do not seek a wife" [1 Cor 7:27]). Similarly, on the topic of slavery Paul asks, "Were you a slave when called," but answers unexpectedly, "Do not be concerned about it" (1 Cor 7:21). Given the diatribal pattern, one would anticipate Paul's saying, *Don't seek to become free*, but instead Paul deliberately softens his imperative's impact, allowing for an exception in the case of slavery. This break from his diatribal pattern suggests that his opening line in 1 Cor 7:20 ("Let each of you remain in the condition in which you were called") does not hold for the case of slavery. When this evidence is laid beside the above mentioned grammatical and syntactical parallels of *mallon chrēsai* in Greek authors, we confront an accumulation of compelling arguments heavily favoring the "use liberty" interpretation.[40]

Social history confirms this conclusion. The city of Corinth in Paul's day was a Roman colony (*colonia*), founded in 44 B.C.E. by Julius Caesar and was at first populated by Italian freedmen. Nothing in the city—families, buildings, or institutions—was over a century old. The previous city of Old Corinth was sacked in 146 B.C.E. (and its inhabitants sold into slavery) when Rome expanded its military influence into the eastern Mediterranean. No other city of Paul operated more under the Roman model and legacy of slavery. Located on the isthmus connecting mainland Greece to the Peloponnesus, Corinth had two seaports with an extensive network of roads: Cenchreae on the Saronic Gulf; and Lechaion on the Corinthian Gulf, one of the largest man-made harbors in the Greco-Roman world. These seaports served as freight way stations that handled high volumes of traffic and vast inventories of merchandise, including human chattel. Paul must have seen or known about the large slave market in the city's northern quarter. Paul may allude to it when he writes, "You were bought with a price; therefore glorify God with your body" (1 Cor 6:20), an exhortation against Christians frequenting prostitutes that compares Christians to purchased slaves (1 Cor 6:12–20). Paul may also be alluding to the sexually seedy reputations of slave dealers in the wider Greco-Roman world.[41] Paul relies on the language of economics and the slave trade also in 1 Cor 7: "For you were bought with a price; do not become slaves of human masters" (1 Cor 7:23), a metaphor of slavery to Christ as the proper condition of the Christian believer. Corinth's marketplace setting, therefore, provides the context against which we should read Paul's exhortation to slaves in 1 Cor 7:21.[42]

When Paul addressed slaves and their possible liberation in 1 Cor 7:21, he spoke to a Roman social context. In that setting, liberation opportunities for slaves would mean manumission in one of the many forms available in Roman practice and not emancipation or abolition in the modern sense of these terms. Paul's acceptance and even encouragement of manumission for slaves are not indications that he opposed slavery as an institution or ideology. By incorporating the Roman institutionalized practice of regular urban manumission into his theology, Paul in 1 Cor 7:21 speaks in ways similar to other Greco-Romans.[43] Yet one might object that Paul was a social conservative and thus was more likely to exhort slaves to remain slaves. To be sure Paul may have been a social conservative: his belief that Christ would return soon and bring the Kingdom of God did not lead him to efforts to change the present society in fundamental ways. But social conservatism in the Greco-Roman world did not include restriction of manumission.

Such a restriction may be typical of modern slave societies, especially in response to abolitionist calls for the political emancipation of slaves. In the decades before the American Civil War, for example, southern apologists defended slavery as the "peculiar institution," a euphemism that reveals a certain uneasiness white Southerners had about the moral legitimacy of slavery as an American and a Christian institution. The rarity of legal manumission in the southern United States served to justify both the peculiarity of and the need for slavery in the modern world. To this perspective, manumission is a "liberal" value that a "conservative" Paul would not hold.

Unlike their modern counterparts, however, Greco-Roman slaveholders saw no need to justify their institution as "peculiar." In fact, Cicero, Augustus, Seneca, and other Roman "social conservatives" did not oppose the manumission of slaves. Quite the contrary, Roman conservatives widely favored and regularly practiced the manumission of deserving urban slaves in their households. Thus to label Paul a "social conservative" based on his advice to slaves concerning manumission is to evaluate Paul from a modern perspective, not from within his ancient context.[44]

Therefore, we find that the nineteenth-century battles for the Bible and slavery have little contact with Paul's original situation.[45] In his extant letters, Paul neither attacked nor defended slavery as a social institution. Rather, he accepted slavery as a given fact of ancient life. He understood the institutional practice of urban manumission, and he knew that slaves were in his Corinthian congregation. Because Corinth was a Roman city, the possibility arose that slaves might become manumitted. So Paul included this possibility as an exception to his general rule of Christians remaining in the situation in which they had their baptismal call.

The second important Pauline text dealing with actual slaves, in this case a specific slave named Onesimus, is the Letter to Philemon. Although the brevity of the work (one page in the NRSV) might encourage readers to assume it easily comprehensible and straightforward, its exegesis is far from certain. Current scholarship offers three different and competing reconstructions of the situation that Paul addresses: (1) the "runaway slave" hypothesis (the standard view); (2) the "intercession" hypothesis; and (3) the "dispatched slave" hypothesis. Unfortunately, none of these proposals solves all the exegetical problems.

The "runaway slave" hypothesis assumes the letter to be what Patristic commentators since John Chrysostom (fourth century) said it was—an epistle requesting the Christian slaveholder Philemon to take back his runaway slave Onesimus who, after doing damage, theft, or some other wrong, had somehow contacted Paul in prison and had been baptized.[46] In such a case, we know that ancient slaves who fled their masters typically sought asylum in a temple or at a statute of the emperor (Achilles Tatius, *Leucippe and Clitophon* 7.13), went underground in a large city (Cicero, *Letters to Quintus* 1.2.14), joined marauding bands of maroon societies in the countryside (Athenaeus 265D–266E), or tried as impostors to enlist in the army (Pliny, *Letters* 10.29–30).[47] Yet Onesimus, it is alleged, took none of these options (or was captured before he had a chance) and either found himself (by remarkable luck) thrown in the same prison as Paul or took refuge among the associates of Paul, wherever he was imprisoned (the location of the prison is not specified; it could be either Rome, Ephesus, or Caesarea in Palestine). Subsequently, Paul prompted Onesimus's conversion, thereby becoming his "father during my imprisonment" (Phlm 10), and then sent Onesimus with the letter, back to the master.

Supporters of the runaway slave hypothesis often draw an alleged parallel with the correspondence of the Younger Pliny (*Letters* 9.21 and 9.24) about an errant freedman being returned to his patron Sabinianus.[48] But Pliny's tone differs markedly from Paul's. After being convinced of the freedman's "genuine penitence," Pliny says he gave the man a very severe scolding and warned him firmly never to make such a request again, in order to frighten the errant runaway (Pliny, *Letters* 9.21). In contrast, Paul does not ask Philemon (as Pliny does of Sabinianus) to forgive or have pity upon the fugitive, the tone one would expect for a runaway situation.[49] These problems cast doubt on the parallel and on the whole runaway slave hypothesis.

The second interpretation, the "intercession" hypothesis, which rejects the runaway slave presupposition, claims that Onesimus was not running away *to freedom* but *to Paul* for intercession after some misdeed. Using the opinions of three classical Roman jurists recorded in the *Digest* of Justinian—who state that a slave running to a friend of the master to seek intercession is not technically a "criminal runaway" (*servus fugitivus*) but merely a "delinquent truant" (*erro*)—scholars in this camp argue that Onesimus was not a *fugitivus* but an *erro* according to Roman slave law. This interpretation, however, suffers the methodological mistake of making monolithic claims about Roman slave law and of relying on law exclusively for one's reconstruction of ancient slavery.[50]

Even if one accepts the intercession hypothesis, it brings us back to the same questions about the runaway-slave theory: Why does not Paul scold and rebuke Onesimus for leaving the household without permission? Why does not Paul's letter share the same tone as Pliny's letter to Sabinianus, which is an explicit example of how a third party could react to a slave request for intercession. Furthermore, the distinction between a runaway *fugitivus* and an intercession-seeking *erro* exists only in the jurists. There was no substantial difference in the actual practice of Greco-Roman slavery. In the end, the intercession hypothesis is but a variation on the runaway-slave hypothesis and leaves still unanswered the original problem, that Paul's tone lacks rebuke of Onesimus.

We are left, then, with the third possibility—the "dispatched slave" hypothesis. In this interpretation, Onesimus did not *run away* but *was sent* to Paul by Philemon.[51] There is encouraging precedent for such a scenario. In Philippians, Paul thanks the congregation for sending Epaphroditus to "minister to my need" (Phil 2:25). Paul acknowledges that "I have been paid in full and have more than enough; I am fully satisfied, now that I have received from Epaphroditus the gifts you sent" (Phil 4:18). Perhaps Onesimus served in a function on behalf of Philemon's congregation similar to that of Epaphroditus on behalf of the congregation at Philippi.[52] In Greco-Roman prisons, guards generally threw the criminal into a prison and left issues like feeding, clothing, and other needs to the criminal to fend for himself.[53] Early Christian congregations would have known the dangers that Paul faced in such a situation and at least on one occasion (recorded in Philippians) sent a minister with money and other gifts to sustain Paul. Onesimus could have served Paul as a scribe, letter-carrier, or personal assistant. The occasion of the letter would be, in this scenario, the delinquency of Paul in not returning the dispatched slave.[54]

We have abundant examples of such cases, especially in the letters of Cicero, who was notorious for keeping his friends' letter carriers too long. "You too," reminds Publius Cornelius Dolabella in a letter to Cicero, "on your part, honourable and courteous as you are, will see that the letter-carrier I have sent to you may be enabled to return to me, and that he brings me back a letter from you" (Cicero, *Letters to Friends* 9.3 [Williams, LCL]). "I have been rather slow," writes Cicero to his friend Atticus, "in sending back your letter-carrier, because there was no opportunity of sending him" (Cicero, *Letters to Atticus* 11.2 [Winstedt, LCL]). In another place, he apologizes: "What is happening here you may gather from the bearer of your letter. I have kept him longer than I should, because every day I am expecting something fresh to happen, and there was no reason for sending him even now, except the subject on which you ask for an answer" (Cicero, *Letters to Atticus* 11:3 [Winstedt, LCL]).[55]

A papyrus letter dated 12 September 50 C.E. provides further support. Mystarion, an Egyptian olive-planter, asks Stotoëtis, a chief priest, for the rapid return of his slave Blastus.

> Mystarion to his own Stotoëtis many greetings.
>
> I have sent to you my Blastus for forked (?) sticks for my olive gardens. See then that you don't detain [κατάσχης, *kataschēs*] him. For you know that I need him every moment [ὥρας, *hōras*].[56]

Two verbal parallels, clear in the original Greek, are immediately apparent. First, Mystarion asks not "to detain" (*katechein*) Blastus, and, similarly, Paul admits that he wants "to detain" (*katechein*) Onesimus (Phlm 13). Second, Mystarion emphasizes that he needs Blastus each "moment" (*hōra*), while Paul, likewise, explains the need ("usefulness"; Phlm 11) to keep Onesimus for a "moment" (*hōra*; Phlm 15). These similarities suggest an analogous social situation: Philemon and his house church sent the slave Onesimus to aid Paul in prison. Having kept the dispatched slave overdue, Paul writes a letter explaining the delay to Philemon and the congregation of which he is member. The fault is Paul's, not that of the slave Onesimus. This explains the absence of any rebuke on the part of Paul for the slave's actions and the lack of remorse on the part of Onesimus for wrongdoing.

Yet exegetical problems remain. One might object, for example, that the pledge Paul makes to "repay" any wrongdoing (Phlm 18) seems to support the runaway slave hypothesis, or at least the idea that the fault lies with Onesimus. Paul could refer to a number of things here—such as the *peculium* that Onesimus had at his disposal (which in law technically belonged to the master), the additional cost of keeping Onesimus from his regular duties at home, or the lost wages that the slave would have earned for his master had he not stayed away so long—but the text is too brief to be certain. One reply to this objection is that the radical change of a slave's religious commitment without his master's permission, and the slave's possible pledge of *peculium* in that conversion, could be taken as a wrong by a slave to the master.[57] Perhaps Paul was anticipating this reaction: Paul does not say that any wrong has taken place but writes in the subjunctive: "*if* he has wronged you at all, or owes you anything, charge that to my account" (Phlm 18) and not the slave's account (*peculium*). Using hypothetical language, Paul might be interpreted as saying that the wrongdoing was a perceived, not an actual, condition.[58] Paul addressed the letter to several people, including the church in Philemon's house (Phlm 2), to raise the honor-shame stakes to that of a public hearing, in the agonistic code of face-to-face rhetorical encounters. Paul pressures Philemon by making a public plea, before the entire house church, to strengthen his hypothetical language.[59]

The exegetical problems are due in part to Paul's diction, which is unusually deferential and circumspect: "I preferred," he writes, "to do nothing without your consent, in order that your good deed might be voluntary and not something forced" (Phlm 14). In this interpretation, the "good deed" that should be "voluntary and not something forced" is manumission and/or granting Paul domestic authority over Onesimus. "Perhaps for this reason [Onesimus] was separated from you for a while, so that you might have him back forever, no longer as a slave but more than a slave, a beloved brother—especially to me but how much more to you, both in the flesh and in the Lord" (Phlm 16). The phrases "more than a slave" and a brother "in the flesh and in the Lord" may imply that Paul hopes to secure the manumission of Onesimus, a possibility that Paul's ending the letter with a note of confidence supports: "knowing that you will do even more than I say" (Phlm 21). Paul first denies the validity of Onesimus's prior slave relationship with Philemon ("no longer a slave") and then substitutes a fraternal bond in its place ("a beloved brother"). Paul wants Philemon to accept Onesimus in accordance with the apostle's terms, making the slaveholder acknowledge Paul's mastery over Philemon's domestic affairs. Paul asserts rhetorical authority over Philemon's legal right to determine the future of his slave Onesimus.[60] If so, then Paul's support of manumission would correspond to what he says in 1 Cor 7:21, revealing once more that Paul shared commonplace Greco-Roman views about the institution of slavery.[61] We find nothing in the letter of Philemon that opposes slavery as an institution or ideology; here the distinction made above between manumission and emancipation is crucial. Manumission was a regular and integral part of Roman slavery. It served to reinforce mastery and social control. Freed slaves remained under the hierarchy and personalized power of their former master, now patron. Manumission was a regular feature of Roman slavery because it suited the master's interests. Often slaves were of more practical use after manumission, because the enfranchised slave had greater legal capacity to administer household affairs.[62] If Paul asks for manumission, he is not condemning slavery but reinforcing its legitimacy by working within its rules and procedures. That Paul may be requesting manumission to gain the services of Onesimus as an enfranchised freedman only strengthens the point.

The third important text dealing with actual slaves is Gal 3:27–28 (parallel in 1 Cor 12:13; cf. Col 3:11): "As many of you as were baptized into Christ have clothed yourselves with Christ. There is no longer Jew or Greek, there is no longer slave or free, there is no longer male and female; for all of you are one in Christ Jesus." The three polarities of circumcision/uncircumcision, slave/free, male/female appear precisely in the same order as in 1 Cor 7:17–28, forming a literary pattern. The pattern reveals a belief that the termination of such social distinctions betokens the eschatological change (or "breakthrough") that the believer experiences by becoming baptized "in Christ."[63] Paul did not coin this baptismal formula but borrowed its language from early initiation rituals that preceded his ministry. These rituals articulated a "new creation" and drew on certain aspects of the Adam legends. In those legends, the first form of humanity was neither male nor female (but both; Gen 1:27), neither Jew nor Greek, neither slave nor free. The sin of Adam represented the loss of the original unity and a change of clothes, from the "image of God" (Gen 1:26) or a "garment of light" to "garments of skin" (Gen 3:21) or the physical body. The ritual of baptism, in which initiates removed their clothes and put on new garments, aimed to recover that unity in paradise where "all are one."[64]

Other Greco-Roman writers could invoke a world without such social distinctions, but usually only to highlight its utopian, unattainable nature. Commenting humorously on the diversity of philosophical sects, Lucian of Samosata compared their professed goal of "virtue" to a fantastic "city all of whose inhabitants are happy": "inferior or superior, noble or common, bond or free, simply did not exist and were not mentioned in the city" (Lucian, *Hermotimus* 24, [Kilburn, LCL]). The impracticality of this ideal city, without distinctions of social rank, shows the absurdity of the multiple philosophical "roads" to it. Earlier Aristotle had tried to imagine a world without slaves in practical terms. He could only envision a fantasy land, where tools performed their work on command (even anticipating what to do), utensils moved automatically, shuttles wove cloth and quills played harps without human hands to guide them, bread baked itself, and fish flipped themselves over in fryers at the appropriate times (Aristotle, *Politics* 1.4 [1253b]; see also Athenaeus 6.267). The satire illustrates how preposterous such a slaveless utopia would be, so integral was slavery to ancient life. One wonders, then, whether any ancient person, even Paul, could imagine the piece of ritual language in Gal 3:28 as a feasible basis for social practice. Furthermore, the difficulty Paul has in sorting out the polarities of circumcised/uncircumcised, married/unmarried, slave/free in 1 Cor 7 illustrates the problem of claiming that Paul advocates some practical program of social reform.

Still, such utopian language had undeniable appeal in a society as hierarchical as classical antiquity, as evidence from other Greco-Roman religions indicates. Some ancient cultic associations advertised, like the baptismal phrase in Gal 3:28, the irrelevance of social distinctions in the enjoyment of their deity's benefits. In ancient Philadelphia (in Asia Minor), a shrine erected in honor of savior gods reads: "The commandments given [by Zeus] to Dionysius [the owner of the house] granting access in sleep to his own house both to free men and women, and to household slaves."[65] This equal access to the Dionysian cult did not lead adherents to become emancipationists, however. There was also the Greco-Roman religious festival of *Saturnalia*, which temporarily inverted the slave and the master roles. Yet the inversion functioned on the level of ritual and play; it was not an attempt to abolish slavery. Slave owners used the *Saturnalia* as a vehicle of social control, to appease slave discontent and reward slave obedience.[66]

Early Christian baptism was a rite of passage that moved a person from the status of stranger to one of family. Some scholars claim that, because the baptismal formula ("neither free nor slave") spoke of all members being one "in Christ," early congregations must have taken this saying not only on the level of theological metaphor but also on the literal level: to erase the slave-free distinction in custom and society.[67] Yet expressions similar to that in Gal 3:28 in the wider Greco-Roman urban culture provide important evidence that slaveholders might believe that slavery could be erased in the ideal but not in daily practice. Roman Stoic morality, for example, blurred the slave-free division in philosophy. According to Stoicism, it was fate and not nature that made people slaves. Every human was a potential slave.[68]

This insight led Stoics to exhort Roman masters to see the humanity of their slaves. In his famous correspondence to Lucilius, a middle-aged politician and wealthy slaveholder, the Stoic philosopher and Roman statesman Seneca writes:

> I am glad to learn, through those who come from you, that you live on friendly terms with your slaves. This befits a sensible and well-educated man like yourself. "They are slaves," people declare. Nay, rather they are men. "Slaves!" No, comrades. "Slaves!" No, they are unpretentious friends. "Slaves!" No, they are our fellow-slaves, if one reflects that Fortune has equal rights over slaves and free men alike. (Seneca, *Letters* 47.1 [Gummere, LCL])

By emphasizing the unity of slave and free in terms of a common humanity, Seneca exhorts his friend further:

> Kindly remember that he whom you call your slave sprang from the same stock, is smiled upon by the same skies, and on equal terms with yourself breathes, lives, and dies. It is just as possible for you to see in him a freeborn man as for him to see in you a slave. As a result of the massacres in Marius's[69] day, many a man of distinguished birth, who was taking the first steps toward senatorial rank by service in the army, was humbled by fortune, one becoming a shepherd, another a caretaker of a country cottage. Despise, then, if you dare, those to whose estate you may at any time descend, even when you are despising them. (*Letters* 47.10 [Gummere, LCL])

Many young Roman officers of equestrian and senatorial families, on a promising career path (*cursus honorum*), instead found themselves slaves of barbarian victors. This military history taught Seneca the precarious character of life, even in high social orders. In Roman Stoic understandings of fortune, there was neither slave nor free: to the powers that be, the terms *slave* and *free* had no stable or intrinsic value for the human condition.

Dio Chrysostom provides one of the longest extant discussions on freedom and slavery and an additional context for how a Greco-Roman audience might have heard Paul's words. He has a hypothetical slave ask his master, "'Is it possible, my good friend, to know who is a slave, or who is free?'" (Dio Chrysostom, *Discourses* 15.2 [Cohoon, LCL]), and declare, "'For of those who are called slaves we will, I presume, admit that many have the spirit of free men, and that among free men there are many who are altogether servile'" (*Discourses* 15.29). Even those not chattel slaves may nonetheless be moral slaves, in bondage to greed, gluttony, or other desires. This belief that all people are potentially bound to slavery in either chattel or moral form renders the slave-free distinction meaningless in Stoic philosophy. "We are all fettered to Fate," writes Seneca, "For some, the chain is made of gold, and is loose; for others it is tight and filthy—but what difference does it make?" Seneca continues:

All of us are surrounded by the same kind of captivity, and even those who hold others bound are in bonds themselves, unless you happen to think that the handcuff the guard wears on his left wrist hurts less than the prisoner's. Public offices hold one man captive, wealth another; some are disadvantaged by high birth, some by humble birth; some have to put up with other people's commands, some with their own. Some have to stay in one place because they've been exiled, others because they've been appointed to a priesthood—all life is slavery. (Seneca, *The Tranquility of Mind* 10.3 [Wiedemann, *Greek and Roman Slavery*])

Seneca expresses the capricious character of life even as he holds one of the highest social ranks in Roman society. Slave owners, he reminds his aristocratic readers, may not possess moral freedom, freedom in the absolute sense. Yet this philosophy did not translate into a program of social reform of slavery at Rome. Seneca was, after all, one of the largest slaveholding senators in the city, and he kept his philosophy and politics separate. He did not care about the slaves' plight for its own sake, but for the sake of the ethical well-being of the slaveholders in general and for strengthening the hierarchy of the upper equestrian and senatorial orders in particular. For example, when the Roman Senate ordered the execution of the four hundred slaves belonging to the murdered Pedanius Secundus (the incident related at the opening of this essay), Seneca as political adviser and minister to the emperor Nero did nothing to stop the slaughter of innocents.[70]

Paul employs metaphors of slavery that cohere with Greco-Roman philosophical discussions on how relative the slave–free distinction is. Any attempt to weigh Paul's place in this Greco-Roman philosophical discussion must take seriously that he made positive and widespread use of slavery as the metaphor for the proper relation of the believer to God. A case in point is 1 Cor 7:22–23: "For whoever was called in the Lord as a slave is a freedperson [*apeleutheros*] belonging to the Lord, just as whoever was free [*eleutheros*] when called is a slave of Christ. You were bought with a price; do not become slaves of human masters." *Slaves of human masters* is a metaphor for yielding to merely human claims and values (cf. Rom 8:12–17; Gal 5:1).[71] To understand Paul's metaphorical language, we need to do close reading of the previous verse. The crucial term is *freedperson* (*apeleutheros*), which biblical commentaries tend not to take seriously. Many exegetes explain the passage in the following way, which has become a standard reading: Paul introduces a leveling of all Christians to one eschatological condition, freedom in Christ, which annuls previous differences in status among Christians.[72] Yet by calling the slave a "freedperson" (*apeleutheros*) rather than a "freeperson" (*eleutheros*) in Christ, Paul stresses precisely what this standard commentary denies—that the status of the person is the issue, not eschatological freedom. Paul is not simply saying that "in Christ" all people hold basically the same, egalitarian position. He introduces an actual reversal of normal status, reinforcing the Roman understanding of slavery as only part of a continuum of domination. In Roman society everyone was subordinated in some sense, even an aristocrat like Seneca. Creating a salvific hierarchy, Paul elevates the slave to the (higher) social order of *freedperson* and demotes the free person to the (lower) rank of slave. Salvation, according to Paul, is not simply an improved individual condition—freedom—but purchase in the market and subsequent relocation as servile domestics in a new hierarchy (the household of the Lord) as slaves and freedpersons of Christ.[73]

This interpretation, however, may seem counterintuitive. It appears to contradict Paul's declarations elsewhere that the Christian condition is freedom and sonship, in direct opposition to slavery. "For you did not receive a spirit of slavery," Paul writes, "to fall back into fear, but you have received a spirit of adoption" (Rom 8:15; cf. Eph 1:5). "For freedom Christ has set us free. Stand firm, therefore, and do not submit again to a yoke of slavery" (Gal 5:1). "For the law of the Spirit of life in Christ Jesus has set you free from the law of sin and of death" (Rom 8:1). Creation "itself will be set free from its bondage to decay and will obtain the freedom and glory of the children of God" (Rom 8:21). "For you were called," he exhorts Gentile converts, "to freedom, brothers and sisters; only do not use your freedom as an opportunity for self-indulgence, but through love become slaves to one another" (Gal 5:13). In his theology, Paul appears to combine the opposing values of slavery and freedom.

Whereas one may dismiss this tension as Pauline inconsistency, or bald doublethink—perhaps the irony of a self-designated "slave of Christ" (Rom 1:1; Phil 1:1; Gal 1:10) preaching the Christian life as "freedom" was lost on Paul—there is another possible interpretation. The alleged contradiction holds only if *slavery* means the same thing when used in these various passages. Identical metaphors, however, do not always point to the same phenomenon when used in different ways. Although both share the same term *slavery*, two distinct metaphors are present, two different *slaveries* betokened: first, a *negative* slavery pointing to the pre- or non-Christian state; second, a *positive* slavery pointing to salvation in Christ. Because the *second* slavery refers to the process by which one is freed from the first slavery (to sin, Satan, and other cosmic forces), Paul can speak of slavery to Christ as "freedom" even though it is not freedom in the sense of the absence of enslavement: "But now that you have been freed from sin and enslaved to God, the advantage you get is sanctification" (Rom 6:22). A beneficial, higher slavery to the divine replaces the lower, pernicious slavery to sin.[74] Whether beneficial or pernicious, slavery remains normative. Important in Paul's metaphors were beliefs in slavery as only part of a continuum of domination—in essence, the Roman cultural understanding of *auctoritas* (mastery). This quintessentially Roman idiom of power distinguished true slavery from other forms of domination by requiring not just compliance to particular commands but total acceptance of the master's will.[75] This view of mastery emphasized patriarchy and personalized power. In such a system of personalized power, "the slave must carry out the master's orders, put the master's interest before his or her own, without compensation or consideration, just because the slave is a slave."[76] When Paul exhorted Christians that slavery was the proper relationship of the believer to God, his words were embedded in this Roman cultural milieu. Paul's words in 1 Cor 7:22–23 did not merely recommend subjection but signaled acceptance of an organic model of human existence for which subjugation was essential. How such language criticized the ideology of the social institution, or suggests some political program for abolition, is difficult to see.

One wonders whether Paul's words in Gal 3:28 translated into some program of political change. Did Paul mean that slave believers were no longer actual slaves in the understanding of the church? Were slaves in the congregations demanding equal rights as a result of this baptismal statement? There is no evidence of such. Nor is there any indication of any unrest or rebellion among slaves in the Pauline congregations. The important clue is 1 Cor 12:13, in which Paul drops the phrase "there is no longer male and female" of Gal 3:28. The change suggests that a conflict did exist over male and female roles in Corinth. But because Paul retains the phrase "slaves or free" in 1 Cor 12:13, it is difficult to prove the presence of any conflict between Christian masters and slaves at Corinth or elsewhere.[77]

We find, then, in the three main Pauline texts addressing actual slaves—1 Cor 7:21, Philemon, and Gal 3:28 (with 1 Cor 12:13)—no call for the end of legalized slavery, or even criticism of the institution itself, though the first passage seems to countenance slaves' seeking their freedom when presented with the opportunity.[78] The advice in 1 Cor 7:21 addresses the institutionalized practice of urban manumission, not emancipation or abolition. The letter of Philemon, seen in light of the third interpretation, noted above, asks a slaveholder for permission regarding his slave, thus operating within the Roman slave system. Galatians 3:28 speaks about the erasure of the slave-free distinction "in Christ," but not in society. In all three instances, Paul accepts the Roman institution of slavery as part of the actualities of daily life. Far from unique, his expressions are similar to those found in wider Roman culture.[79]

Part III. Other Relevant Pauline and Paulinist Texts

Metaphors of Slavery

Paul's self-designation as "slave of Christ." Rom 1:1; Phil 1:1; Gal 1:10 (cf. 1 Cor 9:16–18).

Paul's self-designation as "slave of all" (rhetorical *topos* of enslaved leader). 1 Cor 3:5; 9:19–23; 2 Cor 4:5.

Believers exhorted to become "slaves of Christ" and/or "slaves of all." Rom 12:11; 13:4; 14:4, 18; 1 Cor 7:22–23; Gal 5:13.

Imagery of war captives paraded as slaves. 2 Cor 2:14 (cf. Col 2:15).

Exhortation against servility. 2 Cor 11:20.

Imagery of manumission, redemption. Rom 3:24; 6:6–23; 7:14; 8:12–23; Gal 3:13–14; 4:1–5:1 (cf. Eph 1:5; 2:19).

Christ taking the form of a slave, an image of humiliation. Phil 2:6–11 (cf. 2 Cor 11:7).

Imagery of the ancient slave market and slave trading. 1 Cor 6:12–20; 7:23 (cf. 1 Tim 1:10).

Exhortation against becoming a "slave of desire," advising self-control. Rom 16:18; 1 Cor 9:24–27 (cf. Titus 2:3; 3:3; Eph 2:3).

Possible References to Actual Slaves or Freedpersons in Pauline Congregations

Rom 16:10–11, 23; 1 Cor 1:11, 16; 1:26; 16:17 (cf. 2 Tim 1:16; 4:19; Acts 16:15, 32–34; 18:8); Phil 4:22.

Household Duty Codes for Slaves and Masters

Eph 6:5–9; Col 3:22–4:1; 1 Tim 6:1–2 (cf. 3:4–5, 12); Titus 2:9–10; cf. 1 Pet 2:18–25.

Part IV. Bibliography

Classical Studies

Andreau, Jean. "The Freedman." Pages 175–98 in *The Romans,* edited by Andrea Giardina. Chicago: University of Chicago Press, 1993.

Bradley, Keith R. "Animalizing the Slave: The Truth of Fiction." *JRS* 90 (2000): 110–25.

———. "Slavery." *OCD* 1415–17.

———. *Slavery and Rebellion in the Roman World.* Bloomington: Indiana University Press, 1989.

———. *Slavery and Society at Rome.* Key Themes in Ancient History. Cambridge: Cambridge University Press, 1994.

———. *Slaves and Masters in the Roman Empire: A Study in Social Control.* New York: Oxford University Press, 1987.

Buckland, W. W. *The Roman Law of Slavery: The Condition of the Slave in Private Law from Augustus to Justinian.* 1908. Reprint, New York: AMS Press, 1969.

Duff, A. M. *Freedmen in the Early Roman Empire.* 2d ed. Cambridge: W. Heffer & Sons, 1958.

Finley, M. I. *The Ancient Economy*. Sather Classical Lectures 43. Berkeley and Los Angeles: University of California Press, 1985.

———. *Ancient Slavery and Modern Ideology*. New York: Viking, 1980.

———, ed. *Classical Slavery*. Slavery and Abolition special issue 8. London: Frank Cass, 1987.

———. "Slavery." Pages 307–13 in *International Encyclopedia of the Social Sciences*, vol. 14, edited by David L. Sills. New York: Macmillan, 1968.

———, ed. *Slavery in Classical Antiquity: Views and Controversies*. Cambridge: W. Heffer & Sons, 1960.

Fitzgerald, William. *Slavery and the Roman Literary Imagination*. Roman Literature and Its Contexts. Cambridge: Cambridge University Press, 2000.

Garland, Andrew. "Cicero's *Familia Urbana*." *Greece and Rome* 39 (1992): 163–72.

Garnsey, Peter. *Ideas of Slavery from Aristotle to Augustine*. The W. B. Stanford Memorial Lectures. Cambridge: Cambridge University Press, 1996.

———. "Independent Freedmen and the Economy of Roman Italy under the Principate." *Klio* 63 (1981): 359–71.

Harris, William V. "Demography, Geography, and the Sources of Roman Slaves." *JRS* 89 (1999): 62–75.

———. "Towards a Study of the Roman Slave Trade." Pages 117–40 in *The Seaborne Commerce of Ancient Rome: Studies in Archaeology and History*, edited by J. H. D'Arms and E. C. Kopff. Memoirs of the American Academy in Rome 36. Rome: American Academy in Rome, 1980.

Hopkins, Keith. *Conquerors and Slaves*. Sociological Studies in Roman History 1. Cambridge: Cambridge University Press, 1978.

———. "Novel Evidence for Roman Slavery." *Past and Present* 138 (1993): 3–27.

Manning, C. E. "Stoicism and Slavery in the Roman Empire." Pages 1518–43 in *ANRW* 2.36.3. 1989.

Murnaghan, Sheila, and Sandra R. Joshel, eds. *Women and Slaves in Greco-Roman Culture: Differential Equations*. London: Routledge, 1998.

Pomeroy, Sarah B. *Goddesses, Whores, Wives, and Slaves: Women in Classical Antiquity*. New York: Schocken Books, 1975.

Ste. Croix, G. E. M. de. *The Class Struggle in the Ancient Greek World: From the Archaic Age to the Arab Conquest*. 1981. Reprint with corrections, Ithaca, N.Y.: Cornell University Press, 1989.

Scheidel, Walter. "Quantifying the Sources of Slaves in the Early Roman Empire." *JRS* 87 (1997): 156–69.

Thébert, Yvon. "The Slave." Pages 138–74 in *The Romans*, edited by Andrea Giardina. Chicago: University of Chicago Press, 1993.

Treggiari, Susan. *Roman Freedmen during the Late Republic*. Oxford: Clarendon, 1969.

Vogt, Joseph. *Ancient Slavery and the Ideal of Man*. New York: Oxford University Press, 1974.

Watson, Alan. *Roman Slave Law*. Baltimore: Johns Hopkins University Press, 1987.

Weaver, P. R. C. *Familia Caesaris: A Social Study of the Emperor's Freedmen and Slaves*. Cambridge: Cambridge University Press, 1972.

Westermann, William L. *The Slave Systems of Greek and Roman Antiquity*. Memoirs of the American Philosophical Society 40. Philadelphia: American Philosophical Society, 1955. [Must be read with the critical review by P. A. Brunt in *JRS* 48 (1958): 164–70.]

Wiedemann, Thomas. *Greek and Roman Slavery*. 1981. Reprint, London: Routledge, 1988.

———. "The Regularity of Manumission at Rome." *Classical Quarterly*, n.s., 35 (1985): 162–75.

———. "Slavery." Pages 575–88 in *Civilization of the Ancient Mediterranean: Greece and Rome*, vol. 1, edited by Michael Grant and Rachel Kitzinger. New York: Charles Scribner's Sons, 1988.

———. *Slavery*. Greece and Rome: New Surveys in the Classics 19. Oxford: Clarendon, 1987.

Yavetz, Zvi. *Slaves and Slavery in Ancient Rome*. New Brunswick, N.J.: Transaction, 1988.

New Testament Studies

Barclay, John M. G. "Paul, Philemon, and the Dilemma of Christian Slave-Ownership." *NTS* 37 (1991): 161–86.

Bartchy, S. Scott. "Slavery (Greco-Roman)." *ABD* 6:58–73.

Deming, Will. "A Diatribe Pattern in 1 Cor 7:21–22: A New Perspective on Paul's Directions to Slaves." *NovT* 37 (1995): 130–37.

Frilingos, Chris. "'For My Child, Onesimus': Paul and Domestic Power in Philemon." *JBL* 119 (2000): 91–104.

Glancy, Jennifer A. "Obstacles to Slaves' Participation in the Corinthian Church." *JBL* 117 (1998): 481–501.

Harrill, J. Albert. *The Manumission of Slaves in Early Christianity*. HUT 32. Tübingen: Mohr Siebeck, 1995.

———. "Using the Roman Jurists to Interpret Philemon: A Response to Peter Lampe." *ZNW* 90 (1999): 135–38.

———. "The Vice of Slave Dealers in Greco-Roman Society: The Use of a Topos in 1 Timothy 1:10." *JBL* 118 (1999): 97–122.

Kyrtatas, Dimitris. *The Social Structure of the Early Christian Communities*. New York: Verso, 1987.

Martin, Dale B. "Slavery and the Ancient Jewish Family." Pages 113–29 in *The Jewish Family in Antiquity*, edited by Shaye J. C. Cohen. BJS 289. Atlanta: Scholars Press, 1993.

———. *Slavery as Salvation: The Metaphor of Slavery in Pauline Christianity*. New Haven: Yale University Press, 1990.

Petersen, Norman. *Rediscovering Paul: Philemon and the Sociology of Paul's Narrative World*. Philadelphia: Fortress Press, 1985.

Osiek, Carolyn, and David L. Balch. *Families in the New Testament World: Households and House Churches*. The Family, Religion, and Culture. Louisville: Westminster John Knox, 1997.

Wansink, Craig S. *Chained in Christ: The Experience and Rhetoric of Paul's Imprisonments*. JSNTSup 130. Sheffield, England: Sheffield Academic Press, 1996.

Notes

1. Tacitus, *Ann.* 14.42–45 (two pages in the Teubner edition); Richard P. Saller, "Slavery and the Roman Family," in *Classical Slavery* (ed. M. I. Finley; London: Frank Cass, 1987), 65–66.

2. In part due to this lack of evidence, the secondary literature on classical slavery is enormous and much of it controversial. The best guide is Keith Bradley, "Bibliographical Essay," in idem, *Slavery and Society at Rome* (Key Themes in Ancient History; Cambridge: Cambridge University Press, 1994), 183–85. Helpful reference works include Junius P. Rodriguez, ed., *The Historical Encyclopedia of World Slavery* (2 vols.; Santa Barbara, Calif.: ABC-CLIO, 1997); Joseph C. Miller, ed., *Slavery and Slaving in World History: A Bibliography, 1900–1991* (Millwood, N.Y.: Kraus International, 1993); Joseph Vogt and Heinz Bellen, eds., *Bibliographie zur antiken Slaverei* (new ed., revised by E. Herrmann and N. Brockmeyer; 2 pts.; Bochum: Brockmeyer, 1983); and the annual surveys of scholarship that appear in the journal *Slavery and Abolition*. Advanced students should also be aware of the important monograph series Forschungen zur antiken Sklaverei (Wiesbaden and Stuttgart: Franz Steiner, 1967–). Primary sources on classical slavery in English translation are collected in Thomas Wiedemann, *Greek and Roman Slavery* (1981; reprint, London: Routledge, 1988); and Jo-Ann Shelton, *As the Romans Did: A Sourcebook in Roman Social History* (2d ed.; New York: Oxford University Press, 1998), 163–202.

3. J. Albert Harrill, *The Manumission of Slaves in Early Christianity* (HUT 32; Tübingen: Mohr Siebeck, 1995), 12–13.

4. See P. A. Brunt, "Aristotle and Slavery," in idem, *Studies in Greek History and Thought* (Oxford: Clarendon, 1993), 343–88.

5. Yvon Garlan, *Slavery in Ancient Greece* (revised and expanded edition; Ithaca, N.Y.: Cornell University Press, 1988), 93–98; M. I. Finley, *Ancient Slavery and Modern Ideology* (New York: Viking, 1980), 70–72.

6. Orlando Patterson, *Slavery and Social Death: A Comparative Study* (Cambridge: Harvard University Press, 1982), 1–34. See also Finley, *Ancient Slavery and Modern Ideology*, 67–77, 96.

7. For discipline and corporal punishment defining the boundary between slave and free in the Roman system of honor and shame, see Richard P. Saller, *Patriarchy, Property, and Death in the Roman Family* (Cambridge Studies in Population, Economy, and Society in Past Time 25; Cambridge: Cambridge University Press, 1994), 133–53.

8. See, e.g., Dale B. Martin, *Slavery as Salvation: The Metaphor of Slavery in Pauline Christianity* (New Haven: Yale University Press, 1990), 48.

9. For detailed criticism, see Jennifer A. Glancy, "Slaves and Slavery in the Matthean Parables," *JBL* 119 (2000): 74–75.

10. Beryl Rawson, "Family Life among the Lower Classes at Rome in the First Two Centuries of the Empire," *CP* 61 (1966): 71–83.

11. Peter Garnsey and Richard Saller, *The Roman Empire: Economy, Society, and Culture* (Berkeley and Los Angeles: University of California Press, 1987), 120.

12. Patterson, *Slavery and Social Death*, 299–333.

13. W. V. Harris, "Demography, Geography, and the Sources of Roman Slaves," *JRS* 89 (1999): 65.

14. Walter Scheidel, "Quantifying the Sources of Slaves in the Early Roman Empire," *JRS* 87 (1997): 156–69, claims that natural reproduction provided more new slaves than all other sources combined; however, Harris, "Demography," 62–75, disagrees. See also Keith Bradley, *Slavery and Society at Rome* (Cambridge: Cambridge University Press, 1994), 32–34; Finley, *Ancient Slavery and Modern Ideology*, 80; and Philip D. Curtin, *The Atlantic Slave Trade: A Census* (Madison: University of Wisconsin Press, 1969).

15. M. I. Finley, "The Black Sea and Danubian Regions and the Slave Trade in Antiquity," in idem, *Economy and Society in Ancient Greece* (ed. Brent Shaw and Richard P. Saller; New York: Viking, 1982), 167–75; Keith Hopkins, *Conquerors and Slaves* (Sociological Studies in Roman History 1; Cambridge: Cambridge University Press, 1978), 1–15, 99–115.

16. William V. Harris, "Towards a Study of the Roman Slave Trade," in *The Seaborne Commerce of Ancient Rome: Studies in Archaeology and History* (ed. J. H. D'Arms and E. C. Kopff; Rome: American Academy in Rome, 1980), 117–40; J. Albert Harrill, "The Vice of Slave Dealers in Greco-Roman Society: The Use of a Topos in 1 Timothy 1:10," *JBL* 118 (1999): 97–122.

17. J. Albert Harrill, "Slavery and Society at Corinth: The Issues Facing Paul," *TBT* 35 (1997): 287–88.

18. Harrill, *Manumission of Slaves*, 54–55, 90, 169–72.

19. S. Scott Bartchy, "Slavery (Greco-Roman)," *ABD* 6:71; see also idem, *First-Century Slavery and 1 Corinthians 7:21* (1973; SBLDS 11; reprint, Atlanta: Scholars Press, 1985), 67–72.

20. See Thomas Wiedemann, "The Regularity of Manumission at Rome," *CQ*, n.s., 35 (1985): 162–75, who questions also the alleged epigraphic support for the claim that slaves were regularly freed at age thirty.

21. Shelton, *As the Romans Did*, 187–91; Keith Bradley, *Slaves and Masters in the Roman Empire: A Study in Social Control* (New York: Oxford University Press, 1987), 81–112; Susan Treggiari, *Roman Freedmen during the Late Republic* (Oxford: Clarendon, 1969), 11–20.

22. Apuleius, *The Golden Ass* 9.12; translated in Wiedemann, *Greek and Roman Slavery*, 176–77.

23. Bradley, *Slavery and Society at Rome*, 166–67.

24. Harrill, *Manumission of Slaves*, 42–51; Dale B. Martin, *Slavery as Salvation: The Metaphor of Slavery in Pauline Christianity* (New Haven: Yale University Press, 1990), 11–22; Bradley, *Slavery and Society at Rome*, 57–80; Finley, *Ancient Slavery and Modern Ideology*, 77.

25. Bradley, *Slavery and Society at Rome*, 84. See also Michele George, "*Servus* and *Domus*: The Slave in the Roman House," in *Domestic Space in the Roman World: Pompeii and Beyond* (ed. Ray Laurence and Andrew Wallace-Hadrill; Journal of Roman Archaeology Supplement Series 22; Portsmouth, R.I.: Journal of Roman Archaeology, 1997), 15–24.

26. Harrill, *Manumission of Slaves*, 51–53.

27. Jérôme Carcopino, *Daily Life in Ancient Rome: The People and the City at the*

Height of the Empire (New Haven: Yale University Press, 1968), 70–71; Bradley, *Slaves and Society*, 61–65; Andrew Garland, "Cicero's *Familia Urbana*," *GR* 39 (1992): 163–72.

28. Carolyn Osiek and David L. Balch, *Families in the New Testament World: Households and House Churches* (Louisville: Westminster John Knox Press, 1997).

29. Richard P. Saller, "Symbols of Gender and Status Hierarchies in the Roman Household," in *Women and Slaves in Greco-Roman Culture: Differential Equations* (ed. Sandra R. Joshel and Sheila Murnaghan; London: Routledge, 1998), 90.

30. Harrill, *Manumission of Slaves*, 147–52; Franz Bömer, *Untersuchungen über die Religion der Sklaven in Griechenland und Rom* (4 vols.; Wiesbaden, Germany: F. Steiner, 1958–63).

31. Keith Bradley, *Slavery and Rebellion in the Roman World* (Bloomington: Indiana University Press, 1989); idem, *Slavery and Society at Rome*, 107–31; Harrill, *Manumission of Slaves*, 98; R. H. Barrow, *Slavery in the Roman Empire* (London: Methuen, 1928), 55. For the Saint-Dominque slave revolt, see Lawrence C. Jennings, *French Anti-Slavery: The Movement for the Abolition of Slavery in France, 1802–1848* (Cambridge: Cambridge University Press, 2000), 120–22.

32. *Contra* Bartchy, *First-Century Slavery*, 85.

33. James C. Scott, *Domination and the Arts of Resistance: Hidden Transcripts* (New Haven: Yale University Press, 1990), 2–4, 79.

34. Kathleen McCarthy, *Slaves, Masters, and the Art of Authority in Plautine Comedy* (Princeton: Princeton University Press, 2000), 24–26.

35. The NIV follows the "take liberty" interpretation: "Were you a slave when you were called? Don't let it trouble you—although if you can gain your freedom, do so." The KJV, however, makes no decision on the crux and leaves it ambiguous: "Art thou called *being* a servant? Care not for it: but if thou mayest be made free, use *it* rather" (emphasis in original). The use of italics identifies a word inserted by the translators, which is not in the original Greek; see American Bible Society, Committee on Versions, *Report on the History and Recent Collation of the English Versions of the Bible: Presented by the Committee on Versions to the Board of Managers of the American Bible Society* (New York: American Bible Society Press, 1851), 24. This is why the KJV on this verse was used to support both proslavery and antislavery positions in nineteenth-century American exegesis; see J. Albert Harrill, "The Use of the New Testament in American Slave Controversy: A Case History in the Hermeneutical Tension between Biblical Criticism and Christian Moral Debate," *Religion and American Culture* 10 (2000): 157, 170.

36. Harrill, *Manumission of Slaves*, 74–108.

37. Ibid., 108–21.

38. For diatribe patterns, see Stanley K. Stowers, *The Diatribe and Paul's Letter to the Romans* (SBLDS 57; Chico, Calif.: Scholars Press, 1981), with extensive bibliography; see also idem, "The Diatribe," in *Greco-Roman Literature and the New Testament* (ed. David E. Aune; SBLSBS 21; Atlanta: Scholars Press, 1988), 71–83.

39. Unless otherwise noted, all biblical translations are from the NRSV.

40. Will Deming, "A Diatribal Pattern in 1 Cor 7:21–22: A New Perspective on Paul's Directions to Slaves," *NovT* 37 (1995): 130–37.

41. Cf. Jennifer A. Glancy, "Obstacles to Slaves' Participation in the Corin-

thian Church," *JBL* 117 (1998): 493–96. For Greco-Roman condemnation of prostitution in the slave trade, see Thomas A. J. McGinn, *Prostitution, Sexuality, and the Law in Ancient Rome* (New York: Oxford University Press, 1998), 288–319; Harrill, "Vice of Slave Dealers," 108–15 (see n. 16 for original citation).

42. For the history of Corinth, see James Wiseman, "Corinth and Rome I: 228 B.C.–A.D. 267," in *ANRW* 2.7.1 (1979), 438–548; Jerome Murphy-O'Connor, *St. Paul's Corinth: Texts and Archaeology* (GNS 6; Collegeville, Minn.: Liturgical Press, 1983); Timothy E. Gregory, ed., *The Corinthians in the Roman Period* (Journal of Roman Archaeology Supplement Series 8; Ann Arbor, Mich.: Journal of Roman Archaeology, 1993).

43. Harrill, *Manumission of Slaves*, 69–74.

44. Ibid., 74–75, 121–22. For Roman social conservatives favoring manumission, see Wiedemann, "Regularity of Manumission," 162–75 (see original citation in n. 20).

45. See Harrill, "Use of the New Testament," 149–86 (see n. 35 for the original citation).

46. For an overview of the exegetical issues, see S. Scott Bartchy, "Philemon, Epistle to," *ABD* 5:305–10.

47. On maroon societies, see Bradley, *Slavery and Rebellion*, 4–11, 38–41, 54, 111, 123–24.

48. Eduard Lohse, *Colossians and Philemon: A Commentary on the Epistles to the Colossians and to Philemon,* Hermeneia (Philadelphia: Fortress Press, 1971), 196–97.

49. Paul, furthermore, imbues his letter with kinship imagery, something lacking in Pliny's letter (Chris Frilingos, "'For My Child, Onesimus': Paul and Domestic Power in Philemon," *JBL* 119 [2000]: 92).

50. J. Albert Harrill, "Using the Roman Jurists to Interpret Philemon: A Response to Peter Lampe," *ZNW* 90 (1999): 135–38.

51. Sara C. Winter, "Paul's Letter to Philemon," *NTS* 33 (1987): 1–15.

52. Craig S. Wansink, *Chained in Christ: The Experience and Rhetoric of Paul's Imprisonments* (JSNTSup 130; Sheffield, England: Sheffield Academic Press, 1996), 188–89.

53. Brian Rapske, *The Book of Acts and Paul in Roman Custody* (vol. 3 of *The Book of Acts in Its First-Century Setting*; ed. B. W. Winter; Grand Rapids: Eerdmans, 1993), 195–225.

54. For the renting out of slaves, see Shelton, *As the Romans Did*, 165–66.

55. Ibid., 189–90.

56. My translation; see Adolf Deissmann, *Light from the Ancient East: The New Testament Illustrated by Recently Discovered Texts of the Graeco-Roman World* (1927; reprint, Peabody, Mass.: Hendrickson, 1995), 170. For discussion of this text, see W. Hersey David, *Greek Papyri of the First Century* (New York: Harper & Bros., 1933), 57–59; Norman R. Petersen, *Rediscovering Paul: Philemon and the Sociology of Paul's Narrative World* (Philadelphia: Fortress Press, 1985), 44–53, 78–81; Peter Arzt, "Brauchbare Sklaven: Ausgewählte Papyrustexte zum Philemonbrief," *Protokolle zur Bibel* 1 (1992): 44–55.

57. David E. Garland, *Colossians and Philemon* (Grand Rapids: Zondervan, 1988), 337.

58. Wansink, *Chained in Christ*, 183–88; Clarice J. Martin, "The Rhetorical

Function of Commercial Language in Paul's Letter to Philemon (Verse 18)," in *Persuasive Artistry: Studies in New Testament Rhetoric in Honor of George A. Kennedy* (ed. Duane F. Watson; JSNTSup 50; Sheffield, England: Sheffield Academic Press, 1991), 321–37.

59. See Frilingos, "'For My Child, Onesimus,'" 99.

60. Ibid., 102–3.

61. Cf. the Hebrew Bible prohibition of Deut 23:15–16: "Slaves who have escaped to you from their owners shall not be given back to them. They shall reside with you, in your midst, in any place they choose in any one of your towns, wherever they please; you shall not oppress them." The relevance, however, of this Jewish law for Paul is doubtful; Paul nowhere quotes it and is emphatic about Torah no longer being valid.

62. On the practical benefits of manumission in the Roman slave system, see Harrill, *Manumission of Slaves*, 170–72; for the role of manumission to reinforce slavery's social control, see Bradley, *Slaves and Masters*, 81–122 (see n. 21 for original citation).

63. Bartchy, *First-Century Slavery*, 174.

64. Wayne A. Meeks, *The First Urban Christians: The Social World of the Apostle Paul* (New Haven: Yale University Press, 1983), 88; idem, "The Image of the Androgyne: Some Uses of a Symbol in Earliest Christianity," *HR* 13 (1974): 165–208; Dennis R. MacDonald, *There Is No Male and Female: The Fate of a Dominical Saying in Paul and Gnosticism* (HDR 20; Philadelphia: Fortress Press, 1987), 113–26.

65. Frederick C. Grant, *Hellenistic Religions: The Age of Syncretism* (New York: Liberal Arts Press, 1953), 28–30 (text); Meeks, "Image of the Androgyne," 169.

66. Bradley, *Slaves and Masters*, 41–44.

67. See discussion in Hans Dieter Betz, *Galatians: A Commentary on Paul's Letter to the Churches in Galatia* (Hermeneia; Philadelphia: Fortress Press, 1979), 192–95.

68. See Brent D. Shaw, "The Divine Economy: Stoicism as Ideology," *Latomus* 44 (1985): 16–54.

69. A variant (and more likely) reading is *Varus*, referring to the Roman general whose three legions suffered a disastrous military defeat in Germany (9 C.E.). The "Varian disaster" involved a serious loss of military manpower, and its anniversary was a dark shadow on the Roman calendar (H. H. Scullard, *From the Gracchi to Nero: A History of Rome, from 133 BC to AD 68* [5th ed.; London: Methuen, 1982], 258–59).

70. Miriam Griffin, *Seneca: A Philosopher in Politics* (Oxford: Clarendon 1976), 256–85.

71. Victor Paul Furnish, "First Letter of Paul to the Corinthians," in *The HarperCollins Study Bible* (ed. Wayne A. Meeks et al.; New York: HarperCollins, 1993), 2149, note to 1 Cor 7:23.

72. Hans Conzelmann, *1 Corinthians: A Commentary on the First Epistle to the Corinthians* (Hermeneia; Philadelphia: Fortress Press, 1975), 127–28; Kenneth C. Russell, *Slavery as Reality and Metaphor in the Pauline Letters* (Rome: Catholic Book Agency, 1968), 49–50.

73. Martin, *Slavery as Salvation*, 63–68.

74. Ibid., 60.

75. For Roman understanding of *auctoritas*, see McCarthy, *Slaves, Masters, and*

the Art of Authority, 22–24 (see n. 34 for original citation); Karl Galinsky, *Augustan Culture: An Interpretive Introduction* (Princeton: Princeton University Press, 1996), 12–14.

76. McCarthy, *Slaves, Masters, and the Art of Authority,* 23.

77. Osiek and Balch, *Families in the New Testament World,* 179.

78. Contrary to Peter Garnsey, *Ideas of Slavery from Aristotle to Augustine* (Cambridge: Cambridge University Press, 1996), 53–86.

79. The following works appeared too late for inclusion in this article: *Semeia* (Atlanta: Society of Biblical Literature) 83/84 (1998, published in 2001) (the theme of the issue was "Slavery in Text and Interpretation," edited by Allen Dwight Callahan, Richard A. Horsley, and Abraham Smith); Murray J. Harris, *Slave of Christ: A New Testament Metaphor for Total Devotion to Christ* (Downers Grove, Ill.: InterVarsity Press, 2001); Jennifer A. Glancy, *Slavery in Early Christianity* (New York: Oxford University Press, 2002).

21

PAUL, VIRTUES, AND VICES

Troels Engberg-Pedersen

Here are some traditional problems about the role of virtues and vices in Paul. Together they seem to indicate that Paul was very far from sharing the concern
about virtues and vices that was central to the ancient ethical tradition.[1]

1. There is only one mention of the term "virtue" (ἀρετή, *aretē*) itself in Paul.
Philippians 4:8–9 runs:

> [8] For the rest, brothers, whatever is true, noble, just, pure, pleasing, and
> well spoken of, whichever virtue (*aretē*) there is and whichever object of
> praise (ἔπαινος, *epainos*): have these things in your thoughts; [9] the things
> that you both learned, received, heard, and saw in me: do those things;
> then the God of peace will be with you.[2]

A single occurrence of *aretē* in all the undisputed letters—and a rather inconspic-
uous one at that.

2. It is true that Paul has a number of lists of vices and virtues. See in particular Phil 4:8 (just quoted); 1 Cor 5:10–11 and 6:9–10; 2 Cor 6:6; 12:20–21; Gal 5:19–
21, 22–23 (to be discussed below); and Rom 1:29–31.[3] But they are "traditional"
and "conventional," forming part of the hortatory material that Paul shared with
the Greco-Roman moralists and employed not least in his parenesis (compare Phil
4:8 and Gal 5:19–23). And so they are hardly central to the area that really matters
(to Paul or his exegetes): his theology.[4]

3. Even if we did give *some* importance to the lists in those sections, we would
quickly hit upon features in Paul's handling of them that make them rather different from their Greco-Roman counterparts. The three most important features
are these: (*a*) In Paul, the recommended state is not "self-generated." Rather, it is
brought about by God. (*b*) In Paul, the recommended state is not "individualistic"
or a feature of the single person. Rather, it is communal. (*c*) Finally, it is not even

clear that it is correct to speak of a recommended *state,* namely a state of mind. For Paul is not concerned about states of mind, but rather about action.[5]

4. Finally, there is a difference in social status. In the Greco-Roman tradition, talk about virtues and vices was part of philosophy, an activity engaged in by the very few who belonged to the leisured classes of society. By contrast, the Pauline letters reflect a different social level. It is not clear that Paul had any time for or interest in the kind of theoretical reflection that constituted the essence of Greco-Roman philosophy. Indeed, at one point he explicitly distances himself and his message from the "wisdom" (σοφία, *sophia*) of the Greeks (see 1 Cor 1:22–25). Nor does Paul ever address a "philosophical" issue (as defined by the tradition of Greco-Roman philosophy) directly *as* a philosophical one.[6]

All in all, then, it seems that Paul's engagement with the notion of virtues and vices is only marginal and peripheral. I argue that, quite to the contrary, it is central and goes to the very heart of his thought.[7]

One cannot, however, cover the whole issue in a single essay. I focus on the first two of the four traditional problems by considering the centrality of virtues and vices in Paul's thought at the level of ideas. For that purpose I look at the philosophical core ideas concerning virtue and vice in the ethical tradition inaugurated by Plato, continued by Aristotle, and brought to its conclusion by the Stoics (Part I). That will bring me back to the founding period for Greco-Roman thinking about virtue and vice: the fourth through third centuries B.C.E., when what I call the ancient "virtue system" was fully developed for the first time. Next I compare my findings in this area in some detail with a few test passages in Paul (Part II). Finally, I take brief notice of other Pauline passages in which the Greco-Roman notion of virtues and vices is also relevant (Part III).

One might extend the discussion to consider the two objections voiced in points 3 and 4 above: that Paul's handling of virtues and vices "must" differ from the handling apparent in his Greco-Roman colleagues in the three respects identified (point 3); and that Paul's thought in any case belongs in a different social world from that of the Greco-Roman philosophers (point 4). That discussion would be of general philosophical and theological interest—for point 3—and of broader historical interest, too—for point 4—not least because it would introduce material that is much closer to Paul's own time. Interesting though it would be, this discussion is not necessary to making the basic case. For the line of argument would go the other way around. If it can be established against points 1 and 2 that Paul's engagement with the notion of virtues and vices is central to his thought, then that supposed fact will to a large degree *determine* what we should say on points 3 and 4. The former theme remains basic, therefore.

One caveat needs to be added before we begin. In the present study, I look at

Paul's ideas as he himself wanted them to be understood and put into practice by his addressees. This will leave out topics that employ a "hermeneutics of suspicion" in relation to Paul. I take Paul at his word and bracket the question of whether he deserves to be interpreted in this way. Or to put the point more explicitly: the Paul that will be presented here is very far from being the whole Paul. Just as one should—at some level—go behind the Greco-Roman philosophers and ask about the social function of their ideas, so one should also—at some level—go behind Paul in order to form a full picture of him. But that is not going to happen here.

Part I. The Philosophical Core Ideas (Plato, Aristotle, the Stoics)

The theoretical elaboration of virtue and vice in Greco-Roman philosophy reached a peak at its starting point, in Plato's *Republic*. Two features are of special importance to us. One is substantive, the other is formal. The substantive one is that Plato gave a special place to the virtue of justice (δικαιοσύνη, *dikaiosynē*), that is, to a virtue that is intrinsically directed toward others. The introductory theme of the dialogue is justice (see bk. I). Plato's sketch of the best political state and the best individual mind (or as Plato has it, "soul," ψυχή, *psychē*) is a sketch of the just state and the just mind (see bk. IV). Thus, even though Plato also found room for other virtues, like moderation, courage, and prudence, he understood them all to be, as it were, in the service of justice: the mind whose various "parts" were organized in relation to each other in the way captured under moderation, courage, and prudence—that mind *was* the just mind (bk. IV, 434D–444A).

The other important feature of Plato's account is that, for the purpose of describing justice, Plato looked into the mind. Justice is a state—of mind (bk. IV, 443C–E). It goes without saying that justice will also show itself in certain types of acts. But it is itself a state of mind, one that is further defined in the way Plato spells out in the whole dialogue.[8]

Aristotle took over the two features from Plato's analysis of justice (*Nicomachean Ethics* bk. V). On the substantive side: in Aristotle, too, justice is not just one virtue among others. As he explains, justice is, as it were, "the whole of virtue" (bk. V, 1130a9). For justice is necessarily directed toward others. It is a matter of the individual's relationship with others. And that, as Aristotle thinks, constitutes the core of virtue. It is true that there are aspects of the virtues that are not intrinsically other-directed. For instance, a moderate person may not always display his or her moderation in acts that pertain directly to others. But as Aristotle saw it, there is a continuous line between self-directed aspects of the virtues and other-directed ones. And since it is the latter that are the really difficult aspects, those, namely, that fall specifically under justice, justice is virtue par excellence.[9]

Aristotle also agreed in the formal understanding of virtue (*Nicomachean Ethics* II.v). And he analyzed it in the manner that was to become orthodox in Hellenistic philosophy. As a mental phenomenon (something in the ψυχή, *psyche*) virtue might be one of three things: an affection (πάθος, *pathos*), a proclivity (δύναμις, *dynamis*), or a state (ἕξις, *hexis*). It *is* the latter—for a number of reasons, one of which is that "we are praised and blamed with reference to our virtues and vices" (II.v.3, 1106a1–2—but not to our affections). That is already of some interest for the comparison with Paul, because in the Philippians passage from which we began, he too connected virtue (ἀρετή, *arete*) with praise (ἔπαινος, *epainos*). Another reason why virtue is a state and not an affection is that "with reference to the affections we are said to be moved [namely, to action]; by contrast, we are not said to be moved [to action] with reference to our virtues and vices, but to be disposed [διακεῖσθαι, *diakeisthai*] in some particular way" (II.v.4, 1106a4–6). Here the point is certainly not that a virtue may not move to action, but rather that it is a settled and stable state of mind. It is a settled disposition.

The idea that virtue is a ἕξις, *hexis* (state), has important implications. One is that it is connected with the notion of "activity" (ἐνέργεια, *energeia*). A *hexis* is related to an *energeia* as the possession of something (κτῆσις, *ktesis*) is to its (actual) use (χρῆσις, *chresis*).[10] That too is directly relevant to Paul when he says, in a passage to which we shall return, that the only thing that matters in Christ is faith (πίστις, *pistis*) that is "active" (ἐνεργουμένη, *energoumene*) in ἀγάπη, *agape* (Gal 5:6).

Another point connected with defining virtue as a *hexis* and a settled disposition is that virtue was seen by Aristotle as a state of *character*, an ἠθικὴ ἕξις, *ethike hexis* (see *Nicomachean Ethics* I.xiii.19, 1103a3–7). Ηθος, *ethos* (character), or το ἠθικόν, *to ethikon* (the character "part" of the *psyche*), was a central concept in Aristotle's ethics (see I.xiii–II). Indeed, it gave the discipline its name. It is what makes his particular form of ethical thought a prime specimen of what in modern parlance is called "character ethics."[11] To the extent that Paul's thought about virtue and vice will be seen to fit into the shape given it by Aristotle, that thought, too, will belong under "character ethics."

There is another feature of Aristotle's account of virtue as a *hexis* (state) that will turn out to be of the highest relevance to Paul. Again, Aristotle follows Plato. But again, he has made the point more immediately accessible. It is that because moral virtue is a *hexis,* that is, a settled and stable disposition of the mind, and because, as we must add, "full" or "complete" moral virtue includes all the virtues, therefore if a person has moral virtue (of that kind), he or she will *always and only* act well. In particular, such a person will never have a mind that is divided between wanting and not wanting to do what is right.[12]

Of the latter type of person, by contrast, there are two specimens. One is the person who basically wills what the virtuous person wills (and does). That is the person whom Aristotle called the "strong-willed" person, the one who shows self-mastery, the ἐγκρατής, *enkratēs*. His mind *is* divided, and he does have contrasting desires. But since the "good" side of his mind is stronger, what he actually does reflects that side. But there also is another person with a divided mind in which the contrasting desires are so strong that this person will from time to time—and unpredictably to the person himself—act upon the "bad" side of his mind. That person is the ἀκρατής, *akratēs*, the "weak-willed" person, the one whose profile was most memorably spelled out—by Paul in Rom 7.[13]

We need not go into detail concerning Aristotle's attempt at *explaining* the latter condition. What matters here is the overall set of ideas: of the morally virtuous person as one who always and only does what is right; and of two other people—the ἐγκρατής, *enkratēs* ("strong-willed"), and (most importantly) the ἀκρατής, *akratēs* ("weak-willed")—whose mind is divided.

The Stoics took over the three basic points we have noted in Plato and Aristotle: the substantive point concerning justice and the two formal points concerning virtue as (1) a state of mind, (2) that is, as we may call it, infallible. The point about justice comes out in the Stoic argument for their claim that the "end" (τέλος, *telos*) of action lies in acting in accordance with moral virtue and nowhere else—not in acquiring something, for instance, through one's act.[14] That argument centers on the crucial Stoic notion of οἰκείωσις, *oikeiōsis*, which we may translate as "familiarization." It is the name of a process in which human beings become "familiar" with things outside themselves and come to see such things as "belonging to," and hence being good for, themselves—and next gradually develop that understanding into a complete grasp of what is genuinely good. Though that notion is itself highly relevant to Paul, we leave it on one side here and only note that the Stoics introduced the idea of reaching the complete grasp of the good in two rounds, first to make the basic claim just given about the content of the τέλος, *telos* (end), and a second time to ground the specifically *other*-directed dimension of moral virtue, which is most clearly seen in the virtue of justice.[15] Once more, therefore, and in a manner that closely resembles Aristotle's handling of the point, justice comes out as the paramount moral virtue.

The formal point that virtue is a stable state of mind need not detain us. Here the Stoics accepted Aristotle's idea while also elaborating on it in order to fit it into their own moral epistemology. In that process Aristotle's notion of *hexis* also acquired a new name: διάθεσις, *diathesis* ("disposition").[16] But the overall effect was only to reinforce the Platonic and Aristotelian idea that the morally virtuous person is infallible. He has, as the Stoics said, moral *knowledge*.[17] And because knowledge is itself something absolutely stable, the morally virtuous person, who is identical with the famous Stoic sage or wise man, will always and only do what is right.

This point is closely connected with another well-known point about the Stoic sage: that he has no πάθη, *pathē* ("passions"), but is ἀπαθής, *apathēs* ("passionless," "dispassionate," or "impassive").[18] Does this mean that he has no "emotions" whatever? Certainly not. For in Stoicism there is a set of three generic emotions that are "good emotions" (*eu-patheiai*). And these emotions the sage *will* have.[19] One of them is "joy" (χαρά, *chara*)—a "good emotion" that is highly relevant to the Paul who wrote Philippians. That letter is one of *chara* throughout. The other two emotions are "wish" and "caution." But back to the *pathē*: in what sense is the Stoic sage *apathēs*? In the sense that he has no "emotions" of the kind that risk running out of hand. In other words, he has no "passions." He is neither ἀκρατής, *akratēs* ("weak-willed"), nor *enkratēs* ("strong-willed"): he is good throughout, having the *diathesis* (disposition) that constitutes *knowledge;* he never wishes to do anything other than the acts that spring from his knowledge, and he never does anything else. All that is again highly relevant to the Paul who wrote (Gal 5:24) that "those who belong to Christ Jesus have crucified [that is, "killed" or made wholly inoperative] the flesh together with its 'passions' [παθήματα, *pathēmata*] and 'desires' [ἐπιθυμίαι, *epithymiai*]." Paul's use of the term *epithymia* fits in completely here. For in Stoicism *epithymia* is one of four generic terms for all the "passions."[20]

In sum, the ancient ethical tradition, as founded and brought to completion already in the fourth–third centuries B.C.E. by Plato, Aristotle, and the early Stoics, bequeathed to all ethical thought in later antiquity the following three points, one substantive and two formal: (1) moral virtue is essentially other-regarding, with justice as the virtue par excellence; (2) moral virtue is a state of mind that will be actualized in particular emotions, desires, and acts, those defined by the virtue in question; and (3) as a state of mind, moral virtue is stable and settled— it does not allow for a divided mind and thus differs from ἐγκράτεια, *enkrateia*, and *akrasia*. On the contrary, it is a matter of ἀπάθεια, *apatheia,* in the specific Stoic sense, and so the morally virtuous person will in principle always and only have the right emotions and desires and do the right acts.

I repeat: these points were formulated and given philosophical backing and elaboration in the fourth–third centuries B.C.E. But their relevance extends to the end of antiquity. They are central elements in the ancient "virtue system," which was never challenged. Instead, the virtue system formed the taken-for-granted understanding of moral virtue. That system was presupposed in the less theoretical and more practically oriented ethical thought and practice that is characteristic of the centuries around the turn of the eras and that goes under the term "popular moral philosophy." As such, the virtue system was presupposed by Paul, too.

Part II. The Philosophical Core Ideas in Paul

We have already seen in passing that several individual ideas and concepts in the virtue system also turn up in Paul. But that realization does not in itself answer the two first queries with which we began. A few uses of individual ideas and concepts are hardly enough to make the virtue system of any great relevance to Paul. In any case, such uses would only occur where Paul engages in traditional exhortation. Against this view, analysis of Gal 5:13–26, on which we shall spend some time, will show that Paul drew very extensively on the virtue system, not just for the odd occurrence of this or the other term, and that he did it to make the basic point of the whole letter in one of its two forms. Thus, in drawing on the virtue system, he was not just being traditional or merely parenetic. Instead, he was making the point that constitutes the very raison d'être of the letter, and he was being just as "theological" as anywhere else in Galatians.[21]

Galatians: The Overall Structure

We need initial agreement on the situation behind the letter and its overall structure. We may take it that Paul is writing in order to prevent his immediate addressees, the Galatians, from giving in to an argument that had been presented to them by certain Jewish-oriented "agitators" (as Paul sees them: 1:7 and 5:10) to the effect that the Galatians should let themselves be circumcised (cf. 5:2 and 6:12–13), most likely as a sign that they too were meant to follow the Jewish Law.

Paul emphatically answers "No." The line of his argument is clear enough up until, say, 4:20. Having presented the issue in general terms (1:1–9), Paul goes back to three historical test scenes in which his own attitude to the relationship between non-Jews like the Galatians and the Jewish Law had been made clear: his own call to preach the gospel among Gentiles (1:10–24); his agreement with the apostles in Jerusalem (2:1–10); and his clash with Peter (and probably with representatives of James) in Antioch (2:11–14). The latter leads into a speech (2:15–21) addressed to Peter and purportedly given in Antioch that is also directly relevant to the Galatian situation and indeed to the passage we shall study: if the question is who are sinners (Law-observing Jews or Gentiles?), the answer is that no human being is made just by "works of the Law," that is, by Law-observance, but by Jesus Christ–faith. The basic issue is therefore by what means human beings may escape from sin and become just. "Not by the Law," says Paul, "but by Christ-faith." And he spells out, in a highly suggestive manner (2:19–20), how he has himself moved over from the Law to Christ.

Following this extensive stage-setting, Paul addresses the Galatians directly, recalling his first visit with them (3:1–5 and 4:12–20). These two sections sandwich a section of "theological" argument (3:6–4:11), which aims to give the Law and circumcision a far less crucial role in God's historical relationship with the Jews than had apparently been claimed by Paul's opponents. Indeed, while Paul is far from rejecting the Law (see in particular 3:21),[22] he gives it only a restricted period of validity *until* the arrival of Christ and a function of keeping down the Jews under its guardianship (3:22–24), a function that comes close to an enslavement (cf. 4:3).

With 4:20 one might think that Paul's argument is over. He has stated the issue (1:1–2:21), appealed to the Galatians' original conversion, which in no way involved circumcision and the Law (3:1–5), produced scriptural argument in support of his claim for the restricted role of the Law (3:6–4:11), and amplified his appeal to the Galatians' original conversion (4:12–20). It all adds up to a Pauline *Nein* ("No") to his opponents' call. However, in 4:21–31, Paul again returns to scriptural argument. Why? Galatians 5:1 provides the answer. Based on his earlier intimation of an "enslaving" role for the Law, he now wishes to bring out in the starkest possible terms a contrast between "present Jerusalem" (read: non-Christ-believing Jews) as enslaved (4:25) and the "above Jerusalem" (to which belong *all* genuine Christ-believers) as free (4:26). Galatians 5:1 spells out the point: Christ has *freed* believers for *freedom*. "Stand fast, therefore, and do not once more become entangled under the yoke of slavery." In short, Paul's aim with the almost supererogatory return to scriptural argument is to rephrase his "No" to the Law in what might be called more "positive-negative" terms: not just a "No" to it, but more *positively* a *freedom from* it.

That move is no doubt rhetorically quite effective (witness the phrasing of 5:1 itself). Who, after all, does not wish to be free? So, is Paul just beginning to wind up the letter with this rhetorical sharpening of the issue that he has presented to his addressees? This appears to be the case. Galatians 5:2–6 has the clear air of a summary—of 2:15–4:11 in particular—which brings the whole argument down to the essential question: circumcision or not? And 5:7–12 just as clearly reverts to the direct kind of description of Paul's opponents that he had given in 1:6–9. Add to this that in 6:11, which obviously does introduce the conclusion to the letter, Paul takes up again the reference from 5:2 to *his own* saying or writing to his addressees (introduced by Ἴδε, *Ide,* and Ἴδετε, *Idete,* "See how I . . ."). All this points to a view of the structure of the letter according to which 5:2–12 and 6:11–18 together summarize Paul's basic message, with 6:11–18 *repeating* and *taking up* the earlier passage and thus sandwiching the intervening section. Seen in this perspective, 5:13–6:10 will have less than primary importance. Indeed, it will presumably be primarily "parenetic," with general exhortation in 5:13–26 followed by more particular exhortation in 6:1–10.

However, such an understanding of 5:13–6:10 would be entirely wrong.[23] For 5:13, in particular, shows that Paul's elaboration in 4:21–31 of the strong contrast between freedom and slavery did *not* have the only purpose of serving as a background to the strong, rhetorical statement of 5:1. Nor is the latter statement itself to be taken merely as a rhetorical one based on a move from Paul's merely negative "No" to his "positive-negative" talk of *freedom from*. Rather, 4:21–31 and 5:1 together serve as transitions from merely negative talk, *through* "positive-negative" talk to the genuinely positive talk of 5:13–6:10. To put it differently, in the latter passage Paul spells out what the Christ-faith means in *positive* terms, not just what it means *negatively* (namely, that one should *not* enter under the Jewish Law). He is describing (in hortatory terms)—and now for the first time—what this freedom from the Law is a freedom *for*.

It is of crucial importance to grasp fully this result of our consideration of the letter's overall structure. Galatians 5:13–6:10 is not just "parenesis." Rather, 5:13–26, in particular, spells out in detail the *positive content* of the Christ-faith. And it is that positive content that in the final event *explains* Paul's *negative* claim earlier in the letter to the effect that the Galatians must *not* enter under the Jewish Law. Thus we should take it that 5:13–26 (and 6:1–10) formulates—but now in positive terms—the very same, single point that Paul had up to then been stating only negatively. Far from being a "parenetic" parenthesis, therefore, 5:13–26 constitutes, as has been said, the "culmination" of Paul's argument in the letter as a whole.[24] Here Paul finally spells out what he is himself positively offering in a manner that *explains* his negative stance to circumcision and the Jewish Law earlier in the letter.

Why, then, the sandwiching between 5:2–10 and 6:11–18? Is not 5:13–6:10 after all something of an afterthought? No. It is true that in the letter as a whole the negative side of Paul's point is the more immediately relevant. It therefore deserves the emphatic statement that it is given in the last part of 5:1, in 5:2–12, and in 6:11–18. But 4:21–5:1 certainly leads on to 5:13, as is shown by Paul's play on freedom and slavery in that verse. The same is true of 5:5–6, which comes in the middle of the primarily negative 5:2–12. In fact, the last three of the final four words of 5:6 (πίστις δι' ἀγάπης ἐνεργουμένη, *pistis di' agapēs energoumenē*, "faith that is *active through love*"), which incontestably state Paul's message in positive terms in contrast to the immediately preceding negative statement ("*neither* circumcision *nor* lack of it matters"), obviously announce the essential content of the whole of 5:13–26.

One more question: If 5:13–6:10 is not an afterthought, is it not at least specifically "parenetic"? And is it not therefore also less important? Parenetic, yes. But that it employs imperatives (as in 5:13) or cohortative subjunctives (as in 5:25) does not make it any less important. For imperatives and subjunctives are also employed in passages that do not regularly count as "parenetic." Nor does the fact that its theme is, as we will say, "ethical" make it any less important. Let us accept that "parenetic" passages in the Pauline letters are "ethical" in the sense that they focus on the relationship between human beings, as opposed to the "theological" relationship of God and Christ to human beings, or the converse.

But let us also insist that in Paul the "ethical" perspective can never be separated from the "theological" perspective, nor the other way around. As Paul has himself just said (5:6), what matters in Christ Jesus (clearly a "theological" issue) is faith (another "theological" matter) that is active through love (an "ethical" one). In view of such an intrinsic connection between "theology" and "ethics" in Paul, a parenetic passage like 5:13–26 cannot be deemed "less important." Let us now consider more closely the argument of that passage.

Galatians 5:13–26: The Argument

As so often in Paul, this passage too has sandwich form: 5:13–15 and 5:26 are directly hortatory and address a problem of internal strife (5:15) and rivalry (5:26) among the Galatians. In between comes a section that formulates Paul's direct exhortation more broadly as a matter of living in accordance with the Spirit (5:16a and 25) and *explains*—in a carefully worked-out argument (5:16b–5:24)— why the Galatians should so live. It is this argument that will command our attention.

First I should note, however, that Paul begins the whole passage with two apparent paradoxes. The Galatians have been called in freedom, but they should also "enslave" themselves to one another in love (5:13). Moreover, in doing so they will "fulfill" that Jewish Law (5:14) whose importance Paul has up to this point been so much at pains to deny. Both paradoxes of course serve to tie his earlier argument exceedingly closely into what Paul now intends to say: *not* slavery and the Law—but (now:) *slavery* and *the Law!* Why such paradox-mongering? Clearly the idea is to introduce the new section as giving *another* (but now the *positive*) formulation of the *single* message that the whole letter is intended to convey. *Not* that, but . . . *this!* That we have slavery and the Law on *both* sides of the crucial divide brings out the whole letter's single message particularly clearly.

Galatians 5:16–25 should be paraphrased and analyzed as follows:

16 *Title:* Walk in accordance with the Spirit (that is, let it be applied in practice); then assuredly you will not fulfill the desires of the flesh.

> The verse contains an exhortation and a promise: a thesis concerning the consequences of following the exhortation.
>
> The exhortation (16a) is taken up again in 25b, which concludes the whole argument. The promise (16b) states a thesis to be proven in the following argument. The idea it contains of the eradication of fleshly desire is repeated in 24.

17 *For:*
The flesh desires *against* the Spirit and vice versa.

The two powers wage war over people: they attempt to prevent them from doing what they would (also) wish to do.

> The idea must be that flesh and Spirit are two opposed powers that operate from the outside on human beings, attempting to prevent them from doing what they would do on the basis of the other power. In such a situation it is concretely *up to people themselves* to steer clear of this play of the powers. If they choose the Spirit, then what is stated in 16, 18, and 22–24 will hold, and they will avoid the play of the powers. But if they choose the flesh, then the result will be an internal dividedness: the dividedness spelled out in 19–21.[25]

But if you (then actually) let yourselves be led by the Spirit,

> (A1)   then you are not (no longer)—under *the Law* (**18**).

> (A2)   To that side belongs *the flesh,* namely "*works*" of the flesh = *acts* springing from the flesh (detailed by Paul in **19–21**—more on this below).

>> In this situation one will find a genuine case of internal dividedness: The Law (which one presumably wishes to follow) *prohibits* the acts of the flesh, but cannot altogether *prevent* them. Even if people are under the Law (and hence in principle want to follow it), they will from time to time actually do acts of the flesh. That is the precise import of Paul's speaking of the "works" of the flesh (like in the more frequent "works," ἔργα, *erga, of the Law*): the acts of the flesh are precisely those *prohibited by the Law.*

> (B2)   In contrast with this, the "*fruit*" *of the Spirit* is something quite different (**22–23a**): *attitudes, states* (of mind—more on this below).

> (B1)   Attitudes lie outside the range of *the Law* (**23b**).

>> In this situation there is no room for internal dividedness. The fruit of the Spirit is precisely a set of attitudes or states, as opposed to those acts—or rather act-*types*—that constitute the target field of the Law. When people have the attitudes that are the fruit of the Spirit, they *will* do the acts that spring from the attitudes—and nothing but these acts. Thus when people have the "fruit" of the Spirit, *they will not in fact* "fulfill the desires of the flesh" (16). This is then spelled out explicitly:

Those who belong to Christ (as opposed to those living under the Law) have genuinely "crucified," that is, done away with, the flesh together with its passions and desires (**24**).

In other words, by genuinely letting oneself be guided by the

Spirit or by having "crucified" the flesh, people will overcome any internal dividedness that goes with living under the Law. Such people, therefore, will no longer fulfill the desires of the flesh. Indeed, they cannot do so.

25 *Therefore:* If (or inasmuch as) we live by the Spirit (cf. 22–24), let us also walk in accordance with the Spirit (that is, let it be applied in us in practice).

> As noted, this repeats the exhortation of 16*a*. The promise or thesis of 16*b*—to the effect that application of the Spirit will prevent any concern about fleshly desires—is the position that Paul has argued in 17–24.

In summary, what Paul does in his argument is to *work out the true meaning of living by the Spirit* (as introduced in v. 16): to move *from* verse 17 (which initially seemed to say that there was a stalemate between the flesh and the Spirit) *via* verses 18–23 (with its contrast between what the Spirit may bring about [vv. 22–23] and what *the Law* is able to achieve [vv. 19–21]) *to* verse 24. By bringing out the true power of the Spirit, Paul makes good the claim of verse 16b in relation to verse 16a. And then the road is clear for a repetition in verse 25 of the original exhortation in verse 16a.

Galatians 5:13–26 and the Virtue System

What has all this to do with moral virtue? Very much indeed.

First, Paul's argument in 5:17–24 hinges on the difference between the ἀκρατής, *akratēs* (the "weak-willed" person), on the one side and the fully virtuous person on the other. If one lives under the Law and nothing else, then even if one genuinely wishes to follow the Law, there is always the risk of internal dividedness resulting in action against that wish, namely the action that Paul identifies as falling under "works of the flesh." In other words, there is always the risk of *akrasia* ("weakness of the will"). By contrast, if one lives by the Spirit and lets oneself be guided by that, there is no longer any risk of *akrasia*. Then one is like the fully virtuous person of the ancient virtue system, who always and only does what is right.

Second, Paul even brings out this contrast in a manner that betrays an independent philosophical perceptiveness on his part. The "works" of the flesh that are prohibited by the Law are acts (so we said). The point is that they are not (in themselves) "interior" phenomena, states of mind or passions (even though they obviously spring from such things). Instead they are "external" activities—or, better, act-"types."[26] By contrast, the "fruit" of the Spirit consists of a set of *attitudes* or *states*.[27] It follows that whereas possession of the Spirit is described as a matter of the mind directly, living under the Law is seen as a matter relating to something outside oneself: to such an abstract entity as act-*types,* which are mentioned in *rules*.[28] This difference immediately explains why there is always a risk of *akrasia* ("weakness of the will") in people who relate to the Law, even when they see it as "God's own Law" and basically *will* it as such. Thus Paul's distinction between act-types (as constituting the object of the Law) and attitudes (as the direct result of having the Spirit) immediately fits into the virtue system and the crucial difference it had drawn between *akrasia* and full virtue. But Paul's distinction does more. It even serves to *explain* the difference between living "under" the Law and living "by" the Spirit, and moreover in a manner that had *not* been done within the ancient virtue system itself, for the very good reason that here there was no similar concept of law that had to be taken into account. Here, then, Paul adds to the virtue system while also continuing to work within it.

Third, and very obviously, Paul shows by the way he has constructed his argument that he shares completely what we saw to be an absolutely basic idea in the virtue system: that morally virtuous people are good *through and through,* that they always and only wish to do what is right. This point, which has already been made above, needs emphasizing. For it means that, seen from within Paul's basic perspective, Christ-believers who have the Spirit and let themselves be guided by it are in principle "sinless." Being outside the realm of sin, indeed having been made just through Christ-faith, they no longer sin. They do not even risk sinning (cf. Rom 6).

This conclusion will seem counterintuitive to many Pauline scholars—though the basic argument was made a long time ago.[29] It also immediately raises the question of the relationship between Paul's talk in the "indicative" and "imperative" moods. If his "indicative" talk implies sinlessness, then why is there also an "imperative" (as nobody denies)? What need is there for it? This is not the place to engage in substantial discussion of this issue. Two remarks must suffice.

The first is that Paul himself makes the point quite clear in the passage we are considering. To quote 5:24: "Those who belong to Christ Jesus have crucified the flesh together with its passions and desires." They have crucified it. They *did crucify* it. *Now*, therefore, it is *dead*. The flesh is no longer relevant, no longer operative *at all*. This is altogether unmistakable. And Paul's point should be taken to yield a premise on the basis of which any remaining problems and passages of relevance to this issue must be tackled.

The second remark concerns the next verse in our passage, the famous verse 5:25 on which Bultmann more or less based the whole of his seminal 1924 account of the supposed "problem" of the indicative and imperative in Paul.[30] The verse runs: "If [= inasmuch as] we live by the Spirit, then let us also walk by it." How should it be read? Like this: Paul is not urging his addressees to engage in a moral *struggle*, as if they had both "already" arrived at the final goal and also were "not yet" there.[31] For we have seen that such a struggle is precisely excluded *if* they live by the Spirit, as 5:25 explicitly assumes. Moreover, 5:24 has just stated that they *did* crucify the flesh. Instead, while explicitly presupposing that they have arrived *fully* at the final goal, Paul is now telling them to *show* it in actual practice. Pragmatically, of course, this also presupposes that they may not in fact always have shown it. Moreover, both 5:15 and 5:26 (not to speak of 6:1–5) explicitly state that they did not. But the crucial point is that in his use of the cohortative subjunctive in 5:25, Paul *presupposes* that they did. The "imperative" logically presupposes that the "indicative" has already been fully and completely realized. What it does, therefore, is only to *remind* them of this already-realized fact. The Pauline "imperative" is not a genuine imperative geared to bringing about some real change. Instead, it is a mere reminder that urges its addressees to show in practice what has already been brought about in them. They already know what should be done and wish to do it. And they do not wish to do anything else. If they nevertheless fail to do it, the only available remedy is reminding them once more of what they both know and wish. That is the logic of Paul's parenesis.

There is a fourth point that also makes Paul's argument in 5:13–26 fall squarely within the confines of the virtue system. This point has to do with the substantive content of living by the Spirit. The point has two sides to it.

First, Paul is quite clear throughout the passage on the strongly other-directed shape of living by the Spirit. Enslaving oneself to one another in ἀγάπη, *agapē* (love; 5:15); loving one's neighbor as oneself (5:16); and possessing the set of attitudes (5:22–23) that is headed by *agapē* and followed by such other-regarding attitudes as peacefulness (εἰρήνη, *eirēnē*), forbearance (μακροθυμία, *makrothymia*), kindness, goodness, fidelity, mildness, and self-control (ἐγκράτεια, *enkrateia*)—all these descriptions clearly serve to pinpoint the other-regarding profile of living by the Spirit.[32] Conversely, the catalog of vices (or rather, as we have seen, of vicious act-types) given in 5:19–21 identifies the vices by two features. One is an inordinate directedness toward the body. The other is an inordinate directedness toward the individual himself and a corresponding failure in the appropriate other-directedness (compare sorcery, quarrels, contentiousness, envy, fits of rage, selfish ambitions, dissensions, party intrigues). All this, of course, fits in closely with the ancient virtue system which, as we saw, had the virtue of justice as its paradigm example.

The other side of this general point fits with the other feature of the catalog of vices to which I just alluded. In addition to identifying a lack of concern for others, the list also pinpoints too strong a concern for the individual person's own body (compare fornication, indecency, and several other body-directed types of behavior). The two basic features of vicious behavior (too little concern for others, too much concern for one's own body) are more closely connected than might initially appear. The point cannot be properly argued here. Let it be said that Paul never objected to the human body just as body. What he did object to was self-directedness or (undue) self-concern. That was why he also objected to (undue) body-directedness. For the body is intrinsically connected with the self or individual.[33]

Taken in this way, Paul's catalog of vicious behavior and the converse list of commendable attitudes reinforce each other in showing that the ultimate shape of life in the Spirit was just what Paul had stated it to be in 5:6: a life reflecting a faith that is "active through love," where "active" (ἐνεργουμένη, energoumenē) means actively putting the set of Spirit-generated attitudes or settled states (in Aristotle: ἕξεις, hexeis) to use in actual practice (that is, in Aristotelian energeiai) and "love" is the leading one among those attitudes.

That Paul was not objecting to the body as such but rather to its role as tied to the individual is strengthened by his remark that those who "belong to Christ Jesus" have "crucified the flesh" (5:24). That remark recalls 2:19–20, in which Paul was speaking of himself and his own crucifixion with Christ. There, however, what was crucified was not Paul's body (or flesh), but his ἐγώ, egō, his "I" or self, Paul the individual as a whole—which of course includes his body, but not only that. In short, Paul's target was not primarily the body per se. Rather, the target was everything in the individual person that stands in the way of the kind of other-directedness for which he was arguing.

I suggested above that the point we have now identified, namely the intrinsic connection of Paul's objections to an exaggerated concern for one's own body with a failure of concern for others, constituted a fourth point of convergence between Paul and the ancient virtue system. How? The claim cannot be fully argued here, but we at least need to indicate the direction in which one must go to support it. I noted in Part I that the Stoics developed their notion of oikeiōsis ("familiarization") in two directions: as an argument why the human τέλος, telos (end), consists in living in accordance with moral virtue and as an argument why the moral virtue par excellence is justice. The latter argument is clearly one for other-directedness and concern for others. But the former argument is precisely one for moving away from paying any special attention to oneself as a *bodily* being.[34] Thus we have first a movement away from concern for oneself as a bodily being to moral virtue, and next a movement from self-oriented moral virtue to the other-directed moral virtue of justice. The two arguments differ in that only the second serves to ground a specific concern for *others,* but in Stoicism the second argument should be understood as no more than a specification of the first: from concern for *oneself* as a *bodily* being to moral virtue—*and indeed,* to the *other*-directed virtue of justice. With such a theoretical background in Stoicism, Paul's targets in the list of vices (undue concern for one's own *body and* a failure of concern for *others*) and the list of virtues (the converse) immediately make sense. They provide one more example of the manner in which he presupposed the ancient virtue system.

Galatians 5:13–26 within the Letter as a Whole

It is time to move from the intricacies of the passage to the question from which we began: with the reading of the passage that we now have before us, how does it fit into Paul's overall argument in the letter? We have already seen in some detail that it provides the positive side of Paul's basic message: do *not* enter under the Jewish Law by letting yourselves be circumcised, *but live* by the *Spirit*, that is, *practice* the *virtues*; for that is what Christ-believers (and they alone) both can do and actually do. However, to get the complete picture, we need to add one more item.

Why should Paul bring in virtuous attitudes and virtuous behavior (and Christ-faith and the Spirit as *generating* those attitudes) as his positive solution to the basic issue treated in the letter? One answer imposes itself: because the ultimate issue that lay behind the question whether or not to enter under the Law was *where and how one would escape from sin and become just*. And, in fact, that is just the way Paul sets up his discussion in 2:15–21. Who is a sinner? Who is just? Jews (living under the Law)? Gentile "sinners"? None, at least, is made just "from works of the Law," that is, merely from living under the Law, but through Christ-faith (v. 16). But if that statement applies to Gentile "sinners," too, is Christ then responsible for sin? Never (v. 17)! Indeed, precisely not. The Law, which *defines* Gentiles as "sinners," is *not* a bulwark against sin. Christ is. The last three sentences constitute my gloss on what Paul is saying in the second half of 2:15–21 (from v. 19 onward). Paul has been crucified with Christ. In that way he has come to live for God and to die to the Law. Thus (1) the Law is on the one side of a crucial divide, with God and Christ on the other. And (2) on the other side of that divide, too, is Paul. As he says further: Paul the individual no longer lives. Christ lives "in" him. To the extent that Paul does continue to live "in the flesh," that is, as an individual, bodily being and hence on the bad side of the crucial divide, he lives (and here we again move over to the good side of the divide) "in" the faith of the son of God. But (3) that too is where there is justice—compare the return to δικαιοσύνη, *dikaiosynē* (justice), in verse 21. Justice, as the ultimate alternative to sin around which the whole letter reverberates, has now been generated from above, through God's grace (that is, God's "reaching down" to humankind) and through Christ's loving "Paul" and giving himself up for "Paul's" sake (that is, Christ's "reaching down" to humankind). Justice did not come through the Law. Otherwise Christ would have died in vain! But—and that is the ultimate point—

it only came (to Paul) and only comes (to the Galatians and anybody else) *in* the response to the act of God and Christ that Paul describes, paradigmatically, in 2:19–20. The aim of 5:13–26, then, is to spell out *just how* justice did come fully and completely *through that response.*

Let me spell out the connection as we might hear it from Paul: (2:15–21) You want justice as opposed to sin? Christ is the answer. (5:13–26) And let me now show you in detail (as opposed to my brief pointer in 2:19–20) *how* that is so. The Law prohibits types of behavior, but that is never enough to prevent the risk (which constitutes the essence of "weakness of the will," *akrasia*) of "fleshly" acts (that is, of ἁμαρτία, *hamartia,* "sinning," or acting in the way one would also act if one had a full Aristotelian κακία, *kakia,* "vice," a vice that is undivided and wishes *only* to do the bad thing). Moreover, if you do such things, you will not inherit the kingdom of God. The Spirit, by contrast, generates the proper attitudes or "virtues" in an altogether stable and settled state of mind. In this way the Spirit makes certain that you will always and only do the right acts. You will be just and not sinners. You will inherit the kingdom of God.

Part III. Other Relevant Pauline and Paulinist Texts

It is time to mention other passages in Paul in which ideas and concepts from the virtue system turn up. I cannot go into detail. But I should at least indicate how these ideas and concepts are not there incidentally or haphazardly, but may be seen to inform Paul's whole argument.

The most obvious place to go from Galatians is Romans. A very good case can be made for seeing the ancient virtue system as having a role in Romans that is just as central as—and closely comparable to—the role it had in the earlier letter (Galatians).[35]

One relevant passage is Rom 1:24–32. Paul clearly aims to explain moral vice as a result of a false or insufficient appreciation of God. Some of the terms we have been working with turn up here: ἐπιθυμία, *epithymia* (desire, 1:24); ἀκαθαρσία, *akatharsia* (impurity, 1:24; cf. Gal 5:19); πάθη, *pathē* (passions, 1:26); and the long vice list of 1:29–31. Noteworthy also is the appearance of the Stoic technical term καθήκοντα, *kathēkonta* (appropriate act-types), in the negative form (τὰ μὴ καθήκοντα, *ta mē kathēkonta,* inappropriate act-types) as a sort of title for the vice list that follows.[36] Interestingly, however, the list itself does not mention acts or act-types but rather states of mind or the people who possess them. Perhaps Paul here aims to identify, not cases of *akrasia* ("weakness of the will"), but full-blown sinners, that is, *people* who are κακοί, *kakoi* (vicious), and whose state of mind is one of κακία, *kakia* (vice). One other noteworthy feature is that Paul begins his list with ἀδικία, *adikia,* injustice. That is hardly fortuitous in the light of both 1:18, in which *adikia* was already singled out for special mention, and the overall contrast in 1:17–18 between God's δικαιοσύνη, *dikaiosynē* (justice), and human injustice. Is Paul out to describe how the Christ-event (brought in with full force in 3:21) was designed by the just God to blot out human injustice, as he had described it in so many ways up to 3:20? And does he aim to suggest that God brought about this feat by *making* human beings just and thus, if one so wishes, "virtuous"? Is *that* the sense of Paul's claim in 3:26 that God sent Christ in order to show that "he [God] is himself just and that he *makes* just (δικαιοῦντα, *dikaiounta*) the one who takes his bearings from the faithfulness of Jesus"?[37]

Chapter 2 of Romans abounds no less with ideas and concepts from the ancient virtue system. First, in 2:1–11 Paul is at pains to bring out a point that states indiscriminately for Jews and Greeks that what matters, namely for eschatological glory, honor, and indestructibility, is "doing good" here on earth (ἔργον ἀγαθόν, *ergon agathon*, 2:7, ἐργάζεσθαι τὸ ἀγαθόν, *ergazesthai to agathon*, 2:10) as opposed to "doing evil" (κατεργάζεσθαι τὸ κακόν, *katergazesthai to kakon*, 2:9). We have noted that Paul also produces a summarizing statement of what holds together all the various vices—headed by ἀδικία, *adikia* (injustice)—that went into the vice list of 1:29–31. That single, shared thing is "selfishness" (ἐριθεία, *eritheia*, 2:8).

An earlier point in 2:1–11 also reflects the virtue system and leads to the point about "doing good." God is "kind" (χρηστός, *chrēstos*) and has shown "forbearance" (ἀνοχή, *anochē*) and "patience" (μακροθυμία, *makrothymia*) in order to generate a "change of mind" (μετάνοια, *metanoia*) in human beings (2:4). Clearly, God is described as himself having a character and as being at work to bring about a fundamental change of *character* on the part of human beings. But once more the aim is to generate, or in this case to prevent, a certain kind of *action* (2:13), one that will otherwise fall under God's judgment. Thus here too the basic features of the virtue system are in place: character (which is another word for Aristotle's ἕξις ἠθική, *hexis ēthikē*, "moral state") and the activity (ἐνέργεια, *energeia*) that springs from it. Unfortunately, however, it appears that God's forbearance encounters a "heart that will *not* undergo a change of mind" (an ἀμετανόητον καρδίαν, *ametanoēton kardian*; 2:5). And that is just what explains those cases of "doing evil" that constitute Paul's target.

Romans 2:12–16 also falls immediately into place in the light of the ancient virtue system. The issue is that non-Jews are *doing* what is (also) enjoined by the (Jewish) Law and how that should be explained. Paul's explanation points directly "inside" the human being: the Law's content is written in these people's hearts; their "self-awareness" (conscience, συνείδησις, *syneidēsis*) bears witness on their behalf as does the fact that they are internally divided in their deliberations, with some thoughts accusing (others) and (the) others defending themselves (against the former ones); finally, these "hidden thoughts" of human beings are present *within* them, only to be revealed (and judged) by God on the day of judgment. The reference to dividedness (2:15) is particularly revealing. Apparently, Paul here speaks, with precision, of the figure whom Aristotle called the ἐγκρατής, *enkratēs* (the "strong-willed" one): the one who *is* divided, but in whom the better side is also strong enough to generate the appropriate *doing*. Is there a pointed difference here between Paul's picture of this non-Jewish (and non-Christ-believing, but "good") person, who does practice what the Law requires—and the ἀκρατής, *akratēs* ("*weak*-willed" person), of 7:7–25, who, even though he is Jewish (and non-Christ-believing) and thus *wills* the Law, nevertheless from time to time precisely does *not do* what he wills? And how does either person relate to the one who constitutes the logical end-point of this whole way of thinking: the one who wills through and through what is right—and hence does it? Indeed, how does the *Christ-believing* person fit into this picture?

That question is immediately raised by the way Paul ends chapter 2. He is still concerned with the theme of doing or "performing" (τελεῖν, *telein*) the Law and once more refers to the "hidden," or "internal," prerequisite for this, which is "circumcision of the heart in spirit and not in letter." While this particular metaphor has a distinctly Jewish pedigree that goes far back in Jewish thought, the idea itself immediately translates into that of a full, undivided virtue within the Hellenistic virtue system. But then, of whom is Paul speaking in that final verse? Obviously the "true" Jew. But who is the true Jew? Who else but the Christ-believer?

Thus it is quite possible to see Paul's way of setting up in Rom 1–2 the basic "problem," to which the Christ-event was then taken to provide the "solution," as being permeated by ideas that belong in quite precise ways within the ancient virtue system.[38] That understanding would then also have consequences for understanding both his account of the "solution" itself—the Christ-event (3:21–31) and its intended (faith-)response in human beings as modeled for them by Abraham (ch. 4)—and also his direct attempt (in 6:1–8:13) to spell out what that response would then mean in terms of action (see in particular 8:3–4).[39]

From there it would be possible to move on to the letter's parenetic section proper. Thus, at the beginning of chapter 12, Paul mixes, in a rhetorical tour de force, specifically Christ-believing ideas with Jewish ideas of a broader character—but also with distinctly Hellenistic ideas that form part of the ancient virtue system. His exhortation (12:1) that his addressees engage in a "service" to God that is "rational" (a λογικὴ λατρεία, *logikē latreia*) is one example. And his suggestion that they should undergo a complete metamorphosis through a "renewal of mind" (ἀνακαίνωσις νοός, *anakainōsis noos*, 12:2) is another. A further example is the heading Paul gives to his ethical advice (12:3): that his addressees must not "have thoughts [about themselves] above the proper thoughts [ὑπερ-φρονεῖν, hyper-phronein]; instead they must think [φρονεῖν, *phronein*] in such a way that they will have moderate thoughts [σω-φρονεῖν, *sō-phronein*]." Here Paul is in effect saying, as Aristotle might have said, that his addressees must have the one basic moral (and intellectual) virtue of φρόνησις, *phronēsis* (moral insight), that will include the moral virtue proper of σωφροσύνη, *sōphrosynē* (moderation). The content of this idea is spelled out in the rest of the chapter.

One might continue in a similar way for the rest of chapter 12, chapter 13, and indeed for 14:1–15:13.[40] These scattered suggestions on how one might read Paul's Letter to the Romans in the light of the ancient virtue system have been intended as examples only. In order to convince, they would need to be far more thoroughly developed. But enough has been said to show that Paul's reliance on the ancient virtue system in Galatians was no single event.

Other Pauline and Paulinist letters could be approached to the same effect. Philippians is a prime example. But here, too, it will quickly be seen that it is insufficient to pay attention only to specific terms. For instance, Paul's single explicit reference to "virtue" in the letter (4:8) must be read in its immediate context (4:2–9), and that passage can only be properly understood in the light of 3:1–4:1. Moreover, the moral exhortation of 4:2–8 (cf. 4:2, παρακαλῶ, *parakalō*, "I exhort") harks back to 2:1–5 (cf. 2:1, παράκλησις, *paraklēsis*, "exhortation"), which again must be understood in its context. Similarly, Paul's brief reference to αὐτάρκεια, *autarkeia* (4:11)—another term that is central to the ancient virtue system—can only be understood within its broader context, which at least comprises 4:10–20.

From this result one might move in several directions. I conclude by offering a set of questions worth further reflection:

- What was the function among Paul's addressees of his use of the ancient virtue system?
- How did that use work?
- How does it cohere with ancient "psychagogy" more widely understood?
- How did a group of Christ-believers function socially when virtuous "perfection" stood out as a "goal" (cf. Phil 3:12–16)?
- If Paul's formal use of the system was in fact as "orthodox" as has been suggested here, what difference—if any—did it make to the substantive content of a Christ-believing life that in the Christian case the factor that triggered the change to "virtue" was the experience of the Christ-event focusing on the figure of Christ itself?
- Indeed, where is the difference in content between the "perfect" life of the Christ-believer that Paul has in mind and that of an Aristotelian φρόνιμος, *phronimos*, or—more to the point—of a Stoic sage?

The latter question is obviously of the greatest interest. But it is also a question that should be addressed with the greatest care, not least because of the many vested interests people have in addressing it. My own hunch is that Paul does not differ in any of the areas referred to at the beginning of this essay, but that he does differ on another single point. Paul's "ethics," I would say, are a radicalized version, not only of Aristotelian ethics, but of Stoic ethics, too. Paul did not change what he found in his Jewish and Hellenistic context. But he did radicalize what he found by extending it to what may well be called its logical end: now was the time, not only when what should be done could be done, but also when it could be done in such a way that any relic of the individual, bodily person would be wiped out completely by an exclusive directedness toward Christ.

However, that is only a guess. If we stay with our queries,

- Should we see the possible radicality of Paul's "ethics" as reflecting his "theological" worldview, with its specifically apocalyptic profile that gives a peculiar urgency to his thought?
- Or should we turn the question around and ask whether Paul's use of the virtue system in his "anthropology" sheds any light on his "theology" and "christology," that is, on his constructions of the character of God and Christ and the Christ-event in particular, in which that character is most perspicuously shown?
- Or should we say both? Is it the case both that Paul's specific worldview added to the "ethics" that he found in his context—and also that his "theology" may have been influenced by those "ethics"?

Thus there are plenty of outstanding questions. The claim of this essay has not been that the particular approach to Paul's letters advocated here constitutes the only adequate perspective. The enormous range and density of Paul's thought makes it both possible and necessary to address the letters from many different angles, none of which should be given exclusive preference. The claim has only been that the perspective of the ancient virtue system is both adequate and fruitful for addressing a broad range of traditional issues in the reading of Paul. To go back to the first two traditional claims, we may confidently conclude that Paul's use of the ancient virtue system is not confined to a small group of passages that either mention the very term "virtue" or provide actual virtue or vice lists (point 1 above). Nor is Paul's use of the ancient virtue system just "traditional," that is, basically "dead," and only relevant to a specific segment of his thought, the "parenetic" one (point 2). On the contrary, Paul's use of the ancient virtue system is distinctly alive and goes to the heart of what he aimed to say.

Part IV. Bibliography

Annas, J. *The Morality of Happiness.* New York and Oxford: Oxford University Press, 1993.

Engberg-Pedersen, T. *Aristotle's Theory of Moral Insight.* Oxford: Clarendon Press, 1983.

———. *Paul and the Stoics.* Edinburgh: T. & T. Clark; Louisville: Westminster John Knox, 2000.

———. *The Stoic Theory of Oikeiosis: Moral Development and Social Interaction in Early Stoic Philosophy.* Studies in Hellenistic Civilization 2. Århus, Denmark: Århus University Press, 1990.

Fitzgerald, J. F. "Virtue/Vice Lists." *ABD* 6:857–59.

Furnish, V. P. *Theology and Ethics in Paul.* Nashville: Abingdon, 1968.

Irwin, Terence. *Plato's Ethics.* New York and Oxford: Oxford University Press, 1995.

Kamlah, E. *Die Form der katalogischen Paränese im Neuen Testament.* WUNT 7. Tübingen: Mohr-Siebeck, 1964.

Malherbe, A. J. "Hellenistic Moralists and the New Testament." Pages 267–333 in *ANRW* 2.26.1. Berlin and New York: de Gruyter, 1992.

———. *Moral Exhortation: A Greco-Roman Sourcebook.* LEC 4. Philadelphia: Westminster, 1986.

Popkes, W. *Paränese und Neues Testament.* SBS 168. Stuttgart: Katholisches Bibelwerk, 1996.

Vögtle, A. *Die Tugend- und Lasterkataloge im Neuen Testament, exegetisch, religions- und formgeschichtlich untersucht.* NTAbh 16. Münster, Germany: Aschendorff, 1936.

Wibbing, S. *Die Tugend- und Lasterkataloge im Neuen Testament und ihre Traditions- geschichte unter besonderer Berücksichtigung der Qumran-Texte.* BZNW 25. Berlin: Töpelmann, 1959.

Notes

1. As will become clear, I understand the "ancient ethical tradition" as the way of thinking of central ethical concepts (happiness, virtues and vice, material goods, and more) first fully developed by Plato and Aristotle and then presupposed and elaborated on to the end of antiquity.

2. All translations are the author's.

3. The deutero-Paulines also have several specimens, e.g., Col 3:5–8:10; Eph 4:31; 5:3–5; 1 Tim 1:9–10; 3:2–4; 6:4–5, and more. For an instructive overview see J. T. Fitzgerald, "Virtue/Vice Lists," *ABD* 6:857–59. See also A. J. Malherbe, "Hellenistic Moralists and the New Testament," in *ANRW* 2.26.1 (Berlin and New York: de Gruyter, 1992), 267–333, esp. 325–26.

4. A classic formulation of this viewpoint (though one that does not explicitly mention the virtue and vice lists) is that of Martin Dibelius in his discussion of the literary genre of James: *Der Brief des Jakobus* (11th ed.; Kritisch-exegetischer Kommentar über das Neue Testament [Meyer-Kommentar] 15 [1921]; Göttingen: Vandenhoeck & Ruprecht, 1964), 15–19. For the contrary—and correct—viewpoint

that, e.g., Gal 5:22–23 "amply documents the extent to which the 'virtues' Paul enumerates have their context within his own thought and purpose," see V. P. Furnish, *Theology and Ethics in Paul* (Nashville: Abingdon, 1968), 86 (and 86–89 generally). Unfortunately, however, Furnish's claim is based on the idea referred to in the next paragraph, to the effect that there are crucial differences of a theological kind between virtue talk in the Greco-Roman moralists and in Paul.

5. Once again, the various claims under this point have a very wide currency. They constitute something like a scholarly consensus. I quote a few formulations from a scholar who is more alert than most to the similarity between Paul and the Greco-Roman philosophers, A. J. Malherbe. For point (*a*): "whereas the philosophers stressed the importance of reason and reliance on self in moral growth, Paul refers the moral life to God and the power of the Holy Spirit" (*Paul and the Thessalonians: The Philosophic Tradition of Pastoral Care* [Philadelphia: Fortress Press, 1987], 33). For points (*b*) and (*c*): when in Phil 4:11 Paul uses the notion of "self-sufficiency," which in Stoicism was closely connected with moral virtue, "Paul is essentially concerned with personal relationships [namely, of a social kind: between himself and his readers] rather than introspection." See Malherbe, "Paul's Self-Sufficiency (Philippians 4:11)," in *Friendship, Flattery, and Frankness of Speech: Studies on Friendship in the New Testament World* (ed. J. T. Fitzgerald; NovTSup 82; Leiden: Brill, 1996), 125–39, esp. 138.

6. There is a traditional contrast between Paul the "theologian" and the "philosophers" of the Greco-Roman tradition. The contrast is not without its point, but a figure like the Jewish "theologian"-cum-"philosopher" Philo should make one pause. More interesting is a recent focus on other implications of the difference in social status between Paul and the Greco-Roman philosophers. Thus Dale B. Martin has insisted that the difference matches two different "ideological systems" that are reflected, for instance, in two quite different constructions of desire in relation to self-sufficiency and the possibility (for the philosophers) or impossibility (for Paul) of a "stable self," of "free will," and of "free moral agency"; see Dale B. Martin, "Paul without Passion: On Paul's Rejection of Desire in Sex and Marriage," in *Constructing Early Christian Families: Family as Social Reality and Metaphor* (ed. H. Moxnes; London: Routledge, 1997), 201–15, esp. 210–12. It is indeed true that no matter what their social origin, the Greco-Roman philosophers invariably came into direct contact, *as* philosophers, with the leisured classes and the socially and politically powerful, and hence, to some extent, may have shared their socially based, special "ideology." So too did the Paul of Acts, but hardly that of his own letters. It is another question, however, whether such a strong, dichotomous interpretation as Martin's should be given to the difference.

7. I have argued the case more thoroughly in *Paul and the Stoics* (Edinburgh: T. & T. Clark; Louisville: Westminster John Knox, 2000).

8. For a comprehensive analysis of Plato's argument in *Republic* bks. I–IV, see Terence Irwin, *Plato's Ethics* (New York and Oxford: Oxford University Press, 1995), 169–261.

9. For the general argument see *Nicomachean Ethics* V.i–ii and the discussion in my *Aristotle's Theory of Moral Insight* (Oxford: Clarendon Press, 1983), 53–62.

10. For the distinction see *Nicomachean Ethics* I.viii.9, 1098b31–33: "Perhaps, however, it makes no little difference whether the supreme good is understood to

consist in possessing something [κτῆσις, *ktēsis*] or in using it [χρῆσις, *chrēsis*], or in a state [ἕξις, *hexis*] or an activity [ἐνέργεια, *energeia*]."

11. For a general account of the role of moral virtue in the ancient ethical tradition, viewed as a type of character ethics, see Julia Annas, *The Morality of Happiness* (New York and Oxford: Oxford University Press, 1993), 47–131.

12. For the point about "complete" moral virtue see *Nicomachean Ethics* VI.xiii.6, 1145a1–2, in the context of VI.xii–xiii as a whole. For the undivided mind of the fully virtuous person, see in particular I.xiii.

13. Aristotle introduces the distinction between the ἐγκρατής, *enkratēs*, the ἀκρατής, *akratēs*, and the fully virtuous person in I.xiii.15–18, 1102b13–1103a1. His full discussion of *akrasia* in particular is in VII.iii, 1146b8–1147b19.

14. One central passage to bring this out is Cicero, *De finibus* 3.v.16–18, vi.20–22, vii.23–24. For a comprehensive analysis of these passages, see T. Engberg-Pedersen, *The Stoic Theory of Oikeiosis: Moral Development and Social Interaction in Early Stoic Philosophy* (Studies in Hellenistic Civilization 2; Århus, Denmark: Aarhus University Press, 1990), 64–100.

15. For the first round of the *oikeiōsis* argument, which leads to grasping that the human *telos* lies in acting in accordance with moral virtue, see Cicero, *De finibus* 3.v.16 and vi.20–21. For the second round, leading to seeing that the human *telos* lies, in particular, in acting in accordance with the other-regarding moral virtue of justice, see Cicero, *De finibus* 3.xix.62–64. For discussion, see Engberg-Pedersen, *Stoic Theory of Oikeiosis*, 122–26.

16. The Stoics identified a *diathesis* as a ἕξις, *hexis*, that "does not allow of more or less"; that is, it can never become stronger or weaker but will always remain the same (*Stoicorum Veterum Fragmenta* [ed. H. von Arnim; 4 vols. [1903–24]; Stuttgart: B. G. Teubner, 1964], 3:525; henceforth abbreviated as *SVF*). The virtues are precisely *diatheseis* (see *SVF* 3:104, 3:39).

17. For the virtues as so many forms of knowledge, see *SVF* 2:95–96, 3:214, 202. Plutarch's account in *On Moral Virtue* (3.441B–C) captures the essence of the Stoic idea: "All these men [the old Stoics from Zeno to Chrysippus] take virtue to be a certain disposition [*diathesis*] and power [δύναμις, *dynamis*] of the soul engendered by reason, or rather to be *itself reason* that is internally consistent [ὁμολογούμενος, *homologoumenos*; implicitly also: in accordance with nature], firm and unchangeable."

18. For passages, see *SVF* 3:377–420. For discussion, see Tad Brennan, "The Old Stoic Theory of Emotions," in *The Emotions in Hellenistic Philosophy* (ed. J. Sihvola and T. Engberg-Pedersen; The New Synthese Historical Library 46; Dordrecht, the Netherlands: Kluwer Academic, 1998), 21–70, esp. 22–29, and Engberg-Pedersen, *Stoic Theory of Oikeiosis*, 101–15 and 170–206.

19. For the three "good emotions," see *SVF* 3:431–42.

20. See, e.g., *SVF* 3:391–94.

21. I have set out the argument that follows in more detail in *Paul and the Stoics*, 133–77.

22. Notice Paul's claim in 3:21: "*If* the Law had been given as one that *could* make alive, then justice would *most certainly* [ὄντως, *ontōs*] have come about through the Law." That statement is—and is intended as—high *praise* of the Law.

23. Scholars have gradually come to see this point, though in different ways

that do not add up to the claim I go on to make. See, for instance, John M. G. Barclay, *Obeying the Truth: Paul's Ethics in Galatians* (Edinburgh: T. & T. Clark, 1988), 94–96 and throughout, and F. J. Matera, "The Culmination of Paul's Argument to the Galatians: Gal 5.6–6.17," *JSNT* 32 (1988): 79–91.

24. See Matera, "Culmination of Paul's Argument."

25. For more on this reading of a very difficult verse, see Engberg-Pedersen, *Paul and the Stoics*, 162–63.

26. The basic argument for this claim is derived from Paul's exact choice of words. That he repeatedly uses *plural* nouns (e.g., ἔχθραι, *echthrai, cases of* enmity, θυμοί, *thymoi, cases of* anger)—which cannot refer to states of mind—shows that even where he employs singular nouns, we should interpret them as standing for a type of *act*, as opposed to an "interior" state. Thus, for example, πορνεία, *porneia* (singular), stands for "illicit sexual *behavior*," and so forth.

27. Again the argument is derived from Paul's exact wording. All the items in Paul's "virtue list" here refer very specifically to "interior" states.

28. The Stoics also had the notion of act-types to be mentioned in (general) rules. That is the idea that lies behind their concept of καθήκοντα, *kathēkonta* ("appropriate acts")—or, as in this case, τὰ παρὰ τὸ καθῆκον, *ta para to kathēkon* ("inappropriate acts"; for this term see *SVF* 3:495). For a general account of the Stoic concept of *kathēkonta*, see Engberg-Pedersen, *Stoic Theory of Oikeiosis*, 126–40.

29. See Paul Wernle, *Der Christ und die Sünde bei Paulus* (Freiburg and Leipzig: Mohr [Siebeck], 1897).

30. Rudolf Bultmann, "Das Problem der Ethik bei Paulus," *ZNW* 23 (1924): 123–40.

31. For a general reading of Paul that emphasizes the supposed "tension" between "already" and "not yet" in a manner directly opposed to the reading presented here, see J. D. G. Dunn, *The Theology of Paul the Apostle* (Edinburgh: T. & T. Clark, 1998), 461–98.

32. Notice that Paul does not here use the term *enkrateia* in its specifically Aristotelian sense in which it differs from full virtue; see *Nicomachean Ethics* I.xiii.17, 1102b26–28. Instead, he follows the Stoics, who defined *enkrateia* as a full virtue that "falls under" the virtue of moderation (σωφροσύνη, *sōphrosynē*); see *SVF* 3:264.

33. In Rom 2:8–9, Paul recapitulates the very body-directed vices he has described in 1:18–2:6 and introduces the proper word for self-directedness: ἐριθεία, *eritheia* ("selfishness"; 2:8).

34. Compare Cicero, *De finibus* 3.v.16, and the analysis in Engberg-Pedersen, *Stoic Theory of Oikeiosis*, 66–71.

35. For a far more extensive treatment and argument see my *Paul and the Stoics*, 179–292.

36. Notice that the technical Stoic term is not μὴ καθῆκον, *mē kathēkon*, but παρὰ τὸ καθῆκον, *para to kathēkon*. Paul never strives for technical precision. Indeed, he probably seeks to avoid it. (The phrase [τὸ] μὴ καθῆκον, [*to*] *mē kathēkon*, is found, however, in Epictetus 3.22.43. Philo *Mutat.* 241 speaks of τὰ μὴ προσήκοντα, *ta mē prosēkonta*.)

37. An admittedly tendentious rendering of Rom 3:26, a verse in which the interpretation of almost every word is contested. For discussion, see the commen-

taries, but also the seminal work on "righteousness" (δικαιοσύνη, *dikaiosynē*) and its cognates: J. A. Ziesler, *The Meaning of Righteousness in Paul: A Linguistic and Theological Enquiry* (SNTSMS 20; Cambridge: Cambridge University Press, 1972).

38. See Engberg-Pedersen, *Paul and the Stoics,* 179–216, esp. 200–216.

39. See ibid., 217–55.

40. See ibid., 257–92.

CONTRIBUTORS

Efrain Agosto	*Hartford Seminary*
David L. Balch	*Brite Divinity School*
Will Deming	*University of Portland*
Troels Engberg-Pedersen	*University of Copenhagen*
Benjamin Fiore	*Canisius College*
John T. Fitzgerald	*University of Miami*
Christopher Forbes	*Macquarie University (Sydney)*
David E. Fredrickson	*Luther Seminary in St. Paul, Minnesota*
Clarence E. Glad	*The Reykjavik Academy and The Icelandic Research Council*
J. Albert Harrill	*Indiana University*
Ronald F. Hock	*University of Southern California*
Robert Jewett	*University of Heidelberg*
Edgar Krentz	*Lutheran School of Theology at Chicago*
Peter Lampe	*University of Heidelberg*
Rollin A. Ramsaran	*Emmanuel School of Religion*
J. Paul Sampley	*Boston University*
Stanley K. Stowers	*Brown University*
James C. Walters	*Boston University*
Duane F. Watson	*Malone College*
L. Michael White	*University of Texas*
O. Larry Yarbrough	*Middlebury College*

INDEX OF ANCIENT SOURCES

HEBREW BIBLE

Genesis

1–11	535
1:26	593
1:27	593
3:21	593
15:2–4	76n. 134
48:5	68

Exodus

2:10	68, 76n. 134
4:22–23	76n. 134
19:14	426n. 37
20:3	447
20:4	288n. 44
20:17	532

Leviticus

11	275
11:10	29, 33
18:5	279
18:24–25	542
19:18	443
20:22–25	542

Deuteronomy

5:8	288n. 44
5:21	532
7:2–5	542
14:1	65
20:17–18	542

Judges

2:17	252n.49
7:2	78

1 Samuel

2:2–3	78
8:3	252n. 49

2 Samuel

7:14	42, 76n. 134

1 Kings

3:14	252n. 49
9:4	252n. 49
11:33, 38	252n. 49
20:11	78

1 Chronicles

16:28–29	78
28:6	76n. 134
29:11	78

Esther

2:7	43, 68, 76n. 134
2:15	43, 68

Psalms

2	9
2:7	76n. 134
5:11	78
20:6 (LXX)	564
24:20 (LXX)	564
30:2 (LXX)	564
52:1	78
70:1 (LXX)	564
89:15–18	78
89:26–27	76n. 134
94:3–4	78

Proverbs

25:14	78
27:1	78

Isaiah

43:6	65

Jeremiah

3:19	76n. 134
9:23–24 (9:22–23 LXX)	77, 85, 96
9:23	77
31:9	65

Hosea

1:10	65
11:1	76n. 134

New Testament

Matthew

5:21	288n. 44
5:27	288n. 44
12:2	288n. 44
13:27	482n. 39
13:52	482n. 39
14:21	282
15:4	288n. 44
15:38	282
19:18–19	288n. 44
20:1	482n. 39
20:11	482n. 39
22:20	266
22:21	494
27:9	578

Mark

1:29–35	520n. 51
2:15	520n. 51
14:3	520n. 51
10:2–12	277
10:30	520n. 51
14:14	482n. 39
16:12	40n. 33

Luke

12:39–45	465
12:39	482n. 39
12:42	482n. 40
12:43	465
13:25	482n. 39
14:21	482n. 39

16:1	482n. 40
16:8	482n. 40
22:11	482n. 39

John

15:12–17	320
15:18–25	310

Acts

1:13	265
4:36–37	521n. 64
5:29	494
7:10	486n. 83
9:26	499
9:37	265
9:39	265
10:12	486n. 83
11:14	486n. 83
11:25–26	499
13–14	521n. 65
13:13	521n. 65
15:22	282
15:36–40	500
15:40	521n. 67
16–18	486n. 83
16:1–3	521n. 67
16:3	40n. 37
16:14–15	283, 498
16:15	486n. 83, 599
16:16–24	583
16:31	486n. 83
16:32–34	599
16:33	486n. 83
16:40	260
17:4	498
17:5	498
17:6	483n. 56
17:7	498
17:9	483n. 56
17:12	498
17:14–15	521n. 67
17:28	209
17:33	486n. 83
17:34	498
18	411
18:1–17	426n. 38
18:1–3	483n. 49
18:2–3	499
18:3	218n. 1
18:7	498, 520nn. 52, 60
18:8	486n. 83, 520n. 52, 599

19:9	520n. 49	1:26	277, 278, 534, 535, 540,
19:19	578		542, 624
19:21–22	426n. 40	1:27	277, 278, 537, 545,
19:22	521n. 67		550n. 50
20:4–6	503, 521n. 67	1:28	535, 540, 542
20:4	521n. 68	1:29–31	608, 624, 625
20:8–9	496	1:32	535
20:8	265	2:1–16	211, 535
21:27–40	217	2:1–11	625
21:39	217	2:1–5	13
22:3	215, 218n. 1	2:1	535, 625
24:1–8	216	2:2	535
24:10–21	216	2:3	535, 625
24:17	504	2:4	401n. 31, 625
24:21	216	2:5	625
24:22–27	583	2:6–3:20	152
28:31	522n. 81	2:6–11	565
		2:7–11	13
Romans		2:7	625
1–5	506, 523n. 89	2:8–9	632n. 33
1–3	530	2:8	625, 632n. 33
1–2	626	2:9	190, 625
1	277, 542	2:10	625
1:1	244, 500, 597, 598	2:11–3:20	152
1:3–4	66	2:11	448
1:4	505	2:12–3:20	151
1:5–7	565	2:12–16	565, 625
1:7	472	2:12–13	430
1:9–15	340	2:15	190, 535, 626
1:9	9, 500	2:17–3:8	536
1:13–15	28	2:17–29	211
1:13–14	535	2:17–27	211
1:14	551	2:17–24	565
1:16–17	238	2:17	96, 562
1:16	350	2:18	403n. 66
1:17–18	625	2:20	529
1:18–3:21	536	2:21–21	153
1:18–2:16	535	2:22	426n. 37
1:18–2:6	632n. 33	2:23	96, 562
1:18–32	152, 534, 535, 540	2:25	395
1:18–20	529	2:27–29	153
1:18	506, 559, 624	2:29	12
1:21–28	529	3–5	536
1:21	506	3	559, 561
1:23	507, 523n. 89	3:1–4	154
1:24–32	624	3:1–2	395
1:24–28	542	3:5–8	154
1:24–27	277, 415, 416	3:9–31	536
1:24	278, 535, 540, 542, 624	3:9–20	154
1:25	507	3:19–20	154
1:26–27	544	3:20	559, 625

Romans (*continued*)

3:21–31	626
3:21	560, 625
3:22	402n. 59, 561
3:23	360
3:24	560, 561, 599
3:25–26	280
3:25	506
3:26	625, 632n. 37
3:27–28	95, 98
3:27	561, 562
3:29–30	561
3:30	395
3:37	562
4	626
4:1–3	95
4:3	237
4:9–12	565
4:18–24	565
5–8	169n. 68
5	416, 563
5:1–11	185, 187, 562, 564
5:1–2	95
5:1	14, 436
5:2–3	563
5:2	95, 523n. 88, 562
5:3–5	564
5:3–4	186, 187
5:3	95, 192n. 5, 562, 563
5:5	563, 564
5:6–11	340
5:6–10	339
5:6–8	190
5:6	338
5:7	338, 520n. 58
5:8	338, 506
5:10	9, 337, 338
5:11	95
5:12–21	154, 168n. 57, 169n. 68
5:12–19	505
5:12–17	151
5:14	66
5:15–17	155
5:15	170n. 69
5:16	170n. 69
5:17	66
5:18	170n. 69
5:19	170n. 69
6–8	536
6	620
6:1–8:13	626

6:2	536
6:4	472
6:6–23	599
6:6	536
6:9	473
6:11–12	536
6:11	536, 537
6:12	536
6:13	378n. 108
6:14	473
6:22	597
6:23	378n. 109, 448
6:34	241
7	244, 413, 535, 537, 540, 542, 612
7:1–6	74n. 120, 411
7:1	473
7:2–6	413
7:4–6	413
7:4	505
7:5	534
7:7–25	211, 626
7:7–24	537, 539, 540
7:7–11	211
7:10	279
7:14–24a	211
7:14	537, 599
7:15	526
7:19	526
7:22	527, 543
7:23	353, 543
7:24–25	194n. 41, 244
7:25	211, 543
7:24	190, 537
7:24b	211
8:1–13	539, 540
8:1–8	565
8:1	597
8:3–4	626
8:3	9, 41n. 49, 506
8:4	443
8:7	117
8:12–25	55, 56, 65
8:12–23	599
8:12–17	73n. 88, 473, 596
8:14–17	470, 519n. 47
8:15	9, 42, 65, 73n. 88, 597
8:17	65, 72n. 76, 190
8:18–39	185, 187
8:18–34	189
8:18–25	438

8:18	151, 534	12:3	10, 534, 626
8:19–22	189	12:4–5	36
8:19	519n. 47	12:6–8	124
8:21–23	577	12:8–13	473
8:21	519n. 47, 597	12:8	112, 123, 131
8:23	42, 60, 65, 173, 519n. 47	12:9–21	340
8:24	196n. 63	12:9–18	437, 448, 452n. 46
8:26	173, 189	12:10	497, 522n. 72
8:27	505	12:11	599
8:29	9	12:12	190
8:31–39	565	12:13	467, 497, 520nn. 51, 58
8:31–33	189	12:15–16	565
8:32	9, 190, 472	12:15	36, 190, 339
8:34	189, 190, 505	12:21	190, 353
8:35–39	189, 398	13	523n. 89, 627
8:35	188, 192n. 5	13:1	116, 117
8:37	189, 378n. 105	13:4	599
8:39	188	13:7–10	565
9	153	13:7	448
9:1–3	190	13:8	12
9:4	42, 65	13:11–14	353
9:16	377n. 94	13:11	350, 378n. 107
9:20	237	13:9	426n. 37
9:21	195n. 50	14–16	564
9:25–26	66	14:1–15:13	565, 627
9:30–33	377n. 92, 565	14:1	564
9:30–32	377n. 92	14:4	599
10:1	350	14:5	398
10:3	117	14:6–9	505
10:5	279	14:6–8	398
10:9	350, 505	14:7–8	448, 505
10:10–13	565	14:9	32, 473
10:12–13	394	14:13–19	14
10:12	395, 402n. 59, 436, 448, 505	14:14–17	398
11:11–12	377n. 92	14:14	505
11:11	378n. 104	14:15	14
11:13	535	14:17	436, 448
11:17–32	565	14:18–19	13
11:17	237	14:18	14, 599
11:18	96	14:19	14, 436
11:26–27	377n. 92	14:20	398
11:29	65	14:22	448
11:33–36	338	14:23	448
12–15	452n. 44	15:1–7	35, 340
12	339, 626, 627	15:1–3	190
12:1–15:14	35	15:2	256n. 99
12:1–5	314	15:6	472
12:1–2	14, 36	15:7	564
12:1	626	15:14–21	535
12:2	14, 41n. 49, 447, 626	15:14–16	314
		15:14	340

Romans (*continued*)

15:17	96
15:22–32	340
15:24	502
15:25	265
15:26–27	504
15:26	309
15:27	340, 504
15:28	502
15:30–31	504
15:31	504
15:30	190
16	412, 413, 564
16:1–3	283
16:1–2	110, 111, 113, 122, 125, 127, 340, 467, 483n. 49, 483n. 51, 498, 499
16:1	277, 498, 520n. 52
16:2	112, 123, 124, 467, 473, 499, 518n. 33
16:3–16	125, 340, 565
16:3–15	339
16:3–5	260, 277, 283, 411
16:3–5	116, 565
16:3	482n. 40, 499, 507
16:4	499
16:5–16	467, 483n. 50
16:5	473, 483n. 48, 483n. 49
16:6	112, 277
16:7	467, 507, 521n. 68
16:9	507, 520n. 62, 521n. 61
16:10–11	599
16:10	259, 565
16:11	426n. 42, 565
16:12	112, 277, 467
16:13	278, 498, 521n. 63
16:14	565
16:15	259, 412, 565
16:16	565
16:17–23	240
16:17–20	314
16:17–18	542
16:17	40n. 41, 426n. 41
16:18	599
16:20	363
16:21	426n. 39, 507, 520n. 62, 521n. 67, 522n. 75
16:22–23	520n. 59
16:22	521n. 67

16:23–24	309
16:23	498, 520nn. 52–53, 599
16:23	116, 126, 260, 473, 483nn. 49, 51, 499

1 Corinthians

1–4	244, 340, 521n. 66
1–2	151, 159, 557
1:1	507, 521n. 67, 522n. 75
1:3	472, 505
1:5	304
1:7	304
1:9	9
1:10–31	565
1:10–13	305
1:10	244, 304, 339
1:11	260, 304, 483n. 49, 599
1:12–17	115
1:12	242, 243, 557
1:13–17	131n. 29
1:13–15	115
1:14–17	483n. 53
1:14	483n. 49, 483n. 49, 499, 520nn. 52–60
1:16	260, 520nn. 52–60, 599
1:18–31	431
1:18–25	557
1:20–25	387
1:22–25	609
1:22	557
1:23	30, 32, 216
1:25	431, 448
1:26–31	77, 96
1:26–29	259
1:26–28	557
1:26–27	88, 96
1:26	398, 599
1:29	275
1:30	557
1:31	77, 85, 275, 437, 448
2	456n. 90
2:1–13	565
2:1–5	159
2:1–4	198
2:1	304
2:2	30, 32, 216
2:6–16	430
2:6	255n. 94
2:13	152
2:16	447

3 — 242
3:1–10 — 115
3:1–4 — 305
3:1–2 — 64, 278
3:1 — 74n. 108, 255n. 94
3:2 — 255n. 94
3:4–15 — 565
3:5–6 — 124
3:5 — 599
3:9 — 426n. 39
3:10–15 — 237
3:10 — 85
3:13 — 242
3:14 — 305
3:17 — 244
3:18–23 — 565
3:18 — 41n. 49
3:21–23 — 9, 97, 398, 448, 455n. 87
3:21–22 — 507
3:21 — 275, 448
3:22 — 448
3:23 — 505
4 — 159
4:1–13 — 151, 155, 170n. 71
4:1–7 — 97
4:1–2 — 482n. 40, 500
4:1 — 170n. 76
4:2 — 431, 448
4:5 — 12
4:6–13 — 565
4:6–7 — 155
4:6 — 241, 243, 315n. 2
4:7 — 275
4:8–13 — 88, 305
4:8–11 — 305
4:8 — 170n. 76
4:9–12 — 190
4:9 — 244, 352
4:10–13 — 398
4:12–13 — 83
4:12 — 218n. 1
4:13 — 242
4:14–21 — 64, 470, 471, 473
4:14–16 — 522n. 73
4:14 — 11, 278, 305, 470
4:15 — 9, 216, 255n. 94, 278, 283, 448, 470
4:16–17 — 241, 252n. 49
4:16 — 228, 241, 254n. 68, 470
4:17 — 7, 255n. 94, 278, 470, 521n. 67, 522n. 73

4:20 — 432, 448, 470
4:21 — 190, 470
5–6 — 415
5:1–11:1 — 29
5:1–8 — 40n. 41, 97, 305
5:1–5 — 278, 415
5:1 — 275, 542
5:2 — 186, 190, 275
5:5 — 186, 275
5:6–8 — 187, 255n. 93
5:6 — 225n. 99, 242, 275
5:7 — 2, 447
5:8 — 32
5:9–11 — 40n. 40, 187, 304
5:9–10 — 32
5:9 — 275
5:10–11 — 608
5:11 — 11, 29, 32, 275
5:12 — 31, 242, 243
6:1–11 — 29, 305
6:1–8 — 340
6:1 — 275
6:5 — 522n. 71
6:7–8 — 398
6:7 — 522n. 71
6:7 — 275
6:8 — 275
6:9–10 — 40n. 40, 66, 275, 608
6:9 — 32, 275, 544
6:12–20 — 29, 305, 415, 419, 588, 599
6:12–13 — 398
6:12 — 242, 243, 275, 276, 448, 448
6:13 — 275, 448
6:15–18 — 276
6:16–17 — 255n. 93
6:16 — 2
6:18 — 33
6:19–20 — 32, 72n. 87
6:20 — 428n. 56, 578, 588
7 — 275, 305, 411, 414, 415, 416, 417, 420, 428n. 56, 434, 446, 447, 522n. 71, 536, 541, 542, 543, 588, 594
7:1–16 — 446, 447
7:1–5 — 537
7:1 — 31, 275, 276, 304, 448, 455n. 79, 471, 485n. 73, 543

1 Corinthians (*continued*)

7:2–7	417
7:2–6	471
7:2–5	29
7:2	276, 421, 541
7:3–5	471
7:3–4	276, 277
7:5	275, 416, 428n. 52, 534, 541
7:7–8	243
7:7	277, 420, 486n. 73, 541
7:8–40	417, 418
7:8–16	417
7:8–9	30, 417, 418, 419
7:8	31, 417, 455n. 79
7:9	276, 416, 419, 486n. 73, 534, 537, 541
7:10–16	277
7:10–11	30, 417, 418, 427nn. 44, 57, 447
7:10	29, 281, 455n. 79
7:11	277, 281, 417
7:12–16	30, 33, 278, 417, 418, 447
7:12–13	417
7:12	455n. 79
7:14	277, 419, 448
7:15	277, 281, 436, 446, 448, 455n. 78
7:17–24	30, 417, 446, 447
7:17–28	593
7:17	31, 282, 417, 446, 455n. 79
7:18–20	30
7:18–19	394, 397
7:18	446, 587
7:19	276, 434, 437, 438, 439, 440, 446, 447, 448, 587
7:20–31	41n. 49
7:20–24	586
7:20–23	387, 392, 393, 394, 446
7:20	31, 282, 417, 446, 455n. 81, 587
7:21–24	30
7:21–22	392, 393, 394, 446
7:21	281, 392, 393, 455n. 81, 587, 588, 593, 598
7:22–23	596, 598, 599
7:22	239, 392

7:23	392, 428n. 56, 446, 447, 578, 588, 599
7:24	31, 282, 417, 446, 455nn. 81, 87
7:25–40	417, 446, 447, 455n. 81
7:25–38	387, 390, 392
7:25–31	391
7:25–28	418, 428n. 61
7:25–27	417
7:25–26	417, 455n. 79
7:25	417, 418
7:26–40	417
7:26	31, 281, 448
7:27–28	391, 392, 394
7:27	30, 417, 587
7:28	30, 281, 391, 417, 418, 419
7:29–31	7, 417, 544
7:29	30, 277, 281, 416
7:30	30
7:31	30, 445
7:32–35	391, 416, 417, 448
7:32–34	30, 151, 159, 390
7:32	30, 419
7:34	30, 277
7:35–36	390
7:35	30, 31, 190, 390, 419, 447, 455n. 79
7:36–40	30, 565
7:36–38	391, 417, 418, 428n. 61, 544
7:36	277, 281, 391, 416, 419, 448
7:37	419
7:38	31, 277, 419
7:39–40	417, 418
7:40	417, 448, 455n. 79
8–14	248
8	29, 498, 503
8:1	14, 29, 256n. 97, 304, 448
8:4–13	33
8:4	279, 448
8:8	275, 398, 448
8:10	282
8:13	243
8:4–11	31, 40n. 39
8:6	9, 32
8:13	242
9	31, 306, 503

9:1–23	340	10:23–24	398
9:1–10:13	256n. 100	10:23	31, 432, 448
9:1–23	339, 565	10:26	9
9:1–18	126	10:27–28	33
9:3–7	398	10:27	33
9:4–7	242	10:28–11:1	242
9:5	411, 412	10:31–11:1	306
9:6–18	87	10:31–33	39n. 23
9:6	218n. 1	10:31	448
9:7	119, 255n. 93, 354, 448	10:32–33	31
9:8–10	255n. 93	10:33	28, 242
9:9	448	11–14	305
9:10	448	11:1	33, 127, 228, 237, 241,
9:12–15	242		242, 254n. 68, 255n. 93,
9:13	255n. 93		380n. 134
9:15–18	82, 97, 398	11:2–16	255n. 93, 426n. 37, 565
9:15	242, 448	11:3	9
9:16–18	598	11:4–11	151, 159
9:19–23	26, 28, 29, 40n. 35,	11:4–6	11
	40n. 42, 41n. 49,	11:5–16	277
	242, 599	11:5	277
9:19–27	31	11:9–11	87
9:19–20	2	11:12	448
9:19	28, 448	11:17–34	340, 565
9:20	28	11:17–32	497
9:21	1, 33, 40n. 44	11:17	11
9:22	28, 242	11:18	520n. 53
9:22b	26, 28	11:20	467
9:24–27	216, 351, 538,	11:21–22	10
	540, 599	11:22	12
9:24	216	11:23–26	279
9:25	448, 534	11:29	282
9:27	577	11:33	282
10	503	11:34	455n. 80
10:1–22	447, 549n. 22	12–14	452n. 44
10:1–13	31	12	10, 275, 305, 497
10:1	2	12:1	304
10:4–6	237	12:2–3	447
10:6	380n. 134	12:2	7
10:7	33	12:3	32
10:8	33	12:7	31
10:9–11	159	12:12–27	36
10:13	255n. 93	12:12–13	452n. 44
10:14–22	31, 448	12:13	394, 586, 593, 598
10:14	33	12:14–33	565
10:17	282	12:14–21	237
10:18	255n. 93	12:23–24	237
10:20–22	447	12:25–26	190
10:23–11:1	29, 243,	12:28	497, 507
	256n. 97, 305	12:31–13:3	242
10:23–31	451n. 32	13	151, 160, 243, 498

1 Corinthians (*continued*)

13:1–13	397, 565
13:1–7	96
13:1–3	398
13:3	190
13:6	448
13:11–12	242
13:11	74n. 108
14	275, 497
14:1	14
14:2–25	151, 160
14:8	354
14:11	242
14:14	242
14:16	32
14:18–19	398
14:18	242
14:20	41n. 49, 283
14:21	255n. 93
14:22–25	33
14:23–24	32
14:23	260, 282, 520n. 53
14:24–25	279
14:26–39	565
14:26–28	497
14:26	448
14:29	279
14:30	282, 292n. 117
14:32	117, 292n. 117
14:33	436, 448
14:33b–36	290n. 86
14:34–35	426n. 37
14:34	282
14:35	292n. 117
14:40	378n. 111, 448
15	448
15:3	279
15:8–19	244
15:8–9	500
15:10	112
15:20–22	505
15:23	506
15:24–28	9, 447
15:24	9, 472
15:27–28	117
15:30–33	190
15:30–32	244
15:31	97
15:32–34	33
15:32	255n. 93, 352, 499, 538, 541
15:33	208, 209, 339, 340, 401n. 31
15:34	11, 447
15:35–37	160
15:50	60, 66
15:56	276, 447
15:57–58	354
16:1	303
16:6	502
16:9	411
16:10–11	128, 305, 507, 522n. 73
16:10	521n. 67
16:11	502
16:13–14	448
16:13	354, 447
16:14	354
16:15–20	565
16:15–18	115, 119, 126, 305
16:15–17	473
16:15–16	110, 111, 116, 118, 507
16:15	122, 123, 127, 483n. 49, 520nn. 51–52, 60
16:16–17	260
16:16	112, 122, 127, 497
16:17–18	110, 111, 117, 118
16:17	120, 304, 599
16:18–19	507
16:18	121, 122, 127
16:19–23	115
16:19	116, 259, 260, 283, 473, 483n. 48, 483n. 49, 499, 520n. 52
16:21–34	224n. 94
16:22	447

2 Corinthians

1–9	306, 307, 312, 313, 316n. 26
1–7	179, 182
1:1	507, 521n. 67, 522n. 75
1:3–7	179, 181, 182, 340
1:3	472
1:4	184, 192n. 5
1:5	182
1:6	182, 192n. 5, 195n. 51, 350
1:7	182, 316n. 26
1:8–11	179, 181
1:8–9	182, 192n. 5, 499
1:8	194n. 41
1:9	181

1:11	507	4:10–11	184
1:12–14	97, 340, 566	4:11	353
1:12	339	4:12	184
1:15–24	340	4:14	310
1:15	179	4:15	184
1:16	502	4:16–5:5	179, 184, 195n. 54
1:17	339	4:16–18	8, 353
1:19	507, 521n. 67	4:16–17	184
1:23	179	4:16	527
1:24	339, 426n. 39, 473	5:1–5	184
2	313	5:1–4	160
2:1–11	179	5:2	173, 310
2:1–10	340	5:4	173
2:1–4	182, 306	5:5	485n. 71, 534
2:2–4	306	5:6	534
2:3	316n. 26	5:7	534
2:4	179, 182, 192n. 5, 306	5:8–10	398
2:5–11	180, 183	5:10	13, 15
2:5–7	307	5:11–21	307
2:6–11	306	5:11–13	97
2:8	307	5:11–21	566
2:12–16	179, 190	5:12	8, 97, 195n. 51
2:13	181, 507	5:13	534
2:14–17	566	5:14–21	190
2:14	354, 599	5:14–15	280
2:17	339, 340	5:15	505
3:1–6:13	126, 566	5:18–20	340
3:1–4:6	307	5:18–19	184, 185
3:1–3	86, 110	5:18	337
3:1	110, 507	5:19	337
3:2–3	85, 316n. 26	5:20–21	41n. 49
3:4–6:13	110	5:20	337
3:6	124	6–7	307
3:7–5:10	307	6:3–10	179, 185, 195n. 55, 566
3:7–18	151, 156	6:3	185
3:7	170n. 78	6:4–10	541
3:12	339, 340	6:4–5	124
3:18	41n. 49, 560, 566	6:6–7	195n. 55
4:1	184	6:6	608
4:5–12	566	6:7–10	195n. 55
4.5–6	183	6:11–13	179, 180, 340
4:5	507, 599	6:11	307
4:7–15	183	6:12	180
4:7–12	179	6:13	307
4:7–9	340	6:14–7:1	36, 426n. 37
4:7	184, 337	6:14–18	340
4:8–12	352	6:18	66
4:8–11	181	7:2–4	183, 340
4:8–9	184	7:2	307
4:9	338	7:3	182, 183
4:10–15	184	7:4–7	181

2 Corinthians (*continued*)

7:4	97, 307
7:5–7	307, 313
7:5–6	179
7:6–13	306
7:6–7	507
7:7	340, 354
7:8–12	182, 306
7:8–9	306
7:8	179, 181, 182
7:9b–11a	182
7:9–10	182
7:9	183
7:12	179, 306
7:13–15	507
7:14–16	307
7:14	97
7:16	307
8:1	309
8:2	190
8:6	507
8:9	27, 41n. 49, 256nn. 97, 99, 506
8:13–14	340, 504, 507
8:16–24	128, 566
8:16–19	507
8:17	521n. 67, 522nn. 71, 75
8:18–19	120, 521nn. 67–68
8:19–23	503
8:21	448
8:22–23	507
8:22	521n. 67
8:23	120, 426n. 39, 520n. 62, 521n. 67, 522n. 75
8:24	97
9:1–5	566
9:2–3	97
9:3	507
9:5	507
9:6	436, 448
9:7	225n. 99
9:12	504
9:14	504
10–13	77, 81, 82, 93, 94, 99n. 8, 100n. 13, 132n. 45, 133n. 65, 299, 304, 308, 309, 312, 313, 340
10–12	159
10:1–11	84
10:1	83, 84, 90, 93
10:2	83

10:3–6	84, 308, 354
10:3	119
10:4	90, 92, 93
10:5–18	566
10:5	86
10:7–8	84
10:8	12, 85, 90, 91, 92, 93, 308
10:9–10	90
10:10	83, 84, 90, 93, 151, 215
10:11	84
10:12–28	84, 85
10:12–18	85, 86
10:12	12, 82, 83, 85, 87, 90, 94, 152, 157
10:13–18	84
10:13–16	83, 92
10:13–15	85
10:13	309
10:14	91, 309
10:15–16	85
10:15	308
10:16	85
10:17–18	93
10:17	77, 85
10:18	12, 83, 85, 110
11:1–12:13	85, 166n. 45
11:1–6	86, 132
11:1	85, 86
11:2–6	413
11:2–4	411
11:2	9, 86, 308, 309, 413
11:3–4	92
11:3	91, 92
11:4	82, 86, 92, 93
11:5–11	566
11:5–6	90
11:5	83, 86, 91, 560
11:6	38n. 19, 86, 90, 159, 198, 215
11:7–15	86
11:7–11	83, 91, 97, 126
11:7–10	468
11:7	91, 218n. 1, 309, 507, 599
11:8–9	503
11:8	378n. 109
11:9–12	503
11:9	82, 92, 309, 498, 503
11:10–11	91
11:10	88, 90
11:11	92, 309

11:12–15	132n. 45
11:12	82, 83, 87, 309, 507
11:13–15	41n. 49, 92
11:13	82, 87
11:16–12:13	90
11:16–33	87, 566
11:16–21	90
11:16 –19	85
11:16–18	87
11:18	85, 91
11:19–20	40n. 38
11:20	507, 577, 599
11:21b–12:13	151, 157
11:20–21	82, 91, 92
11:20	92, 309
11:21–12:10	93, 212
11:21	85, 86, 87
11:22–33	190
11:22–23	93
11:22	88
11:23–12:11	91
11:23–33	91, 92
11:23–29	88, 95, 541
11:23	82, 86
11:28–29	507
11:29a	88
11:30–31	88
11:30	88
11:32–33	88, 400n. 23
12:1–13	89
12:1–10	566
12:1	82, 89
12:2–7	89
12:6–10	93
12:6–7	89
12:6	85, 309
12:7–10	92, 190
12:8	93
12:9–10	93
12:9	12, 86, 90, 91, 92, 93, 308, 562
12:10	92, 158, 338, 507
12:11–13	132n. 45
12:11	84, 85, 91, 560
12:12–13	83
12:12	89, 91, 127, 171n. 84, 308, 309
12:13–18	83, 91
12:13	503
12:14–18	83, 91
12:14	309

12:15	87, 91, 92, 309
12:16	82, 91, 92
12:17–18	507
12:17	309
12:19–13:10	92
12:19–13:2	91
12:19–21	566
12:19	82, 91, 92, 93, 309
12:20–21	608
12:20	308
12:21–13:2	179
12:21	190
13:1	308
13:3–4	308
13:3	83, 84
13:4	90, 92, 93, 256n. 97, 507
13:5–7	92
13:5	309
13:8	309
13:9–14	566
13:9	507
13:10	90, 91, 92, 93, 308, 309
13:11	308, 448

Galatians

1–2	300, 302, 303, 441
1:1–9	614
1:1–5	214, 299
1:1	301
1:1 –2	441
1:1–2:21	615
1:2	521n. 67
1:3–4	472
1:3	302
1:4	7, 61, 280
1:6–11	214
1:6–9	214, 299, 615
1:6–7	441
1:6	243, 301, 441, 485n. 71
1:7	614
1:8–9	253n. 62
1:9	299
1:10–6:10	214
1:10–2:21	212, 213, 214
1:10–24	614
1:10–14	566
1:10–12	212
1:10	75n. 123, 238, 239, 253n. 62, 507, 522n. 78, 597, 598
1:11–2:21	215, 442

Galatians (*continued*)

1:11–12	441, 500
1:11	454n. 68
1:12–2:14	212, 214
1:13–2:21	243
1:13–17	212
1:13–14	2, 212, 301
1:13	212, 213
1:14	213, 216, 218n. 2, 558
1:15–17	212
1:15	212, 213, 301
1:16–17	500
1:16	9, 213
1:18–2:10	212
1:18–24	212
1:18–20	212
1:18	265
1:21–24	212
1:23	213, 523n. 85
2	505
2:1–10	212, 300, 301, 441, 614
2:1	265, 500, 507, 522n. 75
2:2	216, 500
2:3	395, 444, 504, 507, 522n. 75
2:4–5	213, 239, 257n. 116
2:4	65, 239, 243, 253n. 62
2:5–9	504
2:5–8	500
2:5	212
2:6–9	398
2:7–9	212, 500
2:7	507
2:9–10	504
2:11–21	212, 239, 300, 301, 566
2:11–14	29, 212, 213, 257n. 116, 282, 441, 614
2:13	500
2:14	209, 444
2:15–4:11	615
2:15–21	212, 214, 614, 623, 624
2:16	395, 442, 506
2:17–21	443
2:19–20	238, 257n. 116, 442, 614, 622, 624
2:19–21	238, 280
2:20	280, 442, 448, 506
2:21	212
3:1–6:10	215
3:1–5	614
3–5	442

3:1–4:31	214
3:1–4:7	55, 56, 65
3:1–5	59, 60, 238, 441, 471, 615
3:1–4	441, 442, 454n. 67
3:1	216, 279, 299, 300, 301
3:2–5	300
3:2–3	64
3:2	397, 441, 485n. 71
3:3	62, 299, 300, 301
3:4	302
3:5	195n. 51
3:6–4:11	614, 615
3:6–4:7	55
3:6–9	60, 566
3:6–29	55, 60, 61
3:6	55, 523n. 85
3:7–29	60
3:7	56
3:9	523n. 85
3:10–14	60, 566
3:13–14	65, 75nn. 130, 131, 599
3:13	41n. 49, 72n. 87, 445
3:15–4:11	151
3:15–18	60
3:15	454n. 68
3:16	60, 209
3:19–22	60
3:20	523n. 85
3:21	614, 631n. 22
3:22–24	615
3:22	58, 442
3:23–4:9	160
3:23–29	60, 61
3:23–25	62, 63, 74n. 118
3:23	302
3:24–25	72n. 75, 216
3:24	58, 60
3:25	58, 239
3:26–29	566
3:26	495
3:27–28	495, 593
3:27–29	36, 55, 442
3:28	72n. 76, 75n. 123, 243, 261, 276, 280, 281, 338, 394, 402n. 59, 436, 448, 497, 502, 519n. 48, 586, 594, 598
3:29	62, 65, 72n. 76, 442
4:1–5:1	599
4:1–11	74n. 105
4:1–9	243, 470

4:1–7	55, 56, 58, 61, 62, 63, 64, 65, 73n. 88, 76n. 132
4:1–5	74n. 105, 473
4:1–3	465
4:1–2	63, 73n. 105, 470
4:1	75n. 123
4:2	58, 63, 482n. 40
4:3–7	63, 74n. 105, 75nn. 123, 131
4:3–5	41n. 49, 302
4:3–4	58, 64
4:3	58, 62, 64, 300, 615
4:4–5	27, 65, 75nn. 130–31
4:4	9, 74n. 118
4:5	42, 56, 58
4:6–7	470
4:6	9, 64, 75n. 129, 471, 485n. 71
4:7	55, 56, 65, 72, 74n. 111, 75n. 123
4:8–11	300
4:8–10	32, 300, 441
4:8–9	64, 301, 441
4:8	75n. 123, 300
4:9	75n. 123, 302
4:11–20	470
4:11	112, 300, 470
4:12–20	302, 340, 442, 614, 615
4:12	1, 228, 238, 302, 441, 448, 454n. 68, 470
4:13–18	507
4:13–15	238
4:13	5
4:14–15	301, 302
4:14	237, 238
4:15	302, 303
4:16–17	238
4:16	303
4:17	302, 303, 444
4:18	448
4:19	41n. 49, 239, 283, 303, 470, 471, 473
4:20	303, 470, 614, 615
4:21–5:1	60, 63, 616
4:21–31	158, 442, 566, 615, 616
4:22–31	243
4:22	65, 75n. 123
4:23	75n. 123, 159
4:25	75n. 123, 615
4:26	615
4:28	454n. 68
4:30	75n. 123
4:31	75n. 123, 454n. 68
5–6	434, 440, 442
5:1–6:10	214
5:1–12	442
5:1	159, 243, 441, 441, 442, 443, 596, 597, 615, 616
5:2–12	446, 615, 616
5:2–10	616
5:2–6	40n. 37, 615
5:2–4	395, 442
5:2	396, 441, 442, 614
5:3–4	395
5:3	73n. 88
5:5–6	442, 616
5:5	443
5:6	13, 14, 397, 434, 437, 439, 440, 441, 444, 445, 448, 611, 616, 617, 622
5:7–12	442, 443, 615
5:7	301, 352, 441, 443
5:8	485n. 71
5:9	225n. 99, 445
5:10	614
5:11–12	444
5:11	442
5:12	300, 395
5:13–6:10	442, 443, 615, 616
5:13–26	614, 615, 616, 617, 619, 621, 623, 624
5:13–15	566, 617
5:13	75n. 123, 243, 443, 454n. 68, 497, 597, 599, 616, 617
5:14	443, 617
5:15	302, 443, 454n. 68, 617, 621
5:16–6:10	60, 443
5:16–26	444
5:16–24	546, 617
5:16–25	617, 618
5:16	301, 444, 454n. 68, 617, 618, 619, 621
5:17–24	619
5:17	619, 623
5:18–23	619
5:18	444, 618
5:19–26	566
5:19–23	608
5:19–21	302, 444, 618, 619, 621
5:19–21	160
5:19	624
5:21	59, 66

Galatians (*continued*)

5:22–24	618, 619
5:22–23	444, 618, 619, 629n. 4
5:23	534, 618
5:24–25	444
5:24	239, 443, 534, 536, 613, 617, 618, 619, 620, 621, 622
5:25–6:10	454n. 68
5:25–26	454nn. 68, 75
5:25	378n. 111, 444, 454n. 68, 616, 617, 619, 620, 621
5:26	302, 444, 454n. 68, 617, 621
6:1–10	444, 615
6:1–5	302, 314, 621
6:1–2	340
6:1	444, 454n. 68
6:2–6	448
6:2	33, 191, 444
6:3–4	566
6:3	444
6:4–5	444
6:6	444, 507
6:7–8	444
6:7–9	59
6:7	225n. 99, 436, 448
6:8	444, 448
6:9	444
6:10	444
6:11–18	61, 214, 215, 442, 444, 615, 616
6:11–17	446
6:11–16	566
6:11–15	75n. 122
6:11	208
6:12–14	444
6:12–13	302, 614
6:13–14	97
6:14–17	239, 442
6:14–16	445
6:14–15	61
6:14	8, 280, 281, 438, 443
6:15	66, 397, 434, 437, 438, 439, 440, 441, 443, 445, 448
6:16	438, 445
6:17	279

Ephesians

1:5	42, 66, 597, 599
1:11	66
1:14	66
1:18	66
1:22	473
2:1–22	36
2:3–4	546
2:3	599
2:8–10	98
2:8–9	95
2:9	98
2:14–18	340
2:16	335
2:19	599
3:10	40n. 33
3:13	191
3:14–19	473
4:1–16	36
4:1–6	314
4:4	473
4:14	74n. 108
4:8–10	40n. 33
4:17–6:9	36
4:19–24	546
4:31	629n. 3
5:1	41n. 50
5:3–5	629n. 3
5:5	66
5:21–6:9	289n. 60, 421
5:22–6:9	473, 516n. 3
5:21	292n. 117
6:5–9	577, 599
6:9	507
6:10–17	191, 195n. 62, 363
6:21–22	521n. 67
6:21	507

Philippians

1:1	241, 360, 507, 521n. 67, 597, 598
1:2	472
1:3–5	126
1:5	310
1:7–26	358
1:7	240, 310
1:8	241, 310
1:9–11	447
1:10	397
1:12–26	119, 241
1:12–19	334
1:12–18	397
1:12	361, 401n. 27

1:13	5, 241, 360
1:14	255n. 95
1:15–18	566
1:15–17	243
1:17–18	255n. 95
1:18–21	397
1:18–26	360
1:19–26	310, 357
1:19	334
1:20–26	387, 388, 389, 390, 391
1:20–21	241, 389
1:20	12, 241, 255n. 95, 357, 390
1:21–26	194n. 41, 340, 361
1:21–24	361
1:21–23	389
1:21	390, 448
1:22	390
1:23	310, 389
1:24	389
1:25–26	97, 355
1:25	310, 361, 389
1:26	361
1:27–4:1	355, 363
1:27–2:18	355
1:27–2:4	362
1:27–30	355, 356, 358, 379n. 118, 566
1:27	311, 332, 340, 355, 358, 361, 362
1:28–30	243
1:28	240, 359
1:29–30	119
1:29	357
1:30	255n. 95, 340
2–3	168n. 59
2:1–3:21	355
2:1–11	119, 566
2:1–5	627
2:1–4	356, 359
2:1	356, 627
2:1–2	356
2:2–4	240, 356
2:2	310, 311, 340
2:4	356
2:6–11	599
2:5–11	27, 41n. 49, 498
2:6–8	506
2:5–8	310
2:5	237, 241, 254n. 75, 338
2:6–11	340
2:6–8	256n. 99
2:6–8	240
2:6–11	280, 356
2:7–8	240
2:7	290n. 84, 310, 506
2:8	241
2:9–11	240, 358
2:11	241, 472
2:12–13	430
2:12	310, 355, 356, 563
2:13	13, 195n. 51, 357
2:14	357
2:16	97, 112, 216
2:17–3:10	338
2:17–18	119, 240, 255n. 95
2:17	120, 241, 310, 357, 378n. 103
2:19–30	361
2:19–24	119, 128, 241
2:19–23	507
2:19	521n. 67
2:20	310
2:22–23	521n. 67
2:21–22	243
2:22	237, 310, 473, 522n. 73
2:23	241
2:25–30	119, 241, 310, 340, 362, 382n. 160, 484n. 65, 503
2:25–28	119, 120, 362
2:25	349, 362, 426n. 39, 484n. 65, 507, 520n. 62, 521nn. 67–68, 522n. 75, 591
2:26	121, 127, 362
2:27	362
2:28	121, 362, 522n. 75
2:28–30	521n. 67
2:29–30	111, 121, 237, 507, 522n. 73
2:29	123, 362, 380n. 132
2:30	120, 127, 241, 243, 310, 501, 521n. 68, 522n. 75
3	244
3:1–4:1	627
3:1–3	121
3:1	311, 357
3:2–11	97, 212
3:2–6	40n. 37
3:2–4	357, 358

Philippians (*continued*)

3:2–3	395
3:3–11	566
3:3–4	95, 255n. 95
3:3	559
3:4–14	310, 358
3:4–8	398
3:4–6	558
3:4	160, 243
3:5–8	395, 396
3:5–6	198, 240
3:5	2
3:6–11	358
3:6	218n. 2
3:7–10	241
3:7–8	390
3:8–14	397
3:8–11	240
3:8–10	559
3:8	254n. 75
3:9	506
3:10–11	254n. 75
3:10	534
3:11	357
3:12–16	398, 627
3:12–15	358
3:12–14	13, 184, 352
3:12	241
3:13	243, 312, 382n. 169
3:14	282, 312, 382n. 162
3:15	240, 254n. 75, 283
3:17–4:1	358
3:17	119, 228, 237, 240, 241, 243, 252n. 49, 254n. 68, 310, 358, 359, 507
3:18–19	241, 358, 542
3:18	191, 240, 340, 358, 359
3:19	359
3:20–4:1	358
3:20	358, 359, 360, 379n. 119
3:21	41n. 49, 358
4:1–3	340, 507
4:1–2	467
4:1	310, 362
4:2–9	627
4:2–8	627
4:2–4	362
4:2–3	111, 311, 356
4:2	277, 311, 627
4:3–5:11	338
4:3	311, 312, 426n. 39, 520n. 62, 521n. 67
4:4–9	448, 454n. 71
4:7–8	168n. 59
4:7	241, 362
4:8–9	382n. 169, 608
4:8	608, 627
4:9–19	507
4:9	241, 311, 363
4:10–20	126, 310, 332, 340, 468, 627
4:10–13	398
4:10	317n. 41, 332, 333, 498, 498
4:11–13	133n. 66, 241
4:11–12	541
4:11	333, 627, 630n. 5
4:12–20	338
4:12	333, 387
4:13	334, 448
4:14–18	498
4:14–16	503
4:14	334
4:15–16	82, 333
4:15	310, 333, 468
4:17	322
4:18	120, 591
4:19	241, 334
4:20	472
4:21	521n. 68
4:22	464, 599

Colossians

1:1	507
1:7–8	521n. 68
1:7	507
1:15–20	281
1:18	473
1:20–22	340, 380n. 136
1:20	335
1:21–23	36
1:22	335
1:24	191
1:28	36
2:6–8	314
2:7	281
2:8–23	73n. 88, 160
2:14–15	378n. 112
2:15	599
3:5–4:6	36
3:5–11	546

3:5–8	629n. 3
3:10	629n. 3
3:11	36, 452n. 44, 497, 593
3:15	473
3:18–4:1	281, 289n. 60, 421, 473,
516n. 3	
3:18	292n. 117
3:22–4:1	599
3:22–25	487n. 85
4:1	507
4:7–14	507
4:7–9	128
4:7–8	521n. 67
4:9–11	521n. 68
4:10	426n. 42, 521n. 67
4:12	521n. 68
4:14	521n. 68
4:15	260, 283, 467, 473, 483n. 48
4:17	507
4:18	224n. 94

1 Thessalonians

1:1	472, 507, 521n. 67
1:2	240
1:3	112
1:5–6	239
1:6–10	240
1:6–7	507
1:6	228, 238, 239
1:7–8	239
1:7	239, 380n. 134
1:8–9	253n. 63
1:9	32
1:10	9
1:14	192n. 5
2:1–12	112, 122, 127, 240, 566
2:2	34, 239, 340, 541
2:5–12	168n. 59
2:5	34, 340
2:6–9	507
2:7	239, 470, 473
2:9	112, 218n. 1, 239, 470
2:10–11	239
2:11	470, 471
2:12	244
2:13	195n. 51
2:14–16	168n. 59, 239
2:14	228, 238
2:15–16	240, 254n. 70
2:17–18	112
2:17	340

2:19–20	97, 566
3:2	426n. 39, 507, 521n. 67
3:3–5	239
3:5–6	507
3:5	112
3:6–8	340
3:8	239
3:11	472
3:12	36
4:1–12	36
4:1–8	566
4:4	537, 542
4:5	534
4:11–12	507
4:3–8	420, 421, 428n. 64
4:3–4	535
4:4	421
4:9–12	340, 452n. 46
4:9	522n. 72
4:10b–12	239, 244
4:12	239
4:13–18	340
4:16	378n. 111
5:1–3	160
5:2–4	237
5:2–3	275
5:3	340
5:7–8	353
5:7	237
5:8	195n. 62
5:11	340
5:12–22	437, 448, 566
5:12–15	340
5:12–14	507
5:12–13	122, 126, 127,
	131n. 32, 497
5:12–13a	111, 113, 116, 121, 123
5:12	112, 113, 127, 467, 473
5:13	122
5:13b–15	36
5:14	113, 239, 244
5:26–28	566
5:27	167n. 55, 520n. 52

2 Thessalonians

1:1	507
1:4–10	191
3:6	40n. 41
3:7–12	507
3:13–15	340
3:14–15	40n. 41

2 Thessalonians (*continued*)
3:14	11
3:17–18	224n. 94

1 Timothy
1:3–20	244
1:8	448
1:9–10	629
1:10	599
1:18–20	191
1:18	195n. 62
2:4–6	448
2:8–3:13	36, 421
2:8–15	516n. 3
2:11–12	292n. 117, 474
2:12	283
2:15	474
3:1–13	407
3:2–13	474
3:2–4	629n. 3
3:2	520n. 51
3:4–5	474, 599
3:5	486n. 81
3:12	474, 599
3:15	486n. 81
4:3	474
4:8	448
4:10	191
4:11–6:2	36
4:12	245
4:13–14	507
4:15	401n. 27
5:1–6:2	421
5:1–2	507
5:4	486n. 81, 507
5:8	507
5:10	520n. 51
5:14	245, 474
5:16–17	507
5:18	448
6:1–2	577, 599
6:1	245
6:2	497
6:4–5	629n. 3
6:6	448
6:9–10	546
6:10	217, 448
6:12	216
6:14	245
6:17–19	36, 507

2 Timothy
1:3–18	244
1:7	546
1:16–18	507, 520nn. 51, 61
1:16	599
1:18–20	191
2:20–3:5	36
2:20	195n. 50, 486n. 81
2:22	546
3:1–4:8	244
3:6	546
3:10–13	191
4:2	36
4:6	363
4:6–8	191, 380n. 127
4:7	216
4:10–12	507
4:19–20	507
4:19	520n. 52, 599

Titus
1:5–9	507
1:7	473, 482n. 40
1:8	520n. 51, 546
1:10–16	245
1:12	217, 546
2	421
2:1–10	516n. 3
2:9–10	599
2:1–3:11	36
2:2	546
2:3	599
2:4–10	473
2:4	216
2:5–7	546
2:7–8	245
2:9–10	577
2:12	546
3:3	546, 599
3:13–13	507

Philemon
1–25	111, 314, 586
1–3	210, 566
1–2	426n. 43
1	210, 501, 502, 520n. 62, 522n. 75
2–3	257n. 118
2	260, 469, 473, 483n. 48, 484n. 65, 520n. 51, 592

3–4	522n. 75	**1 Peter**		
3	257n. 118, 472	1:14	41n. 49	
4–7	210	2:18–3:7	473, 516n. 3	
5–6	484n. 65	2:18–25	577, 599	
5	520n. 51	3:1	292n. 117	
7	126, 210, 339, 340, 520n. 51	4:9	520n. 51	
8–22	210	4:10	482n. 40	
8–10	210			
8–9	522n. 75	**1 John**		
8	210, 244, 501, 520n. 62	3:19–22	192n. 8	
9–14	340			
9	210, 501, 502	**2 John**		
10–20	566	10	520n. 51	
10–11	394			
10	9, 210, 278, 283, 469, 473, 502, 590	**Revelation**		
		3:19	194n. 45	
11	210, 339, 592	5:6	519n. 46	
12	278, 502	7:3	519n. 46	
13–14	210, 484n. 66	11:11	519n. 46	
13	281, 484n. 65, 502, 591	13:2	519n. 46	
14	210, 244, 501, 592	13:3	519n. 46	
15	210, 592	13:4	519n. 46	
16–17	502	13:11	519n. 46	
16	210, 281, 469, 502, 592	13:12	519n. 46	
17	210, 244, 340, 485n. 68, 501, 502	13:14	519n. 46	
		13:15	519n. 46	
18–19	210, 469	13:16	519n. 46	
18	469, 484n. 65, 502, 592	16:13	519n. 46	
19–25	224n. 94	20:10	519n. 46	
19–20	340			
19	210, 339, 469, 485n. 68, 501			
20	339, 501, 522n. 75		**APOCRYPHA**	
21–22	210			
21	501, 592	**2 Maccabees**		
22–25	257n. 118	4:7–15	344	
22	126, 469, 473, 483n. 51, 501			
		4 Maccabees		
23–25	210, 566	2:6	532	
23	426nn. 39, 42, 502, 521n. 68			
		Sirach		
24	520n. 62, 521n. 67	1:11	78	
25	257n. 118	9:16	78	
		10:19	556	
		10:22	78	
Hebrews		10:24	556	
1:1–2	40n. 33	17:9	78	
12:1–2	377n. 97	22:20	336	
12:10–11	194n. 45	22:22	336	
		39:8	78	
James		44:1–13	557	
2:1–5	497	44:1–3	557	

Sirach (*continued*)
44:7   557
44:10–13   557
44:16   557
44:19   557
45:1–2   557
45:4   557
45:16   557
50:20   78

Wisdom of Solomon
8:7   378n. 110
9:7   65

PSEUDEPIGRAPHA

2 Baruch
48:22–24   169n. 64

4 Ezra
7:98   77

Jubilees
1:24–25   65
25:1   542

PHILO

On Agriculture (**Agr.**)
10   539
34   297
110–121   196n. 65

Allegorical Interpretation (**Leg.**)
2.6   539
3.104–106   194n. 48
3.111   192n. 4
3.129   539

On the Change of Names (**Mut.**)
82.1   196n. 65
241   632n. 36

On the Cheribim (**Cher.**)
48   194n. 48
77–78   190

On the Confusion of Tongues (**Conf.**)
69   194n. 48
134–41   39n. 28

171   183
180–182   194n. 45

On the Contemplative Life
(**Contempl.**)
6   288n. 49
11–13   288n. 49
18–19   288n. 49
24–39   273
40–63   273
64–89   273
65   288n. 49
70–71   402n. 51
90   288n. 49

On the Creation of
the World (**Opif.**)
117   539
170–172   279

On the Decalogue (**Decal.**)
142   532
151–53   532
173–74   533

On Dreams (**Somn.**)
1.232   41n. 49
1.147, 232–233   39n. 28
1.91   194n. 45
2.108   336

On the Embassy to
Gaius (**Legat.**)
77–110   143

That Every Good Person Is Free
(**Prob.**)
17–19   392
26–27   196n. 65
47   402n. 42
79   272, 402n. 55
110–112   196n. 65

That God Is
Unchangeable (**Deus.**)
42.91–93   194n. 48

Who Is the Heir?
(**Her.**)
19   315n. 6

Hypothetica (Hypoth.)
11.4	272

On the Life of Abraham (Abr.)
48–49	196n. 66
134–35	545

On the Life of Joseph (Ios.)
32–34	28
73	180
75–79	28
144–146	194nn. 45, 48

On the Life of Moses (Mos.)
2.7	399n. 4

On the Posterity of Cain (Post.)
133	399n. 3

On the Preliminary Studies (Prelim. Studies)
15, 74, 142, 148	269
49, 105, 133	269
65	269
70	254n. 74
79–107	269
133	269

On Rewards and Punishments (Praem.)
137–138	402n. 52

On the Sacrifices of Abel and Cain (Sacr.)
15	532

On the Special Laws (Spec.)
113	533
1.69–70	343n. 38
1.70	321
2.162–63	532
2.61–62	531
2.69	402n. 50
4.55	532
4.92–100	533
4.92	539
4.95	532

On Sobriety (Sobr.)
41.68	194n. 48

On the Virtues (Virt.)
35	343n. 38
66	254n. 74
100	532
152	325

That the Worse Attacks the Better (Det.)
34	165n. 39

JOSEPHUS

Against Apion (C. Ap.)
2.168–71	534
2.193	534
2.234	534
2.282	534

Jewish Antiquities (A. J.)
6.206	341n. 5
6.225	341n. 5
6.228	330, 341n. 5
6.236	341n. 5
6.239	341n. 5
6.275	330
6.276	341n. 5
7.111	341n. 5
10.142	40n. 34
13.380	280
15.5	368
15.93	530
15.259–260	427n. 44
15.267–79	266
18	534
18.21	402n. 51

The Life (Vita)
64–65	266
420	280

Jewish War (B. J.)
2.120–21	534
5.449–50	280

RABBINIC LITERATURE

Mishnah
Abot 1:17	169n. 64

NONCANONICAL EARLY CHRISTIAN LITERATURE

Barnabas
| 10.5 | 33, 40n. 36 |
| 19.5–7 | 516n. 3 |

Basil
Ep.
44.1	177
45	193n. 27
156	193n. 27
204	193n. 27
207	193n. 27
212	193n. 27
223	193n. 27
224	193n. 27
270	193n. 27

1 Clement
| 5 | 522n. 81 |
| 21.6–9 | 516n. 3 |

Clement of Alexandria
Christ the Educator (Paed.)
1.9.87.2	180
1.9.75.1	180
1.9.77.1	180
66.1	37n. 8
Salvation of the Rich (Quis. div.)
| 39 | 174 |
Miscellanies (Strom.)
2.12.55	192n. 8
4.22.143	174
7.9	39n. 30

Didache
| 9.4 | 282 |

Eusebius
Ecclesiastical History
| 5.16.5 | 520n. 56 |

Gregory of Nazianzus
Epistles
| 7.16 | 193n. 27 |
| 40:1–4 | 177 |

Gregory of Nyssa
Homily
| IV on Eccl. 2:7 | 272 |

Ignatius
Letter to the Magnesians
| 6–8 | 520n. 55 |
Letter to the Philippians
| 7–8 | 520n. 55 |

Justin
1 Apology
| 67 | 282 |

Polycarp
Phil.
| 4.2–6.3 | 516n. 3 |

CLASSICAL LITERATURE

Achilles Tatius
The Adventures of Leucippe and Cleitophon
| 7.13 | 589 |
| 8.3.1 | 227n. 152 |

Ad Herennium
4.13.18	232
4.13.19	453nn. 51, 52
4.14.20	453n. 53
4.15.21	452n. 48
4.17.24–25	451n. 23
4.17.24	451n. 27
4.19.27	453n. 50
4.20.27	452n. 49
4.24.54–4.43.56	433
4.27.38	453n. 54
4.42.54–4.44.58	433
4.42.54	433
4.43.56	232
4.44–4.45	165n.36
4.45.59–48.61	232
4.46	165n. 36
4.49.62	232
4.53.66	233
4.57	165n. 36
4.59	165n. 36

Aeschylus
Eumenides
| 296 | 381n. 146 |

Anaximenes
Rhetorica ad Alexandrum
| 1326b.3–7 | 164n. 12 |

1422a.23–27	229
1425b.37–1426a.24	164n. 11
1429a.21	228
1429a.29–31	229
1430a.7–9	229
1430b.3–7	451n. 27
1430b.3–4	451n. 26
1430b.10–11	451n. 23
1431a.26–27	229
1439a.1–5	229
1439a.13–17	229

Antisthenes
Fragments

14.5–6	193n. 15
15.1–3, 9	174
15.5, 9	193n. 15

Appian
Civil Wars

1.15.63	379n. 122
2.73	368
4.90	368
4.117	368
4.119	368

Punic Wars

8.19	368
116	368

Gallic History

1.2	579

Apthonius
Progymnasmata

1	223n. 62
2	223nn. 69–71
8	225n. 116, 226nn. 121, 124–25
11	223nn. 74, 76, 224n. 78
139	252n. 41

Apuleius
The Golden Ass

9.12	603

Aristides Rhetor
Orations

3.668	185

Aristotle
Eudemian Ethics

7.4.1–2	328

7.6.14–15	173
7.9.1	182
1239b10–15	38n. 14
1245b20–26	38n. 14

History of Animals

9.1 608a32–608b18	268

Magna Moralia

2.3.3	38n. 12
1213b3–18	38n. 14

Nichomachean Ethics

1.8.9, 1098b31–33	630n. 10
1.13.15–18, 1102b13–1103a16	31n. 13
1.13.17, 1102b26–28	632n. 32
1.13.19, 1103a3–7	611
1.13–2	611
2.5	611
2.5.3, 1106a1–2	611
2.5.4, 1106a4–6	611
5.1–2	630n. 9
5.1130a9	610
6.13.6, 1145a1–2	631n. 12
7.7.1150b	530
7.3, 1146b8–1147b19	631n. 13
8.2.4	341n. 19
8.3.6–7	194n. 42
8.3.6	326
8.5.1	188
8.6.7	187
8.9.1	182
8.11	576
8.12.1	182, 326
9.1.1	328
9.4.1	178
9.10.2	178
9.12.1	182
1152a17–24	38n. 14
1158a10–14	38n. 14
1170b23–1171a16	38n. 14
1172a2–14	38n. 14
1172a8–14	38n. 13

Politics

1.1–7	576
1.4	594
1.1253b	393
1.1253b 6–7	271
1.1260a 31	292n. 117

Problems

916.26–36	230

Rhetoric

1.2.1–7	37n. 4
1.2.19	229

Aristotle, *Rhetoric* (continued)
1.7.26–28	158
1.9.38	163n. 6, 164n. 13
2.4.26	338
2.13.4	324
2.20	252n. 50
2.20.4	229
2.21.2–16	451n. 15
2.21.2	451n. 16
2.21.3–7	451n. 27
2.21.5	451n. 26
2.21.11	451n. 13
2.21.13–14	325, 433, 451n. 28
2.21.14	451n. 29, 452nn. 36, 37
2.21.113	433
3.12.6	139
1378b23–35	572n. 11

Topics
1.5.102b15	164n. 14
3.4.119a1–11	164n. 15

Arrian
Campaigns of Alexander
2.83	368
5.25	368
7.9	368

Athenaeus
Deipnosophistae
4.159A	163n. 9
5.193D	39n. 29
6.236C–E	321
6.267	594
10.413–14	371n. 28
13.610D	222n. 54
15.694D–E	341n. 8
15.695F	341n. 7
265D–266E	590

Augustus
Res Gestae
13–21	572n. 15
28.1	372n. 47
28.2	372n. 46
49	372n. 47

Bion
Lament for Adonis
35	190

Celsus
On Medicine
1.1.4	266
2.1	266

Chariton
Chaereas and Callirhoe
1.2.2	227n. 145
1.5.2	321
4.4	182

Cicero
To Atticus
1.12.2	518n. 20
11.2	591
11.3	591
12.44.2	464
15.14.3	517n. 12

Brutus
32–35, 138–150	165n. 27
124	166n. 42
138	165n. 38
145	165n. 38
229	143
294	165n. 38

De domo
34–38	71n. 56

De Finibus
3.19.60–61	389
3.21.69	399n. 8
3.27.29	399n. 3
3.58	399n. 12
5.7.18–20	400n. 20

Pro Flacco
37	167n. 55

Letters to Friends
2.4.1	167n. 55
4.13.1	167n. 55
5.5.1	167n. 55
12.2	104
12.2.3	106
12.3	118
13.6	105
13.22	105
13.29	109
13.29.5	109
13.49	104, 114

On Friendship
4.15	321
7.23	338

8.26	338	*De optimo genere oratorum*	
9.3	591	21	165n. 37
16.59–60	325	*Partitiones oratoriae*	
19.69	329	27.96	232
22	178	40	233
23	178	49	142
23.59	196n. 63	55	233
24	178	57	165n. 35
25.93–94	339	66	142
46–48	178	95	142
48.64	182	98	143
50	194n. 42	*Philippic Orations*	
61	178	8.32	581
79, 85	178	*In Pisonem*	
88–100	315n. 6	6	482n. 38
88–89	185	*Epistulae ad Quintum Fratrem*	
90	176	1.2.12–13	182
De Inventione rhetorica		1.2.14	590
1.15	165n. 34	*De Republica*	
1.17	137	2.6.6	251n. 32
1.30.49	232	1.1.4	173
1.51–56	252n. 50	*Pro Sestio*	
1.82	141	9	519n. 41
1.99	141	*Pro Sexto Roscio Amerino*	
1.104	141	19	518n. 20
2.114	164n. 20	*Topica*	
2.72	141	10.41–45	233
2.75	141	18.68–71	141
Pro Lege manilia		18.84–85	141
14.41	530	*Tusculan Disputations*	
De Officiis		1.90	173
1.11.35	519n. 40	2.30–33	190
1.17.54	479n. 7	2.42–50	190
1.38.137	180	2.63	196n. 66
l.121	71n. 71	3.58–61	190
2.27	519n. 39	3.83	173
3.10.42	371n. 30	4	539
De Oratore		4.14	173
1.20	232	4.23–24	195n. 59
1.177	516n. 9, 517n. 12	4.66–67	173
1.31.138	37n. 3	*Verrine Orations*	
22.74	270	2.1.153	71n. 65
2.2.88	250n. 30		
2.13–46	232	**Corpus Inscriptionum**	
2.226	251n. 37	**Latinarum**	
2.341	139	3.6126	518n. 31
3.27.104–105	250n. 27	4.593	518n. 24
3.33	517n. 12	4.822	518n. 24
3.52.201–3.54.208		4.933	518n. 24
3.53.205	165n. 38, 233	4.1011	518n. 24

Corpus Inscriptionum
Latinarum (*continued*)

4.1016	518n. 24
6.1390	518n. 23
12.583.10	516n. 8

Demetrius
Style

223	252n. 44
224	252n. 45
233	168n. 56

Demosthenes
Epistles

2.1, 3, 8, 12	177
2.13, 21–22	177
2.25	177
3.44	177

Orations

23.122	325
27	49
27.4	49, 70n. 41
32.20	49
32.23	49
32.28	49
32.23	49
43	69n. 14
43.13–14	70n. 36
44.49	46
46.14	44, 46

Digest

1.7	71n. 56
7.8.2§§1, 3	518n. 27
9.3.5§1	518n. 27
21.1.17.4–5	522n. 76
21.1.43.1	522n. 76
21.1.17.12	522n. 76

Dio Cassius
Roman History

38.36–46	368
41.27	368
48.44.3	274
50.16–24	368
50.24–30	368
55.2.4	274
55.8.2	274
57.12.5	274
62.9–11	368
67.14	259

Dio Chrysostom
To Diodorus

4	185

Homer

4 in 2 Cor 4	194n. 37

Isthmian Discourse

8	183
9.7–9	175

Kingship

3.100–103	182

Orations

4.10	343n. 38
4.42	321
15.2	595
15.29	595
18.8	222n. 53
31.110	371n. 29
32.5, 7, 11	295
32.39	159
33.9	315n. 6
34.20	379n. 123
36.30	379n. 120
38.11	332, 335
38.15, 45–47	332
38.22	332, 343nn. 32, 38
38.46	343n. 38
40.16	355
40.28	343n. 38
55.4–5	238
57	78
66.5	371n. 29
73	38n. 22
74	38n. 22
77/78.38	315n. 6

To the Nicomedians

11.41.47–48	187

To the People of Alexandria

5.7.11	175
8	175
15	195n. 51
24	175
32.11	175
33	180

First Tarsic Discourse

15	175

Diodorus Siculus

5.38	582
13.15	368
13.98	368

| 16.54.4 | 225n. 96 |
| 18.5 | 368 |

Diogenes Laertius

1.87	324
6.89	377n. 93
7.94	399n. 11
7:98–99	399n. 11, 403n. 60
7.100–101	399n. 3
7.101–102	399n. 2
7.102	403n. 60
7.103	385
7:105–107	399n. 9
7.106	400n. 20
7.107	403n. 60
7.111	180
7.111.118	172
7.122	402n. 49
7.125	399n. 4
7.93	399n. 6
7.95–99	399n. 7
8.23	342n. 17
10.118	266
10.120	178

Dion of Prusa

| Or. 3.55 | 494 |

Dionysius of Halicarnassus

De Compositione Verborum

| 25 | 219n. 13 |

On Epideictic Speeches

258	149
259	149
260	149
266	150
275	150
289	149

Epistula ad Pompeium Geminum

| 6 | 250 |

Fabius

| 9.9 | 368 |

Roman Antiquities

2.9	516n. 8
2.9.2	490, 516n. 9
2.9.3	518n. 18
2.10	517n. 11
2.10.1	517nn. 12–13
2.10.4	491, 516n. 9, 517nn. 11, 15, 518n. 19
2.11.1	519n. 40

2.45.3	335
2.45.4	335
2.46.1	335
2.59.7.4	379n. 123
3.5.4	336
3.7.3	336
3.7.5	336
3.8.3, 5	336
3.8.4	337
3.9.2, 3	337, 377
3.9.3	336
4.20.4.2	379n. 123
4.23.6	518n. 19
5.30.1–5.31.4	343n. 34
5.30.2	342n. 17
5.34.4	343n. 32
5.49.2	335
6.6	368
8.15.1.8	379n. 123
8.34.2	342n. 17
9.41.5	517n. 16
10.18.2	373n. 54
11.9.1	185
11.36	518n. 19
11.43	373n. 54
13.5.1	517n. 11

Dionysius Thrax

Ars. gram.

1	221n. 40
2–4	222n. 50
6–10	221n. 38
11–22	221n. 39
12	221n. 48

Doxaptres

Hom. In Aphth.

2.125, 15–22	223n. 64
2.138, 16–17	223n. 66
2.497, 12–24	224n. 76

Epictetus

Discourses

1.1.12, 22	190
1.2	38n. 21
1.2.25–29, 37	371n. 31
1.4	382n. 155, 401n. 27
1.4.13	371n. 31
1.6.29	190
1.9.16	376n. 84
1.11.11	403n. 63

Epictetus, *Discourses* (*continued*)

1.12.27	194n. 41
1.14.13–17	376n. 84
1.14.15	373n. 52
1.18.21–23	188
1.19	38n. 21
1.20.11	403n. 63
1.24.1–2	196n. 65, 371n. 31
1.28.13	401n. 29
2.9	83n. 21
2.17.29–33	371n. 31
2.27	222n. 57
2.6.16–17	190
2.12.17–25	174
2.9.15	11
2.10.15	403n. 63
2.10.19	403n. 63
2.19.7	221n. 47
2.22.6–7	529
2.22.35	192n. 8
3.1.1, 34	222n. 57
3.1.10–11	175
3.13	39n. 23
3.16	38nn. 18–19, 39n, 29
3.19	38n. 21
3.21	38n. 21
3.22	40n. 38
3.22.37	401n. 29
3.22.43	632n. 36
3.22.45–50	238
3.22.69	391
3.22.94, 97–98	183
3.22.95	170n. 76
3.23.30, 37	175
3.24	38n. 21
3.24.95–99	376n. 84
3.24.95	356
3.25.1–6	196n. 65
3.25.10	403n. 63
3.26.25	401n. 29, 403n. 63
3.26.29	376n. 84
4.1.33–37	272
4.1.76–79	271
4.1.120	403n. 63
4.1.133	400n. 19
4.1.167	400n. 23
4.2	38nn. 18, 20, 39n. 29
4.4.30–32	196n. 65
4.4.32	403n. 63
4.8	38n. 21
4.9.10	403n. 63
4.12.18	403n. 63
4.13	38n. 22
24.24–26	222n. 57

Enchiridion

11	391
16.1	178
19.2	188
34	192n. 8, 196n. 66

Fragments

9	172

Euripides

Hippolytus

1.87	324
252–257	341n. 13

Ion

8	227n. 151

Iphigeneia at Aulis

1375	270
1379–80	280
1379, 1395–1398	270
1395–1401	280
1503, 1533, 1555, 1559–1560	270

Medea

1077–80	525

Orestes

1155–1158	327

Eustathius

1574.18	341n. 8

Sextus Julius Frontinus

Strategemata

4.1.4	373n. 53

Fronto

Ad Amicos

1.1.1	130n. 10
1.1	103
1.3	112
1.4	109, 114, 121
1.5	103, 104

Ad M. Ceas.

5.59	182

Ad Ver. Imp.

2.7.6	106

Gaius

1.190	71n. 66
1.99–107	71n. 56
1.102	54

1.103	54
1.97	53
2.136	53

Gellius
Noctes Atticae

5.13.2	516n. 9
5.13.4	516n. 8
5.13.5	71n. 65
5.13.6	517n. 12
5.19.1–14	71n. 56
5.19.9	53
5.19.10	54
13.20.8	517n. 15
20.1.40	516nn. 8, 9, 517n. 11

Gnomologium Vaticanum

116.487	183
273	182

Greek Anthology

7.10, 142, 241, 268, 292, 328, 393, 468, 476, 481, 547, 549, 599, 633	190
8.3	190

Hermogenes
Progymnasmata

2	147
7	225nn. 114, 116, 226nn. 122, 127
9	223nn. 72, 75, 224n. 77, 225n. 108

Hermogenianus
Digesta

19.1.49 pr.	519n. 35

Herodes Atticus
On Government

6	355

Herodianus

2.10	368
3.6	368
8.3	368

Herodotus

2.91	370n. 17
6.127	370n. 16

Homer
Iliad

1.1	203
1.260–68	78
1.273–74	78
2.23.89–90	329
2.356	553
2.362	379n. 124
2.416	203
4.360–361	321
6.206–10	552
9.648	553
16.21–45	321
22.59	203
22.262–265	321
22.483–499	516n. 2

Odyssey

1.234	516n. 2
6.180–185	321
15.195–198	321

Horace
Epistles

1.7.37	518n. 23
2.1.104	517n. 12

Satires

1.4.103–29	251n. 31
2.2.23	381n. 139
2.8.7	481n. 33
2.8.18–24	481n. 33

Iamblichus
Vit. Pyth.

40	342n. 17
237–239	339

Isaeus

1	69n. 14
1.41	48
2	69n. 14
2.1	45
2.10	50
2.14	48
2.36	72n. 78
2.41–43	50
2.46	45
3	69n. 14
3.59	45
3.60–61	47
4	69n. 14
5	69n. 15

Isaeus (*continued*)

6	69n. 14
6.5	47
6.28	45
6.63	47
7	69n. 14, 70n. 33
7.14–16	48
7.16	47
8.34	69n. 24
9	69n. 14
9.7–8	70n. 38
10	69n. 14
10.10	45
10.17	51, 57

Isocrates
Antidosis

84	231

Concerning Peace

72	37n. 8

Ad Demonicum

1.38	180

Epistles

9.12	185
15.221	525

Evagoras

76	231

Ad Nicoclem

53	192n. 7

Panegyricus

4.130	183
8.72	183

Julian
Ep.

68	193n. 27

Orations

5.171B–C	39n. 29
6.201A–C	315n. 6
8.240A–B	182
8.241C	182

Justin
Dialogue with Trypho

121.2	379n. 122

Justinian
Digest

1.5.4.1	576

Inst.

1.3.2	576

Juvenal
Satires

1.95–102	481n. 27
1.95	518n. 22
3.127–130	481n. 27
13.2 –3	174
13.192–198	192n. 7

Libanius
Progymnasmata

3, Chreia Elaboration 1	327

Livius

5.32.8	517n. 11
34.4.9	517n. 11
38.60.9	517n. 11

Livy

AUC Proem 10	235
5.32.8	517n. 16
5.51.8	250n. 21
26.32.8	519n. 39
37.45.2	519n. 40
38.51.6	518n. 22
40.46.12	337
41.10	250n. 21
45.40.6	250n. 21

Longinus
On the Sublime

33–36	165n. 28

Lucian
Alexander the False Prophet (Alex.)

47	193n. 22

Demonax

6	193n. 26
7	180
55	180

The Downward Journey/ The Tyrant (Cat.)

27	224n. 76

The Fisherman (Pisc.)

20	175, 193n. 16

The Hall (De domo)
4 270
21 270
Hermotimus
24 594
51 185
51 175
Icaromenippus
30 183
The Mistaken Critic (Pseudol.)
3 .... 180, 183
Nigrinus
4.35 176
Parliament of the Gods
(Deor. conc.)
2 183
The Passing of Peregrinus
(Peregr.)
18 174
32 .... 193n. 16
Philosophies for Sale
(Vit. auct.)
7 .... 193n. 26
The Runaways (Fug.)
12 180
18 .... 193n. 26
Salaried Posts in Great Houses
(Merc. Cond.)
12.23 .... 74n. 112
42 .... 192n. 7
Saturnalia
13 273
Slander (Cal.)
12 .... 377n. 95
Symposium
5 .... 222n. 55
6, 26 .... 222n. 55
11 .... 222n. 55
13–14 273
Toxaris
6–7 182
7.9 178
20.36–37 178
46 178
Zeus Rants (Jupp. trag.)
23 180

Lysias
12.40 .... 382n. 168

32.8 49
32.16 49

Macrobius
Saturnalia
1.7.33 .... 518n. 28
Marcus Aurelius
7.9 .... 291n. 102
8.53 .... 192n. 8
9.32 180
11.6.2 183
12.16 .... 192n. 8

Martial
1.55.5–6 .... 518n. 22
1.59 .... 518n. 22
1.108 .... 518n. 22
2.6.1–4 .... 481n. 35
2.18 .... 518n. 22
2.74 .... 518n. 22
3.36 .... 518n. 22
3.38.11 .... 518n. 22
3.60 .... 481n. 34
4.8.1 .... 481n. 27
4.40.1 .... 518n. 22
5.24 .... 371n. 35
6.88 .... 518n. 22
7.32 .... 372n. 39
7.82 .... 372n. 39
9.100.2 .... 518nn. 22, 26
12.68.1–2 .... 518n. 22
14.45–48 .... 372n 39
14.163 .... 371n. 39

Maximus of Tyre
Diss.
1.4 .... 371n. 32
1.5–18.3 29
Or.
1.3 .... 376n. 88
5.3 .... 376n. 87
14 .... 315n. 6
14.3 178
14.5 178

Menander
1.337.31–32 147
2.372.20 .... 164n. 22
2.376.31 .... 164n. 23

Menander (*continued*)

2.377.9	164n. 23
2.380.9	147
2.380.25	148
2.381.5	148
2.381.29–32	148
2.386.10–22	148
2.386.19	163n. 8
2.383.13	148
2.402.21	148
2.404.2	149
2.412.16	149
2.416–17	149
2.421.2–10	166n. 48
2.425.8	166n. 48
2.427.1	166n. 48
575	327
813K	196n. 63

Musonius

Dis.

13A	486n. 77

Frg.

1.32.24–26	401n. 32
3.42.10	401n. 31
8.66.11	401n. 31
9.74.2	403n. 63
10.78.16	401n. 31
13A	267
14.92.31	401n. 31
15.96.19	403n. 63
16.104.33	401n. 31
18B.118.5–7	401n. 32

Nicolaus

Progymnasmata

10	225n. 102

Onasander

The General (Strategicus)

1.1	348
1.5	348
1.6	348
1.10	348
1.13	348
1.14	348
4.1	380n. 131
4.3–6	349
5	380n. 128
24	379n. 124
33.1	374n. 68

36.2	349, 374n. 62
36.23	349, 374n. 62

Paulus

Dig.

38.1.37 pr.	516n. 5
49.15.7§1	519n. 39

Pausanias

Description of Greece

6.13.1–4	552
8.48.2–3	370

Peri epideiktikon

2.9	190

Philodemus

On Frank Criticism (Lib.)

Columns

Ib	183
VIII	297
VIIIb	294, 296, 297
Xb	295
XVa	176
XVIb	176, 295
XVIIb	294, 295
XIXb	294, 303
XXIa	298
XXIIb	176
XXIIIa	295
XXIIIb	295, 298
XXIVa	194n. 38, 298

Fragments

1	295
2	295
7	295, 308
12	176, 295
13	176
14	38n. 22, 317n. 31
16	316n. 20
31	176, 194n. 38
32	295
36	298
37–38	183
37	315n. 8
38	295
39–42	38n. 22
47–49	38n. 22
53–55	38n. 22
58	296

60	295
61–62	176
62	294
70	295
71	297, 304
78	315n. 8
79	315n. 8
82	194n. 38
83	297
84	295

Rhetoric

2.25	39n. 29

Philostratus

Vit. Apoll.

4.22	372n. 42
4.25	252n. 44

Vit. soph.

531, 532–33	224n. 92
542–43	224n. 90
562–563	182
588	220n. 17
616	224n. 92

Plato

Apology

28.d5–29a.1	351
40D–E	401n. 29

Gorgias

472D–479D	192n. 7
473A	269

Ion

540D	373n. 60

Laws

658A	370n. 17

Phaedo

62C	401n. 25

Republic

1.351–352D	269
2.371C	116
2.380D	40n. 33
4.434D–444A	610
4.443C–E	610
9	538
9.588C–591B	526
606E	231
5462B	382n. 160

Symposium

178E	379n. 124
179B–180B	193n. 29
193B	335

Plautus

Menaechmi

574	517n. 16

Pliny the Elder

Natural History

7.12.56	580
7.61	517n. 15
33.153	268
34.17	518n. 23

Pliny the Younger

Epistles

2.13	107
2.13.4	107, 120
2.13.5	107
3.2.5	121
4.1	519n. 41
5.8.4–5	251n. 31
6.8	518n. 30
6.11	232
8.23	232
8.14	251n. 31
8.14.4–6	232
8.32.2	251n. 31
9.21	590
9.24	590
10.2.1	108
10.4	107
10.4.6	105
10.12	108
10.12.2	108
10.87	108
10.87.3	105, 108
10.112–13	43

Panegyricus

2.21	519n. 45

Plutarch

Aem.

1.1–3	251n. 35

An. corp.

500D	194n. 48

An vit.

498D	173

Advice to Bride and Groom

140B	276
144B	268

Amatorius

750D–771C	486n. 79

Plutarch (*continued*)

Amic. mult.

93E	321
95A	188
95F–96D	182
96A	178
96B	178
96C–D	178
96D	182
96E–F	194n. 42, 321
97A	194n. 42

Ant.

60	530

Caes.

15.3	579

Cat. Maj.

3.4	232
24	517n. 15

Cohib. ira

464C–D	183

[*Cons. Apoll.*]

102A	196n. 68
104C–106C, 112D	190
113A	190

De laude

539E–F	92
540A–B	90
540C	90, 91
541A–C	92
541C–F	91
541F–542A	91
542B–C	93
542D–F	92
542E–543A	93
543A–F	93
543F–544B	93
544C	93
544F–545C	90
545A	90
545D–546A	91

Fac.

921–22	377n. 93

How to Study Poetry

14E–37B	268
16A, D	268
17–22,35	269
36A, 36E	269

How to Tell a Flatterer
from a Friend

49F	182
51C	295
51E	194n. 42
52A	298
52B	37n. 7, 298
52B–53A	83–84
55B–E	298
55B	295
56A	303
58F	316n. 9
59C	296, 303
59D	294, 296
59F	317n. 32
61D	294, 298
61E	298
63B	295
64C	295, 304
66A	294
66B	295
66E–67A	295
66F–67A	300, 341n. 6
67A	321n. 6
67B	317n. 41
67E	316n. 15
68C–D	295
68C	297, 303
69A–C	295
69A	175
69E–F	297, 308
69E	295
70D	318n. 42
70F–71C	194n. 40
71A	296
71D	295
71E	297
71F	297
72A	298
72C	303, 312n. 13
72D	298, 312
73A	298, 300, 304
73B	298
73D	294
74A	300
74D	294
74E	309

Lib. Aegr.

1,7	172

[*Lib. ed.*]

13D–E	181

Mar.

5	518n. 19

Mor.

1A–48D	268

243	165n. 30
7.539–47	256n.96
8.14	43
345C–351B	139
446F	529
541–543	170n. 75
562F	57
750C	139
750D	267
751B	139, 267
751C	267
757C–758C	139
760D	139
769A–D	267
834B	72n. 82
843	57
955D–958E	138
959A–985C	138
993A–999B	275
1131B–1147A	268
On Moral Virtue	
3.441B–C	631n. 17
On Praising Oneself	
Inoffensively	
539D	79
539E–F	80
540A–C	79
541A–C	80
541C–542A	80
544D–545C	80
545A	80
545D–546A	80
542B–C	80
542E–543A	80
543A–F	80
544A–C	81
On the Fortune of Alexander	
326D–345B	138
Pel.	
3	329
Pericles	
2.3–4	232
Pyrrh.	
16.7–8	379n. 124
Rec. rat. aud.	
46D	176
47A	176
Rom.	
13	516n. 7, 517n. 11
Sera	
549F–550A	194n. 45

550E–F	183, 194n. 45
551C–E	183
551C	183
554A–B	173
554E–F	173
564B–C	180
566A	173
566E	173
Stoic. rep.	
1046E	399n. 4
Superst.	
168C	180
Table Talk	
615D–619A	273
Tranq. an.	
476E–477B	173
Virt. mor.	
452D	175
Virt. prof.	
82C	176
[*Vit. X orat.*]	
842D	183
Polyaenus	
Strategemata	
2.10.2	376n. 76
3.11.1	374n. 66
8.23.15	382n. 158
8.23.22	382n. 158
Polybius	
1.27	368
2.13.1	382n. 156
2.37.10	382n. 156
3.44	368
3.63–64	368
3.108	368
3.111	368
4.52.6	343n. 32
6.53–55	232
8.21	270
10.21	250n. 20
11.28, 31	368
15.10–111	368
20.10	368
21.16.19	343n. 32
38.4.2–4	185
Proculus	
Dig.	
49.15.7§1	517n. 11

Propertius
  3.11.5–8   235

Pseudo-Aristotle
Mund.
  6 379b 14–15   291n. 102

Pseudo-Crates
Epistle
  35   190

Pseudo-Demetrius
Epistolary Types
  30, 3–4 and 20   37n. 5
Form. Ep.
  6   180

Pseudo-Diogenes
Epistles
  5   196n. 65, 196n. 65
  12   196n. 66, 196n. 66
  29.1, 4   183
  29.2–3   183
  29.14   183
  31   196n. 65
  33   188

Pseudo-Dionysius
  285.5–10   370n. 26
  286.5–9   371n. 27

Pseudo-Heraclitus
Epistles
  4.3   196n. 66
  5.3   193n. 26
  7.2–10   193n. 26
  7.2   183
  7.4   183
  9.3   183
  9.8   183

Pseudo-Hippocrates
Epistles
  17.40   183, 193n. 19
  17.45   175
  17.19–20, 34   175
  17.20–21   175

Pseudo-Libanius
Charact. Ep.
  19   177
  43   193n. 25

  66   177
  90   176

Pseudo-Ocellus Lucanus
  De univ. nat 48   402n. 39

Pseudo-Socrates
Epistles
  1.7   185
  12   183
  24   175

Quintilian
Inst. Or.
  1.1.24–29   219n. 13
  1.1.35   220n. 32
  1.2.4–5   251n. 31
  1.8.1–12   222n. 52
  2.1–8   234
  2.1.35–36   233
  2.2.8   234
  2.4.1–21   163n. 1
  2.4.20   144
  2.13.13   270
  3.7.10–18   129n. 1
  3.8.33–34   137
  3.8.49   166n. 45
  4.1.66–69   166n. 45
  4.2.99   145
  4.2.106   166n. 45
  5.10m73   252n. 50
  5.10.91   145
  5.10.120   163n. 5
  5.11   233
  5.11.1–2   250n. 28
  5.11.7   145
  5.13.12   164n. 21
  5.20.125   144
  7.2.10–11   145
  7.2.22   145
  7.2.25   145
  7.4.12   146
  7.6.2   146
  8.3.71   72n. 84
  8.4.3   144
  8.4.9   145
  8.5.3–34   430
  8.5.9–34   431
  8.5.19   144
  8.5.21   144
  8.6.4   144
  8.6.19   55

8.6.69	144
9.2.2	144
9.2.29–37	225n. 107
9.2.38–39	225n. 111
9.2.100	145
9.2.102	166n. 42
9.3.1	166n. 42
9.3.32	163n. 7
10.1.105	165n. 29
11.1.15–28	78
11.1.17–18	90
11.1.21	90
11.1.23	89, 90, 93
12.2.1	233
12.2.2	251n. 32
12.10.51, 53–55	139

Rhetorica ad Herennium

1.24–25	140
2.50	141
2.6	140

Rufus
Rhet.

1	224n. 81
2	224n. 82
3–41	224n. 83
17	224n. 84
17–20	224n. 85
21–25	224n. 86
27–34	224n. 87

Sallust
Bell. Jug.

4	232

Seneca
Ben.

2.22.1	9
3.18.2	402n. 57
3.28.1–2	402n. 56
4.40.3	333
5.11.1	9
6.33	518n. 22

Brev. vit.

17.5–6	401n. 36

De Clementia

1.9.1	251n. 31
1.24.1	579

De Const.

9.2.27	251n. 32
10.2.16	251n. 31

13.2, 5	11

Controversiae

1 pr. 24	440, 452nn. 34, 41
4 preface 10	272
1.1.3	451n. 20
2.4.9	451n. 19
7.6.15	451n. 19
9.2.23	451n. 19
10.1.14	451n. 19
10.2.10	451n. 19

Dial.

1.2.2	188
2.5.7	189
2.6.6	189
2.10.2–3	180
2.10.4	188

Epistles

4.4	584
5.7	186
6.2	178
6.3	182
6.5	232, 235, 251n. 32
7	38n. 17
9.10–12	193n. 29
9.18–19	189
13.13	186
14.7	195n. 59
23.2	186
24.1	186
24.17–21	195n. 54
32	401n. 27
37.1–2	378n. 101
42.9	401n. 36
47	272, 402n. 42, 576
47.1	595
47.10	402n. 56, 595
47.17	401n. 36, 402n. 45
48.2–4	178
55.8–11	188
59.2	180
59.7–8	376n. 86
63.3	188
64.9	251n. 37
70.19–26	584
70.8–9	401n. 36
71.11–16	190
71.14	186
71.37	189
75	252n. 45
75.1	235
76.22	235
77.14–15	584

Seneca, *Epistles* (*continued*)

78.1–2	400n. 22
78.15–21	189
80.9	580
82.10–11	399n. 12
85.29	188
92.11–13	386
92.30–35	195n. 54
92.31–32	194n. 48
94.10.27, 44	451nn. 26, 27
94.39	180
94.42	235
95.65	235
96.1	401n. 36
96.5	376n. 86
98.13	235
99.2	401n. 36
99.5, 13	186
99.15	173
101.4	186
102.21–30	195n. 54
102.30	235
103	38n. 17
104.3	400n. 22
104.21–22	235
107.9–10	380n. 126
107.9	382n. 160
120.13–19	195n. 54

Helv.

2.2	188
5.5	188

Ira

1.15.1	180
2.6.1	180
2.6.2	183
2.24.2–4	401n. 36
2.30.1	401n. 36
2.30.2	173
3.36.3	174
3.26.2	173

Polyb.

1.1–4	190
12.2	196n. 65
15.3	196n. 65
16.3	196n. 65
17.1–2	188

Prov.

5.5	401n. 36

Tranq.

10.3	596
11.10.12	401n. 36

Vit. beat.

4.2	188
8.3	189
26.5	175

Sextus Empiricus
Math.

2.54	185

Sophacles
Ajax

620	324
678–682	324
683	324
1053	324
1359	324
1376–1377	325
1378–1380	325
1381–1399	325
1383	325

Soranus
Gynecology

1.7.32	266

Stobaeus
Ecl.

2.7.5a	399n. 2
2.7.5a–5b2	399n. 7
2.7.5b2	399
2.7.5b5, 7	399n.4
2.7.5d	399n. 11
2.7.5o	401n. 32
2.7.7	399n. 8
2.7.7b	385
2.7.7d	400n. 20
2.7.7f–g	399n. 9
2.7.7f	385
2.7.7.g	386
2.7.11a	402n. 39
2.7.11i	402n. 43
4.22a.21	401n 26
4.22a.22	391

Flor.

3.13.42	175, 180
3.13.63	183

Stoicorum Veterum Fragmenta

1.51.26–31	172
2.95–96	631n. 17

3.39	631n. 16
3.67.20–22	529
3.67.45–68.2	529
3.94.14–15	172
3.95.17–18	172
3.95.24–25	172
3.95.41–43	172
3.100.29	180
3.100.33	176
3.102.40	195n. 59
3.104	631n. 16
3.105.17–18	180
3.129.9	196n. 66
3.149.18–24	176
3.149.20–24	173
3.150.24–27	176
3.214.202	631n. 17
3.264	632n. 32
3.377–420	631n. 18
3.391–94	631n. 20
3.431–42	631n. 19
3.495	632n. 28
3.525	631n. 16
5.48.16–31	196n. 68

Strabo
Geogr.

1.2.3–8	231
3.4.14	262
4.1.11	262
7.3.9	250
14.5.2	580

Suetonius
Aug.

46	372n. 46
67	578

Nero

16.2	280

Vesp.

2.2	518n. 22

Synesius
Ep.

138	252n. 44

Tacitus
Ann.

3.55	250n. 21
3.55.2	491

4.33	250n. 21
11.5	517n. 12
14.42–45	602
15.44	280
15.57	250n. 21
16.22	518n. 27

Dial.

3	517n. 12, 519n. 41

Hist.

1.4	491
2.13, 47	250n. 21
3.51, 67	250n.21

Aeneas Tacticus
Asclepiodotus Onasander

9.3	381n. 153
350	373n. 58

Terence
The Eunuch

885	516n. 9
1039	516n. 9
2.12.21	339

Theon
Progynnasmata

2.111, 1–3	226n. 128
2.115, 20–22	225n. 102
2.59, 5–11	223n. 61
8.43–50	37n. 6

Themistius
Or.

22.269, 270, 274	178

Theon
Progymnasmata

2.115	374n. 65

Theophylact

3:13	368
22.13–14	368

Thucydides
History of the Peloponnesian War

2.41.5	555
2.43.2–5	555
2.44.4	555
2.60.4	368
2.87	368

Thucydides (*continued*)

2.89	368
3.17	382n. 167
4.10	368
4.93.1	368
4.95	368
4.126.1	368
4.127.1	368
5.9.10	368
5.69.1–2	368
6.68	368
7.28	382n. 168
7.63.3	368
7.66	368
8.76.3	368

Tituli Ulpiani

5.3.5	408

Ulpian
Digest

50.16.195.1–4	478n. 2

Valerius Maximus

2.1.2	274, 282
2.7	376n. 89
4.7 praef.	334
5.10.2	71n. 71
1356a.35–b.6	231

Vegetius
Epitome of
Military Science

1.26	375n. 75
2.11	374n. 71

Velleius

1.15.5	379n. 115

Vetruvius
De architectura

6.7.1–5	274, 282

Xenophon
Anab.

2.3.2	381n. 145

3.1.20–24	368
3.1.37	374n. 70
3.1.42–44	368
3.2.8–32	368

Cyrus

1.4.16	382n. 168
6.3.21	380n. 129, 381n. 146
6.4.12	368
8.2.24–25	381n. 146, 382n. 159
14	368

Memorabilia

1.2.1	525
1.5.1–6	530
2.1.11	116
2.4.1	327
3.1	374n. 68

Symp.

8.32	379n. 124

Xenophon of Ephesus

5.1.2–11	218n. 1

Zaleucus
Prooem.

226.18–21	337, 343n. 36
227.29–31	342n. 35

MISCELLANEOUS

Ostraca

O.ROM inv. 906.8.522	220n. 20
O.Vindob.G.	
285	220n. 21
565	220n. 19

Papyri

PBouriant 1	199, 200, 201, 209, 220nn. 26, 27, 31, 33, 225n. 100
Pgen.Inv. 108	482n. 36
Pgiss. 17	465
P.Vindob.G.	
23624	220n. 22
26011	220n. 24
36016	220n. 24
41103	224n. 93

INDEX OF
MODERN AUTHORS

Achtemeier, P., 522n. 80
Adams, D., 291n. 106
Adinolfi, M., 254n. 70
Agosto, E., 130n. 16
Ahl, F., 315n. 2
Albl, M. C., 253n. 65; 254n. 74
Aletti, J. N., 169n. 68
Alföldy, G., 519nn. 36–37
Allison, P., 425n. 32
Ameling, W., 224n. 80
Anderson, R. D., 129n. 1; 163n. 3;
    165nn. 32, 39; 167nn. 52, 54; 168nn.
    57–58; 169nn. 60, 69; 224n. 79;
    227nn. 140, 142; 252n. 50
Annas, J., 631n. 11
Applebaum, S., 288n. 41
Artz, P., 605n. 56
Ascough, R. S., 482n. 47
Assion, P., 249n. 2
Atherton, K., 221n. 36
Auguet, R., 371n. 35
Aune, D. E., 399n. 15; 486n. 84; 604n.
    38
Avigad, N., 287n. 41
Axelrad, S., 521n. 64

Baasland, E., 252n. 38; 401n. 26
Babut, D., 249n. 12
Bakirtzis, C., 482n. 44
Balch, D. L., 165n. 33, 222n. 54; 285nn.
    1–2, 4; 286nn. 6–8, 13, 15, 19, 20;
    287n. 37; 288nn. 46, 48, 51–55;
    289nn. 73, 75–78; 290nn. 83, 86–87,
    89, 96; 291nn. 99, 105, 108, 110;
    425n. 31 ; 425n. 31; 427n. 49;
    482n. 47; 483nn. 52, 54; 484nn.

65–66; 486nn. 74–75, 79, 84;
    604n. 28; 607n. 77
Baldwin, C. S., 166nn. 43–46
Balsdon, J. P. V. D., 425n. 22
Banks, R., 131n. 31
Barbaglio, G., 256n. 100
Barclay, J. M. G., 288n. 44; 454n. 71;
    632n. 23
Barker, A. D., 377n. 99
Barré, M., 290n. 85
Barrett, C. K., 133n. 55; 171n. 85;
    193nn. 31, 33; 194nn. 46, 48;
    572n. 23
Barrow, R. H., 604n. 31
Bartchy, S. S., 291n. 112; 455n. 86;
    484n. 65; 485nn. 67–68; 603n. 19;
    604n. 32; 605n. 46; 606n. 63
Barton, C. A., 371n. 35; 378n. 101
Basevi, C., 164n. 24
Bash, A., 382n. 160
Bassler, J. M., 133n. 66; 317n. 34
Baumann, R., 522n. 69
Baus, K., 382n. 161
Beare, F. W., 133n. 52
Bek, L., 481n. 32
Beker, J. C., 73nn. 93, 95; 76n. 137
Bellen, H., 602n. 2
Belleville, L., 72n. 85
Benin, S. D., 39n. 31
Benko, S., 574n. 62
Berbuir, E., 521n. 69
Berger, K., 76n. 133
Berry, J., 481n. 29
Berry, K. L., 382n. 170; 484n. 62
Bertram, G., 573n. 53
Best, E., 130n. 20; 131nn. 24, 27–28

Betz, H. D., 72nn. 80, 83; 74nn. 110, 116; 75nn. 126, 129, 131; 99n. 8; 171n. 87; 225n. 95; 226n. 129–33, 136; 291n. 103; 453nn. 61–62; 454nn. 68, 71; 485n. 70–71; 548n. 11; 572nn. 29–30; 606n. 67
Beutler, J., 167nn. 51–52
Bieringer, R., 99n. 8; 454n. 77
Bilde, P. G., 481n. 32
Birch, B. C., 453n. 66
Bishop, M. C., 378n. 106
Black, M., 571n. 1
Blake, M. E., 286n. 6
Blech, M., 382n. 161
Bloomer, W. M., 249n. 15; 250nn. 17–18; 479n. 17
Blue, B., 285n. 1
Blundell, M. W., 342n. 14
Böcher, O., 193n. 31
Bockmuehl, M., 254n. 73
Bömer, F., 291n. 108; 604n. 30
Bonnard, A., 374n. 67
Bonner, S. F., 219nn. 3, 12; 222nn. 50–51, 56
Booth, A., 219n. 10
Borgen, P., 192n. 9; 571n. 2
Borkowski, A., 423n. 5
Bornecque, H., 250n. 16
Borse, U., 253n. 53
Botha, P., 167n. 55
Bowersock, G. W., 371n. 36; 372n. 44
Bowman, A., 69n. 12
Bradley, K. R., 289n. 72; 425nn. 25, 28–29; 602n. 2; 603nn. 21, 23–25; 604nn. 27, 31; 605n. 47; 606nn. 62, 66
Branson, M. L., 453n. 63
Brant, J. A. A., 253n. 65; 255nn. 77, 79, 86; 256n. 97
Braund, S.M., 192n. 2
Brennan, T., 631n. 18
Brewer, D. I., 427n. 44
Brewer, R. R., 380nn 132–33
Breytenbach, C., 343n. 32
Brockmeyer, N., 602n. 2
Brodner, E., 372nn. 38–39
Brooten, B., 427n. 44; 550n. 50
Bruce, F. F., 131n. 24; 227n. 151
Brunschwig, J., 549n. 34
Brunt, P. A., 602n. 4
Buller, J. L., 197n. 73
Bullinger, E. W., 453n. 55

Bultmann, R., 41n. 49; 377n. 94; 572n. 23; 574n. 56; 632n. 30
Burgess, T. C., 371n. 27; 374nn. 63–65; 383n. 176
Burk, E., 251n. 38
Butts, J. R., 166n. 41; 452n. 35
Byrne, B., 73nn. 97, 103; 573n. 51

Callahan, A. D., 607n. 79
Campbell, B., 373nn. 50, 53; 376n. 81
Cancik, H., 251n. 38
Caplan, H., 451n. 33
Carcopino, J., 603n. 27
Carey, C., 69n. 15
Carrié. J. M., 381n. 138
Carter, H. V., 249n. 16
Cartledge, P., 69n. 21; 289n. 59
Casciaro, J. M., 256n. 99
Casels, O., 376n. 83
Castelli, E. A., 254n. 66
Champlin, E., 423n. 7
Chapa, J., 164n. 24
Chow, J. K., 133nn. 65, 67; 484n. 64
Christ, F., 76n. 132
Christoffersson, O., 196n. 71
Christophersen, A., 573n. 52
Clark, D. L., 252n. 43
Clark, J. R., 481n. 31
Clarke, A. D., 520n. 58
Clarke, J. R., 423n. 10
Clarke, M. L., 451n. 9
Classen, C. J., 167n. 55
Cohen, S. J. D., 425n. 36
Cohick, L. H., 286n. 14
Cole, S. G., 222n. 55
Collart, P., 219nn. 3, 14; 220n. 15; 221nn. 41, 43; 379n. 116; 380n. 132; 381nn. 149, 152; 382nn. 163–64
Collins, A. Y., 290n. 82
Collins, J. J., 368n. 1; 369n. 2
Collins, R. F., 253n. 63; 402n. 44; 572n. 22
Connolly, P., 375n. 74
Connor, W. R., 341n. 12
Conzelmann, H., 225n. 97; 291n. 102; 572n. 21; 606n. 72
Cooper, J., 549n. 33
Cosgrove, C. H., 72n. 73; 73n. 92
Cotton, H., 69n. 13; 129n. 2; 130nn. 7, 11, 13–14
Coulston, J. C. N., 378n. 106
Cousar, C., 76n. 131

Cranfield, C. E. B., 76n. 134; 133n. 55; 286n. 10; 426n. 41; 574n. 56

Cribiore, R., 219nn. 4–5; 220nn. 15–16, 21, 23–24, 30; 221nn. 41, 44–46; 224n. 93

Crook, J., 71nn. 50, 53, 60, 67; 423n. 7; 479nn. 11, 14

Croy, N. C., 192n. 14

Culpepper, R. A., 317n. 33

Dahl, N. A., 317n. 41; 483n. 54

D'Angelo, M. R., 426n. 41

Danker, F. W., 379n. 122; 382n. 160; 483n. 58, 485n. 72

D'Arms, J., 481n. 28; 603n. 16

David, W. H., 605n. 56

Davidson, D., 72n. 74

Davies, M., 196n. 64

Davis, B. S., 227n. 148; 291n. 103

Debut, J., 219n. 4; 220n. 28

de Gruyter, W., 252n. 38

Deiss, J. J., 285n. 4

Deissmann, A., 224n. 95; 605n. 56

Deku H., 192n. 8

de Luce, J., 70n. 43

Deming, W., 290n. 81; 401nn. 26, 33–38; 402nn. 40–42, 46; 403n. 66; 423n. 1; 427n. 46–47; 454n. 77; 604n. 40

Derrett, J. D. M., 427n. 44

deSilva, D. A., 100n. 12; 523n. 87; 572nn. 17–20

Devine, A. M., 375n. 72

DeVoto, J. G., 375n. 72

Dewey, A. J., 100n. 13

de Witt, N. W., 316n. 11

Dibelius, M., 380n. 137; 381n. 143; 629n. 4

Dickmann, J. A., 480n. 26

Diller, H., 251n. 38

Dillon, J., 549n. 35

Dilts, M. R., 224n. 79

Dixon, S., 424nn; 13, 16; 425n. 26

Dodd, B. J., 252nn. 47–49; 253nn. 58–59, 61–62; 254nn. 66, 70; 255nn. 80, 82–84 ,87, 91–93, 95–96; 256nn. 106, 109–15; 257nn. 116–23, 125–28

Dodge, H., 369n. 7

Donfried, K. P., 167nn. 51–52; 168n. 59; 426n. 40

Donner, H., 68n. 7

Doran, R., 368n. 1

Dornseiff, F., 251n. 33

Dover, K., 547n. 1

Downing, G. F., 223n. 58; 571n. 3

Droge, A. J., 400n. 21; 401nn. 25, 30

DuBois, P., 424n. 11

Dunn, J. D. G., 73n. 104; 75n. 129; 76n. 131; 169n. 64; 170n. 70; 171n. 86; 454n. 68; 522n. 69; 572n. 36; 573nn. 37, 51; 574nn. 56–57; 632n. 31

Dupont, F., 381n. 139

Eadie, J. W., 251n. 35

Ebner, M., 223n. 58

Eckert, J., 521n. 69

Eddy, P. R., 253n. 65; 254n. 74

Egger, B., 423n. 4

Ehrhardt, A., 379n. 125

Elliott, J. H., 99n. 9

Elliott, N., 455n. 86

Ellis, E. E., 132n. 42

Emonds, H., 376n. 83

Engberg-Pedersen, T., 39n. 27; 166n. 45; 169n. 62; 223n. 58; 225n. 105; 318n. 45; 343n. 30; 400nn. 16, 24; 403n. 67; 548nn. 15–16; 549nn. 21, 23–24, 28, 31; 550nn. 37, 46; 630nn. 7, 9, 631nn. 14–15, 18, 21; 632nn. 25, 28, 34–35; 633nn. 38–40

Engels, D., 372n. 41

Erskine, A., 192n. 2; 548n. 18

Fagan, G. G., 372nn. 39–40

Falkner, T. M., 70n. 43

Farmer, W. R., 130n. 18

Farron, S., 193n. 30

Fatheuer, T., 572n. 12

Fee, G., 131n. 30; 132nn. 35–36, 40, 50; 254n. 74; 255n. 86; 455nn. 78, 88; 572nn. 24–25, 34

Fentress, E., 482n. 44

Ferguson, E., 222n. 54

Finley, M. I., 70n. 43; 289n. 64; 602nn. 1, 5–6; 603nn. 14–15, 24

Fiore, B., 251n. 34; 253nn. 55–56; 254n. 69; 257n. 124 315n. 2

Fiorenza, E. S., 286n. 21; 483n. 55; 486n. 76; 487n. 87

Fisher, N. R. E., 571n. 9; 572n. 10

Fittschen, K., 287n. 41

Fitzgerald, J. T., 38n. 11; 100n. 21;

Fitzgerald, J. T (*continued*)
  133n. 51; 165n. 39; 170nn. 71, 75–76;
  171n. 84; 192nn. 9 –11, 13; 194n. 36;
  195nn., 49, 52–53, 55; 253n. 56;
  288n. 55; 315nn. 2 –3; 317nn. 27, 34;
  342n. 14; 343n. 30; 383nn. 170–172;
  399n. 15; 400n. 24; 479n. 10;
  484n. 62; 485n. 70; 547n. 30;
  550n. 39; 630n. 5–6
Fitzmyer, J., 68nn. 8–9; 402n. 58;
  573n. 50
Flandren, J. L., 478n. 1
Foerster, W., 73n. 96
Foerster, G., 287n. 41
Foley, H., 222n. 55
Forbes, C., 99nn. 2–4; 100nn. 15–16,
  19, 22; 163n. 4; 165n. 25; 170n. 80;
  316n. 22
Fortna, R. T., 485n. 69
Foss, P. W., 286n. 20; 480n. 25
Foucault, M., 424n. 11
Fowler, R. L., 194n. 41
Fraisse, J. C., 249n. 12
Franklin, J. L., 480n. 19
Fredrickson, D., 194nn. 36, 43; 195nn.
  54, 56–57; 288nn. 52–54; 290nn.
  89–95; 316n. 18; 400n. 24; 427nn.
  49–50
Fretheim, T., 194n. 43
Freyne, S., 287n. 39
Friedländer, L., 518n. 25
Friedrich, G., 521n. 69
Friedrich., J. H., 521n. 69
Frilingos, C., 605n. 49; 606nn. 59–60
Frontinus, S. J., 375n. 72
Funk, R., 130n. 18
Furnish, V., 72n. 86; 193nn. 32, 34–35;
  194n. 46; 316n. 24; 378n. 102;
  454n. 70; 606n. 71; 630n. 4
Fürst, A., 316n. 10
Futrell, A., 371n. 35

Gale, H., 74n. 121
Gallant, T., 70n. 29
Gallivan, P., 425n. 33
Galinsky, K., 376n. 80; 607nn. 75–76
Gardiner, E. N., 369n. 8: 370nn. 19,
  21–22; 371nn. 33–34; 377n. 96
Gardner, J. F., 71nn. 48–49, 52, 58–59,
  61–63, 68–70; 72n. 78
Garlan, Y., 602n. 5
Garland, D. E., 605n. 57

Garnsey, P., 289nn. 59, 61–63, 66–71;
  402nn. 42, 47–48, 53 ; 602n. 11;
  607n. 78
Gascó, F., 166n. 47
Gaventa, B., 73n. 102; 253n. 53; 253nn.
  58, 60; 254n. 66; 254n. 70; 485n. 69
Gebhardt, E. R., 376n. 90
Gempf, C., 285n. 1
Geoffrion, T. C., 376n. 86; 379n. 118
George, M., 425n. 32; 480n. 24;
  603n. 25
George, T., 253n. 53
Georgi, D., 100n. 11; 171n. 84
Gerhard, G. A., 193nn. 18, 20; 194n. 47
Gernet, L., 69n. 20
Getty, M. A., 253nn. 63, 65
Giardina, A., 381n. 138
Gilbert-Thirry, A., 192nn. 1, 6
Gill, C., 192n. 2, 547n. 5; 548nn. 8, 13,
  15; 549n. 29
Gill, D. W. J., 285n. 1
Giversen, S., 192n. 9
Glad, C. E., 37nn. 2, 9, 11; 38nn 15–16;
  39n. 26; 40nn. 34–35, 39, 42; 41nn.
  43–44, 47–48, 51–52; 193n. 22;
  195n. 55; 315n. 7; 316n. 11
Glancy, J. A., 290n. 84; 455n. 86;
  602n. 9; 604n. 41; 607n. 79
Gleason, M., 550n. 51
Glockmann, G., 37n. 10
Godet, F., 573n. 39; 574n. 57
Goodenough, E. R., 291n. 101
Gosling, J., 548nn. 7, 13
Graf, D. F., 287n. 39
Grahame, M., 481n. 29
Grant, F. C., 606n. 65
Grassi, J. A., 521n. 69
Gregg, R. C., 196n. 68
Gregory, T. E., 372n. 41; 605n. 42
Griffin, M., 606n. 70
Grimaldi, W.A., 249n. 10
Grosvenor, M., 132n. 46
Gruen, E., 289n. 59
Guijarro, S., 287n. 39
Gundry-Volf, J. M., 454n. 77

Haacker, K., 193n. 31
Hadot, I., 193n. 23; 194n. 38
Hafemann, S., 74n. 105; 75n. 131;
  99n. 8
Haight, E. H., 249n. 16; 250n. 21
Hainz, J, 522n. 69

Hall, D. R., 315n. 2
Hall, E., 550n. 42
Hall, R. G., 73nn. 98–99; 226nn. 135, 138; 452n. 47
Hall, S. G., 289n. 71
Halliwell, S., 249n. 12
Halperin, D., 424n. 11
Hammer, P., 68n. 1; 73n. 96; 76n. 139
Hanson, V. D., 374nn. 67, 70; 375n. 74; 380n. 128
Harrill, J. A., 289n. 68; 291nn. 109, 111, 113–15; 485n. 67; 602n. 3; 603nn. 16–18, 24, 26; 604nn. 30–31, 35–37; 605nn. 41, 43–45, 50; 606n. 62
Harris, H. A., 370n. 21; 371nn. 33–34; 372n. 39
Harris, M. J., 607n. 79
Harris, W. V., 603nn. 13–14, 16
Harrison, A. R. W., 69n. 20; 70nn. 41, 42
Haase, W., 75n. 124; 251n. 35; 256n. 99
Hauck, F., 574n. 54
Hays, R. B., 73n. 101; 75nn. 130–31; 453n. 63; 572n. 26; 573n. 40
Heath, M., 169n. 60; 342n. 15
Heckel, T., 548n. 9
Hendrickson, G. L., 166n. 42
Hengel, M., 218n. 2; 227n. 144; 368n. 2; 450n. 2
Hercher, R., 193n. 19
Herman, G., 341n. 10
Hermann, H.-V., 369n. 8
Herrmann, E., 602n. 2
Herz, P., 291n. 108
Hester, J., 76n. 132
Hilgard, A., 222n. 49
Hills, J. V., 290n. 79
Hock, R. F., 100n. 9; 218n. 1; 225n. 104; 252n. 42; 342nn. 17, 20
Höistad, R., 193nn. 15, 17
Holladay, C., 256n. 97
Holladay, J. S., Jr., 287n. 38
Holland, G. S., 317n. 27
Holloway, P. A., 252n. 50; 400n. 24; 401n. 28; 403nn. 62, 65
Holmberg, A., 249n. 2
Holmberg, B., 131n. 32
Hopkins, K., 71n. 70; 424n. 15; 479nn. 13, 16–17; 603n. 15
Horsley, R. A., 256n. 98; 291n. 98; 450n. 7; 454n. 77; 455n. 84; 607n. 79
Horstmann, A., 571n. 1

Howard, G., 73n. 90
Hübner, H., 75n. 124
Hughes, F. W., 167nn. 52, 55
Hultgren, A. J., 253n. 65
Humphreys, S. C., 69nn. 16, 18
Hunger, H., 223n. 60
Hurd, J. C., 254n. 66
Hurwitt, J. M., 197n. 73
Huskinson, J., 424n. 10
Hutter, H., 341n. 12

Ibbetson, D., 70n. 46
Ilan, Tal, 427n. 44
Ingenkamp, H. G., 193n. 24
Inwood, B., 549n. 34
Irwin, T., 630n. 8

Jameson, M. H., 380n. 128
Jaques, M. V., 254n. 74
Jaquette, J., 317n. 35; 400nn. 18, 21; 403n. 64
Jennings, L. C., 604n. 31
Jervis, L. A., 253nn. 53–54
Jewett, R., 131n. 26; 168n. 59; 285n. 4; 483nn. 57, 59; 571n. 2; 573n. 52
Johann, H. T., 196n. 68; 197n. 72
Johanson, B. C., 254nn. 67, 70–71
Johnson, L. T., 452n. 43
Johnston, D., 70n. 47; 71nn. 54–55, 57, 66; 72n. 72; 423n. 6
Jones, C. P., 371n. 29
Jongman, W., 480n. 19
Joshel, S. R., 604n. 29
Jost, K. T., 252n. 40
Joubert, S., 485n. 72
Jouguet, P., 219n. 14
Judge, E. A., 100nn. 18, 20, 23; 133n. 64; 226n. 129; 227n. 146; 572n. 13
Juel, D. H., 253n. 65

Keck, L., 73n. 98
Kee, H. C., 286n. 14; 571n. 1
Kelly, J. N. D., 291n. 100
Kemp, A., 221n. 37
Kennedy, G. A., 163n. 4; 168n. 59; 170n. 77; 223n. 60; 224n. 79; 226n. 135; 227n. 141; 450nn. 3, 8; 453n. 58: 454n. 74
Kenyon, F. G., 221nn. 42, 48
Keppie, L., 372n. 43; 373nn. 49, 51
Kern, P. H., 226n. 134

Keyes, C., 129n. 2
Kilgallen, J. J., 256n. 100
Kim, C H., 129nn. 2–3; 130nn. 4–6, 12, 17–18; 132nn. 38–39; 133nn. 53–54, 62–63
Kingsbury, J. D., 253n. 65
Klauck, H. J., 482n. 47
Kloppenborg, J. S., 287n. 24
Knox, B., 342n. 14
Knox, J., 484n. 65
Koerte, A., 225n. 96
Koester, H., 285n. 3; 286n. 17; 287n. 33; 482nn. 43–44
Koller, H., 380n. 135
Kondoleon, C., 287n. 41
Konstan, D., 315nn. 3–5, 7, 9; 317n. 36; 340n. 1; 341nn. 3–4, 7, 9–12; 342nn. 18, 22, 24, 27; 383n. 171
Kopff, E.C., 603n. 16
Kornhardt, H., 252n. 39
Koukouli-Chrysantaki, C., 482n. 44
Kraemer, R. S., 426n. 41
Kreitzer, L. J., 376n. 80
Kremer, J., 573n. 48
Krentz, E., 167n. 51; 168n. 59; 376n. 79; 379n. 118
Krentz, P., 375n. 72; 376n. 77
Künzl, E., 376n. 81
Kurylowicz, M., 71n. 60
Kuss, O., 573nn. 44, 51
Kyle, D. G., 371n. 35

Lacey, W. K., 69n. 23; 479n. 7; 482n. 41
Lambrecht., J., 99n. 8
Lampe, P., 286n. 5; 291n. 109; 315n. 2; 426nn. 40–41; 484n. 65; 516n. 1; 518n. 26; 519n. 46; 520nn. 50, 52, 54, 57; 521n. 66; 522nn. 75–76
Laqueur, T., 550n. 44
Larmour, D. H. J., 165n. 31
Laurence, R., 480nn. 21, 24–26; 481n. 29; 603n. 25
Lausberg, H., 37n. 4; 129n. 1; 224n. 79
Lazenby, J., 375n. 74
Le Bohec, Y., 373nn. 48, 55; 376n. 77; 381n. 148
Levick, B., 482nn. 44, 46
Levine, L. I., 288n. 42; 289n. 74
Lewis, A., 70n. 46
Lichtenberger, H., 401n. 26
Liebeschuetz, J. H. W. G., 424n. 12
Lincott, A., 68n. 11

Lintott, A. W., 517nn. 11, 17
Little, J., 74n. 120
Livingston, E. A., 99n. 8
Livingston, N., 221n. 36
Lohse, E., 605n. 48
Long, A. A., 399nn. 2, 10, 13; 547n. 2; 548n. 14; 549n. 32
Longenecker, R.N., 171n. 85
Lovering, E. H., Jr., 256n. 103; 317n. 37; 453n. 59; 523n. 87
Lull, D., 73n. 100; 74nn. 106, 109; 75n. 128; 227n. 149
Lumpe, A., 252n. 40
Lundon, J., 221n. 45
Lührmann, D., 253n. 53
Lyall, F., 68n. 10; 381n. 154
Lyons, G., 253nn. 51, 64; 256nn. 107–8; 316n. 19; 453n. 65

MacDonald, D. R., 37n. 10; 606n. 64
MacDowell, D., 70n. 45
MacMullen, R., 373n. 48
Maiuri, A., 285n. 4
Malherbe, A.J., 37n. 5; 41n. 52; 131n. 31; 168n. 56; 193nn. 16, 21, 25; 194n. 39; 195n. 62;196n. 69; 218n. 2; 222n. 58; 290n. 78; 292n. 119; 317n. 34; 377n. 101; 400n. 24; 428n. 64; 487n. 88 452n. 43; 482nn. 47, 56; 486n. 82; 550n. 38; 629n. 3, 630n. 5
Malina, B. J., 100n. 12; 129n. 1; 225nn. 114–17; 226nn. 118–20, 123; 523n. 87; 571nn. 4–6
Mallwitz, A., 369n. 8
Manning, C. E., 196n. 67
Markschies, C., 548n. 10
Marrou, H. I., 219nn. 3, 12; 221nn. 36, 47; 222nn. 56–57
Marshall, I. H., 130n. 21
Marshall, P., 99n. 8; 100n. 10; 129n. 2; 133nn. 65, 67; 170n. 80; 316nn. 12, 22–23; 484n. 63
Martin, D .B., 68n. 6; 74nn. 110, 114; 425nn. 33–34; 427nn. 48, 50; 428nn. 50, 54, 62; 486n. 73; 549n. 26; 550nn. 45, 47–49, 51; 602n. 8; 603n. 24; 606nn. 73–74
Martin, H. M., Jr., 165, n. 31
Martin, R., 195n. 58
Martinich, A. P., 72n. 74
Mattingly, D. J., 369n. 7, 371n. 35

Martyn, J. L., 72n. 87; 73n. 94; 75nn.
127, 131; 76n. 132; 171n. 87; 453nn.
58, 60–62, 64; 454nn. 68–69, 71–72;
485nn. 69, 71
Matera, F. J., 253nn. 53, 57; 632.nn.
23–24
Mattill, A. J., Jr., 573n. 48
Mayer, R. G., 251nn. 36–37
Mazar, A., 287n. 41
McCall, M. H., Jr., 163n. 3
McCarthy, K., 604n. 34; 606n. 75
McGinn, T. A. J. , 605n. 41
McLean, B. H., 287nn. 24–25;
379n. 118
Meeks, W., 131n. 32; 222n. 54;
290n. 86; 450n. 6; 482n. 47; 483nn.
52, 54; 606nn. 64–65, 71
Meggitt, J. J., 41n. 46
Melick, R. R., Jr., 255n. 77
Merkelbach, R., 518nn. 32, 34; 519nn.
35, 41
Metzner, R., 522n. 77
Michaelis, W., 248n. 1; 254n. 66;
255nn. 75, 96
Michel, O., 574n. 59
Mielsch, H., 287n. 40
Millar, F., 368n. 1
Miller, J. C., 602n. 2
Miller, S. G., 369nn. 4, 11; 370nn.
21–22, 24
Millett, P., 69n. 21
Milne, J. G., 220n. 15
Mitchell, M. M., 39n. 27; 40nn. 32, 35;
130n. 19; 132n. 41; 166n. 45; 170nn.
71, 74; 249nn. 6–9; 255nn. 93–95;
317n. 38; 452n. 42
Mitchell, S., 68n. 11
Moo, D.J., 170n. 70; 573n. 51
Moore, A. M. T., 287n. 38
Moore-Crispin, D. R., 73n. 88; 74n. 116
Morgan, T., 219nn. 4, 6–9, 11–12;
220nn. 15, 25, 29–30, 34–35; 221nn.
36, 41; 222n. 54; 225n. 98
Morris, L., 253n. 53; 573n. 51
Moule, C. F. D., 130n. 18
Moxnes, H., 100n. 12; 285n. 2;
287n. 39; 549n. 26; 573nn. 41–43;
630n. 6
Muensterberger, W., 521n. 64
Murkes, R., 253n. 65; 254n. 74
Murnaghan, S., 604n. 29
Murphy-O'Connor, J., 218n. 2;

225n. 101; 227n. 143; 256n. 100;
572n. 31; 605n. 42

Neiman, D., 41n. 45
Neuenschwander, H. R., 197n. 74
Neumann, A., 373n. 57
Neusner, J., 99n. 8; 171n. 81; 483n. 59
Nevett, L., 425n. 32
Newman, B. M., 574n. 58
Neyrey, J. H., 100n. 12; 129n. 1; 225nn.
114–17; 226nn. 118–20, 123
Nicols, J., 519n. 43
Nida, E. A., 574n. 58
Niebuhr, R. R., 130n. 18
Nielsen, H. S., 479n. 10
Nielsen, I., 481n. 32
Nielsen, M., 481n. 32
Norden, E., 373n. 61
Norris, F. W., 290n. 78
North, H., 547n. 3
Nussbaum, M., 549n. 34

Obbink, D., 317n. 27
Ober, J., 251n. 35
O'Brien, P. T., 132nn. 43, 45–46, 48, 50;
255nn. 75–76, 78, 80–81, 85, 89–90;
572nn. 32–33, 35
Olbricht, T. H., 164n. 24; 165n. 33;
167nn. 52, 55; 168n. 60; 169n. 68;
226n. 134; 479n. 10; 485n. 70;
573n. 45
Oliver, J. H., 375n. 73
O'Neil, E. N., 252n. 42; 342nn. 17, 20
Ortkemper, F. J., 256n. 101
Orton, D. E., 129n. 1; 224n. 79
Osburn, C. D., 131n. 22
Osiek, C., 285nn. 2, 4; 286nn. 6–8, 13,
15, 19–20; 287n. 37; 288nn. 46, 48,
51; 289nn. 73, 75–78; 290nn. 79–80,
83, 86, 96; 291nn. 99, 108, 110, 116;
292n. 118; 482n. 47; 483n. 52; 484nn.
65–66; 486nn. 74, 79; 487nn. 85–86;
604n. 28; 607n. 77

Pack, R. A., 219n. 4
Padilla, C. R., 453n. 63
Palmer, D. W., 401n. 29
Patterson, C. B., 425n. 35
Pattison, S., 572n. 27
Parker, H. D. M., 375n. 74
Parkins, H. M., 481n. 29
Parsons, P. J., 221n. 46

Patterson, O., 602nn. 6, 12
Pawlikowski, J. T., 40n. 31
Perdrizet, P., 219n. 14
Perella, N. J., 574n. 62
Perkins, J., 192n. 12
Perkins, P., 133n. 66
Pesch, R., 521n. 69
Petersen, N. R., 605n. 56
Pfitzner, V. C., 132n. 44
Pickett, R. W., 523nn. 87–89
Pilhofer, P., 379nn. 116–17
Plass, P., 371n. 35
Pleket, H.W., 516n. 6
Pogoloff, S., 131n. 29
Pohlenz, M., 192n. 3
Poliakoff, M. B., 370nn. 15, 20
Pomeroy, S., 69nn. 17, 22, 26; 70nn. 28,
    30, 32; 425n. 35; 482nn. 41–42
Porter, S. E., 163n. 4; 164n. 24;
    165n. 31; 167nn. 52, 54–55; 168n. 60;
    169n. 68; 226nn. 134, 139; 573n. 45
Potter, D. S., 369n. 7; 371n. 35
Price, A., 548nn. 7, 13; 549n. 33
Price, B. J., 249n. 2; 250nn. 26–27
Pulcini, T., 573n. 44

Rabe, H., 223n. 60
Ramsaran, R. A., 224n 94; 225n. 99;
    428n. 55; 450nn. 1, 4–5, 9; 451nn.
    10, 17–18, 21–22, 24–25, 30, 32;
    452nn. 34, 38, 40–41, 45; 454n. 77;
    455nn. 80, 87; 456n. 91
Rankin, H. D., 193n. 15
Rapske, B., 605n. 53
Rathbone, D., 69n. 12
Rawson, B., 423n. 7, 9; 424nn. 10,
    20–21; 425nn. 32–33; 479n. 7;
    481n. 29; 602n. 10
Reader, W., 224n. 91
Reardon, B. P., 423n. 4
Rebell, W., 522nn. 70, 74; 523n. 82
Redlich. B. E., 521n. 64
Reed, J. D., 197n. 73
Reed, N. B., 370n. 15
Reicke, B., 130n. 22; 131n. 24
Reid, J. T., 167n. 55
Reid, M. L., 573nn. 45, 47, 49; 574n. 56
Reinhartz, A., 253n. 65; 254n. 75;
    255n. 76; 256nn. 97, 102
Reinmuth, E., 522n. 75
Renehan, R., 41n. 45; 549n. 36
Renner, T., 221n. 45

Reumann, J., 39n. 29; 317n. 34;
    381n. 144; 383n. 172
Reynolds, J., 369n. 3
Rich, J., 373n. 48; 376n. 83
Richard, E. J., 253n. 65
Richardson, N. J., 369nn. 9–11
Richardson, P., 39n. 27; 254n. 66
Ridderbos, H., 522n.69
Riggsby, A. M., 481n. 30
Rist, J. M., 400n. 21
Robbins, V. K., 100nn. 17, 24
Roberts, W. R., 99n. 3; 165n. 26
Robins, R. H., 221n. 36, 38, 39;
    222n. 49
Robinson, A. W., 250n. 25
Rodriguez, J. P., 602n. 2
Roetzel, C., 218n. 1; 227n. 147;
    377n. 92
Rohrbaugh, R., 100n. 9
Roller, M., 481n. 30
Romano, D. G., 372n. 41; 482n. 44
Rousselle, A., 288nn. 45, 48; 425n. 34
Roussin, L. A., 287n. 41
Rubinstein, L., 69n. 18; 70nn. 34–35,
    37–38, 44; 72n. 78
Russell, D. A., 163n. 5; 164nn. 16–17;
    165n. 40; 166nn. 47, 49; 224n. 88;
    315n. 1; 370n. 26; 371n. 27; 374n. 64
Russell, K. C., 606n. 72

Saller, R. P., 71nn. 51, 64; 74nn. 115,
    117; 130n. 10; 424nn. 15–16; 478nn.
    1, 479nn. 8–9, 11–13, 15; 518n. 29;
    519n. 38; 602nn. 1, 7, 11; 603n. 15;
    604n. 29
Salmon, E. T., 372nn. 45, 47; 379n. 115
Sampley, J. P., 99n. 8; 132nn. 37, 41, 49;
    171n. 81; 256nn. 103–5; 316nn. 21,
    25, 27; 317n. 37; 383n. 173; 403n. 64;
    452n. 39; 453nn. 57, 59; 455n. 83;
    484n. 61
Sanders, B., 256n. 97
Sanders, E. P., 73n. 91
Sansone, D., 369n. 4
Schatkin, M., 41n. 45
Schefold, K., 289n. 56; 291n. 104
Scheidel, W., 603n. 14
Schille, G., 521n. 69
Schissel, O., 223n. 60; 224n. 80
Schlier, H., 75n. 129; 574n. 57
Schmeller, T., 401n. 36; 523n. 84
Schnackenburg, R., 521n. 69

Schoedel, W., 427n. 49
Schoeni, M., 573nn. 45–46
Schrage, W., 522n. 69
Schreiber, A., 521n. 69
Schremer, A.,, 427n. 44
Schütz, J. H., 131n. 32
Schürer, E., 368n. 1
Schwartz, J., 221n. 47
Schwemer, A. M., 450n. 2
Scott, J. C., 604n. 33
Scott, J. M., 68nn. 2, 4–5, 7; 72nn. 79,
    81, 88; 73n. 105; 74nn. 105, 107, 112,
    119; 75n. 131
Scourfield, J. H. D., 196, n. 68
Scroggs, R., 486n. 76
Scullard, H. H., 606n. 69
Sealey, R., 69n. 22; 70nn. 31, 40
Sedley, D. N., 399nn. 2, 10, 13;
    548n. 14; 549n. 32
Seeley, D., 400n. 21
Segal, A. F., 169n. 62
Segal, C., 197n. 73
Seifrid, M., 74n. 105
Sellin, G., 256n. 99
Shaw, B. D., 478n. 5; 479nn. 7, 10;
    603n. 15; 606n. 68
Shelton, J. A., 602n. 2; 603n. 21; 605nn.
    54–55
Sherwin-White, A. N., 287nn. 27–28;
    381n. 142
Shipley, G., 373n. 48; 376n. 83
Sidebottom, H., 376n. 83
Sider, D., 196n. 64
Sihvola, J., 548n. 15; 631n. 18
Silva, M., 255nn. 76, 78, 88
Simpson, J. A., 341n. 2
Skidmore, C., 249n. 13; 250nn. 18–22,
    29; 376n. 89
Smalley, W. A., 571n. 1
Smit, J., 164n. 24; 226nn. 135, 137
Smith, A., 254nn. 70, 72; 523n. 87;
    607n. 79
Smith, D. E., 289n. 75
Smith, R. R. R., 288n. 56
Sontheimer, W., 373n. 57
Stadter, P. A., 251n. 35
Stählin, G., 572n. 28
Stalder, K., 521n. 69
Stambaugh, J. E., 285n. 1
Stanford, W. B., 37n. 10
Stanley, D., 254nn. 66, 70, 75
Stauber, J., 518n. 32

Sterling, G. E., 368n. 1, 369n. 2
Stelton, L. F., 375n. 75
Stewart. A., 287n. 33; 289n. 56
Stowers, S. K., 130nn. 6, 8–9; 163n. 5;
    166n. 45; 169nn. 63, 66–67; 225nn.
    105–10, 112–13; 227n. 142; 252n. 46;
    286nn. 9–11; 317n. 34; 382n. 170;
    401n. 36; 428nn. 51–53; 548nn. 6,
    17, 19–20; 549nn. 27, 30, 36; 550nn.
    41, 48; 604n. 38
Stelton, L. F., 375n. 72
Strange, J. F., 286n. 14
Straub, W., 377nn. 90, 94
Strauss, B. S., 341n. 12
Strubbe, J. H. M., 196n. 68
Stuhlmacher, P., 573n. 40
Suhl, A., 253n. 52
Sumney, J., 100n. 14; 256n. 103;
    317n. 37; 453n. 59
Sussman, L. A., 451nn. 18–19
Swaddling, J., 370nn. 15, 19, 21
Sweet, W. E., 369n. 4; 370n. 25;
    371n. 28; 377nn. 95–96, 98

Tabor, J. D., 400n. 21; 401n. 25
Talbert, C. H., 195n. 60;
Tannenbaum, R., 369n. 3
Tarachow, S., 521n. 64
Tarazi, P. N., 253nn. 53–54
Tatum, J., 423n. 4
Taylor, D., 221n. 37
Theissen, G., 131n. 32; 291n. 107;
    549n. 29
Thiselton, A. C., 399n. 15; 402n. 44
Thompson, C., 194n. 43
Thompson, J. W., 290n. 78
Thompson, M. P., 39n. 24
Thrall, M., 378n. 102
Todd, S., 69nn. 21, 29; 70nn. 27, 45
Too, Y. L., 221n. 36
Trapp, M. B., 249n. 15; 371n. 32
Travis, S. H., 99n. 8
Treggiari, S., 423n. 1; 424nn. 12, 14, 17;
    425nn. 22–24; 428n. 58; 603n. 21
Trümper, M., 287nn. 22, 26, 29–32
Tsekourakis, D., 399n. 14

Valgiglio, E., 251n. 35
van der Horst, P. W., 288n. 50
van Geytenbeek, A. C., 192n. 7
van Hooff, A. J. L., 400n. 21
van Unnik, W. C., 218n. 2

Vermes, G., 368n. 1
Verner, D. C., 486n. 81
Veyne, P., 71n. 55; 289n. 65; 479n. 9
Vittinghoff, F., 516n. 6; 519nn. 44, 46
Vogt, J., 602n. 2
Volkmann, H., 372nn. 46–47
Vollenweider, S., 402n. 42
von Arnim, H., 63ln. 16
von Dobschütz, E, 522n. 69
von Premerstein, A., 517n. 10, 518nn.
    20, 31
Vox, O., 196n. 64

Wallace-Hadrill, A., 285n. 4, 286nn. 8,
    15, 19; 289n. 76; 423n. 9; 480nn.
    21–26; 603n. 25
Wallace, R., 285n. 1
Walter, N., 522n. 75
Walters, H. B., 195n. 50
Walters, J. C., 76n. 136; 131nn. 22–23;
    133nn. 56–61,
Walters, K., 254n. 74
Wanamaker, C. A., 131n. 32; 254nn.
    68, 70
Wansink, C. S., 605nn. 52, 58
Ward, R. B., 289n. 78
Watling, E. F., 342n. 16
Watson, D. F., 39n. 25; 165n. 33;
    168n. 59; 606n. 58
Watson, G. R., 373n. 54; 375n. 75
Weaver, P., 423n. 9; 424n. 10; 425nn.
    32–33; 481n. 29; 482n. 37; 482n. 41
Weber, E., 572nn. 14–15
Webster, G., 373n. 54
Weima, J. A. D., 167n. 52
Weiner, E. S. C., 341n. 2
Wernle, P., 632n. 29
Wettstein, J., 195n. 61
Wheeler, E. L., 374n. 70, 375n. 72
White, L. M., 225n. 104; 285n. 3;
    286nn. 5, 14, 17; 287n. 24; 290n. 97;
    315n. 2; 428n. 63; 479nn. 10, 18;
    480n. 20 482n. 43; 483n. 54;
    484n. 62; 485nn. 70–72; 486n. 83;
    549n. 30
White, P., 342nn. 21, 25–26, 28; 343nn.
    29, 39

Wieacker, F., 70n. 47
Wiedemann,T., 371n. 35; 372nn. 37,
    42; 378n. 101; 602nn. 2, 20; 603n. 22;
    605n. 44
Wilkins, P., 425n. 33
Willert, N., 192n. 9
Williams, D. J., 68n. 10, 227n. 145;
    377nn. 90, 97, 100; 378nn. 102–3,
    111, 113; 379n. 121
Williams, S. K., 289n. 57
Williams, W., 285n. 1
Willms, H., 252n. 40
Wilson, N. G., 163n. 5, 165n. 40;
    166nn. 47, 49; 370n. 26; 371n. 27;
    374n. 64
Wilson, S. G., 287n. 24
Wilson, W. T., 452nn. 38–39
Windisch, H., 574nn. 60–61
Winkler, J. J., 424n. 11
Winter, B. W., 605n. 53; 227n. 150
Winter, J. G., 220n. 18
Winter, S. C., 484n. 65; 605n. 51
Wire, A. C., 290n. 86
Wiseman, J., 605n. 42
Witherington, B., III, 168n. 55; 170nn.
    72–74, 78–79; 171nn. 83–85
Wolff, C., 256nn. 96, 99
Wolter, M., 316n. 14
Wouters, A., 221n. 37
Woyke, J., 486n. 84
Wright, F. A., 373n. 57
Wuellner, W., 256n. 100
Wulf-Rheidt, U., 287nn. 33–35

Yarborough, O. L., 225n. 104; 290n. 97;
    315n. 2; 428nn. 63–64; 483n. 54;
    486n. 83
Youtie, H. C., 220n. 18

Zalateo, G., 221n. 41
Zanker, P., 286nn. 12–13, 16, 18;
    287nn. 22–23, 40; 289n. 78; 290n. 88
Zeibarth, E., 221nn. 41–43, 45, 48
Zerwick, M., 132n. 46
Ziesler, J. A., 550n. 40; 574n. 57;
    633n. 37
Zmijewski, J., 99n. 8

INDEX OF SUBJECTS

Page numbers in bold type indicate a separate article on that topic.

adaptability, **17–41**
adiaphora, 443
adoption, **42–76,** 107
amplification, 134, 146, 156
athletics, *see* games, 188, 540

blame, 296, 301
boasting, **77–100**, 437, 445, 557, 561, 562–63

character, *see* ethos, 19, 22, 101, 103, 107, 174, 176, 186, 234, 326, 390
children, 278, 407–8, 420, 495
chreia, 236
circumcision, 30, 387, 388, 394–97, 417, 437, 445, 446, 587
clients, *see* patrons, 87, 101, 110, 265, 348, 457, 459, 462, 463, 468, **488–533**, 578, 580, 582
commendation, **101–33**
common topics/commonplaces, 31, 146, 178, 185, 186, 435
comparison, 79, 85, 87, 88, 89, 90, 91, 92, **134–71**, 212, 228, 232, 239, 302, 558
conciliatory, 182
conscience, 174, 625

declamations, 207, 430
deliberative, 135, 137, 150, 214, 229, 236–37, 242, 430, 440
desire, 415, 530, 532, 535, 537, 541, 544

divine condescension, 26, 35
divorce, *see* marriage, **404–28**

education, 135, 151, 233, 278, **198–227**, 268
encomium (encomia), 101, 147, 149, 156, 212, 327
enthymeme, 229, 230
epideictic, 135, 137, 141, 204, 235, 349
ethos (character), 18, 103, 106, 112, 113, 114, 118, 121, 122, 126, 127, 209–10, 233, 243, 297, 300, 305, 307, 310, 430–31, 432, 525, 540, 611, 625
exemplification (example), *see* imitation, 117, 118–19, **228–57**, 310, 441

family (familia), *see* household, 10, 50, 52, 102, 104, 107, **258–92**, 436, 457, 461, 464, 466, 583, 594
father, 34, 45, 47, 63, 86, 466
flatterer, 20–22, 34, 83, 84, 330
flattery, 293, 296, 298
forensic, 135, 137, 141, 229
frank speech, 185, **293–318**, 330, 339
friends, 21–23, 34, 101, 180, 181, 186, 189, 190, 298, 463, 492
friendship, 10, 33, 107, 178, 179, 182, 187, 188, 189, 235, 238, 267, 293–94, 297, 298, 301–2, 307–9, 310, 313, **319–43**, 472

games, *see* military, 149, 188, **344–83**
grief, 175–77, 179, 181
guardian, guardianship, 54, 62–63
gymnasium, 216

hardships, see sufferings, 92, 120, 156, 158, **172–97**

honor, see shame, 11, 82–84, 88, 90, 92, 93, 94, 114, 121, 125, **551–74**, 577

household, see family, 116, **258–92**, 488

imitation, see exemplification, 35, **228–57**, 359

impartiality, divine, 152, 154, 536

inclusio, 240, 241, 308, 355, 358, 362

indifferent things (adiaphora), **384–403**, 437, 440, 528

inheritance, 42–76, 457, 458, 459, 524

judicial, 150, 204

manumission, 394, 580, 581, 582, 589, 593

marriage, see divorce, 29–30, 267, 388, 391, **404–28**, 458, 530, 537, 587

mater familias, 459, 466–67, 488

maxims, 201, 208, 217, **429–56**

meals, 273–74, 282–83, 323

military, see games, 188, **344–83**

oaths, 88

passion, 172, 531, 537, 541, 544, 612–13

pater familias, 9, 52, 54, 407, **457–87**, 488

pathos, 19

patronage, 9, 22, 114, 119, 125, 126, 473

patrons, see clients, 87, 101, 105, 110, 113, 116, 123–24, 348, 462, 467, 468, 469–71, **488–523**, 578, 580, 593

peace, 362, 436

praise, 80, 93, 114, 296, 301, 304, 305, 307, 308, 312, 313, 325, 334

progymnasmata, 19, 134, 143, 204, 205, 206, 209, 433

prosopoiia, 211, 233

reconciliation, 335–37

refining, 433

self-commendation (see self-praise), 127, 157

self-mastery (self-control), 330, 416, **524–50**, 612

self-praise (see self-commendation), 78–79, 82, 85, 92

self-sufficiency, 333

sex/sexuality, 266, 275–78, 471, 543–45

shame, see honor, 11, 301, **551–74**, 577

slavery, 28, 64, 159, 388, 392, 393, 442, **575–607**, 615

slaves, 265, 271–73, 280–82, 461, 489

Spirit, 64, 189–90, 239, 300, 305, 430, 441, 443–44, 470, 497, 536, 540, 617, 619–23

strong, 415, 561, 565

suffering, see hardships, 86, 92, **172–97**

vice, see virtue, 32, 59, 175, 235, 384, 388, 392, 396, 440, 444, 535, **608–33**

virtue, see vice, 148, 235, 326, 331, 334, 346, 384, 386, 388, 396, 440, 444, 528, 529, 544, **608–33**

weak/weakness, 28, 31, 86, 88, 89, 90, 91, 93, 94, 158, 420, 561, 565

weddings, 409

well-being, 20, 310